S0-BCP-272

The American System of Criminal Justice
Fourth Edition

The American System of Criminal Justice
Fourth Edition

George F. Cole
University of Connecticut

Brooks/Cole Publishing Company
Monterey, California

Brooks/Cole Publishing Company
A Division of Wadsworth, Inc.

Printed in the United States of America

10 9 8 7 6 5 4 3 2 1

Library of Congress Cataloging in Publication Data

Cole, George F., 1935–
The American system of criminal justice.

Bibliography: p.
Includes indexes.
1. Criminal justice, Administration of—United States. I. Title.
KF9223.C648 1985 345.73'05 85-15169
347.3055

ISBN 0-534-05226-6

Sponsoring Editor: Claire Verduin
Editorial Assistant: Pat Carnahan
Production Editor: Penelope Sky
Production Assistant: Dorothy Bell
Manuscript Editor: Barbara H. Salazar
Permissions Editor: Mary Kay Hancharick
Interior and Cover Design: Victoria A. Van Deventer
Cover Photo: Harold Lambert/Frederic Lewis, Inc.
Art Coordinator: Michèle Judge
Interior Illustration: Art by Ayxa
Photo Editor: Judy Blamer
Photo Researcher: Judy Mason
Typesetting: Bi-Comp, Inc., York, Pennsylvania
Cover Printing: Phoenix Color Corporation, Long Island City, New York
Printing and Binding: R. R. Donnelley & Sons Company, Crawfordsville, Indiana

(*Credits continue on page 677.*)

Preface

An opportunity to write the fourth edition of a book is most gratifying, but it is also humbling. Knowing that students and teachers in a variety of colleges and universities throughout the country have found the first three editions useful makes me keenly aware of the necessity to communicate knowledge accurately and in a readily understandable manner. As an instructor of undergraduates, I have always found teaching criminal justice pleasurable. Students come to the classroom interested in the subject, intrigued by the prospect of understanding the system, and optimistic about the role they may one day play in allocating justice, as practitioners or as citizens.

The present revision has been stimulated by the abundant high-quality research about the criminal justice system that has emerged since the third edition was published. Knowledge about crime and justice has expanded so greatly during the past decade that many of the assumptions in earlier works can no longer serve as the foundation of criminal justice curricula. One has only to compare the 1967 report of the President's Commission on Law Enforcement and Administration of Justice with recent scholarship on the police, courts, and corrections to realize how much the discipline has developed. In such a fast-changing field, instructional materials must be kept up to date. This task requires more than replacing the data in the figures and tables of a book; it demands continued reading of the wide-ranging literature of criminal justice, and the incorporation of significant findings in the text.

In writing this edition I have had much assistance from people who merit particular recognition. Again heading this list is Betty Seaver, who has guided me through the intricacies of the English language. The staff of the Homer Babbidge Library, University of Connecticut, was extremely helpful; especially Isabelle DiCenzo, Lucy DeLuca, and Robert Vrecenak. The project has benefited much from the attention of Claire Verduin, criminal justice editor at Brooks/Cole, whose encouragement and support have been crucial. The many suggestions offered by reviewers and critics in the field have greatly improved this edition. Ultimately, however, the responsibility for the work rests with me alone.

George F. Cole

Acknowledgments

The valuable contributions of the following reviewers, who read parts or all of this book, are here gratefully acknowledged.

Jim Adamitis, *University of Dayton*
Diane Marie Alexander, *Illinois State University, Normal*
William H. Allen, *Belleville Area College*
Joseph Bogan, *Indiana University*
Samuel Chapman, *University of Oklahoma, Norman*
Bob Culbertson, *Eastern Montana University*
John Dombrink, *University of California, Irvine*
Armand Hernandez, *Arizona State University, Tempe*
James L. Jengeleski, *Shippensburg University*
John Klofas, *Illinois State University, Normal*
James Knight, *Memphis State University*
Sue Mahan, *University of Texas, El Paso*
Stephen Mastrofski, *Penn State University*
Annette Means, *El Paso Community College*
Masud Mufti, *University of Wisconsin, La Crosse*
Robert Murillo, *University of Texas, El Paso*
Ken Peak, *University of Nevada, Reno*
Carl Pope, *University of Wisconsin, Milwaukee*
Roxanna Sweet, *California State University, Sacramento*
David Wheaton, *Tennessee State University, Nashville*
David Whelan, *Ocean County College*
Thomas Winfree, *Louisiana State University, Baton Rouge*

To the Reader

Criminal justice emerged during the 1970s as a vital and unique academic discipline emphasizing the professional development of students who plan careers in the field and attracting those who want to know more about a difficult social problem and how this country responds to it. Criminal justice incorporates a broad range of knowledge from a variety of specialties, including law, history, and the social and behavioral sciences, each contributing to our fuller understanding of criminal behavior and of society's attitudes toward deviance.

Because of the vast amount of research that has been done during the last decade, today's students of criminal justice must be familiar with a great deal of up-to-date literature. In preparing this text I have given close attention to monographs, government publications, scholarly journals, papers read at academic meetings, and the popular media. Although reports of research are essential for developing the empirical foundation of criminal justice study, biographies and fiction evoke the system's human dimension far more vividly. Before presenting an interesting and fruitful introduction to the American system of criminal justice, it is appropriate that I discuss some of the assumptions on which this book is based, and describe several of the special features that make this edition especially clear, orderly, and, I hope, exciting.

Multidisciplinary perspective

This introduction to American criminal justice aims at comprehensiveness by describing the system's operational components from a multidisciplinary perspective. Because criminal behavior is human behavior, the key research findings and concepts are drawn from sociology, psychology, and political science, while the efforts of historians allow a comparison of past and contemporary issues and phenomena. Because the institutions of criminal justice compose an organizational system, concepts from the administrative sciences are similarly employed. Criminal justice operates under law; accordingly, its boundaries are formed by jurisprudential responses to society's need for protection and the individual citizen's need for freedom. Because the criminal justice system is an arm of the government, it operates within the political context as well. We recognize both that many criminal justice personnel obtain office by means of politics, and that a form of bureaucratic politics influences how each portion of the system works. It is from this confluence of administration, law, and politics that decisions are made that concern the basis on which behavior is defined as criminal, determine the level of resources given criminal justice agencies, and result in actions that affect the lives of citizens, crime victims, offenders, and officials.

Special features

To make this integrated introduction to American criminal justice informative, enjoyable, and rewarding (a tall order, but one worth attempting), I have included a number of special features.

1. *Running glossary.* One goal of an introductory course is to convey the terminology of a field. Because criminal justice is interdisciplinary, a number of terms employed in law and the social sciences are fully defined in the margin, next to their first appearance in the text.
2. *Graphics.* Great care has been given to preparing tables, figures, and pictures that focus and enliven information so that it can be accurately perceived and easily understood.
3. *Boxed materials.* Scattered throughout the book are excerpts from magazines, newspapers, and other sources that dramatize the topics under discussion and tie the text to the real world with the vivid words of journalists, prisoners, judges, and attorneys.
4. *Biographies.* An introductory course customarily acknowledges many contributors to the development of the field. The book therefore includes succinct descriptions of some of the most important figures in criminal justice. Knowing something about the lives of these leaders will give the student a greater appreciation of their work.
5. *Real-life experience.* The story of Donald Payne, a young man caught in the criminal justice system, is told serially at the end of relevant chapters. "The People versus Donald Payne," first published in *Newsweek,* enables us to see how the system operated in relation to one individual. While reading these selections, students can consider what they would have done in similar circumstances.
6. *Other student aids.* Each chapter opening includes an outline of the topics that follow. Each chapter concludes with a summary, discussion questions, and suggestions for further reading. At the end of the text the running glossary items are arranged alphabetically to facilitate quick reference. An appendix contains the criminal justice portions of the Constitution of the United States. The book concludes with a detailed index.

I want to make it clear that *The American System of Criminal Justice* is neither a radical critique of its subject nor an endorsement of the status quo. I have tried to present an image of current reality, and I hope to challenge those who contemplate careers in this field to work to improve the system. After years of neglect, criminal justice is now in a period of rapid change and development as new concepts and methods come to the fore. The sometimes conflicting needs for freedom and for order in a democratic society create problems and opportunities alike. It is time for a new generation of criminal justice practitioners and scholars to provide leadership that will bring about long-overdue improvements.

Brief Contents

Contents

PART 4

Postconviction Strategies 450

Chapter 13

Sentencing 452

Chapter 14

Corrections 488

Chapter 15

Incarceration 522

The American System of Criminal Justice

Fourth Edition

PART 1

The Criminal Justice Process

Crime is an enduring problem that has required attention since time immemorial. Today we want to understand the dimensions of this problem, how it has been defined, and how society has attempted to deal with it. Is it possible that crime will never be controlled? What types of behaviors does the law define as "criminal"? What legal and administrative requirements must be met before a person can be labeled "guilty"? Part One explores such questions with a twofold aim: to give the reader (1) a sense of the nature of crime and what is currently being done about it and (2) a broad, general framework within which to analyze the more specific materials found in the rest of the book.

Crime and Justice in America

1

Since the mid-1960s, crime in America has been a continuing focus of public attention. Through newspapers, television, and bitter personal experience, Americans have become increasingly aware of the growth of crime and the apparent inadequacy of the criminal justice system to deal with it. One might hope that citizens of the "land of the free" could live without having to devote great physical and psychological energies, let alone resources, to personal protection, but for many Americans the possibility of being victimized by criminals is ever present. When in 1973 the National Advisory Commission on Criminal Justice Standards and Goals set as a target the reduction of crime over the next ten years, it stated that a time would come in the immediate future when

There is much crime in America, more than ever is reported, far more than ever is solved, far too much for the health of the Nation. Every American knows that. Every American is, in a sense, a victim of crime.

PRESIDENT'S COMMISSION ON LAW ENFORCEMENT AND ADMINISTRATION OF JUSTICE

- A couple can walk in the evening in their neighborhood without fear of assault and robbery.
- A family can go away for the weekend without fear of returning to a house ransacked by burglars.
- A woman can take a night job without fear of being raped on her way to or from work.
- Every citizen can live without fear of being brutalized by unknown assailants.[1]

More than a decade later, however, these goals are more elusive than ever, and the important question remains: How may we control crime while maintaining the conditions of justice and freedom appropriate to a democracy?

Crime and justice as public policy issues

Although there is widespread agreement in American society that crime is a serious problem requiring governmental actions, there is no consensus as to the approaches that should be taken. Some people believe that the answer lies in stricter enforcement of the law through the expansion of police forces and the enactment of punitive measures that will result in the swift and certain punishment of criminals. The holders of this conservative view argue that we must strengthen crime control policies, which they assert have been weakened by decisions of the Supreme Court and the liberal dominance of opinion on crime policies through the 1960s and 1970s. In opposition to the conservatives are people who argue that the strengthening of crime control policies would endanger the cherished values of due process and justice. The liberals say that such an approach would also be ineffective in solving the crime problem because the answer lies in reshaping the lives of individual offenders and changing the social conditions from which criminal behavior springs.

We must not overemphasize the distinction between liberal and conservative approaches to crime and criminal justice because the differences between the policies they espouse are not clear-cut. It is important to remember that both crime and criminal justice can be defined in various ways, and a multitude of measures have been proposed to deal with the one and achieve the other. The making of public policies in regard to both issues requires that choices be made. As with other policy choices, political factors influence the decisions that are made.

Speaking before the annual convention of the International Association of Chiefs of Police in 1981, President Ronald Reagan pledged that he would use the "bully pulpit" of the presidency to remind the public of the seriousness of crime, of its causes, and of the importance of those trying to fight it. Defining the crime problem as one that will not be solved by more money, more police, or more prosecutors, the president asserted:

> The war on crime will only be won when an attitude of mind and a change of heart take place in America—when certain truths hold again and plant their roots deep into our national consciousness. Truths like: right and wrong matter; individuals are responsible for their actions; retribution should be swift and sure for those who prey upon the innocent.[2]

Although some readers may regard the speech as typical political oratory before a large and influential group of law enforcement officials, others will note that the values espoused and the solutions recommended summarize a shift in public policy concerning crime and justice.

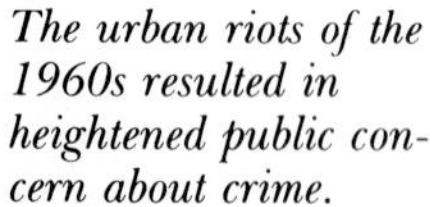
The urban riots of the 1960s resulted in heightened public concern about crime.

It was not many years earlier that a commission appointed by President Lyndon Johnson also looked at the crime problem. In its 1967 report, the President's Commission on Law Enforcement and Administration of Justice declared that crime was caused essentially by disorganization in American society; that agencies concerned with enforcement, adjudication, and corrections lacked resources; and that rehabilitation had been insufficiently used as a means of treating offenders.[3] Throughout, the report recommended eliminating the social conditions that bring about crime, doing away with social and racial injustices to achieve the ideals of the American ethic, and reintegrating into their communities those who commit crimes. To implement these recommendations, Congress, in 1968, created the Law Enforcement Assistance Administration (LEAA) and charged it with conducting research on, experimenting with new approaches to, and providing assistance to the states to deal with criminal justice. Before its demise in 1982, LEAA had spent more than $5 billion.

That these actions by a presidential commission and by Congress were in agreement with the perspective of other presidents, agencies of government, and the American public during the 1960s and 1970s should be emphasized. Richard Nixon, Gerald Ford, and Jimmy Carter held similar views on crime; many state legislatures adopted a moratorium on new prison construction that had been advocated by the National Council on Crime and Delinquency; the United States Supreme Court under Chief Justices Earl Warren and Warren Burger extended the rights of defendants in criminal trials; and social agencies at all levels of government emphasized rehabilitating offenders by reintegrating them into the community.

Shifts in the direction of public policies do not occur suddenly, at specific points in time. With regard to crime, the conservative critique of the liberal policies of the 1960s was constant and contemporaneous, but it gained in credence during the 1970s, in part because of findings by criminal justice researchers that cast into doubt many of the earlier ideas. Debate about "what works," sparked by the reports of Robert Martinson and others, forced a reconsideration of rehabilitation as the primary goal of the criminal sanction.[4] The Police Foundation and scholars whose work was funded by the National Institute of Justice conducted research into the direction of police tactics. Committees of the National Academy of Sciences recommended that greater weight be given to the goals of incarceration and deterrence.[5] Questions were raised about the granting of bail to repeat offenders, the prosecution of career criminals, the lengths of jail and prison sentences, and the broader efforts to reduce crime through social reform.

The election of Ronald Reagan in 1980 and his reelection in 1984 solidified the shift in federal crime control policies that had been evolving for some time. Actions taken by the Reagan administration reinforced the impression that a new approach was being shaped. A 1981 task force on violent crime recommended that $2 billion of federal aid be given to the states to construct additional prisons, that statutes be amended to allow dangerous or recidivist offenders to be held without bail, and that the exclusionary rule be loosened so that it would not hamper law enforcement efforts. The task force report set the tone of the new approach with its critique of the past liberal policies:

> We are not convinced that a government, by the invention of new programs or the management of existing institutions, can by itself re-create those familial and neighborhood conditions, those social opportunities, and those personal values that in all likelihood are the prerequisites of tranquil communities. Finally, we are mindful of the risks of assuming that the government can solve whatever problems it addresses.[6]

In the weeks just before the 1984 elections, bipartisan majorities in Congress passed, and President Reagan signed, the Comprehensive Crime Control Act of 1984, which incorporated many of the proposals advocated by those who urged a new, "tougher" approach to crime.[7] Called "the most far-reaching and substantial reform of the criminal justice system in our history" by Attorney General William French Smith, the legislation provides for a tightening of the insanity defense, abolition of parole release, harsher sentences, and preventive detention of dangerous persons awaiting trial.[8] It should be emphasized that the act affects only the federal justice system and not the state systems, where 95 percent of all crimes are prosecuted. But during the previous decade many of the states had already enacted laws similar to the new federal legislation. It can be expected that other states will reform their systems so as to emulate the new trend in federal policy.

We can see, then, that during the past ten years there has been a definite shift in public policies toward crime, a shift that is perhaps reflected in the increased number of people incarcerated, the longer sentences being served, the greater emphasis on victims' rights, the new "aggressive patrol" policies of the police, and decreased reliance on rehabilitative treatment programs. The point to remember, however, is that defining a crime problem and settling on approaches to it are, in a democracy, issues of public policy. It is in the political arena, at local, state, and national levels, that democratic governments decide how to pursue such a problem. This fact in turn raises a number of questions concerning the importance of crime prevention on the public agenda, the extent to which government agencies pursue certain kinds of criminals, the amounts and types of resources that are allocated for crime control, and the policies that enforcement, adjudication, and corrections officials follow.

Perhaps the most important question confronting American society is how to control crime while preserving the due process and the elements of

In authoritarian systems, legal and political restrictions on the police are minimal.

freedom and justice that quintessentially define a democracy. These intertwined questions are central to the problem of crime. Citizens cannot enjoy their freedom, for example, if they are afraid to walk the streets and must spend a lot to protect themselves against crime. By the same token, freedom is too precious to be infringed upon by unconstitutional actions of law enforcement agencies. Similarly, those wrongly accused of crime do not receive justice if they are convicted, nor do offenders who have paid their debt to society if they are treated as ex-cons rather than as citizens. Though much of our crime problem would disappear if the police were to receive a massive allocation of resources and if limitations on their actions were to be removed, such a public policy would create a police state and a loss of freedom and justice.

Questions for analysis

Although presidential commissions decry the rise in crime and reformers argue that the administration of justice must be drastically changed, it is necessary to address a number of preliminary questions so that we may understand the problem before we attempt to deal with it. First, for example, we must know something about the causes of crime. Of equal importance is knowing something about the justice dispensed by the legal system. Are rich and poor treated alike? Is the constitutional guarantee of a fair and speedy trial upheld? Do correctional programs offer a genuine chance for rehabilitation?

It is also necessary to learn how and why the criminal justice system operates as it does. This means that we must take a hardheaded look at the history and operations of law enforcement, adjudication, and corrections and the social forces that created them. The reality of criminal justice in the United States will shock many people, but only when the way the justice machinery functions is understood can proposals for change be considered.

Description of a social system is important, but criminal justice specialists must also be able to analyze *why* the process operates as it does. They must draw on the literature of a wide range of scholarly disciplines—among them law, history, and the social sciences—to bring together theories and concepts that will help them to comprehend reality and to predict the probable course of future actions. At present, however, the quality of the existing research is uneven; some portions of the criminal justice system have been studied more thoroughly than others. Social analysis is an ongoing search to determine why people act as they do. When the roles played by the multitude of actors in the vast criminal justice system are understood, new and different approaches can be explored to achieve the goal of maintaining both order and human freedom.

Chapter 1 introduces several of the underlying assumptions of the book, looking at such basic themes as the amount and type of crime in America, the present condition of the system, and the role of politics in criminal justice. Conceptual tools for analysis are discussed in the final portion. Succeeding chapters will consider the primary influences of law and administration on the practices of each portion of the system. Some people may view the challenge of crime in a free society as an unpleasantness to be avoided, but the rewards are many for those who are interested in understanding the system, for understanding provides the necessary basis for making appropriate changes.

Crime in America

Emile Durkheim, a nineteenth-century sociologist, made the classic observation that crime is a normal part of society.

> Crime is present not only in the majority of societies of one particular species but in all societies of all types. There is no society that is not confronted with the problem of criminality. Its form changes; the acts thus characterized are not the same everywhere, but, everywhere and always, there have been men who have behaved in such a way as to draw upon themselves penal repression.[9]

In view of the capacity of other eras to produce criminals, villains, deviants, and deeds of violence, ours is neither the best nor the worst of times. There has always been too much crime, and virtually every generation since the founding of the Republic has felt threatened by it. As a 1903 observer wrote:

> Individual crimes have increased in number and malignity. In addition . . . a wave of general criminality has spread over the whole nation. . . . The times are far from hard, and prosperity for several years has been widespread in all classes. Large sums are in unaccustomed hands, bar-rooms are swarming, pool-rooms, policy shops and gambling houses are full, the races are played, licentiousness increases, the classes who "roll in wealth" set intoxicating examples of luxury and recklessness, and crime has become rampant.[10]

References abound to serious outbreaks of violence following the Civil War, after World War I, during the Prohibition Era, and in the midst of the Great Depression. As the President's Commission on Law Enforcement and Administration of Justice pointed out,

> a hundred years ago contemporary accounts of San Francisco told of extensive areas where "no decent man was in safety to walk the streets after dark; while at all hours, both night and day, his property was jeopardized by incendiarism and burglary." Teenage gangs gave rise to the "hoodlum"; while in one central New York City area, near Broadway, the police entered "only in pairs, and never unarmed."[11]

That there has always been a great deal of crime does not mean that the amount and types of crime have been the same. During the labor unrest of the 1880s and 1930s, pitched battles took place between strikers and company police. Race riots occurred in Atlanta in 1907 and in Chicago, Washington, and East St. Louis in 1919. Organized crime became a special focus during the 1930s. The willful homicide rate, which reached a high in 1933 and a low during World War II, has actually decreased to about 20 percent above the postwar-era rate. Violence in the streets, particularly in the form of aggravated assault, is what has skyrocketed during the past decade.

How much crime is there?

One of the frustrations in studying criminal justice is the lack of accurate means of knowing the amount of crime in society. Surveys that ask members of the public whether they have ever committed a breach of the law indicate that much more crime occurs than is reported. Until very recently, the only criminal activities that were counted were those that were known to the police and that made their way into the statistics of the annual *Uniform Crime Reports.*

Since 1972, however, the Law Enforcement Assistance Administration has sponsored ongoing surveys of the public to determine the amount of criminal victimization experienced. A comparison of these studies with the figures published in the *Uniform Crime Reports* reveals a significant discrepancy between the occurrence of crime and offenses known to the police. The large numbers of offenses never brought to the attention of the police, often referred to as the ***dark figure of crime,*** are of concern to the police and to criminal justice planners. Homicide and auto theft are the two offenses whose reported and estimated occurrences correspond. In the case of homicide, this correspondence can be explained by the fact that a body must be accounted for; in the case of auto theft, by the fact that insurance payments require the police to be called in. But the incidence of forcible rape, for example, appears to be more than twice the reported rate; burglary, three times; aggravated assault, half again; and robbery and larceny of $50 and over, more than double. Table 1.1 shows data on reported and unreported crime in the United States.

dark figure of crime A metaphor that emphasizes the dangerous dimension of crime that is never reported to the police.

Many reasons have been advanced to account for nonreporting of crime to the police. Some victims of rape and assault fear the embarrassment of public disclosure and interrogation by the police. Increasing evidence reveals that much violence occurs between persons who know each other—spouses, lovers, relatives—but the passions of the moment take on a different character when the victim is asked to testify against a family member. Another reason for nonreporting is that lower socioeconomic groups fear police involvement. In some neighborhoods, residents believe that the arrival of the law for one purpose may result in the discovery of other illicit activities, such as welfare fraud, housing-code violations, or the presence of persons on probation or parole. In many of these same places the level of police protection has been minimal in the past, and residents feel that they will get little assistance with the current matter. Finally, the value of property lost by larceny, robbery, or burglary may not be worth the effort of a police investigation. Many citizens are deterred from reporting a crime by unwillingness to become "involved," to have to go to the station house to fill out papers, perhaps go to court, or appear at a police lineup. All these aspects of the criminal process may result in lost workdays and in the expense of travel and child care. Even then, the stolen item may go unrecovered. As these examples suggest, multitudes of

TABLE 1.1 Distribution of reported and unreported crime in the United States

Crime	*Percentage of incidents reported to police*	*Percentage of incidents not reported to police*	*Percentage of all nonreported incidents*
Auto theft	68	32	1.7
Robbery	49	51	2.0
Burglary	46	54	14.0
Rape	44	56	0.4
Assault	40	60	8.5
Larceny	18	82	73.0
Total	28	72	99.6

Source: Reprinted, with permission of the National Council on Crime and Delinquency, from Wesley Skogan, "Dimensions of the Dark Figure of Unreported Crime," *Crime & Delinquency* 23 (January 1977): 46.

Uniform Crime Reports
A statistical summary of crimes reported to the police based on voluntary reports to the FBI by local, state, and federal law enforcement agencies; published annually.

people feel that it is rational not to report criminal incidents because the costs outweigh the gains.

Uniform Crime Reports. One of the main sources of crime statistics is maintained by the FBI and published annually: *Uniform Crime Reports* (*UCR*). At the urging of the International Association of Chiefs of Police, Congress in 1930 authorized this national and uniform system of compiling crime data. The *UCR* is the product of a voluntary national network through which local, state, and federal law enforcement agencies transmit information to Washington concerning the twenty-nine types of offenses listed in table 1.2. For eight major crimes—"index offenses"— the collected data show such factors as age, race, and number of reported crimes solved, while for the twenty-one other offense categories the data are not as complete.

The value of the *UCR* has been questioned by a number of scholars. They point out that the data concern only crimes reported to the police, that submission of the data is voluntary, that the reports are not truly uniform because events are defined according to differing criteria in various regions of the country, and that upper-class and so-called white-collar crimes are not included. In addition, they argue that the crime figures are not presented honestly, and such criticism has caused some respected criminologists to declare that the *UCR* is worthless as a research tool. According to another criticism, the reports always seem to emphasize that crime is rampant and that things are getting worse. Finally, because of the shape of the graphs presented in the reports and the choice of baseline data, the untutored eye may not see the potential for distortion. Thus the *Uniform Crime Reports* have limitations and must be used cautiously. But insofar as they contain information about what is known of crime, they are a valuable tool for the criminal justice scholar.

TABLE 1.2 Uniform crime report offenses

Part I (index offenses)	***Part II (other offenses)***
1. Criminal homicide	9. Simple assaults
2. Forcible rape	10. Forgery and counterfeiting
3. Robbery	11. Fraud
4. Aggravated assault	12. Embezzlement
5. Burglary	13. Buying, receiving, or possessing stolen property
6. Larceny-theft	14. Vandalism
7. Auto theft	15. Weapons (carrying, possession, etc.)
8. Arson	16. Prostitution and commercialized vice
	17. Sex offenses
	18. Violation of narcotic drug laws
	19. Gambling
	20. Offenses against the family and children
	21. Driving under the influence
	22. Violation of liquor laws
	23. Drunkenness
	24. Disorderly conduct
	25. Vagrancy
	26. All other offenses (excluding traffic)
	27. Suspicion
	28. Curfew and loitering (juvenile)
	29. Runaway (juvenile)

Source: U.S. Department of Justice, *Crime in the United States* (Washington, D.C.: Government Printing Office, 1984).

Although they are vulnerable, the elderly are less likely than the young to be victimized.

National Crime Surveys National surveys of samples of the U.S. population conducted by the Bureau of Justice Statistics to determine the number and types of criminal victimizations and thus the extent of unreported crime.

National Crime Surveys. In 1972 the U.S. Bureau of the Census began the largest series of interview programs ever conducted to determine the extent and nature of crime victimization. Sponsored by the Department of Justice, these surveys are designed to generate estimates of quarterly and yearly victimization rates for all index offenses except homicide and arson. Unlike the *UCR,* which counts reported crimes committed against all people and all businesses, organizations, and government agencies, the National Crime Surveys (NCS) count only crimes against persons aged twelve or older and against their households. In addition, specialized surveys of twenty-six communities produce rates for many of the nation's largest cities. Separate studies of businesses are made. The results show that for the crimes measured, 41 million victimizations affecting 24 million households (about one-third of all U.S. households) occur each year, a level much higher than that indicated by the number of crimes reported to the police.[12]

Each person interviewed in the national sample is asked a series of questions (for instance, Did anyone beat you up, attack you, or hit you with something such as a rock or a bottle?) to determine whether he or she has been victimized. For each affirmative response to these "incident screen" questions, detail questions then elicit specific facts about the event, characteristics of the offender, and resulting financial losses or physical disabilities. The collection of such data permits the number of crimes that have occurred nationwide to be estimated and yields information on the offenders and indications of demographic patterns that may be emerging.

Data from victimization surveys have thus far helped to validate some hypotheses about the nature of crime. Extensive analysis of the data has disclosed that race is not an important factor in distinguishing those who report crime incidents to the police.[13] Blacks, in fact, are slightly more likely than whites to report their experiences. Sex differences are more consistent with expectations, for women are more likely than men to report victimization to authorities. Age is also a factor: youths between the ages of twelve and nineteen account for a substantial portion of the victims who do not report criminal offenses.

The surveys also shed light on the linkage of sex, age, and race with the probability of victimization. With the exception of rape and personal robbery with contact (purse snatching), men are more likely than women to be victims of crime. An interesting finding is that a majority of the victimizations seem to occur within the lower age group of twelve to twenty-four years. Youths between twelve and fifteen are most likely to be the victims of such crimes as personal larceny without contact, robbery, and simple assault. Race is also an important factor, with blacks and other minorities being more likely than whites to be raped, robbed, and assaulted. In light of the current concern about crimes against the elderly, a notable finding is that they are less likely than the young to be victimized. Clearly, availability, vulnerability, and desirability determine whether someone or something is a likely target. Randomness also contributes to the process. Being near an armed person who is intent on robbing and who perceives an opportunity to do so greatly increases the probability of victimization.

TABLE 1.3 How do the *UCR* and the NCS compare?

	Uniform Crime Reports	*National Crime Survey*
Offenses measured:	Homicide Rape Robbery (personal and commercial) Assault (aggravated) Burglary (commercial and household) Larceny (commercial and household) Motor vehicle theft Arson	Rape Robbery (personal) Assault (aggravated and simple) Household burglary Larceny (personal and household) Motor vehicle theft
Scope:	Crimes reported to the police in most jurisdictions; considerable flexibility in developing small-area data	Crimes both reported and not reported to police; all data are for the Nation as a whole; some data are available for a few large geographic areas
Collection method:	Police department reports to FBI	Survey interviews: periodically measures the total number of crimes committed by asking a national sample of 60,000 households representing 135,000 persons over the age of 12 about their experiences as victims of crime during a specified period
Kinds of information:	In addition to offense counts, provides information on crime clearances, persons arrested, persons charged, law enforcement officers killed and assaulted, and characteristics of homicide victims	Provides details about victims (such as age, race, sex, education, income, and whether the victim and offender were related to each other) and about crimes (such as time and place of occurrence, whether or not reported to police, use of weapons, occurrence of injury, and economic consequences)
Sponsor:	Department of Justice Federal Bureau of Investigation	Department of Justice Bureau of Justice Statistics

Source: U.S. Department of Justice, Bureau of Justice Statistics, *Report to the Nation on Crime and Justice* (Washington, D.C.: Government Printing Office, 1983), p. 6.

Although the victimization studies have added to our scientific knowledge about crime, there are a number of difficulties with these data. Problems associated with the population samples chosen for the studies have been noted, and we must also remember that the surveys are organized to document the victim's perception of an incident. While the latter is perhaps important, it can be argued that lay persons do not have the legal background that would allow them to differentiate criminal from noncriminal behavior. The high number of incidents reported by the young, for example, is thought to be produced by defining schoolyard shakedowns or fights as criminal. Property thought to have been stolen may have been lost. Memories may grow hazy on dates and carry last year's crime into this year's data.

The usefulness of the victimization studies for criminal justice analysts and planners has been somewhat lessened by the time lag between the interviews and publication of the findings. Unlike the *UCR*, which make available each year's data only eight months after the beginning of the following year, NCS data have usually been two years in arrears. Given the recent patterns of stability in ***victimization rates,*** however, this deficiency should not overshadow the analytical value of the studies.

victimization rate The number of victimizations per 1,000 persons or households as reported by the National Crime Surveys.

Crime trends

Despite some skepticism about the accuracy of the data concerning crime, the impression that the U.S. ***crime rate*** has risen during the past two decades is generally accepted as accurate. What remain in dispute are crime trends. The National Crime Surveys showed a general stability of victimization rates until 1979, when significant declines began to occur. The FBI's *Uniform Crime Reports* tell a somewhat different story: a dramatic rise in crime rates beginning in 1964 and continuing increases, generally, until 1980, when the rates began to slack off.

crime rate The number of reported crimes per 100,000 population as published in the *Uniform Crime Reports.*

The differences in the trends indicated by the NCS and *UCR* are explained in part by the different data sources and different population bases on which their computations of crime rates are based. The continuing rise in the number of crimes known to the police, and thus calculated in the *UCR* trend, undoubtedly reflects an increase in citizen willingness to report criminal behavior. The introduction of 911 phone numbers, the augmented presence of police in many communities, and neighborhood watch programs have helped this effort. With regard to one crime, that of rape, more victimizations have been reported to the police. In 1981, 7 percent more rape victims called the police than had done so in 1973. The existence of support groups and the heightened sensitivity of the police to the needs of the victims have been credited with this change. The "dark figure of unreported crime" is an ongoing criminal justice problem, but this figure has declined for all of the index crimes since 1971.

The public most fears crimes of violence—murder, rape, assault—yet such crimes made up only 10 percent of the incidents cited by the *UCR* in 1984. These are also the crimes that have been committed at fairly constant rates over the years, with some rates—that of murder, for one—being lower now than in times past. The most striking increases have occurred among such property crimes as burglary and larceny. Burglary rates may have risen statistically not because there are more burglars but because more things are insured, because there are more opportunities for criminal activity in an affluent society, and because of changes in the urban environment that give thieves greater mobility and access to the enclaves of the well-to-do.

Our knowledge of the amount of crime may also be a function of the heavier use of centralized data processing in metropolitan areas. Most large cities now employ such systems for reporting crimes, dispatching police officers to investigate incidents, and recording the methods used to dispose of the cases. The effect has been to improve reporting methods and thus to add to the crime rate. At the same time, these innovations have reduced the patrol officer's ***discretion,*** and thus the opportunities to dispense informal justice. For example, rather than send a juvenile home to his or her parents, as is often done in the suburbs, the city police officer is compelled to institute formal procedures, with the result that a minor incident becomes a criminal statistic and the youth is turned over to juvenile authorities. The disposition action must be recorded in the computers. Thus the increasing crime rate may be accounted for in part by more accurate reporting measures rather than by more violations of the law.

discretion

The authority to make decisions without reference to specific rules or facts, using instead one's own judgment; allows for individualization and informality in the administration of justice.

A second factor in the crisis of criminal justice is the law explosion—that is, the increasingly complex and demanding pressures placed upon law and legal institutions to resolve conflict in an urban society. To some extent the law explosion is a result of the population explosion, but every technological advance seems to bring with it a multitude of problems that the law is called on to treat. For example, the invention of the automobile may have as much as doubled the burden on the criminal and civil justice systems.

The changing demographic characteristics of the American people constitute a third element in the rise in crime. Age and urbanization are significant factors here. Criminologists have long shown that crime, especially the kinds the public fears most, is largely a function of youth and young adulthood. Young persons in the fourteen-to-twenty-four age category have been the most crime-prone group in the country (See figure 1.1). In 1984, for example, the *UCR* disclosed that 30 percent of those arrested for serious crimes were under the age of eighteen, almost half of those arrested for robbery were under twenty-one, while 60 percent of those arrested for burglary were under twenty-one.[14]

As a result of the post-World War II baby boom, this high-risk crime group (fourteen to twenty-four years old) grew more rapidly during the 1970s than other age groups and almost four times faster than the entire population. Because of this fact, the President's Commission was able to conclude that, "assuming no change in the arrest rate during 1960–65, between 40 and 50 percent of the total arrests during that period could have been expected as the result of increase in population and changes in the age composition of the population." The decline in the crime rate that began in 1979 has been attributed by such criminologists as Marvin Wolfgang to the maturing of the baby-boom generation, which is now moving past the "crime-prone" ages of fourteen to twenty-four. One estimate is that by 1990 there should be a reduction in crime by the fourteen-to-twenty-four age group of 26 percent if other factors affecting crime do not change to a great degree.[15]

The impact of demographic factors on the extent of crime has been disputed by officials of the U.S. Department of Justice, who stress that arrest

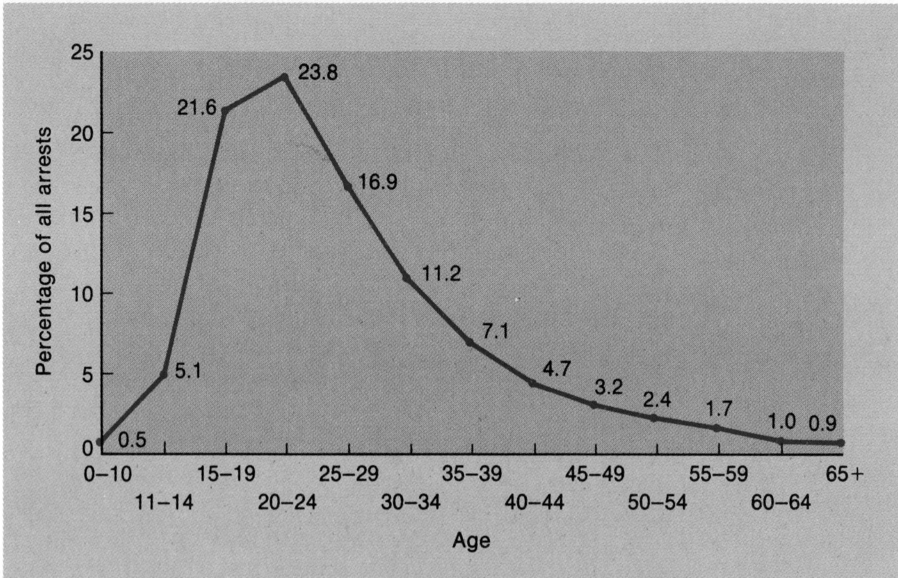

FIGURE 1.1
Arrest curve by age

and sentencing practices play a more important role than age in crime reduction. They say that the government's response to crime should be given greater credit for the decline. It is argued, for example, that in the 1960s crime went up as the probability of being arrested for committing a serious crime and of being sent to prison after arrest went down. As Attorney General William French Smith stated in 1984, "Now we are reaching the midpoint of the 80s. During this decade both the probability of arrest and the probability of incarceration have been increasing. And during this time the crime rates have been falling."[16]

Urbanization has likewise had an impact on the crime rate. Violent crime is primarily a phenomenon of large cities. Of the 12 million index offenses known to the police in 1983, more than 11 million occurred in cities. The greatest proportional increase of serious crimes has taken place in cities whose populations exceed a half million. Although less than 18 percent of the American population live in such cities, they account for more than half the reported index offenses against the person and almost a third of all reported index property crimes. As Norval Morris observed in 1970:

> Though the relationship between crime rates and the degree of urbanization is not a simple one, the increase in the urban population by more than 50 percent since 1930, while the rural population has increased by less than 2 percent, has clearly been a major factor in the rising national crime rates.[17]

Studies have shown that crime rates invariably rise in proportion to proximity to the center of an urban area. The highest incidence is in the physically deteriorating, high-density cores where economic insecurity, poor housing, family disintegration, and transiency are most pronounced. These areas are where the poor (often recent migrants from rural areas) live. Beginning in the 1960s, the populations of such districts tended to become predominantly black as rural southerners moved to the cities to better their lives, but blacks are only the most recent group to follow this pattern. In earlier periods, urban areas

In many urban areas, a lack of community feeling increases the fear of crime.

with the same characteristics were populated by various groups—Irish, Jews, Italians—whichever had arrived most recently. In each period, including the late 1960s, when the words *blacks* and *crime* became synonymous, crime has been most pronounced in these high-density areas. Victims of crimes tend to be neighbors of the criminals.

The growth of urban crime from 1948 to 1978 in 396 American cities has been the subject of research carried out under the direction of Herbert Jacob and Robert Lineberry. They came to the somewhat surprising conclusion that crime "had grown at a rapid rate in American cities, regardless of their size, location, minority populations or whether they are gaining or losing populations."[18] They found that the crime rate was similar in all cities, whether they had declining populations (such as Newark, Philadelphia, and Boston) or dramatic population growth (such as Phoenix, Houston, and San Jose), a low economic base (such as Oakland and Atlanta) or were relatively well off (such as Indianapolis and Minneapolis). Further, it seems that the level of crime control effort did little to differentiate the cities. "Whether local officials engaged in herculean efforts or none at all, the crime wave affected their community."[19]

Given these findings, Jacob and Lineberry suggest that the growth of urban crime results not only from an expansion of the pool of potential offenders, "for reasons not well understood by criminologists,"[20] but also from fundamental changes in the lifestyles of Americans. Greater affluence means that more valuable goods are available for theft, a condition aggravated by the carelessness of Americans, who tend not to guard their property and who expose themselves to dangerous situations as they travel around their cities.

It must be recognized that the United States is not alone in experiencing a rise in crime during the past two decades. As Sir Leon Radzinowicz and others have noted, there seems to be a relationship between affluence and crime.[21] With some exceptions, Switzerland among them, countries of Western Europe have experienced increases in their crime rates, but it should also be taken into account that the rates in Europe are not so high as they are in the United States, especially with respect to crimes of violence. There are as many murders each year in New York's borough of Manhattan as there are in all of England and Wales. Detroit has five times the number of killings that take place in strife-torn Northern Ireland, though their populations are roughly the same size. And it is not only the United States and Europe that are wrestling with more crime than heretofore; Japan's rate of violent crimes has spiraled upward substantially since World War II, though it still is nowhere near the American rate.

Research has suggested that it is extremely difficult to point to specific factors that have caused the rise in crime. It was once thought that the crime problem was amenable to analysis, but social scientists have discovered that it is an extremely complex question, requiring an understanding of some basic influences on human behavior. Does crime occur because of demography, unemployment, housing conditions, and family structure, or is it a result of the multiple interaction of these factors plus others that we are only now beginning to fathom?

Fear of crime

Since 1965 public opinion organizations—Gallup, Harris, and others—have been asking Americans about their reactions to crime to determine whether or not they "feel more uneasy" or "fear to walk the streets at night." The results of these surveys (figure 1.2) show that the incidence of fearfulness closely matches the patterns of victimization and reported offenses. The trend rises sharply from the middle 1960s until about 1973 and then stabilizes. Although we may take heart from the stability in the proportion of people who feel that they cannot walk in their neighborhoods at night or who worry a lot about

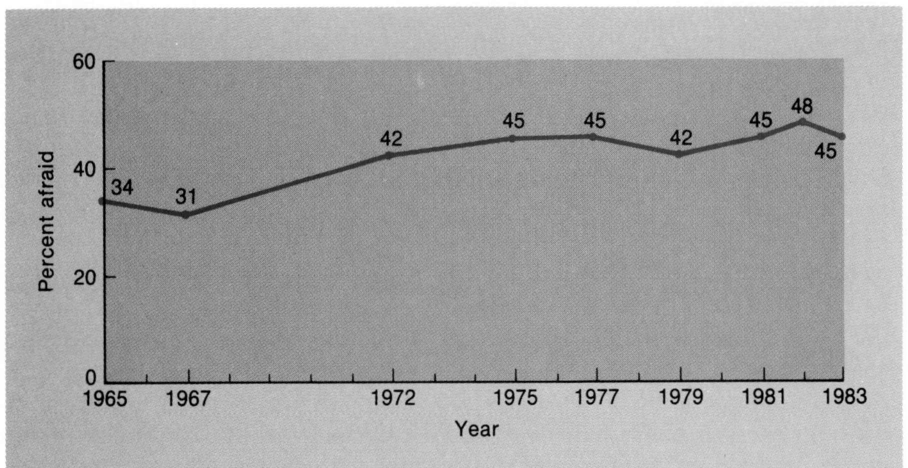

FIGURE 1.2
Trends in fear of crime

being robbed or beaten, the fact remains that the fear of crime limits the freedom of more than 40 percent of the public. Many are forced to confine their activities to "safe" areas at "safe" times. Concern about crime leads people to spend money for protective devices; a national survey found that two-thirds of the populace reported doing something to prevent crime.[22] In addition, fear creates unmeasurable anxieties that have physiological and psychological ramifications. Perhaps most unsettling, some studies have shown that the very persons who have the least chance of being victimized by crime are among the most fearful.

Fear of crime is primarily an urban phenomenon. In small towns and rural areas, less than 30 percent of the residents say that they are afraid to walk through their neighborhoods at night; in large cities this figure is more than 60 percent. One impact of the fact that crime is viewed as urban is that fear of crime stimulates further movement of jobs, businesses, and middle-class people out of the central city, with the result that the core becomes hollow, deserted at night, and lacking in economic and social vitality. When city dwellers are timorous, neighborhood cohesiveness is eroded because residents curtail interactions with others, stop attending public gatherings, and view strangers with trepidation. Wesley G. Skogan and Michael G. Maxfield quote a black woman from South Philadelphia:

> People used to sit on their steps in the evening, doors were open. Now the streets are deserted early in the morning and after dark. My mother used to go to church every morning—she stopped doing it—she is afraid of having her purse snatched. Many church and social activities have stopped—people won't go out at night.[23]

We know that when people talk about such fears, they are talking about street crime and particularly about being victimized by strangers. Robbery is perhaps the crime that citizens have uppermost in mind when they talk about their fears, for it is the violent crime most often committed by strangers (76 percent). But people are also apprehensive about being victimized by criminals when no face-to-face confrontation occurs. Burglary, a property crime without violence, is also fear-provoking because "victims are conscious that there *could* have been a physical confrontation within the intimate setting of their household."[24]

Correlates of fear

What are the individual and social characteristics of fear? One would expect to find a strong relationship between victimization and fearfulness. Surprisingly, with the exception of crime victims who have experienced personal offenses—rape, robbery, mugging—victims in general are no more fearful than nonvictims. Victims of personal offenses have a heightened level of fear, yet a crime of this sort is a rare event in anyone's life (see table 1.4). People evidently do not assess criminal victimization in the same ways that they do other risks, such as those caused by nature or by accident. Most research also shows high levels of fear among nonwhites, people of low income, and those living in urban areas. This finding is not surprising, given the concentration of street crime in sections of cities inhabited by the poor and the nonwhite. Women and the elderly, however—groups that generally have low

TABLE 1.4 How do crime rates compare with the rates of other life events?

Events	*Rate per 1,000 adults per year*
Accidental injury, all circumstances	290
Accidental injury at home	105
Personal theft	82
Accidental injury at work	68
Violent victimization	33
Assault (aggravated and simple)	25
Injury in motor vehicle accident	23
Divorce	23
Death, all cases	11
Serious (aggravated) assault	9
Death of spouse	9
Robbery	7
Heart disease death	4
Cancer death	2
Rape (women only)	2
Accidental death, all circumstances	0.5
Motor vehicle accident death	0.3
Pneumonia/influenza death	0.3
Suicide	0.2
Injury from fire	0.1
Homicide/legal intervention death	0.1
Death from fire	0.03

Source: U.S. Department of Justice, Bureau of Justice Statistics, *Report to the Nation on Crime and Justice* (Washington, D.C.: Government Printing Office, 1983), p. 18.

rates of victimization—are also more frightened than the average citizen.

How do we account for the fearfulness of social groups that have not experienced victimization and do not observe crime in their neighborhoods? Skogan and Maxfield point to vicarious or indirect victimization as an explanation. Some scholars believe that television viewing shapes attitudes in regard to crime. Other researchers think that personal communications networks report and materially magnify the apparent volume of local violence. In all American cities there is extensive newspaper and television coverage of crime and much publicizing of violence. Skogan and Maxfield found that people in low- and high-income neighborhoods were equally attentive to crime stories, but the two researchers place greater weight on interpersonal communication as a factor influencing levels of fear. They write: "Like media coverage of crime, the processes which lead victims' stories of their experience to 'get around' seem to accentuate the apparent volume of personal as opposed to property crime."[25] In particular, television reports and neighborhood conversations focus on and amplify crimes against women and the elderly, two groups perceived as vulnerable. Accounts about the old, frail, and otherwise defenseless who have been victimized seem to heighten perceptions that criminals are rampant.

Although white Americans are fearful of being victimized by black strangers, most violent crime is intraracial; three of every four victims are of the same race as the attacker, as figure 1.3 indicates. Similarly with property crimes: most victims and offenders are of the same race and economic group. Because social and economic factors largely determine where people live, work, and seek recreation, the same factors also influence the probability of coming into close proximity with members of other groups. Blacks and the

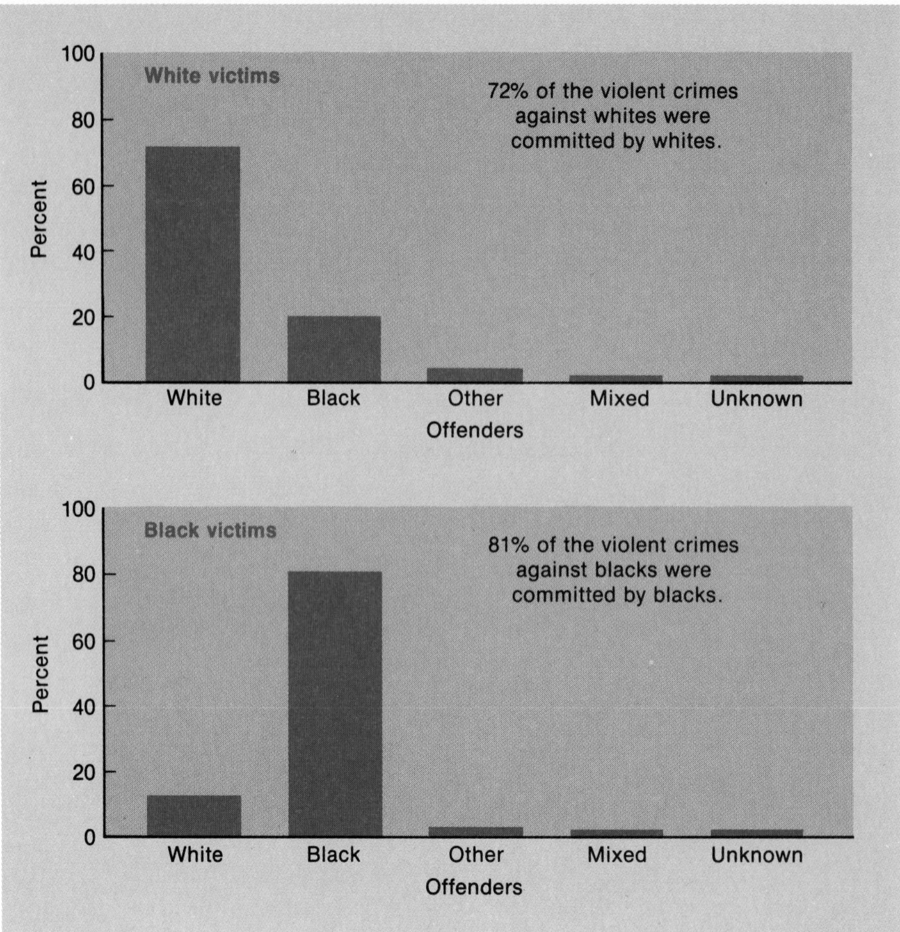

FIGURE 1.3
Victims and offenders are of the same race in three out of four violent crimes.

poor thus bear a disproportionate risk of being victimized, for most are likely to live in the inner-city zones where street crime is greatest.

Responses to fear of crime

What do people do as a result of their fear of crime? As suggested earlier, many take what they believe are precautions by curtailing activities that they think may place them in a dangerous situation. Others may attempt to reduce potential property loss by "target hardening": installing more locks, window grilles, and alarms—systems of one kind or another that turn the home into a fortress. Those who can afford to do so may take refuge in apartment houses or residential enclaves that offer continuous surveillance, doormen or gatekeepers, and patrols. Still others flee to the suburbs or to the countryside, where it seems to them that crime is not a problem.

Most responses to the fear of crime are costly and require adjustments in lifestyle. It is obvious that the economically better off are able to take steps that will help to alleviate their fear and that the poor must endure theirs. It is paradoxical that those who are most vulnerable are also those least able to respond in ways that have a tempering effect.

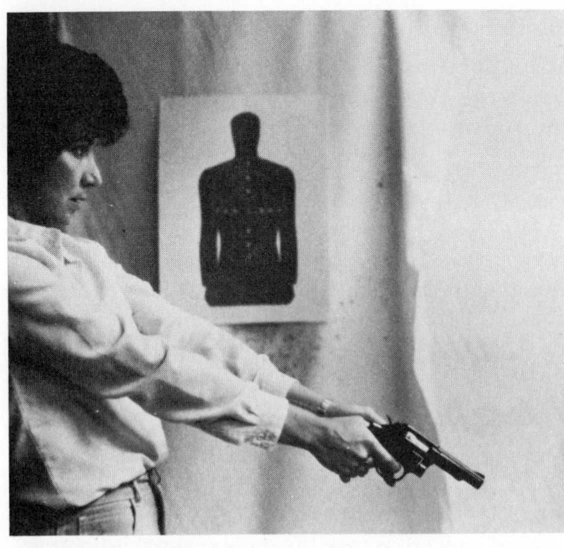

Fear of crime may lead to dramatic personal adjustments.

Criminal justice in America

As crime has increased, the system of criminal justice has been unable to handle the demands made upon it. In an oft-cited 1906 speech titled "The Causes of Dissatisfaction with the Administration of Justice," Roscoe Pound warned that a judicial system created within the framework of a rural America could not meet the needs of an urban society. In 1931 the Wickersham Commission reported that its national survey indicated a need for major reforms in the criminal justice system. It noted that the police were often ineffective in enforcing the law, that the courts were dispensing assembly-line justice, and that the resources allocated to the system were inadequate. More recently, the report of the President's Commission on Law Enforcement and Administration of Justice sounded the same theme: ineffectiveness, assembly-line justice, and inadequate resources. In spite of these warnings, little modernization of the criminal justice system has occurred in this century. The result is that the problems persist.

Effectiveness

Of the 11 million serious crimes reported annually to the nation's law enforcement agencies, barely one in nine results in a conviction. The solution rate varies among crimes. Of the people arrested for murder, which is usually reported and 86 percent of the time leads to an arrest, only 64 percent are prosecuted and 43 percent convicted. Of people arrested for burglary, which leads to an arrest in only 19 percent of reported cases, four out of five are prosecuted, and 56 percent of these are found guilty. These figures mean that for every twelve burglaries reported there is only one conviction. The data may be explained in large part by the nature of the crimes and the difficulty of a successful response by law enforcement agencies. An additional consideration is that unlike the police and courts in an authoritarian governmental system, those in a democracy must act within the law and uphold the civil rights of the accused.

assembly-line justice
The operation of any segment of the criminal justice system with such speed and impersonality that defendants are treated as objects to be processed rather than as individuals.

Assembly-line justice

Assembly-line justice is one highly visible result of our neglect of the criminal justice system. It can be seen in the heavy caseloads processed by metropolitan courts and in the attempt by harassed and overworked staffs to handle cases on a mass-production basis.

> If one enters the courthouse in any sizeable city and walks from courtroom to courtroom, what does he see? One judge, in a single morning, is accepting pleas of guilty from and sentencing a hundred or more persons charged with drunkenness. Another judge is adjudicating traffic cases with an average time of no more than a minute per case. A third is disposing of a hundred or more other misdemeanor offenses in a morning, by granting delays, accepting pleas of guilty and imposing sentences.[26]

For the most part, little attention is paid to the defendants as people. Rather, they are cases to be processed, items on court schedules to be moved.

The number of court officials and the size of facilities have been based on the premise that up to 90 percent of defendants will plead guilty. Lawyers have learned that court congestion can be turned to their clients' advantage: acceptance of guilty pleas to reduced charges and even outright dismissal of charges become attractive alternatives to jury trials when lawyers avail their clients of all the procedural delays the law permits. By invoking due process criteria—that is, the rights that ensure the accused will be prosecuted and tried according to law—lawyers may upset the fine balance that keeps the justice system in equilibrium. Demands for hearings and other formal procedures provided by the law slow down the process and often create turmoil in courts that must dispose of cases as quickly as possible to prevent a backlog of untried defendants. Cases that are delayed usually weaken prosecution efforts, since evidence becomes "stale," witnesses are lost, and public interest lapses. The resulting advantage most often falls to the wealthy, who are able to employ aggressive counsel. Court congestion may seriously impede the due process rights of the poor and less fortunate.

Disposition of Felony Cases

- The most common fate of an arrest for a serious crime is outright dismissal. Roughly 50% to 70% of felony arrests are either refused prosecution or dismissed before trial.
- One of the two principal reasons for this high case mortality is that police officers are not trained in how to collect evidence and lack incentives for making "quality" arrests, i.e., arrests that can stand up in court.
- The other major reason for case mortality is that lay witnesses and victims are not interviewed promptly and, lacking adequate communications, fail to show up when they are supposed to.
- There is a subset of defendants in the courts who are professional or career criminals, who are engaged in such crimes as robbery, burglary, and larceny, and who appear before the same court 10 to 20 times in a decade for different crimes.
- Cases against "career criminals" are just as likely to be dismissed as are cases against other defendants.
- As a medium for disposing of cases in court, trials are statistically insignificant. Except for outright dismissals, the most common medium is a plea bargain.

Source: Reprinted from William A. Hamilton, "Highlights of PROMIS Research," in *The Prosecutor*, ed. William F. McDonald, p. 127, © 1979 Sage Publications, Inc., with permission.

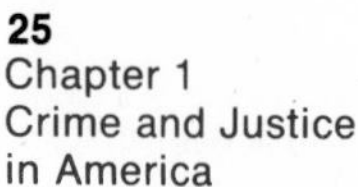

An assembly-line approach to justice results in diminished respect for the system.

The 1982 federal census of city and county jails showed that 60 percent of the inmates had not been convicted but were awaiting the next step in the disposition of their cases.[27] In many cities where defense counsel has been provided for poor defendants, the percentage who plead guilty has been reduced, thereby necessitating a proportional increase in the number of trials, judges, and other court personnel. In Washington, D.C., when the percentage of guilty pleas dropped from 90 to 65, the number of judges working on the criminal calendar had to be quadrupled.[28]

To cope with these pressures, the legal system has placed greater emphasis upon administrative decision making in the pretrial period, when the primary objective of law officials is to screen out cases that do not contain the elements necessary for speedy prosecution and conviction. In a democratic society, administrative practices often create a conflict between the need for order and civil liberties. Maintenance of this sensitive pairing is subject to political influences because various groups hold different conceptions of the rights and duties of judicial actors. The defendant is often

---

Assembly-line Justice

Inside the Manhattan arraignment room, where the defendants' bench is shared by prostitutes, men charged with murder, and youths accused of purse snatching, people are arraigned at the rate of 40 to 50 an hour. Some get 16 seconds—prostitutes and gamblers mostly, whose cases are often dismissed; others get three or four minutes—the "hard cases," a clerk explains. Lawyers stand before the judge and hold hurried, whispered conferences with the district attorney; almost always, they waive their clients' right to a reading of the charges.

Source: *New York Times,* 11 May 1970, p. 29. © 1975 by The New York Times Company. Reprinted by permission.

---

caught between demands for order and the inadequacies of the criminal justice machinery.

Inadequate resources

Too often law enforcement, court, and corrections personnel have not been given the resources to fulfill the constitutional obligation of establishing justice and ensuring domestic tranquillity. Until recently, the number and quality of criminal justice personnel were often inadequate for the job. Police officers were poorly paid, court employees were political appointees, and most courthouses and jails were products of the nineteenth century.

The revolts at New York's Attica Correctional Facility (1971) and the New Mexico State Prison (1980) helped to focus public attention on the most neglected part of America's criminal justice system: corrections. Although conditions in many prisons are at the level of pre-Civil War standards, the fact that up to 65 percent of adult felons are again arrested has earned these institutions the label "universities of crime." The idea of rehabilitation rather than punishment has long been a hallmark of our correctional system, yet too often the resources to prevent offenders from returning through the criminal justice revolving door do not appear to exist.

The problem of the criminal justice system has been described by former attorney general Ramsey Clark.

> If police are not effective in preventing crime, prosecution, courts, and prisons are flooded. If police fail to solve crimes, prosecutions cannot proceed and courts cannot do justice—the rest of the system never has its chance. . . . If courts have backlogs and are unable to reach criminal cases for many months, burdens are placed on police. . . . Prosecution offices face the difficult task of keeping up with witnesses. . . . Jails will be overcrowded with defendants who are not released pending trial. Additional burdens on manpower and facilities are costly, but more costly still is the loss of deterrent effect through delay.[29]

Why has the diagnosis of American justice ills been repeated so frequently without apparent change in the patient's condition? Certainly we have the resources to minimize crime while maintaining the rule of law and the rights of citizens if we really wanted to do so. Is it because public attention has been focused on other issues, such as the environment? Is it because criminal behavior is thought mainly to affect the lower class and therefore the system is not worthy of reform? Is it because the criminal justice bureaucracy has been able to withstand the pressures for change? These questions must be addressed by the makers of public policy. More important, they are questions that should concern all citizens, and they should be of special concern to those who plan careers in criminal justice.

nolo contendere A defendant's formal answer in court in which it is stated that the charges are not contested and which, while not an admission of guilt, subjects the defendant to the same sentencing consequences as a plea of guilty. Often used to preclude civil action against the accused by the victim.

Politics and criminal justice

The vice-president of the United States resigns after a plea of ***nolo contendere*** to charges of income tax evasion. Public officials in "Wincanton, U.S.A."[30] and "Rainfall West"[31] allow gambling syndicates to flourish in return for kickbacks and other favors. A "contribution" of up to $80,000 to the party is the key variable in the awarding of a judgeship in New York City.[32] The secretary of labor in the Reagan administration is indicted by Mario Merola, Democratic district attorney of the Bronx, on charges of grand larceny, falsification of documents, and filing of false documents.[33] In response to demands from owners of businesses, the police agree to keep vagrants and prostitutes on skid row and away from the "better" hotels. Felony charges against a prominent attorney are dropped as a result of pressures on the prosecutor. Candidates for public office use the issue of law and order to gain votes. A city council increases the budget of the police while cutting back on appropriations for social services.

Although the relationship between law and politics has been recognized since ancient times, these dramatic illustrations reawaken us to the fact that the administration of criminal justice does not accord with an image of justice in which the rule of law prevails and equal treatment is accorded each person. Like all legal institutions, the criminal justice system is political—that is, it is engaged in the formulation and administration of public policies in which choices must be made among such competing values as the rights of defendants, protection of persons and property, justice, and freedom. That various groups in society interpret these values differently is obvious. Decisions result from the influence of the political power of decision makers and the relative strengths of competing elites (persons regarded as most powerful or influential). Criminal justice personnel are engaged in the determination of policy in the same sense as are other governmental decision makers whose positions are generally perceived as political. Broadly conceived ***political considerations*** explain to a large extent who gets or does not get—in what amount, and how—the "good" (justice) that is produced by the legal system in the setting of the local community.

political considerations
Matters taken into account in the formulation of public policies and the making of choices among competing values—who gets what portion of the good (justice) produced by the system, when, and how.

The administration of criminal justice is complicated by the fact that laws are often ambiguous, full enforcement of them is both impossible and undesirable, and many still on the books no longer have public support. The result is somewhat of a selective process in which legal actors are given a wide range of discretionary powers to determine who will be arrested, on what charges they will be prosecuted, and how their cases will be administered. Because these decisions are made on a daily basis within the context of the local community, the political aspects of the system are heightened.

Aside from the pervasiveness of politics in the administration of justice, political considerations exist in specific ways throughout the system. That political parties are a weighty ingredient in the recruitment of judges, prosecutors, and other legal personnel has long been recognized. In many American cities the road to a judgeship is paved with tasks performed for the party. Prosecuting attorneys are also recognized as important political actors. Because of their power of discretion and their political ties and obligations, prosecutors are pivotal figures with ties to both the internal politics of the justice system and the local political organizations.

Criminal justice and the community

In many ways the administration of criminal justice is a community affair. Although the FBI is much in the news, the national government plays a relatively minor role in the broad perspective of criminal justice. Most ***crimes*** are violations of state laws, but enforcement is left to a multitude of local-level

crime
A specific act of commission or omission in violation of the law for which a punishment is prescribed.

agencies that have wide discretionary powers so that they may tailor their actions to be consistent with community norms. Most states have no special unit to coordinate activities among law enforcement officials. In any case, the independent election or appointment of judges implies that state appellate courts have little formal authority over the lower trial courts that are staffed by local judges.

Contemporary evidence of the influence of community norms on the machinery of criminal justice may be found by comparing the dispositions of criminal cases in a variety of cities or by contrasting sentences handed out by judges in small towns with those given in metropolitan areas. What rural judges may perceive as crime waves are often viewed as routine by their urban counterparts. Criminal definitions are applied by members of society who have the power to shape the enforcement and administration of criminal law. But it should also be stressed that laws are applied by persons within the context of local conditions.

It is at the local level that people have contact with the legal process. Although most citizens will never appear in court or at the police station, their perception of the quality of justice will greatly affect their willingness to abide by the community's laws. Robert Kennedy noted that "the poor man looks upon the law as an enemy, not as a friend. For him the law is always taking something away."[34] Thus if people widely assume, for example, that the police can be bribed, that certain groups are singled out for harsh treatment, or that lawbreaking will not result in punishment of offenders, the system will lose much of its influence over their behavior. As Roscoe Pound once said, criminal law "must safeguard the general security and the individual life against abuse of criminal procedure while at the same time making that procedure as effective as possible for the securing of the whole scheme of social interests."[35]

Crime control versus due process

Organizations do not exist in a limbo, untouched by the political and social environment. The behavior of criminal justice decision makers is influenced by the administrative structure and also by the values of the American culture. These norms provide legitimacy and justification for the ways criminal behavior is controlled and defendants' cases are judged. Given the organizational context of decision making, what are the goals or values that provide the foundation for the criminal justice system? How do these values influence the police officers, attorneys, and judges who must function within this administrative process? Does an understanding of the social norms underlying criminal justice help us to analyze the activities that lead to the disposition of cases?

Ideally, one might hope to be able to describe a consistent and interrelated set of values that is the rationale for decision making, but such a description does not seem to be possible in the case of the justice system. In such cases, scholars often use models to organize their thinking about a subject and to guide their research, since models are ideal types that clearly characterize the values and goals that underlie a system. In one of the most important recent contributions to systematic thought on the administration of criminal justice, Herbert Packer describes two competing schemes: the Crime Control Model and the Due Process Model.[36] Packer's models are two ways of looking at the goals and procedures of the criminal justice system; they represent

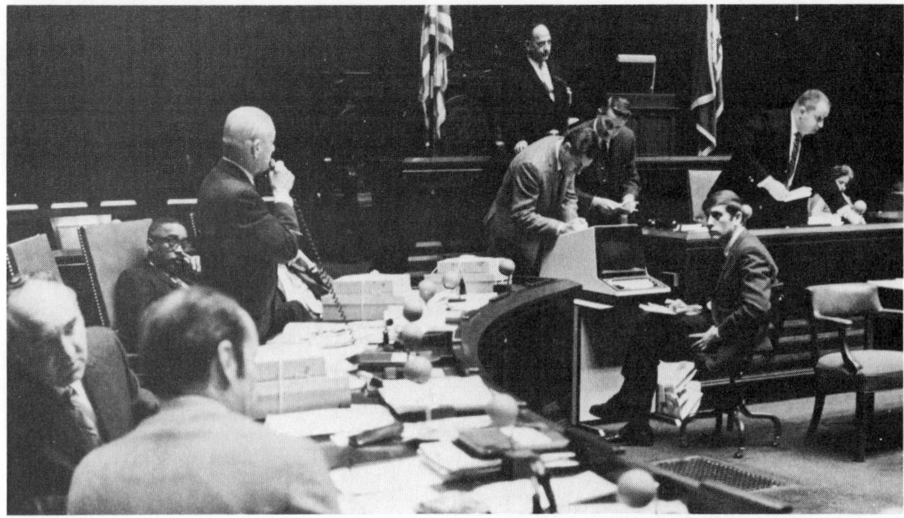

Legislatures define crimes and set penalties in response to political influence.

opposing views of how the criminal law *ought* to operate. He likens the Crime Control Model to an assembly line and the Due Process Model to an obstacle course and describes his models as polar extremes, the end points of a continuum.

Packer does recognize that the administration of criminal justice operates within the contemporary American society and is therefore influenced by cultural forces that in turn determine the models' usefulness. In addition, no one actor or law enforcement subsystem functions totally in accordance with either of the models; elements of both are found throughout the system. The values expressed within the two models describe the tensions within the process.

Crime control: order as a value

Underlying the ***Crime Control Model*** is the proposition that the repression of criminal conduct is the most important function to be performed by the criminal justice system. Law enforcement's failure to control criminals is thought to bring about the breakdown of public order and thus the disappearance of human freedom. If there is a general disregard for laws, the law-abiding citizen is more likely to become a victim of the criminal. As Packer points out, to achieve liberty for all citizens to interact freely as members of society, the Crime Control Model requires that primary attention be paid to efficiency in screening suspects, determining guilt, and applying appropriate sanctions to the convicted.

Crime Control Model A model of the criminal justice system that assumes that freedom is so important that every effort must be made to repress crime; emphasizes efficiency and the capacity to apprehend, try, convict, and dispose of a high proportion of offenders, and also stresses speed and finality.

In the context of this model, efficiency of operation requires that the system have the capacity to apprehend, try, convict, and dispose of a high proportion of criminal offenders whose offenses become known. Because of the magnitude of criminal behavior and the limited resources given to law enforcement agencies, emphasis must be placed on speed and finality. Accordingly, there must be a high rate of arrests, sifting out of the innocent, and conviction of offenders, all of which depends on informality, uniformity, and the minimizing of occasions for challenge. Hence probable guilt is administratively determined primarily on the basis of the police investigation, and those cases unlikely to end in conviction are filtered out. At each successive stage, from arrest to preliminary hearing, arraignment, and courtroom trial, a series of routinized procedures is used by a variety of judicial actors to determine whether the accused should be passed on to the next level. Rather than stressing the combative elements of the courtroom, this model notes that bargaining between the state and the accused occurs at several points. The ritual of the courtroom is enacted in only a small number of cases; the rest are disposed of through negotiations over the charges and usually end with defendants' pleas of guilty. Thus Packer likens decision making under the Crime Control Model to an assembly-line process. That is, an endless stream of cases moves past system actors standing at fixed stations and performing the small but essential operations that successively bring each case closer to being the finished product, a closed file.

Due process: law as a value

Due Process Model
A model of the criminal justice system that assumes that freedom is so important that every effort must be made to ensure that criminal justice decisions are based on reliable information; emphasizes the adversarial process, the rights of defendants, and formal decision-making procedures.

If the Crime Control Model looks like an assembly line, the ***Due Process Model*** resembles an obstacle course. Although likewise valuing human freedom, the Due Process Model questions the reliability of fact finding. Because people are notoriously poor observers of disturbing events, the possibility of the police and prosecutors, the main Crime Control Model decision makers, committing a wrong is very high. Persons should be termed criminal and deprived of their freedom only on the basis of reliable information. To minimize error, hurdles must be erected so that the power of government can be used against the accused only when it has been proven beyond doubt that the defendant committed the crime in question. The best method to determine guilt or innocence is to test the evidence through an adversarial proceeding. Hence the model assumes that persons are innocent until proved guilty, that they have the opportunity to discredit the cases brought against them, and that an impartial judge and jury are provided to decide the outcome. The assumption that the defendant is innocent until proved guilty is emphasized by Packer as having a far-reaching impact on the criminal justice system.

The models stress two very different kinds of guilt: legal and factual. Factual guilt is what people usually mean when they ask, "Did he do it?"—that is, is the person guilty of the crime as charged? Legal guilt, however, involves more than the factual situation—can the state prove in a procedurally regular manner and by lawful authority that the person is guilty of the crime as charged? Judicial actors must therefore prove their cases under various procedural restraints dealing with the admissibility of evidence, the burden of proof, the requirement that guilt be proved beyond a reasonable doubt, and so forth—in short, the person did in fact commit the crime. Forcing the state to prove its case in an adjudicative context functions to protect the citizens from undeserved criminal sanction. In the Due Process Model, the possibility that a few who may be factually guilty will remain free outweighs the possibilities in the Crime Control Model for governmental power to be abused, the innocent to be incarcerated, and society's freedom to be endangered. Table 1.5 compares the basic elements of the two models that lead to these views.

TABLE 1.5 Due Process Model and Crime Control Model compared

	Goal	*Value*	*Process*	*Major decision point*	*Basis of decision making*
Due Process Model	Preserve individual liberties	Reliability	Adversarial	Courtroom	Law
Crime Control Model	Repress crime	Efficiency	Administrative	Police, pretrial processes	Discretion

Reality: crime control or due process?

The public's idea of democracy probably leads to an understanding of the criminal justice system in accordance with the ideals of the Due Process Model. According to this view, principles, not personal discretion, control the actions of police officers, judges, and prosecutors. Criminal justice is thus seen as an ongoing, mechanical process in which violations of laws are discovered, defendants are indicted, and punishments are imposed with little reference either to the organizational needs of the system or to the personalization of justice. This perspective gives little opportunity for discretion in the criminal justice machine, and any attempt to induce flexibility must be carried out *sub rosa*.

Unlike the values expressed in the Due Process Model, in which decisions are made in the courtroom as a result of adversarial conflict, the reality of criminal justice in America is more comparable to the Crime Control Model, in which guilt is administratively determined early in the process and cases are disposed of through negotiation. Rather than emphasis on discovering the truth so that the innocent may be separated from the guilty, the assumption here is that those arrested by the police have committed *some* criminal act. Accordingly, efforts are made to select a charge to which the accused will plead guilty and that will result in an appropriate sentence.

If someone from a foreign country should ask you to describe the way the criminal justice process functions, what would you say? Which of the value models would you use in your explanation?

Summary

Law enforcement and the administration of justice are problems high on the agenda of national priorities. Events of the 1960s awakened Americans to the fact that not only was crime increasing but the forces of law and justice were encountering obstacles in achieving their goals. Even though crime victimization appeared to level off after 1973 and the number of reported crimes began to decline in 1979, the public remains upset by this major social problem. The fear of crime continues to haunt American citizens and causes them to live in ways that restrict their freedoms. Today, as a result of the extensive research carried on during the past two decades, we have a greater understanding of crime and the administration of justice. Many of the assumptions about criminals held by social scientists in the 1960s have been proved to be naive—the problem is much more complicated than was believed at the time.

This chapter has discussed some of the key dimensions of the crime problem in the United States. It has been recognized that crime control is a pressing public policy issue, though measurement of the extent of crime and the reasons for the persistence of high crime rates are not so clear-cut. Although both the *Uniform Crime Reports* of the FBI and the National Crime Surveys have methodological problems, they are still the best sources of information. Chapter 1 has also examined some of the problems of the criminal justice system, particularly questions of effectiveness, the concept of assembly-line justice, and the lack of adequate resources. It has been emphasized that criminal justice operates in a political arena greatly influenced by public opinion, community elites, and competition among differing perspectives.

Two ways of conceptualizing the criminal justice system are described in the Due Process Model and Crime Control Model. These analytic tools help us to focus attention in such a way that we can understand the reasons for decisions concerning the disposition of cases. As one scholar has written:

> It is in the day-to-day practices and policies of the processing agencies that the law is put into effect and it is out of the struggle to perform their tasks in ways which maximize rewards and minimize strains for the organization and the individuals involved that the legal processing agencies shape the law.[37]

This book shows the links among law, politics, and administration in the criminal justice system. This first chapter has introduced the problem and set the direction for the discussions that follow.

For discussion

1. Increased criminal activity seems to come to the attention of the American people at different periods. Is this because more crime is being committed or are other social forces creating this impression?
2. For many years criminal justice resources were neglected. What social and political influences have brought about greater attention to the system?
3. We are most troubled by visible crime. Why?
4. If you had the power and resources to make improvements in America's criminal justice system, what would you do? Why? What values would be enhanced by your decision?
5. What is the major crime problem in your community? What could be done to reduce or eliminate it?

For further reading

Cameron, Mary O. *The Booster and the Snitch.* Glencoe, Ill.: Free Press, 1964.
Clark, Ramsey. *Crime in America.* New York: Simon & Schuster, 1970.
Gardiner, John A. *The Politics of Corruption: Organized Crime in an American City.* New York: Russell Sage Foundation, 1970.
Jackson, Bruce. *A Thief's Primer.* New York: Macmillan, 1969.
Packer, Herbert L. *The Limits of the Criminal Sanction.* Stanford: Stanford University Press, 1968.
President's Commission on Law Enforcement and Administration of Justice. *The Challenge of Crime in a Free Society.* Washington, D.C.: Government Printing Office, 1967.
Silberman, Charles. *Criminal Violence, Criminal Justice.* New York: Random House, 1978.

Notes

1. National Advisory Commission on Criminal Justice Standards and Goals, *A National Strategy to Reduce Crime* (Washington, D.C.: Government Printing Office, 1973), p. 1.
2. U.S. Department of Justice, *Justice Assistance News,* 2 November 1981, p. 1.
3. President's Commission on Law Enforcement and Administration of Justice, *The Challenge of Crime in a Free Society* (Washington, D.C.: Government Printing Office, 1967), pp. v–x.
4. Robert Martinson, "What Works? Questions and Answers about Prison Reform," *Public Interest* 35 (Spring 1974): 22.

5. Alfred Blumstein, Jacqueline Cohen, and Daniel Nagen, eds., *Deterrence and Incapacitation: Estimating the Effects of Criminal Sanctions on Crime Rates* (Washington, D.C.: National Academy of Sciences, 1978).
6. U.S. Department of Justice, Administrative Office of the Courts, *The Third Branch,* 13 September 1981, p. 1.
7. Comprehensive Crime Control Act of 1984 (H.R. 5963; S. 1762).
8. *New York Times,* 15 October 1984, p. B6.
9. Emile Durkheim, *The Division of Labor in Society,* trans. George Simpson (Glencoe, Ill.: Free Press, 1960), p. 102.
10. James M. Buckley, "The Present Epidemic of Crime," *Century Magazine,* November 1903, p. 150.
11. President's Commission on Law Enforcement and Administration of Justice, *Crime and Its Impact: An Assessment* (Washington, D.C.: Government Printing Office, 1967), p. 19.
12. U.S. Department of Justice, Bureau of Justice Statistics, *Bulletin,* November 1981, p. 1.
13. Wesley Skogan, "Citizen Reporting of Crime," *Criminology* 13 (February 1976): 538.
14. U.S. Department of Justice, *Crime in the United States* (Washington, D.C.: Government Printing Office, 1984), p. 143.
15. *Criminal Justice Newsletter,* 2 July 1984, p. 7.
16. Ibid.
17. Norval Morris and Gordon Hawkins, *The Honest Politician's Guide to Crime Control* (Chicago: University of Chicago Press, 1970), p. 202.
18. Thomas O'Toole, "Crime Rate Spiraling in All Cities at Almost Same Rate, Study Says," *Hartford Courtant,* 5 March 1982, p. A3.
19. Ibid.
20. Ibid.
21. Sir Leon Radzinowicz and Joan King, *The Growth of Crime* (New York: Basic Books, 1977), p. 3.
22. Wesley G. Skogan, "On Attitudes and Behaviors," in *Reactions to Crime,* ed. Dan A. Lewis (Beverly Hills, Calif.: Sage, 1981), p. 29.
23. Wesley G. Skogan and Michael G. Maxfield, *Coping with Crime* (Beverly Hills, Calif.: Sage, 1981), p. 48.
24. Ibid., p. 50.
25. Ibid., p. 157.
26. Edward L. Barrett, Jr., "Criminal Justice: The Problem of Mass Production," in *The Courts, the Public, and the Law Explosion,* ed. Harry W. Jones (Englewood Cliffs, N.J.: Prentice-Hall, 1965), p. 87.
27. U.S. Department of Justice, Bureau of Justice Statistics, *Bulletin,* February 1983, p. 1.
28. Warren E. Burger, "State of the Federal Judiciary," *American Bar Association Journal* 56 (1970), p. 929.
29. Ramsey Clark, *Crime in America* (New York: Simon & Schuster, 1970), p. 120.
30. President's Commission on Law Enforcement and Administration of Justice, *Task Force Report: Organized Crime* (Washington, D.C.: Government Printing Office, 1967), p. 94.
31. William J. Chambliss, "Vice, Corruption, Bureaucracy, and Power," *Wisconsin Law Review* 1150 (1971).
32. Martin Tolchin and Susan Tolchin, *To the Victor* (New York: Random House, 1971), p. 145.
33. *New York Times,* 3 October 1984, p. 1.
34. As quoted in James R. Klonoski and Robert Mendelsohn, eds., *The Politics of Local Justice* (Boston: Little, Brown, 1970), p. xxi.
35. Roscoe Pound, *Criminal Justice in America* (New York: Henry Holt, 1930), p. 11.
36. Herbert L. Packer, *The Limits of the Criminal Sanction* (Stanford: Stanford University Press, 1968). For a critique, see John Griffiths, "Ideology in Criminal Procedure or a Third 'Model' of the Criminal Process," *Yale Law Journal* 79 (1970): 359.
37. William Chambliss, ed., *Crime and the Legal Process* (New York: McGraw-Hill, 1969), p. 86.

Defining and Understanding Criminal Behavior

Sources of criminal law
- Consensus: law as an expression of values
  - *Consensus in Puritan Massachusetts*
- Conflict: law as an expression of political power
  - *Conflict in fourteenth-century England*
- Consensus versus conflict: emerging theories

Causes of crime
- Biopsychological explanations
  - *Psychological theory*
- Sociological explanations
  - *Structural theory*
  - *Differential association theory*
  - *Labeling theory*
- Critical criminology
- Victimology
- Female criminals

Types of crimes
- Upperworld crimes
- Organized crime
- Visible crimes
- Crimes without victims
- Political crimes

Too much law?
- Drunkenness
- Prostitution
- Gambling
- Reform

Legislative process and the law
- Interest groups
  - *Interest groups and the law of prostitution*

Summary

2

Rape. The very harshness of the word conveys the violence of the deed and the intensity of the fear and disgust with which society has traditionally viewed this crime. From ancient times, when developing cultures first became concerned about the purity of bloodlines and regulations were created to govern sexual relationships, rape has been a taboo that has evolved into an offense formally labeled by criminal law.

Crime is . . . necessary; it is bound up with the fundamental conditions of all social life, and by that very fact it is useful, because these conditions of which it is a part are themselves indispensable to the normal evolution of morality and law.
EMILE DURKHEIM

Although forcible rape is generally understood to be sexual intercourse by a male with a female who is not his wife against her will and under conditions of threat or force, different countries have variously defined the offense and stipulated the penalties. In England, the woman's consent is no defense if consent was obtained by force.[1] Some state legislatures have recently changed their penal codes to allow wives to accuse their husbands of rape. In some areas of the world rape is not charged if certain classes of women are involved. Robert A. Levine reports that forcible rape is an accepted form of sex relations for unmarried males among the Gusii, a large tribe in Kenya.[2] In Western countries a distinction is often made among rape, forcible rape, and statutory rape, on the basis of such factors as the age of the female, the level of force employed, and the nature of the sexual conduct. Until recently, death was the penalty prescribed for the offense of forcible rape in many American states; life imprisonment is now stipulated in thirty states, although most convicted rapists serve fewer than ten years in prison. Before the rise of the Women's Movement, some states required that the victim's word be confirmed by evidence provided by some other person, and defense counsel could make reference to the victim's past sexual conduct.

Why does the law of rape take the shape it does? Why does the criminal justice system treat rape differently from other assaults? Is something more involved here than the intensity of fear and disgust with which society has traditionally viewed this crime? Are the law's sanctions intended to ensure the maintenance of pure bloodlines? To uphold the sanctity of a husband's "property"? Or is rape a special case because the crime violates the victim's personhood?

The variety of definitions, evidential requirements, and penalties for rape helps to focus the text of this chapter. Societies in various places and at different times have attempted to deal with the problem of crime. Before we can explain the agencies and processes of the criminal justice system, we must first look at the sources of the criminal law, examine theories as to the causes of criminal behavior, and understand the typologies that serve to differentiate crime. An important point to remember is that laws are written by humans and emerge from human experience. Thus disagreements often occur concerning the exact nature of laws defining behavior as criminal. This is especially true in a heterogeneous society in which some groups may not believe that certain behaviors require the criminal sanction while other groups may wish to use the law to maintain the status quo.

Sources of criminal law

Many students ask, "Why is it illegal for me to smoke marijuana but legal for me to consume alcohol?" If the answer is that marijuana might be addictive, could lead to the use of more potent drugs, and is generally thought to be detrimental to health, the student may point out that alcoholism is a major social problem, that drinking beer may whet one's thirst for hard liquor, and that heart and liver disorders, not to mention highway fatalities, are caused by overindulgence in alcohol. If the argument persists, an exasperated "clincher" might be "Because pot smoking is against the law, and that's that!"

Why does the law declare some types of human behavior criminal and not others? What social forces are brought to bear on legislators as they write the criminal code? Why are activities that are labeled criminal during one era found to be acceptable in another? Why is the personal use of marijuana legal in some states but prohibited in others? Such issues need discussing because a theory explaining the sources of the criminal law will have an important impact on assumptions concerning the nature of crime and the sources of criminal behavior.

Why is it illegal to smoke marijuana?

For much of our history we have tended to think of crime as pertaining only to criminals rather than to other units of society. Most Americans do not separate the concept of crime from that of criminal or believe that criminals are separate from the mainstream of society. In Puritan Massachusetts, crime was viewed in theological terms and the criminal was thus considered a creature of the devil. Most provisions of the Puritans' legal code bore notations showing their biblical source. In a later era, the medically oriented professions saw crime as arising from some inherited abnormality. Psychologists in the nineteenth and twentieth centuries, for example, described crime as resulting from mental or personality defects. More recently, sociologists have looked to social situations—neighborhood, school, gang, family—as determining whether persons will be law-abiding citizens or criminals. Throughout these approaches runs the idea that criminality is a characteristic of the person and not a consequence of a label imposed by the community.

A most important point to recognize is that the definition of behavior as criminal stems from a social process and may have little to do with the individual criminal. Social groups create deviance by making the rules whose infraction constitutes deviance and by applying those rules to particular people and labeling them as outsiders. This means that in addition to the person who commits a crime, there must first be a community and a process by which the commission of that act has come to be called criminal. Second, someone must have observed the act or its consequences and applied the community's definition to it. Third, a crime implies a victim. Finally, punishment implies that someone is responsible for carrying out the community's will. Labeling behavior as criminal is thus a social phenomenon that arises from the complex interactions of a number of persons and social institutions. The criminal law is one manifestation of this social and political process.

A number of theories have been developed to explain the focus and functions of criminal laws and the social processes by which they evolve. These ideas may be divided into a consensus model and a conflict model. The ***consensus model*** argues that the criminal law reflects the will or values of society. The conflict model emphasizes the role of political interests in the formulation of the law and points to the dominance of powerful groups in the structuring of law to meet their own needs.

consensus model A legal model that asserts that the criminal law, as an expression of the social consciousness of the whole society, reflects values that transcend the immediate interests of particular groups and individuals.

Consensus: law as an expression of values

The value-consensus position basically is that the criminal law reflects societal values that go beyond the immediate interests of particular groups and individuals and is thus an expression of the social consciousness of the whole society. From this perspective, legal norms (the laws) emerge through the dynamics of cultural processes to meet certain needs and requirements that are essential for maintaining the social fabric. As Jerome Hall, a leading exponent of this approach, has said, "Criminal law represents a sustained effort to preserve important social values from serious harm and to do so not arbitrarily but in accordance with rational methods directed toward the discovery of just ends."[3] This position assumes that the society has achieved a well-integrated and relatively stable agreement on basic values.

> The state of criminal law continues to be—as it should—a decisive reflection of the social consciousness of a society. What kind of conduct an organized community considers, at a given time, sufficiently condemnable to impose official sanctions, impairing the life, liberty, or property of the offender, is a barometer of the moral and social thinking of a community.[4]

Given the multiplicity of racial, ethnic, and religious groups in American society, is there broad agreement as to the moral values that are formalized in the criminal law? A national survey of public opinion concerning the severity of various crimes sheds some light on this question.[5] The people interviewed were asked to rank the seriousness of 204 illegal events. The results showed that the planting of a bomb which exploded in a public building and killed twenty people was rated the most serious offense, and that playing hookey from school was rated the least serious. Among the diverse groups of people who took part in the survey there was generally broad agreement as to the severity of specific crimes. Differences were noted, however, in that crime victims scored the acts higher than did nonvictims, and the severity ratings assigned by blacks and other minority-group members were generally lower than those assigned by whites.

Consensus in Puritan Massachusetts. Kai Erikson argues in *Wayward Puritans* that three serious "crime waves" in seventeenth-century Massachusetts performed the important function of helping the colonists to define the values of their society. During each of these periods—the antinomian controversy of 1636, the Quaker persecutions of the late 1650s, and the witchcraft

The Salem witch trials tightened community bonds.

hysteria of 1692—the Massachusetts Bay colonists labeled certain types of behavior as criminal. As a result, they were better able to set the boundaries of their society, to clarify their doctrines, and to renew community norms.

The theoretical basis for Erikson's fascinating study is Emile Durkheim's idea that crime is a natural kind of social activity and performs an important function in healthy societies. In Durkheim's view, violations of norms unite people in anger and indignation; that is, when a deviant breaks the rules of conduct that the rest of the community holds in high respect, citizens can come together to express their outrage:

> Crime brings together upright consciences and concentrates them. We have only to notice what happens, particularly in a small town, when some moral scandal has just been committed. They stop each other on the street, they visit each other, they seek to come together to talk of the event and to wax indignant in common. From all the similar impressions which are exchanged . . . there emerges a unique temper . . . which is everybody's without being anybody's in particular. That is the public temper.[6]

The deviant act, then, creates a sense of mutuality or community because it supplies a focus for group feeling. Much like a war or some other emergency, deviance makes people more alert to their shared interests and values. Erikson shows that at the time of each of the crime waves, the Puritans were being

Emile Durkheim

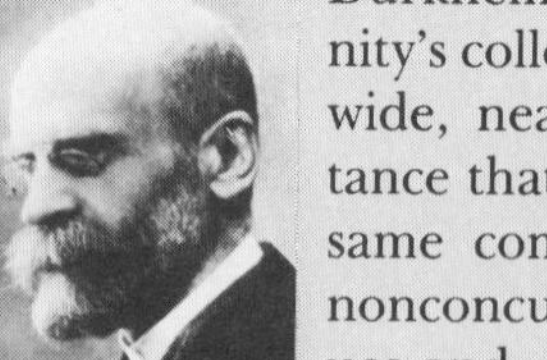

A French sociologist, Emile Durkheim is one of the leading figures in the social sciences. The basic theme of his work is that society is a realm of unique social facts and that order and cohesion are of primary importance. As a criminologist, Durkheim maintained that crime is a normal, not a pathological, factor in society. He did not insist that criminals are always normal but believed that criminal acts reflect the community's dominant values. Crime would disappear, Durkheim asserted, only if the community's collective sentiments reached such a wide, nearly universal degree of acceptance that all persons concurred with the same common values. Crime reflects a nonconcurrence with the dominant values and, as such, is necessary for the cohesion of the broader society. While not condoning crime, Durkheim calls attention to the function that it performs in cementing the ties that bind the members of a society.

confronted with changes in their society and with challenges to existing values. Because of the theological basis of their value system, they interpreted deviant behavior in religious terms.

Also important is Erikson's argument that the amount of deviance a community encounters over time is apt to remain fairly constant. At any given time, a society focuses on people it considers to be criminals, regardless of how serious their behavior may appear according to some universal standards. The number of criminals the society actually deals with, however, is limited by its detection equipment as well as by the size and complexity of its apparatus for control. Thus Erikson found that among the Massachusetts Puritans, even during crime waves the number of criminal offenders did not increase significantly; rather, the crimes that the society used its resources to manage shifted to those with a theological foundation.

Conflict: law as an expression of political power

In contrast to the view of the criminal code as a product of the society's value consensus, a relatively new approach emphasizes that the political power of the dominant social classes influences the content of the code. An articulate spokesman for this ***conflict model*** is Richard Quinney.

conflict model
A legal model that asserts that the political power of interest groups and elites influences the content of the criminal law.

> First . . . society is characterized by diversity, conflict, coercion, and change, rather than by consensus and stability. Second, law is a result of the operation of interests, rather than an instrument which functions outside of particular interests. Though law may operate to control interests, it is in the first place created by interests. Third, law incorporates the interests of specific persons and groups in society. Seldom is law the product of the whole society.[7]

In this view, power, force, and constraint, rather than common values, are the basic organizing principles of society. Since there are unequal distributions of political influence, some groups will have greater access to decision makers and will use their influence to ensure that legislation is enacted to protect their interests. According to this approach, wrongful acts are characteristic of all classes in society, and the powerful not only shape the law to their own advantage but are able to dictate the use of enforcement resources so that certain groups are labeled and processed by the criminal justice system.

Since the political power of groups ebbs and flows, the criminal law, its application, and its interpretation will reflect those tidal alternations.

> New and shifting demands require new laws. When the interests that underlie a law no longer are relevant to groups in power, the law will be reinterpreted or changed to incorporate the dominant interests. The social history of criminal law can be described according to alterations in the interest structure of society.[8]

Conflict in fourteenth-century England. Laws against vagrancy—that is, against wandering idly without means to earn a living—are a part of the penal code of most cities and states. William Chambliss has shown that such laws originated in England and have changed over time to reflect shifts in social concerns. The first vagrancy law was enacted in 1349, when the Black Death—bubonic plague—killed a large part of the population and caused a severe labor shortage. This law regulated the giving of alms to able-bodied unemployed persons. With the need for cheap labor after the breakdown of the feudal system and after the labor force was again decimated by a recurrence of plague in the seventeenth century, the law was changed. Now the statute stated:

> Every man and woman, of what condition he be, free or bond, able in body, and within the age of threescore years, not living in merchandizing nor exercising any craft, nor having of his own whereon to live, nor proper land whereon to occupy himself, and not serving any other, if he in convenient service (his estate considered) be required to service, shall be bounded to serve him which shall him require. . . . And if any refuse he shall on conviction by two true men . . . be committed to gaol till he finds surety to serve.[9]

The rise of commerce and industry in the sixteenth century had brought to life vagrancy laws that had lain dormant during much of the fifteenth century, and directed them against any person who, "being whole and mighty in body, and able to labor, be taken in begging, or be vagrant and can give no reckoning how he lawfully gets his living."[10] Where the earlier law had focused on the idle and was designed to provide labor, the new emphasis was on rogues and others suspected of criminal activities and was designed to protect travelers and goods on the highways. As Chambliss notes, only later did the vagrancy statutes stress the damage to persons or property that might be inflicted by the vagabond. This shift reflected the importance of a new group—the commercial class—and laws were altered to guard its interests.

The English vagrancy laws were adopted in the United States with only minor variations. In all the states, the statutes were written so that they more explicitly focused on the control of criminals and undesirables than was the case in England. Since the 1750s they have been used to clear the streets of people considered nuisances: prostitutes, derelicts, and others who "can be seen as a reflection of the society's perception of a continuing need to control some of its 'suspicious' or 'undesirable' members."[11] In contemporary times, vagrancy laws have been used for such purposes as controlling the movement of migrant laborers in California, civil rights workers in the South, and peace demonstrators in Washington, D.C. Under changing social conditions, dormant laws will often be revived to serve the newly powerful.

Consensus versus conflict: emerging theories

At this point in the study of the social processes involved in the development of criminal law, reaching a conclusion about the theoretical value of the consensus and conflict models is impossible. Certainly with some laws, especially those prohibiting acts that are ***mala in se***—murder, rape, assault—con-

mala in se
Offenses that are wrong by their very nature, irrespective of statutory prohibition.

Labeling Criminals

Those persons or groups that threaten the existing power structure are dangerous. In any historical period, to identify an individual whose status is that of a member of the "dangerous classes," . . . the label "criminal" has been handy. . . . [The] construct, criminal, is not used to classify the performers of all legally defined delicts [offenses against the law], only those whose position in the social structure qualifies them for membership in the dangerous classes.

Source: Theodore R. Sarbin, *The Myth of the Criminal Type* (pamphlet published by the Center for Advanced Studies, Wesleyan University, Middletown, Conn., 1969).

---

sensus exists in most Western societies as to the values expressed in the law. In contrast, the laws prohibiting alcohol consumption, vagrancy, and the sale of pornography—***mala prohibita***—have their source in the political power of special interests. (These distinctions are discussed at greater length in chapter 3.) Since most criminal violations are now of the latter type, attention logically focuses on the conflict model.

mala prohibita Offenses prohibited by statute but not inherently wrong.

Jerome Skolnick has criticized Quinney's assumption that the conflict model explains the source of all criminal law. He argues that in writing the criminal law, we evaluate various acts (heroin possession, robbery, rape) on the basis of some standard of crime. Since Quinney says that the standards of what ought to be criminal reflect various group and class definitions of conduct, an unanswered question remains relating to possible areas of consensus among portions of society. As Skolnick notes: "Surely, there is far greater negative consensus on the 'quality' of the behavior involved in forcible rape and armed robbery than in gambling or marihuana use. Shared definitions of crime exist, albeit variably, depending on the behavior in question, and the fact of sharing is also part of the social reality of crime."[12]

Causes of crime

People have long pondered why some individuals conform to society's norms and values while others do not. References in ancient Greek writings indicate that speculation on this question was prevalent even then. Criminology is primarily concerned with understanding crime, the characteristics of criminals, and how the consequences of crime can be prevented or repaired. It is an interdisciplinary science, with scholars from sociology, political science, biology, economics, and psychology each viewing crime from a particular theoretical perspective.

We can classify the many theories of crime causation into two general models: one looks at the behavior of the individual who commits a crime, the other focuses on the society and its definitions of the behavior that constitutes crime. Attempts to explain criminal behavior on the basis of the individual focus on the offender's biological and psychological characteristics. Theories that focus on crime-creating conditions in the culture attempt to understand criminal behavior by viewing the effects of poverty, social disorganization, and subcultural norms in relation to crime.

Three Italians stand out as the fathers of criminology: Cesare Lombroso (1835–1909), Enrico Ferri (1856–1929), and Raffaele Garofalo (1852–1934). Although Lombroso the physician, Ferri the legal sociologist, and Garofalo the legal anthropologist did not agree on the causes of criminal behavior, they greatly influenced the general development of the scientific study of crime. This Italian school worked to shift the focus from the criminal act to the criminal person. Instead of emphasizing the legal and philosophical ramifications of the deviant act, as had been the tradition, Lombroso and his followers focused on the people who committed crimes, on their behavior, and on the causes of that behavior.

Although this group revolutionized scientific thinking about crime, their approaches diverged considerably. As Stephen Schafer notes, "The disagreements between them proved to be no less significant by branching off this newborn criminology to different orientations, essentially to three avenues: the biological, the psychological, and the sociological."[13] In fact, because there is much overlap between the biological and psychological, it is more appropriate to distinguish a biopsychological from the sociological perspective. In addition, a Marxist orientation has developed during this century, as has the still-emerging field of victimology.

It is important to understand the leading explanations of crime causation because their assumptions significantly affect the ways in which laws are enforced, guilt or innocence is determined, and misconduct is punished. When in Puritan New England the offender's behavior was believed to be the work of the devil, it became the practice for clergymen to use their powers to remove the curse, even if this meant hanging persons thought to be witches. Likewise, if it is believed that poor people are motivated to steal to provide food and clothing for their families, social welfare programs that meet these needs will appear to be the most effective government policy that can be adopted to prevent such crimes.

biopsychological explanations Explanations of crime that emphasize individual biological and psychological conditions as the causes of criminal behavior.

Biopsychological explanations

Lombroso's training in medicine aroused his interest in the physical characteristics that he believed differentiated the criminal from the law-abiding citizen. According to his explanation, criminals are *born* criminal and have characteristics that mark them as more primitive and savage people—"genetic throwbacks" to an earlier stage of evolution. Individuals so disabled have difficulty adjusting to modern society because they are frustrated by their social incompetence and by the rejection arising from it. Down this path the criminal is thrust into illegal activity.

Lombroso supported his theory with data he gathered by measuring the physical characteristics of Italian convicts. He believed that criminals had "stigmata": asymmetric faces, ponderous jaws, eye defects, prominent cheek-

Cesare Lombroso

Born in Verona, Italy, in 1835, Lombroso became one of the most eulogized and attacked criminologists of all time. His work brought about a shift from a legalistic preoccupation with crime to a scientific study of the criminal. A professor of psychiatry and criminal anthropology at the University of Pavia from 1862 to 1876, Lombroso founded what became known as the biological school of criminology, often referred to as the Italian school.

Lombroso maintained that certain people are born criminals. These individuals were biological throwbacks to a more primitive stage of human evolution and could be identified by physical characteristics. He believed, too, that crime was a disease, a disease that could be inherited or brought on by anthropological and social factors. Much of Lombroso's work emphasizes that the study of crime is a study of personality development. The work of Lombroso and his followers encouraged the development of more humane and constructive treatment programs for criminals. Lombroso's ideas are best expressed in his three most important books: *Criminal Man* (1876), *The Female Offender* (1895), and *Crime: Its Causes and Remedies* (1912).

bones, and other such characteristics. These features did not actually cause the illegal behavior but were marks that allowed the scientist to distinguish the criminal type.

With the development of psychology, however, interest shifted from physical characteristics to the importance of inherited traits that affected the intellectual level and mental health of criminals. Some criminologists believed that criminals were morally insane and committed crimes as a means of alleviating the pathological urges they had inherited from mentally defective ancestors. Criminologists with this orientation studied family genealogies to determine the correspondence between these traits and the criminal records of family members.

Two studies of a family given the fictitious name of Jukes and a similar study of a family called the Kallikaks presented evidence that genetic deficiencies reproduced in offspring could condemn succeeding generations to lives of crime.[14] Richard Dugdale located more than 1,000 descendants of the woman he called Ada Jukes, whom he dubbed the "mother of criminals." Among the family were 280 paupers, 60 thieves, 7 murderers, 140 criminals, 40 persons with venereal diseases, 50 prostitutes, and other types of undesirables. Similar data collected by Henry H. Goddard supported the belief that the Kallikak family, a group of relatives linked to the illegitimate son of Martin Kallikak, contained more criminals than the descendants of Martin's later marriage into a "good" family.

These early studies have been greatly criticized, but they were taken seriously in their time. In many states, habitual offenders were sterilized under the assumption that crime could be controlled if hereditary factors were not transmitted. This practice was declared unconstitutional in *Skinner* v. *Oklahoma* (1942).[15]

Although biological explanations of criminal behavior were ignored or condemned as racist during the period following World War II, they have attracted renewed interest in more recent years. In particular, research on nutrition, neurology, genetics, and endocrinology has indicated that these factors may be related to the violent behavior of some people. Studies in the 1960s pointed to the possibility that violence in men may be linked to the presence of an extra male sex chromosome; Richard Speck, who had been convicted of killing eight student nurses in Chicago, was found to have such a chromosomal structure. Additional research, however, has indicated that the smallness of the earlier studies' samples make their findings unreliable. More recently, the defense in a Massachusetts case argued successfully that the accused had an endocrinological dysfunction that caused him to react violently when he consumed even small amounts of alcohol. Likewise, the modern technology of CAT scans, which allows scientists to study portions of the brain, has raised questions about the influence of neurological disorders on violence.

These new perspectives have brought biological explanations of criminal behavior to the fore again, but much more research is needed before theories based on them can be developed. It is also important to emphasize that although current research points to the possibility that the violence of some individuals may be linked to biological factors, there is little evidence to suggest the appropriateness of generalizing such findings to larger populations.

Psychological theory. In the wake of Sigmund Freud's revolution, psychiatrists have related criminal behavior to such concepts as innate impulses, mental conflict, and repression. According to such theories, crime is a form of substitute behavior that compensates for abnormal urges and desires. Although there are great divergences among the practitioners of this school, a main thesis is that personality is formed during early childhood and is a key determinant of later behavior; it is influenced little, if at all, by sociological factors.

Among the theories developed by psychiatrists is that of the person variously described as the "psychopath," "sociopath," and "antisocial personality": a person who is unable to control impulses, cannot learn from experience, and does not experience normal human emotions, such as love. This kind of person is viewed as psychologically abnormal and conforms to the popular image of the crazed killer or sex fiend. During the 1940s, with the rise of psychology and after a number of widely publicized sex crimes, state legislatures were pressured to pass "sexual psychopath laws" designed to remove these "homicidal sex fiends" who stalked the landscape and put them into institutions for treatment of their disorders. Edwin H. Sutherland has shown, however, that such legislation was based on false assumptions and that it reveals the political context within which the criminal law is fashioned.[16]

Psychological theories have been widely and variously criticized. Some critics talk about the difficulty of measuring emotional factors and of isolating persons thought to be ***criminogenic.*** Others point to the variety of theories, some conflicting, that have at their base a psychological approach to crime. Most of these theories have not stood up well when tested.

criminogenic factors
Factors thought to bring about criminal behavior in an individual.

Sociological explanations

The sociological view of crime assumes that the offender's personality and actions are molded by contact with the social environment. People do not live as isolated individuals but as members of social groups, and it is these social influences that shape criminal behavior. This orientation is seen in the work of the nineteenth-century French social thinker Emile Durkheim, who, as we have seen, concluded that a certain level of crime was an intrinsic and natural part of social life. There are occasions, however, when crime rises to such a high level that it becomes dysfunctional. Among the several ***sociological explanations*** of crime, three deserve special mention: structural theory, differential association theory, and labeling theory.

sociological explanations
Explanations of crime that emphasize social conditions that bear on the individual as causes of criminal behavior.

Structural theory. Durkheim emphasized that the structure of society often permits a situation of anomie to develop. By *anomie* he meant social conditions in which rules or norms to regulate behavior have weakened or disappeared. Persons may become anomic or frustrated when the rules are unclear or when they are unable to achieve what they expect. When the balance between cultural aspirations and social opportunities is lost or damaged, antisocial or deviant behavior may result. Thus it is said that American society places great emphasis on individual success but excludes some of its members from the possibility of achieving that goal; hence it follows that those caught in this trap choose crime as a way out. Theorists believe that the movement of some ethnic groups into organized crime has been one way of overcoming such anomic frustrations. Others argue that the social disorganization of urbanized and industrial society brings about conditions in which, among other things, family structure breaks down, alcohol or drug abuse becomes more common, and the incidence of criminal behavior rises. They assert that to reduce crime, poverty must be eradicated and the structures of society reformed.

Differential association theory. Developed by Edwin Sutherland, the theory of differential association states that criminal behavior is learned through interactions with other persons, especially family members and others with whom close associations are maintained.[17] Criminal behavior occurs when an individual encounters strong prescriptions for behavior which are more favorable to than opposed to law violations. If a young person grows up in an environment of violence, in which, say, an older brother is involved in crime, criminal behavior will be learned. If those in the family, neighborhood, and gang believe that illegal activity is nothing to be ashamed of, there is a greater probability that the young person will engage in crime. It is through these close associations that people learn what is expected and allowed. Someone who belongs to a social group that does not frown on criminal activity and has role models who conduct their lives outside the law will almost certainly become involved in crime as well.

Labeling theory. Frank Tanenbaum is the sociologist most frequently associated with the labeling theory because he argued that we should not look for the causes of crime in the individual but should focus on the social process through which certain types of acts are labeled deviant.[18] As Howard Becker notes, social groups create deviance "by making the rules whose infraction constitutes deviance, and by applying those rules to particular people and labeling them outsiders."[19] Social-control agencies, such as the police, courts,

Edwin H. Sutherland

An American criminologist, Edwin H. Sutherland had a profound impact on the development of the theory of crime causation. Born in Nebraska, Sutherland earned his doctorate at the University of Chicago (1913) and for a number of years was a member of sociology departments at leading universities (Illinois, Minnesota, Chicago) before becoming departmental chairman at Indiana University (1935–49). His contribution to criminology was significant in shaping the substantive theory and methodological orientation of the field. His important works include *Criminology* (1924), *The Professional Thief* (1937), and *White Collar Crime* (1949).

A major theme of Sutherland's work was that personality and conduct develop as a result of the incorporation of the perspectives of the dominant culture surrounding the individual. From this view Sutherland developed the theory of differential association, which holds that criminal behavior is learned in essentially the same way as any other aspect of the culture in which a person learns to function. A person becomes a criminal through association with others, usually members of an intimate personal group, whose dominant culture is criminal. For Sutherland, the theory implied that on a societal level the cause of crime is *culture conflict;* that is, a conflict between the behavior patterns and values of different cultures within a society.

and corrections departments, are created to designate certain individuals as outside the normal, law-abiding community. Having been labeled as deviant or criminal, the stigmatized individual comes to believe that the label is true, assumes the identity, and enters into a criminal career.

Labeling theory seems to have certain ideological and policy implications. It suggests that criminals are not very different from other members of the community, except that the agencies of justice have labeled them as deviant. The approach also implies that we would be much better off if government did as little as possible with regard to crime. This theory suggests that the police and courts create criminals by labeling people as such because doing so serves their own bureaucratic-political ends.

Like other explanations of the causes of criminal behavior, the sociological theories have been thoroughly criticized. It has been argued that they are imprecise, are not supported by empirical evidence, and really do not constitute more than observations. Criticism notwithstanding, the fact is that the sociological theories, together with portions of the psychoanalytic orientation, have served as the basis for many attempts to prevent crime and to rehabilitate offenders.

Critical criminology

critical criminology A school of criminology that holds that criminal law and the criminal justice system have been created to control the poor and have-not members of society.

In the mid-1960s a new orientation arose to challenge the biopsychological and sociological explanations of crime. Referred to as ***critical,*** radical, or Marxist ***criminology,*** this perspective claims that criminal law and the criminal justice system are mainly means of controlling society's poor and have-nots. The rich and well educated commit as many crimes as the poor, it is argued, but the poor are more likely to be punished because they are powerless and unsophisticated. The rich use the law to impose their version of morality on the whole of society for the purpose of protecting their property and physical safety. By manipulating the law, elites change the definition of illegal behavior to encompass activities that they view as threatening to the status quo.

The objectives of the critical criminologists may be seen in the newsletter of the Union of Radical Criminologists.

> In this time of domestic and international repression, the activities of the police, the courts, the prison system, and other institutions of "social control" have become an increasingly pervasive and significant factor of life in the United States. At the same time, the conventional approach to these institutions in the academic fields of criminology and sociology has served to mystify their resistance to change. Criminology, in particular, has functioned in the United States and elsewhere as an integral part of the apparatus of state repression.[20]

From the Marxist perspective, then, the American system of criminal justice is used by the powerful to exercise their dominion over the poor and weak. Some critical criminologists view crime as the result of the capitalist economic system because they believe that the law is designed to guard the position of the owners of the means of production against the workers. One result is a deep hostility among the poor toward the social order. This is one factor contributing to criminal behavior. It is argued further that when the status quo is threatened, legal definitions of criminal behavior are altered so as to ensnare those who challenge the system.

Victimology

One of the newest areas of criminology is the subfield of ***victimology.*** There has long been a concern for the victims of crime, and proposals have been made to provide some form of compensation for the wrongs they have suffered. Revived interest in requiring the offender to make restitution to the victim is a contemporary manifestation of this orientation. The ways in which the criminal justice system treats victims will be more fully discussed in chapter 4.

victimology
A subfield of criminology that examines the role played by the victim in precipitating a criminal incident.

Another way of thinking about the victim has surfaced in recent years. Victimology has become concerned with the role the victim plays in the criminal incident. In this view, the crime is precipitated by something that the victim has or has not done. By analyzing the characteristics of a variety of victims, criminologists have advanced the idea that many of them voluntarily act in ways that incite their attackers to commit a violent act against them. The victim may bring about commission of a crime through consent, provocation, enticement, unnecessary risk taking, or carelessness with property.

Let us consider the type of city dweller who is more likely than another to become prey to a mugger. Morton Hunt has listed six elements that may predispose a person to attack.[21] (1) People who are on the sidewalks late at night are three times as likely to be victimized as those who stay indoors after dark. (2) Age and physical disabilities make the elderly more vulnerable to attack than the young and strong. (3) In addition, some people are more vulnerable because they are hampered by things they are carrying, by the attention they are giving to something, or by clothing that may block their view or make defense difficult. (4) Kinds of clothing worn can be a clue to likely amounts of cash being carried or jewelry being worn. (5) Race is a fifth element. Although most street crime is intraracial, more than half the robberies on American city streets are interracial—white victims of nonwhite criminals, strangers to each other. (6) Finally, persons walking alone are more apt to be targets for a mugger than is someone with a companion.

Muggings occur between strangers, but there are other types of violence that occur between people who know each other, and these types add another dimension to the role that victims play in the administration of justice. A study of felony arrests in New York City focuses on the many cases that the prosecution drops because the complainant refuses to provide key testimony. It was found that in a high proportion of crimes of interpersonal violence, a prior relationship existed between offender and victim: manslaughter, 50 percent; rape, 83 percent; assault, 67 percent. When the victim knows the assailant, there is a high probability that an arrest will occur, but in the clarity of the "morning after" the complaint may be dropped. But these occurrences add new information on the causes of crime because we can learn from them about the events leading up to the incident. The New York researchers concluded that much violent conduct is often the "explosive spillover from ruptured personal relations among neighbors, friends, and former spouses."[22] Interpersonal violence seems to result from such incidents as the family argument that escalates until one of the combatants picks up a kitchen knife or gun and commits an assault or homicide. In such circumstances, one can inquire about the responsibility of each of the parties for the final deed.

What do victimology studies tell us? First, there are instances when citizens do not take proper precautions to protect themselves. Acting with common sense and regulating our behavior to prevent criminal attack may be one of the prices of living in contemporary society. Second, under some circumstances, the victim, by some action, may provoke or entice another to commit a criminal act. Third, the victims in certain types of nonstranger crimes are unwilling to assist official agencies in investigation and prosecution activities. All this does not excuse criminal behavior, but it forces us to think about other dimensions of the way the criminal act is perpetrated.

Female criminals

In the past, most criminologists studied the behavior of males. With the exception of such so-called female crimes as prostitution and shoplifting, little research was done on the half of the population that accounted for less than 10 percent of persons arrested. Two assumptions appear to have been operating: first, that most women were incapable of serious criminal activity; second, that those who did commit crimes were "bad" women. For some reason, women were viewed as moral offenders—"fallen." The emergence of the Women's Movement has changed this orientation. Criminologists are focusing

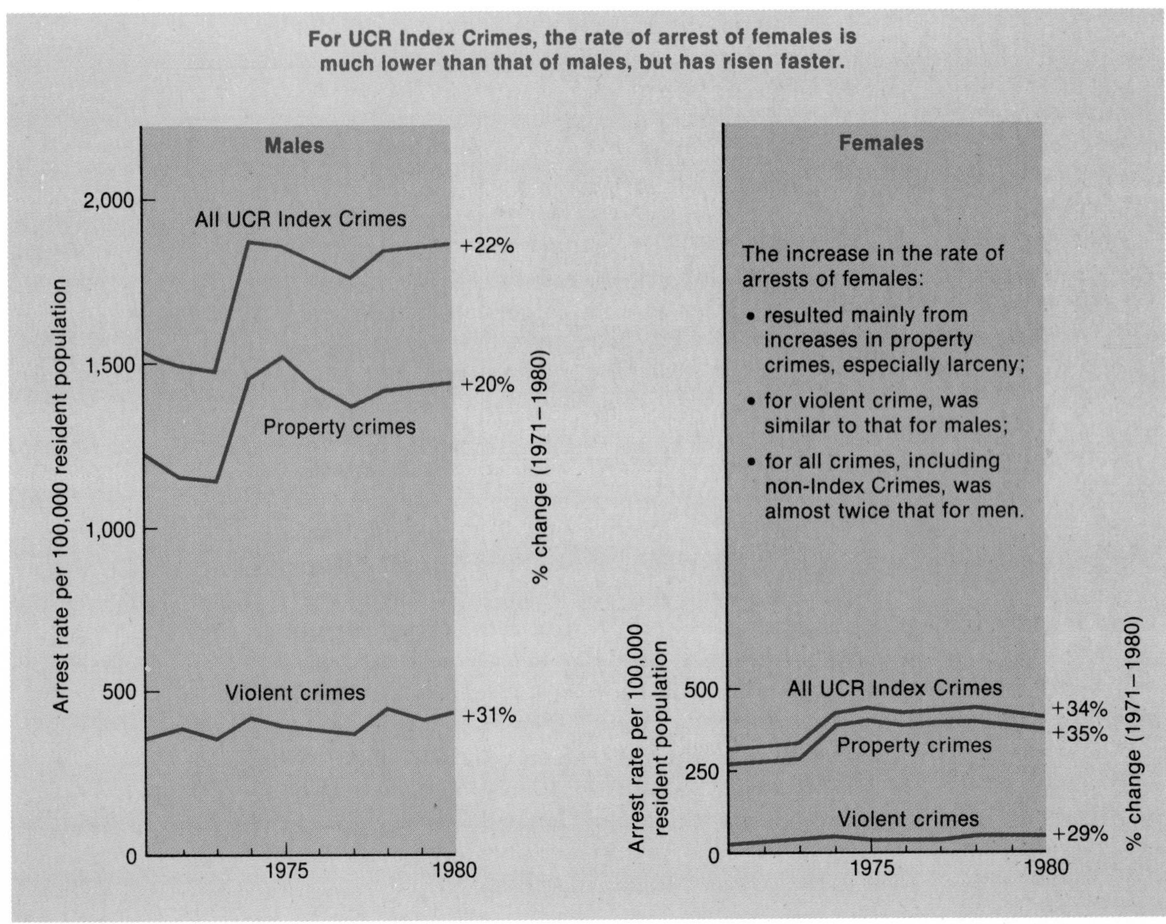

FIGURE 2.1
Male and female arrest rates for *Uniform Crime Reports* Index Crimes

more intently on female offenders, whose arrests for such offenses as fraud, robbery, and larceny, traditionally viewed as the province of males, have increased sharply, though arrest rates for women still lag far behind those for men (figures 2.1 and 2.2).

Why this increase? As Freda Adler has noted: "When we did not permit women to swim at the beaches, the female drowning rate was quite low. When women were not permitted to work as bank tellers or presidents, the female embezzlement rate was low."[23] It is argued that as women take places of equality with men in American society, distinctions of criminality based on sex are diminished. Rita Simon nicely summarizes this trend by stating that because of the changes that have taken place since the 1950s, women are able to enjoy greater freedom, are less likely to be victimized and oppressed by men, and are less likely to be dependent on them.[24] She says that, as a consequence, women will also be less likely to engage in crimes of violence but more likely to commit business-related and property crimes.

Obviously, none of these approaches to the study of crime causation is powerful enough to predict criminality or clinically to link an offender's behavior with a specific cause, yet all contain a kernel of truth. All focus on visible crimes, the illegal activities of the poor. There seems to be little relationship between any of the theories and upper-class or organized crime.

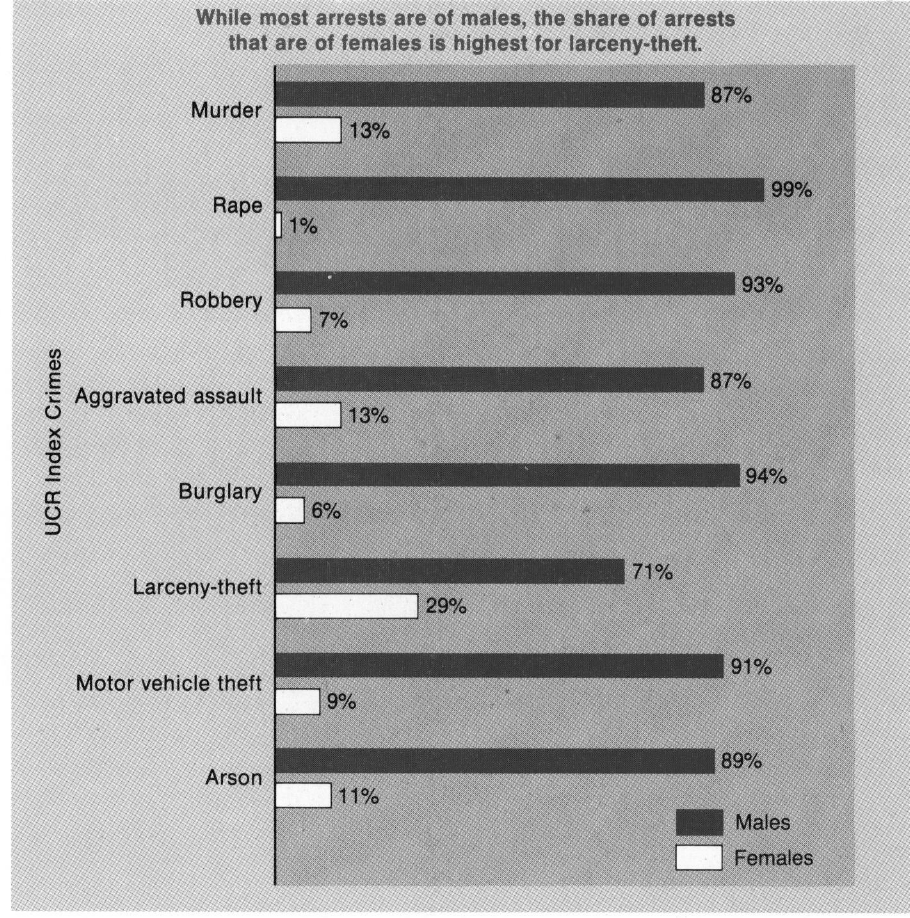

FIGURE 2.2
Proportion of males and females arrested for *Uniform Crime Reports* Index Crimes

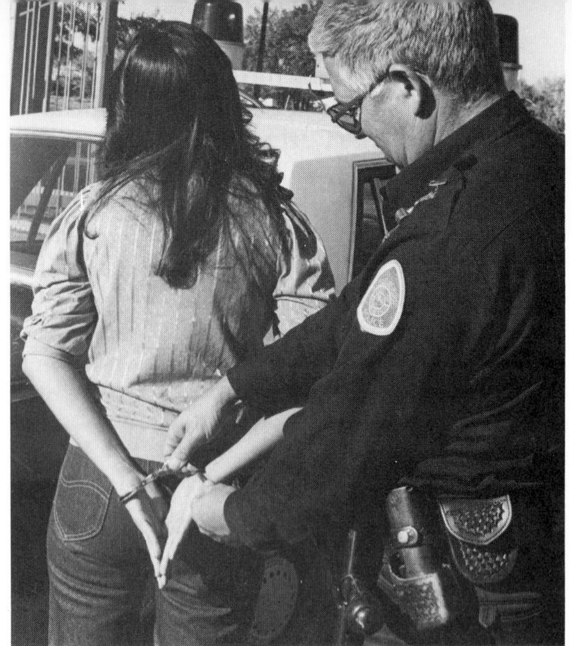

Arrests of females for property crimes have increased during the past decade.

Close-up: Marge: The New Female Criminal?

Marge is forty-three years old, with brown hair headed for gray and muscular legs somewhat the worse for wear. Soft-spoken and hovering just this side of being quite plump, Marge has spent a good many years on those legs earning a living. Since her husband disappeared one day eighteen years ago, she has worked a total of fifteen years either as a waitress or a barmaid. During those years, she supported and raised two sons, one of whom eventually worked his way through a small state college and is currently a teacher. The other one, younger, died four years ago as a result of pumping a bad bag of heroin into his arm.

Deserted, with two small children, Marge was forced to get the first job she had ever had. It was as a barmaid in a small restaurant-lounge. Not long afterward, she gave her first serious thought to being a prostitute—like a fellow barmaid who was developing a very lucrative following among the bar's male clientele.

But soon Marge gave up the idea of prostitution—partly because of her figure, which she didn't feel was suited for the trade, and partly because of her "strong Catholic upbringing." She explained, "I just never felt right in that kind of thing. Now it didn't bother me that other girls I knew were turning tricks; I just couldn't bring myself to stay with it. I guess underneath it all, I was more strait-laced than I knew."

In place of prostitution, Marge found a more acceptable degree of reprehensibility in shoplifting. "Boosting" from department stores became a regular habit with her. At first she began by putting small items, like watches, into her pocket. Later, she progressed to more sophisticated methods. She wore large baggy coats which could conceal things like toasters and radios, then began to sew large bag-like pockets inside the coats to facilitate even larger load handling. She shoplifted for years, and was caught only once. On that occasion she was allowed to go free on her own recognizance and, although threatened with further prosecution, never heard of the incident again.

Five years ago Marge robbed her first bank. The planning took her some months. "It was something that came to me all of a sudden. . . . I had a couple of big debts and I was getting tired of working like I was. . . . I wanted a bit

What is missing and truly needed is an integrating theory that places all these disparate crime-causation ideas together. Perhaps we don't know much about the causes of crime, but notice how many people think they hold the answers!

Types of crimes

It is possible to divide crimes into a number of categories. Scholars interested in the development of societal reaction to crime often use the *mala in se–mala prohibita* distinction. A legal division can also be made, with some crimes labeled as ***felonies*** (those punishable by death or more than a year of incarceration) and others as ***misdemeanors*** (for which a lesser sanction is imposed). Criminologists have developed a third scheme that categorizes crimes according to the nature of the behavior and the type of person most likely to commit specific offenses. This scheme distinguishes five categories of crime: upperworld, organized, visible, crimes without victims, and political. Each type has its own level of risk and profitability, each arouses varying degrees of public disapproval, and each has its own group of offenders with differing cultural characteristics. Though the community potentially can command the energy, resources, and technology to attack all crime, social and political processes

felony
A serious crime that can be penalized up to death or incarceration for more than a year. Persons convicted of felonies lose the right to vote, to hold public elective office, and to practice certain professions and occupations.

misdemeanor
An offense less serious than a felony and usually punishable by incarceration for no more than a year, a fine, or probation.

of easy time. I mean, the kids were getting older and I was still working and, after all those years, I needed a break. I guess maybe I got the idea from watching TV or something, I don't remember. But it surprised me; like, I first thought of it seriously and thought, 'No, I couldn't do that . . . I'm a woman,' you know? But when I thought more about it, what the hell, it didn't seem so bad. The other girls I knew were boosting or [credit] carding. They said I must be crazy when we talked about it one day. We never really thought about a woman hitting a bank before . . . but then soon after that, I heard on the radio of a lady who hit a bank and got away and I figured, what the hell, if she can do it, why can't I?"

After many months of careful planning and observation, Marge attempted to rob one particular bank. That first attempt was a failure. She walked in and approached the teller's window, but was unable to go through with the robbery. "I just asked for change for a ten-dollar bill and felt like a real smacked-ass to myself." Two months later, though, she went through with it and went on to rob two more banks before she was finally caught. After the first one it seemed easy to her. "I just walked in, walked out, and went home to count the money. I always thought it would be a lot harder . . . a lot more dangerous. I did take a gun each time, but it was never loaded and I only really had to show it to one teller. The others just put the money in the bag when I asked them to. . . . I remember that first job. It was like a cheap high afterward. I went home and turned on the radio to see what they would say about me on the news."

To her disappointment, after that first heist, police described her to the news media as a "male dressed in women's clothing." That upset Marge a bit. "Well, I know I'm no beauty queen, but I didn't think I was that bad . . . and who the hell ever saw a man with plucked eyebrows?"

During her third try, Marge was stopped on her way out of the bank by policemen responding to a silent alarm. She gave up peacefully. ("What the hell else could I do, the gun wasn't loaded or anything.") She is currently serving an indefinite prison term for robbery.

Source: Freda Adler, *Sisters in Crime* (copyright © 1975), pp. 6–7. Reissued 1985 by Waveland Press, Inc., Prospect Heights, Ill. Reprinted by permission.

somehow operate so that only certain offenders are thought suitable for processing by the criminal justice system.

Upperworld crimes

upperworld crime
Conduct in violation of the law engaged in during the course of business activity (as tax evasion, price fixing). Such offenses are often viewed as shrewd business practices that are not really criminal.

Upperworld crimes are violations committed in the business world: tax evasion, price fixing, consumer fraud, health and safety infractions. Often viewed as shrewd business practices rather than as legal offenses, they are crimes that, if perpetrated "correctly," are never discovered and no one knows that a crime has in fact been committed. With upperworld crime, then, the problem is less one of catching the offender than of knowing that a crime has been committed. Well-known examples include the 1961 price-fixing convictions of General Electric and Westinghouse executives, the 1972 violations of campaign-financing laws exposed by the Watergate investigations, and the ABSCAM convictions of several congressmen and a senator. Additional examples, with the penalty imposed in each case, are found in table 2.1.

Though highly profitable, upperworld crimes rarely come to public attention, and regulatory agencies, such as the Federal Trade Commission and the Securities and Exchange Commission, are ineffective in their enforcement of the law. Much of society does not view upperworld crime as it views, for example, purse snatching. As the President's Commission on Law Enforcement and Administration of Justice said: "Most people pay little heed to crimes of this sort when they worry about 'crime in America,' because these crimes do not, as a rule, offer an immediate, recognizable threat to personal safety."[25]

Some criminological literature has discussed the prevalence of "white-collar crime." This concept, developed extensively by Edwin H. Sutherland, has recently come under criticism on the grounds that it does not clearly distinguish the criminal activity. Usually "white-collar crime" refers to illegal acts perpetrated by persons of high social status in the course of their professional or business relationships. The accountant who embezzles, the manager who pilfers merchandise, the banker who misuses other people's money—all have been termed white-collar criminals, but this does not help us to differentiate upperworld criminals from those in other crime categories. What is the difference if an accountant embezzles or a dockworker pilfers? Both are involved in theft. What is different is that, if caught, the dockworker will probably be fired and criminally charged, while the accountant may only lose his job on the promise that he will return the stolen money.

Perhaps it is important to differentiate the "white-collar" crimes committed in the workplace that *serve the interests of the organization* (such as antitrust violations, price fixing, pollution of the environment) from those committed on the job by employees that *serve their own interests* (such as theft, embezzlement, forgery).

organized crime
A social framework for the perpetration of criminal acts, usually in such fields as gambling, narcotics, and prostitution, in which illegal services that are in great demand are provided.

Organized crime

The term ***organized crime*** describes a social framework for the perpetration of criminal acts rather than specific types of offenses. Organized criminals provide goods and services to millions of people. They will engage in any illegal activity that provides a minimum of risk and a maximum of profit. Thus

TABLE 2.1 Ten bandits: what they did and what they got

Criminal	*Crime*	*Sentence*
Jack L. Clark	President and chairman of Four Seasons Nursing Centers. Clark finagled financial reports and earnings projections to inflate his stock artificially. Shareholders lost $200 million.	One year in prison.
John Peter Galanis	As portfolio manager of two mutual funds, Galanis bilked investors out of nearly $10 million.	Six months in prison and five years probation.
Virgil A. McGowen	As manager of the Bank of America branch in San Francisco, McGowen siphoned off $591,921 in clandestine loans to friends. Almost none of the money was recovered.	Six months in prison, five years probation, and a $3,600 fine.
Valdemar H. Madis	A wealthy drug manufacturer, Madis diluted an antidote for poisoned children with a worthless look-alike substance.	One year probation and a $10,000 fine.
John Morgan	President of Jet Craft Ltd., John Morgan illegally sold about $2 million in unregistered securities.	One year in prison and a $10,000 fine.
Irving Projansky	The former chairman of the First National Bank of Lincolnwood, Ill., Projansky raised stock prices artificially and then dumped the shares, costing the public an estimated $4 million.	One year in prison and two years probation.
David Ratliff	Ratliff spent his twenty-one years as a Texas state senator embezzling state funds.	Ten years probation.
Walter J. Rauscher	An executive vice-president of American Airlines, Rauscher accepted about $200,000 in kickbacks from businessmen bidding for contracts.	Six months in prison and two years probation.
Frank W. Sharp	The multimillion-dollar swindles of Sharp, a Houston banker, shook the Texas state government and forced the resignation of the head of the Criminal Division of the Justice Dept.	Three years probation and a $5,000 fine.
Seymour R. Thaler	Soon after his election to the New York State Supreme Court, Thaler was convicted of receiving and transporting $800,000 in stolen U.S. Treasury bills.	One year in prison and a fine of $10,000.

Source: Blake Fleetwood and Arthur Lubow, "America's Most Coddled Criminals," *New Times*, 15 September 1975, p. 30.

organized crime involves a network of enterprises, usually cutting across state and national boundaries, that range from legitimate businesses to shady involvement with labor unions to activities that cater to the desires of segments of the population for drugs, sex, and pornography—things forbidden by the criminal code. It has recently become known that with increased regulation of the disposal of hazardous wastes, organized crime has entered into this business as well by finding sites for the illegal disposal of toxic substances for a high fee.

With minor exceptions, organized crime seldom provides inputs to the criminal justice process. Investigations of the crime "families" known as the Mafia and Cosa Nostra by congressional committees and other governmental bodies have provided detailed accounts of the structure, membership, and

The failure to prosecute for the illegal disposing of toxic wastes while prosecuting against crimes committed by the poor has been called an example of the inequities of criminal justice in a capitalist system.

Close-up: Dramatic Crimes the Computer Helped Commit

	The Modus Operandi
The case: Wells Fargo *The date:* 1979–81 *The take:* $21.3 million	L. Ben Lewis, an operations officer for the 11th largest U.S. bank, allegedly produced bogus deposits in an account at one branch belonging to a boxing promotion outfit. He did this by using the bank's computerized interbranch account settlement process to withdraw funds from a different branch. To keep the computer from flagging the imbalance, Lewis created new fraudulent credits to cover the withdrawal—and allegedly kept the rollover going for two years. Lewis denies the charges.
The case: Morgan Guaranty *The date:* 1980 *The take:* Zero	The New York bank reportedly accepted as legitimate a bogus telex from the Central Bank of Nigeria transferring $21 million. In response to subsequent instructions, the money was routed electronically to three banks. When an attempt was made to wire the funds to a new $50 account in a Santa Ana (Calif.) bank, the transfer was refused. This triggered inquiries by the other banks. The Nigerian bank branded the first message as fraudulent, and the funds were never collected.
The case: Dalton School *The date:* 1980 *The take:* Zero	Using a classroom terminal, teenage students at Manhattan's private Dalton School allegedly dialed into a Canadian network of corporate and

activities of these groups, yet few arrests are made and even fewer convictions gained. The FBI has been especially vocal about the impact of organized crime on American society, but it, too, has failed to provide the evidence that would put this particular type of criminal behind bars.

Although the public currently associates organized crime with Americans of Italian ancestry, other ethnic groups have dominated this type of activity before now. Earlier in this century, various organized crime figures came from German, Jewish, and Irish backgrounds. Today there is increasing evidence that blacks and Hispanics have begun to manage these enterprises in some cities.

visible crimes Offenses against persons and property committed primarily by lower-class persons. Often referred to as "street crimes" or "ordinary crimes," these are the offenses most upsetting to the public.

Visible crimes

Visible crimes, often referred to as "street crimes" or "ordinary crimes" and committed primarily by the lower classes, run the gamut from shoplifting

institutional data systems. No funds were diverted—but damage was done to data files.

The case: Security Pacific
The date: 1978
The take: $10.3 million

Stanley Mark Rifkin, who had been a computer consultant for the Los Angeles bank, visited the bank's wire transfer room, where he obtained the electronic funds transfer code. Later, posing as a branch manager, he called from a public telephone and used the code to send money to a Swiss account. By the time the bank's computer flagged the fraud, he had flown to Switzerland, converted the funds into diamonds, and returned to the U.S. Only when he boasted of the feat was he identified, convicted, and sentenced to prison.

The case: Union Dime
The date: 1973
The take: $1.2 million

A teller at the New York City savings bank skimmed money from large new accounts by making a simple computerized correction entry. His embezzlement was discovered when police investigated a gambling parlor he frequented and questioned the source of his betting money.

The case: Equity Funding
The date: 1973
The take: $27.25 million

The insurance holding company used computers to create phony insurance policies that were later sold to reinsurers. Of the company's assets, $143.4 million were found to be fictitious, of which an estimated 19% was the result of computer fraud.

Source: Reprinted from the 20 April 1981 issue of *Business Week* by special permission,

to homicide. For offenders, these crimes are the least profitable violations and, because they are visible, the least protected. These are the crimes that make up the FBI's *Uniform Crime Reports* and are the acts that most of the public regards as criminal. Included are crimes of violence, such as homicide, rape, and assault, as well as crimes against property, such as theft, larceny, and burglary. The extent to which society has allocated law enforcement, judicial, and correctional resources to deal with violators of these laws raises serious questions about the role played by political and social power in determining criminal justice policies. Theorists have argued that the decidedly lower-class characteristics of the inhabitants of American correctional institutions reflect the class bias of a society that has singled out only certain types of criminal activity for attention.

Close-up: Crime and Ethnic Mobility

Social scientists have analyzed the relationships among ethnic groups, organized crime, and politics in American life. Daniel Bell has described how one group of immigrants after another has handed to each newly arriving immigrant group a "queer ladder of social mobility" which has organized crime as the first few rungs. The Irish were the first immigrant groups to become involved in organized criminal activity on a large scale in the United States, and early Irish gangsters began the climb up the social ladder. As more Irish came to American cities and as the Irish gangsters became successful in organized crime and therefore money began flowing into Irish-American communities, the Irish began to acquire political power. As they eventually came to control the political machinery of the large cities, the Irish won wealth, power and respectability by expanding their legitimate business interests and gaining control of construction, trucking, public utilities and the waterfront. The Irish were succeeded in organized crime by the Jews, and the names of Arnold Rothstein, Lepke Buchalter and Gurrah Shapiro dominated gambling and labor racketeering for a decade. The Jews quickly moved into the world of business as a more legitimate means of gaining economic and social mobility. The Italians came last and did not get a commanding leg up the ladder until the late thirties. They were just beginning to find politics and business as routes out of crime and the ghetto and into wealth and respectability in the fifties. . . .

Which is the next group of ethnics that will replace the Italian-Americans—as the Italian-Americans replaced the Irish and Jews before them—in organized crime and how will this new group or groups organize itself to achieve its goals? The answer to the first part of the question is apparent to anyone who would look: Blacks, Puerto Ricans and to a lesser extent Cubans are in fact already pursuing these routes and it is clear Blacks are working their way into higher positions of power in urban politics and also in many cities both Blacks and Puerto Ricans are displacing Italian-Americans in organized crime. The evidence of this displacement is already visible. In New York City, for example, Blacks, Puerto Ricans and Cubans are now displacing Italian-Americans in the policy or numbers rackets. In some cases, particularly in East Harlem and in Brooklyn, this is a peaceful succession as the Italian-American "families" literally lease the rackets on a concession basis. The "family" supplies the money and the protection, the Blacks or Puerto Ricans run the operation. In other cases we know of in Central and West Harlem, however, the transition is not so peaceful and the Italian syndicate members are actually being pushed out.

Source: Francis A. J. Ianni, *Ethnic Succession in Organized Crime*, U.S. Department of Justice (Washington, D.C.: Government Printing Office, 1973), pp. 1–2.

Crimes without victims

Crimes without victims may be defined as offenses involving a willing and private exchange of goods or services that are in strong demand but illegal. These are the offenses against morality: prostitution, gambling, and narcotics sales. The participants in the exchange do not feel that they are being harmed; rather, prosecutions are justified on the grounds that society as a whole is being injured. The use of the criminal law to enforce standards of morality is costly. Not only do these cases flood the courts, but enforcement necessitates the use of police informers.

crimes without victims
Offenses involving a willing and private exchange of goods or services for which there is a strong demand but which are illegal. Participants do not feel that they are being harmed. Prosecution is justified on the grounds that society as a whole is being injured by the act.

Some people feel that classifying goods as prohibited only encourages organized crime to develop an apparatus to supply the desired products. If the sale and possession of heroin, for example, were to be legalized, its price would probably drop immediately, underworld elements would move to more profitable business opportunities, and the crimes perpetrated by users to obtain the money for their costly habit would be reduced. Should individuals be allowed to destroy themselves if they want to? Do drug dealers depend on law enforcement activities to keep profits high? Are the costs of the prohibition worth their impact on the values emphasized? Are there really no victims?

Political crimes

Political crimes include activities, such as treason, sedition (rebellion), and espionage, that are viewed as threats to the government. Political freedom is always qualified, and American history has seen many laws enacted in response to apparent threats to the established order. The Sedition Act of 1789 provided for the punishment of those uttering or publishing statements against the government. The Smith Act of 1940 forbade the advocacy of overthrow of the government by force or violence. During the turmoil surrounding the Vietnam War the government used charges of criminal conspiracy as a weapon to deter the activities of those opposing the administration's policies. Six of the defendants in the trial of the Chicago Eight (prosecutions resulting from the demonstrations at the 1968 Democratic convention) were indicted for violating a quickly enacted federal law prohibiting travel across state lines with the intent to incite to or participate in a riot (defined in the law as an assemblage that involves a threat against or injury to another person or to property). In the 1980s, terrorism, often with international implications, has become a very serious problem.

political crimes
Acts that constitute threats against the state (as treason, sedition, espionage).

Too much law?

The United States has tended to use the criminal law for all sorts of social purposes. Each new technological advance, racial problem, or governmental program has resulted in another set of laws being placed on the books. In 1930 Roscoe Pound wrote that with the accelerated rate at which laws were added, of the 100,000 persons arrested in Chicago in 1912, more than half were arrested for violating laws that had been written since 1887. It has been estimated that the number of crimes for which one may be prosecuted has more than doubled since the turn of the century. More than just the number of offenses is the remarkable range of human activities now subject to the threat of criminal sanctions: "The killing of domesticated pigeons, the fencing of saltpeter caves against wandering cattle, the regulation of automobile traffic, the issue of daylight saving time versus standard time, to give only a few examples, have all, at one place or another, been made problems of the criminal law."[26]

overcriminalization The use of criminal sanctions to deter behavior that is acceptable to substantial portions of society.

One of the current issues of criminal justice policy is that of ***overcriminalization.*** Some theorists have suggested that criminalizing actions that may not be regarded as deviant by substantial portions of the society contributes to disrespect for the law, to unequal enforcement, and to a drain on the resources necessary to control serious misconduct. Especially with regard to such victimless crimes as gambling, marijuana use, drunkenness, and prostitution, there have been calls for decriminalization.

Scholars have increasingly drawn attention to society's failure to distinguish between appropriate and inappropriate uses of criminal sanctions. Because we recognize that the activities mentioned above are crimes without victims, the question arises: Should the criminal law be used to enforce moral-

Close-up: Portrait of a Mugger

His world is small, a whirlpool of lower New York street corners, tense friendships, family problems, small-change business deals, people without last names—and sudden violence. It is an insular world where "uptown" means a girl friend's apartment north of Houston Street and "the Bronx" is your brother's apartment on 287th Street. When it suited him, Jones stayed at his parents' home, a tiny shelter in "the projects," and when it didn't he stayed with one of his women.

One day we decided to play a rather serious game: we would pretend to be muggers.

"I don't know all the rules and answers, but the ones I know I'm sure of," Jones is saying as we begin my guided tour of victimland. "Rule number one is that everything's okay as long as you don't get caught." He is pointing out areas of interest along the way—you and your wallet, for example.

I see a jowly, middle-aged man with wavy hair carrying a grocery bag toward a car. We are about fifty yards from him.

Jones sees the man but does not turn. His eyes seem to be aimed at the pavement.

"Yeah, he'd be good. He's got his hands full. You let him get in the car, and you get in with him before he can close the door. You are right on top of him, and you show him the knife. He'll slide over and go along with it."

"After that?"

"If you think he's gonna chase you, you can put him in the trunk."

We turn toward a cluster of buildings. I see a man in a black suburban coat. He is taller and younger.

"Not him," Jones says, again without looking directly at him. "He looks hard. You could take him off in a hallway, but he would give you trouble in the street." . . .

We walk to Second Avenue, moving among crowds of shoppers—sad faces, tired arms filled with packages, coats, purses, flat hip-pocket wallets in the sunny afternoon . . . so much *money* in this speckled fool's gold afternoon. . . .

He looks across the street.

"There's a precinct house on that block. The check-cashing place near it is a good place to pull rips. Nobody thinks a dude would have the heart to do it so close to a cop station; so nobody watches it very closely."

We walk into a grimy side street between First and Second Avenues and stop across from a storefront. The red-and-blue sign—Checks Cashed/Money Orders Filled—is ringed with light bulbs, and the windows are covered with

ity? Of equal weight is the question: Should behaviors be deemed criminal when there is no consensus about their harmfulness? In a classic statement, John Stuart Mill wrote in 1859: "The only purpose for which power can rightfully be exercised over any member of a civilized community, against his will, is to prevent harm to others. His own good, either physical or moral, is not a warrant."[27] Although Mill's view may sound logical, can it be said that vice does not harm others? A persuasive answer to Mill has been given by Patrick Devlin, who believes that harm does ensue when society fails to bring about adherence to a common morality.[28] From his standpoint, society has the right to use the criminal law to bring about conformity to the majority's moral commitments and values. Further, the criminal law serves to proclaim those values.

Although philosophers and legal scholars will continue to debate these problems, a more concrete and practical question asks: Is the enforcement of laws prohibiting these behaviors consistent with the goals of the criminal justice system? The National Advisory Commission on Criminal Justice Stan-

---

wire and protective devices. Half a block away, the precinct house has patrol cars clustered in front. Brawny plainclothes detectives pass by every few minutes.

Jones looks at my watch and sees that it is two-fifteen.

"It's a little early now. Pretty soon, this place will be doin' business." We lean against a store window and wait.

Jones nudges me. "That dude's got cash. Watch him."

Across the street, I see a tall man with snow-white hair. He walks confidently, head erect, wearing a black cashmere coat; in profile he bears a striking resemblance to the late Chief Justice Earl Warren, the same bright eyes, broad nose, and prominent cheekbones. I mention this to Jones, who laughs, only vaguely familiar with the Warren Court.

Jones's street sense is astounding. The man hasn't moved directly toward the store, only stepped off the curb. He could be headed anywhere on the block.

Jones says he will cash a check.

He passes the storefront, then stops, steps backward, and disappears into the doorway.

"He is being careful. So he's got cash."

"A good victim?"

"Yeah."

Three minutes later, the man emerges and continues walking down the block.

"From the way he walks, I think he lives on this block."

"Why?"

"The way he moves. He looks like he knows where he's going. He's afraid to move too fast, but he looks like he knows where he wants to get to."

As Jones finishes the sentence, the tall old man turns on one foot and walks into a brownstone apartment building.

"When would you move?"

"I'd wait until he gets through the door. The building is old, so the second door won't lock fast. If you time it right, the lock won't stop you."

Jones drags on the cigarette he is holding.

"I'd be in there now. I'd let him start climbing the stairs. Then I'd take him."

And the old man, who looks like a statesman but lives on a bad block, would lose something. His Social Security check? A stock dividend? His life? . . .

Source: James Willwerth, "Portrait of a Mugger," *Harper's Magazine,* November 1974, p. 88. From *Jones: Portrait of a Mugger,* by James Willwerth.

dards and Goals summarizes: "The criminal justice system is ill-equipped to deal with these [morality] offenses. These crimes place a heavy and unwelcome burden on law enforcement resources throughout the nation. And the laws regulating these offenses are open to abuse and, increasingly, to constitutional challenge."[29]

Drunkenness

Almost two million arrests are made each year for the offense of public drunkenness. These represent more than twice the number of arrests for all of the eight serious offenses that the FBI takes as its index crimes. Such a volume places an extremely heavy burden on the operations of the justice system because it requires action by the police, clogs the lower criminal courts, and crowds correctional institutions. As the San Francisco Committee on Crime has noted, the handling of drunks costs that city almost $1 million per year. A conservative estimate places the cost to the nation at more than $100 million.[30] If it could be shown that some social good were being served by laws against drunkenness, it would be easier to justify the costs of enforcing them. Unfortunately, chronic alcoholics go through the doors of the halls of justice repeatedly. It would appear that the criminal sanction not only has been unable to deter drunkenness but has resulted in the diversion of resources to deal with the problem.

In 1966, decisions handed down by the federal courts of appeals in the Fourth Circuit and in the District of Columbia held unconstitutional statutes that punish chronic alcoholics as criminals. In 1968, Congress passed the District of Columbia Alcoholics Rehabilitation Act, repealing the criminal penalties and providing instead for treatment facilities. The National Conference of Commissioners on Uniform State Laws has drafted model legislation calling for the decriminalization of alcoholism and public drunkenness and has provided the states with guidelines for dealing with the problem. These proposals have been endorsed by the American Bar Association and have been incorporated in the laws of at least nine states.

The reforms suggested by these and other groups call for the police or other officials to take a person incapacitated by alcohol into protective custody and then to make available programs for the treatment of the malady. Boston and several other cities have instituted this approach, with social workers assisting the public drunk off the streets to a safe place for sobering up, counseling, and care.

Alcoholism

He has been drinking steadily since his teens, and he lives on Skid Row, that run-down jumble of shabby taverns, insect-infested flophouses, religious missions dispensing free meals and lodging, cafeterias selling cheap soup, and employment agencies that specialize in dishwashers and busboys. John has no ties to anyone, and he has forgotten what trades he ever knew. He panhandles for pennies and wipes the windshields of cars stopped by a red light in hopes of a handout; occasionally he works in a restaurant kitchen hauling out garbage or washing dishes. Whatever he earns goes for cheap wine or rotgut liquor at the cutrate Skid Row bars.

Source: Edwin Kiester, Jr., *Crimes with No Victims* (unpaged pamphlet published by the Alliance for a Safer New York, 1972).

Prostitution

Although the FBI reported 83,000 arrests for prostitution in 1980, the figure is misleading because there were also 700,000 persons arrested for disorderly conduct, a charge often used against prostitutes.[31] In most states the law defines prostitution as the indiscriminate offer by a female of her body for sexual intercourse or other lewdness for the purpose of gain. The penalties imposed are usually fines or brief jail sentences.

Once thought to be the product of bad upbringing, poverty, and seduction at an early age, prostitution is now thought by some researchers to be a chosen profession that is believed to offer greater ease, freedom, and profit than available alternatives. It should be added that because she provides a sexual service for which there is a demand, the prostitute's life is usually one of fear, not only of the police but also of her pimp. The police have justified stiff law enforcement on the grounds that prostitutes are often involved in other types of offenses, particularly robberies.

Enforcement of prostitution laws is carried out in most American cities in a manner that might be called human zoning. It is the visible streetwalker who is arrested, especially if she works in areas of the city where her presence is believed to have a detrimental effect on business. One reason why law enforcement efforts are focused on street solicitation is the extreme difficulty and costliness for the police of gathering the necessary evidence in the hotels, massage parlors, and apartments where the more elite call girls operate. But the police are also under great pressures from segments of the public to keep prostitutes out of sight.

Decriminalization of prostitution has been proposed by a number of authorities; all agree that police efforts to prevent this type of behavior have been both costly and ineffective. On the other hand, there seems to be little political incentive to urge that the laws against it be abolished. Only in Nevada is prostitution legal; throughout the rest of the country, prostitution exists illegally. Police enforcement policies dictate both the extent and the visibility of "the lively commerce."

Gambling

Throughout U.S. history, the law's perspective on gambling has been inconsistent. From the early days, when gambling was permitted for gentlemen but not for laborers, to today, when those with the money can fly to Las Vegas or place a bet in a parlor in Manhattan while others can only illegally play the numbers in Harlem, the law has been riddled with inconsistencies, class bias, and ineffective enforcement.

Gambling in the United States today centers on four kinds of operations: (1) numbers, (2) casino-type operations, (3) lotteries, and (4) pari-mutuel betting at racetracks. Numbers remain illegal throughout the nation; casino gambling is permitted only in Nevada and New Jersey; and state-operated lotteries function in a number of states. The income benefits state governments where legal operations are permitted; but throughout the country, even in states with legalized gambling, gambling is still the greatest source of revenue for organized crime. Estimates ranging from $7 billion to $50 billion a year have been given as the take for illegal operations.

It has been suggested that gambling has been made illegal to emphasize the Puritan ethic—the view that hard work, not luck, is the way to achieve rewards. What is most striking about the enforcement of gambling prohibitions is its class bias and the difficulty of convicting. Playing the numbers has even been justified as a cultural trait of the black ghetto and something that should not be legalized because the operations would be taken over by more powerful interests. Can the law continue to accept the contradiction between a legal bet placed in a state-operated lottery and an illegal bet placed with the corner bookie?

Reform

Numerous commissions and reform groups have suggested reviewing the criminal law with the intention of decriminalizing many aspects of behavior. Although some proposals reflect the humanistic belief that persons should be free to engage in any activity that does not harm others, most decriminalization proposals are based on the assumption that enforcement resources can be utilized more efficiently against "real crime" if they are not spent on crimes without victims.

Thus far, only such nuisance and illness statutes as those on vagrancy and drunkenness have been changed. Laws proscribing certain sexual activities will probably die a slow death through nonenforcement; sexual practices in private between consenting adults will undoubtedly be decriminalized in this

---

Prostitution

Shortly after midnight on May 19, as red neon lights danced in a fine mist on West 85th Street, a policeman watched a man and woman whisper in a darkened doorway and then enter a hotel.

Half an hour later the man left. After briefly questioning him on the street, the policeman walked into the hotel and arrested Matilda F. for prostitution.

When she appeared a few hours later in Women's Court, a clerk called, "Hi, Matilda. Back home again, eh?" Matilda laughed weakly and said, "Yeah, I love you so much I can't stay away."

Matilda's May court appearance was her 81st on prostitution charges since 1943. Age 44 years old [*sic*], she has spent 12 years and 10 months in the Women's House of Detention—most of it in sentences of 10 to 90 days. "She's doing life on the installment plan," a clerk remarked.

Source: J. Anthony Lukas, "City Revising Its Prostitution Controls," *New York Times*, 14 August 1967, p. 88.

Gambling

Joe stands six mornings a week outside a storefront social club in the "Little Italy" area behind Police Headquarters [in New York City]. He is squat. His long gray sweater blends in color with his thinning hair. Housewives on their way to and from the market, men in work clothes, the unemployed and relief clients stop to exchange greetings with a handshake.

A quarter passes hands, or a half dollar, sometimes a dollar bill—but never a slip with a penciled number. If the police were to frisk Joe they'd find no evidence. He carries the number, given orally, into the club inside his head after each encounter. The club interior, where the numbers and amount of play are listed, is forbidden territory to the police without a court-issued search warrant.

Source: "Grocers, Barmaids, Pizza Sellers Help Run Game," *New York Times*, 26 June 1964, p. 17.

---

manner. With the exception of laws prohibiting the possession of marijuana, most of the drug statutes will probably remain on the books and be objects of enforcement activity. As Thurman Arnold has said: "Most unenforced criminal laws survive in order to satisfy moral objections to established modes of conduct. They are unenforced because we want to continue our conduct, and unrepealed because we want to preserve our morals.[32]

Not all observers agree with the assumption that increased law enforcement efficiency will result from decriminalization. Some point out that arrests for such offenses as prostitution, drunkenness, and drug use give the police opportunities to prove their worth. It is much simpler to meet public expectations of crime control by citing the arrests of drug pushers than by publicizing the numbers of people they have managed to arrest for burglary or other visible crimes.

What *are* the likely consequences of decriminalization? To be sure, certain classes of persons would not enter the criminal justice system for the offenses now charged against them, but would other charges be used to impose sanctions on those same individuals? Would decriminalization of particular types of behavior really bring about increased police effectiveness or would it bring about increased frustration? Would the caseloads of the courts become unclogged or is a necessary level of inputs required to meet the organizational needs of the system? With drug offenders currently making up a large part of the prison population, how would correctional authorities react if their clientele suddenly dropped? Such questions must be examined when reform is considered within the conceptual framework of an administrative system.

Legislative process and the law

In a democracy, the people's elected representatives meeting as legislatures are charged with writing the statutes defining crime. Thus in the political arenas of the U.S. Congress and the legislatures of the fifty states, decisions are made as to the types of behavior that will come under the criminal code and the range of punishments that may be imposed on offenders. This is not to dismiss the contributions of constitutions and judicial decisions in the formation of the substantive and procedural aspects of the criminal law but to point to the fact that legislators write the statutes that define crime.

Ideally the legislative process is the instrument through which the public interest is expressed. Rather than being a rational process of decision making in which facts are clear, interests are identical, and unanimous agreement is easily reached as to the nature of the common good, however, the political nature of the legislative process results in clashes, compromises, and bargaining. As a result, proposed statutes are often stated in vague and ambiguous terms to ensure that a majority of lawmakers will vote in their favor.

Statutory specifications of the punishments for criminal offenses demonstrate the ambiguity of the products of the legislative process. While American legislatures have done a good job of defining proscribed behavior, so that most people know the acts that are forbidden, they have not done a good job of specifying punishments. Legislatures grant judges sweeping powers to fashion sentences, and Judge Marvin E. Frankel cites some examples from the federal code: "An assault upon a federal officer may be punishable by a fine and imprisonment for 'not more than ten years.' The federal kidnapping law authorizes 'imprisonment for any term of years or for life.' Rape leads to 'death, or imprisonment for any term of years or for life.' "[33] By giving this type of discretion to judges, legislators may appear to be mandating strong penalties, yet they may trust that more reasonable sentences will be handed down.

Interest groups

interest group
A private organization formed to influence government policies so that they will coincide with the desires of its members. Such organized pressure groups operate at all levels of government.

The few studies of the way legislatures write the criminal law reveal that, other than in connection with such highly publicized and emotional issues as abortion, narcotics traffic, and obscenity, widespread citizen debate with accompanying large, well-organized, and "well-oiled" pressure groups does not exist. Most of the lawmaking activity leading to changes in the criminal code is monopolized by criminal justice professionals—lawyers, police officers, judges, corrections officers—and their occupational associates. However, social scientists have shown that lawmakers are influenced by ***interest groups,*** political leaders, community elites, and on occasion, public opinion. In addition, business interests that might be affected by legislative changes may become vocal.

Interest groups and the law of prostitution. Pamela Roby has described interest-group conflict in a study of the revision of the New York State penal law on prostitution. The new provisions made patronizing a prostitute an offense, restricted the police from using customers as witnesses in prosecutions, and prohibited plainclothesmen from obtaining solicitations from prostitutes. In addition, it reduced the penalty for prostitution from one year to fifteen days in jail. These changes were urged on the Penal Law and Criminal Code Revision Commission by the American Social Health Association, defense attorneys, women's advocates, and some judges.

The new sections of the penal code were passed by the legislature in 1965 almost without notice. Only after they went into effect did New York City business people, politicians, and police, who viewed the revised statute as permissive, become alarmed that there would be a massive influx of prostitutes. In response to this pressure, a cleanup of Times Square was instigated, marking the start of a pitched battle with the police and the district attorney's office on the one side and the Civil Liberties Union, the Legal Aid Society, and certain judges on the other. The number of prostitutes arrested in the raids added fuel to the belief that the revisions had created an intolerable situation from the perspective of such groups as the New York City Hotel Association.

In response to this situation, amendments were submitted to the legislature by the Mayor's Committee on Prostitution. These recommendations would have reclassified prostitution from a violation to a Class A misdemeanor (returning the sentence to one year) and would have extended the loitering section in the penal code to include "loitering for the purpose of prostitution." Nearly ten months after the law had become effective, the legislature rejected these proposed amendments to it and thus left it unchanged, at least temporarily. Roby believes that the Senate Committee on Codes, the group that considered the amendments, turned them down because the law had been in effect for such a short time, because the tougher sentences would fill the jails, and because the senators did not feel that prostitution warranted a one-year jail sentence. In addition, the composition of the committee, whose members were lawyers rather than business people, made it unsympathetic to the proposals.

Roby shows that during the different stages in the formulation and enforcement of the law, power shifted from one interest group to another.

> One group frequently exercised power with respect to one section of the law while another did so with respect to another section. In the final stage of the law's history, civil liberties and welfare groups dominated over businessmen and the police with respect to the clause making prostitution a violation subject to a maximum fifteen day sentence while the police and businessmen dominated over the civil liberties and welfare groups with respect to the nonenforcement of the "patron" clause.[34]

Summary

Behavior that is defined as criminal varies from society to society and from one era to the next. Although it may be shown that throughout history certain crimes considered to be *mala in se* have consistently been part of the penal codes of Western civilization, their interpretation and enforcement have varied. Offenses classified as *mala prohibita* have increased greatly in number as legislatures have responded to pressures from an urbanized and industrial society. Although the criminal code may be thought to reflect the norms of society, we must remember that these laws are enacted by legislatures. They are created in response to the political dynamics of the legislative system. The definition of behavior as offensive, this very basic element of the criminal justice system, is thus a product of the social and political environment.

For discussion

1. Why does the law declare some types of human behavior criminal but not others?
2. Many states are now rethinking the legal status and penal sanctions for the possession and private use of marijuana. Why are these laws being reconsidered?
3. You are a state legislator. The public has called for very stiff penalties for drug sellers. You are aware of studies showing that the police will not make arrests and judges will not punish offenders when the penalties are too harsh. What aspects of the criminal justice system may allow you to remain popular with your constituents yet feel comfortable with new, stiff penalties?
4. Periodically states revise their criminal code. What portions of the penal law in your state need revision? Why?

For further reading

Allen, Francis A. *The Borderland of Criminal Justice.* Chicago: University of Chicago Press, 1964.
Becker, Howard S. *Outsiders: Studies in the Sociology of Deviance.* New York: Free Press, 1963.
Duster, Troy. *The Legislation of Morality.* New York: Free Press, 1970.
Erikson, Kai T. *Wayward Puritans.* New York: Wiley, 1966.
Hall, Jerome. *Theft, Law, and Society.* Indianapolis: Bobbs-Merrill, 1952.
Musto, David. *The American Disease.* New Haven: Yale University Press, 1973.
Quinney, Richard. *The Social Reality of Crime.* Boston: Little, Brown, 1970.
Shur, Edwin M. *Crimes without Victims.* Englewood Cliffs, N.J.: Prentice-Hall, 1965.
Sutherland, Edwin H. *White Collar Crime.* New York: Dryden Press, 1969.

Notes

1. Marshall B. Clinard and Richard Quinney, *Criminal Behavior Systems* (New York: Holt, Rinehart & Winston, 1973), p. 27.

2. Robert A. Levine, "Gusii Sex Offenses: A Study in Social Control," *American Anthropologist* 61 (December 1959): 896–990.
3. Jerome Hall, *General Principles of Criminal Law,* 2d ed. (Indianapolis: Bobbs-Merrill, 1947), p. 1.
4. Wolfgang Friedmann, *Law in a Changing Society* (Berkeley: University of California Press, 1959), p. 165.
5. U.S. Department of Justice, Bureau of Justice Statistics, *Report to the Nation on Crime and Justice* (Washington, D.C.: Government Printing Office, 1983), p. 4.
6. Emile Durkheim, *The Division of Labor in Society,* trans. George Simpson (Glencoe, Ill.: Free Press, 1960), p. 102.
7. Richard Quinney, *Crime and Justice in Society* (Boston: Little, Brown, 1969), p. 25.
8. Ibid.
9. William J. Chambliss, "A Sociological Analysis of the Law of Vagrancy," *Social Problems* 12 (Summer 1964): 67–77.
10. Ibid., p. 68.
11. Ibid., p. 76.
12. Jerome Skolnick, "Perspectives on Law and Order," in *Politics and Crime,* ed. Sawyer F. Sylvester, Jr., and Edward Sagarin (New York: Praeger, 1974), p. 13.
13. Stephen Schafer, *Criminology* (Reston, Va.: Reston Publishing Co., 1976), p. 48.
14. Richard Dugdale, *The Jukes: Crime, Pauperism, Disease, and Heredity,* 4th ed. (New York: Putnam, 1910 [1875]); Arthur Estabrook, *The Jukes in 1915* (Washington, D.C.: Carnegie Institution, 1916); Henry H. Goddard, *The Kallikak Family* (New York: The Macmillan Company, 1902).
15. Skinner v. Oklahoma, 316 U.S. 535 (1942).
16. Edwin H. Sutherland, "The Sexual Psychopath Laws," *Journal of Criminal Law & Criminology* 40 (January–February 1950): 543.
17. Edwin H. Sutherland and Donald Cressey, *Criminology* (Philadelphia: Lippincott, 1970).
18. Frank Tanenbaum, *Crime and the Community* (Boston: Ginn and Company, 1938).
19. Howard S. Becker, *Outsiders: Studies in the Sociology of Deviance* (New York: Free Press, 1963).
20. Union of Radical Criminologists, *Newsletter* 3 (May 1973): 1.
21. Morton Hunt, *The Mugging* (New York: Atheneum, 1972), p. 44.
22. Vera Institute of Justice, *Felony Arrests: Their Prosecution and Disposition in New York City's Courts* (New York, 1977), p. 135.
23. Freda Adler, "Crime, an Equal Opportunity Employer," *Trial Magazine,* January 1977, p. 31.
24. Rita Simon, "Women and Crime Revisited," *Social Science Quarterly* 56 (March 1976): 658.
25. President's Commission on Law Enforcement and Administration of Justice, *The Challenge of Crime in a Free Society* (Washington, D.C.: Government Printing Office, 1967), p. 4.
26. Francis A. Allen, *The Borderland of Criminal Justice* (Chicago: University of Chicago Press, 1964), p. 3.
27. John Stuart Mill, *Utilitarianism, Liberty and Representative Government* (New York: Dutton, 1947), p. 72.
28. Patrick Devlin, *The Enforcement of Morals* (London: Oxford University Press, 1965), p. 13.
29. National Advisory Commission on Criminal Justice Standards and Goals, *A National Strategy to Reduce Crime* (Washington, D.C.: Government Printing Office, 1973), p. 131.
30. Ibid., p. 132.
31. U.S. Department of Justice, *Uniform Crime Reports* (Washington, D.C.: Government Printing Office, 1980), p. 199.
32. Thurman Arnold, *The Symbols of Government* (New York: Harcourt, Brace, 1935), p. 160.
33. Marvin E. Frankel, *Criminal Sentences* (New York: Hill & Wang, 1972), p. 5.
34. Pamela A. Roby, "Politics and Criminal Law: Revision of the New York State Penal Law on Prostitution," *Social Problems* 17 (Summer 1969): 108.

Criminal Justice and the Rule of Law

3

Justice will be universal in this country when the processes as well as the doors of the courthouse are open to everyone.

CHIEF JUSTICE EARL WARREN

Danny Escobedo, a trouble-prone Chicago laborer, was suspected of murdering his brother-in-law. No weapon was found and there were no witnesses. He was held for questioning for fourteen hours, released, and then picked up again. Escobedo had been in enough trouble before to have a lawyer on call, and when he was brought in the second time, he asked to see his attorney but was refused. Meanwhile, his lawyer was in the station house and waited there for more than four hours to see his client. The police told Escobedo that his lawyer was not there and did not want to see him anyway. An alleged accomplice who was apprehended said that Escobedo had offered him $500 to shoot the brother-in-law. When confronted by the accomplice, Escobedo said to him in front of the police that the accomplice had pulled the trigger. By Illinois law, Escobedo was equally guilty. The judge said that the confession had been voluntary and sentenced Escobedo to twenty years in prison.

On appeal to the U.S. Supreme Court, Escobedo's conviction was overturned, not on the basis of a coerced confession but because he had been refused the right to see his counsel during his interrogation. As the opinion of the majority of justices noted, the police viewed Escobedo as the accused, and the purpose of their interrogation was to get him to confess his guilt despite his constitutional right not to do so. The Court said that once an investigation into an unsolved crime begins to focus on a particular suspect, our adversary system with its rights of due process begins to operate, and the suspect has a right to be represented by counsel.[1]

Danny Escobedo's troubles in Chicago serve to remind us that law is at the base of the criminal justice system. Law governs the conduct of officials, and law structures the behavior of citizens. Law thus performs two functions: (1) it defines those behaviors that are labeled criminal and (2) it describes the procedures to be followed under our adversarial system by those with the responsibility for law enforcement, adjudication, and corrections. Persons may not be convicted of committing an illegal act unless the state is able to prove that the conditions specified in the law were met and that the procedures required by the law were followed. We have argued that criminal justice operates as an administrative system influenced by political and social forces; now the third necessary ingredient of our analysis—law—must be examined. This chapter explores the two aspects of criminal law: the substantive criminal law and the law of criminal procedure.

Foundations of criminal law

In our system of justice, violators of society's rules are prosecuted and tried according to laws. As chapter 2 emphasized, not all behavior that is offensive or considered deviant is criminal behavior. Only behaviors proscribed by the criminal code are illegal. We have seen that in different locations and times, different behaviors have been defined as criminal. What is basic to our system, however, is the assumption found in the ancient Latin saying *nullum crimen, nulla poena, sine lege* ("there can be no crime and no punishment except as the law prescribes"). The criminal law, often referred to as the *penal code,* therefore embodies descriptions not only of the forbidden behavior and the punishment to be administered but also of the ways in which justice officials must deal with defendants.

Criminal law is thus divided into substantive law and procedural law. Substantive law embodies a view of the social order that the community desires to achieve. It is the specification, or stipulation, of the types of conduct that are criminal and the punishments to be imposed for such behavior. Substantive law answers the question: *What* is illegal? Procedural law sets forth the rules that govern enforcement of the substantive law. It stipulates the procedures that officials must follow in the enforcement, adjudication, and corrections portions of the criminal justice system. Procedural law limits the activities of police officers, judges, probation officers, and guards. It answers the question: *How* is the law enforced? In brief, the criminal law stipulates the nature of the offenses, thus defining the elements of a violation, and it also specifies the conditions of enforcement and punishment.

Development of criminal law

common law
The Anglo-American system of uncodified law, in which judges follow precedents set by earlier decisions when they decide new but similar cases. The substantive and procedural criminal law was originally developed in this manner but was later codified by legislatures.

stare decisis
The principle that judges should be bound by precedents (decisions made in previous similar cases) when they decide the cases before them.

The earliest known codes of law are the Sumerian (3100 B.C.) and the Code of Hammurabi (1750 B.C.). These were written codes, divided into sections to cover different types of offenses. The Code of Hammurabi, containing 282 clauses, was the first to specify retribution as a sanction. In classical Greece the Draconian Code was promulgated in the seventh century B.C., and the Law of the Twelve Tables existed among the Romans (450 B.C.). Although we can look to these early sources of criminal law, we in the United States look to England as the source of the greater part of our political and legal concepts. Of these concepts, the Anglo-American common law is probably the most important, for it is the major tie that binds the traditions of the two societies and differentiates them from the non-English-speaking world. ***Common law*** developed in England and was based on custom and tradition as interpreted by judges. In continental Europe, a system of civil law developed in which the rules were formulated in codes or specially written stipulations. By contrast, the common law was not written down as a code that one could easily consult to learn what was proper. Rather, it took its form from the collected opinions of the English judges, who looked to custom in making decisions. The judges thus created law when they ruled on specific cases.

These rulings then formed precedents to be followed in later rulings, in accordance with the policy of ***stare decisis*** ("to stand by things [that have been] decided"). Even today *stare decisis* is the basic doctrine followed by American courts. Judges are thus expected to refer to prior opinions for guidance when they decide the cases before them. In other words, the prior decision is part of the law and is used to guide decisions on similar cases. Accordingly, for much of English history it was not possible to learn the law by consulting one source, such as a constitution or statute book. The law was found in many places, most of which were the leading opinions written by judges who had heard earlier cases. As new situations arose and more opinions were written to resolve conflicts, the common law grew. This stability combined with flexibility in the face of new circumstances is the uniquely valuable characteristic of Anglo-American law.

The emergence of criminal law in England paralleled the development of national sovereignty during the twelfth century. With the Norman invasion of 1066, the tribal law of the Saxons yielded to the authority of the central government, the crown. As the blood feud of the tribes had given way under the influence of feudalism and Christianity to a system of compensations for criminal wrongs, the reign of Henry II (1154–1189) marked the emergence of a common law for England. The system of compensations became a system of writs, procedures, and common law developed by a strong centralized court that made general rules for all the realm. This development marked the end of the concept that such offenses as murder were merely regrettable torts (wrongful actions) for which compensation should be paid. Under the common law, crime became an offense to be prosecuted by the community through its chief.

Among the contributions of England to the American colonies was the common law system. Originally the English precedents and procedures were maintained in the New World, but changes in the structure of the common law of crime began to occur with the American Revolution and ratification of a written constitution. Starting in the nineteenth century, state legislatures began to incorporate the common law into written penal codes and rules of criminal procedure. We continue to speak of the United States as having a common law system because the concept of precedent is maintained; yet in most states judges now consult legislatively enacted criminal codes to ascertain how wrongdoing is defined and the punishments to be exacted. At the national level, there was never a common law of crime; rather, from 1789 on, Congress has passed statutes making various behaviors violations of federal law.

Mala in se–mala prohibita. In the course of the development of the English common law, one of the primary distinctions made was between offenses considered *male in se*—"ordinary" crimes, acts wrong in themselves (murder, rape, arson, theft)—and offenses considered *mala prohibita*—acts that are crimes because they are prohibited by law (riot, poaching, vagrancy, drunkenness). Ordinary crimes were considered felonies that could be tried in the central criminal courts; acts labeled *mala prohibita* were proclaimed by legislation, considered misdemeanors, and enforced by justices of the peace. C. Ray Jeffery quotes legal writers of the eighteenth and nineteenth centuries to show these differences.

> Criminal law is related to acts which, if there were no criminal law at all, would be judged by the public at large much as they are judged at present. If murder, theft,

and rape were not punishable by law, the words would still be in use and would be applied to the same or nearly the same actions.[2]

> Which has occasioned some to doubt how far a human legislature ought to inflict capital punishment for positive offences; offences against the municipal law only, and not against the law of nature. . . . With regard to offences *mala in se,* capital punishments are in some instances inflicted by the immediate *command* of God Himself to all mankind; as, in the case of murder. . . .[3]

The distinction between ordinary crimes and those that are prohibited serves the useful purpose of pointing to the sources of the criminal law.

Expansion of mala prohibita. By and large, the types of crimes classified as *mala in se* have remained static while those known as *mala prohibita* have greatly expanded. Modern legislatures have added three major groups to the traditional offenses: crimes without victims, political crimes, and regulatory offenses. Today there are many more arrests and prosecutions for offenses belonging to these latter categories than for the traditional violations of the criminal law. William Chambliss and Robert Seidman make a valid point:

> A common characteristic of these newer offenses [is] that, in one way or the other, the laws defining most of them have abandoned some or all of the devices by which the common law placed restrictions on policemen's discretion. These laws have in fact increased the policeman's opportunity to replace law with "order."[4]

In most of the situations involved in *mala prohibita,* law enforcement authorities are faced with the responsibility of determining not only *who* has committed the offense but, more important, *whether* an offense has been committed. Thus the number of arrests for these crimes is directly related to police efficiency.

The *mala in se–mala prohibita* distinction helps to clarify the principles of the criminal law, but not always. The problem lies in the perceptions or views of those who define criminal behavior. If an asbestos company fails to provide its workers with proper masks, is it violating governmental safety laws or should it be charged with injury to persons? Is rolling back an odometer a commercial fraud or petty theft from a purchaser?

Felony–misdemeanor. Another way of classifying crimes is according to their level of seriousness, though the same crime may be classified as a felony in one state and a misdemeanor in another. Although some might say that a felony is a more serious offense than a misdemeanor, most state laws define these terms with regard to the punishment that may be exacted. Conviction on a felony charge usually means a prison sentence of more than a year; misdemeanants are dealt with more leniently. Some states use place of punishment as the defining criterion—penitentiary for felonies, jail for misdemeanors.

Whether a defendant is charged with a felony or a misdemeanor is important not only in terms of potential punishment but in terms of how the criminal justice system will process the defendant. Certain rights and penalties follow from this distinction. For example, the conditions under which the police may make an arrest, the right of indigents to have counsel provided by the state, and the trial level at which the charges will be heard are determined by whether a felony or misdemeanor is charged. Further, persons convicted of felonies may be barred from certain professions, such as law and medicine, and in many states are barred from other occupations (bartender, police officer, barber) as well. This sort of sanction can be carried to ludicrous extremes. In Connecticut, for example, former felons are prohibited from refereeing professional wrestling matches.

Criminal law versus civil law. It is also important that we clarify the distinctions between criminal law and civil law. A basic distinction is that a violation of criminal law is an offense against society as a whole; civil law regulates relationships between individuals. In the field of civil law known as torts, for example, the major concern is compensation to the individual wronged. If through your negligence your automobile collides with another, the owner of the other car may bring a civil suit against you to recover the amount of damages you have caused. In a separate action the state may charge you with a violation of the criminal law with regard to the operation of motor vehicles because your actions breached society's rules.

Where is criminal law found?

One document that clearly stated the criminal law, both substantive and procedural, would be nice to have. It would allow citizens to know when they might be in danger of committing an illegal act and to know their rights should official action be taken against them. If such a document could be written in simple language, society would probably need fewer attorneys. Compiling such a document would, of course, be impossible, and the criminal law must continue to be found in the four basic sources from which it is derived: constitutions, statutes, court decisions, and administrative regulations.

Constitutions provide the fundamental principles and procedural safeguards that serve as guides for the enactment of laws and the making of decisions. The Bill of Rights of the United States Constitution and that of each state include a number of articles that have direct bearing on the criminal law. The basic protections—those against unreasonable searches and seizures, those requiring due process, and those prohibiting cruel and unusual punishment—were added to the U.S. Constitution immediately after ratification. Most state constitutions also list these protections, and since the early forties the U.S. Supreme Court has required that criminal procedures in the states recognize the protections set forth in the national constitution.

Statutes are laws passed by legislative bodies; the substantive and procedural rules of most states are found in their statutes. Although the law of crime is primarily an activity of state legislatures, Congress and local city and town bodies also play a role. Federal criminal laws passed by Congress deal mainly with violations that occur on property of the U.S. government or with behavior that involves the national interest (treason) or the jurisdictions of more than one state (taking a kidnap victim across state lines). The states give cities and towns some authority to develop laws dealing with local problems. There is often an overlapping of jurisdictions among national, state, and local rules governing some criminal conduct. The possession or sale of narcotics, for example, may violate criminal laws at all three levels of government. In such situations, enforcement agencies may disagree as to which one will prosecute the offender.

statutes
Laws passed by legislatures. Statutory definitions of criminal offenses are embodied in penal codes.

If we want to know the definition of a crime covered by a statute, we consult a state volume known as the penal code; the acts that constitute the crime of robbery in Nevada and the penalty to be imposed there, for example, are clearly specified in Nevada's penal code. For purposes of comparison, we can consult the penal code of Maine. Although the laws of most of the states are similar, there are some differences. To encourage uniformity among the states in the substantive and procedural laws, the American Law Institute has developed a Model Penal code that it urges legislatures to adopt.[5]

Court decisions, often called *case law,* constitute a third source of criminal law. As noted, the major characteristic of the United States' common law system is the principle that judges look to earlier opinions to guide their determinations in the particular cases before them. Although much of the common law of crime has been replaced by statutes, reference to precedent is still very much an aid to lawyers and judges in the interpretation of these codified rules.

Administrative regulations are laws and rulings made by federal, state, and local agencies. Such official bodies as departments of health have been given power by the legislative or executive branch to develop rules to govern specific policy areas. Most such rules have been promulgated during the twentieth century to deal with modern problems: wages and hours, pollution, automobile traffic, industrial safety, pure food and drugs, and the like. Many of the rules are part of the criminal law, and violations are processed through the criminal justice system.

When one talks about the criminal law, then, reference is not being made merely to the penal code or some similar concise statement of rules. The criminal law, both substantive and procedural, is found in the four places described here.

Substantive criminal law

As we have seen, the substantive criminal law defines the misbehavior that is subject to punishment and specifies the punishments for such offenses. Underlying the substantive criminal law is the basic doctrine that no one may be convicted or punished for an offense unless the conduct constituting that offense has been authoritatively defined by the law. In short, the substantive criminal law defines what is illegal. It is a basic principle that people must know in advance what is required of them, but this is more easily said than done because language is often confusing and ambiguous. In such instances, the judiciary is called on to interpret the law so that the meaning intended by the legislature can be understood.

Seven principles

The criteria used to decide whether a specific behavior is a crime are more complicated than one might imagine from the language of the penal code. Jerome Hall has developed a seven-point formalization of the major principles of Western law.[6] This is a system of interlocking legal propositions that recognizes the existence of the same basic ingredients in every crime. Thus, for a behavior to be defined as criminal and subject to the penalties of the law, all seven principles must be present.

1. Legality—the existence of a law defining the crime. Antisocial behavior is not a crime unless it has been prohibited by law before the act is committed. For example, the United States Constitution prohibits *ex post facto* laws.

2. *Actus reus*—behavior of either commission or omission by the accused that constitutes the violation. This principle emphasizes that behavior itself is required, not just bad intentions. In a modern case involving the principle of *actus reus,* the United States Supreme Court declared unconstitutional a California law making it a criminal offense for a person "to be addicted to the use of narcotics."[7] As Justice Potter Stewart, speaking for the Court, said, the California law does not deal with antisocial behavior but rather with a status, that of being addicted, and thus involves no criminal act.

3. Causation—a causal relationship between the act and the harm suffered. If one person shoots another and the victim dies in the hospital from pneumonia, it is difficult to show that the act (shooting) resulted in the harm (death).

4. Harm—damage inflicted on certain legally protected values (such as person, property, reputation) as a result of the act. This principle is often questioned by persons who feel that they are not committing a crime because they may be harming only themselves. Laws requiring motorcyclists to wear helmets have been challenged on this ground. Such laws, however, have been written with the recognition that accidental injury or death may have a harmful effect on others—dependents, for example.

5. Concurrence—the simultaneous occurrence of the intention and the act. If a repairman enters a house to fix an appliance and while there commits a crime, he cannot be accused of trespass. The intent and the conduct are not fused.

6. *Mens rea*—a guilty state of mind. The commission of the act is not itself criminal unless it is accompanied by a guilty mind. This concept is related to *intent*—that is, the person's actions lead to the assumption that the crime was committed intentionally and on the basis of free will. Persons who are insane when they perform a legally forbidden act have not committed a crime because *mens rea* is not present. Again, involuntary behavior is not criminal; there must be an intention to commit the act. (The difficult concept of *mens rea* is discussed further later.)

7. Punishment—the stipulation in the law of sanctions to be applied against persons found guilty of the forbidden behavior.

These principles may be combined in a single generalization: the harm forbidden by a penal law must be imputed to any normal adult who voluntarily commits it with criminal intent, and such a person must be subjected to the legally prescribed punishment.

The simplicity of Hall's formulation has been emphasized by Gerhard Mueller, who summarizes the seven principles defining crime as follows:[8]

1. legally proscribed	(Legality)
2. human conduct,	(*Actus reus*)
3. causative	(Causation)
4. of a given harm,	(Harm)
5. which conduct coincides	(Concurrence)
6. with a blameworthy frame of mind	(*Mens rea*)
7. and which is subject to punishment.	(Punishment)

Criminal theory is concerned largely with the elucidation of this generalization. The seven principles of crime provide the basis for authorities to define individual behavior as being against the law and provide the accused with the basis for defense against the charges. From these principles flow the assumptions of the adversarial process.

Responsibility for criminal acts

Over the course of time, the seven principles that define a crime have been reinterpreted to meet changing conditions. Among the principles, that of *mens rea* is a crucial element of the substantive criminal law because it is the key for establishing the perpetrator's responsibility for the act committed. To obtain a conviction the prosecution must show that the individual not only committed the illegal act charged but did so in a state of mind that makes the imputation of responsibility appropriate. This is a difficult task because it requires that courts inquire into the mental state of the defendant at the time the act was committed.

mens rea
"Guilty mind" or blameworthy state of mind, necessary for the imputation of responsibility for a criminal offense; criminal as distinguished from innocent intent.

In an earlier period, ***mens rea*** was closely linked through the influence of religion to the concept of sin. With the emergence of psychology as a prominent field of knowledge, the definition of *mens rea* as an actual consciousness of guilt has been abandoned "in favor of intentional, or even reckless or negligent conduct."[9] The new doctrine, called "objective *mens rea,*" asks "not whether an individual defendant has consciousness of guilt but whether a reasonable man in his shoes and with his physical characteristics would have had consciousness of guilt."[10] Objective *mens rea* has thus replaced the traditional notion by requiring that the act be voluntary so that responsibility can be assumed, in this way tying the defendant to the act. It is the intentional quality of the illegal behavior that makes it blameworthy.

Although many defendants in criminal cases openly admit that they committed the illegal behavior, they may still enter a plea of not guilty. They do so because they know the state must provide the evidence to prove them guilty and, more important, because they believe they are not responsible for the illegal act because the necessary *mens rea* element was not present. The clearest example of such a situation may occur when the defendant argues that it was an accident that the gun went off and the neighbor was killed or that the car skidded into the pedestrian. As Justice Oliver Wendell Holmes once said, "Even a dog distinguishes between being stumbled over and being kicked."[11]

We label events *accidents* when responsibility is not fixed; *mens rea* is not present because the event was not intentional. But not everything that is claimed to be accidental is so judged by a court. In some situations the perpetrator is so negligent (the gun was kept loaded with the safety catch off) that the court may fix some degree of criminal responsibility.

Note that *mens rea,* or criminal responsibility, may be fixed without showing that the defendant was intent on doing evil. In other words, it is not the quality of one's motives that establishes *mens rea* but the nature and level of one's intention. This is evident in the Model Penal Code, which lists four mental conditions that can be used to satisfy the requirement of *mens rea:*" A person is not guilty of an offense unless he acted intentionally, knowingly, recklessly, or negligently."[12] There are also offenses that require a high degree of intent. For example, the crime of larceny requires that the defendant intentionally took property to which he knew he was not entitled, *intending* to deprive the rightful owner of possession *permanently.*

strict liability
An obligation or duty whose breach constitutes an offense that requires no showing of *mens rea* to be adjudged criminal; a principle usually applied to regulatory offenses involving health and safety.

But there are also so-called ***strict liability*** offenses, acts that require no showing of intent to be adjudged criminal. The majority of such offenses are defined in legislation of a type first enacted in England and the United States during the latter part of the nineteenth century to deal with issues connected with urban industrialization, among them sanitation, pure food, housing, and safety. Often the statutory language did not include a reference to *mens rea.* Some courts ruled that employers were not responsible for the carelessness of their workers because they had no knowledge of the criminal offenses being committed in their establishments. An employer who had not known that the food products being canned by his employees were contaminated, for example, was not held liable for a violation of pure food laws even if people who ate the food died as a result. Other courts, however, ruled that the owners of such industrial firms had a special responsibility to the public to ensure the quality of their products, and therefore could be found criminally liable if they failed to do so.

The concept of strict liability was best described by Justice Robert Jackson in *Morissette* v. *United States* (1952), in which he upheld the right of legislatures to make certain acts criminal even if *mens rea* were lacking. Pointing to the need for health and welfare regulations, he stated that although the offenses did not threaten the security of the state, they were offenses against its authority because their occurrence impaired the efficiency of the controls necessary for social order. "In this respect, whatever the intent of the violator, the injury is the same. . . . Hence, legislation applicable to such offenses does not specify intent as a necessary element."[13]

The reasoning employed by Justice Jackson to uphold the principle of strict liability, however, has not been followed in all circumstances. Some people believe that the principle should be applied only to regulatory offenses that require no incarceration and that carry no social stigma. The Model Penal Code proposes that strict liability be limited to "violations" that are not crimes and that are punishable only by civil sanctions, such as fines or forfeiture. It looks upon regulatory offenses as a special category of quasi-criminal law. In practice the criminal penalty is usually imposed only after many attempts to induce compliance have failed. Some scholars believe that imprisonment would be unconstitutional for some strict liability crimes, but the incidence of such sentences has been so rare that the concept has not been tested.

In a technologically complex society, we may assume that the concept of strict liability will be expanded to a range of other acts in which a guilty mind is not present. It is also likely, however, that courts will restrict the application of the strict liability principle to situations in which recklessness or indifference is present.

The absence of *mens rea,* then, does not guarantee a verdict of not guilty in every circumstance. In most cases, however, it does relieve defendants of responsibility for acts that, if intentional, would be labeled criminal. In addition to the defense of accident, seven defenses based on absence of criminal intent are recognized in appropriate circumstances: self-defense, necessity, duress, immaturity, mistake of fact, intoxication, and insanity.

Self-defense. A person who feels that he or she is in immediate danger of being harmed by another person's unlawful use of force may ward off the attack in self-defense. The laws of most states also recognize an individual's right to defend others from attack, to protect property, and to prevent the commission of a crime. The law also specifies the manner in which one may protect oneself; generally one must use only the level of force necessary. Distinctions are made between deadly and nondeadly force.

One has the right to kill another person in self-defense if one believes that this amount of force is necessary to prevent one's own death, severe bodily harm, kidnapping, or rape. Courts would not uphold the shooting of an assailant armed with a broomstick unless, perhaps, it were shown that the accused thought that the weapon was a gun about to be fired. In most states self-defense is no justification for the use of force to resist arrest, even if it is later shown that the arrest was unlawful.

Necessity. Outlawed acts are often committed because the perpetrators believe that they are necessary for their own preservation or to avoid a greater evil. Necessity is sometimes confused with self-defense. Jerome Hall explains the distinction: a person is acting in self-defense if he "injures the creator and embodiment of the evil situation"; he is acting from necessity if he "harms a person who was in no way responsible for the imminent danger, one who indeed might himself have been imperiled by it."[14] In short, necessity may be claimed as a defense in situations in which the accused was confronted with a choice of evils. The person speeding through traffic lights to get an injured child to the hospital, or someone breaking and entering a building to seek refuge from a snowstorm, is violating the law out of necessity. But there are other, more complex and serious situations in which it is difficult to exonerate the accused completely.

Since 1884, students have been considering the English legal case *The Queen* v. *Dudley and Stephens.*[15] Thomas Dudley and Edwin Stephens were

---

Self-defense Provisions of the Model Penal Code (Excerpts)

Section 3.04. Use of Force in Self-protection.

1. *Use of Force Justifiable for Protection of the Person.* . . . the use of force upon or toward another person is justifiable when the actor believes that such force is immediately necessary for the purpose of protecting himself against the use of unlawful force by such other person on the present occasion.
2. *Limitations on Justifying Necessity for Use of Force.*
   a. The use of force is not justifiable under this Section:
      i. to resist an arrest which the actor knows is being made by a peace officer, although the arrest is unlawful; or
      ii. to resist force used by the occupier or possessor of property or by another person on his behalf, where the actor knows that the person using the force is doing so under a claim of right to protect the property. . . .
   b. The use of deadly force is not justifiable under this Section unless the actor believes that such force is necessary to protect himself against death, serious bodily harm, kidnapping, or sexual intercourse compelled by force or threat; nor is it justifiable if:
      i. the actor, with the purpose of causing death or serious bodily harm, provoked the use of force against himself in the same encounter; or
      ii. the actor knows that he can avoid the necessity of using such force with complete safety by retreating or by surrendering possession of a thing to a person asserting a claim of right thereto or by complying with a demand that he abstain from any action which he has no duty to take. . . .

Source: *Model Penal Code,* Official Draft.

---

indicted for the murder of Richard Parker after the ship on which they were employed sank 1,600 miles from the Cape of Good Hope. The three, together with another seaman named Brooks, managed to get into a lifeboat containing no drinking water and little food. After twenty days, Dudley and Stephens proposed to Brooks that Parker, the cabin boy, be killed and that they eat his remains as a necessity for survival. Brooks would not agree. With Stephens's assent, Dudley then killed the boy and all three ate from his body for four days, at which time a passing vessel picked them up. Dudley and Stephens were committed for trial, but the jury had to inquire of a higher court whether the behavior was murder. It was agreed that

> if the men had not fed upon the body of the boy they would . . . within the four days have died of famine. That the boy, being in a much weaker condition, was likely to have died before them. That at the time of the act there was no sail in sight, nor any reasonable prospect of relief. That under these circumstances there appeared to the prisoners that unless they then fed or very soon fed upon the boy or one of themselves they would die of starvation. That there was no appreciable chance of saving life except by killing some one for the others to eat.[16]

Given these arguments, one might think that the defense of necessity would have carried the day. But Lord Coleridge, the chief justice, argued that regardless of the temptation or the intensity of the suffering, standards had to be maintained and the law not weakened. Dudley and Stephens were given the death sentence, which the Crown later commuted to six months' imprisonment.

Duress (coercion). Closely related to the defense of necessity is that of duress. The distinction is made on the basis of coercion: a person who has been forced or coerced by another into committing an act has acted under duress. Defendants who present this defense are arguing that they are actually the victims, not the criminals. A bank teller who gives deposited money to an armed robber is excused because she was acting under duress and thus should not be held responsible. By contrast, the defense of necessity is used when the environmental situation (natural rather than human forces) was such that a choice was made to commit an illegal act (cannibalism on the high

---

Necessity Provisions of the Model Penal Code

Section 3.02. Justification Generally: Choice of Evils.

1. Conduct which the actor believes to be necessary to avoid a harm or evil to himself or to another is justifiable, provided that:
   a. the harm or evil sought to be avoided by such conduct is greater than that sought to be prevented by the law defining the offense charged; and
   b. neither the Code nor other law defining the offense provides exceptions or defenses dealing with the specific situation involved; and
   c. a legislative purpose to exclude the justification claimed does not otherwise plainly appear.
2. When the actor was reckless or negligent in bringing about the situation requiring a choice of harms or evils or in appraising the necessity for his conduct, the justification afforded by this Section is unavailable in a prosecution for any offense for which recklessness or negligence, as the case may be, suffices to establish culpability.

---

seas). Courts normally uphold the defense of duress when it is shown that the defendant could not have done otherwise without the expectation of imminent bodily harm or death. Thus duress has not usually been allowed when it has been shown that the defendant had opportunities to escape his plight or that there was a span of time between the threat and the act in which help could have been found.

John Charles Green escaped from the Missouri Training Center, where he had been imprisoned for a three-year term. He was apprehended the next day by a state highway patrol officer some distance from the center. Green contended that his escape was justified because

> prior homosexual assaults and threats near noon on the day of the escape of a homosexual assault upon him that night by other inmates caused the conditions of his confinement to be intolerable; and, that these conditions, together with the state's denial to him of access to the courts, made it necessary that he escape in order to protect himself from submission to the threatened assault or the alternative of death or bodily harm.[17]

Green offered evidence to show that he had been attacked previously and had feigned suicide in order to be taken to the prison hospital.

At a meeting of the center's disciplinary board he had been told by a member to "fight it out, submit to the assaults, or go over the fence." The Supreme Court of Missouri did not accept the defense; it said that the defendant was not being closely pursued by his assailants when he escaped and that he could have avoided the threatened consequences if he had reported to the authorities the names of those making the threats. Yet Judge Seiler in dissent noted that

> if the defendant here had been prosecuted for sodomy as a result of the first assault, it would seem clear that a defense of coercion would be available. In this case defendant sought to avoid committing the coerced act by resorting to escape. Because he was a prisoner, this action was a crime. The act of escape was just as much coerced as the prior act of sodomy. It is consistent with the principle underlying the defense to allow it to be asserted here.[18]

Immaturity. Traditionally, Anglo-American law has excused criminal behavior by children under the age of seven on the grounds that they are immature and not responsible for their actions. At common law, it was possi-

---

Duress Provisions of the Model Penal Code

Section 2.09. Duress.

1. It is an affirmative defense that the actor engaged in the conduct charged to constitute an offense because he was coerced to do so by the use of, or a threat to use, unlawful force against his person or the person of another, which a person of reasonable firmness in his situation would have been unable to resist.
2. The defense provided by this Section is unavailable if the actor recklessly placed himself in a situation in which it was probable that he would be subjected to duress. The defense is also unavailable if he was negligent in placing himself in such a situation, whenever negligence suffices to establish culpability for the offense charged.
3. It is not a defense that a woman acted on the command of her husband, unless she acted under such coercion as would establish a defense under this Section.

---

ble to argue against the assumption that children seven to fourteen were not liable for their criminal acts. For example, prosecutors could introduce evidence of a child's criminal capacity by showing that the child had hidden evidence or had attempted to bribe a witness. As a child approached fourteen, the efficacy of the immaturity defense was weakened. Since the development of juvenile courts in the 1890s, children over the age of seven are not tried by the rules and procedures governing adults. There are, however, various situations in which children may be tried as adults—if, for example, they are repeat offenders or are charged with having committed a particularly heinous offense.

Mistake. The courts have consistently upheld the view that ignorance of the law is no excuse, but what if there is a mistake of fact? Can mistake be used as a defense if a person knows the law but believes that it does not apply in the context of a given situation? Certainly a person could not plead ignorance of the fact that stealing is against the law, but he could use the defense that he mistakenly thought the property was his own. Intent to steal would not be present in the latter situation. In many jurisdictions the crime of statutory rape may result in conviction if the man had intercourse with a female under the age of consent even if he believed—because she looked older or had told him so—that she was over that age. The Model Penal Code rejects this position. What if you thought the white substance in your pocket were flour and police analysis showed it to be cocaine?

Intoxication. The law does not relieve an individual of responsibility for crimes committed while voluntarily intoxicated. There are, however, situations in which intoxication can be used as a defense, as when a person has been tricked into consuming a substance without knowing that it may result in intoxication. More complicated are situations in which the law requires it to be shown that a defendant had a specific rather than a general intent to commit a crime. Drunkenness can also be used as a mitigating factor to reduce the seriousness of a charge. The fact of intoxication may be a complete defense against the charge of shoplifting on the grounds that the defendant's condition was such that she simply forgot to pay and had not intended to steal.

Insanity. The defense of insanity has been the object of much judicial soul-searching because of the difficulty of defining the condition and of estab-

---

Immaturity Provisions of the Model Penal Code

Section 4.10. Immaturity Excluding Criminal Conviction; Transfer of Proceedings to Juvenile Court.

1. A person shall not be tried for or convicted of an offense if:
   a. at the time of the conduct charged to constitute the offense he was less than sixteen years of age [in which case the Juvenile Court shall have exclusive jurisdiction]; or
   b. at the time of the conduct charged to constitute the offense he was sixteen or seventeen years of age, unless:
      i. the Juvenile Court has no jurisdiction over him, or,
      ii. the Juvenile Court has entered an order waiving jurisdiction and consenting to the institution of criminal proceedings against him.

M'Naghten Rule
A test of the defense of insanity which requires it to be shown that at the time of committing the act the accused was unable to distinguish right from wrong because of a disease of the mind.

lishing tests to distinguish those who fall into this category. Over time, American courts have followed four tests of criminal responsibility involving insanity: (1) the ***M'Naghten Rule,*** (2) the Irresistible Impulse Test, (3) the Durham Rule, and (4) the Model Penal Code's Substantial Capacity Test. Different states have adopted different tests.

Before 1843 the defense of insanity could be used only by persons who were so deprived of understanding as to be incapable of knowing what they were doing. In that year Daniel M'Naghten was acquitted of killing Edward Drummond, whom he had thought to be Sir Robert Peel, the prime minister of Great Britain. M'Naghten claimed that he had been suffering from delu-

Mistake Provisions of the Model Penal Code

Section 2.04. Ignorance or Mistake.

1. Ignorance or mistake as to a matter of fact or law is a defense if:
   a. the ignorance or mistake negatives the purpose, knowledge, belief, recklessness or negligence required to establish a material element of the offense; or
   b. the law provides that the state of mind established by such ignorance or mistake constitutes a defense.
2. Although ignorance or mistake would otherwise afford a defense to the offense charged, the defense is not available if the defendant would be guilty of another offense had the situation been as he supposed. In such case, however, the ignorance or mistake of the defendant shall reduce the grade and degree of the offense of which he may be convicted to those of the offense of which he would be guilty had the situation been as he supposed.
3. A belief that conduct does not legally constitute an offense is a defense to a prosecution for that offense based upon such conduct when:
   a. the statute or other enactment defining the offense is not known to the actor and has not been published or otherwise reasonably made available prior to the conduct alleged; or
   b. he acts in reasonable reliance upon an official statement of the law, afterward determined to be invalid or erroneous, contained in (i) a statute or other enactment; (ii) a judicial decision, opinion or judgment; (iii) an administrative order or grant of permission; or (iv) an official interpretation of the public officer or body charged by law with responsibility for the interpretation, administration or enforcement of the law defining the offense.
4. The defendant must prove a defense arising under Subsection (3) of this Section by a preponderance of evidence.

Intoxication Provisions of the Model Penal Code

Section 2.08. Intoxication

1. Except as provided in Subsection (4) of this Section, intoxication of the actor is not a defense unless it negatives an element of the offense.
2. When recklessness establishes an element of the offense, if the actor, due to self-induced intoxication, is unaware of a risk of which he would have been aware had he been sober, such unawareness is immaterial.
3. Intoxication does not, in itself, constitute mental disease within the meaning of Section 4.01.
4. Intoxication which (a) is not self-induced or (b) is pathological is an affirmative defense if by reason of such intoxication the actor at the time of his conduct lacks substantial capacity either to appreciate its criminality [wrongfulness] or to conform his conduct to the requirements of law.

sion at the time of the killing, but the public outcry against his acquittal caused the House of Lords to ask the court to define the law with regard to persons suffering mental delusions. The judges of the Queen's Bench answered by saying that a finding of guilty cannot be made if, "at the time of the committing of the act, the party accused was laboring under such a defect of reason, from disease of the mind, as not to know the nature and quality of the act he was doing, or if he did know it that he did not know he was doing what was wrong."[19] This test, often referred to as the "right-from-wrong test," is today accepted by most states.

Over the years the M'Naghten Rule has often been criticized as not conforming with modern psychiatric concepts of mental disorder. It has been argued that individuals may be insane but still able to distinguish right from wrong and that the terms "disease of the mind," "know," and "nature and quality of the act" have not been adequately defined. Some states have supplemented the M'Naghten Rule by allowing defendants to plead that although they knew what they were doing was wrong, they were unable to control an irresistible impulse to commit the crime. The ***Irresistible Impulse Test*** excuses the defendant from responsibility where a mental disease controls his behavior even though he knew that what he was doing was wrong. Fifteen states use this test in combination with the M'Naghten Rule.

Irresistible Impulse Test
A test of the defense of insanity which requires it to be shown that although the accused knew right from wrong, he or she was unable to control an irresistible impulse to commit the crime.

A few states and the District of Columbia use the ***Durham Rule.*** Originally developed in New Hampshire in 1871, it was adopted by the Circuit Court of Appeals for the District of Columbia in 1954 in the case of *Durham* v. *United States.*[20] Monte Durham had a long history of criminal activity as well as of mental illness. At age twenty-six, with two companions, he broke into a house. On appeal of his conviction, Judge David Bazelon rejected the M'Naghten Rule, stating that an accused is not criminally responsible "if an unlawful act is the product of mental disease or mental defect." The Durham Rule is based on the supposition that insanity is a product of many personality factors, not all of which may be present in every case.

Durham Rule
A test of the defense of insanity which requires it to be shown that the accused is not criminally responsible because the act resulted from mental disease or mental defect.

The Durham Rule immediately aroused much controversy. In particular, it was argued that it offered no useful definition of "mental disease or defect." By 1972 (*U.S.* v. *Brawner*) the federal courts had overturned the Durham Rule in favor of a modified version of a test proposed in the Model Penal Code. This rule states that a person is not responsible for criminal conduct "if at the time of such conduct as a result of mental disease or defect he lacks substantial capacity either to appreciate the criminality [wrongfulness] of his conduct or to conform his conduct to the requirements of law."[21] The ***Substantial Capacity Test*** is essentially a broadening and modifying of the M'Naghten–Irresistible Impulse rules. Key terms have been changed to conform better with modern psychological concepts, and the standards lacking in Durham have been supplied. By emphasizing "substantial capacity," the test does not require that a defendant be completely unable to distinguish right from wrong.

Substantial Capacity Test
A test of the defense of insanity which requires it to be shown that the accused, as a result of mental disease or defect, lacked a substantial capacity to appreciate the wrongfulness of his or her conduct at the time of the act.

The insanity defense controversy. The attempted assassination of President Ronald Reagan by John W. Hinckley, Jr., reopened debate over the insanity defense. The facts that television pictures showed Hinckley shoot the president, that he came from a wealthy background and was thus able to enlist the aid of psychiatric experts to substantiate the claim, and that the federal

Close-up: Pitfalls Abundant in Insanity Plea

It was 3:30 A.M. on Jan. 29, 1976. Richard Hilliard Jackson had just taken three hours to explain his theory on the four states of "person" and his concept of death to a detective from the Metropolitan Police Department's homicide squad.

According to a police report, during the interview Jackson claimed that the physical person is guided by a magnet-like, uncontrollable power called The Force. The intellect remains after death, and the soul is the part of the intellect that lives forever. The After Death is a blessing, a state of freedom from pain, heartbreak and defeat.

The Force could do anything, Jackson said, even kill.

The 37-year-old handyman known as "Sweet Pea" and "Slim" was charged with the murder and robbery of an elderly Northeast Washington woman who had been found dead two weeks earlier. Jackson denied any involvement in her death.

Jackson's claims about The Force, his behavior around the time of the slaying, and the testimony of six psychiatrists who said he was mentally ill were recently the focus of an unusually lengthy and complicated trial in D.C. Superior Court. Defense attorneys argued that Jackson was insane on Jan. 14, 1976, when the woman was killed.

The jury, however, did not accept his insanity defense. Last week, after more than 24 hours of deliberation the jury determined that Jackson was sane at the time of the woman's death.

The case typified the problems that prosecutors, defense attorneys and jurors face when law and psychiatry are mixed with the question of criminal responsibility.

In the Jackson case there was a major difficulty "in breaking all this psychiatric testimony down into terms the jury could understand," said one of Jackson's defense attorneys, W. Gary Kohlman. And there is a risk, experts say, that when psychiatric testimony is reduced to layman's terms the significance can be lost.

The psychiatrists "said [Jackson] had a mental problem; OK, we all do," said one juror after the verdict was returned.

The psychiatrists testified that Jackson had symptoms consistent with paranoia and schizophrenia, but, said another juror, "there are other people walking around with these kinds of tendencies who don't commit any violent crime."

"It was really hard to understand," said one juror of the testimony of the psychiatrists. Another juror disagreed.

"It was very understandable," the juror said. The problem, she said, was that the psychiatrists "didn't commit themselves" on whether Jackson was insane or not at the time of the slaying.

Compounding the problems of an insanity defense is jurors' skepticism that the defendant may be faking insanity to escape a severe prison sentence.

In Superior Court the defendant has the burden of proving that he was insane at the time the crime was committed. The strategy for the prosecutor is to expose uncertainties in the testimony of psychiatrists for the defense.

For example, Assistant U.S. Attorney William J. Hardy questioned one psychiatrist who admitted that he was only guessing that Jackson was suffering from a mental illness the day the woman was slain. No witnesses appeared for the government in the insanity trial.

The jurors were instructed in the Jackson case that if they found him not guilty by reason of insanity he would be committed to St. Elizabeth's hospital. After 50 days a hearing would be held to determine whether he was a danger to himself or to the community. If he was found no longer to be a danger, he would be released at the discretion of the judge.

Jurors are inclined "to lock somebody up who was crazy for the rest of his life," according to former public defender Jeffrey Freund. He said jurors may be reluctant to vote for an insanity defense knowing a defendant could be swiftly released. "That's something you've got to overcome," Freund said.

The jurors actually heard two separate trials, which took over a month to complete. The first proceeding was on the merits of the case—whether Jackson in fact murdered and robbed the woman, with the burden of proof being on the government. After the jury found Jackson guilty of second-degree murder and robbery, the same jury then heard a second trial on the issue of whether at the time the offense was committed—Jan. 14, 1976—Jackson was sane and thus responsible for his act. Otherwise the jury could not decide that Jackson was not guilty on the two charges by reason of insanity.

Jackson, a chronic alcoholic who lived out of his 1965 Dodge, went to 1044 Grant St. NE on Jan. 14, in 1976, to repair a fuse box for Dorothia J. King, a 69-year-old cleaning woman. Jackson and a 15-year-old Maryland youth were seen drinking with Mrs. King in her house by a neighbor that evening. The following day Mrs. King was found dead on her living room floor. She had been beaten and strangled.

Jackson claimed that at some point when he was with Mrs. King he blacked out and had no recollection of what happened. The Maryland youth passed out during the evening and remembered nothing.

The medical examiner said Mrs. King died between 3:30 P.M. and 11:00 P.M. on Jan. 14, 1976. A neighbor testified that he saw Jackson's car outside Mrs. King's house at 11:00 P.M. that day. When he was arrested, Jackson had in his possession goods owned by Mrs. King. The Maryland youth testified that Jackson had also shown him other goods which police said were taken from Mrs. King's home.

"If he was insane at the time he committed the crime, why did he steal the property from this lady?" asked one juror. "This is what I think the majority [of the jurors] came around on."

"If he wasn't guilty, why didn't he get up [on the witness stand] and say something?" the juror asked.

On Jan. 16, 1976, two days after Mrs. King's death, Jackson was arrested for disorderly conduct in a Maryland restaurant. According to police, he stood at the salad bar, waved his arms around, and screamed that someone was trying to steal his food. When his money was refunded in an attempt to calm him down, he began to rapidly shove [*sic*] lettuce into his mouth.

On Jan. 29, when he was arrested and charged with Mrs. King's murder, Jackson gave his statement to police about The Force.

"He knew how to become insane at the right times," said one juror, who added that several members of the jury panel thought Jackson was feigning his illness. "I can't say he was faking," said another juror, "but I also thought [Jackson] knew what would be the best defense for him."

Beyond that skepticism, two other factors appeared to militate against the jury's acceptance of the insanity defense.

Jackson had pleaded guilty to manslaughter in connection with the death of his 9-year-old stepson in 1969. The child was slain after Jackson, who had been drinking, had an argument with his wife. He spent about two years in prison for the offense.

The Superior Court jury was told about the earlier killing, according to a defense attorney, because defense psychiatrists thought the 1969 incident had some link to why Jackson killed the elderly Washington woman.

But perhaps the most damaging piece of evidence, and the key to the government's argument that Jackson had fabricated his mental illness, was a letter that Jackson wrote to a friend seven months after his arrest.

". . . be sharp and go along with the insanity moves my attorney and I will make and say nothing about anything else," Jackson wrote.

"That did it," said one juror.

Source: Laura A. Kiernan, "Pitfalls Abundant in Insanity Plea," *Washington Post*, 19 July 1977, p. A-1. Reprinted by permission.

The public was outraged by the decision that John B. Hinckley, Jr. was not guilty by reason of insanity for the attempted assassination of President Reagan. Under federal rules, once the insanity defense is offered, the prosecution must prove beyond a reasonable doubt that the accused was sane at the time of the action.

rules of procedure in the District of Columbia required the government to prove him sane all fed widespread public outcries. In the immediate aftermath of his acquittal several states abolished the insanity defense, and bills were introduced in Congress with a similar objective.

Among the proposed changes is the introduction of a verdict of "guilty but insane." Defendants found guilty but insane would be sent to a mental institution for treatment and then to prison when they were determined to be no longer ill. Norval Morris suggests that it is the defendant's condition after the crime that should be taken into account in the determination of the appropriate place of confinement, a hospital or a prison, but that illness at the time of the crime should enter into the determination of the crime of which a defendant is found guilty: a defendant found to be of diminished capacity would be convicted of manslaughter, for example, rather than murder.[22]

The Comprehensive Crime Control Act of 1984 changed the federal rules on the insanity defense by limiting it to persons who are unable to appreciate the nature and quality or the wrongfulness of their acts as a result of severe mental disease or defect. This legislation seems to eliminate the Irresistible Impulse Test. It also shifts the burden of proof from the prosecutor, who in some federal courts must prove beyond a reasonable doubt that the defendant is not insane, to the defendant, who has to prove his or her insanity. The act also creates a new commitment procedure whereby a person found not guilty only by reason of insanity is required to be committed to a mental hospital until it is determined that he or she no longer poses a danger to society. These provisions apply only to prosecutions in federal courts, but they may serve to promote similar changes in the legal codes of the states.[23]

The problem with these alternatives is that the concept of *mens rea* is deeply rooted in our legal system. In addition, although there is much public discussion of notorious defendants who are found not guilty by reason of insanity, there are in fact few such cases. Persons who are ruled to be incompetent to stand trial because they are unable to assist in their own defense are committed to mental institutions until they are determined to be healthy enough to answer the charges. Civil commitment is also the usual route for defendants who successfully plead insanity. Some observers believe that this defense should be abolished, arguing that it is used to incarcerate legally innocent but dangerous people. Others emphasize that most criminals are somewhat unbalanced and that science cannot adequately measure the level of mental "disease" that allows borderline cases to use this defense. It is charged that the wealthy are able to pay for the testimony of psychiatrists in support of their defense while the poor cannot. It is also erroneously believed that persons who use the insanity defense and are sent to mental hospitals somehow "beat the rap."

Elements of a crime

Legislatures define certain acts as crimes when they are committed in accordance with the principles outlined above and in the presence of certain "attendant circumstances" while the offender is a certain state of mind. Together, these three factors—the act (*actus reus*), the attendant circumstances, and the state of mind (*mens rea*)—are called the *elements of a crime.* Thus the section of the Pennsylvania penal code dealing with burglary reads as follows:

> **Section 3502. Burglary.**
>
> a. Offense defined. A person is guilty of burglary if he enters a building or occupied structure, or separately secured or occupied portion thereof, with intent to commit a crime therein, unless the premises are at the time open to the public or the actor is licensed or privileged to enter.
>
> b. Defense. It is a defense to prosecution for burglary that the building or structure was abandoned.
>
> c. Grading. Burglary is a felony of the first degree.
>
> d. Multiple convictions. A person may not be convicted both for burglary and for the offense which it was his intent to commit after the burglarious entry or for an attempt to commit that offense, unless the additional offense constitutes a felony of the first or second degree.

The elements of burglary are, therefore, entering a building or occupied structure (*actus reus*) with intent to commit a crime therein (*mens rea*) at a time when the premises are not open to the public and the actor is not licensed or privileged to enter (attendant circumstances). For an act to constitute burglary, all three elements must be present.

Even if it appears, according to the formal words of the applicable statute, that the accused has committed a crime, prosecution will be successful only if the elements correspond to the interpretations of the law made by the courts. The Pennsylvania judiciary has, for example, construed the *actus reus* of burglary to include entering a building, such as a store or tavern, open to the public, so long as the entry was "willful and malicious—that is, made with the

---

Insanity Provisions of the Model Penal Code
Section 4.01. Mental Disease or Defect Excluding Responsibility.

1. A person is not responsible for criminal conduct if at the time of such conduct as a result of mental disease or defect he lacks substantial capacity either to appreciate the criminality [wrongfulness] of his conduct or to conform his conduct to the requirements of law.
2. As used in this Article, the terms "mental disease or defect" do not include an abnormality manifested only by repeated criminal or otherwise anti-social conduct.

---

intent to commit a felony therein." Thus one can be convicted of burglary for entering a store with the intent to steal even though entry was made during business hours and without force.

Statutory definitions of crimes

The laws of the United States, collectively and of each of the states individually, often define criminal acts in somewhat different ways. To find out how a state defines an offense, it is necessary to read its particular penal code; this document will give a general idea as to which acts are illegal. But a full understanding of the special interpretations of the code can be gained only by analyzing judicial opinions that have sought to clarify the language of the law, such as the opinion of the Pennsylvania court that interpreted the *actus reus* of the burglary statute.

To clarify the substantive criminal law, the following discussion focuses on two of the eight index crimes of the *Uniform Crime Reports* (*UCR*). The Model Penal Code's definition of each offense is followed by comments that point to critical elements of the crime. Always remember, however, that the elements of a crime may be interpreted somewhat differently in individual states.

Murder and nonnegligent manslaughter. A major problem in categorizing criminal behavior that has brought about death is that legislatures have subdivided the early common law definition of criminal homicide into degrees

---

Homicide Provisions of the Model Penal Code

Section 210.1. Criminal Homicide.

1. A person is guilty of criminal homicide if he purposely, knowingly, recklessly or negligently causes the death of another human being.
2. Criminal homicide is murder, manslaughter or negligent homicide.

Section 210.2. Murder.

1. Except as provided in Section 210.3(1)(b), criminal homicide constitutes murder when:
   a. it is committed purposely or knowingly; or
   b. it is committed recklessly under circumstances manifesting extreme indifference to the value of human life. Such recklessness and indifference are presumed if the actor is engaged or is an accomplice in the commission of, or an attempt to commit, or flight after committing or attempting to commit robbery, rape or deviate sexual intercourse by force or threat of force, arson, burglary, kidnapping or felonious escape.
2. Murder is a felony of the first degree [but a person convicted of murder may be sentenced to death, as provided in Section 210.6].

Section 210.3. Manslaughter.

1. Criminal homicide constitutes manslaughter when:
   a. it is committed recklessly; or
   b. a homicide which would otherwise be murder is committed under the influence of extreme mental or emotional disturbance for which there is reasonable explanation or excuse. The reasonableness of such explanation or excuse shall be determined from the viewpoint of a person in the actor's situation under the circumstances as he believes them to be.
2. Manslaughter is a felony of the second degree.

---

of murder and of voluntary and involuntary manslaughter. In addition, some states have created new categories, such as reckless homicide, negligent homicide, and vehicular homicide. Each of these definitions involves slight variations in the *actus reus* and the *mens rea.* The *UCR* counts murder and nonnegligent manslaughter as index offenses. These classifications correspond to murder and manslaughter in the Model Penal Code.

In legal terminology, the phrase *malice aforethought* is used to distinguish murder from manslaughter. The crime of murder is a deliberate, premeditated, and willful killing of another human being. In most states the definition of murder is also extended to circumstances in which the defendant knew that his behavior had a strong likelihood of causing another person's death, showed indifference to life, and thus recklessly engaged in conduct that resulted in the death of another, or in which his behavior resulted in a death while he was engaged in committing a felony. Mitigating circumstances, such as "the heat of passion" or extreme provocation, would reduce the offense to manslaughter because the requirement of malice aforethought would be absent or diminished. Similarly, manslaughter would include a killing resulting from an attempt to defend oneself that was not fully excused as self-defense, as well as death resulting from a lesser degree of recklessness or negligence.

Rape. There has been a long and almost universal revulsion against the crime of rape. The victim suffers not only assault upon the body but psychological damage as well. Though sexual conduct is in a state of flux in the contemporary United States, in recent years pressure has been brought to bear, especially by the Women's Movement, to ensure strict enforcement of the laws against rape. Successful prosecution for rape is difficult, however, because corroborating evidence is often lacking, and the public humiliation to which victims are often subjected sometimes results in the withdrawal of charges. Some states have reformed their laws by removing the offending word "rape" and classifying the behavior as a sexual offense in an effort to encourage prosecution.

Traditionally, the statutory law has stipulated that the offense has been committed if a male compels by force or threat and against her will a female who is not his wife to have sexual intercourse with him. The charge may also be brought if the act is performed on a woman who is unconscious and therefore unable to resist. If the female is under ten years of age, common law regards her as unable to give consent. Note that this definition of the law does not cover homosexual rape or forced sexual intercourse with one's own wife, though statutory reforms and judicial opinions in some states have dealt with these two situations in recent years.

The charge of rape raises difficult questions of both *actus reus* and *mens rea.* Because the act usually takes place in private, prosecutors may have difficulty showing that sexual intercourse took place without consent; some states require corroborating evidence from someone other than the victim. Force is a necessary element in the crime of rape. In some courts, the absence of injury to the victim's body has been taken to show that there was no resistance, which in some jurisdictions implies that consent was given.

Unlike murder, rape is not usually divided by statutes into degrees; but other offenses are often charged when elements of proof or mitigating circumstances warrant. "Deviate sexual intercourse," "sexual assault," and "statutory rape" are charges that may be used to designate sexual offenses that do not contain all the criminal elements necessary to prove rape.

Briefly, then, the substantive criminal law contains the basic doctrines stipulating the conditions that must be met before a person can be convicted of an offense. The so-called seven principles of Western law categorize these doctrines. Of primary importance are the various conditions that, if present, may relieve an individual of responsibility for committing a crime. Finally, the penal code of each of the states and the laws of the United States define offenses.

Procedural criminal law

The opening of this chapter described the United States Supreme Court's decision that Danny Escobedo, in the Chicago police station, had been denied the right to counsel guaranteed him by the Constitution. This decision was based on the procedural criminal law. Escobedo did not contend that the substantive elements of the case against him had not been met. His legal brief presented to the Supreme Court did not mention the absence of an *actus reus,* attendant circumstances, or *mens rea,* such that he should not have been charged with the murder of his brother-in-law. Rather, improper police procedures were the basis of his appeal. Escobedo argued that he had been denied due process because of a procedural violation.

Although the Supreme Court's opinion in *Escobedo* v. *Illinois* was issued in 1964, its foundation lies in the history of Anglo-American law, with precedent going back to the Magna Carta. In that document, considered to be the first written guarantee of due process, the king promised that "no free man shall be arrested, or imprisoned, or disseized, or outlawed, or exiled, or in any way molested; nor will we proceed against him unless by the lawful judgment of his peers or by the law of the land." Persons must be tried not through the use of arbitrary procedures but according to the process outlined in the law.

due process (procedural)
The constitutional requirement that all persons be treated fairly and justly by government officials. This means that an accused person can be arrested, prosecuted, tried, and punished only in accordance with procedures prescribed by law.

In the United States, ***procedural due process*** of law means that accused persons in criminal cases must be accorded certain rights as protections in keeping with the adversarial nature of the proceedings and that they will be tried according to legally established procedures. As chapter 1 explained, the Due Process Model is based on the premise that freedom is so valuable that efforts must be made to prevent erroneous decisions that would result in an

---

Rape Provisions of the Model Penal Code

Section 213.1 Rape . . .

1. *Rape.* A male who has sexual intercourse with a female not his wife is guilty of rape if:
   a. he compels her to submit by force or by threat of imminent death, serious bodily injury, extreme pain or kidnapping, to be inflicted on anyone; or
   b. he has substantially impaired her power to appraise or control her conduct by administering or employing without her knowledge drugs, intoxicants or other means for the purpose of preventing resistance; or
   c. the female is unconscious; or
   d. the female is less than 10 years old.

---

innocent person's being deprived of it. As Packer puts it, the rules of due process may be likened to an obstacle course in which decisions concerning the accused's guilt or innocence can be made only within the framework of the rules and rights stated in law as applying to all persons. Accordingly, the state may act against accused persons only when it follows due process procedures, thus ensuring that the rights of all are maintained.

From childhood we have been taught that defendants are entitled to fair and speedy trials, to have counsel, to confront witnesses, and to know the charges brought against them. They are protected against having to serve as witnesses against themselves, being subjected to double jeopardy, and enduring cruel and unusual punishment. Underlying procedural criminal law is the assumption that there are limits to the government's powers to investigate and apprehend persons suspected of committing crimes.

Like substantive law, procedural criminal law is found in many places: in

Definition of Offenses in the *Uniform Crime Reports* (Part I)

1. Criminal homicide. a. Murder and nonnegligent manslaughter: the willful (nonnegligent) killing of one human being by another. Deaths caused by negligence, attempts to kill, assaults to kill, suicides, accidental deaths, and justifiable homicides are excluded. Justifiable homicides are limited to: (1) the killing of a felon by a law enforcement officer in the line of duty; and (2) the killing of a felon by a private citizen. b. Manslaughter by negligence: the killing of another person through gross negligence. Excludes traffic fatalities. While manslaughter by negligence is a Part I crime, it is not included in the Crime Index.

2. Forcible rape. The carnal knowledge of a female forcibly and against her will. Included are rapes by force and attempts or assaults to rape. Statutory offenses (no force used—victim under age of consent) are excluded.

3. Robbery. The taking or attempting to take anything of value from the care, custody, or control of a person or persons by force or threat of force of violence and/or by putting the victim in fear.

4. Aggravated assault. An unlawful attack by one person upon another for the purpose of inflicting severe or aggravated bodily injury. This type of assault usually is accompanied by the use of a weapon or by means likely to produce death or great bodily harm. Simple assaults are excluded.

5. Burglary—breaking or entering. The unlawful entry of a structure to commit a felony or a theft. Attempted forcible entry is included.

6. Larceny-theft (except motor vehicle theft). The unlawful taking, carrying, leading, or riding away of property from the possession or constructive possession of another. Examples are thefts of bicycles or automobile accessories, shoplifting, pocket-picking, or the stealing of any property or article which is not taken by force and violence or by fraud. Attempted larcenies are included. Embezzlement, "con" games, forgery, worthless checks, etc., are excluded.

7. Motor vehicle theft. The theft or attempted theft of a motor vehicle. A motor vehicle is self-propelled and runs on the surface and not on rails. Specifically excluded from this category are motorboats, construction equipment, airplanes, and farming equipment.

8. Arson. Any willful or malicious burning or attempt to burn, with or without intent to defraud, a dwelling house, public building, motor vehicle or aircraft, personal property of another, etc.

Source: U.S. Department of Justice, *Crime in the United States* (Washington, D.C.: Government Printing Office, 1980), p. 321.

the U.S. and state constitutions, in statutes, and in judicial opinions. Among these, the Bill of Rights—the first ten amendments to the U.S. Constitution—holds a primary position. In most respects, the due process assumptions found there provide the basis for the implementing procedures that have evolved and that constitute the rules ordering the daily practices of the criminal justice system. In particular, the Fourth, Fifth, Sixth, Eighth, and Fourteenth amendments to the Constitution are especially important and are outlined below. More detailed discussion of each right is presented in the chapter where its operationalization is most appropriate. Thus questions concerning the detailed prohibition of unreasonable searches and seizures and the limitation of self-incrimination are found in chapter 6, the right to counsel is discussed in chapter 9, fair trial in chapter 12, and cruel and unusual punishment in chapters 13 and 15.

Bill of Rights

Although the Bill of Rights was added to the United States Constitution soon after its ratification in 1789, the amendments had little impact on criminal justice until the mid-twentieth century. Under our system of federalism, most criminal acts are violations of state laws, but for most of our history the Bill of Rights has been interpreted as protecting citizens only from acts of the national government. Hence important amendments—such as the Fourth, which guards against unreasonable searches and seizures; the Fifth, which outlines the basic due process rights in criminal cases; and the Sixth and Eighth, which cover procedures for fair trial and punishment—have been viewed as having no bearing on cases that arise out of state law. When it was drafted, the Constitution delegated certain powers to the new federal government, but the power to safeguard the rights of individuals from unjust enforcement of state laws was not among them. Historians have shown that at the time of the addition of the Bill of Rights, it was the power of the new national government that citizens feared; the constitutions of many of the states already contained protections against illegal procedures at the local level. This position was made clear in 1833 when the U.S. Supreme Court ruled in the case of *Barron* v. *Baltimore* that the first ten amendments to the Constitution were limitations only on the federal government and were not binding on the states. As Chief Justice John Marshall said:

> Had the framers of these amendments intended them to be limitations on the powers of state governments, they would have imitated the framers of the original Constitution, and have expressed that intention. . . . These amendments demanded security against the apprehended encroachments of the general government—not against those of the local governments.[24]

This ruling meant that when individual rights had been trampled, only the states, and not the Supreme Court, could interfere.

Fourteenth Amendment

The ratification of the Fourteenth Amendment following the Civil War began a new period in the protection of citizens' rights. This amendment declares that "no state shall make or enforce any law which shall abridge the privileges or immunities of citizens of the United States, nor shall any State deprive any person of life, liberty, or property, without due process of law; nor deny to any person within its jurisdiction the equal protection of the laws."

The idea that the Fourteenth Amendment "incorporated" the first ten amendments and made them applicable to the states was not immediately accepted by the Supreme Court, which realized that it would have to supervise national standards for state justice. Although the Court used the Fourteenth Amendment to uphold property rights against state regulation, not until the 1920s did it begin to require adherence to the protections of the Bill of Rights in state criminal cases. For twenty-odd years a major dispute split the Court: a group led by Justice Hugo Black argued that the due process clause of the Fourteenth Amendment incorporated all the provisions of the Bill of Rights, making them applicable to state proceedings; a majority group led by Justice Felix Frankfurter said that the clause selectively incorporated only those protections necessary to "fundamental fairness." By 1970, however, the two sides had arrived at the same conclusion, and through a piecemeal process, all the major protections of the Bill of Rights have been incorporated.

Initially the justices used the Fourteenth Amendment to require that such fundamental democratic rights as freedom of speech, religion, and assembly, as specified in the First Amendment, be binding on the states. It was not until 1923, in the case of *Moore* v. *Dempsey,* that abuses of due process rights in Arkansas shocked them into reversing a decision of a state criminal court.[25] Five black men had been convicted of murder and sentenced to death in a forty-five-minute trial dominated by a howling lynch mob outside the courtroom. Nine years later the court again invoked the due process clause in the famous Scottsboro case (*Powell* v. *Alabama*), in which nine illiterate young blacks were convicted of raping two white women in an open railroad freight car. Because the defendants had not been given effective counsel, the Court overturned their convictions.[26] In 1936 the justices threw out a confession for

The Scottsboro case led to the expansion of the right to counsel.

the first time (*Brown* v. *Mississippi*) because the statements had been beaten out of two blacks by sheriff's deputies wielding metal-studded belts.[27] In all these early cases, the barbaric nature of the offenses perpetrated by state authorities provided reason for moral outrage and demonstrated that due process had been denied. In the opinions of the Court one finds little legal analysis but rather a feeling that the fundamental requirements of fairness had not been met.

In 1937 Justice Benjamin Cardozo posed a test for determining whether a citizen had been denied due process of law by state action. In *Palko* v. *Connecticut,* upholding that state's rules allowing for the retrial of defendants found not guilty, Cardozo said that the test turned on the question "Does it violate those 'fundamental principles' of liberty and justice which lie at the base of our civil and political institutions?"[28] From *Palko* until the mid-1960s the dominant attitude of the Supreme Court was that the Fourteenth Amendment did not incorporate all the provisions of the Bill of Rights, only those that were fundamental. As Justice Frankfurter had noted, the doctrine of fundamental fairness meant that any state action that included "tactics which offend the community's sense of fair play and decency—conduct that shocks the conscience"—would be a violation of the Fourteenth Amendment's requirement of due process.[29] During those three decades the Court slowly incorporated some of the provisions of the Bill of Rights, but only according to the fairness rule.

The due process revolution

Throughout the years when the fairness doctrine was supported by a majority on the Supreme Court, Justice Hugo Black had argued that all the provisions of the Bill of Rights should be applied to the states through the ***incorporation*** of the due process clause of the Fourteenth Amendment. It was not until 1953, when Earl Warren became chief justice of the United States and a new liberal majority began to form on the Court, that the due process revolution reached its full stride: "The essence of the due process revolution was an attempt by the Supreme Court to reform American justice—and particularly, to police the police of the nation—by imposing rigid constitutional rules from the top and requiring that they be followed in all cases."[30]

incorporation
The extension of the due process clause of the Fourteenth Amendment to make binding on state governments the rights guaranteed in the first ten amendments to the U.S. Constitution (the Bill of Rights).

The Warren Court's revolution refined the meaning of the due process requirements of the Constitution, moving from the dictum that the state must observe "fundamental fairness" to a demand for absolute compliance by state and local officials with most of the specific provisions of the Bill of Rights. Where the fairness test had permitted states to fashion their own procedures, voiding only those that failed the fairness test, the new approach imposed in advance on state police and courts detailed and objective procedural standards. The justices were firm in their determination to void convictions obtained in violation of these rules.

The case of Dolree Mapp. The change in the Supreme Court's attitude was probably first recognized in *Mapp* v. *Ohio* (1961).[31] On 23 May 1957 Cleveland police officers entered the home of Dolree Mapp without a search warrant, saying they were looking for a suspect in a recent bombing who was thought to be hiding there. Miss Mapp demanded to see the search warrant.

One of the officers held up a piece of paper, whereupon Miss Mapp grabbed it and tucked it into her bosom. In an ensuing struggle the officer recovered it. Miss Mapp was then handcuffed—because she had been "belligerent" in resisting the rescue of the "warrant" from her person—and led to her bedroom, where the officers searched a dresser, to other rooms in her apartment, and finally to the basement, where obscene materials were found in a trunk. At her trial no search warrant was produced, yet the Supreme Court of Ohio upheld the conviction because the evidence had not been taken from the defendant's person by the use of brutal or offensive physical force. By a narrow majority the Warren Court overturned Miss Mapp's conviction on the grounds that the Fourth Amendment's injunction against unreasonable search and seizure, as applied to the states by the due process clause of the Fourteenth Amendment, had been violated. In the future, evidence gathered without a proper warrant was to be excluded from state trials.

As in most of the areas where the Warren Court broke fresh constitutional ground, federal procedures already guaranteed the specific right, and most of the states had placed on their books laws that met the Court's contemporary standards. The change was the new stricture that detailed procedural standards be followed by the states to ensure that rights were not violated. This new insistence on the Bill of Rights approach to criminal justice differed from the doctrine of fundamental fairness, which allowed the states to develop their own procedures, voiding only those actions that violated the ideals of fairness.

The significance of the *Mapp* decision lies in the fact not only that the Fourth Amendment was incorporated but that for the first time the Supreme Court of the United States had imposed detailed constitutional restrictions on

Earl Warren

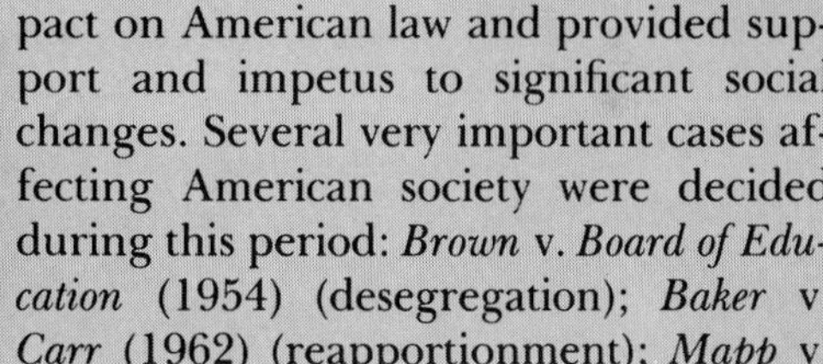

Fourteenth chief justice of the United States (1953–1969), Earl Warren began his public career in 1919 as district attorney of Alameda County, California, a post he held for thirteen years. Having developed a reputation as a crusading, racket-busting prosecutor, Warren was elected California's attorney general in 1938. He was elected governor of California in 1942 and was twice reelected. In 1948 he ran for the office of vice-president of the United States as the Republican nominee.

When Warren was named chief justice, many observers of the Supreme Court expected him to be a moderate jurist with a cautious approach to the use of judicial power. But his appointment marked the beginning of an era of rapid development of the nation's constitutional law. The Warren Court had an enormous impact on American law and provided support and impetus to significant social changes. Several very important cases affecting American society were decided during this period: *Brown* v. *Board of Education* (1954) (desegregation); *Baker* v. *Carr* (1962) (reapportionment); *Mapp* v. *Ohio* (1961) (exclusionary rule); *Gideon* v. *Wainwright* (1963) (counsel); and *Miranda* v. *Arizona* (1966) (confessions).

Warren and his associate justices on the Court were often severely criticized. Critics focused on Warren's abandonment of precedent in favor of what he regarded as fairness and on what some observers saw as the Court's subordination of law to political preference. Others supported Warren's work, arguing that the Constitution must be used to uphold justice.

the actions of state law enforcement officials. It was a milestone opinion in that it breached the precedent against the Court's supervision of the nuts and bolts of state justice. Beyond the Fourth Amendment lay the Fifth, with its protection against self-incrimination, and the Sixth, which guarantees the right to counsel. If these three amendments should be applied by the Court to the states, almost the complete range of activities in the criminal justice system would come under the detailed control of the federal judiciary. With the retirement of Justice Felix Frankfurter in 1962 and the appointment of Arthur Goldberg, a firm liberal majority began to complete the task of incorporation. From 1962 to 1972 the Supreme Court, under the chief justiceships of both Earl Warren and Warren Burger, applied most of the remaining criminal justice safeguards to the states; incorporation was virtually completed.

Fourth Amendment

> The right of the people to be secure in their persons, houses, papers, and effects, against unreasonable searches and seizures, shall not be violated, and no Warrants shall issue, but upon probable cause, supported by Oath or affirmation, and particularly describing the place to be searched, and the persons or things to be seized.

The Fourth Amendment recognizes the right to privacy, but the application of this protection to the daily operations of the criminal justice system has caused a number of problems. First, not all searches are prohibited, only those that are *unreasonable.* Second is the problem of what to do with evidence that is illegally obtained. Should murderers be set free because a vital piece of evidence was seized without a search warrant? The ambiguity of these portions of the amendment and the complexity of some arrest and investigation incidents have created difficulties.

What is unreasonable? With the rise in crime during the 1960s and the Supreme Court's increased interest in protecting the rights of defendants, many states passed laws permitting officers to stop and frisk persons who were thought to be about to commit a criminal act or who were believed to have just engaged in a criminal act. In *Terry* v. *Ohio* (1968), the Warren Court tried to deal with this situation.[32] Three men had been observed prowling in front of some store windows. An officer who believed they were planning a robbery stopped them and after a search found guns on two of them. The state argued that stopping and frisking was not covered by the prohibitions of the Fourth Amendment because such actions were tentative and preliminary procedures that might give rise to evidence that could then be the basis for a lawful arrest. Although the Supreme Court did not accept this argument, it upheld the police officer's action as a reasonable precaution for his own safety.

Since 1968 the Court has tried on numerous occasions to define what is meant by "reasonable" in the context of the search-and-seizure provisions of the Fourth Amendment (see chapter 6). Its conclusion seems to be that a personal search incident to a lawful arrest is legal. But even if it is not incident to an arrest, a search is sometimes legally justified if an officer believes a suspect is armed. The extension of a search to the space surrounding an arrest has been ruled to be restricted to situations in which the suspect may reasonably be expected to obtain a weapon or destroy evidence. After an arrest has been made but before the suspect has been removed from the premises, police have more discretionary power to make a search because the defendant is now in custody.

Problems of the exclusionary rule. Paralleling the development of law in the search-and-seizure area are issues related to illegally obtained evidence. What remedy is available to a defendant who has been the subject of an unreasonable search and seizure? Since 1914 the Supreme Court has held to an ***exclusionary rule:*** illegally seized evidence must be excluded from trials in federal courts. The argument has been that the government must not soil its hands by profiting from illegally seized evidence and that without this rule police would not be deterred from conducting raids in violation of the Fourth Amendment. In *Mapp* v. *Ohio* the exclusionary rule was extended to state courts, yet not all justices have agreed with this solution. Chief Justice Warren Burger, for example, has argued that the rule has not been effective in deterring police misconduct and that it exacts a high price from society—that is, the release of countless guilty offenders. On the other hand, Justice William Brennan has maintained that the justices who developed the exclusionary rule were well aware that it embodied a judgment that it is better for some guilty persons to go free than for the police to engage in forbidden conduct.

exclusionary rule
The principle that illegally obtained evidence must be excluded from a trial.

In sum, of the amendments dealing with criminal justice, the Fourth appears to be the one most likely to undergo continuing interpretation. Not only are several of its provisions ambiguous, but such technological developments as electronic surveillance lead to the need for new interpretations.

Fifth Amendment

> No person shall be held to answer for a capital, or otherwise infamous crime, unless on a presentment or indictment of a Grand Jury, except in cases arising in the land or naval forces, or in the Militia, when in actual service in time of war or public danger; nor shall any person be subject for the same offense to be twice put in jeopardy of life or limb; nor shall be compelled in any criminal case to be a witness against himself, nor be deprived of life, liberty, or property, without due process of law; nor shall private property be taken for public use, without just compensation.

Clearly, the Fifth Amendment provides a number of rights that speak to various portions of the criminal justice process.

Self-incrimination. One of the most important of these rights is the protection against ***self-incrimination***—that is, persons shall not be compelled to be witnesses against themselves. This right is consistent with the assumption of the adversarial process that the state must prove the defendant's guilt. The right does not really stand alone but is integrated with other protections, especially the Fourth Amendment's prohibition of unreasonable search and seizure. The Sixth Amendment's right to counsel has also had an impact on the Fifth Amendment. The Fifth Amendment has its greatest force, however, with regard to interrogations and confessions.

self-incrimination
The act of exposing oneself to prosecution by being forced to answer questions that may tend to incriminate one, protected against by the Fifth Amendment. In any criminal proceeding the prosecution must prove the charges by means of evidence other than the testimony of the accused.

Historically, the validity of confessions has hinged on their being voluntary because self-incrimination is involved. Under the doctrine of fundamental fairness which held sway until the 1960s, the Supreme Court was unwilling to allow confessions that were beaten out of suspects, that emerged after extended periods of questioning, or that resulted from other physical tactics for inducing admission of guilt. In the cases of *Escobedo* v. *Illinois* (1964) and *Miranda* v. *Arizona* (1966), the Court added that confessions made by suspects who had not been notified of their due process rights could not be admitted as evidence. To protect the rights of the accused, the Court emphasized the importance of allowing counsel to be present during the interrogation process.

In sum, the *Miranda* and *Escobedo* decisions fueled criticism of the Warren Court. These decisions shifted attention from due process rights in the courtroom to due process rights during the accused's initial contact with the police. Law enforcement groups claimed that the presence of counsel during interrogation would burden the system and also reduce the number of convictions. Research on this point has shown, however, that the fears of the police have not been realized. Confessions do not seem to be as important as the police stated, and informing suspects of their rights does not seem to have greatly impeded the police's ability to secure admissions of guilt.

Double jeopardy. Because of the limitations of the Fifth Amendment, a person charged with a criminal act can be subjected to only one prosecution or punishment for that offense in the same jurisdiction. As previously noted, illegal acts often violate both state and federal laws, so the prohibition against ***double jeopardy*** does not necessarily rule out prosecution in successive jurisdictions. The Supreme Court upheld this position in the case of *Bartkus* v. *Illinois* (1973).[33] Another question often raised concerning double jeopardy asks, At what point in the criminal process does it attach? There have been a number of cases on this point, but generally the provision has been held to mean that if a case is dismissed before trial commences, a subsequent prosecution for the offense is not prohibited.

double jeopardy
The subjecting of a person to prosecution more than once for the same offense, prohibited by the Fifth Amendment.

The state must prove its case by using lawfully gathered evidence.

Sixth Amendment

In all criminal prosecutions, the accused shall enjoy the right to a speedy and public trial, by an impartial jury of the State and district wherein the crime shall have been committed, which district shall have been previously ascertained by law, and to be informed of the nature and cause of the accusation; to be confronted with witnesses against him; to have compulsory process for obtaining witnesses in his favor, and to have the assistance of counsel for his defense.

Right to counsel. Although the accused's right to counsel in a criminal case had long prevailed in the federal courts, not until the landmark decision in *Gideon* v. *Wainwright* (1963) was this requirement made binding on the states. In prior cases, relying on the doctrine of fundamental fairness, the Supreme Court had ruled that states must provide indigents (poor people) with counsel only when the special circumstances of the case demanded such assistance. Thus, when conviction could result in death, when the issues were complex, or when the indigent defendant was either very young or mentally handicapped, counsel had to be provided.

At the time of the *Gideon* decision, only five states did not already provide attorneys for indigent defendants in felony cases, but the decision led to issues concerning the extension of this right. The next question concerned the point in the criminal justice process at which a lawyer had to be present. Beginning in 1963, the Supreme Court extended the right to counsel to preliminary hearings, to appeals, to a defendant out on bail after an indictment, to identification lineups, and to children in juvenile court proceedings. Although the *Gideon* case demanded counsel for indigents charged with felonies, this right was extended in 1972 to persons charged with misdemeanors when imprisonment might result (*Argersinger* v. *Hamlin*). The effect of these cases was to ensure that poor defendants would have at least some of the protections that had always been available to defendants with money. In sum, the rulings of the Court with regard to the right to counsel have been generally accepted throughout the nation with little criticism. Under most circumstances, counsel is made available, but the effectiveness of that counsel may still be open to question.

Speedy and public trial. The founders of this country were aware that in other countries the accused often languished in jail awaiting trial and was often convicted in the seclusion of the judge's chambers. At the time of the American Revolution, the right to a speedy and public trial was recognized in the common law and had been incorporated into the constitutions of six of the original states. But the word *speedy* is vague, and the Supreme Court has recognized that the interest of quick processes may be in conflict with other interests of society as well as with interests of the defendant. It has not demanded rigid guarantees, although in *Barker* v. *Wingo* (1972) it made note of the injustice when delays occur. It adopted a balancing test designed to give judges guidance in determining when the right to a speedy trial had been violated: "We can do little more than identify some of the factors which courts should assess in determining whether a particular defendant has been deprived of his right. Though some might express them in different ways, we identify four such factors: length of delay, the reason for the delay, the defendant's assertion of his right, and prejudice to the defendant."[34]

The right to a public trial is intended to protect the accused against arbitrary conviction. The assumption is that if justice must be done in the open, judges and juries will act in accordance with the law. As with the matter of speed, the Supreme Court has recognized that there may be circumstances in which the need for a public trial has to be balanced against other interests. For example, the right to a public trial does not mean that all members of the public have the right to attend the trial. The seating capacity and the interests of a fair trial, free of outbursts from the audience, may weigh heavily. Likewise in trials concerning sex crimes when the victim or witness is a minor, courts have temporarily barred the public to spare the child embarrassment.

Impartial jury. The right to a jury trial was as well established in the American colonies at the time of the Revolution as it had been in England for centuries. In their charters, most of the colonies specifically guaranteed trial by jury, and thus references to this essential process are found in the debates of the First Continental Congress in 1774, the Declaration of Independence, the constitutions of the thirteen original states, and the Sixth Amendment to the U.S. Constitution.

From a historical and philosophical perspective, the jury constitutes a barrier between an accused individual and the power of the state. As Justice Byron R. White wrote in 1968, "A right to jury trial is granted to criminal defendants in order to prevent oppression by the government."[35] Because the crucial decisions in criminal—and civil—trials are made by an impartial jury of one's peers, a safeguard is erected against corrupt or overzealous officialdom.

The question of how to create juries that are representative of the community and inclusive of its various elements has not been answered with the unanimity expressed in regard to the principle itself. The Magna Carta stipulated that juries should be drawn from "peers" of the accused, and later, during the time of Henry II, members were selected from the immediate vicinity of the crime. Because *peer* and *community* in medieval England may have had meanings different from today's, scholars and the Supreme Court have advanced a number of definitions to clarify the nature and impartial composition of juries. Jon Van Dyke asserts that impartiality can best be achieved when jurors are drawn at random from the broadest possible base, thereby balancing the different biases in the community against one another.[36] The jury is expected to perform a representative function, and representativeness thus becomes the crucial concept permeating all aspects of jury administration. Because courts have prohibited the systematic exclusion of any identifiable group of prospective jurors, random selection is the basis on which most trial juries in the United States are chosen.

State laws specify the kinds of offenses that can be tried by a jury, the size of the jury, and the types of decisions that can be made. The Supreme Court ruled in *Duncan* v. *Louisiana* (1968) that states must make jury trials available to defendants who are charged with serious offenses. This rule was further refined in *Baldwin* v. *New York* (1970) to mean that the option may be used when a crime carries a sentence of more than six months.[37] In other rulings, the Supreme Court has said that the size of the jury is left up to the state (*Williams* v. *Florida* [1970])—six-person juries are thus allowed—and that a

Trial by an impartial jury is a basic element of our criminal justice system.

unanimous verdict is not required in any criminal trial.[38] In a number of states, primarily in the South, the jury not only decides matters of fact but is also charged with determining the type and length of punishment—a requirement that takes this vital decision away from the judge. The practice has been greatly criticized, principally because the brevity of jury service does not give citizens a perspective that would allow them to recommend sentences that are realistic and consistent with the goals of the criminal sanction.

Eighth Amendment

Excessive bail shall not be required, nor excessive fines imposed, nor cruel and unusual punishment inflicted.

Release on bail. The purpose of bail is to allow for the release of the accused while he or she is awaiting trial. The Eighth Amendment does not require that release on bail be granted to all defendants, only that the amount of bail shall not be excessive. Many states do not allow bail to persons charged with some offenses, such as murder, and there appear to be few restrictions on the amount that can be demanded. As reformers have noted, the bail system discriminates against the poor because persons with money are able to gain release so that they can prepare their cases.

The issue of capital punishment. During recent decades the spotlight of public attention has focused on the Eighth Amendment's prohibition against cruel and unusual punishment—in particular, on the issue of capital punishment. In the case of *Furman* v. *Georgia* (1972), the Supreme Court ruled that the death penalty, as administered, constituted cruel and unusual punishment. Only Justices Marshall and Brennan argued that the death penalty was per se cruel and unusual punishment, but a five-member majority could agree with Justice Potter Stewart that the death sentences being considered were cruel and unusual, "in the same way that being struck by lightning is cruel and unusual. For, of all the people convicted of rapes and murders in 1967 and 1968, many just as reprehensible as these, the petitioners are among a capriciously selected random handful upon whom the sentence of death has in fact been imposed."[39]

Following this decision, many states passed laws designed to maintain the death penalty by removal of the arbitrary aspects of the proceedings. These new laws were tested in the 1976 case of *Gregg* v. *Georgia;* the Court upheld those statutes that permitted a sentencing judge or jury to take into account specific aggravating or mitigating circumstances in deciding whether a convicted murderer should be put to death.[40] Since that decision, the death row population has exceeded 1,400, yet very few persons have been executed. It seems that the death penalty is a continuing problem that the Court will be called on to face again.

Warren versus Burger

With the retirement of Chief Justice Earl Warren and the appointment of Warren Burger in June 1969 as the fifteenth chief justice of the United States, liberals feared that the recent policies of the Supreme Court would be reversed. Their fear was intensified with the resignations of Justices Hugo Black and John Harlan and the appointments of Lewis Powell and William Rehnquist in 1971. Through the three resignations and that of William O. Douglas, who was replaced by John Paul Stevens in 1975, President Richard Nixon was able to remake the court. But has the Burger Court brought the due process revolution to a halt and begun a counterrevolutionary retrenchment in defendants' rights?

Yale Kamisar believes that the Warren Court was perhaps not so defense-oriented as its critics said and that the Burger Court has not catered primarily to the prosecution.[41] Scholars generally accept the fact that a continuity between the Courts can be found with regard to the right-to-counsel and speedy-trial provisions of the Sixth Amendment but that differences can be seen in the police-interrogation and search-and-seizure cases that followed *Miranda* and *Mapp.* These developments will be explored in detail in chapter 6. Kamisar notes, for example, that in the *Miranda* decision, the Warren Court did not take "the final step" to require that a "suspect *first* consult with a lawyer, or actually have a lawyer present, in order for his waiver of constitutional rights to be deemed valid."[42] Whatever the intended impact of the *Miranda* decision may have been, suspects in custody who have been given the required warnings continue to confess with great frequency.

But has the Court under Chief Justice Burger "gutted" the advances made by the Warren Court? Kamisar believes that one must recognize that there was an initial assault on those advances, particularly with regard to decisions concerning the rights of suspects in police lineups, and that the Court "soon dealt heavy blows to the Fourth Amendment, appeared to be stalking the exclusionary rule, and seemed to be laying the groundwork to overrule *Miranda.*"[43] But in later years, he says, the "second" Burger Court gave a "fairly generous reading" to *Miranda,* and although *Miranda* and *Mapp* did not survive the 1970s unscathed, they now seem to be more secure than in earlier years. Summing up, Kamisar writes:

> A Warren Court admirer probably would say that the new Court did retreat on a number of search and seizure fronts but that it held firm on others and even advanced on some. In the confessions area, again viewed from the perspective of a Warren Court supporter, the Burger Court did inflict substantial damage, especially in the earlier years, but much less than it had been threatening to do.[44]

Summary

This discussion of substantive and procedural criminal law has attempted to describe only some of the basic assumptions found in the U.S. and state constitutions, statutes, and judicial opinions. For every criminal charge, it must be shown that the behavior of the accused was such as to be consistent with the seven principles that define crime. Such defenses as self-defense, necessity, and insanity may be used to show that the accused was not legally responsible for the offense.

Substantive law concerns the question: What is illegal? Procedural law focuses on how the law is enforced. The manner in which evidence is collected, the admission of witnesses' statements at trial, the judge's charge to the jury, the rights of prisoners—these are only a few of the matters in which the procedural law stipulates what can and cannot be done. In most states, attorneys may consult a practice book that describes the operational rules that must be followed in regard to the rights of defendants.

Many people believe that the substantive law and the rules of procedure have become so intricate that criminals escape punishment, court proceedings are unnecessarily drawn out, and the police are unable to do their job. Others contend that law and due process are essential for a just society. These positions remind us of the values summarized in Packer's Due Process and Crime Control models and of the tensions existing between the rule of law and the administration of justice.

For discussion

1. We often talk about the rights of the accused, but what are the rights of the victim?
2. If very few persons have taken advantage of the rights enunciated by the Supreme Court, what is the importance of the Court's opinions?
3. You are a police officer. You have every reason to believe that if you search a certain automobile you will find evidence that will result in an arrest, thereby solving a recent burglary. What actions can you take without violating the rights of the automobile owner, the suspect in the case?
4. You are a suspect. You have just been read the *Miranda* warnings by the arresting officer. What will be your response to the questions asked by officers at the station house? Why? Will your response help your treatment by the police and your case when it comes to court?
5. How far can the rights of due process be extended? Are there any limits?

For further reading

Gillers, Stephen. *Getting Justice.* New York: Basic Books, 1971.
Graham, Fred P. *The Self-Inflicted Wound.* New York: Macmillan, 1970.
Katkin, Daniel. *The Nature of Law.* Monterey, Calif.: Brooks/Cole, 1982.

Levy, Leonard W. *Against the Law: The Nixon Court and Criminal Justice.* New York: Harper & Row, 1974.

Lewis, Anthony. *Gideon's Trumpet.* New York: Vintage Books, 1964.

Notes

1. Escobedo v. Illinois, 364 U.S. 478 (1964).
2. J. F. Stephen, *A History of the Criminal Law of England,* vol. 2 (London: Methuen, 1883), p. 75, quoted in C. Ray Jeffery, "The Development of Crime in Early English Society," *Journal of Criminal Law, Criminology & Police Science* 47 (March–April 1957): 660.
3. William Blackstone, *Commentaries on the Laws of England,* 8th ed. (Oxford: Clarendon Press, 1778), 4:9, quoted in Jeffery, "Crime in Early English Society," p. 660.
4. William J. Chambliss and Robert B. Seidman, *Law, Order, and Power* (Reading, Mass.: Addison-Wesley, 1971), p. 230.
5. American Law Institute, *Model Penal Code* (Philadelphia, 1962).
6. Jerome Hall, *General Principles of Criminal Law,* 2d ed. (Indianapolis: Bobbs-Merrill, 1947), p. 18.
7. Robinson v. California, 370 U.S. 660 (1962).
8. Jerome Hall and Gerhard O. W. Mueller, *Cases and Readings on Criminal Law and Procedure,* 2d ed. (Indianapolis: Bobbs-Merrill, 1965), p. v.
9. Chambliss and Seidman, *Law, Order, and Power,* p. 202.
10. Ibid.
11. Oliver Wendell Holmes, Jr., *Common Law* (Boston: Little, Brown, 1881), p. 3.
12. American Law Institute, *Model Penal Code,* p. 32.
13. Morissette v. United States, 342 U.S. 246 (1952).
14. Hall, *General Principles of Criminal Law,* p. 348.
15. The Queen v. Dudley and Stephens, 14 Q.B.D. 273 (1884).
16. Ibid.
17. Missouri v. Green, 470 S.W. 2d 565 (1971).
18. Ibid.
19. M'Naghten's Case, 8 Eng. Rep. 718 (H.L. 1843).
20. Durham v. United States, 94 U.S. App. D.C. 228, 214 F. 2d 862 (1954).
21. U.S. v. Brawner, 471 F. 2d 969 (1972).
22. Norval Morris, *Madness and the Criminal Law* (Chicago: University of Chicago Press, 1982), esp. chap. 2.
23. Comprehensive Crime Control Act of 1984 (H.R. 5963; S. 1762).
24. Barron v. Baltimore, 32 U.S. 243 (1983).
25. Moore v. Dempsey, 261 U.S. 86 (1923).
26. Powell v. Alabama, 287 U.S. 45 (1932).
27. Brown v. Mississippi, 297 U.S. 278 (1936).
28. Palko v. Connecticut, 302 U.S. 319 (1937).
29. Rochin v. California, 342 U.S. 172 (1953).
30. Fred P. Graham, *The Self-Inflicted Wound* (New York: Macmillan, 1970), p. 16.
31. Mapp v. Ohio, 367 U.S. 643 (1961).
32. Terry v. Ohio, 394 U.S. 1 (1968).
33. Bartkus v. Illinois, 411 U.S. 423 (1973).
34. Barker v. Wingo, 407 U.S. 530 (1972).
35. Duncan v. Louisiana, 391 U.S. 155 (1968).
36. Jon M. Van Dyke, *Jury Selection Procedures* (Cambridge, Mass.: Ballinger, 1977), p. 92.
37. Baldwin v. New York, 399 U.S. 66 (1970).
38. Williams v. Florida, 399 U.S. 78 (1970).
39. Furman v. Georgia, 408 U.S. 238 (1972).
40. Gregg v. Georgia, 96 S. Ct. 2909 (1976).
41. Yale Kamisar, "The Warren Court (Was It Really So Defense-Minded?), The Burger Court (Is It Really So Prosecution-Oriented?), and Police Investigatory Practices," in *The Burger Court,* ed. Vincent Blasi (New Haven: Yale University Press, 1983), pp. 62–91.
42. Ibid., p. 67.
43. Ibid., p. 91.
44. Ibid.

The Administration of Criminal Justice

4

In the course of the investigations and prosecutions that accompanied the Watergate scandal, Americans were given an elementary education in the functions and processes of the criminal justice system. With the help of the news media, persons who had never before paid attention to the activities of their local police and courts were soon debating issues of parole and pardon, conspiracy, and plea bargaining. Other citizens may have been confused by the fact that so many different agencies of government at both the national and state levels participated in the three functional divisions of the justice system: law enforcement, adjudication, and corrections. Although most of the Watergate-related activity involved violations of federal laws, simultaneous investigations were begun in several states (California and Florida, for example) in connection with possible violations of their laws. Even the convictions of the Watergate defendants puzzled many citizens, as some offenders were given long sentences while others were ordered to serve only short terms in prison. President Ford's pardon of Richard Nixon for any offenses that he might have committed in office raised further questions about the nature of the administration of justice.

Any criminal justice system is an apparatus society uses to enforce the standards of conduct necessary to protect individuals and the community. It operates by apprehending, prosecuting, convicting, and sentencing those members of the community who violate the basic rules of group existence.

PRESIDENT'S COMMISSION ON LAW ENFORCEMENT AND ADMINISTRATION OF JUSTICE

Before we examine the subsystems of criminal justice, it is helpful to take an overview of the system's administration and to confront several crucial questions. What are the purposes of the criminal justice system? What organizations make up this system? What are the procedures by which a citizen may be arrested, found guilty, and imprisoned? What analytic tools can we use to understand the system better? This chapter focuses on the operation of the criminal justice system, its agencies, and its processes. It is hoped that the description of formal relationships in this broad and complex system will add meaning to the theoretical and analytic chapters that follow. At the end of the chapter, several social science concepts are examined to determine whether they are useful in furthering our understanding of the way the system really works.

Criminal justice and society

The concept of society implies that interpersonal relations are governed by rules. Violations of these rules are followed by reactions that take a variety of forms, ranging from expressions of mild disapproval to the severest penalties, or sanctions, of the law. Although many of the actions of our fellow citizens may appear unpleasant, antisocial, or immoral, only certain types of behaviors have been labeled illegal. The criminal law specifies formal methods to enforce rules and a range of distinctive sanctions for violations. Of special importance is the fact that the criminal law and its agencies are authoritative—that is, the citizenry has given them certain legitimate rights and duties, including the ultimate sanctions that restrict freedom or even bring about death.

Crime is found in all societies, and each culture has developed some mechanism to control it. But the ways in which different peoples of the world attack crime vary considerably. Not only do dissimilarities exist in what is considered illegal, but a great variety of instruments are used to judge and penalize criminals. In many respects, a society's way of confronting its crime problem reflects its political and cultural values.

Because the United States is a democracy, the way we control crime represents a basic test of our ideals. The administration of justice in a democracy may be distinguished from that in an authoritarian state by the extent and form of protections provided for the accused as guilt is determined and punishment imposed. Although the United States may have one of the highest crime rates in the world, the efficiency of crime control may have to be sacrificed to preserve the rights of individual citizens. As Chief Justice Warren once observed:

> When society acts to deprive one of its members of his life, liberty or property, it takes its most awesome steps. No general respect for, nor adherence to, the law as a whole can be expected without judicial recognition of the paramount need for prompt, eminently fair and sober criminal law procedures. The methods we employ in the enforcement of our criminal law have aptly been called the measures by which the quality of our civilization may be judged.[1]

Every year more than four million persons in the United States are arrested. Although most of these arrests are for relatively minor violations, the fact remains that a sizable portion of the population (especially if we add the victims and witnesses) has direct contact with the official processes of criminal justice. Yet the system that the United States has developed to deal with crime is not uniform, and some critics say it is not consistent. What is important is that the system is used to enforce the standards reflected in the laws we have developed to protect the individual citizen and the community.

Goals of criminal justice

For most Americans, the goals of the criminal justice system appear obvious: the prevention and control of crime; but such a broadly phrased statement does not tell us much about how these goals may be achieved. As the epigraph to this chapter notes, the criminal justice system operates to apprehend, prosecute, convict, and punish those members of the community who do not live according to the law. These functions are enhanced by the effect the sanctions imposed on one person have on the general population—that is, by observing the consequences of criminal behavior, others may be encouraged to live according to the law. Finally, we must recognize that our society can prevent and control crime only within the framework of law. The criminal law defines what is illegal and prescribes the procedures that officials must use as they attempt to achieve these goals. The rights of citizens are carefully outlined in the law.

In any city or town one may see the goals of the criminal justice system being actively pursued: a police officer speaking to elementary schoolchildren, a patrol car quietly moving through a darkened street, an arrest being made outside a neighborhood bar, lawyers walking into the courthouse, neon signs flashing the word "BAIL," the forbidding gloom of the county jail. While these images exemplify the broadly stated goals of the criminal justice system, they also point to nuances of meaning in the definition of these goals that require examination. It can be argued, for example, that prevention and control so overlap that they cannot be described as truly separate functions. The arrest outside the bar not only controlled the behavior but may have prevented future violations by the offender and had a similar influence on bystanders.

In addition, questions may be raised about the boundaries of the criminal justice system. To what extent are criminal justice agencies responsible for pursuing the system's goals? If we believe that poverty causes crime, are the police and courts charged with curing poverty as a means of preventing crime? How do the stated goals of prevention and control shape the daily operations of the criminal justice system?

Control of crime

One of the best ways to gain an understanding of crime control is to look at the processes by which offenders are apprehended, convicted, and punished. But a knowledge of how criminal justice agencies function tells us little about their contribution to the goal. Measures of effectiveness are needed so that observers can determine which activities are related to the achievement of this goal. This is where value conflicts occur among competing measures of effectiveness and among competing operational styles.

For example, is the police department that makes many arrests more

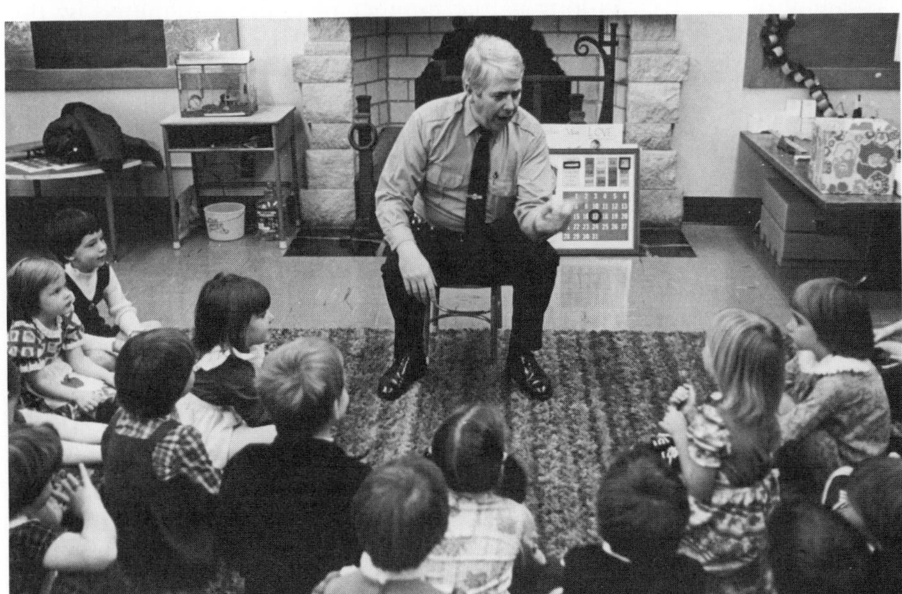

Education about crime and justice should begin at an early age.

effective than one that tolerates certain types of behavior in order to maintain an ordered community? Is the crime control goal of criminal justice better served by judges who sentence according to the letter of the law or by those who reduce the allowable sentences because of the characteristics of the individual offender? Are long periods of imprisonment under maximum-security conditions more effective than the rehabilitative setting of a halfway house? The variety of ways in which criminal justice agencies can operate in the pursuit of crime control present value dilemmas that must be faced not only by the individual patrol officer, judge, or correctional guard, but by citizens and legislators as well. Those who influence the making of public policy must face these choices.

Prevention of crime

deterrence
Discouragement of criminal behavior on the part of known offenders (special deterrence) and of the public (general deterrence) by the threat of punishment.

The goals of criminal justice also include crime prevention—that is, preventing or deterring criminal behavior. ***Deterrence*** means two things: (1) deterring offenders with whom the system has direct contact from committing further crime (special deterrence) and (2) deterring the public from committing crimes in the first place (general deterrence). As with the value choices that influence crime control operations, options may be chosen in the pursuit of deterrence.

Considerable evidence indicates that criminal sanctions have not been particularly effective when it comes to special deterrence. Too many offenders continue in their former ways after they are released from prison. In addition, when some first offenders are "sent up" they often become embittered and better skilled in criminal pursuits while imprisoned. Instead of being an effective institution for special deterrence, prisons have often been referred to as schools for thieves.

But even if the evidence should show that the criminal justice system had failed as a special deterrent, it might still perform the very important function of general deterrence. As long as the number of crimes committed by the public at large is smaller proportionally than the number of crimes committed by former convicts, general deterrence may be judged to have succeeded.

The use of criminal sanctions for punishment or for rehabilitation provides the sort of value choice that will influence the deterrent effect of the criminal justice system. If the emphasis of a correctional institution is on the treatment and rehabilitation of offenders, the criminal justice system's capacity to act as a general deterrent may be diminished. The most obvious reason is that successful treatment programs must be conducted in an atmosphere in which the unpleasant aspects of prison life have been lessened or done away with altogether. To the extent that treatment is conducted in such an environment, rehabilitation efforts may succeed in deterring individual offenders from pursuing criminal careers. However, the general population may not be deterred from committing illegal acts because the way the rehabilitation process is conducted does not seem especially unpleasant.

In the pursuit of criminal justice goals

The ways in which American institutions have been developed in order to achieve the goals of crime prevention and control lead to a series of choices. In the pursuit of criminal justice goals, decisions must be made that reflect legal, political, social, and moral values. As we try to understand the system, we must be aware of possible conflicts among these values as well as of the implications of choosing one value over another. The task of preventing and controlling crime would be eased considerably if the means of doing so could be clearly determined, so that citizens and officials were able to act with a forthright understanding of their responsibilities and obligations. Making such easy translations of wishes into reality is not characteristic of human institutions.

Criminal justice in a federal system

Since this book is about American criminal justice, we must consider the political system of the United States as it influences the enforcement of the law and the trying of defendants. Of primary importance is the federal governmental structure created in 1789 with the ratification of the U.S. Constitution. This instrument created a delicate political agreement: the national government was given certain powers—to raise an army, to coin money, to make treaties with foreign countries, and so forth—but all other powers were retained by the states. Nowhere in the Constitution does one find specific reference to criminal justice agencies of the national government, yet we all are familiar with the Federal Bureau of Investigation (FBI), recognize that criminal cases are often tried in United States district courts, and know that the Bureau of Prisons operates institutions from coast to coast.

Two justice systems

For conceptual purposes, thinking of two distinct criminal justice systems—national and state—is useful. Each performs enforcement, adjudication, and correctional functions, but they do so on different authority and their activities vary greatly in scope. Criminal laws are written and enforced primarily by agencies of the states, yet the rights of defendants are protected by the constitutions of both state and national governments. Although approximately 85 percent of criminal cases are heard in state courts, certain offenses—narcotics violations and transportation of a kidnap victim across state lines, for example—are violations of *both* state and federal laws.

As a consequence of the bargain worked out at the Constitutional Convention, general police power was not delegated to the federal government. No national police force with broad enforcement powers may be established in the United States. The national government does have police agencies such as the Federal Bureau of Investigation and the Secret Service, but they are authorized to enforce only those laws prescribed under the powers granted to Congress. Since Congress has the power to coin money, it also has the authority to detect and apprehend counterfeiters, a function performed by the Secret Service of the Department of the Treasury. The FBI, a part of the Department of Justice, is responsible for investigating all violations of federal laws with the exception of those assigned by Congress to other departments. The FBI has jurisdiction over fewer than two hundred criminal matters, including such offenses as kidnapping, extortion, interstate transportation of stolen motor vehicles, and treason.

Jurisdictional division. The role of criminal justice agencies following the assassination of President John F. Kennedy in November 1963 illustrates the federal–state division of jurisdiction, or territory. Because Congress had not made killing the president of the United States a federal offense, Lee Harvey Oswald, had he lived, would have been brought to trial under the laws of Texas. The U.S. Secret Service had the job of protecting the president, but apprehension of the killer was the formal responsibility of the Dallas police and other Texas law enforcement agencies.

As the constant movement of people and goods across state lines has become an integral part of American life, federal involvement in the criminal justice system has increased. The assumption that acts committed in one state will have no effect on the citizens of another state is no longer useful. Especially in the area of organized crime, for example, gambling and drug syndicates are established on a national basis. Congress has passed laws designed to allow the FBI to investigate situations in which local police forces are likely to be less effective. Thus, under the National Stolen Property Act, the FBI is authorized to investigate thefts exceeding $5,000 in value when the stolen property is likely to have been taken across state lines. In such circumstances, disputes over jurisdiction may occur because the offense is a violation of *both* state and national laws. The court to which a case is brought may be determined by the law enforcement agency that makes the arrest. In some cases, a defendant could be tried under state law and then retried in the federal courts for a violation of the laws of the national government. In most instances, however, the two systems respect each other's jurisdictions.

It is important to emphasize that the American system of criminal justice is decentralized, or not concentrated at, for example, the federal level of government. As table 4.1 notes, two-thirds of all criminal justice employees work for county and municipal units of government. This large proportion is not a result of the fact that any one subunit of the system, such as the police, functions primarily at the local level. With the exception of corrections employees, the majority of workers in all of the subunits of the criminal justice system—police, judicial, prosecution, public defense—are tied to local government. Likewise, as figure 4.1 indicates, the costs of criminal justice are distributed in varying proportions among the federal, state, county, and mu-

TABLE 4.1 Total number and percentage of criminal justice employees at each level of government

	Number				*Percentage*		
Activity	*All governments*	*Federal*	*State*	*Local*	*Federal*	*State*	*Local*
Total criminal justice systems	1,226,209	105,423	322,046	800,730	8.6	26.2	65.2
Law enforcement	697,039	75,182	98,651	523,206	10.8	14.1	75.1
Judicial	163,154	8,266	43,625	111,263	5.1	26.7	68.2
Legal services and prosecution	75,937	7,811	18,974	49,152	10.3	25.0	64.7
Public defense	8,680	230	3,256	5,194	2.7	37.5	59.8
Corrections	273,566	12,192	153,770	107,594	4.5	56.2	39.3
Other criminal justice	9,833	1,742	3,770	4,321	17.7	38.3	44.0

Source: U.S. Department of Justice, *Sourcebook of Criminal Justice Statistics, 1980* (Washington, D.C.: Government Printing Office, 1981), p. 21.

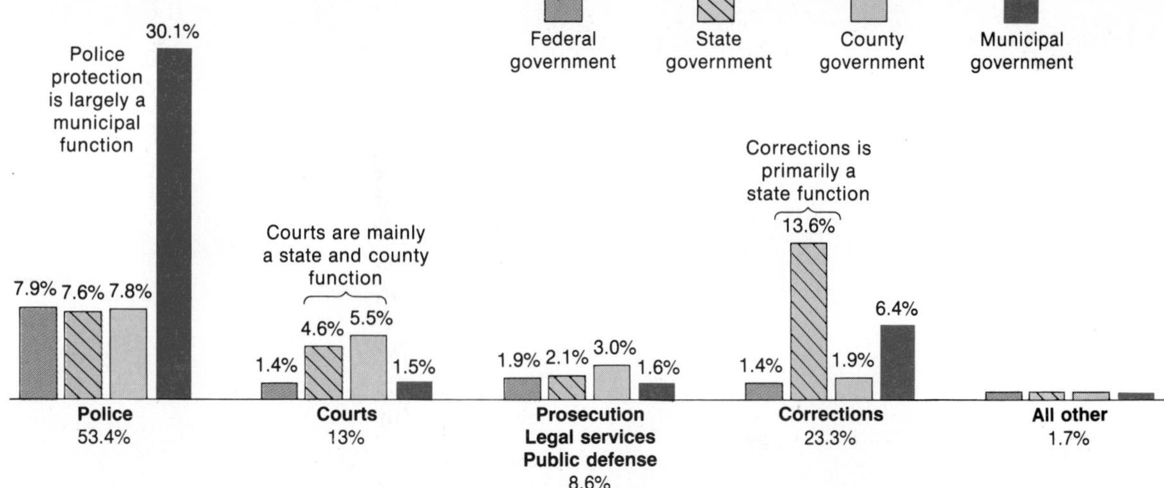

FIGURE 4.1 Percentage of costs of criminal justice services borne by each level of government

nicipal governments. It is in the states and communities that laws are enforced and violators brought to justice. Consequently, the formal structure and actual processes are greatly affected by local norms and pressures—that is, by the needs and demands of influential local people and by the community's interpretation of the extent to which the laws should be enforced.

Agencies of criminal justice

Society has commissioned the police to patrol the streets, prevent crime, arrest suspected criminals, and enforce the law. It has established courts to determine the guilt or innocence of accused offenders, to sentence those who are guilty, and to "do justice." It has created a system of prisons to punish convicted persons and programs to try to rehabilitate them so that they may eventually become useful citizens. These three components—law enforcement, adjudication, and corrections—combine to form the system of criminal justice. We would be incorrect, however, to assume that system to be either uniform or even consistent. It was not fashioned in one piece at one time. Rather, various institutions, principles, and procedures that are parts of the system were built around the core assumption that people may be punished by government only if it can be proved by an impartial process that they violated specific laws. Some of the parts, such as trial by jury and bail, are of ancient origin; others, such as juvenile courts and community-based corrections, are relatively new. The system represents an adaptation of the institutions of the English common law to the American social and political environment.

Law enforcement

The complexity and fragmentation of the criminal justice system is perhaps best seen with regard to the number and jurisdiction of the approximately 20,000 public organizations in the United States engaged in law enforcement activities. The police function is dominated by local governments, as may be seen in the fact that the federal government has only 50 law en-

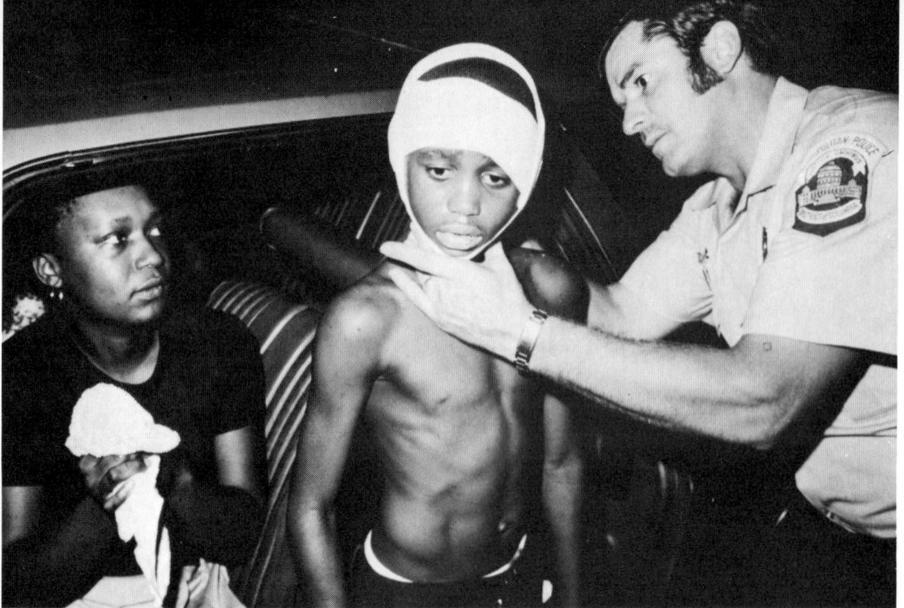

We expect the police to provide a wide variety of services.

forcement agencies while the states have about 200; the remainder are dispersed throughout the counties, cities, and towns. Altogether, these agencies have 700,000 employees and a total annual budget in excess of $13 billion.

The responsibilities of law enforcement organizations fall into four categories. First, they are called on to keep the peace. This broad and most important mandate, or command by the people, involves the protection of rights and persons in a wide variety of situations, ranging from street-corner brawls to domestic quarrels. Second, the police must apprehend law violators and combat crime. This is the responsibility the public most often associates with law enforcement work, though it accounts for only a small proportion of law enforcement agencies' time and resources. Third, law enforcement agencies are expected to engage in their own special form of crime prevention. By educating the public about the threat of crime and by reducing the number of situations in which crimes are most likely to be committed, the police can lower the incidence of crime. Finally, the police are charged with providing a variety of social services. In fulfilling these obligations, a police officer recovers stolen property, directs traffic, provides emergency medical aid, gets cats out of trees, and helps people who have locked themselves out of their apartments.

Federal agencies. Entrusted with the enforcement of a list of specific federal laws, police organizations of the national government are part of the executive branch. The FBI has the broadest range of control, which encompasses investigation of all federal crimes not the responsibility of other agencies. Units of the Treasury Department are concerned with violations of laws related to the collection of income taxes (Internal Revenue Service), alcohol and tobacco taxes and gun control (Bureau of Alcohol, Tobacco, and Firearms), and customs (Customs Service). Other federal agencies concerned with specific areas of law enforcement include the Drug Enforcement Administration of the Justice Department, the Secret Service Division of the Treasury (concerned with counterfeiting, forgery, and protection of the president), the

Bureau of Postal Inspection of the Postal Service (concerned with mail offenses), and the Border Patrol of the Department of Justice (concerned with violations of immigration laws).

State agencies. Each state has its own police force, yet here again may be seen the traditional emphasis on the local nature of law enforcement. State police forces were not established until the turn of the century and then primarily as a wing of the executive branch of state government that would enforce the law when local officials did not. In all the states these forces are charged with regulation of traffic on the main highways, and in two-thirds of the states they have been given general police powers. In only about a dozen populous states, however, are they adequate to the task of general law enforcement outside the cities. Where the state police are well developed—as in Pennsylvania, New York, New Jersey, Massachusetts, and Michigan—they tend to fill a void in rural law enforcement. The American reluctance to centralize police power has kept state forces generally from replacing local officials. For the most part they operate only in areas where no other form of police protection exists or where local officers request their expertise or the use of their facilities.

County agencies. Sheriffs are found in almost every one of the more than 3,000 counties in the United States. They have the responsibility for law enforcement in rural areas, but over time many of their functions have been assumed by the state or local police. This is particularly true in portions of the Northeast. In parts of the South and West, however, the sheriff's office remains a well-organized force. In thirty-three of the states, sheriffs have broad

J. Edgar Hoover

Born in Washington, D.C., J. Edgar Hoover received his LL.B. and LL.M. degrees from George Washington University in 1917. After admission to the bar, he began a career with the Justice Department and served as special assistant to the attorney general from 1919 to 1921.

President Calvin Coolidge appointed Hoover director of the Federal Bureau of Investigation in 1924, when that agency was racked by dissension and rife with politics. Hoover set out to eliminate politics from the FBI appointment process and to establish better training programs for new agents. Very early he recognized the importance of improved technical methods of police work and instituted such aids as a national fingerprint filing system and coordinated development of the Uniform Crime Reporting System.

In his early career, Hoover became well known to the public as a G-man, pursuing such notorious criminals as Ma Barker, Machine Gun Kelley, Bonnie and Clyde, and John Dillinger, using these exploits to create an image of the FBI agent as the ultimate crime fighter. During the 1940s and 1950s, when Hoover became noted for his anticommunist views, the subversive control functions of the FBI became prominent.

Hoover's long career sustained many criticisms of his management of the FBI, including accusations that the Bureau exceeded its jurisdiction, manipulated crime data, exaggerated reports of subversive activities, and tried to block activities in support of the civil rights movement. Nevertheless, Hoover's contributions to improved management of police work and to the effectiveness of the FBI are widely recognized.

authority, are elected, and occupy the position of chief law enforcement officer in the county. Even when the sheriff's office is well organized, it may lack jurisdiction over cities and towns. In addition to having law enforcement responsibilities, the sheriff is often an officer of the court and is charged with holding prisoners, serving court orders, and providing the bailiffs who are responsible for maintaining order in court. In many counties, local politics determines appointments to the sheriff's office, while in other places, such as Los Angeles County (California) and Multnomah County (Oregon), the department is staffed by professional, trained personnel.

Local agencies. Though police departments exist in more than 1,000 cities and 20,000 towns, only in the cities can they be said to perform all four of the law enforcement functions. Although established by local government, the police of the cities and towns are vested by state law with general authority. Usually, the larger the community, the more police workers. Nearly one-third of the police personnel in the United States are employed by the 55 cities with populations exceeding 250,000. The resulting ratio of officers to residents is 2.9 per 1,000, which is almost twice the average ratio for cities of fewer than 100,000. In a metropolitan area the law enforcement function may be divided among agencies at all governmental levels, and jurisdictional conflict may inhibit the efficient use of police resources. America is essentially a nation of small police forces, each of which operates independently within the limits of its jurisdiction.

Adjudication

dual court system
A court system consisting of a separate judicial structure for each state in addition to a national structure. Each case is tried in a court of the same jurisdiction as that of the law or laws broken.

Although we may talk about *the* judiciary and speak of *the* opinions—that is, of *the* Supreme Court—the United States has a ***dual court system,*** consisting of a separate judicial structure for each state in addition to a national structure. Each system has its own series of courts, and the U.S. Supreme Court is the body where the two systems are "brought together." It should be emphasized that the Supreme Court, although commonly referred to as the highest court in the land, does not have the right to review all decisions of state courts in criminal cases. It will hear only cases involving a federal law or those in which a right of the defendant under the Constitution is alleged to have been infringed—that is, a case in which the accused claims that one or more rights were denied during the state criminal proceeding.

With a dual court system, interpretation of the law can vary from state to state. Although states may have laws that are similarly worded, none of them interprets the laws in exactly the same way. To some extent these variations reflect varying social and political conditions. They may also represent attempts by state courts to solve similar problems by different means. But primarily the diversity of legal doctrine results simply from fragmentation of the court system. Within the framework of each jurisdiction, judges have discretion to apply the law as they feel it should be applied until they are overruled by a higher court. The criminal law of auto theft, for example, thus depends not only on the laws written by the fifty state legislatures or by Congress but also on the development of interpretation in the judicial system of each state in addition to that of the federal government.

Each state's adjudicatory procedures have evolved through a blend of legislative enactments and judicial interpretation of both state and federal laws. Decisions made by criminal justice actors may be challenged as in violation of defendants' rights under the laws or constitution of the particular state or under the U.S. Constitution.

Federal courts. Figure 4.2 shows the national court system arranged in a hierarchical manner, with the district courts at the base, the courts of appeals at the intermediate level, and the Supreme Court at the top. Ninety-four *U.S. District Courts* are the courts of original jurisdiction, or of first instance, where federal cases are first heard and decisions of fact are made. Distributed throughout the country, with at least one in each state, they hear the great majority of civil and criminal cases arising under federal law.

Above the federal district courts are twelve *U.S. Courts of Appeals*, each with jurisdiction for a geographic portion of the country and one for the District of Columbia. Created in 1891 as a means of reducing the case burden of the Supreme Court, this intermediate level of the judiciary hears appeals from the district courts and from such administrative bodies as the U.S. Tax Court and the National Labor Relations Board. From three to nine judges are assigned to each court of appeals, and normally three jurists sit as a panel.

The Constitution gives original jurisdiction to the *U.S. Supreme Court* in only a few types of cases—suits between states, for example. The primary task of the high court is to hear appeals from the highest state courts and the lower federal courts. But as the highest court of appeals in the United States, it still retains discretion over the cases it will hear. Each year it rejects as unworthy of review 90 percent of the 2,000 cases that reach it. With nine justices appointed

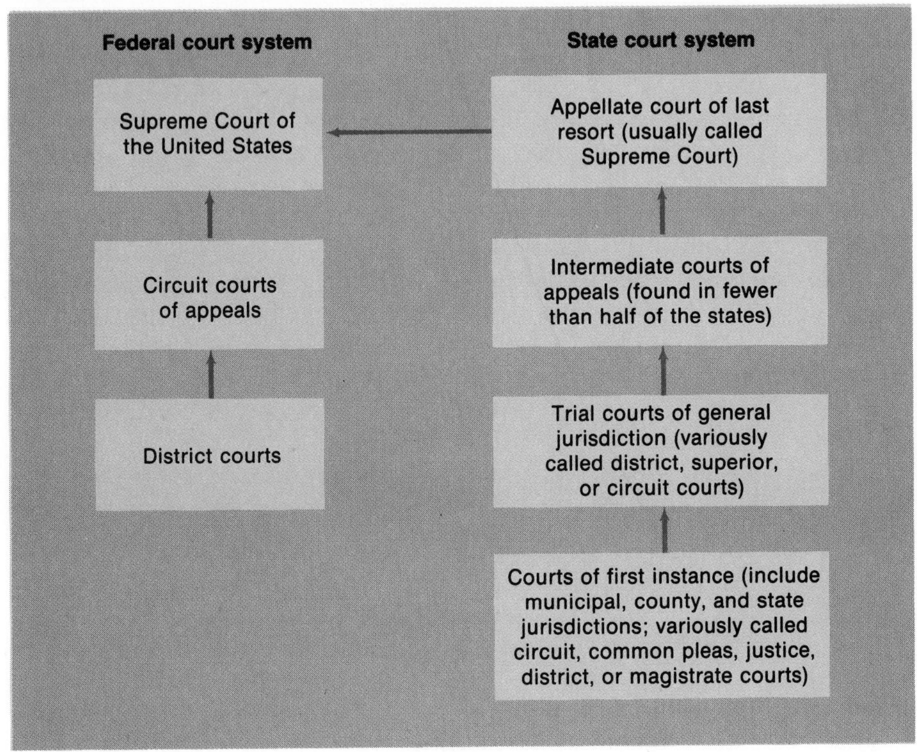

FIGURE 4.2
Dual court system of the United States and routes of appeal

for life, the Supreme Court is probably the most influential judicial tribunal in the world. It reviews and attempts to maintain consistency in the law within the federal structure of the United States.

State courts. One of the difficulties in describing the structure of state courts is that while they are all somewhat alike, they are all somewhat different. The laws of each state determine the organization of these courts; thus their names, their relationships to one another, and the rules governing their operation vary considerably. Still, one usually finds three levels of courts and a close resemblance between the pattern in the states and the organizational framework of the national judiciary. Note that state courts operate under the authority of state constitutions and should not be considered "inferior" to comparable courts in the national structure.

The powers of the state *courts of first instance,* often referred to as the "inferior" trial courts, are limited to hearing the formal charges against accused persons in all cases, holding preliminary hearings involving crimes that must be adjudicated at a higher level, and conducting summary trials (where a jury is not allowed) and, in some states, trials of persons accused of some minor offenses. Generally, the law defines the court's jurisdiction according to the maximum jail sentence that may be imposed. Commonly, six months in jail is the greatest penalty that these courts may impose.

Especially in urban areas, the observer at these courts will find very little that resembles the dignity and formal procedures of higher courts. These are not courts of record (no detailed account of the proceedings is kept), and the activities are carried out in an informal atmosphere. In most urban areas, endless numbers of people are serviced by these courts, and each defendant gets only a small portion of what should be his or her day in court.

The *courts of general jurisdiction* are above the courts of first instance and have the authority to try all cases, both civil and criminal. They are courts of record and follow formal procedures specified by law. In large metropolitan areas, they commonly have divisions that specialize in different kinds of cases. In addition to the original jurisdiction such courts exercise, which is their principal function, they also act on appeals, by hearing defendants who contest decisions made at the inferior level.

The *appellate courts* have no trial jurisdiction but hear only appeals from the lower courts. In some states only the state's supreme court—an appellate court of last resort—is found at this level; in others, an intermediate appellate court may exist in addition to the state's highest judicial body.

Corrections

On any given day approximately 2.5 million offenders are under the care of America's system of corrections. Through a variety of institutions and treatment programs at all levels of government, attempts are made to restore people to society. Of interest is the great number of approaches employed by correctional personnel to rehabilitate offenders. The average citizen probably equates corrections with prisons, but only about one-third of convicted offenders are actually incarcerated; the remainder are under supervision in the community. The use of probation and parole has increased dramatically, as has the creation of community-based centers where offenders who have been incarcerated may maintain ties with families and friends so that their reintegration into society can be more successful.

The federal government, all the states, most counties, and all but the smallest cities are engaged in corrections. In small communities, facilities are usually limited to jails used to hold persons awaiting disposition of their cases. As in the police and court functions, each level of government acts independently. Although the states operate prisons and parole bodies, probation is frequently tied to the judicial departments of counties or municipalities.

The flow of decision making

Although the flow chart of criminal justice decision making shown in figure 4.3 may appear streamlined, with cases entering at the top and moving swiftly toward their disposition at the bottom, the route is long and has many detours. At every point along the way decision makers have the option of moving a case on to the next point or dropping it from the system. The chart shows only the various processes involved at various points in the system. It is a blueprint of

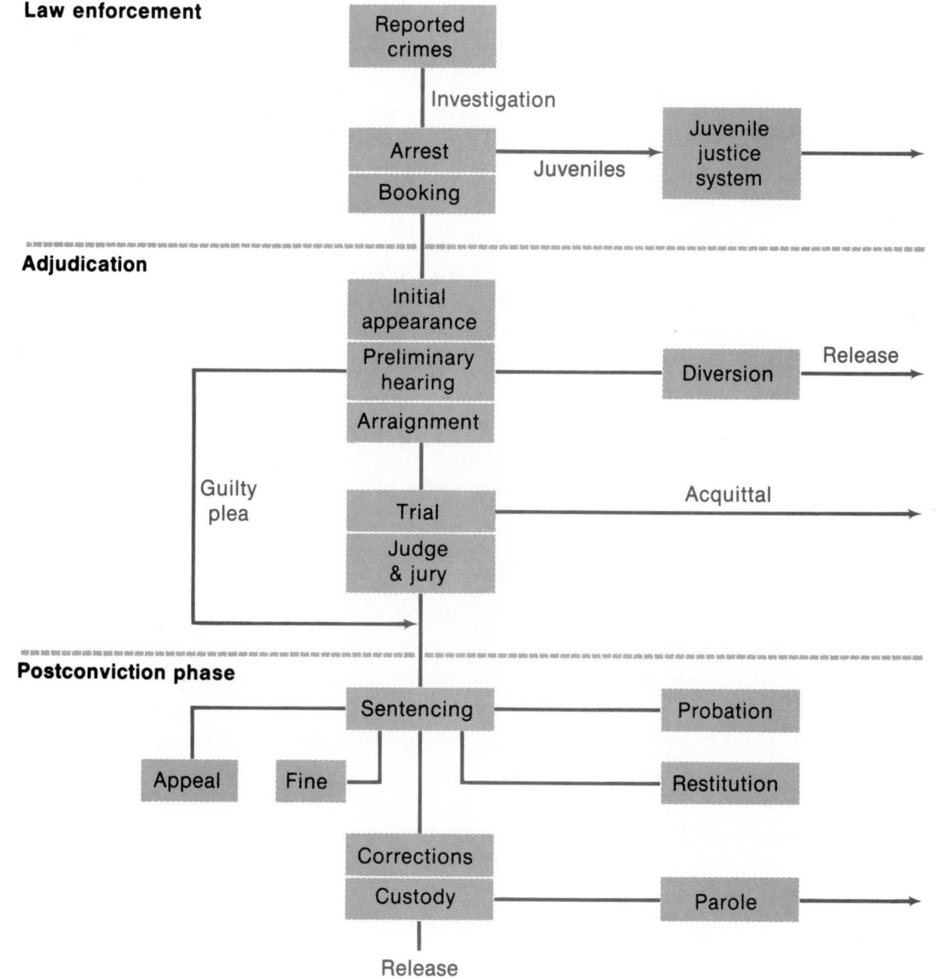

FIGURE 4.3
An overview of the criminal justice system

the criminal justice system, but it does not include the influences of the social relations of the actors or the political environment within which the system operates.

The popular Perry Mason image of an adversary system—in which the facts are determined in a public "battle" between defense and prosecution with the judge acting as arbitrator of the contest—and even lawbook conceptions of due process goals are consistent with the ideal flow through the system presented in figure 4.3. The police arrest a person suspected of violating the law and promptly bring the suspect to a judge. If the offense is minor, the judge disposes of the case immediately; if it is serious, the accused is held for further action and perhaps later released on bail. The case is next given to the prosecutor, who charges the offender with the specific crime after a preliminary hearing of the evidence. The defendant who pleads not guilty to the charge is held for trial. In the courtroom, the "fight" supervised by the judge is staged between the adversaries—defense counsel and prosecutor—so that the truth may become known. If the jury finds the defendant guilty, the judge announces the sentence, which is then carried out by corrections officials.

Although many cases do proceed in this way, this conception of the criminal justice flow is based on assumptions that do not correspond to the reality of most cases. It fails to take note of the many informal arrangements that are made through negotiation among the principal actors. Only a small number of cases ever reach the trial stage. Rather, decisions are made early in the process on the basis of discretion so that cases that may not result in conviction are filtered out by the police and prosecutor. In addition, in some jurisdictions up to 90 percent of defendants plead guilty, thus eliminating the need for a trial. Through ***plea bargaining*** between the prosecutor and defendant, a guilty plea is exchanged for reduction of the charges or for a recommendation of a reduced sentence. The enormous size of the prison population can be cited as justification of such practices.

plea bargaining
A defendant's pleading of guilty to a criminal charge with the reasonable expectation of receiving some consideration from the state for doing so, usually a reduction of the charge. The defendant's ultimate goal is a penalty lighter than the one formally warranted by the offense originally charged.

Many observers claim that these deviations from the formal blueprint have been brought about by the need to adapt a system created for a rural society to the realities of urban America, in which cases overload the system. More important, the use of shortcuts and other informal procedures reflects the adaptation of the criminal justice system to the personal and organizational needs of the administrators.

The criminal justice wedding cake

A flow chart such as figure 4.3 is a linear depiction of the criminal justice process. Cases are shown entering the system after a crime is reported and proceeding through the enforcement, adjudication, and postconviction phases. Some of the cases are shown to be filtered out, but flow charts give the impression that all are treated equally. What is not revealed by such presentations is the third dimension of the system: the degrees of importance accorded to cases by the agencies and actors in the process, and the ways in which this factor influences the allocation of justice.

Samuel Walker has suggested that although the flow chart is a notable aid to our understanding of the criminal justice system, an alternative model, the ***criminal justice wedding cake,*** is also enlightening.[2] According to this model, shown in figure 4.4, criminal justice can be thought of as a set of layers, with

criminal justice wedding cake
A model of the criminal justice process in which criminal cases form a four-tiered hierarchy with a few celebrated cases at the top, each succeeding layer increasing in size as its importance in the eyes of officials and the public diminishes.

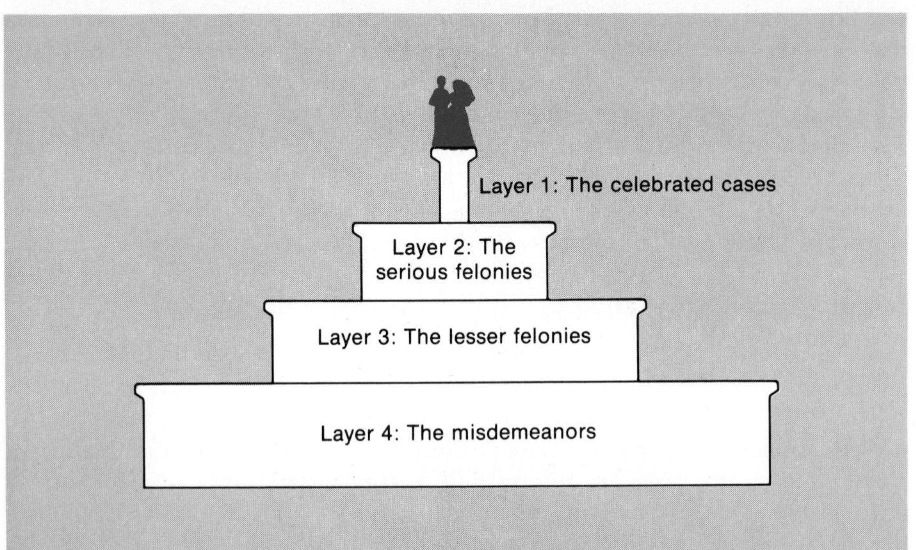

FIGURE 4.4
The criminal justice wedding cake

different kinds of cases being handled in different fashions. The nature of a case has much to do with the way in which criminal justice officials and the public react to it. Walker describes four layers of the criminal justice wedding cake.

Layer 1 consists of those very few "celebrated" cases that are exceptional, get great public attention, result in a jury trial, and often run on in extended appeals. The cases of Leopold and Loeb, the Rosenbergs, Patty Hearst, John Hinckley, and Jean Harris are in this category. Not all cases in Layer 1 achieve national notoriety; from time to time local crimes, especially cases of murder and rape, are treated in this manner. The importance of the celebrated cases lies in the fact that they are like morality plays; too often the public assumes that all criminal cases are handled in this manner.

Layer 2 consists of felonies that are deemed to be serious by officials—crimes of violence committed by persons with long criminal records against victims unknown to them. These are the cases that the police and prosecutors consider important from the perspective of crime control and that result in "tough" sentences.

Layer 3 also consists of felonies, but the crimes and the offenders are seen as of lesser concern than those in Layer 2. When such cases occur, the primary goal of criminal justice officials is to dispose of them quickly. For this reason many are filtered out of the system and plea bargaining is encouraged. It is at this level that we really begin to see the administrative rather than the adversarial system in operation.

Layer 4 is made up of misdemeanors. About 90 percent of all cases handled in the criminal justice system are found in this layer. They concern such offenses as public drunkenness, shoplifting, prostitution, disturbing the peace, and motor vehicle violations. Looked upon by officials as the "garbage" of the system, these cases are adjudicated in the lower courts, where speed is essential, trials are rare, processes are informal, and fines, probation, or short jail sentences result. Assembly-line justice reigns.

The concept of the criminal justice wedding cake is a useful corrective to the flow-chart perception of the system. Cases are not treated equally; some are viewed as very important by criminal justice officials, others as merely part of a mass that must be processed. When one knows the nature of a case, one can predict with some degree of confidence the way it will be handled and its outcome. In later portions of this book emphasis will be placed on the differential treatment of cases, but for our immediate purposes figure 4.5 underscores for us the fact that officials' conceptions of what is "important" determine how cases are dealt with.

Movement of cases

As we have seen, there are formal procedures for the handling of criminal cases, yet some offenders are given higher priority by justice officials because of the nature of their cases. One must recognize that at each step of the justice system officials are able to exercise discretion in ways that influence the defendant's fate. Many cases are filtered out of the system, others are forwarded with various charges, and still others go through informal processes. Figure 4.5 shows the funneling effect that results from these decisions.

It has been emphasized that criminal justice is basically a function of local governments. Criminal justice policies and programs reflect local attitudes and values, and they change as attitudes and values change. The influence of these variations in five states can be seen in table 4.2, which shows the percentage of arrests for serious crimes that result in prosecution, conviction, and incarceration. Some of the differences can be explained by the laws and formal procedures of the several states; other differences may relate to the resources allocated to justice agencies; and still others arise because of special programs that have been developed in particular systems. Pennsylvania's use of pretrial diversion, for example, is believed to account in part for the fact that its convic-

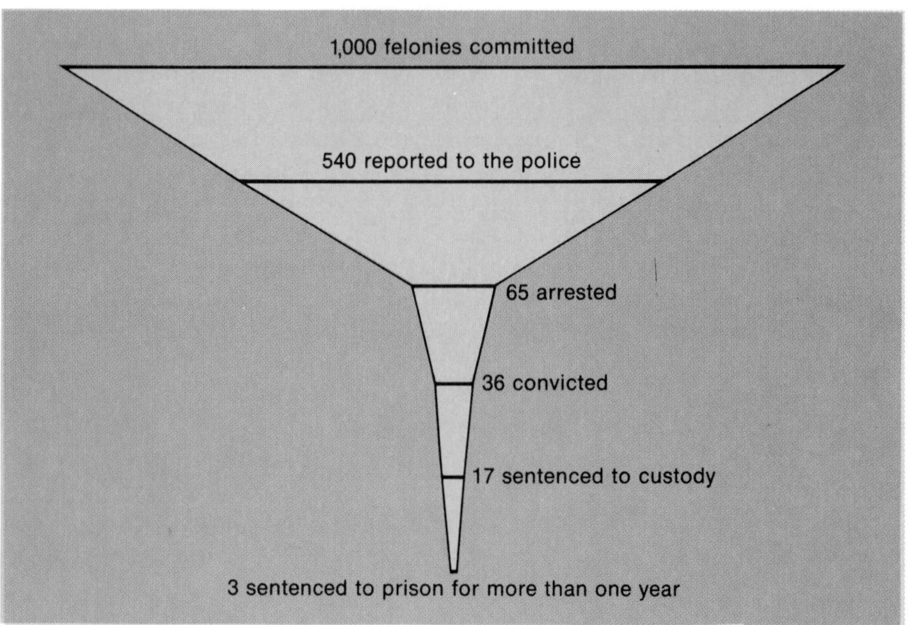

FIGURE 4.5
Funneling effect from committed felonies through prison sentences

TABLE 4.2 Processing of felony cases in five states

	Percentage of arrests for serious crimes that result in . . .		
	Prosecution	*Conviction*	*Incarceration*
New York	97%	56%	25%
California	76	57	39
Pennsylvania	76	39	15
Oregon	73	49	22
Arkansas	61	40	18

Source: U.S. Department of Justice, Bureau of Justice Statistics, *Report to the Nation on Crime and Justice* (Washington, D.C.: Government Printing Office, 1983), p. 45.

tion rate is lower than that of any of the other states analyzed.

The process by which criminal justice agencies handle reported crime may be thought of as consisting of ten major steps of law enforcement, adjudication, and corrections. Although the terms used and the sequence of the steps vary in some parts of the United States, the flow of decision making shown in table 4.3 is illustrative.

Law enforcement

We may hold to the ideal of full enforcement, with resources allocated so that all criminal acts are discovered and all offenders caught, but the reality falls short of the ideal. Only a small portion of the crimes reported result in an investigation followed by arrest. And as we have seen, victimization studies indicate that about twice as many offenses occur that are classified as serious than are known to the police. To achieve a policy of full enforcement, it is essential to have the cooperation of a citizenry willing to report violations of the law.

During periods of low community tension, however, the public appears little concerned about enforcement policies.

> So long as the vagrants are kept off the streets, the burglars away from the financial district, commercialized vice and organized racketeering away from the middle-class suburbs and the occasional spectacular case is somehow "cracked," the community does not seriously object to inefficiency and even graft in the lower echelons of officialdom . . . at least as long as things are not brought so closely to the community's attention as to be disturbing.[3]

TABLE 4.3 Flow of decision making and responsible agency

Criminal justice agencies	*Process*
1. Police	1. Investigation 2. Arrest 3. Booking
2. Prosecution and defense	4. Initial appearance 5. Preliminary hearing 6. Arraignment
3. Court	7. Trial or guilty plea 8. Sentencing
4. Corrections	9. Probation or prison 10. Parole or release

Under these circumstances, decision makers tend to accommodate the preferences of community elites and the pressures of interest groups in the formation of law enforcement policy. As a result, certain laws are enforced and others are ignored.

The community's enforcement policy and the allocation of police resources in support of it will determine the amount and kind of criminality discovered. Since the public is unable or unwilling to allow a policy of full enforcement (because it would be intolerable and expensive), decisions must be made as to the level of police resources desired and their distribution to various parts of the city. Although the size of a city and the number of police it employs are closely correlated, measuring the level of needed law enforcement resources is difficult, while predicting the increase in protection that would result from the addition of police to the force is virtually impossible. A policy of concentrating patrol officers in sections of the city perceived as high-crime areas may become a self-fulfilling prophesy: more crimes may be discovered, thereby indicating a need for more officers. An independent study might reveal that any area with a large number of police officers will show a correspondingly high crime rate. The policies of law enforcement decision makers have an important influence on the number of criminals caught and the types of cases solved.

Investigation. The flow of decision making begins when the police believe that a crime has been committed and an investigation is initiated. In this sense the police are the front-line agency charged with determining whether the criminal justice process should be invoked. This exercise of discretion is significant because a decision to do nothing may be as important as a decision to launch a full-scale probe.

Only under special circumstances are the police able to observe illegal behavior. Thus law officers usually must react after receipt of information from a victim or other citizen who reports an incident. The fact that most crimes have already been committed and their perpetrators have left the scene before the police arrive places the police at an initial disadvantage. Since they have not witnessed the event, they must examine physical clues, question witnesses, determine whether a crime has been committed, and begin a search for the offender. Only in the case of certain categories of crimes, particularly those involving vice, can the police initiate the use of investigative techniques—for example, the use of informers, electronic surveillance, and undercover agents—to catch the criminal in the process of committing the illegal act.

Arrest. If a police officer finds enough evidence indicating that a particular person has committed a crime, an arrest may be made. From an administrative standpoint, arrest involves taking a person into custody, which not only restricts the suspect's freedom but constitutes the initial steps toward prosecution.

What are the legal grounds for seizing citizens and putting them through the frightening experience of being taken into custody? Under some conditions, arrests may be made on the basis of a warrant—that is, an order issued by a judge who has received information pointing toward a particular person as the offender. In practice, most arrests are made without warrants. In some states, police officers may issue a summons or citation that orders a person to appear in court on a particular date, thus eliminating the need to hold the suspect physically until the case is disposed of.

Booking. The immediate effect of arrest is that the suspect is usually transported to a police station for booking, the procedure by which an administrative record is made of the arrest. When booked, the suspect may be fingerprinted, interrogated, and placed in a lineup for identification by the victim or witnesses. All suspects must also be warned that they have the right to counsel, that they may remain silent, and that any statement they make may later be used against them. Bail may be set.

Adjudication

"Innocent until proved guilty" is a key concept of our criminal justice system. Although we tend to focus attention on the courts as the determiners of guilt or innocence, the process really begins when the police decide a law has been violated and identify a suspect. These decisions provide the inputs to the adjudicatory process, where the evidence is closely examined by the prosecutor, judge, and jury. Throughout this process, the defendant, through counsel, may challenge the evidence, thereby creating adversarial tensions so that the case must be proved within the requirements of the law. Like the police, prosecutors and members of the bench may drop or dismiss the charges at any point in the process, thus filtering unsupported or doubtful cases out of the system.

Prosecuting attorneys provide the key link between the police and the courts. Their responsibility is to take the facts of the situation provided by the police and determine whether there is reasonable cause to believe that an offense was committed and whether the suspect committed it. The decision to prosecute is crucial because it sets in motion adjudication of the case.

Initial appearance. Within a reasonable time after arrest, suspects must be brought for an initial appearance before a judge to be given formal notice of the charge for which they are being held, to be advised of their rights, and to be given the opportunity to post bail. Statutes usually specify that bail may not be allowed for certain crimes, such as murder, but most suspects are told the amount of their bail at the initial appearance. Here the presiding judge may determine that there is not sufficient evidence to warrant holding the suspect for further criminal processing and the case may be dismissed. In some states, the initial appearance is also the point at which such minor offenses as drunkenness are disposed of through a summary trial.

Bail. The purpose of bail is to permit the accused to be released while awaiting trial. That is, to ensure that the person will be in court at the appointed time, surety (or pledge), usually in the form of money or a bond, is required. In almost all jurisdictions, the amount of bail is based primarily on the judge's perception of the seriousness of the crime and the defendant's record. In part, this emphasis stems from a lack of information about the accused. Because a suspect must be allowed to post bail within twenty-four to forty-eight hours after an arrest, the judge does not have time to seek out background information on which to base a fair bail determination. The result is that judges have developed standard rates that are used in both the courtroom and station house: so many dollars for such-and-such an offense. For accused persons who lack the necessary money for bail, a bondsman (a person who lends such cash) will provide the financing. Increasingly suspects are being released on their own recognizance—a promise to appear in court at a later date—when the crime is minor and when it can be shown that they have ties in the community.

Preliminary hearing. Even after suspects have been arrested, booked, and brought before a magistrate to be notified of the charge and advised of their rights, the evidence and probability of conviction must be evaluated before a decision is made that they should be held for prosecution. The preliminary hearing, used in about half of the states as an alternative to the grand jury, is theoretically held to determine whether the evidence is sufficient to justify holding the accused person for arraignment on formal charges. The prosecutor may use the hearing to test the value of the evidence and the reliability of witnesses. In some cases, especially those involving morals violations, there may be no victim, or the victim may be unwilling to cooperate with the prosecution. Often the victim swears out a complaint against the accused, only to have second thoughts about reciting the facts in a courtroom.

In addition to its function as a means of formally deciding whether a crime has been committed and whether there is reasonable cause to believe that it was committed by the accused, the preliminary hearing affords prosecutor and defense counsel alike an opportunity to get a glimpse of the cards held by their opponent. During the preliminary hearing, the prosecutor may decide that the probability of conviction is slight and that efforts directed against the accused would be more effectively expended elsewhere. Likewise, defense counsel may see that the accused does not have much of a case and thus may be more willing to seek a negotiated plea.

Information or indictment. In the United States, people must be formally accused by means of either an indictment or an information before they can be required to stand trial on a felony criminal charge; the stated legal purpose of both is to make a preliminary finding that there is sufficient evidence to warrant further action by the state. The major difference between these procedures is that an information may be filed by the prosecutor on the basis of the findings of the preliminary hearing, while an indictment needs the concurrence of a grand jury. In states where the information is used, the grand jury proceeding is absent. The use of one form rather than the other is related in part to historical development. One finds the use of the information throughout most of the states west of the Mississippi River, while the indictment persists largely in the eastern states.

The grand jury is drawn especially for the purpose of hearing the evidence amassed by the prosecutor and issuing the indictment. The practice originated in England as a device to gain knowledge from local people concerning matters of interest to the crown. It gradually became an instrument for the protection of the people against arbitrary accusation by the crown. This evolution brought about a reduction of the number of baseless allegations (statements without proof) presented to judges and allowed a degree of local control of prosecution.

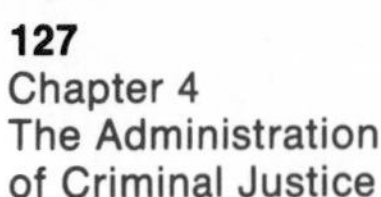

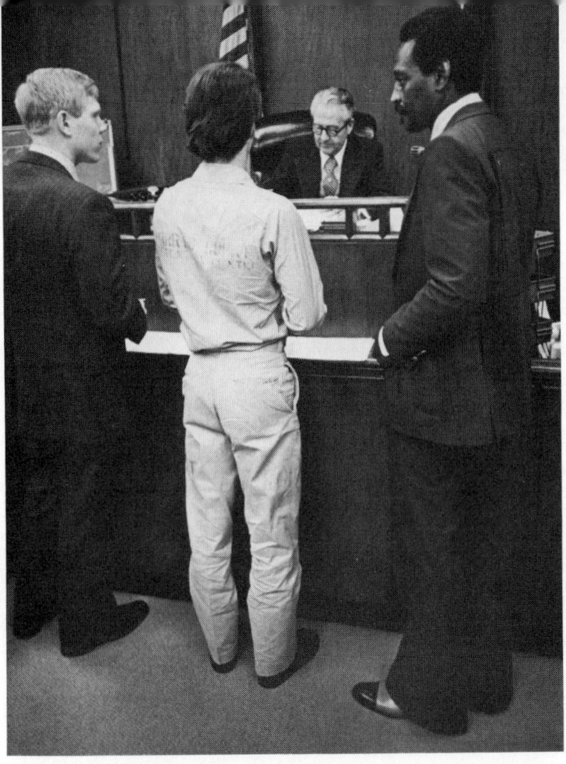

At a preliminary hearing, the judge determines whether there is sufficient evidence to hold a person.

Indictment through grand jury action has been criticized as costly and wasteful, yet the institution survives in twenty states and in the federal judicial system as the sole means of bringing criminal charges against a person. The grand jury's independence from the prosecutor has been questioned. As the only lawyer in the room, the prosecutor defines legal terms for the citizens on the grand jury and instructs them concerning their function. Not surprisingly, the relationship between them tends to be strongly influenced by the prestige and influence of the prosecutor on the one hand and the inexperience of the jurors on the other. The assembly-line aspects of the judicial process usually result in the waiving (giving up) of the right to a grand jury hearing in approximately 80 percent of cases; in the remainder, the prosecutor is usually able to secure the desired indictment. One study in Montgomery County (Philadelphia metropolitan area), Pennsylvania, found that indictments were issued in 95 percent of cases.[4] To the extent that the prosecutor is able to lead the members of the jury to feel that they are participating in the war against crime, he or she will be successful in securing the desired indictments.

From the defendants' standpoint, the information, with its requirement of a preliminary hearing, may have advantages over the indictment. They have the right to appear before the examining magistrate with counsel, to cross-examine witnesses, and to produce their own witnesses—rights they do not have before a grand jury. At the preliminary hearing, counsel is allowed to see the prosecutor's evidence against the defendant. With this knowledge, counsel is in a better position to structure plea negotiations.

Arraignment. During the arraignment phase, accused persons are taken before a judge to hear the formal information or indictment read and are asked to enter a plea. In addition, they are notified of their rights, a determination is made as to their competence to stand trial, and counsel is appointed if they can establish their inability to pay for a lawyer. Defendants may enter a plea of guilty or not guilty, or in some states may stand mute. In some states they also have the option of pleading *nolo contendere* ("no contest"), which is the same as guilty except that the plea may not be used against them in later civil suits.

If a defendant enters a guilty plea, the judge must determine whether it is made voluntarily and whether the person has full knowledge of the possible consequences of the action. A judge who is not satisfied in these respects may refuse to accept the plea and enter "not guilty" in the record. The importance of the guilty plea will be commented on extensively in chapter 10 of this book. Here we should recognize that when it is made, the accused is immediately scheduled for sentencing. It should also be understood that at any time during the trial phase the prosecutor may reduce the charge to a lesser offense that carries a correspondingly lighter sentence or may recommend that the judge deal leniently with the defendant in return for a plea of guilty, which eliminates the need for the time-consuming processes of a trial.

Courtroom. Most Americans who visit a criminal court in a metropolitan area find it an educational experience. They confront noise and confusion in dramatic contrast to the dignified and precise judicial machinery they expected. The courtroom is often a cavernous space crowded with lawyers, defendants, and relatives. It is presided over by a judge sitting at one end, going through a procedure that can be heard only by those directly in front of the bench. Especially in misdemeanor cases, the informality and speed are startling to the observer and must be confusing to the defendant. The President's Commission on Law Enforcement and Administration of Justice found that

> speed is the watchword. Trials in misdemeanor cases may be over in a matter of 5, 10, or 15 minutes; they rarely last an hour even in relatively complicated cases. Traditional safeguards honored in felony cases lose their meaning in such proceedings; there is still the possibility of lengthy imprisonment or heavy fine.[5]

For the relatively small percentage of defendants who plead not guilty, the right to a trial by an impartial jury is guaranteed by the Sixth Amendment, but this right has been interpreted as an absolute requirement only when imprisonment for more than six months may result. In many jurisdictions,

---

Arraignment

It is 3:00 P.M. now, and Alvin, who was arrested for burglary at 11:30 the previous night, has not slept for thirty-one hours. He hunches forward and hides his face in his hands to shut out the sight of the iron bars, the guard and the door to the courtroom.

"I don't know," he mutters when someone asks him what the next step in his case will be. "I don't know," he mutters again when asked the name of his lawyer. Alvin has just been arraigned in Manhattan Criminal Court, and like many other defendants who filter each week through the same procedure, he understands almost nothing of what has happened to him.

Source: *New York Times,* 11 May 1970, p. 29.

---

lesser charges do not command a jury. The use of juries is required in only a small number of cases; most trials are summary or bench trials—that is, they are conducted solely before a judge. In Detroit Recorder's Court during 1965, a total of 5,258 felony cases were heard, but only 13 percent (708 cases) were by trial, and only about 5 percent (299 cases) were heard by juries.[6] In felony cases the choice of a jury or bench trial is generally left to the defendant, with the nature of the crime, community norms, and the past record of the judge influencing the choice. Juries are waived in approximately 30 percent of murder prosecutions but in 90 percent of forgeries. Defendants in Wisconsin waive the right to a jury trial in roughly 75 percent of criminal cases; in Utah only 5 percent prefer bench trials.[7] Further, it seems to be widely assumed that because of court congestion, judges normally penalize defendants who do not waive their right to a jury trial by imposing longer sentences on the convicted.

Trial. Whether a criminal trial is held before a judge alone or before a judge and jury, the procedures are similar and are prescribed by law. A defendant may be found guilty only if the evidence proves beyond a reasonable doubt that he or she committed the offense. Rules prescribe the type of evidence that may be introduced, the way it may be obtained, and the way it is interpreted. The prosecutor's role is to present proof to substantiate the charge. The defense has an opportunity to challenge this proof by presenting alternative evidence or by questioning the validity of the prosecutor's case according to the rules of procedure. In a jury trial, the judge instructs the jurors concerning the laws applicable to the case before they depart to decide the defendant's fate.

Sentencing. Judges have the responsibility of imposing sentences, but in the case of felonies they are usually assisted by an investigation and a presentence report prepared by the probation department. The report covers the offender's personal and social background, criminal history, and emotional characteristics, and studies show that judges usually follow its recommendation. In the sentencing phase, attention is focused on the offender; the intent is to make the sentence suitable to the particular offender within the requirements of the law and in accordance with the retribution (punishment) and rehabilitation goals of the criminal justice system. Although criminal codes place limitations on sentences, the judge still has leeway to consider alternatives: suspension, probation, prison, or fine. The level of the sentence also gives the trial judge tremendous choice because legislatures typically set minimum and maximum limits but still allow for discretion.

Appeals. Defendants found guilty may appeal their conviction to a higher court. An appeal is based on claims that the rules of procedure were not properly followed by criminal justice officials or that the law forbidding the behavior that resulted in the charge is unconstitutional. Under some conditions, an appeal is automatically granted by the higher court; however, most law codes specify that the granting of an appeal is discretionary. The number of criminal trial verdicts appealed is very small in comparison with the total number of convictions, and most such appeals are dismissed. Appeals are extensive, and most defendants in criminal trials do not have the resources to appeal their convictions.

Corrections

Execution of the court's sentence is the responsibility of the correctional subsystem. Apart from fines, which are collected by officers of the court, probation and incarceration are the sanctions most generally imposed to achieve the goals of deterrence, retribution, and rehabilitation.

The deterrent effect of punishment on both the specific offender and the general public has been offered as its justifications. Although contemporary society does not like to think of the retributive aspect of corrections, this function of the system does have an effect on the offender. At the same time, rehabilitation has been the overriding goal of corrections during most of this century. Rather than punishment for the sake of punishment, the objective of corrections became rehabilitation so that offenders could be successfully reintegrated into society. Through counseling, job training, education, and therapy the goal of changing behavior has been pursued.

The goals of corrections are now being reexamined. The effectiveness of treatment programs has been questioned. The United States incarcerates offenders for much longer terms than most other Western countries. The high rates of recidivism—that is, the rate at which offenders return to crime after imprisonment—and the prison explosions typified by the 1971 riots at Attica have caused correctional officials, social scientists, and citizens to rethink the functions performed by the system.

Probation. Probation is a device to allow convicted offenders to serve their sentences in the community under supervision. Probation is used instead of incarceration primarily for the young, first offenders, and offenders convicted of minor violations. The conditions of probation generally include restrictions on the use of alcoholic beverages, possession of firearms, and leaving the court's jurisdiction without permission. Probation officers are assigned to help offenders to make their way in society and to see that the rules are followed. Violations of the conditions of probation may result in its cancellation by the judge and the imposition of a prison sentence.

Incarceration. Regardless of the reasons offered for incarceration, prisons exist to segregate the criminal from the rest of society. Offenders convicted of misdemeanors usually serve their time in city or county jails, which probably make up the most discouraging portion of the United States criminal justice system. Often poorly run, most local jails have few recreational opportunities or programs for rehabilitation. The type of prison to which felons are assigned depends on the degree of security considered necessary to keep them incarcerated. In addition to maximum-security prisons characterized by high walls, gun turrets, and locked doors at every turn, there are medium- and minimum-security facilities where offenders are granted more privileges.

Isolation from the community is probably the most overbearing characteristic of incarceration. Not only are visits from family members and correspondence restricted, but supervision and censorship are ever present. In the name of internal security, prison officials justify unannounced searches and the maintenance of rigid discipline among the inmates. These characteristics of a total institution have brought about a reconsideration of the rehabilitative goal. Thoughtful observers have asked: Can behavioral ills be treated in such an atmosphere?

Community corrections. As a consequence of the seeming inconsistency of attempts to rehabilitate within penal institutions, the idea of community corrections has attracted the interest of penologists during recent years. This concept emphasizes that the goal of reintegrating the offender into society cannot be achieved behind granite walls. As a more realistic means toward this end, programs have been devised to give inmates opportunities to remake their ties to the community. Educational release, work release, and halfway houses are among the numerous alternatives to incarceration that are being explored.

Parole. Instituted in the United States near the turn of the century, parole is today under attack. However, release on parole is still a feature of the criminal justice system of more than half the states, and a period of supervision is provided for in most. After a portion of the prison sentence has been served, parole allows the offender to live in society under conditions similar to those of probation. Prisoners are eligible for parole after they have served the minimum sentence imposed on them; the decision to release them, however, is left to the parole board. Parolees remain under supervision until the length of time represented by their maximum sentence has expired. Parole may be revoked and the person returned to prison if the conditions of parole are not fulfilled or if the parolee commits another crime.

Juvenile justice

Thus far attention has been focused on the processes by which adult offenders are arrested, judged, and punished. Until the turn of this century little effort was made to separate juvenile from adult offenders. With the rise of the Progressive movement in the early years of the century, however, Illinois, Massachusetts, New York, and later other states instituted separate criminal justice systems for juveniles. The focus of the reforms was on the courts, but special police units, detention facilities, and reformatories were also created to deal with juvenile delinquency.

Until very recently a central emphasis of the juvenile courts was the appropriateness of a humanistic rather than legal perspective on the individual child accused of crime. Stress was placed on dealing with the juvenile much as a parent would deal with a child, searching for the reasons for the criminal behavior and working out treatment programs that would be in the best interests of the individual. It was argued that the formal and adversarial aspects of the adult system, with its emphasis on rules, impeded efforts to reach the goals of juvenile justice. Thus juvenile courts were run in an informal manner, without attorneys, rules of evidence, juries, or observers. These elements of adult courts were to be replaced by a caring judge, a social worker, and the parents, who would work together to understand the child's problem and devise ways to prevent future waywardness.

Beginning in the 1960s, changes demanded by the U.S. Supreme Court began to reshape juvenile justice. Today the rules of due process are increasingly finding their way into the juvenile court. Attorneys may now be present during proceedings to protect the interests of the child. In addition, the penal codes of many states have been revised with respect to "status" offenses—acts that are not considered criminal when they are committed by adults but that bring children into conflict with the law. Changes in the corrections system have also been made with respect to juveniles. Several states have closed their reformatories. And throughout the nation group homes and other community facilities are increasingly taking the place of the more traditional correctional institution.

Chapter 17 is devoted to a description and analysis of the juvenile justice system; here the reader is only being alerted to its separate existence. As you examine the remaining chapters, bear in mind that it is adult crime and the systems that deal with it that are being discussed.

Impact on the victim

In the concern about crime control and the administration of justice, the victims are often forgotten. After crimes have been committed, victims repeatedly are heard to complain that they not only suffer loss, injury, and emotional trauma but are poorly treated by the agencies of criminal justice. Some say that they have been doubly victimized: by the criminal and by the system. Once the crime has been reported to the police, victims frequently say, they are interrogated as if they themselves were responsible for the offense; officials are rude to them; they are called to appear in court repeatedly, only to be told that the case has been postponed, or, alternatively, they never hear another word about the incident and do not know if the criminal is still at large and ready to strike again. In addition to these aspects of the victim's dealings with the police, prosecutor, and courts, victims usually incur economic costs. Earnings may be lost because of court appearances, transportation must be paid for, and access to recovered property is denied pending trial. Unlike some European countries where the victim may take part in the prosecution of the accused, the United States makes no provision for the victim's participation in the adjudicatory process other than as a provider of information to the police and prosecution or as a witness at the trial. It is society's interests that are being taken care of by the system, not the needs or desires of the victim.

During the past decade justice agencies have become increasingly sensi-

Many people are demonstrating an increasing concern for the rights of victims.

tive to the interests of victims of crime. This sensitivity has resulted in part from the recognition that victims are often the only witnesses to the event in question, and their help is necessary if a conviction is to result. If economic and emotional costs are involved in assisting law enforcement and judicial officials, many citizens will not cooperate.

This awakened concern about the victims of crime is evident in the 1982 report of the President's Task Force on Victims of Crime.[8] The task force stressed the importance of achieving a balance between the needs and rights of the victim and those of the defendant. It urged that both be protected against intimidation, that restitution be required by the courts, and that the Sixth Amendment to the Constitution be changed so that the victim would have a right to participate in all of the critical judicial proceedings. In 1982 California voters passed Proposition 8, known as the "Victim's Bill of Rights." As a result, California law now places greater emphasis on restitution, involves the victim more closely in the criminal justice process, and gives correspondingly less weight to the rights of the accused.

Programs of information, assistance in time of crisis, and compensation have been inaugurated in many states to help meet the needs of crime victims. Information programs are designed to accomplish two goals: first, to sensitize justice officials to the need to treat crime victims courteously in order to secure their effective cooperation; second, to develop ways to let victims know what is happening at each stage of the case. In some states the investigating officer at the scene hands the crime victim a booklet containing information about the steps that will be taken and telephone numbers that can be called should questions arise. Assistance in time of crisis is most important when the victim faces medical, emotional, or financial problems as a result of a crime; rape

Crime Victim's Bill of Rights

Victims of crimes have the right:

1. To protection from criminal violence
2. To be kept informed by law enforcement agencies of their investigation of a crime
3. To be kept informed by the district attorney as to the progress of a criminal case
4. To be notified of any discretionary disposition of a case
5. To be notified of any release of the defendant after conviction
6. To be notified of any change in the defendant's status
7. To be informed of financial and social services available to crime victims
8. To be provided with appropriate employer intercession services
9. To be provided with adequate witness compensation
10. To be provided with a secure waiting area during court proceedings
11. To receive adequate protection from threats of harm arising out of cooperation with law enforcement personnel
12. To have any stolen or other personal property held by law enforcement offices returned as soon as possible
13. To be represented by an attorney for certain types of cases
14. To be made whole through restitution and/or civil law recovery
15. To have perpetrators prevented from being enriched by their crimes at the victim's expense

crisis centers, prosecutors' victim assistance programs, and family shelters are among the means that have been adopted. Compensation programs in most states (see table 4.4) now supplement the assistance offered to victims of violent crime by crisis centers and provide for payment of the medical expenses of those who cannot meet them without help. When property has been stolen or destroyed, compensation programs serve to encourage judges to order restitution.

Criminal justice in an organizational setting

A major factor that distinguishes modern from traditional or primitive societies is the domination of the contemporary world by large, complex, formal

TABLE 4.4 Range of financial awards available to victims of violent crime and qualifications to be met, by state

		To qualify, victim must—		
State	*Financial award*	*show financial need*	*report to police within:*	*file claim within:*
Alaska	$0–40,000	No	5 days	24 months
California	$100–23,000	Yes	*	12 months
Colorado	$25– 1,500	No	3 days	6 months
Connecticut	$100–10,000	No	5 days	24 months
Delaware	$25–10,000	No	*	12 months
D.C.	$0–25,000	Yes	7 days	6 months
Florida	$0–10,000	Yes	3 days	12 months
Hawaii	$0–10,000	No	*	18 months
Illinois	$0–15,000	No	3 days	12 months
Indiana	$100–10,000	No	2 days	3 months
Iowa	$0– 2,000	No	1 day	6 months
Kansas	$100–10,000	Yes	3 days	12 months
Kentucky	$100–15,000	Yes	2 days	12 months
Louisiana	$250–10,000	No	3 days	12 months
Maryland	$100–45,000	Yes	2 days	6 months
Massachusetts	$100–10,000	No	2 days	12 months
Michigan	$100–15,000	Yes	2 days	1 month
Minnesota	$100–25,000	No	5 days	12 months
Missouri	$200–10,000	No	2 days	12 months
Montana	$0–25,000	No	3 days	12 months
Nebraska	$0–10,000	No	3 days	24 months
Nevada	$100– 5,000	Yes	5 days	12 months
New Jersey	$100–25,000	No	90 days	24 months
New Mexico	$0–12,500	No	30 days	12 months
New York	$0–20,000†	Yes	7 days	12 months
North Dakota	$100–25,000	No	3 days	12 months
Ohio	$0–25,000	No	3 days	12 months
Oklahoma	$0–10,000	No	3 days	12 months
Oregon	$250–23,000	No	3 days	6 months
Pennsylvania	$100–25,000	No	3 days	12 months
Rhode Island	$0–25,000	No	10 days	24 months
South Carolina	$300–10,000	No	2 days	6 months
Tennessee	$100–10,000	No	2 days	12 months
Texas	$0–50,000	Yes	3 days	6 months
Virginia	$100–10,000	Yes	2 days	6 months
Washington	$200–15,000†	No	3 days	12 months
West Virginia	$0–20,000	No	3 days	24 months
Wisconsin	$0–12,000	No	5 days	24 months

* Must report but no time limit specified.
† Plus unlimited medical expenses.
Source: U.S. Department of Justice, Bureau of Justice Statistics, *Report to the Nation on Crime and Justice* (Washington, D.C.: Government Printing Office, 1983), p. 26.

organizations. Modern society, characterized by a highly advanced division of labor and bureaucratization, places a premium on rationality, effectiveness, and efficiency. Organizations are designed to coordinate human activity in specific areas in ways that will enhance these qualities without producing unsatisfactory consequences. Analysis of bureaucracy's unique characteristics—hierarchical structure, division of labor, rules, and career employees—has so influenced our understanding of formal organizations that the terms ***bureaucracy*** and *organization* are often used synonymously.

bureaucracy
A form of administrative organization characterized by depersonalized, rule-bound, and hierarchically structured relationships that efficiently produces highly predictable, rationalized results.

The criminal justice system has not escaped the tendency toward the creation of formal organizations. To achieve the goals of criminal justice, many and varied organizational subunits, each with its own personnel, functions, and responsibilities, have been developed so that administration of the system is presumably an orderly continuum in which a variety of professionals act upon the accused in the interests of society.

But it is not enough merely to describe formal structures. If we are to understand the criminal justice system, we must know more than the way an organization chart says it is *supposed* to work. To assist us in this task, we can use concepts that social scientists have developed to analyze other public organizations. These concepts can help us to understand both how the criminal justice system functions and why it works as it does. We can then discuss possibilities of change in the administration of criminal justice.

System perspective

Too often critics have said that criminal justice is a "nonsystem." They have made this charge because they do not think that the administration of justice in America conforms with the formal blueprints or organization charts that outline the process, or with the traditional notions of the way the system is *supposed* to work. Typical of these criticisms is that of the National Commission on the Causes and Prevention of Violence.

> A system implies some unity of purpose, an organized interrelationship among component parts. In the typical American city and state, and under federal jurisdiction as well, no such relationship exists. There is, instead, a reasonably well-defined criminal process, a continuum through which each accused offender may pass. . . . The inefficiency, fallout, and failure of purpose during this process is notorious.[9]

While the concept of ***system*** does imply some unity of purpose and an interrelationship among parts, it does not assume that organizations will act as rationally ordered machines. Criminal justice is a living system made up of a number of parts, or subsystems, each with its own goals and needs. The concept of system focuses attention on the fact that the parts of an organization are interdependent—that is, changes in the operation of one unit will bring about changes in other units. An increase in the number of felony cases processed, for example, will affect the work not only of the clerks and judges of the criminal court but also of the police, prosecution, probation, and correctional subsystems. As a system, therefore, criminal justice is made up of a set of interacting parts—all the institutions and processes by which criminal justice decisions are made—and for criminal justice to achieve its goals, each must

system
A complex whole consisting of interdependent parts whose operations are directed toward goals and which are influenced by the environment within which they function.

Close-up: For Some Victims of Crimes, the Fear Never Leaves

Blossom Jackson will never forget that November night when—at 10 minutes to 9—her sister-in-law pounded on the door of her small Brooklyn house screaming, "They've killed Jackson."

"I remember thinking, 'No. No. It's not Jackson, it's not my husband, it's not my Jackson,' " she said. "But it was. He was lying in the street, right across from our house. The police said a man shot him over a parking space."

Thousands . . . have had their lives shaken by violent crime, according to police statistics. And whether they have suffered through the murder of a husband or they themselves have survived an attack by [a] knife-wielding robber or a purse snatcher, the victims say in interviews that they have found their lives changed.

Some say fear and caution are now a part of their daily routine. For others, there is anger at a criminal justice system they believe has failed them. Still others say there is disappointment in their own cherished beliefs about people and a city they once loved.

Then there are . . . [those] who have been victimized so often that they have lost their fear and anger. Instead, they say, they have learned to live with threats and blows and thievery, as if these things were as natural as air and sun and rain.

For most, the crime itself is just the beginning.

It has been more than a year since Alfred Jackson, a 38-year-old Brooklyn plumber, was shot and killed by a neighbor because Mr. Jackson wanted to park in the spot where the man was walking his dog.

Mrs. Jackson can still remember her sister-in-law's screams, the cold night air and the swarm of neighbors and policemen.

In the weeks that followed her husband's killing, Mrs. Jackson said, she was numbed by shock. But gradually, the shock wore away, replaced by fear.

"I know now that anything can happen in this city," she said. "My husband was a good, hard-working man. He never carried a gun, he was never in trouble. But that didn't matter."

Mrs. Jackson said fear is now a part of her most ordinary days and her quietest nights. "I'm scared," Mrs. Jackson, the mother of five children, said. "I'm scared when I go to work, or go out shopping, or take the kids to school. I can't wait to get back home and lock the door.

"It's very hard," she said, sitting in the living room of her home. "Sometimes I feel like I'm falling apart.

"I have no social life," the young woman said. "Nothing. I'm just here."

The man who shot Alfred Jackson pleaded guilty to first-degree manslaughter, and last month he was sentenced to five to 15 years in prison. With good behavior, he will serve 10 years at the most.

Mrs. Jackson now works six days a week at two jobs to make ends meet. She lives in fear, and she worries about her children, who she said "spend too much time just staring at the walls and asking questions about Jackson's death."

Three months ago, Jan Chytillo, who works for the city, was mugged on a quiet street in a residential section of Queens. She said she and a friend had gone out to dinner that night, and were walking home together at about 10 o'clock, when a "very big, very tall man" accosted them and demanded their purses. When her friend resisted, he shoved her in the bushes, grabbed both purses, and then ran to a waiting car. He was never captured.

Today, just walking on a city sidewalk in broad daylight is a small ordeal that makes Mrs. Chytillo jumpy, nervous. "I feel very, very vulnerable," she said, "and I'm anxious, afraid, suspicious of almost everybody I see."

The 28-year-old woman said that for two months her husband had to meet her at the subway because "I was too frightened to walk home alone." Now, she said, "I'm always very aware of everything that's going on around me on the street, even in my own neighborhood, where I used to feel safe.

"When I leave the house, I watch out," she said. "I won't walk past a car that is double parked, and I won't walk on the side of the street where it happened.

"I'm convinced," she added, "that this is a very scary city, and you have to have a lot more energy to live here—you have to be a lot tougher."

Edward Tede, a retired postman who lives in the Bronx, was attacked a month ago at a subway entrance in his neighborhood. It was late afternoon, he said, and he was returning home after visiting his wife in the hospital.

Suddenly, three young men jumped him. They grabbed his watch and his wallet, then hit him in the face. The blow sent him crashing to the ground and, when he got up, his glasses were smashed and a tooth was knocked out. Doctors later found that several of his cheekbones had been fractured.

Mr. Tede, a tall, strapping man even at age 76, said that before the mugging, he went where he wanted, when he wanted, without fear.

Even though he said he is "determined not to dwell on this," he admitted, "I'm leery now when I go out." He said, "I try to stick with crowds of people. I don't want to be alone on the street or in the subway.

"I guess I'm more nervous," Mr. Tede said. "There is a tension—you can't get it out of your mind."

His wife, Jeanette, said the whole episode has left her "frightened and angry." She added: "You work hard all your life and try to be honest, then you get this."

She and her husband have lived in the same neighborhood for most of their lives. "And in one afternoon, those boys destroyed the sense of security we had here," she said.

"You know," she added, "they never caught them. That means they are still out there . . . and that's hard to live with."

For Louise Brooker of Manhattan, it is just as hard to live with the fact that her husband's killer was caught, and sentenced to "only seven to 30 years in jail. I mean, a man kills in cold blood—and he could be out of prison in seven years?" she asked.

Her husband, Eugene Brooker, was in a supermarket when five armed men came in to rob the place. When Mr. Brooker, who had a license to carry a gun, drew his pistol to try to stop the robbers, one of them fired a shot that killed him.

"The police were marvelous," Mrs. Brooker recalled. "They caught three of the men the night after it happened. But it was two years before they were sentenced to prison. There was no trial, just plea bargains."

Mrs. Brooker said she was "bitter about the judicial system."

"We will never be protected as long as people know they can commit a crime and be out in a few years," she said. "There is something very wrong with a system like that."

Her husband's murder shook her faith not only in the legal system, but in people as well.

"My husband and I were liberal people—giving the benefit of the doubt to everyone, bending over backwards to be fair," she recalled. "We used to believe that some groups of people—because of circumstances—couldn't help what they did. Now I think everyone must take responsibility for what they do. There is no excuse for them."

She said her grown son and daughter were "devastated" by the murder. Although they were raised in New York and loved it, she said, "both left, and they will never be back." They, too, she said, "lost all their liberal feelings."

Mrs. Brooker said she was careful of the city before her husband's death, and is even more careful now. Like Mrs. Chytillo, she now has little rituals that she follows each time she stirs from the house—streets she avoids, jewelry she won't wear, house keys she hides in a pocket.

Last month, Mrs. Brooker sold the family store, and she is now thinking of moving to another city.

Source: Barbara Basler, *New York Times*, 5 May 1981, p. B6.

make its own distinctive contribution. None can function without at least minimal contact with at least one other.

Before we continue to develop this conceptual framework, it is necessary to clarify certain assumptions. First, the system is an open one; new cases, changes in organizational personnel, and shifting conditions in the political system mean that the criminal justice system is forced to deal with constant variations in its environment. Second, a state of scarcity exists within the system. The shortages of resources (time, money, information, personnel) characteristic of bureaucracies here prevent the system from processing every case in accordance with formally prescribed criteria. The subunits of law enforcement—police, prosecutor, courts, corrections—are forced to compete with one another for available resources. Central to these ideas is the politics of administration: the range of interactions between an agency and its environment that augment, retain, or diminish the basic resources needed to attain organizational goals.

Although understanding the dynamics of an operating system is important, we must also see how individual actors play their parts. The criminal justice system is, of course, made up of a great many persons whose jobs require them to perform specific roles. Therefore, the focus at this microlevel is on individual and group behavior. A key tool for analysis of the relationships among individual decision makers is the concept of ***exchange.*** Developed mainly by social psychologists, exchange theory views interpersonal behavior as resulting from the weighing by individuals of the values and costs of alternatives. A central position of exchange theory is that of reciprocity, according to which behavior responds to the rewards and punishments the individual receives.

exchange
A mutual transfer of resources; hence, a balance of benefits and deficits that flow from behavior based on decisions as to the values and costs of alternatives.

When an agreement is made between a defense attorney and prosecutor in regard to the terms of a guilty plea, presumably an exchange takes place—that is, their decision results from some trade of valued resources. In this example, the exchange was probably a guilty plea in return for a reduction of charges. Such face-to-face relationships are found throughout the criminal justice system. The concept of exchange makes us aware that decisions are the products of interactions among individuals and that the major subsystems—police, prosecutor, court, and corrections—are tied together by the actions of individual decision makers.

The concepts of system and exchange are closely linked, and their value as tools for the analysis of criminal justice cannot be overemphasized. In this book, these concepts will serve as the organizing framework within which individual subsystems and actors will be described. Organizations do not exist in a vacuum, untouched by the forces around them. With this emphasis, we can hope to understand the nature of the American system of criminal justice, evaluate its components, and work toward its improvement.

System characteristics

As noted above, an organization can be described in terms of the functions it performs, the names of the actors, the value of the resources it produces, or the special ways its tasks are pursued. We have already discussed many of the agencies of criminal justice but we have not yet looked at their methods of operation. Three special attributes—discretion, resource dependence, and sequential tasks—characterize the work of the criminal justice system. Other organizations contain one or more of these features, but few contain all three.

Discretion. At all levels of the justice process there is a high degree of discretion—the ability of officials to act according to their own judgment and conscience. The fact that discretion exists throughout the criminal justice system may seem odd since our country is ruled by law and has created procedures to ensure that decisions are made in accordance with that law. However, instead of a mechanistic system in which law rather than human decision making prevails, criminal justice is a system in which the participants—police officer, prosecutor, judge, and correctional official—may consider a wide variety of circumstances and exercise many options as they dispose of a case. The need for discretionary power has been justified primarily on two counts: resources and justice. If every violation of the law were to be formally processed, the costs would be staggering. Additionally, the belief exists that in many cases justice can be more fully achieved through informal procedures. Any system that professes to promote individualized justice must allow for the use of discretion.

Resource dependence. Like other service organizations, the criminal justice system does not produce its own resources but is dependent on others for them. This resource dependence means that it must develop special links with people responsible for the allocation of resources—that is, the political decision makers. Criminal justice actors must be responsive to the legislators, mayors, and city council members who hold the power of the purse. Further, the system relies on citizens for its raw materials. Too often we think of citizens

TABLE 4.5 Who exercises discretion?

These criminal justice officials . . .	*. . . must often decide whether or not, or how, to:*
Police	Enforce specific laws Investigate specific crimes Search people, vicinities, buildings Arrest or detain people
Prosecutors	File charges or petitions for adjudication Seek indictments Drop cases Reduce charges
Judges or magistrates	Set bail or conditions for release Accept pleas Determine delinquency Dismiss charges Impose sentence Revoke probation
Correctional officials	Assign to type of correctional facility Award privileges Punish for infractions of discipline
Paroling authority	Determine date and conditions of parole Revoke parole

primarily in the role of violator, with the police in the role of enforcer. In fact, the discretionary decisions of citizens to report crime to the police are a principal input of the system and constitute a resource that helps to maintain it.

Sequential tasks. Every part of the criminal justice system has distinct sequential tasks. This means that each subunit is granted jurisdiction over particular decisions and each has discretion over what to create or accept as inputs and whether to send these inputs on to the next level as outputs. Performance of the tasks must flow efficiently from police to prosecutor to judge to corrections or probation officer. Since a high degree of interdependence exists, the actions of one part directly affect the work of the others. The courts can deal only with the cases brought to them by the prosecutor, who can deal only with persons arrested by the police. Not every person arrested, however, arrives in the courtroom. On the contrary, a filtering process removes those cases that the relevant person—police officer, prosecutor, or judge—feels should not be passed on to the next level.

Decision making in an exchange system

The concept of system emphasizes that organizations are made up of parts that are purposefully linked for the accomplishment of a common end. Yet systems exist in a social and political environment, which thus influences such factors as the level of resources allocated, the laws to be enforced, and the internal decisions of each of the various parts. Accordingly, the administration of criminal justice may be viewed as a system in which law enforcement, prosecution, judicial, and correctional subunits are integrated to achieve an overriding objective, while the work of each is affected by the conditions and interests specific to its own portion of the process.

Because the criminal justice system is a continuum, with the actions of each component dependent on the work of prior units, decisions are greatly affected by the system's interrelated activities. Prosecution cannot proceed without an arrest and evidence, the judge requires the cooperation of the prosecution and defense, the correctional caseload is influenced by the judge's sentencing practice. From this perspective one might ask: Why do these agencies cooperate? What might happen if the police refused to transfer information to the prosecutor concerning the commission of a crime? What are the tensions existing between the police and the court? Do agencies maintain a form of "bureaucratic accounting" that, in a sense, keeps track of favors owed? How are cues transmitted among agencies to influence decision making? These are some of the questions posed when decisions are viewed as resulting from an exchange system.

The basis for exchange

The concept of exchange is based on the concept of the marketplace, in which inputs and outputs, or resources and products, are traded among persons and systems. Exchange is thus a bargaining activity that involves the transfer of certain resources among organizations and individual people and that has consequences for common goals. The person who furnishes rewarding services (favors) to another acquires a debtor; to discharge the obligation, the debtor must return some benefit. Continued exchange relationships generate a sense of trust between the system's participants, which in turn promotes a cooperative attitude that is strengthened by the organization's reward structure. For example, the help the prosecutor receives from the defense attorney who has encouraged a client to plead guilty produces benefits for both because the case is the more speedily moved.

Instead of assuming that a criminal justice agency such as the police needs to use only its statutory authority as it works in the bureaucratic world, we should recognize that each agency interacts with many clients on whom it depends for resources. In an exchange system, an organization owes its power and influence largely to its ability to develop clients that will support and enhance its needs. While the justice system is characterized by the interdependence of its parts, each subunit is in competition with other public agencies outside the system. Since criminal justice agencies operate in an economy of scarcity and are faced with more claims than they can fulfill with available resources, the system must thus occupy a favorable power position vis-à-vis its clientele. Many of the exchange relationships between agencies within the system are necessitated not only by statutes mandating their participation in decision making but by the system's needs.

The concept of an exchange system also helps to clarify the influence of decisions made in one justice agency on the relationships and decisions made in the other parts of the judicial process. Figure 4.6 illustrates the exchange relationships between the prosecutor and other units in the system. Figure 4.7 indicates that lateral relationships are necessary because the outputs of one subsystem become the inputs of the next. A judge's verdict in a felony case affects the arresting officer's record, the prosecutor's conviction rate, and the credibility of the probation officer's sentencing recommendation. An official's decisions are often made in anticipation of a judge's reaction. For example, knowledge that a judge customarily gives lenient sentences or fines for certain types of offenses may discourage the police from making arrests in such cases.

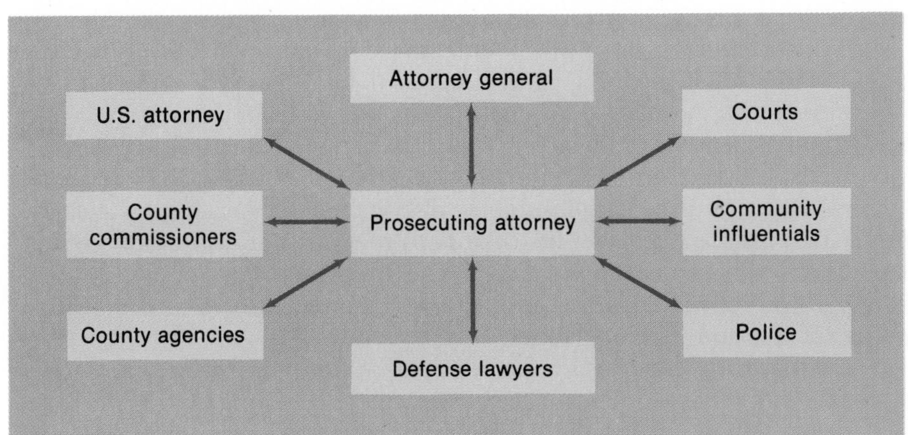

FIGURE 4.6 Exchange relationships between prosecutors and others

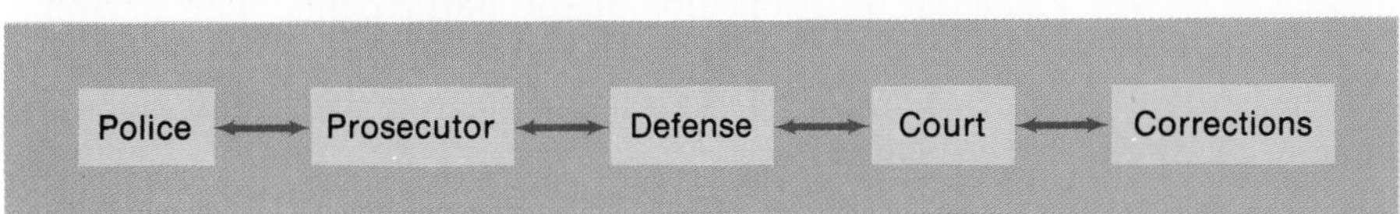

FIGURE 4.7 Selected lateral relationships in the administration of justice

An interesting example of this type of interdependence was given by a district court judge who noted that when the number of prisoners reached the riot point, the warden urged the courts to slow down the flow. Accordingly, men were let out on parole, and the number of persons given probation and suspended sentences increased. One could speculate that the prosecutor viewing this behavior by the judges would reduce the inputs to the courts either by not preferring charges or by increasing the pressure for guilty pleas through bargaining. Adjustments of other parts of the system could be expected to follow. For instance, the police might sense the prosecutor's reluctance to accept charges and hence be willing to present only airtight cases for indictment. One of the consequences of the 1970 prison riots in New York City was an immediate decrease in the population of correctional facilities. Because overcrowding had been one of the primary reasons for the uprising, the system was modified so that fewer prisoners were held. This modification had repercussions throughout the system.

Remember that interactions within organizations result from the decisions and actions of real persons; exchanges do not simply sail from one subsystem to another but take place in an institutionalized setting. Agreements are made between persons occupying boundary-spanning roles who set the conditions under which the exchange will occur. How decisions are made depends on how the actors play their roles and their perceptions of the others in the interaction.

Although the formal structures of the judicial process stress antagonistic and competitive subunits, exchange relationships strengthen cooperation within the system, thus deflecting it from its adversarial goals. For example, although the prosecutor and defense counsel play roles that are prescribed as antagonistic, continued interaction on the job, in professional associations, and in political and social groups may produce a friendship that greatly alters the way they play their roles. Combat in the courtroom, as ordained by the formal structure, may not only endanger the personal relationship but also expose the actors' personal weaknesses to their own clienteles. Neither the judge, the prosecutor, nor the defense attorney wants to look unprepared in public. Rather than encouraging the unpredictability and professional insecurity stressed by the system, decisions on cases may be made in such a way as to bring mutual benefits to the actors in the exchange.

Exchange relationships are enhanced by the fact that each actor in the administration of justice has substantial discretionary power. Each patrol officer is able to make his or her own decisions regarding arrest in most circumstances involving minor crimes. The decision to prosecute is frequently in the hands of the individual prosecutor as a result of exchanges with individual police officers and criminal lawyers.

Thus far, this section has indicated that the justice system is composed of a number of interdependent subunits and that the work of each influences the activities of the others. Decisions concerning the operation of the system are influenced by the exchange relationships of the participants. The personal and organizational needs or goals of each member of the relationship may supersede the formally prescribed rules and procedures. Accommodations are made to maintain these relationships.

Criminal justice as a filtering process

The President's Commission on Law Enforcement and Administration of Justice has referred to the criminal justice process as a continuum—that is, as having an orderly progression of events. As in all legally constituted structures, there are formally designated points at which certain decisions are made. To speak of the system as a continuum, however, may be to ignore the complexity and the flux of relationships within it. Although the administration of criminal justice is composed of a set of subsystems, there are no formal provisions for the subordination of one unit to another. Each has its own clientele, goals, and norms, yet the output of one unit constitutes the inputs of another.

The criminal justice system is better likened to a ***filtering process*** through which cases are screened: some are advanced to the next level of decision making, while others are either rejected or the conditions under which they are processed are changed. The President's Commission declared, "The limited statistics available indicate that approximately one-half of those arrested are dismissed by the police, a prosecutor, or a magistrate at an early stage of the case."[10] Other evidence corroborates this finding.

filtering process A screening operation; hence, a process by which criminal justice officials screen out some cases while advancing others to the next level of decision making.

A study by the Rand Institute of the flow of defendants through the New York City criminal courts is one of the most detailed examinations of the administration of justice in a single city. As figure 4.8 shows, approximately 330,000 cases were processed, yet more than 90,000 never went beyond the preliminary examination because the cases were dismissed (60,868) or because the defendants were transferred to other jurisdictions (4,033), were acquitted (10,659), or were not located (15,565). Only 7 percent of the 195,000 convicted received a trial; sentences were imposed on the rest following a plea of guilty. Commenting on the report, Nathan Sobel noted, "The system has been almost totally directed toward disposing of cases without trial. We cling to the due process idea of justice, and it doesn't exist any more."[11]

The system in operation. Organizations exist within a social context in which the subunits and personnel find some activities rewarding and others tension-producing. The policies followed in an exchange system will evolve to maximize gains and minimize stress. The administration of justice is greatly affected by the values of decision makers whose careers, influence, and positions may be more important to them than consideration for the formal requirements of the law. Thus when decisions that might be disruptive are contemplated, accommodations are sought within the exchange system. Because they fear they will be criticized for committing "work crimes," the members of the criminal justice system are bound together into an effective network of complicity. This network consists of a work arrangement in which patterned, secretive, informal breaches and evasions of due process are institutionalized but are nevertheless claimed not to exist. A whole language with meanings known only to system actors has emerged within the administration of justice: "Thus *cooperation* implies an understanding of the requirements of the other functionaries in the system, *ability* implies the capacity to fulfill those needs, and *rationality* or *reasonableness* suggests the acceptance of prevailing assumptions."[12]

Prosecuting attorneys play a central role in the administration of criminal

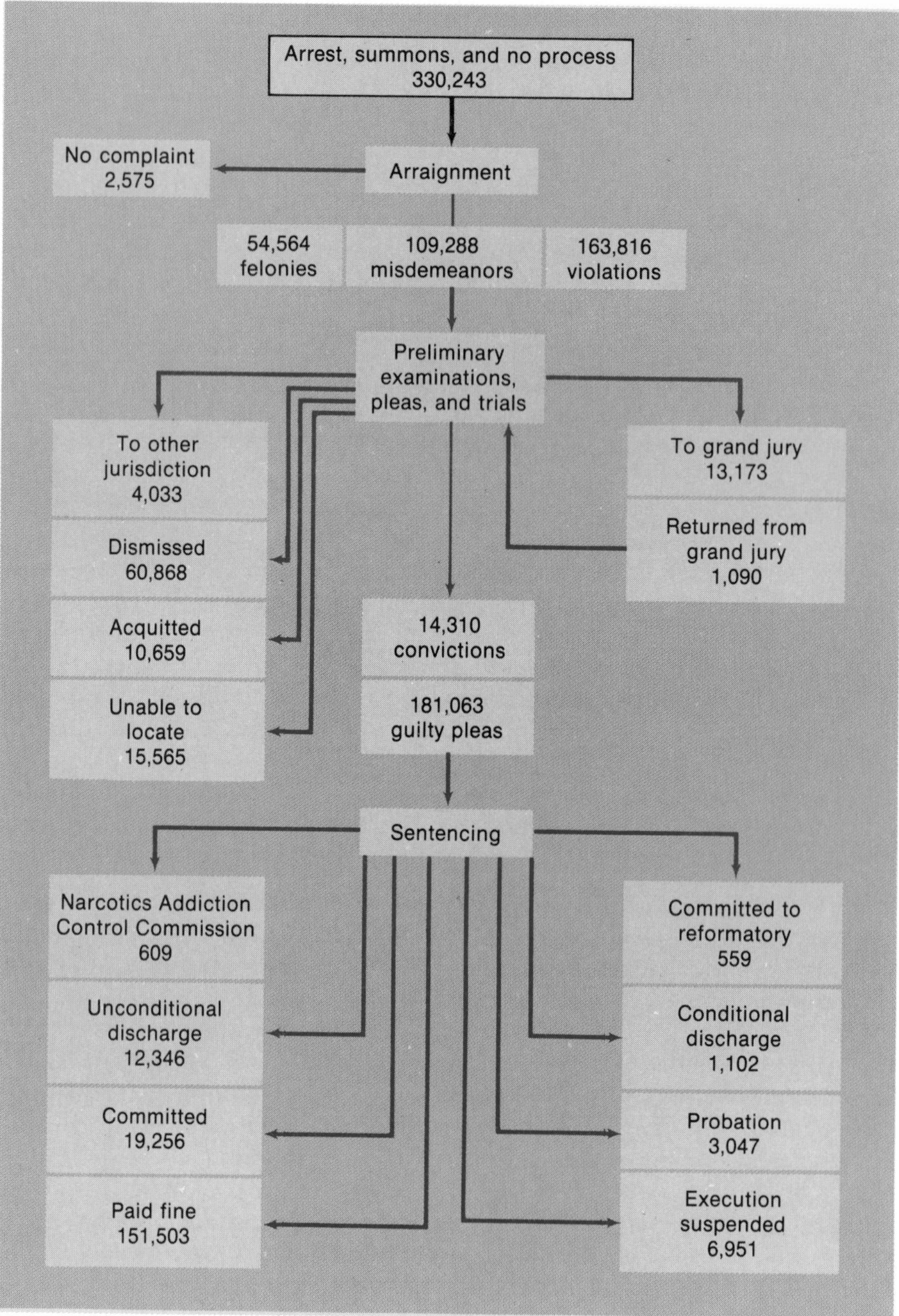

FIGURE 4.8
The flow of defendants through the New York criminal courts

justice. Theirs are the strategic moves: they recommend bail, select the charges, and determine whether a lesser plea will be accepted. Although discretion is a formal power of the prosecutor, it is exercised within the exchange framework of a bureaucratic system. In addition, the highly partisan nature of the office can mean that political considerations play a prominent part in decision making. Therefore, exchange relationships, the norms of efficiency, good public relations, and the maintenance of harmony and esprit de corps among underlings will have a great effect on the power the prosecutor can wield.

The place of the defendant. Of central concern is the place of defendants in the administrative process. Because they pass through the system while judicial actors remain, they may become secondary figures in the bureaucratic setting. The judicial actors may view defendants and their cases as challenges or as temporarily disruptive influences. The tensions that individual cases may produce are repressed because system personnel must be able to interact on the basis of exchange in the future. Because these relations must be maintained, pressures may be brought to dispose of cases in a manner that will help to sustain the existing linkages within the system.

Social scientists have expressed fears that defendants with certain social characteristics who are accused of certain types of crimes receive unfair treatment because of the bureaucratic rather than the adversary emphasis within the justice process. One suspects that those persons who can be handled without creating tension will receive harsher treatment than those whose status may cause them to be viewed as a threat to productive exchange relationships. As William Chambliss suggests, "those persons are arrested, tried, and sentenced who can offer the fewest rewards for nonenforcement of the laws and who can be processed without creating any undue strain for the organizations which comprise the legal system."[13]

Evidence from major cities demonstrates that a disproportionate number of defendants in criminal cases are under twenty-five years of age, are poor, and are members of racial or ethnic minorities. Such defendants may be vulnerable to the actions and manipulations of both counsel and criminal justice officials. The typical defendant is unable to cope effectively with the system. It is complex, and the disadvantaged do not understand its intricacies. The low visibility of the entire system shields it from the public and even from other officials. Judges and other criminal justice actors work with a great deal of independence from supervision.

The disposition of a case depends to a great extent on the negotiating skill of the accused's counsel. By exposing weaknesses in the state's case, counsel may convince the prosecutor of the futility of proceeding to trial. Alternatively, counsel may help to convince the defendant of the strength of the prosecution's case and urge bargaining for a lesser charge in exchange for a guilty plea. In some jurisdictions the filtering process works so well that, statistically, if the prosecutor says a person is guilty, the person is guilty. From the standpoint of the Crime Control Model, the courts increasingly become tribunals of last resort after the administrators of the system have made their decisions.

Most research indicates that the values of the administrative or Crime Control Model are widely held by police, prosecutors, court officials, and even defense attorneys. The tenor of comments by these actors reveals that the conditions under which decisions are made contribute to the assumption and reinforcement of those values. As one experienced prosecutor told the author, "We know that more than 80 percent of these guys are guilty. After a while you get so that you can look at the sheet [case record] and tell what is going to happen." Similar attitudes have been expressed by judges of the lower trial courts and by attorneys who depend on criminal cases for a major portion of their work. A startling example is the judge who says that he assumes that defendants who have survived the scrutiny of the police and prosecutor must be guilty.

Summary

Society has charged the criminal justice system with prevention and control of crime within the framework of law and of our cultural values. Although this goal may seem clear, a view of the criminal justice system in operation reveals that a number of value decisions must be made at each point in the law enforcement, adjudication, and corrections process as to the best way to fulfill the purpose of criminal justice.

In the United States, the operations of criminal justice are distributed among federal, state, and local agencies. Most criminal justice agencies, including the special agencies created to deal with juvenile crimes, operate at the local level, under the authority of counties and municipalities. The federal government has jurisdiction over only a limited number of crimes, primarily those affecting the national interest and some offenses involving the crossing of state lines. At each level of government, the law specifies the jurisdiction of the agencies and the procedures that must be followed throughout the process. The Constitution of the United States is the major tie that binds the activities together.

As the latter part of this chapter emphasizes, the criminal justice system may be viewed as an organization with goals antagonistic to those posited by the Due Process Model. Decisions concerning the disposition of cases are influenced by the selective nature of a filtering process in which administrative discretion and interpersonal exchange relationships are extremely important. At each level of decision making, judicial actors are able to determine which types of crimes will come to official notice, which kinds of offenders will be processed, and the degree of enthusiasm that will be brought to the effort to secure a conviction:

> It is in the day-to-day practices and policies of the processing agencies that the law is put into effect and it is out of the struggle to perform their tasks in ways which maximize rewards and minimize strains for the organization and the individuals involved that the legal processing agencies shape the law.[14]

For discussion

1. In recent years, increased stress has been placed on the accumulation of crime and personal data in national computer banks. What are the implications of this development for crime control? for civil liberties?
2. In our increasingly urbanized society, increased coordination among law enforcement agencies may be desirable. What problems would such a development present?
3. What means could prevent the misuse of discretion?
4. Organization of the police in metropolitan areas is often a hodgepodge of overlapping jurisdictions, with lack of cooperation among city, county, and local forces. Although some may argue that one law enforcement agency for an entire metropol-

itan area would be more effective, what arguments can be offered in support of the continuation of the present arrangement?

5. What are the goals of the criminal justice system? Which goals seem most important?

For further reading

Blau, Peter M., and Scott, Richard. *Formal Organizations.* San Francisco: Chandler, 1962.
Davis, Kenneth Culp. *Discretionary Justice.* Baton Rouge: Louisiana State University Press, 1969.
Holt, Dan. *The Justice Machine.* New York: Ballantine, 1972.
Jacob, Herbert. *Justice in America.* 3d ed. Boston: Little, Brown, 1978.
Karmen, Andrew. *Crime Victims.* Monterey, Calif.: Brooks/Cole, 1984.
Smith, Bruce. *Police Systems in the United States.* New York: Harper & Row, 1960.
Walker, Samuel. *Sense and Nonsense about Crime.* Monterey, Calif.: Brooks/Cole, 1985.

Notes

1. Coppedge v. U.S., 369 U.S. 449 (1962).
2. Samuel Walker, *Sense and Nonsense about Crime* (Monterey, Calif.: Brooks/Cole, 1985), chap. 1.
3. William J. Chambliss, ed., *Crime and the Legal Process* (New York: McGraw-Hill, 1969), p. 99.
4. Walton Coates, "Grand Jury, the Prosecutor's Puppet: Wasteful Nonsense of Criminal Jurisdiction," *Pennsylvania Bar Quarterly* 33 (1962): 311.
5. President's Commission on Law Enforcement and Administration of Justice, *Task Force Report: The Courts* (Washington, D.C.: Government Printing Office, 1967), p. 30.
6. Ibid., p. 134.
7. Harry Kalven and Hans Zeisel, *The American Jury* (Boston: Little, Brown, 1966), pp. 26–32.
8. President's Task Force on Victims of Crime, *Final Report* (Washington, D.C.: Government Printing Office, 1982).
9. James S. Campbell, Joseph R. Sahid, and David P. Stang, *Law and Order Reconsidered* (New York: Bantam, 1970), p. 263.
10. President's Commission on Law Enforcement and Administration of Justice, *Task Force Report: The Courts,* p. 130.
11. As quoted in Lesley Oelsner, "Criminal Courts: Statistical Profile," *New York Times,* 28 March 1970, p. 23.
12. Jerome Skolnick, "Social Control in the Adversary System," *Journal of Conflict Resolution* 11 (March 1967): 63.
13. Chambliss, ed., *Crime and the Legal Process,* p. 84.
14. Ibid., p. 86.

An 18-year-old named Donald Payne came handcuffed and sullen into the [courthouse] building last year—a tall, spidery, black dropout charged with the attempted armed robbery and attempted murder of a white liquor-store owner in a "changing" fringe neighborhood. The police report told it simply: ". . . At 2100 [9 P.M.] . . . August 4, 1970 . . . victim stated that two male Negroes entered his store and the taller of the two came out with a gun and announced that this is a holdup, 'give me all of your money.' With this the victim . . . walked away from the area of the cash register. When he did this, the smaller offender shouted 'shoot him.' The taller offender aimed the pistol at him and pulled the trigger about two or three times. The weapon failed to fire. The offenders then fled. . . ." It was a botched job—nobody was hurt and nothing stolen—and so Payne in one sense was only another integer in the numbing statistics of American crime.

Donald Payne's passage from stick-up to station house to jail to court and finally into the shadow world of prison says more than any law text or flow chart about the realities of crime and punishment in America. The quality of justice in Chicago is neither very much better nor very much worse than in any major American city. The agents of justice in Chicago are typically overworked, understaffed, disconnected, case-hardened, and impossibly rushed. Payne protested his innocence to them every step of the way, even after he pleaded guity. There is, given the evidence, no compelling reason to believe him, and no one did—least of all the lawyer who represented him. So the agents of justice handed him and his case file along toward a resolution that satisfied none of them wholly. "That we really have a criminal-justice system is a fallacy," remarked Hans Mattick, co-director of the Center for Studies in Criminal Justice at the University of Chicago Law School. "A system is artificially created out of no system. What we have is a case-disposition system." In the winter of 1970–71, the system disposed of *People* v. *Payne*—and the sum of Donald Payne's case and tens of thousands more just like it across the nation is the real story of justice in America.

The defendant

They fought over Donald Payne, home against street, a war of the world recapitulated ten thousand times every day in the ghetto; only, when you live in a ghetto, you can never get far enough away from the street to be sure of the outcome. Payne's mother tried. Her first husband deserted her and their four kids when Donnie, the baby, was still little. But she kept them together and, thirteen years ago, was married to Cleophilus Todd, a dark, rumbly-voiced man who preaches Sundays in the storefront Greater Mount Sinai M. B. (for Missionary Baptist) Church and works weekdays to keep his family and his ministry afloat. She bore two more children and worked some of the time to supplement the family's income; and two years ago they were able to put enough together to escape the gang-infested section where Donald grew up and move into a little green-and-white frame house in a fringe working-class neighborhood called Roseland. . . . But it may have come too late for Donald. He had already begun sliding out of school: it bored him ("They'd be repeatin' the same things over and over again, goin' over the same thing, the same thing") so he started skipping, and when the school called about him, he would pick up the phone and put it back on the hook without saying anything. *Maybe I thought it was too much happenin' out there in the streets to be goin' to school.* Or church either. "They have to go to church long as they live with us," says Cleophilus Todd. For years, Donald did: he spent his Sunday mornings in the peeling, blue-curtained storefront, shouting gospel in the choir, listening to his stepfather demanding repentance of a little congregation of women and small children in the mismatched, second-hand pews and hardwood theater seats. But it got claustrophobic on Mount Sinai. "I just slowed down," Payne says. "I started sayin' I'd go next Sunday, and then I wouldn't. And then I just stopped."

The street was winning. Payne showed a knack for electricity; he made a couple of lamps and a radio in the school shop before he stopped going and brought them home to his mother, and she would ask him why he didn't think about trade school. "He could fix everything from a light to a television set," she says. "He was all right as long as he was busy. Only time you had to worry about him was when he had nothin' to do." He did work sometimes, two jobs at once for a while, and once he talked to a man working on a house about how you get into electrical work. The man told him about apprenticeships and gave him the address of his union. "But I just hated to travel. It bored me even when I was workin'—I just hated to take that trip. So I kept puttin' it off and puttin' it off." . . .

Nobody knows, really, why the street swallows up so many of them. Poverty in the midst of affluence is surely part of it, and color in the midst of whiteness; so are heroin and broken homes and the sheer get-it-now impulsiveness of life in so empty and so chancy a place as a ghetto. But no one can say which ones will go wrong—why a Donald Payne, for example, will get in trouble while three brothers and two sisters come up straight. "I told 'em all," says Todd. "I'm not going to be spending all my time and money on jail cases for you doing something you don't need to get into." Only Donald got into it. . . .

Still, he did get run in a few times for disorderly conduct, routine for kids in the ghetto street. And, in 1968, he was arrested for burglary.

It was a kid-stuff, filling-station job, two tires and a sign, and Payne was caught with the tires a few blocks away. He insisted he was only trying to help a friend sell them, but Todd says he confessed to the family ("Sometimes it makes no difference how good a kid is or how good he is brought up") and he wound up pleading guilty in a deal for a few days in jail and two years on probation. It came to little: probation in theory is a means to rehabilitation, but probation officers, in fact, in Chicago and around the country, tend to have too many cases and too little time to do much active rehabilitating. Payne's papers were lost for several months until he finally got scared and came in to find out why no one had called him. After that, he reported once every month, riding two hours on buses to see his probation officer for ten minutes. "We talked about was I workin' and how was I doin' out on the street—that was all." Once the probation officer referred him to a job counselor. Payne never went, and no one seems to have noticed.

And now, at 18, he is in big trouble. . . .

Source: Peter Goldman and Don Holt, "How Justice Works: The People vs. Donald Payne," *Newsweek*, 8 March 1971, pp. 20–37.

PART 2

Law Enforcement

Because the police are the most visible agents of the criminal justice system in American society, Part Two deals exclusively with the role of law enforcement as the critical subunit of the system that must confront crime at the community level. Most of us have gained an image of the police from movies and television, but we shall see that law enforcement differs greatly from the exploits of the cops on "Hill Street Blues." Police work often takes place in a hostile environment with crucial questions of life and death, honor and dishonor at stake. Officers are given discretion to deal with these situations, and how that discretion is used has an important effect on the way society views law enforcement. Chapter 5 closes with an account of how one citizen, Donald Payne, faced the police; chapter 6 examines the daily operations of the police; and chapter 7 analyzes some of the current issues and trends in law enforcement.

Police

A historical perspective
- The English tradition
- Development of the police in the United States
  - *Professionalism and reform*
  - *Rethinking policing*

Law enforcement policy
- Levels of enforcement
- Selective enforcement
- Community influence on enforcement policy

Police functions
- Order maintenance
- Law enforcement
- Service
- Implementing the mandate

Police action and decision making
- Encounters between police and citizens—"Call the cops!"
- Discretion

Police work
- Qualifications
- On the job
  - *Danger*
  - *Authority*
- Subculture of the police
- Working personality
- Isolation of the police
- Job stress
- The making of a police officer
  - *Preentry*
  - *Admittance*
  - *Change*
  - *Continuance*
- Operational styles
  - *Crime fighter*
  - *Service agent*
  - *Watchman*
  - *Legalist*

Summary

The People versus Donald Payne

5

A democracy, like all other societies, needs order and security, but it also and equally requires civil liberty. This complexity of needs creates difficult theoretical and practical problems.

JEROME HALL

Law and order is a seemingly elementary phrase that politicians and others have used frequently in recent years to express certain values. Some people use the phrase in response to the rise in violent crime; for others it reflects a concern for social change; for still others, it may be a code that masks racial prejudice. Yet from philosophical, historical, and administrative perspectives, law and order is not a simple concept but one that has wide implications for the preservation of civil liberties and the rule of law. A key question in a democratic society is: For what social purpose do police exist? Herman Goldstein points out that the police, "by the very nature of their functions, are an anomaly in a free society." They are given a great deal of authority—to arrest, to search, to detain, and to use force (all actions disruptive of personal freedom)—yet democracy requires police to maintain order so that the free society may be possible. As Goldstein notes, "The strength of a democracy and the quality of life enjoyed by its citizens are determined in large measure by the ability of the police to discharge their duties."[1]

Yet if we depend on the "thin blue line" to protect democratic society, the police and the public must clearly understand the duties and functions of law enforcement. Research shows that there are still many questions about the role of police in a democracy and the best methods that they can use to achieve their goals.

History gives little help in defining police functions because the agencies of law enforcement have played a great variety of often contradictory roles.

> Are the police to be concerned with peacekeeping or crime fighting? The blind enforcers of the law or the discretionary agents of a benevolent government? Social workers with guns or gunmen in social work? Facilitators of social change or defenders of the "faith"? The enforcers of the criminal law or society's legal trash bin? A social agency of last resort after 5:00 P.M. or mere watchmen for business and industry?[2]

This chapter addresses the role of the police in a democratic society. By focusing on the historical development of law enforcement, the policies of law enforcement, the functions of the police, the nature of decision making, and the subculture of the police, the chapter shows that the activities of law enforcement are greatly influenced by social and political factors. The police are but one organization within the closely integrated system of criminal justice.

Their work provides the essential inputs of the other subsystems. How the police pursue their goals greatly influences the operation of the rest of the system. Because the police are the most visible representatives of the criminal justice process, citizens necessarily form judgments about them, and those judgments have a strong impact on the way order is maintained under law.

Not only is order to be maintained under law but enforcement is performed within the context of an organizational exchange system. Thus a third dimension is added to the concept of law and order. Jerome Skolnick summarizes the problems that flow from this situation:

> The police in democratic society are required to maintain order and to do so under the rule of law. As functionaries charged with maintaining order, they are part of the bureaucracy. The ideology of democratic bureaucracy emphasizes initiative rather than disciplined adherence to rules and regulations. By contrast, the rule of law emphasizes the rights of individual citizens and constraints upon the initiative of legal officials. This tension between the operational consequences of ideas of order, efficiency, and initiative, on the one hand, and legality, on the other, constitutes the principal problem of police as a democratic legal organization.[3]

A historical perspective

Law and order is not a new concept; it has been a focus of discussion since the formation of the first police force in metropolitan London, in 1829. Looking even farther back in history to the Magna Carta, one recognizes that limitations were placed on the constables and bailiffs of thirteenth-century England. By reading between the lines of this ancient document, one can surmise that problems of police abuse, the maintenance of order, and the rule of law were similar to those encountered today. What is surprising is that the same remedies—recruiting better police, stiffening the penalties for official malfeasance, creating a civilian board of control—were suggested in that earlier time to ensure that order was kept in accordance with the rule of law. Having given power to the police to arrest and incarcerate citizens, society must control this power so that civil liberties are not infringed. The potential for misuse of power by law enforcement agencies led many thoughtful American citizens of the nineteenth century to contend that such a power was alien to democracy and would lead to an end of freedom.

It is also from the English tradition that the three major characteristics of American policing have flowed: limited authority, local control, and fragmentation. Like the British police but unlike the Continental police, the American police have limited authority—their powers and responsibilities are closely circumscribed by law.[4] England, like the United States, has no national police force; each unit is under local community control. Tied to this characteristic is the fact that law enforcement is fragmented: there are many types of police agencies, each with its own special jurisdiction and responsibilities—constable, sheriff, urban police, the FBI, and so on.

The 20,000 public law enforcement agencies that are today dispersed throughout the counties, cities, and towns of the United States have their origins in the second quarter of nineteenth-century England, during the early phases of the Industrial Revolution. Arguing for establishment of a police force in metropolitan London, Sir Robert Peel cited statistics indicating that the crime rate was increasing more rapidly than the population rate. Moreover, the city's slum residents were rioting and had to be kept from destroying property and life in the "respectable" neighborhoods. Yet even in the face of these conditions, the fear of centralization of power in a military-style body was so great that only after seven years of lobbying was Peel able to persuade Parliament of the necessity of an organized police force. As with so many other public institutions, the English example quickly spread to the United States. Police organizations were established in the principal urban centers, while leading citizens contended that a paid professional police force would spell the end of freedom and democracy.

The English tradition

Although Peel is often credited with helping to establish the first professional police force in England, historians have shown that organizations to protect local citizens and property had existed before the thirteenth century. In this early period, however, peacekeeping was primarily a responsibility of groups of citizens who volunteered to pursue lawbreakers. The voluntary nature of these efforts was changed in 1285 by the Statute of Winchester, which required all citizens to pursue criminals under the direction of the local constable, the primary law enforcement officer in every town in England, if he needed their assistance.

This traditional system of community law enforcement was maintained well into the eighteenth century. With the onset of the Industrial Revolution, policing became more complex. What had worked for a rural and feudal society was inadequate in the growing cities, where community ties and the influence of the lord of the manor were greatly reduced. Inevitably, with urban growth, established patterns of life changed and social disorder resulted. As a consequence, there was an almost complete breakdown of law and order in London.

In the 1750s Henry Fielding (author of *Tom Jones*) and his brother Sir John Fielding led efforts to improve the police in England. Through the pages of the *Covent Garden Journal* they sought to educate the public on the problem of increased crime. They also published *The Weekly Pursuit,* a one-page flyer carrying descriptions of known offenders. Henry Fielding became a magistrate of London in 1748 and organized a small group of "thief-takers," men with previous service as constables who became a roving band dedicated to breaking up criminal gangs, pursuing lawbreakers, and making arrests. So impressed was the government by this Bow Street Amateur Volunteer Force (known as the "Bow Street Runners") that a salary was provided each member and an attempt was made to extend the concept to other areas of London. But Henry Fielding died in 1754, and his brother John was unable to maintain the high level of integrity of the original group. Effectiveness waned. Riots broke out in the summer of 1780, and for nearly a week mobs ruled much of the city. That a new approach to law enforcement was necessary had become obvious.[5]

During the first years of the new century various attempts were made to create a centralized police force for London. Patrick Colquhoun, a Glasgow businessman who had been appointed a magistrate in London, developed and advanced the concept of "preventive policing," and urged creation of an organized force for Greater London.[6] When his ideas were rejected, he followed the Fieldings' example and in 1792 created a special force to patrol the Thames. Much of the opposition to a centralized force came from "men of goodwill in all classes who genuinely believed, with the example of France before them, that police of any kind were synonymous with tyranny and the destruction of liberty."[7] Finally in 1829, under the prodding of Home Secretary Sir Robert Peel, Parliament established the Metropolitan Constabulary in London. Structured along the lines of a military unit, the 1,000-man force was commanded by two magistrates, later called "commissioners," who were given administrative but not judicial duties. The ultimate responsibility for maintaining and to a certain degree supervising "bobbies" was vested in the home secretary. Because he was accountable to Parliament, this first regular police force was in essence controlled by the democratically elected legislature.

Peter Manning has analyzed the rise of the police in England during the early part of the nineteenth century and has described their four-part mandate: (1) to prevent crime without the use of repressive force and to avoid intervention by the military in community disturbances; (2) to manage public order nonviolently, using force to obtain compliance only as a last resort; (3) to minimize and reduce conflict between the police and the public; and (4) to demonstrate efficiency by means of the absence of crime and disorder rather than by visible evidence of police actions in dealing with problems. The mandate was to keep a low profile while maintaining order. Because of fears by political leaders that a national force might emerge that would threaten civil liberties, every effort was made to keep direction of the police at the local level. As Manning says:

> The first "bobby" who walked the streets of London could not have foreseen the present American pattern of highly organized, politically active, rationalized, mechanized, and mobile policing, nor could he have anticipated the centrality of weaponry and the direct force applied by American police. It is unlikely that he would have had much sympathy for the crime-fighting rhetoric, for at that time in London it was neither possible nor very wise to seek out criminals and attempt to combat them.[8]

Development of the police in the United States

Before the Revolution, Americans shared the English belief that community members had a basic responsibility to help maintain order. The offices of constable, sheriff, and night watchman were easily transferred to the New World. With the birth of the new nation with a federal structure in 1789, police power remained with the states, again in response to the fear of centralized law enforcement activity. However, the development of the police and their mandate in the United States emerged as a response to conditions unlike those in England. Ethnic variety, local political control, the opening up of the continent, and the more violent tradition of American society were some of the factors that brought about a different development in peacekeeping forces.

The westward expansion of the United States during the nineteenth century presented circumstances that were quite dissimilar to those in the urbanizing East and the agricultural South. As Samuel Walker has noted, "settlement preceded society, and individuals with a vested interest in 'law and order' often had to take the law into their own hands."[9] In the absence of effective government, vigilante groups imposed law and order.

One of the first official positions to be created in rural areas was that of sheriff. Although the sheriff had responsibilities similar to those of his counterpart in seventeenth-century England, the American officer was chosen by popular election and had broad powers to enforce the law. Sheriffs depended on the men of the community for assistance, and the "posse comitatus," borrowed from fifteenth-century Europe, came into being. This institution required local men to respond to the sheriff's call for assistance. As governments were formed in the territories, marshals appointed by federal authority helped to enforce the law. Although the federal marshal has become a law enforcement folk hero, his duties were primarily judiciary; he was responsible for maintaining order in the courtroom and for holding prisoners for trial.

In the United States as in England, the growth of cities led to pressures for modernization of law enforcement. Social relations in the cities of the nineteenth century were quite different from those in the towns and countryside. In fact, from 1830 to 1870 there was unprecedented civil disorder in the major cities. Ethnic conflict as a consequence of massive immigration, hostility toward nonslave blacks and abolitionists, mob actions against banks and other institutions of property during economic declines, and violence in settling questions of morality created fears that democratic institutions would not survive.[10]

It was during this period that the major cities began to take steps to create constabularies. Boston and Philadelphia became the first cities to add a daytime police force to supplement the night watchmen. In 1837 Mayor Samuel Eliot of Boston adopted crime prevention as a major goal of police activity. As

Sir Robert Peel

One of the outstanding British statesmen and politicians of the nineteenth century, Sir Robert Peel had a tremendous impact on the development of policing. Appointed to the position of secretary of state for the Home Department in 1822, Peel subsequently set out to reform the criminal law through the consolidation and rewriting of all offenses. His work with the criminal law and the rise in crime led him to believe that legal reform must be accompanied by improved methods of crime prevention. In 1829, over much opposition, he was able to persuade Parliament to pass the Metropolitan Police Act, establishing the first disciplined and regular police force in the Greater London area. As a result, the patchwork of private law enforcement systems in use at the time was abolished.

Committed to governmental service, Peel sought to reduce the costs of administering justice by establishing an efficient full-time civil service that could be relied on to serve the state, not local interests. He advocated full-time careers for the police and urged enhancement of the deterrent capacity of law enforcement. The core activity of the police, he said, should be preventive patrol by officers who were part of a civilian force, who did not carry arms, and who had been trained to prevent crime by being present in the community. He felt that effective prevention and enforcement of the laws could be substituted for harsh penalties. England's "bobbies" or "Peelers" are the legacy of Sir Robert Peel.

he said, the police should "prevent trouble by actively seeking it out on their own, before it had time to reach serious proportions."[11] The inefficiency of separate day and night forces was soon recognized, and in 1844 the New York legislature passed a law to create a unified force for cities under the command of a chief appointed by the mayor and council. By the middle of the century, most major American cities had followed this pattern.

One of the problems that plagued law enforcement in the United States during the nineteenth and early twentieth centuries was political control of the police.

> Rotation in office enjoyed so much popular favor that police posts of both high and low degree were constantly changing hands, with political fixers determining the price and conditions of each change. . . . The whole police question simply churned about in the public mind and eventually became identified with the corruption and degradation of the city politics and local governments of the period.[12]

To alleviate these problems, various reforms were set in motion to create police administrative boards and to eliminate political patronage—that is, to take law enforcement appointments and ensuing control out of the hands of the mayors and city councils. In some states, appointed or elected commissions were created to oversee law enforcement and to keep it out of politics. In other states the legislatures took control of the urban police forces by retaining the authority to appoint the chief and to control the internal affairs of the departments. This latter reform reflected the rural domination of the legislatures and the widespread belief that the cities harbored vice and corruption. Although these efforts were designed to eliminate the unsavory aspects of politics from law enforcement, it can also be argued that they resulted in the elimination of legitimate civic influences on the police and the need to make them accountable to the public.

Professionalism and reform. Like the judiciary and corrections, law enforcement was greatly influenced by the reform movement that marked the turn of the twentieth century. Stimulated mainly by a group known as the Progressives, attempts were made to create a truly professional police force. The Progressives were for the most part upper-middle-class, educated Americans who were interested in two goals: efficient operation of government and provision of governmental services to improve the conditions of the less fortunate. They hoped at the same time to rid government of undesirable political influences, such as machine politics and patronage. It has been argued that their calls for efficient government run on a businesslike basis and their concern for the downtrodden arose from elitist worries about the effect of the newer immigrant groups on local government and social control in the city.

The key to understanding the Progressives' concept of professionalism in law enforcement is found in the slogan "The police have to get out of politics and politics has to get out of the police." A professional force was to be a nonpartisan agency of government committed to the highest ideals of public service. It was asserted that departments should be run by trained people, that law enforcement executives should have job security so that they would not have to worry about shifts in political power, and that command within the police organization should be centralized so that policies would be carried out in a consistent manner. Those who advocated professionalism also pushed for adoption of new law enforcement techniques: better training, the employment of women officers, and the development of juvenile bureaus.

Law enforcement professionalism also brought about a redefinition of the police mission. The major shift was from the maintenance of order to crime control, but professionalism also emphasized the use of police resources to prevent crime by helping individuals, diverting them from the criminal justice system. Speaking before the International Association of Chiefs of Police in 1919, August Vollmer, probably the leading advocate of professionalism, said that the police had "far greater obligations than the mere apprehending and prosecuting of law breakers"; they should follow "the stream a little further and dam it up at its source."[13] The police were to work with private and public social work agencies to help prevent crime by identifying predelinquents and directing them away from wrongdoing.

Eric Monkkonen has shown that the period from the end of the Civil War to the 1920s was marked by a shift in the focus of the urban police from control of the "dangerous classes" to control of crime. With this shift the police gave up many of their service functions, such as providing shelter for the homeless and returning lost children to their parents. As Monkkonen says, "between the 1890s and the end of World War I, the important public service functions that police departments had practiced disappeared or were substantially diminished, and police systems presenting viable alternatives to the subsequent system disappeared. Cops were now to be crime fighters."[14]

Building on the precepts of Vollmer and of the Progressive tradition of civic reform, the professional model of police organization and activity became dominant and went largely unchallenged until the 1960s. The profes-

August Vollmer

August Vollmer was born in New Orleans, the son of German immigrants. Despite a lack of formal education, Vollmer became a prominent figure in the history of American police reform. His career began in Berkeley, California, after his election as police marshal in 1904. He was made chief in 1909 and remained in that office until 1932.

Vollmer was an outspoken advocate of a professionalized police force staffed by dedicated crime fighters who were expertly trained and able to use science and technology in all phases of police work. In general, his desire to develop professional police forces grew out of the Progressive civic reform movement of the early twentieth century. Among the reforms that Vollmer instituted in the Berkeley Police Department were the creation of a motorcycle patrol force and the installation of a fingerprint and handwriting classification system. His advancement of police technology and administration paralleled his concept of the police officer as social worker. Accepting the belief that crime was a product of social and psychological problems, he urged that the police intervene in the lives of individuals before they entered crime.

Following his retirement in 1932, Vollmer taught and trained police professionals. His book *The Police and Modern Society* (1936), which details his vision of the professional police officer, remains a classic statement of this ideal.

sional model has stressed that the force should stay out of politics, that members should be well trained and disciplined, that advantage should be taken of technological developments, and that the crime-fighter role should be made prominent. A preventive style of policing, accenting the importance of the patrol officer's presence as a deterrent to crime and as a means of responding to the community's needs, has also been important.

But as Robert Fogelson has noted, even with the prodding of the state and federal governments, policing has remained under local control.[15] This means that in many large cities political considerations still influence law enforcement. Yet even as the model of professionalism has become widely accepted, questions have been raised about the validity of this conventional wisdom. It can be argued, for example, that since the police have been given such wide powers of discretion under the law, they must be held accountable to some political authority for the manner in which they exercise them. The community cannot give the police carte blanche to investigate and arrest without input from the citizenry.

Rethinking policing. The rise of crime in the 1960s, the urban riots, racial confrontations, and problems associated with drugs—all placed strains on the performance of law enforcement agencies. With the vast research effort that followed the creation of the Law Enforcement Assistance Administration (LEAA) and the National Institute of Justice, the crime-fighter model of police professionalism soon came under scrutiny. Traditional policing was found to be a source of tension in the community (particularly among minority groups) and to be less effective than it was claimed to be in regard to catching and deterring criminals. The police were found to be unable to respond to criminal events in ways that could greatly affect the incidence of most types of crime. In addition, renewed recognition was given to the importance of informal means of social control through the family, schools, and neighborhoods.

Stuart Scheingold has described the reform proposals advanced in the 1980s as a "crime attack" strategy and a "community service" strategy.[16] Behind the crime attack approaches is the idea that the police should seize the initiative against crime through the deployment of patrol resources against specific targets. These methods focus on aggressive seeking out of criminals by means of decoys, sting operations, and stakeouts. The community service approach operates on the assumption that the police are in need of information about crimes and offenders, and that the people in the community are the best source of such information. To achieve the necessary cooperation, officers should be assigned to particular neighborhoods on a long-term basis so that they can become as much a part of the community as possible.

By emphasizing the crime-fighter role, the U.S. police have presented themselves as professionals using advanced technology to attack crime. A crucial question is the extent to which this orientation is viable and meaningful in modern society.

Law enforcement policy

Although the criminal law is written as if every infraction were expected to result in arrest and punishment, such is not the case. Limitations imposed by the law, legislatures, courts, and community greatly reduce the number of criminal acts that may become a focus of police activity. In addition, the police have wide discretion in determining how they deploy their resources, which types of behaviors are overlooked, and the particular circumstances in which officers do or do not make an arrest. Because the criminal justice system is organized as a continuum, from the police to prosecutor to court to corrections, law enforcement policies determine the extent to which agencies of adjudication and corrections function. The police are thus in a crucial position with regard to regulating the flow of cases through the system. Changes in law enforcement policy—for example, increasing the size of the night patrol or tolerating certain types of vice—influence the amount of crime that comes to official attention and the system's ability to impose sanctions on offenders.

It must be emphasized that in a modern democratic society it is the police that have been designated by the community to use force against lawbreakers. The use of force by citizens acting in their private capacity is strictly circumscribed. As chapter 3 has indicated, the private use of force is restricted in the main to situations of self-defense. There are also occasions when a person may hold a lawbreaker until the police arrive, but public law enforcement has a virtual monopoly on the right to use force to maintain order and uphold the criminal law. As later chapters will make clear, the police are accountable to the community for their actions.

total enforcement
A policy whereby the police are given the resources and support to enforce all laws without regard to the civil liberties of citizens.

As figure 5.1 illustrates, various levels of enforcement and discretion exist within the area of police decision making. The criminal code describes acts that are prohibited, but a policy of ***total enforcement***—in accordance with which the police are expected to carry out all laws without regard to civil liberties or the requirements of due process—is not a legitimate goal of American criminal justice. Such a policy might exist in a totalitarian regime, but police in a democracy are directed to work within the confines of the law, to respect the liberties of all citizens, and to proceed against suspects in accordance with the concept of due process.

full enforcement
A policy whereby the police are given the resources and support to enforce all laws within the limits imposed by the injunction to respect the civil liberties of citizens.

Thus the police are expected to follow a policy of ***full enforcement,*** in accordance with which they not only are authorized but are bound to enforce fully the criminal law. It would be possible for them to do so if they had the necessary resources and if they had community support. But the policy would make life intolerable. Although every illegal act would be noted and every violator caught, the freedom of all citizens would be greatly restricted because

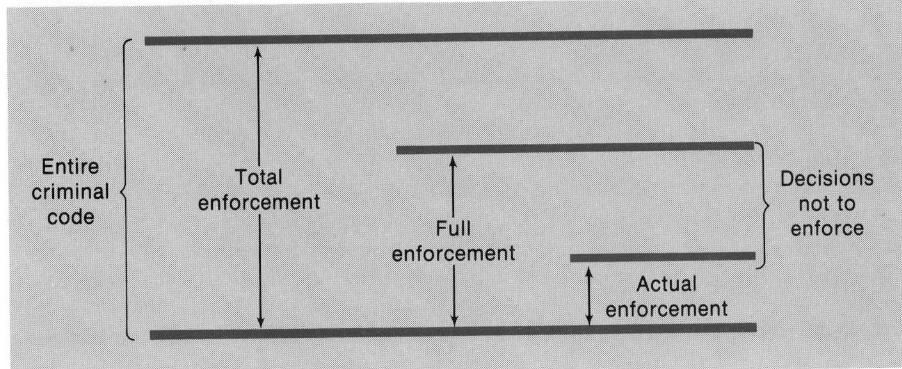

FIGURE 5.1
Discretionary factors influencing law enforcement

the police would be constantly searching, patrolling, inspecting, and observing in order to root out criminals. As we know, however, communities do not allocate their resources in such a way that law enforcement is clearly a dominating goal. The police and other agencies of criminal justice must compete for resources with such other public needs as education, recreation, and municipal services.

actual enforcement Enforcement of the law at a level that reflects such factors as civil liberties, discretion, resources, and community values.

In reality, though legislators write laws as if full enforcement were the norm, and though every officer solemnly swears to uphold every law, the police determine the ***actual enforcement***—the proportion of crimes that are reported and that result in the offender's conviction. The difference between full and actual enforcement reflects such factors as the difficulty of making arrests, the availability of resources, community disagreement on whether certain acts are to be considered unlawful, and pressure from influential persons who desire that certain laws not be rigidly enforced. Law enforcement agencies are required to fulfill their obligations but in ways that will retain community and organizational support. They resolve the dilemma by establishing procedures that minimize tension and give the greatest promise of reward for the organization and the persons involved.

Levels of enforcement

The functions of the police are more complex than most of us assume. The police are charged with maintaining order, enforcing the law, and providing a variety of social services, but the policies they follow dictate the persons and offenses that will be labeled deviant. The policies that allocate resources and set criteria for law enforcement goals are also an important variable. This consideration was well stated by the President's Commission: "The police must make important judgments about what conduct is in fact criminal; about the allocation of scarce resources; and about the gravity of each individual incident and the proper steps that should be taken."[17]

In a mixed society like the United States, there are bound to be differing interpretations of deviance. Should criminal justice resources be used primarily to cope with such upperworld crimes as stock fraud and government corruption, with the organized crime of supplying narcotics, or with less serious but high-visibility crimes such as public drunkenness and shoplifting? Each of these and other categories involves a different social class, a different perception of deviance, and a different mode of enforcement. Each category of crime has its own political and administrative threats and rewards for enforcement organizations.

Enforcement Oath

Enforcement of all Criminal Laws and City Ordinances is my obligation. There are no specialties under the Law. My eyes must be open to traffic problems and disorders though I move on other assignments, to slinking vice in back streets and dives though I have been directed elsewhere, to the suspicious appearance of evil wherever it is encountered. . . . I must be impartial because the Law surrounds, protects, and applies to all alike, rich and poor, low and high, black and white. . . .

Source: Rules and Regulations of the Atlanta, Georgia, Police Department.

Selective enforcement

The focus of law enforcement policy is well reflected in the categories that make up the index crimes of the FBI's *Uniform Crime Reports:* homicide, rape, aggravated assault, robbery, burglary, car theft, larceny, and arson. These are the crimes that make headlines and to which politicians can point when they ask for increases in the police budget. They are also the crimes generally committed by the poor. Nowhere among the crimes the FBI labels as major or serious does one find activities of the upper class: violations of industrial safety rules and housing codes, stock manipulation, tax fraud. In sum, law enforcement policy is primarily directed toward certain types of criminal acts usually performed by a specific class of people—the poor. White-collar crime is usually committed by persons of high status and reputation in the course of their work, and the full force of the criminal sanction is rarely brought to bear on them.

Much of the discussion of crime rates shows the influence of law enforcement policy and the role of the police in the criminal justice system. As we have seen, the incidence of crime known to the police is a small portion of that committed. Presumably they are aware that their position is politically enhanced by the way certain types of offenders are processed. In terms of volume and the generation of public support, arrests of narcotics offenders and prostitutes have more payoff in an organizational sense than does the pursuit of white-collar criminals of upper-class social status, who may be able to challenge police decisions and whose cases may require a considerable expenditure of departmental resources.

Such a basic decision as to how police resources will be deployed has an important effect on the types of persons arrested. Given the mixed social character of a metropolitan area, police administrators have to decide where they are going to send their troops and what tactics are to be employed. In part, decisions concerning the distribution of police resources are made in the light of demands of certain community groups, such as the demands of business people for special protective services. In most cities, patrol officers are expected to check the doors of downtown stores at night to make sure they are locked. Vagrancy policy is often developed in response to the desires of certain groups to keep derelicts out of the "better" areas. The use of foot patrols rather than prowl cars in such neighborhoods may also be a response to community pressures.

Community influence on enforcement policy

An important factor in the deployment of resources is the police administrator's perceptions of the style of law enforcement the community desires. The community's power and value structures, which are supported by the police, in turn set boundaries to the spheres of police action. James Q. Wilson found that the political culture, reflecting the socioeconomic characteristics of a city and its organization of government, exerted a major influence on whether the police acted in accordance with the watchman, legalistic, or service style of operation.[18] Table 5.1 shows the relationship between governmental structure and type of police behavior.

TABLE 5.1 Varieties of police behavior

Style	*Defining characteristics*	*Style/Structure*	*Examples*
Watchman	Emphasis on order maintenance role	Partisan/mayor-council	Albany, Amsterdam, and Newburgh, New York
Legalistic	Emphasis on law enforcement role	Good government/ council-manager	Oakland, California; Highland Park, Illinois
Service	Balance between order maintenance and law enforcement; less likely to make arrest than legalistic departments	Amenities-seeking/ mayor-council or council-manager	Brighton and Nassau County, New York

Source: James Q. Wilson, *Varieties of Police Behavior* (Cambridge: Harvard University Press, 1968), drawn from chapters 5–8.

In the declining industrial town of Amsterdam, New York, which had a partisan elected mayor-council form of government, Wilson found the watchman style of police behavior, which emphasizes the order-maintenance activities of patrol officers. With this orientation, the administrator allowed officers to ignore minor violations, especially those involving traffic and juveniles, and to tolerate a certain amount of vice and gambling. The police were to use the law to maintain order rather than to regulate conduct and were expected to exercise discretion in judging the requirements of order, depending on the character of the group in which a violation took place.

Emphasis on professionalism and good government in Highland Park, Illinois, led to the development of a style of police work in which the police detained a high proportion of juvenile offenders, acted vigorously against illicit enterprises, and made a large number of misdemeanor arrests. In this legalistic style of enforcement, the police acted as if there were a single standard of community conduct—that which the law prescribed—rather than different standards for juveniles, blacks, drunks, and the like.

In suburban communities, where the service style predominates and police work is oriented toward providing amenities, such matters as burglaries and assaults are taken seriously, while arrests for minor infractions tend to be avoided when possible and replaced by informal, nonarrest sanctions. In some suburbs, where citizens feel they should be able to receive individualized treatment from their local police, plans for the development of metropolitan-wide police forces have come under strong attack.

From the vantage point of the police, their business is to control crime and keep the peace. The connection between social and economic inequality, on the one hand, and criminality, on the other, is not their concern. The problem is that by distributing surveillance and intervention selectively, they contribute to the existing tensions in society. "That the police are widely assumed to be a partisan force in society is evident not only in the attitudes of people who are exposed to greater scrutiny; just as the young-poor-black expects unfavorable treatment, so the old-rich-white expects special consideration from the policeman."[19]

Thus, even before an arrest is made, the police have formulated rules that will influence the level and type of enforcement. Since the police are the entry point to the criminal justice system, the total picture is shaped to a large extent by the decisions made by officials as to the allocation of resources and their perception of the level of law enforcement desired by the community.

Police functions

One of the most critical needs facing the criminal justice system in the United States is for a definition of the role of the police in a modern and urban democracy. Not only must the public understand the purpose of the police officer's job but the officer must be able to operate from a position that is not in conflict with society's expectations. Until the role of the police is defined and understood by both criminal justice officials and the general public, the police will continue to function under what has been called "the impossible mandate," with citizens' expectations about police work at dramatic variance with daily reality. Although the public and many police officers may believe that the job revolves around the excitement of crime fighting, police work is often tedious, dirty, sometimes technically demanding, and more dull than dangerous. Unfortunately, the occasional shootout or act of bravery is used as an index to measure how well a department is accomplishing its mission.

Police functions and responsibilities are extremely broad and complex. The police are expected not only to maintain the peace, prevent crime, and serve and protect the community but also to direct traffic, handle accidents and illnesses, stop noisy gatherings, find missing persons, administer licensing regulations, provide ambulance services, take disturbed or inebriated people into protective custody, and so on. The list is long and it varies from place to place. It is evident that much police work has little to do with the penal code. Some criminal justice planners have even suggested that the police have more in common with agencies of municipal social service than with the criminal justice system.[20]

The American Bar Association developed a list of the objectives and functions of the police as a first step in understanding that the police are concerned with more than maintaining order, enforcing the law, and serving the public. The breadth of the police's responsibility is impressive. Among their duties are these:

1. To prevent and control conduct widely recognized as threatening to life and property (serious crime).
2. To aid individuals who are in danger of physical harm, such as the victim of a criminal attack.
3. To protect constitutional guarantees, such as the right of free speech and assembly.
4. To facilitate the movement of people and vehicles.
5. To assist those who cannot care for themselves: the intoxicated, the addicted, the mentally ill, the physically disabled, the old, and the young.
6. To resolve conflict, whether it be between individuals, groups of individuals, or individuals and their government.
7. To identify problems that have the potential for becoming more serious problems for the individual citizen, for the police, or for government.
8. To create and maintain a feeling of security in the community.[21]

How did the police acquire such broad responsibilities? Three answers have been given: first, that the police are about the only public agency that is available seven days a week, twenty-four hours a day, to respond to citizens' need for help; second, that the police constitute the agency of government best able to perform the initial investigations required for the tasks listed above; and finally, that the capacity of the police to use force is a unifying theme of all their activity. Some commentators, however, have offered a political explanation for the breadth of the police function. It has been suggested that since the police have been unable to control crime as their original mandate expected, they have agreed to every request that they perform a new service rather than attempt to help define their crime control mandate realistically.

To aid in conceptually organizing the functions of the police, three primary categories have been developed over the years: maintenance of order, law enforcement, and service. Although we usually think of the police in relation to arrests following the breaking of laws passed to protect persons and property, the argument may be made that their principal function is peacekeeping. Certainly history tells us that the police were initially more involved in maintaining order than in catching criminals. Indeed, during the mid–nineteenth century, apprehension of thieves, robbers, and murderers was not considered a responsibility of the police; the victim was expected to find the guilty party.

Order maintenance

order maintenance Role of the police function of preventing behavior that disturbs or threatens to disturb the public peace or that involves face-to-face conflict among two or more persons. In such situations the police exercise discretion in deciding whether a law has been broken.

The ***order-maintenance*** function is a broad mandate to prevent behavior that either disturbs or threatens to disturb the public peace or that involves face-to-face conflict among two or more persons. A domestic quarrel, a noisy drunk, loud music in the night, a panhandler soliciting on the street, a tavern brawl—all are examples of disorder that may require the peacekeeping efforts of the police. Whereas most criminal laws specify acts that are illegal, laws in regard to disorderly conduct deal with ambiguous situations that may be variously interpreted in accordance with the social environment and the perceptions and norms of the actors. Law enforcement comes into play when a law has been violated and only guilt must be assessed; order maintenance calls for intervention in situations in which the law may have been broken but which require the law to be interpreted and standards of right conduct and assignment of blame determined.

When we study the work of patrol officers, the most numerous officers on the force, we can see that they are concerned primarily with behavior that either disturbs or threatens to disturb the peace. In these situations they confront the public in ambiguous circumstances and have wide discretion in matters of life and death, honor and dishonor. Walking the streets, patrol officers may be variously required to help persons in trouble, to manage crowds, to supervise various services, and to assist people who are not fully accountable for what they do. In all of these actions, patrol officers are not subject to direct external control, and they have the power, if necessary, to arrest but also the freedom not to arrest. The order-maintenance function is further complicated by the fact that the patrol officer is normally expected to "handle" a situation rather than to enforce the law, and in such cases the atmosphere is likely to be emotionally charged.

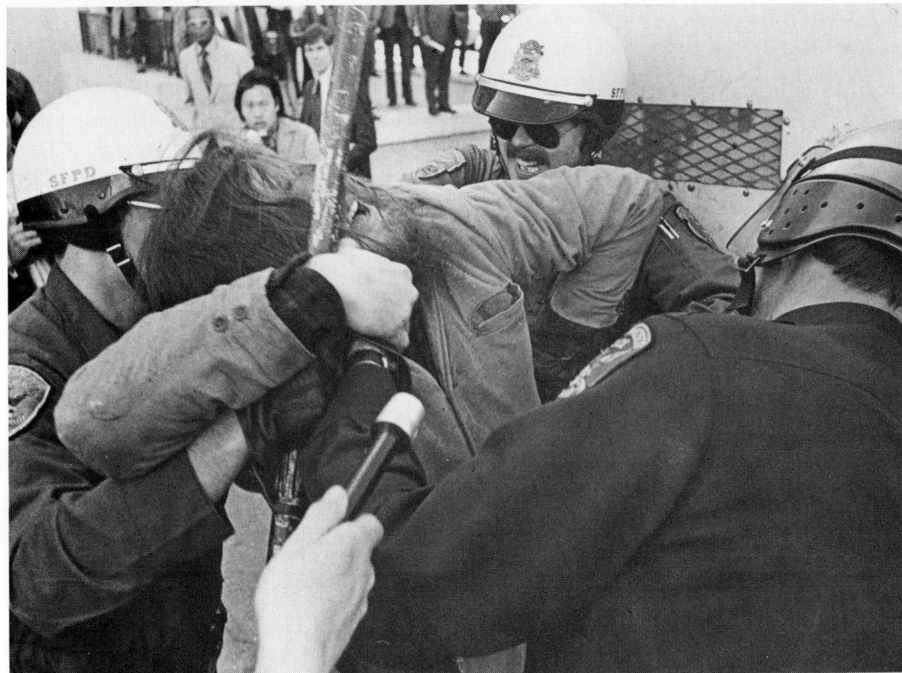

The order-maintenance function requires officers to "handle" various situations.

Some people may argue that separating the law officer and peace officer roles is impossible. As Wilson says, however, "to the patrolman, 'enforcing the law' is what he does when there is no dispute—when making an arrest or issuing a summons exhausts his responsibilities."[22] When Jesse Rubin asked patrol officers in Miami what their job consisted of, they answered in police academy fashion, "Protection of life and property and the preservation of peace," thus confirming what they believe to be their primary role—that of peacekeeper.[23]

Studies of citizen complaints and requests for service justify this emphasis on the order-maintenance function. In his study of Syracuse, New York, Wilson found that 30.1 percent of the calls concerned maintenance of order and only 10.3 percent concerned law enforcement, the remainder being service calls.[24] In describing a Baltimore police district, Irving Wallach says that

> the bulk of police activity . . . does not relate to the crime control function. The vast majority of police activities . . . do not involve crimes and most of the crime-related contacts are really after-the-fact report-taking from crime victims. . . . The vast majority of all resident requests sampled was related to the maintenance of order, the settling of interpersonal disputes and the need for advice and emergency assistance.[25]

law enforcement The police function of controlling crime by intervening in situations in which it is clear that the law has been violated and only the identity of the guilty needs to be determined.

Law enforcement

The ***law enforcement*** function of the police is concerned with situations in which the law has been violated and only the identity of the guilty needs to be determined. Police officers charged with major responsibilities in these areas are in the specialized branches of modern departments, such as the vice squad and the burglary detail. Although the patrol officer may be the first officer on the scene of a crime, in serious cases the detective usually prepares the case for prosecution by bringing together all the evidence for the prosecuting attorney. When the offender is identified but not located, the detective conducts the search; if the offender is not identified, the detective has the responsibility of analyzing clues to determine who committed the crime.

Although the police emphasize their law enforcement function, their efficiency in this area has been questioned. Especially when crimes against property are committed, the perpetrator usually has a time advantage over the police. Their efficiency is further decreased when the crime is an offense against a person and the victim is unable to identify the offender or delays notifying the police beyond the time in which apprehension might reasonably be expected.

Service

service
The police function of providing assistance to the public, usually with regard to matters unrelated to crime.

In modern society the police are increasingly called on to perform services for the population. This ***service*** function—providing first aid, rescuing animals, and extending social welfare, particularly to lower-class citizens and especially at night and on weekends—has become the dominant area of police activity. As table 5.2 shows, analysis of more than 26,000 calls to twenty-one police departments confirms the long-held belief that about 80 percent of citizens' requests for police intervention involve matters unrelated to crime. Because the police department is usually the only representative of local government readily accessible twenty-four hours every day, this is the agency to which people turn in times of trouble. Many departments provide information, operate ambulance services, locate missing persons, check locks on vacationers' homes, and stop would-be suicides. In cities, the poor and the ignorant—groups that few are eager to serve—rely almost solely on the police to perform service functions.[26]

It is apparent that the police perform an important referral function. Especially in urban areas, people who call the police are often directed either to specialized units of government or to community agencies that deal with the kinds of problems they present. People who want directions, crime victims who need information, persons who seek particular social services may all contact the police for guidance.

TABLE 5.2 Problems prompting citizens' calls to 21 police departments (N = 26,418)

Type of problem	*Percentage of calls*
Violent crime: homicide, robbery, assault, sexual attack	2
Nonviolent crime: burglary, theft, vandalism, arson	17
Interpersonal conflict: argument, threat, fight	7
Medical assistance needed: death, medical help, transportation	3
Traffic problem: accident, flow, abandoned vehicle	9
Dependent person: drunk, missing, runaway, mentally disordered	3
Public nuisance: harassment, noise, trespassing, morals, alcohol-drug violation	11
Suspicious circumstances: person, property, situation	5
Assistance needed: animal, property, escort, utility problem, property discovery	12
Information needed: police related, nonpolice related, road directions	21
Information offered: general, complaint against police, false alarm	8
Internal operations: internal legal procedures, officer gives information, officer wants information	2

Source: Adapted from Eric J. Scott, *Calls for Service: Citizen Demand and Initial Police Response*, U.S. Department of Justice (Washington, D.C.: Government Printing Office, 1981), pp. 26–37.

TABLE 5.3 Percentage of patrol activities engaged in by police, by type of department

Activity	*Urban department (Midwest City) (N = 2,835)*	*Suburban department (Smithville) (N = 264)*	*Suburban department (Pinewood) (N = 214)*	*State police station (East Coast) (N = 150)*	*Township department (N = 168)*	*Total (N = 3,631)*
Information gathering	8%	6%	5%	19%	12%	9%
Service	13	23	10	12	5	13
Maintenance of order	24	29	16	13	26	24
Law enforcement	33	19	13	19	27	30
Traffic	18	21	52	29	30	21
Other	3	3	4	8	0	3
Total	99	101	100	100	100	100

Adapted from Richard J. Lundman, "Police Patrol Work: A Comparative Perspective," in *Police Behavior: A Sociological Perspective*, ed. Richard J. Lundman, p. 56. Copyright © 1980 by Oxford University Press. Reprinted by permission.

Although it may appear that valuable resources are being expended for police work unrelated to crime, it has been claimed that such services do have ramifications that help in crime control. In general, it is thought that through the service function the officers gain knowledge of the community, and citizens in turn grow to rely on and trust the police. Checking the security of buildings is the service that most obviously helps prevent crime, but dealing with runaways, drunks, and interpersonal disturbances may help to solve problems before they can lead to criminal behavior.

Implementing the mandate

The list of police functions on page 165 may give the impression that each is of equal importance; in practice, however, the work of law enforcement agencies requires that choices be made as to the importance of law enforcement, maintenance of order, service, and other functions. The choices will be made in accordance with community need as citizens request action and with departmental policy as various styles of police work are emphasized.

In a comparison of police patrol work in five jurisdictions, Richard Lundman found that the level of activity varied greatly with the function performed, as table 5.3 indicates. In the urban department of the community called Midwest City, 33 percent of all activities were classified as law enforcement; in the suburban department of Pinewood, only 13 percent. Similarly, the levels of activity concerned with maintenance of order, service, traffic, and other functions varied.

The findings of this and other studies demonstrate that although the public may depend on the order-maintenance and service functions of the police, citizens act as if law enforcement—the catching of lawbreakers—were the most important function. That the crime-stopping image is widely held is shown by public opinion polls and the reasons given by recruits for joining the force. Police administrators have learned that public support can be gained for budgets when the law enforcement function is stressed, an emphasis demonstrated by the internal organization of metropolitan departments, where high status is accorded the officers who perform this function. This focus leads to the creation of specialized units within the detective division to deal with such crimes as homicide, burglary, and auto theft. The assumption seems to be that all other requirements of the citizenry will be handled by the patrol division. In some departments, this arrangement may create morale problems because of the allocation of disproportionate measures of resources and prestige to the function that is concerned with a minority of police problems. Police are occupied with peacekeeping but preoccupied with crime fighting.

Police action and decision making

reactive
Occurring in response to a stimulus, as police activity in response to notification that a crime has been committed.

proactive
Occurring in the absence of a specific external stimulus, as an active search for offenders on the part of police in the absence of reports of violations of the law. Arrests for crimes without victims are usually proactive.

Police efforts to carry out their functions in a democracy are mainly ***reactive*** (citizen-invoked) rather than ***proactive*** (police-invoked). Only in the vice, narcotics, and traffic divisions of the modern police department does one find law officers acting in response to information gathered internally, by the organization. Because most criminal acts occur at an unpredictable time and in a private rather than a public place, the police respond to calls from persons who telephone, who signal a patrol car or officer on foot, or who appear at the station to register their need or complaint—all of which circumstances greatly influence the way the police fulfill their duties. In addition, the police are usually able to arrive at the scene only after the crime has been committed and the perpetrator has fled; the job of finding the guilty party is hampered by the time lapse and the frequent unreliability of the information the victim supplies. To a large extent, reports by victims define the boundaries of law enforcement.

As part of his work for the President's Commission, Albert Reiss directed a team of observers who examined police–citizen transactions in Boston, Chicago, and Washington, D.C. His analysis of police mobilizations revealed that 81 percent resulted from citizen telephone calls, 14 percent were initiated in the field by an officer, 5 percent were initiated by persons who walked into a station to ask for help, and 5 percent were initiated by people who requested service in the field. Such a distribution not only influences the organization of a department but to a great extent also determines the response to a case. In almost one-third of the cases, for example, no citizen was present when the police arrived to handle the complaint. In addition, because the patrol division of any department is organized to react to citizen requests, differences may develop between the police and citizens as to what constitutes a criminal matter and the appropriate action to be taken. As Reiss comments: "Police regard

Service in Urban Areas

The widest array of police services is reported in the congested and depressed areas of the large cities, for here the combination of poverty, unemployment, broken homes, poor education, and other elements of social disorganization results in the police officer often being called upon to serve as surrogate parent or other relative, and to fill in for social workers, housing inspectors, attorneys, physicians, and psychiatrists. It is here, too, that the police most frequently care for those who cannot care for themselves: the destitute, the inebriated, the addicted, the mentally ill, the senile, the alien, the physically disabled, and the very young.

Source: Reprinted with permission from Herman Goldstein, *Policing a Free Society* (Cambridge, Mass.: Ballinger, 1977), p. 25.

it as their duty to find criminals and prevent or solve crimes. The public considers it the duty of the police to respond to its calls and crises: The police should render assistance when citizens request it."[27]

All this is not to say that the police do not employ proactive strategies—relying on surveillance and undercover work to obtain the required information—but that they do so only in connection with specific types of offenses, such as vice, which can be detected by these means. Because of the lack of complainants, the police must rely on informers, stakeouts, wiretapping, and raids. To deal with those offenses known as crimes without victims, which supposedly offend society rather than a particular person, proactive tactics are used. Thus proactively produced crime rates are nearly always rates of arrest rather than rates of known criminal acts. The result is a direct correlation between the crime rate for these proactive operations and the allocation of police personnel.

Encounters between police and citizens—"Call the cops!"

Encounters between police and citizens in situations that may be labeled criminal are structured by the roles each participant plays, by the setting, and by the attitudes of the victim toward legal action. Studies have shown that victims report offenses in only about half of all cases of victimization. As table 5.4 shows, most often the police were not called because of the feeling that they could not or would not do anything. In other incidents, the relationship

TABLE 5.4 Victims' primary reason for not notifying police

		Reasons for not notifying police				
Crimes[a]	*Percent of cases in which police not notified*	*Felt it was private matter or did not want to be bothered*	*Police could not be effective or would not want to be bothered*	*Did not want to take time*	*Too confused or did not know how to report*	*Fear of reprisal*
Robbery	35%	27%	45%	9%	18%	0%
Aggravated assault	35	50	25	4	8	13
Simple assault	54	50	35	4	4	7
Burglary	42	30	63	4	2	2
Larceny ($50 and over)	40	23	62	7	7	0
Larceny (under $50)	63	31	58	7	3	0[b]
Auto theft[c]	11	20	60	0	0	20
Malicious mischief	62	23	68	5	2	2
Consumer fraud	90	50	40	0	10	0
Other fraud (bad checks, swindling, etc.)	74	41	35	16	8	0
Sex offenses (except forcible rape)	49	40	50	0	5	5
Family crimes (including desertion, nonsupport)	50	65	17	10	0	7

[a] Willful homicide, forcible rape, and a few other crimes had too few cases to be statistically useful, and they are therefore excluded.
[b] Less than 0.5%.
[c] Auto theft was not reported in only five instances.
Source: President's Commission on Law Enforcement and Administration of Justice, *Crime and Its Impact: An Assessment* (Washington, D.C.: Government Printing Office, 1967), p. 18.

of the offender to the victim discouraged reporting. Studies have shown that the accessibility of the police to the citizen, the complainant's demeanor and characteristics, and the type of violation structure official reaction and the probability of arrest. Although most citizens may believe that they have a civic obligation to assist the police by alerting them to criminal activity, an element of personal gain or loss exerts an important influence. Many people fail to call the police because they think it is not worth the effort and cost—filling out papers at the station, appearing as a witness, confronting a neighbor or relative. Clearly, then, citizens exercise control over the work of the police by their decisions to call or not to call them.

clearance rate The percentage of crimes known to the police that they believe they have solved through an arrest; a statistic used as a measure of a police department's productivity.

The ***clearance rate***—the percentage of crimes known to the police that they believe they have solved through an arrest—varies with each category of offense. In such reactive situations as burglary, the rate of apprehension is extremely low, only about 15 percent; much greater success is experienced with violent crimes (46 percent), in which the victims tend to know their assailants.[28] Arrests made through proactive police operations against prostitution, gambling, and drug traffic have a clearance rate, theoretically, of 100 percent.

The arrest of a person often results in the clearance of other reported offenses because police make it a practice to connect arrested persons with similar, unsolved crimes when they can. Interrogation and lineups are standard procedures, as is the lesser-known operation of simply assigning unsolved crimes in the department's records to the defendant. Acknowledgment by offenders that they committed prior but unsolved crimes is often part of the bargain when guilty pleas are entered. Professional thieves know that they can gain favors from the police in exchange for "confessing" to unsolved crimes that they may or may not have committed.

Citing the curbs placed on many police tactics by the Supreme Court plus the rise in urban street crime, some metropolitan departments have shifted their emphasis from law enforcement to reduction of crime. In the proactive technique of "aggressive patrol," some large cities have developed specially trained squads that are sent to high-crime areas to "show the flag." This strategy is also based on the assumption that the public judges the police by the crime rate and that few people know the conviction rate. But we must remember that the primary focus of police energy is attributable to the reactive nature of their work.

Discretion

Discretion is a characteristic of organizations. Whether in the corporate structure of General Motors or the bureaucracy of a state welfare department, officials are given the authority to base some decisions on their own judgment rather than on a formal set of rules. Thus executives and managers, but not workers on the assembly line, are given the power to make discretionary decisions. Within the police bureaucracy, this relationship is reversed: discretion increases as one moves *down* the organizational hierarchy. Patrol officers, the most numerous and lowest-ranking officers and the ones who are newest to police work, have the greatest amount of discretion. In addition, they deal with clients in isolation and are charged primarily with maintaining order and enforcing highly ambiguous laws—laws concerning disorderly conduct, public drunkenness, breach of the peace, conflicts among citizens, and other situations in which the offensiveness of the participants' conduct is often open to dispute. Wilson has caught the essence of the patrol officer's role when he describes it as one that "is unlike that of any other occupation . . . one in which subprofessionals, working alone, exercise wide discretion in matters of utmost importance (life and death, honor and dishonor) in an environment that is apprehensive and perhaps hostile."[29]

In the final analysis, the police officer exercises discretion through nonenforcement, arrest, or some more informal way of handling a dispute. The individual officer has the responsibility of deciding whether and how the law should be applied and is sensitive to a variety of cues. Wayne LaFave suggests that the decision not to arrest is particularly likely in four categories of cases: trivial offenses, offenses involving conduct that is thought to be representative of a racial or ethnic group, offenses that victims are unwilling to prosecute, and offenses in which illegal conduct of the victim has also been involved. "Because the application of law depends to a large measure on the definition of a situation and the decision reached by the officer, he, in effect, makes the law; it is his decision that establishes the boundary between legal and illegal."[30]

Figure 5.2 combines the types of situation with the types of police response in order to designate the offenses that belong to each category. Each type of situation offers the officials a different degree of discretion, and each has a different probability of being cleared through some kind of formal action. As mentioned earlier, law enforcement involves a situation in which the law has been violated and only the identity of the violator needs to be determined. The maintenance of order often calls for intervention in situations in which the law may have been broken but which require the law to be interpreted and standards of right conduct determined.

In encounters between citizens and police, the matter of fairness to the citizen is often intertwined with departmental policy. When should the patrol officer frisk? When should a deal be made with the addict-informer? Which disputes should be mediated on the spot and which left to adjudicatory personnel? Surprisingly, these conflicts between the demands of justice and policy are seldom decided by heads of departments but are left largely to the discretion of the police, who often act illegally without disapproval from superiors. In fact, departmental control over police actions is lacking in certain types of activities. In categories I and IV, for example, the patrol officer has great

FIGURE 5.2
Discretion situations

Nature of situation	Type of police response: Police-invoked (proactive) response	Type of police response: Citizen-invoked (reactive) response
Law enforcement	I. Crimes without victims	II. Crimes against persons, property
Order maintenance	III. Drunkenness, disorderly conduct	IV. Calls for assistance —public disorder

discretion, but in the former category it can be brought under departmental control and in the latter it cannot. Further, departments must resort to an internal intelligence network to suppress police corruption associated with discretion in crimes-without-victims cases. In category II, patrol officers have the least amount of discretion (except when juveniles are involved), and the departmental policies and organization are instruments of control. Category III presents an intermediate relationship between the amount of discretion and the possibility of departmental control.

Herbert Jacob lists four factors that seem particularly important in affecting the exercise of discretion by police officers:

> 1. Characteristics of the crime. Some crimes are considered trivial by the public, so, conversely, when the police become aware of a serious crime, they have less freedom to ignore it.
>
> 2. The relationship between the alleged criminal and the victim. The closer the personal relationship, the more variable the exercise of discretion. Family squabbles may not be as grave as they appear, and police are wary of making arrests since a spouse may on cool reflection refuse to press charges.
>
> 3. The relationship between the police and the criminal or victim. A respectful complainant will be taken more seriously than an antagonistic one. Likewise, a respectful alleged wrongdoer is less likely to be arrested.
>
> 4. Departmental policies. The preferences of the chief and the city administration as reflected in the policy style will influence the exercise of discretion.[31]

In sum, police officers are street-level bureaucrats, since their encounters with citizens allow for extensive independence. Further, they are concerned primarily with order-maintenance situations, in which the law is not cut and dried and citizens are often hostile. Because of the situational environment, they must mobilize information quickly and make decisions through the tactics of simplification and routinization, basing their perceptions of the clients on prior cases and experiences. Such a process often leads to error.

Although some people advocate the development of detailed instructions to guide the police officer, such an exercise would probably be fruitless. No matter how detailed the formal instructions, the officer will still have to fit rules to cases. As Egon Bittner observes: "In the final analysis, we can send even the most completely instructed patrolman out on his round only if we have grounds for believing that he will know what the instructions mean when he faces a situation that appears to call for action."[32]

In the end, police administrators must decide what measures they will take to influence the way their officers use discretion. Given the variety of functions the police are asked to perform and the influence of such factors as the nature of crime and citizen response, administrators must develop policies that can serve to guide their officers. Controlling the actions of subordinates, according to one social scientist, "depends only partly on sanctions and inducements; it also requires instilling in them a shared outlook or ethos that provides for them a common definition of the situations they are likely to encounter and that to the outsider gives to the organization its distinctive character or 'feel.' "[33]

Police work

Although we may define the formal position and legal mandate of police officers according to the duties stated in a job description, such a definition tells us little about the way individual officers act in everyday settings when they meet citizens face to face. Even if we accept the myth of the police officer as philosopher, guide, and friend, he or she plays a variety of roles according to the work situation and the persons encountered in it. The behavior of the patrol officer who arrests a boisterous young man inside a bar is very unlike that officer's behavior when an injured victim needs assistance at the scene of an accident. In both encounters the officer occupies the position of patrol officer yet plays dissimilar roles and acts differently toward the others in the interpersonal exchanges. We should not generalize even to this extent but recognize that the ways in which individual officers play their roles depend on such factors as personality, goals, and previous experiences. The actual behavior of police officers—their actions, perceptions, and norms—is the important dimension for discussion rather than the formal description of their duties.

Qualifications

The policies that determine the type of person recruited and retained in law enforcement will greatly structure the behavior of the almost 700,000 persons who serve in police departments around the country. If pay scales are low, educational requirements minimal, and physical standards unrealistic, police work will attract only those from certain socioeconomic groups with certain personalities, attitudes, and objectives. At a time when police work calls for persons who are sensitive to the complex social problems of contemporary society, a majority of departments offer entrance salaries of less than $15,000 and require of new members only a high school education, good physical condition, and the absence of a criminal record. The last requirement is often cited as the reason the police have had little success in recruiting in the ghetto, where the probability of having had some brush with the law is much higher than in the suburbs.

Qualifying standards vary greatly and depend to a large extent on a community's level of urbanization. The fact that much of the research on the characteristics of police officers has been carried on in such major departments as those of New York City and San Francisco may have provided a false picture because the patrol officers in rural areas and small cities may have lower education levels. Between 1969 and 1980, police officers and preservice students were encouraged to earn a college degree through LEAA's Law Enforcement Education Program (LEEP). Although various presidential commissions have supported higher education for police officers, the vast majority of law enforcement agencies do not require a college degree.

The pay in relation to that of comparable occupations is one of the outstanding problems of police work. Although a top-grade patrol officer in a highly paid department such as New York City's receives more than $20,000, this income is much less than that of an electrician or plumber. Pay levels influence the personnel situation in at least three ways. Obviously, low pay scales will not attract recruits who have invested money and effort to gain additional education or skills. A second influence is more psychological. Because police officers may interpret the level of compensation as society's estimate of their worth, their self-esteem is dealt a blow. And relatively small paychecks may lead a police officer to "moonlight"—a practice that places added physical and emotional burdens on the officer and his or her family—

or to yield to the temptation of corruption in order to achieve the living standard of the middle class.

On the job

What factors have an impact on the police officer's lot? Skolnick believes that the principal variables of the police officer's role are danger and authority.[34] Training takes place on the job, and respect comes from colleagues. Unlike other specialists, however, the police work in an environment charged with apprehension or hostility to provide a service whose value is not easily judged.

Danger. The danger of their work makes police officers especially attentive to signs of potential violence and lawbreaking. Throughout the socialization process the recruit is warned against incautious actions and is told about fellow officers who were shot and killed while trying to settle a family squabble or write a ticket for speeding. In 1983 alone, 82 officers were killed in the line of duty, an average yearly number. The folklore of the corps emphasizes that officers must always be on their guard. Thus police officers become suspicious of everyone and all situations.

The element of unexpected danger creates such tension in police that they are constantly on edge and worried about the possibility of attack. People stopped for questioning may sense this tension. A suspect may not intend to attack an officer, but the latter's gruffness may be seen as uncalled-for hostility. If the suspect shows resentment, the officer may in turn interpret it as animosity and be even more on guard. Because the work demands continual preoccupation with potential violence, the police develop a perceptual shorthand to identify certain kinds of people as possible assailants—for example, persons who use gestures, language, and attire that the officer has come to recognize as a prelude to violence: long hair, motorcycle jackets, "jiving."

Authority. The police represent authority, but, unlike workers whose clients have learned to recognize their professional prerogatives (such as doctors, psychiatrists, or social workers), a law enforcement officer must *establish* authority. Certainly the symbols of police authority—the uniform, badge, gun, and nightstick—help, but more important is the way police officers act within the social setting of each encounter. The officer must gain control of a situation by intervening, for example, but the right to intervene may be challenged because the patrol officer is concerned primarily with order maintenance, an area of the law in which there may be a great deal of disagreement. The maintenance of order requires that the police stop fights, arrest drunks, and settle domestic quarrels—situations in which the pertinent laws are inexact and the presence of an officer may be welcomed by neither the offender nor onlookers.

In law enforcement situations, the officer can usually expect the victim's support; the shopkeeper will be pleased by the officer's arrival and will assist by describing the burglar. But when officers are dispatched to investigate a report of juveniles causing trouble in a public place, a neighborhood disturbance, or a victimless crime, they usually do not find a cooperative complainant and must contend not only with the perpetrators but with others who may gather and expand the conflict. These are the kinds of circumstances that require them to "handle the situation" rather than to enforce the law—that is, to assert authority without becoming emotionally involved. Further, they must regulate a public that, while often denying recognition of the police's authority, stresses their obligation to respond to danger. Even when verbally challenged by citizens on their personal conduct and right to enforce the law, they are expected to react in a detached or neutral manner.

The police officer, a symbol of authority with low occupational status, must at times give orders to people of high status. According to William Westley, "he expects rage from the underprivileged and the criminal but understanding from the middle classes: the professionals, the merchants, and the white-collar workers. They, however, define him as a servant, not as a colleague, and the rejection is hard to take."[35] Given the blue-collar background of the cop, maintaining self-respect and refusing to take "crap" may be impor-

Close-up: Field Interrogation and the Symbolic Assailant

A. Be suspicious. This is a healthy police attitude, but it should be controlled and not too obvious.

B. Look for the unusual.
   1. Persons who do not "belong" where they are observed.
   2. Automobiles which do not "look right."
   3. Businesses opened at odd hours, or not according to routine or custom.

C. Subjects who should be subjected to field interrogations.
   1. Suspicious persons known to the officer from previous arrests, field interrogations, and observations.
   2. Emaciated-appearing alcoholics and narcotics users, who invariably turn to crime to pay for cost of habit.
   3. Person who fits description of wanted suspect as described by radio, teletype, daily bulletins.
   4. Any person observed in the immediate vicinity of a crime very recently committed or reported as "in progress."
   5. Known trouble-makers near large gatherings.
   6. Persons who attempt to avoid or evade the officer.
   7. Exaggerated unconcern over contact with the officer.
   8. Visibly "rattled" when near the policeman.
   9. Unescorted women or young girls in public places, particularly at night in such places as cafes, bars, bus and train depots, or street corners.
   10. "Lovers" in an industrial area (make good lookouts).
   11. Persons who loiter about places where children play.
   12. Solicitors or peddlers in a residential neighborhood.
   13. Loiterers around public rest rooms.
   14. Lone male sitting in car adjacent to schoolground with newspaper or book in his lap.
   15. Lone male sitting in car near shopping center who pays unusual amount of attention to women, sometimes continuously manipulating rearview mirror to avoid direct eye contact.
   16. Hitchhikers.
   17. Persons wearing coat on hot days.
   18. Car with mismatched hub caps, or dirty car with clean license plate (or vice versa).
   19. Uniformed "deliverymen" with no merchandise or truck.
   20. Many others. How about your own personal experiences?

Source: Thomas F. Adams, "Field Interrogation," *Police*, March–April 1963, p. 28. Reprinted by permission of Charles C Thomas, Publisher.

tant ways of resolving this problem. A major emphasis of law enforcement work is on the need to assert authority on arrival at the scene when arrival itself may generate hostility. The emphasis on authority may lead to use of excessive force or violence by officers who feel that their status has been placed in question by a person who represents a danger to them and to the community. Cries of police brutality often spring from such a circular chain of events.

Subculture of the police

subculture
The aggregate of symbols, beliefs, and values shared by members of a subgroup within the larger society.

The ***subculture*** of the police helps to define the "cop's world" and each officer's role in it. A subculture is a subdivision of a national culture defined by such social factors as ethnicity, class, and residence, which in combination form a functioning unity that shapes the beliefs, values, and attitudes of the group's members. The police share a set of expectations about human behavior that they carry into professional contacts because they are members of the police community. Like the subculture of any occupational group that sees itself as distinctive, the subculture of the police is based on a set of value premises stemming from their view of the nature of their occupational environment and their relationship to that environment and to other people. Entry requirements, training, behavioral standards, and operational goals combine to produce a similarity of values.

socialization
The process by which the rules, symbols, and values of a group or subculture are learned by its members.

The norms and values of the police subculture are learned. From the time recruits make their first contact with the force, they become aware of the special ways they are expected to act. This process of ***socialization*** makes police officers attuned not only to the formally prescribed rules of the job but, more important, to the informal ways in which the subculture dictates their actions. They learn that loyalty to fellow officers, professional esprit de corps, and respect for police authority are esteemed values. Although the formal training given at the police academy teaches recruits a portion of their new occupation, by actually working as police officers they become socialized by fellow officers to the "real" way the job should be performed.

Like soldiers, patrol officers work in an organizational framework in which rank carries responsibilities and privileges; yet the success of the group depends on the cooperation of its members. All patrol officers are under direct supervision and can be punished if they fail to recognize that their performance is measured by the contribution they make to the group's work. They are also influenced by the pressure exerted on them directly by their colleagues, buddies who work alongside them. Patrol officers, however, have territorial constraints dictating that they be solitary workers, dependent on their own personal skills and judgment. They move onto a social stage with an unknown cast of characters and are expected to perform in a setting and plot that can never be accurately predicted. They must be ever ready to act and to do so according to law. From arresting a fleeing assailant to protecting a fearful wife from her drunken husband to assisting in the search for a lost child, the patrol officer meets the public alone.

Although the police bureaucracy allocates duties among officers on the basis of rank and ability, the police subculture overrides these differentiations because, as organizational specialists believe, of the practice of promoting from within. There are few opportunities for lateral entry into supervisory positions; all members begin at the rank of patrol officer. Upward movement depends on the recommendations of supervisors, with the result that adherence to the rules of the occupational subculture is strengthened. The idealism of young police academy graduates may be shattered when they realize that they must operate within the structure and norms of a bureaucracy. To advance above the boredom of patrol work to the law enforcement work of the detective division may require connections (often political) and a record for acting in accordance with departmental norms. These requirements can mean that arrests that may cause fellow officers extra work are not made or that various unlawful practices within the department are not brought to the chief's attention.

The impact of the police community on the behavior of the individual officer is enhanced when situations develop that produce conflict between the group and the larger society. To endure their work, the police find they must relate to the public in ways that protect their own self-esteem. As former New Haven police chief James Ahern has stated, most job routines in law work are boring; the idealistic recruit soon begins to question the worth of the profession.[36] If the police view the public as essentially hostile and police work as aggravating that hostility, they will segregate themselves from the public by developing strong attitudes and norms that will ensure that all members of the police community will conform to the interests of the group.

As these examples indicate, the subculture of the police exerts a strong impact on law enforcement operations. Further, even with the increased amount of formal training that is given to the police, law enforcement is an art, not a science. There is no body of generalized, written knowledge, theory, or rules that can chart the police officer's way. The recruit learns on the job, as an apprentice, and is thus molded to a great extent by fellow officers and the culture within which they operate.

Working personality

Social scientists have demonstrated that there is a decided relationship between one's occupational environment and the way one interprets events. An occupation may be seen as a major badge of identity that a person acts to protect as an aspect of his or her self-esteem and person. Like doctors, teachers, janitors, and lawyers, the police as a group develop their own particular ways of perceiving and responding to their work environment. The police officer's ***working personality*** is thus developed in response to the occupational environment. Because the police role contains two important variables, danger and authority, officers develop a distinctive perspective from which they view the world. Because they operate in dangerous situations, law enforcement officers are especially attentive to signs of potential violence and lawbreaking. Hence they become suspicious persons, constantly on the lookout for indications that a crime is about to be committed or that they may become targets for lawbreakers.

working personality The complex of emotional and behavioral characteristics developed by a member of an occupational group in response to the work situation and environmental influences.

As Skolnick has said, "the element of danger isolates the policeman socially from that segment of the citizenry which he regards as symbolically dangerous and also from the conventional citizenry with whom he identifies."[37] The element of authority reinforces the element of danger because the officer is typically required to direct the citizenry, whose typical response denies recognition of this authority and stresses the officer's obligation to respond to danger.

In sum, working personality and occupational environment are so interlocked that they reinforce each other in a way that greatly affects the daily work of the police. Procedural requirements and the organizational structure of law enforcement are overshadowed by the perceived need to establish authority in the face of danger.

Isolation of the police

National studies of occupational status have shown that the public nowadays ascribes more prestige to the police than it did in earlier decades. Surveys conducted for the President's Crime Commission and numerous public opinion polls indicate that the overwhelming majority of Americans have a high opinion of the work of the police. Even in economically depressed inner-city areas where the police may be viewed as the tools of an unjust society, most of the inhabitants see them as protectors of their persons and property. But despite these findings, the police do not believe that the public regards their vocation as honorable or their work as just. Westley notes that although they are expected to offer efficient assistance in times of crisis, the police feel that they are looked upon with suspicion, probably because they must "discipline those whom they serve" and are given the authority to use force to ensure compliance.[38] Because they believe the public is hostile to them and that the nature of law work aggravates the hostility, the police tend to separate themselves from the public and develop strong in-group ties. As Michael K. Brown suggests, the police culture also encourages the strong bonding that commonly occurs among people who deal with violence. This solidarity "permits fallible men to perform an arduous and difficult task, and . . . places the highest value upon the obligation to back up and support a fellow officer."[39]

Throughout the publications of police organizations runs the theme that the public is extremely critical of law enforcement agents. But the public is not the only group that is unappreciative of the police; other actors in the criminal justice system are often cited. By failing to treat the police with professional respect and by not dealing seriously with offenders whose behavior may have endangered the patrol officer, lawyers, prosecutors, and judges demean the

---

Values Shared by the Police

1. People cannot be trusted; they are dangerous.
2. Experience is better than abstract rules.
3. You must make people respect you.
4. Everyone hates a cop.
5. The legal system is untrustworthy; the police officers make the best decisions about guilt or innocence.
6. People who are not controlled will break laws.
7. Police officers must appear respectable and be efficient.
8. Police can most accurately identify crime and criminals.
9. The major jobs of the police are to prevent crime and to enforce the laws.
10. Stronger punishment will deter criminals from repeating errors.

Source: Adapted from Peter K. Manning, "The Police: Mandate, Strategies, and Appearance," in *Criminal Justice in America: A Critical Understanding*, ed. Richard Quinney (Boston: Little, Brown, 1974), p. 175.

---

officer's status. Part of the burden of being a police officer is that one is beset by doubt about one's professional status and worth in the public mind. This burden heightens the pressures on individual officers to isolate themselves within the police community.

The world of few other occupational groups is so circumscribed by the job's all-encompassing demands as that of police officers. The situational context of their position limits their freedom to isolate their vocational role from other aspects of their lives. From the time they are first given badges and guns, they must always carry these reminders of the position—the tools of the trade—and be prepared to use them. The requirements that they maintain vigilance against crime even when off duty and that they work at odd hours, together with the limited opportunities for social contact with persons other than fellow officers, reinforce subculture values.

Even more important is the fact that the police uniform and membership in the force are social liabilities. Wherever they go, the police are recognized by bartenders, bookies, and waitresses who want to talk shop; others harangue about the inadequacies of police service. The result of these occupational hazards is that officers tend to interact primarily with their families and with other cops.

> When he gets off duty on the swing shift, there is little to do but go drinking and few people to do it with but other cops. He finds himself going bowling with them, going fishing, helping them paint their house or fix their cars. His family gets to know their families, and a kind of mutual protection society develops which turns out to be the only group in which the policeman is automatically entitled to respect.[40]

Job stress

The working environment and subculture of the police expose members of the force to situations that affect their physical and mental health. This hazard has been fully recognized by law enforcement officials only during the past decade. One study of 2,300 officers in twenty departments found that 37 percent had serious marital problems; 36 percent, health problems; 23 percent, problems with alcohol; 20 percent, problems with their children; and 10 percent, drug problems.[41] Newspaper and magazine articles with such titles as "Time Bombs in Blue" discuss the effects of the pent-up emotions and physical demands of the job.

Many of the factors that produce stress in law enforcement officers have been identified by psychologists and other behavioral scientists, who have noted four general categories of stress to which police officers are subject:

1. *External stress,* produced by real threats and dangers, such as the necessity of entering a dark and unfamiliar building, responding to a "man with a gun" alarm, and pursuit of lawbreakers at high speeds.
2. *Organizational stress,* produced by elements that are inherent in the paramilitary character of police forces: constant adjustment to changing schedules, working at odd hours, requirements that detailed rules and procedures be complied with.
3. *Personal stress,* which may be generated by an officer's racial or gender status among peers, with consequent difficulty in getting along with individual

fellow officers and in adjusting to group-held values not in accordance with one's own values, perceptions of bias, and social isolation.

4. *Operational stress,* the total effect of the need to confront daily the tragedies of urban life; the need to deal with thieves, derelicts, and the mentally deranged; being lied to so often that all citizens become suspect; being required to place oneself in dangerous situations to protect a public that appears to be unappreciative; and the constant awareness of the possibility of being held legally liable for one's actions.[42]

Police departments have been slow to deal with stress, but now some of the larger departments provide psychological and medical counseling for officers. As in industry, an individual is often referred to a counselor only after a problem has been identified as resulting from a work-related incident. Stress is the type of debilitating problem that may not be identified for a long time because it is usually internalized. In popular terminology, it gets "bottled up" until finally it is manifested in the person's health, habits, or behavior. Programs of prevention, group counseling, liability insurance, and family involvement have been undertaken. The legislatures of many states have instituted more liberal disability and retirement rules for police than for other public employees because their jobs are recognized to be more stressful and potentially debilitating.

The making of a police officer

Are the values and attitudes of police officers brought with them to the force or are those values and attitudes shaped by the unique demands of the job? How does a new recruit learn the subcultural norms of the police? How does the working personality form? John Van Maanen has described four stages that a police officer goes through as he or she becomes a part of the law enforcement subculture.[43]

When Cops Crack Up

Boston policeman Eddy Donovan, 49, drives a black Ford LTD with a license plate that reads STRESS. For Donovan, the letters are highly appropriate. He runs the department's police stress program, and sees in his fellow cops all too much of the emotion-frayed side of police work. Perhaps even more to the point, Donovan, after 23 years on the force, can identify with stress. A recovered alcoholic and the divorced father of seven children, he recalls his past with utter frankness: "I was getting paranoid and cynical under the pressure. I was afraid of showing fear because that didn't go with the macho image. I've put a cocked gun to my head. I've put one in my mouth."

Lots of cops feel that way. Shot at, jumped on, menaced by hostile crowds, threatened by community watchdogs and politicians seeking a scapegoat, the policeman can be excused for thinking he is Target Blue. The strain is often too much. Recently an off-duty Philadelphia policeman was shot by officers in Camden, New Jersey, after he opened fire on the driver of a bus. In Buffalo, two policemen were sentenced to four years in prison for stomping an 18-year-old boy to death. On Long Island, an off-duty New York City police officer shot and killed a police sergeant while they were riding home together after celebrating St. Patrick's Day. In Providence, the chief of police shot himself to death in his office with his service revolver.

Source: John Langone, "When Cops Crack Up," *Discover,* May 1981, pp. 84–87.

Preentry. What sort of person is attracted to police work? Early studies emphasized that law enforcement tended to attract persons with authoritarian and conservative values. Later research, however, has shown that police recruits differ very little from persons who seek other civic jobs, such as fire fighters. The attraction of police work lies less in the opportunity to exert authority and use a gun than in the security and economic gains a government job offers and the opportunity to do something of worth for the community. When Van Maanen interviewed recruits in Union City, he found that "virtually all recruits alluded to the opportunity afforded by a police career to perform in a role which was perceived as consequential or important to society."[44] The opportunity to work out of doors in a nonroutine job was another important factor. Knowledge of police work through contact with family members or friends who are officers was also found to be instrumental.

Admittance. Upon joining a police department, the new recruit immediately faces the reality of the organization. He or she may have a citizen's understanding of the work but little knowledge of the procedures and tactics it entails. Throughout a probationary period, the recruit learns aspects of the work and is tested. In most cities, new officers must attend a formal course of training at a departmentally run academy. Such courses range from two-week sessions in which the handling of weapons and target practice are emphasized to more academic four-month programs followed by fieldwork, such as those developed by the Los Angeles police and sheriff's departments. In the latter courses, recruits hear lectures on social relations, receive language training, and learn emergency medical treatment. As increasing emphasis has been placed on the professionalization of the police, formal training programs have been developed and expanded throughout the country.

The typical training program focuses on technical components of the job; it is outside the classroom, in interaction with fellow cadets and experienced officers, that the real socialization to departmental norms takes place. Van Maanen quotes one recruit who values the "war stories" and nuances of policing that instructors can share:

> "I want them to tell me what police work is all about. I could care less about the outside speakers or the guys they bring out here from upstairs who haven't been on the street for the last twenty years. What I want is for somebody who's gonna level with us and really give the lowdown on how we're supposed to survive out there."[45]

Change. Some critics place little value on the formal instruction of the academy, for they believe that the officer is introduced to the reality of police work on the street and not in books. This attitude is often impressed on recent academy graduates the first day on the job when they are placed under the supervision of an experienced officer—often called a field training officer—whose opening remark may be "Now, I want you to forget all that stuff you learned at the academy."

It is during the first encounters with real police work that new officers learn about the culture of their chosen occupation. "Learning the ropes" includes learning the informal ways, rather than the rulebook ways, in which law enforcement operates. It includes learning about shortcuts, how to be

Physical training is an important part of the police academy program.

"productive," what to avoid, and a host of other bits of wisdom, norms, and folklore that define the job in a particular department.

Continuance. From the initial shock at the realization that police work is not exactly what it seemed to be, the officer settles into departmental routine. He or she readily recognizes that the crime-fighting image of television and recruiting posters bears little resemblance to reality: most police work consists of routine service and administrative tasks. The patrol officer is predominantly an order taker—a reactive member of a service organization. There are enough unpredictable elements to police work to make it interesting, however, and enough opportunities for actions that provide the self-esteem and gratification necessary to go on doing one's job well, whatever one's occupation. Thus the new police officer is "made" on the job. In the making of the police officer this socialization process far outweighs in importance either the formal criteria for recruits or the background characteristics of those who seek law enforcement work.

Operational styles

The actual behavior of police officers on the job varies from individual to individual, depending on the extent to which the officer internalizes the norms of the subculture, the lessons of the recruitment process, and the experiences that typically go into the formation of the working personality. Job assignment, community environment, and departmental structure also influence the way an individual carries out police duties. Social scientists have tried to categorize the various approaches to police work by describing operational styles. By clustering behaviors, one can create "ideal types" that serve to emphasize the different ways in which individuals act on the job. These are composite portraits. James Q. Wilson, William K. Muir, and Michael K. Brown each have their own labels for these operational styles, but there are commonalities among them.[46] Four operational styles are described here: crime fighter, service agent, watchman, and legalist.

Crime fighter. Interested in dealing with the more serious crimes, individuals who adopt the *crime-fighter style* emphasize taking tough actions against lawbreakers. For them the sole function of police work is to enforce the law, and they have little regard for policies that dilute this goal. On the job, they are more interested in preventing crime and making arrests than in conforming their actions with decisions of the Supreme Court, which they see as "handcuffing" the police. They are supercops who have little sympathy for the common citizen and the social conditions of the common citizen's life. Using what have been called "old-style" crime-fighting tactics, they have little hesitation in employing force to maintain control of the streets. Crime fighters look upon individuals and groups who do not conform with their rigid views of proper behavior as dangerous or threatening.

Service agent. The values of the police officer who assumes the *service-agent style* contrast markedly with those of the crime fighter. Often a younger member of the force, this officer recognizes that the police have responsibilities that go beyond fighting crime and enforcing the law. The agent may define policing operations as assisting others because such service not only helps a fellow citizen but has an influence on crime prevention. Unlike the crime fighter, who looks upon minorities as potentially dangerous, the service agent may believe that the conditions of lower-class neighborhoods are the basis for much illegal behavior. This is not to say that officers who adopt the service-agent style are "soft" on crime; they are just as interested in law enforcement and maintenance of order as are other members of the force, but they see the problem in a broader context. As Brown says, service agents "argue that the police should take a positive role in assisting people to solve their problems."[47]

Watchman. For the person who adopts the *watchman style,* the maintenance of order is the primary goal of police work. For the watchman, crime fighting and service are less important than maintaining order. The traditional patrol officer "on the beat" who knows the neighborhood, exercises discretion by overlooking some infractions, and is concerned with "keeping a lid on things" typifies this operational style. Critics of this style say that it does not meet the requirements of a modern, professional police force. Too often, they argue, the watchman uses discretion in an illegal manner ("knocking heads") and avoids responsibilities under pressure. As Wilson says, the watchman not only emphasizes order over law enforcement but judges "the seriousness of the infractions less by what the law says about them than by their immediate and personal consequences."[48]

Legalist. The *legalist style* conforms closely to the model of police professionalism. Officers who adopt this style believe that control of crime is the major function of the police but that the mission also has service and other goals. The legalist recognizes the seriousness of crime and is intent upon law enforcement but pursues that goal according to the rules. Less prone than the watchman or service agent to consider the characteristics of the individual offender, the legalist exercises discretion with restraint. Such officers tend to place greater emphasis on the statutes that have been broken, the legal rights of the suspect, and the departmental procedures to be followed. Brown argues, however, that such individuals, while legalistic, are not rigid, and that by the same token their flexibility does not mean that they overlook infractions or avoid conflict.[49] To enforce the law, the legalist believes, is to serve the public, but to be carried out successfully the law enforcement must be done in the right way.

Summary

As the Gilbert and Sullivan operetta observes, "a policeman's lot is not a happy one." Much of the unhappiness of the police may be traced to the public's misunderstanding of the role of law enforcement in a democratic society. Citizens evaluate the effectiveness of police work with respect to the function of law enforcement—solving crimes—though the maintenance of order and community service take the major share of the police's time and resources. Because police response is reactive, law officers depend on citizens to notify them that an offense has been committed. The reluctance of many citizens to give timely notification reduces the ability of the police to prevent and control crime. In addition, the police are required to exercise discretion in situations in which decisions must be made carefully and quickly, a factor that further complicates the performance of their role.

Although some people may say that the police have a simple assignment—to maintain order through law enforcement—such is not the case. Legislators may write the laws as if full enforcement were expected, but to a large extent the police determine the extent of actual enforcement. Police administrators must make choices about the types of criminal behavior to which they will respond, the allocation of enforcement resources, and the policies governing the relationship of officers to citizens. The police are expected to perform three functions: law enforcement, maintenance of order, and service. Social and political forces will shape the extent to which each department emphasizes one or another of these functions.

As in other professions, there is a link between the work situation, the social bonds that unite police officers, and their interpretations of the world around them. Recruited because of a belief that the work will be an interesting way to serve the community, the officers often find that the assigned tasks are dull. More important, they feel that the work is not appreciated by the citizenry. On the job they are constantly aware of the danger that goes with their career and the authority they must exercise. These pressures further strengthen the bonds among officers. They may seriously interfere with the effectiveness of law enforcement in a democratic society.

For discussion

1. You are a police chief. What are some of the assumptions that will guide your decisions as to the allocation of your resources?

2. You are a police chief. How will the community's social and political characteristics influence the style of law enforcement that you will create?
3. What changes could be made to enable police officers to feel that theirs is a respected profession and to integrate the police more effectively with the community?
4. The police officer is taught to be on guard and watchful for suspicious activity. What influence might this stance have on encounters with the public?
5. How might police departments be reorganized to improve career opportunities for members of the force?

For further reading

Ahern, James F. *Police in Trouble.* New York: Hawthorn Books, 1972.
Bordua, David J. *The Police: Six Sociological Essays.* New York: Wiley, 1967.
Muir, William K., Jr. *Police: Streetcorner Politicians.* Chicago: University of Chicago Press, 1979.
Repetto, Thomas A. *The Blue Parade.* New York: Free Press, 1978.
Rubinstein, Jonathan. *City Police.* New York: Farrar, Straus & Giroux, 1973.
Skolnick, Jerome H. *Justice without Trial: Law Enforcement in a Democratic Society.* New York: Wiley, 1966.
Uhnak, Dorothy. *Law and Order.* New York: Simon & Schuster, 1972.
Westley, William. *Violence and the Police.* Cambridge: M.I.T. Press, 1970.
Wilson, James Q. *Varieties of Police Behavior.* Cambridge: Harvard University Press, 1968.

Notes

1. Herman Goldstein, *Policing a Free Society* (Cambridge, Mass.: Ballinger, 1977), p. 1.
2. Bernard I. Garmire, "The Police Role in an Urban Society," in *The Police and the Community,* ed. Robert F. Steadman (Baltimore: Johns Hopkins University Press, 1972), p. 2.
3. Jerome H. Skolnick, *Justice without Trial: Law Enforcement in a Democratic Society* (New York: Wiley, 1966), p. 6.
4. Samuel Walker, *The Police in America* (New York: McGraw-Hill, 1983), p. 2.
5. Thomas A. Critchley, *A History of Police in England and Wales* (London: T. A. Constable, 1967), p. 36.
6. Philip John Stead, "Patrick Colquhoun," in *Pioneers in Policing,* ed. Philip John Stead (Montclair, N.J.: Patterson Smith, 1977), p. 48.
7. Charles Reith, *The Blind Eye of History: A Study of the Origins of the Present Police Era* (London: Faber & Faber, 1952), p. 128.
8. Peter Manning, *Police Work* (Cambridge: M.I.T. Press, 1977), pp. 82–83.
9. Samuel Walker, *Popular Justice* (New York: Oxford University Press, 1980), p. 57.
10. Manning, *Police Work,* pp. 82–83.
11. Roger Lane, *Policing the City: Boston 1822–1885* (Cambridge: Harvard University Press, 1967), p. 26.
12. Bruce Smith, Sr., *Police Systems in the United States,* 2d rev. ed. (New York: Harper & Row, 1960), pp. 105–6.
13. Walker, *Popular Justice,* p. 137.
14. Eric H. Monkkonen, *Police in Urban America, 1860–1920* (Cambridge: Cambridge University Press, 1981), p. 127.
15. Robert M. Fogelson, *Big-City Police* (Cambridge: Harvard University Press, 1977), p. 223.
16. Stuart Scheingold, *The Politics of Law and Order* (New York: Longman, 1984), p. 118; George L. Kelling, "On the Accomplishments of the Police," in *Control in the Police Organization,* ed. Maurice Punch (Cambridge: M.I.T. Press, 1983), pp. 152–68; James Q. Wilson, *Thinking about Crime,* 2d ed. (New York: Basic Books, 1983).
17. President's Commission on Law Enforcement and Administration of Justice, *Task Force Report: The Police* (Washington, D.C.: Government Printing Office, 1967), p. 14.
18. James Q. Wilson, *Varieties of Police Behavior* (Cambridge: Harvard University Press, 1968).
19. Egon Bittner, *The Functions of the Police in Modern Society,* National Institute of Mental Health Center for Studies of Crime and Delinquency (Washington, D.C.: Government Printing Office, 1970), p. 12.
20. Goldstein, *Policing a Free Society,* p. 15. Copyright © 1976 Ballinger Publishing Company. Reprinted by permission.
21. Ibid., p. 35.
22. Wilson, *Varieties of Police Behavior,* p. 16.
23. Jesse Rubin, "Police Identity and the Police Role," in *Police and the Community,* ed. Steadman, p. 24.
24. Wilson, *Varieties of Police Behavior,* p. 18.

25. Irving A. Wallach, *Police Function in a Negro Community* (McLean, Va.: Research Analysis Corp., 1970), 1:6.
26. Thomas E. Bercal, "Calls for Police Assistance: Consumer Demands for Governmental Service," *American Behavioral Scientist* 13 (1970): 681.
27. Albert J. Reiss, Jr., *The Police and the Public* (New Haven: Yale University Press, 1971), pp. xiii, 70.
28. U.S. Department of Justice, *Crime in the United States* (Washington, D.C.: Government Printing Office, 1983), p. 159.
29. Wilson, *Varieties of Police Behavior,* p. 30.
30. Wayne LaFave, *Arrest: The Decision to Take a Suspect into Custody* (Boston: Little, Brown, 1965), p. 29.
31. Herbert Jacob, *Urban Justice* (Boston: Little, Brown, 1973), p. 27.
32. Bittner, *Functions of the Police,* p. 4.
33. Wilson, *Varieties of Police Behavior,* p. 33.
34. Skolnick, *Justice without Trial,* pp. 42–70.
35. William Westley, *Violence and the Police* (Cambridge: M.I.T. Press, 1970), p. 56.
36. James F. Ahern, *Police in Trouble* (New York: Hawthorne Books, 1972), p. 27.
37. Skolnick, *Justice without Trial,* p. 44.
38. Westley, *Violence and the Police,* p. 110.
39. Michael K. Brown, *Working the Street* (New York: Russell Sage Fondation, 1981), p. 82.
40. Ahern, *Police in Trouble,* p. 14.
41. John Blackmore, "Are Police Allowed to Have Problems of Their Own?" *Police Magazine* 1 (1978): 47–55.
42. Robert J. McGuire, "The Human Dimension in Urban Policing: Dealing with Stress in the 1980s," *Police Chief* 46 (November 1979): 27.
43. John Van Maanen, "Observations on the Making of Policemen," *Human Organization* 32 (1973): 407–18.
44. Ibid.
45. Ibid.
46. Wilson, *Varieties of Police Behavior;* William K. Muir, Jr., *Police: Streetcorner Politicians* (Chicago: University of Chicago Press, 1977); Brown, *Working the Street.*
47. Brown, *Working the Street.*
48. Wilson, *Varieties of Police Behavior,* p. 141.
49. Brown, *Working the Street.*

The victim

A voice said, "I want that." Joe Castelli looked up from the till, and there across the counter stood this tall colored kid with an insolent grin and a small-caliber, blue-steel automatic not 4 feet from Castelli's face. . . .

And finally the tall one with the blue-steel .25 and the scornful half-smile—the one Castelli identified later as Donald Payne. He and another, smaller youth came in the out door that cool August evening, just as Castelli was stuffing $250 or $300 in receipts from cash register No. 2 into his pocket. "I want that," the tall one said. Castelli edged away. "Shoot him! Shoot him!" the small one yelled. The tall one started at Castelli and poked the gun across the counter at him. "Mother f——er," he said. He squeezed the trigger, maybe once, maybe two or three times.

The gun went *click.*

The two youths turned and ran. Castelli started after them, bumped against the end of the counter and went down. He got up and dashed outside, but the youths disappeared down a dark alley. An old white man emptying garbage saw them go by. The tall one pointed the pistol toward the sky and squeezed again. This time it went off.

A clerk from across the street came over and told Castelli that a woman had seen the boys earlier getting out of a black Ford. "People around here notice things like that," Castelli says. "They watch." Castelli found the car parked nearby and wrote down the license number. The driver—a third Negro youth—followed him back to the store. "What you taking my license for?" he demanded. "I was just waiting for my wife—I took her to the doctor." He stood there yelling for a while, but some of Castelli's white neighbors crowded into the store, and the black youth left. Castelli went back into the street, flagged down an unmarked police car he recognized and handed over the number, and the hunt was on.

The cops

The evening was clear and mellow for August, a cool 67° and breezy. Patrolman Joe Higgins nosed his unmarked squad car through the night places of the Gresham police district, watching the alleys and storefronts slide past, half-listening to the low staccato of the radio, exchanging shorthand grunts with his partner, Tom Cullen, slouched low in the seat beside him. They had been riding for three humdrum hours when, shortly after 9 P.M., they picked up the call: gunfire in the street up in the north reaches of the district. The two cops glanced at one another. Cullen got the mike out of the glove compartment and radioed: "Six-sixty going in." Higgins hit the accelerator and snaked through the sluggish night traffic toward Shop-Rite Liquors—and the middle of his own neighborhood.

. . . Higgins lives just a few blocks from Shop-Rite; he has traded there for twenty years, and when he saw Joe Castelli waving in the streets that August evening, he forgot about the shooting call and hit the brakes fast. Castelli blurted out the story and gave Higgins the license number of the black Ford. But it checked out to a fake address—a schoolyard—and Higgins and Cullen spent the next six hours cruising the dark, fighting drowsiness and looking.

It was near first light when they spotted the car, parked in a deserted industrial area with two Negro runaways, 13 and 17 years old, curled up asleep inside. The two patrolmen rousted the boys out, searched the car—and found the blue-steel .25 under a jacket in the front seat. One of the boys, thoroughly scared, led them to a 17-year-old named James Hamilton* who admitted having driven the car but not having gone into the store. Hamilton led them to his kid cousin, Frank, who admitted having gone into the store but not having handled the gun or clicked the trigger. And Frank Hamilton led them to Donald Payne.

And so, red-eyed and bone-weary, Higgins and Cullen, along with a district sergeant and two robbery detectives, went to the little green-and-white frame house in Roseland at 9 A.M. and rang the bell. Payne's sister let them in and pointed the way upstairs.

Payne was sleeping when the cops crowded

into his little attic bedroom and he came awake cool and mean. "Get moving," someone said. "You're under arrest." The police started rummaging around while Payne, jawing all the while, pulled on a pair of green pants and a red jacket. "You don't have no warrant," he said. As Payne told it later, one of the cops replied, "We got a lawyer on our hands." But Higgins insists he misunderstood—"What I said was we'd *get* him a lawyer."

They marched him out in handcuffs past his mother, took him to the district station and shackled him to a chair while one of the officers started tapping out an arrest report: "PAYNE DONALD M/N [for male Negro] 18 4-19-52. . . ." Higgins got Castelli on the phone. "It's Joe," he said, "come in—we think we've got the man." Castelli came in with DeAngelo. The cops put Payne into a little back room with a few stray blacks. Castelli picked him out—and that, for the cops, was enough. Payne was taken to the South Side branch police headquarters to be booked, then led before a magistrate who set bond at $10,000. The bounty is a paper figure: the Chicago courts require only 10 percent cash. But Payne didn't have it, and by mid-afternoon he was on his way by police van to the Cook County Jail.

Joe Higgins and Tom Cullen by then had worked twelve hours overtime; in four hours more, Tac Unit 660 was due on patrol again. They talked a little about Donald Payne. "He had a head on him," Cullen said in some wonder. "Maybe if he didn't have a chip on his shoulder. Maybe—"

* The names of Hamilton and his cousin have been changed since both are juveniles.

Source: Peter Goldman and Don Holt, "How Justice Works: The People vs. Donald Payne." *Newsweek*, 8 March 1971, pp. 20–37.

Police Operations

6

When you need a cop you can't find one.

POPULAR SAYING

About eight o'clock on the morning of August 9, 1969, Winifred Chapman got off the bus at the intersection of Santa Monica and Canyon Drive in the Bel Air section of Los Angeles to begin her day's work as a housekeeper at 10050 Cielo Drive. Walking past a white Rambler parked at an odd angle in the driveway, she entered the house and went to the living room. Blood was spattered over the walls, pools of blood had collected on the flagstone porch, and a body could be seen on the front lawn. As Mrs. Chapman ran screaming toward a neighbor's house, she saw there was a body in the Rambler.

With the arrival of officers from the West Los Angeles Division of the LAPD, a search was begun of the entire house and three more bodies were found. One, a male, was near the front door—the head and face battered and the torso punctured by dozens of wounds. Behind the couch in the living room was the blood-smeared body of a young pregnant woman with a rope looped around her neck. The rope extended across the room to a dead man whose clothes were blood-drenched and whose face was covered by a towel.

The homicides at 10050 Cielo Drive became known to the American public as the Tate murders, one of the most bizarre and gruesome incidents in modern law enforcement. Investigation of the multiple murders led to the conviction and life imprisonment of Charles Manson, self-styled god and commune leader who had spent seventeen of his thirty-two years in prison. The story of the investigation and prosecution of members of the Manson "family" is well told by Vincent Bugliosi, deputy district attorney of Los Angeles, in *Helter Skelter*.[1] His account provides an excellent case study of police operations and realistically describes many of the problems that face law enforcement agencies as they seek to marshal their resources against crime.

Chapter 5 explored the broad dimensions of the police role in a democratic society: the police are expected to perform a number of functions, including order maintenance, law enforcement, and service, within a framework of democratic culture, institutions, and rules. Emphasis was placed on the discretionary aspect of police activity and the influences that are brought to bear on individual police officers as they work. Chapter 6 will focus on police operations—the actual work of law enforcement agencies as they pursue offenders and prevent crimes. Because of the demands on them, the police must be organized so that enforcement efforts may be coordinated, investigations conducted, arrests made, evidence assembled, and crimes solved.

Organization of the police

The police clearly have many varied responsibilities, and they have been given the resources to carry them out by special organizational structures that have been created to ensure efficient and effective operation. Tailored to meet the special needs of and demands on the police, these structures are different from those created for other organizations.

The highly decentralized nature of policing in the United States is underscored by the fact that departments vary in organization and service activities. Although a majority of police officers are employed by departments with more than a thousand officers, a majority of departments have fewer than thirty officers each. Most departments patrol, investigate, direct traffic, and provide other services, yet others are involved in only one or two of these functions. Some communities have an officer-to-resident ratio of 4.55 : 1,000; in others (usually smaller cities) the ratio is 2.01 : 1,000. Even when cities are similar in size, the ratios may differ (Detroit, with 1.3 million residents, has 4.2 : 1,000; Houston, with about the same population, has only 1.9 : 1,000). The size and nature of police departments, then, vary around the country. Only through the manipulation of statistics can a model of the "typical" law enforcement agency be drawn.[2]

Traditionally the police have been organized in a military manner. A structure of ranks from patrol officer to sergeant, lieutenant, captain, up to chief helps to designate the authority and responsibility of each level within the organization. Like that of the military, this operations model is designed to emphasize superior–subordinate relationships so that discipline, control, and accountability are primary values. This emphasis is thought to be important both as a means of efficiently mobilizing police resources to combat crime and as a way of ensuring that civil liberties are protected. The belief is that police objectives can be achieved most easily, effectively, and satisfactorily when the principles related to this framework are applied. The structure of a well-organized police department, shown in figure 6.1, is designed to fulfill five functions:

1. Apportion the work load among members and units according to a logical plan.
2. Ensure that lines of authority and responsibility are as definite and direct as possible.
3. Specify a unity of command throughout so that there is no question as to which orders should be followed.
4. Place responsibility accompanied by commensurate authority. If the authority is delegated, the user is held accountable.
5. Coordinate the efforts of members and units so that all will work harmoniously to accomplish the mission.[3]

Allocation of resources

In large cities, not all law enforcement activities can physically be carried out from a central office. As a result, districts or precincts are created so that most operations affecting particular geographical areas can function within them. Accordingly, the patrol and traffic divisions tend to be dispersed throughout the city, while specialized units work out of headquarters. The

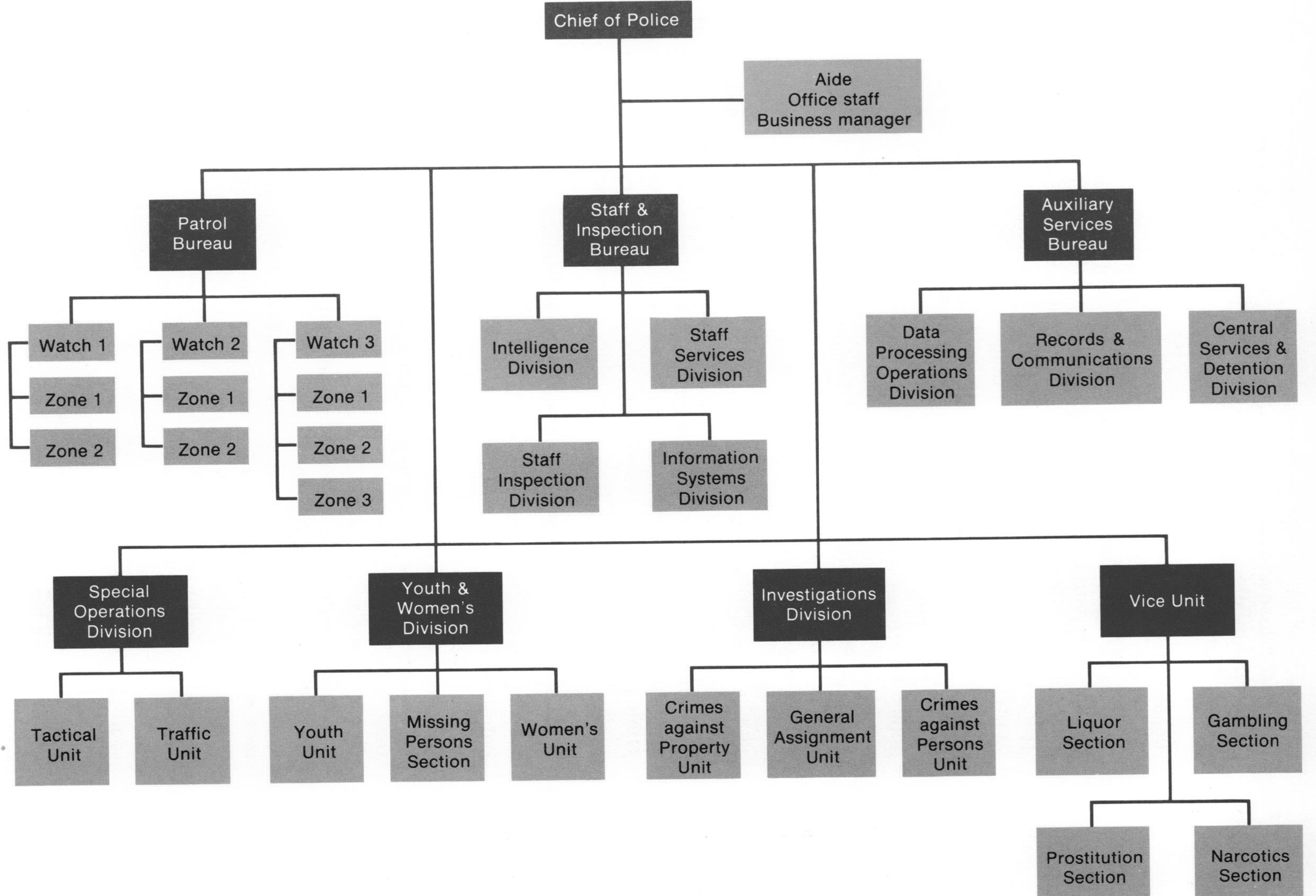

FIGURE 6.1
Structural organization chart for a police department serving a city of 500,000

advantage of having law enforcement units already positioned in the field carries the disadvantage of lessened control by headquarters. However, modern communications technology has done much to diminish the independence of district units.

The operations bureau, the major law enforcement section of a police department, contains a separate functional division for each of the line units: patrol, investigation, traffic, vice, and juvenile. Line units are the direct-operations components and perform the basic law enforcement tasks of crime prevention and control. The patrol and investigation (detective) units are the core of the modern department. Patrol is traditionally the basic action arm of the police and deals with a wide range of functions, including preventing crime, apprehending offenders, arbitrating domestic quarrels, helping the ill, and assisting at the site of accidents. The investigation division is a specialized unit that is concerned primarily with apprehension and conviction of the perpetrators of the more serious crimes. The separation of patrol and investigation sometimes complicates the definition of objectives, functions, and responsibilities of each unit. While the investigation unit usually concentrates on murder, rape, and major robberies, the patrol division has joint responsibility for investigating those crimes and also is responsible for investigation of lesser crimes, which of course are far more numerous.

Many departments have a traffic unit, but usually only police forces in middle-sized to large cities maintain specialized vice and juvenile units. Vice is sometimes kept as part of the investigation unit, but because operations in this field present the risk of corruption, the specialized unit reports directly to the chief in some departments. The juvenile unit is concerned primarily with crime prevention as it relates to young people. As with the other specialized units, the carrying out of its responsibilities depends on the patrol division.

Influences on decisions: bureaucratic politics

Several factors characterize the organizational context within which law enforcement decisions are made. First, the police stand as the essential gateway to the justice system, through which raw materials enter to be processed. They have the discretion not to arrest or to filter out cases they feel should not be forwarded. Those cases sent to the prosecutor for charging and then on to the courts for adjudication have their beginning with an individual officer's decision that probable cause exists to arrest. How the officer makes the arrest and collects supporting evidence to justify the action greatly influences the decisions of the prosecutor and judge.

Second, the administrative decision making of the police, unlike that of most other formal organizations, is structured by the fact that the ultimate fate of one group of clients (the accused) rests with other clients (prosecutor and judge). The police may introduce clients into the system, but the outcome of a case is largely in the hands of others. That the others are members of the legal profession and of higher social status than the police creates a potential for conflict.

Third, the police are in an odd situation because their work includes all the elements essential to qualify as a profession. Like medical doctors, for example, they have acquired a body of technical knowledge, are expected to act in accordance with a code of ethics, have a moral duty to respond to the needs of others, possess authority, and may use discretion to decide the fate of clients. Yet the police must function within a chain of command. As part of a bureaucracy, they are expected to observe rules, follow the orders of superiors, and *also* exercise professional discretion. They are duty-bound both to stay in line and to be responsible for independent choices. To understand the impact of these organizational factors on the daily activities of the police, it is necessary to examine certain of their aspects.

Exchange relationships. Besides being influenced by the interpersonal relationships among decision makers, police actions are influenced by external groups, such as other governmental agencies, interest groups, and citizens. This penetration of the police organizational environment results from the overlapping jurisdictions of city, county, state, and national law enforcement agencies and the political context of criminal justice decisions.

In his study of enforcement of traffic regulations in four Massachusetts towns, John Gardiner found that city officials with budgetary powers, individual citizens, and such groups as the safety council all insisted that the police conform with *their* perceptions of the way the law should be enforced. Attempts to fix tickets through the intervention of politicians or of police officials of other communities were common. Massachusetts police chiefs believe that enforcement of traffic regulations can jeopardize public relations more than any other phase of their work. If ticket-writing campaigns are too active, they fear for their budget and for community support. As traffic policies must be

Orlando Winfield Wilson

O. W. Wilson, police official and criminologist, was born in South Dakota. After his family moved to Berkeley, California, Wilson enrolled in the university and completed a degree in criminology in 1924. While taking courses, Wilson became a patrolman with the Berkeley police department and in the process became a protégé of Chief August Vollmer, who was, in addition, a professor at the university. After his graduation, Wilson became chief of police of Fullerton, California, on Vollmer's recommendation, and thereby launched his career as a law enforcement official and innovator.

As chief of police in Wichita, Kansas (1928–1939), Wilson attracted national attention by reorganizing the department and introducing such innovations as clearly marked police vehicles, lie detectors, and mobile crime laboratories. He gained a reputation for ridding the police of corruption and was made superintendent of the Chicago Police Department in 1960 to meet that objective. He saw corruption as a by-product of poor organization, scant planning, and tangled lines of command.

Between the periods he spent in Wichita and Chicago (1939–1960), Wilson was professor of police administration at the University of California at Berkeley. Here he developed a theory concerning the relationship of law enforcement to crime control: the police could not prevent crime because they had little control over its social causes—poverty, neglect, and the like; the police could, however, repress and control the criminal through such aggressive tactics as preventive patrol. His most important works are *Police Records* (1942), *Police Administration* (1950), and *Police Planning* (1957).

made in a context of sporadic citizen demands and group pressures, they tend to be decided by a process of "vague picking and choosing among public values."[4]

Many of the exchange relationships between the police and their clientele are cooperative. The extensive communications network between the Federal Bureau of Investigation and local police forces is a good example. The FBI performs important and helpful services for local agencies by publicizing the names of wanted criminals, providing background information on offenders, and completing technical operations such as fingerprint analysis for departments that lack such expertise. At the same time there are organizational and political benefits to be gained by the FBI. Presumably the political support of local officials is the payment made for the services rendered.

Jurisdictional disputes. Within the criminal justice system, the police have a peculiar connection to the prosecution and judicial subsystems. Although the police have the power to introduce clients into the larger system, they are formally required to allow other professionals to evaluate their work. Police officers' professional right to decide which clients should enter the system is thus infringed on by the bureaucratic context. Conflict among the police, prosecutor, and courts is inevitable and may lead officers to impose their own brand of justice outside the system. When the court sends accused violators back to the community, the police may take the law into their own hands. "The continuing conflict between the police and the courts over admissibility of evidence, techniques of interrogation, the status of the confession, and the use of force, together with their separate definitions of justice, are likewise consequences of the separation of powers."[5] Because the traditional index of police effectiveness has been the number of arrests rather than either the number of convictions or the nature of the sentences imposed, the police may be motivated primarily to generate information that links a person with a criminal event rather than to ensure that evidence is admissible or that other criteria of due process are met.

Prosecutors, on the other hand, may be motivated to ensure that each case brought to them by the police will easily pass the scrutiny of the judge and result in a conviction that will enhance the D.A.'s record. In certain cases, they may require that the police develop exceptionally strong evidence before they will consider acting. Since prosecutors know that they have more to lose than just the case if the victim refuses to cooperate, if the evidence is skimpy, and if the judge is known to dislike a certain type of case, they may persuade the police to handle the offender in some other way. The filtering system gives the police this opportunity to drop cases without the need to secure the approval of other judicial units.

Bargaining between police and court personnel is thus characterized by an inequality and reversal of roles. Police officers who interrogate a suspected offender are in a superior position and are able to use tactics that assert their authority in the situation. In contacts with the prosecutor and courts, however, officers' behavior must reflect the fact that their formal and social status is lower than that of the officials with whom they must deal. Under trial conditions, the officer may even be interrogated by a member of the bar. Such officers of the court as probation and juvenile personnel are of lower social status than attorneys or judges, but they, too, are formally superior to the police.

In all the bargaining relationships within the criminal justice bureaucracy, the police must interact with persons who may view law enforcement with hostility. In fact, many are hired because of their adversarial stance toward the police. Yet these exchange relationships are not completely one-sided; the police, too, have tactics that they may use in their dealings with prosecutor and judge. Often these tactics take the form of informal and sub rosa practices, such as inducing suspects to plead guilty to a host of prior unsolved offenses in return for leniency, thus increasing the clearance rate.

Organizational response. Although the police depend primarily on citizens for inputs into the law enforcement system, the nature of the police response is greatly influenced by the organizational character of the police bureaucracy. Through the functional structure of the operational divisions (patrol, vice, investigation, and so on), the quasi-military command system, and the various incentives used to induce the desired responses, the administrative environment affects the way calls for actions are processed as well as the nature of the police response.

Police organizations are increasingly being shaped by innovations in communications technology. These developments have led to growing centralization of both command and control in departments, a centralization of decision making. The core of modern police departments is the communications center, where decisions are made to activate officers. This means that line officers are in constant touch with headquarters and are required to report each of their actions. Extensive use of the two-way radio has been a primary means for police administrators to limit the discretion of the officer in the field. Where in former times patrol officers might have administered their own version of on-the-spot justice to a mischievously behaving juvenile, they may now be expected to file a report, take the delinquent into custody, and initiate formal proceedings.

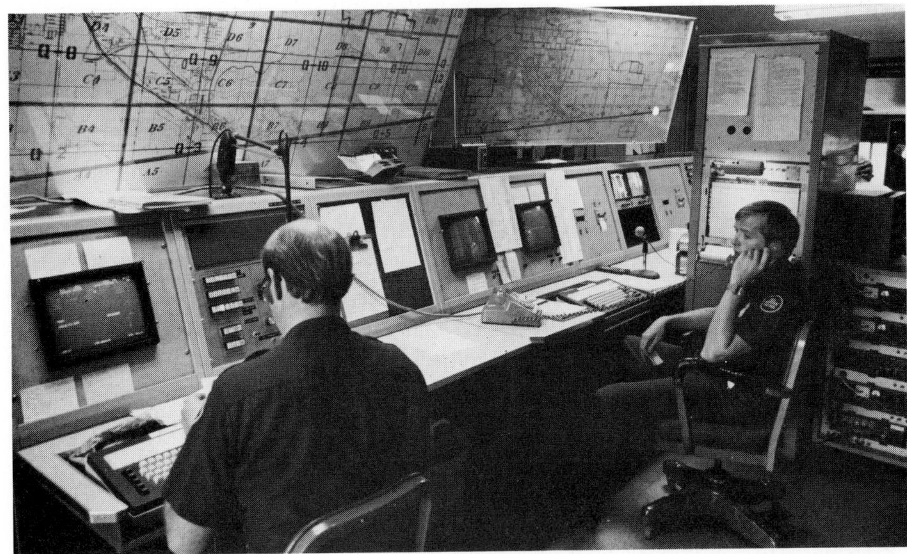

The communications center of a metropolitan police station directs officers to respond to calls.

Productivity. Like other organizations, the modern police department is interested in maintaining quality control. Thus it is not uncommon to hear a weary patrol officer say when scanning the log at the end of a busy day, "Well, we worked tonight but we didn't get any activity for the sergeant." As Jonathan Rubinstein asks:

> How can a man who has taken fifteen assignments from the radio dispatcher, patiently listened to complaints, and steered his car through clogged and steamy streets say he has had no activity? His shirt is soaked with sweat and filth, his arms ache from wrestling the heavy steering of a car that quickly ages beyond recognition under constant wear and occasional mistreatment. He is tired from no activity.[6]

Activity is the bureaucratic measure of police work. It is the statistic used by sergeants to judge the productivity of their officers, by lieutenants to assure themselves that the sergeants are properly directing their officers, by captains to show their superiors that their districts are in capable hands, and by the chief to prove to the public that tax money is not being squandered. In most departments, effectiveness is based on such things as the number of parking meters tagged, illegally parked cars ticketed, suspects stopped for questioning, and arrests made, and the value of stolen goods recovered. It is obvious that such activity is more easily produced when it is police-invoked (proactive) than when it is citizen-invoked (reactive). Thus departmental policies concerning such offenses as traffic violations, public drunkenness, and crimes without victims greatly influence the record of police effectiveness.

Although an organization chart may display the formal connections among portions of a police department, informal relationships shape the actual operations. Like other organizations structured by formal rules and roles, the police department functions according to a more flexible arrangement held together at many points by individual and group linkages characterized by bargaining, cooperation, and discretion. The influence of these informal factors shapes the ongoing activities of the organization. Recruitment, socialization, and the working personality are also important factors that remold the formal organization to meet the goals and needs of the individual people operating within it.

Delivery of police services

A distinction is often made between line and staff functions. *Line functions* are those that directly involve operational activities; *staff functions* supplement or support the line. Staff functions are found in the administration and service bureaus as well as in the internal investigation and community relations sections (see figure 6.1). The efficient police department must have a proper balance between line and staff duties so that they may be coordinated into an effective crime control and prevention force. The distribution of personnel in a department of the size and structure suggested by figure 6-1 would probably be: administrative bureau, 7.5 percent; operations bureau, 84.0 percent; service bureau, 8.5 percent. Within the operations bureau, the patrol unit accounts for 55 percent of the personnel; the investigation unit, 17 percent; traffic, 12 percent; and the specialized units of vice and juvenile, the remaining 16 percent.[7] The allocation of personnel should *not* be used as an index of importance because within a department the number of persons required to fulfill a function varies.

This section directs attention to the line activities of the operations bureau, including the patrol, investigation, traffic, and vice units. As each operational unit is described, consider not only the work of the unit but its contribution to the overall effectiveness of law enforcement.

Patrol

Patrol is often called the backbone of police operations. The patrol officer's work can be traced to the time when Sir Robert Peel established the first organized police force in London and even to the watchmen of an earlier period in English history. The mission of Peel's bobbies was to walk through the streets of London so as to be seen in every part of the beat every ten or fifteen minutes, and thus to be available to assist citizens in need, to become acquainted with inhabitants, and to be a deterring presence for criminals. This crime-prevention strategy was adopted by police in the United States throughout the nineteenth century. The foot patrol officer in urban areas provided a "highly informed and socially integrated kind of watching; while he was watching his beat, the beat was watching him."[8]

Every modern police department has a patrol unit; even in large specialized departments, patrol officers constitute up to two-thirds of all sworn officers. In small communities, police operations are not specialized and the patrol force *is* the department. The patrol officer is the law enforcement generalist and must be prepared to assume a wide variety of responsibilities. The word *patrol* is thought to be derived from a French word, *patrouiller,* which roughly means "to tramp about in the mud." This translation clearly establishes what one authority has called a function that is "arduous, tiring, difficult, and performed in conditions other than ideal."[9]

The patrol function has three components: answering calls for assistance, maintaining a police presence, and probing suspicious circumstances. Patrol officers are well suited to these activities because they are near the scene of most situations and can render timely help or speedily move to apprehend a suspect. When not responding to calls, they engage in preventive patrol—that is, making the law enforcement presence known—on the assumption that doing so will deter crime. Walking the streets of a neighborhood or cruising in a vehicle through the beat, the patrol officer is constantly on the lookout for suspicious people and behavior.

The object of the patrol function is to disperse the police in ways that will eliminate or reduce opportunities for lawbreaking and increase the likelihood that a criminal will be caught while committing a crime or soon thereafter. Patrol officers also perform the important function of helping to maintain smooth relations between police and community. As the most visible members of the criminal justice system, they can have a decisive effect on the willingness of citizens to cooperate in an investigation. In addition, their effective work can help to create a sense of security among citizens.

As the essential action arm of law enforcement, patrol forces are engaged in a variety of activities, including preventing crime, maintaining order, arresting offenders, and giving aid to citizens. Performing these activities as part of their basic responsibility to respond to calls and to make rounds on the streets may sound fairly straightforward but in practice turns out to be complex.

> With the patrol force deployed throughout the community and able to respond rapidly to calls for service, one or more of these men usually arrive first at the scene of a crime or disaster. But merely reaching the scene of an incident does not mark the end of a patrolman's mission; it is just beginning. The measures a patrolman takes to confront a situation, the discretionary decisions he makes, the way he interacts with citizens, the skill and imagination he applies to conducting investigations, questioning suspects, interviewing complainants and witnesses, and the techniques he follows in searching crime scenes and preserving physical evidence are the hallmarks of his job. Hence, the work of a patrolman is of far-reaching importance and the quality of service rendered by the whole department is largely dependent upon his competence.[10]

One of the problems of modern police administration is that too often the patrol unit is taken for granted. Because the rank of patrol officer is the entry level for recruits, greater status is accorded detectives in the investigation unit. In addition, patrol work is viewed as cold, sometimes dirty, boring, and thankless. Yet patrol officers must carry the major burden of the criminal justice system. They must "confront the enraged husband, the crazed drug addict, the frightened runaway, the grieving mother, the desperate criminal, and the uninformed, apathetic, and often hostile citizen."[11]

A number of studies have shown, however, that most officers, on most duty tours, do not make even one arrest. This finding helps us to realize that taking formal measures against lawbreakers is only a small part of patrol activity. Patrol officers are expected to be constantly "on guard," watching for suspicious persons and behaviors, providing information and assistance to the public. Because of their ability to exercise discretion, officers can handle situations without invoking formal processes. Patrol officers are important because they serve the public's need for security and assistance. Contemporary research has shown that patrol officers' presence in a neighborhood or community, especially if they are on foot, is a major factor in reducing the fear of crime.

Methods of patrol. Historically, patrolling was done on foot, but with the development of the automobile, much patrol work is now carried out in squad cars. Methods of allocating patrol officers and arriving at decisions concerning various means of transportation and communications have been a subject of research during the past decade. Though the results of these studies are not definitive, they have caused law enforcement specialists to rethink some traditional aspects of patrol. Increased emphasis is being placed on foot patrol as a way of reducing the fear of crime. But attempts to change some current law enforcement practices have not always been successful because patrol methods that may appear to researchers to be the most efficient often run counter to the desires of departmental personnel. The following pages will discuss allocation of patrol personnel, response time, foot patrol versus motorized patrol, one-person versus two-person patrol units, and team policing.

Allocation. Traditionally it has been assumed that patrol officers should be assigned where and when they will be most effective in preventing crime,

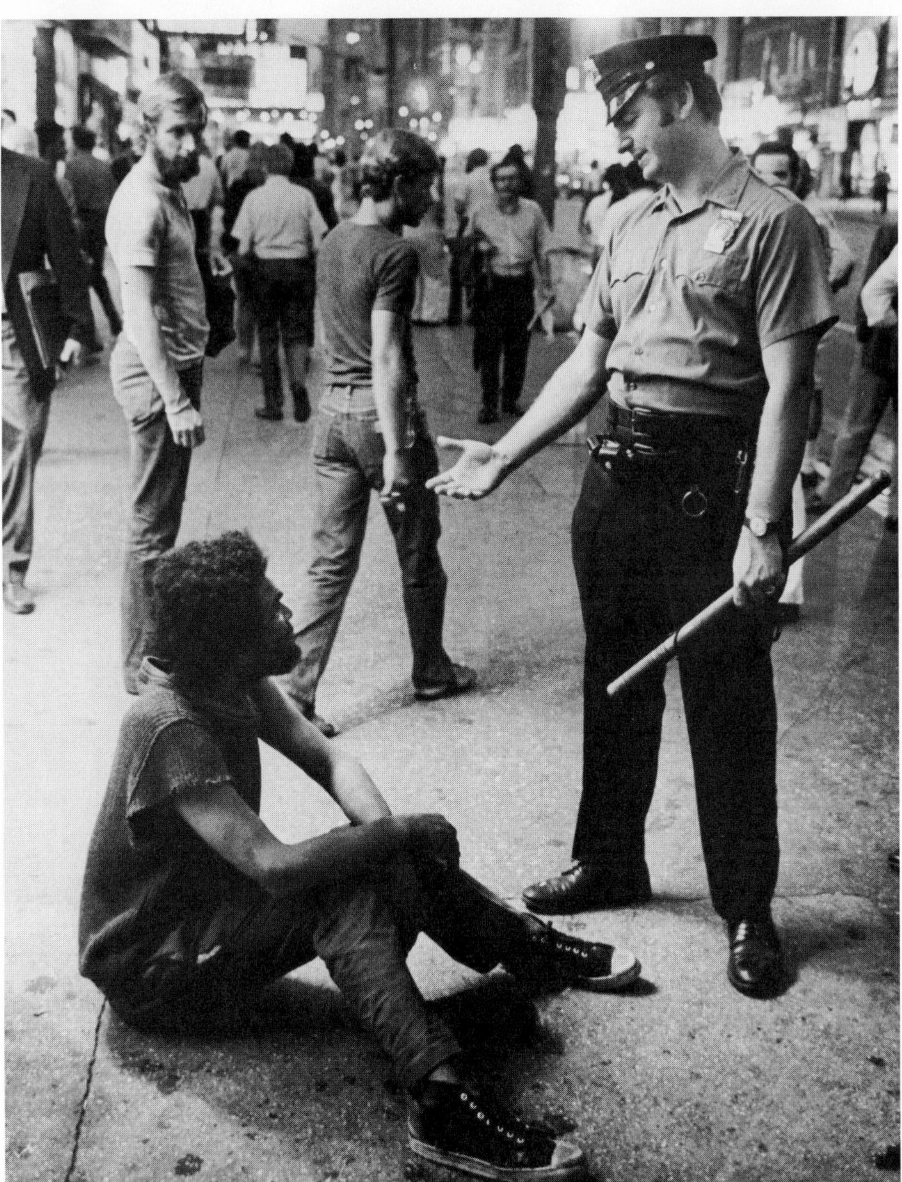

Foot patrol requires the police to confront citizens who are not at their best.

but this assumption poses a basic problem for the police administrator: Where do you send the troops and in what numbers? There are no precise guidelines that help to answer this question, and most allocation decisions seem to be based on the assumption that patrol should be concentrated where the crime is occurring. Thus crime statistics, the degree of industrialization, pressures from business people, ethnic composition, and socioeconomic characteristics are the major factors determining the distribution of police resources. Decisions based on such factors may lead to a self-fulfilling prophecy: the more patrol officers in an area, the more criminal behavior they will find.

preventive patrol The activity of providing regular protection to an area while maintaining a mobile police presence for the purpose of deterring potential criminals from committing crimes.

Preventive patrol has long been held to be an important deterrent to crime. In 1972 this assumption was tested in Kansas City, Missouri, with surprising results. A fifteen-beat area was divided into three sections, with careful consideration given to ensure similarity in crime rates, population characteristics, income levels, and calls for police service. In one area, designated "reactive," all preventive patrol was withdrawn and the police entered only in response to citizens' calls for service. In another, labeled "proactive," preventive patrol was raised to four times the normal level, and all other services were provided at the preexperimental levels. The third section was used as a control, and the department maintained the usual level of services, including preventive patrol. The Kansas City project concluded that there were no significant differences in the amount of crime reported, the amount of crime measured by citizen surveys, and the extent to which citizens feared criminal attack.[12]

The authors of the study emphasized the tentative nature of their finding that although 60 percent of officer time in all three areas was available for active patrolling, only 14.2 percent was spent in this manner. The officers were engaged instead in such administrative chores as report writing and in other matters unrelated to patrolling. This and other studies of preventive patrol have been strongly criticized as attacking the heart of police work. What the research did was to call into question the inflexibility of traditional preventive patrol, and its findings have led some departments to try new approaches.

Response time. The image of the patrol officer on the beat is enshrined in American folklore. During the last twenty years, however, with increased use of the squad car, the foot patrol officer has almost disappeared from many cities. With most officers in squad cars and with most citizens having ready access to a telephone, modern patrol tactics are based on the assumption that calls for assistance will come to a central dispatching section of the depart-

Patrol in Baywood

In a city of 400,000 persons with a police force of 900 sworn officers, a study was conducted of the 599,211 individual assignments of the patrol division during a fifty-four-week period. Each assignment to which a patrol officer was dispatched—be it a homicide, abandoned vehicle, barking dog, or rest break—was recorded and timed. A total of 109 types of events were reduced to six categories.

	Frequency (percentage)	*Consumed time (percentage)*
Crimes against persons	2.82	2.96
Crimes against property	13.76	14.82
Traffic	7.16	9.20
On-view (officer-initiated)	19.68	9.10
Social services	17.27	13.70
Administration (includes coffee breaks, meals, taking reports, running errands, attending court, serving warrants)	39.28	50.19

Source: John A. Webster, "Police Task and Time Study," *Journal of Criminal Law, Criminology, and Police Science* 61 (March 1970): 95.

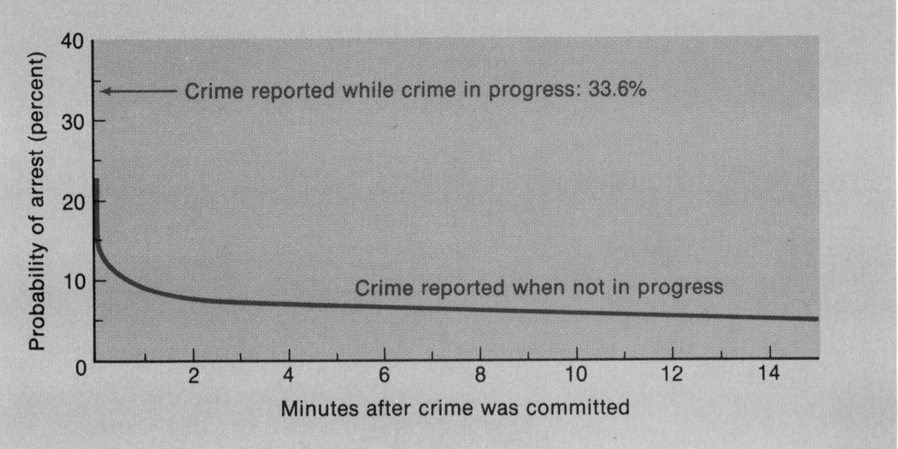

FIGURE 6.2
The probability of an arrest declines sharply if the incident is not reported to the police within seconds after a confrontational crime.

ment, and from there officers will be directed to the site of the incident. It has been argued that because motorized officers are patrolling an area, they can respond rapidly to a call for help.

A study completed in Kansas City in 1977 and since replicated in Peoria (Illinois), Jacksonville (Florida), Rochester (New York), and San Diego (California) measured the impact of police response time on the ability of officers to intercept a crime in progress and arrest the criminal. The researchers found that the police were successful in only 29 of 1,000 cases, and it made little difference whether they arrived in two minutes or twenty: as figure 6.2 indicates, the crucial factor was the speed with which citizens called the police.[13]

Detractors of motorized patrol say that the value of the automobile's range, flexibility, and speed is lost if citizens are the delaying factor. As Lawrence W. Sherman says, the rise of motorized patrol and telephone dispatch has changed the older strategy of "watching to prevent crime" to "waiting to respond to crime."[14] He believes that the officer in the patrol car is not attentive to the beat and is isolated from citizen contact. If it is also shown that the value of rapid response is lost because victims or observers do not call quickly, the entire strategy is brought into question.

If the problem of response time is one of citizen delay, it might be possible to develop education programs or technological innovations that would reduce reporting time, but it appears that such strategies would not appreciably improve crime control through arrest. As William Spelman and Dale Brown point out, there are three reasons for delay in calling the police. Some people find the situation *ambiguous*—they want to make sure that the police should be called. Others are too busily engaged in *coping activities*—taking care of the victim, directing traffic, and generally helping out—that they are unable to leave the scene. Still others experience *conflict* that they must first resolve—they may avoid making an immediate decision or may seek the advice of someone else before placing a call. In addition to these decision-making delays, there are communications problems: a phone may not be readily available, the person may not know the correct number to call, the police complaint taker may not be cooperative. But as figure 6.3 shows, the elimination of these problems would only marginally increase the police's ability to make an arrest.

Close-up: Saturday Night in a Squad Car

Car 120 covers an area one-half mile wide by one mile long in the heart of downtown Minneapolis. Bisecting the district along its long axis is Hennepin Avenue, a street lined with bars, nightclubs, and movie theaters. South of Hennepin Avenue lie the shopping and business areas of Minneapolis; north of Hennepin are warehouses and older office buildings. At the east end of the district lies the Mississippi River, and along it, just north of Hennepin Avenue, is the Burlington Northern Railway Station. That portion of the district is heavily populated with derelict alcoholics.

6:45 We saw some derelicts drinking wine, and the officers forced them to pour the wine out.

7:00 9____ West Franklin, Apt. ____, unwanted guest. The caretakers of the apartment building advised us that the ex-husband of one of their tenants was threatening harm to the tenant and abduction of the tenant's child. He had also threatened the babysitter. We determined the kind of car that the ex-husband was driving. The tenant then returned with a friend and asked us to keep out of the area so that her husband would not be afraid to find her. She then hoped to tell him that the divorce was final and that he ought not to bother her any more.

7:50 Cassius Bar, fight. It had been settled by the time we arrived.

7:58 ____ Cafe, domestic. A 20-year-old girl and her sister-in-law met us and advised us that the girl's stepfather, the proprietor of the cafe, had let the air out of the tires of the girl's car. He had also pulled loose some wires under the hood and then blocked their car with his. All of this had occurred in the cafe's parking lot. She also claimed that he had hit her. We talked to the stepfather and mother of the girl, and they said that they had taken this action in order to prevent the girl from driving to Wisconsin until she had cooled down. They claimed that she had had a fight with her husband, that she wanted to get away by driving to see her grandmother in Wisconsin, and that she was too emotionally upset to drive. This was apparently evidenced by the fact that she was willing to take her baby with her in only a short-sleeved shirt. The mother also told us that the girl was a bad driver with many arrests and that the car wasn't safe. The officers advised the girl that she could call a tow truck and that, if she wished, she could sign a complaint against her parents in the morning. We then left.

8:28 ____ Cafe, "settle it this time." The sister-in-law claimed that she had been verbally abused by the stepfather. The officers decided to wait until the tow truck arrived. The stepfather moved the car that was blocking. The parents of the girl began to criticize the officer in sarcastic terms, saying such things as, "Isn't it a shame that the police have nothing better to do than to spend hours helping to start a car." They also threatened not to give half-price food to police officers any more. The tow truck arrived and reinflated the tires of the car. However, the tow truck driver was unable to start the car. The stepfather, although advised by one of the officers not to do so, tried to move his car in a position to block his daughter's car. The officer at that point booked him for reckless driving and failure to obey a lawful police order. The officer had the stepfather's car towed away. Another squad car came to sit on the situation until the tow truck had moved the girl's car to a service station. We took the stepfather to jail, where he immediately arranged to bail himself. The stepfather said that he was going right back. The officer replied, "We can book you more than you've got money." As soon as we left the police station, we went back to the parking lot and found that the girl's car had been started and that she had left town.

9:55 ____ Spruce, Apt. ____ unwanted guest. The tenant told us that she had been ill and that she had not opened the door when her landlady knocked. The landlady then had opened the door and walked in. The girl tenant was upset. The officers went to talk to the landlady and told her, "You can't just walk in. You are invading her privacy." The landlady replied, "The hell I can't, you damned hippie-lover. I'm going to call the mayor." "Go ahead," the officer said. He then added, "The next time this happens, we will advise the tenant to use a citizen's arrest on you."

10:35 We saw a woman crying outside a downtown bar and a man with his hands on her. We stopped but were told by both that this was merely a domestic situation.

10:50 The officers saw a drunk in an alley, awakened him and sent him on his way.

10:55 We saw a door open in a downtown automobile dealership. When we checked, we learned that all the employees were there to carry out an inventory.

11:15 As we drove by an area near the University, which was known as a gathering place for the disaffected young, we noticed an elderly man in a car talking to a number of rather rough-looking motorcycle types. We stopped and learned from the motorcyclists that the man was very intoxicated. They offered to drive the car for him to a parking spot, and the officers allowed them to do this. The man was told by the officers to sleep off his drunk condition, and the officers took the keys from the car and threw them into the trunk so that he would be unable to drive further that evening.

11:45 15th and Hawthorne, gang fight. When we arrived, the officers from two other squad cars were busy booking some young men. The officers believed that occupants of the top floor of the building adjoining this corner had been throwing things at them. When the landlord refused admittance to that building, the officers broke the door down. The apartment from which the objects had been thrown was locked, and the tenants refused admittance. Again, the officers broke down the door and booked the occupants.

12:25 Nicollet Hotel, blocked alley. By the time we arrived, the car which had blocked the alley had been driven away.

12:55 11th and LaSalle, take a stolen [police radio slang]. We made a report of a stolen automobile.

1:22 As we were driving through a lower-class apartment neighborhood, we saw one woman and two men standing outside an apartment building. The men appeared to be fighting. One man and the woman said that the other man was bothering them. We sent him away. The couple then went into an apartment building. As we drove away, we saw the man who had been sent returning and trying to obtain entrance to the apartment building. We returned and booked him as a public drunk.

1:45 Continental Hotel, see a robbery victim. We took a report from a young man who had been robbed at knife point. We drove around the neighborhood looking, without success, for his assailant.

Source: Joseph M. Livermore, "Policing," 55 *Minnesota Law Review* 672–74 (1971). Reprinted by permission.

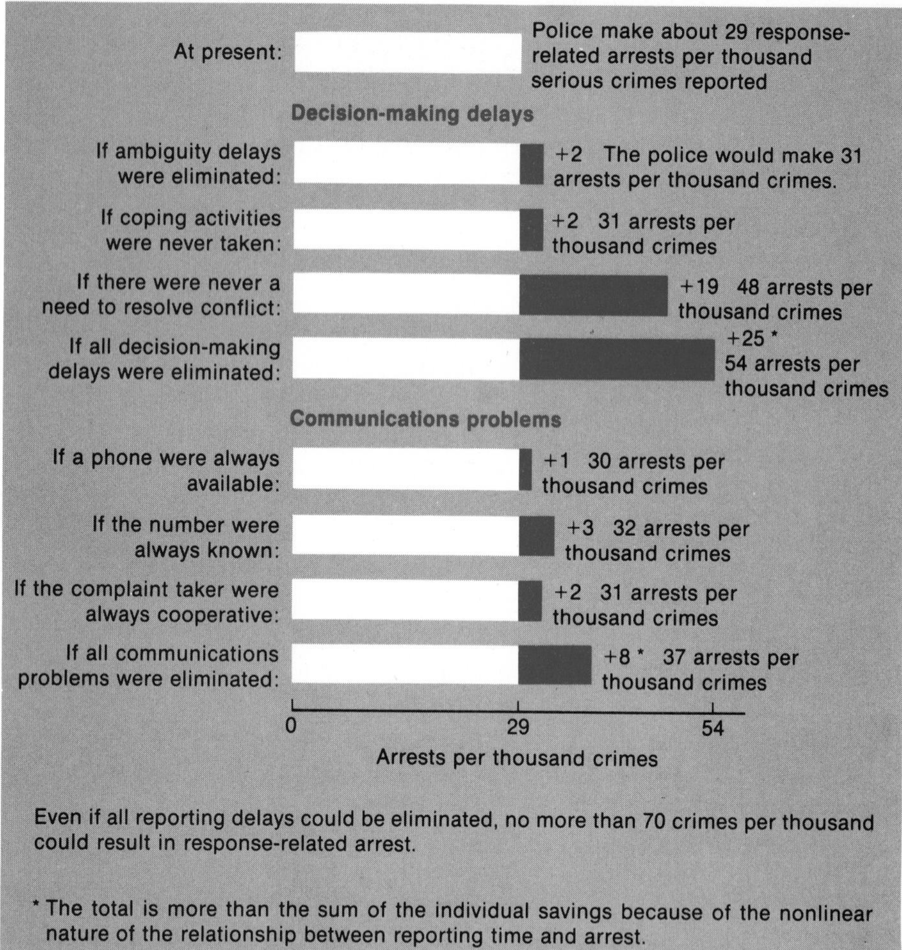
At present:
Police make about 29 response-related arrests per thousand serious crimes reported
Decision-making delays
If ambiguity delays were eliminated:
+2 The police would make 31 arrests per thousand crimes.
If coping activities were never taken:
+2 31 arrests per thousand crimes
If there were never a need to resolve conflict:
+19 48 arrests per thousand crimes
If all decision-making delays were eliminated:
+25 * 54 arrests per thousand crimes
Communications problems
If a phone were always available:
+1 30 arrests per thousand crimes
If the number were always known:
+3 32 arrests per thousand crimes
If the complaint taker were always cooperative:
+2 31 arrests per thousand crimes
If all communications problems were eliminated:
+8 * 37 arrests per thousand crimes
0
29
54
Arrests per thousand crimes
Even if all reporting delays could be eliminated, no more than 70 crimes per thousand could result in response-related arrest.
* The total is more than the sum of the individual savings because of the nonlinear nature of the relationship between reporting time and arrest.

FIGURE 6.3
Potential increases in response-related arrests as a result of elimination of important causes of delay

In the majority of cases the police are in a reactive situation, and the environmental context of the illegal act greatly hampers their ability to respond to it.[15]

Recognition that giving a high priority to rapid response to all calls for police assistance is unproductive has led to the development of differential response strategies. Such strategies are based on the premise that it is not always necessary to rush a patrol car out when a call is received. When calls are classified by immediacy of need, priorities can be assigned. It has been found that a delayed response is often just as effective as a very prompt one, and that callers are satisfied as long as they know what to expect. It is also recognized that a patrol car on the scene is not always essential, for there can be alternative ways of handling a problem, such as referral to another agency, a telephone response, or the sending of nonsworn personnel to the scene.

Studies carried out in Garden Grove (California), Greensboro (North Carolina), and Toledo (Ohio) have shown the effectiveness of differential police response. In Greensboro, 46.4 percent of all calls were categorized as eligible for a response other than the immediate dispatch of a patrol car; similar results were found in the other test sites.[16] Differential police response permits resources to be saved because patrol units are not diverted to nonemergency situations.

Foot patrol versus motorized patrol. One of the most frequent requests of citizens is that the officer be put back on the beat. They claim that patrol officers in squad cars have become remote from the people they protect. During the 1960s such cries were especially strong because racial upheavals were thought to have been intensified in part by the fact that white officers and the residents of black neighborhoods did not have close physical contact. Because patrol officers were not familiar faces, they were perceived as symbols of oppression. Many people believe that the patrol officer on foot is at home in the neighborhood and can more readily spot circumstances and people that warrant investigation. When patrol officers are close to the daily life of the beat, they are in a better position to detect criminal activity and to apprehend those who have violated the law.

There are, however, definite limitations to the exclusive use of foot patrol officers. Not only are they unable to cover as great an area as their motorized counterparts but they take longer to respond. In heavy snow and rain they are almost ineffective. Increasingly cities are using a mixed force, assigning foot patrols to high-crime and downtown areas, where their presence is an important deterrent. With development of the compact walkie-talkie, foot patrol officers on the beat can now be linked to the communications center at headquarters and directed to wherever they are needed.

The past decade has seen a revival of foot patrol. Part of the new interest may be a reaction to the research discussed above and the annual cost of keeping a patrol car on the street twenty-four hours a day ($180,000 for a two-officer car, with salaries around $15,000), but citizens' demands for a familiar figure walking their neighborhoods have perhaps been a greater factor.[17]

The best evidence that citizens want foot patrols is probably seen in the experience of Flint, Michigan, where despite the highest unemployment rate in the nation, citizens voted in 1981 to increase taxes in order to extend an experimental program to the entire city. In 1979 fourteen city beats had been designated for foot patrol. The three-year results showed that crime on those beats went down about 19 percent overall. And although robberies and burglaries increased in the city as a whole, even these crimes did not increase at the same rate on the experimental beats. Foot-beat residents rated their officers more effective than car-bound patrol officers, rating the motorized division higher only in its ability to respond quickly in emergencies. Sixty-four percent of the foot-beat residents were happy with the patrol program, and 70 percent said that they felt safer in their neighborhoods because of it. But as

A View from a Patrol Car, A View of a Patrol Car

What the patrol car officer sees is familiar buildings with unfamiliar people around them. What the public sees is a familiar police car with an unfamiliar officer in it. The public has little chance to tell the officer what is going on in the community: who is angry at whom about what, whose children are running wild, what threats have been made, and who is suddenly living above his apparent means. Stripped of this contextual knowledge, the patrol car officer sees, but cannot truly observe.

Source: Lawrence W. Sherman, "Patrol Strategies for Police," in *Crime and Public Policy*, ed. James Q. Wilson (San Francisco: ICS Press, 1983), p. 149.

Robert Trojanowicz, evaluator of the Flint experiment, points out, "if an officer's walking along [the beat] in the traditional way, he won't affect the crime rate. Patrolmen who operate that way are just motorized officers without a car. Basically, they're doorshakers. But when the officer becomes actively involved in the community, that's when crime problems begin to be solved."[18]

One- versus two-person patrol units. As in the controversy over beat patrol officers, the question of one- or two-person patrol units has raged in law enforcement circles. Although the two-person squad car appears to be uneconomical, patrol officers and their union leaders argue that officer safety requires the second person. On the other side, police administrators claim that the one-person squad car is so much more cost-effective that more such squad cars can be deployed and thus each car can cover a smaller geographical sector, more sectors of the city can be covered, and response time can be decreased. A further belief is that an officer operating alone is more alert, as he cannot be distracted by idle conversation with a fellow officer. Research supports the conclusions of both sides. This matter is clearly one that needs to be settled practically, through negotiations between individual police chiefs and the leadership of the patrol officer's unions.

Team policing. During the 1960s, police administrators were confronted by community demands for more sensitive police and at the same time for better crime control. Because of the increased use of motorized patrols tied to a centralized communications system, many leaders felt that the police had

---

The One-Man—Two-Man Debate

On June 6, 1975, Police Officer Leland Anderson was shot to death with his own gun, in broad daylight, in downtown Austin, Tex., while attempting to arrest a suspect on a traffic warrant.

Anderson was the first officer killed in the line of duty in Austin since 1966, and his death caused an uproar. He was working alone at the time of his death. His fellow officers—and their wives—attributed his murder to this fact. After less than three weeks of newspaper publicity and negotiations with department administrators, city and police officials agreed to a 60-day experiment with two-man cars.

On July 9, the Austin Police Department converted overnight from all one-man to all two-man units. By September, the department brass had concluded that the experiment was not working. Using two-man cars had cut the number of units on the street in half, decreasing visibility, increasing response time and causing numerous other administrative problems. A mixture of one- and two-man units was adopted. But within a few weeks, that too was abandoned; all officers found themselves patroling their beats "solo" again. Police Association leaders argue to this day that two-man cars were not given a fair test in Austin. To properly test the concept would have required more manpower, more equipment, more flexibility in assignments and more training, they say. But they don't argue too long or too loud, because it turned out that a substantial number of Austin police officers didn't like two-man cars. The return to one-man units met no resistance.

The controversy over one- and two-man cars is dormant in Austin now. But it will no doubt arise again the next time an officer is hurt or killed who might—and the word is almost always "might"—have been saved if he had had a partner to protect him.

Source: Michael S. Serrill, "The One-Man, Two-Man Debate," *Police Magazine*, March 1978, pp. 20–21. Reprinted by permission of the Edna McConnell Clark Foundation.

become isolated from the community. ***Team policing*** (also known as neighborhood police team, basic car plan, and beat commander project) has been tried as a means of creating ties to the community that avoids both the inefficiencies of the traditional cop on the beat and the perceived insensitivity to neighborhood values of the motorized patrol. It is a community service model of patrol.

team policing
A police organizational strategy by which teams of generalists and specialists are assigned to defined geographical areas (neighborhoods).

Team policing means something different in almost every city in which it has been tried, but it universally contains four elements: (1) geographical stability of patrol, (2) the combining of patrol and investigative functions in one unit, (3) maximum interaction among team members, and (4) maximum communication between team members and the community. The patrol force is organized in one or more semi-independent teams, each based in a particular neighborhood. A team has primary responsibility for the delivery of police services to its neighborhood. The belief is that because a team is permanently assigned to a small area, citizens will identify with "their" police officers and the team will identify with "its" citizens. Thus team policing emphasizes interaction among team members and citizens for the exchange of information about the neighborhood. Informal sessions develop a team spirit that furthers effectiveness. In meetings with community members, the team passes on information to the citizenry in an attempt to bring about community involvement in the police function.

Because team policing departs greatly from traditional models of police organization, it has met with resistance in some quarters. It has been especially criticized by officers in middle-management positions who feel that development of the team encroaches on their influence and authority. The concept of team policing has been used as a basis for experimentation, but it has not been widely adopted on a sustained basis.

Aggressive patrol. In contrast with the community service model of team policing is the crime attack model of ***aggressive patrol.*** This strategy takes a wide variety of forms, from programs to encourage citizens to identify their valuables to "sting" operations. James Q. Wilson and Barbara Boland have shown that patrol tactics that increase the risk of arrest are associated with crime reduction.[19] They argue that the effect of the police on crime depends less on how many officers are deployed in a particular area than on what they do while they are there. Following an aggressive strategy, officers maximize the number of interventions and observations in the community. This does not mean that they are encouraged to patrol in a hostile manner, for such tactics could have the effect of merely arousing the community.

aggressive patrol
A patrol strategy designed to maximize the number of police interventions and observations in the community.

In San Diego it was found that an aggressive patrol strategy of field interrogations and street stops was associated with a significant decrease in certain "suppressible" crimes: robbery, burglary, theft, auto theft, assault, sex crimes, malicious mischief, disturbances. "It was concluded that field interrogations deterred potential offenders, especially young, opportunistic ones."[20] Officers in an "anticrime patrol" in New York worked the streets of high-crime areas in civilian clothes. Although these officers represented only 5 percent of the men and women assigned to each precinct, during one year they made over 18 percent of the felony arrests, including more than half of the arrests for robbery and about 40 percent of the arrests for burglary and auto theft. The Kansas City force adopted procedures to distribute information about the most active burglars and robbers to officers before they went on patrol and created a specialized unit to stake out locations known to be likely targets of criminal activities (say, the back room of a liquor store).

The most cost-effective strategy seems to be to create incentives so that officers on patrol will increase the number of field interrogations and traffic stops. As Wilson and Boland note, "to achieve an aggressive patrol strategy a police executive will recruit certain kinds of officers, train them in certain ways, and devise requirements and reward systems (traffic ticket quotas, field interrogation obligations, promotional opportunities) to encourage them to follow the intended strategy."[21]

The future of patrol. It is obvious that a great deal of research and thinking are going on with regard to patrol—the essential element of American policing. Preventive patrol and a rapid response to calls for assistance have been the hallmarks of policing in the United States for the past half century. Because of this orientation, most patrol officers have been placed in squad cars that are linked to a dispatcher at the station house. But the police are still highly dependent on the community to report the occurrence of a crime, to cooperate with police investigations, and to appear in court as witnesses. With-

Close-up: Split-Force Patrols Boost Efficiency

Police productivity went up and crime went down during an experimental police patrol program in Wilmington, Delaware.

The program—called "Split-Force"—is so promising that Wilmington Police Chief Harry F. Manelski and Wilmington Mayor William McLaughlin are continuing it with city funds now that LEAA [Law Enforcement Assistance Administration] seed money has run out.

Two units formed

Under the experiment, the patrol force—which comprised two-thirds of the Wilmington Bureau of Police total manpower—was split into two units.

The basic patrol unit—or call-for-service unit (CFS)—was assigned about 65 percent of the manpower. The remaining 35 percent of the patrol force was welded into a "structured force" or preventive patrol unit.

The police bureau conducted a crime analysis survey to determine when most of the calls came in, where the highest crime areas were, and what types of crimes were being most frequently committed in what areas.

Patrols reapportioned

By restructuring the twenty-four-hour day into a closer relationship to the crime patterns and calls for service, the police bureau reduced the number of cars assigned to patrol from 45 to 27, and went from two-man patrol car units to one-man cars without loss of safety. . . .

The 65 percent of the patrol force assigned to calls-for-service, the so-called basic patrol unit, handled only those calls except in emergencies, when the nearest units, including the preventive patrol units, moved in. Nonemergency calls were ranked according to priority, and the caller was told in advance when an officer would arrive.

When the basic patrol was not actually on calls-for-service, they stayed in geographical areas where they were most likely to receive calls. They might, for example, station themselves near a park or playground where there had been several child-molesting complaints.

Meanwhile, the structured force, or so-called prevention detail, concentrated on a directed, detailed assignment schedule that allowed them to work uninterrupted on cases.

"We might put a man in the back of a liquor

out the public's voluntary participation, the police may patrol indefinitely and have little impact on crime. The police's heavy orientation toward dispatch and preventive control may have narrowed the roles they play in the community.

The research conducted during the past twenty years has perhaps raised as many questions as it has answered. It is apparent, however, that police forces in large cities need to consider a mix of patrol tactics that fit the demographic and criminogenic characteristics of various neighborhoods. Many researchers also believe that patrol operations have focused too narrowly on crime control in recent decades, to the neglect of the order-maintenance activities for which the police were originally formed.

Investigation

The fictional Sherlock Holmes has long epitomized the detective in the public's eyes. With a minimum of clues, an intuitive mind, and a careful application of logic, he and his counterparts in thousands of dramas stalk the criminal until an arrest is made in the final moment. In the real world, how-

store that has been held up several times," said Nicholas Valiante, inspector of operations for the Wilmington Bureau of Police and project director. "He was to be there eight hours a day and that was that. We knew where he was."

"We would find that a lot of citizens band radios were being stolen out of cars in a certain area. So we would set up a decoy car with a large, conspicuous antenna on it. As soon as the thief moved in, our structured force moved in. We would not only get him for that theft, but through his fingerprints often clear up a lot of similar CB thefts."

Inspector Valiante said officer productivity went up 20.6 percent. He said for the four months preceding the formation of the structured preventive patrol force, Part I crime levels increased 10 percent in Wilmington (Part I crimes consist of about 90 percent of all the felony offenses).

He said for the last eight months of the experiment, Part I crimes decreased 25 percent. During 1976, Part I crimes decreased 18.6 percent. Comparing the first eight months of 1977 with the first eight months of 1976, there was another 2 percent decrease in Part I crime.

Productivity increased

Dr. James M. Tien, [responsible for evaluation of] the experiment, said he felt the two most significant results were that productivity by the officers was up 20 percent—less manpower doing the same amount of work—and that the structured force has the potential to bridge the traditional gap between basic police patrol and detectives.

"You have more immediate follow-up by your structured force and your clean-up rate on the cases naturally goes up," he said. . . .

In his conclusions, Dr. Tien said: "The split-force patrol approach causes significant increase in call-for-service response productivity. The very act of forming a dedicated, prevention-oriented patrol force causes the remaining, response-oriented basic force to be more efficient, without compromising its effectiveness."

Source: *LEAA Newsletter 6* (December 1977): 10–11.

TABLE 6.1 Percentage of convictions by elapsed time from offense to arrest

Elapsed time	*Robbery*	*Larceny*	*Burglary*
0–5 minutes	38%	34%	43%
6–30 minutes	36	30	45
30 minutes to 24 hours	30	29	40
More than 24 hours	26	26	38

Source: U.S. Department of Justice, Bureau of Justice Statistics, *Report to the Nation on Crime and Justice* (Washington, D.C.: Government Printing Office, 1983), p. 51.

ever, the investigative function is not the sole responsibility of one bureau in a police department, let alone of one detective. Patrol, traffic, vice, and sometimes juvenile units contribute to this process. In fact, the patrol unit, because it is normally represented at the scene of the crime, accomplished much of the preliminary investigative work. The patrol unit's investigation can be crucial; as table 6.1 indicates, successful prosecution in cases of robbery, larceny, and burglary is closely linked with the speed with which a suspect is arrested. In many incidents, however, the criminal is not immediately apprehended, and investigation must be continued to determine who committed the crime and where the person is. This section looks at the investigative function—the special police units set up to achieve two objectives: the identification and apprehension of offenders and the collection of evidence with which to prosecute them.

A survey by the Rand Corporation revealed that every city with a population in excess of 250,000 and 90 percent of the smaller cities have officers specially assigned to investigative duties.[22] Traditionally, detectives have enjoyed a prestigious position in police departments. The pay is higher, the hours are more flexible, and the supervision is more permissive than those of patrol officers. Detectives do not wear uniforms, and their work is considered more interesting than the patrol officer's. In addition to these incentives, they are engaged solely in law enforcement rather than in order-maintenance or service work; hence their activities correspond more closely to the image of the police as crime fighters.

Detective responsibilities. Investigative units are normally separated from the patrol chain of command. Within the unit, detectives are frequently organized according to the type of crime they investigate—homicide, robbery, forgery—or by geographical area. Reported crimes are automatically referred to the appropriate investigator. One argument against separating investigation from patrol is that it results in duplication of effort and lack of continuity in the handling of cases. It often means that vital pieces of information held by one branch are not known to the other.

Detectives are concerned primarily with law enforcement activities after a crime has been reported and a preliminary investigation held. Their investigative activities depend on the circumstances of the case:

1. When a serious crime occurs and the offender is immediately identified and apprehended, the detective prepares the case for presentation to the prosecuting attorney.
2. When the offender is identified but not apprehended, the detective tries to locate the individual.

3. When the offender is not identified but there are several suspects, the detective conducts investigations aimed at either confirming or disproving his suspicions.
4. When there is no suspect, the detective starts from scratch to determine who committed the crime.[23]

In performing the investigative function, detectives depend not only on their own experience but on the technical expertise in their department or in a cooperating police force. They require information and must therefore rely on criminal history files, laboratory technicians, and forensic scientists. Many small departments turn to the state crime laboratory or the FBI for such information when serious crimes have been committed. Detectives are often pictured as working alone, but in fact they are members of a departmental team.

The apprehension process. Discovery that a crime has been committed is likely to set off a chain of events leading to the capture of a suspect and the gathering of the evidence required for the suspect's conviction. Unfortunately, it may also lead to a number of dead ends ranging from a decision by the victim not to report the crime to the absence of clues that point to a suspect or of evidence that links the suspect to the crime. Where some crimes are concerned, the probability is remote that the offender will be found, especially if there is delay between commission of the crime and arrival of the police.

As figure 6.4 shows, the felony apprehension process may be viewed as a sequence of actions taken in response to the commission of a crime. The actions are designed to mount the resources of criminal justice to bring about the arrest of a suspect and to assemble enough supporting evidence to substantiate a charge.

FIGURE 6.4
The apprehension process

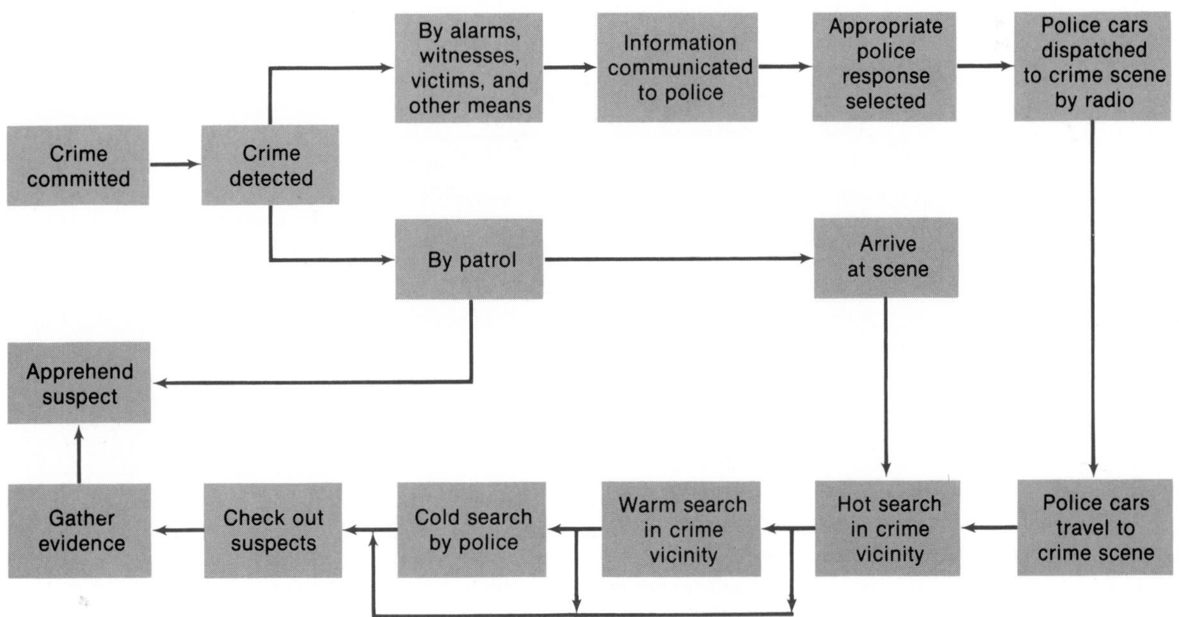

1. *Crime detected.* Information that a crime has been committed usually comes in the form of a telephone call by the victim or complainant to the police. The patrol officer on the beat may also come upon a crime, but usually the police are alerted by others. In some cities, police are alerted to crime in business premises by automatic security alarms that are connected to police headquarters so that response time can be shortened. Studies have shown that in cases of such crimes as burglary and robbery, the likelihood of apprehending the perpetrator declines rapidly as the elapsed time passes eight minutes.

2. *Preliminary investigation.* The first law enforcement official on the scene is usually a patrol officer who has been dispatched by radio. The officer is thus responsible for providing aid to the victim, for securing the crime scene for later investigation, and for beginning to document the facts of the crime. If a suspect is present or in the vicinity, the officer conducts a "hot" search and possibly apprehends a suspect. This work is crucial because the information gathered during this initial phase is essential. These data concern the basic facts of the crime, including identity of the victim, description of the suspect, and names of witnesses. After the information is collected, it is transmitted to the investigation unit.

3. *Follow-up investigation.* After a crime has been brought to the attention of the police and a preliminary investigation has been made, further action is determined by a detective. In the typical big-city department, incident reports from the previous day are analyzed the first thing in the morning. Assignments are distributed to individual investigators in accordance with their specialties. These investigators study the information, weigh each informational factor in accordance with a formula, and determine whether the factors present are sufficient to indicate that the crime can be solved.

In Fremont, California, a disposition decisional rule was created for burglaries.[24] As table 6.2 indicates, if the total score of the informational factors was 10 or less, further action on the case was suspended. A study of the Kansas City (Missouri) Police Department showed that although homicide, rape, and suicide received considerable attention, less than 50 percent of all reported crimes received more than a minimal half-hour's investigation by detectives. In many of these cases, detectives merely reported the facts discovered by the patrol officers during the preliminary investigations.[25]

TABLE 6.2 Case disposition decision rule: burglary

Information element	*Weighting factor*
Estimated range of time of occurrence	
Less than 1 hour	5
1 to 12 hours	1
12 to 24 hours	0.3
More than 24 hours	0
Witness' report of offense	7
On-view report of offense	1
Usable fingerprints	7
Suspect information developed—description or name	9
Vehicle description	0.1
Other	0
Total Score	

Note: If the sum is less than or equal to 10, suspend the case; otherwise, follow up the case.
Source: Peter B. Bloch and Donald R. Weidman, *Managing Criminal Investigations* (Washington, D.C.: Government Printing Office, 1975), p. 33.

Detectives must make a number of discretionary decisions concerning any investigation. As already noted, a decision must be made about whether the preliminary investigation has produced enough information to warrant a follow-up investigation. Decisions have also to be made about the crime categories that should receive special attention and when an investigation should be discontinued.

When a full-scale investigation is thought warranted, a wider search—referred to as a "cold" search—for evidence or weapons is undertaken: witnesses may be reinterviewed, contact made with informants, and evidence assembled for analysis. The pressure of new cases, however, often requires an investigation in progress to be shelved so that resources may be directed at "warmer" incidents.

4. *Clearance and arrest.* The decision to arrest is a key part of the apprehension process. In some cases, additional evidence or links between suspects and their associates are not discovered if arrests are premature. Once in custody, suspects may be interrogated to determine whether they can provide information that will clear additional crimes. As previously discussed, police departments use the clearance rate as a measure of their effectiveness in solving crimes. A crime is cleared when evidence supports the arrest of a suspect or when a suspect admits to having committed other unsolved offenses in department files. Clearance, then, does not mean that the suspect will eventually be found guilty. Clearance rates are easily manipulated for administrative purposes and must be read with caution.

Evaluating investigation. During the past few years a number of studies have raised important questions about the value of investigations and the role detectives play in the apprehension process. This research tends to downplay the importance of investigation as a means of solving crimes and shows that most crimes are cleared because of arrests made by the patrol force at or near the scene. The President's Commission notes, "If a suspect is neither known to the victim nor arrested at the scene of the crime, the chances of ever arresting him are very slim."[26] Response time—the speed with which police can arrive at a crime scene—becomes an important factor in the apprehension process. Table 6.3 shows that detectives investigate practically all serious crimes, but, as figure 6.5 indicates, large numbers of crimes against persons and a great majority of crimes against property are never cleared. Not only is response time important; the information given by the victim or witnesses to the responding patrol officer is crucial.

A Rand Corporation study of 153 large police departments found that the major determinant of success in solving crimes was information identifying the perpetrator supplied by the victim or witnesses at the scene. Of those cases not immediately solved but ultimately cleared, most were cleared by such routine procedures as fingerprint searches, receipt of tips from informants, and mug-shot "show-ups." The report emphasizes that special actions by the investigating staff were important in only a very few cases. In summary, the study indicates that about 30 percent of the crimes were cleared by on-scene arrest and another 50 percent by the identification of victims or witnesses when the police arrived. Thus only about 20 percent could have been solved by detective work. But even among this group, the study found that most "were also solved by patrol officers, members of the public who spontaneously provide further information, or routine investigative practices."[27]

If the accumulating evidence should force a reassessment of the role of

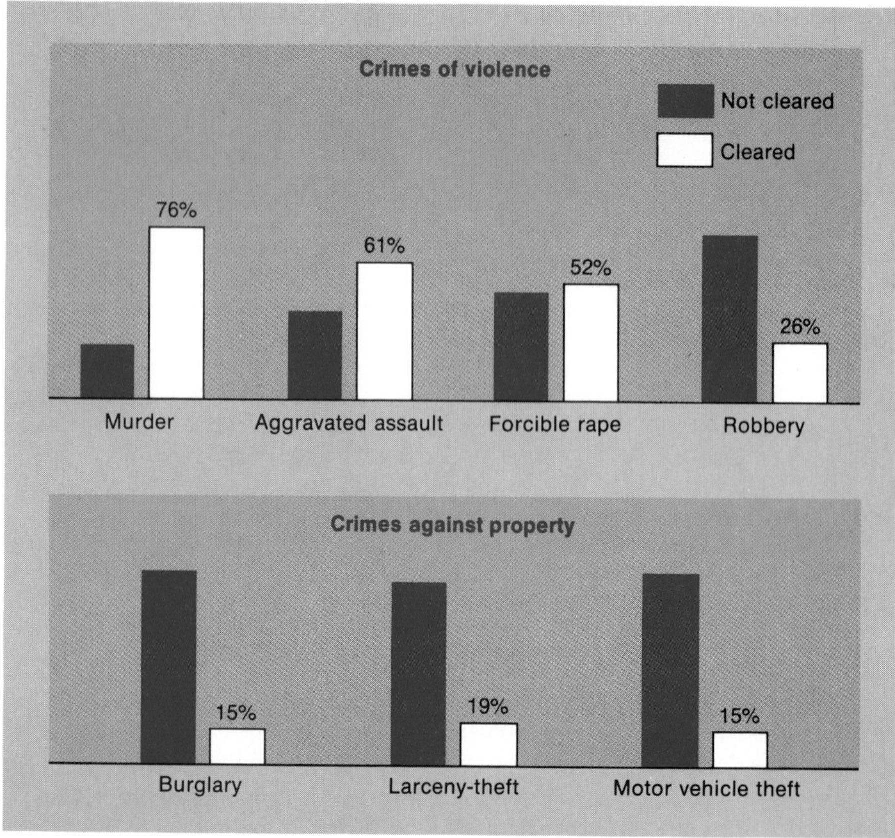

FIGURE 6.5
Crimes cleared by arrest

TABLE 6.3 Percentage of reported cases worked on by detectives

Type of incident	*Percentage*
Homicide	100.0
Rape	100.0
Suicide	100.0
Forgery/counterfeiting	90.4
Kidnapping	73.3
Arson	70.4
Auto theft	65.5
Aggravated assault	64.4
Robbery	62.6
Fraud/embezzlement	59.6
Felony sex crimes	59.0
Common assault	41.8
Nonresidential burglary	36.3
Dead body	35.7
Residential burglary	30.0
Larceny	18.4
Vandalism	6.8
Lost property	0.9
All above types together	32.4

Source: Peter W. Greenwood and Joan Petersilia, *The Criminal Investigation Process*, vol. 1: *Summary and Policy Implications* (Washington, D.C.: Government Printing Office, 1975), p. 14.

investigation, what policies might law enforcement officials adopt? The Rand research team suggests a number of reforms, including the following six:

1. Reduce follow-up investigation on all cases except those involving the most serious offenses.
2. Assign generalist-investigators (who would handle the obvious leads in routine cases) to the local operations commander.
3. Establish a major-offenders unit to investigate serious crimes.
4. Assign serious-offense investigations to closely supervised teams rather than to individual investigators.
5. Employ strike forces selectively and judiciously.
6. Initiate programs designed to impress on the citizen the crucial role he plays in solving crimes.[28]

Whether or not such changes are made, of what importance is the detective to police operations? The detective's role is important in at least two respects (apart from the ability to solve crimes). First, the prestigious rank of detective provides a goal to which the patrol officer may aspire. Second, citizens expect investigations to be carried out. As Herman Goldstein says: "One cannot dismiss lightly the public-relations value of detective work. It may fully justify the police resources that are invested. Persons treated sympathetically may offer greater assistance to the police in the future."[29]

It is clear that the realities of detective work do not match the myth, and to a large extent the belief that the investigator is the most important member of a police agency can have damaging repercussions. As a result of this myth, patrol officers may feel that their only job is to take reports, improper practices may be used to satisfy public expectations, and the citizenry may be lulled into believing that nothing more needs to be done once detectives take over. The realities of the crime problem, however, demand new responses to the traditional roles of law enforcement personnel.

Specialized operations

Patrol and investigation are the two largest and functionally most important units within a police department. In metropolitan areas, however, specialized units are set up to deal with particular types of problems; traffic, vice, and juvenile units are the most common, but in some cities separate units are also created to deal with organized crime and narcotics. The work of the specialized units should not be permitted to overshadow the fact that patrol and investigation also have a responsibility to deal with the same problems.

Traffic. Because almost everyone in the community is a pedestrian, passenger, or driver, almost everyone is affected by the problems associated with the use of the automobile. The police are required to regulate the flow of vehicles, to investigate accidents, and to enforce traffic laws. This work may not seem to fall within the category of crime fighting or maintenance of order, but certain dimensions of the task of traffic control lend themselves to these objectives. Enforcement of traffic laws contributes to the maintenance of order; it also educates the public in safe driving habits, and it provides a visible community service. As an enforcer of traffic laws, the patrol officer has an opportunity to stop vehicles and interrogate drivers, with the result that stolen property and suspects connected with other criminal acts are often discovered.

Most departments are now linked to communications systems that permit the checking of automobile and operator license numbers against lists of wanted vehicles and suspects.

Basically, the traffic-control function includes accident investigation, traffic direction, and enforcement. These functions overlap with the broader goal of public safety and accident prevention. For example, accident data and observations made by the patrol officer while on duty may contribute to the pinpointing of traffic hazards that require new safety devices or even highway reconstruction.

Authorities differ with regard to the work of a specialized unit dealing solely with traffic. Most suggest that traffic control is primarily a responsibility of the patrol division and that personnel of the traffic unit should be limited to educational and preventive functions. Some argue that overemphasis on traffic-control work through specialized line units can lead to morale problems owing to the privileged nature of motorcycle work and can drain resources from more important patrol duties. In some cities, the police have hired civilians to deal with nonmoving and parking violations as a way to make better use of resources. Nevertheless, in many cities police units that are assigned primarily to traffic-control duties concurrently perform patrol functions.

Enforcement of traffic regulations provides one of the best examples of police discretion. This work is essentially proactive, and the level of enforcement may be considered a direct result of departmental policies and norms. Selective enforcement is the general policy, since the police have neither the desire nor the resources to enforce all traffic laws. As a consequence, many departments target particular intersections or highways for stiff enforcement, maintaining a visible presence as a deterrent to speeding motorists. As table 6.4 shows, Wilson found a wide range in the number of tickets for moving violations issued by the eight departments he studied.[30] Although some differences may be explained by the physical conditions and highway patterns of a city, the range also results from the resources allocated to traffic control and the importance that a police chief places on this function, which in turn is a reflection of community and political values.

TABLE 6.4 Tickets issued for moving traffic violations by eight departments and rate per 1,000 population

	Tickets for moving violations	
City	*Number*	*Rate per 1,000*
Albany	1,368	11.4
Amsterdam	460	16.4
Newburgh	1,226	40.9
Brighton	1,829	61.0
Nassau County	68,375	61.0
Highland Park	2,933	97.8
Syracuse	23,465	109.1
Oakland	90,917	247.7

Source: James Q. Wilson, *Varieties of Police Behavior* (Cambridge: Harvard University Press, 1968), p. 95.

Traffic law enforcement is one of the areas in which police departments employ measures of productivity. Although few administrators will admit that they employ quota systems, officers seem to understand what is expected of them; that is one reason why traffic work is preferred to patrol. As Wilson notes, the traffic officer "has clearer, less ambiguous objectives, he need not 'get involved' in family fights or other hard-to-manage situations, and he need not make hard-to-defend judgments about what people deserve."[31] One traffic patrol officer told an interviewer:

> I was in patrol for nine years, and as far as I'm concerned you can have it. You've got all those messy details; you're called in on cheatings and stabbings, family fights and quarrels; you're chasing kids. You never know what's going to happen next, and not all of it is very pleasant. When you get in a traffic enforcement unit you know exactly what's expected of you, and what you have to do; then you can do your work and that's it.[32]

Vice. Enforcement of laws against vice—prostitution, gambling, narcotics, and so forth—is dependent on proactive police work that is itself often dependent on the use of undercover agents and informers. Because of the nature of the crimes, political influence is sometimes brought to bear to dampen law enforcement efforts. At the same time, vigorous enforcement of the laws against vice requires that individual police officers be given wide latitude in the exercise of discretion. Often they are obliged "to engage in illegal and often degrading practices that must be concealed from the public."[33] The potential for corruption in this type of police work presents a number of administrative dilemmas.

A specialized vice-control unit is a part of most large city departments. Regardless of the department's size, however, it is important that the police chief closely supervise this unit and that adequate controls be maintained to ensure that the department's integrity is not compromised. The special nature of vice work requires the members of the unit to be well trained in the legal procedures that must be followed if arrests are to lead to convictions. In addition, personnel are subject to transfer when their identities become known and their effectiveness is lost.

Officers engaged in vice-control operations depend heavily on informants. Thus one of the major problems with these operations is that a mutually satisfactory relationship may develop between the law enforcer and the law violator. In the field of narcotics control, addicts may provide information on sellers. Frequently they are also used as decoys to help trap sellers—a practice that is of questionable legality. In exchange for cooperating with the police, addicts are sometimes rewarded by being given small amounts of drugs, freedom from prosecution for possession, or police recommendations for leniency should they be sentenced. These practices result in a paradox: the police tolerate certain levels of vice in exchange for information that will enable them to arrest other people for engaging in the same behavior they tolerate in the informant.

Police actions and the rule of law

To repeat, in a democratic society the police are expected to control crime within the framework of the law. Throughout the law enforcement processes of detection, apprehension, and arrest, police officers are required to perform their tasks in ways that conform to the law as specified in the United States Constitution, individual state constitutions, statutes passed by legislatures, and the interpretations of the courts. As chapter 3 explained, the ideals of the rule of law and due process aim to ensure that justice is accorded to all citizens and that officials of the state do not use their power to thwart the law. Three police practices—search and seizure, arrest, and interrogation—are specially structured to ensure that the rule of law is upheld and that the rights of citizens are protected. Although many police officers complain that they have been handcuffed by the courts, this may be one of the prices to be paid to maintain freedom in a democratic society.

The Fourth and Fifth Amendments and to some extent the Sixth are the major articles of the Constitution that bear directly on police activities. The Fourth protects citizens from unreasonable searches and seizures, the Fifth protects them from being compelled to testify against themselves, and the Sixth upholds the right to counsel. While Earl Warren was chief justice of the

Close-up: Police Decoys Shield the Helpless

That derelict slumped in the dank doorway, her purse spilled open, may have a pistol in her pocket. Since 1970 the streets of New York City have been infiltrated by police decoys. The program has paid off, with a drop in crime against the elderly and against taxi drivers, and an arrest rate that is rising.

There are 250 men and women in the decoy program. All alternate between decoys and back-up or defense officer. Scheduling consists of a few procedural films and lectures, but most of it is conducted on the street itself, as trainees accompany a real decoy team.

A night's tour of duty begins at headquarters on Randall's Island. There decoys such as Officer Maureen DeStasio pick up their disguises. Officer DeStasio, one of ten women in the program and a decoy with eighty arrests so far this year, joined the squad four years ago after she herself was mugged. Her eighteen-year-old daughter hopes to follow in her professional footsteps.

Later that evening decoys and back-up teams will emerge from dusty, unmarked police cars or taxicabs all over the city as convention delegates, foreign sailors in uniform, Con Edison employees, street toughs, ice cream vendors, and a host of other characters familiar to the city's night scene. Decoys are no longer allowed to impersonate American servicemen or the clergy—"two of our best marks," one policeman said wistfully.

At 10:15 three officers are on the street, looking for a good spot on a deserted block in the theater district. "There's a beautiful doorstep," Officer DeStasio says, "I've got to set up there one night, no doubt about it." Her usual decoy's step has a drunken student stretched across it. "That's Bert," Officer Monahan says. Officer Bert Salerno, a fledgling decoy, is reluctant to move. "He wants to get hit once," Officer DeStasio says sympathetically. But Officer Salerno is persuaded to take his turn as a back-up. "Suit up, Mo," Officer Monahan says to Officer DeStasio.

The policewoman pulls a disheveled wig from her shopping bag and crams it over her reddish curls. A dingy scarf follows, hiding her gold earrings. Then come a decrepit coat and flopping shoes, and an aging woman derelict staggers from the station wagon, lurches past a seedy midtown hotel and collapses into a corner doorstep, newspapers fluttering at her feet, her purse open at her side with a lone dollar bill protruding from its flap.

Several pairs of eyes watch covertly as the

United States, the Supreme Court interpreted these rights to require the states to uphold these protections.

To make certain that the police would observe the provisions of the Bill of Rights, the Supreme Court emphasized two devices: the exclusionary rule and the Sixth Amendment's right to counsel. The exclusionary rule, first developed by the Court in 1914 (*Weeks* v. *United States*), stipulates that illegally seized evidence or improperly given confessions shall be excluded from trials. The argument is made that the government must not soil its hands by profiting from police abuses of the law. It is further stated that because of the rule, the police will be deterred from acting improperly. As an additional protection, the Sixth Amendment's provision of the right to counsel has been interpreted to mean that the defendant may have a lawyer not only in the courtroom but during the earlier proceedings, such as arraignment, even during interrogation in the station house. The provisions of the Bill of Rights, the decisions of the Supreme Court, and state laws may appear clear, but enough ambiguities exist to keep the police constantly aware that their actions in the

evening wears on. Two youths bounce down the block and a back-up man lounging casually against a parked truck whispers, "Looks like it." But the two youths pass by. Several minutes later a middle-aged couple stop. "Are you all right?" the man asks, bending over Officer DeStasio. His wife tucks the dollar bill back into her purse, clamps it shut and pushes it further under the derelict's arm and the couple walk on, shaking their heads. The policewoman quietly reopens the purse and slides it back to its original exposed position. . . . But twenty minutes later a figure emerges from the gloom, darts his hand into the purse and removes the protruding dollar bill.

Moving as quietly and as quickly as shadows, three back-ups converge on the slight, stoop-shouldered young man (his name is Ray) who will admit only that he is an unemployed truck driver. After searching him, Officer Abe Walton, a back-up man who has newly joined the team, drives the young man off to be booked.

By 12:10 A.M., sideline conversation turns to weekend fishing and the Broadway plays the officers have seen. A young couple passes Officer DeStasio and the man stops beyond her, turns back and suddenly dips into her purse. The back-ups press around him and surprised, he flattens against the wall. His teenaged girl companion clings to the edge of his leather jacket, her eyes open wide with fear, as he is searched and led away. Officer DeStasio removes her disguise and climbs into the back seat of the station wagon with the two others.

"Can't we make a deal?" the young man, Luis, an auto mechanic, asks as they pull up in front of the police station. "My wife Marta just arrived in New York. She doesn't even speak English." Officer DeStasio offers to drive the young weeping wife to her hotel, but she pleads to remain with her husband, then decides to wander off into the night alone, shoulders hunched. Luis screams after her. He is taken upstairs to be booked.

"You going to lock me up for this?" he asks incredulously. "I thought she was just a bum. You must catch people all the time who do like me."

"Not really," Officer Walton responds. "Only those who have larceny in their hearts."

Source: Jennifer Dunning, "Police Decoys Shield the Helpless," *New York Times*, 30 June 1977.

field or station house may jeopardize the building of a case strong enough to be prosecuted successfully.

Search and seizure

Evidence collected by the police in the course of an investigation must be gathered in accordance with the Fourth Amendment's strictures against unreasonable searches and seizures. It must be emphasized that the Supreme Court has prohibited *unreasonable* searches and seizures. This means that there are circumstances in which the police may indeed invade the privacy of a home or person. One such circumstance is the issuance of a search warrant.

A search warrant is an order from a court official allowing a police officer to search a designated place. The officer must go to the court, give *reasons* for the search, and describe the particular place to be searched and the persons or things to be seized. Searches conducted under the authority of a warrant are not unreasonable, but before a judge may grant the authority the officer must provide reliable information indicating that there is *probable cause* to believe that a crime has been or is being committed. In addition, the *particular* premises and pieces of property to be seized must be identified, and the officer must swear under oath that the facts given are correct. The police cannot obtain a search warrant that vaguely describes the evidence sought or the property to be searched.

In some circumstances, however, the interests of crime control dictate that the police conduct a search without a warrant, and it is here that the courts have been most active in defining the term *unreasonable.* Searches of five kinds may be conducted without a warrant and still be in accord with the Constitution: (1) searches incident to an arrest, (2) searches during field interrogation, (3) searches of automobiles under special conditions, (4) seizures of evidence that is in "plain view," and (5) searches when consent is given.

Incident to an arrest. When an officer has observed a crime or believes that one has been committed, an arrest may be made and a search conducted without a warrant. This does not mean that an arrest can be made as a pretext for a search. As the Supreme Court explained in *United States* v. *Robinson* (1973): "It is the fact of the lawful arrest which establishes the authority to search and we hold that in the case of a lawful custodial arrest a full search of the person is not only an exception to the warrant requirement of the Fourth Amendment, but is also a 'reasonable' search under that Amendment."[34]

In part, the rationale for this exception is the possibility that the suspect will destroy evidence unless swift action is taken. But in *Chimel* v. *California* (1969) the Supreme Court also said that such a search is limited to the person of the arrestee and the area within the arrestee's "immediate control," defined as that area "from within which he might [obtain] a weapon or something that

---

Fourth Amendment

The right of the people to be secure in their persons, houses, papers, and effects, against unreasonable searches and seizures, shall not be violated, and no Warrants shall issue, but upon probable cause, supported by Oath or affirmation, and particularly describing the place to be searched, and the persons or things to be seized.

---

could have been used as evidence against him" in order to destroy it.[35] Thus, if the police are holding a person in one room of a house, they are not authorized to search and seize property in another part of the house, away from the suspect's physical presence.

Field interrogation. Searches may be made without a warrant during field interrogations. The police often stop and interrogate persons without knowing any facts to justify an arrest. Clearly, much police activity involves interrogating people who are acting suspiciously or who are disturbing the public order. These street encounters, often called "threshold inquiries," allow for brief questioning and frisking to ascertain whether the person is carrying a weapon.

In the case of *Terry* v. *Ohio* (1968), the Supreme Court upheld the stop-and-frisk procedure.[36] In this case, a police officer noticed two men taking turns looking into a store window and then conferring. A third man joined them. Suspecting that a crime was about to be committed, the officer confronted them, removed pistols from two of the men, and charged them with carrying concealed weapons. The court ruled that this was a constitutional search since the officer had stopped them for the purpose of detention and/or interrogation and that, because he believed he was dealing with armed and dangerous individuals, the search could be conducted for his own safety or that of others.

On the basis of *Terry* and subsequent decisions, it is now accepted that a police officer is justified in stopping and questioning an individual if it is reasonable to assume that a crime has been committed. The individual may be frisked for a weapon if the officer fears for his or her life, and the officer is justified in going through the individual's clothing and person if the frisk has indicated something that might be a weapon. The courts have concluded that an officer may conduct this form of field interrogation in order to investigate suspicious persons without first showing probable cause.

Automobiles. A third special circumstance in which a warrantless search can be made is when there is probable cause to believe that an automobile contains criminal evidence. The Supreme Court has distinguished automobiles from houses and persons on the grounds that a car that has been involved in a crime can be moved and evidence lost. First developed by the Supreme Court in 1925 (*Carroll* v. *United States*), this doctrine emphasizing the mobile nature of motor vehicles has been accepted, though the police must have reason to believe that the particular case is linked to a crime.[37]

In recent years, however, two new questions have confronted the justices: whether impounded automobiles are subject to warrantless search and whether searches may be made of automobiles stopped in routine traffic inspections. In *Preston* v. *United States* (1964) the Court ruled that once the police had towed a car to a police garage after arresting its occupants at a different location, they could not then conduct an incidental search of the automobile.[38] The Court said that because the search was remote in time and place from the point of arrest, it was not an incidental search and thus was unreasonable.

A ruling in *Harris* v. *United States* (1968), however, upheld the right of the police to enter an impounded vehicle subsequent to an arrest in order to inventory its contents.[39] Building on this decision, the Court in 1970 (*Chambers*

Automobiles and their occupants may be searched pursuant to an arrest of the driver or passenger.

Close-up: The Case of Dolree Mapp

Mapp v. *Ohio*, 367 U.S. 643 (1961)

In the early afternoon of 23 May 1957 three Cleveland police officers went to the home of Miss Dolree Mapp to check on an informant's tip that a suspect in a recent bombing episode was hiding there. They also had information that a large amount of materials for operating a numbers game was being kept on the premises. Miss Mapp lived on the top floor of the two-story brick dwelling with her fifteen-year-old daughter. Upon arrival at the house, the officers knocked on the door and demanded entrance, but Miss Mapp, after telephoning her lawyer, refused to admit them without a search warrant.

Some three hours later, the officers again sought entrance. When their knocking went unanswered, they forcibly entered the house. Miss Mapp came down the stairway, confronted the officers, and demanded to see a search warrant. One of the policemen waved a piece of paper, claimed to be the warrant, in the air. Immediately Miss Mapp snatched the paper and placed it in her bosom. One of the officers asked, "What are we going to do now?" The other replied, "I'm going after it."

"No, you're not," said Miss Mapp, but the officer went after it anyway. In the ensuing struggle, Miss Mapp was handcuffed. At about that time her attorney, Walter Green, arrived at the house and saw the policemen kicking down a door. He heard Miss Mapp scream, "Take your hand out of my dress!" Green was not permitted to enter the house nor to see his client.

Meanwhile, Miss Mapp was forcibly taken upstairs to her bedroom where her belongings were searched. A photo album and personal papers along with her child's bedroom and a trunk in the basement were included in the widespread hunt. When one officer found a brown paper bag containing books, Miss Mapp yelled, "Better not look at those. They might excite you." Disregarding the warning, he looked at the books and proclaimed them to be obscene. The trunk held additional materials that were thought to be obscene.

Miss Mapp was charged with violation of Section 2905.34 of the Ohio Revised Code, which makes illegal the possession of obscene, lewd, or lascivious materials. In the trial that followed, the state sought to show that the materials belonged to Miss Mapp, while the defense contended that they were the property of a former boarder who had just moved and left his things behind. The trial judge was unimpressed

v. *Marony*) upheld a warrantless search of an in-custody automobile, saying that because the police had probable cause to believe the car might yield evidence of a crime and because it could be easily moved, it made little difference whether a warrant was sought or an immediate search conducted.[40] The justices appear to have equated the older *Carroll* decision, in which the car was on a highway, with *Chambers,* in which it was in police custody. By 1974 (*Cardwell* v. *Lewis*), the Court seemed to be saying that citizens have lesser expectations of privacy in an automobile because it has "little capacity for escaping public scrutiny [since] it travels public thoroughfares where both its occupants and its contents are in plain view."[41] This position was advanced in *South Dakota* v. *Opperman* (1976), in which the Court said that a validly impounded car may be searched without probable cause or warrant on the grounds that it is reasonable for an inventory of the contents to be taken as a protection against theft or charges of theft while the car is in police custody.[42]

Automobiles may also be searched pursuant to the arrest of the driver or another occupant. On the basis of the permissibility of a search incident to an

by the defense contentions and instructed the jury that under Ohio law unlawfully obtained evidence (evidence gathered without a proper search warrant) could be introduced into the court. The jury found Miss Mapp guilty, and she was sentenced to an indefinite term in the Ohio Reformatory for Women. The effect of the sentence was that Dolree Mapp could serve between one and seven years behind bars.

On 27 May 1959 Miss Mapp appealed to the Ohio Supreme Court. She claimed first, that the materials found in the trunk were not in her possession; second, that the evidence had been obtained through an illegal search and seizure; and third, that the statute under which she had been charged was unconstitutional. The majority opinion found that the boarder had left the trunk with Miss Mapp for safekeeping and thus it was in her possession. In regard to Miss Mapp's second claim, the court found that while evidently no search warrant had been issued, Ohio law nevertheless allowed the admission of evidence obtained through an illegal search and seizure. Finally, concerning her claim about the obscenity statute, the court ruled that it was an unconstitutional infringement on free speech and press. However, the 4–3 ruling did not make the statute invalid because the Ohio Constitution requires that all but one of the justices must be in the majority to overturn a law. Because of this peculiarity in the Ohio Constitution, Miss Mapp's conviction stood. Her attorneys wasted no time in appealing the case to the U.S. Supreme Court.

Decision

On 11 June 1961 a narrow majority of the Supreme Court overturned Miss Mapp's conviction on the grounds that the Fourth Amendment's prohibition against unreasonable search and seizure, as applied to the states by the due process clause of the Fourteenth Amendment, had been violated. Speaking for the majority, Justice Tom Clark reviewed the history of the Court's interpretation of the amendment and then said that as

> the right to be secure against rude invasions of privacy by state officers is . . . constitutional in origin, we can no longer permit that right to remain an empty promise. . . . We can no longer permit it to be revocable at the whim of any police officer who, in the name of law enforcement itself, chooses to suspend its enjoyment.

arrest as developed in *Chimel* v. *California,* the Court ruled in *New York* v. *Belton* (1981) that the entire interior of the car, including containers, may be examined even if the items are not within reach.[43] This principle was further developed in *United States* v. *Ross* (1982), which states that a warrantless search of an automobile and its contents is permissible if there is probable cause to believe that it contains evidence of a crime.[44] The right to search the containers follows from the right to search the vehicle.

The warrantless search of a car's occupants is still a cloudy legal area. Currently it appears that automobiles are seen as different from other areas considered private. Because of the importance of the automobile in American society, there will undoubtedly be additional interpretations of the Fourth Amendment with regard to unreasonable search and seizure.

"Plain view." Another exception to the requirement of a warrant occurs when officers seize items that are in "plain view" when they have reason to believe that the items are connected with a crime. If an officer has a warrant to search a house for cocaine, for example, and during the course of the search comes upon drug paraphernalia, the paraphernalia may also be seized. Issues of probable cause and the place where items are found may be raised to invalidate the seizure. Whether or not the finding of the item was inadvertent may be the basis of a challenge as well.

Consent. A citizen may waive the rights granted by the Fourth Amendment and allow the police to conduct a search or to seize items without a warrant and in the absence of special circumstances. The prosecution must be able to prove, however, that the consent was given voluntarily by the correct person. In some circumstances, as when airplane passengers' belongings are searched by airline employees before they board a plane and by customs agents, consent is implied. But in the absence of such circumstances, as the Supreme Court ruled in *Wren* v. *United States* (1965), consent must be clearly voluntary and not given as a consequence of duress or coercion.[45] Moreover, the consenting person must understand his or her right to deny the search. Questions about who may give consent center on permission given by persons other than the defendant—for example, landlords, cohabitants, or relatives.

Future of the exclusionary rule. Critics of the Supreme Court's interpretation of the Fourth Amendment and the rule excluding illegally seized evidence have argued that police officers often act in good faith, in the belief that they are following the law. It is said that the Court's interpretations are so varied and so complex that even professors of law have difficulty understanding them.

In a move likely to create a "good-faith exception" to the exclusionary rule, the Supreme Court has declared that evidence can be used even though it has been obtained under a search warrant that later is proved to be technically invalid. In *United States* v. *Leon* (1984), a 6–3 majority of the Court agreed with Justice Byron White that evidence obtained by law enforcement officers acting in reasonable reliance on a search warrant issued by a detached and neutral magistrate but ultimately found to be unsupported by probable cause could be used at trial. In dissent, Justice William Brennan, Jr., objected to the majority's effort to balance the costs and benefits of the exclusionary rule. The majority, he said, ignored the fundamental constitutional importance that was at stake in the case, and he seemed to despair: "It now appears that the Court's victory over the Fourth Amendment is complete."[46]

The Court has yet to determine the applicability of a good-faith exception to evidence seized by police officers during a warrantless search. Does the exclusionary rule apply to evidence obtained by officers who reasonably but incorrectly believe they have a proper basis for a search?

Arrest

Arrest is the seizure of an individual by a governmental official with authority to take the person into custody. It is more than a field interrogation or threshold inquiry, since the normal consequence of arrest is that the suspect is taken to the station house and there proceedings begin that will eventually lead to prosecution and trial. The law of arrest mixes the Fourth Amendment's protections and local rules regarding procedure. Generally this means that the arresting officer must be able to show that there is probable cause to believe (1) that a crime has been committed and (2) that the person taken into custody has committed the crime. Although this is sometimes difficult for the police to prove, the restrictions prevent them from randomly taking people into custody or using their power to limit the freedom of those whom, for one reason or another, they do not like.

arrest
The physical taking of a person into custody on the grounds that there is probable cause to believe that he or she has committed a criminal offense. Police may use only reasonable physical force in making an arrest. The purpose of arrest is to hold the accused for a court proceeding.

Although the courts have not specifically *required* arrest only upon presentation of a warrant, they have implied that for felony arrests this is the preferred method. As Wayne LaFave has noted, however, it is routine to make

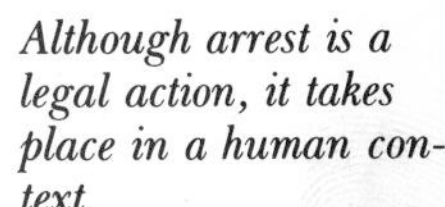

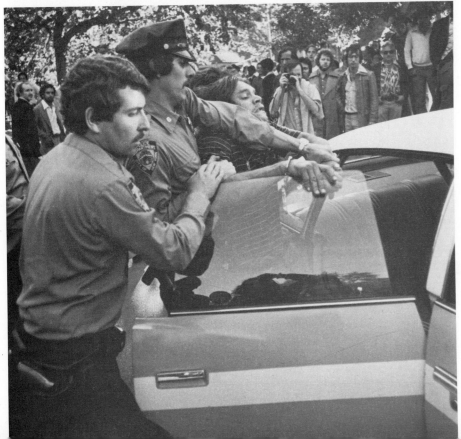

Although arrest is a legal action, it takes place in a human context.

arrests without a warrant "and thus without the prior approval of a judicial officer, even though there is adequate opportunity to obtain a warrant."[47] In general, courts have upheld the common law rule stated in *Carroll* v. *United States* (1925) that "a police officer may arrest without a warrant one believed by an officer upon reasonable cause to have been guilty of a felony and he may only arrest without a warrant one guilty of a misdemeanor if committed in his presence."[48]

Interrogation

Among the rights guaranteed by the Fifth Amendment, one of the most important is the protection against self-incrimination: persons shall not be compelled to be witnesses against themselves. This right is consistent with the assumption on which the adversarial process is based: that the state must prove the defendant's guilt. Although closely linked to the Fourth Amendment's prohibition of unreasonable search and seizure, the right has most force with regard to interrogations and confessions. The court will exclude from the evidence presented to the jurors any confession illegally obtained; further, because of the Sixth Amendment, the suspect has the right to counsel during the interrogation process.

The Supreme Court ruled in *Escobedo* v. *Illinois* (1964) and *Miranda* v. *Arizona* (1966) that confessions made by suspects who have not been notified of their constitutional rights cannot be admitted as evidence.[49] To protect the rights of the accused, the Court emphasized the importance of allowing counsel to be present during the interrogation process. In addition, the Court said in effect that as soon as the investigation of an unsolved crime begins to focus on a particular suspect and when the suspect has been taken into custody, the so-called *Miranda* warnings have to be read aloud before interrogation can commence.

Handcuffing the police?

No sooner was the *Miranda* opinion announced than a hue and cry arose over the propriety of the new judicial rules. Criticism of the Supreme Court came from a number of sources but especially from the law enforcement community, which said that it would be hamstrung in its pursuit of criminals, and from those public figures who were concerned about crime in the streets. Prominent among the officials who felt that the police had been handcuffed by the Court was Quinn Tamm, executive director of the International Association of Chiefs of Police: "I believe our citizens are fully aware of the situation,

Fifth Amendment

No person shall be held to answer for a capital, or otherwise infamous crime, unless on a presentment or indictment of a Grand Jury, except in cases arising in the land or naval forces, or in the Militia, when in actual service in time of war or public danger; nor shall any person be subject for the same offense to be twice put in jeopardy of life or limb; nor shall be compelled in any criminal case to be a witness against himself, nor be deprived of life, liberty, or property, without due process of law; nor shall private property be taken for public use, without just compensation.

Close-up: Rape on the Desert

***Miranda* v. *Arizona*, 384 U.S. 436 (1966)**

While walking to a bus on the night of 2 March 1963, after leaving her job as a candy counter clerk at the Paramount Theater in Phoenix, Arizona, eighteen-year-old Barbara Ann Johnson was accosted by a man who shoved her into his car, tied her hands and ankles, and took her to the edge of the city, where he raped her. The man then drove Miss Johnson to a street near her home, where he let her out of his car and asked that she say a prayer for him. After piecing the girl's story together, officers of the Phoenix Police Department picked up Ernesto Miranda and asked him whether he would voluntarily answer questions about the case. In a lineup at the station Miranda was picked out by two women: one identified him as the man who had robbed her at knifepoint on 27 November 1962, and Barbara Johnson thought he was the rapist.

Ernesto Arthur Miranda was a twenty-three-year-old eighth-grade dropout with a police record going back to his arrest at the age of fourteen for stealing a car. Since that time, he had been in trouble as a peeping Tom in Los Angeles, had been given an undesirable discharge by the Army for the same offense, and had served time in a federal prison for driving a stolen car across a state line. When Phoenix police officers Cooley and Young told Miranda that he had been identified by the women, he made a statement in his own handwriting that described the incident. He also noted that he made the confession voluntarily and with full knowledge of his legal rights. Miranda was soon charged with robbery, kidnapping, and rape.

At Miranda's trial, his court-appointed attorney, Alvin Moore, got Officers Cooley and Young to admit both that during the interrogation the defendant was not told of his right to have counsel and that no counsel was present. Over Moore's objections the judge admitted Miranda's confession into evidence. After more than five hours of jury deliberations, Miranda was found guilty and later was given concurrent sentences of from twenty to thirty years for kidnapping and rape. In a separate trial, he was given a sentence of from twenty to twenty-five years for robbery, that term to commence after the kidnapping and rape sentences had been served. Miranda thus faced a minimum of forty and a maximum of fifty-five years in prison.

Following an unsuccessful appeal to the Arizona Supreme Court, the United States Supreme Court agreed to review Miranda's case. His counsel asked the Court to decide whether "the confession of a poorly educated, mentally abnormal, indigent defendant, not told of his right to counsel, taken when he is in police custody and without assistance of counsel, which was not requested, can be admitted into evidence over specific objection based on the absence of counsel."

Decision

On 13 June 1966 Chief Justice Earl Warren announced the decision of the Supreme Court in *Miranda* v. *Arizona.* In clear terms he outlined detailed procedures that the police must use when questioning an accused person. As the chief justice said in explaining the reasons for the decision:

> The current practice of incommunicado interrogation is at odds with one of our Nation's most cherished principles—that the individual may not be compelled to incriminate himself. Unless adequate protective devices are employed to dispel the compulsion inherent in custodial surroundings, no statement obtained from the defendant can truly be the product of free choice.

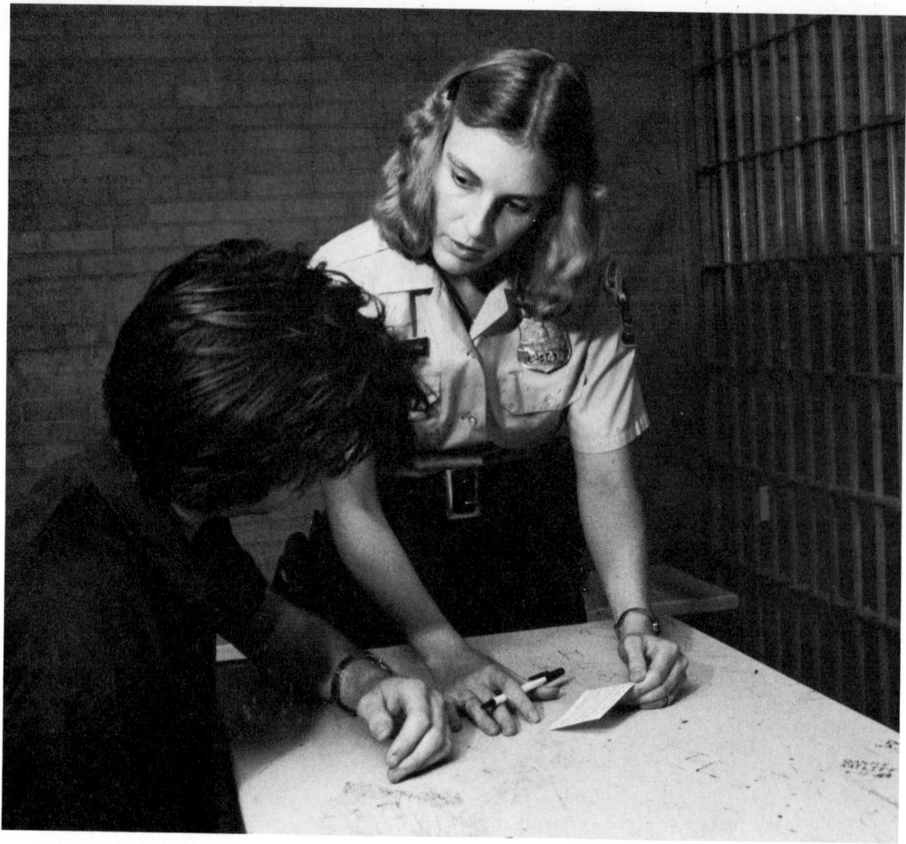

The "Miranda warning" must be read to any individual taken into custody.

and I predict that if there is not a turning point reached soon toward more realistic Supreme Court decisions, we are going to witness one of the greatest surges of outraged citizenship that we have ever seen."[50] In Congress, Senators Sam Ervin, Strom Thurmond, and John McClellan were especially outspoken. Standing before a chart showing the crime rate rising in parallel with decisions of the Supreme Court, McClellan proclaimed: "The Supreme Court has set a low tone in law enforcement and we are reaping the whirlwind today! Look at that chart! Look at it and weep for your country—crime spiralling upward and upward and upward. Apparently nobody is willing to put on the brakes."[51] Several constitutional amendments were introduced with the specific aim of punishing the Court by legislatively taking away some of its powers. The Omnibus Crime and Safe Streets Act of 1968 was designed to circumvent the *Miranda* decision by allowing trial judges in federal proceedings to determine whether confessions had been made voluntarily.

Criticism of the decisions seems to have been based on three assumptions: (1) that confessions are essential for the apprehension and conviction of law violators, (2) that informing suspects of their rights would greatly reduce the ability of the police to secure confessions, and (3) that the police would actually give the required warnings. All of these assumptions have been challenged both by law enforcement officials and by social scientists studying the impact of the new rulings. The most extensive of these studies focused on felony cases in California between 1976 and 1979. It was found that less than 1 percent of the cases that reached the courts were dismissed because of the exclusionary rule.[52] Similar findings were reported by the General Accounting Office in a study of the rule's impact on the federal courts.[53] It appears that the rule has been used to exclude evidence only in drug cases.

When Peter Nardulli reviewed 7,500 cases in nine counties in three states, he found that motions to suppress evidence were filed in only a small percentage of cases.[54] Motions to suppress physical evidence were filed in 5 percent of the cases (largely those involving drugs and weapons), to suppress identifications in 2 percent, and to suppress confessions in 4 percent. The success rates for these motions were equally marginal: 69 percent or less for each type, and even then—with the evidence excluded—not all defendants escaped conviction. In sum, only 46 cases (0.6 percent of those studied) were lost because of the exclusionary rule, and most of those involved offenses that might have resulted in incarceration for less than six months. Nardulli believes that these findings show that the exclusionary rule has had only a marginal impact on the criminal court system.

In most cities the police depend on either catching the accused in the act or locating witnesses who will testify. Almost all departments have limited resources for scientific investigation and so are hampered in their efforts to amass enough evidence to arrest a suspect. In the usual situation, a suspect is not arrested until the crime is solved and conviction assured. Interrogation becomes unnecessary under these circumstances.

Although police officials, politicians, and others felt that the *Miranda* rules would stifle efforts to control a rising crime rate, no such impact occurred. Neither was *Miranda* the boon that the Supreme Court and its de-

---

Interrogation: Advice of Rights

Your rights

Before we ask you any questions, you must understand your rights.

You have the right to remain silent.

Anything you say can be used against you in court.

You have the right to talk to a lawyer for advice before we ask you any questions and to have him with you during questioning.

If you cannot afford a lawyer, one will be appointed for you before any questioning if you wish.

If you decide to answer questions now without a lawyer present, you will still have the right to stop answering at any time. You also have the right to stop answering at any time until you talk to a lawyer.

Waiver of rights

I have read this statement of my rights and I understand what my rights are. I am willing to make a statement and answer questions. I do not want a lawyer at this time. I understand and know what I am doing. No promises or threats have been made to me and no pressure or coercion of any kind has been used against me.

Signed ______________________

Witness ______________________
Witness ______________________
Time: ______________________

---

fenders suggested it might be. Because of noncompliance during field and station-house interrogation, the difficulties of developing schemes to provide effective counsel for indigent suspects, and distrust and misunderstanding on the part of suspects, the new protections had much less effect than had been anticipated.

Modifications by the Burger Court

In the years since Ernesto Miranda's case was heard, a flow of cases to the Supreme Court of the United States has raised further questions about specific aspects of that opinion. As the number of conservative justices increased, some people expected the court to overturn *Miranda.* Though it has not done so, the new conservative majority seems intent on halting the liberal thrust of previous decisions and shaping them to meet the complex demands of law enforcement. Decisions in recent cases have modified *Miranda* to such an extent that civil libertarians have complained that the exclusionary provisions are all but dead. They are not dead, but they have been modified by rulings in regard to particular circumstances in which interrogations of suspects have been conducted.

Notable among the cases modifying *Miranda* was *Harris* v. *New York* (1971), in which the Court ruled that statements that are trustworthy (not coerced) may be used to attack the credibility of a defendant who takes the stand even though they have been obtained in violation of the rule.[55] The prosecution charged that Harris had lied during his trial, and the Court ruled that his statements to the police before trial could be introduced as evidence to prove the contention. In *Michigan* v. *Mosley* (1975) the Court ruled that a second interrogation session held after the suspect had initially refused to make a statement did not violate *Miranda.*[56] In *Rhode Island* v. *Innis* (1980), however, the Court broadened the applicability of *Miranda* by ruling that the safeguards against self-incrimination must be observed "whenever a person in custody is subjected to either express questioning or its equivalent."[57] In that case the suspect, riding with police officers in a squad car after being picked up in a murder investigation, heard one officer worry aloud to the other that because the murder had occurred near a school for handicapped children, some child might find the gun and be injured by it. At that the suspect told the officers where the gun could be found.

Two doctrines modifying the rule excluding evidence gathered during interrogation in violation of the normal requirements of *Miranda* have been enunciated by the Burger Court. In the case of *New York* v. *Quarles* (1984), Justice William H. Rehnquist established a "public safety exception" to the suspect-warning doctrine.[58] Benjamin Quarles was charged with criminal possession of a weapon after a rape victim described him to the police. The officers located him in a supermarket. In response to the officers' question as to the gun's whereabouts, Quarles indicated that it was behind some cartons. Although the *Miranda* warnings had not been read to Quarles, Rehnquist said that the case presented a situation in which concern for public safety must take precedence over adherence to the literal language of the rules. The police were justified in asking the question by "immediate necessity."

A second doctrine, called the "inevitability of discovery exception," was stated by the Court in *Nix* v. *Williams* (1984).[59] This decision followed an earlier case, *Brewer* v. *Williams* (1977).[60] Robert Williams had been convicted of the murder of a ten-year-old girl. During the investigation, detectives searching for the body had given Williams what became known as the "Christian burial speech." Though they had promised his lawyer not to ask questions during a drive across the state with the suspect, they had asked Williams to think about the fact that the parents of the girl were entitled to have an opportunity to provide a Christian burial for their child. Williams had then told them where to find the body. In 1977 the Supreme Court ruled that the detectives had violated the suspect's rights by inducing him to incriminate himself outside the presence of counsel. However, the Court left open the possibility that in a retrial the state could introduce the evidence of the body's discovery if it could be shown that it would have been found even without the defendant's testimony. Applying the "inevitability of discovery exception," the Iowa courts found Williams guilty, and in 1984 the Supreme Court upheld the conviction. The chief justice said that the doctrine was designed to put the police "in the same, not a *worse,* position than they would have been in if no police error or misconduct had occurred."

Given the conservative majority on the Court, it can be expected that as more cases linked to the *Miranda* decision and the exclusionary rule come before the justices, the standard first enunciated by Chief Justice Warren in 1966 will be further eroded.

Law and law enforcement

As we have seen in this examination of the three major elements of the law enforcement process—detection, apprehension, and arrest—the law stipulates the actions that may be taken at each stage. Many people believe that the Supreme Court has gone too far and that criminals have gone free on technicalities as a result. Others emphasize that the Constitution protects all Americans against the unbridled exercise of power by the government, and that the benefits of freedom are worth the price of letting some criminals go.

Is either position entirely valid? Research supports the contentions of both sides, particularly with regard to confessions, search and seizure, and the exclusionary rule. Yale Kamisar has argued that "when the police obtain evidence in violation of the Constitution, the courts must exclude it to assure the people that the government cannot profit from its lawlessness."[61] Malcolm Wilkey counters, "If we want to reduce crime, we ought to admit all the evidence into the trial—and punish the police later if they obtained any of it illegally."[62] On the question "Does the rule really deter police from making illegal searches?" Bradley Canon argues that the evidence is inconclusive; in some cities the rule deters, in others it doesn't.[63] Steven Schlesinger responds that the rule's proponents bear the burden of proving that it is effective, and they have not provided such proof.[64] It seems likely that this debate will continue and that the relationship of police actions to the rule of law will always be a subject of contention.

Summary

In a most thoughtful essay, Peter Manning writes that the police agree with their audiences and their professional interpreters—the American family, criminals, and politicians—in at least one respect: they have an "impossible" mandate.[65] Society gives various occupational groups license to carry out certain activities that others may not. Indeed, groups that achieve professional status, such as medical doctors, have formal rules and codes of ethics that not only set standards for their conduct but also define their occupational mandate. The police in contemporary society, however, have been unable to define their mandate; rather, it has been defined for them. As a result, citizens have a distorted notion of police work.

> The public is aware of the dramatic nature of a small portion of police work, but it ascribes the element of excitement to all police activities. To much of the public,

Close-up: Police Legal Liaison

Since the careers of today's senior administrators began, police work has become more difficult, more complicated, more professional. A large part of that change is the result of rapidly unfolding legal developments, including new statutes, court decisions, and reform in court procedures. The most publicized aspect of these developments is the creation of a system of strict safeguards of the constitutional rights of the accused—the *Miranda* warning; strict scrutiny of the existence of probable cause to justify arrest, search, and seizure of evidence; tough testing of the sufficiency of warrants; and restrictions on the use of tape recordings and wiretaps.

In the midst of these legal developments—and facing a generally rising incidence of reported crime—stand the police officers. If they fail to keep pace with legal changes, if their judgment in a difficult street incident is in error, both the rate of crime and the police image may suffer.

To prevent and correct legal error by the police, the Dallas Police Legal Liaison Division, a special unit of the Dallas Police Department, provides training and legal counsel to staff-level police officers and investigators. Assistant city attorneys are assigned around the clock to provide line officers with expert counsel, to screen all cases for legal sufficiency, and to conduct comprehensive case follow-up.

By successfully linking two parts of the criminal justice system that often operate in isolation—the police and the prosecutor—the Dallas project has created a stronger, more cohesive law enforcement team. The results? Fewer cases rejected by a grand jury or dismissed by a judge, more informed decision making by police, and greater respect for citizens' constitutional rights.

Duties of the legal advisers

Dallas's legal advisers perform four major functions for the department.

Review case documents. The key element is the review of legally important case documents. All prosecution reports prepared by police officers (except traffic cases and petty misdemeanors) are routinely sent to the Legal Liaison Office for review. Those free of legal error are submitted to the District Attorney's Office for filing with the appropriate court. Deficient reports are returned to the police officer for revision. The total number of reports checked often exceeds 2,000 per month.

Review warrants and affidavits. Warrant activity in the department is centered in the investigative unit. Investigators are not required to confer with the Legal Liaison Division before seeking a warrant, but they are encouraged to use the lawyers in any unusual or troublesome

the police are seen as alertly ready to respond to citizen demands, as crime-fighters, as an efficient, bureaucratic, highly organized force that keeps society from falling into chaos.[66]

In addition, sociopolitical influences have added to tensions between the mandate of the police "that claims to include the efficient, apolitical, and professional enforcement of the law" and their ability to define and fulfill it.[67] Police operations not only are shaped by the formal organizational structures created to allocate law enforcement resources in an efficient manner but also are influenced by social and political processes both within and outside the department.

The police are organized along military lines so that authority and responsibility can be located at appropriate levels of the structure. Within the modern police department, operational divisions are responsible for activities

case. When consulted, the lawyers generally review the entire case with the investigators and draft the documents themselves. The police attorneys help prepare about a tenth of the total number of affidavits for warrants drawn up by the department.

Monitor police error. The effort to reduce legal error does not stop when prosecution reports and warrants have been approved for submission. The lawyers follow all major cases through the grand jury and court systems, both to check on the effectiveness of the documents review system and to pinpoint areas in which improvements by the police or the Legal Division are needed.

General legal counsel. Acting as general "house counsel" is one of the most vital (and probably the most time-consuming) services the legal advisers perform. The Legal Liaison Office gives fast, over-the-phone advice to practically any member of the department who requests it. Usually the caller is an investigator asking for a legal analysis of a specific incident that resulted in an arrest.

Impact of the Dallas legal advisers

Have the Dallas legal advisers helped the police to build better cases? The proportion of failures attributed to police errors in cases submitted both to grand juries and to courts has declined substantially—about 1,170 more cases per year are meeting the requirements of grand juries and judges as a result of decreased police error.

But statistics are only part of the story. The Police Department and District Attorney's Office have never worked together more productively. The District Attorney's Office lauds the police for prosecution reports that are easily of the highest quality in Dallas County. Although it cannot be measured statistically, the general benefit to the department of having in-house legal counsel should not be overlooked. It matters significantly when a field officer takes an individual into custody after a turbulent street incident but is unsure whether a charge is justified, and needs to know at once; or when the chief of police can turn to his lawyer for advice on how to respond to a mass demonstration or a sit-in on City Hall steps.

An increase in convictions is not the only—and perhaps not even the most important—result of correct police behavior. It also reflects increased observance of constitutional safeguards and enhanced respect for the rights of individuals.

Source: Adapted from U.S., Department of Justice, National Institute of Law Enforcement and Criminal Justice, *The Dallas Police Legal Liaison Division* (Washington, D.C.: Government Printing Office, 1976).

designed to achieve the goals of crime prevention and control. Although organization charts appear to show that police operations run like a well-adjusted machine, administrative leadership, recruitment, socialization of recruits to norms and values of the system, and the perspectives of the general public serve to shape the ways these activities are conducted. Police operations can likewise be influenced by pressures from community political leaders who want law enforcement resources to be allocated in ways that will further their own interests. Other portions of the criminal justice system may also shape law enforcement activities. The police are the system's crucial entry point for the disposition of offenders, and law enforcement officers are under pressure to get the evidence the prosecution needs. Yet their operations must be carried out according to law.

The traditional functions and operations of the police are being reassessed. Although the crime-fighting image is widely held, research has shown that the police are engaged in a wider variety of activities. One view suggests that the modern police department has been given so many responsibilities that it is really a public service organization. New technologies, especially those of communication, have helped to alter police operations, yet research continues to describe the patrol officer as the multipurpose officer who is equipped to meet the many demands that the public places on the police. But the mandate that the police have been given is impossible. The situation cannot be changed so long as both police and public harbor misunderstandings in regard to the nature of law enforcement work, unrealistic estimates of the potential for success in efforts to control crime, and misconceptions of the role of law in a democratic society.

For discussion

1. The use of patrol cars instead of police officers on foot has been extensively debated. What do you see as the conflicting values underlying this argument?
2. You are a patrol officer. What things can you do to win high effectiveness ratings from your boss?
3. The military-style organization of the police is often criticized as inhibiting effective law enforcement. Do you feel this emphasis enhances or detracts from police efficiency?
4. You are a police chief. How would you allocate the personnel resources in your city?
5. Modern communications have greatly altered patrol work. What are some of the changes that a central command post has brought to police operations?

For further reading

Brown, Michael K. *Working the Street.* New York: Russell Sage Foundation, 1981.
Bugliosi, Vincent. *Helter Skelter.* New York: Norton, 1974.
Goldstein, Herman. *Policing a Free Society.* Cambridge, Mass.: Ballinger, 1977.
LaFave, Wayne. *Arrest: The Decision to Take a Suspect into Custody.* Boston: Little, Brown, 1965.
Manning, Peter K. *Police Work.* Cambridge: M.I.T. Press, 1977.
Wambaugh, Joseph. *The Onion Field.* New York: Delacorte, 1973.
Wilson, Jerry. *Police Report.* Boston: Little, Brown, 1965.

Notes

1. Vincent Bugliosi, *Helter Skelter* (New York: Norton, 1974).
2. Gordon P. Whitaker, Stephen Mastrofski, Elinor Ostrom, Roger B. Parks, and Stephen L. Percy, *Basic Issues in Police Performance,* U.S. Department of Justice (Washington, D.C.: Government Printing Office, 1982), p. 23.

3. President's Commission on Law Enforcement and Administration of Justice, *Task Force Report: The Police* (Washington, D.C.: Government Printing Office, 1967), p. 46.
4. John Gardiner, *Traffic and the Police: Variations in Law Enforcement Policy* (Cambridge: Harvard University Press, 1969), p. 116.
5. Albert J. Reiss, Jr., and David J. Bordua, "Environment and Organization: A Perspective on the Police," in *The Police: Six Sociological Essays*, ed. David J. Bordua (New York: Wiley, 1967), p. 33.
6. Jonathan Rubinstein, *City Police* (New York: Farrar, Straus & Giroux, 1973), p. 47.
7. J. F. Elliott and T. J. Sardino, *Crime Control Team* (Springfield, Ill.: Charles C Thomas, 1971), p. 87.
8. Lawrence W. Sherman, "Patrol Strategies for Police," in *Crime and Public Policy,* ed. James Q. Wilson (San Francisco: ICS Press, 1983), p. 148.
9. Samuel G. Chapman, *Police Patrol Readings,* 2d ed. (Springfield, Ill.: Charles C Thomas, 1970), p. ix.
10. Samuel G. Chapman, "Police Patrol Administration," in *Municipal Police Administration,* ed. George D. Eastman and Esther Eastman, 7th ed. (Washington, D.C.: International City Management Association, 1971), p. 77.
11. Charles D. Hale, *Fundamentals of Police Administration* (Boston: Holbrook Press, 1977), pp. 105–6.
12. George Kelling, Tony Pate, Duane Dieckman, and Charles E. Brown, *The Kansas City Preventive Patrol Experiments: A Summary Report* (Washington, D.C.: Police Foundation, 1974).
13. William G. Spelman and Dale K. Brown, *Calling the Police: Citizen Reporting of Serious Crime* (Washington, D.C.: Police Executive Research Forum, 1981), p. xxix.
14. Sherman, "Patrol Strategies for Police," p. 149.
15. Spelman and Brown, *Calling the Police,* p. 4.
16. Marcia Cohen and J. Thomas McEwen, "Handling Calls for Service: Alternatives to Traditional Policing," *NIJ Reports,* September 1984, p. 4.
17. Kevin Krajick, "Does Patrol Prevent Crime?" *Police,* September 1978, p. 6.
18. Ben Davis, "Foot Patrol," *Police Centurian,* June 1984, p. 41.
19. James Q. Wilson and Barbara Boland, *The Effect of the Police on Crime,* U.S. Department of Justice (Washington, D.C.: Government Printing Office, 1979).
20. James Q. Wilson, *Thinking about Crime,* 2d ed. (New York: Basic Books, 1983), p. 71.
21. Wilson and Boland, *Effect of the Police,* p. 4.
22. Peter W. Greenwood and Joan Petersilia, *The Criminal Investigation Process,* vol. 1: *Summary and Policy Implications* (Santa Monica: Rand Corporation, 1975). The entire report is found in Peter W. Greenwood, Jan M. Chaiken, and Joan Petersilia, *The Criminal Investigation Process* (Lexington, Mass.: D. C. Heath, 1977).
23. Herman Goldstein, *Policing a Free Society* (Cambridge, Mass.: Ballinger, 1977), p. 55. Copyright © 1977 Ballinger Publishing Company. Reprinted by permission.
24. Peter B. Bloch and Donald R. Weidman, *Managing Criminal Investigations* (Washington, D.C.: Government Printing Office, 1975), p. 33.
25. Greenwood and Petersilia, *Summary and Policy Implications,* p. 19.
26. President's Commission on Law Enforcement and Administration of Justice, *Task Force Report: The Police,* p. 58.
27. Greenwood, Chaiken, and Petersilia, *Criminal Investigation Process,* p. 227.
28. Greenwood and Petersilia, *Summary and Policy Implications,* pp. x–xiii.
29. Goldstein, *Policing a Free Society,* p. 57. Copyright © 1977 Ballinger Publishing Company. Reprinted by permission.
30. James Q. Wilson, *Varieties of Police Behavior* (Cambridge: Harvard University Press, 1968), p. 95.
31. Ibid., p. 53.
32. Ibid.
33. Rubinstein, *City Police,* p. 375.
34. United States v. Robinson, 414 U.S. 218 (1973).
35. Chimel v. California, 395 U.S. 752 (1969).
36. Terry v. Ohio, 392 U.S. 1 (1968).
37. Carroll v. United States, 267 U.S. 132 (1925).
38. Preston v. United States, 376 U.S. 364 (1964).
39. Harris v. United States, 390 U.S. 234 (1968).
40. Chambers v. Marony, 399 U.S. 42 (1970).
41. Cardwell v. Lewis, 417 U.S. 583 (1974).
42. South Dakota v. Opperman, 428 U.S. 364 (1976).
43. New York v. Belton, 453 U.S. 454 (1981).
44. United States v. Ross, 102 S.Ct. 2157 (1982).
45. Wren v. United States, 352 F. 2d 617 (1965).
46. United States v. Leon, 52 L.W. 5155 (1984).

47. Wayne LaFave, *Arrest: The Decision to Take a Suspect into Custody* (Boston: Little, Brown, 1965), p. 16.
48. Carroll v. United States, 267 U.S. 132 (1925).
49. Escobedo v. Illinois, 378 U.S. 478 (1964); Miranda v. Arizona, 384 U.S. 436 (1966).
50. Richard Harris, *The Fear of Crime* (New York: Praeger, 1969), p. 38.
51. Fred P. Graham, *The Self-Inflicted Wound* (New York: Macmillan, 1970), p. 12.
52. U.S. Department of Justice, National Institute of Justice, *The Effects of the Exclusionary Rule: A Study in California* (Washington, D.C.: Government Printing Office, 1982).
53. Controller General of the United States, *Impact of the Exclusionary Rule on Federal Criminal Prosecutions,* Report GGD-79-45, 19 April 1979.
54. Peter Nardulli, "The Societal Cost of the Exclusionary Rule: An Empirical Assessment," *ABF Research Journal,* Summer 1983, pp. 585–609.
55. Harris v. New York, 401 U.S. 222 (1971).
56. Michigan v. Mosley, 423 U.S. 93 (1975).
57. Rhode Island v. Innis, 446 U.S. 291 (1980).
58. New York v. Quarles, 52 L.W. 4790 (1984).
59. Nix v. Williams, 52 L.W. 4732 (1984).
60. Brewer v. Williams, 430 U.S. 387 (1977).
61. Yale Kamisar, "Is the Exclusionary Rule an 'Illogical' or 'Unnatural' Interpretation of the Fourth Amendment?" *Judicature* 62 (August 1978): 68.
62. Malcolm Richard Wilkey, "The Exclusionary Rule: Why Suppress Valid Evidence?" *Judicature* 62 (November 1978): 215.
63. Bradley Canon, "The Exclusionary Rule: Have Critics Proven that It Doesn't Deter Police?" *Judicature* 62 (March 1979): 398.
64. Steven R. Schlesinger, "The Exclusionary Rule: Have Proponents Proven that It Is a Deterrent to Police?" *Judicature* 62 (March 1979): 404.
65. Peter K. Manning, "The Police: Mandate, Strategies, and Appearances," in *Crime and Justice in American Society,* ed. Jack D. Douglas (Indianapolis: Bobbs-Merrill, 1971), p. 149.
66. Ibid., p. 157.
67. Ibid., p. 158.

Law Enforcement Issues and Trends

7

The rise of crime that caught general public notice in the mid-1960s brought immediate governmental response. After many decades during which the police functioned outside the public limelight and the dimensions of their work were of significance only to law enforcement professionals, the impact of the war on crime was great. For the first time many law enforcement agencies were forced to reevaluate treasured assumptions about the ways crimes are committed, police resources allocated, and suspects captured. In retrospect, we can see that one result of LEAA and other federally funded programs was a thorough shaking of the criminal justice system. Still, some people feel that little was changed and that performance did not improve.

The demise of LEAA through congressional action in 1981 brought a shrinkage of federal dollars for crime control and reductions in public spending by states and municipalities. Law enforcement is now being forced to face a number of issues and trends, which chapter 7 will discuss. Most of these issues and trends do not have a direct impact on police operations but rather affect the links of law enforcement agencies to the broader society and some of the enduring problems associated with police work. This does not mean that such matters as corruption, unionism, hiring practices, and accountability do not influence the effectiveness of law enforcement; they do. Their effect, however, is indirect because they concern police personnel and the reaction of citizens to law enforcement.

The police in the United States are not separate from the people. They draw their authority from the will and consent of the people, and they recruit their officers from them. The police are the instrument of the people to achieve and maintain order; their efforts are founded on principles of public service and ultimate responsibility to the public.

NATIONAL ADVISORY COMMISSION ON CRIMINAL JUSTICE STANDARDS AND GOALS

Politics and the police

Descriptions of the relationship between politics and the police have generally centered on links among the police, partisan politics, and corruption. From the beginning of this century, when Lincoln Steffens exposed corruption in American cities, to more recent times, when police scandals have rocked departments in New York City, Chicago, and Denver, politics has been shown to be entwined in the relationships that often bind criminals and police officers. In addition, issues concerning allocation of enforcement resources, appointment of administrators, determination of enforcement policies that attract public attention—all have a political dimension. Thus it is a plain fact that police corruption occurs and that partisan politics is often the basis for it.

A number of studies have provided examples of the relationship between politics and the police. Circumstances such as those described by John Gardiner as existing in "Wincanton" and those cited by William Chambliss in "Rainfall West" show how organized crime can forge direct links to government officials and influence the daily operations of the police.[1] The reaction of Mayor Richard Daley's administration to the Walker Commission report of the police riot in Chicago during the 1968 Democratic National Convention indicates that politicians felt there were political gains to be gotten from a public defense of the police. In a number of cities police officials have been elected to the position of mayor as "law and order" candidates.

But the relationship between politics and law enforcement policy goes beyond such well-publicized incidents as these. In a heterogeneous and pluralistic society such as ours, there is often disagreement about the role of the police, the activities that should be labeled criminal, and the enforcement practices that should be followed. Some communities may achieve consensus regarding the policies that should be followed. In others, the heterogeneity of the population and existing political divisions may lead portions of the community to be antagonistic to certain police activities. For example, Wilson found that in Oakland, California, what appeared to whites to be a sound police strategy to deter crime—intensive surveillance of public places—was viewed as "harassment" by a substantial part of the black community.[2] Public controversy may develop over such matters as the treatment of juveniles, charges of police brutality, policies concerning strict or tolerant enforcement of gambling laws, and the level of protection maintained in certain neighborhoods. When such matters come to the fore in the arena of public opinion, they attract the attention of political leaders.

Although controversial issues may engender a high degree of citizen influence over decisions, studies have shown that the true nature of police work is of little interest to most citizens. Police protection is an exceptional service that may be called upon to prevent things from happening; it is largely invisible, and the average citizen comes into contact with it only in the exceptional case. For most citizens, police service is difficult to evaluate. Thus, while police brutality, traffic-safety crackdowns, and the flagrant flouting of vice laws may bring a public outcry, most police activities are known only to people who have direct contact with the law.

Wilson's examination of the police in eight communities disclosed that law enforcement activities were governed by the dominant values of the local political culture rather than by direct political intervention.[3] Such values were reflected in the police force's budget, pay levels, and organization, but explicit political decisions were not made about the routine handling of situations by the men and women on the force. The police were found to be sensitive to the political environment but were not governed by it in their day-to-day activities. In short, the prevailing style of law enforcement in each community was not explicitly determined by political decisions, although a few elements were shaped by those considerations.

Police administrators are the key figures in law enforcement politics because they link the department to other decision makers, public officials, and community elites. Through the choice of a particular type of administrator, the values of the local political culture are translated into law enforcement policies. If conflict develops between the police chief and a politically powerful figure such as the mayor, the police department may find its operations hampered by cuts in its budget. Such political battles may even result in the firing of the chief.

During the past decade the position of police chief has become professionalized in many major U.S. cities. It used to be customary to award the job to an insider as a patronage plum; now it is becoming increasingly common to conduct a national search for the best-qualified person to fill the position. But however the chief is chosen, it is apparent that the department reflects the chief's policies, and that the chief's approach to law enforcement must conform to the expectations of dominant local groups.

Police and the community

To carry out complicated law enforcement and service tasks with efficiency and discretion is a formidable assignment even under the best circumstances—that is, when the police have the public's support and cooperation. The "best circumstances" may have existed in our rural past and may exist in some suburban communities today, but they definitely do not exist in metropolitan areas, especially those populated by the poor and minorities. In city slums and ghettos—the neighborhoods that need and want effective law enforcement—there is much distrust of the police; accordingly, citizens fail to report crimes and refuse to cooperate with investigations. Encounters between individual police officers and members of these communities are often charged by animosity and periodically turn into large-scale disorders. Yet, as Wilson has said, "The single most striking fact about the attitudes of citizens, black and white, toward the police is that in general these attitudes are positive, not negative."[4]

The relationship of the police to the urban community has been given increased attention since the long hot summers of the late 1960s. Initially emphasis was placed on the special problems associated with the relations between the mostly white police officers and the mostly black inner-city residents. Until the mid-1970s, the phrase "police–community relations" essentially meant attempts to improve police–minority relations. To this end, the recruitment of minority members and the creation of programs designed to put law enforcement in a good light before community members were stressed.

Policing a Ghetto

The only way to police a ghetto is to be oppressive. None of the Police Commissioner's men, even with the best will in the world, have any way of understanding the lives led by people they swagger about in twos and threes controlling. Their very presence is an insult, and it would be, even if they spent their entire day feeding gumdrops to children. They represent the force of the white world, and that world's criminal profit and ease, to keep the black man corraled up here, in his place. The badge, the gun in the holster, and the swinging club make vivid what will happen should his rebellion become overt.

Source: James Baldwin, *Nobody Knows My Name* (New York: Dell Publishing Co., 1962), p. 65.

The concept of police–community relations has undergone a shift of emphasis in recent years. As we have seen, researchers have begun to shed light on the connection between the amount of crime and the fear of crime. It is argued that the consequence of an exaggerated fear of crime is a decline in the quality of life. Citizens, George Kelling writes, have "armed themselves, restricted their activities, rejected cities, built fortress houses and housing complexes both inside and outside the cities, and panicked about particular groups and classes of citizens."[5] Strategies to reduce the fear of crime are now viewed as an important element of police–community relations. The reappearance of foot patrols and enhancement of the order-maintenance function of the police have been cited as measures that may be taken to reassure citizens that an arm of government cares about their needs and is determined to provide the safety that will allow for civility in their neighborhoods.

Citizen crime-watch groups have proliferated in many communities. It has been estimated that more than 5 million Americans are now members of such organizations, which often have direct channels to police departments. In Detroit, Neighborhood Watch is organized on 4,000 of the city's 12,000 blocks; in New York, the Blockwatchers are 70,000 strong, and are "trained at precinct houses to watch, listen and report accurately"; and in Dade County, Florida, the 175,000-member Citizens Crime Watch has extended its operations into schools in an effort to reduce drug use.[6]

One group that has gained national publicity is the Guardian Angels, which originated in New York City but now has chapters across the country. The Angels are young people in distinctive apparel—red berets and T-shirts—who patrol buses, subways, and streets as self-appointed peacekeepers. Although the Angels have held lawbreakers until a police officer has arrived and have broken up fights, their main function is to act as an intimidating force against people who would otherwise be disruptive. As a consequence, the mere presence of the Guardian Angels has a reassuring effect on people who must travel in what they believe to be a dangerous area of the city. The Angels have gained official recognition in several large cities other than New

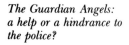

The Guardian Angels: a help or a hindrance to the police?

York—Boston and Los Angeles among them—but their presence in some other parts of the country has been less welcome. As the Atlanta Public Safety commissioner said, "There's going to be only one police department around here."[7] The thought has been expressed that the peace can be kept only by well-trained police officers, and that the presence of the Angels may provoke trouble in some situations.

The control of criminal and deviant behavior is a task that cannot be the sole responsibility of the police. Law enforcement agencies require the support and assistance of the community: support when they take actions that are consistent with neighborhood values and that help to maintain order; assistance in the form of information about wrongdoing and cooperation with police investigation. The police and residents of a community must collaborate in maintaining standards of communal life, with the aim of reducing not only crime but—perhaps more important—the fear of crime.

The police: a link to government

Police officers provide the only direct contact many people have with government, so the way the officers do their work affects the citizen's sense of the fairness of the political system. When Herbert Jacob studied attitudes toward the police in black, white working-class, and white middle-class neighborhoods of Milwaukee, he found that blacks judged the police to be more corrupt, less fair, tougher, and more excitable than did respondents in white neighborhoods. Yet Jacob found that race was not the sole factor that determined attitudes toward the police. Rather, race and personal experience with the police may have interacted to produce different results in the several areas. Jacob found, in addition, that the attitudes toward the police shown in table 7.1 may have been associated with dissatisfaction about the quality of life in particular neighborhoods. When residents were asked whether "people in

TABLE 7.1 How people perceive the police: mean scores in three neighborhood samples

Scales (1 . . . Score . . . 7)	*Black (N = 71)*	*White working class (N = 71)*	*White middle class (N = 73)*
Corrupt . . . Honest	3.70	4.75	5.16
Bad . . . Good	4.10	6.04	6.10
Unfair . . . Fair	3.76	5.56	6.03
Excitable . . . Calm	3.42	5.69	4.97
Lazy . . . Hardworking	4.62	5.86	5.85
Dumb . . . Smart	4.24	5.07	4.97
Unfriendly . . . Friendly	3.37	4.94	4.92
Cruel . . . Kind	3.18	4.86	4.90
Weak . . . Strong	4.34	4.96	4.88
Harsh . . . Easygoing	3.04	3.86	3.68
Tough . . . Softhearted	2.49	3.24	2.70

Source: Adapted from Herbert Jacob, "Black and White Perceptions of Justice in the City," *Law and Society Review* 6, no. 1 (1971): 73. Reprinted by permission of the Law and Society Association.

TABLE 7.2 Ratings of police treatment of neighborhood residents by respondents in ten cities

Response	*Albuquerque (N = 471)*	*Atlanta (N = 469)*	*Baltimore (N = 500)*	*Boston (N = 507)*	*Denver (N = 357)*	*Kansas City, Kansas (N = 193)*
Very good	47%	37%	30%	29%	44%	44%
Good enough	34	38	48	44	29	42
Not so good	6	7	16	12	8	7
Not good at all	2	5	5	6	4	2
Not ascertained	11	13	1	9	15	5
Total	100%	100%	100%	100%	100%	100%

Source: Floyd F. Fowler, Jr., *Citizen Attitudes toward Local Government Services and Taxes* (Cambridge, Mass.: Ballinger Publishing Co., 1974), p. 167. Reprinted by permission.

this neighborhood are treated as well as people living in other sections of the city," 40 percent of the ghetto blacks, 15 percent of the white working-class respondents, and 7 percent of the white middle-class respondents answered no.[8] Thus law enforcement policies and police actions clearly have a significant effect on the attitudes of some citizens toward the fairness of the political community. Yet as table 7.2 and figure 7.1 show, there is wide variation among cities in public ratings of the way the police treat people. Blacks consistently rate the police lower than whites, but in Kansas City, Kansas, and San Diego, California, 86 percent of those interviewed said that the police's treatment of people in their neighborhoods was either "very good" or "good enough."

Studies have shown that permissive law enforcement on the one hand and brutality on the other are the two basic reasons why residents of the urban community resent the police. The police are charged with failure to give adequate protection and services in minority-group neighborhoods and with abusing residents physically or verbally. In a survey of New York's Bedford-Stuyvesant area, respondents listed eight elements of conflict and antagonism

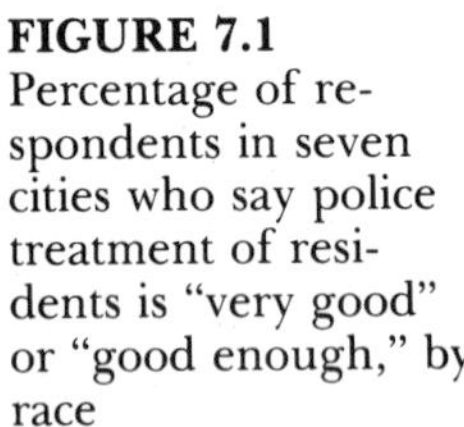

FIGURE 7.1
Percentage of respondents in seven cities who say police treatment of residents is "very good" or "good enough," by race

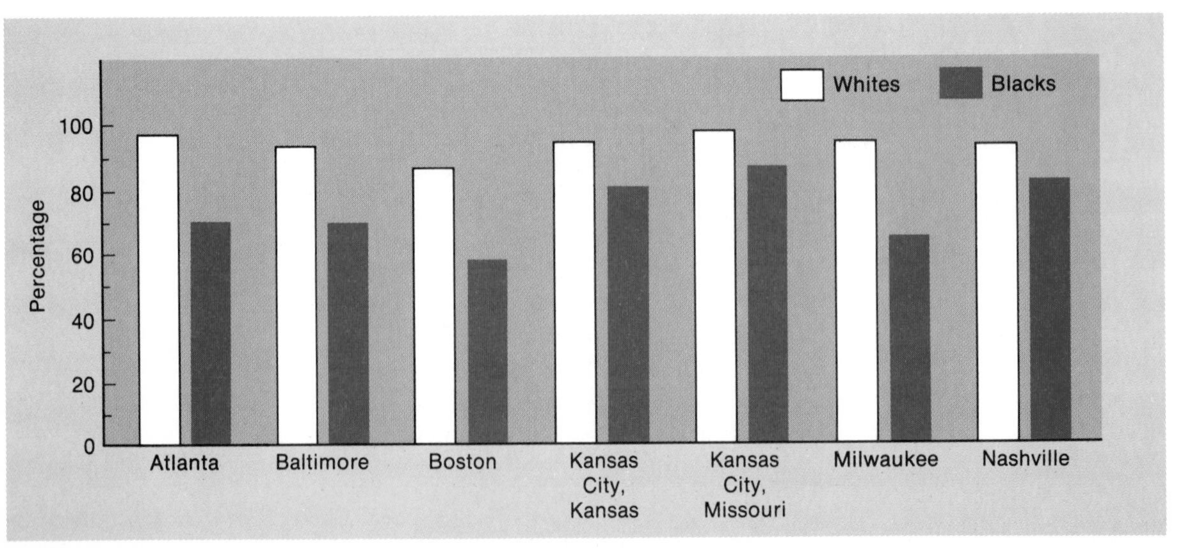

Kansas City, Missouri (N = 383)	*Milwaukee (N = 443)*	*Nashville (N = 426)*	*San Diego (N = 517)*
50%	52%	40%	51%
35	32	41	34
3	5	6	4
3	4	2	3
9	7	11	8
100%	100%	100%	100%

between them and the police: abrasive relationships between the police and black juveniles, police toleration of narcotics traffic, the small number of black patrol officers stationed in black neighborhoods, inefficient handling of emergencies, lack of respect toward black citizens, low police morale, not enough patrol officers, and inadequate patrol in black neighborhoods.[9]

Law enforcement is seen as permissive when an officer treats an offense committed against a person of the same ethnic group as the offender more lightly than a similar incident in which offender and victim are members of different groups. The police often explain such differential treatment as a result of working in a hostile environment. The white patrol officer may fear that breaking up a street fight among members of a minority group will provoke the wrath of onlookers, while community residents may in fact view such negligence as a further indication that the police do not care about their neighborhood. It is said that the police do not work effectively on such crimes as dealing in narcotics, gambling, petty thievery, and in-group assault, although these are the crimes that are most prevalent in the community and cause the greatest insecurity and apprehension among residents.

For too long the lack of adequate protection in urban lower-class neighborhoods has been obscured by the public attention given to police brutality, disorders in the ghetto, and white perceptions of black citizens. Only in recent years have black leaders addressed the black crime rate and the fact that most crimes of violence occur among members of the same racial group. As *Ebony* noted in a special 1979 issue, "black on black crime has reached a critical level that threatens our existence as a people."[10] The seventy-year-old black woman coming home from church who is robbed by two young blacks; the twenty-six-year-old black woman who is dragged by her hair behind a hedge by a young black man in Brooklyn; the ten-year-old black boy who is robbed of $3 in front of Harlem Hospital by two middle-aged black women—all are typical victims of ghetto crime and have the right to be critical of the agents of law enforcement for not providing better security in their community. Obviously, people in such circumstances may believe that they are not receiving equal protection of the law, and this perception contributes to their distrust of their neighbors, their lack of confidence in public leaders, and their disgust with due process—a concept that in their minds is just a defense for successful white (and sometimes even black) criminals.

Interpersonal relations

Law enforcement is one of the few public services that is delivered via face-to-face encounters with citizens in each community and neighborhood. One might think that through the experience of their interactions, police and citizens would develop more accurate pictures of the behavior each can expect of the other. In every situation, each must judge whether the other, in the specific social context, is hostile, friendly, or indifferent, and act accordingly. Most police–community relations programs are based on this assumption, with the thought that cordial relations will develop if police officers are known to the neighborhood and have learned the special characteristics of the people among whom they work.

However, behavior also results from perceptual processes that are influenced by attitudes. These attitudes may affect the extent to which police officers can become a part of a neighborhood and may prevent them from developing a network of acquaintances. As Eugene Groves and Peter Rossi write in their study of police perceptions of a ghetto,

> minor incidents, or even harmless street corner gatherings, may be blown out of proportion, and interpreted as exceptionally hostile in confirmation of the policeman's preexisting mental set. The policeman may then assault a person who used incautious phrases, or may summarily order a group to disperse, thus engendering the actual hostility he initially imagined.[11]

Because of residential segregation, the black urban community is more heterogeneous than the nonblack outsider understands—that is, blacks of differing degrees of law-abidingness and different social class, family background, and aspirations live in close proximity. To the police, the heterogeneous, densely settled ghetto thus makes perceiving or acting on differences in social position difficult. For many officers, skin color conceals important differences in class and lawfulness among black Americans. Thus, as citizens living near or in high-crime areas, innocent blacks not only become victims of crime but objects of police suspicion as well.

Practically all studies have documented prejudicial attitudes on the part of the police toward blacks. Albert Reiss, for example, found that a majority of white officers in Boston, Chicago, and Washington held antiblack attitudes, noting that "in the predominately Negro precincts, over three-fourths of the white policemen expressed prejudiced or highly prejudiced sentiments towards members of the Negro race."[12] Interviews with 522 police officers in thirteen major central cities disclosed that only 31 percent felt that "most

---

The Police Officer as a Symbol

The policeman in the ghetto is a symbol not only of law, but of the entire system of law enforcement and criminal justice. As such, he becomes the tangible target for grievances against shortcomings throughout the system. Against assembly-line justice in teeming lower courts; against wide disparities in sentences; against antiquated correctional facilities; against the basic inequities imposed by the system on the poor—to whom, for example, the option of bail means only jail. The policeman in the ghetto is a symbol of increasingly bitter social debate over law enforcement.

Source: *Report of the National Advisory Commission on Civil Disorders* (New York: Bantam Books, 1968), p. 299.

Will cordial relations between the police and the community develop through increased contact?

Negroes regard police as on their side." These attitudes lead many police officers to see all blacks as slum dwellers and thus as potential criminals, and as a result they tend to exaggerate the extent of black crime. If both the police and citizens view each other with intense hostility, personal encounters will be strained and the potential for explosions great. In such circumstances it is little wonder that the ghetto resident thinks of the police as an army of occupation and that the police think of themselves as combat soldiers.

An organizational factor also influences citizen–police encounters in lower-class neighborhoods. Just as most city school systems assign the inexperienced and incompetent to teach in the slums, job assignment and opportunity for transfer in most police departments is organized so that those with the least training and time on the job are sent to the precincts with the highest crime rates. Only with seniority and good effectiveness ratings do officers win transfers to more desirable middle-income (white) neighborhoods where crime rates are low and service calls less demanding. Reiss found that slum precincts were assigned deviant policemen of two types—"those who basically did excellent police work but were against the system, taking every opportunity to show their disregard for it, and those who both were poor police officers and had been reprimanded previously for infractions of the rules."[13]

Police brutality

The rising voices of excluded groups have brought incidents of police brutality to public attention. Although the poor have suffered these indignities for generations, only recently has an awakened citizenry focused attention on the illegal use of violence by the police. At a time when the political system is most vulnerable to complaints, most citizens are aware of their rights and are prepared to defend them. In 1901 Frank Moss, a former police commissioner of New York, said:

> For three years, there has been through the courts and the streets a dreary procession of citizens with broken heads and bruised bodies against few of whom was violence needed to effect an arrest. Many of them had done nothing to deserve an arrest. In a majority of such cases, no complaint was made. If the victim complains, his charge is generally dismissed. The police are practicing above the law.[14]

More recently there have been published accounts of narcotics agents breaking into private homes and holding the residents at gunpoint while pulling apart the interiors in what have proved to be vain searches for drugs. That these have been cases of mistaken identity is no excuse. No citizen, drug peddler or not, should be placed in such circumstances.

Definition

Such dramatic incidents easily serve to define police brutality, but citizens use the term to encompass a wider range of practices, including:

1. The use of profane and abusive language.
2. Commands to move on or get home.
3. Stopping and questioning people on the street or searching them and their cars.
4. Threats to use force if orders are not obeyed.
5. Prodding with a nightstick or approaching with a pistol.
6. The actual use of physical force or violence.

Indeed, citizens object to any practice that debases them, restricts their freedom, annoys or harasses them, or entails the use of unnecessary physical force. Charges of police brutality may result when citizens are not accorded the rights and respect due them in a democratic society.

Behavior that serves only to degrade a citizen's sense of self was found to be most upsetting in surveys conducted among blacks in Watts, Newark, and Detroit. Belittling names were particularly objectionable: "They talk down to me as if I had no name—like 'boy' or 'man' or whatever, or they call me 'Jack' or by my first name. They don't show me no respect." One out of every five blacks surveyed in postriot Detroit reported that the police had "talked down" to him; more than one in ten said a policeman had "called me a bad name."[15]

Violence has been committed by the police from time to time throughout American history, but it was not until the 1960s that the issue of misconduct by law enforcement personnel was treated seriously. The 1968 report of the Kerner Commission, which looked into the causes of the riots that shook Detroit, Los Angeles, Newark, New York, and other cities, focused on the extent to which police actions in dealing with citizens had triggered the disorders.[16] The report pointed to aggressive patrol, police brutality, and the unwarranted use of deadly force as sources of minority-group hostility.

Dealing with officer misconduct has become an item of high priority on the agenda of professional police administrators. It has been shown that when the top leadership of a department disciplines officers who disregard the professional code, a standard is set and notice given that such conduct will not be tolerated.

Low visibility

We can never know the amount of force used illegally because of the low visibility of police–citizen interactions and the reluctance of victims to file charges against their assailants. Police officers are authorized by law to use the force necessary to make arrests, but there is no agreement on the amount of

---

Response to Police Misconduct

Two Minneapolis police officers were suspended for 30 days without pay for kicking and breaking the ribs of a man in June 1982, Minneapolis Police Chief Tony Bouza said Thursday.

Both officers, Sgt. William Chaplin and Patrolman James Thernell, were acquitted of the same criminal charge by separate Hennepin County District Court juries last year. Bouza said the jury verdicts were wrong.

"The reality is the evidence was overwhelming," Bouza said yesterday in an interview. "As I read the transcripts of the criminal trials, I came to the inescapable conclusion that they should have been found guilty."

Chaplin and Thernell denied at their trials that they assaulted the man.

"I'm being punished for something I didn't do," Thernell said yesterday.

Bouza said he was persuaded by the testimony of two other Minneapolis policemen who said Chaplin and Thernell kicked 19-year-old Steve Goodwin when he was lying face down on the ground. . . .

The chief said the primary reason the juries voted for acquittal was that Goodwin "was a terrible witness. He's a street guy. He was hostile to the police. He made silly statements on the stand," Bouza said.

In addition, he said the acquittals reflected the reluctance of juries to convict police officers.

When Chaplin was acquitted, Bouza said he probably would not initiate disciplinary action. Later he said he made a mistake and moved for a departmental hearing.

Bouza said that the criminal process, the civil process and the internal disciplinary process "are distinct and separate. They might influence one another, but they are three separable events."

"This is an important symbolic case," because "it centers on one of the last holdouts of the old system, Bill Chaplin," Bouza said. "He is one of the leaders of this department. He has many admirable qualities and he has some qualities that make him a menace in the police world.

"He has been among the last to receive my message that brutality will not be condoned. He mistakes aggressive policing for doing anything you want on the streets." . . .

Chaplin, a 17-year veteran, previously was found guilty of "wanton and malicious" behavior in the beating of a suspect he arrested eight years ago.

Chaplin, an officer in the Second Precinct, was disciplined twice for incidents that occurred in 1979. He was suspended for a few days following allegations of misuse of vice-squad funds. He was reprimanded after a fight in a northeast Minneapolis bar.

Chaplin could not be reached for comment yesterday.

Thernell, a 14-year veteran, had no disciplinary record.

Bouza said he expects the Minneapolis Police Federation to inform him today that it will appeal the discipline. If the union appeals, the suspensions will be stayed until the appeals are resolved.

Source: Dennis J. McGrath, "Bouza Suspends 2 Officers Whom Juries Acquitted," *Minneapolis Star and Tribune*, 27 April 1984, p. 38. Reprinted with permission from the *Minneapolis Star and Tribune*.

---

force that is necessary. Is it better to let the suspect escape than to employ "deadly" force?

Although it is widely believed that police brutality is a racial matter between white police and black victims, Reiss found that lower-class white men were as likely to be brutalized by the police as lower-class black men, and that both were the likeliest victims. Observers who accompanied patrols for seven weeks in Boston, Chicago, and Washington, D.C., witnessed police assaults on forty-four citizens, yet only twenty-two arrests were made. What is most disturbing about Reiss's findings is that 37 percent of the instances of excessive force took place in settings controlled by the police—in the patrol car and station house. In half of the situations, a police officer did not participate but did not restrain his or her colleague. Although official police codes forbid such practices, the police culture does not.

Following a two-year study of police practices in New York City, Paul Chevigny concluded that taking officers to task for unprofessional behavior is virtually impossible. Police have a variety of ways of camouflaging misconduct. If a false arrest is made, there is a great temptation for police to make some charge against the citizen to avoid a possible lawsuit or the displeasure of superiors. In instances of physical abuse, the lack of witnesses, the code of secrecy, and the powerlessness of the victim prevent the disciplining of the abuser. Chevigny documents incidents that can only lessen respect for the law. He notes, "There is no more embittering experience in the legal system than to be abused by the police and then to be tried and convicted on false evidence."[17]

In addition to the fact that many police actions occur in situations of low visibility, such as the back seat of the squad car and the inner recesses of the station house, there is the tendency for other citizens to avoid becoming involved in cases of police brutality. Attempts to bring formal charges against the police are often frustrated by lack of witnesses. Chevigny reports further

Police Deviance

Evidence of the fraternal bond was found in a study of the police force in South City, a southern community of more than 25,000 inhabitants located east of the Mississippi River.

QUESTION: How often would a policeman in your department report another policeman for these kinds of acts? (*N* = 43)

Deviant pattern	*Responses*			
	Every time	*Some-times*	*Rarely*	*Never*
Sleeping on duty	6(14%)	21(49%)	10(23%)	6(14%)
Police brutality (excessive force)	5(12%)	18(42%)	16(37%)	4(9%)
Sex on duty	8(19%)	11(26%)	15(35%)	9(21%)
Police perjury	12(28%)	8(19%)	12(28%)	11(26%)
Drinking on duty	24(56%)	14(33%)	1(2%)	4(9%)

Source: Thomas Barker, "An Empirical Study of Police Deviance Other than Corruption," *Journal of Police Science and Administration* 6 (September 1978): 271. Reprinted with permission of the International Association of Chiefs of Police, P.O. Box 6010, 13 Firstfield Road, Gaithersburg, Maryland 20878.

that the courts are reluctant to give credence to civilian complainants, since impeachment of a police officer may be viewed as an assault against the entire criminal justice system.

The code of secrecy among the police has been documented by William Westley in *Violence and the Police.* Westley found that eleven out of fifteen men indicated their adherence to the code of secrecy when they said that they would not report another officer for taking money from a prisoner, and ten out of thirteen said they would not testify against an officer accused by a prisoner. Lying by police officers to protect themselves and one another is justified by the bonds among officers and the fear of outsiders.

Throughout their socialization, officers are reminded that every police activity may be the basis for two legal actions: one in which they are the complainant and one in which they are the defendant. The potential for a civil suit charging false arrest, usually the citizen's only recourse, is impressed upon the officer. Victims of brutality or false arrest who feel strongly enough about their case to register a formal complaint or to bring a civil suit encounter great difficulty in doing so. In one eastern city, the police department used to charge citizens who complained of police misconduct with filing false reports. In Philadelphia, the police review board found that it was standard practice to lodge a charge of resisting arrest or disorderly conduct against anyone who accused the police of brutality.

How much force?

Basic to the issue of police brutality is the question of the use of physical force. By law the police have the right to use force if necessary to make an arrest, to keep the peace, or to maintain public order. But just how much force is necessary and under what circumstances it may be used is an extraordinarily complicated and arguable question. In particular, the use of deadly force in the apprehension of suspects has become a deeply emotional issue with a direct connection to community relations. "There is no occurrence between the police and the community that causes more outrage [and] demoralization [or] precipitates [more] tension in a community [than] the police shooting of a civilian."[18] Estimates of the number of citizens killed annually by the police

---

Model Penal Code: Use of Deadly Force

Section 307(2)(B)

The use of deadly force is not justifiable under this Section unless:

i. the arrest is for a felony
ii. the person effecting the arrest is authorized to act as a peace officer or is assisting a person whom he believes to be authorized to act as a peace officer
iii. the actor believes that the force employed creates no substantial risk of injury to innocent persons
iv. the actor believes that:
   1. the crime for which the arrest is made involved conduct including the use or threatened use of deadly force
   2. there is a substantial risk that the person to be arrested will cause death or serious bodily harm if his apprehension is delayed.

---

range between 300 and 600, with about 1,500 more wounded.[19] It has become clear during the past decade that "the typical victim of deadly force employed in police–civilian contacts has been a young black male."[20] Deadly force has therefore become one of the major sources of strain between the police and the minority community.

Most states place limits on the use of deadly force, and departmental rules specify the circumstances in which it may be used. But there are still cities in which the formal police policy with regard to gun use is nothing more than "Never take me out in anger, never put me back in disgrace."[21] It is difficult to show that deadly-force policies have been violated when it is claimed that the victim was attempting to flee or that the officer killed in self-defense. When is it better to let the suspect flee than to employ deadly force?

By no means do all cases of the use of force by police officers involve the use of *unnecessary* force. Reiss lists six situations in which physical assault on a citizen should be judged improper or unnecessary:

1. If a policeman physically assaulted a citizen and then failed to make an arrest; proper use involves an arrest.
2. If the citizen being arrested did not, by word or deed, resist the policeman; force should be used only if it is necessary to make the arrest.
3. If the policeman, even though there was resistance to the arrest, could easily have restrained the citizen in other ways.
4. If a large number of policemen were present and could have assisted in subduing the citizen in the station, in lockup, and in the interrogating rooms.
5. If an offender was handcuffed and made no attempt to flee or offer violent resistance.
6. If the citizen resisted arrest, but the use of force continued even after the citizen was subdued.[22]

Arthur Kobler studied the deaths of 1,500 civilians killed by the police and discovered that the officer was punished for criminal misconduct in only three cases.[23] Richard Kania and Wade Mackey found that statewide rates of persons killed by the police ranged from a low of 2.97 per 100,000 population in New Hampshire to a high of 37.97 in Georgia.[24] In a study of police shootings in New York City, James Fyfe found that many incidents occurred when the officers themselves were either injured or killed, and that racial minority groups are more likely to be involved in weapons assaults than whites.[25] Lawrence Sherman reports that nationally most such incidents occur at night in central cities, that the victims are almost all males between the ages of seventeen and thirty, and that about half are black.[26] It is also clear that a high proportion of deadly-force incidents occurs in those large-city precincts where forms of criminal violence are most prevalent.

What can be done about this situation? Policies have been developed on the use of firearms by police officers, but no state law is as restrictive as the regulation of the Federal Bureau of Investigation, which says basically that an agent may kill someone only in self-defense or in the defense of another person against an immediate threat of physical violence. A number of states have adopted the provisions of the Model Penal Code, which emphasize that the officer must evaluate the danger before any action is taken. In twenty-four states, however, the Common Law Rule, enacted before the development of accurate firearms, remains the policy. This rule allows the police to shoot a fleeing felon even if there is no clear and present danger to the officer.

Policies and guidelines notwithstanding, as long as law enforcement officers carry weapons, such incidents will occur. Training, internal review of incidents, and disciplining or discharging of trigger-happy officers may help to reduce the use of unnecessary force, but the problem will undoubtedly erupt from time to time as an issue separating the community from the police.

Corruption

Police corruption is an enduring problem. The nature of some laws, especially those concerning victimless crimes, place the police in positions in which favors may be extended, bribes accepted, and arrests made in the pursuit of individual goals rather than the goals of law enforcement. Police corruption is not new to America. Earlier in the century, numerous city officials actively organized liquor and gambling businesses to provide personal income and to enhance political operations. In many cities a link was maintained between politicians and police officials so that favored clients would be protected and competitors harassed. Much of the movement to reform the police was designed to block such associations. Although political ties have been cut in most cities, corruption is still present.

One of the difficulties in discussing police corruption is that of definition. Sometimes corruption is defined so broadly that it ranges from accepting a free cup of coffee to robbing unlocked business establishments. Herman Goldstein suggests that corruption includes only those forms of behavior designed to produce personal gain for the officer or for others.[27] This definition, however, excludes the misuse of authority that may occur in a case of police

---

Should Patrolman G.K. Have Fired?

T.O. . . . was killed on December 28, 1968, by Patrolman G.K. in Prince Georges County, Maryland. T.O. had driven to the Mount Pleasant police station at about 1:45 A.M., parked his car, and told the police he was too drunk to drive and wanted them to drive him home. He refused a police offer to call a cab for him, became boisterous and unruly, and was charged with being drunk and disorderly. As he was being taken to a cell he hit officer G.K. and ran outside to the parking lot. G.K. followed, fired two warning shots and then a third shot which hit T.O. in the neck; he died in a hospital intensive care ward six days later.

G.K. was suspended and the case presented to the county grand jury. The state's attorney noted that the patrolman had "apparently deviated" from the prosecutor's guidelines on police use of firearms and that there may have been a "violation of the law." Maryland law indicated that a policeman should avoid firing at a person fleeing from arrest on a misdemeanor such as a disorderly conduct charge. The grand jury, however, brought no indictments. A police board was convened to evaluate Patrolman G.K.'s action and concluded that "O. became a felon when he escaped from K.'s custody, regardless of the charge on which he had been arrested." The board quoted Article 27, Section 139, of the Annotated Code of Maryland, which holds that: "If any offender legally detained and confined in the penitentiary, jail, . . . or station escapes, he shall be guilty of a felony." They added that police regulations permit firing at fleeing felons. On February 26, 1969, Patrolman G.K. was reinstated with back pay and vacation time.

Source: Arthur L. Kobler, "Police Homicide in a Democracy," *Journal of Social Issues* 31 (1975): 166–67. Reprinted by permission.

Close-up: Serpico

When Serpico started working with Gil Zumatto, his partner in the 7th Division, his imagination wasn't overly taxed as to what Zumatto and Stanard had discussed after he had left them in front of the Bronx County Criminal Courthouse.

Almost at once Zumatto asked him, "How do you feel about the money?"

Serpico repeated his litany of seeming indifference. "I don't care what you do, as long as I'm not involved," he said. "I don't want to get into any trouble."

Zumatto did not appear at all fazed by this. "Ah, don't worry about it. I'll tell you what. I'll take your share and save it for you, and whenever you make up your mind, it'll be there."

As Serpico soon observed, the main function of the division plainclothesmen was to protect the entire pad while servicing their racketeer clients. A principal safeguard was always to produce a minor arrest for the record whenever a complaint about illegal activity came down to the division for investigation. One day Zumatto said, "Come on, I got to check out some action."

A ghetto mother had reported wide-open gambling in her neighborhood and was afraid her teen-age son was being sucked into becoming a policy runner, the lowest level in the numbers racket. Policy is one of the most lucrative underpinnings of organized crime. A runner dashes around from apartment to apartment and helps take bets for a collector in a particular area; next in the intricately structured racket is the pickup man, who brings the "work"—the betting slips—from various collectors to a controller. He in turn passes it on to a "banker," the money man. The spiral continues upward with many banks interlocked into still larger ones. Playing the numbers may be basically a "poor man's game," but it is still big business, and hundreds of millions of dollars are milked annually out of ghetto areas by the underworld.

When Serpico and Zumatto arrived on the block cited in the woman's letter, it was not long before they spotted the local collector. He was a "mover," going from place to place—an alley, a tenement, a candy store—to take his action. Zumatto watched him with some amusement until he finally said, "Let's grab him." They stopped the man, frisked him, and found enough slips and money on him to make an iron-clad felony arrest. The collector was puzzled. "What's the matter?" he asked. "What's the problem? Ain't you from the division? You know, we're friends with the division. We're on."

The collector gave the name of the banker he worked for, and Zumatto said, "That's easy to check out. But we have a complaint from downtown, and we got to do something about it."

"Hey, that's cool, man. I understand, but I'm losing money just talking to you. I can't go in now. This is prime time, you know. What say I meet you at the precinct at four-thirty?"

Zumatto smiled.

"I'll bring some work," the collector said. "I'll even bring my own work, and you won't have to worry about nothing."

"OK. Four-thirty, remember."

"No use breaking his chops," Zumatto said to Serpico afterward. "The guy he works for is good people. He's never late."

The incident had taken place in the 42nd Precinct, and later in the day Zumatto brought Serpico to a bar called the Picadilly, across from the station house. Zumatto asked him if he wanted the collar. When Serpico said no, he didn't want this one, Zumatto looked around the bar, spied another plainclothesman, and offered it to him. He was delighted to take it, and they all adjourned to the sidewalk in front of the station house. Promptly at four-thirty, the collector, whose name Serpico learned was Brook Sims, walked up, smiling, clutching a handful of slips, although only enough for a misdemeanor arrest. The third plainclothesman marched Sims up to the desk and booked him. The case was dismissed the next day in court, but if anyone checked the record, the complaint had been investigated and an arrest had been made.

brutality when personal gain is not involved. The distinction is often not easy to make.

"Grass eaters" and "meat eaters"

Corrupt police officers have been described as falling into two categories: "grass eaters" and "meat eaters." "Grass eaters" are persons who accept payoffs that the circumstances of police work bring their way. "Meat eaters" are persons who aggressively misuse their power for personal gain. "Meat eaters" are few, though their exploits make headlines; "grass eaters" are the heart of the problem.[28] Because "grass eaters" are many, they make corruption respectable, and they encourage adherence to a code of secrecy that brands anyone who exposes corruption as a traitor.

In the past, poor salaries, politics, and recruitment practices have been cited as reasons that some police officers engage in corrupt practices, but corruption in some departments has been shown to be so rampant that the rotten-apple theory does not adequately explain the situation. An explanation based on organizational factors adds another dimension. Much police work involves the enforcement of laws in situations where there is no complainant or where there may be doubt as to whether a law has actually been broken. Moreover, most police work is carried out at the officer's own discretion, without direct supervision. If corruption takes place, the norms of a department and the code of the force may shield the bad cop from detection.

Enforcement of vice laws creates formidable problems for police agencies. In many cities the financial rewards to the vice operators are so high that they can easily afford the expense of protecting themselves against enforcement. More important, police operations against victimless crimes are proactive; no one complains and no one requests enforcement of the law. In seeking out vice, police often depend on informants—persons who are willing to steer a member of the squad toward gamblers, prostitutes, or narcotics dealers in

---

Policy in Regard to Gifts, Gratuities, and Favors

Section 310.70: Gifts, Gratuities, Fees, Rewards, Loans, etc., and Soliciting

Members and employees shall not under any circumstances solicit any gift, gratuity, loan, or fee where there is any direct or indirect connection between solicitation and their departmental membership and employment.

Section 310.71: Acceptance of Gifts, Gratuities, Fees, Loans, etc.

Members and employees shall not accept either directly or indirectly any gift, gratuity, loan, fee, or any other thing of value arising from or offered because of police employment or any activity connected with said employment. Members and employees shall not accept any gift, gratuity, loan, fee, or other thing of value the acceptance of which might tend to influence directly or indirectly the actions of said member or employee or any other member or employee in any matter of police business; or which might tend to cast any adverse reflection on the department or any member or employee thereof. No member or employee of the department shall receive any gift or gratuity from other members or employees junior in rank without the express permission of the chief of police.

—Oakland, California, Police Department

Source: President's Commission on Law Enforcement and Administration of Justice, *Task Force Report: The Police* (Washington, D.C.: Government Printing Office, 1967), p. 213.

---

exchange for something of value, such as money, drugs, information, or tolerance. Once the exchange is made, the informant may gain the upper hand by threatening to expose the cop for offering a bribe.

Ellwyn Stoddard, who studied "blue-coat crime," contends that a measure of role ambivalence is inevitable among the police in a democratic society. Officers are responsible for protecting community members but are not given the powers necessary to carry out this mandate. As a result, conscientious police officers must often violate the law in order to perform their duties. Minor infractions by fellow officers are overlooked; but what may begin as a small departure from the rules can grow until it becomes routine: "If these reference group norms involving illegal activity become routinized with use they become an identifiable informal 'code.' "[29] Stoddard says that police offi-

Terms Used in the "Code"

Bribery. The receipt of cash or a "gift" in exchange for past or future assistance in avoidance of prosecution, as by a claim that the officer is unable to make a positive identification of a criminal or by being in the wrong place at a time when a crime is to occur, or by any other action that may be excused as carelessness but not offered as proof of deliberate miscarriage of justice. Distinguished from *mooching* by the higher value of the gift and by the mutual understanding in regard to services to be performed upon the acceptance of the gift.

Chiseling. Demanding price discounts, free admission to places of entertainment whether in connection with police duty or not, and the like.

Extortion. A demand for placement of an advertisement in a police magazine or purchase of tickets to a police function; the practice of holding a "street court" where minor traffic tickets can be avoided by the payment of cash "bail" to the arresting officer, with no receipt given.

Favoritism. The practice of issuing license tabs, window stickers, or courtesy cards that exempt users from arrest or citation for traffic offenses (sometimes extended to wives, families, and friends of recipients).

Mooching. Accepting free coffee, cigarettes, meals, liquor, groceries, or other items, justified as compensation either for being in an underpaid profession or for future acts of favoritism the donor may receive.

Perjury. Lying to provide an alibi for fellow officers apprehended in unlawful activity approved by the "code."

Prejudice. Treatment of minority groups in a manner less than impartial, neutral, and objective, especially members of such groups who are unlikely to have "influence" in City Hall that might cause the arresting officer trouble.

Premeditated theft. Planned burglary, involving the use of tools, keys, or other devices to force entry, or any prearranged plan to acquire property unlawfully. Distinguished from *shakedown* only by the previous arrangements made in regard to the theft, not by the value of the items taken.

Shakedown. The practice of appropriating expensive items for personal use during an investigation of a break-in, burglary, or unlocked door and attributing their loss to criminal activity. Distinguished from *shopping* by the value of the items taken and the ease with which former ownership of items may be determined if the officer is caught in the act of procurement.

Shopping. Picking up small items such as candy bars, gum, and cigarettes at a store where the door has been accidentally left unlocked at the close of business hours.

Source: Adapted from Ellwyn R. Stoddard, "The Informal 'Code' of Police Deviancy: A Group Approach to Blue-Coat Crime," *Journal of Criminal Law, Criminology, and Police Science* 59 (1968): 205.

cers become socialized to the code early in their careers. Those who deviate by "snitching" on their fellow officers may become objects of ridicule. If, however, corruption comes to official attention, if it exceeds the limits of the code, other members of the force will distance themselves from the accused, in this way protecting the code.

One of the most highly publicized investigations into police corruption was launched by the Knapp Commission, a group appointed in 1970 by New York City Mayor John Lindsay. In its 1972 report, the commission said that it had found corruption to be widespread in the New York City Police Department. In the areas of gambling, narcotics, prostitution, and the construction industry, payments to police officers were a regular occurrence. Not only did patrol officers on the beat receive these "scores," they shared them with superior officers. The amounts ranged from a few dollars in minor shakedowns to a narcotics payoff of $80,000. What most concerned the commission was the fact that although most police officers were not themselves corrupt, they tolerated the practices and took no steps to prevent what they knew or suspected was happening.

Impact of corruption

Police corruption has multiple effects on law enforcement: criminals are left free to pursue their illegal activities, departmental morale and supervision drop, and the image of the police suffers. The credibility of a law enforcement agency is extremely important in light of the need for the citizenry's cooperation. When there is a generally prevalent belief that the police are not much different from the "crooks," effective crime control is impossible.

What is startling is that many people do not equate police corruption with other forms of criminal activity. That officers may proceed forcefully against minor offenders yet look the other way if a payoff is forthcoming seems acceptable to some. As Goldstein notes, however, "this absurdity is not lost on those who live where petty offenses are common. Black citizens in particular consistently rate the integrity of police officers much lower than whites do and

---

Findings of the Knapp Commission

We found corruption to be widespread. It took various forms depending upon the activity involved, appearing at its most sophisticated among plainclothesmen assigned to enforcing gambling laws. In the five plainclothes divisions where our investigations were concentrated we found a strikingly standardized pattern of corruption. Plainclothesmen, participating in what is known in police parlance as a "pad," collected regular bi-weekly or monthly payments amounting to as much as $3,500 from each of the gambling establishments in the area under their jurisdiction, and divided the take in equal shares. The monthly share per man (called the "nut") ranged from $300 and $400 in midtown Manhattan to $1,500 in Harlem. When supervisors were involved they received a share and a half. A newly assigned plainclothesman was not entitled to his share for about two months, while he was checked out for reliability, but the earnings lost by the delay were made up to him in the form of two months' severance pay when he left the division.

Source: City of New York, Commission to Investigate Allegations of Police Corruption and the City's Anti-Corruption Procedures, *The Knapp Commission Report on Police Corruption* (New York: George Braziller, 1973), p. 1.

---

react with understandable disdain when urged to have greater respect for the law by officers whom they know to be corrupt."[30] Further, some citizens believe that police corruption is tolerable as long as the streets are safe. This attitude is unreasonable because police officers "on the take" are pursuing personal rather than community goals.

Controlling corruption

As with other problems in a free society, the power of public opinion is crucial for the control of police corruption. The public, however, knows only about the major police scandals that are publicized in the newspapers and on television and radio, such as those that in the past have infected the police departments of such cities as Chicago, Denver, and New York. When corruption reaches this level of notoriety, government agencies other than the police—prosecutors, attorneys general, grand juries, special investigating bodies, and others—step in to solve the problem by means of indictments and organizational reforms. But to a great extent the American political and legal systems have charged the police with keeping their own house in order. It is through mechanisms internal to law enforcement organizations that the more pernicious daily acts of corruption must be exposed and corrected.

It is well recognized in police leadership circles that the top administrators of a department must set the tone with regard to corruption. Successful police officials, such as Patrick Murphy, O. W. Wilson, Clarence Kelley, and Wyman Vernon, all took much-publicized stands that let the general public and law enforcement employees know that they would not tolerate even the slightest act of corruption, and would take swift action when any such acts came to their attention.

Improving community relations

Law enforcement requires the active cooperation of all citizens. The police depend on citizens to report crimes and to assist officers in the conduct of investigations but are too often hampered by the fear and distrust exhibited by the residents of high-crime areas. One might suppose that people who are constantly being victimized would be the most outspoken in their demands for efficient law enforcement; yet the police commonly face closed mouths and blank stares when they seek information about an event.

Improvement in community relations has become one of the foremost goals of criminal justice personnel, particularly in localities where members of minority groups live. Large sums have been expended to improve the image of the police and to educate the public about the need for cooperation in the war against crime. Recruitment of racial-minority and female officers and attempts to augment civic accountability are two means by which cities have moved toward this goal.

Minority police officers

Historically, the American criminal justice system has recruited few police officers among racial minorities. Though the major metropolitan areas have become increasingly populated by black and Hispanic citizens, law enforcement positions are still held predominantly by whites. In no major city does

TABLE 7.3 Percentages of black and Hispanic police officers and of black and Hispanic residents in the twenty largest U.S. cities

City	*Percentage of black officers*	*Percentage of community black*	*Percentage of Hispanic officers*	*Percentage of community Hispanic*
New York	10.2	25.2	7.2	19.9
Chicago	20.1	39.8	3.4	14.0
Los Angeles	9.4	17.0	13.6	27.5
Philadelphia	16.5	37.8	0.6	3.8
Houston	9.7	27.6	8.6	17.6
Detroit	30.7	63.1	0.7	2.4
Dallas	8.2	29.4	4.6	12.3
San Diego	5.5	8.9	7.8	14.9
Phoenix	2.8	4.8	9.3	14.8
Baltimore	17.5	54.8	0.3	1.0
San Antonio	4.6	7.3	32.9	53.7
Indianapolis	13.1	21.8	0.1	0.9
San Francisco	8.1	12.7	8.1	12.3
Memphis	22.0	47.6	0.0	0.8
Washington, D.C.	50.1	70.3	1.0	2.8
Milwaukee	11.6	23.1	4.5	4.1
San Jose	2.1	4.6	17.3	22.3
Cleveland	11.3	43.6	0.2	3.1
Columbus	11.1	22.1	0.0	0.8
Boston	13.2	22.4	2.1	6.4

Source: Adapted from Samuel Walker, "Black and Hispanic Police Officers: Employment Trends in the Fifty Largest Cities," *Review of Applied Urban Research* 11 (October 1983): 3.

the number of nonwhites in blue approximate the proportion of nonwhites in the community. In Washington, D.C., and in Atlanta, both with populations about 70 percent black, only 50 percent and 46 percent, respectively, of the police forces are black. A national survey revealed that the percentage of black and Hispanic members of the police forces of the fifty largest cities was on the average only half the percentages of blacks and Hispanics in the cities' populations.[31] Thus, as table 7.3 indicates, if 60 percent of a city's population is minority, it can be expected that only 30 percent of the police force will be minority. As political power shifts toward minorities in some American cities, however, the composition of their police forces can be expected to reflect the change. But the election of a black or Hispanic mayor need not signal a change in the composition of the police force. Again, it is political power that is crucial, and in many cities the police are able to protect their turf from outsiders even when the outsiders are elected officials. Recruitment of minorities to the force requires a commitment by law enforcement officials.

The effort to recruit more minority police officers was initially spurred by the 1968 report of the National Advisory Commission on Civil Disorders, which identified police—minority relations as a major factor contributing to ghetto riots. The problem received renewed emphasis with passage by Congress of equal opportunity legislation and with court decisions promoting affirmative action. The 1972 Equal Employment Opportunity Act, the 1973 Amendment to the Omnibus Crime Control and Safe Streets Act, and the 1976 Crime Control Act all contain language designed to further the recruitment of minority criminal justice personnel and to penalize those agencies that do not cooperate in this effort.

At the prodding of the federal government, most city police forces have undertaken extensive campaigns to recruit more minority officers. To a large extent, however, these efforts have failed, perhaps because departments have not been aggressive enough in their search, because young blacks have a negative view of law enforcement work, or because a poor educational background has left them unable to pass the entrance examination. An equally strong factor is prejudice within departments, which often assign black police officers to the dirty jobs and subject them to slurs by fellow officers.

In a study of New York City police officers, Nicholas Alex found that black police officers are only partially integrated into the law enforcement subculture. *Black in Blue* describes the position of black police officers as one of "double marginality," of not being fully accepted in either their social or their professional world.[32] Black officers must deal with the fact that members of their own race may expect more sympathetic treatment from them while at the same time they must face racism among their white colleagues. In a later book titled *New York Cops Talk Back,* however, Alex reported that black police officers are becoming more aggressive and self-assured.[33] As members of minority groups form a larger proportion of the urban police force, they may be expected to be increasingly unwilling to put up with discriminatory practices.

The experience of black officers in some large police forces has encouraged them to become politicized and to form separate organizations. The Afro-American Patrolman's League (AAPL) of Chicago, the Afro-American Police (AAP) of New York, and the Black Guardians of Bridgeport, Connecticut, have appealed to the courts to rule on such employment issues as seniority, minority recruitment, and discriminatory practices.

Efforts to add minority members to police forces have met with difficulty, and even when such officers are recruited, they must face the problem of becoming integrated into a department's social system. White officers have resented the hiring of minority officers to fulfill affirmative action quotas, and such reactions can have a detrimental effect on attempts to maintain a

The Black Cop: A Man Caught in the Middle

It was an incident just waiting to explode. Three flights up in a Chicago ghetto tenement, six white policemen were surrounding a furious, cursing Negro. "I didn't fire no shots," he railed. "Get your hands off me!" Neighbors, curious and uncooperative, had gathered in the hallway. A suspicious crowd was forming outside on the street. As the cops debated their next move, black patrolman George Owens and his white partner, John Bacus, rushed up the stairs from radio car 1315. Almost immediately, the elderly Negro manager of the building sought out Owens and reported having seen the suspect fire the shots. That was enough. The white cops quickly stepped aside for Owens as he approached the alleged gunman, ignoring the obscenities and racial appeals ("I'm a black man!") the man shouted at him. "We've got a complaining witness," Owens announced firmly. "He says he saw the gun, saw him fire it. Book him."

As the suspect was led away, the Negro policeman mused to his partner about the thick hide needed to absorb the abuse he had taken from a fellow black. "It's when a guy starts developing that outer skin," said Owens, "that he really becomes a policeman."

Source: "The Black Cop: A Man Caught in the Middle," *Newsweek,* 16 August 1971, p. 19.

smoothly operating law enforcement organization. As public organizations continue to face limited resources in the 1980s, there may be continued reductions in the number of officers serving many financially strapped cities. Because of the important role played by seniority in layoff procedures, minority officers may be the first to go and the gains of the past decade may thus be lost.

The importance of minority police officers cannot be overemphasized. It is not only a question of equal access to an economically desirable governmental position; it is also a question of effective law enforcement. It is extremely difficult for members of an underrepresented group to view the police as being responsive to their needs, free of prejudice, and interested in the cause of justice if they do not see members of their group on the force. The importance of ethnic identification in American society makes it essential that the agents of justice reflect the characteristics of the community.

Civic accountability

Relations between citizens and the police depend to a great extent on the level of confidence people have that officers will behave in accordance with the law and with departmental guidelines. Rapport is enhanced when citizens feel secure in the knowledge that the police will protect their persons and property and the civil liberties guaranteed by the Constitution. Permissive enforcement is as great a concern as police brutality in some metropolitan areas. The problem of making the police accountable to civilian control without thereby destroying their effectiveness has aroused increasing public concern.

Traditionally, Americans have relied on locally elected officials to ensure that the police carry out their tasks in accordance with the law and as the citizenry desires. Indeed, civic accountability is one reason why law enforcement has been kept primarily a responsibility of municipal government. As chapter 5 noted, the appointment of the police chief by the mayor or legislature has served as one way to ensure that the uniformed force is responsible to political authority. During the last half century, however, these formal ties between the police and the community have been weakened by the development of the law enforcement bureaucracy and the job security created by the civil service personnel system, which fills positions on the basis of scores obtained in competitive public examinations. More recently, the growth of urban areas has brought demands that local police units give way to centralized law enforcement agencies for the entire metropolitan region. These changes have diminished the ability of individual citizens, political leaders, and neighborhood groups to influence the way the police work.

Civilian review boards. The dismal record of ***civilian review boards*** illustrates the frustrations encountered in attempts to maintain civic accountability. Set up originally in the early 1960s, these boards were organized so that complaints about police malpractice would be channeled through a publicly constituted committee of citizens. The boards were to review the way the police departments disposed of these complaints and to recommend remedial action; they did not have power to investigate or to discipline. It was expected that the boards would be most attuned to complaints about police brutality, racial or religious discrimination, and abuse of authority.

civilian review board
A citizen board independent of the police, established to receive and investigate complaints against law enforcement officers.

The operating civilian boards have shown many of the same weaknesses as the internal police boards. Citizens have difficulty filing complaints, procedures are time-consuming, and staff is lacking. The results are not impressive. From 1958 to 1965 the Philadelphia Civilian Review Board processed 704 complaints but recommended penalties against the police officers involved in only 38 cases. Wilson may be correct in stating that review boards will have little effect on substantive police policies, partly because objectionable behavior results from "styles created by general organizational arrangements and departmental attitudes and partly because grievance procedures deal with specific complaints about unique circumstances, not with general practices of the officers."[34] In fact, the review of police actions occurs after the incident has occurred and usually comes down to a question of the officer's word against that of the complainant. Given the low visibility of the incidents that lead to complaints, a great many complaints are destined to be found to be unsubstantiated.

Internal control. Policing the police is really an internal matter that must be given top priority by administrators. The community must feel confident that the department has developed procedures to ensure that personnel will act in ways that preserve the rights of citizens and that those procedures are effective. Unfortunately, many departments have no formal complaint machinery, and when such machinery does exist, it often seems designed to discourage citizen input. Internal investigators may assume that a citizen's grievance is an attack on the police as a whole and reflexively move to shield individual officers. In such a situation, administrators may be deprived of valuable information and so may be unable to correct the problem. The public, in turn, may be led to believe that the questioned practices are condoned or even expected.

internal affairs unit A segment of a police department designated to receive and investigate complaints against officers alleging violation of rules and policies.

Depending on the size of the department, a single officer or an entire section may be designated an ***internal affairs unit*** to investigate wrongdoing. An officer who is charged with misconduct may face criminal prosecution or departmental disciplinary action that may lead to resignation, dismissal, or suspension for a period of time. Officers assigned to the unit carry responsibilities similar to those of the inspector general's staff in the military. They investigate complaints of misconduct, reports of the discharge of weapons by officers, allegations of corruption, and the wounding or killing of an officer by a citizen or of a citizen by an officer.

The internal affairs unit must be provided with sufficient investigative resources to carry out its mission and must have direct access to the chief. Even when the top administrator supports the rooting out of misconduct, however, it is often difficult to persuade officers to testify against fellow officers. But maintenance of a "clean" force is essential if the crime prevention and law enforcement goals are to be met. When the police department demonstrates to the community that it is professionally responsible for the actions of its members, demands for review by an external body fade away.

Women on the force

Traditionally defined as "man's work," policing is increasingly attracting women into its ranks. Although Lola Baldwin, the first policewoman in the United States, was made an officer in the Portland, Oregon, Police Depart-

Only in recent years has there been an increase in the number of women who are sworn police officers.

ment in 1905, the number of women officers remained small—about 1.5 percent of all officers—until 1970. At that time, as a result of prodding by LEAA, passage of equal opportunity legislation, and the rise of the Women's Movement, police departments began actively to recruit female officers. Even now, however, only 5 percent of sworn officers (about 19,000) are women, as figure 7.2 indicates, though in some cities their proportion exceeds 7 percent.[35] As sociologist Susan Martin notes, it is in the cities with large black populations, such as Atlanta, Detroit, and Washington, D.C., that sexual and racial integration of the police department has gone the furthest: "in strongly [white] ethnic-group dominated cities (Buffalo, Boston, Philadelphia, and Minneapolis) the forces of traditionalism and resistance to change . . . have retarded the hiring of policewomen."[36]

Unfortunately, since Martin concluded her research many of these cities have been hard hit by fiscal crises and as a result have been laying off police officers rather than trying to attract new ones. Because women and racial minorities have been the latest hired, they have also been the first to lose their jobs. It is the new population centers of the South and Southwest that have been expanding their departments during the past few years, and there the percentage of female officers has increased most strikingly.

Despite increases in their numbers on police forces, women still have difficulty breaking into this traditionally male stronghold. Cultural expectations of women often conflict with ideas about behavior appropriate for officers. As newcomers to the force, women have often found their upward mobil-

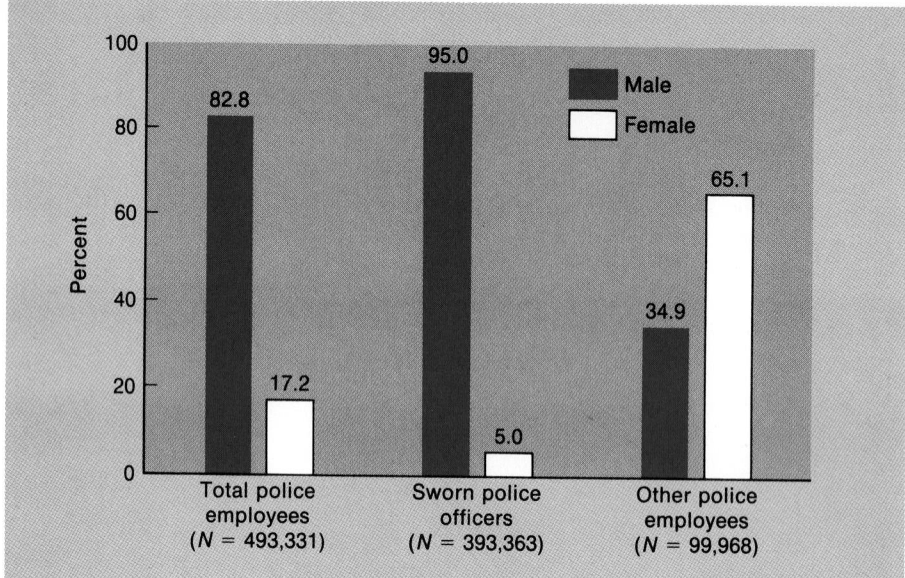

FIGURE 7.2 Percentage of male and female full-time police employees

ity blocked and that they must contend with prejudice against their pioneering activities. Especially with regard to the assignment of women to patrol duty, such questions as the following are frequently raised:

- Can women handle situations involving force and violence?
- What changes in training and equipment must be made?
- Do women resent the loss of the "specialist" role they previously played in police work?
- Should women and men be treated equally in regard to promotion?
- Does putting men and women together on patrol as partners tend to break up families?

Martin studied female officers in Washington, D.C., by becoming a member of the police reserve. As she explains, women officers are required to learn a new set of behaviors and their fellow officers and citizens must become accustomed to their presence in their new role. In addition to mastering the technical details of arrest, weaponry, and self-defense, policewomen must learn to take control of situations assertively, to wield power, and to act authoritatively, skills seldom acquired in the socialization process most of them have undergone.

Policemen have low expectations of the law enforcement abilities of women officers but insist that they be treated just like men. Questions are raised about the physical strength of women, their willingness to take risks, and their ability to control a situation. Some are criticized for being timid in trying circumstances; if they are not timid, they are labeled bossy and unfeminine. Policemen also complain that women undermine the "emphasis on crime fighting and the masculine image that accompanies it."[37] Because of these attitudes, some departments continue to segregate female officers in specialized juvenile or women's details, while others keep them in the station house in clerical roles.

Although most policewomen have easily met the performance expectations of their superiors, it is at the social level that they have had to overcome the greatest resistance to change. In particular, they have encountered unpredictable resistance to their exercise of authority, and are often subjected to sexist remarks and more overt forms of sexual harassment designed to undermine their authority. Interaction with their male counterparts has brought further problems. Police work takes place in the social context of an occupational fraternity. Great emphasis is placed on the bonds that tie fellow officers together so that they will come to one another's aid, shield the force from the prying eyes of outsiders, and uphold the traditions of police work. A woman's entrance into this male domain is upsetting to many policemen. They complain that if their patrol partner is a woman, they cannot be sure of her ability to lend assistance in times of danger—that she simply lacks the physical stature to act effectively when the going gets rough.

Although women have encountered barriers to their acceptance as equals of men in law enforcement work, studies conducted by the Police Foundation

Close-up: "People Are Always Asking Me What I'm Trying to Prove . . ."

Patrol Officer Cristina Murphy

Jim Dyer was drunk out of his mind when he called the Rochester Police Department on a recent Saturday night. He wanted to make a harassment complaint; a neighbor, he claimed, was trying to kill him with a chair. Off. Cristina Murphy, 27, a petite, dark-haired, soft-spoken three-year veteran of the Rochester P.D., took the call.

"What's the problem here?" she asked when she arrived at the scene. A crowd had gathered. Dyer's rage was good local fun.

"You're a *woman*!" Dyer complained as Murphy stepped from her squad car. "All they send me is *women*. I called earlier and they sent me a Puerto Rican and *she* didn't do nothing either."

"Mr. Dyer, what exactly is the problem?"

"Dickie Burroughs is the problem. He tried to kill me." Through a drunken haze, Dyer made certain things clear: He wanted Dickie Burroughs locked up. He wanted him sent to Attica for life. He wanted it done that night. Short of all that, Dyer hoped that the police might oblige him by roughing up his foe, just a little.

"We don't do that sort of thing," Murphy explained in the voice she uses with drunks and children. "Mr. Dyer, I can do one of two things for you. I can go find Mr. Burroughs and get his side of the story; I can talk to him. The other thing I can do is take a report from you and advise you how to take out a warrant. You'll have to go downtown for that."

Later, in her squad car, Murphy would say that she isn't usually so curt to complaining citizens. "But it's important not to take crap about being a female. Most of the stuff I get, I just let slip by. This guy, though, he really did not want service on his complaint, he wanted retribution. When he saw a woman taking his call, he figured that I wouldn't give it to him; it never struck him that no male officer would either. You know, *everyone* has an opinion about women being police officers—even drunks. Some people are very threatened by it. They just can't stand getting orders from a woman. White males, I think, are the most threatened. Black males seem the least—they look at me and they just see blue. Now women, they sometimes just can't stand the idea that a woman exists who can have power over them. They feel powerless and expect all women to feel that way too. As I said, everyone has an opinion."

Source: Claudia Dreifus, "People Are Always Asking Me What I'm Trying to Prove . . . ," *Police Magazine*, March 1980, p. 19. Reprinted by permission of the Edna McConnell Clark Foundation.

and by other researchers point to a more positive reception. Research in Washington, D.C., in which a group of female recruits was compared with a group of male recruits, found that gender "is not a bona fide occupational qualification for doing police patrol work."[38] This study, corroborated in other cities, found that most citizens had generally positive things to say about the work of policewomen.

The future role of women in police work will evolve in tandem with changes in the nature of policing, the cultural values of society, and the organization of law enforcement. As citizens become used to women on patrol and in other nontraditional roles, it will probably become less difficult for them to assert their authority and to gain the compliance required in law enforcement work. Finally, there are signs that more and more citizens and policemen alike are beginning to take it for granted that women will be found on patrol as sworn officers of the law.

Unionism

collective bargaining Negotiation between management and a labor union in regard to compensation, working conditions, and other aspects of employment. An agreement is set forth in a contract binding on both parties.

During much of this century, police employee organizations were mainly fraternal associations designed to provide opportunities for fellowship, to serve the welfare needs (death benefits, insurance) of police families, and to promote charitable activities. In some cities, however, the police were organized for the purpose of ***collective bargaining,*** and by 1919 thirty-seven locals had been chartered by the American Federation of Labor. The famous Boston police strike of 1919 was in fact triggered by the refusal of the city to recognize one of these AFL affiliates. Not until the 1950s did the police, along with other public employees, begin to join labor unions in large numbers. During the past fifteen years the unionization of the police has become what Samuel Walker has called a "hidden revolution." Today nearly three-fourths of all American police officers are members of unions.[39]

The dramatic rise in membership in police unions has been attributed to several factors: job dissatisfaction, especially with regard to pay and working conditions; the perception that other public employees were improving their positions through collective bargaining; the belief that the public is hostile to police needs; and an influx of young officers who hold less traditional views on relations between officer and police commissioner.[40] Another factor is strong recruitment efforts by organized labor, which sought to make up for a decline in membership as employment opportunities shifted from the industrial to the service sectors of the economy by enrolling public employees.

The growth of police unionism has alarmed many law enforcement administrators and public officials. Police chiefs fear they will be unable to manage their departments effectively because they believe that various aspects of personnel administration (transfers, promotions) will become bound up in arbitration and grievance procedures. Thus many administrators view the union as interfering with their law enforcement leadership and with the officers in the ranks. Public officials have recognized the effectiveness of unions in gaining financial advantages for their members and are thus wary of the demands that will be placed on government resources. No politician likes to raise taxes. Some commentators have also expressed the view that the police, as the public embodiment of law enforcement, should not engage in such job actions as strikes, slowdowns, and sickouts (the "blue flu"). They wonder about the impact on the practical and symbolic aspects of criminal justice should picket lines be thrown around public buildings and the police refuse to work.

Police unions today

Most officers are today members of a labor union, but unlike the steelworkers and other trade unionists, they have no national organization representing all police. There are, in fact, different types of organizations at the local, state, and national levels. Police unions are locally based, in the main, because the key decisions in regard to law enforcement are made at this level. There is also the feeling among some officers that the organized police of a city can achieve their ends without the need to affiliate with and pay dues to a national labor union. As Hervey Juris and Peter Feuille observe, the local character of the employment relationship helps to explain why "the relatively centralized national police organizations . . . have failed to enroll large numbers of police officers as members."[41]

The state is the next higher level of police unionism. Again, this structure is related to the need to bring pressure on the state government in regard to such issues as pensions, disability benefits, and the rights of public employees. Thus state federations of the local police organizations function essentially as lobbyists in the state capital.

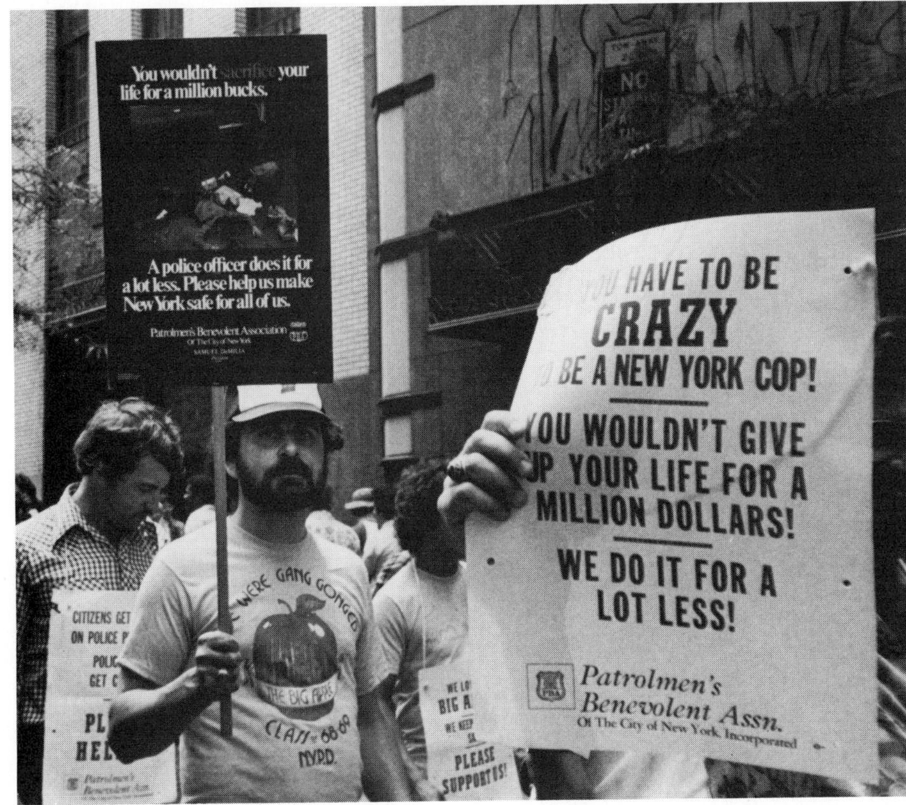

A number of cities have experienced job actions by their police.

On the national level, the International Conference of Police Associations (ICPA) is the largest organization, with more than 100 local and state units representing more than 200,000 officers. In 1978 this organization asked its members to approve application for entrance into the AFL-CIO, but this move was rejected by the rank and file. Subsequently, a large part of the membership broke away and formed the International Union of Police Associations (IUPA), to which the AFL-CIO then granted a charter. The Fraternal Order of Police (FOP) and the International Brotherhood of Police Officers (IBPO) are other major organizations representing law enforcement interests. Police officers are also members of such national unions as the American Federation of State, County, and Municipal Employees (AFSCME), a group with members among occupational groups in all sectors of public service, and the Teamsters.

Impact of police unions

Clearly, the police are little different from union members in other sectors of society: they are concerned primarily about wages, hours, and working conditions. Broader issues of changes in operating procedures have been touched on only when they affect these three elements. Abuses of collective bargaining procedures have occurred, according to Juris and Feuille, when union leaders have appealed directly to the public or city council after failure to get police administrators to discuss contract terms in accordance with normal procedures.[42]

Of concern to some police administrators is the inclusion in union contracts of terms specifying policies and procedures that they believe interfere with their ability to run their departments. Restrictions on management's exercise of discretion in determining patrol officers' work shifts, criteria for promotion, and procedures for disciplining employees are sometimes upsetting to leadership. Officers in some localities have succeeded in having a "police bill of rights" written into their contracts, specifying the procedures that will be followed when an officer must submit to an investigation that could eventuate in disciplinary action, demotion, or expulsion. Included are terms specifying the right to counsel, the right to confront accusers, the keeping of verbatim transcripts of questioning, and the conditions under which interrogation may take place.

Police unions have been antagonistic to changes in law enforcement organization and techniques when they affect the membership. For example, attempts to shift from two-person to one-person patrol cars were opposed by unions in at least two of the twenty-two cities studied by Juris and Feuille. In addition, police unions opposed efforts to employ civilians in clerical positions, on the grounds that civilians constituted a potential security risk and that all police jobs required personnel who had street experience and authority to arrest. Although the stated reasons may seem plausible, they are consistent "with the traditional trade union protectionist goal of safeguarding bargaining-unit work for incumbents."[43] In response to calls for increased recruitment of women and minorities, police unions have again tried to maintain the status quo. Affirmative action efforts, especially with regard to promotion, have been resisted by the unions because such practices threaten the prerogatives attached to seniority.

Job actions

Slowdowns, sickouts, and other disruptive tactics are the more common means that police unions use to exert pressure on employers. The strike has been used sparingly. It is illegal for most public employees to strike, and it was more than fifty years after the famous Boston Police Strike of 1919 before there was another such job action in a major American city. During the past decade, however, New Orleans, San Francisco, Tucson, Oklahoma City, Las Cruces (New Mexico), and Youngstown (Ohio) have all experienced strikes by law enforcement officers.[44] In some of these actions, the police returned to work within days; in others, they stayed out for as long as a month. In some cities, strikers lost their jobs; in others, they won pay raises. Aside from the legal prohibitions against such actions, individual members have ambivalent feelings about deserting their responsibilities for a strike that would leave a city to be preyed upon by criminals.

In analyzing the causes of police strikes, researchers for the International Association of Chiefs of Police concluded that a combination of factors was operating in each situation.[45] Among these factors the municipal financial crisis stands out. Beginning in the mid-1970s, American cities were faced with reduced federal allocations, local taxpayer revolts, and inflation. Since personnel costs make up as much as 85 percent of a city's operating budget, public employees usually bear the brunt of budget reductions. Many police departments had been expanded earlier in the decade because of the public clamor for increased protection—an expansion aided by the large amounts of federal money then being distributed by LEAA and by revenue sharing. When the inflow of federal funds started to dwindle, public expenditures could not keep pace with inflation and reduced municipal revenues.

Future of police unions

The increase in the use of collective bargaining by public employees during the past decade has been phenomenal. Although most police officers have preferred to join local organizations rather than to become members of an affiliate of the AFL-CIO or some other national union, the strength of police unions has increased greatly in many cities. Clearly, collective bargaining is a concept whose time has come, and police officials are going to have to recognize this new influence on law enforcement administration. At the same time, note that in a public sector whose resources have diminished, state and local governments may not have the funds to increase salaries to keep pace with inflation. Already New York City and Boston have reduced the sizes of their police forces as one way of reducing budget deficits. But in other cities, particularly those in regions undergoing economic and population growth, and in the more affluent suburbs police unions are making greater headway and can be expected to retain their influence. There are still, however, crucial questions about the role that unions should play in determining police department policies and the methods they can legitimately use to influence bargaining agreements.

Private security

In the past ten years or so, Americans have become aware of the increased number of privately organized, uniformed security agents in stores, shopping malls, industrial plants, and airports. Private policing existed in Europe and the United States before the public organization of law enforcement, as witness Fielding's Bow Street Runners in England and the bounty hunters of the American West. Then, during the industrialization of the United States at the end of the nineteenth century, the Pinkerton National Detective Agency provided industrial spies and strikebreakers to thwart labor union activities, and Wells, Fargo & Company was formed to provide security for banks and other businesses. It is only in recent years that businesses have felt the need to employ private security forces to deal with shoplifting, employee pilfering, robbery, and airplane hijacking. As figure 7.3 indicates, retail and industrial/manufacturing establishments spent nearly as much for private protection in 1980 as all localities had spent for police protection in 1979. Many private groups, too—especially residents of upper-income suburbs—have engaged private police to patrol their neighborhoods.

Private security services are classified as either contract or proprietary. Contract security services are provided by agencies and private practitioners for a fee. Such practitioners include locksmiths, alarm specialists, and polygraph examiners; such organizations as Brink's, Burns, and Wackenhut provide guards and detectives. States and municipalities often require contract personnel to be licensed and bonded. Similar services are provided by proprietary security personnel, who are employed directly by the organization they protect. Regulation by the state or municipality is not the norm for proprie-

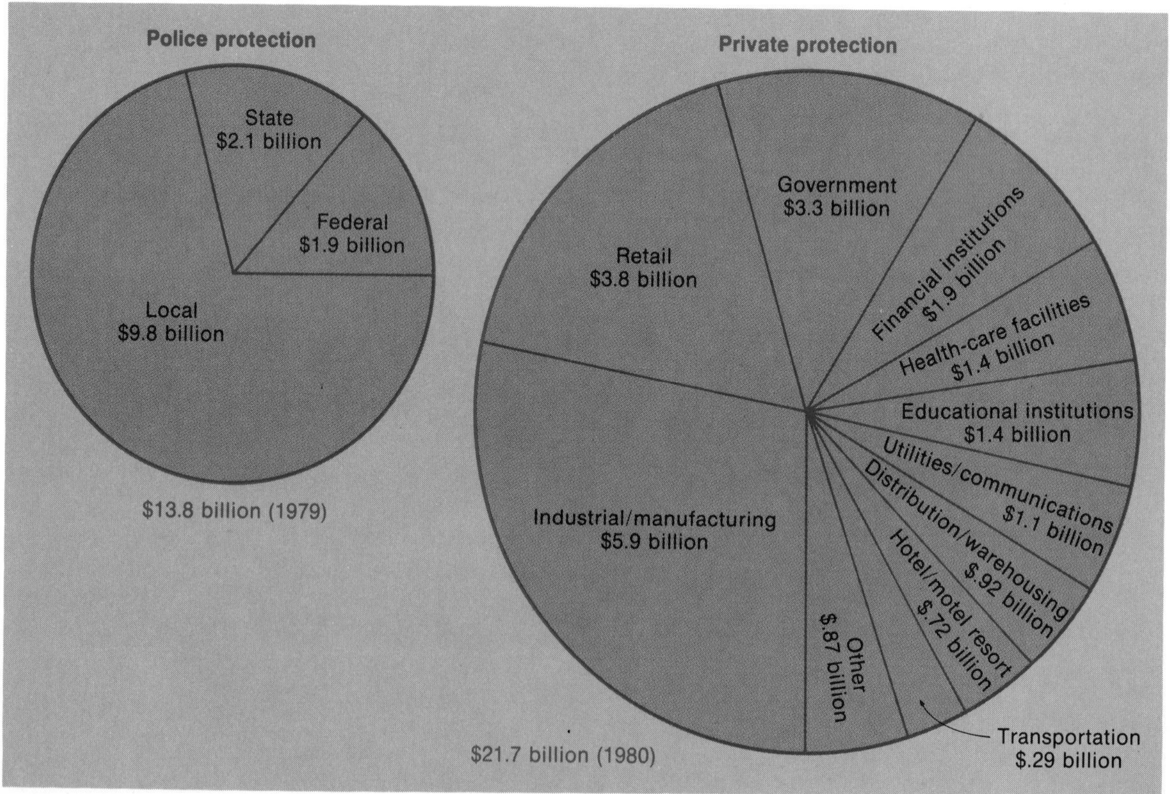

FIGURE 7.3
Gross expenditures for police and private protection in the United States, 1979 and 1980, by economic sector

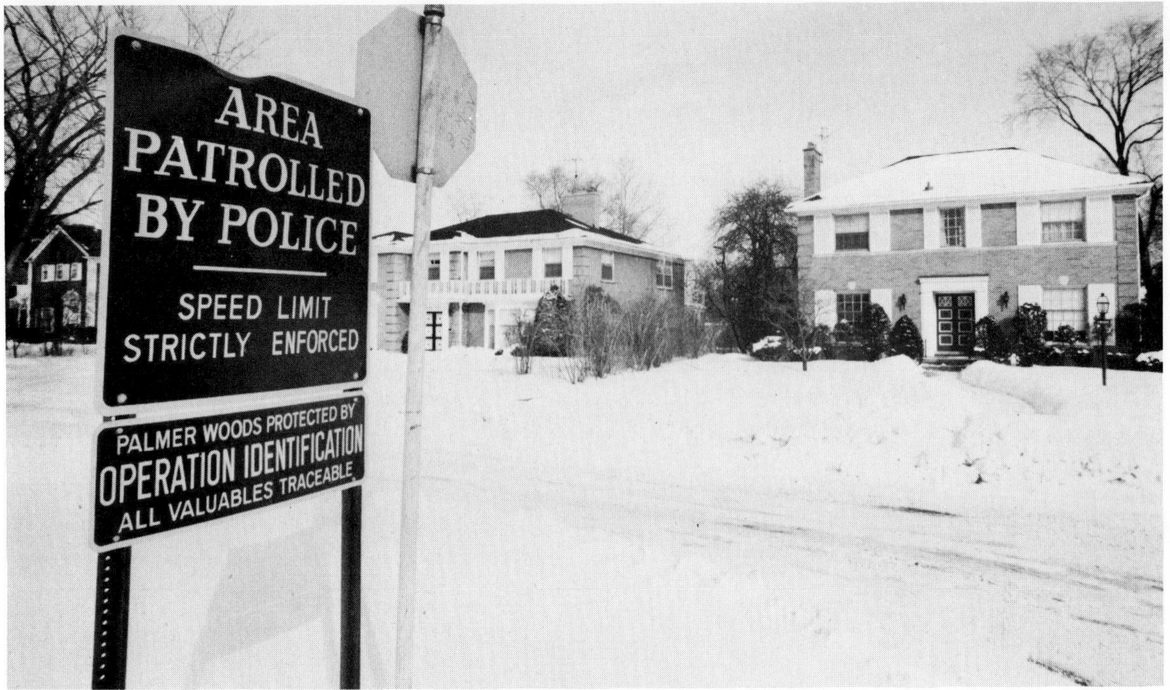

Private security firms are hired to supplement police patrol in some neighborhoods.

tary security operations, except for those individuals required to carry weapons.

Private policing has become a very large enterprise; the United States has an estimated four thousand agencies that in the aggregate have upwards of a million employees and payrolls of over $21 billion.[46] The private security field is thus larger in both personnel and resources than the federal, state, and local public police forces combined. As figure 7.4 indicates, private security is a growth industry.

Functions

The activities of private security personnel vary greatly: some employees merely act as watchmen, and call the police at the first sign of trouble; others are deputized by public authority to carry out patrol and investigative duties as police officers do; and still others rely on their presence and willingness to make a "citizen's arrest" to deter lawbreakers. In most instances, private persons are authorized by law to make an arrest only when a felony has been committed in their presence. Thus even though private police function in a security occupation, they or their company face the possibility of being held civilly or even criminally liable for false arrest and the violation of an individual's civil rights. Some states have passed antishoplifting laws to give civil immunity to store personnel who reasonably but mistakenly detain people suspected of larceny. More ambiguous is the issue of a private guard's search of the person or property of a suspect. The suspect may resist and file a civil suit against the guard; if the search yields evidence of a crime, the evidence may not be admitted in court. Yet the Supreme Court has not applied the

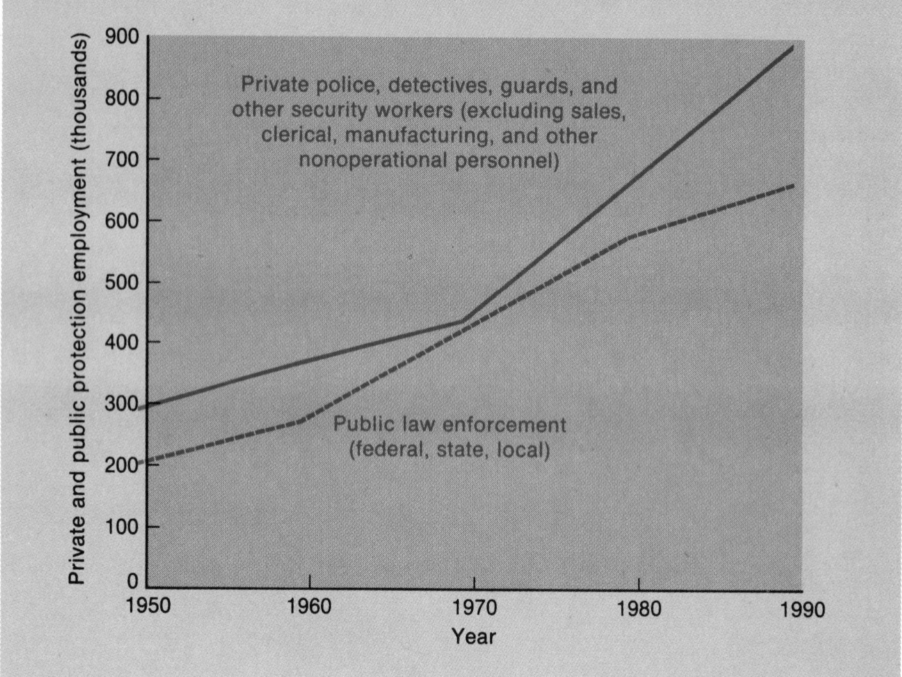

FIGURE 7.4 Employment in private and public protection, 1950–1990 (projected)

Miranda ruling to private police. Federal law prohibits private individuals from engaging in wiretapping, and information gathered by this means cannot be entered as evidence at trial.

A study sponsored by the National Institute of Justice indicated the willingness of proprietary and contract security managers to accept increased responsibility for minor criminal incidents that occur within their jurisdictions.[47] It was suggested that such tasks as responding to burglar alarms, investigating misdemeanors, and initiating preliminary investigations of other crimes could be undertakings that they would accept. Their counterpart law enforcement administrators indicated willingness to discuss the transfer of some of these responsibilities to private security firms. They cited a number of police tasks "potentially more cost-effectively performed by private security," such as provision of security in public buildings and courthouses and enforcement of parking regulations. Some of these tasks are already being performed by personnel provided by private firms in some parts of the country.

Public–private interface

The interface between public and private law enforcement is a matter of concern to professionals charged with crime control under law. As Clifford Shearing and Philip Stenning have noted, most private security organizations have the prevention of crime as their goal; others, however, adopt "police-like methods" and engage in investigation, apprehension, and prosecution.[48] Private security agents work for the people who employ them, and their goals may not always coincide with the public interest. Questions have been raised about the authority of private security personnel to make arrests, to conduct searches, and to participate in undercover investigations. Of crucial importance is the issue of the boundary between the work of the police and that of private agencies. Lack of communication between public and private organizations has resulted in botched investigations, destruction of evidence, and overzealousness—all to the detriment of crime control. Yet most firms that provide private policing services stress that their chief concern is the prevention of crime and therefore their activities do not conflict with the work of the public police.

Law enforcement officials criticize private security firms for hiring an estimated 150,000 police officers to provide security services in their off-duty hours. These police officers, they say, are "hired guns," inasmuch as they can carry weapons while other private security personnel may have difficulty in obtaining a license to do so. Another problem is that of liability: is the police force or the off-duty employer legally responsible for the acts of moonlighting officers? Other conflict-of-interest problems arise when a police officer operates a private security firm as a sideline and when an officer wears a police uniform and badge while in private employment.

These and other questions are seen to have impeded cooperation between the public and private forces. Security managers do report some sharing of information and equipment. Cooperative efforts have been reported with regard to such tasks as the transportation of hazardous materials, protection of dignitaries, crowd control, and investigation of economic crimes.

Security managers have said that they generally report UCR index crimes to the police. However, incidents of employee theft, insurance fraud, industrial espionage, commercial bribery, and computer crime tend *not* to be reported to public authorities. Thus an interesting question arises: To what extent does a parallel system of private justice exist with regard to some offenders and some crimes? In such situations the chief concern of private companies is to prevent loss and protect assets. Although some such incidents are reported to the public prosecutor for action, the majority of them are resolved through internal procedures ("private justice") within the victimized company. Most businesses consider employee theft to be their greatest single crime problem. When such offenses are discovered, the offender may be "convicted" within the company and punished by forced restitution through payroll deductions or the loss of the job and the dissemination of information about the incident throughout the industry.

Private organizations often bypass the public criminal justice system in an effort to avoid the need to cope with changing prosecution policies, administrative delays in prosecution, discovery rules that would open the internal affairs of the company to public scrutiny, and bad publicity. A survey by the United States Chamber of Commerce in 1979 revealed that half of 446 business executives interviewed believed that law enforcement and the criminal justice system do a poor job of fighting crimes against business.[49]

Recruitment and training

A major concern of law enforcement officials and civil libertarians is the recruitment and training of private security personnel. Studies have shown that such personnel are generally recruited from among persons with minimal education and training; because the pay is low, the work often attracts only people who cannot find other jobs or who seek only temporary work. Thus most of the work is done by the young and the retired. A study by the Rand Corporation found that fewer than half of the private security guards surveyed had a high school education, and their average age was fifty-two. Perhaps more important, although "almost half of the respondents were armed, less than one-fifth reported having received any firearms training." Ninety-seven percent of the respondents failed to pass a "simple examination designed to test their knowledge of legal practice in typical job-related situations."[50]

As the private security industry has grown, there have been calls for the examination and licensing of its personnel. Fewer than half of the states have such requirements. The National Council on Crime and Delinquency and the Private Security Advisory Council of LEAA have offered model licensing statutes that specify periods of training and orientation, the wearing of uniforms that permit citizens to distinguish public from private police, and the prohibition of employing any person who has a criminal record. In some states security firms are licensed, often by the attorney general, while in others the local police have this authority. In general, however, there is little regulation of such firms.

The private security industry arose in response to a need; it grew because the product it offered was in demand. The perceived need for the product may have resulted from the growth of crime, but it may also have developed because of the perception that the public police could not carry out a particular task. It is important that citizens distinguish between the actions of the forces of the public and private sectors. More important, private police must not hamper the work of law enforcement.

Summary

This chapter has explored a number of the trends and issues that confront law enforcement today. These topics make us realize that the police exist not only as part of the criminal justice system but also as part of the larger community. Changes in society influence the operations and internal organization of the police. The police have been forced to respond to external pressures; the emphases on community relations and civic accountability exemplify that response. The police are now under pressure to reassess their traditional practices, but this is easier said than done. The administrator who attempts to bring about change in an organization must contend with elements that are afraid of becoming losers. Law enforcement cannot remain static, however. It must evaluate suggested innovations and adopt those that appear to lead in the most promising directions.

For discussion

1. Community relations are important because police depend on citizens to report crimes. What actions might be taken to improve community relations? What is meant by "community relations"?
2. You are a police officer. You learn that some of your fellow officers are accepting gifts from local business people. What will you do?
3. How should police administrators confront the issue of unionism?

4. If you feel that a police officer has been rude or has otherwise mistreated you, what actions may you take?
5. How are the issues discussed in this chapter linked to the effective functioning of the police?

For further reading

Alex, Nicholas. *New York Cops Talk Back.* New York: Wiley, 1976.
Banton, Michael. *The Police in the Community.* New York: Basic Books, 1964.
Chevigny, Paul. *Police Power.* New York: Vintage Books, 1969.
Juris, Hervey A., and Peter Feuille. *Police Unionism.* Lexington, Mass.: Lexington Books, 1973.
Maas, Peter. *Serpico.* New York: Bantam Books, 1973.
Reiss, Albert J., Jr. *The Police and the Public.* New Haven: Yale University Press, 1971.
Scharf, Peter, and Arnold Binder. *The Badge and the Bullet.* New York: Praeger, 1983.

Notes

1. John Gardiner, "Wincanton: The Politics of Corruption," in President's Commission on Law Enforcement and Administration of Justice, in *Task Force Report: Organized Crime* (Washington, D.C.: Government Printing Office, 1967), pp. 61–79; William Chambliss, "Vice, Corruption, Bureaucracy, and Power," 4 *Wisconsin Law Review* 1150 (1971).
2. James Q. Wilson, *Varieties of Police Behavior* (Cambridge: Harvard University Press, 1968), pp. 191–99.
3. Ibid., chap. 8.
4. James Q. Wilson, *Thinking about Crime,* 2d ed. (New York: Basic Books, 1983), p. 91.
5. George L. Kelling, "On the Accomplishments of the Police," in *Control in the Police Organization,* ed. Maurice Punch (Cambridge: M.I.T. Press, 1983), p. 164.
6. *New York Times,* 30 August 1982, p. 1.
7. Ibid., 15 February 1981, p. 46.
8. Herbert Jacob, "Black and White Perceptions of Justice in the City," paper presented at the annual meeting of the American Political Science Association, Chicago, September 1970.
9. "A National Survey of Police and Community Relations," in President's Commission on Law Enforcement and Administration of Justice, *Field Surveys, V* (Washington, D.C.: Government Printing Office, 1967), p. 14.
10. *Ebony,* August 1979, p. 31.
11. W. Eugene Groves and Peter H. Rossi, "Police Perception of a Hostile Ghetto," *American Behavioral Scientist* 13 (1970): 741.
12. Albert J. Reiss, Jr., "Police Brutality: Answers to Key Questions," *Transaction,* July–August 1968, pp. 10–19.
13. Albert J. Reiss, Jr., *The Police and the Public* (New Haven: Yale University Press, 1971), p. 168.
14. Frank Moss, "National Danger from Police Corruption," *North American Review* 173 (October 1901): 470–80, as cited in Reiss, *Police and the Public,* p. 152.
15. Reiss, "Police Brutality," p. 12.
16. National Advisory Commission on Civil Disorders, *Report* (Washington, D.C.: Government Printing Office, 1968).
17. Paul Chevigny, *Police Power* (New York: Vintage Books, 1969), p. 238.
18. Amitai Schwartz, " A Role for Community Groups and Human Rights Agencies," in U.S. Department of Justice, *Police Use of Deadly Force* (Washington, D.C.: Government Printing Office, 1978), p. 54.
19. Lawrence Sherman and Robert Langworthy, "Measuring Homicide by Police Officers," *Journal of Criminal Law and Criminology* 4 (1979): 546–60; William Geller, "Deadly Force: What We Know," *Journal of Police Science and Administration* 10 (1982): 151–77.
20. Wilson, *Thinking about Crime,* p. 102.
21. James J. Fyfe, "Reducing the Use of Deadly Force: The New York Experience," in U.S. Department of Justice, *Police Use of Deadly Force,* p. 28.
22. Reiss, "Police Brutality," p. 14.
23. Arthur L. Kobler, "Police Homicide in a Democracy," *Journal of Social Issues* 31 (1975): 166.
24. Richard Kania and Wade Mackey, "Police Violence as a Function of Community Characteristics," *Criminology* 15 (1977): 27–48.
25. James Fyfe, "Toward a Typology of Police Shootings," paper presented at the annual meeting of the Academy of Criminal Justice Sciences, Oklahoma City, March 1980 (mimeo).
26. Lawrence W. Sherman, "What Do We Know about Homicides by Police Officers?" in U.S. Department of Justice, *Police Use of Deadly Force,* p. 9.
27. Herman Goldstein, *Policing a Free Society* (Cambridge, Mass.: Ballinger, 1977), p. 190.

28. City of New York, Commission to Investigate Allegations of Police Corruption and the City's Anti-Corruption Procedures, *The Knapp Commission Report on Police Corruption* (New York: Braziller, 1973), p. 4.
29. Ellwyn R. Stoddard, "The Informal 'Code' of Police Deviancy: A Group Approach to Blue-Coat Crime," *Journal of Criminal Law, Criminology and Police Science* 59 (1968): 204.
30. Goldstein, *Policing a Free Society,* p. 190. Copyright © 1976 Ballinger Publishing Company. Reprinted by permission.
31. Samuel Walker, "Employment of Black and Hispanic Police Officers," *Review of Applied Urban Research* 11 (October 1983): p. 1.
32. Nicholas Alex, *Black in Blue* (New York: Appleton-Century-Crofts, 1969).
33. Nicholas Alex, *New York Cops Talk Back* (New York: Wiley, 1976).
34. Wilson, *Varieties of Police Behavior,* p. 229.
35. U.S. Department of Justice, *Sourcebook of Criminal Justice Statistics 1982* (Washington, D.C.: Government Printing Office, 1983), p. 43.
36. Susan Ehrlich Martin, *Breaking and Entering* (Berkeley: University of California Press, 1980), p. 27.
37. Ibid., p. 95.
38. Peter Bloch and Deborah Anderson, *Policewomen on Patrol: Final Report* (Washington, D.C.: Police Foundation, 1974), pp. 1–7.
39. Samuel Walker, *The Police in America* (New York: McGraw-Hill, 1983), p. 285.
40. Hervey A. Juris and Peter Feuille, "Employee Organizations," in *Police Personnel Administration,* ed. O. Glenn Stahl and Richard A. Staufenberger (Monterey, Calif.: Duxbury Press, 1974), p. 206.
41. Ibid., p. 216.
42. Ibid., p. 214.
43. Ibid., p. 222.
44. William D. Gentel and Martha L. Handman, *Police Strikes: Causes and Prevention,* in U.S. Department of Justice (Washington, D.C.: Government Printing Office, 1980), p. 5; Richard M. Ayres, "Case Studies of Police Strikes in Two Cities—Albuquerque and Oklahoma City," *Journal of Police Science and Administration* 5 (1977): 19–30; L. Thomas Winfree and Frieda Gehlen, "Police Strike: Public Support and Dissonance Reduction during a Strike by Police," *Journal of Police Science and Administration* 9 (1981): 451–62.
45. Ibid., p. 22.
46. James S. Kakalik and Sorrell Wildhorn, *Private Police in the United States: Findings and Recommendations* (Washington, D.C.: Government Printing Office, 1972), and *The Private Police: Security and Danger* (New York: Crane Russak, 1977); William C. Cunningham, "Security–Law Enforcement Relationships: An Update of the Hallcrest Report" (Annandale, Va.: Washington Crime News Services, 1982).
47. William C. Cunningham and Todd H. Taylor, "The Growing Role of Private Security," in U.S. Department of Justice, Bureau of Justice Statistics, National Institute of Justice, *Research in Brief* (Washington, D.C.: Government Printing Office, 1984).
48. Clifford D. Shearing and Philip C. Stenning, "Modern Private Security: Its Growth and Implications," in *Crime and Justice,* vol. 3, ed. Michael Tonry and Norval Morris (Chicago: University of Chicago Press, 1981), pp. 193–245.
49. Cited in Cunningham and Todd, "Growing Role of Private Security."
50. Kakalik and Wildhorn, *Private Police,* p. 155.

PART 3

Adjudication

The arrest of an individual in a democracy is only the first part of a complex process designed to sift the guilty from the innocent. Part Three examines this process, by which guilt is determined in accordance with the law's requirements. Here we shall look into the work of prosecutors, defense attorneys, bondsmen, and judges to understand the contribution each makes toward the ultimate decision. It is in the adjudicatory stage that we learn how the goals of an administrative system blunt the force of the adversarial process prescribed by law. Although our eyes may be focused on courtroom activities, most decisions relating to the disposition of a case are made in less public surroundings. After studying these chapters, we should ask ourselves whether justice is served by processes that are more akin to bargaining than to adversarial combat.

Prosecuting Attorney

Roles of the prosecutor
Discretion of the prosecutor
Exchange relations
Police
Narcotics arrests: an example of exchange
Victim
Courts
Community
Decision-making policies
Legal sufficiency
System efficiency
Trial sufficiency
Implementing prosecution policy
Decision to prosecute
Accusatory process
Crime construction
Intake
Charging
Evidential considerations
Pragmatic considerations
Organizational considerations
Prosecution management
Career criminal
Diversion: alternatives to prosecution
Assessment of diversion programs
Politics and prosecutors
Summary

8

Although the criminal justice system is frequently said to consist of three subsystems—police, courts, and corrections—the categories fail to take note of the most powerful figure in the administration of justice: the ***prosecuting attorney.*** Prosecutors (also known in some states as district attorneys, county attorneys, or state's attorneys) have been immortalized in novels and motion pictures, on radio and television, so that they have become almost folk heroes who secure conviction of the guilty while upholding justice for the innocent. For many years the radio serial "Mr. District Attorney" held audiences spellbound as its namesake sought "not only to prosecute to the limit of the law all persons accused of crime within this county, but to defend with equal vigor the rights and privileges of all its citizens." In real political life there are counterparts to the crusading prosecutors of fiction. Earl Warren, Hugo Black, and Thomas E. Dewey, along with hundreds of others, came into prominence as fighting prosecutors and often based their campaigns for higher political office on a reputation gained from a widely publicized investigation or trial.

Nowhere is it more apparent [than in the prosecuting attorney's office] that our government is a government of men, not of laws. Nowhere do the very human elements of dishonesty, ambition, greed, lust for power, laxness or bigotry have more room for development. Also, there is no office where an able and honest public servant can be more effective.
LEWIS MAYERS

prosecuting attorney A legal representative of the state with sole responsibility for bringing criminal charges. In some states referred to as district attorney, state's attorney, county attorney.

The influence of prosecutors flows directly from their legal duties, but it must be understood within the context of the system's administrative and political environment. Of the many positions in the legal system, that of the prosecuting attorney is distinctive because it is concerned with all aspects of the system: from the time of arrest to final disposition of a case, prosecutors can make decisions that will determine to a great extent the cases that are to be prosecuted, the charges that are to be brought into the courtroom, the kinds of bargains that are to be made with the defendant, and the enthusiasm with which a case will be pursued. Throughout the justice process, prosecutors have links with the other actors in the system, and their decisions are usually affected not only by the types of relationships they maintain with these officials but by the level of the public's awareness of their own actions. In most states, the prosecutors are elected officials who are able to accumulate considerable power in partisan politics, so they must be conscious of public reaction.

The office of prosecutor typifies the decentralization of criminal justice. Traditionally, prosecutors have been responsible only to the voters, and they enjoy an independence from the formal checks usually placed on American public officials. (Only in Alaska, Connecticut, Delaware, New Jersey, and Rhode Island are they not elected.) Although they commonly must submit to the electoral process every four years, there are few other public restraints on their actions. In most states, neither the governor nor the attorney general is authorized to investigate suspected illegal activity without the permission of the local prosecutor. Prosecutors' freedom to pursue their own vision of justice, unhampered by the formal powers of higher officials, can be seen in the attempt of New Orleans prosecutor Jim Garrison to overturn the Warren Commission's findings concerning the assassination of John F. Kennedy and the almost holy aura that surrounded the thirty-two-year reign of Frank Hogan, district attorney of New York County.

Not only is there a lack of structural elements tying the prosecutors' decision-making power to that of other criminal justice officials, but the confidential nature of their decisions diminishes the visibility of their actions. For example, a decision may take the form of an agreement reached in the course of conversation between a prosecutor and a defense attorney over a cup of coffee or in the hall outside the courtroom. Such an agreement may mean the reduction of a charge in exchange for a guilty plea or the dropping of a charge if the defendant agrees to seek psychiatric help.

Rarely is the scope of the prosecutor's discretionary power either publicly recognized or defined by statute. Generally, state laws are explicit in requiring the prosecution of offenders, yet nowhere in the laws are there specific descriptions of the elements that must be present before the prosecutor can take action. Most laws describe the prosecutor's responsibility in such vague terms as "prosecuting all crimes and civil actions to which state or county may be party." On occasions when the prosecutor's decisions have been challenged, they have been shielded from judicial inquiry by an almost magical formula in

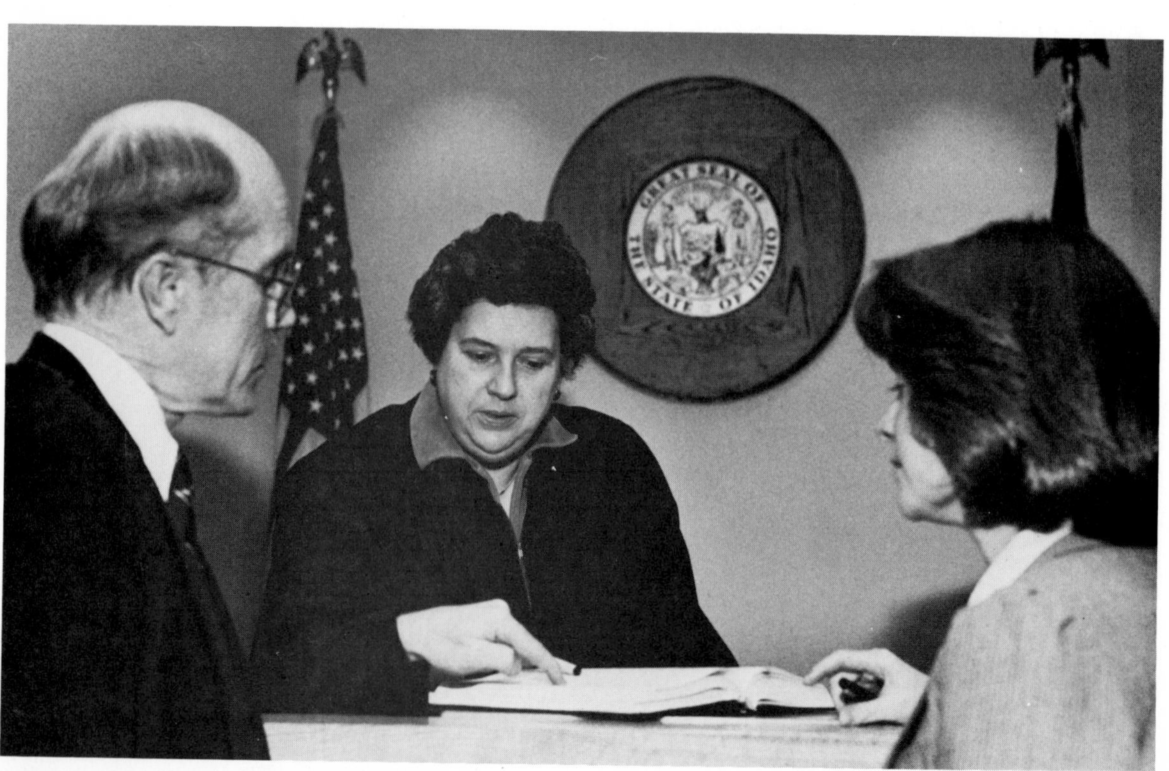

Prosecutors must maintain constant relationships with a variety of "others".

the law: "within the prosecutor's discretion." In essence, the American people have placed district attorneys in a position in which they have to make choices but have not given them principles of selection.

When prosecutors feel that the community no longer considers that an act proscribed by law constitutes criminal behavior, they will probably refuse to prosecute or will expend every effort to convince the complainant that prosecution should be avoided. In this sense, they are like father-confessors of the community. But, like other government officials, prosecutors are sensitive to the force of public opinion. Often they must take measures to protect themselves when they believe that a course of action is likely to arouse antipathy toward agencies of law enforcement rather than toward the accused. If they hold to an exaggerated notion of duty, they can arouse a storm of protest that may gain them reputations as "persecutors" and cost them the cooperation of the community. The fact that about three-fourths of American prosecutors serve counties with populations of fewer than 100,000 accentuates the potential influence of public opinion. Local pressures may bear heavily on the single prosecution official in a community. Without the backing of public opinion, law enforcement and prosecution officers are powerless; especially with regard to victimless crimes, such as marijuana smoking, petty gambling, and prostitution, prosecutors develop policies that reflect community attitudes. A New York prosecutor has remarked, "We are pledged to the enforcement of the law, but we have to use our heads in the process."

Roles of the prosecutor

References to the "prosecutor's dilemma" are often found in legal writings. Prosecutors face a dilemma because, as "lawyers for the state," they are expected to do everything in their power to win the public's case; yet they are also members of the legal profession and are expected to engage in prosecution not to win convictions but to see that justice is done. The conditions under which they work are thought to create a "prosecutor's bias," sometimes called a "prosecution complex": they consider themselves to be instruments of law enforcement, although theoretically they are supposed to represent all the people, including the accused. This point is well made in the Canon of Ethics of the New York State Bar Association: "The primary duty of a lawyer engaged in public prosecution is not to convict, but to see that justice is done. The suppression of facts and the secreting of witnesses capable of establishing the innocence of the accused is highly reprehensible."[1] Thus, by combining the professional dimensions of their work with the political context of their office, prosecutors will individualistically define their roles.

Role definition is complicated by the fact that prosecutors must maintain constant relationships with a variety of "others"—police officers, judges, defense attorneys, party leaders, and so forth—and these actors may have competing ideas about what the prosecutor should do. The prosecutor's decisions will vitally affect the ability of the others to perform their duties and to achieve their objectives. Because the district attorneys are at the center of the adjudicative and enforcement functions, if they decide not to prosecute, the judge and jury are helpless and the police officer's word is meaningless. If they decide to launch a campaign against gambling, there will certainly be repercussions in the political as well as the criminal justice arenas.

Close-up: For the Assistant D.A., It's Nothing Like on TV

An 8-year-old boy, his voice soft but steady, told how he had seen robbers shoot his father to death in front of the family's Brooklyn grocery store.

"He had the key and was opening the car," the child said in a small interview room in State Supreme Court in downtown Brooklyn, absently playing with the buttons of his sweater. "Then they came, the four men. They told him if he moved they would kill him. One man had a gun."

He looked down at his feet. His mother, a woman of about 30, stared straight ahead in the chair next to him. "What was your father doing before he got shot?" asked Steven Samuel, a young assistant district attorney.

"He screamed."

There was a moment of silence. A detective who had arrested a suspect in the murder, which occurred several weeks before, pursed his lips. The widow shifted in her seat. Mr. Samuel gazed at the pen poised in his fingers, contemplating the latest of the many murder cases he has handled.

Mr. Samuel, who is 30 and five years out of law school, is typical of the 318 A.D.A.s—assistant district attorneys—in the office of District Attorney Eugene Gold of Brooklyn, the largest local prosecutor's office in the country behind those of Chicago and Los Angeles.

"All right," said Mr. Samuel, breaking the stillness. "Now I'm going to take you into a room," he said to the boy, "and I want you to tell what you told me to the people in that room. They like to hear little boys tell stories."

As he strode down the corridor to where the child and other witnesses would repeat their accounts before a grand jury—which later would vote a murder indictment—Mr. Samuel described his own feelings in such a case. "It used to rattle me, the tragedy of it," he said. "But now I try to keep myself as emotionally detached as possible. When you're presenting a case, it helps to be as objective as possible."

Mr. Samuel, like many of his colleagues, views his job as a chance to pursue interesting work and gain valuable experience before moving on.

"I've been bitten by the trial bug—I don't think I could satisfy it sitting behind a desk," said Mr. Samuel, a lean, dark-haired six-footer.

Most of Mr. Gold's assistants stay with the office about five years before entering private or corporate practice or switching to other government agencies.

But perhaps the way in which Mr. Samuel most typifies his colleagues is that he and his routine often bear little resemblance to the portrayals of prosecutors on television and in the movies.

"My image of a prosecutor as a young kid was of Hamilton Burger, the District Attorney in 'Perry Mason,' " said Mr. Samuel. "He never had a guilty defendant."

Mr. Samuel, on the other hand, has won 25 convictions in the last three years, during which he has exclusively handled homicides. But he has also had three defendants who, the jury decided, were not guilty, despite his best efforts.

Then, too, in the television and movie scenarios, prosecutors generally spin their oratory in crowded, hushed courtrooms, unraveling plots complicated or clever, exciting or exotic. . . .

"Murders committed during grocery and bar holdups, during disputes among acquaintances—two guys get into a fight over a dice game—these are typical of the cases I've had," Mr. Samuel said. . . .

The bachelor son of a Jewish refugee couple from Nazi Germany—his parents sometimes come to court to watch him in action—Mr. Samuel was attracted to the Brooklyn District Attorney's office by recruiters who visited the Albany Law School while he was a student there. With a turnover rate of 12 to 14 percent a year among his assistants, Mr. Gold each year sends representatives to law schools throughout the

East, so that he can replenish his staff every fall.

Senior assistants, like Mr. Samuel, generally earn $30,000 a year, according to a Gold aide.

The day before, he had won a conviction in the robbery-murder of a drug addict in East New York. But with his average workload of 15 cases awaiting trial, this simply meant that Mr. Samuel could now focus on some of his other cases. So, at 10 A.M. in the Brooklyn branch of State Supreme Court, where the borough's felony crimes are prosecuted, he was scurrying from one courtroom to another, juggling appearances in several of his cases.

In one of the wood-paneled courtrooms, Mr. Samuel and a defense lawyer, Lewis Cohen, agreed to begin the next day to try the case of a man charged with killing an off-duty corrections officer. The officer had interrupted the defendant's attempt to hold up a Crown Heights bar, Mr. Samuel said as he scurried the single block back to his office, already calculating how he would prepare his evidence and line up his witnesses on such short notice.

Mr. Samuel had hardly begun reviewing the graphic police photographs of the murder scene and other evidence in the case when the phone rang. Detective Lambert Roessner had just arrived at Supreme Court with the witnesses in the case of the grocer whose son had seen him slain.

Shunted aside was the trial beginning tomorrow; Mr. Samuel would have to work on that at home at night. Now he had to hurry back to the court and prepare the witnesses in the case of the murdered grocer for their scheduled appearance before the grand jury that afternoon.

When the trial in the killing of the corrections officer was past the jury selection stage, Mr. Samuel rose to deliver his opening statement. "The people will prove," he declared in resonant, self-assured tones, "that Leon Taft killed Rudolph Smith during the holdup of the bar at 162A Utica Avenue."

As he presented the case against Mr. Taft, the young prosecutor rarely glanced at the defendant, a man hardly older than himself, with a shaved head, sitting at the defense table only a few feet away. All the witnesses were cooperative—the defense called none of its own—and Mr. Samuel, with detailed and systematic questioning, drew forth their moment-by-moment recollections of the fatal shooting.

Within a week, the verdict was in: guilty of murder.

"Justice was served," Mr. Samuel said, pausing only briefly before turning to the next case on his still-large agenda.

Source: Joseph P. Fried, "For the Assistant D.A., It's Nothing Like on TV," *New York Times*, 18 October 1979, p. B1.

A clearer understanding of the work of prosecutors and their place in an exchange system may be achieved through use of the concept of role. A person may occupy a socially defined *position,* in this case that of prosecuting attorney, yet hold a conception of the role—the manner of action on a daily basis—that differs from those of other persons in the same position. A person's role, therefore, is a function not only of the formal aspects of the position but also of such other important factors as the individual player's personality, the environment within which he or she operates, and the individual's expectations concerning the attitudes of others with whom he or she interacts.

Four role conceptions are found among prosecutors. Some think of themselves primarily as "trial counsel for the police"—that is, as reflecting departmental views in the courtroom and taking a crime-fighter stance in public. Others view their role as that of "house counsel" for the police—they are there to give legal advice so that arrests will stand up in court. In both of these role conceptions, prosecutors appear to believe that the police are the clients of their legal practices. A third role is that of "representative of the court." Here prosecutors consider their primary responsibility to be enforcement of the rules of due process to ensure that the police act in accordance with the law and uphold the rights of defendants. Finally, prosecutors may view their role primarily as that of elected official and thus be most responsive to community opinion. The possible political content of their decisions is a major concern of this type of prosecutor.[2]

Discretion of the prosecutor

Because of the decentralized nature of their office, their broad discretionary powers, and the low visibility of their decisions, prosecutors are able to structure their role so that they can play it in ways that are consistent with the political environment, their own personalities, and the interests of the others who are linked to the office.

Their wide power of discretion allows prosecutors to make decisions at each of the essential steps in the criminal justice process. One can readily understand that the type of case that eventually reaches the courtroom and its disposition depend to a large extent on a prosecutor's conception of his or her role within the criminal justice system as influenced by the larger political and social structure of the community. From the time the police turn a suspect's case over to the prosecutor, there are major decisions over which he or she has almost undisputed control.

That the police may arrest a person does not necessarily mean that the prosecutor will accept the charges against the suspect. Prosecutors can screen out cases they do not want to prosecute at their own discretion. While the proportion of such dismissals varies from place to place, estimates indicate that in most cities up to half of all arrests do not lead to the filing of formal charges. Prosecutors may decide not to press charges because of factors related to a particular case or because they have established policies dictating that charges will not be brought for certain offenses.

Having decided that a crime should be prosecuted, the prosecutor has great freedom in determining the types of charges to be lodged. Incidents of criminal behavior often involve the breaking of a variety of laws, so the prosecutor can bring a single charge or multiple charges. Suppose that Smith, who is armed, breaks into a grocery store, assaults the proprietor, and robs the cash drawer. What charges may the prosecutor file? By virtue of having committed the robbery, the accused can be charged with at least four violations: breaking and entering, assault, armed robbery, and carrying a dangerous weapon. Other charges may be added depending on the circumstances of the incident—whether the robbery was carried out during the day or night, for example.

The concept of ***necessarily included offense*** helps us further to understand the position of the prosecutor.[3] We can ask: Could Smith have committed crime *A* without committing crime *B*? If the answer is yes, *B* is not a necessarily included offense. In the example of the grocery store, Smith has committed the necessarily included offense of carrying a dangerous weapon in the course of the robbery. The prosecutor may charge Smith solely with the armed robbery or may include any number of other charges and combinations of charges in the information. By including as many charges as possible, the prosecutor increases his or her position in plea negotiations.

necessarily included offense
An offense committed for the purpose of committing another offense; for example, trespass committed for the purpose of committing burglary.

Selection of the charge or charges requires the prosecutor to decide also on the number of counts to be brought against the individual for the same offense. Each ***count*** named in an indictment or an information deals with a specific criminal act, and under some conditions repeated acts result in multiple charges. A forger, for instance, may be charged with multiple counts, each carrying the potential for a similar penalty, for every act of forgery committed. It is because the prosecutor may charge multiple counts of the same criminal act that newspapers often announce that the accused may be liable for unrealistically long sentences—for example, five years for each of twenty counts. This is misleading, however, because judges may stipulate that the twenty terms of five years each are to be served concurrently. In other words, the offender will serve only a total of five years, not the hundred years he would serve if the judge had stipulated consecutive terms (to be served one after another).

count
Each separate offense of which a person is accused in an indictment or an information.

The prosecutor's discretion may be limited by the procedure known as ***discovery***—a legal requirement that some information in the case file be made available to the defense counsel. Although this procedure may suggest that the law unnecessarily limits the ability of the prosecution to win a case, the procedure is justified by the fact that the state has an obligation to act impar-

discovery
a prosecutor's pretrial disclosure to the defense of facts and evidence to be introduced at trial.

Felony Prosecutions in New York City

- 43% of the cases connected by felony arrest and disposed of in the Criminal Court were dismissed.
- 98% of the cases that ended in conviction were disposed of by guilty pleas rather than trial.
- 74% of the guilty pleas were to misdemeanors or lesser offenses.
- 50% of the guilty pleas were followed by "walks," 41% by sentences to less than a year in prison.
- Only 9% of the guilty pleas were followed by felony time sentences.
- Only 2.6% of cases were disposed of by trial.

Source: *Felony Arrests: Their Prosecution and Disposition in New York City's Courts* (New York: Vera Institute of Justice, 1977), p. 134.

nolle prosequi
An entry made by a prosecutor on the record of a case and announced in court to indicate that the charges specified will not be prosecuted. In effect, the charges are thereby dismissed.

tially and should not win a conviction through the use of deceit. The prosecutor has an obligation to secure justice, and knowledge of the evidence against the accused should help the accused to prepare an effective defense.

After the charge has been made, the prosecutor may reduce it in exchange for a guilty plea or enter a notation of ***nolle prosequi*** (*nol. pros.*), indicating a freely made decision not to press the charge, either as a whole or as to one or more count. In our system of public prosecution there is no recourse to this decision. On conclusion of a case in which a conviction is obtained, the prosecutor can exert influence over the impending sentence by submitting a recommendation concerning its nature.

Exchange relations

Formal rules of a bureaucracy do not completely account for the behavior of the actors within it; there also exists an informal structure that arises from the social environment, personal relationships, and their interaction. Thus we can assume that the decisions made by the office of prosecuting attorney will reflect its clientele—those persons and organizations with whom it interacts. The influence of a particular client group will depend on such things as its role in the criminal justice process, friendship, the amount of contact it has with the office, and its ability to impede the work of the prosecutor if it should choose to do so. This section examines several exchange relationships.

Although statutes define the formal relationships among portions of the criminal justice system, research has shown that the actual ways in which the system operates are always in flux, often blurred, and usually open to negotiation. As a result, prosecutors in some jurisdictions do control the charging decision; others are mere rubber stamps for the police. Some prosecutors wield extensive influence over the operations of the court by their ability to control the calendar, to appoint counsel for indigents, and to dominate the sentencing decisions; others are beholden to the judiciary and obediently respond to directions from the bench. What must be emphasized is that the role conceptions of individual prosecutors and their clientele and the customs of particular criminal justice systems cause variations in the operation of the office. When a prosecution operation is described, it should be understood to be a picture of the exchange relations in one city at one time.

Police

Although prosecuting attorneys have discretionary power to determine the disposition of cases, they are dependent on the police to produce the raw materials with which they work. Because of the low visibility of police decisions and their own lack of investigative resources, prosecutors are unable to control the types of cases brought to them for disposition. The police may be under pressure to establish an impressive crime-clearance record and so may make many arrests without the substantiating evidence required to ensure conviction. No prosecutor wants to have poorly developed cases. They would not stand up in court and would be a wasteful expenditure of valuable resources.

In relationships with the police, prosecutors are not without means of exercising control. Their main check is the ability to return cases for further investigation and to refuse to approve arrest warrants. The police depend on the prosecutor to accept the output of their system. Rejection of too many cases can seriously affect the morale and discipline of the force.

Police requests for prosecution may be turned down for a number of reasons unrelated to the facts of the case. First, prosecutors serve as the regulators of caseloads, not only for their own office but for the rest of the judicial bureaucracy as well. Constitutional and statutory time limits prevent them and the courts from building a backlog of untried cases. Prosecutors may also reject the police's requests for prosecution because they do not want to take forward cases that will place them in an embarrassing position in the courtroom. Finally, prosecutors may return cases in order to check on the quality of police work. As one deputy told this author, "You have to keep them on their toes, otherwise they get lazy." Rather than expend the resources necessary to find additional evidence, the police may dispose of a case by sending it back to the prosecutor on a lesser charge, may implement the "copping-out machinery" that leads to a guilty plea, or may drop the case.

David Neubauer reports that a third of all arrests in Prairie City were changed by the charging decision of the prosecutor. There was a general downward trend, with the prosecutor filing charges more serious than those recommended by the police in only 3 percent of the cases. Yet Neubauer saw significant differences in the prosecutor's evaluation of the recommendations made by the police department and those made by the sheriff's office. Whereas the prosecutor *agreed* with the police assessment of a case 75 percent of the time, he *disagreed* with the sheriff's arrest designation 75 percent of the time. These differences were related to the prosecutor's perceptions of the value of the work done by the two departments.[4]

In most cases a deputy prosecutor and the assigned police officer occupy the boundary-spanning roles in this exchange relationship. After repeated contacts, deputies get to know the police officers they can trust, and these perceptions may be an important consideration in the decision to prosecute. Sometimes the police perform the ritual of "shopping around" for a deputy prosecutor whose past experience has led them to believe is likely to be sympathetic to their point of view on a case. Some prosecution offices prevent this practice by stipulating that only the prosecutor, not deputies, can make primary decisions.

Narcotics arrests: an example of exchange. The major organizational requirement of narcotics policing is the presence of an informational system. Without a network of informers, addicts and peddlers cannot be caught with evidence that can bring about convictions. One pool of informers is made up of people who have been arrested for narcotics violations. Through promises to reduce charges or even to *nol. pros.*, arrangements can be made to return the accused to the narcotics community to gather information for the police. Bargaining observed between the head of the narcotics squad of the Seattle force and the deputy prosecutor who specialized in drug cases involved the question of charges, promises, and the release of an arrested peddler.

In the course of postarrest questioning by the police, a well-known drug dealer intimated that he could provide evidence against a pharmacist suspected of illegally selling narcotics. Not only did the police representative want to transfer the case to the friendlier hands of a certain deputy, he wanted to arrange for a reduction of charges and bail. He believed that it was important that the accused be let out on bail in such a way that the narcotics community would not realize that he had become an informer. He also wanted to ensure that the reduced charges would be processed so that the informer would be kept "on the string" and the narcotics squad would retain control over him. The deputy prosecutor, on the other hand, insisted on procedures that would not discredit his boss. He "suggested" that the police work a little harder on another pending case.

Victim

Until a very few years ago, the victim of a crime was the forgotten participant in the criminal justice process. One reason for this state of affairs lies in the nature of prosecution in the United States. In our system, a complainant depends on the prosecuting attorney to bring charges. If the prosecutor refuses, a private citizen cannot bring an indictment against a fellow citizen, as is possible in England.

Victims generally play a passive role in the criminal justice process, yet their cooperation is essential for successful prosecution. They must assist the police and prosecuting attorney by identifying the offender, and the basic evidence to be considered often depends on their testimony. In many types of cases, the nature of a victim's prior relations with the accused, the victim's actions at the time of the offense, and the victim's personal characteristics are deemed important if the case is to come to a successful conclusion before judge and jury.

The relationship of the accused to the victim has strong bearing on a case having to do with violent crime, and thus can present a major problem to the prosecutor. In one study of crimes by persons who were not strangers to their victims, difficulties with the complaining witness accounted for 61 percent of

The victim is too often the forgotten participant in the criminal justice system.

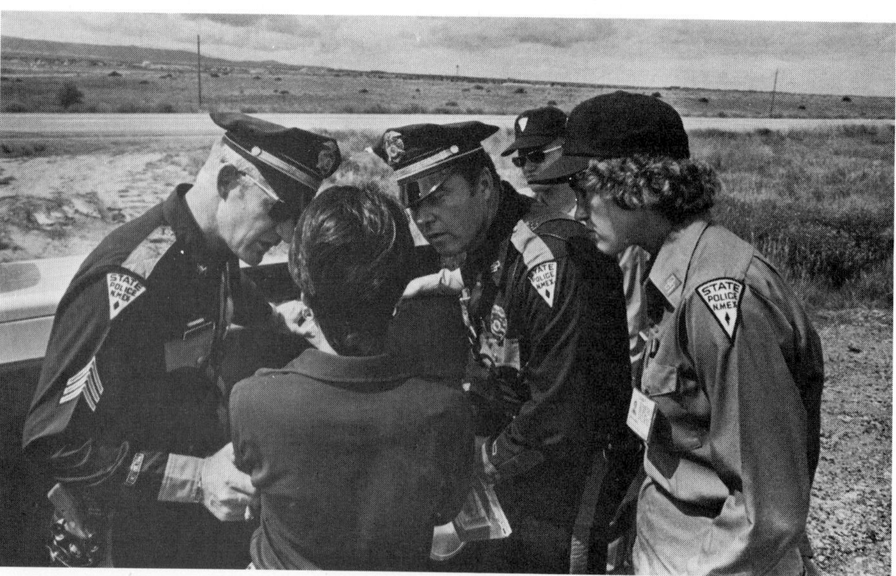

the refusals to prosecute and 54 percent of the dismissals. Barbara Boland found that the conviction rate in New Orleans for crimes of violence committed by strangers was 48 percent; by friends or acquaintances, 30 percent; and by family members, 19 percent.[5] As the closeness of the accused's relationship to the victim increased, the likelihood of conviction decreased.

A study of the prosecution and disposition of felony arrests in New York City emphasizes the crucial role of the victim and the exchange relationships that may exist in the prosecution process. By analyzing a sample of felony arrests, researchers learned that a high percentage of crimes in every category, from murder to burglary, involved victims with whom the accused had had prior and often close relations. This finding was particularly true with respect to crimes of interpersonal violence: 83 percent of rape victims, 50 percent of manslaughter and attempted homicide victims, and 69 percent of assault victims knew their assailants.

Such findings are to be expected: suspects known to their victims are more likely to be arrested than strangers, since they can more easily be identified by the complainants. The fact that the victim and the accused knew each other, however, led to the dropping of a large number of cases. Complainants were often reluctant to pursue prosecution. As the study noted, "tempers had cooled, time had passed, informal efforts at mediation or restitution might have worked, or in some instances, the defendant had intimidated the complainant."[6] Thus the relatively close defendant–victim relationship was felt to be responsible for dismissal of felony charges, their reduction to misdemeanors, or lenient sentences even when evidence of guilt was plentiful. Prosecutors are aware of all such situations and are usually reluctant to press charges fully when there is a possibility that victims will have second thoughts as they begin to realize that the sanctions of the criminal law will be brought to bear on the offender.

In some types of cases the victim's personal characteristics and attitudes may influence the decision to prosecute. Prostitutes who claim rape, drug users who are assaulted by pushers, and children who may be unable to testify under pressure are viewed by prosecutors as victims whose characteristics make the securing of a conviction difficult.

Courts

The influence of the courts on the decision to prosecute is very real. The sentencing history of each judge gives prosecutors, as well as other enforcement officials, an indication of the treatment a case may receive in the courtroom. Prosecutors' expectations of the court's action may affect their decision to prosecute or not to prosecute. In the words of one prosecutor interviewed by the author: "There is great concern as to whose court a case will be assigned. After Judge Lewis threw out three cases in a row in which entrapment was involved, the police did not want to take any cases to him."

Prosecutors depend on the plea bargaining machinery to maintain the flow of cases from their office. If guilty pleas are to be successfully induced, the sentencing actions of judges must be predictable. If the defendants and their lawyers are to be influenced to accept a lesser charge or a promise of a lighter sentence in exchange for a plea of guilty, there must be some basis to believe that the judges will fulfill their part of the arrangement. Since judges are unable to announce formally their agreement with the details of the bargain, their past performance influences the actors.

Within the limits imposed by law and by the demands of the system, prosecutors may regulate the flow of cases to the court. They can regulate the length of time between accusation and trial, holding cases until they have the evidence that will convict. They may also seek repeated adjournments and continuances until the public's interest dies down, witnesses become unavailable, or other difficulties make their requests for dismissal of prosecution more easily justifiable. In many cities the prosecutor is able to determine the court that will receive a case and the judge who will hear it.

In most jurisdictions, persons arrested on felony charges must be given a preliminary hearing within ten days. For prosecutors, the preliminary hearing is an opportunity to evaluate the testimony of witnesses, to assess the strength of the evidence, and to try to predict the outcome of the case should it go to trial. Subsequently, prosecutors have several options: they may recommend that the case be held for trial, seek a reduction of the charges to those of a misdemeanor, or conclude that they have no case and drop the charges.

Community

As a part of the wider political system, the administration of criminal justice responds to its environment. Exchange relationships between community and prosecutor may be analyzed at several levels. First, the general public is able through regulations to have its values translated into policies that law enforcement officers follow. Through the political process, especially in the election of prosecutors and in decisions concerning the resources to be placed at their disposal, the electorate may affect decision making.

The public's influence is particularly acute in those "gray areas" of the law where full enforcement is not expected. Legislatures may enact statutes that define the outer limits of criminal conduct, but this does not necessarily mean that the laws will be fully enforced. Some statutes may be passed as expressions of desirable morality, while others are kept deliberately vague. Finally, some existing laws proscribe behavior that the community no longer considers criminal. Prosecutors' charging policies will reflect the public's attitude toward the legislation. They usually will not prosecute violations of laws regulating some forms of gambling, certain sexual practices, or Sunday "blue laws."

Alternatively, the community may insist that charges be brought against people who flout its dominant values: groups with unorthodox political views may be harassed; activists may be prosecuted for a wide variety of violations. The public is also prone to press for selective prosecution of persons who engage in some forms of "immoral" activity—for example, streetwalkers may be arrested while calls girls and "hostesses" are immune.

Studies have shown that the public's level of attention to the activities of the criminal justice system is low. Still, the community remains a potential source of pressure that opinion leaders may activate against the prosecutor. The prosecutor's office always has the public in mind when it makes its decisions. It is recognized that some crimes will bring forth a vocal public reaction. Sexual molestation of a child, for instance, is bound to cause a hue and cry.

In sum, although prosecutors are free from statutory checks on their power, they must make decisions within an organizational framework and are thus subject to the influence of other actors. Because the criminal justice system requires that a number of officials participate in the disposition of each case, bargaining occurs. Prosecutors—as the link between the police and the courts—hold a strategic position in this regard because all cases must pass through their office. Accordingly, they are able to regulate not only the flow of cases but also the conditions under which they will be processed. Given the caseload in metropolitan areas and the scarcity of resources to deal with it, officials are pressed to dispense justice efficiently. The prosecutors' influence over other actors is based on these stresses within the criminal justice environment. In addition, there is the dramatic aspect of their work, which can command public attention, which in turn can be used as a weapon against the police, the courts, or other actors who do not cooperate with the efforts of their office.

Decision-making policies

In view of the differences in role conceptions, exchange relationships, and sociopolitical factors that influence the decisions made by prosecutors, is it possible to generalize about how this vital sector of criminal justice operates? Research indicates that throughout the pretrial phase the prosecutor and the prosecutor's assistants are involved in a screening process to determine what action should be taken with regard to a particular case. Pretrial screening is designed to remove from the system cases that do not meet the legal test of probable cause, to divert cases that the prosecutor believes could be better handled by another agency, and to prepare appropriate charges.

Studies show that there is great variation in the ways of conducting this portion of the prosecutorial process. Some offices make extensive use of screening; those prosecutors decline to charge twice as many cases as other prosecutors decline to charge. Pleas of guilty are the primary dispositional vehicle in some offices, while in others pleas of not guilty strain the courts' trial resources to their limits. Some offices remove cases soon after they are brought to the prosecutor's attention by the police; in others, disposition occurs as late as the first day of trial. The period from receipt of the police report to the trial is thus a time of review in which the prosecutor exercises discretion to determine what charging actions should be taken.

Joan Jacoby has completed extensive research on prosecutors through national surveys and case studies. Her research has focused on the types of policies that prosecutors try to implement to achieve specific goals during the pretrial process and the ways in which individual offices are managed toward those ends. On the basis of data from more than 3,000 prosecutors, she has found three policy models: Legal Sufficiency, System Efficiency, and Trial Sufficiency. She assumes that a prosecutor's choices with regard to the handling of cases are guided by a policy set forth in one of the models. The choice of policy is shaped by personal considerations of the prosecutor, by such external factors as crime levels, and by the relationship of prosecution to the other portions of the criminal justice system.[7]

It is important to recognize that the operative policy affects the decisions made by the prosecutor and the prosecutor's assistants as to how cases are to be screened and dispositions made. To accomplish the basic goals stated in the model, the prosecutor adopts strategies with regard to discovery, diversion, plea bargaining, and allocation of resources. It is assumed that only a certain proportion of cases the police make available will go to trial. Each model thus alerts us to the point in the process at which some types of cases are filtered out of the system. These models are valuable for our understanding of criminal justice and as management tools that the prosecutor can use to ensure implementation of a particular policy choice.

legal sufficiency The presence of the minimum legal elements necessary for prosecution of a case. When a prosecutor's decision to prosecute a case is customarily based on legal sufficiency, a great many cases are accepted for prosecution but the majority of them are disposed of by plea bargaining or dismissal.

system efficiency Operation of the prosecutor's office in such a way as to effect speedy and early disposition of cases in response to caseload pressures in the system. Weak cases are screened out at intake, and other nontrial alternatives are used as primary means of disposition.

trial sufficiency The presence of sufficient legal elements to ensure successful prosecution of a case. When a prosecutor's decision to prosecute a case is customarily based on trial sufficiency, only cases that seem certain to result in conviction at trial are accepted for prosecution. Use of plea bargaining is minimal; good police work and court capacity are required.

Legal sufficiency

Some prosecutors believe that if a case is legally sufficient, they have a responsibility to accept it for prosecution. They ask: Are the minimum legal elements present so that charges should be brought? In a breaking-and-entering case, for example, if there is evidence of forcible entry and if the accused was found to have the stolen items in his possession, the case would be prosecuted because it is legally sufficient—the required elements are there. But the force of these surface characteristics may be diminished if the police accumulated the evidence by unconstitutional tactics that would be exposed in court. Under the ***Legal Sufficiency*** Model, cases are initially screened merely for evidentiary defects before they are given a preliminary court hearing. Thus a great many cases are accepted for prosecution, and various operational strategies are employed to prevent overload of the system. Under this model, assistant prosecutors, especially those assigned to misdemeanor courts, have little time to prepare individual cases, must use plea bargaining to the utmost, and expect many dismissals and acquittals.

System efficiency

The ***System Efficiency*** Model aims at a speedy and early disposition of cases. A prosecutor in an office that adheres to this policy asks: What charges should be made in view of the caseload pressures on the system? Here the same breaking-and-entering case would be rejected because emphasis is placed on screening as the major technique to reduce workload. If the same unconstitutional search-and-seizure elements were present, they would be spotted and the case rejected. If the case did not appear defective, a prosecutor operating under a system-efficiency policy might charge the defendant with a felony but agree to reduce the charge to a misdemeanor—perhaps unlawful trespass or larceny—in exchange for a guilty plea. According to Jacoby's research, this model is usually followed when the trial court is backlogged and the prosecutor has limited resources. Thus the prosecutor must not only screen out weak cases at the intake point but also use other nontrial alternatives to minimize the number of trials.

Trial sufficiency

Under the ***Trial Sufficiency*** Model, cases are accepted and charges made only at the level that can be sustained in court. The prosecutor asks: Will this case result in a conviction? This does not mean that the prosecutor accepts only sure cases; it does mean that when the facts are present to sustain a conviction, every effort is made to secure that outcome. In the breaking-and-entering example, given the evidence and if the constitutional problem of the police search could be overcome, the defendant would be charged with a felony, and the goal would be conviction on that charge. This model requires good police work, a prosecution staff experienced in trial work, and—because plea bargaining is minimized—court capacity. Rejected cases must be diverted from the system by alternative means.

Implementing prosecution policy

As this description of the three models shows, the policy choice dictates that prosecutors select certain points in the process for disposition of the vast majority of the cases presented to them by the police. With a policy of legal sufficiency, many cases are accepted for prosecution but are then disposed of through plea negotiation and diversion after the preliminary hearing and before trial. With a policy of system efficiency, the prosecutor rejects the majority of requests for prosecution and diverts appropriate cases from the system. With a policy of trial sufficiency, most cases do not get beyond the point of intake, and the prosecutor proceeds with only those cases that will result in conviction.

Each policy requires the prosecutor to use strategies and deploy assistants in ways that are consistent with the overriding goal of the office. Accordingly, it is important for offices operating under the System Efficiency Model to have well-trained personnel at the intake point so that the critical decision to charge can be based on experience; offices operating under the Trial Sufficiency Model require skilled courtroom advocates; and offices operating under the Legal Sufficiency Model may use less-experienced personnel at the intake point but need good plea negotiators.

Decision to prosecute

Deciding whether to prosecute and what will be the nature of the charge may be considered the focus of the formal aspect of prosecuting attorneys' work. These determinations can legally be made by them alone, and the consequences have a great impact not only on the defendants but also on the other agencies that participate in the administration of justice.

As the Due Process Model emphasizes, a decision to label a citizen a defendant in a criminal action should be undertaken only with full and serious understanding. Once a suspect becomes a defendant, the entire weight of the criminal justice process is brought to bear on the individual. The state may restrain the person's liberty; economic burdens are imposed by the requirement that bail be posted and a lawyer hired; and there is the nontangible penalty of damage to the person's reputation. Though the public gives lip service to the idea of "innocent until proved guilty," it may also subscribe to the notion that where there's smoke, there's fire. There are negative aspects to being arrested, but there are even greater penalties attached to being charged with a crime.

The decision to prosecute is not made at only one point in the criminal justice process. While a decision to file charges is made during the initial phase, prosecutors may alter the charges at any time as they learn new facts about the case and as they interact with police, grand jury, defense attorneys, defendant, and judge. As Frank Miller points out, the charging decision is complex:

> The decision to charge, unlike the decision to arrest, is not a unitary decision made at a readily identifiable time by a specific individual. It is, instead, a process consisting of a series of interrelated decisions, and the steps in the process do not always occur in the same sequence. Most often the decision is made after a suspect has already been taken into custody. In some instances, the effective decision is made when the police decide not to ask the prosecutor to charge, but to release a suspect instead. Of greater significance are the decisions made by prosecutors, acting through their assistants, whether to charge suspects already in custody, in response to requests made by the police that they do so.[8]

Accusatory process

accusatory process The series of events that take place from the arrest of a suspect to the filing of a formal charging instrument (indictment or information) with the court.

We may define the ***accusatory process*** as the series of activities that take place from the moment a suspect is arrested and booked by the police to the moment the formal charging instrument—indictment or information—is filed with the court. During this process the activities of the police, grand jury, bail agency, and court are linked to those of the prosecuting attorney. Here the government must show only that there is a prima facie (that is, at first sight) case that a crime has been committed and that it was committed by the accused. Two issues are addressed by decision makers: (1) Is there probable cause to restrict the liberty of the individual? (2) Under the circumstances, would a reasonable person believe that the defendant committed the crime? If a grand jury or judge answers the questions affirmatively, a formal accusation instrument is presented and the defendant is arraigned on the charges. All of these procedures are carried out within a relatively brief span of time, but the decisions made have an important effect on the accused: personal liberty may be taken away, and the beginnings of a defense may have to be mounted. It is during the accusatory process that we can best see the way prosecutors in various parts of the United States conduct their formal duties.

As chapter 4 explained, the legal instrument by which charges are brought against a person is either an indictment handed down by a grand jury or a prosecutor's bill of information ruled upon by a judge at a preliminary hearing. In some states the prosecutor must present the facts of the case to a grand jury; if the jurors agree that the facts warrant formal charges, they will vote a "true bill" authorizing an indictment. In other states, primarily in the West, there is no grand jury; the prosecutor files an information directly with the court at a preliminary hearing. In addition to this difference in formal accusatory procedure between the areas, generally speaking, east and west of the Mississippi River, there are local variations in the responsibilities of the police and of the prosecutor at the several stages between an arrest and the filing of charges. These differences greatly influence the prosecutor's ability to exercise independent judgment in regard to the disposition of a case.

Although the formal description of the two charging processes discussed above and illustrated in figure 8.1 seems to be clear-cut, there are operational variations that mix the roles of the city police, prosecutor, and court. The variations influence the "domain" of the prosecutor, that is, the decisions over which the prosecutor lays claim. In some places the prosecutor really controls the charging decision; in others, the police informally make the decision,

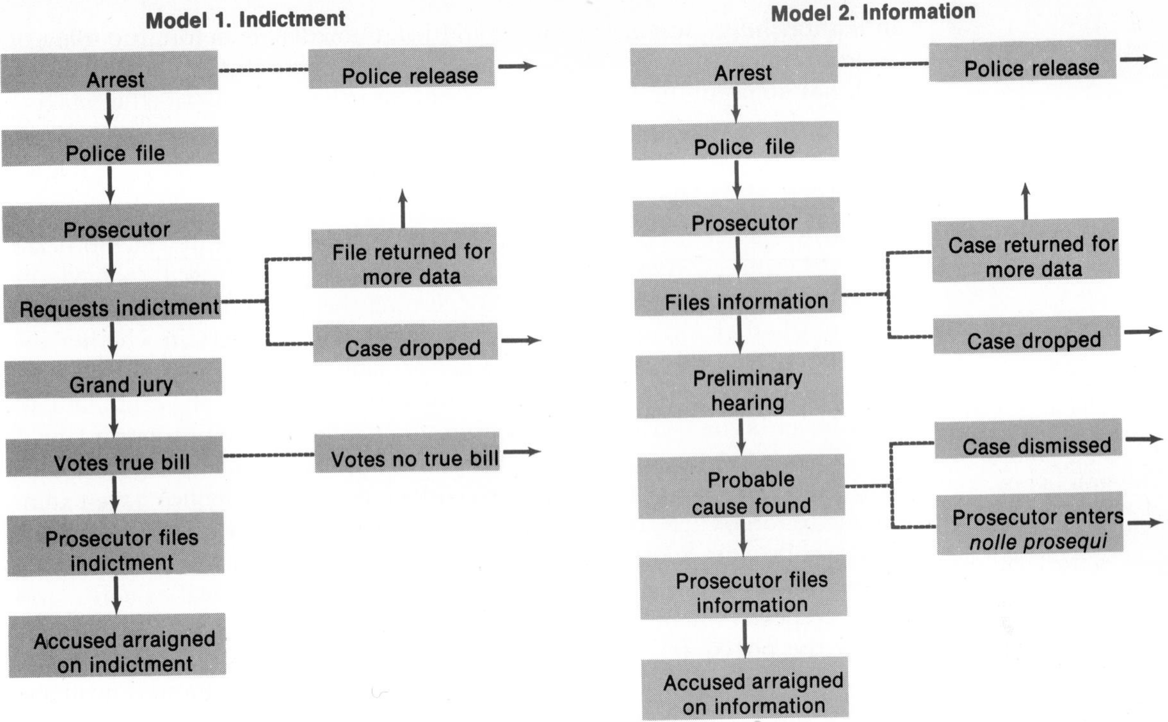

FIGURE 8.1
Two models of the accusatory process

which is then rubber-stamped by the prosecutor; and in still others, the prosecutor not only controls the charging process but is greatly involved in such judicial functions as determining the court calendar, appointing defense counsel for indigents, and sentencing.

The prosecutor's power is enhanced by the capability to screen cases early and to make accusatory decisions with the cooperation (or compliance) of the police. If, however, the police are able to hold cases until just before the filing of the information or the presentation of charges to the grand jury, the prosecutor's opportunity to assert authority is diminished.

In some cities, such as Detroit, the charging decision is made early in the process. The police decide to book a suspect and then bring the case file to the prosecutor's office for review and the institution of charges. These actions are taken within twelve hours after arrest, well before the case is filed in court. At this early point the prosecutor makes the charge that, unless it is dropped at the preliminary hearing, will become the formal charge eventually filed. This arrangement puts the prosecutor in a position to influence the bail recommendation at the defendant's initial appearance. In other jurisdictions, however, portions of the accusatory process are outside the prosecutor's domain.[9] In New Orleans, for example, the case does not reach the prosecutor's office until after initial charges, made by the police, are filed in court. With "police charges" already formalized, the prosecutor not only has little influence on the bail decision but has less ability to exercise discretion. In still other jurisdictions (Greenville, South Carolina; Knox County, Tennessee; and Delaware County, Pennsylvania, for example) the prosecutor is unable to review cases until after the preliminary hearing and just immediately before the filing of the information or presentation to the grand jury. With this system, the prosecutor has no input to the bail decision and is further circumscribed in making the charging decision.

Crime construction

Boyd Littrell has described the charging process as one in which officials construct crimes.[10] By this he means that the police and prosecutors have the authority to interpret information concerning the accused's behavior, to determine whether a crime has been committed, and to ascertain whether the legal elements necessary to prosecute are present. Naturally, not all "bad acts" are deemed to be crimes, and, among those that do violate the criminal law, many never become crimes because they go undetected, are unreported, or—even though they are detected and reported—are not prosecuted.

In the early stages of the criminal justice process, the police have extensive discretion to determine whether formal actions will be taken against law violators. Because most crimes occur before the police arrive at the scene, officers must reconstruct the situation on the basis of physical evidence and witness reports. There is considerable ambiguity in most sets of circumstances, so that the police, relying on their training, experience, and work routines, evaluate the crime as to its potential for an arrest and prosecution. If an arrest is made and a formal complaint filed, the prosecutor is then in a position to evaluate the police reports, as well as information from other sources, in order to arrive at the exact charges.

The prosecutor's task is not simple. He or she must keep uppermost in mind that behaviors must conform to the elements of a crime—the ingredi-

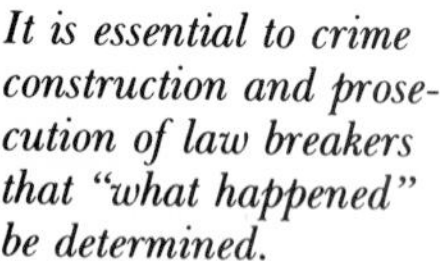
It is essential to crime construction and prosecution of law breakers that "what happened" be determined.

ents that must be present before a person can be convicted. The law defines robbery, for example, as an act in which there is (1) forcible taking (2) of goods of another person (3) by an individual who (4) employs violence or puts victims in fear as a means to accomplish the theft. These elements also show what must be done to prove a case of robbery. The prosecutor must thus organize the evidence and witnesses so that each element can be proved to the satisfaction of judge and jury. If the prosecutor believes that this cannot be done, lesser included charges may be filed—for example, "assault with intent to rob" or "larceny from the person." The prosecutor's ability to make these decisions, however, depends not only on the evidence but also on the organizational context within which he or she operates.

Intake

In a study of twenty-one urban prosecution offices throughout the United States, Jacoby found two distinct types of intake and charging processes. In the first, the charging function is transferred to the police and the court because the prosecutor does not review cases after they have been filed in court. As a result, prosecutors in such systems can only react to the actions of others and have limited discretion. They may not decide *whether* to charge the suspect but only *at what level* to go forward with the prosecution—felony or misdemeanor. Prosecutors operating under a "transfer" system may only correct, modify, or dismiss police arrest charges; they do not have the power to decline cases for prosecution. Jacoby's survey found that in a small but significant minority of jurisdictions, prosecutors did not exercise discretion at intake, this most crucial gatekeeping function.[11]

In most jurisdictions, cases are screened in the prosecutor's office on the basis of police reports before charges are filed. Here the prosecutor exercises the greatest amount of discretion. Here crimes are "constructed" to determine whether the required legal elements are present and whether such factors as the strength of the evidence and the believability of victims or witnesses will substantiate the police report so that a conviction may be expected.

Elizabeth Stanko observed the intake and screening process in the Early Case Assessment Bureau (ECAB) of a large metropolitan prosecutor's office. Here two assistant prosecutors examined forty to eighty felony arrests each day and determined the disposition of each case—drop or charge. To determine whether a case was "solid," prosecutors not only assessed the legal factors of an arrest but also evaluated extralegal factors that might influence the outcome of the case. Of importance is the prosecutor's assessment of the victim's credibility.

> Not only does the credibility of the victim become an essential organizational question—i.e., whether or not someone's story is credible is essential information when one is predicting the probable conviction of the defendant—but a victim's credibility is integrally linked to social stereotyping which predicts what *kinds* of individuals are likely to tell the truth.[12]

The examples that follow will show that case evaluation is more than just a process of matching the police arrest report with the criminal code. It is an attempt by the prosecutor to determine whether the reported crime will appear credible and meet legal criteria in the eyes of judge and jury.

Charging

Determining the exact motivation of prosecutors when they select one charge over another is impossible. They can identify the factors that consciously entered into their choice, but they are seldom able to pinpoint the conversations they had or the words they read that were responsible for injecting these ideas, reinforcing them, and turning them into final decisions. Studies of the decision to prosecute, however, show a remarkable agreement on the broad elements considered (table 8.1). These considerations may be classified as evidential, pragmatic, and organizational. We cannot tell whether one of these categories is more important than another, but we can note that at the initial stage, when a decision to file is made, the type and amount of evidence reflected in the police report appear to be dominant factors. As a former

Close-up: Case Assessment

Robbery in the first degree

The complainant is a professional man who works for the Better Business Bureau. He entered the Early Case Assessment Bureau with his Sunday *New York Times* tucked under his arm. His recall of the incident was clear, and he presented his story articulately. After the complainant had received instructions to appear before the grand jury the next morning and had then left the room, the ADA [Assistant District Attorney] remarked to the arresting officer [A/O]:

ADA: Do you think the defendants know the complainant is a homosexual?
A/O: No.
ADA: Would have been a great alibi. They could claim that they had met and the complainant invited them up for a drink.

Robbery in the second degree

A young black complainant was accosted by two males. The defendants stopped the complainant and told him they wanted money. One put his hand on the complainant's chest and told him if he didn't produce "they could 'cap' him." The prosecutor asked the complainant what "cap" meant. The complainant replied that he didn't know. All he knew was that he didn't want to be hurt and he assumed that whatever capping was, he didn't want to find out. He gave them his money (included was one $10 bill torn in half, which was found in the possession of the defendant). One defendant reached inside the coat of the complainant. Then they left. The prosecutor reduced the charges from robbery in the second degree to grand larceny in the third degree. The prosecutor stated that if the grand jury asked [the complainant] what "cap" meant he couldn't answer and therefore wouldn't be able to prove the threat of force in the robbery charge.

Robbery in the first degree

ADA: How long have you known the defendant?
C/W [Case Worker]: I was a counselor in a drug program—Neighborhood Thing—in 1971–72 and I met her there. I've seen her around since then. She was a Muslim and had a boyfriend and I didn't see her much then. But since she split I've seen her around.
. . . ADA then asks the complainant to go out to the waiting room while he draws up the affidavit in the presence of the A/O.
A/O: He's the best complainant I've had in two years.
ADA: The people in the Supreme Court don't like prior-relationship cases. I think he was going out with her. The jury wouldn't like this. It's just a feel for the case. I don't like it.

Source: Elizabeth A. Stanko, "The Impact of Victim Assessment on Prosecutors' Screening Decisions: The Case of the New York County District Attorney's Office," paper presented at the annual meeting of the Northeastern Political Science Association, New Haven, Connecticut, November 20–22, 1980. Reprinted by permission.

deputy prosecutor told this author, "If you have the evidence, you file, then bring the other considerations in during the bargaining phase."

Evidential considerations. Is there a case? Does the evidence warrant the arrest of an individual and the expense of a trial? These are major questions that prosecutors ask when they think about whether to prosecute. Legally, a prosecution cannot hope to be successful without some proof that the required elements of a criminal act are present in the case, that the suspect has committed it, and that he or she formulated some intent to commit the act. Aside from the precise legal definition of the crime, prosecutors must decide whether the act is viewed as criminal within the local political context. Many offenses committed under borderline circumstances do not result in prosecution.

The nature of the crime may require the presentation of evidence that can prove such a vague charge as neglect. Prosecutors must be certain that the evidence will coincide with the court's interpretation of the term. In addition, evidence must be introduced that will connect the defendant with the criminal act: a confession, statement of witnesses, physical evidence. All these requirements must be met within the context of the rules of evidence and guarantees of due process.

The nature of the complaint, the strength of the testimony of witnesses, and the attitude of the victim must also be evaluated. Thought has to be given to whose interests are being served by prosecution. Often when complaints are based on marital or neighborhood quarrels or quasi-civil offenses (for example, debt claims), the prosecutor must ensure that a violation of the criminal law has occurred and that the victim is not using the law for his or her own purposes. Evidence is weak when it is difficult to use in proving charges, when the value of a stolen article is questionable, when a case results from a brawl or other order-maintenance situation, or when corroboration (supporting testimony) is lacking.

Pragmatic considerations. The prosecutor is able to individualize justice in ways that can benefit both the accused and society. Especially when the offense arises from mental illness, prosecutors may feel that psychiatric treat-

TABLE 8.1 Number and percentage of cases rejected by prosecutors in seven jurisdictions, by reason for rejection

		Percent of cases rejected						
Jurisdiction	*Number of cases rejected*	*Evidence*	*Witness*	*Office policy*	*Due process*	*Diversion*	*Other*	*Total*
Golden, Colo.	49	20%	18%	45%	2%	4%	10%	100%
Indianapolis, Ind.	155	40	12	19	3	0	25	100
Los Angeles, Calif.	19,197	70	12	7	7	1	3	100
Manhattan, N.Y.	1,062	50	26	13	6	0	4	100
New Orleans, La.	3,315	40	31	12	10	7	0	100
Salt Lake City, Utah	702	65	20	10	2	1	2	100
Washington, D.C.	1,442	22	16	12	1	0	49	100

Note: Percents may not add to 100% because of rounding.
Source: Adapted from Barbara Boland, Elizabeth Brady, Herbert Tyson, and John Bassler, *The Prosecution of Felony Arrests*, U.S. Department of Justice, Bureau of Justice Statistics (Washington, D.C.: Government Printing Office, 1983), p. 9.

ment is more desirable than imprisonment. Diversion of the accused from the criminal justice system to a treatment facility may be a more realistic disposition of the case. Concern for the welfare of the victim may also be a reason for deciding against prosecution. In cases involving the sexual molestation of a child, prosecution may not be sought if conviction hinges on the victim's testimony because the requirement of reciting the facts in court may be considered too great a psychological burden to place on the child.

The character of the accused persons, their status in the community, and the impact of prosecution on their families may likewise influence the charges filed. Prosecutors may not invoke the full weight of the law when they believe that to do so would unduly punish the offender. Where the law is not flexible (mandatory sentences, for example), the prosecutor may believe that the gravity of the crime does not warrant such severe treatment. The rehabilitative potential, the seriousness of the offense, and the benefits to be gained by keeping a suspect's record clean weigh heavily in the decision to prosecute.

Organizational considerations. The exchange relationships among units of the criminal justice system, court congestion, community pressures, and the demands placed on the system's resources all affect the decision to prosecute. The prosecuting attorney is the one criminal justice actor who has significant interactions with every other major actor. Thus the personal relationships of the participants are more influential in decision making than the written report of an incident. A prosecutor may be reluctant to turn down a police officer's request for an arrest warrant even though the evidentiary

Decision Making

The defendant was drinking in the bar and a heated argument erupted. He claimed the bartender hadn't paid up on a debt. The defendant started to storm out, the victim made some gratuitous remark. The defendant pulled out a gun and shot him. There was a lot of confusion after that. We had only one witness who could make the identification. It was enough, but it weakened the case. The bar was dark, and the witness made the ID when he was shown just one picture—of the defendant. To do it right there should have been a lineup, or we should have brought fifteen pictures for the witness to choose from. There was the shaky ID and a plausible self-defense argument—a jury might have believed the victim had pulled a weapon. I had no question about this defendant's guilt, but there were these evidentiary weaknesses. I figured there was a 60–40 chance of winning a conviction at trial. And also, juries will not convict on first-degree murder unless it's a gangland premeditated murder—they hand down first-degree manslaughter convictions instead, particularly where the crime is committed in the heat of passion. So, already, you're down to manslaughter one. The question of time [sentence] is important here. Because this guy had a bad record—a homicide arrest, and prison on aggravated assault and weapons charges—I was set on a ten- to fifteen-year sentence. That would be covered by a second-degree manslaughter plea. And he was 47; the older a man gets, the less necessary it becomes to sentence him to a long prison term. In the end, the judge pushed me down from ten to seven years. I wouldn't have compromised those three years except I was about to leave the job. The case would have been even weaker if it got transferred to a new ADA [assistant district attorney].

Source: Vera Institute of Justice, *Felony Arrests: Their Prosecution and Disposition in New York City's Courts* (New York, 1977), pp. 55–56.

aspects of the case may be weak. At the same time, prosecutors develop a sensitive awareness of the types of cases likely to lead to convictions in the local courts. They may refrain from filing a case that a judge may regard as a waste of time because the judge may doubt the prosecutor's judgment in future cases.

The expected public reaction is a factor in most decisions. Especially if the crime is of a heinous nature, such as child rape, if publicity has aroused the electorate, and if the victim is well known, the prosecutor's discretion may be limited. In one instance, a prosecutor abandoned the practice of charging escapees from the county jail with misdemeanors and brought in felony charges instead after the newspapers publicized a rash of jailbreaks.

As has often been said, justice must "be seen publicly to be done." The public's respect for the criminal justice process is greatly affected by the behavior of prosecutors. Prosecutors must decide whether the community's regard for the law will be harmed if a person is brought to trial and is not convicted. Some people may feel that too many acquittals call into question the validity of the judicial process and undermine respect for law. Is it better to let a guilty person go free than to attempt a prosecution that is bound to fail?

The expenditure of organizational resources may be another reason for withholding prosecution. If the matter is trivial or if the accused must be extradited from another state, the costs may be too high to warrant action. If the accused is on parole or has a prior deferred or suspended sentence, a prosecutor may feel that the best decision is merely to go before a judge and seek revocation of the parole.

Organizational influences on the decision to prosecute are many. Certainly the exchange relationships between the police and the prosecutor, congestion within the system, and community pressures are considered at this juncture. Prosecutors must decide which charge is appropriate to the facts of the case, the needs of the defendant, and the needs of society. They may decide to throw the book at the defendant, only to have it boomerang when they are unable to prove the case in court. They may charge the defendant with serious or multiple offenses to increase their own latitude in plea bargaining. These options are available to prosecutors from the time the police originally file a case with them until the judge pronounces sentence, as figure 8.2 indicates.

Factors to Be Considered

In determining whether prosecution should be declined because no substantial federal interest would be served by prosecution, the attorney for the government should weight all relevant considerations, including:

1. federal law enforcement priorities;
2. the nature and seriousness of the offense;
3. the deterrent effect of prosecution;
4. the person's culpability in connection with the offense;
5. the person's history with respect to criminal activity;
6. the person's willingness to cooperate in the investigation or prosecution of others; and
7. the probable sentence or other consequences if the person is convicted.

Source: U.S. Department of Justice, *Principles of Federal Prosecution* (Washington, D.C.: Government Printing Office, 1980), p. 7.

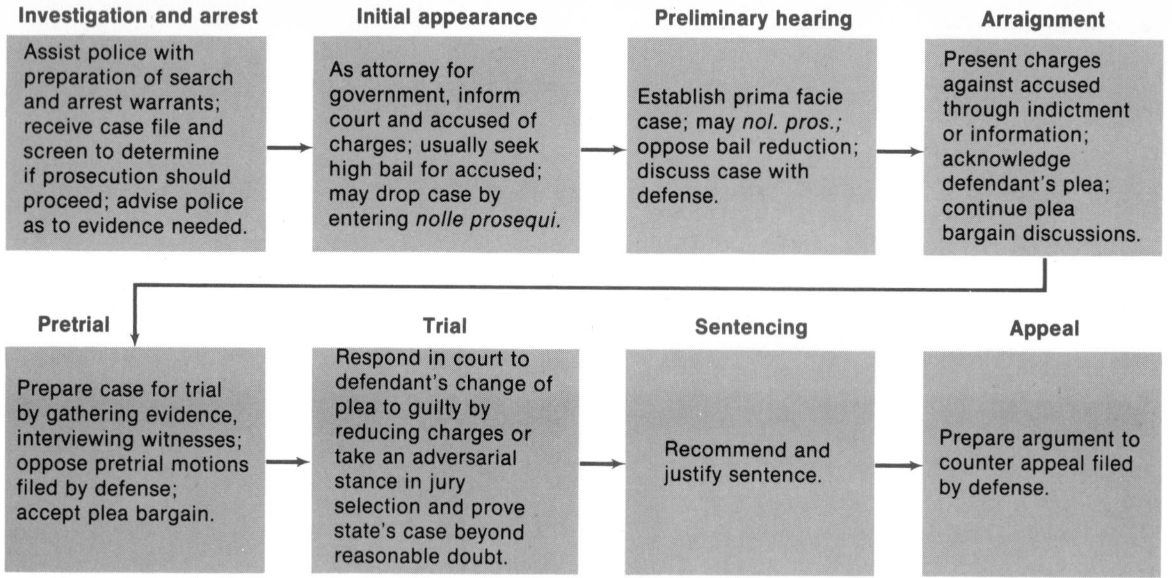

FIGURE 8.2 Typical actions of a prosecutor in processing a felony case

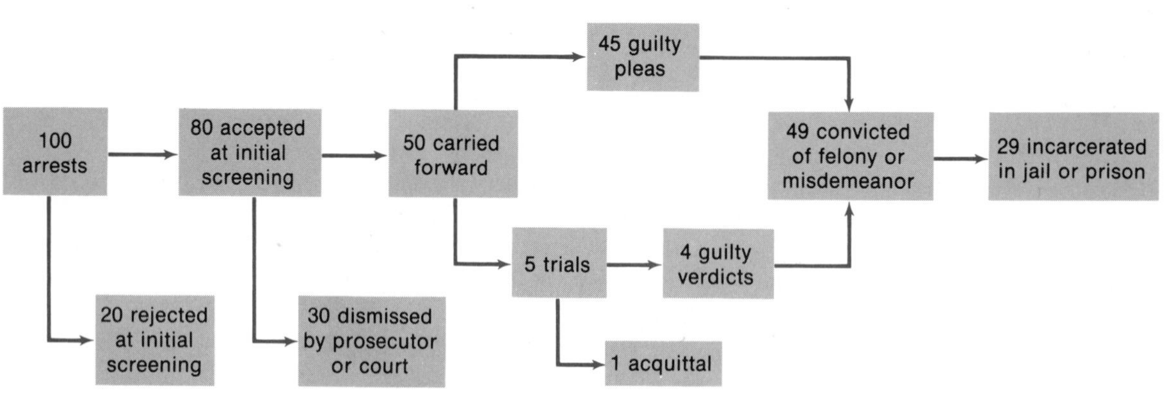

FIGURE 8.3 Outcome of 100 "typical" felony arrests

Prosecutors—the link between the police and the courts—hold a strategic position because all cases must pass through their office. Accordingly, they are able to regulate not only the flow of cases but also the conditions under which the cases will be processed. Given the caseload that burdens the contemporary legal system and the scarcity of resources to deal with it, officials are hard pressed to dispense justice efficiently. And as figure 8.3 indicates, of 100 typical felony arrests, fewer than half result in conviction. The prosecutor's influence over other actors is based on the stresses within the organizational environment.

Prosecution management

The volume of cases and the multitude of details in regard to each offender and incident that flood most prosecutors' offices made it obvious to criminal justice planners in the early 1970s that effective crime control required efficient management practices. Too often a case was lost because a vital piece of information was missing from the file; too often a recidivist was sentenced as a first-time offender because a record was not known to the prosecution or judge; too often the prosecutor was overwhelmed by the sheer volume of cases. In addition, the deterrent effect of certain punishment was minimized by long delays in final disposition, often because cases were misplaced. A variety of management practices based on use of computers and data systems have made it increasingly possible for prosecuting attorneys to have at their disposal the information on cases and offenders necessary to accomplish their task.

One of the most prominent management tools is the Prosecutor's Management Information System (PROMIS), which stores information on pending cases in a computer and ranks them according to seriousness, the accused's criminal record, the strength of the evidence, and the age of the case.[13] Prosecutors are able to call up a list of pending cases that accord with these variables, thereby ensuring that important matters are not neglected and that facts necessary for conviction are not overlooked. With the aid of PROMIS, prosecutors can allocate their resources more effectively and efficiently. PROMIS has been installed in more than a hundred state and local prosecution and court agencies.

Career criminal

career criminal
An individual for whom criminal activity is a way of life; such individuals are thought to be responsible for a large proportion of all crimes.

Recognition that a small group of ***career criminals*** is responsible for a disproportionate share of some offenses caused prosecutors to develop management programs that concentrate resources to ensure the conviction and incarceration of offenders for whom criminal activity is a way of life. The programs were developed in response to studies showing that in Washington, D.C., for example, 7 percent of all persons arrested accounted for 25 percent of all cases.[14] Marvin Wolfgang found that chronic offenders constituted 23 percent of all male offenders he reviewed in Philadelphia but they had committed 61 percent of all the crimes.[15] The heavy caseload pressures facing prosecutors and the normal two-year delay between felony indictment and trial in some urban courts often work to the advantage of repeat offenders.

Many prosecution offices with career criminal programs ensure continuity of a case by holding one individual responsible for it from arrest to conviction, by allocating additional resources to the prosecution of chronic offend-

Prosecution as Lovemaking

Man's greatest experience is the art of lovemaking. I sometimes wonder if the moment when the jury foreman rises to utter those sweet words of the verdict—"We the jury find the defendant guilty as charged"—is not as satisfactory an experience.

Source: Maurice Nadjari, "Case Trial Preparation," lecture presented at National College of District Attorneys, University of Houston, summer 1971; quoted in Marvin Frankel, *Partisan Justice* (New York: Hill & Wang, 1980), p. 32.

ers, and by limiting plea bargaining. At sentencing, prosecutors are expected to emphasize to the judge the seriousness of the charges and the long prior record of the offender.

One such career criminal program, the Major Offense Bureau (MOB) of the Bronx County District Attorney's Office, was established in 1973 to concentrate exclusively on the prosecution of serious crimes and repeat offenders. A staff of experienced prosecutors armed with such management tools as PROMIS pursues full-time serious cases involving career criminals. From 1973 to 1976, MOB filed 842 indictments for the prosecution of 1,238 defendants. The majority of the cases involved armed robbery and various types of aggravated assault. More than half of the defendants had two or more previous felony convictions. With the special focus of MOB, these cases—which would otherwise have been handled in a routine and less effective manner—were identified as serious and given high priority. MOB cases were disposed of in an average of ninety days, with an overall conviction rate of 96 percent. The operations of the Bronx MOB have been copied in other parts of the country.

What have been the results of the special attention given to career criminals? Evaluations of these programs have been carried out, and it appears that conviction rates have been increased only marginally. In Kalamazoo, Michigan, the conviction rate went from 66.6 percent to 73.4 percent; in New Orleans, from 81.8 percent to 88.7 percent; and in Columbus, Ohio, from 73.9 percent to 76.4 percent. Incarceration rates increased in two of the cities, but went down in New Orleans.[16] This experience seems to indicate that factors other than the resources of the prosecutor's office are important in achieving the desired results.

Diversion: alternatives to prosecution

When prosecuting attorneys believe that the ideals of justice can be better served if they do not seek formal adjudication, they may seek alternatives that divert the offender from the criminal justice system.

> Diversion refers to formally acknowledged . . . efforts to utilize alternatives to . . . the justice system. To qualify as diversion such efforts must be undertaken prior to adjudication and after a legally proscribed action has occurred. . . . Diversion implies halting or suspending formal criminal or juvenile justice proceedings against a person who has violated a statute, in favor of processing through a noncriminal disposition.[17]

diversion An alternative to adjudication by which the defendant agrees to conditions set by the prosecutor (such as to undergo counseling or drug rehabilitation) in exchange for withdrawal of charges.

Although ***diversion*** from the criminal justice system is a traditional American custom—"get out of town" or "join the Army"—it has become formalized only during the past two decades. Cases may be dropped at the prosecutor's discretion at any time up to the moment the verdict is pronounced. As we have seen, the police often warn persons that they face arrest if they continue a particular behavior, "handle" family crises without formal action, and take individuals directly to treatment facilities. The extent of the diversionary activities of the police is unknown because they are never recorded, but it is believed to be substantial. We have more knowledge about programs developed to divert accused individuals from the criminal justice system during the accusatory process, when the prosecutor is dominant.

In most systems, such efforts are directed at diverting certain types of

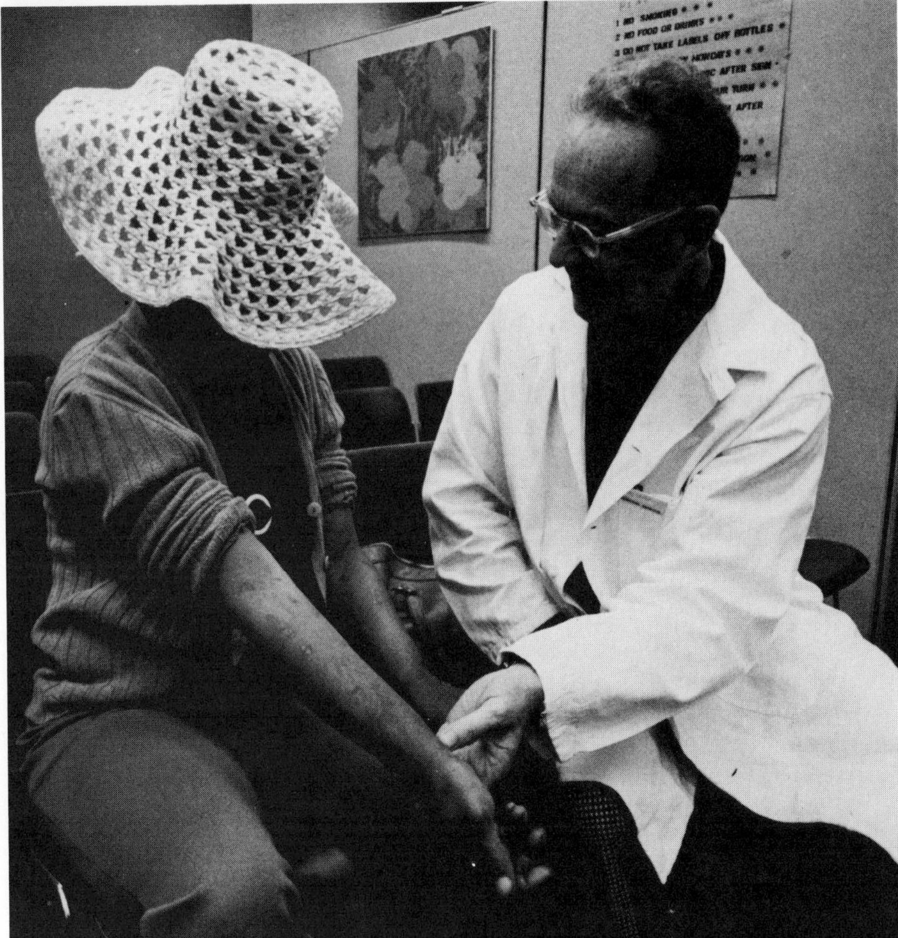

A realistic alternative to prosecution may be to divert the accused out of the system for treatment.

offenders to treatment programs for drug or alcohol abusers, to mental hospitals, or into voluntary public service, or at persuading them to make restitution to their victims. Pretrial diversion consists of informal administrative efforts to provide alternatives to adjudication by which accused persons may receive help—medical, psychological, or social—to deal with the problems thought to be at the root of their criminal behavior. Pretrial diversion is also justified as a way to avoid the damage caused by labeling an individual as a criminal. The case of a first-time offender accused of committing a minor infraction may be informally disposed of. In some states the case is screened out of the system by the prosecutor with only minimal restrictions, or none at all; or the prosecutor may place a charge "on hold" for a specified time (say, a year), at the end of which it is dropped if the individual has not been rearrested. In other states such informal dispositions are made in court at the recommendation of the prosecutor, and so-called accelerated rehabilitation is granted. As in the case of other informal practices, the fact of the arrest, prosecution, and disposition is expunged from the record at the expiration of an arrest-free period.

Pretrial diversion may be either unconditional, in that there is no follow-up, or conditional, in that the person is monitored to ensure that the required activity has been carried out. If it has been, the defendant's case is dismissed and a criminal record avoided. Should the required activity not take place, prosecution may be reinstituted.

Several factors are considered to determine whether diversion is appropriate: the age of the offender; the willingness of the victim not to press for conviction; the likelihood that the offender has physical or psychological difficulties that are at the root of the criminal behavior and for which treatment is available; and the likelihood that the crime was related to a condition, such as unemployment or a family problem, that may be changed through rehabilitative measures. In addition, diversion is generally used only for certain types of crimes, usually those classified as misdemeanors or property felonies. Prosecutors do not usually divert an offender who has committed a crime of violence. As with other aspects of the decision to prosecute, evidential, pragmatic, and organizational factors can determine the prosecutor's action.

Assessment of diversion programs

Pretrial diversion programs, developed with LEAA funds, proliferated throughout the United States during the early 1970s. Pretrial diversion was viewed as a simple and appealing idea at that time. As the President's Commission said in 1967, efforts should be directed toward "early identification and diversion to other community resources of those offenders in need of treatment, for whom full criminal disposition does not appear required."[18] The concept was applauded by many people as offering the promise of the best of all worlds; it would result in cost savings, rehabilitation, and more humane treatment. Some pretrial diversion programs, such as the Manhattan Court Employment Project, Operation Crossroads (Washington, D.C.), and Project Intercept (San Jose, California), gained wide publicity and were emulated.

Just as quickly as pretrial diversion programs rose, their gloss began to fade. Few remained by the end of the decade, and many of those had altered their direction. Even by 1975 evaluations of some of the original experimental programs had raised serious questions about their effectiveness. Researchers had discovered that many accused persons refused to participate in pretrial diversion programs. Either because of their past experience or upon the advice of counsel, they preferred to try to "beat" the formal adjudicatory process rather than accept the probation-like conditions of diversion. Almost 50 percent of the Manhattan project's eligible defendants in 1974–1975 chose this path. In addition, evaluators alleged that the programs were doing little to reduce prosecutorial and judicial caseloads because pretrial diversion had the effect of merely "widening the net": with some accused persons diverted, prosecutors could spend more time on cases that previously they would have dropped as minor and not worth the expenditure of resources. Other studies challenged the reported success of some pretrial programs in reducing recidivism. An overriding theme of the evaluations is that even in the absence of diversion programs the same individuals would have been treated leniently by the prosecutor.

Malcolm Feeley asks the important question: "Why, despite serious efforts and substantial funds, has diversion had so little success?" He believes that the developers of the programs erroneously assumed that the major actors in the criminal justice system would respond positively to the goals of the programs.

> Defendants were supposed to welcome diversion as a benign alternative to an alienating courtroom. Prosecutors were expected to divert less serious cases so they could spend more time on more serious cases. Judges were expected to divert people because diversion led to rehabilitation.[19]

It appears that diversion became for many officials a further device to achieve their goals. Feeley charges that defendants learned that they could wait out the system; prosecutors used diversion as a weapon to wield against defense attorneys; and judges resented the intrusion of "outside" diversion agencies into their domain.

Most federal funding of diversion programs has ended, and few have been able to discover steady and secure alternative sources of revenue. After a decade of enthusiasm, the remaining programs seem to have changed their focus, taking on goals not directly linked to criminal justice and diversion. This is not to say that prosecutors do not use their discretion to divert offenders out of the system; they do. In fact, the long-range impact of the diversion programs may have been to legitimize alternative courses of action. It is now clear that prosecutors have power to take such actions and should use it. In addition, pretrial diversion may have helped the police, too, to understand that it is legitimate to find alternative means to deal with some types of deviants.

Politics and prosecutors

The powers that accrue to prosecutors from their legal duties may be further developed through political partisanship. Prosecutors are often able to mesh their own ambitions with the needs of a political party. The appointment of deputies to the prosecutor's office, for example, may serve the party's desire for new blood and the prosecutor's need for young lawyers. Also, prosecutors may press charges in ways that enhance their own and the party's objectives. Cases may be processed so that only the few that are certain to be successful come to trial and hence help to maintain the prosecutor's conviction record. Investigations may be initiated before elections to embarrass the opposition. Charges may be pressed against public officials for political gain. It is significant that certain groups and persons may receive less than impartial justice because of the prosecutor's determinations.

The political potential of the district attorney's office may not be realized in communities whose culture demands nonpartisanship in the system. A study of a New Orleans prosecutor's office under a reform administration and then of a prosecutor tied to a political machine found only insignificant differences in the way most cases were handled, suggesting that disposition of most cases may be unaffected by direct political pressures. Indirectly, however, the part played in prosecution by political pressure may be important. Brooklyn prosecutor John J. Meglio has noted that when politics is a factor in the administration of justice, the prosecutor's office displays an intimate awareness of the problems and concerns of society which translates into a greater effectiveness in the courtroom, where testimony often needs interpretation and a grasp of different social contexts and meanings. . . . Being attuned to the people and the community also contributes to a better use of discretion in meting out justice. Such knowledge is built into a political office, where assistant prosecutors are expected to keep their fingers on the pulse of the community attitudes and needs.[20]

The office of prosecuting attorney has long been viewed as a stepping-stone to higher office. Because they deal with dramatic materials, prosecutors can use the communications media to create favorable public opinion. Their discretionary powers may be exercised so that voters will be impressed by their abilities. Many prosecutors have attained prominence in other political arenas, such as the judiciary and the governor's mansion. Each session of Congress includes numerous senators and representatives who have been prosecutors.

Although successful prosecutor-politicians are numerous, in some areas of the country the record of upward mobility from the prosecuting attorney's office is unimpressive. Further, with the recent emphasis on improving the salaries and tenure of criminal justice personnel, more lawyers may decide to embark on long-term careers in prosecution.

Summary

With justification, the prosecuting attorney is called the central actor in the criminal justice system. Prosecutors not only are responsible for the decision to bring charges against defendants, but in the vast majority of cases they also

Close-up: Lloyd Meeds: The Office as a Stepping-stone

On the night of August 21, 1959, a small band of deputy sheriffs, led by Deputy Prosecuting Attorney Lloyd Meeds, raided a suspected house of prostitution in Snohomish County, Washington. In the course of this action they arrested two deputy sheriffs who were enjoying the comforts of the premises. The fact that the raid was conducted without the knowledge of either Prosecutor Arnold Zempel or Sheriff Robert Twitchell resulted in the call for a grand jury to look into charges of corruption in county government because of the implication that law enforcement officials were protecting the vice operations. The investigation brought about the indictment and ultimate conviction of Twitchell on charges of willful neglect of duty and the hasty resignation of Zempel.

Appointed to fill Zempel's unexpired term, Meeds ran successfully for prosecutor as the "man who stopped vice in Snohomish County." Two years later, in November 1964, Meeds defeated Republican incumbent Jack Westland to become congressman from Washington's Second District. During the campaign the image of the reformer for good government was widely publicized, with references made to Meeds's success as a fighting prosecutor.

In the rise of Meeds, we find almost a classic example of the stepping-stone thesis, in which a bright young lawyer bent on a career in the public sector is able to use the opportunity resources of the prosecutor's office—publicity, personnel, and organization—to his political benefit: from energetic deputy, to interim appointment as prosecutor, to election to the office in his own right, and then on to the United States House of Representatives.

Source: George F. Cole, "The Politics of Prosecution" Ph.D. diss., University of Washington, Seattle, 1968, chap. 6.

participate in negotiations concerning the outcome. Thus the extent of prosecuting attorneys' influence is obvious, but the fact remains that throughout the United States little public attention is given to their role. Even where the office is elective, the amount of interest generated by the campaign for it is usually low. In many ways the prosecutor's decisions have a potentially greater impact than those of the mayor or city council. The level of law enforcement and therefore a vital aspect of the quality of life is directly related to the actions of the prosecutor.

The office of prosecuting attorney typifies decentralization in the justice system; there are few structural checks on the powers of prosecutors, and the confidentiality of their decisions lessens the visibility of their actions. Because the decision to prosecute is the focus of their work, prosecutors are able to exercise discretion at various points in the justice process. The decision to file charges is made at the initial phase, but the charges may be altered, reduced, or dropped at a number of points for reasons pertaining to evidence, for pragmatic considerations, or in the interests of the organizational needs of the system.

For discussion

1. You are the prosecutor. How may factors—such as an overcrowded jail, a backlog of cases, and a shortage of staff—influence your decisions? Is this justice?
2. Which policy would you follow if you were prosecutor of your county: legal sufficiency, trial sufficiency, system efficiency? Why?
3. How can the prosecutor's decisions be made more visible? What effect would increased visibility have on the system?
4. You are the prosecutor. The director of a local business group asks you to spearhead a drive to move "undesirables" away from the sidewalks in front of the downtown stores. Should you grant the request? What should be considered?
5. You are the prosecutor. The daughter of a local minister has been caught using narcotics. The minister promises that the girl will undergo therapy at a private hospital if the case is dropped. What will you do?

For further reading

Botein, Bernard. *The Prosecutor.* New York: Simon & Schuster, 1956.
Heuman, Milton. *Plea Bargaining.* Chicago: University of Chicago Press, 1977.
Jacoby, Joan E. *The American Prosecutor: A Search for Identity.* Lexington, Mass.: Lexington Books, 1979.
McDonald, William F., ed. *The Prosecutor.* Beverly Hills, Calif.: Sage, 1979.
Miller, Frank W. *Prosecution: The Decision to Charge a Suspect with a Crime.* Boston: Little, Brown, 1969.
Moley, Raymond. *Politics and Criminal Prosecution.* New York: Minton, Balch, 1929.

Notes

1. Alexander B. Smith and Harriet Pollack, *Crimes and Justice in a Mass Society* (New York: Xerox, 1972), p. 165.
2. Wayne LaFave, *Arrest: The Decision to Take a Suspect into Custody* (Boston: Little, Brown, 1965), p. 515.
3. David Sudnow, "Normal Crimes: Sociological Features of the Penal Codes in a Public Defender's Office," *Social Problems* 12 (Winter 1965): 255–76.
4. David W. Neubauer, *Criminal Justice in Middle America* (Morristown, N.J.: General Learning Press, 1974), p. 116.
5. Barbara Boland, Elizabeth Brady, Herbert Tyson, and John Bassler, *The Prosecution of Felony Arrests,* U.S. Department of Justice, Bureau of Justice Statistics (Washington, D.C.: Government Printing Office, 1983), p. 9.

6. Vera Institute of Justice, *Felony Arrests: Their Prosecution and Disposition in New York City's Courts* (New York, 1977), p. 135.
7. Joan E. Jacoby, "The Charging Policies of Prosecutors," in *The Prosecutor,* ed. William F. McDonald (Beverly Hills, Calif.: Sage, 1979), p. 75.
8. Frank W. Miller, *Prosecution: The Decision to Charge a Suspect with a Crime* (Boston: Little, Brown, 1969), p. 11.
9. William F. McDonald, "The Prosecutor's Domain," in *The Prosecutor,* ed. McDonald, p. 16.
10. W. Boyd Littrell, *Bureaucratic Justice* (Beverly Hills, Calif.: Sage, 1979), p. 29.
11. Joan E. Jacoby, "The Effects of Intake Policy and Procedures on the Prosecutor's Charging Decision," paper presented at the annual meeting of the Law and Society Association, Madison, Wis., June 5–7, 1980.
12. Elizabeth A. Stanko, "The Impact of Victim Assessment on Prosecutors' Screening Decisions: The Case of the New York County District Attorney's Office," paper presented at the annual meeting of the Northeastern Political Science Association, New Haven, November 20–22, 1980.
13. William A. Hamilton, "Highlights of PROMIS Research," in *The Prosecutor,* ed. McDonald, p. 125.
14. Jacqueline Cohen, "The Incapacitative Effects of Imprisonment: A Critical Review of the Literature," in *Deterrence and Incapacitation: Estimating the Effects of Criminal Sanctions on Crime Rates,* ed. Alfred Blumstein et al. (Washington, D.C.: National Academy of Sciences, 1978), p. 201.
15. Marvin E. Wolfgang, Robert M. Figlio and Thorsten Sellin, *Delinquency in a Birth Cohort* (Chicago: University of Chicago Press, 1972), p. 65.
16. Eleanor Chelimsky and Judith Dahmann, *National Evaluation of the Career Criminal Program: Final Report* (McLean, Va.: Mitre Corp., 1979).
17. National Advisory Commission on Criminal Justice Standards and Goals, *Task Force Report: Corrections* (Washington, D.C.: Government Printing Office, 1973), p. 50.
18. President's Commission on Law Enforcement and Administration of Justice, *The Challenge of Crime in a Free Society* (Washington, D.C.: Government Printing Office, 1967), p. 134.
19. Malcolm M. Feeley, *Court Reform on Trial* (New York: Basic Books, 1983), p. 103.
20. John J. Meglio, "Comparative Study of the District Attorney's Offices in Los Angeles and Brooklyn," *Prosecutor* 5 (1969): 238.

Defense Attorney

9

Have you a criminal lawyer in this burg? We think so, but we haven't been able to prove it on him.

CARL SANDBURG

Standing before Judge Robert L. McCrary, Jr., in the Circuit Court of Bay County, Florida, on 4 August 1961, was Clarence Earl Gideon, drifter, former convict, and now charged with breaking and entering with the intent to commit a felony under Florida law. Although his case may sound like any of the thousands of felony and misdemeanor cases that are heard daily in America's courtrooms, Clarence Gideon made a request that eventually produced a path-breaking opinion from the U.S. Supreme Court. As the trial transcript in the Bay County court shows, Gideon misunderstood the law, a misunderstanding that was to make history. "The United States Supreme Court," he proclaimed, "says I am entitled to be represented by Counsel."[1] It had not said so, but it shortly would remedy that oversight.

The 1963 opinion by the Supreme Court in *Gideon* v. *Wainwright* began a movement that extended the right of counsel not only to persons accused of felonies but, with the case of *Argersinger* v. *Hamlin* (1972), to any defendant charged with commission of a crime punishable by a prison sentence. The importance of legal counsel was underscored by Justice Hugo Black when he wrote for the majority in *Gideon:*

> The right of one charged with crime to counsel may not be deemed fundamental and essential to fair trials in some countries, but it is in ours. From the very beginning, our state and national constitutions and laws have laid great emphasis on procedural and substantive safeguards designed to assure fair trials before impartial tribunals in which every defendant stands equal before the law. This noble ideal cannot be realized if the poor man charged with crime has to face his accusers without a lawyer to assist him.[2]

The rise of crime in recent decades and the requirement that counsel must be provided for indigents have brought about a major shift in the way defendants are legally represented. Since nearly two-thirds of all persons charged with crimes are found to be indigents unable to pay for a lawyer, government has had to devise ways for defense counsel to be provided. Defendants in criminal cases may avail themselves of three types of legal representation: (1) those who are financially able may hire a private attorney; (2) indigents are furnished with a public defender, a full-time staff lawyer employed by the government to represent the poor; or (3) a private attorney may be assigned by the court, which is reimbursed by the state according to a standard fee scale. The 1970s saw a great expansion in the number of public defenders, especially in urban areas, where sometimes up to 90 percent of defendants receive free counsel. Private counsel is assigned more often in rural areas, where the caseload does not warrant a full-time public defender; but this system is also used in some cities (Houston, for example) where local conditions and tradition favor this approach. As can be imagined, with the great expansion of publicly funded counsel, the number of lawyers who represent defendants in criminal cases on a private basis has diminished.

This chapter examines the world of the criminal lawyers. It will be shown that the structure of the American bar influences the type of person who enters criminal practice. Since both private and public lawyers are encouraged to handle many cases in an impersonal, bureaucratic manner, the adversarial norm of a vigorous defense is often lacking. Counsel seeks to move cases as quickly as possible by persuading clients to plea bargain in order not to upset the ongoing routine of the courthouse.

The defense attorney: image and reality

defense attorney The lawyer who represents the accused and the convicted offender in their dealings with criminal justice officials.

Most Americans have seen a ***defense attorney*** in action on television; the much-rerun "Perry Mason" program has shown the investigative, challenging, probing defense attorney at his best, to the constant chagrin of District Attorney Burger. Through television, motion pictures, and literature, images of the great defense attorney—Clarence Darrow, Jerry Giesler, F. Lee Bailey, Melvin Belli—have become familiar.

Counsel is essential for the defense of a person accused of a crime. Criminal lawyers are advocates—that is, they are understood to support the defendant by their investigative ability before trial and by their verbal skills in the courtroom, by their knowledge of the law, and by their ability to knit these talents together in a constant creative questioning of decisions at every stage of the judicial process. The stakes are high not only because the defendant's freedom is at stake but also because the essence of the adversary system assumes that well-qualified and active defense counsel keeps the system honest. A defense attorney keeps the other actors on their toes so that they do not relax into the lethargy often associated with bureaucracy.

Role of the defense attorney

Defense attorneys represent their clients. Although this concept is not altogether clear, counsel is generally assumed to be responsible for both the strategy and tactics of the defense. Thus the defense attorney must explain to the client the legal consequences of the facts of the case and devise tactics for the defense. The client–counselor relationship is crucial; the qualities of respect, openness, and trust between the two are indispensable. If the defendant refuses to follow the attorney's advice, the lawyer may feel obliged to withdraw from the case in order to protect his or her own reputation.

What specific functions does the defense attorney perform as an advocate or representative of the accused? Figure 9.1 describes the actions of counsel in a typical felony case. In addition to these formal activities, the defense attorney also provides psychological support to the defendant and the defendant's family. Although the figure deals with a case that may proceed to trial, it should be remembered that normally counsel would begin discussion of a plea

Close-up: The Persistent Defendant

Gideon v. *Wainwright*, 372 U.S. 335 (1963)

Clarence Earl Gideon, fifty-one years old, petty thief, drifter, and gambler, had spent most of his adult life in jails serving time for burglary and larceny. On 4 June 1961 he was arrested in Panama City, Florida, for breaking into a poolroom to steal coins from a cigarette machine, beer, and soft drinks. After arraignment on 31 July for "unlawfully and feloniously" breaking and entering with intent to commit a misdemeanor—petty larceny—Gideon was held for trial in what appeared to be a routine case.

Standing before Judge Robert L. McCrary on 4 August, Clarence Gideon surprised the court by requesting that counsel be appointed to assist with his defense.

The Court: What says the Defendant? Are you ready to go to trial?

The Defendant: I am not ready, Your Honor.

The Court: Why aren't you ready?

The Defendant: I have no Counsel.

The Court: Why do you not have Counsel? Did you know that your case was set for trial today?

The Defendant: Yes, sir, I knew that it was set for trial today.

The Court: Why, then, did you not secure Counsel and be prepared to go to trial?

The Defendant: Your Honor, . . . I request this Court to appoint Counsel to represent me in this trial.

The Court: Mr. Gideon, I am sorry, but I cannot appoint . . . Counsel to represent you in this case. Under the laws of the State of Florida, the only time the Court can appoint Counsel to represent a Defendant is when that person is charged with a capital offense. I am sorry, but I will have to deny your request to appoint Counsel to defend you in this case.

The Defendant: The United States Supreme Court says I am entitled to be represented by Counsel.

Acting as his own counsel, Gideon was unable to interrogate witnesses and present his defense in the way required by the law. The jury found him guilty, and on 25 August he was sentenced to five years in the Florida State Prison.

From his prison cell Gideon prepared a handwritten petition of appeal to the Florida Supreme Court. On 30 October it was denied without hearing. Despite the setback, Gideon persisted and filed a petition for review with the U.S. Supreme Court. On 4 June 1962 the Court granted the petition and appointed Attorney Abe Fortas, later to become a Supreme Court justice, to represent Gideon.

Fortas argued that an accused person cannot effectively defend himself and thus cannot receive due process and a fair trial. Without counsel, the accused cannot evaluate the lawfulness of his arrest, the validity of the indictment, whether preliminary motions should be filed, whether a proper search was carried out, whether the confession is admissable as evidence, and so on. Fortas noted that the indigent defendant is almost always in jail and cannot prepare his defense and that the trial judge cannot adequately perform the function of counsel. As he said, "To convict the poor without counsel while we guarantee the right to counsel to those who can afford it is also a denial of equal protection of the laws."

Decision

On 18 March 1963 a unanimous Supreme Court said that Gideon was entitled to counsel and that the Sixth Amendment obligated the states to provide counsel to indigent defendants. Speaking for the Court, Justice Hugo Black said:

> In our adversary system of criminal justice, any person hauled into court, who is too poor to hire a lawyer, cannot be assured a fair trial unless counsel is provided for him. This seems to us to be an obvious truth.

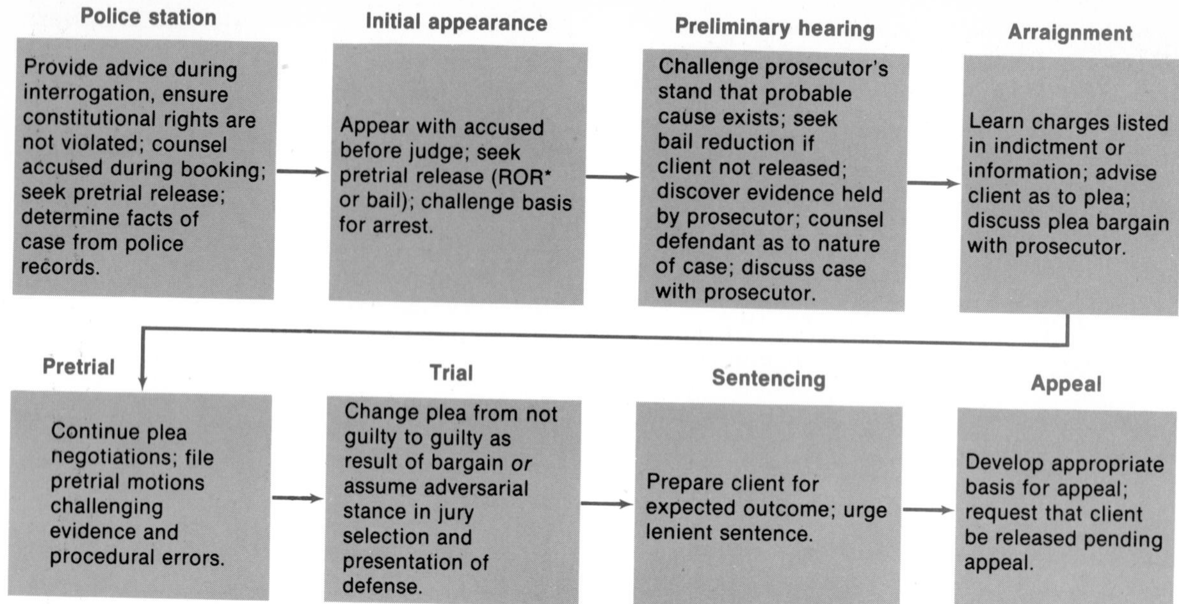

Police station
Provide advice during interrogation, ensure constitutional rights are not violated; counsel accused during booking; seek pretrial release; determine facts of case from police records.
Initial appearance
Appear with accused before judge; seek pretrial release (ROR* or bail); challenge basis for arrest.
Preliminary hearing
Challenge prosecutor's stand that probable cause exists; seek bail reduction if client not released; discover evidence held by prosecutor; counsel defendant as to nature of case; discuss case with prosecutor.
Arraignment
Learn charges listed in indictment or information; advise client as to plea; discuss plea bargain with prosecutor.
Pretrial
Continue plea negotiations; file pretrial motions challenging evidence and procedural errors.
Trial
Change plea from not guilty to guilty as result of bargain *or* assume adversarial stance in jury selection and presentation of defense.
Sentencing
Prepare client for expected outcome; urge lenient sentence.
Appeal
Develop appropriate basis for appeal; request that client be released pending appeal.
* Release on recognizance.

FIGURE 9.1
Typical actions of a defense attorney in processing a felony case

bargain soon after the facts were known and would continue negotiations until an acceptable agreement had been reached. Even after the trial has begun, a plea of not guilty may be changed to guilty as a result of bargaining.

The opinions of the Supreme Court and the values of the Due Process Model are based on a conception of the defense attorney as a combative element in an adversarial proceeding. How closely does this conception square with reality? The adversary system will be realized only if the exchange process and organizational setting enhance the role of the criminal lawyer. Merely to require the provision of counsel may not help if the attorney provided is ill educated and poorly paid, and if the principles that structure the role of the defense attorney have been compromised by the values of the system. Rather than act as the adversary—challenging the decisions made at each step in the process—defense counsel may, in fact, play the role of mediator for the defendant, prosecutor, and judge. Possibly a defendant with an attorney who is attuned to the administrative system will interfere with its smooth operation less than a defendant who has no counsel and whose notion of criminal justice has been formed by "Perry Mason." The latter defendant may be unwilling to cooperate because he does not know the ropes. The defense attorney may help the prosecutor and judge to pull the loose ends together so that a bargain can be worked out. In whose interest the bargain is made remains an open question.

Traditionally, defense attorneys have been caught between divergent concepts of their position. According to the Perry Mason image, they owe their client a full defense at every stage of the criminal process. Too often, however, the general public feels that defense lawyers are somehow soiled by their clients and are not so much engaged in freeing the innocent as in letting the guilty escape by exploiting technical loopholes in the law. Because most defense lawyers are continually on the losing side, they must also suffer the

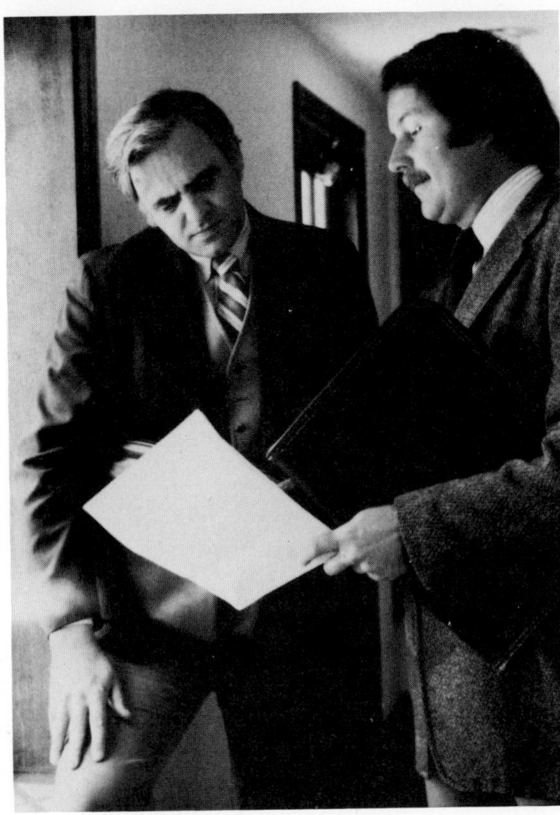

It is important for the defense attorney to negotiate with the prosecutor.

discontent of clients who feel that they did not work hard enough. The public defender is the special focus of such complaints. In some prisons, PD is an abbreviation not for "public defender" but for "prison deliverer."

The Defense Never Rests

Specializing in criminal law makes me a rebel by profession; our system requires that mavericks stand for the defense. Otherwise, pity the poor accused. Kids in grade school are told by their teachers that we have the most impeccable system of criminal justice in the world. Our educators and leaders have been saying so for years, and most people believe it. I see a lot of these people. It is with a good deal of indignation, fright, and consternation that they walk into my office and say, "I have an indictment here that falsely accuses me of such and such. I'll pay you a big retainer, and I'd like to know how soon I'm likely to be acquitted." I tell them that because they spend too much time reading the newspapers and watching Perry Mason, they think they're hiring a magician instead of a lawyer. And I usually add something like "I suppose you think that your innocence is a factor in the probable outcome of this case?" Invariably, the answer is "yes." Whereupon I explain that not only is innocence less than a guarantee that there will be a favorable outcome, but, as the wheels of justice grind on, innocence becomes progressively less relevant.

Source: From *The Defense Never Rests* by F. Lee Bailey. Copyright © 1971 by F. Lee Bailey and Harvey Aronson. Reprinted by arrangement with The New American Library, Inc., New York, N.Y.

Private counsel: an endangered species?

The number of lawyers who regularly take criminal cases constitutes a serious problem. Of an estimated 400,000 practicing lawyers in the United States, only between 10,000 and 20,000 accept criminal cases on a "more than occasional" basis, and of these about 4,000 are employed as public defenders. In the only contemporary national study of the criminal bar, Paul Wice found that the number and quality of privately retained lawyers varied among cities, with legal, institutional, and political factors accounting for much of the variance.[3]

Three general groups of lawyers take criminal cases on a regular basis, and these might be called specialists in their field. The first group is composed of nationally known attorneys—for example, Melvin Belli, F. Lee Bailey, and Edward Bennett Williams—who have built their reputations by adhering to the Perry Mason pattern. But there are few of them, they are expensive, and they usually take only the dramatic, widely publicized cases; they do not frequent the county courthouse. A second group of lawyers practice in major metropolitan areas and are retained by professional criminals, such as narcotics dealers, gamblers, pornographers, and those in organized crime: specialists working for specialists. In some cities—Miami, for one, with its large drug traffic problem—lawyers who fit this category make a profitable living. But this group is fairly small because of its relatively limited clientele.

The largest group of attorneys in criminal practice consists of lawyers who accept many cases for small fees and who daily participate in the criminal justice system. Surrounding most courthouses in large cities are the offices of attorneys like those called the Fifth Streeters in the District of Columbia, the Tulane Avenue bunch in New Orleans, and the Bryant Streeters in San Francisco. They routinely prowl the urban criminal courts searching for clients who can pay a modest fee. These criminal defense "regulars" are, according to Abraham Blumberg,

> highly visible in the major urban centers of the nation; their offices—at times shared with bondsmen—line the back streets near the courthouses. They are also visible politically, with clubhouse ties reaching into judicial chambers and the prosecutor's office. The regulars make no effort to conceal their dependence upon police bondsmen, jail personnel, as well as bailiffs, stenographers, prosecutors, and judges.[4]

Rather than prepare their cases for disposition through the adversary process, they negotiate guilty pleas and try to convince their clients that they have received exceptional treatment. Such lawyers cease to be true professionals and instead act as fixers. They operate in a relatively closed system where there are great pressures to process a great many cases for small fees, and they depend on the cooperation of judicial actors. These practitioners usually are less well educated, must work harder, and are financially less secure than lawyers who take the cases of business corporations.

In addition to these specialists in criminal practice are many private practitioners who are willing on occasion to take criminal cases. Often they are members of or connected with a law firm whose upper-class clients have run afoul of the law. Although this group of attorneys is fairly substantial, its members have little experience in trial work and do not have well-developed relationships with the actors in the criminal justice system. As they lack inside know-how, their clients might be better served by a courtroom regular.

Thus far we have been describing the practice of the criminal bar in big cities. In middle-sized and small cities a greater proportion of the legal profession appears to do criminal defense work as part of general practice. For example, studies of Prairie City, an Illinois community of 90,000 residents, indicated that the bar was not specialized. But even though a greater proportion of Prairie City attorneys took defense work than one would find in Chicago or New York, criminal law was not important either in terms of time spent or as a principal source of income. Unlike their metropolitan counterparts, the attorneys most active in the defense of criminals were viewed as competent by fellow lawyers in Prairie City and none had reputations as makers of shady deals.[5]

The private criminal bar

Urbanization and specialization have clearly influenced the type of legal talent available during the past quarter-century. Although law has always been an urban profession, the small-town lawyer who handled a wide variety of cases was once more typical of the majority of lawyers. With the need for legal talent shifting to the centers of population, attorneys have drifted to the cities. The rise of the modern industrial state has also greatly affected the structure of the legal profession so that the more financially rewarding practices stem from associations with large public or private organizations. As American society grows increasingly complex, lawyers can no longer be jacks-of-all-trades but must try to be masters of one specialty or of a limited few legal areas. Major law firms now assemble specialists who are well versed in segments of the law. Solo practitioners and small firms with a more generalist orientation still exist, particularly in rural areas, but their ranks are gradually thinning.

One result of the increased specialization and urbanization of the bar is that persons engaged in the practice of criminal law are considered to occupy a low-status position both by their profession and by the community. As in other professions, members of the bar are ranked in relation to the "cleanliness" and financial worth of the functions they perform. To be the brilliant advocate in court, the criminal lawyer must engage in duties (gathering evidence, dealing with informants and criminals, negotiating with the prosecutor's office) in which guile and force are needed but not admired. These characteristics of criminal practice, in addition to the relatively low pay, mean that most defense specialists are accorded little professional status.

The membership of the urban bar appears to be divided into three parts. An inner circle handles the work of banks, utilities, and large commercial concerns; another circle includes lawyers who represent business interests opposed to those of the inner circle; and finally, an outer group scrapes out a living by haunting the courts in the hope of picking up crumbs from the judicial table. With the exception of a highly proficient few who have made a reputation by winning acquittals in difficult, highly publicized cases, most of the lawyers who deal with criminal justice belong to the third group.

Membership of the criminal bar. Recognizing the place of criminal practice within the legal profession, we might ask: Who does take criminal cases? What are the qualifications of the practitioners? How were they recruited to the lowest rung of the legal ladder? Social scientists interested in this matter say that the average criminal lawyer is a solo practitioner, not a member of a law firm; comes from a middle-class, nonprofessional background; graduated from a lesser law school; and entered private criminal practice after some experience as a public lawyer. Only an estimated 4 percent are women. Wice found that 38 percent of his sample of private criminal lawyers had been prosecutors, and an additional 24 percent had been public defenders, had worked for legal services (civil law work), or had held civil service positions.[6]

When these background characteristics are tied to the recruitment patterns of the profession, certain problems follow. For many upwardly mobile persons, law provides the easiest and cheapest avenue to professional status; yet once they have become members of the bar, these same persons may find that the higher ranks of corporate practice are all but closed to them. Thus the positions they do manage to achieve are often marginal and their role in the profession is doubtful. In a real sense, members of the criminal bar may feel that they are not true members of the legal profession since they rarely interact with lawyers in the large firms and their practice does not conform to the adversary style taught in law school.

Again, we are speaking of urban areas. Very possibly the small-town lawyer who engages in a general practice may be well rewarded by the standards of the local community. But in the metropolitan areas of the United States where more than 70 percent of the population lives, the judicial process is under the greatest stress.

Environment of criminal practice

Other aspects of the criminal lawyers' practice help to explain their lower status within the profession. Criminal cases, as well as those concerned with matrimonial problems, tend to involve attorneys in emotional situations. Much of the service that the defense counsel renders involves preparing clients and their relatives for possible negative outcomes of their cases. Thus the client's troubles are an emotional drain. Even the lawyer's exposure to "guilty knowledge" may be a psychological burden. Lawyers have explained that they may easily become emotionally entangled because they are the only judicial actors to view the defendant in the context of social environment and family ties. Sympathy for the client is psychologically too heavy a burden for many attorneys.

Criminal lawyers must also interact continually with a lower class of clients and with police officials, social workers, and minor political appointees. They may be required to visit such depressing places as the local jail at all hours of the day and night, and after winning a case may find themselves unable to collect the fee. Even an appearance in court may be viewed as a disadvantage. As Thomas M. O'Malley, an attorney in Washington, D.C., has said, "it is . . . more comforting to work in the friendly atmosphere of one's office than in an unfriendly court where otherwise discerning people sometimes miss the subtle distinctions between the criminal and the defense attorney."[7] The work setting of most criminal lawyers is thus a far cry from the mahogany paneling, plush

Close-up: Criminal Defenders: Law's Outcasts

The criminal lawyer's work goes far afield from what happens in court. It is the "getting around" which is important.

And getting around Richard Daly does.

By 8:30 A.M., on any given court day, his Thunderbird is parked on Market Street in front of the courthouse and he's soon into the flow.

A prostitute who had once been helped by Daly gladeyes him in the corridor, tapping her lavender thick-soled shoes in a tattoo on the bare floor. "Stay cool, Mr. Richard," she says. Daly gives her his Jimmy Cagney smile; lots of teeth, briefly.

A clerk with a sheaf of traffic violations whispers something and Daly says thanks, which seems to please the clerk.

One after another, a variety of people move toward him like pieces of metal attracted to a magnet.

By 9 A.M., he is in the office of George Solomon, clerk of the Circuit Court of Criminal Causes. Solomon is a cousin of Sarkis Webbe, who shares Daly's office.

In Solomon's office, there is the special coterie gathered for morning coffee. The talk is easy. It's about cases. Solomon is there. And Daly. And Sidney Faber, the associate prosecuting attorney for the city of St. Louis, and Robert Wendt, an associate of Daly, and Norman London, and another lawyer, Gordian S. Benes.

Staying "tight" with Solomon's office is important to Daly because much of the processing flows through the clerk's hands. The better the relationship, the fewer the snarls and hassles.

He also is "tight" with Sidney Faber, the prosecutor. It is a mutual feeling. From Daly's point of view, he can pretty well talk out a case with Faber, and get something favorable for his client. From Faber's point of view, it is profitable because by reaching an accord he doesn't have to fight Daly in court.

At 10 A.M., court opens and Daly is working the courthouse. This does not necessarily mean that he may be arguing a case. Mostly, it is filing of motions, seeing that certain things get done, seeing that he stays "tight" with the right people. James Lavin, for example. Lavin is clerk for two judges.

"Say I need a copy of all search warrants in cases I'm involved in," explains Daly. "It is proper that I get them, but getting them can be achieved efficiently and cooperatively, or can be full of hassles and delays. Of course, I want to get along with Lavin."

Which also means getting along reasonably well with the twenty or so others in the clerk's office.

At noon, the Daly coterie assembles near the chambers of Judge David Fitzgibbon. Lunch time. Cold cuts, coffee and Coke and conversation.

The talk got around to fame and what it does to the lawyer and to his client ultimately, how it affects the performance of the criminal justice system.

"Frankly," Daly said, "becoming as well known as Morris Shenker or F. Lee Bailey or Percy Foreman could hurt my professional activity. I'd have to do something altogether different.

"Now, you might say that I have the courthouse wired. That is, I know how it works to the Nth degree. I have things functioning very smoothly. I'm not a big star, I don't draw outside attention. I'm able to accomplish a very good job as a defense lawyer."

Source: Bernard Gavzer, "Criminal Defenders: Law's Outcasts," *The Washington Post*, 18 February 1973. Reprinted by permission.

carpets, and stimulating conversation of the "inner circle" law firm.

The fact that criminal practice does not pay well is probably the key variable of the defense attorney's environment and one that influences other aspects of criminal practice. For the most part, criminal defendants are poor, and losing the case is likely to reduce their earning capacity even further. Thus most attorneys must make every effort either to get their fees in advance or somehow to tie defendants and their families to them financially.

> "The lawyer goes out and tries to squeeze money from the defendant's mother or an aunt," explains Judge Charles W. Halleck, of the local trial court in Washington, D.C. "Sometimes, he asks a jailed defendant, 'You got $15 or $25? Here, let me hold it for you.' And later that becomes part of the fee."[8]

Such financial circumstances generally force most attorneys to handle a multitude of cases for modest fees. A fifteen-minute conference with the prosecutor and a five-minute appearance in court may earn the lawyer the same fee as a three-day trial. Criminal lawyers frequently say, "I make my money on the phone or in the prosecutor's office, not in the courtroom." Wice's national survey of urban criminal law specialists revealed that income was represented by a bimodal curve, with "many lawyers bunched at the lower end of the scale netting between $15,000 and $25,000 and several fortunate ones in the top earning annual salaries in excess of $100,000."[9]

Defense attorneys face the possibility of "losing by winning." An attorney who secures the release of a defendant accused of a heinous crime by mounting a zealous defense may be censured by the community for using "technicalities" to defeat justice.

> This is a game that cannot be won by the attorney: if he loses deliberately, he violates the lesson of virtually all of his training and surrenders his client to the passions of the community. If he presses his opportunities to win when all others are convinced of his client's guilt and brings victory, he risks being accused of "shyster" behavior.[10]

In such cases, the defense attorney faces the additional risk of embarrassing the prosecution or the judge, thus reducing the possibility of future considerations from them. The environment of criminal practice, then, involves extensive physical, psychological, and social pressures. Many attorneys get "burned out" after only a few years of such practice; few criminal law specialists are older than fifty.

Counsel for indigents

An unidentified prisoner in a Connecticut jail contributed one of the legal profession's favorite remarks when he was asked whether he had had a lawyer when he went to court. "No," he said, "I had a public defender."[11] The quality of defense counsel available to the poor is a major national problem, especially since the Supreme Court brought it to public attention. In urban areas an increasing percentage of those arrested are being represented by counsel provided by the state. As early as 1964, Judge J. Edward Lumbard reported that more than 60 percent of all defendants charged with serious crimes did not have the resources to retain counsel. In such large cities as New York and Chicago the proportion reached 75 percent.[12] The Supreme Court's requirements that counsel be appointed early in the criminal justice process and that it be provided to all indigents accused of crimes punishable by prison sentences have drastically raised the percentage of defendants who become clients of publicly supported defender programs. In some jurisdictions, up to 90 percent of the accused must be provided with counsel.

Under ideal conditions, well-qualified counsel would be appointed early in the criminal justice process to pursue each case with zeal in the best adversary tradition. Too often, however, the right to counsel is mocked by the assignment of a lawyer in the courtroom, a brief conference with the defendant, and a quick guilty plea. These factors—the quality of counsel, conditions of defense practice, and administrative pressures to move the caseload—are major concerns of those who are committed to the principle of due process. The adversary process can be realized only if an attorney has incentives to defend an indigent with the same skill and vigor brought to bear for a client who is paying his or her own bill.

Although the *Gideon* decision required counsel to be provided, it did not set standards for indigency. The concept of indigency has been variously defined throughout the country; often the ability to make bail is taken to be an indication the defendant is able to afford counsel. Thus the defendant must choose between freedom before trial and an attorney's services at no charge. A jail stay can have serious effects on the defendant's job and family. Even with

The Right to Counsel: Major Supreme Court Rulings

Case	*Ruling*
Gideon v. *Wainwright* (1963)	The Fourteenth Amendment requires that defendants in state noncapital felony cases have the right to counsel.
Escobedo v. *Illinois* (1964)	The accused has the right to counsel during interrogation by the police.
Miranda v. *Arizona* (1966)	The right to counsel begins when investigation of a crime focuses on a suspect. The suspect must be informed of the right to remain silent and to have counsel, and that any statement made may be used against him or her.
United States v. *Wade* (1967)	The defendant has the right to be assisted by counsel during a police lineup. (Extended to state defendants in *Gilbert* v. *California* [1967]).
Coleman v. *Alabama* (1970)	Counsel must be present at a preliminary hearing.
Argersinger v. *Hamlin* (1972)	Whenever a criminal charge may result in a prison sentence, the accused has the right to counsel.
Ross v. *Moffitt* (1974)	States are not required to provide counsel for indigents beyond one appeal.
Moore v. *Illinois* (1977)	The defendant has the right to counsel at a preliminary court hearing at which he or she appears to be identified by a witness.
United States v. *Henry* (1980)	Government agents may not solicit a statement from a defendant covertly and then introduce the statement at trial.

widespread judicial knowledge of the Supreme Court's ruling on counsel, in some parts of the country an indigent is not given a lawyer unless the charge is sufficiently serious.

Methods of providing indigents with counsel

In the United States there are three basic methods of providing counsel to indigent defendants: the assigned counsel system, by which a court appoints a private attorney to represent a particular accused; the contract system, by which an individual attorney, a bar association, or a private law firm contracts with a local government to provide legal services to indigent defendants for a specified dollar amount; and public defender programs, established as public or private nonprofit organizations with full-time or part-time salaried staff. Although the public defender system is growing rapidly, 1,833 counties (60 percent) still use the assigned counsel system and 6 percent contract for defender services. The public defender system is the dominant form in 43 of the 50 most populous counties, however, and overall such programs serve 68 percent of the U.S. population. Figure 9.2 shows the system in use in the majority of counties in each of the fifty states. In addition to the three major legal defense systems for indigents, some areas use a so-called mixed system in which the state provides counsel but a lawyer may be assigned under certain circumstances. Each system has its advantages and disadvantages, all of which have been endlessly argued in law journals.

assigned counsel An attorney in private practice who is assigned by a court to represent an indigent and whose fee is paid by the government that has jurisdiction over the case.

Assigned counsel. Through the ***assigned counsel*** system, the court appoints a lawyer in private practice to represent an indigent defendant. This system is widely used in small cities and in rural areas, but even some urban areas with public defender systems follow the practice of assigning council in

FIGURE 9.2 Type of counsel provided to indigents by the majority of counties in fifty states

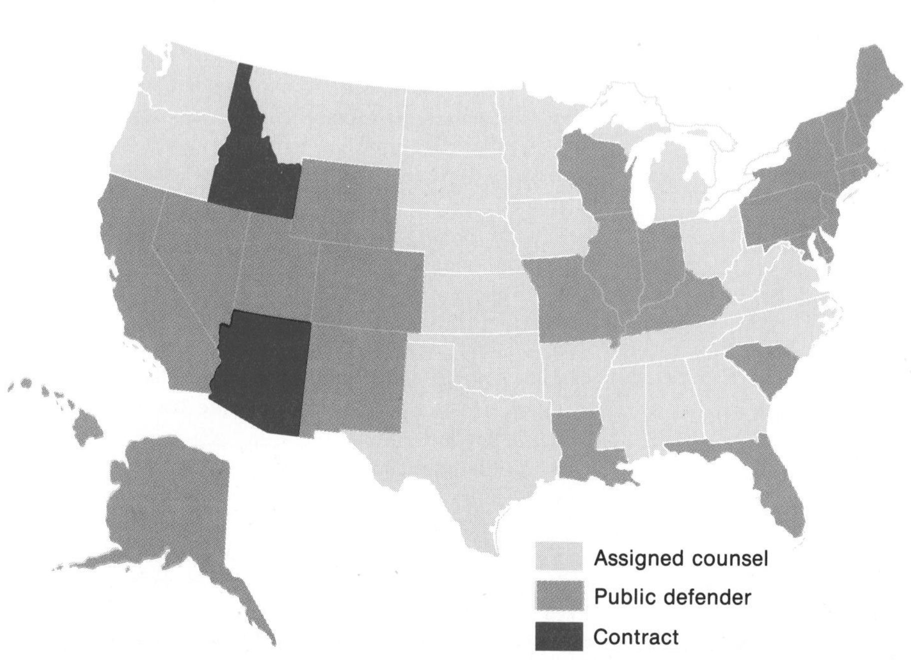

some circumstances, as when a case has multiple defendants and a conflict of interest might result if one were to be represented by a public lawyer. In cities with mixed systems, some appointments are reserved for private attorneys. Where the assigned counsel system is followed, private attorneys indicate to the judge that they are willing to take the cases of indigent defendants. The judge then either assigns lawyers in rotation from a prepared list or selects among attorneys who are known and present in the courtroom. It has been argued that the assigned counsel system leads to favoritism in the selection process and that the lawyers chosen are so beholden to the judges that they temper their adversarial stance.

The competence of attorneys who are willing to be assigned cases is sometimes questionable. In many urban areas where the assigned counsel system is used, such lawyers are largely recent law school graduates or has-beens. A study of lawyers in Oregon revealed that those appointed were younger, less experienced, and rated by other members of the bar as less competent than retained counsel. Just as important as the quality of legal talent is the fact that a "courthouse regular" may become co-opted to serve the organizational needs of the system.[13]

In many cities the fee schedule for defenders of indigents may be an inducement for counsel to persuade the client to plead guilty to a lesser charge. Albert Alschuler asked attorneys throughout the nation how large a fee would have to be before they could regard even the simplest trial as profitable. More than half mentioned $1,000.[14] In Washington, D.C., Wice

Clarence Seward Darrow

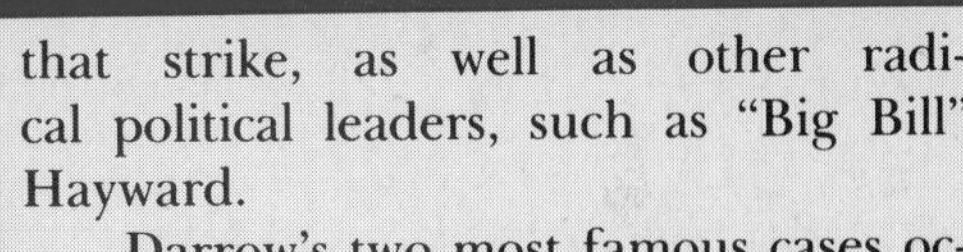

Born in Kinsman, Ohio, Clarence Darrow studied law for one year at the University of Michigan Law School. He was admitted to the Ohio bar in 1878 and, after practicing law in Ohio for nine years, moved to Chicago and embarked on a career that would make him one of the most famous defense attorneys in the United States.

Darrow devoted much of his career to political and labor cases. Shortly after moving to Chicago he associated himself with those who sought amnesty for the Haymarket Square defendants, a group indicted in connection with a bomb thrown into the ranks of police attempting to control a labor demonstration. Because of his political beliefs, Darrow resigned his position as corporate counsel for the Chicago and Western Railway during the Pullman strike of 1894. He defended socialist Eugene V. Debs against a charge of contempt of court in connection with that strike, as well as other radical political leaders, such as "Big Bill" Hayward.

Darrow's two most famous cases occurred within a year of each other. In 1924 he became defense counsel in the famous trial of Richard Leopold and Nathan Loeb for the "thrill" murder of Bobby Franks. By basing his defense on a plea of temporary insanity and emphasizing the two defendants' abnormal conduct and personality development, Darrow was able to save them from the death penalty. In 1925 Darrow became defense attorney in the famous Scopes "monkey trial" in Tennessee. Here he found himself pitted against William Jennings Bryan, a long-time adversary, and though Darrow lost the case, his defense refuted the fundamentalist assertions that were at the basis of Bryan's antievolution argument.

found that about fifty regulars dominated the assignment system, receiving $20 per hour for out-of-court work and $30 an hour in court.[15] In many cities, lawyers who are assigned the cases of indigents find that they can make more money by collecting a preparation fee. Such a fee usually amounts to about $50 and is payable when an indigent client pleads guilty rather than go to trial. Handling a large number of cases on this basis is more profitable than spending an entire day in the courtroom at trial, for which the fee may be only $200. One member of the Seattle bar had developed this practice to such a fine art that a deputy prosecutor said, "When you saw him coming into the office, you knew that he would be pleading guilty." Michael Moore quotes a district attorney who commented that "counsel for indigents very often display an attitude of 'let's get it over with.' The same lawyer, whom I know to be a veritable tiger for a paying client, is in many cases a pussy cat when representing the indigent client. Such are the economic facts of life."[16] Table 9.1 indicates the pattern of compensation paid to assigned counsel nationwide.

Contract system. In the newest system for providing defense services to poor people, the government enters into a contract with an individual attorney, a bar association, or a private law firm. The majority of counties that have chosen this method are not heavily populated. Some places use public defenders for most cases but contract for services in multiple-defendant situations that might present conflicts of interest or when a case is considered to be

TABLE 9.1 Pattern of compensation paid to assigned counsel

Method of establishing fees	***Number of states***[1]	
Judicial discretion	34	
Statute	27	
Statewide court rule	11	
Public defender	9	
Custom in jurisdiction	23	
Type of fee schedule used	***Percentage of assigned counsel counties***	
Separate out-of-court/in-court hourly rates	70%	
Flat fee per case	11	
Type of appearance	7	
Flat fee per appearance	3	
Other	9	
Maximum amount stipulated		
Felonies	40%	
Misdemeanors	50	
Hourly fees	***Range***	***Most frequent***
For felonies		
In-court	$12.50–65	$30–40
Out-of-court	$10–50	$20–30
For misdemeanors		
In-court	$12.50–50	$30–40
Out-of-court	$10–50	$20–30
Maximum fees		
Felonies (not including capital case)	$200–2,500	$500–1,000
Misdemeanors	$100–2,500	$200–500

[1] Because the survey question permitted multiple responses, the number of states exceeds 50.
Source: U.S. Department of Justice, Bureau of Justice Statistics, *Special Report*, August 1984, p. 5.

extraordinarily complex or to require more time than the government's salaried lawyers can give to it.

The terms of contracts vary. The most common provision is for a block grant: a private law firm agrees to provide representation in all cases for a fixed amount. Fixed-price contracts are the second most frequently used type. Under such agreements lawyers agree to provide representation for a specified number of cases for a fixed amount per case. Some systems enter into a cost-plus arrangement: representation is provided at an estimated cost per case until the dollar amount of the contract is reached, at which point a new contract is negotiated.

public defender
An attorney employed on a full-time, salaried basis by the government to represent indigents.

Public defender. The ***public defender*** is a twentieth-century response to the legal needs of the indigent. Started in Los Angeles County in 1914, when attorneys for the defense were first hired by an American government, the system has spread to many populous cities, as well as to a number of states, including Minnesota and Connecticut. In 1967 the President's Commission on Law Enforcement and Administration of Justice reported that defender systems were operating in 272 counties that had almost one-third of all felony defendants in the country.[17] By 1982 defender systems were serving 68 percent of the population.

Criminal defense programs were initially funded by public and private agencies, but most of their costs have been gradually assumed by government. The public defender system is often viewed as superior to the assigned counsel system because the attorneys are full-time specialists in criminal law. In addition, public defenders are thought to be more efficient attorneys who do not create lengthy delays or make frivolous technical motions. Salaried public defenders represent a break with the hallowed tradition of the attorney as a private professional serving individual clients for a fee.

The style of defense in the typical public defender program is in marked contrast to the personalized relationship between client and privately retained attorney. As with most public services, the crush of cases bears heavily on the attorney's resources, and procedures become as impersonal as those on an assembly line. Public defense is often handled on a "zone" rather than on a person-to-person basis: public defenders are assigned to particular courtrooms and take all the cases of indigent defendants there. Thus the defendant has several attorneys, each of whom handles only a portion of the process: one the preliminary hearing, another the arraignment, and still another the trial, if there is a trial; no one attorney is solely responsible for defending the individual accused. In a study of Chicago felony cases, Janet Gilboy and John Schmidt found that 47 percent of defendants received such sequential representation by public defenders.[18] One effect of the dispersion of responsibility is that cases are handled routinely, and many of the special elements of an individual defense are lost. More important, because the defendant is passed from one attorney to another, no relationship of trust is developed.

Critics point out that the defender's independence is undermined by daily contact with the same prosecutors and judges. Private counsel has brief, businesslike encounters in the courtroom, but the public defender has a regular work site in the courtroom and thus presents himself or herself as one of its core personnel. He or she arrives at the defense table in the morning with case files for the day and only temporarily leaves this post when a private attorney's case is called. As the noted criminal lawyer Edward Bennett Williams has said,

> the public defender and the prosecutor are trying cases against each other every day. They begin to look at their work like two wrestlers who wrestle with each other in a different city every night and in time get to be good friends. The biggest concern of the wrestlers is to be sure they do not hurt each other too much. They don't want to get hurt. They just want to make a living.[19]

An equally difficult problem for public defenders is the tendency to routinize decision making. Typically confronted by overwhelming caseloads, they develop strategies to make decisions quickly and with a minimum expenditure of resources. Cases are standardized as much as possible and the defense is conducted in accordance with repetitive or routinized processes, so that there is little individualized treatment of the special facts of each case. With experience, defenders develop mental images of typical clients so that the characteristics of the accused will help them to "place" the case in an established category and follow a standard procedure for disposition. Since the public defender has little time to interview clients and investigate each charge, negotiations with prosecutors and courtroom proceedings cover groups of cases. Under these circumstances, with a public defender who assumes that most of his or her clients are guilty of something, the atmosphere is different from the case of an attorney who believes clients to be innocent until the state proves them guilty.

Defendant's perspective. Defendants interviewed by Jonathan Casper saw the criminal justice process as not much different from life on the streets as they knew it—a harsh reality divorced from the abstract values of due process. As one prisoner said, the public defender was

> just playing a middle game. You know, you're the public defender, now you, you don't care what happens to me, really . . . you don't know me and I don't know you . . . this is your job, that's all, . . . so, you're gonna go up there and say a little bit, you know, make it look like you're trying to help me, but actually you don't give a damn.[20]

They perceived a gamelike quality to the system, with the police, prosecutors, defenders, and judges manipulating the defendants and each other for their own ends. From the defendants' perspective, this was true even of their lawyers, the public defenders. As Casper comments, "most of those who were represented by public defenders thought their major adversary in the bargaining process to be not the prosecutor or the judge, but rather their own attorney, for he was the man with whom they had to bargain. They saw him as the surrogate of the prosecutor—a member of 'their little syndicate'—rather than as their own representative." In the view of one defendant, "a public defender is just like the prosecutor's assistant. Anything you tell this man, he's not gonna do anything but relay it back. . . . They'll come to some sort of agreement, and that's the best you're gonna get."[21]

Private versus public defense. Are there differences in the quality of legal services provided to defendants who can afford to retain their own counsel and those who cannot? The available evidence is not definitive. A study in Cook County (Chicago), for example, found that the public defender generated more guilty pleas than did lawyers who had been either privately retained or assigned to cases.[22] But these differences may only reflect the type of defendant associated with each category of counsel. Because a major portion of the criminal defendants in a city are poor, the public defender handles cases for clients charged with such crimes as assault and robbery, which reflect their social environment. Retained counsel may serve upper-class defendants who are charged with white-collar crimes, which are more difficult to detect and prosecute. In his study of Prairie City, David Neubauer found that "while the majority of defendants with private attorneys (66 percent) have been charged with property crimes (forgery, burglary, theft, robbery), almost 90 percent of the public defender clients have been charged with these offenses."[23] Perhaps the scholarly debate in the law journals is pointless. Following a national study of legal services for the poor, Lee Silverstein reported that "no firm conclusions can be drawn as to whether assigned counsel systems are better than defender systems, or vice versa."[24]

Defense counsel in the system

Most of the criminal lawyers in metropolitan courts work in a precarious professional environment. They work very hard for small fees in unpleasant surroundings and are not rewarded by professional or public acclaim. In a judicial system in which bargaining is a primary method of decision making, defense attorneys believe they must maintain close personal ties with the police, prosecutor, judges, and other court officials. An attorney's ability to establish and continue a pattern of informal exchange relations with these persons is essential not only for professional survival but for the opportunity to serve the needs of clients. An experienced attorney described his work as "getting along with people—salesmanship. That's what this young lawyer in my office right now doesn't know anything about. He's a moot court champion—great at research. But he doesn't know a damn thing about people."[25]

At every step of the criminal justice process, from the first contact with the accused until final disposition of the case, defense attorneys are dependent on decisions made by other judicial actors. Even such seemingly minor activities as visiting the defendant in jail, learning the case against the defendant from the prosecutor, and setting bail can be difficult unless defense attorneys have the cooperation of others in the system. Thus their concern with preserving their relationships within that system may have greater weight for them than their short-term interest in particular clients.

We should not assume, however, that defense attorneys are at the complete mercy of judicial actors. At any phase of the process, the defense can invoke the adversary model with its formal rules and public battles. The effective counsel can use this potential for a trial with its expensive, time-consuming, and disputatious features as a bargaining tool with the police, prosecutor, and judge. A well-known tactic of defense attorneys, certain to raise the ante in the bargaining process, is to ask for a trial and to proceed as if they meant it.

Some attorneys play the adversary role skillfully. They have developed a style that emphasizes the belligerence of a professional who is willing to fight the system for a client. Such lawyers are experienced in the courtroom and have built a practice around defending clients who can afford the expense of a trial. Further, some clients may expect their counsel to play the combatant role in the belief that they are not getting their money's worth unless verbal

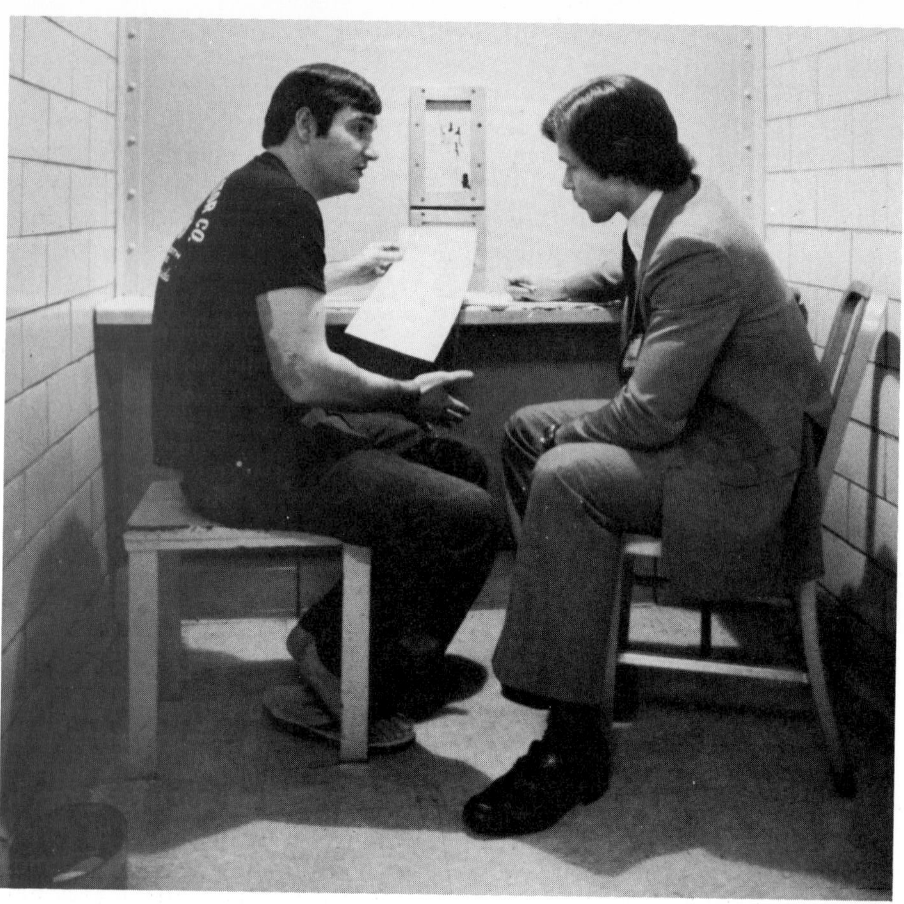

Counsel for the poor is usually provided by public defenders.

fireworks are involved. The costs of this kind of practice are not only financial. The attorney must be willing to gamble that the trial results will benefit the accused and counsel more than a bargain arranged with the prosecutor. Once having broken the informal rules of the system, however, combative attorneys may find that they have jeopardized future cooperation from the police and prosecutor.

Even when verbal fireworks do occur, one cannot be certain that the adversaries are engaged in a meaningful contest. Studies in some cities have shown that attorneys with clients who expect to get a vigorous defense may engage in the form of courtroom drama commonly known as the "slow plea of guilty." Although negotiations have already determined the outcome of a case, a defense attorney with a paying client who expects a return for the fee may arrange with the prosecutor and even the judge to stage a battle that is designed to culminate in a sentence agreed on previously.

> We had to put on one of these shows a few months ago. Well, we were all up there going through our orations, and the whole time the judge just sat there writing. Finally the D.A. reduced his charge, and the judge looked up long enough to say "Six months probation." Afterwards in the coffee shop my partner told the judge, "Jesus, man, can't you try to look a little more interested while you're filling out

your docket sheets?" The judge said, "What in the hell am I supposed to be interested in? You come to me with this scheme all planned out, you tell me exactly what you're going to do, then you tell me exactly what I'm going to do—and now you expect me to have acted interested."[26]

For the criminal lawyer who depends on a large volume of petty cases from poor clients and assumes they are probably guilty of some offense, the incentives to bargain are strong. If the attorney is to secure cases, to serve clients' interests, and to maintain status as a practitioner, friendship and influence with judicial officials are essential. Specific benefits can be obtained from these sources: informal discovery of charges and plea bargaining from the prosecutor, fact finding and favorable testimony from the police, sentencing discretion and courtroom reception by the judge, and the influence of all three on the bail decision. For these courtesies, however, a price must be paid: information elicited from the client, a less than vigorous defense, the cultivation of active social relationships, political support, and a general attitude of cooperativeness.

Securing cases

As in other professions in which a potential exists for client exploitation, the American bar has rigid strictures against the solicitation of clients. Lawyers with reputations as "ambulance chasers" soon find that colleagues hold their conduct in low regard. Unlike clients of the medical profession (which has similar rules of conduct), most citizens do not have a "family lawyer" and in exceptional circumstances must seek out legal services. To a great extent, persons in need of lawyers depend on the recommendations of others; hence an attorney's reputation in the community is important. For both the lawyer trying to make a living and the accused who is in need of counsel, the difficulties of establishing contact may be severe.

While some criminal lawyers may chase patrol wagons, many depend on a broker—a person who is able to identify and channel potential legal business to the attorney. The broker may be a bondsman, police officer, fellow attorney, prison official, or member of the clergy. Criminal lawyers seeking clients have the problem of making themselves known to a broker and creating a climate so that cases will be referred to them. Participation in social or political groups is one way to make contact with brokers. Favors to law enforcement actors, such as free legal advice on personal matters, can bring about a climate of indebtedness, but these arrangements can lead the lawyer to become more obligated to the broker than to the client. A police officer is less likely to hand the attorney's business card to a prisoner if past experience has revealed that the lawyer is not cooperative.

Relations with clients

If criminal lawyers are not advocates using technical skills to win a case, what is the service that they perform for the accused? One of the assets they sell is their influence within the judicial system: their ability to telephone the sheriff, enter the prosecutor's office, and bargain for their clients with judicial officials. On the basis of knowledge of the accused, the charge, the evidence, and the possible sanctions, defense attorneys may view their role as getting a client's penalty set at the lowest end of the range provided by statute. All these activities are played out in such a way that clients believe they are getting their money's worth. Professional confidence, an aura of influence, and having the "inside dope" are essential.

Often the first arraignment is the greatest boon to the defense attorney. In this proceeding, the accused is told what the maximum penalty is for the charges made. When his lawyer negotiates a sentence of three to five years in prison, the client is grateful that he has been spared the potential sixty-five years that the law prescribes for the multiple charges originally lodged against him. Thus, in one attorney's view, "the lawyer's fee is money charged for getting his client the normal penalty, which is substantially less than the maximum penalty under the law. Clients have no way of knowing what to expect from the system and one imagines attorneys do not go overboard in stressing 'I did what any attorney could do.' "[27]

Agent-mediators. A criminal lawyer is not only an advocate for the client but also an agent-mediator—that is, an adviser who explains the judicial process and lets the accused know what to expect.[28] This facet of the attorney's role may evolve into a confidence game in which the lawyer prepares the accused for defeat and then "cools him out" when it comes, as it is likely to do. Defense attorneys help clients redefine their situation and restructure their perceptions and thus prepare them to accept the consequences of a guilty plea. In the process of cooling out a client, the lawyer is often assisted by the defendant's kin, the probation officer, the prosecutor, and the judge: all try to emphasize that they want the accused to do the right things for his own good. The defendant finds himself in a position similar to that of a sick person on whom various treatments are urged by people who proclaim that they are all working on the patient's behalf.

The interrelatedness of these services is evident: success in one venture depends on success in the other. If a client balks at the bargain that has been struck, the attorney's future influence with the prosecutor may be jeopardized. At the same time, the lawyer does not want to get a reputation for selling out clients; such a reputation may quickly end a career.

Public defenders have a special problem of client control. Defendants who have not selected their own counsel may not accept the bargain but insist that a trial be held. Because public defenders may fear a charge of misleading a client, they may have to invoke the "slow plea of guilty" drama. Thus the extent to which the defender *represents* the accused is open to question, for the trial may be used to impress on other defendants the fact that a cooperative attitude is important.

Criminal lawyers in their role as agent-mediators may in fact be viewed as double agents. With obligations to both client and court, they are agents seeking to effect a satisfactory outcome for both. As Abraham Blumberg notes, the position is filled with conflicts of interest.

> Too often these must be resolved in favor of the organization which provides him with the means of his professional existence. Consequently, in order to reduce the strains and conflicts imposed in what is ultimately an overdemanding role obligation for him, the lawyer engages in the lawyer-client "confidence game" so as to structure more favorably an otherwise onerous role system.[29]

Summary

The role of defense attorney is structured by the occupational environment within the criminal justice system. Recruitment into criminal practice, financial considerations, interpersonal relations, and the demands of the system for a speedy disposition of each case in a huge caseload create needs that are met through a process of bargaining. As a result, criminal lawyers participate in a number of exchange relationships that influence case disposition. Most cases are disposed of by plea bargaining, in which the various perspectives of the defendant, prosecutor, defense lawyer, and judge play their parts. As one judge told the author, "lawyers are helpful to the system. They are able to pull things together, work out a deal, keep the system moving." But we must ask whether that is the purpose of defense work.

For discussion

1. You are the defendant. How will you select an attorney? What criteria will you use? Where will you obtain the information necessary to make this decision?
2. Chief Justice Burger has suggested that only lawyers with special qualifications be allowed to argue cases in court. Should the United States adopt the British distinction between solicitor and barrister?
3. You are the defense attorney. You have just learned that your client committed the crime charged. What are your responsibilities to your client? to the court?
4. We place much emphasis on the adversarial characteristics of the defense attorney. How can we create a situation so that lawyers will not be co-opted by the system?
5. If every person accused of committing a crime had access to the legal talents of a Melvin Belli or F. Lee Bailey, how would the criminal justice system be affected?

For further reading

Bailey, F. Lee. *The Defense Never Rests.* New York: Stein & Day, 1971.
Mayer, Martin. *The Lawyers.* New York: Harper & Row, 1966.
Moldovsky, Joel, and DeWolf, Rose. *The Best Defense.* New York: Macmillan, 1975.
Oaks, Dallin H., and Lehman, Warren. *A Criminal Justice System and the Indigent.* Chicago: University of Chicago Press, 1968.
Wice, Paul B. *Criminal Lawyers: An Endangered Species.* Beverly Hills, Calif.: Sage, 1978.
Wood, Arthur. *Criminal Lawyers.* New Haven, Conn.: College & University Press, 1967.

Notes

1. Anthony Lewis, *Gideon's Trumpet* (New York: Vintage Books, 1964), p. 10.
2. *Gideon* v. *Wainwright,* 372 U.S. 335 (1963).
3. Paul B. Wice, *Criminal Lawyers: An Endangered Species* (Beverly Hills, Calif.: Sage, 1978), p. 29.
4. Abraham S. Blumberg, "Lawyers with Convictions," *Transaction,* July 1967, p. 18.
5. David W. Neubauer, *Criminal Justice in Middle America* (Morristown, N.J.: General Learning Press, 1974), p. 70.
6. Wice, *Criminal Lawyers,* p. 75.
7. As quoted in Leonard Downie, Jr., *Justice Denied* (New York: Praeger, 1971), p. 172.
8. Ibid., p. 173.
9. Wice, *Criminal Lawyers,* p. 123.
10. John E. Crow, "A Professional's Dilemma: The Criminal Law," unpublished manuscript, University of Washington, Seattle, 1963.
11. Jonathan D. Casper, "Did You Have a Lawyer When You Went to Court? No, I Had a Public Defender," *Yale Review of Law and Social Action* 1 (Spring 1971): 4–9.
12. J. Edward Lumbard, "Better Lawyers for Our Criminal Courts," *Atlantic Monthly,* June 1964, p. 86.
13. Michael Moore, "The Right to Counsel for Indigents in Oregon," 44 *Oregon Law Review* 255 (1965).
14. Albert Alschuler, "The Defense Attorney's Role in Plea Bargaining," 84 *Yale Law Journal* 1201 (1975).
15. Wice, *Criminal Lawyers,* p. 208.

16. Moore, "Counsel for Indigents in Oregon," p. 283.
17. President's Commission on Law Enforcement and Administration of Justice, *Task Force Reports: The Courts* (Washington, D.C.: Government Printing Office, 1967), p. 59.
18. Janet A. Gilboy and John R. Schmidt, "Replacing Lawyers: A Case Study of the Sequential Representation of Criminal Defendants," *Journal of Criminal Law and Criminology* 70 (1979): 2.
19. Edward Bennett Williams, *The Law,* interview by Donald McDonald (New York: Center for the Study of Democratic Institutions, n.d.), p. 10.
20. Casper, "Did You Have a Lawyer?" p. 5.
21. Ibid., pp. 5, 6.
22. Dallin H. Oaks and Warren Lehman, *A Criminal Justice System and the Indigent* (Chicago: University of Chicago Press, 1968), p. 176.
23. Neubauer, *Criminal Justice in Middle America,* p. 158.
24. Lee Silverstein, *Defense of the Poor* (Chicago: American Bar Foundation, 1965), p. 73.
25. Jackson B. Battle, "In Search of the Adversary System: The Cooperative Practices of Private Criminal Defense Attorneys," 50 *University of Texas Law Review* 66 (1971).
26. Ibid., p. 108.
27. Neubauer, *Criminal Justice in Middle America,* p. 75.
28. Abraham Blumberg, "The Practice of Law as a Confidence Game," *Law and Society Review* 1 (1967): 11–39.
29. Ibid., p. 38.

The defender

Connie Xinos disliked Donald Payne from the beginning. They met in October in the prisoners' lockup behind Judge Fitzgerald's courtroom, and all Xinos had to go on then was the police report and Payne's public-defender questionnaire ("All I know is I was arrested for attempted murder on August 5") and that insinuating half smile. *He did it,* Xinos thought; all of them except the scared children and the streetwise old pros swear they are innocent, but you get a feeling. And that smile. *He's cocky,* Xinos thought. *A bad kid.* Xinos has been at it less than four years, but four years in the bullpens is a long time. He thinks Chicago is dying. And he thinks thousands of black street kids much like Donald Payne—his clients—are doing the killing.

Xinos is 30, the son of a Greek cafeteria owner bred in the white Chicago suburbs, a stumpy young bachelor with quizzical eyes, a shock of straight, dark hair and a Marine Reserve pin glinting gold in the lapel of his three-piece suit. He came to the building a year out of John Marshall Law School, hoping for a job as an assistant state's attorney ("It seemed to be glamorous—you don't get parking tickets and you carry a gun") but hungry enough for steady pay and trial experience to settle for what he could get.

The state's attorney had no openings, so he went upstairs to see public defender Gerald Getty. . . .

Ideals die young in a public defender's office. Chicago's is one of the oldest and best in the U.S.; it was organized in 1930, three decades before the Supreme Court asserted the right of the poor to counsel in any felony case, and its staff now numbers 68 mostly young and energetic lawyers. But they remain enormously overworked, partly because crime rates keep rising, partly because all the defendants' rights announced by the High Court in the 1960s have vastly increased and complicated their caseload. Xinos and his colleagues, squeezed in four desks to a cubicle, handle more than half of Cook County's yearly 3,700 criminal cases; their clients are 70 percent black and typically too poor either to hire private lawyers or to make bail pending trial. At any given time, says Xinos, "I got a hundred guys sitting over there in County Jail wondering if Xinos is working on my case out there." And he knows the most he will be able to do for 90 percent of them is "cop them out"—plead them guilty—"and look for the best deal you can get."

That they are all nominally innocent under the law is little more than a technicality: public and private defenders learn quickly to presume guilt in most cases and work from there. "I tell 'em I don't have to presume innocence," says one senior hand in the office. "That's a legal principle, but it doesn't have to operate in a lawyer's office." It stops operating when a rookie lawyer discovers that practically all his clients come in insisting that they didn't do it. "You can almost number the stories," says one of Xinos's colleagues, Ronald Himel. " 'I walked into the alley to urinate and I found the TV set.' 'Somebody gave me the tires.' Well, God forbid it should be true and I don't believe you. My first case out of law school, the guy told me he walked around the corner and found the TV set. So I put that on [in court]. The judge pushed his glasses down his nose, hunched up and said, 'Fifty-two years I have been walking the streets and alleys of Chicago and I have never, ever found a TV set.' Then he got me in his chambers and said, 'Are you f——ing crazy?' I said, 'That's what he told me.' The judge said, 'And you *believed* that s——? You're goofier than he is!' "

Xinos learned fast. . . . "It's our court," Xinos says. "It's like a family. Me, the prosecutors, the judges, we're all friends. I drink with the prosecutors. I give the judge a Christmas present, he gives me a Christmas present." And you learn technique. The evidence game. The little touches: "The defendant should smile a lot." The big disparities: which judge gives eighteen months for a wife-killing and which one gives twenty to forty years. How to make time and the caseload work for you. "The last thing you want to do is rush to trial. You let the case ride. Everybody gets friendly. A case is continued ten to fifteen times, and nobody cares any more. The victims don't care. Everybody just wants to get rid of the case." Then you can plead your man guilty and deal for reduced charges or probation or short time. You swing.

Xinos took an apartment in the distant suburbs, . . .

And, like any commuter, he tries to leave it all at the office. The ones you can't are the few you plead guilty when you really believe they are innocent: "When you're scared of losing. When they've got a case and you believe your guy but you lose your faith in the jury system. You get scared, and he gets scared and you plead him." But the Donald Paynes—the great majority of his cases—are different. Xinos never liked Payne; Payne fought him, and Xinos much prefers the pros who tell you, "Hey, public defender, I killed the f——er, now get me off." Xinos thought Payne should plead guilty and go for short time. But Payne clung to Standard Alibi Number Umpty-one ("I was home at the time this was supposed to have broke out") and demanded a trial, so Xinos gave him the best shot he could. He had to lay aside his misgivings—his upset at crime in the streets and his suspicion that Payne was part of it. "Me letting ten or twenty guys out on the street isn't going to change that," he says. "This violence—it's like Niagara Falls. You can't stop it."

The jail

He clambered down out of the van with the rest of the day's catch and was marched through a tunnel into a white-tiled basement receiving area. He was questioned, lectured, classified, stripped, showered, photographed, fingerprinted, X-rayed for TB, bloodtested for VD and handed a mimeographed sheet of RULES OF THE COOK COUNTY JAIL. (". . . You will not escape from this institution. . . . You will be safe while you are in this institution. . . .") He says he was marked down as a Blackstone Ranger over his objections—"I told them I was a little old to be gang-bangin' "—and assigned to a teen-age tier, E–4. He was issued a wristband, an ID card and a ceiling ticket, led upstairs and checked into a tiny 4-by-8 cell with an open toilet, a double bunk, two sheets, a blanket and a roommate. The door slammed shut, and Donald Payne—charged with but still presumed innocent of attempted robbery and attempted murder—began nearly four and a half months behind bars waiting for his trial.

Jails have long been the scandal of American justice; nobody even knew how many there were until a recent federal census counted them (there are 4,037)—and found many of their 160,000 inmates locked into what one official called "less than human conditions of overcrowding and filth." And few big-city jails have had histories more doleful than Cook County's. The chunky, gray fortress was thought rather a model of penology when Anton Cermak started it in 1927. But its first warden hanged himself, and its last but two, an amiable patronage princeling named Jack Johnson, was sacked when a series of investigations found the jail ridden with drugs, whisky and homosexual rape and run by inmate bully boys.

Johnson gave way to warden (and now director of corrections) Winston Moore, 41, a round black buddha with wounded eyes, short-shaven hair, a master's and a start on a doctorate in psychology and some iron-handed notions about managing jails and jail inmates. Moore's mostly black reform administration has tamed the inmate tier bosses, cleaned up the cells and the prisoners, repainted the place for the first time, hired more guards at better pay, started some pioneering work and work-training programs, opened an oil-painting studio in the basement room where the county electric chair used to be and begged free performances by B. B. King, Ramsey Lewis, Roberta Flack, and even, minus the nude scene, the Chicago company of *Hair*. But there has never been enough cash, and lately the John Howard Association, a citizens' watchdog group that gave Moore top marks for the first year, has turned on him with a series of reports charging a miscellany of cruelties within the walls. And worst of all is the desperate overcrowding. The rise in crime and the slowing processes of justice have flooded Moore's 1,300 claustrophobic cells with 2,000 prisoners, most of them doubled up at such close quarters that if one inmate wants to use the toilet, the other has to climb on the bunk to let him by.

Roughly 85 percent of the inmates are Negro, and most, like Donald Payne, are stuck inside because they are too poor to make bail—not because they have been convicted of crimes. But the presumption of guilt infects a jail as it does so much of American justice, and Moore squanders little sympathy on his charges. He came up in black New Orleans, the son of a mailman struggling for decency, and when any of his inmates blames his troubles on hard times or bad conditions, Moore explodes: "Bulls——! Don't give me that—I was there too, I know what it's like and I made it. You got in trouble because you *wanted* to get in trouble."

. . . He has small pity for the Donald Paynes and enormous scorn for those white liberals who seem more concerned with explaining them than with punishing them. It is there that he sees the real racism of the system—"These bleeding liberals who have so much guilt that they can justify blacks killing blacks because we're immature. They're the ones that want to keep you immature. Quit justifying why I kill my buddies on Saturday night and try to stop me from doing it."

Moore has no such tender feelings; he lays on rock concerts and painting classes but he also maintains The Hole—a tier of isolation cells into which the hard cases are thrown with no beds, no day-room privileges, no cigarettes, no candy bars, no visitors, nothing to do but lie or sit or squat on a blanket on the floor and wait for the days to go by. "You will always have to have a place like The Hole," Moore says without a hint of apology. "Much of the problem of crime is immaturity, and the greatest reflection of immaturity is rage—blind rage. There is no other way to contain it." The Hole nevertheless is a degrading place for people on both sides of the bars. The men crouch like caged animals, eyes glinting in the half light. The guards in The Hole wear white because the men throw food at them and white is easier to launder.

It took Donald Payne less than twenty-four hours to get there.

He came onto tier E–4 angry at being put with the gang kids and shortly ran into a youth from his block who had been a member of the Gangsters. "He had me classified as a Gangster, too," Payne says. "He thought I was just scared to say 'cause we were on a Blackstone tier. He ran up in my face and wanted to fight. We had a fight and I went to The Hole for thirty days and he got fifteen."

So they gave Payne a cage, and he sat it out. What do you do? "You sit on the toilet. You wait for the food to come around." What do you think about? "Gettin' out." How do you feel about The Hole leaving it? "It didn't matter much." Not enough, in any case, to keep him out: he went straight back in four days for sassing a guard, emerged with a reputation as a troublemaker with a "quick attitude" and later did thirty more when Moore's men put down a noisy Blackstone hunger strike on E–4. After that, Payne was transferred to a men's tier and did a bit better. "Those Rangers," he says, "they keep talkin' about killin' up people. What they did when they was outside. What they gonna do when they get out." The older men by contrast idled away their time in the daytime playing chess and cards and dominoes. They taught Payne chess and let him sit in. "People over here been playin' five and six years," he says, grinning a little. "They're pretty good, too. But I don't wanta be that good."

All the while, his case inched through the courts. Illinois requires that the state bring an accused man to trial within 120 days or turn him loose—a deadline that eases the worst of the courthouse delays and the jailhouse jam-ups that afflict other cities. But the average wait in jail still drags out to six or seven months, occasionally because the state asks for more time (it can get one sixty-day extension for good cause), more often because delay can be the best defense strategy in an overloaded system. Evidence goes stale; witnesses disappear or lose interest; cases pile up; prosecutors are tempted to bargain. "You could get twenty years on this thing," Constantine Xinos, the assistant public defender who drew Donald Payne, told him when they met. "Don't be in a hurry to go to trial."

Waiting naturally comes easier to a man out on bail than to one behind bars, but Payne sat and waited. On August 24, nineteen days after his arrest, he went from The Hole down to the basement tunnel to the courthouse, stripped naked for a search, then dressed and was led upstairs for a hearing in Room 402—Violence Court. Room 402 is a dismal, soot-streaked place, its business an unending bleak procession of men charged with armed robbery, rape and murder, its scarred old pews crowded with cops, witnesses, wives, mothers and girl friends jumbled uncomfortably together. Payne waited in the lockup until a clerk bellowed his name, then stood before Judge John Hechinger in a ragged semicircle with his mother, the cops, the victims, an assistant state's attorney and an assistant public defender and listened to the prosecution briefly rehearse the facts of the case.

Frank Hamilton—Payne's alleged accomplice—by then had been turned over to the juvenile authorities, and Hechinger dismissed the case against James, the driver of the car, for want of evidence that he had had anything to do with the holdup. But he ordered Payne held for the grand jury. The day in court lasted a matter of minutes; Payne was shuffled back through the lockup, the nude search, the basement tunnel and into The Hole again. On September 18, word came over that the grand jury had indicted him for attempted armed robbery (gun) and attempted murder, and the case shortly thereafter was assigned to Circuit Judge Richard Fitzgerald for trial.

So Payne waited some more, and the rhythm and the regularity of the life inside crept into his blood. Connie Xinos, appalled by the surge in black crime, thinks it might help a little to put one of those tiny cells on display on a street corner in the middle of the ghetto as an object lesson. But, talking with Donald Payne, one begins to wonder about its power as a deterrent. Payne was irritated by the days he spent in court; nobody brings you lunch there. "I sort of got adjusted to jail life," he says. "It seem like home now."

Source: Peter Goldman and Don Holt, "How Justice Works: The People vs. Donald Payne." *Newsweek,* 8 March 1971, pp. 20–37.

Pretrial Processes

From arrest to trial or plea
  Pretrial motions
Bail: pretrial release
  Methods and purposes of bail
  Bondsmen: beneficiaries of bail
  Bail setting: an example of exchange
  Reform of the system
    Citation
    Release on recognizance (ROR)
    Ten percent cash bail
    Preventive detention
Jail
  Pretrial detention
  Impact of pretrial detention
Plea bargaining
  Exchange relationships in plea bargaining
    Tactics
    Pleas without bargaining
  "Copping out"
  Justification for plea bargaining
    Individualized justice
    Administrative necessity
  Criticisms of plea bargaining
  Reforming plea bargaining
    Abolition
    Preplea conferences
  Evaluating plea bargaining
Summary

10

For a number of years "Arrest and Trial" was a popular television drama in which audiences were permitted to see an arrest, the trial, and the sentencing. Most viewers probably assumed that arrest and trial were linked and that all persons taken into custody ended up facing a judge and jury. But most people arrested will never face trial because a major portion of cases are dropped through the discretionary action of the police, prosecutor, or judge. Up to 90 percent of people who are arraigned on an indictment plead guilty and thus do not have a trial. The filtering process operates in such a way that only a very small portion of those who come to the attention of the police for wrongdoing are eventually given a sentence. Many who are sentenced appeal their convictions and some have them overturned.

From the time I first meet my client until we leave the courthouse, I have to be ready to bargain. Bail, charge, plea, and sentence—they all result from my ability to deal with the system.

DEFENSE ATTORNEY

The concept of the "criminal justice wedding cake," discussed in chapter 4, alerts us to the fact that different kinds of cases are handled in somewhat different fashions. The interest of the public, the nature of the case, the character of the defendant, the tactics of the opposing attorneys—all help to determine whether a case is given routine treatment and results in a plea bargain, becomes one of the few highly publicized trials that occur in a jurisdiction each year, or falls somewhere in between. The vast majority of cases are handled in ways that bear little resemblance to the adversarial processes described by the Due Process Model.

Chapter 10 focuses attention on the pretrial period, when most major decisions concerning the fate of persons arrested are made. It is in this portion of the criminal justice system that we can best see the links among the police, prosecution, defense, and court. Of particular importance are the subjects of bail and plea bargaining, practices and procedures that are here examined in detail.

From arrest to trial or plea

Following the arrest, booking, and initial appearance of a defendant, the pretrial processes begin. It is at this time that the prosecution and defense prepare their cases, an indictment or information is presented to the court, and a formal ***arraignment*** on the charges is held. More important, this is the time for screening and filtering out of the system those cases that the prosecution believes will not pass judicial scrutiny. As we have seen, prosecutors can

arraignment the act of calling an accused person before the court to hear the charges lodged against him or her and to enter a plea in response to those charges.

TABLE 10.1 Major dispositional points of felony cases in six jurisdictions

	Cook County (Chicago) (population: 5,500,000)	*Los Angeles County (population: 7,200,000)*	*Kings County (Brooklyn) (population: 2,600,000)*	*City of Detroit (population: 1,700,000)*	*City of Baltimore (population: 980,000)*	*Harris County (Houston) (population: 1,800,000)*
Number of felony arrests	22,000	69,000	15,000	20,000	8,000	16,000
Police screening	In all jurisdictions studied there were no records kept on the number of releases or "dropped charges" at the police level. Unofficial estimates from police officials, however, indicate there is relatively little screening of felony cases after arrest; estimates ranged from 1% to 2% in Chicago to around 10% in Baltimore and New York.					
Prosecutor screening	Only in major cases, business frauds, and white-collar crimes	Extensive screening; approximately 50% of cases are rejected	Only in major cases or highly publicized ones	All cases are reviewed; approximately 30% are rejected	Only in major cases or highly publicized ones	Review at examining trial (preliminary hearing) reduces caseloads 25%
Preliminary hearing	Major disposition point; approximately 80% of cases receive final disposition	10% dropout; hearing is formal and designed to produce transcript for later trial	Major disposition point; approximately 65% of cases receive final disposition	Majority of defendants waive preliminary hearing	Little screening; no records available; prosecutor usually not present	25% of cases screened out (see above)
Grand jury	Approves virtually all of prosecutor's recommendations	Less than 1% of cases are referred to G.J. (information used)	Rejects about 5% of cases, mostly on recommendation of D.A.	None (information used)	Approximately 3% of cases are rejected	Approximately 10% of cases are rejected
Indictment or information	5,000	21,400	3,000	9,000	6,500	7,000
Guilty plea	2,300 Conference with judge and prosecutor available on request	9,400 Little judicial participation in bargaining	2,500 Mandatorily referred to "conference and discussion" court before docketing	4,800 Mandatory pretrial conference without judicial participation	900 No practice of encouraging plea	5,500 Heavy emphasis on plea negotiations between prosecutor and defense
Dismissal and nol. pros.	1,300 Mostly superfluous charges	1,500	200	3,500 Mostly superfluous charges	1,300	400
Contested non-jury	600	9,500 Majority are adjudicated on transcript of preliminary hearing	100	600	5,000 Juries are traditionally waived	60
Contested jury	300	900	200	300	125	300

Source: Donald M. McIntyre and David Lippman, "Prosecutors and Early Disposition of Felony Cases," 56 *American Bar Association Journal* 1156 (1970). Reprinted by permission.

drop the cases of some defendants, return other cases to the police for further investigation, and recommend diversion for still others.

Table 10.1 shows that the amount of screening that takes place during the pretrial period varies from city to city. Roughly comparable categories and volumes of persons and offenses enter the system through police arrest in city after city, and at the sentencing end of the continuum the same kinds, categories, and numbers of persons are sent to penal institutions. But some differences do exist; the felony arrest rate in Cook County, Illinois, for example, is 545 per 100,000 and in Los Angeles County it is 990. Though the uniformity of intake and outputs is striking, of more direct relevance to our concerns are the dramatic variations in the screening-out and settlement processes. In the cities studied, these crucial decisions were made by different criminal justice actors and at different points in the process.

Considerable variation may be seen among jurisdictions as to when and by whom the important dispositional choices are made. In Los Angeles and Detroit, once the police feel they have enough evidence to press charges, they take their cases to the prosecutor for a formal decision about whether to do so. The result is that about half the felony cases are either dropped or routed to lower courts to be prosecuted as misdemeanors. In Chicago, Brooklyn, and Baltimore, the police file cases directly in the lower courts without clearance from the prosecutor's office. Thus the judges at preliminary hearings are given primary responsibility to decide whether to prosecute. The study shows that 80 percent of the felony cases in Chicago are terminated by the judge at the preliminary hearing, while in Houston a magistrate seems to follow the recommendations of the prosecutor assigned to the court.

The methods by which guilty pleas are negotiated and accepted also vary. In Detroit and Houston, negotiations take place directly between the prosecutor and defense counsel, without participation by the court. Detroit has so formalized the process that there is a special room in the courthouse where these negotiations are conducted. In Brooklyn and Chicago, however, the courts fully participate in the process. A trial judge in Chicago listens to the facts of each case and indicates to counsel the type of sentence that would be imposed in exchange for a plea. In Brooklyn there is a special Conference and Discussion Court with the sole function of reviewing felony cases and giving recommendations as to reductions and settlements. In Baltimore, 80 percent of indicted defendants go to trial, but waiver of a jury and expeditious methods of presenting evidence permit what may be termed "mass production" of felony trials.

These permutations in pretrial processes may result because, as in any organizational system, responses by the various actors in the criminal justice system are influenced by exchange relations, the power of particular actors, and the community's political environment. One might suggest that in a county like Los Angeles, where the prosecutor's staff has little turnover and where individuals have stepped down from positions as judges to run for district attorney, bureaucratic power may be accumulated in that office. The prosecutor's bargaining position in relation to other criminal justice actors may be enhanced by such factors. Staff turnover is very high in Chicago, whereas judges enjoy long tenure and have close ties to the political machine.

Judges there have more influence on the criminal justice process than they have in Los Angeles.

More important is the fact that *somewhere* in the system cases are screened and either are removed or undergo alterations in the charges. In all the examined cities, the criminal justice system was under pressure to reduce the number of cases requiring formal trial by jury. Donald McIntyre and David Lippman report that 80 percent of the felony cases initiated in Chicago, for example, had to be eliminated. In Los Angeles the prosecutor rejected 50 percent of the cases, while another 10 percent were removed at the preliminary hearing. In Brooklyn, 65 percent of the final dispositions were made at preliminary hearings, while another 5 percent were filtered out by the grand jury at the recommendation of the prosecutor.[1] Table 10.1 indicates that the great bulk of felony cases end with a conviction on the original charge and that most such dispositions are made very early in the process. The maintenance of the system requires this type of administrative decision making.

Pretrial motions

motion
An application to a court requesting that an order be issued to bring about a specified action.

The defense uses the pretrial period to its own advantage. Through pretrial **motions** to the court, counsel may attempt to suppress evidence or to learn about the prosecutor's case. A motion is an application to a court requesting that an order be issued to bring about a specified action. A court hearing is held on the motion and the presenting attorney must be able to support the contention made about procedures used in the arrest, the sufficiency of the evidence, or the exclusion of evidence. Typical pretrial motions by the defense include:

1. Motion to quash a search warrant.
2. Motion to exclude evidence, such as a confession.
3. Motion for severance (separate trials in cases with more than one defendant).
4. Motion to dismiss because of delay in bringing the case to trial.
5. Motion to suppress evidence illegally obtained.
6. Motion for pretrial discovery of the evidence held by the prosecutor.
7. Motion for a change of venue because a fair and impartial trial cannot be held in the original jurisdiction.

Aggressive use of pretrial motions has strategic as well as substantive advantages. They can become part of the jockeying for position between the prosecution and defense. One Houston lawyer listed the following reasons for the filing of numerous motions:

1. It forces a partial disclosure of the prosecutor's evidence at an early date.
2. It puts pressure on the prosecutor to consider plea bargaining early in the proceeding.
3. It forces exposure of primary state witnesses at an inopportune time for the prosecution.
4. It raises before the trial judge early in the proceedings matters the defense may want called to his or her attention.
5. It forces the prosecutor to make decisions before final preparation of the case.
6. It allows the defendant to see the defense counsel in action, which has a salutary effect on the client–attorney relationship.[2]

Although pretrial motions are entered in only about 10 percent of felony cases and in less than 1 percent of misdemeanors, they can be used not only to secure the defendant's release but also to bargain, since the defense may want to give every indication that it is going to trial. A second, equally important function of the pretrial processes for the defense is to secure release of the defendant on bail. As the next section will explain, the defendant who is out on bail has enormous advantages over the defendant awaiting trial in jail.

Bail: pretrial release

Although the Eighth Amendment prohibits excessive bail and most state statutes are written in a way intended to ensure that the system is administered in a nondiscriminatory manner, judicial personnel have a great deal of discretion in determining the conditions of a defendant's release. Studies have shown that individuals with certain racial or economic characteristics or who have unconventional lifestyles are required to post higher bonds than are those who conform more closely to middle-class norms. This finding may merely reflect the fact that crimes committed by lower-class persons tend to be more serious than those perpetrated by persons with white-collar status. Yet as early as 1835 the Supreme Court ruled that the purpose of bail is to ensure the presence of the accused in court to answer the indictment and to submit to trial.[3] Along with our assumption that accused persons are innocent until proved otherwise, we believe that they should not suffer hardship while awaiting trial. Bail should not be used as punishment, for the accused has not been found guilty. The amount of bail should therefore be sufficient to ensure the defendant's presence for trial, but no more.

Methods and purposes of bail

The practice of allowing defendants to be released from jail pending trial originated in Anglo-Saxon law. In a period when the time between arrest and trial was lengthy and the cost of detention burdensome, bail was used as a convenience to the sheriff, allowing him to release a prisoner from his responsibility and yet be fairly certain that he or she would be in court at the appointed time. As today, some form of surety was required, to be forfeited if the accused did not show up as promised. This concept was transferred across the Atlantic with modifications, so that now the right to bail is guaranteed and excessive bail is prohibited.

The reality of the bail system is far from the ideal. The question of bail may arise at the police station, during the initial court appearance in a misdemeanor case, or at the arraignment in most felony cases. In almost all jurisdictions, the amount of bail is based primarily on the judge's perception of the seriousness of the crime and the defendant's record. In part, this emphasis stems from a lack of information about the accused. Because bail must be allowed within twenty-four to forty-eight hours after an arrest, there is no time to seek out background information on which to make a more just bail determination. The result is that judges have developed standard rates that are used in both courtroom and station house: so many dollars for such-and-such an offense. A judge may in certain instances set high bail in response to the police's wish to keep a defendant in custody. Defense attorneys have reported that bail of any amount has the effect of scaring the defendant but that a high bail implies that the judge believes the crime was vicious or that the defendant may not otherwise appear in court.

The amount of bail and the number and type of charges are set at the discretion of judicial actors. Unpopular defendants, those who are "down and out," political dissenters, and members of a minority may have bail set at levels out of proportion to either the crime or the probability that they will appear in court. Bail is often used to punish through confinement in the absence of evidence to convict. In Des Moines such a device was used against people suspected of operating a motor vehicle while intoxicated (OMVI). As Captain Wendell Nichols told reporter Howard James, "The boys figured the defendant would at least be rapped for the bond [defendants pay a bail bondsman $25 to write a $300 bond for OMVI] and also spend a night in jail."[4]

Ronald Goldfarb, whose book *Ransom* criticizes the bail system, has shown that the emphasis on monetary bail operates to penalize the poor and to punish in advance of trial those whom society does not like: "The financial emphasis of the American bail system raises provoking and perplexing problems about the equality of the administration of justice. What if a man has no money? Should he be denied a chance for freedom before trial simply because he is poor? What if a man has a little money, but cannot afford to use it for bail?"[5] It is not difficult for big-time racketeers to make bail and continue their criminal activities while awaiting trial; a poor person arrested for a minor violation such as vagrancy will spend the pretrial period in jail. Should the dangerous rich be allowed out on bail and the undangerous poor kept in?

> How can it be that members of Brooklyn's notorious Gallo gang, who were charged with murdering a policeman in the course of a gang war, were released on bail, while at the same time in that same city 17- and 18-year-old defendants were kept in jail over a year because they could not afford bail? The two teenagers were acquitted.[6]

To post bail, a prisoner is required to give the court some form of monetary surety, usually cash, property, or a bond from a bonding company. On some occasions, persons who are highly placed in the community are released on their own recognizance, but such actions are rare for all but the pettiest of misdemeanors. The effect of the system on the poor may be seen in figure 10.1, which indicates that more than half of felony defendants studied in New York City could not raise the money to pay a bondsman to provide bail. Meanwhile, the more affluent and the professional criminal have no difficulty. In some metropolitan night courts one may see lawyers for syndicate-connected prostitutes concluding with fistfuls of money the arrangements to ensure that their clients are quickly released and back on the job.

The inequity of the system is further shown by the fact that those who cannot make bail must remain in jail, where they are treated the same as convicted prisoners. In New York, which has a median delay of thirty-two days between arraignment and trial, the effect on both defendants and their families can be disastrous. Not only is their freedom impinged upon, but they almost always lose their jobs and their family relationships are jeopardized. Following a period in jail, almost half the persons held in lieu of bail in Philadelphia were released after trial, through either acquittal, suspended

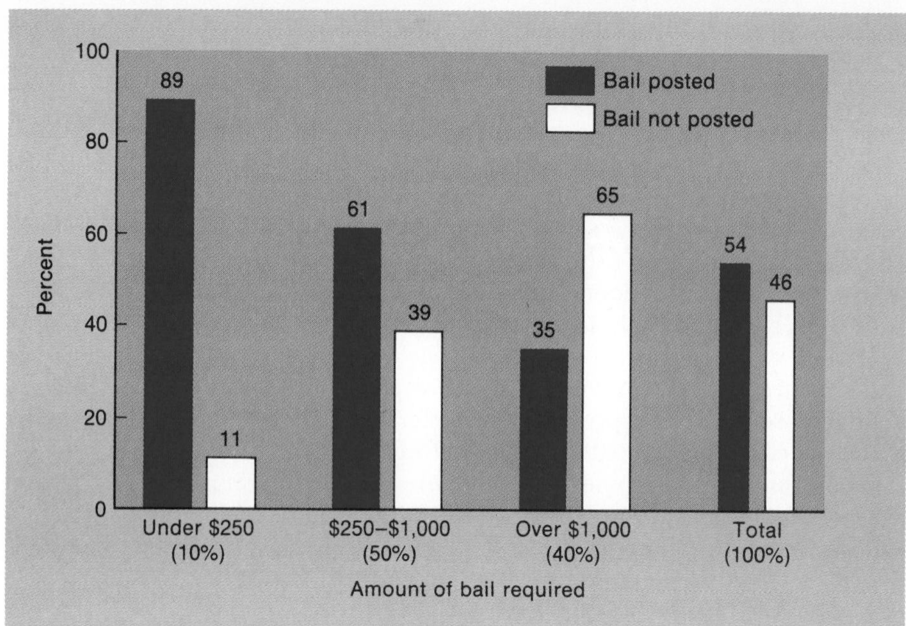

FIGURE 10.1 Percentage of persons accused of felonies released pending trial in New York City, by amount of bail required ($N = 840$)

sentence, or probation. Judges commonly give suspended sentences to the guilty because of the time already spent in jail awaiting trial.

Bondsmen: beneficiaries of bail

A central figure in the bail system is the professional bondsman, whose services are available twenty-four hours a day to those who need to produce sufficient cash to be released. Across from most courthouses his bright neon sign spells out BONDS, a reminder of the freedom that can be had for a price.

Using their own assets or those of an insurance company, bondsmen will provide the surety required for a fee of between 5 and 10 percent. They are licensed by the state, choose their own clients, and can set their own collateral requirements. In addition, they may track down and return bail jumpers without extradition and by force if necessary. Bondsmen are in a financially rewarding occupation: 10 to 12 million Americans need bail bonds each year, which translates into total profits for the trade of almost $30 million.[7]

Like other actors who have an interest in the judicial system, bondsmen exert a strong influence on the court of justice through their ability to cooperate with police officers who recommend their services rather than those of another bondsman. In return they may refuse to provide bail for defendants whom the police do not wish to see released. Bondsmen are viewed as a cardinal flaw in the bail system because although they are private individuals with no formal ties to the judicial process, they still have the power to overrule in effect a judge's decision. Bondsmen may withhold their services arbitrarily. Bondsmen, as Judge J. Skelly Wright succinctly said,

> hold the keys to the jail in their pockets. They determine for whom they will act as surety—who in their judgment is a good risk. The bad risks, in the bondsmen's judgment, and the ones who are unable to pay the bondsmen's fees, remain in jail.

The court and the commissioner are relegated to the relatively unimportant chore of fixing the amount of bail.[8]

Although the bonding profession has an unsavory reputation, these business people of criminal justice facilitate court operations. Their most important function is to maintain social control over the defendant during the pretrial period. Bondsmen stress to their clients the importance of appearing in court on the correct date, and emphasize the penalties that may result if they fail to do so. Often pressure on friends and relatives, as well as telephone calls and mailed reminders, are used to ensure appearance. Like defense attorneys, bondsmen help to prepare their clients for the probable fate in store for them, often encourage a plea of guilty, and usually forecast the sentence quite accurately. Bondsmen also share responsibility with judges for the defendant's release, thus providing a buffer should the defendant upset the public by committing further crimes before trial. In this era of crowded jails, bail bondsmen relieve some of the pressure.[9] Table 10.2 shows who sets bail in eleven large cities, where the process is carried out, and how the amount is determined.

Bail setting: an example of exchange

The judge or magistrate determines the amount of bail but is influenced by the prosecutor, defense counsel, and police. Sometimes the bondsman will also participate in the exchange. Inevitably the prosecutor supports high bail and the defense attorney asks that it be low, pointing out that the defendant must "take care of his family," "has a good job," or "is well liked in the neighborhood." The police may be particularly active in some settings in urging high bail, especially if they have expended extensive resources to apprehend the suspect or have had contact with the victims.

> Detectives sometimes enter the judge's chamber before the arraignment to inform the judge of any unusual aspects of the case that cannot be brought out in open court. In one instance where the judge, at arraignment on the warrants, posted $500 bonds against each of three defendants under investigation, the detective immediately contacted a prosecutor, explained the facts of the case, and went with him to the judge's chambers, where a conference was held with the judge. The bonds were raised to $5,000.[10]

Donald McIntyre reports a murder case in which both the defense and a bondsman brought pressure on a judge to set bail.

> The attorney and a professional bondsman were in the judge's chamber pleading for a bail bond to be fixed. The bondsman said that he had known the defendant for 10 years, and he would be happy to vouch for her character. The judge, however, continued in his refusal to fix a bond. After the men left, the judge stated that one consideration in not fixing the bond at this point was the presence of the professional bondsman, pleading desperately to have the bond fixed so that he would be able to get a $300–$400 fee.[11]

Frederic Suffet studied bail settings in Part 1A of the New York County Criminal Court. Recording the interactions of the prosecutor, defense attorney, and judge, Suffet noted the way norms emerged and guided the decision. The acknowledged standards or "rules of the game"—seriousness of the charge, prior record, defendant's ties to the community—provided the accepted boundaries for the interactions. With these standards accepted by the participants, negotiations could proceed with a minimum of conflict. Of the 1,473 bail settings Suffet observed, the judge made a decision in 49 percent without discussing the matter with the attorneys. Thirty-eight percent resulted from a suggestion by either the prosecution or defense that the judge accepted. In only 12 percent was there a conflict among the role players; only 3 percent went beyond the original sequence of suggestion–objection–decision and occasioned additional argument.[12]

The study showed that the prosecutor had more prestige in the courtroom than did the defense attorney. The latter was less likely to make the initial bail suggestion and had less chance of getting the judge to accede to it if he did make it. As table 10.3 shows, the prosecutor's request for higher bail was granted in more than four out of five cases, no matter who had made the original suggestion. By contrast, the defense attorney, when arguing against the first suggestion of the prosecutor, got the bail lowered only a little over half the time (57.8 percent). In a direct conflict with the judge, the defense attorney affected the bail decision a little more than a fourth of the time (28 percent). Suffet's further analysis shows that the judge and prosecutor hold similar conceptions as to the level of bail required and are reciprocally supportive.

Although the "manifest," or formal, purpose of setting bail is to stipulate an amount that will ensure the defendant's appearance in court, the latent purpose, or by-product, of this interaction is to spread responsibility for the defendant's release. By including the prosecutor and defense counsel in the process, the judge can create a buffer between the court and the outraged public if an accused criminal released from custody pending his court appearance should commit a crime.

In addition to interpersonal influences, the local legal and political culture have been found to be important factors in the setting of bail. In a study of Detroit and Baltimore, Roy Flemming learned that the two cities approximated the extremes of pretrial treatment of felony defendants among larger American cities. In Detroit's Recorder's Court, nearly 48 percent of felony defendants arraigned were freed on their own recognizance, the median bail for the remainder was $2,000, and 32 percent were detained for the entire

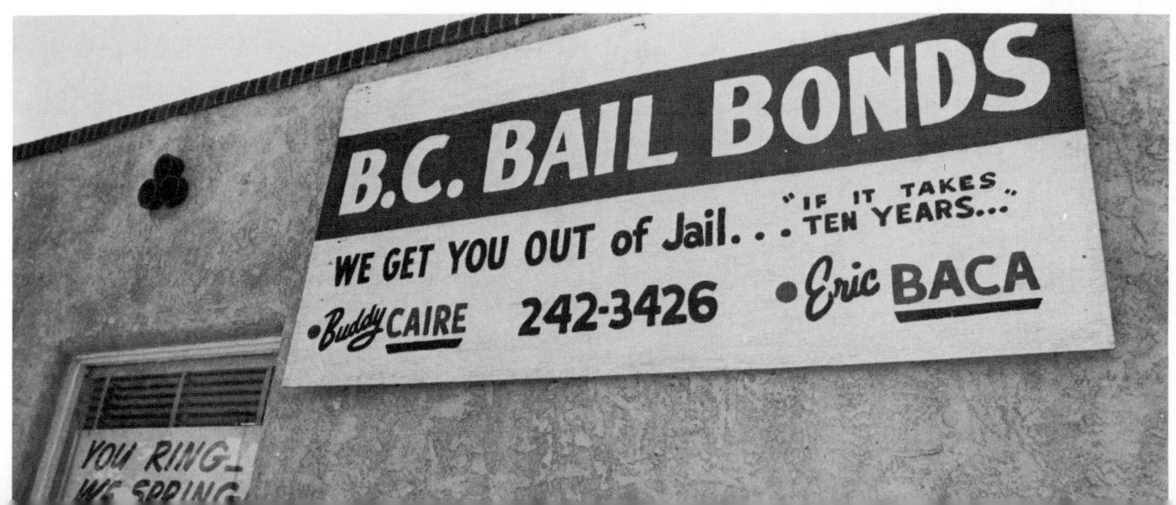

TABLE 10.2 Who sets bail for defendants accused of misdemeanors and of felonies in eleven cities, where, and how

City	*Who sets the bail*		*Where it is done*		*How it is done*	
	Misdemeanor	*Felony*	*Misdemeanor*	*Felony*	*Misdemeanor*	*Felony*
Washington	Desk sergeant	Judge	Station house	Court of Gen'l sessions	Schedule	Discretion
San Francisco	Clerk of criminal court	Judge	Hall of Justice	Hall of Justice	Schedule	Discretion
Los Angeles	Police captain	Judge	Station house	Regional	Schedule	Discretion
Oakland	Police captain	Judge	Station house	Courthouse		
Detroit	Desk sergeant Arresting magistrate	Arresting magistrate	Police station	Hall of Justice	Schedule	Discretion
Chicago	Desk sergeant	Judge of bond court	Police station	Bond court or electronically	Schedule	Discretion
St. Louis	Desk sergeant	County circuit court judge	Police station	Police station or courthouse	Schedule	Flexible schedule
Baltimore	Desk sergeant	Judge	Police station	Police court	Schedule	Schedule
Indianapolis	Turnkey	Turnkey	City jail	City jail	Schedule	Schedule
Atlanta	Police	Police	Police head-quarters	Police head-quarters	Discretion schedule	Discretion schedule
Philadelphia	Desk sergeant	Magistrate and district attorney	Station house	Police head-quarters	Schedule	Discretion

From *Freedom for Sale*, by P. B. Wice, p. 26. Copyright © 1974 by D. C. Heath and Company. Reprinted by permission of Lexington Books.

TABLE 10.3 Bail differential according to person disagreeing and person making first bail suggestion

	Prosecutor asks higher bail				*Defense attorney asks lower bail*			
	1st suggestion by judge		*1st suggestion by def. attorney*		*1st suggestion by judge*		*1st suggestion by prosecutor*	
Differential	*Percent*	*Number*	*Percent*	*Number*	*Percent*	*Number*	*Percent*	*Number*
Lower	0.0		2.3	1	28.0	7	57.8	26
None	15.8	3	14.0	6	72.0	18	40.0	18
Higher	84.2	16	83.7	36	0.0	—	2.2	1
	100.0	19	100.0	43	100.0	25	100.0	45

Source: Frederic Suffet, "Bail Setting: A Study of Courtroom Interaction," *Crime and Delinquency* 12 (October 1966): 325.

predisposition period. In Baltimore's District Court, only 12 percent of the accused were freed on their own recognizance, the median bail was $4,650, and 41 percent awaited disposition in jail.[13]

Among the influences contributing to these differences was the political climate in Detroit, described as "prodefendant" following reforms instituted after the riots in 1967, when thousands of black citizens were detained by means of exorbitant bail; a formal limit on the Wayne County Jail population; and bail-setting judges who held secure positions. In Baltimore, in contrast, bail was set by "low-status court officials or commissioners with insecure tenure who were more highly vulnerable" to criticism of bail reforms on the part of the police and other public officials; thus there was a high level of uncertainty among the people responsible for setting bail. And there were no population limitations on detention facilities.

From a constitutional viewpoint, it has been argued that bail should be set in accordance with six presumptions: (1) that the accused is entitled to release on his or her own recognizance, (2) that nonfinancial alternatives to bail will be used when possible, (3) that the accused will receive a full and fair hearing, (4) that reasons will be stated for the decision, (5) that clear and convincing evidence will be offered to support a decision, and (6) that there will be a prompt and automatic review of all bail determinations. Many people will claim that requiring bail to be set in accordance with these criteria will greatly hamper the ability of the justice system to deal with offenders and to protect society. Others will counter just as strongly that personal freedom is so precious that failure to afford a person every opportunity to remain at large is a greater injustice.

Both Financial Bonds and Alternatives Release Options Are Used Today

Financial bond

Fully secured bail. The defendant posts the full amount of bail with the court.

Privately secured bail. A bondsman signs a promissory note to the court for the bail amount and charges the defendant a fee for the service (usually 10% of the bail amount). If the defendant fails to appear, the bondsman must pay the court the full amount. Frequently, the bondsman requires the defendant to post collateral in addition to the fee.

Percentage bail. The courts allow the defendant to deposit a percentage (usually 10%) of the full bail with the court. The full amount of the bail is required if the defendant fails to appear. The percentage bail is returned after disposition of the case although the court often retains 1% for administrative costs.

Unsecured bail. The defendant pays no money to the court but is liable for the full amount of bail should he fail to appear.

Alternative release options

Release on recognizance (ROR). The court releases the defendant on his promise that he will appear in court as required.

Conditional release. The court releases the defendant subject to his following of specific conditions set by the court such as attendance at drug treatment therapy or staying away from the complaining witness.

Third-party custody. The defendant is released into the custody of an individual or agency that promises to assure his appearance in court. No monetary transactions are involved in this type of release.

Source: U.S. Department of Justice, Bureau of Justice Statistics, *Report to the Nation on Crime and Justice* (Washington, D.C.: Government Printing Office, 1983), p. 58.

Reform of the system

In response to the inadequacies of the bail system, several alternative methods have been developed to facilitate pretrial release.

citation
A written order issued by a law enforcement officer directing an alleged offender to appear in court at a specified time to answer a criminal charge; referred to as a "summons" in some jurisdictions.

Citation. The police have long been accustomed to issuing a ***citation*** or summons to appear in court—a "ticket"—to a person accused of committing a traffic offense or some other minor violation. By issuing the citation, the officer avoids the need to take the accused to the station house for booking and to court for arraignment and determination of bail. Such citations are being used with increasing frequency for more serious offenses, in part because the police want to reduce the amount of time they must spend booking minor offenders and waiting in arraignment court for their cases to come up for decision. One study in California showed that only 4.5 percent of defendants given citations failed to appear.[14] In some cities bail bondsmen have opposed this threat to their livelihood.

Release on recognizance (ROR). Pioneered by the Vera Institute of Justice in New York City, the ROR approach is based on the assumption that judges will grant releases if they are given verified information about defendants' reliability and roots in the community. Court personnel talk to defendants soon after their arrest about job, family, prior criminal record, and associations and then determine whether release should be recommended. In the first three years of the New York project, more than 10,000 defendants were interviewed and approximately 3,500 were released. Only 1.5 percent failed to appear in court at the appointed time, an appearance rate almost three times better than the rate for those being released on bail.[15] Comparable programs instituted in other cities have had similar results. The forfeiture rate in San Francisco is 2.3 percent, compared with the bondsman's rate there of 5.4 percent. St. Louis and Indianapolis have had corresponding experiences.[16]

Ten percent cash bail. Although ROR has been quite successful, judges are unwilling to release many defendants on their own recognizance. For this group, some states have inaugurated bail programs in which the defendants deposit with the court cash equal to 10 percent of their bail. When they appear in court as required, 90 percent of this collateral is returned to them. Begun in Illinois in 1964, this plan is designed primarily to release as many defendants as possible without enriching the bondsmen.

Preventive detention. Reforms have been suggested not only by those concerned with inequities in the bail system but also by those concerned with crime. Critics point to a relationship between release on bail and commission of crimes, arguing that the accused may commit other illegal acts while awaiting trial. As one more reflection of the due process–crime control debate, "prevention detention" has been proposed so that judges can hold suspects without bail if they are accused of committing a dangerous or violent crime and locking them up is deemed necessary for community safety. Civil libertarians, however, call preventive detention a threat to basic constitutional values. This approach was authorized by Congress in the District of Columbia Court Reform and Criminal Procedure Act of 1970 and the Comprehensive Crime Control Act of 1984.

Under the 1984 legislation, federal judges may consider whether the defendant poses a danger to the community in deciding whether (and under what conditions) to release him or her before trial; the legislation allows outright detention on the basis of presumed danger to particular persons or the community at large. This decision is made at a hearing to consider the prosecution's contention that (1) there is a serious risk that the person will flee; (2) the person will obstruct justice or threaten, injure, or intimidate a prospective witness or juror; or (3) the offense is one of violence or one punishable by life imprisonment or death.

The major evaluation of preventive detection was carried out during the first ten months after the District of Columbia law went into effect. It was found that only 10 of 6,000 felony defendants were detained, and that prosecutors made only 20 requests that judges invoke the law.[17] Prosecutors evidently felt it unnecessary to turn to the law because they were able to hold selected defendants in jail by obtaining the cooperation of judges in the setting of high bail. They also were reluctant to invoke the preventive detention provisions because in some cases they would have had to disclose evidence they possessed. Some said, too, that the hearing procedure was too clumsy.

Proponents of preventive detection point to the fact that eight studies have shown that somewhere between 7 and 20 percent of persons under pretrial release commit crimes, and for some crimes the figure is as high as 34 to 70 percent. Martin Sorin argues that "pretrial criminals may account for as

San Francisco Bail Project: Pretrial Release Criteria

To be recommended for release on own recognizance, a defendant needs:

A Bay Area address where he can be reached, and a total of five points (verified by references) from the following:

Residence

3 Present address one year or more
2 Present residence 6 months, or present and prior 1 year
1 Present residence 3 months, or present and prior 6 months
1 Five years or more in nine Bay Area counties

Family ties

3 Lives with family, and has contact with other family members in area
2 Lives with family, or has contact with family in the Bay Area
1 Lives with a nonfamily person

Employment

3 Present job one year or more
2 Present job 3 months, or present and prior job 6 months
1 Current job, or intermittent work for 1 year
1 Receiving unemployment compensation or welfare
1 Supported by family or savings

Prior record

2 No convictions
1 One misdemeanor conviction
0 Two misdemeanor convictions, or one felony conviction
−1 Three or more misdemeanor convictions, or two or more felony convictions
−2 Four or more misdemeanor convictions, or three or more felony convictions

Source: San Francisco Commission on Crime, *Staff Reports: The Criminal Courts, 1970,* p. 138.

much as one-fifth of our nation's total crime problem."[18] Such findings have led planners to argue that there is a small but identifiable group of defendants who are immune to the imposition of stringent release conditions and the prospect of revocation of their bail: they are not deterred. A 1980 study by the Institute for Law and Social Research revealed that in the District of Columbia the nature and seriousness of the charge, a history of prior arrests, and the presence of drug addiction all have a strong bearing on the probability that a defendant will commit a pretrial criminal act.[19]

It will be instructive to track the federal courts' use of preventive detention in the late 1980s—a time when interest in crime control is on the rise. The extent to which states adopt the federal procedures will also be a factor that criminal justice scholars will follow with interest.

Jail

Individuals who are unable to secure bail or to be released on their own recognizance are remanded to jail to await their court appearance. Although popularized in folksong and in fiction, American jails have been called "the ultimate ghetto." Most of the more than 200,000 people in the jails are poor. About half are in pretrial detention, and the remainder are serving sentences (normally of less than one year) or awaiting transfer to prison or to another jurisdiction. Traditionally jails have been the dumping ground not only for the criminal but also for the public drunk, the mentally ill, the vagrant, and the moral deviant. Uniformly jam-packed and generally brutalizing, jails are almost never life-enhancing. They seem to be the oldest, most numerous, and most resistant to reform of all criminal justice processes and institutions.

The 1983 National Jail Census confirms that although people are being held in jail for a range of reasons, most of them share at least one condition: poverty. As we would expect, about 93 percent are men, most are under thirty years of age, only a little more than half are white, and most have very low incomes.[20] In some ways the demographic characteristics of the jail population diverge from those of the national population: people in jail are younger and disproportionately black, and most are unmarried.

Most of the 3,300 jails in the United States are locally administered by elected officials (sheriffs or county administrators). Only in Alaska, Connecticut, Delaware, Hawaii, Rhode Island, and Vermont are they run by the state government. Traditionally jails have been run by law enforcement agencies,

Most Unconvicted Jail Inmates Have Had Bail Set

Of 66,936 unconvicted jail inmates surveyed in 1978—

- 81% had bail set.
- 46% could not afford the bond that had been set.
- 17% had not had bail set.
- 6% were held on nonbailable offenses such as murder.
- 3% had not yet had a bail hearing.
- 2% were held on detainers or warrants.

Source: U.S. Department of Justice, Bureau of Justice Statistics, *Report to the Nation on Crime and Justice* (Washington, D.C.: Government Printing Office, 1983), p. 58.

though about half of the inmates are sentenced offenders under correctional authority. It seems reasonable that the agency that arrests and transports defendants to court should also administer the facility that holds them, but generally neither sheriffs nor their deputies have much interest in corrections. They think of themselves as police officers and of the jail as merely an extension of law enforcement activities. Remember, though, that about half of the inmates are sentenced offenders under correctional authority.

Pretrial detention

For most suspects the period immediately after arrest is the most frightening. Imagine yourself in such circumstances. After being fingerprinted, photographed, and questioned, you are taken to the detention section of the jail. In some newer facilities you may be asked further questions about your background, physical condition, and mental health so that treatment may be provided if necessary. More than likely, there is no formal intake procedure and you are simply put in a holding "tank." If you are a man, there are probably three or more strangers in the cell with you, men whose stories you do not know and whose behavior you cannot predict. If you are a woman, you are probably by yourself. In either case, the guard leaves and you are on your own. You now have time to think and to worry about your situation.

For most people, this is a threatening fantasy because they might approach panic in such circumstances. That is why the initial hours following arrest are often referred to as a period of crisis for the defendant. The vulnerability, the sense of hopelessness and fright, the ominous future that includes potential loss of freedom are never more stressful than in those first few hours of confinement. During 1983, 53 percent of deaths that occurred in jail were suicides. It is understandable that most jail suicides occur within the first six to

The period immediately after arrest is extremely stressful.

ten hours of detention, and that most psychotic episodes occur during or just after intake.

The crisis nature of arrest and detention can be exacerbated by other factors. Often the newly arrested person is intoxicated by alcohol or another drug; indeed, intoxication may have contributed to the very crime for which the person is being held. Sometimes the criminal behavior that has put the accused in jail stems from an emotional instability that may become more severe in detention. For young offenders, the oppressive threat and reality of personal violence can set off debilitating depression. Without question, one of the most crucial times for the administrator and the offender comes immediately after arrest.

Impact of pretrial detention

The fact that a defendant is being held in jail seriously affects the ultimate disposition of his or her case. Consider the effect on a judge and jury of two hypothetical defendants: one steps neatly dressed from among the onlookers to the counsel's table; the other, in prison garb, is escorted by guards from a nearby cell to the counsel's table. What would you think if you were on the bench or in the jury box? Although it would be difficult to prove that these contrasting scenes affect the justice dispensed, various theories of human behavior suggest that the accused who has been detained is more likely to be labeled guilty. As Erving Goffman has written, the ways we present ourselves to others have important effects on their actions toward us.[21]

A study by Eric W. Single revealed that defendants held for trial in lieu of bail are more often convicted and, when convicted, go to prison more often and receive longer sentences than those who post bail. Using data from 857 files of persons accused of felony or misdemeanor offenses in New York City, Single performed an analysis that overcame many of the methodological flaws of similar investigations. He found that among people charged with a felony, 24 percent of the detainees were not convicted, compared to 59 percent of those on bail. Among those convicted, 21 percent of the detainees received no prison time, compared to 27 percent of the releasees; and 26 percent of the detainees received a long prison sentence, compared to 4 percent of those released.[22]

One of the most startling facts about U.S. jails is that although half of the persons in them have not been convicted of the crimes for which they are being detained, the conditions under which they are held are deplorable. For a goodly number, their pretrial detention is long—in many states the average delay between arrest and trial is six months or more. The hardship of detention before trial is serious, for it creates pressures on defendants to waive their rights and to plead guilty.

Plea bargaining

The Supreme Court has ruled that plea bargaining is constitutional. Other courts, and prosecutors, say it is absolutely necessary. Defense lawyers say it is often a boon to their clients. Chief Justice Warren Burger has said, "It is an elementary fact, historically and statistically, that the system of courts—the number of judges, prosecutors, and of courtrooms—has been based on the premise that approximately 90 percent of all defendants will plead guilty, leaving only 10 percent, more or less, to be tried."[23] By contrast, the National Advisory Commission on Criminal Justice Standards and Goals called for the abolition of plea bargaining.

The process of plea bargaining—also called negotiating a settlement or "copping a plea"—was for many years one of the best-kept secrets of criminal justice practitioners; only in relatively recent years has the public become aware of it as the method by which the great bulk of criminal offenders are sanctioned. It was little discussed earlier because there were doubts about its constitutionality and because it did not seem appropriate to a system committed to the adversary procedure.

But recent decisions by the Supreme Court have clearly acknowledged the legitimacy of plea bargaining. In *Blackledge* v. *Allison* (1976), for example, the justices said: "Whatever might be the situation in an ideal world, the fact is that the guilty plea and the often concomitant plea bargain are important components of this country's criminal justice system. Properly administered, they can benefit all concerned."[24] The Court has noted that plea bargaining flows from "the mutuality of a vantage" to defendants and prosecutors, each with his or her own reasons for wanting to avoid trial.

In the broadest sense, plea bargaining is a defendant's agreement to plead guilty to a criminal charge with the reasonable expectation of receiving some consideration from the state for doing so. Some defendants plead guilty without entering into negotiations but expect to receive some benefit nevertheless. This practice has been called *implicit* plea bargaining, as distinguished from *explicit* plea bargaining, an arrangement between the prosecutor and defendant—sometimes with the participation of the judge—whereby a plea of guilty is exchanged for the prosecutor's agreement to press a charge less serious than that warranted by the facts and perhaps to recommend leniency to the judge.

The defendant's usual objective is to be charged with a crime carrying a lower potential maximum sentence, thus limiting the judge's discretion in sentencing. A plea may also be entered on one charge on agreement that the prosecutor will drop other charges in a multicount indictment. Another reason for seeking a lesser charge may be the wish to avoid charges with legislatively mandated sentences or stipulations against probation or to escape a charge that carries an undesirable label, such as rapist or homosexual. The prosecutor seeks to obtain a guilty plea to avoid combat in the courtroom. Although the imposition of the sentence remains a function of the court, the prosecutor draws up the indictment and usually has an important influence on the judge's sentencing decision. Clearly, plea bargaining is the most crucial stage in the criminal justice process and is the primary example of "bargain justice."

According to the traditional conception of adversarial justice, criminal cases are not "settled," as in civil law; the outcome is determined by the symbolic contest of the state versus the accused. Yet as Donald Newman found in Wisconsin, and as others have documented elsewhere, "most of the convictions (93.8 percent) were not convictions in a combative, trial-by-jury sense, but merely involved sentencing after a plea of guilty has been entered."[25] Although variation exists among jurisdictions, estimates are that up to 90 percent of all defendants charged with crimes before state and federal courts plead guilty rather than exercise their right to go to trial. Table 10.4 shows the percentage of guilty pleas in several states according to the population of the jurisdiction. In this table, and consistent with the findings of other studies, there is little difference between jurisdictions and little correlation between guilty plea rate and population size. It is generally accepted that up to 90 percent of felony defendants in the United States plead guilty.

Exchange relationships in plea bargaining

Plea bargaining is essentially a series of exchange relationships in which the prosecutor, the defense attorney, the defendant, and sometimes the judge participate. All enter the contest with particular objectives; all attempt to structure the situation to their own advantage and come armed with a number of tactics designed to improve their position; and all will see the exchange as a success from their own perspective. The exchange may be considered successful by the prosecutor who is able to convict the defendant without trial; by the defense attorney who is able to collect a fee with a minimum of effort; and by the judge who is able to dispose of one more case from a crowded calendar. Yet Jonathan Casper found that defendants felt they could not win: "It is a game in which they can, should they choose to play and be skillful or lucky, lose less than they would if they failed to play at all."[26]

Tactics. Plea bargaining between defense counsel and prosecutor bears a striking resemblance to a formal ritual in which friendliness and joking mask the forceful advancement of antagonistic views. The pattern is a familiar one: initial humor, the stating of each viewpoint, resolution of conflict, and a final

TABLE 10.4 Percentage of guilty pleas to felony charges in selected states, by population of jurisdiction

	Population of jurisdiction			
State	*Up to 100,000*	*100,000–250,000*	*250,000–500,000*	*500,000 & over*
Idaho	87.8	94.5	—	—
Illinois	91.4	86.5	82.6	84.0
Kansas	71.0	69.3	69.8	—
Louisiana	72.0	92.8	86.4	85.1
Michigan	86.4	88.8	90.4	93.5
Minnesota	83.6	89.3	85.5	85.4
Missouri	73.8	79.6	—	87.6
New Jersey	96.2	92.3	88.1	88.2
New York	92.1	89.9	94.5	92.7
North Dakota	89.7	—	—	—
Ohio	68.9	80.4	88.8	78.5
Oklahoma	67.3	89.0	90.7	80.9
Pennsylvania	82.3	86.6	85.5	65.6
South Carolina	95.8	97.3	—	—
South Dakota	91.5	—	—	—
Texas	90.9	89.6	92.7	91.6
Utah	71.5	78.8	80.4	—
Vermont	95.2	100.0	—	—
Wyoming	55.4	—	—	—

Source: Adapted from Herbert S. Miller, William F. McDonald, and James A. Cramer, *Plea Bargaining in the United States,* U.S. Department of Justice (Washington, D.C.: Government Printing Office, 1978), p. 19, by permission of the Georgetown University Law Center.

period of cementing the relationship. Throughout the session, each side tries to impress the other with its confidence in its own case, while indicating weaknesses in the opponent's presentation. During the discussion, there appears to be a norm of openness and candor designed to maintain the relationship. Little effort seems to be made to conceal information that may later be useful to the adversary in the courtroom. There seems to be a standing rule that confidences shared during negotiations will not be used in court.

Some attorneys, of course, do not conform to this norm. One prosecutor said: "There are some attorneys with whom we never bargain, because we can't. We don't like to penalize a defendant because he has an ass for an attorney, but when an attorney cannot be trusted, we have no alternative." Defense attorneys often feel that prosecutors are insulated from the human factors of a case and are thus unwilling to individualize justice. Since defense lawyers get to know the defendants, their problems, and their families, they may become emotionally attached to cases. As one defense lawyer told this author: "We have to impress [the chief deputy prosecutor] with the fact that he is dealing with humans, not with just a case. If the guy is guilty he should be imprisoned, but he should get only what's coming to him, no more."

A tactic that prosecutors commonly bring to plea bargaining sessions is the multiple-offense indictment. One defense attorney commented: "Prosecutors throw everything into an indictment they can think of, down to and including spitting on the sidewalk. They then permit the defendant to plead guilty to one or two offenses, and he is supposed to think it's a victory."[27]

Types of Bargaining

1. *Bargain concerning the charge.* A plea of guilty was entered by the offenders in exchange for a reduction of the charge from the one alleged in the complaint. This ordinarily occurred in cases where the offense in question carried statutory degrees of severity such as homicide, assault, and sex offenses. . . .

2. *Bargain concerning the sentence.* A plea of guilty was entered by the offenders in exchange for a promise of leniency in sentencing. The most commonly accepted consideration was a promise that the offender would be placed on probation, although a less-than-maximum prison term was the basis in certain instances. All offenses except murder, serious assault, and robbery were represented in this type of bargaining process. . . .

3. *Bargain for concurrent charges.* This type of informal process occurred chiefly among offenders pleading without counsel. These men exchanged guilty pleas for the concurrent pressing of multiple charges, generally numerous counts of the same offense or related violations such as breaking and entering and larceny. This method, of course, has much the same effect as pleading for consideration in the sentence. The offender with concurrent convictions, however, may not be serving a reduced sentence; he is merely serving one sentence for many crimes. . . .

4. *Bargain for dropped charges.* This . . . involved an agreement on the part of the prosecution not to press formally one or more charges against the offender if he in turn pleaded guilty to (usually) the major offense. The offenses dropped were extraneous law violations contained in, or accompanying, the offense alleged in the complaint such as auto theft accompanying armed robbery and violation of probation where a new crime had been committed. . . .

Source: Donald J. Newman, "Pleading Guilty for Considerations: A Study of Bargain Justice," *Journal of Criminal Law, Criminology, and Police Science* 46 (March–April): 780–90. Reprinted by special permission of the *Journal of Criminal Law, Criminology, and Police Science.*

Multiple-offense charges are especially important to prosecuting attorneys when they are faced with difficult cases—cases in which, for instance, the complainant is reluctant, the value of the stolen item is in question, and the reliability of the evidence is in doubt. Narcotics officers often file sale charges against defendants when they know they can convict only for possession. Since the accused persons know that the penalty for selling is much greater, they will be tempted to plead guilty to the lesser charge.

Defense attorneys may approach these negotiations by threatening to ask for a jury trial if concessions are not made. Their hand is further strengthened if they have filed pretrial motions that require a formal response by the prosecutor. Another tactic is to seek rescheduling of pretrial activities, in the hope that, because of the delay, witnesses will become unavailable, public interest will die, and memories of the incident will be weakened by the time of the trial. Rather than resort to such legal maneuverings, some attorneys prefer to bargain on the basis of friendship. An Oakland attorney once commented:

> I never use the Constitution. I bargain a case on the theory that it's a "cheap burglary" or a "cheap purse-snatching" or a "cheap whatever." Sure, I could suddenly start to negotiate by saying, "Ha, ha! You goofed. You should have given the defendant a warning." And I'd do fine in that case, but my other clients would pay for this isolated success. The next time the district attorney had his foot on my throat, he'd push too.[28]

Often the bargain is struck in ways that might go unnoticed by the casual observer. To maintain some psychological distance between the adversaries, vague references are often made to disposition of the case. Such statements as "I think I can sell this to the boss" or "I'll see what can be done" signal the completion of a bargaining session and are interpreted by the actors as an agreement on the terms of the exchange. On other cases, negotiations are more specific, with a direct promise made that certain charges will be altered in exchange for a guilty plea.

Because negotiations are conducted primarily between the prosecutor

Should the Government Agree to Plea Bargain?

In determining whether it would be appropriate to enter into a plea agreement, the attorney for the government should weigh all relevant considerations, including:

1. The defendant's willingness to cooperate in the investigation or prosecution of others.
2. The defendant's history with respect to criminal activity.
3. The nature and seriousness of the offense or offenses charged.
4. The defendant's remorse or contrition and his willingness to assume responsibility for his conduct.
5. The desirability of prompt and certain disposition of the case.
6. The likelihood of obtaining a conviction at trial.
7. The probable effect on witnesses.
8. The probable sentence or other consequences if the defendant is convicted.
9. The public interest in having the case tried rather than disposed of by a guilty plea.
10. The expense of trial and appeal.
11. The need to avoid delay in the disposition of other pending cases.

Source: U.S. Department of Justice, *Principles of Federal Prosecution* (Washington, D.C.: Government Printing Office, 1980), p. 23.

Judges frequently take part in plea bargaining.

and the defense attorney, the interests of the public and even of the defendant may become secondary considerations. Without the possibility of a trial where evidence gathered in a legal manner must be presented, plea bargaining can shield unconstitutional practices by justice system actors from public view. The police, for example, may abuse the rights of certain defendants, but a guilty plea does not give the defendants or their attorneys the opportunity to make such practices public. Thus persons who are not "legally" guilty—whose guilt cannot be proved given the constraints supposedly imposed on police conduct—are in fact convicted with their own silent or expressed consent.

Neither the prosecutor nor the defense attorney is a free agent. Each must count on the cooperation of both defendants and judges. Attorneys often cite the difficulty they have convincing defendants that they should uphold their end of the bargain, while experienced defendants have expressed the opinion that they are better off without a lawyer because they can then deal directly with the prosecutor. Judges must cooperate in the agreement by sentencing the accused according to the prosecutor's recommendation. Although their role requires that they uphold the public interest, judges may be reluctant to interfere with a plea agreement in order to maintain future exchange relationships. Thus both the prosecutor and defense attorney usually confer with the judge regarding the sentence to be imposed before agreeing on a plea. At the same time, however, the judicial role requires that judges hold in reserve their power to reject the agreement. Because uncertainty is one of the hazards of the organizational system, prosecutors and defense attorneys will use each judicial decision as an indication of the judge's future behavior.

Pleas without bargaining. Recent studies have alerted scholars to the fact that in many courthouses the marketplace tactics of plea bargaining do not exist in certain types of cases, yet guilty pleas remain as high as the national average.[29] It appears that in many lower, misdemeanor courts there is consensus among judges, prosecutors, and defense attorneys as to "going rates," or the usual sentences given for offenses. The shared expectations as to the going rate and the ways that a defendant can obtain it may be referred to as implicit bargaining. Douglas Maynard found that many cases are concluded when one party offers a disposition and the other simply agrees to it. Because courthouse actors know the going rate, the exchange relationship is limited. In only a small number of cases did Maynard discover extensive bargaining carried out visibly and unambiguously. As he notes, the sharing of expectations means simply that participants are able to read situations in like manner and infer what resolution will be mutually acceptable. Such a process in plea bargaining is surely aided by the participants' knowledge of the courtroom subculture. The establishment by legal practitioners of "going rates" for run-of-the-mill, "normal" crimes . . . in local jurisdictions and the administration of these rates as a matter of course . . . is a well-documented practice.[30]

We should expect to find implicit plea bargaining in courtrooms where the going rates are known to the participants. If there is much turnover among the actors, uncertainty would be likely to reduce the number of guilty pleas offered without negotiation. We should also expect bargaining to be more explicit over serious offenses, when the possible sentence would be incarceration. But underlying both the implicit and explicit models of plea bargaining is the assumption that there is a penalty for going to trial. The nature of that penalty may be an added factor that looms over all plea considerations.

We should also be alert to the fact that the local courtroom culture has a decided impact on the bargaining process; similar issues are not decided in the same manner from courthouse to courthouse. Particular ways of disposing of cases develop in each setting. In some courts a "slow plea" process will be the dominant method: defendants initially plead not guilty but change their pleas as the trials progress. In other courts, various portions of the caseload may be filtered out by the prosecutor through the dropping of cases or the diversion of offenders. The variety of routines, norms, and expectations may be much greater than was originally thought, and observers of any one courthouse discover patterns that are not exactly like the textbook description.

"Copping out"

Although decisions by the Burger Court have removed most of the constitutional doubts about plea bargaining, judges are still required to learn whether the defendant understands the implications of an agreement to plead guilty. The plea must be made voluntarily, and if the prosecutor has given a promise of leniency, it must be kept. In *Santobello* v. *New York* (1971), the Supreme Court ruled that "when a [guilty] plea rests in any significant degree on a promise or agreement of the prosecutor, so that it can be said to be part of the inducement or consideration, such promise must be fulfilled."[31] Thus when a plea is given, the judge is required to ask a series of questions to ensure that the method by which the bargain was struck adheres to these principles. At one time, this charade of the "***copping out*** ceremony" was one of the regular features of the courtroom day. But judges are increasingly discussing plea bargaining openly in their courts and admitting on the record that they are aware of plea negotiations. In many cases, they themselves have entered into plea discussions with respect to sentences.

copping out
Entering a plea of guilty, normally after bargaining (slang). The "copping out ceremony" consists of a series of questions that the judge asks the defendant as to the voluntary nature of the plea.

Justification for plea bargaining

As early as the 1920s the legal profession was united in opposition to plea bargaining. Roscoe Pound, Raymond Moley, and others associated with the crime surveys of the period stressed the opportunities for political influence as a factor in the administration of criminal justice. Today, under the pressures generated by crime in an urban society and the reality of bargaining, a shift has occurred so that professional groups are primarily interested in procedures that will allow for the review of guilty pleas and for other safeguards. Thus the American Bar Association has proposed minimum standards for the acceptance of guilty pleas. In a series of decisions beginning in 1970, the Supreme Court under Chief Justice Burger has legitimized the practice and has begun to stipulate the procedures that may be used to elicit a guilty plea.

Individualized justice. One of the most common justifications for plea bargaining is that it is necessary to individualize justice. Traditionally, judges have performed this function. Some people have argued, however, that developments in the system have limited the discretion of the judge while increasing the opportunity for the prosecutor to allocate justice. This view suggests that if the criminal law is to be even minimally fair, the prosecutor's office must become a ministry of justice by being able to determine case outcomes administratively.

One factor that promotes the guilty plea is related to the legislatures that have dictated extreme sentence lengths. As Arthur Rosett and Donald Cressey have suggested, legislatures fix severe punishments in order to appease the public.[32] Criminal justice personnel soften the punishments through the plea bargaining process in the interests of justice, to serve the needs of the bureaucracy, and to gain the acquiescence of the accused. In this way, courthouse practitioners develop shared norms as to the sentencing value attached to a particular offense. Courthouse regulars are convinced that defendants who insist on a trial and are then found guilty and those who refuse to cooperate receive harsher sentences than those who "go along." Legislatures see that most criminals do not receive the punishments prescribed and so increase them—and the severity-softening round begins again. Although the organizational needs of criminal justice personnel may be at the heart of plea bargaining, it can also be claimed that the acceptance of the guilty plea by the prosecutor and judge may help to soften the occasional overharshness of the law.

Pressures to Plead?

Willie Jones, a 22-year-old city man who pleaded guilty on June 20 to one count of sale of a cannabis substance and one count of possession of a controlled substance, was given the opportunity in Superior Court to withdraw his guilty pleas today by Superior Court Judge Joseph F. Dannehy.

The surprising move came when Dannehy, referring to an addition to the presentence investigation report, said it had been brought to his attention that "Mr. Jones claims he is innocent and has apparently convinced others who represent substantial interests in the community" in connection with the charges.

"Under these circumstances, Mr. Jones can withdraw his pleas and have his case tried before a jury," Dannehy said.

Dannehy set the trial date for Tuesday if Jones decides to withdraw the guilty pleas.

At press time, Jones had not yet decided to withdraw his pleas.

State's attorney Harry S. Gaucher said today that if the original guilty pleas were withdrawn he would request that Jones be put to plea for three other counts.

Those three counts are possession of marijuana, sale of marijuana and possession of a narcotic substance, according to Gaucher.

Source: *The Chronicle* (Williamantic, Conn.), 19 July 1974.

Close-up: Plea Bargaining in Detroit Recorder's Court

The elderly lawyer pushed through the swinging gate in the dark wood railing that separates court officials from the public and walked up and down past packed rows of spectators. He was dressed for the race track, where he intended to spend the afternoon, in an orange and green sport coat, bright green slacks, and soft white leather shoes, and his clothes were a flash of unexpected color in the drab, stuffy, downtown courtroom.

It was 10 o'clock on an August morning in Recorder's Court, which is the criminal court for the city of Detroit. In many ways, the scene could have been any criminal courtroom in the United States.

"Jackson," the lawyer called out. "Sam Jackson."

He was trying to find a client he had seen only once before, months ago, when he had been appointed to defend the man for a $100 fee paid by the state of Michigan. On the first day, he stood briefly beside his client as Jackson was arraigned and a date was set for his trial. Until this morning, when a courtroom clerk handed him a copy of the official court "paper" for the case, the lawyer had done nothing more.

"Jackson," he called again.

A slightly built black man in a polo shirt and work pants rose hesitantly a few rows back in the audience. Sam Jackson, a sometime laborer and truck driver, had, his record showed, been connected on and off with gambling and dope. He had been arrested nearly a year earlier for possession of a concealed pistol, which was found when a police detective stopped and searched his car, and he had been free on bail since then, waiting for his trial. That day, he was one of many defendants, mostly black, crowded together with relatives and friends in the worn wooden pews of Courtroom 8.

To these benches and to the barred cells hidden behind the courtroom are brought each day scores of men and women charged with such felonies as murder, rape, robbery, burglary, serious assault, the sale or possession of narcotics, or the illegal possession of a weapon. Many, like Jackson, wait a year or longer to be tried. But, for most of them, trial before a judge and jury never comes.

"Jackson?" the lawyer asked, pushing down his glasses to peer at his client. "Okay, okay. Sit back down. I'll be with you in a minute."

Turning, he walked through the gate again toward a cluster of policemen, all in street clothes, standing and gossiping idly near the empty jury box on the left side of the courtroom. In the confusion and cacophony that characterize the criminal-courtroom scene, the policemen, numbering about thirty, were balanced by a swirling, changing mass of as many men opposite them. These are the criminal lawyers, most of whom work in Courtroom 8 every day. Their only clients, whose fees are usually paid by the state, are those assigned to them by the court. Some keep dingy offices in squat, grimy buildings across narrow Clinton Street from the courthouse; others have no offices at all and operate out of the courtroom itself. Known collectively as the "Clinton Street bar," they carry no brief cases and seldom consult lawbooks; their case preparation consists of marking trial dates in dog-eared date books and scanning court papers hurriedly on the day a case comes up. Jackson's lawyer is one of the more flamboyant Clinton Street barristers.

By this time, as the lawyer passed by, the judge was seated on his perch atop a two-tiered wooden platform, surrounded by clerks, bailiffs, and other functionaries shuffling through and stamping papers just below him. Save for the few persons standing immediately before him to conduct business, nobody seemed really aware of the judge's presence. Lawyers, policemen, clerks, and others criss-crossed noisily in front of his bench, streamed back and forth through the swinging gate, and generally kept up a roar of conversation that crashed around the pronouncements of the judge, occasionally drowning out his words altogether.

"Detective Sanders," Jackson's lawyer said, "You got the Jackson case?" The policeman, recognizing the attorney, nodded. "Good," said the lawyer. Then, ignoring the judge nearby, the lawyer shouted the question that, in Recorder's Court, takes the place of trials, juries, legal rules, and the rest: "Hey, Sanders, what can you do for me today?"

Coming together in the middle of the courtroom, the lawyer and policeman began to haggle amiably over what reduction the government might make in its charge against Jackson if he agreed to plead guilty rather than go to trial. If convicted of the felony charge by a jury, Jackson would be given a prison sentence of several years. The law required it. The policeman suggested that the charge might be reduced to "failure to present a gun for licensing," a misdemeanor carrying a penalty of only ninety days in jail, *if* Jackson pleaded guilty immediately. Together, the lawyer and Detective Sanders then joined a line of other attorneys and policemen that stretched to a back room occupied by the prosecutor—an official who is himself seldom seen in the courtroom.

Case by case, the prosecutor and each lawyer, usually joined by the policeman involved, hammer out a bargain for a guilty plea, similar to the one that Jackson's lawyer was seeking. If the accused agrees to admit guilt rather than insisting on a trial by jury, the government reduces the charge against him, often assuring a lighter sentence. Thus, a man charged with armed robbery, which carries a mandatory twenty-year prison sentence, might plead guilty to unarmed robbery or attempted robbery and receive a much shorter sentence. Another, charged with burglary, might "admit" to attempting "unlawful entry." The changes are not made simply to fit the facts of the crimes involved; usually, in fact, the robber *had* used a gun or the burglar *had* succeeded in entering a house and stealing valuables. Instead, the change is made to induce the defendant to trade the possibility of a long prison term (against the chance for freedom if acquitted by a jury) for the promise of a shorter sentence.

In Sam Jackson's case, the prosecutor readily agreed to the bargain offered by the lawyer and policeman. The lawyer took Jackson into the bustling hallway outside the courtroom.

"I got you ninety days," he told Jackson enthusiastically. He did not refer at all to the crime itself or to his client's actual guilt or innocence. "It's a good deal. You have a record. You go to trial and get convicted on the felony and you're in trouble."

Jackson nodded in agreement.

"Remember," the lawyer cautioned as they returned to the courtroom, "don't hem and haw in front of the judge, or he might insist on a trial."

Jackson's turn came quickly. He stood mute, while the judge sorted through papers and read out the defendant's name and address and the charge originally placed against him. A court stenographer recorded everything.

"The prosecutor has signed a statement that he will accept your plea of guilty to a lesser charge," the judge announced. Then, like a clergyman reading a litany, with Jackson responding at appropriate pauses, he intoned, "You are pleading guilty because you are guilty?"

"Yes, sir."

"No one has threatened you or promised you anything?"

"No."

"No one has induced you to plead guilty?"

"No."

"You understand your constitutional right to a trial, and you are freely waiving that right?"

"Yes."

Turning sideways to stare out a window, the judge wearily recited, as he had again and again already that morning, "Let the record show that counsel was present, that the defendant was advised of his rights and that he understood them, and that the defendant waived his right to trial by jury or this court, and that he freely withdrew his plea of not guilty and entered a plea of guilty."

The court stenographer took down every word. The judge swiveled around again and sentenced Jackson to ninety days in jail.

Our legal tradition maintains that a judge should retain sentencing discretion so that the punishment can be fitted to the individual defendant. When the legislature has preempted the judicial power by requiring that a mandatory, nonsuspendable sentence be imposed, the only way the defendant's counsel can help a guilty client is to negotiate for a lesser charge. Only under such circumstances may the defendant be given a sentence that takes into account mitigating circumstances (no prior record, youth, and so forth).

Administrative necessity. A second justification for plea bargaining is administrative necessity. As we have seen, the problem of criminal justice is that of mass production. In our increasingly complex society, the demands on the judicial process are overwhelming. Calendar congestion, the size of the prison population, and strains on judicial personnel have been cited as shortcomings in the system. One Los Angeles trial judge caught the essence of the matter when he told an investigator, "We are running a machine. We know we have to grind them out fast."[33] A Manhattan prosecutor has said, "Our office keeps eight courtrooms extremely busy trying 5 percent of the cases. If even 10 percent of the cases ended in a trial, the system would break down. We can't afford to think very much about anything else."[34] Yet there are courts in large urban areas where guilty pleas are not used.

Recent studies cast doubt on the assumption that plea bargaining is a contemporary practice that developed as a response to increased caseloads. Milton Heumann, in a study of case dispositions in Connecticut, found that plea bargaining was practiced extensively in both high- and low-volume courts as early as 1880, and that trials have constituted less than 10 percent of indictments since that time.[35] Others have shown that plea bargaining has been a major feature of American criminal justice at least since the Civil War.

Malcolm Feeley argues that the prevalence of plea bargaining has increased in direct proportion to the adversariness of the system. From a historical perspective, he says, the modern criminal justice system has expanded requirements of due process, has allocated increased resources to both the prosecution and the defense, has developed a substantive criminal law, and has increased the availability of defense counsel. If one looks at conditions in the nineteenth century, a period often referred to nostalgically as the "golden era of trials," one finds

> a process that is difficult for the contemporary observer to recognize; those accused of criminal offenses—misdemeanor or felony alike—were typically rushed through crowded and noisy courts either subject to a perfunctory trial lasting an hour or two or pressured to plead guilty by overbearing prosecutors whose practices were condoned by judges. All this took place without benefit of counsel.[36]

In the contemporary system, Feeley believes, the relationship between the state and the accused is more evenly balanced. It is this new relationship—"a relationship that did not hold in a great many criminal cases when trials were more prevalent but the accused more dependent"—that has increased the adversariness of the system, and thus the opportunity for negotiation.[37]

Criticisms of plea bargaining

Although plea bargaining is pervasive in the American criminal justice system, its practice has been deplored by a number of scholars and by such

Institutionalizing Plea Bargaining

IN THE SUPERIOR COURT OF THE STATE OF WASHINGTON FOR KING COUNTY STATE OF WASHINGTON,

	)	
Plaintiff,	)	No.
v.	)	STATEMENT OF
	)	DEFENDANT ON
	)	PLEA OF GUILTY
________,	)	
Defendant.	)	

1. My true name is ________________.
2. My age is ______.
3. My lawyer is ________________.
4. The court has told me that I am charged with the crime of ________________, the maximum sentence for which is ________.
5. The court has told me that:
   a. I have the right to have counsel (a lawyer) and that if I cannot afford to pay for counsel, one will be provided at no expense to me.
   b. I have the right to a trial by jury.
   c. I have the right to hear and question witnesses who testify against me.
   d. I have the right to have witnesses testify for me. These witnesses can be made to appear at no expense to me.
   e. The charge must be proved beyond a reasonable doubt.
   f. I have the right to appeal.
   g. By entering a plea of guilty, I give up the rights listed in (b) through (f) and I will be sentenced on the basis of my plea.
6. I plead ________ to the crime of ________________ ________________ as charged in the information, a copy of which I have received.
7. I make this plea freely and voluntarily.
8. No one has threatened harm of any kind to me or to any other person to cause me to make this plea.
9. No person has made promises of any kind to cause me to enter this plea except as set forth in this statement.
10. I have been told the Prosecuting Attorney will take the following action and make the following recommendation to the court: ________________ ________________.
11. I have been told and fully understand that the court does not have to follow the Prosecuting Attorney's recommendation as to sentence. The court is completely free to give me any sentence it sees fit no matter what the Prosecuting Attorney recommends.
12. The court has told me that if I am sentenced to prison the judge must sentence me to the maximum term required by the law, which in this case is ________. The minimum term of sentence is set by the Board of Prison Terms and Paroles. The judge and Prosecuting Attorney may recommend a minimum sentence to the board but the board does not have to follow their recommendations. I have been further advised that the crime with which I am charged carries a mandatory minimum of ____ years. If not applicable, this sentence shall be stricken and initialed by the defendant and the judge.
13. I understand that if I am on probation or parole, a plea of guilty to the present charge will be sufficient grounds for a judge or the parole board to revoke my probation or parole.
14. The court has asked me to state briefly in my own words what I did that resulted in my being charged with the crime in the information. This is my statement: ________________ ________________.
15. I have read or have had read to me all of the numbered sections above (1 through 15) and have received a copy of "Statement of Defendant on Plea of Guilty." I have no further questions to ask of the court.

____

prestigious groups as the American Bar Association and the National Advisory Commission on Criminal Justice Standards and Goals. The criticisms are mainly of two kinds. The first emphasizes due process considerations and argues that plea bargaining does not provide procedural fairness to individual defendants because they forfeit the exercise of some of their constitutional rights, especially the right to trial by jury. The second emphasizes sentencing policy and points out that society's interest in awarding appropriate sentences for criminal acts is diminished by plea bargaining. It is believed that in urban areas where caseloads are burdensome, harried prosecutors and judges make concessions on the grounds of administrative expediency, with the result that sentences are lighter than those required by the penal code. Such a sentence may have little relationship either to the seriousness of the crime or to the rehabilitation and deterrence of the offender. Thus plea bargaining is criticized by both civil libertarians and law-and-order advocates, groups that usually are not on the same side of the fence.

Plea bargaining also comes under fire because it is hidden from judicial scrutiny. Since the agreement is most often made at an early stage of the proceedings, the judge has little information about the crime or the defendant and cannot evaluate the prosecutor's appraisal of each. Nor can the judge make a knowledgeable review of the terms of the bargain—that is, a check on the amount of pressure applied to the defendant to plead guilty. The result of "bargain justice" is that the judge, the public, and sometimes even the defendant cannot know for certain who got what from whom in exchange for what.

Another criticism leveled at plea bargaining is that it is inconsistent with the espoused values of the adversarial system. Some critics feel that overuse of plea bargaining breeds disrespect and even contempt for the law. It is said that criminals look at the judicial process as a game or a sham, little different from other "deals" that one makes in life.

Critics also contend that it is unjust to penalize persons who assert their right to a trial and are convicted by giving them stiffer sentences than they would have received if they had pleaded guilty. The evidence in this regard is unclear, although courthouse mythology upholds the view that a penalty is exacted from defendants who take up the court's time. James Eisenstein and Herbert Jacob's data from their study of the criminal courts of Baltimore, Chicago, and Detroit indicate that going to trial was only a minor factor in accounting for the sentences defendants received.[38] David Brereton and Jonathan Casper, however, found in their analysis of robbery and burglary data from three California counties that a greater proportion of defendants who went to trial received prison sentences than of those who pleaded guilty.[39]

Finally, there is concern that innocent people will plead guilty to acts they did not commit. Although it is difficult to substantiate such suspicions, evidence exists that some defendants have indeed entered guilty pleas when they have committed no criminal offense. In 1973 the Colorado courts overturned a sentence on the grounds that the defendant had been coerced by the judge's statement that he would "put him away forever if he did not accept the bargain."[40] Benjamin M. Davis, a San Francisco attorney, represented a man charged with kidnapping and forcible rape. Though Davis was confident that the defendant was not guilty, the defendant elected to plead guilty to the lesser charge of simple battery. When Davis informed him that conviction on the original charges seemed improbable, he simply replied, "I can't take the chance."[41]

Such cases often arise from the confusion of inexperienced offenders or from the reluctance of hardened criminals to risk a trial. When faced with the possibility that a jury may find them guilty of murder, innocent defendants with a record may plead guilty to the lesser charge of manslaughter. In fact, the utility of this position was underscored by the Supreme Court in the 1969 case of *Alford* v. *North Carolina,* when it approved in principle a pleading of guilty by an innocent defendant for the purpose of obtaining a lesser sentence.

Reforming plea bargaining

Abolition. In a number of jurisdictions, the prosecutor has acted to end plea bargaining. The most noteworthy instance was in Alaska, where the state attorney general instructed district attorneys to stop the practice as of 15 August 1975.[42] Attorney General Avrum Gross emphasized that he wanted to restore to the courts their proper role in sentencing. Criminal justice practitioners feared that the courts would be immediately flooded and that there would be a massive slowdown in moving the docket. Neither fear was realized.

The impact of the abolition of plea bargaining in Alaska has been extensively studied, and it was found that the courts had not been inundated and their business had not been impeded. In fact, disposition time actually decreased. Also unexpected: young defendants without prior records who were accused of property crimes received sentences that were more severe than those received by such defendants when plea bargaining had been practiced. More serious offenders received approximately the same sentences as before. Yet, although plea negotiation was greatly reduced, the number of guilty pleas decreased only from 94 percent to 92 percent of all cases. Defense attorneys learned that a guilty plea from a "clean defendant" was a sign of a "cooperative attitude," a factor that did not go unnoticed by the judges. "Resourceful attorneys tried to perfect techniques for judge-shopping, initiated discussions with victims, police, and presentence investigators, and sought more elaborate sentencing hearings when they could find receptive judges."[43] These activities benefited some defendants, but others pleaded guilty even without the assurance that they would receive a lighter sentence. Direct negotiation seems to have been eliminated in most Alaskan cases, yet a form of "implicit" bargaining remains.

Preplea conferences. To meet many of the criticisms of plea bargaining, several jurisdictions have instituted the ***preplea conference,*** in which all the parties—judge, victim, defendant, police, and prosecutor—take part.[44] For the purpose of the conference, the defendant's guilt is assumed and the discussion is of issues that may contribute to a settlement. This approach holds that many of the charges against plea bargaining will be blunted if there is full and open participation by all concerned. The presence of the judge ensures that the facts and the defendant can be fully evaluated before sentence is passed.

preplea conference A discussion, in which all parties openly participate, of ways to bring about an agreement on a sentence in return for a plea of guilty.

The best experimental use of this approach took place in Dade County, Florida, in 1974.[45] From 1,000 cases, the researchers assigned more than 300 to a preplea conference; the remainder were designated as the control group.

Seventy-six percent of the experimental cases resulted in a conference, with settlement being achieved in 26 percent and tentative settlement in 46 percent. The conference assumed the characteristics of an administrative proceeding in which the goals were to determine the facts of the case, to fit the case into a category, and then to apply existing legal rules. The researchers found that the conference shortened the length of time required to close cases but had no effect on the overall proportion of cases litigated or on the proportion of defendants found guilty. It can be said, however, that the preplea conference opens up bargaining so that it is no longer hidden in the prosecutor's office or judge's chambers.

Evaluating plea bargaining

Pleading guilty, either in the expectation of a lighter sentence or as part of a bargain, is one of the most typical phenomena of the American criminal justice system. The guilty plea occurs in up to 90 percent of felony cases before state and federal courts. Although often explained in terms of the heavy caseloads being processed through the system, plea bargaining can be shown to be in the interests of all the participants: the prosecutor secures a guilty plea and does not have to go to trial; the defense attorney is able to use time more efficiently; the judge moves the caseload; and the defendant receives a sentence that is less than the law could impose.

Attempts to abolish or limit plea bargaining have not altered the results: consideration in sentencing in exchange for a guilty plea. The system appears to require some means of serving the interests of the participants. With the recent decisions of the Supreme Court and the increased public awareness of plea bargaining, the practice will continue and will be increasingly aboveboard.

Summary

Until the chief justiceship of Earl Warren, most Supreme Court decisions focused on the trial in efforts to ensure an impartial jury and courtroom procedures in accordance with the Constitution. That the period from arrest to acceptance of a guilty plea is most crucial in our system has been recognized only during the last two decades. Chapter 10 has discussed the pretrial processes with emphasis on bail setting and plea bargaining. These processes offer some of the best insights into the making of administrative decisions that affect the future of criminal defendants within the context of law.

For discussion

1. The Constitution prohibits the levying of excessive bail. Should money be the sole determinant of whether someone is forced to await trial in jail? What other criteria might be used?
2. You are the judge. When you set bail, how may the nature of the crime, the characteristics of the defendant, and community pressure influence your decision?
3. Is discovery fair? Should the defense be allowed to see information held by the state?
4. Is plea bargaining really necessary? Whom does it help?
5. You, the defendant, have been arrested and charged with a crime. Your attorney has begun to bargain with the prosecutor for a reduction of the charges. Do you feel

that you will be able to resist the temptation to cop a plea if you did not commit the offense charged? What will be weighing in your mind as you decide?

For further reading

Casper, Jonathan D. *American Criminal Justice: The Defendant's Perspective,* Englewood Cliffs, N.J.: Prentice-Hall, 1972.
Goldfarb, Ronald. *Ransom: A Critique of the American Bail System.* New York: Harper & Row, 1965.
Heumann, Milton. *Plea Bargaining.* Chicago: University of Chicago Press, 1978.
Mather, Lynn M. *Plea Bargaining or Trial?* Lexington, Mass.: Lexington Books, 1979.
Trebach, Arnold. *The Rationing of Justice.* New Brunswick, N.J.: Rutgers University Press, 1964.
Wice, Paul. *Freedom for Sale.* Lexington, Mass.: Lexington Books, 1974.

Notes

1. Donald M. McIntyre and David Lippman, "Prosecutors and Early Disposition of Felony Cases," 56 *American Bar Association Journal,* p. 1156 (1970).
2. Paul Wice, *Criminal Lawyers: An Endangered Species* (Beverly Hills, Calif.: Sage, 1978), p. 148.
3. Ex Parte Milburn, 34 U.S. 704 (1835).
4. Howard James, *Crisis in the Courts* (New York: David McKay, 1968), p. 113.
5. Ronald Goldfarb, *Ransom: A Critique of the American Bail System* (New York: Harper & Row, 1965), p. 16.
6. Ibid., p. 33.
7. Goldfarb, *Ransom,* p. 96.
8. Pannell v. U.S., 320 F. 2d 698 (D.C. Cir. 1963).
9. Mary A. Toborg, "Bail Bondsmen and Criminal Courts," *Justice System Journal* 8 (Summer 1983): 144.
10. Donald McIntyre, ed., *Law Enforcement in the Metropolis* (Chicago: American Bar Foundation, 1967), p. 120.
11. Ibid., p. 121.
12. Frederic Suffet, "Bail Setting: A Study of Courtroom Interaction," *Crime and Delinquency* 12 (October 1966): 318.
13. Roy B. Flemming, *Punishment before Trial* (New York: Longman, 1982), pp. 136–38.
14. Alan Kalmanoff, *Criminal Justice: Enforcement and Administration* (Boston: Little, Brown, 1976), p. 191.
15. Goldfarb, *Ransom,* p. 157.
16. Paul B. Wice, "Bail Reform in American Cities," paper presented at the 1973 annual meeting of the Midwest Political Science Association, Chicago, p. 23.
17. Wayne H. Thomas, *Bail Reform in America* (Berkeley: University of California Press, 1976), pp. 231–32.
18. Steven R. Schlesinger, "Criminal Procedure in the Courtroom," in *Crime and Public Policy,* ed. James Q. Wilson (San Francisco: Institute for Contemporary Studies, 1983), p. 188; Martin D. Sorin, "How to Make Bail Safer," *Public Interest* 76 (Summer 1984): 102–10.
19. *Pretrial Release and Misconduct in the District of Columbia* (Washington, D.C.: Institute for Law and Social Research, 1980).
20. U.S. Department of Justice, Bureau of Justice Statistics, *Bulletin,* November 1984, p. 1.
21. Erving Goffman, *The Presentation of Self in Everyday Life* (Garden City, N.Y.: Doubleday, 1959).
22. Eric W. Single, "The Consequences of Pretrial Detention," paper presented at the 1972 annual meeting of the American Sociological Association, New Orleans.
23. Warren Burger, "Address at the American Association Annual Conference," *New York Times,* 11 August 1970, p. 1.
24. Blackledge v. Allison, 431 U.S. 63 (1976), 71.
25. Donald J. Newman, "Pleading Guilty for Considerations: A Study of Bargain Justice," *Journal of Criminal Law, Criminology, and Police Science* 46 (March–April 1956): 780–90.
26. Jonathan D. Casper, *American Criminal Justice: The Defendant's Perspective* (Englewood Cliffs, N.J.: Prentice-Hall, 1972), p. 78.
27. Albert W. Alschuler, "The Prosecutor's Role in Plea Bargaining," 35 *University of Chicago Law Review* 54 (1968).
28. Ibid., p. 79.
29. Malcolm Feeley, *The Process Is the Punishment* (New York: Russell Sage Foundation, 1979), p. 462; Peter F. Nardulli, Roy B. Flemming, and James Eisenstein, "Criminal Courts and Bureaucratic Justice: Concessions and Consensus in the Guilty Plea Process," unpublished paper, 1984.
30. Douglas Maynard, "The Structure of Discourse in Misdemeanor Plea Bargaining," *Law and Society Review* 18 (1984): 81.
31. Santobello v. New York, 404 U.S. 257 (1971).

32. Arthur Rosett and Donald Cressey, *Justice by Consent* (Philadelphia: Lippincott, 1976), p. 157.
33. Alschuler, "Prosecutor's Role in Plea Bargaining," p. 54.
34. Ibid., p. 55.
35. Milton Heumann, "A Note on Plea Bargaining and Case Pressure," *Law and Society Review* 9 (1975): 515.
36. Malcolm M. Feeley, "Plea Bargaining and the Structure of the Criminal Process," in *Criminal Justice: Law and Politics*, ed. George F. Cole, 4th ed. (Monterey, Calif.: Brooks/Cole, 1984), p. 405.
37. Ibid.
38. James Eisenstein and Herbert Jacob, *Felony Justice: An Organizational Analysis of Criminal Courts* (Boston: Little, Brown, 1977), p. 270.
39. David Brereton and Jonathan D. Casper, "Does It Pay to Plead Guilty? Differential Sentencing and the Function of Criminal Courts," *Law and Society Review* 16 (1981–82): 56–61.
40. People v. Clark, 515 2d 1242 (Colorado, 1973).
41. Alschuler, "Prosecutor's Role in Plea Bargaining," p. 61.
42. Michael L. Rubinstein and Teresa J. White, "Alaska's Ban on Plea Bargaining," *Law and Society Review* 13 (1979): 367.
43. Ibid., p. 389.
44. "Restructuring the Plea Bargain," 82 *Yale Law Review* 300 (1972).
45. Anne M. Heinz and Wayne A. Kerstetter, "Pretrial Settlement Conference: Evaluation of a Reform in Plea Bargaining," *Law and Society Review* 13 (1979): 349.

Court

11

Yet trial-court fact-finding is the toughest part of the judicial function. It is there that court-house government is least satisfactory. It is there that most of the very considerable amount of judicial injustice occurs. It is there that reform is most needed.

JEROME FRANK

The traditional image of the courthouse is of a building standing prominently on the central square of a town or city. It usually has a marble exterior, and it often is in the style of a Greek temple. The courthouse's location and structure symbolize the prominence of the rule of law in the American social and governmental system. But not all judicial decisions are made in this idealized version of the courthouse. The buildings vary from community to community. In some large cities it is difficult to distinguish the courthouse from the office buildings that surround it. In rural areas "court" is often held in a small office or even in the converted living room of the justice of the peace. A visitor might be at a loss to find a particular court, for courts are given a somewhat bewildering collection of names—municipal court, superior court, county court, district court, justice court, and so on. Further, these names rarely tell us much about what the courts do. Upon entering one of these buildings, we would probably be still further confused by signs that read "Clerk of Court," "Criminal Division, Part I," "Arraignment Court," "Juvenile Court." Venturing ahead, we might come upon a crowded and noisy room in which groups of people appear before a judge and then move on in rapid succession; or we might watch a trial in progress that has all the dignity of our image of the administration of justice; or we might see a circular table around which four or five adults and a fourteen-year-old girl are seated.

It is obvious that *court* refers to a variety of physical structures, names, functions, processes, and settings. Because of the fragmented and local nature of American governmental units, our courts have developed in a somewhat irregular fashion. Each has been influenced by political and cultural aspects of its community's history. Although all courts are alike in that they follow the basic patterns of the Anglo-American legal tradition, each is distinctive in the way it is structured to perform particular functions and to deal with certain problems.

Differences aside, courts in the United States have many problems in common. Court congestion is one of them. Governmental and civic groups deplore the fact that defendants in criminal cases often wait in jail for months before they come to trial. Yet the conditions in the criminal courts also point up the reality of the filtering process, the administrative determination of guilt, and the exchange relationships that characterize the system. The additional judges and courtrooms that are demanded will not serve to emphasize

Courthouses come in many shapes and sizes.

due process as long as the system is able to function in a way that is consistent with the needs of the actors within it.

As they say at the ball park, you can't tell the players without a scorecard. Chapter 11 examines the structure of the American court system and looks at the conditions that influence decision making within it. It focuses on the key player—the judge—but it also shows that decisions on guilt or innocence, probation or prison are essentially made collectively by a small group. As you read this chapter, put yourself in the position of each of the courtroom players. Is justice being served?

Structure and management of American courts

Before we can analyze the problems of American criminal courts, we must understand the structure and management of these essential instruments of justice. As chapter 4 emphasized, the United States has a dual court system—one for the federal government and one for each of the state governments. Although the United States Supreme Court oversees both systems and the Constitution protects the rights of defendants in criminal cases, most crime is processed in state systems. Within the state systems, it is the trial courts of limited and general jurisdiction—the judicial workhorses of county and city governments—that deal with most of the criminal business.

American courts are strikingly decentralized. Throughout our history it has been felt that courts should be close to the people and responsive to them. Only in a few relatively small states is the court system completely unified on a statewide basis, centrally administered, and funded by state government. In the rest of the country, the criminal courts operate under the state penal code but they are staffed, managed, and financed by county or city government. Thus local political influences are brought to bear on the courts, local officials determine the resources to be allocated to the judiciary, and there is a lack of coordination among the courts of a given state. This situation leads to overstaffing in some courts while others have tremendous case backlogs, to leniency toward offenders in some courts and severity in others, and to the processing of cases in ways that accord with local practices.

The movement for reform

In 1906 Roscoe Pound, one of the nation's greatest judicial thinkers, delivered a speech to the American Bar Association (ABA) with the memorable title "The Causes of Popular Dissatisfaction with the Administration of Justice."[1] Later referred to as "the spark that kindled the white flame of progress," the speech was a broadly based analysis that struck mainly at the organizational inadequacies of the judicial system.[2] Pound claimed that there were too many courts and, in consequence, duplication and inefficiency; further, there was a great waste of judicial power because of rigid jurisdictional boundaries, poor use of resources, and the frequent granting of new trials.

Calls for the upgrading of the organization and administration of the state courts have continued. What is the malady that affects the courts and what are the proposed remedies? Although a range of symptoms is usually cited, such as insufficient resources and the poor quality of politically appointed judges, the reform literature generally points to the fragmented and decentralized structure of state courts as impeding the effective administration of justice. The remedy most often prescribed: creation of a unified court system. This conventional wisdom generally stipulates four objectives:

1. Elimination of overlapping and conflicting jurisdictional boundaries (of both subject matter and geography).
2. A hierarchical and centralized court structure, with administrative responsibility vested in a chief justice and court of last resort. Its proposed range of authority often includes assignment of judges, promulgation of rules, designation of presiding judges of local trial courts, and general administrative proce-

Roscoe Pound

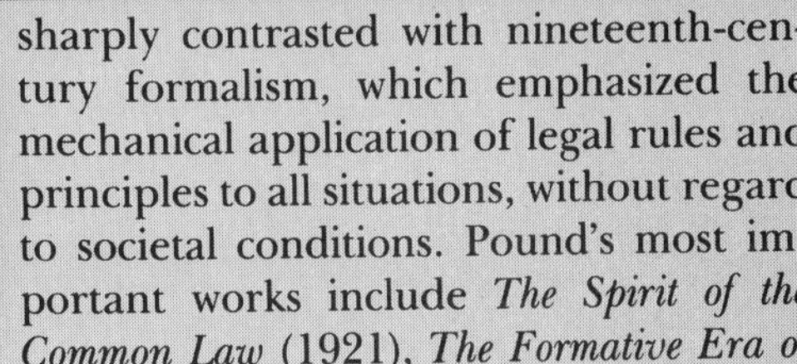

As jurist and educator, Roscoe Pound had a profound influence on American jurisprudence and court reform. Born in Lincoln, Nebraska, he studied botany at the University of Nebraska, then attended Harvard Law School and in 1890 was admitted to the Nebraska bar. From 1916 to 1936 he served as dean of Harvard Law School and retired from that institution as a professor in 1947.

Pound is principally known as the most prominent American exponent of a theory of law known as *sociological jurisprudence,* which asserts that the law must recognize contemporary social conditions, and therefore rules must be adapted to a changing world. This theory sharply contrasted with nineteenth-century formalism, which emphasized the mechanical application of legal rules and principles to all situations, without regard to societal conditions. Pound's most important works include *The Spirit of the Common Law* (1921), *The Formative Era of American Law* (1938), and *Jurisprudence* (1959).

As a court reformer, Pound is remembered for his 1906 speech "The Causes of Popular Dissatisfaction with the Administration of Justice" to the American Bar Association. This speech called attention to the organizational inadequacies of the judicial system and helped to spark reform efforts by the ABA and the American Judicature Society.

dures relating to jury selection, case processing time standards, monitoring techniques, and collection of statistics.
3. Financing of the courts at the state level.
4. A separate personnel system centrally run by a state court administrator covering the full range of personnel functions (recruitment, selection, promotion) and encompassing all employees.

These themes—(1) structure, (2) centralization of administrative authority, (3) funding, and (4) a separate personnel system—have been at the forefront in the movement to reform the state courts. They parallel ideas identified with the Progressive movement of the early part of the twentieth century, which sought to apply business principles to government through emphasis on efficiency, simplicity, unification, coordination, and a distaste for politics.

The court reformers were influential in bringing about changes in certain states and cities, particularly in the West, but they made little headway in the more populous sections of the country, where politics was more entrenched and presumably the need was greatest. In emphasizing structural change, they neglected political realities and were often unable to bring about their proposed programs. When successful, they were often disheartened later to see their efforts scuttled by pressures from the existing judicial bureaucracy. As Geoff Gallas notes, the failure to achieve the objectives of court reform may be laid to the "belief that simple structural and process reforms will solve complex behavioral problems."[3] Where judicial reform has succeeded, its architects have recognized the system's political nature and been able to move the system in the necessary direction.

The structure of state courts

The basic structure and organization of American state courts were borrowed, with some modification, from the English heritage. During the prerevolutionary period, each of the American colonies adapted the English court system to the local customs, religious practices, needs, and nature of its commerce. With the coming of the Revolution, the courts became identified in the popular mind with the royal governors, who had exerted a great influence on judicial operations. Indeed, one of the complaints listed in the Declaration of Independence is that George III had made "judges dependent on his will alone, for the tenure of their offices, and the amount and payment of their salaries." The colonists maintained that the crown's insistence that judges serve at the governor's pleasure rather than during good behavior threatened the impartiality of the courts.

Because of the colonial experience, the judiciary was not very popular, and during the postrevolutionary period efforts were made to ensure that the courts would be responsive to the local community. Legislatures viewed the courts as potential extensions of the governor's power and attempted to prevent the development of a strong, independent judiciary. They created court systems that were decentralized, linked to the local political system, and dependent for resources on the other branches of government.

The growth of commerce and population during the nineteenth century brought new types of disputes requiring judicial attention. Litigation increased and there were more specialized cases. The states and localities responded to this challenge mainly by creating new courts with particular legal or geographical ***jurisdictions.*** Small claims courts, juvenile courts, and family relations courts were added in many states. In the larger cities, more courts of general jurisdiction were added, in part to meet the demands of the increased population and in part to create jobs that could be filled through patronage appointments beneficial to the political machines. In most states these changes produced a confusing structure of multiple courts with varying jurisdictions, overlapping responsibilities, and intercounty differences.

The current situation. The courts of all fifty states are organized into three tiers: ***appellate courts*** (courts of last resort and those with intermediate appellate jurisdiction), ***trial courts of general jurisdiction,*** and ***trial courts of limited jurisdiction.*** Although this basic structure is found throughout the United States, the number of courts, their names, and their specific functions vary widely. Table 11.1 contrasts the court structure of Alaska, a reformed state, with that of Georgia, where the court structure has not been reformed. Both are organized according to the three-tier model, but Georgia has more courts and greater jurisdictional complexity, with two appellate courts and multiple courts of limited jurisdiction.

At the heart of reform efforts is the wish to consolidate and simplify court structures. A simple court structure is appealing because it creates an impression of clarity of purpose and efficiency. It must be recognized, however, that the presence of various courts within one structure provides desirable alternatives. Overlapping jurisdictions may be of benefit to some litigants. Likewise, the existence of courts in many locations means that decisions of appellate courts may conflict with those handed down by trial judges. Without the authority to enforce uniformity, members of the appellate courts have to put up with a fair amount of independence by the trial court judges, which means conflicting judicial policies within the state. Further, judicial decentralization

jurisdiction
The territory or boundaries within which control may be exercised; hence, the legal and geographical range of a court's authority.

appellate court
A court that does not try criminal cases but hears appeals of decisions of lower courts.

trial court of general jurisdiction
A criminal court that has jurisdiction over all offenses, including felonies, and that may in some states also hear appeals.

trial court of limited jurisdiction
A criminal court of which the trial jurisdiction either includes no felonies or is limited to some category of felonies. Such courts usually have jurisdiction over misdemeanor cases and probable-cause hearings in felony cases, and sometimes over felony trials that may result in penalties below a specified limit.

TABLE 11.1 Court structures of Alaska (reformed) and Georgia (unreformed)

Alaska	*Georgia*
Appellate courts	
Supreme Court	Supreme Court
	Court of Appeals
Trial courts of general jurisdiction	
Superior courts	Superior courts
Trial courts of limited jurisdiction	
District courts	Justice of the peace courts
Magistrates' courts	County courts, also known as city courts (Dougherty and Washington counties)
	Probate courts, also known as: courts of ordinary (probate)
	Traffic courts
	Juvenile court
	Magistrates' courts (Clarke and Glynn counties)
	Municipal and civil courts
	Small claims courts
	State courts

Source: U.S. Department of Justice, *National Survey of Court Organization: 1977 Supplement to State Judicial Systems* (Washington, D.C.: Government Printing Office, 1977).

and autonomy make it possible for local courts to become integral parts of the local political systems, thus providing community interest groups with access to judicial decision makers.

Centralization of administrative authority

Who runs the courts? Who is in charge? These questions address not only the issue of authority within the court structure but also the autonomy of the judiciary. In decentralized court systems there is no overall authority to ensure continuity in procedures, to supervise, or to protect the judiciary from encroachment by the legislative and executive branches of government. Contemporary proponents of a unified court system argue that the supreme court of the state as a collectivity, or the chief justice, should be given both policy-making and administrative authority. They believe it to be essential that there be one head of a hierarchical chain of command with the power to assign judges, set rules, and institute systemwide procedures.

Centralized management. The day-to-day administration of a state judiciary necessitates that some person or body handle such matters as assignment of judges, assignment of cases, record keeping, personnel, and financing. Roscoe Pound proposed that supervisory power for a state court system be given to the chief justice. He noted that traditionally the judiciary had never had control over its clerical force, often because such positions were elective or separately appointive. Pound was one of the first to enunciate the need for a court administrator, a professionally trained individual.

Today each of the fifty states has a central court administrator. The office is legislatively created for the most part, and its holders are appointed either by the chief judge of the state or by a committee of the state's highest court. In many states an analogous position exists in the trial courts. During the rush to increase the courts' resources following the rise of crime in the 1960s, a number of academic programs were created to train court administrators; the National Center for State Courts and the Institute for Court Management offer two of the leading programs.

Court management as a professional career has come a long way since 1947, when Chief Justice Arthur Vanderbilt of New Jersey appointed the first administrative director of the courts. The persons occupying this position vary considerably across states: some are judges, others are attorneys who have moved from private practice, and still others are persons trained primarily in public administration. Resistance to court administrators by court staff whose tenure predated the reform has been reported, and many administrators do not have enough power to direct the system as Pound proposed. Some states exhibit continuing competition between the state court administrator and the trial court administrators over the degree of local policy-making autonomy.

Although the movement toward centralized rule making and management continues, experience has shown that the granting of these powers to a supreme court does not necessarily ensure the expected results. In most states the local judges, clerks, and administrators are still able to resist dominance by the centralizing authority. Systems may look unified on an organization chart but be operationally fragmented nevertheless.

State funding

Of all the elements that make up the ideal unified state court system, the method of funding is probably the most influential in determining the extent to which the judiciary will be able to function according to the centralized administration model. Control of the purse strings is a crucial ingredient of power in any organization. Funding involves both the amount of resources that come from the state (as opposed to the local treasury) and the procedure by which the needs of the judiciary are made known to the funding body. It is on this portion of the unified court model that reformers have been most consistent during the past two decades; they have proposed that the state fully fund the courts and that the court administrator, under the direction of the chief justice, prepare for the legislature a budget for the entire system.

In the most extensive study of judicial funding, Carl Baar found that while the state share of funding varied from 11 percent to 100 percent, the court systems of thirty-one states (62 percent) received less than a third of their budget from the state.[4] During fiscal year 1979 almost $3.5 billion was spent on the judiciary by state and local governments: 33 percent by state governments, almost twice the amount spent by local governments.[5] A more striking fact is that the larger a state's population, the lower its percentage of court funding by state government. Thus, as table 11.2 shows, five of the ten largest states (California, Texas, Ohio, Michigan, Massachusetts) are among the fourteen with the lowest percentage of state funding. States smallest in area and population show the highest levels of funding by the central government: Connecticut, Hawaii, Delaware, Rhode Island, Vermont, and New Mexico all provide more than 80 percent.

TABLE 11.2 State court systems, ranked by state share of total state-local judicial expenditures, fiscal year 1976 (percent)

Lowest percentage state funding		*Lower than average state funding*		*Average state funding*		*Highest percentage state funding*	
Arizona	9.4	New Jersey	26.0	Illinois	41.0	New Mexico	82.2
California	11.2	Oregon	26.7	Kansas	43.3	Delaware	86.7
South Carolina	12.6	Wisconsin	27.2	Oklahoma	43.5	Vermont	89.5
Minnesota	14.1	Tennesee	27.2	Virginia	45.8	Rhode Island	96.6
Ohio	14.7	Louisiana	27.8	Nebraska	46.8	Connecticut	99.1
Texas	15.4	North Dakota	28.4			Alaska	99.5
Georgia	17.9	Alabama	28.6	*Higher than average state funding*		Hawaii	100.0
Washington	17.9	New Hampshire	30.1				
Michigan	18.2	Utah	30.8	West Virginia	53.1		
Massachusetts	19.0	Arkansas	30.9	Idaho	53.8		
Nevada	19.3	Iowa	32.2	Maryland	56.4		
Montana	22.7	Florida	33.1	Maine	64.4		
Indiana	23.2	New York	33.2	South Dakota	66.2		
Mississippi	24.1	Missouri	34.9	North Carolina	67.1		
		Wyoming	35.5	Colorado	68.0		
		Kentucky	37.6				
		Pennsylvania	39.3				

Source: U.S. Department of Justice and U.S. Department of Commerce, *Expenditure and Employment Data for the Criminal Justice System: 1976* (Washington, D.C.: Government Printing Office, 1978). Adapted from Carl Baar, *Separate but Subservient* (Lexington, Mass.: Lexington Books, D. C. Heath and Co., 1975) p. 6.

During the past few years there has been a slow but significant move toward increased funding by a number of states. In 1973 the Temporary Commission on the New York State Court System recommended that state government assume full financial responsibility for the courts. Following the passage of legislation in 1976, the state assumed the costs of the New York courts in accordance with a formula based on a gradual decrease of local appropriations. With passage of reforms in July 1978, Massachusetts joined the states now fully funding their courts. Additional efforts in this direction are under way in Michigan, New Jersey, and Pennsylvania. As court costs rise in an increasingly litigious society, local political leaders seem willing to let the state government assume them.

Separate court personnel system

It is logical that the judiciary should have its own personnel system. Without a separate civil service system for judicial employees, a statewide unified court system cannot come into being and the courts are beholden to local political powers. The 1974 ABA Standards Relating to Court Organization recommended a system of position classification, levels of compensation, and procedures for personnel evaluation. Though it suggested that the usual civil service system may be appropriate for some jurisdictions, the ABA warned that some of its aspects, particularly rigid seniority arrangements and elaborate dismissal procedures, are burdensome and inefficient.

Identifying the employees of the court is not so simple an undertaking as it may seem. There are many persons, such as sheriffs, probation officers, and social workers, whose work is closely tied to the judicial process but who report to other officials and agencies. With the growth of the unified court concept, especially with regard to state funding, separate personnel rules for the judicial branch have been developed in a number of states. In other states, however, court employees are still subject to the rules that cover all public workers.

Trend toward unified court systems

In recent years, deficiencies in the administration of justice have received much attention from state and federal governments. The rise in crime and the caseload problems of the courts have led to increased funding, particularly from the federal government, as a means of improving the administration of justice. Judicial expenditures in the states almost doubled between 1971 and 1976. Several populous states have moved toward a unified court system, and employment in state and local courts has increased.

While these facts may portend eventual realization of the reformers' dream, questions are now being raised about the impact of the unified court system. Gallas argues that "the conventional wisdom of centralized management of state court systems is out of date both in fact and theory."[6] He says, as do other commentators, that the traditional model does not deal adequately with the reality of administration because it is based on a closed-system model, which assumes that formal structures determine behavior. Many fear that the emphasis on centralization and unity through structural change neglects the need for better management of the courts. A tidy organization chart in no way reflects either a more efficient or more equitable administration of justice.

To be a judge

Of the many actors in the criminal justice process, judges are perceived to hold the greatest amount of leverage and influence over the system. Decisions of the police, defense attorneys, and prosecutor are greatly affected by their rulings and sentencing practices. Although we tend to think of judges primarily in connection with trials, their work is much more varied. They are a continuous presence throughout the activities leading to the disposition of each case. Many portions of a judge's work—signing warrants, fixing bail, arraigning defendants, accepting guilty pleas, scheduling cases—fall outside the formal trial process.

More than any other person in the system, the judge is expected to *embody* justice, thereby ensuring that the right to due process is respected and that the defendant is fairly treated. The black robes and gavel symbolize the impartiality we expect from our courts. The judge is supposed to act within and outside the courthouse according to a well-defined role designed to prevent involvement in anything that may bring the judiciary into disrepute. Yet such are the pressures of today's justice system that the ideals of the judge's position have often been relegated to a back seat while the need to dispose of cases speedily takes priority.

Judges of the criminal courts have socioeconomic characteristics very different from those of judges in the upper appellate courts, and they operate in a different organizational environment. One national survey of trial judges revealed that they were overwhelmingly white and male, had an average age of 53.4 years, and came from families connected to the local legal-political community. A majority (53.8 percent) had been in private legal practice, while 24 percent became trial judges after serving in lower courts—municipal, juvenile, or probate.[7]

In most cities, criminal court judges occupy the lowest place in the judicial hierarchy. Lawyers and citizens alike fail to accord them the prestige that is part of the mystique usually surrounding members of the bench. Even their peers who hear civil cases may look down on them. As in other professional relationships, the status of criminal trial judges may be linked to the status of the defendants. The judges are so close to the type of client they serve and work under such unpleasant conditions that, while they may retain some of the charisma of the judiciary, their reputation becomes tarnished and somewhat mundane.

Functions of the judge

With so much public discussion about case backlogs in the criminal courts, many citizens who have visited the local courtroom have been surprised to find the bench empty, the judge and staff absent. As figure 11.1 indicates, a study of the criminal courts in New York City revealed that, on the average, judges were on the bench only three hours and three minutes a day. Although this period is shorter than that prevailing in most parts of the country, it does highlight questions about the work and function of the criminal court judge. If the judge is on the bench less than half a workday, how does he or she spend the rest of it? What *do* judges do?

We tend to think that the judge's functions are primarily concerned with

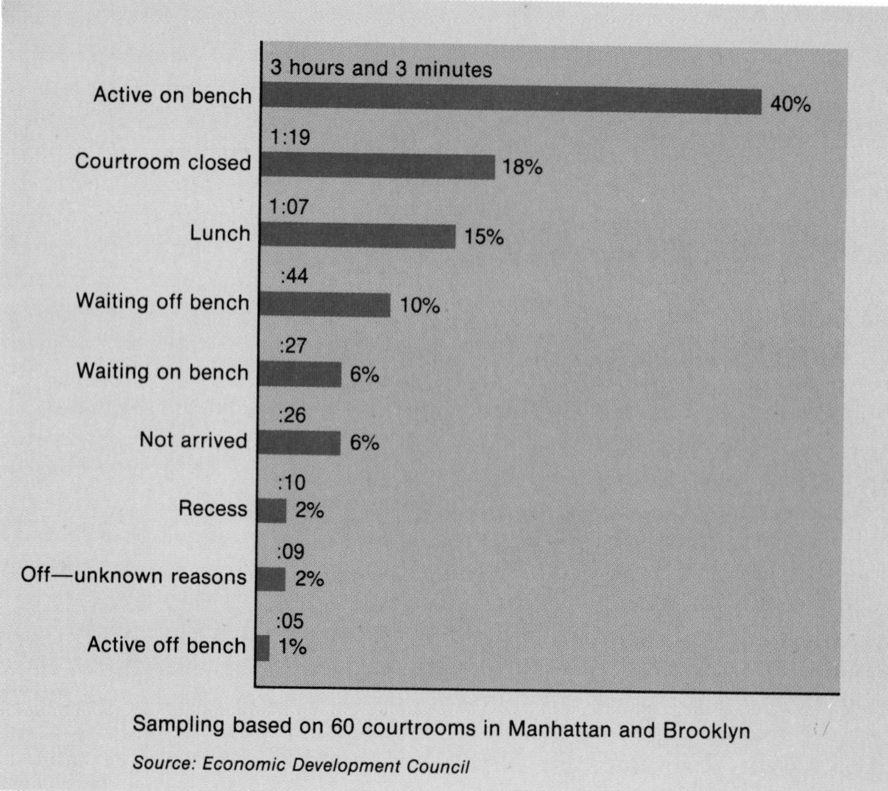

FIGURE 11.1
How a judge spends a seven-and-a-half-hour day

Black Judges

What special ingredient do the background and experience of a black judge add to judicial decision making? Judge George W. Crockett, Jr., who presides over Detroit's Recorder's Court, gives his perception:

We who are products of the American common law are always extolling the virtue of a common law system and its ability to adapt to the growing needs of the people. In the past, white judges have really made the common law adaptable to what they conceive to be the desires of the American people. We black judges have to take a page from that book. If the common law is so adaptable, let's get down to books and find the remedies, and apply them to the old evils that have plagued the poor and the underprivileged in our society for so long. The answers are there. The special role of the black judge is to see what justice requires and then go to the books and get the remedies to apply to it. Most people assume that the law is something that is clear cut, it's written out, it's black and white; it's not so. Most of the law is a matter of discretion. What is discretion? Discretion is whatever the judge thinks it is as long as he can give a sound reason for it. A judge is a product of his own experiences, of his own history, of the people from whom he came. So a black judge's exercise of discretion is not going to be necessarily the same as that of a white judge. But as long as it is reason, and the law made by precedent established by white people, that discretion stands.

Source: George W. Crockett, Jr., "The Role of the Black Judge," *Journal of Public Law* 20 (1971): 398–399. Reprinted by permission of the *Journal of Public Law* of the Emory University School of Law.

presiding at trials, but the work of most judges extends to all parts of the judicial process. Defendants see a judge whenever decisions about their future are being made: when bail is set, when pretrial motions are made, when pleas of guilty are accepted, when a trial is conducted, when sentence is pronounced, and when appeals are entered. But in addition to responsibilities directly related to the processing of defendants, judges have functions that are performed outside the courtroom and that are related to the administration of the judicial system. Judges are adjudicators, negotiators, and administrators, as figure 11.2 makes clear.

Adjudicator. In a criminal justice system based on the ideals of due process and the adversary system, judges must play a role of neutrality between the prosecution and the defense. They must apply the law to ensure that the rights of the accused are upheld as decisions are made concerning detention, plea, trial, and sentence. In discharging these responsibilities, judges are given a certain amount of discretion—for example, in setting the level of bail—but they must also conduct the proceedings according to law. Judges are the final arbiters of the law in the cases before them unless, on appeal, they are overruled by a higher court. If a nonjury trial is held, the judge not only rules on the issues of law but decides issues of fact and ultimately determines the defendant's guilt or innocence. Judges may exercise discretion in the sentencing of convicted persons. If a felony has been committed, most states require that the judge be given a report of a presentence investigation conducted by a probation officer to help in the determination of the most appropriate penalty.

Negotiator. Much of the criminal justice process is carried out through

FIGURE 11.2
Typical actions of a trial court judge in processing a felony case

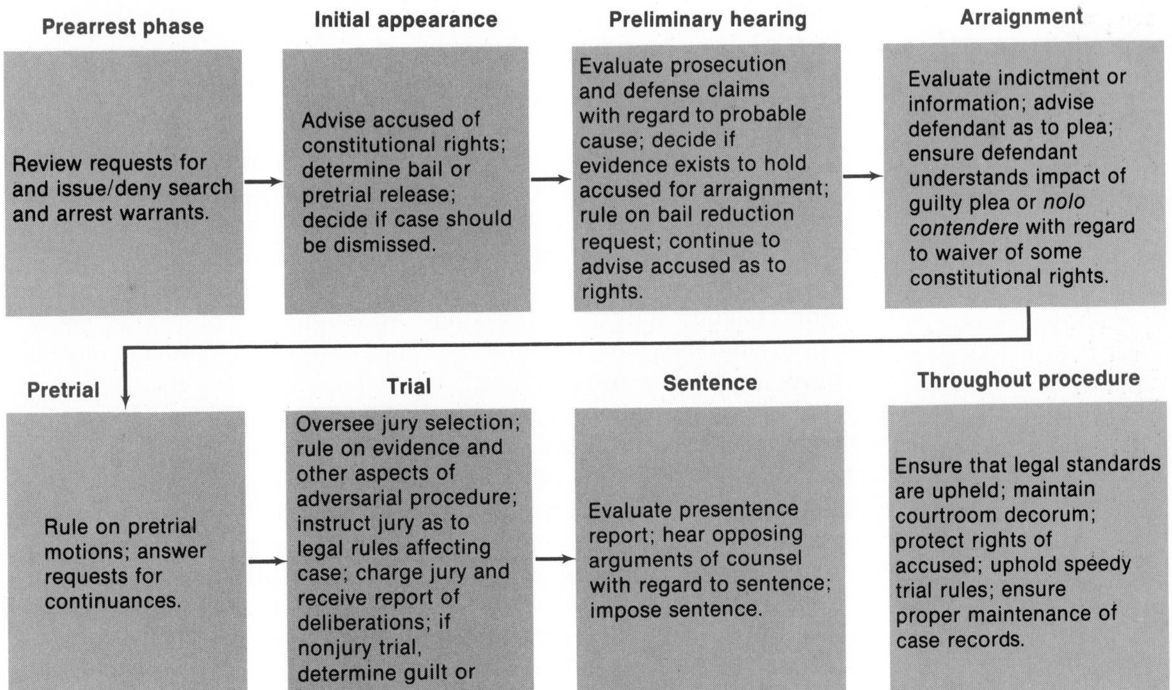

negotiation in the privacy of areas shielded from public view. Judges spend much of their time in their chambers talking with prosecutors and defense attorneys and often encourage the litigants to compromise or to agree to conduct proceedings in a specific manner. Although judicial ethics generally prohibit judges from directly discussing a pending case with the victims, witnesses, defendants, and arresting officers, members of the bench often are called on to mediate disputes that have not yet escalated to a formal trial. In lower misdemeanor courts, the remarks of the judge from the bench often take the form of advice to the disputants rather than formal points of law. It is in the plea bargaining process that many judges act as negotiators. Although there is a new openness toward this practice, the court rules in seven states and in the federal jurisdiction prohibit judicial participation in these discussions. In other states, case law and dicta place additional restraints on the role that judges may play in plea bargaining.

Administrator. A seldom recognized function of most judges is the administration of the courthouse. In urban areas a professional court administrator may direct the personnel who are assigned to record keeping, case scheduling, and the many logistical operations that keep a system functioning. Even in cities, however, judges are responsible for the administration of their own courtroom and staff. In rural areas, the administrative responsibilities of judges may be more burdensome because professional court administrators are not usually employed. In discharging these duties, judges must be concerned not only with the administration of the judicial process itself but with the operation of the courthouse and with its personnel. Budgeting, labor relations, and the maintenance of the physical plant may all come under their supervision. As administrator, the judge is required to maintain contact with such nonjudicial political actors as county commissioners, legislators, and members of the state executive bureaucracy.

Judicial selection

The quality of justice depends to a great extent on the quality of those who dispense it. As the American jurist Benjamin Cardozo once said, "in the long run, there is no guarantee of justice except the personality of the judge."[8] Because government has been given the power to deprive a citizen of his or her liberty, good judges are essential. Because society wants protection from wrongdoers, good judges are essential. Although the connection between these needs and the character and experience of those appointed to our highest courts has long been recognized, less interest has been focused on trial judges of the criminal courts. Yet it is in the lower courts that citizens most often have contact with the judiciary, and the public's impression of the criminal justice system is shaped to a great extent by the trial judge's behavior in the courtroom. When a judge is rude or inconsiderate or allows the courtroom to become a noisy, crowded dispensary of rapid-fire justice, public confidence in the fairness and effectiveness of the criminal justice process is diminished.

All judges are addressed as "Your Honor," and we deferentially stand whenever they enter or leave the courtroom, yet too often they are chosen in the smoke-filled political clubhouse for reasons that have very little to do with either their legal qualifications or their judicial temperament. The variety of

Close-up: The Judge of Criminal Assignment: Time Management and the Flow of a Typical Day

A typical day for the judge of criminal assignment began around 9:00 A.M., when the judge arrived in chambers, read his mail, and skimmed the day's case files. The call of criminal cases generally started soon after but might be delayed if the judge were in conference with lawyers, or if lawyers were in conference with each other. More times than not, the judge and the court were forced to wait while lawyers concluded bargains, talked with clients, or hurried from an appearance in another courtroom. In many courts the call itself tended to be a rather chaotic process, with attorneys coming in and out of court, whispered plea negotiations continuing throughout the room (and sometimes back in chambers), and a variety of people approaching the clerk's desk (usually immediately adjacent to the bench) for one reason or another. In most instances, the criminal call not only served an attendance-taking function but afforded a review of the status of each case. The call could also assume some legal importance as defense lawyers jockeyed for advantageous (i.e., later) trial dates, while the judge used the threat of immediate trial as his own form of bargaining leverage. Often, short hearings, arraignments, the taking of guilty pleas, sentencings, and probation violations were disposed of in the criminal call.

After the completion of the call (or the first round), the judge might attend to some minor administrative matters, socialize with attorneys or court personnel, take a coffee break, or participate in case-related discussions with attorneys. Then, the judge might begin formal court proceedings—a motions hearing, a bench trial, or (most likely) a jury trial. These proceedings would continue for the rest of the morning, with adjournment around noon for a lunch break. While some judges gulped sandwiches at their desks and worked through lunch, most criminal judges lunched with court or law enforcement personnel, lawyer acquaintances, former political associates, or other judges. Occasionally judges attended bar luncheons, spoke at civic meetings, or participated in more specialized meetings such as judicial seminars, advisory board meetings of a halfway house, and the like. Frequently lunch conversations included mention of past and current cases, and from time to time some judicial business of a minor nature was transacted (usually pertaining to scheduling). However, politics, financial affairs, and travel plans were also common topics of conversation.

Returning to chambers somewhere between one hour and ninety minutes later, the judge might meet with some lawyers, catch up on correspondence, sign orders, or glance through the "advance sheets" (early publication of recent appellate cases) before the afternoon court session. After the court was reconvened, unfinished matters of the morning might again be taken up, whether continuation of the call or of a bench or jury trial. Jury proceedings were planned to begin and end for juror convenience; but while there might be a half-hour comfort break during the afternoon, many judges preferred to finish as much of the scheduled proceedings as possible before leaving for the day. Departure ranged anywhere from 3:00 to 6:00 P.M. or later, though the majority probably left sometime around 4:30 or so. The judge might attend to some minor matters after adjourning court or go to a meeting of the judiciary before leaving the building, but such activities were generally infrequent and not very lengthy. Most of the criminal judges whom we observed did not take case files or journals home, though some may have read the latter at home.

Source: Reprinted with permission of The Free Press, a Division of Macmillan Publishing Co., Inc., from J. P. Ryan, A. Ashman, B. D. Sales, and S. Shane-Dubow, *American Trial Judges* (The American Judicature Society, 1980), pp. 18–19.

processes by which judges are selected may reflect confusion about their work and about the justice system as a force in society. On the one hand, there is a strong reform movement to place men and women of quality on the bench. Such groups as the American Judicature Society have labored to create procedures that will take the selection of judges "out of politics," emphasizing instead their legal and scholarly capacities. Reformers argue that judges should be experts and believe that selection on a nonpolitical basis will produce higher quality, more efficient, more independent, and consequently more impartial and just members of the judiciary.

In opposition are those who argue that in a democracy the voters should elect the people charged with carrying out public policies, including judges. The attorney who earned a degree at a less prestigious law school and whose general practice has focused on the representation of people rather than of corporations, they contend, would have a better sense of the justice to be meted out in the lower criminal courts than the Harvard graduate who can discuss the philosophy behind the elements of a fair trial but may be ill equipped to handle the steady stream of human problems confronting the judges of the nation.

nonpartisan election An election in which candidates who are not endorsed by political parties are presented to the voters for selection.

partisan election An election in which candidates endorsed by political parties are presented to the voters for selection.

Methods of selection. The methods used to select judges have greatly concerned advocates of reform. The states and the federal government use essentially six methods to select trial court judges: appointment by the executive, selection by the legislative body, appointment by other judges, merit selection, ***nonpartisan election,*** and ***partisan election.*** Table 11.3 shows the methods used in each of the states. Throughout all the arguments advanced in support of one method or another runs a persistent concern about the desired qualities in a judge and the assumption that the type of selection process will lead to a particular judicial style. On the one hand is the view that judges should be concerned only with the law; on the other, the view that they must feel the pulse of the people in order to render justice. Each approach heightens opportunities for certain people and interests and diminishes them for others.

Judges are popularly elected in more than half the states. Selection by the electorate seems to go against the traditional notion that the function of the judge is to "find the law," but choice by the community has long been part of the American tradition. Campaigns for judgeships, however, are generally low-keyed, low-visibility contests marked by little controversy: usually only a small portion of the voters participate, judicial positions are not prominent on the ballot, candidates are constrained by ethical considerations from discussing issues, and public attention is centered on executive and legislative races. The situation was well summarized by Judge Samuel Rosenman of New York:

> I learned at first hand what it meant for a judicial candidate to have to seek votes in political clubhouses, to ask for support of political district leaders, to receive financial contributions for his campaign from lawyers and others, and to make nonpolitical speeches about his own qualifications to audiences who could not care less—audiences who had little interest in any of the judicial candidates, of whom they had never heard, and whom they would never remember.[9]

Although popular election of judges may be an important part of our political heritage, these elections rarely capture the voters' notice.

TABLE 11.3 Methods used by states for interim appointments of trial judges, by initial selection method used

Partisan election		*Nonpartisan election*		*Gubernatorial selection*	
State	**Interim appointment**	**State**	**Interim appointment**	**State**	**Interim appointment**
Alabama	G or M	California	G	Connecticut	G
Arkansas	G	Florida	M	Delaware	G-M
Georgia	G-M	Idaho	M	Hawaii	G
Illinois	SC	Kentucky	M	Maine	G
Louisiana	SC[a]	Maryland	G-M	Massachusetts	G-M
Mississippi	G	Michigan	G	New Hampshire	G
New Mexico	G	Minnesota	G	New Jersey	G
New York	G-M	Montana	M	Rhode Island	G
North Carolina	G-M	Nevada	M		
Pennsylvania	G-M	North Dakota	M		
Tennessee	G	Ohio	G		
Texas	G	Oklahoma	G-M		
West Virginia	G	Oregon	G		
		South Dakota	G-M		
		Washington	G		
		Wisconsin	G		

Merit system		*Legislative selection*		*Hybrid selection*	
State	**Interim appointment**	**State**	**Interim appointment**	**State**	**Interim appointment**
Alaska	M	South Carolina	G or LS[b]	Indiana[c]	G
Colorado	M	Virginia	G	Kansas[c]	G
District of Columbia	M			Missouri[c]	G or M
Iowa	M			Arizona[d]	G
Nebraska	M				
Utah	M				
Vermont	M				
Wyoming	M				

Note: G = gubernatorial appointment; G-M = gubernatorial appointment, but merit system currently in effect by executive order; G or M = gubernatorial appointment or merit, depending on locale; SC = state supreme court appointment; LS = legislative selection.

[a] In Louisiana the supreme court fills vacancies until an election is called by the governor, but the interim appointee is ineligible to run in the election.

[b] In South Carolina, if the unexpired term is less than one year, the governor appoints; if more than one year, the legislature selects.

[c] Partisan or merit, depending on locale.

[d] Nonpartisan or merit, depending on locale.

Source: Adapted with permission of The Free Press, a Division of Macmillan Publishing Co., Inc., from J. P. Ryan, A. Ashman, B. D. Sales, and S. Shane-Dubow, *American Trial Judges* (The American Judicature Society, 1980), p. 123. Copyright © 1980 by The American Judicature Society.

The selection of judges is complicated by the regular occurrence of vacancies owing to deaths and retirements. In most states, the governor has the power to fill these judicial posts, and the person appointed normally wins a full term in the next election. In California, for example, although nonpartisan election is the formal selection system, 88 percent of the trial court judges were initially selected by the governor to fill a vacancy. One study has shown that in states where nonpartisan elections are held, only 43 percent of the judges initially assumed the bench following election,[10] a finding that indicates the importance of political connections in obtaining the position.

In many cities judgeships provide much of the fuel for the party machine. Because of the honors and material rewards that may be gained from a place on the bench, parties are able to secure the energy and money of attorneys who seek a judgeship as the capstone of their career. In addition, a certain amount of courthouse patronage may be involved because clerks, bailiffs, and

Missouri merit selection plan
A reform plan by which judges are nominated by a committee and appointed by the governor for a given time period. When the term expires, the voters are asked to signify their approval or disapproval of the judge for a succeeding term. If the judge is disapproved, the committee nominates a successor for the governor's appointment.

secretaries—all jobs that may be filled by active party workers—are appointed by the judge.

The ***Missouri Plan of merit selection,*** combining appointment and election, was first instituted in 1940 and has now spread to eight states. When a vacancy occurs, a nominating commission of citizens and attorneys for the empty bench sends the governor the names of three candidates from among whom the replacement is selected. After one year, a referendum is held to determine the judge's retention. The voter is asked, "Shall Judge *X* remain in office?" With a majority vote, the judge serves out the term and can then come before the citizens on another ballot. This plan has been backed by such groups as the American Bar Association and the American Judicature Society. Designed to remove partisan politics from the judiciary, it is also supposed to have the advantage of giving the electorate an opportunity to unseat judges.

Despite the impressive support of bar groups, the Missouri Plan has not gone unchallenged. Many lawyers regard it as a system favoring "bluebloods" (high-status attorneys with ties to corporations) to the detriment of the "little guy." One study has shown that party politics has merely been replaced by bar politics. Under the Missouri Plan, membership on the nominating commissions is a key to influence within the process. In both Kansas City and St. Louis, seats are competed for by rival organizations of attorneys representing the basic plaintiff–defendant cleavage in the profession—that is, those lawyers who are primarily counsel for the banks, utilities, and insurance companies are "defendant's lawyers," and those whose clients are primarily persons who sue such companies are "plaintiff's lawyers." Thus their choices reflect

How to Become a Judge

When interviewed by a *Chicago Tribune* reporter, Cook County Circuit Court Judge Herbert R. Friedlund, aged 63, gave a classic account of the role of politics in judicial selection. In 1956 Friedlund ran for county clerk as a Republican against Democrat Edward Barrett, a close associate of Mayor Richard J. Daley.

"You see, all the newspapers predicted that Eddie Barrett would beat me by 500,000 votes in the county clerk's race," Friedlund explained. "Well, he won by only 147,000 votes and I got a million votes.

"Later on, Barrett said to Mayor Daley, 'Any guy that can get a million votes against me should be on my side.' And Daley said that he was right, anybody that could do that should be on his side. So, when 1960 came along, he asked me if I wanted to be a Democrat. I said I did."

Then came the crucial conversation with Daley that would lead to a seat on the bench. Friedlund recalls it this way:

Daley: "What do you want?"
Friedlund: "I'd like a judgeship."
Daley: "You do good work for us and you will be a judge. I think you should be one. I think you're qualified for it. Anyone who can poll a million votes against Eddie Barrett deserves to be on the bench if he wants to."
Friedlund: "That's my ambition."
Daley: "I'll back you."

"And the Mayor stuck by that," said Friedlund. "He was the only politician who ever kept his promise to me."

Source: *Chicago Tribune,* 17 May 1971. Reprinted courtesy of the *Chicago Tribune.*

the social status, political affiliations, and types of practice within the bar. "The stakes of these elections for lawyers relate both to the perceived policy 'payoffs' in terms of judges' rulings that affect their clients' economic interests and to symbolic 'payoffs' for the contending bar groups involving matters of prestige and ideology."[11]

Output of selection methods. What are the dynamics and consequences of using one selection method over another? Does each have class implications, as some believe, so that judges of only a certain social background reach the bench? Do some methods favor the choice of politically oriented judges as opposed to legally oriented judges? If each method has built-in biases, do these biases find their way into judges' decisions? Does one method elevate judges who sentence lawbreakers more leniently than judges chosen by a different method?

Martin Levin's comparison of the criminal courts of Pittsburgh and Minneapolis is the major investigation of the relationship between selection methods and judicial decisions. He singled out those two cities because of major differences in their political systems and methods of judicial selection, and consequent differences in judges. In Pittsburgh, judges are chosen through the highly politicized environment of a city controlled by the Democratic machine: "Public and party offices are filled by party professionals whose career patterns are hierarchical and regularized. They patiently 'wait in line' because of the party's needs to maintain ethnic and religious 'balance' even on a judicial ticket."[12] Partisan politics is so much a part of the culture of that city that the public accepts the idea that the courts should be staffed by party workers; the bar association plays a very limited role in judicial selection. There has been little enthusiasm for efforts to reform the selection process.

Minneapolis has a system that is formally nonpartisan. The parties have almost no place in the selection of judges, but the bar association is influential. Before a judicial election, the Minneapolis Bar Association polls its members and publicizes the results. The winner in this straw vote among lawyers almost always wins in the general election. When vacancies occur, Minnesota governors have traditionally appointed judges according to the preference of the attorneys. Out of the Minneapolis system come judicial candidates who are usually members of large, business-oriented law firms and who have not been active in partisan politics.

The differing selection methods and political settings of these two cities produce judges with opposing judicial philosophies and, as a result, contrasting sentencing decisions in the criminal courts. In general, judges in Pittsburgh are more lenient than those in Minneapolis. Not only do white and black defendants receive more sentences of probation and shorter terms of incarceration in Pittsburgh, but the pattern is maintained when the defendants' prior records, pleas, and ages are held constant. The relationship between selection method and judicial philosophy holds in regard to all nine offenses analyzed. A portion of Levin's findings, illustrated in table 11.4, demonstrates this relationship. Among white defendants with prior records, the percentage of those convicted who received probation rather than incarceration was higher in Pittsburgh than in Minneapolis.

This analysis suggests that Minneapolis judges approximate a model of judicial decision making that emphasizes the facts developed through the adversary system. In addition, they stress the need to maintain an emotional distance from the defendant and to affirm the importance of procedures. They maintain an image of detached objectivity and exercise little effort to individualize justice. As Judge Edwards told the interviewer, "If the crime involves violence—like robbery or rape—then the defendant is a danger to society, and I won't place him on probation." Typically the Minneapolis judge is more concerned with the legal requirements of "the law," conceived as an abstract ideal, than with producing "just" settlements of individual cases. Judge Slovack noted: "There are only a few situations in which I will give a fellow extra consideration. I had one in here on burglary and his attorney made a very emotional plea about the fellow's wife going blind and that he had to raise some money to help her. So I gave him probation."[13]

By contrast, Pittsburgh judges approximate a model of administrative decision making that emphasizes the exercise of discretion in order to reach a decision that seems a solution that is "just" even though it may be at variance with the formal rules. Decisions are made on the kind of evidence on which reasonable people usually base day-to-day choices. In this case, the evidence is frequently gathered by the judges' own investigation and colored by their perspective. They feel that they must remain in touch with the real world in order to make just decisions. Thus the Pittsburgh courts are run informally so that personal and individualistic aspects of cases may be considered. Rather than emphasizing the written law, judges place greater stress on practical value judgments. The comments of Judge Bloom relay this approach: "A judge should feel a kinship with the people that come into criminal court. Through my thirty years of active political work I worked with Negroes and other poor persons, and I developed a kinship with them and an awareness of their problems."[14]

The background of judges and the method of their selection seem to exert strong influence on their decisions. An elimination process may operate so that only certain types of persons who have had certain kinds of experiences are available for selection in each judicial system. Levin believes that any relationship between judges' background and their decisions is indirect. What is crucial is the variable of the city's political culture and its influence on judicial selection methods.

The courtroom: how it functions

The usual image of the courtroom stresses the individuality, aloofness, and loneliness of the judge, sitting in robed splendor above the battle to control the actors before the bench. The law emphasizes the crucial role of the judge: within hours after arrest, accused persons shall be brought before a judge and informed of their rights. From that moment until final disposition of the case, accused persons face a judge whenever decisions affecting their future are made: bail, arraignment, preliminary hearing, pleading, trial, and sentencing. Because the courtroom trial is primarily a process of fact finding, judges function as lawgivers. They interpret legal precedents and apply them to the specific circumstances of the case. They are believed to be isolated from the social context of the courtroom participants and to base their decisions on their own interpretation of the law after thoughtful consideration of the issues.

TABLE 11.4 Percentage and number of white defendants with prior records receiving probation, Pittsburgh and Minneapolis, by charge

	Burglary	*Grand larceny*	*Aggravated assault*	*Aggravated robbery*	*Simple robbery*	*Indecent assault*	*Aggravated forgery*	*Nonsufficient funds*	*Possession of narcotics*
Pittsburgh									
Percent	59.4%	62.1%	47.4%	26.1%	33.3%	72.4%	54.6%	56.2%	77.8%
Number	227	103	19	23	21	47	11	16	9
Minneapolis									
Percent	22.0%	34.8%	15.4%	2.8%	27.8%	28.6%	25.5%	35.7%	55.6%
Number	159	69	13	36	18	28	106	70	9

Source: Martin A. Levin, "Urban Politics and Policy Outcomes: The Criminal Courts," in *Criminal Justice: Law and Politics,* ed. George F. Cole (Monterey, Calif.: Brooks/Cole, 1972), p. 335.

Like patrol officers, lower court judges have many of the attributes of street-level bureaucrats. They are able to exercise discretion in the disposition of summary offenses without the constant supervision of a higher court, and they have wide latitude in fixing sentences. Although judges are popularly portrayed as forced to decide complex legal issues, in reality their courtroom tasks are routine. Because of the unending flow of cases, they operate with assembly-line precision, and, like workers on an assembly line, many judges soon tire of the repetition. Bored judges paying little attention to the arguments of the lawyers before them can often be observed in the courtroom.

Judges may feel threatened by the gap between the due process values they have sworn to uphold and the reality of administrative decision making. They may be concerned that the legal rules do not furnish adequate guidelines for their behavior. They must depend to a great extent on exchange relationships to maintain their position in the system and to meet the needs of a variety of actors and publics. Negotiations and efforts to minimize the adversarial nature of the trial are undertaken to ensure that all will benefit. The exchange relationships of the pretrial period continue as the defendant is brought before the court. Judges must play their part according to the script and be consistent in their sentencing practices. Doing so does not mean that they will enter directly into negotiations, but they may stop a trial and call the attorneys to the bench to ask, "Can't you get together on this?" Even for the few defendants who choose a trial by jury, the values of bargain justice may work a special twist: those found guilty may receive harsher sentences for not following the norms of the system and pleading guilty.

The courtroom workgroup

The traditional picture of the courtroom emphasizes adversarial attitudes, but a more realistic picture, emphasizing the major actors' continuing interaction and common goals, would reveal many of the collective characteristics associated with a ***workgroup.*** Some scholars see the courtroom as analogous to a formal bureaucracy in which the judge uses his or her authority to direct the staff, defense attorneys, and prosecutors so that the overriding task—disposition of cases—proceeds according to the law. Others see the courtroom in terms of an assembly line, in which cases flow past and the actors dispense justice in a mechanical fashion. Both conceptions have been criticized. It has been argued that the courtroom does not function according to the bureaucratic model because it lacks a hierarchical authority structure, well-defined

workgroup
A collectivity of individuals who interact in the workplace on a continuing basis, share goals, develop norms in regard to the way activities should be carried out, and eventually establish a network of roles that serves to differentiate this group from others.

Since they must interact constantly, courtroom participants form a workgroup.

rules, and positionally defined tasks. Likewise, although some may view the courtroom as an assembly line, studies have shown that consideration *is* given to individual cases, that the actors recognize their interdependence, and that it would not be possible to computerize the courtroom.

Merely placing the major actors in the courtroom does not instantly make them into a workgroup. Such a collectivity—judge, prosecutor, defense attorney, defendant, and others—might be called a ***grouping,*** a conglomerate of persons. It is only when the following conditions are met that a workgroup exists:

grouping
A collectivity of individuals who interact in the workplace but because of shifting membership do not develop into a workgroup.

1. There must be *interaction* of the members.
2. The members share (that is, have the same attitudes about) one or more *motives* or *goals* that determine the direction in which the group will move.
3. The members develop a set of norms that determine the boundaries within which interpersonal relations may be established and activity carried out.
4. If interaction continues, a set of roles becomes stabilized and the group differentiates itself from other groups.
5. A network of interpersonal relationships develops on the basis of the members' likes and dislikes for one another.[15]

The degree to which these conditions is met distinguishes a workgroup from a grouping. We might think of this as a continuum, as illustrated in figure 11.3.

Given this conceptual framework, research might place different sets of courtroom actors at different points on the continuum. For example, a rotation of judges in the courtroom may limit the opportunity to develop workgroup norms and roles. Although the same prosecutors and defense attorneys

FIGURE 11.3
The courtroom social system as a continuum

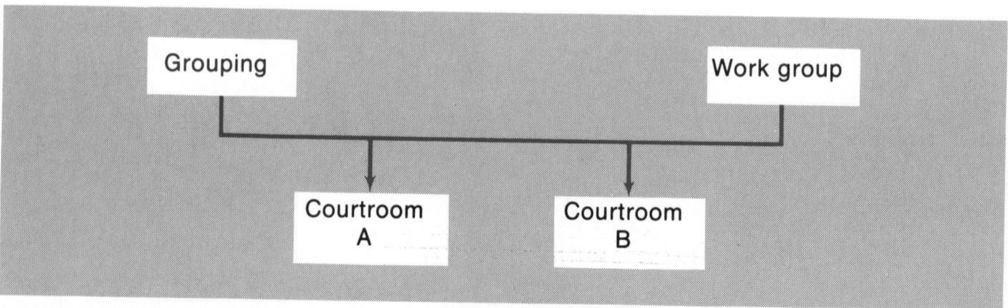

may be present every day, bringing in a new judge, perhaps on a weekly basis, will require them to learn and accommodate to the various special ways that the judges on the circuit expect the proceedings to be run. The position of this set of courtroom actors at point *A* on the continuum indicates that there is some basis for shared norms and role stability because some of the actors are regularly present but that there is enough interruption in this social network to keep strong relationships from developing. Cases proceed more formally, with less reliance on agreed-upon routines, than with a workgroup that has a well-developed pattern of interactions.

Alternatively, if the same actors are in the courtroom on a continuing basis, we may expect that, through interaction, the cooperative relationships among the judge, prosecutor, and defense attorney, along with those of the supporting cast (clerk, reporter, bailiff), will shape the manner in which decisions are made. Thus the defendant, a person from outside the workgroup, will confront "an organized network of relationships, in which each person who acts on his case is reacting to or anticipating the actions of others."[16] Through cooperation it is possible for each member to achieve individual goals as well as for the group to achieve its collective goals.

Although norms and goals are shared, each member of the courtroom workgroup occupies a specialized position and is expected to fit into the socially accepted definition of that status. Because the occupant of each position has specific rights and duties, there is no exchange of roles. When a lawyer moves from the public defender's office to the prosecutor's and ultimately to the bench, each status mandates a different role in the courtroom workgroup. Because each actor is expected to conform to certain role prescriptions, there can be a high degree of stability in the interpersonal relations among members: each member can become proficient at the work routines associated with his or her role, and the group can develop stable expectations about the actions of the members. Thus the business of the courtroom proceeds in a regularized, informal manner, with many understandings among the members that are never recorded but that ease much of the work.

In addition to sharing norms with the other members of the courtroom group, each actor represents a sponsoring organization and must fulfill its expectations when in the courtroom.[17] Workgroup members come from several distinct organizations. One organization, loosely called the court, sends judges; the prosecuting attorney's office sends assistant prosecutors; the public defender's office sends counsel for indigents. Sponsoring organizations determine and provide the resources for the courtroom workgroup and—perhaps more important—they attempt to regulate the behavior of their representatives in the courtroom. Policies of a particular sponsoring organization may stipulate rules to be followed, may encourage or discourage plea bargaining, or may insist that police evidence conform strictly to formal requirements. Thus the judge, prosecutor, or public defender must meet the needs and goals of the workgroup while at the same time satisfying superiors in the sponsoring organization. The degree to which the chief judge, prosecuting attorney, or chief public defender oversees the work of the representative greatly influences the degree to which the courtroom member can adjust his or her practices to meet the workgroup's goals.

Finally, the courtroom actors must keep in mind those others with whom they have ties. Prosecutors must not endanger their relationships with the police; defense attorneys know that the accused persons and their families expect a defense; judges must be alert to reactions to their decisions on the part of the news media as well as of members of higher appellate courts. These pressures may have two effects. First, they may require that the actors give "performances" to satisfy their clients and that the dramatizations in turn have the support of other members of the courtroom cast. Second, they may bolster the shared norms of the group—that is, the secrets of stage technique must be shielded from the audience's view—with the effect that cohesion is increased.

Playing supporting roles in the courtroom drama, the judge's staff has access to vast amounts of confidential information. This resource, as well as their access to the judge, may be used to enhance their own power within the group. Lower court judges, because they are often ill equipped to handle the decision-making and administrative routine, must rely heavily on the know-how of their staff of bureaucrats. New judges are "broken in" by the clerks and other civil service workers, who socialize them in terms of the practical side of the organizational features, goals, and requirements. Regardless of their own preferences, judges soon learn to accept and adapt to the routines and rituals preferred by their socializers. Judges who are unwilling to conform to the needs of the bureaucracy soon become quite frustrated.

Physical setting

The work site of the courtroom group strengthens the interaction patterns of its members and separates them from their clientele groups. The physical surroundings separate the individual courtroom from other social spaces so that communications with those outside the group are limited. Opportunities for social interaction occur during recesses, but the irregularity of these breaks means that refreshment and conversation are shared with other members of the group, not with members of other courtroom teams working in adjoining space.

The low visibility of courtroom activities to both the public and government officials is an additional characteristic of the judicial system. Judges enjoy a great deal of independence from supervision because few are watching. The members of the courtroom team could be an important instrument for quality control, but they are bound into the process and depend on the judge for favors. The higher courts may supervise the administration of justice, but only about 1 percent of criminal cases are appealed. Civic organizations or members of the general public may observe, but perhaps because most defendants are poor, their interest is not aroused. In a few cities, Quaker groups have assumed the function of "court watching," believing that the presence of middle-class citizens will cause officials to treat defendants with greater consideration.

Although the bench is usually elevated to symbolize the judge's authority, it faces the lawyers' table so that persons in the audience, and sometimes even the defendant, are unable to observe all the verbal and nonverbal exchanges. In some courts the attorneys for both sides sit at either end of a long table—the furniture does not define them as adversaries. Throughout the proceedings, lawyers from both sides periodically engage in muffled conversations with the judge out of the hearing range of the defendant and spectators. When judges call the attorneys into their chambers for private discussion, the defendants remain in the courtroom. In most settings, the defendants sit isolated either in the "dock" or in a chair behind their counsel to symbolize their status as silent observers with no power to negotiate their own fate.

Since public defenders often represent as many as 90 percent of the court's clients, they occupy a "permanent" place in the courtroom and only temporarily relinquish their desks to the few lawyers who have been privately retained. While the courtroom encounters of private attorneys are brief, businesslike, and temporary, public defenders view the courtroom as their regular workplace and thus give the impression that they are core members of the courtroom group. From the defendants' perspective, the adversarial system must appear to be a myth as these agent-mediators decide their fate.

Role of the judge

When asked about the job of the judge, one prisoner said, "The judge's job is to sit on his ass and do what the prosecutor tells him to do." Another prisoner responded: "I don't really know what the judge's job is. All I know is that my lawyer went to the prosecutor and told him my story, and he came back and told me the prosecutor was going to give me the suspended. I don't even know what the judge's job is."[18] Many defendants and probably most judges would not agree with these assessments, but in the view of some defendants the judge is a peripheral figure who does not play an important part in determining the outcome of their case. From their perspective, the judge's behavior shows the ultimate failure of the system and the complete submission of due process ideals to bureaucratic goals.

Judges are not only leaders of the courtroom team who are supposed to ensure that procedures are correctly followed, they are also administrators who are responsible for coordinating the process. Even within the definition of the judicial position there is latitude for each judge to play the role somewhat differently. Some judges run a "loose ship" and others run a "tight ship." Judges who run a loose administrative ship see themselves as somewhat above the battle. They give other members of the team considerable freedom to discharge their responsibilities and will usually ratify decisions made by the group. One might expect that although the task goals of the organization, in terms of the number of cases processed, would be low, the social relations within the courtroom group would be high.

More aggressive judges see themselves as necessary leaders of the courtroom team. They anticipate problems, provide cues for other actors, threaten, cajole, and move the group toward an efficient accomplishment of goals. Such a judge commands respect and fully participates in the ongoing courtroom drama.

> "Where is your witness, Mr. District Attorney?" the judge asks. "On his way." "He should be here—you know this was scheduled for 9:00 A.M.," the judge admonishes. "We'll take the next case, notify me when your witness is here—93854, State v. Jones." And on and on. Like a symphony director, the judge goes down his board, calling cases, allowing brief postponements when necessary.[19]

Because of their position within the judicial process, judges possess the potential leadership resources to play their role according to these polar types or somewhere in between. The way they define their role will greatly influence the structure of interpersonal relations within the courtroom. As a consequence, the way the group performs its task, as measured by the output of its case decisions, is influenced by the role of the judge.

Encounters: the labeling process

The criminal court provides a social context for encounters between the defendant and the agents of the law who fasten the label "criminal" onto the guilty. The courtroom appearance of the accused, the plea of guilty, and the process of sentencing may be viewed as containing many of the elements of a degradation ceremony. Harold Garfinkel has said:

> The work of the denunciation effects the recasting of the objective character of the perceived other. The other person becomes in the eyes of his condemners literally a different and new person . . . the former identity stands as accidental; the new identity is the "basic reality." What he is now is what, "after all," he was all along.[20]

We should emphasize, however, that the new label on the defendant is the culmination of a process that began at the time of arrest (some would argue even before). From civilian to accused to defendant to convict, the entire journey through the criminal justice system may be viewed as a "moral career"—a sequence of changes in the person's conception of self and the framework within which he or she interacts with others and they, in turn, react to the person. Erving Goffman explains:

> Each moral career, and behind this, each self, occurs within the confines of an institutional system, whether a social establishment such as a mental hospital or a complex of personal and professional relationships. The self, then, can be seen as something that resides in the arrangements prevailing in a social system for its members. The self in this sense is not a property of the person to whom it is attributed, but dwells rather in the pattern of social control that is exerted in connection with the person by himself and those around him. This special kind of institutional arrangement does not so much support the self as constitute it.[21]

The courtroom is a meeting place for professionals (lawyers, probation officers, and social workers) who proclaim that they work in the service of accused persons, supposedly to treat their needs and those of society. These are the agent-mediators who help the defendants redefine themselves and prepare them for the next phase of the moral career.

Dress may communicate the role each performer plays. Group members wear appropriate uniforms: the judge in robes, the attorneys, both male and female, in conservative suits. One may even observe differences between the clothing of the prosecutor and the defense attorney. Prosecutors dress in more somber colors (to identify their role with that of the judge?), while some defense attorneys tend toward more flamboyant outfits (to conform to their clients' expectations?). Even the defendants may be dressed in a uniform—jail garb—if they are being detained for lack of bail. Because most defendants are poor, their clothing helps to define their role and differentiates them from the group of court actors.

The role played by defendants in courtroom encounters will greatly influence the perceptions of the agent-mediators and guide their decisions. Defendants are expected to present themselves according to the "ideal form" as conceived by the other persons along the moral career journey. If the defense attorney, social worker, family members, and other agent-mediators have been successful during the pretrial phase in getting the accused to redefine himself, he should understand how he must act out his part. Ideally, he will act guilty, repentant, silent, and submissive. Further, the "copping out ceremony" allows others in the courtroom to meet administrative needs within a legal context. For example, when the accused acknowledges his guilt in public and testifies that he enters his plea willingly and voluntarily, acceptance of the plea can be followed by a brief lecture from the judge about the seriousness of the wrongful act or the unhappiness the defendant has caused his family. Thus the defendant's presentation of himself to the court as contrite and ready for rehabilitation allows the judge to justify the lesser sentence that has been negotiated by the prosecutor and defense lawyer. The judge can "give him a break" because he has cooperated.

The defendant who pleads not guilty or who otherwise gives an inappropriate performance may incur severe sanctions. Maureen Mileski observed that the judge's harsh manner in encounters was not related to the seriousness of the charge; the courtroom is removed from tension and emotional reaction to wrongful behavior. More important, a minor disruption in the courtroom or a show of disrespect for its personnel led to reprimands from the judge or sentences that were more severe than usual. But as she notes, there were few cases in which the defendant's behavior was not according to form; only 5 percent elicited a harsh response from the judge. The vast majority conformed to the expectations of a routine bureaucratic encounter.[22]

Felony justice: the impact of courtroom workgroups

The most extensive development of the concept and study of courtroom workgroups has been carried out by James Eisenstein and Herbert Jacob.[23] Their research on the felony disposition process in the courtrooms of Baltimore, Chicago, and Detroit gives us important insights into the influence of the workgroup on decisions in felony cases and provides comparative evidence showing differences in the criminal justice systems of three cities. They found that the same type of felony case was handled very differently in each, yet the dispositions were remarkably similar for those defendants who reached the trial court. It was not the law, rules of procedure, or crime rate that produced the variation but rather the structure of the courtroom workgroups, the influence of the sponsoring organizations, and the sociopolitical environment of each city.

Before examining the trial courtroom dispositions discussed by Eisenstein and Jacob, we must first look at the screening process that occurred in the felony defendants' preliminary hearings. And we note a basic fact of American criminal justice: the courts convict few of the persons the police arrest. Many felony defendants never reach a trial court because their cases are dismissed, charges against them are reduced, or they are diverted at a preliminary hearing. As table 11.5 shows, the preliminary hearings in the three cities had quite different functions.

TABLE 11.5 Outcomes of probable-cause proceedings in three cities

	Baltimore[a]	*Chicago*[b]	*Detroit*[c]
Dismissed	21.0%	63.4%	5.1%
Findings of innocence or no probable cause	4.0	10.8	14.2
Findings of guilt	7.9	4.5	0
Guilty pleas	.3	8.6	0
Sent to grand jury but not indicted	4.0	0	N.A.
Indicted by grand jury or information	62.6	12.7	80.5
	99.8%	100%	99.8%

[a] Based on weighted file sample: N = 1,577.
[b] Based on weighted preliminary hearing observation samples: N = 982.
[c] Based on preliminary examination observation sample: N = 350.
Source: James Eisenstein and Herbert Jacob, *Felony Justice: An Organizational Analysis of Criminal Courts*, p. 191. Copyright © 1977 by Herbert Jacob and James Eisenstein. Reprinted by permission of the publisher, Little, Brown, and Company.

In Chicago about two-thirds of the cases presented were dismissed, while in Baltimore and Detroit three-fifths and four-fifths, respectively, were moved on to the trial courtroom after probable cause was found. Although these differences are striking, they do not tell the entire story. Bail and pretrial motion decisions are also made at preliminary hearings, and bail outcomes disagree substantially. About half of Baltimore defendants remained in jail, compared to two-fifths in Chicago and Detroit. Baltimore released 21 percent on recognizance but levied high money bail for the remainder; practically no one was let out on recognizance in Chicago, but money bail was kept low; in Detroit, almost half were released on recognizance, and when money bail was required it was fairly low. Pretrial motions concerning the state's evidence were also treated variously. Since most Baltimore defendants went directly to a trial courtroom without a preliminary hearing, there was little opportunity to present pretrial motions to suppress evidence. The preliminary examination was conducted in an adversarial fashion in Detroit, less so in Chicago.

What influence did the courtroom workgroups have on these preliminary hearings? Eisenstein and Jacob found that the stable courtroom workgroups in Chicago developed informal procedures for screening cases. Because of the groups' close links to the trial courtrooms, they felt pressure to screen out many cases, hence the very high dismissal rate. Baltimore was characterized as having unstable workgroups, in part because members were frequently rotated and the sponsoring organizations exercised little supervisory control. As a result, most defendants were forwarded to the grand jury and ultimately to the trial courts. In Detroit, also a city with unstable workgroups, the prosecutors had already screened cases before they reached the courtroom; thus most of the defendants who appeared at preliminary hearings were sent to trial.

Findings in regard to the trial court stage were similar to those in regard to the preliminary hearing: the conviction rates of the cities were similar (table

11.6) but the methods used to produce the dispositions differed substantially. It must be remembered, however, that Baltimore processed largely unscreened cases, while 40 percent of felony arrests in Detroit and 85 percent in Chicago had been pruned at the preliminary hearing. The data also make it apparent that each of the cities arrived at the results in a different way. Detroit operated at a pace three times faster than that of Chicago and Baltimore. Chicago and Detroit relied primarily on guilty pleas, while Baltimore processed more cases through trials than through a "copout." But in all three cities the workgroups shunned the jury trial: fewer than 10 percent of the cases were disposed of in this manner.

As Eisenstein and Jacob note, differential dispositions among the cities were reflections of, among other things, the organizational structure of the courtroom workgroups.

> Where workgroup members were familiar with one another and the workgroups were stable (as in Chicago and Detroit), plea negotiations occurred frequently; where they were not (as in Baltimore), fewer guilty pleas appeared. But Baltimore workgroups could and did reduce uncertainty with bench trials. Detroit trial workgroups had a higher proportion of adversarial defense attorneys who made greater use of jury trials in those few cases which were not pleaded.[24]

The way the workgroups dealt with cases was also influenced by defendants' characteristics, the strength of the evidence, and the nature of the offense—factors that were inputs to the ongoing social system of the courtroom.

TABLE 11.6 Trial courtroom dispositions of felony defendants in three cities

	Baltimore[a]	*Chicago*[b]	*Detroit*[c]
Defendants sent to trial whom court convicted	68.0% (*N* = 549)	75.5% (*N* = 519)	72.2% (*N* = 1,202)
Median number of days between grand jury indictment or information and trial courtroom disposition	178 (*N* = 459)	151.5 (*N* = 626)	56 (*N* = 1,114)
Median number of days between arrest and trial courtroom disposition	226 (*N* = 451)	267.5 (*N* = 604)	71.2 (*N* = 1,114)
Disposition methods			
guilty pleas	34.7%	61.7%	63.9%
bench trials	33.9%	19.9%	6.8%
jury trials	9.4%	6.7%	7.3%
dismissals	22.0%	11.7%	22.0%
	100.0% (*N* = 549)	100.0% (*N* = 519)	100.0% (*N* = 1,208)

[a] Unweighted file sample.
[b] Indictment sample used except for estimates of disposition time, which are based on combination of indictment and information samples.
[c] Trial court sample.
Source: James Eisenstein and Herbert Jacob, *Felony Justice: An Organizational Analysis of Criminal Courts*, p. 233. Copyright © 1977 by Herbert Jacob and James Eisenstein. Reprinted by permission of the publisher, Little, Brown, and Company.

The disposition of felony cases results from the interaction of the courtroom members. The tasks that they perform require full participation, but they in turn are influenced by the policies of their sponsoring organizations. The degree to which the interdependence of these factors affects the processes of felony justice varies "from jurisdiction to jurisdiction, over time in each jurisdiction, and even from courtroom to courtroom."[25] The stability of workgroup interactions can be upset by such changes as a new docket system, a shift by the public defender's office from a zone to a person-to-person strategy, or a decision by the prosecutor to institute policies reflecting the Trial Sufficiency Model. When such shifts occur, new factors are brought to bear on the courtroom, and its members must adapt, with the result that an altered felony disposition configuration will evolve.

Delay in the courts

One of the oldest concepts of the common law is that justice delayed is justice denied. Ever since the English nobles forced King John to sign the Magna Carta and promise not to "deny or delay right or justice," there has been concern over the slowness with which courts process cases. In the United States a speedy trial is guaranteed by the Sixth Amendment to the Constitution, and the Supreme Court has characterized adherence to swift justice as "an important safeguard to prevent undue and oppressive incarceration prior to trial, to minimize anxiety and concern accompanying public accusation and to limit the possibilities that long delay will impair the ability of an accused to defend himself."[26]

Nowadays the pace of the criminal courts is usually assumed to be slowed by the huge caseloads thrust upon mismanaged and inefficient operations. Because of the courts' deficiencies, defendants must wait unreasonably long for trial (often in jail) and prosecution is hampered by victims' loss of interest and witnesses' fading memories of crucial facts as time passes.

Delay is usually described as an aberration and dysfunction of the system. According to the President's Commission on Law Enforcement and Administration of Justice, "the causes of delay are manifold: lack of resources, inefficient management and an increasing number of cases. . . . Internal management tends to be archaic, inefficient, and wholly out of tune with modern improvements in management and communications."[27] Much of the research on delay has emphasized structural and resource problems associated with the organization of the courts. It has been suggested that the problems would go away if the numbers of judges and courtrooms were increased, if professional administrators were hired, and if sound management were instituted.

A study by the National Center for State Courts questions assumptions about the causes of delay and about the remedies traditionally advanced.[28] When researchers examined the size, caseload, and management procedures of twenty-one courts in major American cities, they found major exceptions to the expectation that criminal cases are disposed of expeditiously only in courts that have a small volume of cases that are neither serious nor complex (see table 11.7). The court in Philadelphia is larger and slower than the small-volume courts of Portland and New Orleans, but the Pontiac and Newark courts are substantially slower than might be expected for their size, and the large Pittsburgh court processes criminal cases at a faster pace than others like

TABLE 11.7 Court structure and case delay

	Median upper-court disposition time for criminal cases (days)	*Total judges*[a]	*Criminal judges*[b]	*1976 criminal filings*[c]	*1975 population (thousands)*	*1976 felony filings per judge*[d]
Wayne County, Mich.	33	33	7	4,244	2,537	575
San Diego, Calif.	45	28	9	4,254	1,588	473
Atlanta, Ga.	45	11	*	5,296	584	*
New Orleans, La.	50	10	10	7,525	564	275
Portland, Ore.	51	17	*	3,627	536	*
Seattle, Wash.	56	24	*	4,567	1,149	*
Pittsburgh, Pa.	58	31	14	7,949	1,517	471[e]
Oakland, Calif.	58	24	10	2,711	1,088	265
Minneapolis, Minn.	60	17	6	2,369	926	384
St. Paul, Minn.	69	12	*	1,051	476	*
Cleveland, Ohio	71	26	*	6,632	1,603	*
Pontiac, Mich.	78	11	*	4,921	968	*
Miami, Fla.	81	43	12	11,741	1,439	*
Phoenix, Ariz.	98	31	10	7,294	1,218	522
Ft. Lauderdale, Fla.	99	27	7	4,081	863	583
Houston, Tex.	99	38	15	15,086	1,964	*
Newark, N.J.	99	26	16	7,083[e]	885	443[e]
Dallas, Tex.	102	25	9	10,457	1,399	*
Philadelphia, Pa.	119	60	43	9,122	1,825	233
Boston, Mass.	281	19	9	3,989	723	218
Bronx County, N.Y.	328	39	29	3,518	1,377	121

* Data unavailable or not applicable.
[a] Total number of judges authorized for general jurisdiction court in civil and criminal divisions.
[b] Judges assigned to criminal matters.
[c] Total criminal matters filed in 1976. Because of significant differences in statistical procedures across courts, these figures are not strictly comparable.
[d] Felony cases (defendant incidents) filed per judge assigned to criminal matters, 1976.
[e] Estimate.
Source: Adopted from Thomas Church, Jr.; Alan Carlson; Jo-Lynne Lee; and Teresa Tan, *Justice Delayed* (Williamsburg, Va.: National Center for State Courts, 1978), tables 3.1, 3.2, and 3.4, by permission.

it. The courts of Boston and the Bronx are not particularly distinguished by the numbers of their filings, judges, or populations, yet they are the slowest of those examined.

Delay is often attributed to overworked judges and understaffed courts, but research has failed to discover a link between the criminal caseloads of judges and the pace of litigation. For example, fifty-one judgeships were added to the criminal courts of New York City between 1972 and 1974, with accompanying increases in prosecution and public defender staffs. After a survey of the impact of these additions, the commissioner of criminal justice services said that the new expenditures had "not solved the problem of delay and backlog."[29] The research conducted by the National Center for the State Courts uncovered very little relationship between processing time and either the number of felony filings per judge or the number of pending felonies per judge. The data show that the courts with the largest caseloads are not those with the slowest disposition times, nor are the comparatively underworked courts speedier.

Why, then, do some courts process cases much more quickly than others? The answer appears to be that it is not the formal, structural elements of courts that are important in this regard but rather the local legal culture and the social organization of the criminal justice system. The participants become adapted to a certain pace of litigation, and these expectations are translated into others in regard to the way cases should proceed. What is viewed as the normal speed for the disposition of criminal cases in one system may be viewed as undue haste in another. As this book has emphasized throughout, decisions are made in the context of an organization in which discretion is widely exercised. This means that local norms, role relationships, and the incentives of the major actors determine the manner in which cases are processed. Unless the defendant is being held without bail while awaiting trial, there is little incentive for speed.

Continuances: accommodations in the system

continuance
An adjournment of a scheduled case until a future date.

The ***continuance*** is a prime example of the type of accommodation that causes delay. From a legal standpoint, the judge has the discretion to grant continuances so that the defense will have an opportunity to prepare its case. The need for time to obtain counsel, to prepare pretrial motions, to obtain evidence, or to find a witness can be used as a reason for postponement. The prosecution can also request continuances, but in most states such adjournments are constitutionally limited by the requirements that the defendant must be brought to trial within a set period—usually 120 days—unless the delay is caused by the defense. Although the law is specific, the granting and denial of motions for continuances go on almost unaffected by the legal framework. The important rules that the system follows are rules of administrative practice rather than of law, and thus continuances are accommodations to the goals of judicial actors rather than to technical factors of a case.

Using data gathered from five urban court systems, Martin Levin estimated that the percentage of cases in which continuances are granted ranges from 10 in Minneapolis District Court to more than 70 in Chicago Criminal Division Court.[30] Research also shows that continuances have the effect of decreasing the number of guilty dispositions as the number of court appearances increases. Defendants with retained counsel are often able to induce judges to put off a trial as a way of wearing out witnesses, of remaining out on bail as long as possible, or of waiting for community interest to die. This tactic has the additional effect of discriminating in favor of defendants who can afford counsel. The poor, represented by the public defender, do not receive the same treatment, in part because they must await disposition of their cases in pretrial detention.

Rules for speedy trials

One answer to the problem of delay has been the enactment of rules for speedy trials by Congress and several states. The rules typically require that cases be moved from arrest to trial within certain strict time limits, and provide for the dismissal of charges if the case is not brought to trial within the time specified. Many federal and state courts have long had such requirements, and in 1974 Congress passed the Federal Speedy Trial Act, which provided for a five-year planning period during which the new rules were to be phased in and time limits were to be applied at various points during the pretrial period. The maximum limits established by the act are thirty days from arrest to

Close-up: Making Things Happen: The Genius of Judge Harold Rothwax

Seated behind an elevated desk in the high-ceilinged courtroom, Judge Harold Rothwax does not look at all pleased. His broad face, an appealing face with something of the lumpy quality of an old prizefighter's, is set and pale, and his head is pulled down between his shoulders. The two lawyers before him—a young assistant district attorney clutching a confusion of documents and a defense counsel whose brown toupee gleams in contrast to his own dull sideburns—place their hands on the massive desk and seem to brace themselves against his next words. A few spectators stare from the high-backed wooden benches, and in the well of the court, the clerks and uniformed officers are still.

At a table perhaps 20 feet from the judge and behind the lawyers, the defendant stands waiting. He is a handsome white man in his early thirties, and his face above the light turtleneck projects a kind of distaste, as if his straight nose were picking up bad odors at this tawdry proceeding. But he has been in such surroundings many times before. As his record attests, he is a specialist in burglarizing the rooms of first-class hotels, and he often carries a gun to impress anyone unfortunate enough to discover him. He is, in short, a dangerous thief whose devotion to his work led most recently to his capture on one job while he was out on bail after another. He uses different names for different occasions, and he is in bad trouble this morning.

"Tell the defendant," says Judge Rothwax to the defense attorney, in a voice that cannot be heard beyond his desk, "that this is the last day for three and a half to seven. After this, it goes up. If he's going to take the offer, he has to decide now. If he doesn't take it, he's going to trial. We've had enough of this delay. Either he takes the plea, or we set a trial date *today*."

The lawyer looks at the judge for a moment without speaking and then turns and walks back to his client. It is clear that Rothwax is not going to tolerate further stalling. The defendant either must plead guilty to the reduced burglary charge offered by the district attorney—for which Rothwax had earlier indicated he would hand down a sentence of no more than three and a half to seven years in prison—or must prepare to go to trial. Then if a jury convicts him on the original charge (and the prosecution's case seems very good), the trial judge will surely give him a much heavier sentence. And if the defendant wants to delay now and enter a plea later, to avoid trial, the bargain offered today will be unavailable. This is the hard moment of truth in the plea-bargaining process for the handsome burglar, and his face, empty now of any disdain, is taut and angry. He speaks in a rapid whisper to his attorney, stares at Rothwax, shrugs and whispers to his lawyer again.

The lawyer comes back to the bench. "This guy is crazy," he says to Rothwax. "We'll go to trial."

"All right, gentlemen," the judge says briskly. "Let's settle on a date certain for trial."

"Judge, I'd like to be relieved of this case," says the defense lawyer. "This guy won't listen."

Rothwax shakes his head. "No," he replies. "You're the fourth lawyer he's had. That's enough. Let's pick a trial date." It is clear that there is no more room for discussion on this matter. A day two weeks later is selected. The defendant is taken out of the courtroom and back into detention. His case, of course, may still never go to trial, but it has been brought one step closer, largely because of pressure brought by Judge Rothwax. The calendar proceeds.

Source: Loudon Wainwright, "Making Things Happen: The Genius of Judge Harold Rothwax," 10 June 1978.

indictment and seventy days from indictment to trial. Cases that do not meet these requirements may be dismissed either with or without the option of reinstatement of the charges, but it is expected that charges will not be reinstated without good reason. Although defendants may waive their right to a speedy trial under the rules, the prosecution can get an extension of the limits only if the ends of justice will thus be served or if there is a "judicial emergency."[31]

In assessing the results of the 1974 act, Malcolm Feeley found that it has not been taken seriously by most federal judges.[32] The legislation has had some indirect effects, however: the planning process has spurred administrative modernization of the courts and procedures have been tightened in the interest of improved allocation of resources. The backlog of civil cases has grown as the courts have worked to bring criminal cases to trial before the charges have to be dismissed. In many courts it appears that only the formal requirements of the act have been met and that the problem of delay remains, because the "ends of justice" exception is used extensively.

Although speedy-trial statutes give the impression of having caused a revolution in some state courts, the policies at that level also contain enormous loopholes. Surveys have discerned "no correlation between the stringency of provisions in state speedy trial rules and actual disposition times."[33] Feeley notes, "The state pattern is similar to that of the federal courts: expression of high-minded ideals coupled with symbolic responses."[34]

Assessing delay

Delay benefits not only defendants seeking lenient treatment but defense attorneys, prosecutors, and judges. The major goals of defense attorneys are to collect their fees and to minimize their court time per case. They are further motivated to avoid a conviction or severe punishment for their clients. Thus delay not only is in the defendants' interest but also helps the attorneys to maximize their fees, please their clients, and enhance their reputations for skill. Although a move to delay a case is usually initiated by the defense attorney, it cannot succeed without the cooperation of the prosecutor and judge. Levin found that prosecutors generally did not oppose motions for continuances. Presumably prosecutors understand the need to reach accommodations that will result in a bargained plea. Judges also realize that postponement usually helps to prevent a full-length trial that would tie up the courtroom for an extended period. Both the prosecutor and judge recognize that by assisting the defense attorney, they ensure the attorney's cooperation in turn.

Although formal changes have been proposed to reduce delay in the criminal courts, such changes will not be successful unless it is recognized that courtroom actors have individual and multiple goals. The personal needs of the defense attorney, prosecutor, and judge have been shown to be stronger than the broader goal of processing offenders quickly. Thus system goals may not be expected to dominate the criminal court until incentives are provided that are more rewarding to the actors than the fulfillment of their current needs.

Summary

Assembly-line justice is the means that enables court administrators to move the enormous caseloads with which they must contend. Judicial decisions are dispensed in wholesale lots because actors in the system work on the basis of three assumptions: (1) that any person who is brought before the court is probably guilty; (2) that the vast majority of defendants will plead guilty; (3) that those charged with minor offenses will be processed in volume. This chapter has examined the conditions that influence decision making in the criminal courts. Although attention has been focused on the judge, we have also seen that guilt or innocence, probation or prison are usually decided by a small group of courtroom actors.

The judge is the most important figure in the criminal court. Decisions of the police, defense attorneys, and prosecutors are greatly affected by judges' rulings and sentencing practices. The socioeconomic characteristics of judges in the lower criminal courts are very different from those of judges in the upper courts. In most cities the criminal court judge occupies the lowest rung in the judicial hierarchy.

In more than half the states, judges are popularly elected, which usually means that candidates must be active in politics and are often nominated for a judgeship as a reward for party work. In twenty states judges are appointed by either the executive or the legislature, while in seven they are selected by merit under the Missouri Plan. Arguments have been advanced in support of each method, but the important question concerns the decisions made by the judges once they are seated. Levin's comparison of the criminal courts of Pittsburgh and Minneapolis provides an opportunity to examine the types of persons selected to be judges under each system and the types of decisions that they make.

The concepts of "role" and "group" help to clarify the operations of courtroom actors. Although norms and goals are shared, each member of the courtroom group—judge, prosecutor, defense attorney, defendant, bailiff, clerk—occupies a specialized position and is expected to fit into the socially accepted definition of that status. The cohesion of the group is enhanced by the physical setting and by the delineation of roles. The delays in the courts result from the conflicts between the goals of the system and the personal needs of the members of the courtroom team. The criminal court provides a social context for personal encounters between the defendant and the agents of the law who fasten the label "criminal" onto the guilty.

For discussion

1. Case overload is one of the major problems facing the criminal courts. Is multiplication of judges and facilities likely to solve this problem?
2. Discuss the effects that partisan election of judges may have on the administration of justice. Which system of judicial selection do you prefer?
3. The judge plays several roles. What are they? Do any of them conflict?
4. What does the phrase "a jury of one's peers" mean in the context of contemporary society? Are ghetto residents given the equal protection of the laws if they are judged by upper-middle-class persons? Do white upper-class persons receive equal protection if they are judged by juries composed of lower-class blacks?

For further reading

Balbus, Isaac D. *The Dialects of Legal Repression.* New York: Russell Sage Foundation, 1973.
Blumberg, Abraham S. *Criminal Justice.* Chicago: Quadrangle Books, 1967.
Botein, Bernard. *Trial Judge.* New York: Simon & Schuster, 1952.
Eisenstein, James, and Jacob, Herbert. *Felony Justice.* Boston: Little, Brown, 1977.
Feeley, Malcolm M. *Court Reform on Trial.* New York: Basic Books, 1983.
——. *The Process Is the Punishment.* New York: Russell Sage Foundation, 1979.

Notes

1. Roscoe Pound, "The Causes of Popular Dissatisfaction with the Administration of Justice," *Journal of the American Judicature Society* 20 (1937): 178–87.
2. John H. Wigmore, "Roscoe Pound's St. Paul Address of 1906," *Journal of the American Judicature Society* 20 (1937): 176.
3. Geoff Gallas, "The Conventional Wisdom of State Court Administration: A Critical Assessment and an Alternative Approach," *Justice System Journal* 2 (Summer 1976): 54.
4. Carl Baar, *Separate but Subservient* (Lexington, Mass.: Lexington Books, 1975).
5. U.S. Department of Justice, *Sourcebook of Criminal Justice Statistics, 1982* (Washington, D.C.: Government Printing Office, 1982), pp. 2, 3.
6. Gallas, "Conventional Wisdom," p. 55.
7. John Paul Ryan, Allan Ashman, Bruce D. Sales, and Sandra Shane-Du Bow, *American Trial Judges* (New York: Free Press, 1980), p. 128.
8. Benjamin N. Cardozo, *The Nature of the Judicial Process* (New Haven: Yale University Press, 1921), p. 149.
9. Samuel I. Rosenman, "A Better Way to Select Judges," *Journal of the American Judicature Society* 48 (1964): 86.
10. Ryan et al., *American Trial Judges,* p. 124.
11. Richard A. Watson and Rondal G. Downing, *The Politics of the Bench and the Bar: Judicial Selection under the Missouri Nonpartisan Court Plan* (New York: Wiley, 1969), p. 42.
12. Martin A. Levin, "Urban Politics and Policy Outcomes: The Criminal Courts," in *Criminal Justice: Law and Politics,* ed. George F. Cole (North Scituate, Mass.: Duxbury Press, 1972), p. 332.
13. Ibid., p. 359n, 343.
14. Ibid., p. 360n.
15. A. Paul Hare, *Handbook of Small Group Research* (New York: Free Press of Glencoe, 1962), pp. 9–10.
16. Edward J. Clynch and David W. Neubauer, "Trial Courts as Organizations," *Law and Policy Quarterly* 3 (1981): 69–94.
17. James Eisenstein and Herbert Jacob, *Felony Justice* (Boston: Little, Brown, 1977), p. 43.
18. Jonathan Casper, *American Criminal Justice: The Defendant's Perspective* (Englewood Cliffs, N.J.: Prentice-Hall, 1972), p. 140.
19. William M. Beaney, "Relationships, Role Conceptions, and Discretion among the District Court Judges of Colorado," paper presented at the 1970 annual meeting of the American Political Science Association, New York, September 1970, p. 19.
20. Harold Garfinkel, "Conditions of Successful Degradation Ceremonies," *American Journal of Sociology* 61 (1956): 421.
21. Erving Goffman, *Asylums* (Garden City, N.Y.: Doubleday, 1961), p. 169.
22. Maureen Mileski, "Courtroom Encounters," *Law and Society Review* 5 (1971): 524.
23. Eisenstein and Jacob, *Felony Justice,* pp. 19–39.
24. Ibid., pp. 258–59.
25. Ibid., p. 294.
26. United States v. Ewell, 283 U.S. 116 (1966).
27. President's Commission on Law Enforcement and Administration of Justice, *Task Force Report: The Courts* (Washington, D.C.: Government Printing Office, 1967), p. 80.
28. Thomas Church, Jr.; Alan Carlson; Jo-Lynn Lee; and Teresa Tan, *Justice Delayed* (Williamsburg, Va.: National Center for the State Courts, 1978).
29. Ibid., p. 25, n. 6.
30. Martin A. Levin, "Delay in Five Criminal Courts," *Journal of Legal Studies* 4 (1975): 83.
31. Title 18 U.S.C. 3166.
32. Malcolm M. Feeley, *Court Reform on Trial* (New York: Basic Books, 1983), p. 173.
33. Church et al., *Justice Delayed,* pp. 48–49, 78.
34. Feeley, *Court Reform on Trial,* p. 178.

Trial and Posttrial Processes

Trial: the deviant case
- Jury selection
  - *Creation of the pool*
  - *Voir dire*
- Opening statements
- Presentation of the prosecution's evidence
- Presentation of the defense's evidence
- Presentation of rebuttal witnesses
- Closing arguments by each side
- Judge's instructions to the jury
- Decision by the jury
- Jury duty
- Assembly-line justice: the lower courts

The sentencing process
- Sentencing behavior of judges
  - *Who receives unfavorable treatment?*
- Prison or probation?
  - *Presentence report*
  - *Judge's perspective*

Appeals
- Habeas corpus

Summary

The People versus Donald Payne

> *"For instance, now [the Queen says to Alice] . . . there's the King's Messenger. He's in prison now, being punished; and the trial doesn't even begin till next Wednesday; and of course the crime comes last of all." Alice replies, "Suppose he never commits the crime?" "That would be all the better, wouldn't it?" the Queen responds.*
>
> LEWIS CARROLL

Throughout the fall of 1980 the national media closely followed the daily activities surrounding the trial of Mrs. Jean Harris. Mrs. Harris was charged with the murder of Dr. Herman Tarnower, author of the best-selling *Complete Scarsdale Medical Diet,* in the bedroom of his house in an exclusive section of Westchester County, New York. The prosecution argued that Mrs. Harris, Tarnower's lover for more than fourteen years, had shot him in a jealous rage because he had become involved with a younger woman. Like other dramatic trials of the past, such as those of Bruno Hauptmann, Leopold and Loeb, Joan Little, Patty Hearst, and Sacco and Vanzetti, the Harris trial contained all the ingredients of soap opera—love, sex, violence, betrayal, glamour—and the public was eager for every tantalizing tidbit. Meanwhile, judges were handing out hundreds of sentences to less famous defendants whose crimes were perhaps no less heinous but who did not receive the trial by judge and jury guaranteed by the Bill of Rights. As we have seen, the vast majority of defendants plead guilty or are judged in a bench trial without jury. The number of full-fledged trials with a judge and jury is tiny compared with the total number of cases processed by the judicial system.

Trial: the deviant case

According to the assumptions underlying the adversarial system, a trial by ***jury*** is a search for the truth. In reality, however, many other values, some of them in conflict, combine in a jury trial. It must be remembered that the search must be conducted within the framework of the constitutionally guaranteed protections accorded the defendant. Thus the search for truth must step aside when the process conflicts with the individual's rights against self-incrimination, unlawful searches and seizures, and other abuses of governmental authority. A trial by a jury composed of members of the community is one of the greatest safeguards against arbitrary and unlawful actions by criminal justice officials.

jury
A panel consisting of a statutorily defined number of citizens selected according to law and sworn to determine matters of fact in a criminal action and to render a verdict of guilty or not guilty.

A trial is also a contest, a symbolic combat between the prosecution and the defense in which one party normally emerges the winner. The spirit of rivalry permeates the proceedings, with the result that the determination to win may override the search for the truth.

Because trials are conducted in public, they are also a kind of stylized drama, though the totality of this living theater often assumes proportions greater than those intended.

> It is also politics, in both the noblest and the basest senses of the word. A criminal trial is an almost primordial confrontation between the individual and society. At stake are values no less important than individual liberty on the one hand, and the need for social order on the other. It is also pragmatic, grass-roots clubhouse politics in its rawest form. Trial by jury is publicity, the news media, and the making and unmaking of reputations. Many a political career has begun or ended in a criminal courtroom.[1]

Who goes to trial? What are the characteristics of defendants who demand and receive the constitutionally stipulated trial by jury? Because the data on which to base answers to these questions have not yet been accumulated, we must respond broadly that trials result when other forms of disposition (dismissal, diversion, plea negotiation) fail or are not sought. Often a dispute over the facts of a case is so irreconcilable that either the prosecutor or defense attorney seeks a trial. The fact-finding function of the jury trial serves to resolve such a dispute. The defendant's prior record may also play a part in the state's decision to go to trial. If the evidence against a repeat offender is weak, the prosecutor may prefer to have a jury find the accused innocent rather than strike a bargain that would yield only a minimal sanction. The state may lose the trial but still convey to the defendant the message that "we are after you."

The seriousness of the charge is probably the most important factor influencing the decision to go to trial. A trial is rarely demanded by defendants charged with property crimes; murder, armed robbery, or drug sales, all of which bring long prison terms, are more likely to require judge and jury. When the penalty is harsh, defendants seem willing to take the risk inherent in a trial.

Since the adversarial process is designed to get to the truth, the rules of criminal law, procedure, and evidence govern the conduct of the trial. Trials are based on the idea that the prosecution and defense will compete before a judge and jury so that the truth will emerge. Above the battle, the judge sees to it that the rules are followed and that the jury impartially evaluates the evidence and reflects the community's interest. The jury is the sole evaluator of the facts in a case.

Traditionally twelve citizens constitute a jury in a criminal trial, but some states now allow as few as six persons. This reform was recommended as a way to modernize court procedures and reduce expenses. It was upheld by the Supreme Court in *Williams* v. *Florida* (1970) and has been extended nationally,[2] although twelve-person juries are still required in capital cases. In *Burch* v. *Louisiana* (1979) the court ruled that in juries of six a unanimous vote for conviction is required, but with larger juries a majority verdict is enough for conviction.[3] The change to six-person juries has its critics, who charge that the smaller group is less representative of the conflicting views in the community and too quick to bring in a verdict.

Although the right to trial by jury is one of the most ingrained features of the American ideology—it is mentioned in the Declaration of Independence, three amendments to the Constitution, and countless opinions of the Supreme

Court—only about 8 percent of criminal cases are decided in this manner, and fewer than half of all trials are conducted before a jury. But although jury trials account for such a small fraction of prosecutions, they have a decided impact on decisions made throughout the criminal justice system. We have already indicated that the anticipated reactions of juries play a major role in plea bargaining, but even at the point of arrest the question "Would a jury convict?" enters the decisional thinking of police officers. The decision to prosecute and even the sentencing behavior of judges are influenced by the potential call for a jury.

> Thus the jury is not controlling merely the immediate case before it, but the host of cases not before it which are destined to be disposed of by the pretrial process. The jury thus controls not only the formal resolution of controversies in the criminal case, but also the informal resolution of cases that never reach the trial stage. In a sense the jury, like the visible cap of an iceberg, exposes but a fraction of its true volume.[4]

Juries perform vital functions in the judicial system in other ways as well. First, as a symbol of the rule of law, the citizen membership of the jury reinforces the idea that sanctions in the justice process evolve from the community. The fact that a convicted person has been found guilty by a jury of his or her peers makes for greater stability in the system than would a decision that could be viewed as merely an act of the government. Second, juries provide citizen input in adjudication. Since the members are drawn from the community, the attitudes of the majority may cause the terms of the written law to be selectively applied. Civil libertarians, for example, are often afraid that local juries will discriminate against minorities or against those who pursue a "different" lifestyle, while law enforcement officials often believe that a jury will not convict except when the evidence leaves no other possibility. A third function of juries is educational. Because citizens have an obligation to serve when they are called, jury duty provides an important opportunity to learn about the processes of criminal justice. Citizens' perceptions of how the law functions have a significant impact on their behavior and attitudes toward the judicial process.

Apart from legal stipulations, the choice of trial by jury is left to the accused, and the option becomes a major strategy of the defense. If the ac-

---

State Provisions on Size of Criminal Justice

Twelve-member juries required
Alabama, Hawaii, Illinois, Maine, Maryland, New Jersey, North Carolina, North Dakota, Rhode Island, Vermont, West Virginia, Wisconsin.

Juries of fewer than twelve specifically authorized
Alaska, Arizona, Colorado, Connecticut, Florida, Georgia, Idaho, Indiana, Iowa, Kansas, Kentucky, Louisiana, Massachusetts, Michigan, Minnesota, Mississippi, Missouri, Montana, Nebraska, New Hampshire, New Mexico, New York, Ohio, Oklahoma, Oregon, South Carolina, South Dakota, Tennessee, Texas, Utah, Virginia, Washington, Wyoming.

Juries of fewer than twelve permitted by agreement
Arkansas, California, Delaware, Nevada, Pennsylvania.

Source: David W. Neubauer, *America's Courts and the Criminal Justice System,* 2d ed. (Monterey, Calif.: Brooks/Cole, 1984), p. 286.

TABLE 12.1 Percentage of felony trials by jury in five cities

	Percentage of trials that were trials by jury	*Total number of trials*
Los Angeles	53%	922
Detroit	60	983
Indianapolis	68	206
New Orleans	57	255
District of Columbia	98	262

Source: U.S. Department of Justice, *A Cross-City Comparison of Felony Case Processing* by Kathleen B. Brosi (Washington, D.C.: Government Printing Office, 1979), p. 48.

cused waives the right to trial by jury (in some states the prosecutor must agree), the case is decided by the judge, who serves as finder of fact and determines issues of law. Such trials are called *bench trials*. As table 12.1 indicates, considerable variation in the division of jury and bench trials was found in one five-city study of case processing, but about 40 percent of felonies are decided by judges alone.

The decision to avoid a jury trial by having the case resolved solely by the bench varies considerably according to the offense and to regional customs. A principal consideration is the question: Will a jury believe the defendant's story? In addition, attorneys must estimate whether a harsher penalty will be incurred if a guilty verdict is returned by a jury rather than handed down by a judge. A defense lawyer in Prairie City said: "No question there is a harsher penalty if there is no plea. An unwritten rule of practice here is that if you go

Most Cases That Go to Trial Result in Conviction

The conviction rate at trial varies by jurisdiction because:

- Screening policies vary.
- So many defendants with strong cases plead guilty that the remaining mix of cases that go to trial is relatively weak.

	Felony cases tried (1979)	
	Resulted in conviction	***Number tried***
Geneva, Ill.	96%	24
Salt Lake City, Utah	84	137
Louisville, Ky.	77	296
Indianapolis, Ind.	77	226
Los Angeles, Calif.	73	1,966
Milwaukee, Wis.	73	198
New Orleans, La.	70	690
Manhattan, N.Y.	70	675
Washington, D.C.	68	629
Kalamazoo, Mich.	68	68
St. Louis, Mo.	64	157
Rhode Island	64	111
Golden, Colo.	64	63

Source: U.S. Department of Justice, Bureau of Justice Statistics, *The Prosecution of Felony Arrests*, 1979 (Washington, D.C.: Government Printing Office, 1983), p. 17.

to trial and lose, there will be a harsher penalty. Maybe in one case in 500 there will be an exception and the defendant will get the same after the trial as he would have with a plea. Otherwise the penalty is always more."[5]

Although variations are found among the states, the trial process generally follows eight steps: (1) selection of the jury, (2) opening statements by prosecution and defense, (3) presentation of the state's evidence and witnesses, (4) presentation of the defense's evidence and witnesses, (5) presentation of rebuttal witnesses, (6) closing arguments by each side, (7) instruction of the jury by the judge, and (8) decision by the jury. Though the number of trials may be proportionately small, it is essential to understand each step in the process and consider the broader societal impact of this institution.

Jury selection

The problem of selecting a fair and impartial jury received widespread publicity during the early 1970s with the trials of the Black Panthers and other political radicals. These minority activists persistently claimed that they could not receive a fair trial because American juries were composed not of their "peers" but of middle-class whites with racist attitudes who were predisposed to find them guilty. As can be easily demonstrated, jury selection methods discriminate against the lower occupational groups by excluding them from consideration for jury duty. Not only does such a practice create juries that are unrepresentative of the community, but the class bias influences decision making within the jury room. Studies have shown that regardless of the supposed equality of the jury members, upper-status males tend to dominate the deliberations and are most likely to find defendants guilty.

Creation of the pool. Theoretically, every citizen of the community should have an equal chance of being chosen for jury duty in accordance with the process shown in figure 12.1; but various stipulated qualifications have the effect of keeping certain citizens out of the jury pool. In most states, jurors are

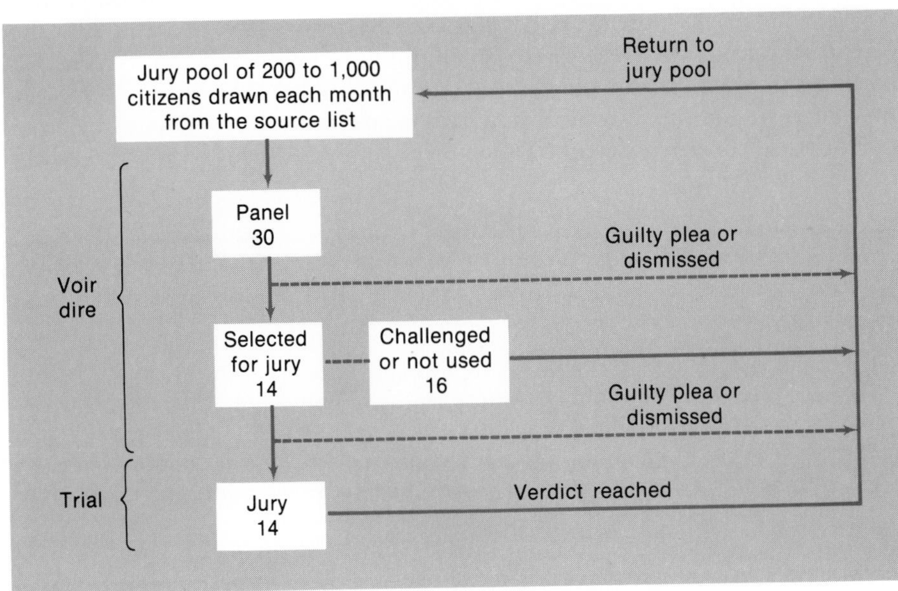

FIGURE 12.1 Jury selection process, twelve-person jury. Potential jurors are drawn at random from a source list. From this pool a panel is selected and presented for duty. The voir dire examination may remove some, while others will be seated.

FOR BY IT THE CITIZEN PARTICIPATES IN THE
ADMINISTRATION OF JUSTICE BETWEEN MAN AND MAN
AND BETWEEN GOVERNMENT AND THE INDIVIDUAL."
HARLAN F. STONE

Individuals are randomly selected to serve in specific juries.

drawn from the list of registered voters, but research has shown that nonwhites, the poor, and the young register to vote at substantially lower rates than the remainder of the population. In addition, the Bureau of the Census has reported that only about 70 percent of those eligible actually register to vote and that in some areas the rate is as low as 40 percent. Over the past decade, the proportion of registered voters has continued to decrease.

Researchers agree that jury unrepresentativeness can best be attacked by the use of a comprehensive list from which citizens are randomly selected for duty.[6] Supplementary pools of citizens—for instance, licensed drivers, utility users, taxpayers—would bring new names to the roster. Ideally, a cross-section of the community could be found if the jury were randomly and scientifically selected from an up-to-date list of all adult citizens.

The number of potential jurors may be further reduced. Persons in some occupations—doctors, lawyers, teachers, police officers—are not called because their professional services are needed; others are not called because of their connection with the criminal justice system. Some legislatures, particularly in states where jurors are required to serve thirty days, have added other categories because of pressures for exemption. In many localities, citizens may be excused if jury duty would cause economic or physical hardship. Because of this narrowing of the sources of potential jurors, there is a tendency for retired persons and those who would not be inconvenienced by the duty to be overrepresented on juries.

Only 15 Percent of American Adults Have Ever Been Called for Jury Duty

The limited number of adults who have served as jurors results from several factors, including:

- The age limits on prospective jurors set by many states.
- The use of voter registration lists, which represent only a portion of eligible voters (71% at the 1976 presidential election).
- The replacement of names of jurors in the jury pool at too frequent intervals.
- The number of exemptions to service permitted by law or granted by the court.

Source: U.S. Department of Justice, Bureau of Justice Statistics, *Report to the Nation on Crime and Justice* (Washington, D.C.: Government Printing Office, 1983), p. 67.

"Hard Questioning Is Screening Out Tarnower Jurors"

Each of the 31 prospective jurors in Westchester County Court who have been examined so far in the murder trial of Jean S. Harris has been asked the same question, and usually at the end, by the defense lawyer, Joel Aurnou: "Have you used the Scarsdale diet?"

The question about the diet has brought murmurs of recognition in the courtroom and smiles to members of the jury panel, many of whom have had to describe their attitudes about suicide, depression, drugs, sex, religion and other things that Mr. Aurnou and the prosecutor, George Bolen, say will emerge in the trial.

It is not clear why Mr. Aurnou asks the diet question. He never follows it up, as he does with other questions, to examine the attitudes of those who have used the diet—nine of the 13 women and one of the 18 men. Nor does it seem to be a factor in selection; one of the women who tried it was among the first five picked for the jury. As of today, eight jurors have been selected.

Going beyond integrity

It is in the replies to other questions, however, that the prosecution and defense seem most interested, reaching beyond the integrity and absence of bias that Judge Russell R. Leggett has told the prospective jurors both sides are seeking.

Mr. Aurnou asked a Mamaroneck school employee and auxiliary policeman about his friends, and then quickly changed the subject:

"This relationship crossed religious lines," he said, and then asked, "You won't punish my client for that, will you?"

The man said no.

"It was a relationship between two adults who were not married. You won't hold that against her because she's a woman?"

Again the reply is no.

"She grew up in Grosse Point, Mich., and was the headmistress of a very exclusive girls' school. That won't mean you would impose a higher standard on her than anyone else?"

Again no.

Jury selection, where many lawyers say cases often are won or lost, provides an opportunity for both sides to gain crucial first impressions and to begin formulating arguments that will be expanded during the trial. But basically it is attitudes that are being examined with great care in this case, because, as Mr. Aurnou told one panel member yesterday, "it is hard for us to look into the mind of a juror."

The trial of Jean Harris attracted wide public attention.

Source: James Feron, "Hard Questioning Is Screening Out Tarnower Jurors," *New York Times*, 13 November 1980, p. B2.

voir dire
An examination of prospective jurors by means of which the prosecution and defense screen out persons who might be biased or incapable of rendering a fair verdict.

challenge for cause
To question formally a prospective juror's competency to render a fair verdict by showing bias or some other legal disability. Prospective jurors so challenged are excused. The number of such challenges permitted is unlimited.

peremptory challenge
Removal of a prospective juror without assignment of any cause. The number of such challenges permitted is limited.

Voir dire. As a protection against bias, prosecution and defense are allowed to challenge the seating of some jurors. This process of ***voir dire*** ("to speak the truth") examination is designed for the constitutional purpose of ensuring a fair trial. Attorneys for each side and/or the judge may question each potential juror about background, knowledge of the case, or acquaintance with the persons involved. If it appears that the juror will be unable to be fair, he or she may be ***challenged for cause.*** The challenge must be ruled on by the judge, and if it is sustained the juror will be excused from participation in that specific case. There is usually no limit to the number of challenges for cause that both lawyers can make, and in some complex or controversial cases the voir dire is extremely time-consuming.

The ***peremptory challenge*** has a more important influence on the composition of the jury. It is used to exclude a person from service, and no reason need be given. An attorney may exercise this prerogative because of a hunch or because someone appears to be unsympathetic. Normally the defense is allowed eight to ten peremptory challenges and the prosecution six to eight.

Instances of "jury stacking" raised questions about voir dire. In several highly publicized trials, especially those involving political radicals such as the Harrisburg Seven, Angela Davis, and the American Indians indicted because of the episode at Wounded Knee, the assistance of social scientists has been sought. Lawyers for the defense reasoned that if they could determine the social and attitudinal characteristics of persons who would be most likely to sympathize with the accused, they could use such knowledge to select a sympathetic jury. That radicals do not have a monopoly on the use of social science was demonstrated in the trial of Ford Motor Company executives in their criminal prosecution resulting from defective gasoline tanks in Pinto automobiles. The defendants hired jury scholar Hans Zeisel, who advised them that their interests would best be served with older men who remembered that FMC had put American industry on the world map.[7]

Whether these methods may become standard practice is still not known. In the past, voir dire was attacked as too time-consuming. If investigation of potential jurors' backgrounds and exclusion of those whose attitudes are deemed to be not in the interest of one side become widespread, the opportunity for challenge may be limited by future changes in the law. One suggested reform holds that only the judge should examine the jurors for bias; another, that the number of challenges allowed should be sharply reduced.

Opening statements

After the jury has been selected, the trial begins. The clerk reads the complaint (indictment or information), and the prosecutor and the defense attorney may, if they desire, make opening statements to the jury to summarize the position that each side intends to take. They are not evidential, and judges normally keep tight control so that no prejudicial or inflammatory remarks are made. Lawyers use this period of trial to establish themselves with the jurors and emphasize points they intend to make later.

Presentation of the prosecution's evidence

One of the basic protections of the American criminal justice system is the assumption that the defendant is innocent until proved guilty. The prosecution has the burden of proving beyond a reasonable doubt, within the demands of the court procedures and rules of evidence, that the individual named in the indictment committed the crime. This does not mean that absolute certainty is required, only that the evidence is such that there is no reasonable doubt.

By presenting evidence to the jury, the state must establish a case showing that the defendant is guilty. Evidence is classified as real evidence, testimony, direct evidence, and circumstantial evidence. *Real evidence* might include such objects as a weapon, records, fingerprints, or stolen property; most evidence in a criminal trial, however, consists of the *testimony* of witnesses. Witnesses at a trial must be legally competent; thus the judge may be required to determine whether the witness whose testimony is challenged has the intelligence to tell the truth and the ability to recall what was seen. *Direct evidence* refers to eyewitness accounts—for example, "I saw John Smith fire the gun"; *circumstantial evidence* requires that the jury infer a fact from what the witness observed. Thus: "I saw John Smith walk behind his house with a gun. A few minutes later I heard a gun go off, and then Mr. Smith walked toward me holding a gun." The witness's observation that Smith had a gun and that he heard a gun go off does not provide the direct evidence that Smith fired his gun; yet the jury may link the described facts and infer that Smith fired his gun. After a witness has given testimony, he or she may be cross-examined by counsel for the other side.

The rules of evidence govern the facts that may be admitted into the case record. Real evidence that has been illegally seized, for example, may be excluded under the Fourth Amendment's protection against unreasonable searches and seizure. Likewise, statements by the defendant given outside the Supreme Court's requirements developed by the *Miranda* decision may also be excluded. Testimony that is hearsay or opinion cannot become a formal part of the trial record. It is the judge who decides, with reference to these rules, what evidence may be heard. In making such decisions, the judge must weigh the importance of the evidence and balance it against the need for a fair trial. Because the purpose of an adversary proceeding is to get the truth, the attorney for each side contests the presentation of evidence with reference to the rules, to the trustworthiness of statements, and to the relevance of the information presented to the points at issue.

Once the prosecution has presented all of the state's evidence against the defendant, the court is informed that the people's case rests. It is common for

The prosecution must prove the case against the defendant beyond all reasonable doubt.

the defense then to ask the court to direct the jury to bring forth a verdict of not guilty. Such a motion is based on the defense contention that the state has not presented enough evidence to prove its case; it has not established all the elements of the crime charged. The judge rules on this motion, sustaining or overruling it. If the motion is sustained (it rarely is), the trial is ended; if it is overruled, the defense has its chance to present its evidence.

Presentation of the defense's evidence

There is no requirement that the defense answer the case presented by the prosecution. Since it is the state's responsibility to prove the case beyond a reasonable doubt, it is theoretically possible—and in fact sometimes happens—that the defense rests its case immediately. Usually the accused's attorney employs one strategy or a combination of three strategies: (1) contrary evidence is introduced to rebut or cast doubt on the state's case, (2) an alibi is offered, or (3) an affirmative defense is presented. If the last strategy is employed, the attorney presents a legal excuse that permits the jury to find the defendant not responsible for the crime. The affirmative defenses include self-defense, insanity, duress, and necessity.

One of the most important questions that the defense must consider is whether the accused shall take the stand. The Fifth Amendment protection against self-incrimination means that the defendant does not have to testify. In *Griffin* v. *California* (1965), the Supreme Court ruled that the prosecutor may not comment on, nor can the jury draw inferences from, the defendant's decision not to appear in his or her own defense.[8] The decision is not taken lightly because if the defendant does testify, the prosecution may cross-examine. Cross-examination is broader than direct examination, and the prosecutor may question the defendant not only about the crime but about his or her past, and often is able to introduce testimony about prior convictions. In addition, many criminal lawyers believe that juries expect to hear both sides of what happened; to deny them this opportunity may prejudice them against the client. Given the suspiciousness of human nature, jurors wonder what the defendant who chooses not to testify is hiding.

Justice Warner's Definition of Reasonable Doubt in *People* v. *Richardson*

A reasonable doubt is a doubt based upon reason . . . a doubt for which the juror . . . can give a reason . . . if called upon to do so. [It] . . . is not a mere . . . surmise that the accused may not be guilty [nor] . . . a doubt based upon sympathy, or the reluctance of a juror to perform a disagreeable task. . . .

If you are satisfied to a moral certainty that this defendant . . . is guilty of any one of the crimes charged here, you may safely say that you have been convinced beyond a reasonable doubt. If your mind is wavering, or if you are uncertain . . . you have not been convinced beyond a reasonable doubt and must render a verdict of not guilty. . . .

The People are not required to prove the guilt of the defendant beyond *all* doubt. The question of punishment, members of the jury, is one for the Court. You have no right to discuss . . . or speculate about punishment in any way. . . . Your working function is to determine . . . the guilt or innocence of the defendant. Punishment is the duty of the Court. . . .

Source: Steven Phillips, *No Heroes, No Villains*, p. 214.

Presentation of rebuttal witnesses

On completion of the defense's case, the prosecution may present witnesses whose testimony is designed to discredit that of preceding witnesses. Evidence previously introduced by the prosecution may not be rehashed, but new evidence may be presented. Should the prosecution bring rebuttal witnesses, the defense has the opportunity to examine them and also to present new witnesses in surrebuttal.

Closing arguments by each side

When each side has completed its presentation of the evidence, prosecution and defense make closing arguments to the jury. The attorneys lay out the facts of the case in a manner that is most favorable to their side. The prosecutor may use the summation to tie together the evidential and legal elements and to try to show that isolated bits of evidence form a cohesive whole that proves the accused to be guilty. The defense, on the other hand, may set forth the applicable law and try to show that the prosecution has not proved its case, that the testimony raised questions instead of providing answers, and that the need to prove beyond a reasonable doubt is very demanding. Each side reminds the jury of its duty not to be swayed by emotion and to evaluate the evidence impartially.

Veteran attorneys feel that the closing argument is a major chance to appeal directly to the members of the jury. Some lawyers use the emotional and spellbinding techniques of experienced actors in making their summations in an attempt to sway the jury. But for many it is also an opportunity to show the defendant, the agent-mediators, or their supervisors that they really put their full effort into the task.

Judge's instructions to the jury

The jury decides the facts of the case but the judge determines the law. Before the jurors retire to consider the defendant's fate, the judge instructs them about the manner in which the law bears on their decision. The judge may discuss such basic legal principles as proof beyond a reasonable doubt, the legal requirements necessary to show that all the elements have been proved by the prosecution, or the rights of the defendant. More specific aspects of the law bearing on the decision, such as complicated court rulings on the nature of the insanity defense or the manner in which certain types of evidence have been gathered, may be included in the judge's instructions.

Clearly, this experience may become an ordeal for the jurors, who must assimilate perhaps two or three hours of instruction without taking notes. It is assumed that somehow they will be able to absorb these details so that when they are in the jury room they will be able to draw on their instant expertise. Finally, the judge explains the charges and the possible verdicts. Trials usually involve multiple charges, and the judge must instruct the jurors in such a way that their decisions will be consistent with the law and the evidence.

Decision by the jury

After they have been instructed, the jurors retire to a room where they have complete privacy. A foreman to run the meeting is elected from among them and deliberations begin. Until now, the jurors have been passive observers of the trial, unable to question witnesses; now they can discuss the facts that have been presented. Throughout their deliberations the jurors may be sequestered; if they are allowed to spend nights at home, they are ordered not to discuss the case with anyone. The jury may request that the judge reread to them portions of the instructions, ask for additional instructions, or seek portions of the transcript.

In almost every state and in the federal courts, the verdict must be unanimous. If the jury becomes deadlocked and cannot reach a verdict, the trial ends with a hung jury. When a verdict is reached, the judge, prosecution, and defense reassemble in the courtroom to hear it. The prosecution or the defense may request that the jury be polled: each member tells his or her vote in open court. This procedure presumably ensures that there has been no pressure by other members. If the verdict is not guilty, the defendant is immediately freed. If the verdict is guilty, the judge may continue bail or may incarcerate the convicted person to await a presentence report.

The question of which factors in a trial lead to the jurors' verdict is always intriguing. Major research on this question has been conducted at the University of Chicago Law School, which has found that, consistent with theories of group behavior, participation and influence in the process are related to social status: men were more active than women, whites more active than minority members, and the better educated more active than those less educated. Much of the discussion in the jury room was not directly concerned with the testimony but rather with trial procedures, opinions about the witnesses, and personal reminiscences.[9] In 30 percent of the cases, a vote taken soon after sequestration was the only one necessary to reach a verdict; in the rest of the cases, the majority on the first ballot eventually won out 90 percent of the time.[10] Because of group pressures, only rarely did a lone juror produce a hung jury.

In evaluating the jury system, researchers have tried to discover whether juries and judges view cases differently. Harry Kalven and Hans Zeisel attempted to answer this question by examining more than 3,500 criminal trials in which juries played a part. They found that the judge and jury agreed on the outcome in 75.4 percent of the trials, but that a jury is more lenient than a judge: the total conviction rate by juries is 64.5 percent; that by judges, 83.3 percent.[11] The very high rate of conviction supports the idea that the filtering process removes doubtful cases before trial.

Analysis of the factors that caused disagreement between the judge and jury revealed that 54 percent of disagreements were attributable to "issues of evidence," about 29 percent to "sentiments on the law," about 11 percent to "sentiments on the defendant," and about 6 percent to other factors. Thus juries clearly do more than merely deal with questions of fact. Much of the disagreement between the judge and jury was favorable to the defendant, an indication that citizens recognize certain values that fall outside the official rules. In weighing the evidence, the jury was strongly impressed by a defendant who had no criminal record and took the stand, especially when the charge was serious. Juries tend to take a more liberal view of such issues as self-defense and are likely to minimize the seriousness of an offense if they are impressed by some attribute of the victim. Presumably because judges have more experience with the process, they are more likely to confer the guilty label on defendants who survive the examination of the police and prosecutor.

Jury Duty

Jury duty is
a. Interesting
b. A pain in the ass
c. Boring
d. All of the above
Answer: d

Jury duty

The *Juror's Manual* of the U.S. District Court says that jury service is "perhaps the most vital duty next to fighting in the defense of one's country." Every year nearly two million Americans respond to the call to perform this civic duty even though doing so usually entails personal and financial hardships. Unfortunately, most jurors experience great frustration with the system as they wait for endless hours in barren courthouse rooms to be called for actual service. Often they are placed on a jury only to have their function preempted by a sudden change of plea to guilty during a portion of the trial. The result is wasted juror time and wasted money. Compensation is usually minimal, and not all employers pay for time lost from the job. What could be an important part of a civic education is often sacrificed to boredom. Misleading impressions of the entire criminal justice system may be the result.

To deal with some of the more distasteful aspects of jury duty, some courts have introduced the one-day/one-trial system. Citizens are traditionally asked to be jurors for a thirty-day term, and although only a few may be needed for a particular day, the entire pool may be present in the courthouse for the full thirty-day period. In the new system, jurors serve either one day or for the duration of one trial. Prospective jurors who are challenged at voir dire or not called to a courtroom are dismissed at the end of their first day and have thus fulfilled their jury duty for the year. Those who are accepted on a jury are required to serve for the duration of that trial, normally about three days. The consensus of jurors, judges, and court administrators is that the one-day/one-trial system is a great improvement.

The value of the jury system has long been debated. Judge Jerome Frank noted in the 1930s that "jury-made law" was the best example of something that is capricious and arbitrary. From time to time public interest has been aroused by this controversy. When juries in highly publicized trials reach verdicts that accord with community sentiment, great praise is heaped on the system; when the outcome is unpopular, questions are raised about the value of this method of fact finding. What must be kept in mind is that juries are a factor in only a small number of the decisions in the administration of criminal justice. Our due process ideals may have obscured this fact.

Assembly-line justice: the lower courts

"The court! All rise, please," shouted an official as Judge Elija Adlow of the Boston Municipal Court entered and began to process a seemingly endless stream of defendants charged with everything from vagrancy, drunkenness, and prostitution to armed robbery and murder. The courtroom is large and crowded with defendants, spectators, lawyers, police officers, and witnesses. In the front row sit about a half-dozen of the "courthouse regular" attorneys waiting to be assigned to the defense of indigents. Adlow parcels out the assignments among them so that they can make up to $200 a week from the state, but only if they follow his rules: no motions for continuances and no delays.

The judge, who recently retired after nearly forty-five years on the bench, ran his court informally—that is, by settling marital and neighborhood quarrels, sending alcoholics to the state farm to dry out, slowing proceedings to encourage a young man charged with statutory rape to marry the woman, committing persons to mental hospitals, arraigning persons charged with felonies, setting bail, and conducting summary trials (without a jury). All this was done in a manner combining the role performance of disciplinarian, father-confessor, sage, and autocrat. As one Boston lawyer said, "His lawbook contains no Constitutions, no rules of evidence, no legal niceties like presumption of innocence or due process. Instead it says only 'You are here to keep your calendar clean.' " *(From "Annals of Law," Part I of "In Criminal Court" by Richard Harris, in the April 14, 1973* New Yorker. *© 1973 The New Yorker Magazine, Inc. Reprinted by permission.)*

Judge Adlow's is an old-fashioned brand of justice but one that is representative of the more than 13,000 lower courts (often referred to as misdemeanor or "inferior" courts) of the country, where order-maintenance violations arising from the problems of living in a complex urban environment flood the system. In small towns and rural areas the lower courts may not be under the same caseload pressure, but here, too, cases are handled in an informal and speedy fashion. The lower courts are of limited jurisdiction because the law restricts the level of punishment that they can allocate. In a sense they are "people's courts." The judges hear the full range of infractions, but most cases involve defendants who have committed minor violations of the law. It is here that about 90 percent of criminal cases are heard either for arraignment and preliminary hearing or through to completion in the form of dismissal or sentence. As table 12.2 shows, only a minority of cases that are adjudicated in lower courts end in jail sentences.

Because the courts are overloaded, the time allotted an individual case is minimal; acceptance of a guilty plea takes no more than fifteen minutes and a summary trial following a plea of not guilty typically lasts less than thirty minutes. When lesser offenses are involved, groups of defendants are often arraigned and processed en masse so that the judicial machine can keep moving.

TABLE 12.2 Choice of sanction in four misdemeanor courts

	Austin, Texas (N = 1,216)	*Columbus, Ohio (N = 1,281)*	*Mankato, Minnesota (N = 803)*	*Tacoma, Washington (N = 565)*
Probation	15.0%	NA	5.6%	3.0%
Jail	6.7	5.1	10.7	4.2
Fine	6.7	57.2	62.7	54.4
Fine and probation	49.0	NA	4.4	4.8
Fine and jail	22.2	29.6	2.0	3.2
Other combinations	0.4	—	4.8	2.1
None of above	—	8.1[a]	9.8[b]	28.3[c]
	100.0%	100.0%	100.0%	100.0%

[a] Includes fines and jail terms suspended in their entirety; possibly also probation sentences, for which data are unavailable.
[b] Includes fines and jail terms suspended in their entirety, as well as community work and counseling/treatment programs.
[c] Includes court costs imposed in lieu of fines, as well as community work.
Source: Anthony J. Ragona and John Paul Ryan, "Misdemeanor Courts and the Choice of Sanctions: A Comparative View," *Justice System Journal* 8 (Summer 1983): 203.

Judicial decisions are mass-produced because actors in the system work on the basis of three assumptions. First, there is a high probability that any person brought before a court is guilty; doubtful cases will be filtered out of the system by the police and prosecution. Second, the vast majority of defendants will plead guilty. Third, those charged with minor offenses will be processed in volume. Thus all the defendants charged with a particular offense will be herded before the bench, the citation will be read by the clerk, and sentences will be pronounced by the judge. Although disposition of vagrancy and drunkenness cases is probably the most blatant example of assembly-line justice, other misdemeanors are often handled with equal dispatch.

We would like to believe that courtroom overload may be relieved by the addition of more judges and the construction of new facilities, but other factors, including poor management, the rise in crime, and the surfeit of lawyers, contribute to the situation. Some people argue that the procedural requirements laid down by the Supreme Court have lengthened processing time, yet observers point out that, typically, persons accused of similar offenses are informed en masse of their rights by a bailiff who drones on in a steady monotone. In addition, studies have shown that most defendants waive their right to a trial, and many do not wish the services of an attorney. Assembly-line justice may also result from the fact that the major players are working to achieve their own individual goals. What may strike outside observers as a sham of due process may in fact be preferred by attorneys, judges, and even defendants.

Although the lower criminal courts have been criticized because of their assembly-line characteristics, social scientists are now beginning to reassess this view. Susan Silbey argues, for example, that the informality, availability, and diversity of the lower courts are their most valuable qualities. As she points out, the lower courts have a unique capacity to resolve cases effectively because they are placed at the entry point of the system, are dispersed throughout the nation, and are embedded within local communities. "They are the place where all problems come that may require certification that someone [will] do something forcefully about this 'trouble.' "[12] These courts are less rule-bound than other courts and more oriented toward individualized justice that is responsive to the community. They appear to be more interested in responding to "problems" than to formally defined "crimes." Thus they seek to achieve substantive justice rather than formal justice, as defined by the criteria of due process.

The sentencing process

Most criminal court judges are "men of no longer tender years who have not associated much with criminal defendants, who have not seemed shrilly unorthodox, who have not lived recently in poverty, who have been modestly or more successful in their profession."[13] While selection procedures may be designed to ensure the presence of qualified persons on the bench, special attributes that would assist the sentencing decision are not usually among the prerequisites, even though in the final analysis the judge alone makes the decision. As the distinguished jurist Irving A. Kaufman has said:

Close-up: Quiet, Efficient Justice in a Small City Court

City Court in this quiet upstate community [Saratoga Springs] sometimes looks very much like Criminal Court in New York City. The Public Defender meets his clients for the first time in the courtroom. Much of the judicial action takes place briskly before the bench. And the prosecutor is amenable to "down charging" for first offenders.

But on the whole, Saratoga Springs, like many other small cities around the state, is a place where justice is being done, according to those who work in City Court.

The process is efficient, the atmosphere is dignified and case disposition is fairly predictable, with dismissals and adjournments granted on merit. And as Judge Lawrence J. LaBelle puts it, "Our 'don't shows' amount to only 1 percent."

The differences of scale, of course, are enormous. The 100 cases that represent a month's work in this historic wood-paneled courtroom in City Hall are equal to a single day's calendar for many judges in Criminal Court in Manhattan. Misdemeanors are handled only twice a week, on Mondays and Thursdays.

The contrast between the court here and in New York City is well known to defendants.

"They'll say that in the city they wouldn't bother with this," said the Public Defender, John P. Pastore. He tells them, "Wrong county, Charlie."

Judge LaBelle, a practicing lawyer, works part time in the $21,000-a-year post of City Court judge, as his father did from 1934 to 1950.

"When I began in 1970," he said, "there was less than an hour and a half's work a day. Today, it's 60 percent of my time. We're bordering on a full-time judgeship."

The judge described courtroom conditions as "horrendous," but they seemed orderly and efficient on a recent day, when the court handled more than two dozen cases.

The day began, as it often does in most courts, with informal discussions in chambers. Judge LaBelle's court assistant, Ann Armstrong, went over some of the cases as Frank B. Williams, an assistant district attorney, and the Public Defender discussed the scheduled trial of a woman charged with welfare fraud. It seemed that the charges might be dropped.

The judge looked up. "Are you telling me it was a bad arrest?" he asked. Mr. Williams said the city's Social Services Department was backing off. Although the defendant "had not given notice that her husband had moved back in," he said, she had accurately reported the number of family members living with her, making it difficult to prove intentional fraud.

There were roughly 30 people in the courtroom, a few sitting inside the railing after being escorted from the local jail. The rest, in the rows of wooden benches, were other defendants, family members or friends, lawyers and potential jurors.

In the first cases the defendants were defended by Mr. Pastore. Then Judge LaBelle said, "Now we'll take cases where attorneys are ready." They included traffic violations, petty larceny, disorderly conduct and aggravated harassment—with many offenses including intoxication.

Judge LaBelle was relatively tough on drunken drivers. One man who pleaded guilty to speeding and failing to keep to the right, but with no drinking charges, was fined $45. The next case, a man who was charged with driving while intoxicated, received a $250 fine, a civil surcharge of $10 and was required to attend a course for drunken drivers.

One by one, the defendants appeared before the bench, the majority pleading guilty to reduced charges, many paying fines ranging from $25 to $50 and none going to jail that day. Cases were put over, defendants were encouraged to settle civil disputes and, finally, the case of the People v. Debbie Millington, the woman who had been charged with wrongfully acquiring welfare funds, was "dismissed in the interests of justice," as Judge LaBelle put it.

The potential jurors filed out, the judge returned to his chambers and Mrs. Millington left, passing a sign behind the bench that reads, "Not All Are Guilty."

Source: James Feron, "In an Upstate City Court, a Feeling of Quiet, Efficient Justice," *New York Times*, 30 June 1983, p. B4.

> If the hundreds of American judges who sit on criminal cases were polled as to what was the most trying facet of their jobs, the vast majority would almost certainly answer "sentencing." In no other judicial function is the judge more alone; no other act of his carries greater potentialities for good or evil than the determination of how society will treat its transgressors.[14]

In the administrative context of the criminal courts, judges often do not have the time to consider all the crucial elements of the offense and the special characteristics of the defendant before imposing a sentence. Especially when the violation is minor, judges tend to routinize decision making and announce sentences to fit certain categories of crimes without too much attention to the particular offender. When the defendant pleads guilty, judges may essentially leave the sentencing decision to the prosecutor and defense attorney. The sole function of the judge may be to legitimize their plea bargaining in open court. When a plea of guilty has been made in a serious case, for example, the prosecutor is asked to outline the facts briefly to the judge and to recommend a sentence. If the plea is to be accepted as voluntarily made, the defense is unable to challenge the prosecutor's story, so the best the defense attorney can do is plead for mercy, stressing the defendant's repentance and the need for a just decision. In such situations prosecutors usually keep their end of the bargain and make their presentations accordingly. Thus, in the eyes of many defendants, "the prosecutor is the person who gives the time," not the judge.

Sentencing behavior of judges

That judges exhibit different sentencing tendencies is taken as a fact of life by criminal lawyers and most recidivists. As early as 1933 one report noted that "some recidivists know the sentencing tendencies of judges so well that the accused will frequently attempt to choose which is to sentence them, and further, some lawyers say they are frequently able to do this."[15]

The disparities among judges can be ascribed to a number of factors: the conflicting goals of criminal justice, the fact that judges are products of different backgrounds and have different social values, the administrative pressures on the judge, and the influence of community values on the system. Each of

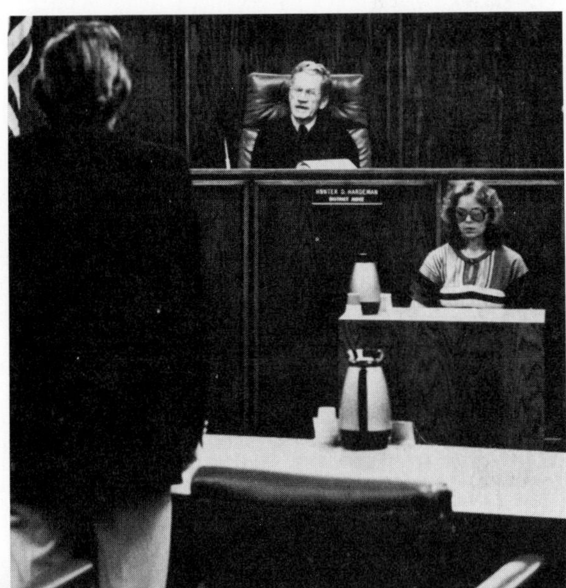

It is during sentencing that the judge imposes punishment.

these factors to some extent structures the judge's exercise of discretion in sentencing offenders. In addition, a judge's perception of these factors is dependent on his or her own attitudes toward the law, toward a particular crime, or toward a type of offender.

Martin Levin's study of the criminal courts of Pittsburgh and Minneapolis revealed the impact of judges' social backgrounds on their sentencing behavior. He found that Pittsburgh judges from humble backgrounds showed greater sympathy toward defendants than did judges with upper-class backgrounds on the Minneapolis bench. Where the Pittsburgh judges tried to base

Close-up: Criminal Court or Sausage Factory?

The nerve center of Criminal Court is Part 1-A. Through it, during daytime and evening sessions, passes a daily procession of 200 to 500 defendants arrested that day or the night before for every kind of crime. Most are represented at this initial hearing by lawyers from the Legal Aid Society, a quasi-public defender supported by the city and private donors. Those who can afford it hire their own lawyers—frequently from the Baxter Street bar—before their next date in court, if there is one.

The pandemonium in Part 1-A is unique even for a criminal court. Defendants on bail, victims of and witnesses to crimes, and others crowd the wooden benches and line the walls. Dozens of police in street clothes, with badges pinned on suits, sport shirts, and windbreakers, scurry about, retrieving defendants for their cases from the public pews or the lockup behind the court, bringing them and their papers before the judge, and returning them after each case. The scene in front of the judge is a constant jumble of people bumping into one another, as defendants, policemen, and witnesses for each case come and go. The pace is so rapid that the judge himself often has time only to check his calendar and set dates for cases to be continued to another day. Most of the talking is done by a bailiff called the "bridgeman," who, in each courtroom of Manhattan's Criminal Court, stands just below the judge on the bottom level of the two-tiered platform.

"Numbers 104, 105, 106, 107, 108, and 109, step up here," a swarthy, dark-haired, gruff-voiced bridgeman shouts, in calling a case with six defendants arrested for possession of narcotics. "Hurry it up. Hurry it up."

The defendants squeeze between the prosecutor and the Legal Aid lawyer in front of the judge. Policemen and witnesses crowd around them. The two lawyers operate in shifts with other prosecutors and defenders. Each stands for about an hour in front of the judge, taking cases as they come. The prosecutor knows nothing about a case until it is called and he sees the court papers on it for the first time. Sometimes, the Legal Aid lawyer has interviewed defendants briefly through the bars in the lockup, or he is given a scanty fact sheet by another defender who saw the prisoner.

In a tobacco-auctioneer's rapid, singsong style, the bridgeman reads the formal charge against the defendants so fast it can barely be understood.

"Put up your hands," the bridgeman orders the policemen who made the arrest. Under New York law, they must swear to the veracity of the charge they filed. They stick up their right hands, but they are not really paying attention to the bridgeman; they are explaining their case in whispers to the prosecutor. The Legal Aid lawyer leans over to try to overhear them. The bridgeman rattles off the oath: "Officers, do-you - swear - that - this - is - the - affadavit - you - signed?" No response, but it doesn't matter. "Put your hands down," the bridgeman growls.

"All right, QUIET in here," he interrupts himself to shout. "Shut that door back there."

their decisions on what they believed was best for the defendant, Minneapolis judges were more legally oriented and considered society's need for protection from criminal behavior. The result of these differing approaches was that white and black defendants received both a greater percentage of probation and a shorter length of incarceration in Pittsburgh, even when Levin accounted for such factors as prior record, plea, age, and offense. In both cities, whites received a greater percentage of probation than blacks, but on the whole sentencing decisions were more favorable for blacks in Pittsburgh than in Minneapolis, both in absolute terms and in relation to whites.[16]

"Howdya plead? howdya plead?" the bridgeman demanded of the Legal Aid attorney, a young blonde woman, on one typical day. She asked a few whispered questions of some of the defendants and turned to the prosecutor to confer with him.

"Let's go. Let's go," the bridgeman barked. "Officers, number 110, Stanton, is next. Have the prisoner ready. We've got to move along."

After a few more words with the Legal Aid lawyer, the prosecutor announced that charges against four of the men would be dropped. There was no explanation why. A date was set for the trial of the other two, who pleaded not guilty.

"All right, all right, you can go," the bridgeman told the four who were let go. "Hurry it up."

The other two men were returned to the lockup, but the bridgeman first had to advise them of their rights. This is his most practiced speech, a series of rapid sentences, each recited as if it were one word and delivered without looking up as he sifts through his papers for the next case: "You-understand-you-have-the-right-to-an-attorney-or-the-right-to-an-adjournment-to-procure-the-services-of-one. If-you-do-not-have-the-financial-resources-to-afford-an-attorney-the-court-will-appoint-one-for-you. You-also-have-the-right-to-communicate-free-of-charge-by-telephone-or-mail-with-any-officer-of-the-court."

His voice rose, "All right, put the prisoners away. Take them away."

Already, he was calling the next case. "Number 110. Stanton. Let's go. Step to the other side of your attorney, mister. Hands out of your pockets. Officer, put your hand up."

Frequently, defendants and witnesses are rushed away by the bridgeman before they understand what has been decided about the case or when and where they are to return to court for the next hearing. In many cases, nothing more is done than the setting of a date for trial. Other cases are dismissed by the prosecutor, usually with no reason given. Occasionally, a guilty plea is arranged on the spot after a whispered conference in front of the judge. The judge passes sentence right away.

In one case, the Legal Aid lawyer announced that her client wanted to plead guilty to assaulting a policeman. But the defendant said he "didn't hit nobody." The judge ordered a date set for trial.

No case lasts more than five minutes. Many are over in sixty seconds.

During a break, one young prosecutor just out of law school said he likes the system. "It becomes routine," he explained with some pride. "You can look at the first couple of lines on the [police] complaint and tell what the case is about, what the state can prove. The defense attorney is equally skilled. You just learn to think quickly on your feet. It's fascinating. I enjoy it."

Who receives unfavorable treatment? Our initial impression may be that blacks and poor people receive the longest prison terms, pay the highest fines, and are placed on probation the fewest times. Although some investigations sustain these assumptions, the evidence is not totally conclusive. The prison populations of most states are more heavily black than the general population. Is this situation a result of the prejudicial attitudes of judges, police officers, and prosecutors? Are poor people more liable to commit violations that elicit a strong response from society? Are enforcement resources distributed so that certain groups are subject to closer scrutiny than other groups?

One study of sentencing in Texas found that blacks received longer prison terms than whites for most offenses but shorter terms than whites for others. Blacks received longer sentences when they were convicted of burglary (largely an interracial offense) but shorter sentences when they were convicted of murder (a predominantly intraracial offense). Intraracial rape, too, elicits short sentences when blacks are the offenders. Although the popular mind may retain the stereotype of the black rapist and the white woman, in reality the victim and assailant are usually of the same race. Thus these racial attitudes concerning property and morals show the important role played by local and regional values. As the author concludes, "those who enforce the law conform to the norms of the local society concerning racial prejudice, thus denying equality before the law."[17]

Analysis of a sample of 2,366 sentencing files for blacks and whites drawn from 50,000 felony convictions in "Metro City" also indicated discrimination on the basis of race. When Cassia Spohn, John Gruhl, and Susan Welch took into account prior record, charge, legal representation, and severity of sentence, they found that black men received harsher sentences than white men, but that this disparity could be accounted for primarily by the fact that blacks were charged with more serious offenses and had more serious prior criminal records. They also found that defendants who had private attorneys or had been released pending trial received less severe sentences. Because of the racial link to social class, these factors were an indirect form of racial discrimination. But even after both legal and extralegal factors were taken into account, the researchers found that the incarceration rate for black men was 20 percent higher than that for white men. Whites were more likely to receive long periods of probation; blacks were more likely to receive short prison terms.[18]

Prison or probation?

One of the most significant developments in the criminal justice system during the last thirty years has been the increased use of probation rather than incarceration. Widely employed today, probation accounts for more than half of the dispositions of felony cases. The judge's decision as to whether an offender should be incarcerated has thus become a crucial part of the sentencing process. The laws of many states stipulate that probation may be given only when mitigating circumstances warrant it.

The American Bar Association, however, has urged that probation be considered the sentence of choice. According to the ABA's Project on Minimum Standards for Criminal Justice, incarceration should be imposed only if the sentencing court determines one of the following factors:

1. Confinement is necessary to protect the public from further criminal activity of the offender.
2. The offender is in need of correctional treatment that can most effectively be provided if he or she is confined.
3. A sentence of probation would unduly depreciate the seriousness of the offense.[19]

Presentence report. Even though sentencing is usually the judge's responsibility, other persons may participate in the decision-making process. In many states the ***presentence investigation*** has become an important ingredient in the judicial mix. Usually a probation officer investigates the convicted person's background, criminal record, job status, and mental condition in order to suggest a sentence that is in the interests both of the person and of society. In some areas, however, probation officers present only factual material to the judge and make no sentencing recommendation. The probation officer may weigh hearsay as well as firsthand information. The defendant usually has no opportunity to challenge the contents of the report or the probation department's recommendation to the judge.

presentence investigation An investigation into the background of a convicted offender, which forms the basis of a report prepared to help the judge determine an appropriate sentence.

One of the criticisms of the presentence report is that probation officers, because of case overload, do not have time to gather adequate evidence to make an informed recommendation. More serious perhaps is the lack of a technical body of knowledge in the corrections field; reports are not diagnostic statements but primarily reflections of the middle-class values of probation officers. Such terms as "immature," "weak-willed," and "shiftless," found in many reports, may seem to arise from hard data, but they are primarily labels applied within a bureaucratic context to influence decision making. In addition, because some probation officers are asked to make a "risk assessment" of the offender, they tend in borderline cases to overpredict on the side of community protection.

The presentence report is one means by which judges ease the strain of decision making: they shift responsibility to the probation department. Because a substantial number of sentencing alternatives are open to them, they often rely on the report for guidance. As table 12.3 shows, after studying sentencing decisions in California, Robert Carter and Leslie Wilkins found a high correlation (96 percent) between a recommendation for probation in the presentence report and the court's disposition of individual cases.[20] When the probation officer recommended incarceration, there was a slight weakening of this relationship, an indication that the officers were more punitive than the judges.

Given the crucial role of the presentence report and the manner in which the information it contains is collected, one might expect that the offender would have a right to examine it and to challenge the contents. In 1949 the Supreme Court ruled in *Williams* v. *New York* that a convicted person did not have a Sixth Amendment right to cross-examine persons who supplied the information in the report.[21] Since then, however, the Court (in *Gardner* v. *Florida*) has ruled that a defendant is denied due process if a sentence is based on information that the defendant is not given the opportunity to deny or explain.[22]

TABLE 12.3 Probation officers' recommendations and subsequent court dispositions, northern district of California, September 1964 to February 1967

		Disposition								
Recommendation	***Total***	***Mandatory***	***Probation***	***Fine only***	***Jail only***	***Imprison-ment***	***Observation and study***	***Continuance***	***Deferred prosecution***	***Other***
All cases	1,232	45	671	30	27	337	73	18	2	29
No recommendation	67	—	44	2	2	14	1	—	—	4
Mandatory	45	45	—	—	—	—	—	—	—	—
Probation	601	—	551	5	3	15	17	2	—	8
Fine only	38	—	14	22	—	1	—	—	—	1
Jail only	35	—	5	1	19	8	2	—	—	—
Imprisonment	334	—	31	—	2	281	13	5	—	2
Observation and study	51	—	3	—	—	9	38	1	—	—
Continuance	16	—	6	—	—	—	—	10	—	—
Deferred prosecution	3	—	—	—	—	—	—	—	2	1
Federal Juvenile Delinquency Act	2	—	1	—	—	—	—	—	—	1
Other	40	—	16	—	1	9	2	—	—	12

Source: Robert M. Carter and Leslie T. Wilkins, "Some Factors in Sentencing Policy," *Journal of Criminal Law, Criminology, and Police Science* 58 (December 1967): 507. Reprinted by special permission of the *Journal of Criminal Law, Criminology, and Police Science*.

In keeping with the privatization of some aspects of the criminal justice system, a number of courts have begun the practice of contracting with private firms for the conduct of presentence investigations. It is argued that such arrangements cost less and provide a more independent assessment of the defendant because the private consultant is not so closely tied to the judiciary as probation officers are. These programs will be watched with interest.

From an organizational standpoint, the probation department is independent of other parts of the criminal justice system; yet from the standpoint of the politics of administration, it is tied to the court structure. In a great number of jurisdictions the probation department is part of the judiciary and under the institutional supervision of the judges. Its budgetary, recruitment, and supervision policies all flow through the court structure; hence it is not as independent as one might expect. A close relationship between the probation officers and the members of the court is often justified on the grounds that judges will place greater trust in the information provided by staff members under their immediate supervision. Rather than presenting an independent and impartial report, probation officers may be more interested in second-guessing the judge. Yet one should also be concerned that because of the pressure of their duties, judges may rely totally on the presentence recommendations and merely ratify the suggestions of the probation officers without applying their own judicial perspective to the decisions.

Judge's perspective. Given the information contained in the presentence report (p. 440), what elements most influence the judge to specify probation rather than incarceration? Interviews with the judges of the Connecticut superior courts indicated that a prior record was a major, often *the* major, consideration. Eighty percent of all offenders with no prior record received probation, while 70 percent with a major criminal record (felonies or a large number of arrests and some convictions) received a prison sentence. Of secondary importance was the nature of the offense. According to the interviews, a good candidate for probation had no substantial prior record, committed the crime in neither a violent nor a particularly outrageous manner, had been a good steady worker, and was likely (according to the presentence report and the judge's own intuition) to be rehabilitated.

The impression of the offender that the presentence report conveys is a very important factor. The probation officer's use of language is crucial. Summary statements may be written in a totally noncommital style or may convey

Presentence Report

PROBATION
FORM 2
FEB 65

UNITED STATES DISTRICT COURT
Central District of New York
PRESENTENCE REPORT

NAME
John Jones

ADDRESS
1234 Astoria Blvd.
New York City

LEGAL RESIDENCE
Same

AGE DATE OF BIRTH 2-8-40
33 New York City

SEX RACE
Male Caucasian

CITIZENSHIP
U.S. (Birth)

EDUCATION
10th grade

MARITAL STATUS
Married

DEPENDENTS
Three (wife and 2 children)

SOC. SEC. NO.
112-03-9559

FBI NO.
256 1126

DETAINERS OR CHARGES PENDING:
None

CODEFENDANTS (Disposition)
None

DATE
January 4, 1974

DOCKET NO.
74-103

OFFENSE
Theft of Mail by Postal
Employee (18 U.S.C.
Sec. 1709) 2 counts

PENALTY
Count 2: 5 years and/or
$2,000 fine

PLEA
Guilty on 12-16-73 to
Count 2
Count 1 pending

VERDICT

CUSTODY
Released on own
recognizance. No time
in custody.

ASST. U.S. ATTY
Samuel Hayman

DEFENSE COUNSEL
Thomas Lincoln
Federal Public Defender

Drug/Alcohol Involvement:
Attributes offense to
need for drinking money

DISPOSITION

DATE

SENTENCING JUDGE

the notion that the defendant either is worth saving or is unruly. Judges say they read the report to get an understanding of the defendant's attitude. A comment such as "the defendant appears unrepentant" can send a person to prison.

> In one sentencing hearing a seventeen-year-old first offender was sent to the Correctional Institution at Cheshire (reformatory) in large measure because he was reported to be unrepentant and unconcerned with what he had done. His father protested that the probation officer who drafted the report had talked to the boy twice for no longer than two minutes each time and could not have formed a reasonable impression of the boy's attitude. This protest had no effect on the judge.[23]

Presentence Report

Offense: official version. Official sources reveal that during the course of routine observations on December 4, 1973, within the Postal Office Center, Long Island, New York, postal inspectors observed the defendant paying particular attention to various packages. Since the defendant was seen to mishandle and tamper with several parcels, test parcels were prepared for his handling on December 5, 1973. The defendant was observed to mishandle one of the test parcels by tossing it to one side into a canvas tub. He then placed his jacket into the tub and leaned over the tub for a period of time. At this time the defendant left the area and went to the men's room. While he was gone the inspectors examined the mail tub and found that the test parcel had been rifled and that the contents, a watch, was missing.

The defendant returned to his work and picked up his jacket. He then left the building. The defendant was stopped by the inspectors across the street from the post office. He was questioned about his activities and on his person he had the wristwatch from the test parcel. He was taken to the postal inspector's office where he admitted the offense.

Defendant's version of offense. The defendant admits that he rifled the package in question and took the watch. He states that he intended to sell the watch at a later date. He admits that he has been drinking too much lately and needed extra cash for "drinking money." He exhibits remorse and is concerned about the possibility of incarceration and the effect that it would have on his family.

Prior record

Date	*Offense*	*Place*	*Disposition*
5-7-66 (age 26)	Possession of Policy Slips	Manhattan CR. CT. N.Y., N.Y.	$25.00 Fine 7-11-66
3-21-72 (age 32)	Intoxication	Manhattan CR. CT. N.Y., N.Y.	4-17-72 Nolle

Personal history. The defendant was born in New York City on February 8, 1940, the oldest of three children. He attended the public school, completed the 10th grade and left school and was active in sports, especially basketball and baseball.

The defendant's father, John, died of a heart attack in 1968, at the age of 53 years. He had an elementary school education and worked as a construction laborer most of his life.

The defendant's mother, Mary Smith Jones, is 55 years of age and is employed as a seamstress. She had an elementary school education and married defendant's father when she was 20 years of age. Three sons were issue of the marriage. She presently resides in New York City, and is in good health.

Appeals

Imposition of a sentence does not mean that it must be served immediately. In most jurisdictions the defendant has the right to appeal the conviction to a higher court. An ***appeal*** is based on a contention that one or more errors of law were made during the criminal justice process. A defendant might base an appeal, for example, on the contention that evidence was improperly admitted, that the judge did not charge the jury correctly, or that a guilty plea was not made voluntarily. Note that appeals are based on questions of procedure, not on the defendant's guilt or innocence. It is for the government to prove, in the ways required by the law, that the individual is guilty. If mistakes were made by the prosecution or judge, a conviction may be reversed. The convic-

appeal
A request to a higher court that it review actions taken in a completed trial.

Defendant's brother, Paul, age 32 years, completed 2½ years of high school. He is employed as a bus driver and resides with his wife and two children in New York City.

Defendant's brother, Lawrence, age 30 years, completed three semesters of college. He is employed as a New York City firefighter. He resides with his wife and one child in Dutch Point, Long Island.

The defendant after leaving high school worked as a delivery boy for a retail supermarket chain, then served 2 years in the U.S. Army as an infantryman (ASN 123 456 78). He received an honorable discharge and attained the rank of corporal serving from 2-10-58 to 2-1-60. After service he held a number of jobs of the laboring type.

The defendant was employed as a truck driver for the City of New York when he married Ann Sweeny on 6-15-63. Two children were issue of this marriage, John, age 8, and Mary, age 6. The family has resided at the same address (which is a four-room apartment) since their marriage.

The defendant has been in good health all of his life but he admits he has been drinking to excess the past eighteen months which has resulted in some domestic strife. The wife stated that she loved her husband and will stand by him. She is amenable to a referral for family counseling.

Defendant has worked for the Postal Service since 12-1-65 and resigned on 12-5-73 as a result of the present arrest. His work ratings by his supervisors were always "excellent."

Evaluative summary. The defendant is a 33-year-old male who entered a plea of guilty to mail theft. While an employee of the U.S. Postal Service he rifled and stole a watch from a test package. He admitted that he planned on selling the watch to finance his drinking which has become a problem resulting in domestic strife.

Defendant is a married man with two children with no prior serious record. He completed ten years of schooling, had an honorable military record, and has a good work history. He expresses remorse for his present offense and is concerned over the loss of his job and the shame to his family.

Recommendation. It is respectfully recommended that the defendant be admitted to probation. If placed on probation the defendant expresses willingness to seek counseling for his domestic problems. He will require increased motivation if there is to be a significant change in his drinking pattern.

Respectfully submitted,

Donald M. Fredericks
U.S. Probation Officer

Source: "The Selective Presentence Investigation Report," *Federal Probation* 38 (December 1974): 53–54.

tion is then set aside and the defendant may be retried. Many states provide for an automatic appeal in capital cases.

Unlike most Western countries, the United States does not allow the terms of the sentence to be appealed in most circumstances. An appeal may be filed when it is contended that the judge selected penalties that did not accord with the law or that were violations of either due process or equal protection. But if the law gives the judge the discretion to impose a sentence of, for example, ten years in a particular case and the defendant thinks that his actions warranted only eight, it would be quite unusual for the sentence to be overturned on appeal unless some procedural defect could be shown. It would be necessary to show that the decision was illegal, unreasonable, or unconstitutional.

A case originating in a state court is usually appealed through that state's judicial system. If a state case involves a constitutional question, however, it may be appealed to the U.S. Supreme Court. Almost four-fifths of all appeals are decided by state courts, yet in 1982 4,767 criminal appeals were filed in the federal courts.

Habeas corpus

habeas corpus
A writ or judicial order requesting that a person holding another person produce the prisoner and give reasons to justify continued confinement.

Known as "the great writ," ***habeas corpus*** is a command by a court to a person holding a prisoner in custody requiring that the prisoner be brought before a judge. This procedure permits a judge to decide whether the person is being legally held. Article III of the U.S. Constitution extends the application of habeas corpus to federal prisoners, and over time the use of the writ led to a kind of appellate review of the conviction. The right was extended by Congress in 1867 to state prisoners, allowing review of their convictions in federal court after state remedies had been exhausted.

Although very few habeas corpus petitions are successful in federal court (about 3 percent), the number filed has increased by almost 700 percent during the past twenty years. This increase has caused concern among federal judges, who find their criminal caseloads greatly expanded. Various tactics, such as allowing magistrates to review petitions and eliminate the frivolous, have been used to deal with this problem.

Frustrated by the problems of crime, some conservatives have argued that opportunities for appeal should be limited. It is said that too many offenders delay imposition of their sentences and that others completely evade the sanctions by filing appeals endlessly. This practice not only increases the workload of the courts but puts the concept of the finality of the justice process at risk. It is thought that punishment should be swift and certain.

Much of the concern about the leakage caused by the appellate process seems to result from a few highly publicized cases. What goes unnoticed is the fact that relatively few cases reach this stage. Since up to 90 percent of defendants plead guilty, very few are able to appeal; the guilty plea substantially reduces the legal grounds for reversal of a conviction. Of the remaining group who plead not guilty to a felony charge, about two-thirds are convicted and perhaps 30 percent of those may appeal. Thus if, say, 100 defendants were to plead not guilty at trial, probably 66 would be convicted, and of those perhaps 19 would appeal. Of the 19, 4 (about 20 percent) would have their convictions reversed.[24]

A successful appeal for the defendant, one that results in reversal of the conviction, normally means that the case is remanded to the lower court for a new trial. At this point the state must consider whether the procedural errors in the original trial can be overcome and whether it is worth additional expenditure to bring the defendant into court again.

Summary

The public's assumptions about the criminal justice system are greatly influenced by the newspapers and by television. Most people are exposed to only the most noteworthy cases—the criminal trials that become public dramas. Chapter 12 has explained the processes of the trial from jury selection to decision. The sentencing process, introduced here, will be explored further in chapter 13. Throughout, this book has argued that the sanction imposed by the court—"the time to be served"—is a factor that heavily influences the actions of many portions of the system. The judge's crucial decision concerning whether the offender will receive probation or prison is evaluated by the prosecutor, the defense attorney, and the defendant. The final portion of this chapter introduced the appellate process. Offenders may appeal their convictions on legal grounds, but in most jurisdictions in the United States it is not possible to appeal the sentence. This, then, is the final chapter in the section on adjudication. Part Four focuses on postconviction strategies.

For discussion

1. Since there are so few jury trials, what types of cases would you expect to find adjudicated in this manner? Why?
2. If most cases are decided through a guilty plea or a bench trial, what is the purpose of appellate courts? Who is likely to use them?
3. How might your counsel's knowledge of the judge's sentencing behavior influence decisions in your case?
4. Should probation officers be required to make a presentence investigation and report in plea-bargained cases?

For further reading

James, Howard. *Crisis in the Courts.* New York: David McKay, 1968.
Kalven, Harry, Jr., and Zeisel, Hans. *The American Jury.* Boston: Little, Brown, 1966.
Neubauer, David. *America's Courts and the Criminal Justice System.* Monterey, Calif.: Duxbury Press, 1979.
Phillips, Steven. *No Heroes, No Villains.* New York: Random House, 1977.
Villaseñor, Victor. *Jury: The People vs. Juan Corona.* Boston: Little, Brown, 1977.

Notes

1. Steven Phillips, *No Heroes, No Villains* (New York: Random House, 1977), p. 109.
2. 399 U.S. 78 (1970).
3. 441 U.S. 130 (1979).
4. Harry Kalven, Jr., and Hans Zeisel, *The American Jury,* pp. 31–32.
5. David Neubauer, *Criminal Justice in Middle America* (Morristown, N.J.: General Learning Press, 1974), p. 229.
6. David Kairys, Joseph B. Kadane, and John P. Lehoczky, "Jury Representativeness: A Mandate for Multiple Source Lists," 65 *California Law Review* 776 (1977).
7. Paula D. Perna, *Juries on Trial* (New York: Dembner Books, 1984), p. 137.
8. *Griffin* v. *California,* 380 U.S. 609 (1965).
9. Fred Strodtbeck, Rita James, and Gordon Hawkins, "Social Status in Jury Deliberations," *American Sociological Review* 22 (1957): 713–19.

10. David W. Broeder, "The University of Chicago Jury Project," 38 *Nebraska Law Review* 774–80 (May 1959).
11. Kalven and Zeisel, *American Jury,* p. 62.
12. Susan S. Silbey, "Making Sense of the Lower Courts," *Justice System Journal* 6 (Spring 1981): 20.
13. Marvin E. Frankel, *Criminal Sentences* (New York: Hill & Wang, 1972), p. 13.
14. As quoted in Ronald L. Goldfarb and Linda R. Singer, *After Conviction* (New York: Simon & Schuster, 1973), p. 138.
15. Frederick J. Gaudet, G. S. Harris, and C. W. St. John, "Individual Differences in Sentencing Tendencies of Judges," *Journal of Criminal Law and Criminology* 23 (1933): 814.
16. Martin A. Levin, "Urban Politics and Policy Outcomes: The Criminal Courts," in *Criminal Justice: Law and Politics,* ed. George F. Cole, 2d ed. (North Scituate, Mass.: Duxbury Press, 1976), p. 372.
17. Henry A. Bullock, "Significance of the Racial Factor in the Length of Prison Sentence," *Journal of Criminal Law, Criminology, and Police Science* 52 (1961): 411.
18. Cassia Spohn, John Gruhl, and Susan Welch, "The Effect of Race on Sentencing: A Reexamination of an Unsettled Question," *Law and Society Review* 16 (1981–82): 85.
19. American Bar Association, *Project on Minimum Standards for Criminal Justice Standards Relating to Probation* (Chicago, 1970).
20. Robert M. Carter and Leslie T. Wilkins, "Some Factors in Sentencing Policy," *Journal of Criminal Law, Criminology, and Police Science* 58 (1967): 503.
21. 337 U.S. 241 (1949).
22. 430 U.S. 349 (1977).
23. Rosemary B. Zion, "Sentencing Practices in the Superior Courts of Connecticut," study prepared for the Judicial Department, State of Connecticut, 1972, p. 51.
24. Peter W. Lewis and Kenneth D. Peoples, *The Supreme Court and the Criminal Process* (Philadelphia: Saunders, 1978), p. 90.

The trial

Everybody kept trying to talk him out of his trial. "Plead guilty, jackass, you could get ten to twenty for this," Xinos whispered when they finally got to trial. *Ain't no need for that,* said Payne. "You really want a jury?" the assistant state's attorney, Walter Parrish, teased him. "Or you want to plead?" *I want my trial,* said Payne. Everything in the building says cop out, make a deal, take the short time. "They ought to carve it in stone over the door," an old courthouse hand, then a prosecutor and now a judge, told a friend once. "NO CASE EVER GOES TO TRIAL HERE." The People vs. Donald Payne did get to trial, halfway at least. But then his case went sour, and the deal got sweeter, and in the end Donald Payne copped out, too.

Practically everybody does: urban justice in America would quite simply collapse if even a major fraction of the suspects who now plead guilty should suddenly start demanding jury trials. The Payne case was only one of 500 indictments on Judge Richard Fitzgerald's docket last year; it would have taken him four years to try them all. So 85 to 90 percent of them ended in plea bargaining—that backstairs haggling process by which pleas of guilty are bartered for reduced charges or shorter sentences or probation. "Plea bargaining used to be a nasty word," says Fitzgerald; only lately have the bar and the courts begun to call it out of the closet and recognize it not as just a reality but a necessity of the system. "We're saying, 'You're doing it, we know you're doing it and you have to do it; this is the way it has to be done.'"

The pressures to plead are sometimes cruel, the risks of going to trial high and well-advertised. There is, for waverers, the cautionary tale of one man who turned down one to three years on a deal—and got 40 to 80 as an object lesson when a jury convicted him. Still, Payne insisted, and Xinos painstakingly put a defense together. He opened with a pair of preliminary motions, one arguing that the pistol was inadmissible because the evidence tying it to Payne was hearsay, the other contending that the police should have offered Payne a lawyer at the line-up but didn't. The witnesses straggled in for a hearing on December 1. Joe Castelli took the stand, and Patrolman Cullen, and, for a few monosyllabic moments, Payne himself. Had anyone advised him of his rights to a lawyer? "No." Or let him make a phone call? "No." But another of the arresting officers, Robert Krueger, said that Payne had been told of his rights—and such swearing contests almost always are decided in favor of the police. Everybody admired Xinos's energy and craftsmanship. Nevertheless, Fitzgerald denied both of the defense motions and docketed the case for trial on December 14.

And so they all gathered that wintry Monday in Fitzgerald's sixth-floor courtroom, a great dim cave with marbled and oak-paneled walls, pitted linoleum floors and judge, jury, lawyers, defendant and a gallery so widely separated that nobody could hear anything without microphones. Choosing a jury took two hours that day, two the next morning. Parrish, an angular, Ivy-cut Negro of 41, worked without a shopping list. "I know some lawyers say fat people are jolly and Germans are strict," he says, "but none of that's true in my experience. If you get twelve people who say they'll listen, you're all right."

But Xinos is a hunch player. He got two blacks on the jury and was particularly pleased with one of them, a light-skinned Urban League member who looked as if she might be sympathetic. And he deliberately let one hard hat sit on the panel. Xinos had a point to make about the pistol—you couldn't click it more than once without pulling back the slide to cock it—and the hard hat looked as if he knew guns.

That afternoon, slowly and methodically, Parrish began to put on his case. He opened with the victims, and Castelli laid the story on the record: "About ten after 9, the gentleman walked in. . . . He had a small-caliber pistol. . . . I edged away. . . . The other lad came up to me and he said, 'Shoot him, shoot him, shoot him.' . . . [The first youth] pointed the gun at me and fired three times or four—at least I heard three clicks." And the gunman—did Castelli see him in court?

"Yes I do, sir."

"And would you point him out, please?"

Castelli gestured toward the single table shared by the prosecution and defense. "That," he said, "is Donald Payne."

But Xinos, in his opening argument, had promised to alibi Payne—his mother was prepared to testify for him—and now, on cross-examination, he picked skillfully at Parrish's case. Playing to his hard hat on the jury, he asked Castelli whether the stick-up man had one or two hands on the gun. "Only one, sir," said Castelli. "And was that trigger pulled in rapid succession—click-click-click?" Xinos pressed. "Yes, sir," said Castelli, and Xinos had his point: it takes two hands to keep pulling the slide and clicking the trigger. Next came Patrolman Joe Higgins, who remembered, under Xinos's pointed cross-examination, that Castelli had described the gunman as weighing 185 pounds—30 more than Payne carries on his spindly 6-foot-1 frame. Payne had nearly botched that point by wearing a billowy, cape-shaped jacket to court, but Xinos persuaded him to fold it up and sit on it so the jurors could see how bony he really was. The 30-pound misunderstanding undercut Castelli's identification of Payne—and suddenly the People and their lawyer, Walter Parrish, were in trouble.

Parrish didn't show it: he is a careful, phlegmatic man born to striving parents in the Chicago ghetto and bred to move smiling coolly through the system. He came into it with a Howard law diploma, a few years' haphazard practice and the right sort of connections as counsel to and precinct captain for the 24th Ward regular Democratic organization. He figured on the job only as an apprenticeship for private practice, but he has stayed six years and seems rather comfortable where he is. The black kids over in the County Jail call him "The Devil," and he likes that; he fancied that the edgy hostility he saw in Donald Payne's eyes was a tribute to his hard-guy reputation. He likes his public law firm, too. It pays him $18,000—he guesses he would have to gross $50,000 in private practice to match that—and it puts all the enormous resources of the state at his service. Investigators? The state's attorney has 93 to the public defender's six. Police, the sheriff, the FBI? "All you got to do is call them." Pathology? Microanalysis? "Just pick up the phone. You've got everything at your beck and call."

What he had in People vs. Payne was the Hamilton boys, the two cousins through whom the police had tracked Payne. Parrish had hoped he wouldn't have to put them on the stand. "It was a risk," he said later. "They could have hurt us. They could have got up there and suddenly said Donald wasn't there." But he was behind and knew it. He needed Frank Hamilton to place Payne inside the store, James to connect him with the car and the pistol. So, that afternoon, he ordered up subpoenas for the Hamiltons. "We know how to scramble," said his young assistant, Joe Poduska. "That's the name of the game."

The subpoenas were being typed when Connie Xinos happened into the state's attorney's office to socialize—*it's like a family*—and saw them in the typewriter. Xinos went cold. He had talked to the mother of one of the Hamiltons; he knew their testimony could hurt. So, next morning, he headed first thing to Parrish's austere second-floor cubicle—and found the Hamiltons there. "We're going to testify," they told Xinos, "and we're going to tell the truth."

Xinos took Parrish aside. "Let's get rid of this case," he said.

"It's Christmas," Parrish said amiably. "I'm a reasonable man."

"What do you want?" Xinos asked.

"I was thinking about three to eight."

"One to five," said Xinos.

"You got it."

It's an absolute gift, Xinos thought, and he took it to Payne in the lockup. "I can get you one to five," he said. Payne said no. Xinos thought fast. It was a dead-bang case—the kind Clarence Darrow couldn't pull out—and it was good for a big rattle, maybe ten to twenty years. Xinos went back downstairs, got the Hamiltons and sat them down with Payne in Fitzgerald's library. "They rapped," he remembers, "and one of them said, 'Donald—you mean you told them you weren't *there?*' I told him again I could get him one to five. They said, 'Maybe you ought to take it, Donald.' I said, 'You may get ten to twenty going on with the trial.' And he said, 'Well, even if I take one to five, I'm not guilty.' That's when I knew he would go."

But would Fitzgerald buy it? Xinos was worried. The judge is a handsome 57, with a pink Irish face rimmed with silver hair and creased to smile. "He looks like God would look and acts like God would act if God were a judge," says Xinos. "He doesn't take any s——." He was a suburban lawyer in Calumet City when Mayor Richard Daley's organization slated him for judge seven years ago, a reward for having backed a Daley man for governor once when it was tough to do so. He started in divorce court and hated it: "I think I'd rather have 150 lashes than go back down there. Jeez—it's a lot easier to give a guy the chair than it is to take five kids away from a mother." He is happier where he is, and he has made a considerable reputation in the building as a solid, early-rising, hard-working judge—no scholar but conscientious and good on the law. He can be stern as well: he isn't the hanging type, but he does think the pendulum has swung pretty far lately in the defendant's favor. "We've clothed 'em in swaddling clothes," he says, "and laid 'em in a manger of bliss." So Xinos fretted. "The judge is the judge," he told Payne while they waited for an audience with Fitzgerald. "He might give you three to eight. You better think about that."

But Fitzgerald agreed to talk, and the ritual began to unfold. Xinos led Payne to the bench and announced for the record that they wanted to discuss pleading—"Is that correct, Donald?" Payne mumbled, "Correct," and, while he went back to the lockup to wait, the lawyers followed the judge into chambers. A bailiff closed the door behind them. Fitzgerald sat at his desk and pulled a 4-by-6 index card out of a box; he likes to keep his own notes. Parrish dropped into a deep, leathery sofa, his knees coming up almost to his chin. Xinos sat in a green guest chair in a row along the wall. There were no outsiders, not even a court stenographer. The conference, not the courtroom, has become the real focus of big-city criminal justice, but its business is transacted off the record for maximum flexibility.

Fitzgerald scanned Parrish's prep sheet, outlining the state case. Xinos told him glumly about the Hamiltons. "We look beat," he conceded.

"Walter," asked the judge, "what do you want?"

"I don't want to hurt the kid," Parrish said. "I talked to Connie, and we thought one to five."

They talked about Payne's record—his jobs, his family, his old gas-station burglary rap. "Two years' probation," Xinos put in hopefully. "That's nothing." Fitzgerald pondered it all. He had no probation report—there isn't time or manpower enough to do them except in major cases—and no psychological workup; sentencing in most American courts comes down to a matter of instinct. Fitzgerald's instincts told him one to five was a long time for Payne to serve—and a wide enough spread to encourage him to reform and get out early. "Up to five years," he feels, "that's the area of rehabilitation. Beyond five, I think they get saturated." So he made up his mind.

"Will he take it?" the judge asked Xinos.

"I'll go back and see," Xinos replied. He ducked out to the lockup and put the offer to Payne.

"Let's do it," Payne said. "Right now."

A light snow was falling when they brought him back into court, grinning slightly, walking his diddybop walk. A bailiff led him to a table below Fitzgerald's high bench. His mother slipped into place beside him. He spread his fingers out on the tabletop and looked at them. The judge led him through the prescribed catechism establishing that he understood what he was doing and that no one had forced him to do it. Payne's "yesses" were barely audible in the cavernous room.

The choice now was his, Fitzgerald told him. He could go to the pen and cooperate and learn a trade and come out on parole in eleven months; or he could "go down there and do nothing at all and sit on your haunches . . . and you will probably be going [back] down there for twenty or thirty years." Payne brushed one hand across his eye and studied the tabletop. "I'm giving you the first break you probably ever got in your life," the judge said. ". . . The rest of it, Donald, is up to you. Do you understand that?"

"Yes," said Payne.

And then it was over. Fitzgerald called the jurors in and dismissed them. They knew nothing of the events that had buried Donald; they sat there for a moment looking stunned. Xinos slipped back to the jury room to see them before they scattered. "But you were *ahead,*" one told him.

Payne's mother walked out to a pay phone, eyes wet and flashing. "They just pressed Donnie," she insisted, "until he said he did it." Parrish packed up. "An hour, a day—even that's punishment," he said. "One to five is enough." Joe Higgins went back to Tac Unit 660. "Donald," he said, "is a very lucky man." Winston Moore heard about it in his office at the jail. "One to five?" he snorted. "S——. That's no sentence for armed robbery." Xinos went home to his apartment in the suburbs. "One to five," he said. "Fantastic. Payne *should* go to the penitentiary. He's a bad kid, he's better off there. He's dangerous. He'll be back."

And Payne was sulky sore. He shook hands with Xinos and grinned broadly when the deal went down, but when Xinos told him later what the juror said—*you were ahead*—he felt cheated. A break? "The best break they could have given me was letting me go." But there was nothing for him to do just then but go brooding back down to the tunnel and to jail. "Everybody do something wrong," he told himself. "Maybe my time just caught up with me."

Source: Peter Goldman and Don Holt, "How Justice Works: The People vs. Donald Payne," *Newsweek,* 8 March 1971, pp. 20–37.

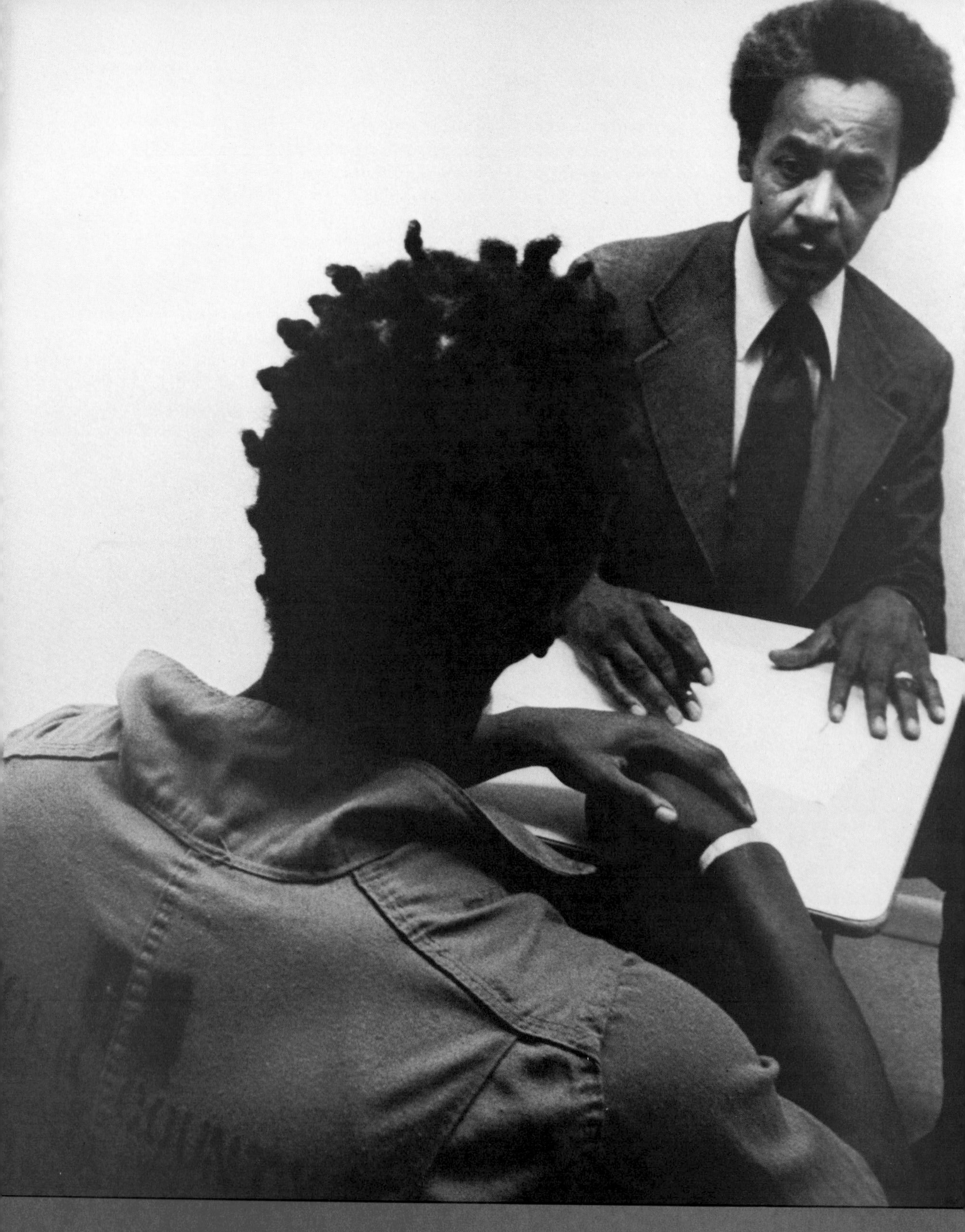

PART 4

Postconviction Strategies

Part Four looks at the various ways in which the American system of criminal justice deals with offenders. The processes of sentencing and corrections are believed to meet a number of needs: to penalize the individual found guilty and also to impress upon others that those who transgress the law will be punished. Historically, there has been no agreement about the best measures to use against law-breakers. Unfortunately, over the course of time the corrections system has risen to peaks of excited reform, only to drop to valleys of despairing failure. Chapters 13–16 will discuss how offenders are treated and the various influences that have structured our correctional system. As these chapters unfold, recall the processes that have occurred before the imposition of sentence, especially as they determine the goals of the correctional portion of the criminal justice system.

Sentencing

- **Purpose of the criminal sanction**
  - Retribution (deserved punishment)
  - Deterrence
  - Incapacitation
  - Rehabilitation
  - Criminal sanctions: a mixed bag?
- **Forms of the criminal sanction**
  - Fines
  - Incarceration
    - *Indeterminate sentences*
    - *Determinate sentences*
    - *Mandatory sentences*
    - *Good time*
    - *The sentence versus actual time served*
  - Probation
  - Death
  - Restitution
  - Informal sanctions: the process is the punishment
- **Legislative responsibility**
- **Sentencing reform**
- **Toward rationality in sentencing**
  - Sentencing institutes
  - Sentencing councils
  - Sentencing review
  - Sentencing guidelines
- **Summary**

13

The rationale of the criminal justice system rests on concepts that symbolize the three basic problems in the law: offense—what conduct should be designated as criminal?; guilt—what determinations must be made before a person can be found to have committed a criminal offense?; punishment—what should be done with persons who are found to have committed criminal offenses? Earlier chapters have emphasized the first two problems, but, as we have seen, the assumptions a society makes about any of the three problems greatly affect the interpretation and focus of the others. They are inextricably bound together. The answers given by the legal system to the first question comprise the basic norms of the society: do not murder, rob, sell drugs, commit treason. The process of determining guilt or innocence is stipulated by the law and is greatly influenced by the administrative and interpersonal considerations of criminal justice actors. The remainder of this book will focus primarily on the third problem: the sanctions or punishments specified by the law.

You sit on the bench . . . and you get this terrible sense that you can't help anyone who could be helped. Sometimes you look at a young man or woman and you feel that if someone could really get hold of them maybe something good could come of their lives.

JUDGE JOEL L. TYLER, MANHATTAN NIGHT COURT, CITY OF NEW YORK

Sentencing, or the specification of the sanction, may be viewed as both the beginning and the end of the criminal justice system. When guilt has been established, a decision must be made concerning what to do with the convicted person. Public interest seems to wane at this point; usually the convicted criminal is out of sight and thus out of mind as far as society is concerned. This is certainly not the case with the offender or with the decision makers in the criminal justice system, however. For the offender, the passing of sentence is the beginning of corrections, with its restriction of freedom and its promise of rehabilitation.

For the regular participants and observers of the criminal justice system, the terms of the sanction will to some degree determine their future behavior. As we have seen, a great part of the efforts of the defendant, prosecutor, and defense attorney during the presentencing phase is based on assumptions concerning the sanction that may follow conviction. Although police officers are generally removed from the courtroom at the time of sentencing, they, too, will be influenced by the judge's decision. Law enforcement officials may wonder whether arresting certain types of violators is worthwhile if their effort is not reflected in the sentences imposed. For the general population, punishment is expected to perform a deterrent function that reinforces societal values by serving as a warning of the consequences of wrongdoing.

Purpose of the criminal sanction

Throughout the history of Western civilization, punishment for violations of the criminal law has been shaped by philosophical and moral orientations. Although the ultimate purpose of the criminal sanction is assumed to be the maintenance of social order, different justifications have emerged in different eras to legitimize the punishment imposed by the state. The ancient custom of severing a limb of a thief who stole was once justified as an act of retribution; in later periods, similar penalties were exacted—capital punishment, for example—on the grounds of incapacitation or deterrence. Over time, Western countries have moved away from the imposition of physical pain as a form of retribution and toward greater reliance on social and psychological sanctions imposed for the purpose of rehabilitation.

From the Middle Ages through the mid–eighteenth century, sanctions were severe and no attempt was made to fit the punishment to either the offense or the offender. Under the leadership of the German philosopher Immanuel Kant, efforts were made to create a balance between the gravity of the offense and the degree of punishment. In the context of the times, his slogan "Make the punishment fit the crime" was a humanistic advance, since it sought to do away with the horrible punishments given for trivial offenses. Later, with the development of the Italian school of criminology and Cesare Lombroso's belief that the "born criminal" could be identified by certain physical characteristics, the emphasis of sanctioning theory shifted to the offender. No longer was the level of punishment expected to reflect the crime; rather, "the punishment should fit the criminal."

In the United States today the term "punishment" often has an ideological connotation that links it to retribution and not to the other justifications for the criminal sanction. It is difficult for some people to reconcile the goal of rehabilitation with punishment. Are individuals being punished if they are in a correctional facility that emphasizes therapy? Is probation a punishment?

Herbert Packer argues that punishment may be described as any way of dealing with people that is marked by these elements:

1. The presence of an offense.
2. The infliction of pain on account of the commission of the offense.
3. A dominant purpose that is neither to compensate someone injured by the offense nor to better the offender's condition but to prevent further offenses or to inflict what is thought to be deserved pain on the offender.[1]

Note that Packer emphasizes two major goals of criminal punishment: the deserved infliction of suffering on evildoers and the prevention of crime.

In the twentieth century the United States has acknowledged four goals of the criminal sanction: retribution (deserved punishment), deterrence, incapacitation, and rehabilitation. Although no one goal is the sole reason for a particular sentence, until a decade ago most legislatures stipulated that rehabilitation was to be given priority. That judges often acknowledged the importance of other goals and that legislatures did not appropriate money to implement the rehabilitative goal did not strike many people as odd.

Retribution (deserved punishment)

"An eye for an eye, a tooth for a tooth" has been a purpose of the criminal sanction since biblical times. Although the ancient saying may sound barbaric, it can be thought of as a definition of ***retribution:*** those who do a wrong should be punished alike, in proportion to the gravity of the offense or to the extent to which others have been made to suffer. Retribution is punishment that is deserved. Andrew von Hirsch, a leading contemporary writer on punishment, has described "someone who infringes the rights of others" as one who "does wrong and deserves blame for his conduct. It is because he deserves blame that the sanctioning authority is entitled to choose a response that expresses moral disapproval: namely, punishment."[2] He argues further that deserved punishment should be applied only for the wrong inflicted and not primarily to achieve utilitarian benefits (deterrence, incapacitation, rehabilitation). Offenders should be penalized for their wrongful acts because fairness and justice dictate that they deserve punishment.

retribution (deserved punishment)
Punishment inflicted on a person who has infringed the rights of others and so deserves to be penalized. The severity of the sanction should fit the seriousness of the crime.

Some people claim that the desire for retribution is a basic human emotion. If the state does not provide criminal sanctions so that the community may express its revulsion at offensive acts, citizens will take the law into their own hands. Retribution is thus an expression of the community's disapproval of crime. This view argues that if retribution is not exacted, the disapproval may also disappear. A community that is too ready to forgive a wrongdoer may end up approving the crime.

One of the developments in criminal justice in recent years has been the resurgence of interest in retribution as a justification for the criminal sanction. Using the concept of "just deserts," some theorists have advanced the idea that one who infringes the rights of others does wrong and deserves blame for that conduct.[3] The argument is that criminals should be penalized because they deserve to be punished, not in the form of treatment and not to prevent crime but rather because sanction is demanded by justice. This development and the implications of "just deserts" as a goal of the criminal sanction will be discussed later in this chapter.

Deterrence

The eighteenth- and nineteenth-century reformers called utilitarians, followers of Jeremy Bentham, were struck by what seemed to be the pointlessness of retribution. Holding that human behavior was governed by the individual calculation of the excess of pleasure over pain to be derived from an act, the Benthamites argued that punishment by itself is unjustifiable unless it can be shown that more "good" results if it is inflicted than if it is withheld. The

---

Retribution in the Bible

When one man strikes another and kills him, he shall be put to death. Whoever strikes a beast and kills it shall make restitution, life for life. When one man injures and disfigures his fellow-countryman, it shall be done to him as he has done; fracture for fracture, eye for eye, tooth for tooth; the injury and disfigurement that he has inflicted upon another shall in turn be inflicted upon him.

Leviticus 25:17–22

---

presumed good was the prevention of the greater evil, crime. The basic objective of punishment, they said, was to deter potential criminals by the example of the sanctions laid on the guilty. This purpose is well stated by one of the leaders of the movement: "When a man has been proved to have committed a crime, it is expedient that society should make use of that man for the diminution of crime; he belongs to them for that purpose."[4]

general deterrence Punishment of criminals intended to serve as an example to the general public, and thus to discourage the commission of offenses.

special deterrence Punishment inflicted on criminals with the intent to discourage them from repeating their illegal behavior.

Modern ideas of deterrence have incorporated two subsidiary concepts: ***general deterrence,*** which is probably most directly linked to Bentham's ideas, and ***special deterrence.*** General deterrence is the idea that the general population will be dissuaded from criminal behavior by observing that punishment will necessarily follow commission of a crime and that the pain will be greater than the benefits that may stem from the illegal act. The punishment must be severe enough so that all will be impressed by the consequences. For general deterrence to be effective, the public must be informed of the equation and continually reminded of it by the punishments of the convicted. Public hanging was once considered to be important for its effect as a general deterrent.

Special deterrence (often called specific or individual deterrence) is concerned with changes in the behavior of the convicted and is individualized in that the amount and kind of punishment are calculated to deter the criminal from repeating the offense. "What does the criminal need?" becomes the most important question here.

There are some obvious difficulties with the concept of deterrence. In many cases, for example, the goals of general and special deterrence are incompatible. The level of punishment necessary to impress the populace may

Jeremy Bentham

Born in London, Jeremy Bentham was the foremost writer on jurisprudence and criminology of his time. He earned a master's degree in law at Oxford and was admitted to the bar in 1767 but spent little time in the practice of law. Instead, he soon became well known for pursuit of his three major interests: politics, jurisprudence, and criminology.

Wishing to depart from the social-control jurisprudence of his day, Bentham substituted a new theory termed *utilitarianism.* He believed that human beings are essentially hedonistic calculators of the relative values of pleasure and pain, and that all laws should therefore be guided by a principle of rational utility. Law is a balance between what society demands and what humanity needs. When applied to punishment, the principle of utility demands that a relationship be established between the value of committing a crime and the punishment to be expected for it. A person who chose a course of crime rationally would be deterred by the likelihood of a quick, certain, and commensurate penalty.

Bentham applied utilitarian principles to prison management and discipline as well. His *Principles of the Penal Code* contains the basis for many reforms in the treatment of prisoners, including reform of their morals, preservation of their health, and the provision of education so that society would be relieved of their burden. His planned "panopticon" prison was of circular design to reduce the number of guards required (they were to be able to keep all prisoners in view from the center of the circle) and was to be operated by a manager who would employ the convicts in contract labor. The prison at Stateville, Illinois, built between 1916 and 1924, was modeled on Bentham's design.

be inconsistent with the needs of an individual offender. The public disgrace and disbarment of an attorney, for example, may be effective in preventing him from committing criminal acts, but the sanction may seem inconsequential to many persons who cannot believe he has been sufficiently punished.

A more important problem with the goal of deterrence is that of obtaining proof of its effectiveness. General deterrence suffers because social science is unable to measure its effects; only those who are *not* deterred come to the attention of criminal justice researchers. Thus a study of the deterrent effects of punishment would have to examine the impact of different forms of the criminal sanction on various potential lawbreakers. An additional factor to be considered is how the criminal justice system influences the effect of deterrence through the speed, certainty, and severity of the allocated punishment. While deterrence is believed to play a prominent role as a purpose of the criminal sanction, the exact nature of that role and the extent to which sentencing policies may be altered to meet the purpose are still matters that rest on an unfirm scientific foundation.

Incapacitation

"Lock them up and throw away the key!" Such sentiments are heard often from citizens outraged by some illegal act. The assumption of ***incapacitation*** is that a crime may be prevented if criminals are physically restrained. In primitive societies, banishment from the community was the usual measure taken to prevent a recurrence of forbidden behavior. In early America, agreement by the offender to move away or to join the army was often presented as an alternative to some other form of punishment. Prison is the most typical mode of incapacitation since offenders may be kept under control, even placed in solitary confinement, so that they cannot violate the rules of society. In some states, castration of sexual offenders is permitted on the assumption that it will prevent a future violation of the criminal law. Capital punishment is the ultimate method of incapacitation.

incapacitation Deprivation of capacity to commit crimes against society by detention in prison.

Any policy that incarcerates or in some way physically restricts the offender has some incapacitative effect, even when retribution, deterrence, or rehabilitation is the espoused goal. But the incapacitative sanction is different from these other goals in that it is future-oriented (unlike retribution); is based on personal characteristics of the offender, not on characteristics of the crime (unlike general deterrence); and is not intended to reform the criminal. Incapacitation is thus imposed because a person of a certain type of personality has committed a particular type of crime and is believed to be likely to repeat the offense. It is important to note that we are really dealing with a policy of

---

Deterrence

If I were having a philosophical talk with a man I was going to have hanged (or electrocuted) I should say, "I don't doubt that your act was inevitable for you but to make it more avoidable by others we propose to sacrifice you to the common good. You may regard yourself as a soldier dying for your country if you like."

Source: Oliver Wendell Holmes, *Holmes–Laski Letters, 1916–1935,* ed. Mark DeWolfe Howe (Cambridge: Harvard University Press, 1963), p. 806.

---

selective incapacitation, not general incapacitation which would require the incarceration of all offenders.

One of the problems of this concept is that of undue severity. If the object is prevention, imprisonment may be justified for both a trivial and a serious offense. More important is the question of the length of incarceration. Presumably offenders are not released until the state is reasonably sure that they will no longer commit crimes. Not only is such a prediction difficult to make, but the answer may be that they can never be released.

> What this means, pushed to its logical conclusion, is that offenses that are universally regarded as relatively trivial may be punished by imprisonment for life. It means that, at least, unless we have some basis for asserting that lengthy imprisonment is a greater evil than the prospect of repeated criminality.[5]

The extreme of the incapacitative position may seem foolish, but many states do have habitual-offender laws that seem to be based on this assumption. Under such statutes, people who have committed two or more serious offenses at different times can be sentenced to extended imprisonment, even for life, on the grounds that they have not learned from their past mistakes and so society must be protected from them.

In recent years greater attention has been paid to the concept of selective incapacitation. Research has suggested that a relatively small number of offenders are responsible for a large number of violent and property crimes. Burglars, for example, tend to commit many offenses before they are caught, so it is argued that they should receive long terms in prison. Self-reports of prison inmates have been used to develop individual offense rates for several specific types of crime. Under the assumption that offenders commit only one type of crime, it has been estimated that an individual commits between 2 and 3.5 robbery offenses per year, 6 or 7 burglaries, or 3 to 3.5 auto thefts. Sentencing policies, it is asserted, should be so directed that such career criminals will be locked up for long periods of time.[6]

James Q. Wilson declares that imprisonment should follow conviction for certain crimes. "Were we to devote resources . . . to incapacitating a larger fraction of the convicted serious robbers—then not only is a 20 percent reduction possible, but even larger ones are conceivable."[7] The costs of such a policy, however, are worth considering: correctional facilities would have to be expanded; it would be more difficult to obtain convictions if the accused were aware that a long prison term would result; and policing activities would have to be upgraded to catch and convict these serious offenders.

Rehabilitation

rehabilitation The process of restoring a convicted offender to a constructive place in society through some form of vocational, educational, or therapeutic treatment.

Rehabilitation is undoubtedly the most appealing modern justification for use of the criminal sanction. That the offender may be treated and resocialized while under the care of the state is not an entirely new idea and is even found in some of Bentham's writings. What is new is the belief that techniques are available to identify and treat the causes of the offender's behavior. If the criminal behavior is assumed to result from some social, psychological, or biological imperfection, the treatment of the disorder becomes the primary goal of corrections. Because rehabilitation is oriented solely toward the offender, no relationship can be maintained between the severity of the punishment and the gravity of the crime.

In the ***Rehabilitation Model*** of the criminal sanction, offenders are not being punished, they are being treated and will return to society when they are well. One principle of the Rehabilitation Model is the indeterminate sentence and parole. The assumption that offenders are in need of treatment, not punishment, requires that they remain in custody only until they are "cured." Consequently, the judge should set not a fixed sentence but rather one with maximum and minimum terms so that correctional officials, through the parole board, may release inmates when they have been rehabilitated. The indeterminate sentence is also justified by the belief that if prisoners know when they are going to be released, they will not make an effort to engage in the treatment programs prescribed for their cure.

Rehabilitation Model A model of the criminal sanction based on the view that the criminal is suffering from some physical or psychological defect that can be corrected.

Until a decade ago, the rehabilitative ideal was so widely shared that it was almost assumed that matters of treatment and reform of the offender were the only questions worthy of serious attention in the whole field of criminal justice and corrections.[8] Since then, however, the model has come under closer scrutiny and in some quarters has been discredited. Indeed, some social scientists have wondered whether the causes of crime can be diagnosed and treated. Researchers holding different theoretical orientations have proclaimed what they identify as the cause and have recommended their pet solutions for curing the condition. Others have asked whether rehabilitation really influences the rate at which released offenders return to crime. Some have pointed out that California, where the Rehabilitation Model was most completely incorporated, also had one of the highest recidivism rates in the United States. Still others raise civil libertarian issues by pointing out that although the law dictates the type of sanction, its duration is often left open-ended. The power of determination is given to nonjudicial officials (parole boards, psychiatrists, social workers, and so forth) whose decisions are made in private and according to imprecise criteria.

Objections to the dominance of rehabilitation in American corrections reached a peak in the 1970s, when its detractors pointed to the failure of treatment programs to lower the recidivism rate; the lengthy incarceration of offenders in states where the treatment philosophy was most pronounced; and the misuse of discretion by parole and other correctional officials. The criticisms and the resulting reform of sentencing will be discussed later in this chapter.

Criminal sanctions: a mixed bag?

Although the goals and justifications of criminal sanctions may be discussed as if they were distinct concepts, there is great overlap among most of the objectives.

> The difficulty of the sentencing decision is due in part to the fact that criminal law enforcement has a number of varied and often conflicting goals: the rehabilitation of offenders, the isolation of offenders who pose a threat to community safety, the discouragement of potential offenders, the expression of the community's condemnation of the offender's conduct, and the reinforcement of the values of law-abiding citizens.[9]

A sentence of life imprisonment may be philosophically justified in terms of its primary goal of incapacitation, but the secondary functions of retribution and deterrence are also present. Deterrence is such a broad concept that it mixes well with all the other purposes, with the possible exception of rehabilitation, where logically only specific deterrence applies. Bentham's notion that the pain of criminal punishment must be present as an example to others cannot be met if the prescribed treatment for the rehabilitation of offenders requires a therapeutic environment.

For the trial judge, the burden of determining a sentence that accommodates these values as applied to the particular case is extremely difficult. In one case, a forger may be sentenced to prison as an example to others despite the fact that he is no threat to community safety and is probably not in need of correctional treatment. In another case, the judge may impose a light sentence on a youthful offender who, although he has committed a serious crime, may be a good risk for rehabilitation if he can move quickly back into society.

A historian of social values might suggest that justifications for punishment have varied to fit the dominant ethical ideals of the day. In our century, humanitarian and practical motives have promoted the Rehabilitation Model of corrections. Given the special position of science in the twentieth century, it is not surprising that the diagnosing and curing aspects of the Rehabilitation Model have had wide appeal. In reality, however, the public may respond emotionally to the criminal sanction, as if retribution were the goal, and only give lip service to the importance of treatment and special deterrence.

Among the stated goals of the sanctioning process, only rehabilitation, if carried out according to its model, does not present opportunities for overlap with the objectives of the other purposes. The emphasis on treatment and rehabilitation may diminish the capacity of the criminal justice system to serve as a general deterrent to crime: "to the extent that imprisonment is unpleasant, it will be less than an ideal environment in which to conduct treatment. To the extent that the correctional system becomes a therapeutic environment, it will be less than an ideal institution for general crime deterrence."[10] A problem with the rehabilitative goal itself is that there is necessarily little correspondence between the gravity of the offense and the kind of treatment an offender may need. Studies have shown that murderers do not usually murder again and may be very good parole risks. A drug addict, however, may require extensive incarceration and treatment and be an unlikely prospect for successful parole. But to release a murderer before an addict would probably strike the general public as unjust.

The reality of corrections may indicate that the highly praised goals of rehabilitation have served primarily as window dressing for a system that has deterrence, incapacitation, and retribution as its functioning objectives. Certainly, legislative appropriations for correctional institutions are not yet lavish enough to provide environments that may be compared with privately funded treatment centers. More important, we may not know how to change human behavior or may not fully understand the causes of a criminal's actions. The restrictions imposed in the name of treatment may be as extensive and painful as those supported in the name of retribution or deterrence. But because such measures are taken in the name of humanity, we are slower to recognize and defend against encroachments on human freedom. When freedom is at stake, we must have a clear understanding of what we are doing and of the consequences that the criminal sanction has not only for the offender but for the general population as well.

Forms of the criminal sanction

Fines, incarceration, and probation are the basic forms of criminal sanction imposed in the United States. These apparently simple categories of legally authorized punishments do not reveal the complex problems associated with their application. The penal code defines the behaviors that are considered illegal and specifies the punishments. Unfortunately, the legal standards for sentencing—applying the punishment—have been less well developed than the definitions of the offenses or the procedures used to determine guilt. Because of the complexity of the goals of the criminal sanction and because of our insistence that the punishment should be related to the criminal, judges are given vast discretion to determine the appropriate sentence. As a result, observers have raised certain questions about the rationality and fairness of sentencing practices.

Although sentencing is generally considered to be the judge's province, many states place the responsibility on the jury or on an administrative agency. In some states the defendant is given the choice of having the task carried out by either judge or jury. Until a recent change in the law, the guilty in California were not sentenced to a term of imprisonment by a judge but were committed to the custody of the California Adult Authority, an administrative body. After interviews, testing, and observation, the Authority had the power to determine the actual length of incarceration and to determine when the prisoner was ready for parole.

That judges have wide powers of discretion with regard to sentencing is reflected in the combining of forms to tailor the punishment to fit the offender. The judge may stipulate, for example, that the prison terms for two charges are to run either concurrently or consecutively or that the entire period of imprisonment is to be suspended. In other situations, the offender may be given a combination of a suspended prison term, probation, and a fine. Execution of the sentence may be suspended as long as the offender stays out of trouble, makes restitution, or seeks medical treatment. The judge may also delay imposing any sentence but retain power to set penalties at a later date if conditions warrant. The variety of choices emphasizes the fluidity of sentencing, especially if bargaining is a part of the process. This condition, too, has come under fire. Critics charge that such wide discretion leads to

---

Sentencing: A Problem for Judges

The prisoner is apt to think of himself as being at the mercy of the judge; actually it is the judge who is at the mercy of forces over which he has little control—tradition, precedent, and lack of information, especially the last. On the basis of what someone has written years ago and on the basis of what somebody—a lot of somebodies—has said in court, the poor judge must decide—within limits—where the prisoner goes next on his roundabout route back to society. All this the judge is obliged to decide with a minimal amount of scientific information as to what kind of a man he is dealing with.

Source: Karl Menninger, *The Crime of Punishment* (New York: Viking Press, 1968), p. 63.

---

disparity of treatment: offenders of upper-status backgrounds are given less severe sanctions than members of minority groups and the lower class.

Fines

fine
A sum of money to be paid to the state by a convicted person as punishment for an offense.

Although ***fines*** were leveled in the nineteenth century primarily in connection with crimes of a financial character, they are routinely imposed today for offenses ranging from traffic violations to felonies. Often a fine is leveled in conjunction with some other form of the criminal sanction, particularly probation. A 1983 study by the Vera Institute of Justice and the Institute for Court Management revealed that the fine is used very widely as a criminal sanction and that probably well over $1 billion is collected annually by courts across the country. Judges in the lower courts were found to be more positively disposed to them than judges of higher courts, yet, as table 13.1 shows, fines are extensively imposed even by courts that handle only felonies. It was also found that the use of fines varies regionally, especially in relation to the source of funding for the judiciary. Where courts are dependent largely on the fines they collect to fulfill their budget requirements, this monetary sanction is used heavily.[11] Serious questions must be raised, of course, as to the amount of a fine when a crime of violence is involved. There are also problems of collection; some officials believe that offenders will merely engage in additional criminal activity to gather the money necessary to pay the fine.

Until 1971 it was common for judges to sentence offenders to a fine or a prison term. This practice came under scrutiny by the Supreme Court because state laws usually specify imprisonment for a period thought to be of greater value than the amount of the fine, such as sixty days or $150. Obviously poor people who cannot pay the fine suffer excessive punishment, as the period of imprisonment is a much harsher penalty than the fine. In the case of *Tate* v. *Short* (1971), the Supreme Court ruled that it was unconstitutionally discriminatory to imprison offenders at such an excessive rate solely because of indigency. Citing the Fourteenth Amendment, the Court ruled that the Constitution "requires that the statutory ceiling placed on imprisonment for any substantive offense be the same for all defendants irrespective of their economic status."[12]

There is also concern that fines exact a heavier toll from the poor than from the wealthy. Sweden and the Federal Republic of Germany have attempted to solve this problem by the use of a "day fine." Under this system, fines are levied on the basis of a specified number of days contingent on the severity of the offense. The amount of money paid is equal to the individual's daily income. Thus, for example, a person making $36,500 a year and sentenced to pay a day fine of 10 would pay $3,650; a person making $3,650 and receiving the same penalty would pay $365.

The Use of Fines

Properly employed, the fine is less drastic, far less costly to the public, and perhaps more effective than imprisonment or community service.

Source: National Advisory Commission on Criminal Justice Standards and Goals, Task Force on Corrections, *Report* (Washington, D.C.: Government Printing Office, 1973), p. 154.

TABLE 13.1 Numbers of fines imposed by courts of limited and general jurisdiction, by type of offense

Type of offense	Courts of limited jurisdiction (N = 74)	Courts of general jurisdiction: Felony, misdemeanor, and ordinance violation (N = 28)	Courts of general jurisdiction: Felony only (N = 24)	All courts (N = 114)
Driving while intoxicated/driving under the influence	54	22	2	78
Assault	29	14	5	48
Drug-related offenses (including sale and possession)	23	10	11	44
Disturbing the peace/breach of the peace/disorderly conduct	32	8	1	41
Reckless driving	30	9	0	39
Other theft	19	9	8	36
Violation of fish and game laws and other regulatory ordinances	24	3	0	27
Shoplifting	17	3	0	20
Loitering/soliciting for prostitution	15	4	0	19
Drinking in public/public drunkenness/carrying an open container	14	5	0	19
Bad checks	14	2	0	16
Vandalism/criminal mischief/malicious mischief/property damage	9	3	3	15
Burglary/breaking and entering	2	6	6	14
Criminal trespass	10	2	1	13
Weapons (illegal possession, carrying concealed weapon, etc.)	6	2	1	9
Forgery/embezzlement	2	3	2	7
Fraud	1	4	1	6
Robbery	0	1	3	4

Source: Adapted from Sally T. Hillsman, Joyce L. Sichel, and Barry Mahoney, *Fines in Sentencing: A Study of the Use of the Fine as a Criminal Sanction* (Washington, D.C.: National Institute of Justice, 1984), p. 41.

Incarceration

Imprisonment is the most visible penalty imposed by U.S. courts. Though probation is increasingly used as an alternative, incarceration remains the almost exclusive means for punishing those who commit serious crimes, and it is also widely used against misdemeanants. Because of its severity, imprisonment is thought to have the greatest effect in deterring potential offenders, but it is expensive for the state to carry out and may prevent the offender's later reintegration into society.

The imprisonment sanction is more complicated than a statutory rule specifying a certain number of years based on the gravity of the crime and the characteristics of the offender. Usually legislatures provide a range of terms that the judge may prescribe. The offender convicted of more than one charge may receive a sentence for each. The judge stipulates whether sen-

tences are to be served concurrently (all at one time) or consecutively (one after the other).

Penal codes vary as to the structure of the sentences permitted. Sentences may be indeterminate, determinate, or mandatory. Each structure makes certain assumptions about the goals of the criminal sanction and each allocates discretionary authority. It is also from the structure of the sentences authorized by the legislature that the problems of disparity, unchecked discretion, and excessive terms derive. As this chapter will discuss later, the move away from rehabilitation as the primary goal of the criminal sanction has brought about a rethinking of the nature of the sentences to be imposed and the amount of discretion to be accorded judges.

indeterminate sentence
A period set by a judge in which there is a spread between the minimum date for a decision on parole eligibility and a maximum date to completion of the sentence (five to ten years). In holding that the time necessary for treatment cannot be set, the indeterminate sentence is closely associated with the rehabilitative model.

Indeterminate sentences. In accord with the goal of rehabilitation, which dominated corrections for much of the past half-century, state legislatures also adopted ***indeterminate*** (often termed *indefinite*) ***sentences.*** On the basis of the notion that correctional personnel must be given the discretion to make a release decision on the grounds of successful treatment, penal codes with indeterminate sentences stipulate a minimum and maximum amount of time to be served in prison: one to five years, three to ten years, ten to twenty years, one year to life, and so on. At the time of sentencing, the offender knows only the range and that he or she will probably be eligible for parole at some point after the minimum term (minus "good time") has been served.

State penal codes vary in the degree of sentencing discretion they permit judges. Court discretion may be described as narrow if the range of sentencing options available to the judge is restricted by law to less than a third of the statutory maximum sentence for each offense. Thus for a person convicted of a crime carrying a twelve-year statutory maximum, judges with narrow discretion must select a sentence from within, at most, a four-year range (six to ten years, say, or eight to twelve). As figure 13.1 indicates, eleven states give judges narrow discretion. Although judicial discretion is broad in the remaining states, the sentences imposed may bear little relation to the amount of time actually served because parole boards in most of these states also have broad discretion in making release decisions.

Determinate sentences. Growing dissatisfaction with the rehabilitative goal has led to efforts in support of determinate sentences based on the

Narrow court discretion and no discretionary parole board release	Narrow court discretion and discretionary parole board release
California (CDC)[a] Colorado Minnesota New Mexico North Carolina	Arizona California (CYA)[b] Iowa Ohio Pennsylvania Utah West Virginia

Broad court discretion and no discretionary parole board release	Broad court discretion and discretionary parole board release
Connecticut Illinois Indiana Maine	Alabama Alaska Arkansas Delaware Dist. of Columbia Federal system Florida Georgia Hawaii Idaho Kansas Kentucky Louisiana Maryland Massachusetts Michigan Mississippi Missouri Montana Nebraska Nevada New Hampshire New Jersey New York North Dakota Oklahoma Oregon Rhode Island South Carolina South Dakota Tennessee Texas Vermont Virginia Washington Wisconsin Wyoming

This column includes the nine determinate sentencing states

[a] California Department of Corrections.
[b] California Youth Authority.

FIGURE 13.1
Breadth of judicial and parole discretion, January 1983

determinate sentence
A sentence that fixes the term of imprisonment at a specified period of time.

assumption of deserved punishment. With a ***determinate sentence,*** a convicted offender is given a specific length of time to be served rather than a range of years or months (two years, five years, ten years). At the end of this term, again minus credited "good time," the prisoner is automatically freed (there is no parole board); hence release is not tied to participation in a treatment program. As states have moved toward determinate structures, some have adopted penal codes that stipulate a specific term for each crime category; others still allow the judge to choose from a range the time to be served. Some states emphasize a determinate presumptive sentence; the legislature or often a commission specifies a term from a range into which it assumes most cases will fall. Only in special circumstances should judges veer from the presumptive sentence. Whichever variant is used, however, the offender knows at sentencing the amount of time to be served. One result of determinate sentencing is that legislatures have tended to reduce the discretion of the judiciary as a means of limiting sentencing disparities and ensuring that terms will correspond to those deemed appropriate by the elected body.

Mandatory sentences. Recent years have brought allegations that many offenders are being set free by lenient judges and that the objective of crime control requires greater certainty that criminals will be incapacitated. During the past ten years more than thirty legislatures have responded by stipulating that persons convicted of selected crimes must be confined a minimum of some specified amount of time; no consideration may be given to the circumstances of the offense or to the background of the individual—the judge has no discretion and is not allowed to suspend the sentence.

The Massachusetts gun law, which decrees that anyone convicted of pos-

mandatory sentence
A type of sentence by which statutes require that a certain penalty shall be imposed and executed upon certain convicted offenders.

sessing an unregistered firearm *must* spend one year in jail, is one such piece of legislation requiring a ***mandatory sentence.*** Like the 1973 Rockefeller drug law of New York, the Massachusetts law has had no deterrent or incapacitative effects.[13] In the New York case, the draconian sentences prescribed by the law merely raised the stakes for the defendant so high that the prosecution had to bargain to move cases. Research in several states shows that the mandatory sentence is imposed in only a small portion of the cases in which it could be used. What appears to happen is that in exchange for a guilty plea, the charge is changed to avoid the mandatory sentence. Table 13.2 shows the categories of offenses carrying mandatory prison terms in the federal and state systems.

Good time. Although not a type of sentence, good time and its impact on sentencing should be mentioned here; it is more fully discussed in chapter 16. In all but four states, days are subtracted from prisoners' minimum or maximum term for good behavior or for participation in various types of vocational, educational, and treatment programs. Correctional officials consider these sentence-reduction policies necessary for the maintenance of institutional order and as a mechanism to reduce overcrowding. Good time is also taken into consideration by prosecutors and defense attorneys during plea bargaining.

TABLE 13.2 Categories of offenses carrying mandatory prison terms in the federal and state systems

Key
V Violent crime
H Habitual offender
N Narcotic/drug law violation
G Handgun/firearm

	V	H	N	G		V	H	N	G
Federal system	—	—	—	—	Dist. of Columbia	—	—	N	G
Alabama	V	H	N	—	Montana	V	—	N	G
Alaska	V	H	N	G	Nebraska	V	H	—	—
Arizona	V	H	N	G	Nevada	V	H	N	G
Arkansas	V	H	—	G	New Hampshire	V	—	—	G
California	V	H	N	G	New Jersey	V	—	—	G
Colorado	V	H	—	—	New Mexico	V	H	—	G
Connecticut	V	—	N	G	New York	V	H	N	G
Delaware	V	H	N	G	North Carolina	V	—	N	G
Florida	V	—	N	G	North Dakota	V	—	—	G
Georgia	V	H	N	G	Ohio	V	H	N	G
Hawaii	V	H	N	—	Oklahoma	—	H	N	—
Idaho	V	H	N	G	Oregon	V	—	—	G
Illinois	V	H	N	G	Pennsylvania	V	H	—	G
Indiana	V	H	N	G	Rhode Island	—	H	N	G
Iowa	V	—	N	G	South Carolina	V	H	N	—
Kansas	—	—	—	G	South Dakota	V	—	N	—
Kentucky	—	H	—	G	Tennessee	V	H	N	—
Louisiana	V	H	N	G	Texas	V	H	—	—
Maine	V	—	—	G	Utah	—	—	—	—
Maryland	V	H	—	G	Vermont	—	—	—	—
Massachusetts	V	H	N	G	Virginia	—	—	—	G
Michigan	V	—	N	G	Washington	V	—	N	G
Minnesota	V	—	—	G	West Virginia	V	H	—	G
Mississippi	V	H	—	G	Wisconsin	V	—	—	—
Missouri	V	—	N	G	Wyoming	V	H	N	—

Source: "Setting Prison Terms," U.S. Department of Justice, Bureau of Justice Statistics, *Bulletin*, August 1983.

The amount of good time that can be earned varies among the states, from five days a month to forty-five a year. The amounts are written into the penal codes of some states, stipulated in department of corrections policy directives in others. In some states, once ninety days of good time are earned, they are vested, that is, they cannot be taken away because of misbehavior. Prisoners in those systems risk losing only days not vested if they violate the rules.

The sentence versus actual time served. Newspapers often headline sentences given by judges that seem to indicate that the United States prescribes long periods of incarceration for serious crimes. What the public does not recognize is that there is a great difference between the length of the sentence announced in the courtroom and the amount of time actually served by offenders. Credit for time spent in jail awaiting the sentence, the application of good time, and in most states release to the community on parole greatly reduce the period of incarceration. Table 13.3 shows the average (mean) time actually served in prison by felony offenders in selected states. The figures give credibility to the belief that the average felony offender spends about two years in prison.

Because of the variation in sentencing and releasing laws, it is difficult to compare the amount of time served with the length of sentence imposed throughout the United States. It is possible, however, to make comparisons in regard to different offenses in the same state. The Bureau of Justice Statistics has brought to light an interesting phenomenon: the more serious the offense, the smaller the proportion of the sentence served. An auto thief, say, may be sentenced to twenty-four months in prison but actually serve twenty months, or 83.3 percent of the sentence; a murderer may well be sentenced to thirty years but be released after fifteen years, or 50 percent of the sentence. These examples are not atypical. In states with indeterminate sentences, release on parole is possible after good time and jail time credit have been deducted from the minimum term. (Chapter 16 provides an illustration.)

TABLE 13.3 Mean time served in prison by felony offenders in eleven states (months)

State and release period	*All felonies*	*Serious violent crimes*[a]	*Serious property crimes*[b]
Delaware, 1980–82[c]	17.8	32.5	10.3
Illinois, 1978–82	23.1	34.0	*
Iowa, 1979–83[c]	32.8	48.6	26.1
Maryland, 1982[c]	29.5	50.5	21.7
Ohio, 1980–81	24.6	40.5	20.9
Oklahoma, 1982	15.4	28.3	13.5
Oregon, 1979–82	17.2	28.4	14.0
Pennsylvania, 1981–82[c]	26.7	38.1	21.1
Washington, 7/81–6/82	26.9	41.3	21.0
Wisconsin, 1/80–5/83	29.2	39.7	25.2
Wyoming, 7/80–6/83	22.9	39.0	20.1

[a] Murder, nonnegligent manslaughter, rape, robbery, aggravated assault.
[b] Burglary, larceny, auto theft, arson.
[c] Includes credited jail time.
* Data not available.
Source: U.S. Department of Justice, Bureau of Justice Statistics, *Time Served in Prison,* Special Report (Washington, D.C.: Government Printing Office, 1984), p. 3.

Probation

probation
A sentence allowing the offender to serve the sentence imposed by the court in the community under supervision.

Unlike incarceration, ***probation*** is designed as a means of simultaneously maintaining control and assisting offenders while permitting them to live in the community under supervision. Because probation is a judicial act and is given by grace of the state, and not extended as a right, conditions are imposed that specify how the offender will serve the term. If the conditions are not met, the supervising officer may bring the offender back to court and recommend that the probation be revoked and that the sentence be served in prison.

Probation gives hope for the rehabilitation of the offender who has not committed a serious crime or whose past record is clean. It is viewed as less expensive and more effective than imprisonment, which may not only embitter youthful or first-time offenders but also mix them with hardened criminals so that they learn more skillful criminal techniques. Probation is granted to more than 60 percent of the offenders sentenced in the United States, and the proportion is increasing. There are almost five times as many probationers as adult prisoners.

Although most probationers serve their sentences in the community and not in prison, the sanction is often tied to incarceration. Judges may set a prison term but suspend it upon successful completion of a period of probation. In some jurisdictions the court is authorized to modify an offender's prison sentence after a portion is served by changing it to probation. Ohio, for example, has tried "shock probation" (called "split probation" in California), by which an offender sentenced to incarceration is released after a period of incarceration (the shock) and resentenced to probation. An offender on probation may be required to spend intermittent periods, such as weekends or nights, in jail. Whatever the specific terms of the probationary sentence, its emphasis is on guidance and supervision in the community.

The success of probation in preventing recidivism is hard to document, but there are optimistic reports. A Michigan study found that of 2,411 offenders, only 20.9 percent had failed after three years of probation.[14] Other studies have placed the success rate at between 60 and 90 percent. When you compare these data with recidivism rates of incarcerated offenders, remember that normally it is those most likely to live a crime-free life who are given probation in the first place. Many reform advocates urge that this form of community-based corrections be the disposition of choice for almost all first-time offenders.

In the case of *Gagnon* v. *Scarpelli* (1973) the Supreme Court ruled that before probation is revoked the state must hold a two-stage hearing and provide the probationer with specified elements of due process.[15] When a probationer is taken into custody for violating the conditions of probation, a preliminary hearing must be held to determine whether probable cause exists to believe that the incident occurred. If there is a finding of probable cause, a final hearing, where the revocation decision is made, becomes mandatory. At these hearings the probationer has the right to cross-examine witnesses and to be given notice of the alleged violations and a written report of the proceedings. The Court ruled, though, that there is no automatic right to counsel; this decision is to be made on a case-by-case basis.

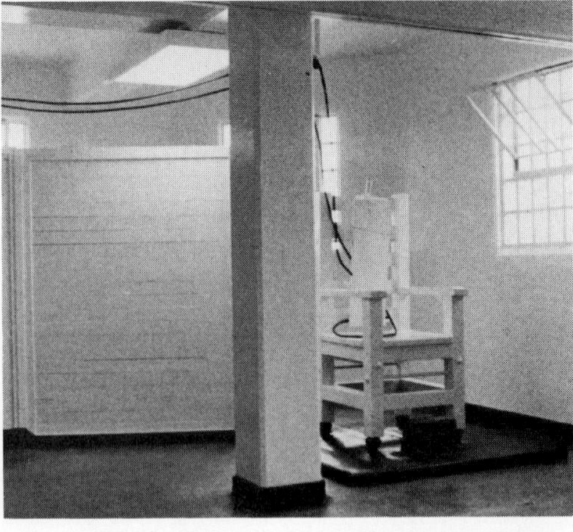

Only a small number of those sentenced to death are executed.

Death

Between 1930 and 1967, when the Supreme Court ordered a stay of executions pending a hearing on the issue, more than 3,800 men and women were executed in the United States. In 1935, a particularly active year for use of this sanction, 199 persons were executed. During recent decades, however, public attention has focused on capital punishment and the question of its consistency with the Eighth Amendment's prohibition against cruel and unusual punishment.

In the 1972 case of *Furman* v. *Georgia,* the Supreme Court ruled for the first time that the death penalty, as administered, constituted cruel and unusual punishment, thereby voiding the laws of thirty-nine states and the District of Columbia.[16] Every member of the Court wrote an opinion, for, even among the majority, agreement could not be reached on the legal reasons to support the ban on the death penalty. Three of the five members of the majority emphasized that judges and juries had used their discretion with regard to imposition of capital punishment in such an arbitrary, capricious, and discriminatory manner that it constituted cruel and unusual punishment. Justices Marshall and Brennan argued that capital punishment per se was cruel and unusual, in violation of the Eighth Amendment.

Although headlines declared that the Court had banned the death penalty, many legal scholars felt that state legislators could write capital punishment laws that would remove the arbitrariness from the procedure and thus pass the test of constitutionality. By 1976 thirty-five states had enacted new legislation designed to eliminate the faults cited in *Furman* v. *Georgia.* These laws took two forms. Some states removed all discretion from the process by mandating capital punishment on conviction for certain offenses; other states provided specific guidelines for judges and juries to use in deciding whether death is the appropriate sentence in a particular case. The new laws were tested before the Supreme Court in June 1976 in the case of *Gregg* v. *Georgia.*[17]

Eighth Amendment

Excessive bail shall not be required, nor excessive fines imposed, nor cruel and unusual punishments inflicted.

The Court struck down the mandatory death penalty provisions of the new laws but upheld those that required the sentencing judge or jury to take into account specific aggravating and mitigating factors in deciding which convicted murderers should be sentenced to death. Many state legislatures, citing public opinion polls showing that a great majority favored the death penalty for murder, quickly revised their laws to accord with those of Georgia. By 1984, thirty-eight states and the federal government had enacted such laws. The methods of execution employed in these states are shown in table 13.4.

The number of persons under sentence of death has increased dramatically in the past decade, as figure 13.2 shows. About 1,400 incarcerated persons are currently awaiting execution in thirty-three of the death penalty states. Two-thirds of those on death row are in the South, with the greatest

Close-up: Death by the Highway

***Gregg* v. *Georgia*, 428 U.S. 153 (1976)**

As they stood trying to hitch a ride from Florida to Asheville, North Carolina, on 21 November 1973, Troy Gregg and his sixteen-year-old companion Sam Allen watched car after car whiz past. Finally, as they were beginning to lose hope, one came to a stop, the door was opened, and they entered and were off. Fred Simmons and Bob Moore, both of whom were drunk, continued toward the Georgia border with their passengers. Soon, however, the car broke down. Simmons purchased another, a 1960 Pontiac, using a large roll of cash. Another hitchhiker, Dennis Weaver, was picked up and then dropped off in Atlanta about 11 P.M. as the car proceeded northward.

In Gwinnett County, Georgia, just after Simmons and Moore got out of the car to urinate, Gregg told Allen, "Get out, we're going to rob them." Gregg leaned against the car to take aim at the two men, and as they were climbing up an embankment to return to the car, he fired three shots. Allen later told the police that Gregg circled around behind the fallen bodies, put the gun to the head of one and pulled the trigger, and then quickly went to the other and repeated the act. He rifled the pockets of the dead men, took their cash, and told Allen to get into the car. Then they drove away.

The next morning the bodies were discovered beside the highway. On 23 November, after reading about the discovery in an Atlanta newspaper, Weaver—the other hitchhiker—called the police and described the car. The next afternoon Gregg and Allen, still in Simmons's car, were arrested in Asheville. A .25-caliber pistol, later shown to be the murder weapon, was found in Gregg's pocket. After receiving the *Miranda* warnings, Gregg signed a statement in which he admitted shooting and then robbing Simmons and Moore. He justified the slayings on the grounds of self-defense.

Georgia uses a two-stage procedure in which one jury decides questions of guilt or innocence and a second jury determines the penalty. At the conclusion of the trial, the judge instructed the jury that charges could be either felony murder or nonfelony murder, and either armed robbery or the lesser included offense of robbery by intimidation. The jury found Gregg guilty of two counts of armed robbery and two counts of murder. At the penalty stage, the judge instructed the jury that it could not authorize the death penalty unless it first found that one of three aggravating circumstances was present: (1) that the murder was committed while the offender was engaged in committing two other capital felonies; (2) that Gregg committed the murders for the purpose of acquiring the money and automobile; (3) that the offense was outrageously and wantonly vile, horrible, and inhuman, and showed the depravity of the mind of the defendant. The jury found the first and second circumstances to be present and returned verdicts of death on each count.

TABLE 13.4 Methods of execution used in thirty-eight states

Method	States that use method
Electrocution	Alabama, Akansas*, Connecticut, Florida, Georgia, Indiana, Kentucky, Louisiana, Massachusetts*, Nebraska, New York, Ohio, Pennsylvania, South Carolina, South Dakota, Tennessee, Vermont, Virginia
Lethal injection	Arkansas*, Idaho*, Illinois, Massachusetts*, Montana*, Nevada, New Jersey, New Mexico, North Carolina*, Oklahoma, Texas, Utah*, Washington*
Lethal gas	Arizona, California, Colorado, Maryland, Mississippi, Missouri, North Carolina*, Wyoming
Hanging	Delaware, Montana*, New Hampshire, Washington*
Firing squad	Idaho*, Utah*

*Provides for two methods of execution.
Source: "Capital Punishment 1983," U.S. Department of Justices Bureau of Justice Statistics, *Bulletin*, July 1984, p. 5.

The sentence was affirmed by the Supreme Court of Georgia in 1974. Gregg appealed to the United States Supreme Court, arguing that imposition of the death penalty was cruel and unusual punishment in violation of the Eighth Amendment.

Decision

On 2 July 1976 the Supreme Court upheld the Georgia law under which Gregg had been sentenced. In a widely split opinion, seven of the justices said that capital punishment is not inherently cruel and unusual and thus upheld the laws in those states where the judge and jury had discretion to consider the crime, the particular defendant, and mitigating or aggravating circumstances before ordering death.

In recent years the Supreme Court has addressed a number of questions concerning the constitutionality of the death penalty statutes. Thus far these opinions have mainly refined issues dealt with earlier in *Furman* and *Gregg*. In 1984, however, the Court ruled in *Pulley* v. *Harris* that there is no constitutional requirement that judges view the proportionality of a death sentence in comparison with punishment given for similar crimes committed by offenders with similar characteristics. Among the issues still pending before the Court are the effectiveness of counsel in capital cases, the practice of trial judges of overriding a jury's sentence recommendation, and research findings of racial discrimination in the imposition of the death penalty.

Although the decision in *Gregg* v. *Georgia* upheld a process that was thought to have overcome the discriminatory aspects of the death penalty found unconstitutional in *Furman* v. *Georgia*, recent studies have raised new questions about the arbitrariness that results from the procedures. David Bruck analyzed cases of murder committed during robbery from 1977 to 1981 in South Carolina, where such crimes may be punished by death. Of the 286 defendants arrested for such murders, prosecutors sought the death penalty against 37. It was imposed on only 4; 33 received life imprisonment.[18] David Baldus analyzed more than 230 factual circumstances related to more than a thousand Georgia homicides, including 253 death penalty proceedings under the law validated by *Gregg*. His findings

confirmed that among defendants convicted of murdering whites, blacks are substantially more likely to go to death row than are whites. Although blacks account for some 60 percent of Georgia homicide victims, Baldus found that killers of black victims are punished by death less than one-tenth as often as are killers of white victims.[19]

It seems clear that a selection process is at work at every point in the justice system from the arrest of a murder suspect until sentencing, moving some defendants toward the death penalty while others receive alternative treatment and are given life imprisonment.

concentration in Florida, Georgia, and Texas. Since 1976, when the Georgia law was upheld, until 1984, however, there were never more than five executions during any one year. The slow rate at which sentences were being carried out provoked the displeasure of Chief Justice Burger at the time of the 1983 execution of Robert Sullivan, who had been able to delay the carrying out of his sentence for ten years while appeals wound their way through the courts. During 1984, twenty-two prisoners were executed. More than 250 new death sentences are now being given out each year, and the number of states where capital punishment is permitted continues to mount, yet executions are comparatively few. Is this situation the result of a complicated and time-consuming appeals process or lack of will on the part of both political leaders and a society that is perhaps uncertain about the taking of human life? Is the death penalty consistent with the Eighth Amendment's prohibition of cruel and unusual punishment if only a minuscule number of those sentenced to death are executed?

Restitution

restitution
Compensation for injury one has inflicted, in the form of either a payment of money to the victim or the performance of service to the community.

In its simplest form, ***restitution*** is repayment to a victim who has suffered some form of financial loss as a result of the offender's crime. This is an idea that is receiving new attention, having received the endorsement of the National Advisory Commission on Criminal Justice Standards and Goals, the American Bar Association, and the American Law Institute. Iowa and Colorado have enacted laws recommending restitutive sanctions, and programs have been inaugurated in additional states.

Restitution has always been a part of the American criminal justice system

Close-up: "I Didn't Like Nobody"

On the night of June 3, 1973, a Chevrolet Caprice, driven by a woman, was forced off Interstate 57 in southern Cook County, Ill., by a car carrying four men. One of them pointed a 12-gauge pump shotgun at her, ordered her to strip and then to climb through a barbed-wire fence at the side of the road. As she begged for her life, her assailant thrust the shotgun barrel into her vagina and fired. After watching her agonies for several minutes, he finished her off with a blast to the throat. Less than an hour later, the marauding motorists stopped another car and told the man and woman inside it to get out and lie down on the shoulder of the road. The couple pleaded for mercy, saying that they were engaged to be married in six months. The man with the shotgun said, "Kiss your last kiss," then shot both of them in the back, killing them. The total take from three murders and two robberies: $54, two watches, an engagement ring and a wedding band.

The man ultimately convicted of the "I-57 murders" now sits confined in the Menard Condemned Unit, the official name for death row in the Illinois prison system. Yet Henry Brisbon Jr., 28, does not face execution for those three killings nearly ten years ago. Illinois' death penalty was invalidated in 1972 and was not restored until 1977, the year that Brisbon was finally brought to trial. At that time, the judge sentenced him to a term of 1,000 to 3,000 years in prison. It took Brisbon less than one year to kill again, this time stabbing a fellow inmate at Stateville Correctional Center with the sharpened handle of a soup ladle. At the trial for this murder, Will County State's Attorney Edward Petka described Brisbon as "a very, very terrible human being, a walking testimonial for the

but a largely unpublicized one, effected by informal agreements between enforcement officials and offenders, at the station house and during plea bargaining, and by sentence recommendations. It is only during the past decade that it has been institutionalized in many areas. In 1972, Minnesota inaugurated what has become the most highly publicized restitution program. Prison inmates are paroled to the Restitution Center, a residential halfway house, under a formally negotiated agreement to make restitution. A similar program has been extended to probationers in Georgia, and a recent survey shows that there are now more than forty such programs throughout the country.

Restitution is usually carried out as one of the conditions of probation. In addition to payments to specified victims for damages incurred, restitution may take the form of community service—work in a social service agency for a specified period of time, for example. Although restitution has many supporters, some theorists believe that if it is used as the sole sanction, it may allow some offenders to purchase a relatively mild punishment. Other theorists point out that although it can be a useful criminal justice sanction in consequence of a property crime, it is of little value if violence figured in the offense.

Informal sanctions: the process is the punishment

In addition to the formal sanctions prescribed by law, other punishments are imposed on persons who get caught in the criminal justice system, even on those who ultimately are not convicted. If one is arrested and released without

death penalty." The jury agreed.

Brisbon's eleven months on death row have been quiet, compared with his Stateville years, when he took part in 15 attacks on inmates and guards, instigated at least one prison riot, trashed a courtroom during a trial and hit a warden with a broom handle. "I'm no bad dude," he says, "just an antisocial individual." The third of 13 children, Brisbon thinks that his upbringing by a strict black Muslim father made him different: "I was taught to be a racist and not like whites. As I grew up, I decided I didn't like nobody."

Brisbon has 90 well-supervised minutes each day outside his small (7 ft. 7 in. by 5 ft. 10 in.) cell. He works out with weights keeping his 155 lbs. (on a 5-ft. 9-in. frame) in shape. He complains about his confinement: "Can't take two steps in this cage. It's inhuman. And that dull-ass color blue on the walls in no way brightens my life." He has devised a novel idea about judicial reform: "All this talk about victims' rights and restitution gets me. What about my family? I'm a victim of a crooked criminal system. Isn't my family entitled to something?" The shadow of the death penalty does not faze him: "I don't see that happening to me. What would killing me solve? Isn't that just another murder? If I got to die, it's going to be of natural causes." The state of Illinois thinks otherwise. Says Michael Ficaro, who prosecuted the I-57 case: "On the day he dies in the chair at Stateville, I plan to be there to see that it's done. Nobody I've heard of deserves the death penalty more than Henry Brisbon."

Source: *Time,* 24 January 1983, p. 30.

Current Sentencing Alternatives Reflect Multiple Objectives

What types of sentences are usually given to offenders?

Death penalty. In some states, for certain crimes such as murder, the courts may sentence an offender to death by electrocution, exposure to lethal gas, hanging, lethal injection, or other method specified by state law.

- 36 states have death penalty provisions in law.
- Most death penalty sentences have been for murder.
- About 1,400 inmates in 31 states are under a sentence of death.

Incarceration. The confinement of a convicted criminal in a federal or state prison or a local jail to serve a court-imposed sentence. Custody is usually within a jail, administered locally, or a prison, operated by the state or the federal government. In many states, offenders sentenced to less than one year are held in a jail; those sentenced to longer terms are committed to the state prison.

- More than 4,300 correctional facilities are maintained by federal, state, local governments, including 43 federal facilities, 791 state-operated adult confinement and community-based correctional facilities, and 3,500 local jails which are usually county-operated.
- On any given day in recent years, approximately 412,000 persons were confined in state and federal prisons and approximately 210,000 persons were confined in local jails.

Probation. The sentencing of an offender to community supervision by a probation agency, often as a result of suspending a sentence to confinement. Such supervision normally entails the provision of specific rules of conduct while in the community. If the terms of probation are violated, a judge may impose a sentence to confinement. It is the most widely used correctional disposition in the United States.

- State or local governments operate more than 2,000 probation agencies. These agencies supervise nearly 1.6 million adults and juveniles on probation.

Split sentences and shock probation. A penalty that explicitly requests the convicted person to serve a period of confinement in a local state or federal facility (the "shock"), followed by a period of probation. This penalty attempts to combine the use of community supervision with a short incarceration experience.

- Recent California data reveal that by far the most common disposition in felony cases was a combined sentence of jail and probation.

Restitution. The requirement that the offender provide financial remuneration for the losses incurred by the victim.

- Nearly all states have statutory provisions for the collection and disbursement of restitution funds. In 1982, a restitution law was enacted at the federal level.

Community service. The requirement that the offender provide a specified number of hours of public service work, such as collecting trash in parks or other public facilities.

- Nearly a third of the states authorize community service work orders. Community service is often imposed as a specific condition of probation.

Fines. An economic penalty that requires the offender to pay a specific sum of money within the limit set by law. Fines are often imposed in addition to probation or as an alternative to incarceration.

- Many laws that govern the imposition of fines are undergoing revision. These revisions often provide for more flexible means of ensuring equality in the imposition of fines, flexible fine schedules, "day fines" geared to the offenders' daily wage, installment payment of fines, and a restriction on confinement to situations that amount to intentional refusal to pay.

Source: U.S. Department of Justice, Bureau of Justice Statistics, *Report to the Nation on Crime and Justice* (Washington, D.C.: Government Printing Office, 1983), p. 73.

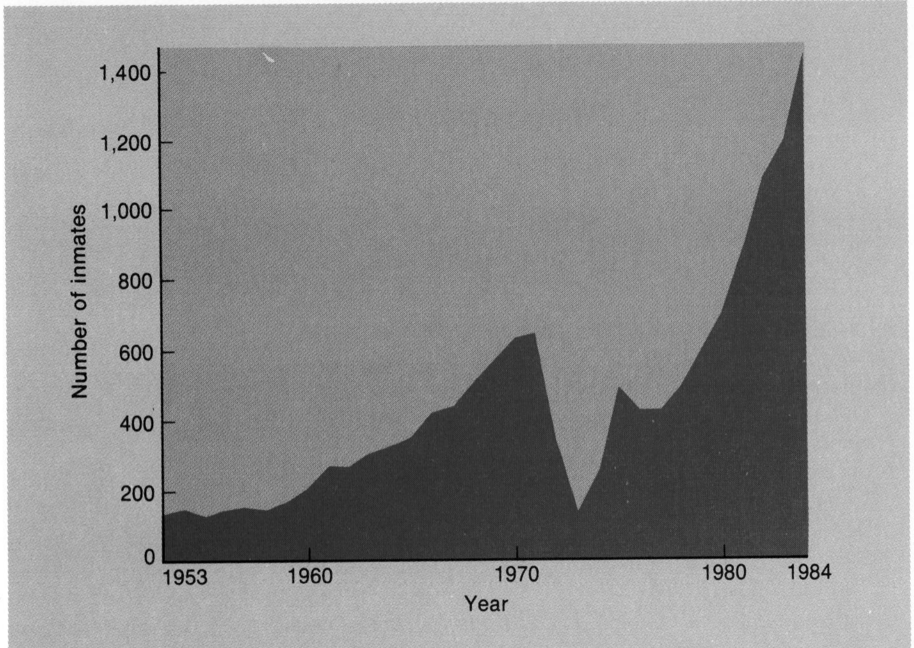

FIGURE 13.2
Number of persons under sentence of death in the United States, 1953–1985

having been charged, if the case is dismissed at a preliminary hearing or nolled at trial, various tangible and intangible costs are still to be borne. Social scientists have become increasingly aware of these costs; indeed, one book describing sentencing in a misdemeanor court is titled *The Process Is the Punishment.*[20] In a study of felony courts in Baltimore, Chicago, and Detroit, James Eisenstein and Herbert Jacob found that considerable penalties were imposed on unconvicted defendants.[21]

For most people, simply being arrested is a frightening and costly experience. It is impossible to measure the psychic and social price of being stigmatized, separated from family, and deprived of freedom. Even on release, one's associates may have lingering suspicions about one's alleged participation in a criminal act. Many employment applications ask whether you have ever been arrested. Other costs are more easily measured: the amount of time the case took, the sum of money posted to obtain bail, the defense attorney's fee, and lost wages. Some of the costs for unconvicted defendants are shown in table 13.5.

Although the law decrees that only those the court finds guilty are to be punished under the penal code, many citizens find the process of criminal justice expensive. It might be argued that such costs are part of the price we pay for having an adversarial system under law and that inconvenience or financial drain for a few is unavoidable. But law enforcement officials recognize that the punishment is the process and use this fact to extract some level of discomfort or cost when evidential requirements for conviction cannot be met. If, for example, a police officer illegally stops and searches a car on suspicion and finds that it contains drugs, conviction of the car's occupants is probably not possible, given the exclusionary rule. The arresting officer and the prosecutor are aware that, even so, some punishment can be dealt out merely by an arrest that will eventually be dismissed or nolled at trial.

TABLE 13.5 Sanctions imposed on unconvicted defendants in three cities

	Baltimore	*Chicago*	*Detroit*
Percentage not released on bail	38.1%	19.2%	33.8%
Percentage of those released on bail who spent a week or more in jail	48.2%	22.9%	n.a.
Percentage with bond set at $5,000 or more	31.6%	19.4%	25.1%
Median number of days from arrest to disposition	42.0	102.0	65.5
Estimated number of unconvicted defendants in 1972 or 1973	2,100	21,100	7,700

Source: Adapted from James Eisenstein and Herbert Jacob, "Sentences and Other Sanctions," in *Criminal Justice: Law and Politics*, ed. George F. Cole, 4th ed. (Monterey, Calif.: Brooks/Cole, 1984), p. 260.

Malcolm Feeley believes that the pretrial costs not only have an impact on the unconvicted but encourage rapid and perfunctory practices in the courtroom and guilty pleas. As he notes, the costs to the individual defendant of the pretrial process may serve to answer a number of puzzling questions: "why so many waive their right to free appointed counsel; why so many people do not show up for court at all; and why people choose the available adversarial options so infrequently."[22] In addition, many defendants do not "take advantage" of diversion programs designed for their benefit because they perceive them as simply increasing their contact with the criminal justice system. All told, defendants seem to have as their principal goal getting out from the control of the police and courts as rapidly as possible—perhaps a rational strategy in view of the exactions of the process. In short, a series of costly informal punishments is inflicted on those arrested, whether they are quickly released, plead guilty, are found guilty or innocent. Some of these penalties are unavoidable in an adversarial system, while others serve the needs of the principal actors in the system to move cases and to achieve organizational goals.

Legislative responsibility

Legislatures have generally neglected the second portion of the ancient Latin rule *Nullum crimen, nulla poena, sine lege* (there can be no crime *and no punishment* except as a law prescribes). This neglect has led to two disturbing characteristics of the criminal law: crazy-quilt statutory patterns and blank-check powers of judges. In most states the penal code has been enacted in a piecemeal fashion, with new crimes and new penalties added as circumstances warrant. Often laws are placed on the books in response to public pressures following a particularly upsetting act; thus the emotions of the day have an important effect on decision makers.

Recent studies have provided examples of illogic and inconsistency in the law:

. . . a Colorado statute providing a ten-year maximum for stealing a dog, while another Colorado statute prescribed six months and a $500 fine for killing a dog; in Iowa, burning an empty building could lead to as much as a twenty-year sentence, but burning a church or school carried a maximum of ten; breaking into a car to steal from its glove compartment could result in up to fifteen years in California, while stealing the entire car carried a maximum of ten.[23]

It must be recognized that legislators operate in a political world and respond to pressures that may not correspond to sentencing or correctional theory. When Albert Price surveyed members of the legislatures of four states undergoing sentencing reform—Minnesota, Indiana, Illinois, and Connecticut—he found that they had difficulty differentiating among the four traditional goals of the criminal sanction, and could really distinguish only between two basic sets: one encapsulating the values of retribution, deterrence, and incapacitation; the other, the values of rehabilitation. Most of the legislators were interested primarily in responding to public pressures for stiffer punishment rather than in developing sentencing laws tied to theories of punishment. As a result, sentencing structures tended to conflict with correctional goals.[24]

In a most perceptive book, Arthur Rosett and Donald Cressey suggest that sentencing policy is influenced by a severity–softening–severity process in which legislators and criminal justice officials each attempt to achieve their own ends. They believe that to a considerable degree the legislature becomes an agency of harshness, especially for defendants who do not acquiesce to pressures from the courthouse to plead guilty. The six steps of this process of legislative action and reaction seem to follow an established pattern.

Step I. Laws calling for severe punishments are passed by legislatures on the assumption that fear of pain will terrorize the citizenry into conformity.

Step II. Criminal justice personnel soften these severe penalties for most offenders (a) in the interests of justice, (b) in the interests of bureaucracy, and (c) in the interests of gaining acquiescence.

Step III. The few defendants who then insist on a trial and are found guilty, or who in other ways refuse to cooperate, are punished more severely than those who acquiesce.

Step IV. Legislatures, noting that most criminals by acquiescing avoid "the punishment prescribed by law," (a) increase the prescribed punishments and (b) try to limit the range of discretionary decision making used to soften the harsh penalties.

Step V. The more severe punishments introduced in the preceding step are again softened for most offenders, as in Step II, with the result that the defendants not acquiescing are punished even more severely than they were in Step III.

Step VI. The severity–softening–severity process is repeated.[25]

What Rosett and Cressey have explored is the systemic relationship between the criminal justice and legislative systems. Each system has certain needs and goals. Legislators are responsive to public opinion and are expected to do something about the crime problem. Criminal justice officials, however, must work together within a different organizational framework. Although they operate under formal rules laid down by the legislature, the legislature is not a continuing presence; it is the members of the courthouse staff who are responsible for implementing sentencing policy. They not only find a need to encourage guilty pleas and other actions that do not conform strictly to the rules but often find no agreement in society on the goals of the criminal sanction and the requirement that every offender be treated exactly as the law prescribes. As we have seen before, the conflict between the Due Process Model and the Crime Control Model causes tension throughout the criminal justice system.

Sentencing reform

During the past decade serious questions have been raised about the assumptions of the Rehabilitation Model of the criminal sanction and the sentencing forms linked to it. An accumulating literature points to both the ineffectiveness of rehabilitative programs and mounting concern about the degree of discretion required by the treatment model. Many people believe that rehabilitation has made little impact on the control of crime but has greatly interfered with due process, increased the length of incarceration, and widened the boundaries of the criminal justice system. To deal with these criticisms, more than thirty state legislatures have considered major changes in the sentencing process by "toughening" criminal penalties, making greater use of definite terms of incarceration, and ending or limiting the parole release decision.

Robert Martinson's research is probably one of the most influential factors in current efforts to reform sentencing practices. Using rigorous standards, Martinson surveyed all studies of rehabilitation programs in correctional systems written in English and published between 1945 and 1967; 231 met his criteria. The studies used various measures of offender improvement—recidivism, adjustment to prison life, vocational success, educational achievement, personality and attitude change—to compare the results for offenders who received treatment with results for those who did not. Included in his analysis were such standard rehabilitative programs as educational and vocational training, individual counseling, group counseling, milieu therapy, medical treatment (plastic surgery, drugs), parole, and supervision. Martinson's findings: "With few and isolated exceptions, the rehabilitative efforts that have been reported so far have had no appreciable effect on recidivism."[26]

Current reforms are based on the assumption that deserved punishment should be the goal of the criminal sanction. Advocates of this approach say that justice should be humane and simple and that it can be achieved if discretion is harnessed by the specification of definite sentences. Unlike rehabilitation, which emphasizes that the sanction should fit the needs of the individual offender, "just deserts" focuses on the seriousness of the crime that the offender has committed and the number of his or her prior convictions. "Seriousness" depends on the harm done by the act and the degree of the offender's responsibility for it.

Although the various reforms advocated differ in some respects, their aim is the narrowing of sentencing discretion. Advocates have recognized that for both officials and offenders, the amount of time to be served and the manner in which it is to be calculated are at the heart of the matter. With these factors in mind, reformers have urged legislatures to adopt definite sentences whose certainty is designed to achieve the objectives of impartiality, predictability, and visibility within the context of deserved punishment. The reasoning is that the offender should know, when he or she is being sentenced, the amount of

Sentencing laws are reformed through the political processes of legislatures.

time to be served. Discretionary release on parole is viewed as incompatible with determinate sentences. Release should be automatic following expiration of the specified time to be served.

One of the interesting aspects of the push for determinate sentences was the broad coalition that supported the idea of deserved punishment. Backing came from groups across the ideological spectrum: conservatives applauded the certainty of punishment and what they thought would be longer prison terms, and liberals were attracted by the equity and fairness that were likely to result. Thus, during the legislative debate in California, persons representing the American Civil Liberties Union, the National Prisoners Union, and the District Attorneys and Peace Officers Association spoke in favor of ending indeterminate sentencing and parole. In Illinois, *The Blue Light,* a publication "for and about Chicagoland Police Officers," emphasized the benefits to law enforcement of the shift, and so did Willie Holder of the National Prisoners Union.[27]

It was when legislatures in the pioneering states of California, Illinois, Indiana, and Connecticut started to specify new prison terms under definite sentencing laws that the interest-group coalition broke apart. Now the liberal–conservative dichotomy was again apparent. Liberals argued that the new sentences should be similar to the actual time now being served for each offense; conservatives, shocked by what they thought was too little punishment, pushed for longer terms. Parole officers in some states feared that there would be no need for their supervisory services under a model of deserved punishment. In all states but Maine, officers were able to convince the legislatures that all former prisoners should receive a period of supervision of at least two years. It was one thing for activists to promote a rational scheme dedicated to a particular sanctioning model, but quite another to turn the scheme into law.

The new penal codes in the first four states to move to determinate sentences (see table 13.6) differ with regard to the amount of discretion given judges, the simplicity of the offense categories, and the opportunities for consideration of such factors as prior criminal record, heinousness of offense, length of sentence, amount of good time, and release mechanism. The results were not pleasing to the supporters of reform, who had thought that the terms

TABLE 13.6 Sentencing ranges for selected felony offenses in Maine, California, Indiana, and Illinois

Offense	*Maine*	*California*	*Indiana*	*Illinois*
Forcible rape (2 prior nonviolent felony convictions)	0–20 years	4–6 years	6–50 years	6–60 years
Forcible rape (first offense)	0–20 years	3–5 years	6–20 years	6–60 years
Narcotics dealing (first offense)	0–10 years	3–5 years	20–50 years	4–30 years
Simple burglary (2 prior felony convictions)	0–5 years	28–48 months[a]	2–38 years	6–60 years[b]
Simple burglary (first offense)	0–5 years	16–36 months	2–8 years	3–14 years

[a] Under the California code, one year is added to the base term for each prior prison term for a nonviolent offense; three years are added for violent offenses if the current offense is also violent. This example assumes that one prior prison term was served for a nonviolent felony.

[b] Persons convicted of a class 1 or 2 felony with two prior convictions of class 1 or 2 felonies are sentenced as class X offenders under Illinois law.

Source: Stephen P. Lagoy, Frederick A. Hussey, and John H.Kramer, "A Comparative Assessment of Determinate Sentencing in the Four Pioneer States," *Crime and Delinquency* 24 (October 1978): 399. Reprinted by permission of Sage Publications, Inc.

of determinate sentences would be equal to the amount of time then being served. The attempt to harness the discretion of parole boards and judges appears to have shifted power to prosecutors and corrections departments.

The speed with which the goals of corrections shifted from rehabilitation to deserved punishment in about thirteen states caused some observers to argue for caution. As Todd Clear has warned, "the fact that correctional planners spend much of their time attempting to 'reform' earlier reforms should lend a note of caution to the neo-retributionist movement."[28] Some people argue that it is because of fixed sentences without the possibility of parole that prison populations have skyrocketed. Other commentators suggest that when accused persons know the terms they will have to serve if they are convicted, prosecutors are in a better position to bargain. Still others believe that on the demise of the rehabilitation goal, public support for the provision of resources to corrections will falter. Finally, it may be argued that discretion is an essential ingredient in criminal justice—as it is in any system—and that even with such structural reforms as definite sentences, the informal mechanisms of the administrative organizations will adapt to the new criteria and eventually the new sentences will fit the organization's needs.

Toward rationality in sentencing

sentence disparity
Divergence in the lengths and types of sentences imposed for the same crime or for crimes of comparable seriousness when no reasonable justification can be discerned.

To a certain degree, a lack of uniformity in sentences is justifiable given rehabilitative goals and the command that the punishment should fit the criminal. The sentence imposed for a given offense may also vary among jurisdictions because of statutory limitations on judicial discretion. Differences in regional norms in regard to types of violations may result in variations in the sentences given in different geographical areas. ***Sentence disparity*** becomes a problem when no reasonable basis for it can be adduced. Individualized sentencing is abused when the type and length of sentence depend on the presence of a particular trial judge who exercises unchecked judicial discretion within a wide range of statutory sentencing alternatives.

Sentence disparity among forty-one New York judges is shown in figure

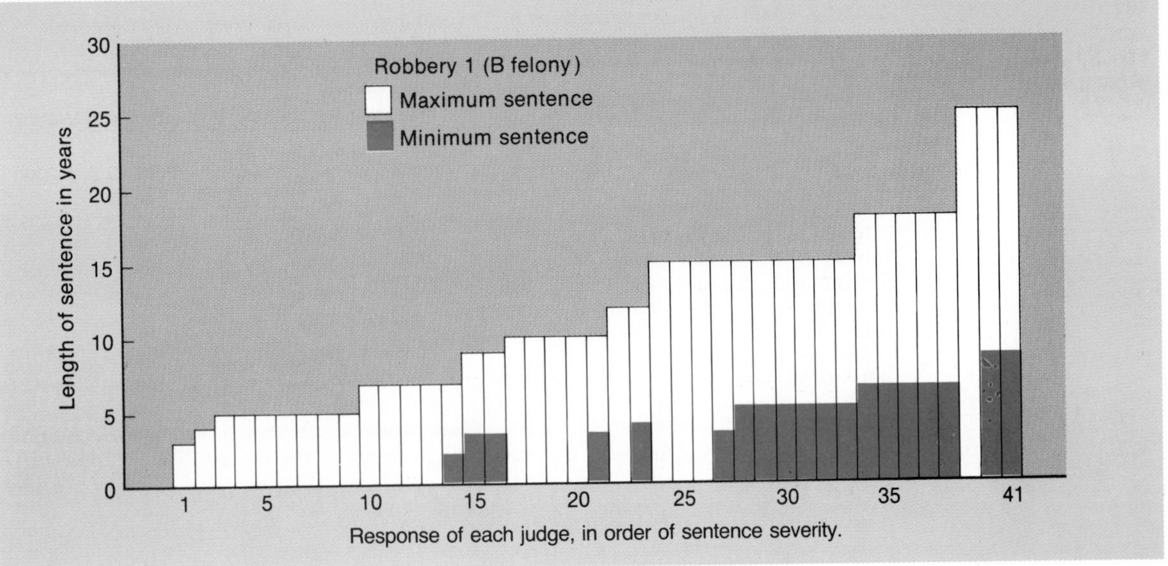

FIGURE 13.3
Minimum and maximum sentences hypothetically imposed in a case of first-degree robbery by forty-one New York judges

13.3. The judges were asked to review files of actual cases and to indicate the sentences they would impose. In the example shown, an elderly man was robbed at knifepoint by a heroin addict. The defendant was convicted of first-degree robbery. He was unemployed, lived with his pregnant wife, and had a minor criminal record. He had received an actual sentence of incarceration for a minimum of no time to a maximum of five years. Each bar on the chart represents the sentence that would have been given by one judge if the case had come to his or her courtroom. Note that the sentences range from zero to three years to the statutory maximum of eight and one-third to twenty-five years.

Data from the Federal Bureau of Prisons, shown in table 13.7, reveal great differences in sentence length and release time when violations are the same. With identical statutory choices, federal judges in North Carolina sentenced narcotics law violators to an average of 77.6 months in prison, while judges in South Carolina sentenced others for the same offense to 56.3 months. Forgers were punished in the Federal District Court for the Western District of Texas by prison terms of 43.0 months; in the Southern District of Texas by 27.2 months; in Indiana's Northern District by 36.0 months; and in the Southern District of Indiana by 19.6 months.[29] In general, sentences are harsher in the South than in the North, in rural areas than in urban.

Sentencing disparities not only present a constitutional issue that challenges the ideal of equal justice under law but create problems that interfere with rehabilitative goals. Prisoners compare sentences. Those who feel they have been the victims of prejudice become embittered and less responsive to treatment. In many cases, serious disciplinary problems have erupted because of perceived injustices. Consistent differences among judges within an urban court system interfere with the scheduling and processing of cases when defense attorneys request continuances in the hope that they can bring a client's case to a more lenient judge.

The sentencing decision demands considerable expertise on the part of judges. They must have knowledge of the wide range of sentencing alterna-

TABLE 13.7 Average sentences of federal prisoners, in months, by selected offense and judicial circuit (fiscal year ended June 30, 1972)

Judicial circuit	*Narcotics laws*	*Forgery*	*Robbery*	*All offenses*
1st (Me., Mass., N.H., R.I., P.R.)	68.0	19.7	133.5	52.5
2d (Conn., N.Y.)	58.8	30.4	114.7	44.3
3d (Del., N.J., Penna., V.I.)	77.4	27.3	128.3	67.7
4th (Md., N.C., S.C., Va., W.Va.)	77.0	36.4	158.8	57.3
5th (Ala., Fla., Ga., La., Miss., Tex.)	74.8	36.7	144.0	41.3
6th (Kent., Mich., Ohio, Tenn.)	54.0	39.3	134.4	52.8
7th (Ill., Ind., Wisc.)	75.6	38.2	114.4	50.4
8th (Ark., Iowa, Minn., Mo., Neb., N.D., S.D.)	103.3	36.6	155.8	52.4
9th (Alaska, Ariz., Calif., Hawaii, Idaho, Mont., Nev., Ore., Wash., Guam)	70.8	42.9	131.1	40.5
10th (Colo., Kansas, N.M., Okla., Utah, Wyo.)	85.7	56.5	134.9	54.3
All circuits	69.7	37.3	134.6	46.8

Source: U.S. Department of Justice. Federal Bureau of Prisons, *Statistical Report, Fiscal Years 1971 and 1972* (Washington, D.C.: Government Printing Office, 1973), pp. 96–101.

tives and their usefulness in treating the variety of offenders who appear before them. They must be able to evaluate the diagnostic information that is made available in the presentence report. Each must have a sense of others' sentencing norms. To improve the sentencing proficiency of judges and to ensure that the ideal of equal justice under the law is achieved, several innovations, including sentencing institutes, sentencing councils, sentencing review, and sentencing guidelines, have been advocated.

Sentencing institutes

sentencing institute A seminar designed to acquaint judges with sentencing laws and practices with the objective of reducing disparity in sentences.

Sentencing institutes for federal judges were inaugurated under a 1958 act of Congress for the purpose of promoting uniformity in sentencing procedures. Some states, notably New York, California, and Pennsylvania, have begun their own programs. Sentencing institutes are judicial seminars in which papers are presented and discussions held on topics designed to increase the participants' familiarity with new provisions of the law, special problems (such as those of the mentally disordered offender), and new correctional methods. At the seminars, usually of one or two days' duration, mock sentencing experiments are held on the basis of actual presentence reports and hypothetical cases. The judges individually stipulate the sanctions they would impose, which are then compared with those of other judges in the group. Not surprisingly, there are huge divergences in the suggested dispositions.

In addition to providing a forum for the dissemination of new information, sentencing institutes enable judges to compare norms with their peers and also remind them of the sentencing options that are available to them. Yet sentencing institutes act only as an informal pressure on judges; the law still emphasizes judicial independence. Some argue, however, that "judicial independence" has been used too often to justify the unpredictability and inequality of sentences, even though no one trained in law would accept a decisional crazy quilt of this kind in any other context.

sentencing council A seminar at which judges discuss particular cases before their courts. Recommendations for an appropriate sanction are made to the sentencing judge, who may follow them or not in sentencing the offender.

Sentencing councils

First begun by the judges of the United States District Court for the Eastern District of Michigan, ***sentencing councils*** have spread to several other federal and state jurisdictions. Under this concept, judges meet on a regular basis to discuss particular cases before their courts. Meeting in panels of three, which include the judge charged with handing down the actual sentence, they talk about the facts of the case, elements in the presentence report, and treatment alternatives. Each makes a recommendation, which may or may not be used by the sentencing judge when the sanction is formally prescribed. The decision is then relayed to the panel at the next meeting, where it may be further discussed.

Like sentencing institutes, the councils exemplify the use of peer pressure to create greater uniformity in sentences. Individual extremes of harshness and leniency tend to be tempered. Marvin Frankel reports that the net effect of sentencing councils has been that "the participating judges give shorter prison terms and make increased use of probation rather than confinement."[30] One criticism notes that the panel sessions are held before the sentencing hearing. It is felt that the influence of other judges may inhibit the sentencing judge from keeping an open mind as additional information is presented by the prosecutor, defense attorney, and defendant.

Sentencing review

Unlike criminal offenders in most Western countries, those in the United States normally do not have the right to review of their sentences. It is possible to appeal a sentence on constitutional grounds if, for example, it is not authorized by law, if it is a violation of equal protection, or if the terms are so disproportionate to the seriousness of the crime that it "shocks the conscience" or is "cruel and unusual." Only fifteen states have some system by which appellate courts may affirm or reduce a sentence. In some of these states, only the defendant may ask for a review of a sentence, while in others the prosecution may also seek a change. As the American Bar Association's Committee on Minimum Standards for Criminal Justice observes, "judicial review should be available for all sentences imposed in cases where provision is made for review of the conviction."[31]

In the states authorizing ***sentencing review,*** two methods are used. In seven states, special panels of trial judges are convened to review the propriety of sentences in individual cases. On hearing an appeal, the panel may increase or decrease the original sentence. In the other eight review states, requests

sentencing review
A process whereby a board of review may consider the propriety of sentences appealed to it in individual cases. After hearing an appeal, the board may increase or decrease the original sentence.

Sentence Disparity

At the Georgia Industrial Institute at Alto, I found prisoners between 14 and 19 years old. Many were first offenders.

James W was sentenced to life from a court in Taylor County, after being charged with rape. Harvey J is serving three years for the same offense from Paulding County. David J was accused of *attempted* rape in Bibb County and is in for three years. Elmer E, from Baldwin County, is also serving for attempted rape—17 years.

Yet about 100 miles east, in Greenville, S.C., almost nobody is charged with rape, according to B. O. Tomason, Jr., the county solicitor. He asserts that very few grown girls or women are really raped, and that in most cases the act is the result of the girl's leading the man on and then regretting it later.

Source: Howard James, *Crisis in the Courts* (New York: David McKay, 1971), p. 145.

---

may be brought to a regular appellate court. In all fifteen states, reformers have sought to require trial judges to provide a written explanation of each sentence they impose.

The major argument against appellate review is that it would greatly increase the amount of litigation; but experience in states where review is allowed shows that most defendants do not appeal the trial court's decision. In Massachusetts, where an average of 300 sentences per year are appealed, the review division sits for only fifteen days. In Connecticut there have been few sentence modifications, and the Sentence Review Division of the courts has not published its opinions to guide lower trial judges. The division has occasionally indicated that a sentence imposed by a trial judge will be affirmed "so long as it meets a 'reasonable judge' test." Observers believe that judges are extremely reluctant to criticize publicly the sentences rendered by a fellow judge, and a study by the American Judicature Society of five states with review panels revealed that none of the chief justices believed that sentencing criteria were developed as a result of panel actions.[32]

Sentencing guidelines

sentencing guidelines An instrument developed to indicate to judges the usual sanction given in the past in particular types of cases.

In recent years, ***sentencing guidelines*** have been established on a statewide basis in three states (Minnesota, Pennsylvania, Utah) and in selected jurisdictions in six others.[33] Guidelines are designed to constrain the discretion of judges. Although statutes provide a variety of sentencing options for particular crimes, the guidelines attempt to direct the judge to more specific actions that *should* be taken. Sentence ranges provided for most offenses are based on the seriousness of the crime and the criminal history of the offender.

For sentencing guidelines, as for parole guidelines (discussed in chapter 16), a grid is constructed on the basis of two scores, one related to the serious-

TABLE 13.8 Suggested sentencing guidelines for felony 4 offenses, Denver, Colorado
The Colorado Penal Code contains five levels of felonies (Felony 1 is the most serious) and three levels of misdemeanors; the Felony 4 category includes crimes such as manslaughter, robbery, and second-degree burglary. The legislated maximum sentence for a Felony 4 offense is ten years; no minimum period of confinement is to be set by the court. "Out" indicates a nonincarcerative sentence such as probation, deferred prosecution, or deferred sentence.

Offense score (severity of crime)[a]	***Offender score (likelihood of recidivating)***[b]				
	−1 −7	0 2	3 8	9 12	13+
10–12	Indet. min., 4–5-year max.	Indet. min., 8–10-year max.	Indet. min., 8–10-year max.	Indet. min., 8–10-year max.	Indet. min., 8–10-year max.
8–9	Out	3–5-month work project	Indet. min., 3–4-year max.	Indet. min., 8–10-year max.	Indet. min., 8–10-year max.
6–7	Out	Out	Indet. min., 3–4-year max.	Indet. min., 6–8-year max.	Indet. min., 8–10-year max.
3–5	Out	Out	Out	Indet. min., 4–5-year max.	Indet. min., 4–5-year max.
1–2	Out	Out	Out	Out	Indet. min., 3–4-year max.

[a] The higher the offense score, the more serious the crime.
[b] The higher the offender score, the higher the likelihood of recidivism.
Source: Jack M. Kress, Leslie T. Wilkins, and Don M. Gottfredson, "Is the End of Judicial Sentencing in Sight?" *Judicature*, December 1976, p. 221.

ness of the offense, the other to characteristics of the offender that indicate the likelihood of recidivism. The offender score is arrived at by summing the points allocated to each of the following factors: the number of juvenile, adult misdemeanor, and adult felony convictions; the number of times incarcerated; whether the accused was on probation or parole or had escaped from confinement at the time of the last offense; and employment status or educational achievement. As table 13.8 indicates, the judge locates the recommended sentence by finding the appropriate cell. Although no jurisdiction now requires that judges follow the guidelines, they are expected to provide a written explanation when they depart from them.

Sentencing guidelines are expected to be reviewed and modified periodically so that decisions in the most recent past will be included. Some critics argue that because the guidelines reflect only what has happened, they in no way really reform sentencing. Others question the choice of characteristics included in the offender scale and wonder whether some are used to mask racial criteria. Unlike some reforms designed to limit the discretion of judges, guidelines attempt to structure it so as to reflect the collective experience of sentencing in a particular city. Some prefer the use of guidelines to legislative enactment of a penal code based on mandatory or definite sentences.

Summary

Sentencing—the specification of the sanction—may be viewed as both the beginning and the end of the criminal justice system. With guilt established, a decision must be made concerning what to do with the person who has been convicted. Much of the effort of the defendant, prosecutor, and defense attorney during the presentencing phase is based on assumptions about the sanction that may follow conviction. This chapter has looked at the justifications for the criminal sanctions that have been given in succeeding eras to legitimize the punishment imposed by the state. Although the goals of retribution, deterrence, incapacitation, and rehabilitation may be viewed as distinct, there is a great deal of overlap among them. Rehabilitation appears to be the one goal that, if carried out according to its model, does not overlap with the other objectives.

When a judge sentences an offender in open court, the effect is felt not only by the individual facing the bench but by the official actors in the criminal justice system and by the general public as well. Each person will view the sentence through his or her own perceptual screen and evaluate its contents as one element to be considered when personal decisions are made. So much of the emphasis of the values and culture of the criminal justice system is on the sentence that its impact is felt throughout the system. So long as judges are given discretion in sentencing, disparities will exist. So long as the corrections process is expected to serve the multiple goals of rehabilitation, deterrence, and retribution, disparities will exist. So long as it is agreed that the punishment should fit the criminal, disparities will exist. The excesses are what concern those bothered by the "sentencing wonderland."

For discussion

1. You are the judge. What personal characteristics do you feel justify you in giving different sanctions to offenders who have committed the same crime?

2. In some states the jury not only decides guilt but also fixes the sentence. What problems do you see with this approach?
3. Many white-collar offenders are given short terms that they serve in minimum-security institutions with extensive recreational facilities and campus-like surroundings. Poor persons who are found guilty of committing property crimes serve long terms in the "big house." Is this justice?
4. You are the judge. The law in your state sets terms of five to fifteen years for the offense of armed robbery. The parole board usually releases individuals when half their sentence has been served. How might these facts influence your sentencing decisions?
5. You have been commissioned by your state legislature to devise a criminal sanction that will deter crime yet treat offenders humanely. What will you suggest?

For further reading

American Friends Service Committee. *Struggle for Justice.* New York: Hill & Wang, 1971.
Feeley, Malcolm M. *The Process Is the Punishment.* New York: Russell Sage Foundation, 1979.
Frankel, Marvin E. *Criminal Sentences.* New York: Hill & Wang, 1972.
Gaylin, Willard. *Partial Justice.* New York: Knopf, 1974.
——. *The Killing of Bonnie Garland.* New York: Simon & Schuster, 1982.
Goldfarb, Ronald, and Singer, Linda R. *After Conviction.* New York: Simon & Schuster, 1973.
Hirsch, Andrew von. *Doing Justice.* New York: Hill & Wang, 1976.
Menninger, Karl. *The Crime of Punishment.* New York: Viking Press, 1966.

Notes

1. Herbert L. Packer, *The Limits of the Criminal Sanction* (Stanford: Stanford University Press, 1968), pp. 33–34.
2. Andrew von Hirsch, *Doing Justice* (New York: Hill & Wang, 1976), p. 49.
3. Ibid.; Twentieth Century Fund, Task Force on Criminal Sentencing, *Fair and Certain Punishment* (New York: McGraw-Hill, 1976); David Fogel . . . *We Are the Living Proof* . . . (Cincinnati: W. H. Anderson, 1975).
4. As quoted in Leon Radzinowicz and J. W. C. Turner, "A Study in Punishment: Introductory Essay," 21 *Canadian Bar Review* 89 (1943).
5. Packer, *Limits of the Criminal Sanction,* p. 51.
6. Peter Greenwood, "Controlling the Crime Rate through Imprisonment," in *Crime and Public Policy,* ed. James Q. Wilson (San Francisco: ICS Press, 1983), p. 258.
7. James Q. Wilson, *Thinking about Crime* (New York: Basic Books, 1975), pp. 202–3.
8. Francis A. Allen, *The Borderland of Criminal Justice* (Chicago: University of Chicago Press, 1964), p. 28.
9. President's Commission on Law Enforcement and Administration of Justice, *Task Force Report: The Courts* (Washington, D.C.: Government Printing Office, 1967), p. 14.
10. Leroy Gould and J. Zvi Namenwirth, "Contrary Objectives: Crime Control and Rehabilitation of Criminals," in *Crime and Justice in American Society,* ed. Jack D. Douglas (Indianapolis: Bobbs-Merrill, 1971), p. 247.
11. Sally T. Hillsman, Joyce L. Sichel, and Barry Mahoney, *Fines in Sentencing* (New York: Vera Institute of Justice, 1983).
12. Tate v. Short, 401 U.S. 395 (1971).
13. U.S. Department of Justice, *Mandatory Sentencing: The Experience of Two States,* Policy Briefs (Washington, D.C.: Government Printing Office, 1982).
14. State of Michigan, Department of Corrections, *Criminal Statistics* (Lansing, 1972), p. 9.
15. Gagnon v. Scarpelli, 411 U.S. 778 (1973).
16. Furman v. Georgia, 408 U.S. 238 (1972).
17. Gregg v. Georgia, 428 U.S. 153 (1976).
18. *New Republic,* 12 December 1983, pp. 18–25.
19. Ibid.
20. Malcolm M. Feeley, *The Process Is the Punishment* (New York: Russell Sage Foundation, 1979).
21. James Eisenstein and Herbert Jacob, *Felony Justice* (Boston: Little, Brown, 1977).
22. Feeley, *Process Is the Punishment,* p. 200.
23. Marvin E. Frankel, *Criminal Sentences* (New York: Hill & Wang, 1972), p. 8.
24. Albert C. Price, "The Politics of Definite Sentencing in Four American States," Ph.D. dissertation, University of Connecticut, 1980.

25. Arthur Rosett and Donald R. Cressey, *Justice by Consent: Plea Bargains in the American Courthouse* (Philadelphia: Lippincott, 1976), p. 159.
26. Robert Martinson, "What Works?: Questions and Answers about Prison Reform," *Public Interest* 35 (Spring 1974): 22.
27. George F. Cole, "Will Definite Sentences Make a Difference?" *Judicature* 61 (August 1977): 58.
28. Todd R. Clear, "Correctional Policy, Neo-Retributionism, and the Determinate Sentence," in *Criminal Justice: Law and Politics,* ed. George F. Cole, 3d ed. (Monterey, Calif.: Brooks/Cole, 1980), p. 469.
29. Julian C. D'Esposito, Jr., "Sentencing Disparity: Causes and Cures," *Journal of Criminal Law, Criminology, and Police Science* 60 (1969): 183.
30. Frankel, *Criminal Sentences,* p. 69.
31. American Bar Association, *Standards on Appellate Review of Sentences* (Washington, D.C.: American Bar Association, 1968), p. 7.
32. "Appellate Review of Primary Sentencing Decisions: A Connecticut Case Study," *69 Yale Law Journal* 1453 (1960).
33. "Setting Prison Terms," U.S. Bureau of Justice Statistics *Bulletin,* August 1983.

Corrections

14

Sunday night, September 12, 1971, was a sleepless one for the 1,250 inmates holed up in D Yard of New York State's Attica Correctional Facility. They realized that the revolt that had begun on Thursday with the taking of forty-three hostages was nearing its end. On Saturday night the men had shouted down "Twenty-eight Points" for reform of the institution, and Commissioner Russell Oswald had agreed to them after negotiating with the prisoners, with the help and protection of thirty-three civilian observers. These citizens had been assembled at the request of the inmates and with the agreement of the prison authorities. Most were public figures known for their work in politics or journalism or for their affiliation with various social reform groups. Their political and social attitudes ranged from radical to reform. On Friday and Saturday, acting as negotiators, they had moved back and forth between the inmates and the authorities. As dawn approached on Monday, the convicts and their hostages tried to dry themselves over campfires in the yard while state troopers armed with .270s and shotguns assembled in front of the administration building. The beginning of the end of the four-day prison uprising was at hand.

When a sheriff or a marshal takes a man from a courthouse in a prison van and transports him to confinement for two or three or ten years, this is our act. *We have tolled the bell for him. And whether we like it or not, we have made him our collective responsibility. We are free to do something about him; he is not.*

CHIEF JUSTICE WARREN BURGER

At 7:40 A.M. Oswald delivered to the inmate spokesmen a written ultimatum calling for release of the hostages in exchange for implementation of the "Twenty-eight Points." It was read aloud in the yard, but only one inmate spoke in favor of acceptance. Some of the hostages were blindfolded and led to the catwalks in full view of the authorities; eight were held by at least one inmate each, most with knives at their throats. The hostages were told that they would be killed when the authorities made their move. By 9 o'clock troopers had taken positions on the walls surrounding the enclosure. At 9:44 electric power was turned off and immediately a National Guard helicopter rose in front of the administration building and began to drop CS gas (an incapacitating agent) on the inmates.

> As the gas descended, there was movement by the inmates and hostages on the catwalks, and the riflemen on A and C roofs—troopers and three corrections officers—commenced firing. Then troopers and correction officers on the third floor of A and C blocks joined in the firing. . . .
>
> Within about three minutes, the catwalk teams had cut through the barricades and moved on to B and D catwalks overlooking D yard. The rescue detail proceeded behind the A catwalk team to B catwalk, dropped its ladders, descended into D yard, and moved toward the hostage circle.[1]

At 9:50, four minutes into the assault, a state police helicopter began circling the yard, broadcasting a message for the inmates to surrender. In the six minutes of heavy fire, ten hostages and twenty-nine inmates were killed by bullets from guns in the hands of the authorities. Another three hostages and eighty-five inmates were wounded. No hostages were killed by the inmates during the attack. The bloodiest encounter between Americans in the twentieth century had ended.

Public reaction to the harsh methods used to put down the rebellion was immediate. The large proportion of black and Puerto Rican inmates in Attica confirmed for some people the system's racial repressiveness. For those concerned about the safety of the correctional officer hostages, the action was justified as necessary to end the uprising. In the weeks that followed, a blue-ribbon commission was appointed to determine what had happened and the causes of the revolt. With attention focused on the way the encounter was suppressed, little emphasis was placed on the fact that negotiations between prisoners and authorities over conditions at the institution had taken place throughout the four-day occupation.

The United States has had prison riots before. During the 1920s and 1930s in particular, bloody insurrections were suppressed immediately and hostages lost their lives. Prison guards are well aware of this risk, for a cardinal rule taught every recruit is that no guard is ransomable. Why was Attica different? Why were negotiators from the outside flown in and proposals and counterproposals exchanged? David Rothman, a leading scholar of the history of penology, believes that the failure to act immediately and with confidence at Attica points to the loss of legitimacy of prisons in American society. Most of the convicts' demands were not unreasonable in light of contemporary public attitudes: better food, pay for work, communications with families, and so forth. Since even Commissioner Oswald had agreed that these reforms were necessary and should be instituted, why did the National Guard repress the revolt in such a savage manner? Guards may be sacrificed if there is belief in the system, but if there are doubts, a compromise is attempted. When negotiations failed, the rebellious prisoners were put down "with a rage and force that in part reflects the urge to obliterate the questions and the ambivalence."[2]

Rothman's analysis of the frustrations at Attica is shared by a number of penologists and corrections officials who increasingly doubt our ability to rehabilitate prisoners and are uncertain of the goals of incarceration. With prison populations continually growing, some observers believe that all that can be offered is humane custody. From this perspective, existing educational, vocational, and treatment programs should operate on a completely voluntary basis; without the promise of rehabilitation, however, many correctional planners believe that appropriations for such programs would be minimal. Others believe that decarceration should be the goal, and would broaden the alternatives of probation, parole, bail, and halfway houses. Their argument is that this reform should be undertaken not in the hope that criminals would be redeemed or that crime would be reduced but because decarceration would be no worse than the present system, and the human, financial, and social costs would be considerably less. American corrections is at a crucial stage. Many paths are available, and it is uncertain which will be chosen.

The penitentiary: an American invention

Few Americans realize that their country gave the world the modern prison system, and still fewer know that it was brought about in response to concern for the humanitarian treatment of criminals. During the first decades of the nineteenth century the creation of penitentiaries in Pennsylvania and New York attracted the attention not only of legislators in other states but also of investigators from Europe. In 1831, France sent Alexis de Tocqueville and Gustave Auguste de Beaumont, England sent William Crawford, and Prussia dispatched Nicholas Julius. Travelers from abroad with no special interest in penology made it a point to include an American penitentiary in their travel plans, much as they planned visits to a southern plantation, a textile mill in Lowell, Massachusetts, or a town on the frontier. The American penitentiary had become world-famous by the middle of the century.

An age of reform

The latter part of the eighteenth century stands out as a remarkable period, one in which scholars and social reformers in Europe and America engaged in an almost complete rethinking of the nature of society and the place of the individual in it. The Enlightenment, as the philosophical movement was called, challenged traditional assumptions by emphasizing the individual, limitations on government, and rationalism. It was the major intellectual force behind the American Revolution and had a direct impact on views of the way the criminal law should be administered and on the goals and practices of corrections. Questions were raised about such matters as the procedures used to determine guilt, the limits on government's power to punish, the nature of criminal behavior, and appropriate means to correct offenders. At a time of overcrowded and unmanaged jails, brutal corporal punishment, and rising levels of crime, the great period of correctional reform was launched.

During the colonial and early postrevolutionary years, Americans used physical punishment, a legacy from Europe, as the main criminal sanction. Fines, stocks, flogging, branding, and maiming were the primary means used to control deviancy and to maintain public safety. For more serious crimes, the gallows was used with frequency. In New York about 20 percent of all crimes were capital offenses, and criminals were regularly sentenced to death for picking pockets, burglary, robbery, and horse stealing.[3] Recidivists especially usually ended on the gallows during the early years of the republic. Jails existed throughout the country, but they served only the limited purpose of holding people awaiting trial or punishment or those unable to pay their debts. Jails were not a part of the correctional scheme.

The early American preference for physical punishment was reinforced by the Puritans' belief in human depravity and the ever-present temptations of the devil. The Calvinist notion of predestination—that is, that people had no control over their fate in the next life—did not encourage efforts to rehabilitate offenders in this one.

The French scholar Michel Foucault has chronicled the spread of humanistic ideas during the latter portion of the eighteenth century. In Europe, the period following the French Revolution led to the disappearance of torture as a public spectacle and the adoption of "modern" penal codes that emphasized adapting punishment to fit the individual offender. Most important, those decades "saw the disappearance of the tortured, dismembered, amputated body, symbolically branded on face or shoulder, exposed alive or dead to public view." As punishment moved away from the infliction of pain, the offender's body was no longer the major target of penal policy. Now the body served as the instrument for correctional intervention to change the individual and set him or her on the right path. Foucault notes, "The expiation that once rained down upon the body must be replaced by a punishment that acts in the depths of the heart."[4]

Of the many persons who actively promoted the reform of corrections, John Howard (1726–1790), sheriff of Bedfordshire, England, stands out. His book, *The State of Prisons in England and Wales* (1777), led to the development of the penitentiary.[5] It is an unsentimental, factual account of his observations of the prisons that he visited. He found the conditions to be horrible, and he was particularly concerned about the lack of discipline. The book aroused the interest of certain members of Parliament, who sought passage of the Penitentiary Act of 1779. The act called for the creation of a house of hard labor in which people convicted of crimes would be imprisoned for up to two years. The institution would be based on four principles set down by Howard: (1) a secure and sanitary structure, (2) systematic inspection, (3) the abolition of fees, and (4) a reformatory regime. During the night prisoners were to be confined to solitary cells, and during the day they were to labor silently in common rooms. The regimen was to be strict and ordered. Perhaps influenced by his Quaker friends, Howard believed that the new institution should be not merely a place of industry but also one for contrition and penance. The purpose of the penitentiary was to punish and to reform.

Howard was to see the legislation passed but not implemented. The war in the American colonies diverted English public attention, and the resources to carry out the changes were not appropriated. It was not until 1842, with the opening of Pentonville in North London, that Howard's plan came to fruition. Meanwhile, however, his conception of the penitentiary had traveled across the Atlantic and was planted in the more fertile soil of Pennsylvania and New York, where it blossomed.

Reform in the United States

During the first fifty years after the birth of the new American republic, a revolution occurred in the conception of criminal punishment. Part of the impetus for change came from the postrevolutionary patriotic fervor that blamed recidivism and criminal behavior on English laws. Still more, however, the new correctional philosophy coincided with ideals found in the Declaration of Independence, with its optimistic view of human nature and its implied belief in each person's perfectibility. Accordingly, social progress was seen to be possible through reforms carried out according to the dictates of "pure reason." Emphasis shifted from the assumption that deviance was part of human nature to a belief that crime was a result of forces operating in the environment. Historian Alice Felt Tyler points to the incompatibility of a primitive penal system based on retribution in a nation committed to the idea of human perfectibility: "If American statesmen were to give more than lip service to the humane and optimistic idea of man's improvability, they must remove the barbarism and vindictiveness from their penal codes and admit that one great objective of punishment for crime must be the reformation of the criminal."[6]

The Pennsylvania system

Reform of the penal structure became the goal of a number of humanist groups in the United States. The first of these groups was the Philadelphia Society for Alleviating the Miseries of Public Prisons, formed in 1787. Under the leadership of Dr. Benjamin Rush, this group, which included a large number of Quakers, urged replacement of capital and corporal (bodily) punishment by incarceration. The Quakers believed that criminals could best be reformed if they were placed in solitary confinement so that, alone in their cells, they could consider their deviant acts, repent, and reform themselves. The word *penitentiary* is rooted in the Quaker idea that criminals need an opportunity for penitence (sorrow and shame for their wrongs) and repentance (willingness to change their ways).

In a series of legislative acts in 1790, Pennsylvania provided for the solitary confinement of "hardened and atrocious offenders" in the existing three-story, stone Walnut Street Jail in Philadelphia. This plain building, forty feet by twenty-five feet, housed eight cells on each floor, and there was an attached yard. Each cell was small and dark (only six feet by eight feet, and nine feet high). Inmates were alone in their cells, and from a small, grated window high on the outside wall they "could perceive neither heaven nor earth." No communications of any kind were allowed.

Pressed by the Philadelphia Society, the legislature was persuaded to build additional institutions: Western Penitentiary on the outskirts of Pittsburgh and Eastern Penitentiary near Philadelphia. The opening of Eastern in

Benjamin Rush

Benjamin Rush (1745–1813), physician, patriot, signer of the Declaration of Independence, and social reformer, was born in Pennsylvania and began practicing medicine in Philadelphia in 1769. While widely recognized for his work in medicine, particularly his insistence on the importance of personal hygiene, Rush was also a humanitarian. He helped to organize the Pennsylvania Society for the Abolition of Slavery and served as surgeon general under Washington during the Revolutionary War.

Following his military career, Rush became active in various reform movements, especially those dealing with treatment of the mentally ill and with prisoners. His interest in methods then being used to punish criminals led him to protest laws assigning such punishments as shaved heads, whippings, and other public displays. In *An Enquiry into the Effects of Public Punishment upon Criminals* (1787) he maintained that such excesses served only to harden criminals. Opposed to capital punishment, he wrote *On Punishing Murder by Death* (1792), condemning the practice as an offspring of monarchical divine right, a principle contrary to a republican form of government. He is probably best known for advocating the penitentiary as a replacement for capital and corporal punishment.

1829 marked the culmination of forty-two years of reform activity by the Philadelphia Society. On 25 October 1829 the first prisoner arrived. Charles Williams, eighteen years old and sentenced to a two-year term for larceny, was assigned to a cell twelve by eight by ten feet that had an individual exercise yard some eighteen feet long. Designed according to the segregate system, the prison isolated inmates not only from the community but from one another. In each cell was a fold-up steel bedstead, a simple toilet, a wooden stool, a workbench, and eating utensils. Light came from an eight-inch window in the ceiling. Solitary labor, Bible reading, and reflection were the keys to the moral rehabilitation that was supposed to occur within the prison walls. Although the cell was larger than most in use today, it was the only world the prisoner would see for the duration of his sentence. The only other human voice he heard would be that of a clergyman who would visit him on Sundays. Nothing was to distract the penitent prisoner from the path toward reform.

As described by Robert Vaux, one of the original Philadelphia reformers, the Pennsylvania system was based on the following principles: (1) prisoners should be treated not vengefully but in ways to convince them that through hard and selective forms of suffering they could change their lives; (2) to prevent the prison from being a corrupting influence, solitary confinement of all inmates should be practiced; (3) in seclusion offenders have an opportunity to reflect on their transgressions so that they may repent; (4) solitary confinement is a punishing discipline because humans are by nature social animals; (5) solitary confinement is economical, because prisoners do not need long periods of time to acquire the penitential experience, fewer keepers are needed, and the costs of clothing are reduced.[7]

Unfortunately for Vaux and the Quakers, their ideals were short-lived. The Walnut Street Jail became overcrowded as more and more offenders were held for longer periods of time. It turned into a warehouse of humanity dominated by Philadelphia politicians, who took over its operation. The Western Penitentiary was soon declared outmoded because isolation was not complete and the cells were too small for solitary labor. Like the other institutions, it became overcrowded and was recommended for demolition in 1833.

The Auburn system

In 1819 the Auburn system of New York evolved as a rival to Pennsylva-

---

A Foreign View of Eastern Penitentiary, 1831

Generally, their hearts are found ready to open themselves, and the facility of being moved renders them also fitter for reformation. They are particularly accessible to religious sentiments, and the remembrance of their family has an uncommon power over their minds. . . . Nothing distracts, in Philadelphia, the mind of the convicts from their meditations; and as they are always isolated, the presence of a person who comes to converse with them is the greatest benefit. . . . When we visited this penitentiary, one of the prisoners said to us: "It is with joy that I perceive the figure of the keepers, who visit my cell. This summer a cricket came into my yard; it looked like a companion. When a butterfly or any other animal happens to enter my cell, I never do it any harm."

Source: Gustave de Beaumont and Alexis de Tocqueville, *On the Penitentiary System in the United States and Its Application to France* (Carbondale, Ill.: Southern Illinois University Press, 1964), p. 83.

The Pennsylvania system incorporated the time for reflection and penance that the Quaker reformers believed important.

nia's. The use of incarceration was not questioned, only the regimen to which the prisoners were to be exposed. Under the Auburn system, prisoners were kept in individual cells at night but congregated in workshops during the day. In this congregate system, however, inmates were forbidden to talk to one another or even to exchange glances while on the job or at meals. One of the advantages of the Auburn system was that it cost less because one guard could supervise an entire group of prisoners. In addition, Auburn reflected some of the growing emphases of the Industrial Revolution: the men were to have the benefits of labor as well as meditation. They were to live under tight control, on a simple diet, and according to an undeviating routine, but they would work to pay for a portion of their keep.

American reformers saw the Auburn approach as a great advance in penology, and it was copied throughout the land. At an 1826 meeting of prison reformers in Boston, the Auburn system was described in terms so glowing that they are now hard to understand.

> At Auburn, we have a more beautiful example still, of what may be done by proper discipline, in a Prison well constructed. . . . The unremitted industry, the entire subordination, and subdued feeling among the convicts, has probably no parallel among any equal number of convicts. In their solitary cells, they spend the night with no other book than the Bible, and at sunrise they proceed in military order, under the eye of the turnkey in solid columns, with the lock march to the workshops.[8]

During this period of reform, advocates of both the Pennsylvania and Auburn plans debated on public platforms and in the nation's periodicals. Although both approaches seem similar in retrospect, an extraordinary amount of intellectual and emotional energy was spent on the arguments. Often the two systems have been contrasted by noting that the Quaker

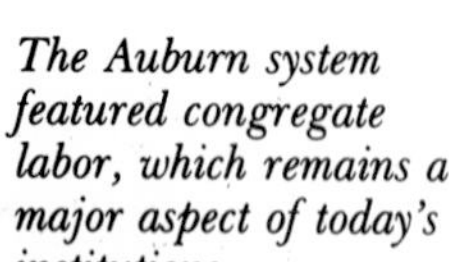
The Auburn system featured congregate labor, which remains a major aspect of today's institutions.

method aimed to produce honest persons while the New York system sought to mold obedient citizens. Advocates of both the congregate and solitary systems agreed that the prisoner must be isolated from society and placed on a disciplined routine. They believed that deviancy was a result of corruption pervading the community and that such institutions as the family and the church were not providing a counterbalance. Only when offenders were removed from these temptations and subjected to a steady and regular regimen could they become useful citizens. The convicts were not inherently depraved, but rather the victims of a society that had not protected them from vice. As the word *penitentiary* connotes, while offenders were being punished, they would become penitent, see the error of their ways, and want to place themselves on the right path.

> The penitentiary, free of corruptions and dedicated to the proper training of the inmate, would inculcate the discipline that negligent parents, evil companions, taverns, houses of prostitution, theaters, and gambling halls had destroyed. Just as the criminal's environment had led him into crime, the institutional environment would lead him out of it.[9]

How to Construct a Prison: circa 1824

Prisons should be so constructed that even their aspect might be terrific, and appear like what they should be—dark and comfortless abodes of guilt and wretchedness. No mode or degree of punishment . . . is in its nature so well adapted to purposes of preventing crime or reforming a criminal as close confinement in a solitary cell, in which, cut off from all hope of relief, the convict shall be furnished a hammock on which he may sleep, a block of wood on which he may sit, and with such coarse and wholesome food as may be suited to a person in a situation designed for grief and penitence, and shall be favored with so much light from the firmament as may enable him to read the New Testament which will be given him as his sole companion and guide to a better life. There his vices and crimes shall become personified, and appear to his frightened imagination as co-tenants of his dark and dismal cell.

Source: First warden of the Maine State Prison quoted in Walter F. Ulmer, "History of Maine Correctional Institutions," *American Journal of Corrections* 27 (July–August 1965): 33.

The Cincinnati Declaration

By the middle of the nineteenth century, reformers had become disillusioned with the results of the penitentiary movement. Deterrence and reform had been achieved in neither the Auburn nor the Pennsylvania system nor in their copies. The failure of the penitentiaries, however, was seen as a problem of poor administration rather than as an indictment of the concept of incarcerative penalties. Within forty years of their advocates' optimistic proclamations, penitentiaries had become overcrowded, understaffed, and minimally financed. Discipline had become lax, administrators were viewed as corrupt, and the institutions had become places of brutality. At Sing Sing in 1870, investigators discovered that

> dealers were publicly supplying prisoners with almost anything they would pay for; convicts sitting and lying about under the trees, or congregated in groups in cool places, without keepers, [were] playing all sorts of games, reading, scheming, trafficking. . . . Numerous shanties [were] scattered about the grounds, affording lounging places for convicts.[10]

In 1870 the newly formed National Prison Association, meeting in Cincinnati, issued a Declaration of Principles, which sounded the trumpet for a new round of penal reform. Although exponents of the Pennsylvania system continued to condemn congregate prisons and looked with suspicion on the advocates of a new order, they were outnumbered by such progressive penologists as Franklin Sanborn, Enoch Wines, and Zebulon Brockway. The association advocated a new design for ***penology***. The goal should be the treatment of criminals through their moral regeneration: the reformation of criminals, "not the infliction of vindictive suffering." To achieve this goal, corrections should provide for progressive classification of prisoners, the indeterminate sentence, and the development of the inmate's self-respect. Penitentiary practices as developed during the first half of the nineteenth century—the fixed sentence, lockstep, rules of silence, and isolation—were now seen as debasing, humiliating, and destructive of initiative.

penology
A branch of criminology dealing with the management of prisons and treatment of offenders.

The Declaration of Principles asserted that prisons should be operated in accordance with a philosophy of inmate change that would reward reformation with release. Peremptory sentences should be replaced by sentences of indeterminate length, and proof of reformation should replace the "mere lapse of time" in bringing about the prisoner's freedom. This reformation program should be encouraged through a progressive classification of prisoners based on character and improvement. But in this connection it should be remembered that, like the Quakers, these progressive reformers looked to institutional life as the way to effect rehabilitation. Inmates should be made into well-adjusted citizens, but the process should be done behind walls. The declaration could thus in good faith insist: "Reformation is a work of time; and a benevolent regard to the good of the criminal himself, as well as to the protection of society, requires that his sentence be long enough for reformatory processes to take effect."[11]

Elmira Reformatory

The new progressive approach, which had an early advocate in the person of Zebulon Brockway, a career prison administrator, took shape at Elmira,

New York, in 1876. According to Brockway, the key to reform and rehabilitation lay in education.

> The effect of education is reformatory, for it tends to dissipate poverty by imparting intelligence sufficient to conduct ordinary affairs, and puts into the mind, necessarily, habits of punctuality, method and perseverance. . . . If culture, then, has a refining influence, it is only necessary to carry it far enough, in combination always with due religious agencies, to cultivate the criminal out of his criminality, and to constitute him a reformed man.[12]

Brockway's approach at Elmira Reformatory was supported by legislation passed by New York providing for indeterminate sentences, permitting the reformatory to release inmates on parole when their reform had been assured. At Elmira, attempts were made to create a schoollike atmosphere with courses in both academic and moral subjects. Inmates who performed well in the courses and who lived according to the reformatory discipline were placed in separate categories so that they could progress to a point where they were eligible for parole. Poor grades and misconduct extended the inmates' tenure. Society could reform criminals, Enoch Wines said, only "by placing the prisoner's fate, as far as possible, in his own hands, by enabling him, through industry and good conduct, to raise himself, step by step, to a position of less restraint; while idleness and bad conduct, on the other hand, keep him in a state of coercion and restraint."[13]

By 1900 the reformatory movement had spread throughout the nation, but by World War I it was already in decline. In most institutions the architec-

Zebulon Brockway

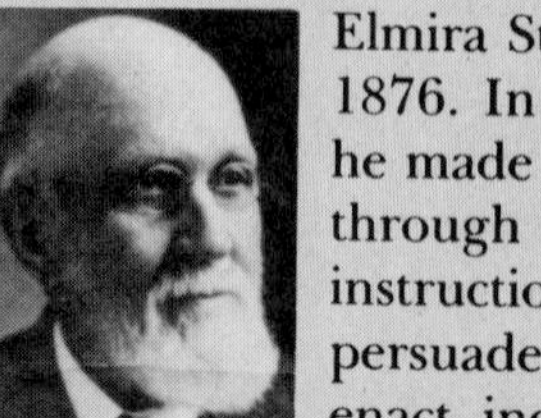

Zebulon Brockway of Connecticut began his distinguished career in penology at the age of twenty-one as a clerk at the Wethersfield Prison. In 1852 he became superintendent of the Albany Municipal and County Almshouse, where he founded the first county hospital for the insane. In 1854, at the age of twenty-seven, he became superintendent of the Monroe County Penitentiary in Rochester, New York, where he began to experiment with ideas on making prisons more humane and rehabilitative. Believing that his energies should be devoted to youthful offenders, who offered the greatest possibility for reformation, Brockway moved to Detroit in 1861 to head the Michigan House of Correction, an institution for young men between the ages of sixteen and twenty-one.

Brockway welcomed the opportunity to put his theories into practice as superintendent of Elmira State Reformatory, New York, in 1876. In the following twenty-five years he made it a model for other institutions through the development of educational instruction and training for trades. He persuaded the New York legislature to enact indeterminate sentences and ran Elmira on a graded system that rewarded inmates for their progress. He believed that incarceration had one purpose—to protect society against crime—but that reform of the criminal should be the ultimate goal.

Brockway retired from Elmira in 1900 and served in a variety of public and charitable offices for the next twenty years. He was a charter member of the National Prison Association (predecessor of the American Correctional Association) and was its president in 1898. His autobiography, *Fifty Years of Prison Service,* was published in 1912.

ture, attitudes of the guards, and emphasis on discipline differed little from orientations of the past. Too often the educational and rehabilitative efforts took a back seat to the traditional punitive emphasis. Even Brockway admitted difficulty in distinguishing between inmates whose attitudes had changed and those who superficially conformed to prison rules. Being a good prisoner, the traditional emphasis, became the way to win parole in most of these institutions.

Reforms of the Progressives

The first two decades of the twentieth century were also a period of reform as social and political thought confronted such modern developments as industrialization, urbanization, and the advancement of science. This was the era of the Progressives, who attacked the excesses of urban society, in particular those of big business, and advocated state action to deal with the social problems of slums, adulterated food, vice, and crime. They believed that civic-minded people could apply the findings of science to social problems in ways that would be of benefit to all. Application of the concepts of the social and behavioral sciences was believed to be the means by which criminals could be rehabilitated.

David Rothman characterizes the Progressive programs as being epitomized in two words: "conscience" and "convenience."[14] The reforms were promoted by benevolent and philanthropic men and women who aimed to understand and cure crime through a case-by-case approach. Knowledge of the life history of the offender could lead to the fashioning of treatment programs that would be specific to the offender's needs. However, to diagnose each criminal, to prescribe treatment, and to determine when release to the community was possible, correctional administrators had to be permitted to exercise discretion.

Because discretion was required for the day-to-day operation of the new penology, Rothman shows, correctional administrators responded favorably to it. Discretion made it more convenient for administrators to carry out their daily assignments. He also notes that although the Progressives were not committed to incarceration, as supporters of the penitentiary were, and in fact were instrumental in promoting acceptance of probation and parole, the factor of discretion served to expand the size of the prison population.

Many of the reforms advocated by the Progressives were first stated in the 1870 Declaration of Principles, but the new activists looked to the social sciences, biology, and psychology both for explanations of the causes of crime and for therapies to treat it rather than to religious or moral precepts. They relied on the developments of modern criminology associated with a scientific approach to crime and human behavior known as the positivist school, which focused on the behavior of the offender.

Armed with this positivist view of criminal behavior and faith in the efficacy of state action to reform offenders, the Progressives fought for changes in correctional methods. Their efforts centered on two strategies: one designed to improve conditions in the environments they believed to be breeding grounds of crime, the other emphasizing ways to rehabilitate the individual deviant. The presentence report, with its extensive personal history, could enable judges and correctional officials to analyze the individual's problem and take action toward rehabilitation. Probation, the indeterminate sentence and parole, and treatment programs became the instruments of this new approach to crime.

Although the Progressives were instrumental in advancing the new penology, it was not until the 1930s that attempts were made to implement fully what became known as the medical model of corrections. Then penologists operating under the banner of the newly prestigious social and behavioral sciences helped to shift the emphasis of the postconviction sanction to treatment of criminals, whose social, intellectual, or biological deficiencies were seen as the causes of their illegal activities. With the essential structural elements of parole, probation, and the indeterminate sentence already in place in most states, incorporation of the medical model required only the addition of classification systems to diagnose offenders and treatment programs that would make them well. Following World War II this approach won new adherents, with California leading the way. Group therapy, behavior modification, counseling, and numerous other approaches all became part of the "new penology." Yet even during the 1950s, when the medical model was at its zenith, only a small proportion of state correctional budgets was allocated for rehabilitation. What frustrated many persons committed to treatment was that although states adopted the rhetoric of the medical model, the institutions were still being run with custody as an overriding goal. The failure of these new techniques to stem crime, the changes in the characteristics of the prison population, and the misuse of the discretion required by the medical model prompted another cycle of correctional reform, so that by 1980 rehabilitation as a goal had become discredited.

The fruits of prison reform: a summary

Although each of the reform movements of American corrections was the work of well-intentioned people working in the name of humanity, their ideals were never achieved, and the changes that were made often produced unsatisfactory results. In most cases, political and bureaucratic influences constituted a more powerful force than the reformers' ideals, and the prisons, quickly overpopulated and poorly managed, functioned as factories for crime. As society changed, the assumptions underlying the approach to corrections likewise changed from one period to the next. What remained was the stone walls of the prisons.

Although the 1870 Declaration of Principles continued to embody the espoused goal of American penology, the fortress prison remained the dominant type of institution. Except in the South, where prisons were organized to provide inmate labor for agriculture, most correctional facilities emphasized industrial-type work inside the walls. Overcrowding and idleness became problems after World War I. The prison industries developed in emulation of Auburn were restricted by political pressure brought by business and the labor movement. Although penologists and humanitarians continued to advocate rehabilitation, they made little headway during the first half of the century.

Until the end of World War II the "big house" dominated the penological landscape. The big house was a walled prison with an average population of 2,500 men housed in one- or two-man cells stacked in three or more tiers in large cell blocks.

> This granite, steel, cement, and asphalt monstrosity stood as the state's most extreme form of punishment, short of the death penalty. It was San Quentin in California, Sing Sing in New York, Stateville in Illinois, Jackson in Michigan, Jefferson City in Missouri, Canon City in Colorado, and so on. It was the place of banishment and punishment to which convicts were "sent up." Its major characteristics were isolation, routine, and monotony. Its mood was mean and grim, perforated here and there by ragged-edged vitality and humor.[15]

Periodically, charges of corruption or brutality in the prisons reached the press. Such reports often prompted state legislative investigations, which focused public attention on the situation but produced few lasting reforms. More often, legislatures dismissed complaints that appropriations were not at a level commensurate with the institutions' goals.

By the beginning of the 1970s the prison reform movement seemed so dispirited that many penologists threw up their hands in despair. The belief that prisons were mainly training institutions for criminal careers, that rehabilitative efforts were not reflected in recidivism rates, and that alternatives to prison were less costly began to influence a growing number of concerned citizens. The events at Attica in 1971, followed by those in New Mexico State Prison in 1980, seemed to lend weight to these latest straws in the wind for prison reform. Yet by the 1980s the size of the prison population in the United States had risen to a new high.

Organization of corrections in the United States

The administration of the corrections system is fragmented, with the federal government, all fifty states, the District of Columbia, most of the 3,047 counties, and most cities each having at least one facility. Correctional facilities range from the numerous overnight lockups that are often part of town police headquarters to 550 prisons and more than 4,000 jails. The prisoners in these institutions are fed, treated, and guarded by about 100,000 full-time employees. What Jessica Mitford has called "the prison business" costs more than $7 billion a year.[16]

Although we tend to think of corrections with reference to institutions, fewer than a third of the persons under correctional supervision live in them. Persons under probation supervision constitute more than twice the population that is maintained in prisons and jails, while 11 percent of the total are being supervised on parole in the community (see figure 14.1). Prisons and jails make up the popular image of corrections, yet, as we shall see, this portion of the American criminal justice system includes a variety of programs and facilities.

The correctional institutions in the federal and state systems are widely diverse. Closed correctional facilities—usually called prisons, penitentiaries, or reformatories—are those best known to the public through novels, films, and television. But there are also correctional farms and camps, especially in the South and West, where inmates engage in agriculture, forestry, or road

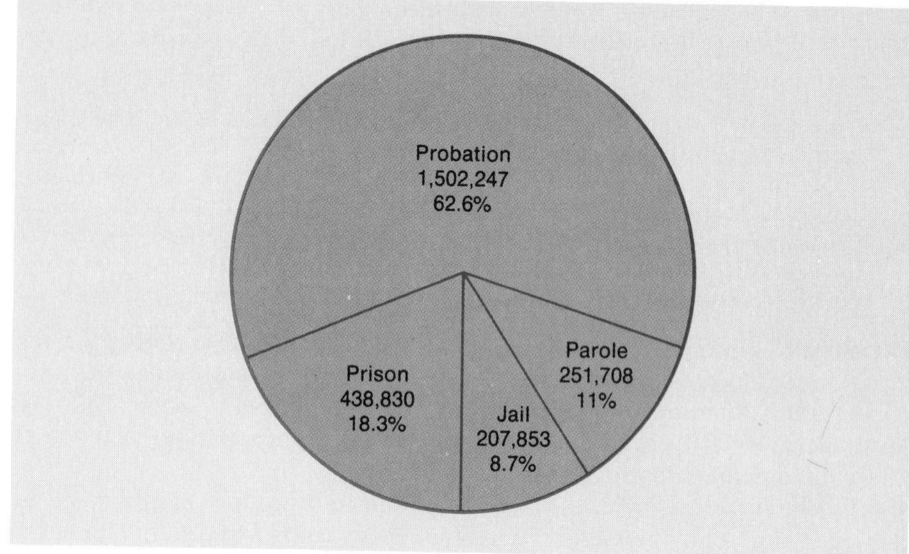

FIGURE 14.1
Number and percentage of persons under correctional supervision in all categories of supervision

repair. Community corrections has brought into being a range of halfway houses and treatment centers.

Each level of government has some responsibility for corrections, and often one level exercises little supervision over another. The federal government has no formal control over corrections in the states. In most areas, maintaining prisons and parole is the responsibility of the state, while counties have some misdemeanant jails but no authority over the short-term jails operated by towns and cities. In addition, there is a division between juvenile and adult corrections. The fragmentation of corrections forces us to remember that within the physical boundaries of a state there are many correctional systems, each with its own special orientation.

The federal prison system

The United States Bureau of Prisons was created by Congress in 1930. Before that time, the administrators of the seven federal prisons then in operation functioned with relative freedom from control. Since 1930 the Bureau of Prisons has grown until it operates an integrated system of prisons containing about 32,000 inmates. These facilities include eight correctional categories: youth and juvenile institutions, young adult institutions, adult penitentiaries, adult correctional institutions, short-term camps, institutions for women, community treatment centers, and a medical treatment center. Because of the nature of federal criminal law, prisoners in most of these facilities are quite different from those in state institutions. In general, the population contains more inmates who have been convicted of white-collar crimes, although drug offenders are increasing. There are fewer who have committed crimes of violence than are found in most state institutions. The quality of the federal prisons is considered to be higher than that of prisons in most states. Some differences between federal and state prisons are suggested by table 14.1.

TABLE 14.1 Characteristics of federal and state prisons

	Federal	*State*
Number of prisons	38	521
Security level		
Maximum	13	140
Medium	17	207
Minimum	8	174
Inmate population		
Less than 500	10	366
500–999	18	80
1,000 or more	10	75
Year built		
Before 1875	0	25
1875–1924	3	76
1925–1949	16	125
1950–1969	8	156
1970–1978	11	139
Prisoners housed		
Males	31	460
Females	2	40
Coed	5	21
Prison employees		
Number	8,626	83,535
Percent administration	2.2	2.2
Percent custodial	42.4	62.9
Percent service	23.0	15.9
Percent office	32.4	19.0

Source: U.S. Department of Justice, Bureau of Justice Statistics, *Report to the Nation on Crime and Justice* (Washington, D.C.: Government Printing Office, 1983), p. 79.

State corrections

Until very recently, the operation of corrections in the states was one of the least visible aspects of the criminal justice system because of the nature of its function and its clientele. In the past ten years the role of state government in corrections has become more widely known, in part because of the new range of programs and institutions and the movement to shift more of these activities into the community.

Every state has a centralized department of the executive branch that administers corrections, but the extent of these departments' responsibility for programs varies. In some states, for example, probation and parole programs are operated by the department of corrections, while in other states probation is under the judiciary and parole is handled separately. Wide variation also exists in the way correctional responsibilities are divided between the state and local governments. The differences can be seen in the proportion of correctional employees who work for the state. In Connecticut, Rhode Island, and Vermont, for example, the proportion is 100 percent, while in California it is only 44 percent.

Some states have formed alliances with neighboring states to share responsibility for the confinement and rehabilitation of offenders. Such compacts customarily designate one facility in a region to receive certain types of offenders from a multistate area. The New England Correctional Compact is the oldest and most extensively applied of such agreements.

State correctional institutions for adult felons include a great range of facilities and programs, including prisons, reformatories, industrial institutions, prison farms, conservation campuses, forestry campuses, and halfway houses. Despite this variety, most state prisons are generally old and large. Over half of the nation's inmates are in institutions with average daily populations of more than 1,000, and about 61 percent are in prisons built more than thirty years ago. More than 11 percent of the inmates are held in facilities built before 1875, and most of these structures house upwards of 1,000 inmates. Some states have created facilities that are small and are designed to meet individual correctional needs, but most inmates are in very large "megaprisons" that are antiquated and have many of the maintenance and operational deficiencies associated with other old, intensively used buildings.

Correctional institutions are classified according to the level of security they afford, and the type of population shifts according to the special needs of the offenders. The security level is easily recognized by the physical characteristics of the buildings: the massive stone walls of maximum security prisons are topped by barbed wire and strategically placed guard towers; minimum security institutions are often indistinguishable from college campuses or apartment complexes.

The maximum security prison (52 percent of state inmates). Built like a fortress, surrounded by stone walls with guard towers, the maximum security prison is designed to prevent escape. Inmates live in cells that have plumbing and sanitary facilities. The barred doors may be operated electronically so that an officer can confine all prisoners to their cells with the flick of a switch. The purpose of the maximum security facility is custody and discipline; there is a military-style approach to order. Prisoners wear uniforms, march to meals and work, and follow a strict routine. Some of the most famous prisons, such as Stateville, Attica, Yuma, and Sing Sing, are maximum security facilities.

The medium security prison (37 percent of state inmates). Although in appearance it resembles the maximum security prison, this prison is organized on a somewhat different basis, with the result that its atmosphere is less rigid and tense. Prisoners have more privileges, and contact with the outside through visitors, mail, and access to radio and television is freer. One may expect to find a greater emphasis on rehabilitative programs in the medium security prison because, although in most states the inmates of this type of facility have probably committed serious crimes, they are not perceived to be hardened criminals.

The minimum security prison (11 percent of state inmates). Housing the least violent offenders, principally white-collar criminals, the minimum security prison does not have the guard towers and walls usually associated with correctional institutions. Often the buildings are surrounded by Cyclone fencing. Prisoners usually live dormitory style or even in small private rooms rather than barred cells. There is a relatively high level of personal freedom—inmates may have television sets, choose their own clothes, and move about casually within the buildings. Particular reliance is placed on treatment programs in minimum security institutions, and there are opportunities for education and for work release. Although outsiders may sometimes feel that little punishment is associated with the minimum security facility, it is still a prison, restrictions are placed on inmates, and they remain segregated from society.

Jails: local correctional facilities

Although recent penological thinking has emphasized that treatment programs in the community are a constructive alternative to custody, local jails and short-term institutions in the United States are generally held to be poorly managed custodial or caretaking institutions. A 1982 survey of inmates of local jails found 3,493 locally administered jails with the authority to detain prisoners for more than forty-eight hours. At the time of the survey, they held 209,582 inmates, of whom 1,729 were juveniles (see table 14.2). The jail population had increased by one-third since the immediately preceding survey, in 1978; this increase matches that of the prison population over the same period. Even when the short terms of confinement in jails are considered, the 7 million commitments to jails each year make a staggering figure, and more than half of the adults included in that number have not yet been convicted but are awaiting disposition of their cases. Of special interest is the fact that 40 percent of inmates are held in the hundred largest jails, whose populations range from 400 (Kern County, California) to more than 6,000 (Los Angeles County Central Jail).[17]

Functions. The primary function of jails is to hold persons awaiting trial and those who have been sentenced as misdemeanants to terms of no more than one year. In some states, however, convicted felons may serve terms of more than one year in jail rather than in prison. Others held in jail are those awaiting transportation to prison, those convicted of parole or probation violations, and those housed there because of prison overcrowding. In 1982 more than 8,200 persons were in the last category.

Jails and police lockups have increasingly had to shoulder responsibility for housing not only criminal defendants and offenders but also those persons viewed as problems by society. Here we can see how the criminal justice system is linked to other agencies of government. The deinstitutionalization of mental patients in particular has shifted a new population to criminal justice. The development of psychotropic drugs (those that act on the mind) has permitted institutions for the mentally ill to release many patients to live in the commu-

TABLE 14.2 Number of male and female inmates of U.S. jails, by detention status, 30 June 1982

	Total	*Male*	*Female*
All inmates	209,582	195,730	13,852
Adult	207,853	194,153	13,700
Awaiting arraignment or trial	118,189	110,078	8,111
Convicted	89,664	84,075	5,589
Juvenile	1,729	1,577	152
Awaiting preliminary hearing or adjudication	1,274	1,145	129
Adjudicated	455	432	23

Source: U.S. Department of Justice, Bureau of Justice Statistics, *Bulletin*, February 1983, p. 1.

nity. Like offenders in community corrections programs, many former mental patients can find housing only in deteriorating neighborhoods. Many such people are unable to cope with urban living and come to the attention of the police upon reports that they are acting in a deviant manner that, although not illegal, is upsetting to the citizenry (urinating in public, appearing disoriented, shouting obscenities, and so on). The police must handle such situations, and temporary confinement in the lockup or jail may be necessary if no appropriate social service facilities are immediately available. In Denver, for example, the situation has been described as a revolving door that shifts these "street people" from the police station to the mental wing of the jail, often to court, and then back to the street.

Most inmates spend relatively brief periods in jail. The 1982 National Survey of Jails found that the average stay was about eleven days, but this figure masked a wide range. In some states jail inmates serve sentences of more than a year but a high proportion are there only a few days or less. Because of the great turnover and because local control provides an incentive to keep costs down, correctional services are usually lacking. The Bureau of

Close-up: Specific Strategies for Reducing Jail Populations

Reducing bookings

Diversion for alcoholics. To keep the jail from being an expensive drunk tank, communities must do more than merely decriminalize public drunkenness, which most states have already done. The community must provide detoxification centers, and these must be designed to meet the needs of police and health officials as well as alcoholics. After San Diego revitalized its detoxification program by making booking a simple two-minute procedure and allowing health personnel to exclude violent inebriates, referrals jumped from 3,000 to 24,000 a year. Treatment costs only $6 per visit. A study of two cities in Kentucky showed that Lexington had a jail population two and a half times larger than Louisville's because Louisville used a diversion program for alcoholics, while Lexington did not.

Taking care of the mentally ill. Community mental health centers can provide support to keep people from getting into trouble in the first place, and can be a refuge for those picked up on nuisance charges or for minor crimes. Many of these are people who have been released from mental hospitals but not given outpatient treatment. In Galveston, Texas, specially trained deputies identify mental health arrestees and divert them to special facilities.

Keeping juveniles out of jail. Juveniles end up in jail not because authorities think they belong there, but because there is nowhere else to put them. Even for communities without separate juvenile institutions, there are many options. . . . Police can find a bed for runaway or troubled youths in hospitals, nursing homes or mental health facilities. Foster families can be trained to take in juveniles on short notice. Using a network of these and other resources, Pennsylvania has kept all juveniles out of adult facilities since 1980.

Citation release. For those charged with misdemeanors, there is often no need to book into jail at all; a police officer can issue a summons or citation. The pioneer project in this area, the Manhattan Summons Project, established by the Vera Institute of Justice, saved $6.7 million in police time in its first four years and had a low failure-to-appear rate of 5 percent.

Getting inmates out of jail quickly

Release on recognizance. Known as ROR, this system . . . uses a point scale that

Justice Statistics found that 86.4 percent of the institutions surveyed had no recreational facilities, 89.2 percent had no educational programs, and 49 percent provided no medical services.[18] Such conditions are at odds with the philosophy of community corrections.

The mixture of offenders of widely diverse ages and criminal histories is another of the problems most often cited when the conditions in the U.S. jails are discussed. Because most inmates are viewed as temporary residents, little attempt is made to classify them for either security or treatment purposes. Horror stories of the mistreatment of young offenders by older, stronger, and more violent inmates occasionally come to public attention. The physical condition of most jails aggravates this situation because most are old, overcrowded, and often lacking in basic facilities.

Institutions for women

Because so few women are sent to prison, the number and adequacy of facilities for them are limited. Although the ratio of arrests is approximately

counts ties to the community, including job, family, and length of residence, to determine which defendants are most likely to show up for trial; they can be released on their own without posting cash bond. Across the country, 135 formal programs do such screening; in smaller jurisdictions, probation officers often handle it. . . .

Percentage bail. Under this option, a defendant can post 10 percent of the amount of bail with the court, rather than with a bail bondsman. If he shows up for trial, he gets most or all of his money back, unlike the fee he pays a bail bondsman. If he does not show up, he owes the other 90 percent, plus he is charged with a separate offense for bail-jumping. Philadelphia estimated that it saved $1 million a year and reduced its jail population 29 percent by using this system.

Conditional release. For those who cannot be released on their own recognizance, but do not present a major threat to the community, judges can impose special conditions, such as requiring that the defendant attend a drug-treatment program or call the probation office every day.

Speeding up the courts. By introducing measures to reduce court delays, Providence, Rhode Island, was able to reduce the median time a case was in court from 277 days to 61 days. These measures included bringing in extra judges to clear up a backlog, enforcing strict time limits, and introducing new management practices. . . .

Warrants and detainers. Many jurisdictions automatically keep people in jail even on petty charges if they have a warrant lodged against them. Investigating these warrants and discriminating between types of warrants can speed releases from jail.

Programs for sentenced inmates. Alternative programs such as restitution, community service, intensive probation, work-release and halfway houses can be run on a county level. These programs keep convicted petty offenders from taking up jail space for months on minor charges.

Source: *Time to Build?* Copyright © 1984 by Edna McConnell Clark Foundation, pp. 40–41. Reprinted by permission.

six men to one woman, the admission to state and federal correctional institutions is a ratio of twenty-one men to one woman. Of 432,000 inmates in state and federal prisons in 1983, only about 19,000 were women, who were being held in three federal and forty state institutions. The proportion is low, but the number of women in prison is increasing annually at the rate of 6 percent, while the growth of the male correctional population is 4 percent. During the ten-year period 1974–84, the number of incarcerated women rose 133 percent, compared to 86 percent for men.

The woman in prison has been called the forgotten offender. Because so few women are sentenced to prison, some critics say that those incarcerated are given a low priority for educational and vocational training programs. In many states no distinctly separate facilities exist for them and they are assigned to a section of the state prison for men. Here, as some have argued, they are subjected to the abuse of male prison officials and are expected to keep busy in such "female" pursuits as sewing for the entire penal system.

The first prison intended exclusively for women was built in Indiana in 1873. Within fifty years, thirteen other states had followed this lead. By 1975, twenty-eight states had separate women's prisons; others send their female offenders out of state on a contractual basis.

Conditions in correctional facilities for women are more pleasant than those of similar institutions for men. Usually the buildings are attractive, without gun towers and barbed wire. Because of the small population, however, most states have only one facility, and that is located in a rural setting far removed from urban centers. Thus women prisoners may be more isolated from their families and communities. This is a special problem when one considers that an estimated 70 percent of incarcerated women are mothers with an average of two children. Pressure from the Women's Movement and the apparent rise in the incidence of crime among women may bring about a greater equality in corrections for men and women. A full discussion of life in correctional institutions for women is found in chapter 15.

Co-corrections

Separation of the sexes in penal institutions was one of the major reforms of the nineteenth century. Until recently sexual segregation of offenders has been an overriding rule. From the early 1960s some juvenile homes and drug rehabilitation centers have been operated on a gender-neutral basis, but it was not until 1971, with the opening of the Federal Correctional Institution at Fort Worth, Texas, housing both male and female inmates, that co-corrections became a reality. In addition to county jails, twenty-one state and five federal institutions are now being operated on this basis.[19]

Co-corrections has been advanced for a number of reasons, among them the need to narrow the disparity between the programs available to men and those available to women, reduce the tensions and violence of single-sex institutions, to prepare prisoners for return to a heterosexual society, and to use facilities in a cost-effective manner. It is the last consideration that has made the possibility of housing men and women together attractive to some correctional administrators. With the female incarceration rate at a fairly stable 4 percent and the number of male inmates greatly expanding, co-corrections has been instituted in many states as a way to postpone or avoid new construction; male inmates are assigned to unused space in the women's prison. Although the wider variety of vocational programs and the increased resources to meet the social needs of female offenders afforded by co-corrections have attracted reform attention, the economical use of available space seems to have been a primary motivation for co-corrections.[20]

Co-corrections can mean different things in different contexts. In the federal system, the term means more than merely putting male and female prisoners in the same facility. A determined effort is made to ensure that programs and social contacts are integrated in a minimum security setting. Restrictions are placed only on the presence of inmates in the living quarters of the opposite sex, and the rules limit physical contact to hand-holding. By 1984 approximately 61 percent of adult female federal inmates were in co-correctional facilities. In the state systems, *co-corrections* can mean that prisoners of both sexes are housed in one facility but may have only minimal contacts, such as sharing the dining room or sitting together in classrooms. At the Albion Correctional Facility in New York, for example, the 116 women and 332 men are segregated except for work assignments, classes, and special programs. The women "are always escorted whenever they leave their housing block, which is surrounded by a chain link fence." Physical contact between members of the opposite sex can result in a transfer.[21]

As prison crowding continues to be a problem for most systems, it can be expected that co-corrections will be increasingly used as a means of maximizing spatial resources rather than for programmatic reasons. But even with this innovation some observers are concerned that the interests of female inmates will still be drowned in a sea of men's interests.

Private prisons

One response to prison crowding has come from private entrepreneurs who argue that they can build and run prisons at least as effectively, safely,

The Framingham (Massachusetts) Reformatory for Women is one of many co-correctional institutions.

and humanely as any level of government can. Their efficiency, they believe, can lower costs for taxpayers while allowing a profit for themselves. The contracting of correctional services on a piecemeal basis is not new and varies

Contracting Activity for the Management of Corrections Facilities, 1984

Federal contracts

Immigration and naturalization service

- 4 facility contracts for aliens awaiting deportation were operating (in San Diego, Los Angeles, Houston, Denver), providing a total capacity of 625 beds.
- 3 facility contracts were nearing award (in Las Vegas, Phoenix, San Francisco), providing another 225 beds.
- 2 additional facility contracts offering a total of 270 beds were planned in the near term (Laredo and El Paso, Texas).

U.S. Marshal's service

- 2 small (30-bed) facilities operated under contract in California.
- Plans to open a larger (100- to 150-bed) contracted facility in Los Angeles for alien material witnesses.

Federal bureau of prisons

- Plans to operate a 400- to 600-bed contracted facility for sentenced aliens in Southwest region. (Project delayed due to siting difficulties.)

State corrections contracts

Secondary adult facilities

- 28 states reported the use of privately operated prerelease, work-release, or halfway house facilities. Largest private facility networks found in California, Massachusetts, Michigan, New York, Ohio, Texas, and Washington.

Primary adult facilities

- No contracts reported for the confinement of mainstream adult populations; most private proposals still focused on community corrections facilities.
- One interstate 720-bed facility for protective custody prisoners planned by private contractor. (Project delayed due to siting difficulties.)

Juvenile facilities

- A 1982/83 survey of private juvenile facilities found 1,877 privately operated residential programs holding a total of 31,390 juveniles, 10,712 of whom were held for delinquency. Only 47 institutions were classified as strict security and 426 as medium security.
- Departing from the small, less secure settings characteristic of contracted juvenile facilities, a private contractor operates the Okeechobee (FL) Training School for 400 to 500 serious juvenile offenders.

Local jail contracts

- Legislation enabling private jail operations was pending in Colorado and had passed in New Mexico and Texas.
- While the National Sheriff's Association registered formal opposition to privately operated jail facilities, corporate providers reported significant interest and a number of pending proposals for jail operations in the Southern and Western regions.

Shared facilities

- One private organization in Texas is planning to construct and operate a facility that would serve local detention needs as well as the needs of Federal agencies responsible for confining illegal aliens.
- Other proposals have called for the development of regional jail facilities that would serve multicounty detention needs.

Source: Joan Mullen, "Corrections and the Private Sector," U.S. Department of Justice, *Research in Brief*, October 1984, p. 4.

from jurisdiction to jurisdiction; such services as food and medical care, educational and vocational training, maintenance, security, and industrial programs are provided by private businesses. But the idea of running entire institutions for adult felons under private contract is new.

The first correctional institution privately operated was the Intensive Treatment Unit, a twenty-bed high-security, dormitory-style training school for delinquents opened in 1975 by RCA in Weaversville, Pennsylvania. The second, the Okeechobee School for Boys in Florida, was turned over to the Eckerd Foundation to operate beginning in 1982, as was a prison for youthful offenders near San Francisco, contracted by the U.S. Bureau of Prisons to Eclectic Communications, Inc., in 1983. Other private facilities include those for the detention of illegal aliens in Arizona, California, Colorado, and Texas operated under contract from the U.S. Immigration and Naturalization Service (INS); jails run by Southwest Detention Facilities in Texas and Wyoming; and a 250-bed medium-security facility operated by Corrections Corporation of America in Chattanooga, Tennessee.[22]

The major advantages cited by advocates of privately operated prisons are that such prisons provide more cheaply and flexibly the same level of care provided by the states. The private enterprise is so new that there are few empirical data to support or disprove these arguments. Comparisons of costs under private and public management are difficult to make because among the "true costs" are some (fringe benefits, contracting supervision, federal grants) that are not taken into consideration. The quoted rates of existing private facilities range greatly. A report for the National Institute for Corrections, for example, cites a cost of $30 a day at Okeechobee, $110 a day at the Weaversville facility. The INS facilities for illegal aliens operate on average daily rates of $23 to $28.[23] In regard to the issue of care, we have only the evaluation of juvenile justice expert James Finkenauer that the Weaversville facility is "better staffed, organized, and equipped than any program of its size that I know."[24] In regard to flexibility, it is argued that because correctional space requirements rise and fall, private entrepreneurs can provide additional space when it is needed, and their contracts can go unrenewed when space is in oversupply.

A number of political, fiscal, and administrative issues must be considered and resolved before corrections can become too heavily committed to the private ownership and operation of prisons. The political issues, including ethical questions of the propriety of delegating social-control functions to persons other than the state, may be the most difficult to overcome. Some people believe that the administration of justice is one of the basic functions of government and that it should not be delegated. There is also concern that correctional policy would be skewed because contractors would use their political influence to continue programs not in the public interest; would press for the maintenance of high occupancy levels, thus widening the net of social control; and would be interested only in skimming off the "cream of the crop," leaving the most troublesome inmates to the public correctional system. Though it is not yet possible to demonstrate the fiscal value of private corrections, labor unions have opposed these incursions into the public sector, pointing out that the salaries, benefits, and pensions of workers in such other spheres as private security are lower than those of their public counterparts. Finally, there are questions about quality of services, accountability of service providers to corrections officials, and problems related to contract supervision. Opponents cite the many instances in which privately contracted services in group homes, day-care centers, hospitals, and schools have been terminated upon reports of corruption, brutality, and provision of only minimal services.

The idea of privately run correctional facilities has stimulated much interest among the general public and within the criminal justice community. There may be further privatization of criminal justice services, or privatization may become only a limited venture that was spawned at a time of prison crowding, fiscal constraints on governments, and revival of the free-enterprise ideology. The controversy about privatization has, however, forced corrections to rethink some strongly held beliefs. In this regard the possibility of competition from the private sector may be a positive factor.

Who is in prison?

For a brief period dring the early 1970s the trend in correctional circles was to stress deinstitutionalization and community corrections for all but violent offenders. More recently, however, penologists have been jolted by the realization that the American prison population is at a record level and still climbing. The Bureau of Justice Statistics found in its 1984 survey that the number of men and women incarcerated in state and federal prisons had jumped to a new high of more than 463,866.[25] The rate of incarceration per 100,000 persons has risen each year since 1973 and today stands at 188 (see figure 14.2). The increase continues a trend that began in 1973 after almost a decade during which the number of prisoners declined. In many states the influx of new adult inmates crowded already bulging institutions; some offenders had to be held in county jails and temporary quarters, while others made do in

FIGURE 14.2
Incarcerations per 100,000 population, 1940–1984

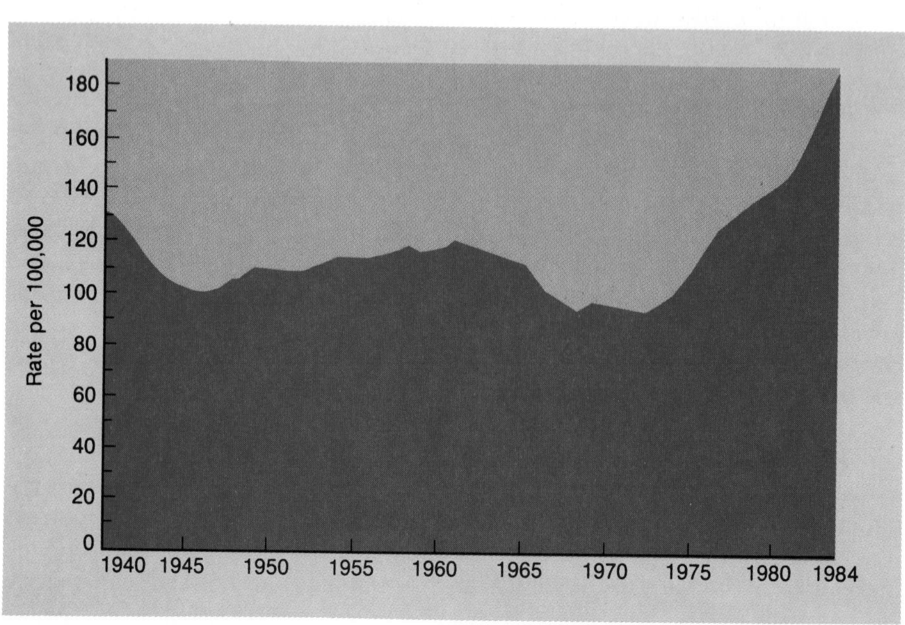

corridors and basements. Faced with such conditions, courts in several states demanded that changes be made because they viewed the overcrowding as a violation of the equal protection and cruel-and-unusual-punishment portions of the Bill of Rights.

Why this increase? Who is in prison? Several hypotheses have been advanced to explain the surge. Some people argue that regional attitudes toward crime and punishment account for much of the increase. As figure 14.3 shows, the highest ratio of prisoners to the civilian population is in the southern states. That region incarcerated at the rate of 231 persons for each 100,000 inhabitants, a ratio much higher than the national average of 188. The penal codes in many southern states provide for the longest sentences, and inmates there have spent extended periods in institutions. But there are exceptions to the thesis that the upswing is largely a regional phenomenon. Texas, California, New York, Michigan, North Carolina, Ohio, Georgia, and Illinois each increased its prison population during 1984. But California had the largest prison population, with 43,314 persons incarcerated, thus surpassing the size of the entire federal prison system.[26]

A second hypothesis is that a hardening public attitude toward criminals is reflected in longer sentences, in a smaller proportion of those convicted being granted probation, and in fewer being released at the time of their first

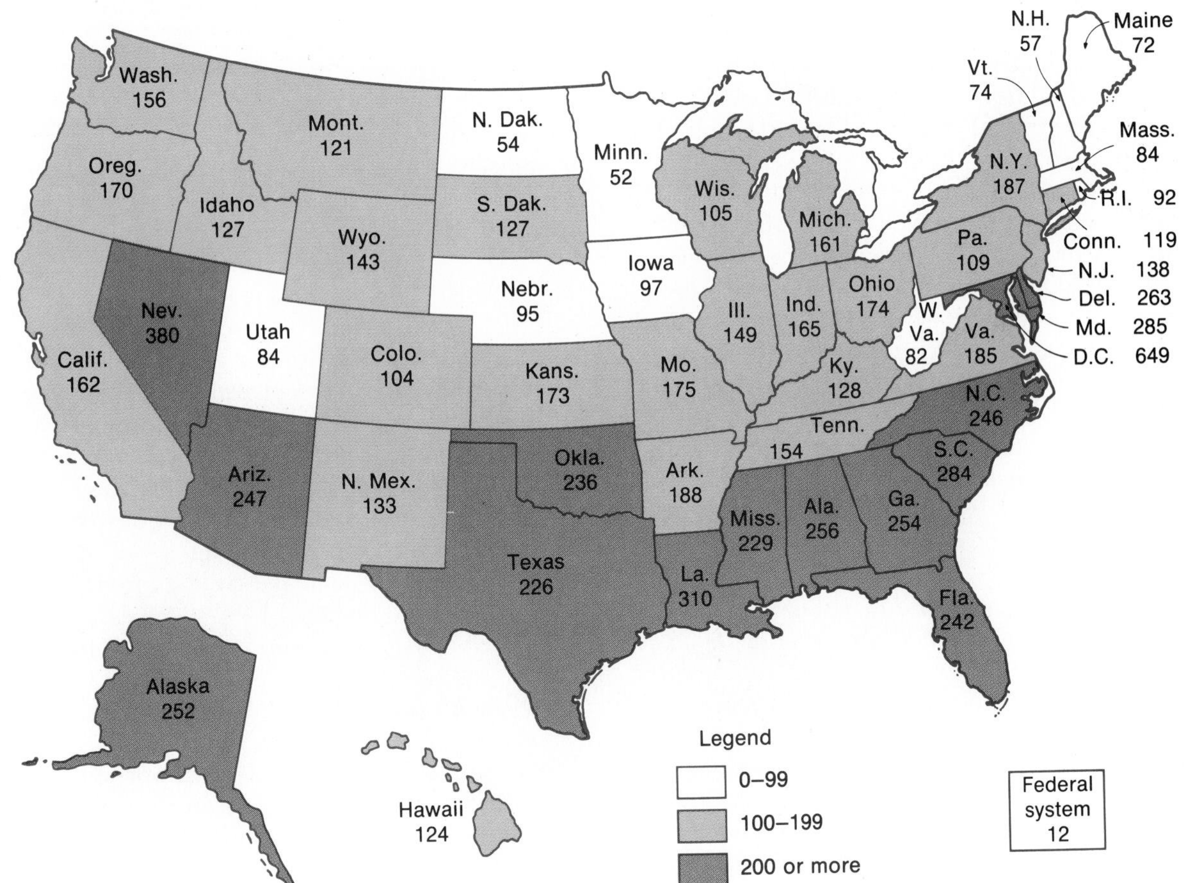

FIGURE 14.3
Sentenced prisoners in state institutions per 100,000 civilian population at year end 1984

parole hearing. Some states have passed penal codes that greatly limit the discretion of judges in regard to probation and sentencing for offenders who have committed certain types of crimes. In addition, the shift to determinate sentences has removed the safety valve of parole release, so important to corrections administrators when prison populations have risen in the past. The change in public opinion may have resulted in the allocation of increased resources to the law enforcement and adjudication portions of the criminal justice system. The billions that LEAA spent on the national crime problem may be paying off. Accordingly, the impact of the successes of the police and prosecution is being felt by the corrections subsystem. As Kansas Commissioner of Corrections Robert Raines has said, "police beef up, prosecution beefs up, courts beef up—and corrections catches the crunch."[27]

A third hypothesis is that increases in the prison population are influenced by the number of persons "at risk"—that is, those who are most likely to commit crimes and be sent to prison. Many social scientists and demographers explain the rise of crime in terms of the number of persons in the "crime-prone" age group of eighteen to twenty-four years. That group, numbering about 25 million, grew by about 48 percent after 1960 but is leveling off in the

Close-up: Overcrowding in South Carolina: "Don't Be Afraid of Public Opinion"

"I've been in politics for a long time," said State Senator John Drummond, a conservative Democrat from Greenwood, South Carolina. "If there's one thing I've learned, it's that ignorance will beat you every time."

Drummond is a powerful figure in South Carolina state affairs; he is the chairman of the State Reorganization Committee, a joint executive-legislative commission with far-reaching authority. He is also the chairman of the South Carolina Prison Overcrowding Project. The project, a panel of key state and local officials and private citizens, was created in 1981 to find solutions to the state's severe prison overcrowding problem. Dispelling ignorance about that problem, both in the legislature and among the citizens of the state, was one of the panel's primary tasks.

"When we started out, I was probably the most conservative member of the Senate," Drummond said. "I was in favor of putting more of these s.o.b.'s in jail, not turning them loose." That has certainly been the prevailing attitude about imprisonment in South Carolina for the last decade. The number of state inmates there tripled between 1972 and 1982; at the end of 1982, the prison population was 9,161. The state's incarceration rate of 270 per 100,000 is one of the highest in the nation.

But a closer look at the inmates serving time in the state's prisons surprised Drummond and other members of the prison overcrowding panel. South Carolina sends everyone sentenced to 90 days or more, including misdemeanants, to state prison. This was originally a reform measure designed to remove lesser offenders from the harsh and primitive conditions of county road camps. Although corrections officials are unable to say precisely how many misdemeanants are in state facilities, a survey made for the ovecrowding panel showed that more than 400 inmates were admitted to the corrections system during fiscal 1982 for the offenses of writing bad checks and failing to make child support payments. About 40 percent of the state's prisoners have been convicted of non-violent property offenses.

"When I got the facts," Drummond said, "I was solidly sold on going the other way," that is, finding punishments other than imprisonment. "I could see that we had been totally wrong in the direction we had been going. I didn't see any

mid-1980s. The effect of this ballooning may have been felt only during the late 1970s and early 1980s. An adage among many observers is that "committing crime is a young man's game, but serving time is an old man's." Studies have brought out that only after successive periods on probation or of incarceration in youth facilities or in jail does the average youthful offender graduate to state or federal felony prison. Correctional planners have been heartened by an evident slowing of the growth rate of the incarcerated population. The 1983 census found an increase of only 5.9 percent in the total prison population, compared with a 12 percent increase during each of the prior two years. This slowing of the rate of increase, however, may reflect only the fact that facilities in most states are now so tight that judges have responded by sending fewer offenders to prison.

Impact of prison population on corrections

The size of the inmate population directly affects the ability of correctional officials to do their work because crowding reduces the placing of offenders in rehabilitative programs, increases the potential for violence, and greatly strains staff morale. In addition, the makeup of the inmate community

point in ruining someone's life by sending him to prison for a first-time minor offense."

The panel eventually produced two short-term remedies for overcrowding that would require legislative action. One was an emergency powers act that would legally establish a capacity for the state prison system of 7,630 inmates, and permit the release of inmates when that capacity was reached or exceeded. The other was the creation of a sentencing guidelines commission. It will report to the legislature . . . on a proposed sentencing system that will set up uniform sentencing standards that take the prison system's capacity into account.

All of the panelists fulfilled pledges to lobby for the measures; they travelled throughout the state, speaking before civic clubs and newspaper editorial boards. "We wanted to take the fire away from the opposition before these measures went to the floor," Drummond said. "We wanted to let the people know that we were not talking about turning rapists loose, or turning murderers loose."

The support of one panel member in particular became especially important. Bill Traxler is a tough law and order "solicitor" (the South Carolina term for state prosecutor) from Greenville. Roughly 25 percent of the inmates in South Carolina prisons have been prosecuted by his office. "I personally picked him for the panel," Drummond said. "He has been a great voice for building more prisons. I knew I would rather have him on the inside with us than on the outside against us." Drummond's foresight paid off in the final hours of the legislative session, when Traxler made last-minute phone calls to members of the House of Representatives, persuading them to lift objections to bills drafted from the panel's recommendations. The measures passed in the House in the final hours of the last day of the session.

Drummond has some advice for legislators in other states who want to change the direction of their corrections systems. "First," he said, "arm yourself with the facts. And don't be afraid of public opinion. The public will be with you if you give them the facts. I don't know of a more conservative state than South Carolina, and we were able to get the public behind us."

Source: *Time to Build?* Copyright © 1984 by Edna McConnell Clark Foundation, pp. 12–13. Reprinted by permission.

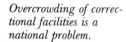

Overcrowding of correctional facilities is a national problem.

in terms of age, race, and criminal record has a determining impact on the operation of correctional institutions.

Researchers have shown that over time the proportional size of the prison population in the United States has remained fairly stable. Between 1930 and 1970 the rate of imprisonment averaged 110 per 100,000 population (it is now 179). Comparison with other industrialized nations indicates that the United States not only incarcerates more persons than does any other nation, but relies more and more on incarceration.

The contemporary rise in the incarceration rate has brought increased pressures to build more prisons. With courts sentencing more and more offenders to imprisonment, some people argue that space must be made available. For reasons of both health and security, the crowded conditions in existing facilities cannot be tolerated or permitted to worsen. But others say that, once built, prisons will stay filled because of the organizational needs of the correctional bureaucracy. Cells will not remain empty. Society, it is said, "penalizes less serious offenses at times when serious crime is not viewed as a problem and lets off minor offenders when serious crime has become endemic." [28] Thus, if murder is relatively uncommon, criminal justice resources will be diverted to shoplifters, drug abusers, or prostitutes. Similarly, when violent offenses are more prevalent, there may be proposals to decriminalize the victimless crimes, such as drug use, prostitution, and gambling.

Perhaps building costs are one of the greatest deterrents to prison expansion. Typically legislatures discuss new construction in terms of $25,000 to $125,000 per cell, but recent analyses by economists have shown that these levels are very low. One study computed the true cost of constructing and operating a hypothetical 500-bed medium security prison, using real designs and construction estimates. In addition to the base cost of $61,015 per bed, or approximately $30 million for the facility, hidden (but expected) costs such as architects' fees, furnishings, site preparation expenses, and so on pushed the estimate to $82,246 per bed ($41 million for the facility). At a conservative estimate of $14,000 per inmate per year, the operating cost would be $7 million a year. Thus the thirty-year bill to the taxpayers for construction and operation would be $350 million—"all for the '$30,000,000 prison.'"[29]

When we look at the contemporary situation in our nation's prisons, we must also examine the social characteristics of the inmates. Following a survey of state prisons, the Bureau of Justice Statistics said that this population is predominantly made up of

> poor young adult males with less than a high school education. Prison is not a new experience for them; they have been incarcerated before, many first as juveniles. The offense that brought them to prison was a violent crime or burglary. On the average they have already served 1½ years on a maximum sentence of 8½ years. Along with a criminal history, they have a history of drug abuse and are also likely to have a history of alcohol abuse.[30]

These data are further described in table 14.3. It is clear that over time the composition of the prison population has become blacker and has committed more serious crimes. Now about half of all prisoners are black; in 1960 only

TABLE 14.3 Selected characteristics of state inmates

Characteristic		*Percent*
Age at survey		
Under 30		63.0
30 and over		37.0
Median	27.3	
Sex		
Male		96.0
Female		4.0
Race		
White		49.6
Black		47.8
Other		2.5
Ethnicity		
Hispanic		9.4
Non-Hispanic		90.6
Prior incarceration record		
With prior incarceration		63.9
Juvenile only		7.9
Adult only		29.0
Both		22.8
Not available		4.3
Without prior incarceration		35.6
Not available		0.4
Current offense		
Violent		57.5
Murder and attempted murder		13.6
Manslaughter		4.0
Sexual assault		6.2
Robbery		24.9
Assault		6.4
Other		2.4
Property		31.1
Burglary		18.1
Larceny		4.7
Auto theft		1.9
Forgery, fraud, embezzlement		4.3
Other		2.1
Drug		7.1
Public order		4.0
Unspecified		0.3
Maximum sentence length		
Less than 5 years		20.6
5 to 9 years		23.2
10 to 14 years		14.2
15 to 19 years		8.8
20 to 97 years		16.8
98 years or more		0.8
Median (months)	103.6	
Life		10.1
Death		0.5
Not available		5.0
Time served on current offense		
Less than 1 year		34.8
1 to 1.9 years		23.2
2 to 2.9 years		14.6
3 to 3.9 years		8.8
4 to 4.9 years		6.0
5 to 9.9 years		10.0
10 years or more		2.2
Median (months)	18.0	
Not available		0.4
Education		
Less than 12 years		58.0
12 years or more		42.0
Median	11.2	
Prearrest employment status		
Employed		70.2
Full-time		60.3
Part-time		9.9
Not employed		29.5
Looking for work		13.9
Not looking for work		15.5
Not available		0.1
Not available		0.3
Prearrest annual income		
With income		77.8
Less than $3,000		19.2
$3,000–9,999		30.2
$10,000 or more		24.9
Don't know		3.5
Median	$6,660	
Without income		22.2

Source: Adapted from U.S. Department of Justice, Bureau of Justice Statistics, *Bulletin* (Washington, D.C.: Government Printing Office, 1982), p. 2.

one-third were black. Today 57.5 percent are incarcerated for a crime of violence whereas twenty years ago only about 40 percent were in prison for such an offense.[31]

In the context of overcrowded facilities, the contemporary inmate population presents correctional workers with a challenge. Even if resources are not available to provide rehabilitative programs for most inmates, the goal of maintaining a safe and healthy environment may tax the ability of the staff. Corrections is being asked to deal with a different type of inmate, one who is more prone to violence, and in a prison society where racial tensions are great. Further, there are the problems inherent in trying to deal with individuals in crowded, out-of-date facilities. How well this correctional challenge is met will have an important impact on crime in American society.

Rethinking correctional policy

After decades of neglect, the American system of corrections is undergoing an intense critical reappraisal. A wide-ranging group of critics—academics, prisoners, humanists, and politicians—has raised questions not merely about conditions in the prisons and the use of various treatment methods but about fundamental assumptions concerning the goals of corrections, the causes of recidivism, and the place of treatment in a system of crime control. The scrutiny has been encouraged by evidence published during the last few years showing that the array of correctional treatments used by modern penologists has had no appreciable effect on the recidivism of convicted offenders. In addition, evidence indicates that the very act of incarcerating offenders greatly reduces the possibility that they will have a crime-free future. The fact that a high proportion of released felons can be expected to be convicted for another serious crime within ten years has caused corrections officials to despair and political leaders to debate the value of an expensive system. Attica has become a symbol of the many problems besetting corrections and other subsystems of criminal justice.

Further, research has shown that the likelihood of recidivism is more strongly related to the characteristics of the offender than to the characteristics of the treatment program. Age, race, prior criminal record, and the presence or absence of a drug habit appear to be among the best predictors of whether an offender will continue to break the law. These factors have a special impact on judges, correctional officials, and parole boards. How much weight should they give these factors when they make decisions about freedom or incarceration? Should a judge sentence a person to an institution when to do so may have only a detrimental effect? Should a correctional official place a murderer who is elderly, white, and a first offender in a halfway house because research has shown that such a person is unlikely to commit another crime? Should parole boards use certain characteristics as a basis for decision making? These questions warrant consideration because they challenge many of the assumptions on which correctional policy has been built.

Now that the goal of correctional rehabilitation is in eclipse, greater stress is being placed on the incarceration of offenders. The growth in the prison population during the past few years has added to pressures on the correctional subsystem. As a result, criminal justice planners are caught between the need to expand the capacity of prisons as a means of making them more habitable and the demands of some critics for a moratorium on construction as a way of limiting intake. Those who point to community corrections as the wave of the future have been disappointed by the resistance of most neigborhoods to the placement of facilities in their midst. The expected limited expansion of community corrections in the near future cuts off one means by which pressures of the prison population can be released. There has been a general awakening to the fact that very little is known about the causes of criminal behavior and the best methods of dealing with it. Confusing the issue is the fact that such a key measurement concept as recidivism has been poorly used, for statistical analysis of correctional performance can often be interpreted in both positive and negative directions. Besides questions about the effectiveness of treatment to prevent or control criminal behavior, civil libertarian issues have arisen to challenge the influences on decision making within the justice system. Of primary concern is the amount of discretion accorded officials—correctional administrators, parole boards, and judges—in the postconviction process and the ways in which decision making can be restructured to conform to the due process ideal.

For the past thirty years, the rehabilitative ideal has dominated corrections in most states, and this has been the major theme among academics and administrators concerned about corrections. If the new emphasis is on deserved punishment, what directions should be taken in attempts to implement this goal? How do diversion, probation, fixed sentences, the end of release on parole, community corrections, and voluntary access to rehabilitative services all fit together into a coherent policy that serves the need for crime control with due process and meets the political realities of the times?

Summary

This chapter has introduced the correctional subsystem of criminal justice. At various times in the history of the United States, alternative methods of imposing criminal sanctions have been considered appropriate. With the development of the penitentiary at the beginning of the nineteenth century, incarceration was chosen as the primary means of dealing with offenders. Several different emphases have been brought to corrections, but the prison has remained a dominant feature. During the most recent period, when the rehabilitative ideal that dominated corrections was found to be unsatisfactory in many ways, penologists have looked to other models for the administration of justice. The chapters that follow will first examine the internal structure of prison society and then consider the community corrections alternative.

For discussion

1. If prisons don't work, why do we use them?
2. You are the administrator of a local jail. What are some of the management problems that you face?
3. Correctional officials must compete with other public agencies for resources. What are some of the special problems that they face in this quest?
4. Is reintegration a viable alternative or is it a passing fad?

For further reading

Foucault, Michel. *Discipline and Punish.* Translated by Alan Sheridan. New York: Pantheon, 1977.
Mitford, Jessica. *Kind and Usual Punishment.* New York: Knopf, 1973.

Morris, Norval. *The Future of Imprisonment.* Chicago: University of Chicago Press, 1974.
Nagel, William G. *The New Red Barn.* New York: Walker, 1973.
Rothman, David J. *Conscience and Convenience.* Boston: Little, Brown, 1980.
——. *The Discovery of the Asylum: Social Order and Disorder in the New Republic.* Boston: Little, Brown, 1971.

Notes

1. *Official Report of the New York State Special Commission on Attica* (New York: Bantam Books, 1972), p. 373.
2. David J. Rothman, "Prisons, Asylums, and Other Decaying Institutions," *Public Interest* 26 (Winter 1972): 16.
3. David J. Rothman, *The Discovery of the Asylum: Social Order and Disorder in the New Republic* (Boston: Little, Brown, 1971), p. 49.
4. Michel Foucault, *Discipline and Punish,* trans. Alan Sheridan (New York: Pantheon, 1977), pp. 8, 16.
5. John Howard, *The State of Prisons in England and Wales* (London: J. M. Dent, 1929).
6. As quoted in William G. Nagel, *The New Red Barn* (New York: Walker, 1973), p. 7.
7. Thorsten Sellin, "The Origin of the Pennsylvania System of Prison Discipline," *Prison Journal* 50 (Spring–Summer 1970): 15–17.
8. Ronald L. Goldfarb and Linda R. Singer, *After Conviction* (New York: Simon & Schuster, 1973), p. 30.
9. Rothman, *Discovery of the Asylum,* p. 82.
10. David J. Rothman, *Conscience and Convenience* (Boston: Little, Brown, 1980), p. 18.
11. Ibid., p. 32.
12. Goldfarb and Singer, *After Conviction,* p. 40.
13. As quoted in ibid., p. 41.
14. Rothman, *Conscience and Convenience,* p. 5.
15. John Irwin, *Prisoners in Turmoil* (Boston: Little, Brown, 1980), p. 5.
16. Jessica Mitford, *Kind and Usual Punishment* (New York: Knopf, 1973), p. 169; U.S. Department of Justice, *Sourcebook of Criminal Justice Statistics* (Washington, D.C.: Government Printing Office, 1980), p. 4.
17. U.S. Department of Justice, Bureau of Justice Statistics, *Bulletin,* February 1983, p. 1.
18. Ibid.
19. U.S. Department of Justice, Bureau of Justice Statistics, *Sourcebook, 1982,* p. 145; John O. Smykla, ed., *Co-ed Prison* (New York: Human Sciences Press, 1980).
20. Claudine Scheber, "Beauty Marks and Blemishes: The Coed Prison as a Microcosm of Integrated Society," *Prison Journal* 64 (Spring–Summer 1984): 5.
21. Ibid.
22. Kevin Krajick, "Prisons for Profit: The Private Alternative," *State Legislatures* 10 (April 1984): 9–14; Philip E. Fixler, Jr., "Behind Bars We Find an Enterprise Zone," *Wall Street Journal,* 29 November 1984, p. 34.
23. Camille G. Camp and George M. Camp, *Private Sector Involvement in Prison Services and Operations,* Report to National Institute of Corrections (Washington, D.C., February 1984).
24. Cited in Kevin Krajick, "Punishment for Profit," *Across the Board* 21 (1984): 25.
25. "Prisoners in 1984," U.S. Department of Justice, Bureau of Justice Statistics, *Bulletin,* April 1985.
26. Ibid.
27. "U.S. Prison Population Again Hits New High," *Corrections* 3 (March 1977): 5.
28. James Q. Wilson, "Who Is in Prison?" *Commentary,* November 1976, p. 56.
29. *Time to Build?* (New York: Edna McConnell Clark Foundation, 1984), pp. 18–19.
30. U.S. Department of Justice, Bureau of Justice Statistics, *Bulletin,* December 1982, p. 1.
31. Wilson, "Who Is in Prison?" p. 57.

Incarceration

15

Born in this jailhouse
Raised doing time
Yes born in this
jailhouse
Near the end of the line

MALCOLM BRALY, *On the Yard*

The camera follows the blue van as it moves through a rural countryside aglow with autumn colors. It passes through a small town and then veers off the highway onto a secondary road where only occasional houses punctuate the fields and woods. We are heading toward a looming fortress. As we approach it we see gray stone walls, barbed-wire fences, gun towers, steel bars. The van moves directly to the entrance, passes through opened gates, and comes to a stop. Blue-uniformed guards move briskly to the rear doors, and in a moment four men, linked by wrist bracelets on a chain, stand on the asphalt and look about nervously.

Although this description may read like the beginning of the scenario of one of the 1940s "big house" movies starring James Cagney, Pat O'Brien, or George Raft, it could be filmed today at Brushy Mountain, Tennessee; Ossining, New York; or Soledad, California. Incarceration in contemporary American prisons for adult felons may appear to the casual eye to have changed from what it was in the 1940s: the characteristics of the inmates are different, rehabilitative personnel are employed in addition to guards, and the time to be served is shorter. The physical dimensions of the fortress institution remain the same, however, and the society of captives within may be only slightly changed.

Incarceration—what does it mean to the inmates, the guards, and the public? What goes on in our prisons? Is prison society a mirror image of American culture? How does incarceration fit with the goals of the criminal sanction? Are correctional institutions really training schools for criminals? These are a few of the questions that this chapter will explore. Because we will be emphasizing the social dimensions of prison life, assume that you are anthropologists attempting to understand the culture and daily activities of people in a foreign society. In many ways the interior of the American maximum security prison is like a foreign land, and we observers need guidance as we try to gain an awareness of its traditions, the roles played there, and the patterns of interpersonal relations that prevail. Although the walls and guns may give the impression that everything goes by strict rules and with machine-like precision, a human dimension exists that we may miss if we study only the formal organization and routines. This human element and the lives of the incarcerated—both inmates and keepers—are the subjects of this chapter.

The modern prison: legacy of the past

For someone schooled in criminal justice history, entering most American penitentiaries of today is like entering a time machine. Elements from each of the major prison reform movements can be seen within the walls. In accord with the early notion that the prison should be located away from the community, most correctional facilities are still found in rural areas—Somers, Connecticut; Stateville, Illinois; Attica, New York—far from the urban residences of the inmates' families. The fortress style, built to secure the population, remains typical of today's prison architecture. Prison industries, founded on the principles of the Auburn system, occupy many inmates. Treatment programs, including vocational education, group therapy, and counseling, are available. While modern penology has stressed rehabilitation and treatment, a prison remains a prison whatever it's called.

John Irwin makes the important point that to understand the contemporary American prison "we must clear the air of a lot of old concepts and images which surround it like a fog and blur our vision."[1] Hollywood's picture of the "big house" is still the image in the minds of most citizens, even though it is no longer realistic, if indeed it ever was. More important, Irwin wants us to realize that a great deal of the social science literature about incarceration is based on studies conducted in big houses during the 1950s. The pioneering of such scholars as Donald Clemmer and Gresham Sykes laid the conceptual and theoretical basis for much research that has followed.[2]

Irwin notes that American correctional institutions have always been more variegated than one might suspect from viewing films or reading some of the landmark prison studies. Although big houses predominated in much of the country during the first half of this century, some prisons, especially in the South, did not conform to this model. There, racial segregation was maintained, prisoners were involved in farm labor, and the massive walled structures were not so dominant a form. In many other states the correctional systems had not emerged from the cruelty and corruption, silence systems, hard labor, and corporal punishment that had characterized American prisons during the late nineteenth century.

The big house was a walled prison made up of large, tiered cell blocks, a yard, shops, and industries. The prisoners, averaging about 2,500, came from both urban and rural areas, were poor, and, outside the South, were predomi-

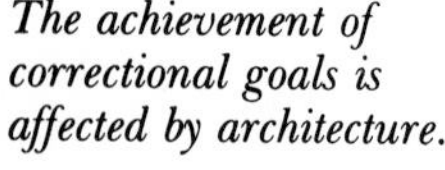
The achievement of correctional goals is affected by architecture.

nantly white. The prison society was essentially isolated; access to visitors, mail, and other kinds of communication was restricted. Prisoners' days were strictly structured, with rules enforced by the guards. There was a basic division between inmates and staff; rank was observed and discipline maintained. In the big house there was little in the way of treatment programs; custody was the primary goal.

Since World War II many changes have come to American prisons. It is now difficult to find an institution that conforms exactly to the big house depicted in films and analyzed by such social scientists as Clemmer and Sykes. During the 1950s and early 1960s most penologists accepted the Rehabilitation Model of corrections. Many states built new facilities and converted others into "correctional institutions." Although the new name was often the principal evidence of an alternative philosophy, in some states the medical model was widely accepted and treatment programs became a major part of institutional life. Indeterminate sentences, classification, treatment, and parole, the chief emphases of this approach, brought changes to the prison. In particular, treatment personnel—counselors, educators, and psychologists—were added to the staff. Often conflict erupted over the competing claims of the treatment and custody goals. As James Jacobs' study of Stateville Penitentiary in Illinois has documented, the shift toward rehabilitation occurred at a time when outside forces were beginning to penetrate the prison walls.[3]

The ending of corrections' isolation from the wider community has had the most far-reaching influence on correctional institutions during the past two decades. As the population of the United States changed, so did that of the inmate population. The proportion of black and Hispanic inmates increased, and inmates from urban areas became more numerous, as did inmates convicted of drug-related and violent offenses. The average age was younger. The civil rights movement of the early 1960s had a profound effect on minority prisoners. There was an infusion of political activism during this period, with demands that prisoners be more fully integrated into the society, and that there be greater sensitivity to their needs. With a shift in judicial policy, the courts began to take notice of the legal rights of prisoners. Legal services were extended to corrections, and the hands-off policy of the past gave way to directions from the judiciary that institutions be run according to constitutional mandates. In a number of states former street gangs regrouped

inside prisons when their members became incarcerated. These gangs disrupted the existing inmate society, raising the levels of violence in many institutions. Finally, with the rise of public employees' unions, correctional officers were no longer willing to accept the paramilitary work rules of the warden.

As prisons have responded to community influences, they have shifted away from the Treatment Model of corrections during the past decade. The rehabilitative programs so highly touted in the 1960s have been either deemphasized or abandoned. The determinate sentence has replaced the indeterminate sentence in about a third of the states, with the consequence that releasing mechanisms have been altered. On top of these policy shifts there has been a great increase in the number of persons being held in prisons, so that most are overcrowded and under increased tension. Humane incarceration seems to have become the contemporary goal of correctional administrators.

There is much variety in the functions, social systems, and organization of American prisons. Most research, however, has been conducted in maximum security prisons for adult male felons. Studies of institutions with lower levels of security, of institutions for women and for juveniles, have taken the big house literature as the standard of comparison. We must use the best available research as the means of describing incarceration so that we can appreciate the way these institutions operate and the problems they face.

Goals of incarceration

Various parts of the correctional subsystem tend to emphasize one or a combination of the broad goals of the criminal sanction: punishment, deterrence, incapacitation, and rehabilitation. It is natural to regard security as the dominant purpose of a prison, given the nature of the inmates and the need to protect the staff and the community. High walls, barbed-wire fences, searches, checkpoints, and regular counts of inmates serve the security function because few inmates escape; but more important, they set the tone and strongly color the daily operations. As the President's Commission on Law Enforcement and Administration of Justice has noted, "these measures also serve the idea that deterrence requires extremes of deprivation, strict discipline and punishment, all of which, together with considerations of administrative efficiency, make institutions impersonal, quasi-military places."[4]

In the same way that justifications for criminal sanctions have been incorporated in models that have influenced sentencing decisions, correctional models have been developed to describe the purposes and approaches that

---

The Goals of Prison Administrators

Wardens must store inmates. They must feed, clothe, and protect inmates, must offer them vocational and recreational activities, must provide educational, medical, and mental health services, must permit access to mail, visits, and libraries (including law libraries), and must furnish basic amenities. The goal of wardens and other officials is to deploy their staff and resources to service inmates to the extent budgetary constraints permit. The *bottom line* is storage. Whatever the prison does, it must retain and restrain inmates.

Source: Robert Johnson and Hans Toch, eds., *The Pains of Imprisonment* (Beverly Hills, Calif.: Sage, 1982), p. 15.

---

should be used in handling prisoners in an institutional setting. Although models may provide a set of rationally linked criteria and aims, the extent to which a given model is fully implemented is a question for empirical investigation. As with the stated purpose of the criminal sanction, the operationalization of a particular model may have little relation to the ongoing process of corrections and the experience of the inmates. The language used to describe the key elements of each model may be adopted by a correctional system to signify changes in day-to-day practices, yet the new terminology may have no relationship to actual conditions. Two decades ago, for example, it became customary for state legislatures to decree that prisons be referred to as "correctional facilities" and that guards be designated "correctional officers" to signify a shift in goals from a custodial to a rehabilitative model (table 15.1). Too often, however, these same legislatures have not provided the resources to implement the accompanying essential shifts in facilities and personnel required by the new model.

There are three models of correctional institutions: custodial, rehabilitative, and reintegrative. Each model may be viewed as an ideal type that summarizes the assumptions and characteristics associated with that style of correctional organization. In the ***Custodial Model,*** inmates of the prison are assumed to have been incarcerated for the protection of society. Emphasis is on maintenance of security and order through the subordination of the prisoner to the authority of the warden. Discipline is strictly enforced and most aspects of behavior are regulated. A caretaking purpose is evident rather than an attempt to help the inmates reform their lives.

Custodial Model
A model of corrections that emphasizes security, discipline, and order.

The prison that emphasizes the ***Rehabilitation Model*** is organized to provide the therapeutic treatment required by each inmate. The prison's security and housekeeping activities are viewed primarily as a framework in which rehabilitative activities may take place. Professional treatment specialists enjoy superior status over other employees in accordance with the idea that all aspects of the organization should be directed toward rehabilitative efforts. Only restrictions that are absolutely necessary are imposed on inmates in the rehabilitative institution, and they are encouraged to work toward a solution to their problems.

Rehabilitation Model (institutions)
A model of corrections that emphasizes the provision of treatment programs designed to reform the offender.

The ***Reintegration Model*** is linked to the structures and goals of community corrections. Although inmates are confined in a prison during the early part of their sentences, they may gradually be given greater freedom and responsibility, and often move to a halfway house or community correctional

Reintegration Model
A model of corrections that emphasizes maintenance of the offender's ties to family and the community as a method of reform.

TABLE 15.1 Nomenclature associated with correctional models

Custodial model	*Rehabilitative model*	*Reintegrative model*
Prison	Correctional facility	Community correctional facility
Guard	Correctional officer	Counselor
Prisoner	Inmate	Resident
Solitary confinement	Adjustment center	n/a

center before being released to supervision. The Reintegration Model is based on the assumption that it is important for the offender to maintain or develop ties with the free community. It is believed that without strong bonds to family, church, and workplace, people are more likely to commit criminal acts; hence their reintegration with these groups is necessary if they are going to resume a normal life. The structures of the Reintegration Model—community corrections, probation, and parole—will be extensively discussed in chapter 16.

This chapter will describe the operation of the vast majority of prisons in the United States that fall between the extremes of the highly authoritarian custodial institution and those designed to maintain a purely therapeutic or rehabilitative atmosphere. An assumption of this chapter is that in the long run the two goals of custody and rehabilitation cannot be equally served in the same institution. Both may be pursued, but one will predominate and the other will be relegated to secondary status. The goal that predominates is almost invariably custody. But because all but a few inmates may be expected to return to society at some point, even the most thoroughly custodial institution cannot neglect the reintegrative needs of prisoners.

Prison organization

The prison differs from almost every other institution or organization in modern society. Not only are its physical features different from those of most institutions, but it is a place where a group of persons devotes itself to managing a group of captives. Prisoners do not come voluntarily; they are brought forcibly through the gates and are prevented from leaving by the guards, walls, and fence. Alternatively, prison administrators cannot select their clients and have little or no control over their release. Prisoners are required to live according to the dictates of their keepers, and their movements are sharply restricted. Over and above these features, three important organizational characteristics dictate the administrative structure, and these factors influence the nature of prison society—that is, the interactions among the inmates, between inmates and guards, and among the guards.

Total institution

total institution
An institution (such as a prison) that completely encapsulates the lives of those who work and live within it. Rules govern behavior, and the group is split into two parts, one of which controls all aspects of the lives of the other.

Much research on prisons has assumed that they share with some other organizations, such as the mental hospital and the monastery, the characteristics of a ***total institution.***[5] This concept, developed by Erving Goffman, emphasizes that the prison completely encapsulates the lives of those who work and live there. It is a total institution in the sense that whatever prisoners do or do not do begins and ends in the prison; every minute behind bars must be lived according to the institution's rules as enforced by the staff. Adding to the totality of the prison is a basic split between the large group of persons (inmates) who have very limited contact with the outside world and the small group (staff) who supervise on an eight-hour shift within the walls and are socially integrated with the outside world where they live. Each sees the other in terms of stereotypes. Staff members view inmates as secretive and untrustworthy, while the inmates view them as condescending and mean. Staff members feel superior and righteous, inmates inferior and weak.

This view of the prison has been challenged by social scientists who have noted the extent to which the modern correctional institution has been permeated by outside influences. They argue that today's inmates have a greater political awareness and greater access to news of the outside world than they once did, that racial and ethnic cliques have divided the prison population, and that community advocacy groups using the power of the law have dented the total power of institutional administrators. Given these changes, we must use the total institution concept cautiously; yet the contemporary prison is still far enough removed from the free world so that Goffman's term remains useful for purposes of analysis.

Management

The administrative structure of prisons is organized down to the lowest level.[6] Unlike the factory or the military, where there are separate groups of supervisors and workers or officers and enlisted personnel, the lowest-status prison employee (the guard) is both a supervisor *and* a worker. The guard is seen as a worker by the warden but as a supervisor by the inmates. Guards are thus subject to role conflict that makes them susceptible to corruption by the inmates. The warden judges their efficiency on the basis of their ability to manage the prisoners, which often depends in large part on their ability to secure at least some cooperation by the inmates. Thus the guards have to ease up on some rules so that the inmates will be willing to follow others.

Multiple goals

Most prisons are expected to carry out a number of goals related to keeping (custody), using (working), and serving (treating) inmates. Because individual staff members are not equipped to perform all functions, there are separate organizational lines of command for the groups of employees that fulfill these different tasks. One group is charged with maintaining custody over the prisoners, another group supervises them in their work activities, and a third group attempts to rehabilitate them.

The custodial employees are normally organized along military lines, from warden to captain to guard, with accompanying pay differentials and job titles that follow the chain of command. The professional personnel associated with the using and serving functions, such as clinicians and teachers, are not

---

Unlike other government agencies, corrections:

1. Cannot select its clients.
2. Has little or no control over release of its clients.
3. Services clients who are there against their will.
4. Relies on clients to do most of the work in the day-to-day operation of the institution and to do so by coercion and without fair compensation for their work.
5. Usually has no clear, comprehensive law defining what it should do with its clients.
6. Can have its capacity grossly overloaded.
7. Depends upon the maintenance of satisfactory relationships between its clients and its staff.

Source: M. Robert Montilla, *Prison Employee Unionism: Management Guide for Correctional Administrators*, U.S. Department of Justice, National Institute of Law Enforcement and Criminal Justice (Washington, D.C.: Government Printing Office, 1978), pp. 13–14.

---

part of the regular custodial organizational structure, and they have little in common with the others. All employees are responsible to the warden, but the treatment personnel and the civilian supervisors of the workshops have their own salary scales and titles. They are not part of the custodial chain of command, and their responsibilities do not include the provision of specialized advice to the custodial employees. The formal organization of staff responsibilities in a typical adult prison is shown in figure 15.1.

As a result of multiple goals and separate employee lines of command, the administration of correctional institutions is often filled with conflict and ambiguity. Under these circumstances, how do prisons function? What are the means by which prisoners and staff attempt to meet their own distinct goals? In view of the conflicting purposes and the complex set of role relationships within the prison society, it is amazing that prisons are not a chaotic mess of social relations. Although the U.S. prison may not conform to the ideal goals of corrections and although the formal organization of staff and inmates may bear little resemblance to the ongoing reality of the informal relations, order *is* kept and a routine *is* followed.

Classification: the way in

classification
The act of assigning a new inmate to a type of custody and treatment appropriate to his or her needs.

The idea that prisoners should be diagnosed and then classified according to their custodial and treatment needs can be traced to the Elmira Reformatory and Zebulon Brockway. In the modern prison, this process has been developed so that it plays a major role in determining the inmate's life. Most states now have diagnostic and reception centers that are physically separated from the main prison facility. All new prison-bound offenders pass through such a center, where they are received for evaluation and ***classification*** so that a decision can be made as to which correctional facility they will be sent to. During the classification process, specialized clinical personnel, such as psy-

FIGURE 15.1
Formal organization of a prison for adult felons

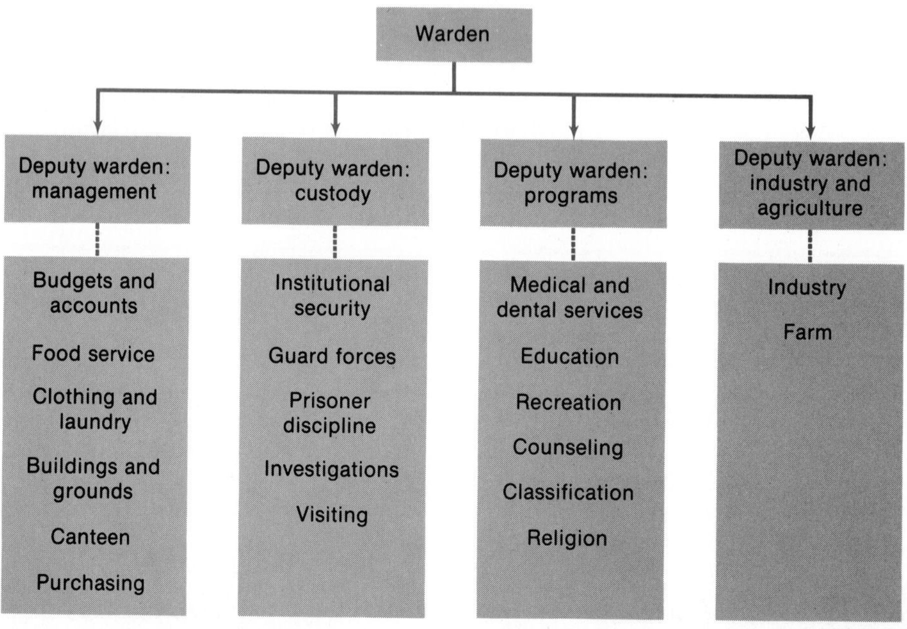

chologists, physicians, and counselors, determine the inmates' treatment needs and the level of custody they require. An inmate with a drug, alcohol, or educational problem may be assigned to a program within the correctional facility that is organized to meet such a need. During the period of incarceration, prisoners may be brought back to the center for reclassification if their needs and goals change or if transfer to another institution is desired.

Reception and classification have been likened to a process of mortification. As the army recruit is socialized by basic training, the sentenced felon is introduced to a new status as convict. The reception process deliberately exaggerates inmates' new status as they are stripped of their personal effects and given uniforms, rulebooks, medical examinations, and showers.

Classification decisions are often made on the basis of administrative needs rather than inmate needs. Certain programs are limited, and the demand for them is great. Thus inmates may find that the few places in the electrician's course are filled and that there is a long waiting list. Another problem is that the institution's housekeeping work must be carried out by the inmates. Inmates from the city may be assigned to farm work because that is where they are needed. What is most upsetting to some prisoners is that release on parole often depends on a good record of participation in treatment or educational programs. They have difficulty explaining to the parole board that they really did want to learn plumbing but that there was no opportunity to do so.

The society of captives

A view widely held by the public is that prisons are operated in an authoritarian manner. In such a society of captives, guards *give* orders and inmates *follow* orders. Rules specify what the captives may and may not do, and these rules are strictly enforced. Because the guards have a monopoly on the legal means of enforcing rules and can be backed up by the state police and the National Guard if necessary, many people believe that no question should arise as to how the prison is run. Members of the staff have the right to grant rewards and to inflict punishment, and, in theory, any inmate who does not follow the rules should end up in solitary confinement.

We could imagine a prison society made up of hostile and uncooperative captives ruled in an authoritarian manner. Prisoners can legally be isolated

Close-up: . . . *On the Yard*

A man walked by carrying a cardboard box and sporting parole shoes. Red knew he had made his date and was heading out. By ten he'd be free, on his way to the city, and before the day was over some fish would be coming in to replace him. This happened every day. The gradual turnover was constant. Only lifers and a few other longtimers stood outside this process.

For a moment Red thought about the men waiting somewhere in some county jail, still unaware they'd be hitting the big yard before the day was out. Then he saw the bookmaker he worked for, and walked over to take his station beside him.

Source: Malcolm Braly, *On the Yard* (Boston: Little, Brown, 1967). Reprinted by permission of Knox Burger Associates.

from one another, physically abused until they cooperate, and put under continuous surveillance. While such a regime is theoretically possible, however, a prison would probably not be run long in this fashion because the public expects correctional institutions to be run humanely. Besides, there are defects in the view that the guards have total power over the captives. As Gresham Sykes has noted, "the ability of the officials to physically coerce their captives into the paths of compliance is something of an illusion as far as the day-to-day activities of the prison are concerned and may be of doubtful value in moments of crisis."[7] Forcing people to follow commands is basically an inefficient method of making them carry out complex tasks, and efficiency is further diminished when the realities of the usual 1 to 40 guard-to-inmate ratio and the potential danger of the situation are understood. Thus correctional officers' ability to threaten the use of physical force is limited in practice.

Rewards and punishments. Faced with the necessity of running the prison, correctional officers often rely on a system of rewards and punishments to induce cooperation. In keeping with the concept that the prison is a total institution and a society of captives, extensive rules of conduct are imposed on prisoners, and rewards in the form of privileges may be offered for obedience: ***"good time"*** allowances, choice job assignments, favorable parole reports. Informers may be rewarded and administrators may purposely ignore conflicts among inmates on the assumption that such dissension prevents the prisoners from organizing to work together as a united force against the authorities.

good time
A reduction of a convict's prison sentence awarded for good behavior at the discretion of the prison administrator.

The reward and punishment system also has limitations, however. One of the problems is that the punishments for rule breaking do not represent a great difference from the prisoners' usual status. Because they are already deprived of many freedoms and valued goods—heterosexual relations, money, choice of clothing, and so on—the punishment of not being allowed to attend a recreational period does not carry much weight. Further, the system is often defective because the authorized privileges are given to the inmate at the start of the sentence and are taken away only if rules are broken. Thus few additional authorized rewards may be granted for progress or exceptional behavior, although a desired work assignment or transfer to the honor cell block will induce some prisoners to maintain good behavior.

In recent years the ability of correctional officials to discipline prisoners who resist authority has been somewhat weakened by the prisoners' rights movement and the demands of the courts for due process. The extent to which these forces have actually limited official sanctions is not known, but wardens are undoubtedly aware of the fact that their actions may be subject to legal action or censure by groups outside the prison.

Exchange relations. One way that correctional officers obtain inmates' cooperation is through the types of exchange relationships described in earlier chapters. The guard is the key official in the exchanges within the custodial bureaucracy.

> It is he who must supervise and control the inmate population in concrete and detailed terms. It is he who must see to the translation of the custodial regime from blueprint to reality and engage in the specific battles for conformity. Count-

ing prisoners, periodically reporting to the center of communications, signing passes, checking groups of inmates as they come and go, searching for contraband or signs of attempts to escape—these make up the minutiae of his eight-hour shift.[8]

Thus the guards are in close and intimate association with the prisoners throughout the day: in the cell block, workshop, or recreation area. Although

---

Rules of General Conduct, Michigan Department of Corrections

1. All residents are expected to obey directions and instructions of members of the staff. If a resident feels he/she has been dealt with unfairly, or that he/she has received improper instructions, he/she should first comply with the order and then follow the established grievance procedure outlined later in this booklet.
2. Any behavior considered a felony or a misdemeanor in this state also is a violation of institutional rules. Such acts may result in disciplinary action and/or loss of earned good time in addition to possible criminal prosecution.
3. Any escape, attempt to escape, walk-away or failure to return from a furlough may result in loss of good time and/or a new sentence through prosecution under the escape statute. At one time or another, most persons in medium or minimum custody have felt restless and uneasy. When this happens, we urge you to see your counselor or the official in charge for guidance and advice. Occasionally, the department has asked that those who have walked away impulsively not be prosecuted when they have turned themselves in immediately after the act, realizing their mistake.
4. Any residents may, if they feel they have no further recourse in the institution, appeal to the Director of Corrections, Deputy Director, the Attorney General, state and federal courts, Michigan Civil Rights Commission or the Governor in the form of sealed and uncensored mail.
5. Reasonable courtesy, orderly conduct and good personal hygiene are expected of all residents. Standards for haircuts, beards and general appearance are listed later in this rule book.
6. Residents cannot hold any group meetings in the yard. Meetings for all legitimate purposes require staff approval; facilities, if available, will be scheduled for this purpose and necessary supervision provided.
7. While residents are permitted to play cards and other games, gambling is not allowed. In card playing areas there shall be no more than four persons at a table. Visible tokens or other items of value will be sufficient evidence of gambling. Games are prohibited during working hours on institutional assignments.
8. All typewriters, calculators, radios, TV's, electric razors and other appliances, including musical instruments, must be registered with the institutional officials by make, model and serial number.
9. Items under Para. 8 cannot be traded, sold or given away without written approval of the Deputy Warden or Superintendent.
10. Residents cannot operate concessions, sell services, rent goods or act as loan sharks or pawnbrokers.
11. All items of contraband are subject to confiscation.
12. When residents desire to go from one place to another for a specific and legitimate reason, they should obtain a pass from the official to whom they are responsible, such as the housing unit supervisor, work foreman, teacher, etc.
13. No resident is allowed to go into another resident's cell or room unless specifically authorized.

Source: Michigan Department of Corrections, *Resident Guide Book* (Lansing, n.d.).

---

the formal rules stipulate that a social distance must be maintained between guards and inmates and that they speak and act toward each other accordingly, their closeness makes them aware that each is in many ways dependent on the other. The guards need the cooperation of the prisoners so that they will look good to their superiors, and the inmates depend on the guards to relax the rules or occasionally look the other way. Even though the guard is backed by the power of the state and has the formal authority to punish any prisoner who does not follow his orders, he "often discovers that his best path of action is to make 'deals' or 'trades' with the captives in his power."[9] As a result, the guard exchanges or "buys" compliance or obedience in some areas by tolerating violation of the rules elsewhere.

Correctional officers must be careful not to pay too high a price for the cooperation of their charges. Sub rosa (secret) relationships that turn into manipulation of the guards by the prisoners may result in the smuggling of contraband or other illegal acts. The guards are under public pressure to be humane and not to use coercion—in short, to be "good guys"—yet there are risks to the use of the carrot rather than the stick.

By working through the leaders of the inmate social system—the convict society—correctional administrators secure their cooperation in helping to maintain order.

> Far from systematically attempting to undermine the inmate hierarchy, the institution generally gives it covert support and recognition by assigning better jobs and quarters to its high-status members provided they are "good inmates." In this and other ways the institution buys peace with the system by avoiding battle with it.[10]

Being a "good" inmate does not mean withdrawing from the convict society but rather maintaining a position that permits one to control other inmates. The convict society leader tends to be a person with extensive prison experience who has been "tested" through relationships with other inmates so that he is neither pushed around by his fellows nor distrusted by them as a stool pigeon. Because the staff can also rely on him, he serves as the essential communications middleman between the two. With his ability to acquire inside information and his access to decision makers, the inmate leader is in a position to command respect from other prisoners. He benefits from the corruption of the formal authority of the staff by receiving illicit privileges and favors from the guards. In turn, he can distribute these benefits to other prisoners, thus bolstering his influence within the society.

In sum, there is a striking difference between the formal chain of command as displayed on an organization chart of the prison and the reality of the existing social relationships. The prison conforms to an authoritarian model of control only in a formal sense; an informal network of social and exchange relationships maintains order and secures correctional goals. Riots may occur as a result of forces that disrupt the social equilibrium of the prison. Changes in the institution's leadership, attempts to shift from custodial to treatment goals, and political pressures to tighten discipline have all been cited as forces that destroy the stability of the ongoing system. Struggles for leadership within the convict society and the racial antagonisms of the contemporary prison have likewise caused unrest.

One of the amazing aspects of prisons is that they "work" in the sense that order is maintained, chaos is avoided, and activities are carried out. Edwin Sutherland and Donald Cressey have noted that any prison is made up of

> synchronized actions of hundreds of people, some of whom hate and distrust each other, love each other, fight each other physically and psychologically, think of each other as stupid or mentally disturbed, "manage" and "control" each other, and vie with each other for favors, prestige, power, and money.[11]

Despite these conditions and the organizational problems described here, the prison society does not fall into disarray. Staff and prisoners are bound together so that potential conflicts and misunderstandings are generally avoided, the routine is followed, and the institution functions.

The convict world

What is it like to be incarcerated? Most of us rely on films, novels, and the accounts of former prisoners to picture life in the convict world. Because a prison population is made up of felons, many of whom are prone to violence, one might expect much rebellion if it were not for the discipline imposed by the authorities. As we have seen, however, there are definite limits to the ability of correctional administrators to impose their will on inmates. Scholars have looked at the convict world to try to understand the prison subculture

Close-up: . . . *On the Yard*

The yard was growing crowded. Hundreds of men were now walking steadily from one end to the other, pounding the blacktop, and a great many more were gathered under the rain shed in small groups, exchanging the idle topics of a thousand mornings. All wore blue denims, but the condition of their uniforms varied greatly, the tidy, the slovenly, and the politicians in their pressed pants—starched overalls, Red thought mockingly—their polished free-world shoes, and expensive wristwatches.

Red was waiting for his hustling partner, but he rapped to anyone who passed by. He liked to bulls—, play the dozens, and when some clown stopped to call him "old tops and bottoms" he quickly said, "Your mammy gives up tops and bottoms."

"I heard yours was freakish for billy goats."

"She used to sport a light mule habit," Red returned, his yellow eyes shining with pleasure. "But she wrote and told me she was trying to quit."

The clown smiled. "Red, you think you'll ever amount to anything?"

"Next time out I figure to file my pimp hand."

"Next time? You've already beat this yard long enough to wear out two murder beefs and a bag of robberies."

Red shrugged. "Off and on, I've been around a while."

"The big yard's a cold place to f——off your life."

Red's eyes began to grow vague as he lost interest in the conversation. Cons busted into jail, then spent half their time crying. And all the sniveling didn't make anyone's time any easier to do, any more than it shortened the length of a year. You did it the easiest way you could and hard-assed the difference. The big yard was an undercover world if you knew how to check the action, and something was always coming down. You could make a life of this yard, and you could die on it.

Source: Malcolm Braly, *On the Yard* (Boston: Little, Brown, 1967). Reprinted by permission of Knox Burger Associates.

and the means by which prisoners adapt to their social and physical environment. Many studies of prison behavior have attempted to describe the relationships and perceptions of the inmates.

A widely recognized fact is that the inmate population is *not* made up of persons who serve their terms in internal isolation. Rather, prisoners form a society with traditions, norms, and a leadership structure. Some members may choose to associate with only a few close friends, while others form cliques along racial or "professional" lines. Still others may be the politicians of the convict society: they attempt to represent convict interests and distribute valued goods in return for support. Within this society the inmate lives. Just as there is a social culture in the free world, there is a prisoner subculture on the "inside."

inmate code
The system of values and norms of the prison social system that define for inmates the characteristics associated with the model prisoner.

As in any society, the convict world has certain norms and values. Often described as the ***inmate code,*** the values and norms emerge within the prison social system and help to define the inmate's image of the model prisoner. The code also helps to emphasize the solidarity of all inmates against the staff. Although some sociologists believe that the code is something that emerges from within the institution as a way to lessen the pain of imprisonment, others believe that it is part of the criminal culture that prisoners bring with them. The inmate who follows the code can be expected to enjoy a certain amount of admiration from other inmates. He may be thought of as a "right guy" or a "real man." Those who break the code are labeled "rat" or "punk." Members of this group will probably spend their prison life at the bottom of the convict social structure, alienated from the rest of the population and preyed upon.[12]

Because contemporary prison society has become more heterogeneous, a single, overriding inmate code may not exist in some institutions. "The variety of cultural and subcultural orientations [ethnic, class, and criminal], the variety of preprison experiences, and the intense, open hostility between segments of the prison population may preclude this."[13] In particular, as the American prison population has become blacker, race has become a key variable dividing convict society. Perhaps reflecting tensions in the broader community, many prisons have been plagued during the past decade by racially motivated violence, the formation of organizations based on racial symbolism, and the voluntary segregation of inmates by race whenever possible (recreation areas, dining halls). John Irwin has called this formation of exclusive friendship groups "ordered segmentation."

For its members the group affords mutual protection from theft and physical assault, serves as the basis of wheeling and dealing activities, and provides a source of cultural identity. In the absence of a single code accepted by the entire population, however, administrators find their task more difficult. They must be aware of the variations that exist among the groups, recognize the norms and rules that members hold, and deal with the leaders of many cliques rather than with a few inmates who have risen to top positions in the inmate society.

Adaptive roles

On entering prison, a newcomer ("fish") is confronted by the question: How am I going to do my time? Some may decide to withdraw into their own world and isolate themselves from their fellow prisoners. Others may decide to become full participants in the convict social system, which, "through its solidarity, regulation of activities, distribution of goods and prestige . . . helps the individual withstand the 'pains of imprisonment.' "[14] In other words, some inmates may decide to identify mainly with the outside world while others may orient themselves primarily toward the convict world. As John Irwin has emphasized, this choice of identity is influenced by prisoners' values. Are they interested primarily in achieving prestige according to the norms of the prison culture, or do they try to maintain or realize the values of the free world? Their preference will influence the strategies that they will follow during the prison sentence.

Four categories have been used to describe the lifestyles of inmates as they adapt to prison. "Doing time" and "gleaning" are the choices of those who try to maintain their links with the free world and its perspectives. "Jailing" is the style used by those who cut themselves off from the outside and try to construct a life within the prison. The fourth category, "Disorganized criminal," includes those who are unable to develop role orientations to prison life. Often of low intelligence or afflicted with a psychological or physical disability, they have difficulty functioning within the prison society—they are the human putty of the prison social world who are exploited by others. Irwin believes the great majority of imprisoned felons may be classified according to these orientations.[15]

"Doing time." The "doing time" lifestyle is adopted by those who see the period in prison as a temporary break in their outside careers. They tend to be professional thieves—that is, criminals who look at their "work" as a legitimate businessman would. A prison sentence to these inmates is one of the risks or "overhead" costs of the way they make their living. Such inmates come to prison to "do time." They try to serve their terms with the least amount of suffering and the greatest amount of comfort they can manage. They avoid trouble by adhering to the inmate code, find activities to fill their days, form friendships with only small groups of other convicts, and generally do what they think is necessary to get out as soon as possible.

The Inmate Code, circa 1960

1. *Don't interfere with inmate interests*
   Never rat on a con. Don't be nosy. Don't have a loose lip. Don't put a guy on the spot.
2. *Don't quarrel with fellow inmates*
   Play it cool. Don't lose your head. Do your own time.
3. *Don't exploit inmates*
   Don't break your word. Don't steal from the cons. Don't sell favors. Don't be a racketeer. Don't welsh on bets. Be right.
4. *Maintain yourself*
   Don't weaken. Don't whine. Don't cop out. Don't suck around. Be tough. Be a man.
5. *Don't trust the guards or the things they stand for*
   Don't be a sucker. Guards are hacks or screws. The officials are wrong and the prisoners are right.

Source: Adapted from Gresham M. Sykes and Sheldon L. Messinger, "The Inmate Social System," in *Theoretical Studies in the Social Organization of the Prison*, ed. Richard A. Cloward, Donald R. Cressey, George H. Grosser, Richard McCleery, Lloyd E. Ohlin, Gresham M. Sykes, and Sheldon L. Messinger (New York: Social Science Research Council, 1960), pp. 6–8. Reprinted by permission.

"Gleaning." With the prevalence of rehabilitative programs, some prisoners decide to spend their time "gleaning"—taking advantage of opportunities to change their lives by trying to improve themselves, improve their minds, or "find themselves." They use every resource at hand: library, correspondence courses, vocational training programs, school. Some prisoners make a radical conversion to this prison lifestyle. Irwin's study of San Quentin shows that such persons tend to be those who are not committed to a life of crime.[16]

"Jailing." Some convicts never acquire a commitment to the outside social world. While in prison, they adopt a "jailing" lifestyle and make a world out of the prison. They are likely to be "state-raised youth," persons who have known foster homes, juvenile detention facilities, reformatories, and finally adult prisons for most of their lives. Because they know the institutional routine, have the skills required to "make it," and view the prison as a familiar place, they often aspire to leadership within the convict society. These are the inmates who seek positions that carry power and influence in the larger prison society. An assignment as a runner for a staff member means that the convict has greater freedom of movement within the institution and thus has access to information. Assigned a job as clerk in the kitchen storeroom, he is able to steal food that he can exchange with other prisoners for cigarettes, the prison currency. By constantly dealing in goods that are valued—food, clothes, information, drugs—he can live more comfortably in prison. This lifestyle has its rewards: "first, there is the reward of consumption itself, and second, there is the reward of increased prestige in the prison social system because of the display of opulence."[17]

Although we have described only four of the potential adaptive models chosen by inmates, we can see that prisoners are not members of an undifferentiated mass; individual members choose to play specific roles in the convict society. These models reflect the physical and social environment of the prison and contribute to the development of the system that maintains the institution's ongoing activities.

Making it

In prison, as in the outside world, individuals desire goods and services that are not freely provided. Although the state feeds, clothes, and houses all prisoners, amenities are sparse; institutional life is a type of enforced destitution in comparison with contemporary American living standards. In prison one is deprived of everything but bare necessities and subjected to monotony in diet and routine, loss of individual identity due to uniformity of treatment, scarcity of recreational opportunities, and lack of responsibility. It is true that during the past two decades the items that a prisoner may purchase or receive through legitimate channels have increased. In some institutions, inmates may own television sets, civilian clothing, and hot plates; the prison community remains unique, however, in that it has been deliberately designated "an island of poverty in the midst of a society of relative abundance."[18]

Offenders bring to the institution needs and desires for goods and services other than those provided. Television and magazines reinforce their appetite. In addition,

> there are many things not provided by the state that most prisoners regard as even more necessary than people on the outside do—for example, talcum powder and deodorant because of the prisoner's more limited bathing facilities. [They crave] store-bought cigarettes, instant coffee, immersion coils for heating water and between-meal snacks. . . .[19]

At the same time, the state has decreed that a life of extreme simplicity is part of the punishment of incarceration; and correctional administrators feel that rules must be enforced so that all prisoners are treated alike and none can gain higher position or status or comfort because of wealth or access to goods. Thus prisoners are limited as to what they may have in their cells, visitors are restricted as to the gifts that they may bring into the institution, and money may not be in the inmate's possession.

Recognizing that prisoners do have some needs that are not met, officials have created a formal economic system in the form of a commissary or "store" in which inmates may, on a scheduled basis, purchase a limited number of items—toilet articles, tobacco, snacks, and other food items—in exchange for credits drawn upon their "bank accounts." The size of a bank account depends on the amount of money deposited on the inmate's entrance, gifts sent by relatives, and amounts earned in the low-paying prison industries. In some prisons, the amount that may be spent weekly is limited.

But the peanut butter, soap, and cigarettes of the typical prison store in no way satisfy the consumer needs and desires of prisoners, and in consequence an informal, sub rosa economy exists as a major element in the society of captives. Many items taken for granted on the outside are inordinately valued on the inside. Vergil Williams and Mary Fish note:

> Truncated supply results in prison demand for goods and services inconsequential or even bizarre to the free world denizen. Goods and services that would not be consumed at all outside prison can attain exaggerated importance inside the prison simply because the inmates are denied the use of things that constitute a normal part of their living standard outside.[20]

As examples they cite offenders who, unable to enjoy their accustomed drink of bourbon, will find that somewhat the same effect can be achieved by sniffing glue; or those who, to distinguish themselves from others, pay laundry workers to iron a shirt in a particular way, a modest version of conspicuous consumption.

The informal economy reinforces the norms and roles of the social system, influences the nature of interpersonal relationships, and is thus one of the principal features of the culture. The extent of the economy and its ability to produce desired goods and services—food, drugs, alcohol, sex, preferred living conditions—vary according to the extent of official surveillance, the demands of the consumers, and the opportunities for entrepreneurship. Much inmate activity revolves around the "hustle."

The standard medium of exchange in the prison economy is cigarettes. Because possession of coins or currency is prohibited and a barter system is somewhat restrictive, "cigarette money" is a useful substitute. Cigarettes are not contraband, are easily transferable, have a stable and well-known standard of value, and come in denominations of singles, packs, and cartons. Further, they are in demand by smokers. Even those who do not smoke keep cigarettes for trading purposes.

As in the outside world, there are positions in the prison society that provide opportunities for entrepreneurs. Access to food, clothing, materials, and information allows inmates assigned to work in such places as the kitchen, warehouse, and administrative office to ply their trade. As Susan Sheehan found in Green Haven, almost every job offered possibilities for "swagging" (stealing from the state).

> The kitchen is another first-rate place to swag. Supervision is limited, and kitchen workers can take far more food than they can eat, and sell it or swap it. One of Malinow's friends, who receives five cartons of cigarettes a month from a crime partner he didn't rat on, doesn't smoke but loves to eat. His recent purchases from a kitchen worker have included a dozen eggs (two packs of cigarettes), a pound of rice (one pack), a pound of coffee (one pack), and several steaks (three packs apiece). He also has a contract with his friend in the kitchen for a daily loaf of soft bread (one carton a month). Kitchen workers have access to the various ingredients used at Green Haven to make booze—yeast, raw dough, sugar, fruit, potatoes, cereal—and either sell the raw ingredients or make and sell the finished product.[21]

It is important to recognize that "sales" in the economy are one to one and are also interrelated with other sub rosa transactions. Thus the exchange of a dozen eggs for two packs of cigarettes may result in the reselling of the eggs in the form of egg sandwiches made on a hot plate for five cigarettes each, while the kitchen worker who swagged the eggs may use the income to get a laundry worker to starch his shirts or a hospital orderly to provide drugs or to pay a "punk" for sexual favors. The economic transactions wind on and on.

Disruptions of the economy may occur when correctional officials conduct periodic "lockdowns" and inspections. Confiscation of contraband may result in temporary shortages and, as in the free economy, price readjustments, but gradually hustling will return. The laws of supply and demand will be back in force.

One must acknowledge that the economy of the prison society meets the members' needs for goods and services. It permits some inmates to live better than others and to exert power over them. Economic transactions may lead to violence when goods are stolen, debts are not paid, or agreements are violated. The guards may also become enmeshed in the prison economy as they, too, see opportunities to provide goods for payment. The prison economy, like that of the outside world, allocates goods and services, rewards and sanctions, and is closely linked to the cultural and social systems of the society it serves.

Prison programs

One of the major ways in which modern correctional institutions differ from those of the distant past is in the number and variety of programs that are available. While prison industries were a part of such early penitentiaries as Auburn, under the stimulus of the rehabilitative goal many educational, vocational, and treatment services have been added to the correctional institution. In some states such programs have not been well developed, and prisoners spend their time working at tasks that do not prepare them for jobs on the outside. During the 1960s, often with the help of funds from the Law Enforcement Assistance Administration, the number of programs devoted to rehabilitation increased dramatically. Even with these new opportunities, however, many correctional administrators are not able to provide enough activities to occupy all inmates most of the time. Idleness and boredom are facts of prison life.

Educational programs

Most state and federal correctional facilities offer academic programs. Often the department of corrections is designated as a school district so that courses passed by inmates are credited in accordance with state requirements. Since a great majority of adult felons lack a high school diploma, it seems natural that many could make good use of their prison time in the classroom. In many institutions, inmates without at least an eighth-grade education are assigned to school as their main occupation. In some facilities, college-level courses are offered in the evening through an association with a local community college. Studies have shown that inmates who were assigned to the prison school are good candidates to achieve a conviction-free record after release. Evidence has also suggested, however, that this outcome may be due largely to the type of inmate selected for schooling rather than the schooling itself.[22]

Vocational education

The idea that inmates can be taught a trade that will be of service to them in the free world has great appeal. In view of the educational level and social backgrounds of most prisoners, they might be expected to be eager to learn a skilled trade. Indeed, programs in modern facilities are designed to teach a variety of skills: plumbing, automobile mechanics, printing, computer programming. One of the weaknesses of most such programs is that they are unable to keep abreast of technological advances and needs of the free market. Too many programs are designed to train inmates for trades that already have an adequate labor supply or in which new methods have made the skills taught

Most prisons offer educational and vocational programs.

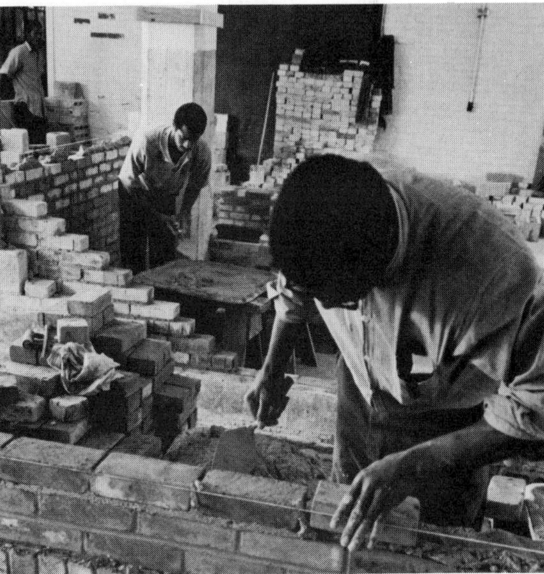

obsolete. Some vocational programs are even designed to prepare inmates for careers on the outside that are closed to former felons. The restaurant industry, for example, might be a place where former felons might find employment, yet in many states they are prohibited from working where alcohol is sold.

Prison industries

Early prison reformers felt that good work habits should be developed in inmates, and that prisoners should be productive so that their labor would help to pay the costs of their incarceration. Others cited the usefulness of work in keeping inmates out of mischief and declared that work is consistent with the goal of incapacitation. Some scholars now point to the early industries established at Auburn as a reflection of the industrialization of the United States and the need for prison to instill good work habits and discipline in potential members of the labor force.

Traditionally, prisoners have been required to work at tasks that are necessary to maintain and run their own and other state facilities. Accordingly, food service, laundry, and building maintenance jobs are assigned. In some states, prison farms produce food for the institution. Industry shops make furniture, repair office equipment, and fabricate items. Prisoners receive a nominal fee (perhaps 50 cents an hour) for such work.

The prison industries system has had a checkered career. During the nineteenth century, prisoners were often engaged in the manufacture of items that were sold on the open market. With the rise of the labor movement, however, state legislatures passed laws restricting the sale of prison-made goods so that they would not compete with those made by free workers. Whenever unemployment became extensive, political pressures mounted to prevent prisons from engaging in enterprises that might otherwise be conducted by private business and free labor. In 1940 Congress passed an act prohibiting the interstate transportation of convict-made goods, but with the outbreak of World War II, President Franklin Roosevelt issued an executive order permitting the federal government to procure goods for the military effort from state and federal prisons. Under labor pressure, the wartime order was revoked in 1947 by President Harry Truman and prisoners returned to the idleness so characteristic of U.S. corrections.[23] By 1973 the National Advisory Commission found that throughout the correctional system "only a few offenders in institutions have productive work."[24]

The past decade has seen renewed interest in the channeling of prison labor into revived industrial programs that would relieve idleness, allow inmates to earn wages that they could save until their release, and reduce the costs of incarceration to the state. In 1979 Congress lifted restrictions on the

---

Those Who Wait

When it happened, my whole life came crashing down. I couldn't bring myself to believe that *my* husband was actually in prison. Two years seemed like a lifetime. No one understood how I felt—not my family, not my friends, not even myself. That place terrified me. I had no money. My head was spinning with questions and I was so very confused.

Source: Women in Crisis, *Third Annual Report* (Hartford, Conn., 1980).

---

interstate sale of prison-made products and urged correctional administrators to explore with the private sector the possibilities for improving prison industry programs.[25] Under the LEAA Free Venture program, funds were extended in 1979 to seven states to develop industries that would operate according to six principles: a full workweek for inmate employees; wages based on productivity; private-sector productivity standards; the vesting of industries staff with responsibility for hiring and firing inmate workers; self-sufficient or profitable shop operations; and a postrelease job placement mechanism. The Prison Industries Enhancement program (PIE) has also been started on a pilot basis in seven other states. The program requires the actual involvement of private business in the correctional industry. The best example is Zephyr Products, Inc., of Leavenworth, Kansas; prisoners receive the wage being paid in the company's private-sector plant for assembling metal parts for the electronics industry.[26]

The change in attitude toward prison industries may be related to the fact that many large U.S. firms have moved their operations to the Third World in search of cheap labor. Because of increased shipping costs and problems related to the running of plants overseas, some manufacturers may be recognizing that prison labor is abundant and an attractive alternative to foreign workers. Union opposition may weaken if it can be shown that prisoners are not taking jobs away from tax-paying free workers.

These innovations, the decline of treatment programs, the high costs of incarceration, and the change in public attitudes with regard to the role of private enterprise may portend a reinvigoration of prison industries.

Treatment services

Reports by Robert Martinson, Walter Bailey, and others in the mid-1970s cast doubt on the ability of treatment programs to stem recidivism and raised questions about the ethics of requiring inmates to participate in such programs in exchange for the promise of parole.[27] Their findings led to a rethinking of rehabilitation as an element of sentencing decisions. Treatment programs still have their supporters, as can be seen in the work of Ted Palmer, director of research for the California Youth Authority, and of Francis Cullen and Karen Gilbert.[28] Palmer's main argument is that certain programs work for certain offenders, but such happy outcomes require more accurate diagnosis and fine-tuned sentencing by judges than are now possible.

Undoubtedly treatment services will remain a part of correctional institutions, but the overemphasis of the past has diminished. Incarceration's current goal of humane custody implies no effort to change inmates.

On guarding

A survey of American teenagers by pollster Louis Harris revealed that only 1 percent had considered a career in corrections. This finding is not surprising because a prison guard or correctional officer has no opportunity to acquire the prestige accorded the Secret Service agent, who may come to share in the glamour of the person he guards. The correctional officer's occupational prestige is tarnished by the company he must keep—the felon. The prisoner, of course, is not pleased at being guarded, while the community, the benefactor

The correctional officer works in close contact with prisoners and has the greatest potential for inducing behavioral changes.

of the guard's activities, seems not to care except when a riot or escape occurs. Guards make up more than half of all correctional employees. Their hours are long, their pay is low, entry requirements are minimal, and turnover is very high.

Role

Lucien X. Lombardo has used the concepts of "people worker" and "bureaucrat" to analyze the role of the correctional officer.[29] As a "people

---

Gaining Respect

The hardnose, thick-headed, bull correctional officer of the movies in the Jimmy Cagney era doesn't exist. And if he comes in here, he doesn't last very long. Your first goal ought to be to gain the respect of an inmate.

You can't gain respect from an inmate from being an easy mark. They don't respect easy marks. You don't gain respect through bully tactics, then everyday he comes into the joint it's going to just wear him down a little bit more. Things just don't work that way anymore.

You gain respect by attempting to treat everyone the same . . . equally . . . no matter what they're in for. As a matter of fact, myself, I try not to find out what a man's in here for. It might change me a little bit . . . I might not feel that it showed, but it shows. Now, someone will ask me to do something, send a request out to the visiting desk or something like that . . . his request might sit in my pocket where someone else's request would be expedited right off the bat because of maybe what he did on the street . . . so I try not to even know what he's here for. . . .

Source: Edgar May, "Prison Guards in America: The Inside Story," *Corrections Magazine*, December 1976, p. 36. Reprinted by permission of Edna McConnell Clark Foundation.

---

worker," the guard must cope "with the human problems of inmates on a personal level," that is, treat prisoners as individuals and help them with their institutional and personal problems. But the officer also functions as a member of a complex bureaucratic organization and thus is expected to deal with clients impersonally and to follow formally prescribed procedures. Fulfilling these contradictory role expectations is difficult in itself, and the difficulty is exacerbated by the physical closeness of the officer and inmate over long periods of time.

Although prison work is widely perceived to be largely routine, guarding is not an undifferentiated occupation as James Jacobs and Norma Crotty describe it:

> Guards supervise the cell houses, dining areas, and shops; transport prisoners to hospitals and courts; take turns serving on the disciplinary board; sit perched with rifles in the towers on top of the walls; and protect the gates leading into and out of the interior. Unscheduled activities range from informal counseling to breaking up fights to escorting prisoners on family visits in the community.[30]

Of all the correctional staff, the officers in the cell blocks have the closest contact with the prisoners, and one might assume that they would have the greatest potential for inducing behavioral change in their charges. One of the problems that has faced most correctional systems during recent decades has been the unclear role that the guard is expected to play in an institution that combines both custodial and treatment goals. Officers are held responsible for preventing escapes, for maintaining order, and for the smooth functioning of the institution. At the same time, they are expected to cooperate with treatment personnel by counseling inmates and assuming an understanding attitude. Not only are those roles incompatible, but the rehabilitative ideal stresses attempts to deal with each person as a unique being, a task that seems impossible in a large people-processing institution. Guards are expected to use discretion yet somehow to behave both custodially and therapeutically. As Cressey notes, "if they enforce the rules, they risk being diagnosed as 'rigid,' " whereas "if their failure to enforce rules creates a threat to institutional security, orderliness or maintenance, they are not 'doing their job.' "[31]

Guards complain that the rules are constantly changing, and neither they nor the inmates know where they stand. Many guards look back with nostalgia to the days when their purpose was clear, their authority unchallenged, and they were respected by the inmates. One Stateville guard told Jacobs:

> During Ragen's days you knew every day what you were supposed to do and now you are in a position where there are too many supervisors and too many changing rules. First one will come and tell you it's got to be done this way and then somebody else comes along and says to do something different. In the old days we knew what our job was.[32]

The position of correctional officer is more complicated than may be realized. The guard is both a manager and a worker—a low-status worker in

---

On Guarding

"We're all doing time, some of us are just doing it in eight-hour shifts."

A MASSACHUSETTS PRISON GUARD

---

relationships with supervisors but a manager of the inmates. Placed in an environment where most interactions while on duty are with the prisoners, the guard is nevertheless expected to maintain a formal distance from them. As the member at the lowest level of the correctional staff, the guard is constantly under scrutiny by superiors in the same way that the inmate is under surveillance. Because of the fear of trafficking in contraband, guards are often shaken down, just as inmates are. As guards write disciplinary reports on inmates, captains write up rule infractions of the guards. Jacobs comments that even "the disciplinary board for guards is quite similar to the tribunal that hears inmate cases."[33]

Prison personnel issues

Recruitment. As we know, employment as a correctional officer is not one of the glamorous, sought-after occupations. The work is thought to be boring, the pay is low, and career mobility is almost nonexistent. Studies have shown that one of the primary incentives for becoming a guard is the security civil service status provides. In addition, prisons offer better employment options than most others available in the rural areas where most correctional facilities are located. As correctional officers are recruited locally, most of them are rural and white, while the majority of prisoners come from urban areas and are either black or Hispanic. In 1972 the commission investigating the Attica riots found that only 2 percent of the 500 employees were members of minority groups, but 63.5 percent of the inmates were black and 9.5 percent were Puerto Rican. More recently, a report following a disturbance at Brushy Mountain State Penitentiary noted that 55 percent of the prisoners were black and 100 percent of the officers were white.[34]

The need for correctional workers has increased in recent years, and in most states recruitment of good personnel has been given high priority. Salaries have been increased so that now the yearly average pay runs between $15,000 and $20,000.[35] Special efforts have been made to recruit women and minorities. Women are no longer restricted to working with female offenders, and the number of correctional officers from minority groups has increased dramatically, though not in proportion to the inmate population in most states.

Female correctional officers may now work in prisons that house adult males.

Collective bargaining. The unionization of prison guards is a fairly recent phenomenon. It was not until the 1970s, when many states passed laws permitting collective bargaining by public employees, that the unions made inroads in prisons. By 1981 correctional employees in twenty-nine of fifty-two jurisdictions (state, federal, and District of Columbia) were unionized.[36] Like other labor organizations, unions representing prison employees seek better wages and working conditions for their members. Because the members are public employees, most are prevented by law from engaging in strikes, but work stoppages have occurred in a number of prisons nonetheless.

The unionization of prison employees has added one more ingredient to the mix of corrections: inmates, administration, employees, and now unions. As a result, relationships between employees and administration are now more formalized, with the rights and obligations of each side stipulated by contract.

The correctional officer: linchpin

One of the most curious aspects of modern corrections is "the way in which the custodial officer, the key figure in the penal equation, the man on whom the whole edifice of the penitentiary system depends, has with astonish-

Close-up: . . . *On the Yard*

The prison is never at rest. The incident rate slows at night, but it doesn't ever cease. It slows because with the exception of a few trusted to watch over the vitals of light and heat, the entire inmate body is confined in cells from 10 P.M. to 7 A.M. It doesn't cease because they are locked two to a cell. They gamble, fight, build fires, practice various perversions and sometimes kill one another.

At night the guard staff is reduced by two-thirds and the ratio then runs at approximately one guard to a hundred and seventy-five convicts. The night bulls would find themselves in a desperate minority if the cons ever broke loose, but they never have, and first watch is considered an easy turn reserved for young and inexperienced officers, or old screws pushing retirement, or the cowards afraid to beat the yard shoulder to shoulder with the enemy in the blue uniform.

These first-watch officers walk the gun rails, their flashlights lingering over the barred gloom of the lightless cells, tier on tier, five tiers high, one hundred cells long. From the gun rail the block looks like a metal honeycomb, or perhaps more accurately like a huge multiple trap, sprung now on its unimaginable quarry while the will-o'-the-wisp of the trapper's flash moves from snare to snare in quiet approval. Other night bulls sit out in the towers above the floodlit walls and blocks. They sip black coffee, read girlie magazines, or watch the moonlight slowly shifting on the empty concrete seventy-five feet below them. The prison seems like a walled city, smothered under a rigid curfew, governed by an alien army.

The gun rail guards are required to wear crepe-soled shoes, and they try to move silently, not, as any con is quick to say, out of consideration for inmate sleep, but to cause those who might plot at night to think of the gun bull as drifting like a shadow—a phantom who in as many imaginations could silently keep all the thousand cells under simultaneous surveillance. In dull fact their approach is betrayed to those who have reason to listen by the creaking of the leather harness that supports the guns, both rifle and pistol, they are required to carry.

Source: Malcolm Braly, *On the Yard* (Boston: Little, Brown, 1967). Reprinted by permission of Knox Burger Associates.

ing consistency either been ignored or traduced or idealized but almost never considered seriously."[37] Correctional officers are asked to do an almost impossible task without proper training, for low pay, and at great risk. Further, the current emphasis on humane custody requires that guards be of a quality that permits them to influence their charges.

Women in prison

Women constitute only a small portion of the entire prison population. For every twenty-five men convicted as felons, only one woman is convicted. Perhaps because the number of women among both prisoners and corrections researchers has been so small, the literature on women's institutions is sparse. In general, it compares life in women's prisons with that in men's and indicates that women's prisons both resemble and differ from those housing men. They are smaller; security is less tight; the relationships between inmates and staff are less structured; physical aggression seems less common; the sub rosa economy is not so well developed; and female prisoners appear to be less committed to the convict code. Women serve shorter sentences, and there is perhaps more fluidity in the prison society as new members join and others leave.

Like male prisoners, incarcerated women may be viewed as "the disadvantaged losers in our complex and competitive society." A study of the backgrounds of women imprisoned in Michigan from 1968 to 1978 found that almost 70 percent had not finished high school; about half had been unemployed or had held unskilled jobs; 90 percent came from families described as "working poor"; and about 73 percent were nonwhite.[38] Nearly half were caring for dependents when they were admitted, yet most had no male companion. Few had alcohol problems but about half were drug abusers. The predominant offenses for which they were incarcerated were larceny and forgery.

The women prisoners in Michigan are probably typical of those incarcerated throughout the country. Their background characteristics are much like those of male prisoners, but most have the added problem of being responsible for dependents. Because many have been concerned with child rearing during their early adult years, most do not have the skills necessary to enter the job market on their release from prison. Whatever their crime, women prisoners as a group tend to be dependent, and it is argued that the prison environment increases this weakness.

Separate institutions for women

It was not until the end of the nineteenth century that separate prisons for women were created in the United States. Although women had been housed in penitentiaries since the 1820s, they were usually segregated from men in out-of-the-way areas where they had no access to exercise yards, visiting rooms, or even fresh air and light. In 1873 the Indiana Women's Prison, the first physically separate women's institution, was opened. It was followed by other such institutions in Massachusetts (1877), New York (1887), and New Jersey (1913). There are now 42 institutions for women (40 state, 2 federal) in the United States, compared to 490 for men and 26 that house both men and women.[39]

Although institutional facilities for women are generally smaller, better staffed, and less fortress-like than those for men, these advantages may disappear when the problems of remoteness and heterogeneity are considered. Because only three states operate more than one prison for women and some operate none, inmates are generally far removed from their families, friends, and attorneys. In addition, because the number of inmates is small, there is less pressure to design programs to meet an individual offender's security and treatment needs. Rehabilitation programs are few, and dangerous inmates are not segregated from those who have committed minor offenses. The vocational and educational opportunities available to women prisoners tend to conform to class and sex stereotyping, with programs offering cooking, sewing, cosmetology, and housekeeping.

Social relationships

Researchers have been most interested in the types of social relationships that women prisoners maintain. As in all types of penal institutions, homosexual relationships are found, though among women they appear to be more voluntary than coerced. More important, female inmates tend to form pseudofamilies in which they adopt various roles—father, mother, daughter, sister—and interact as a unit. Esther Heffernan views these "play" families as a "direct, conscious substitution for the family relationships broken by imprisonment, or . . . the development of roles that perhaps were not fulfilled in the actual home environment."[40] Such interpersonal links help to relieve the

Elizabeth Fry

Born in Norwich, England, Elizabeth Fry was second only to John Howard as a nineteenth-century advocate of prison reform in Europe. She came from an old Quaker family that had long been active in efforts to improve society. Her devotion to her religion was strengthened in 1798 under the fiery influence of the American Quaker William Severy.

Elizabeth Fry devoted much of her life to caring for the poor and neglected, and her most notable work was in prison reform. In April 1817 she helped to organize the Association for the Improvement of Female Prisoners in Newgate, then the major prison in London. The group was made up of the wives of Quaker businessmen who believed that prison to be a "den of wild beasts." Their aim was to establish prison discipline, separation of the sexes, classification of criminals, female supervision for the women inmates, adequate provision for religious and secular instruction, and the useful employment of prisoners. The positive results at Newgate were dramatic.

Largely through the personal effort of Mrs. Fry, methods similar to those at Newgate were rapidly extended to other prisons in England and abroad. Publication of the notes that she took while visiting the prisons of Scotland and northern England in 1818 brought her recognition on an international scale. Her *Observations on Visiting, Superintendence, and Government of Female Prisons* (1827) was influential in the movement to reform American prisons for women. She made personal inspection tours of prisons throughout Europe: Ireland in 1827; France and Switzerland in 1838; Belgium, Holland, and Prussia in 1840; and Denmark in 1841. By the time of her death in 1845, her reform approaches had been widely accepted.

tensions of prison life, to assist the socialization of the new inmate, and to allow individuals to act according to clearly defined roles and rules.

Rose Giallombardo believes that in most respects the subcultures of prisons for males and females are similar, with one major exception: the informal social structure of the female prison helps inmates to "resist the destructive effects of imprisonment by creating a substitute universe—a world in which the inmates may preserve an identity which is relevant to life outside the prison." The orientation of female inmates is somewhat collectivist, with warmth and mutual aid being extended to an extended network of "family" members. This emphasis, Giallombardo contends, is in sharp contrast to male inmates' strategy of combating the pains of imprisonment through the development of a convict code and by the showing of solidarity with other inmates.[41]

Adaptive roles. Esther Heffernan discovered three argot roles—"square," "cool," and "in the life"—corresponding to the noncriminal, professional, and habitual offenders in the women's correctional institution. "Square" is a term used there as it is used in the larger community: to describe a person who holds conventional norms and values. A square is a noncriminal who perhaps killed her husband in a moment of rage. She attempts to maintain a conventional life while incarcerated, strives to gain the respect of officers and fellow inmates, and seeks to be a "good Christian woman." Female prisoners are "cool" if they make a "controlled, pleasurable, manipulative response to a situation." They are the professionals who "keep busy, play around, stay out of trouble, and get out." They attempt to manipulate others and intend to get through this term of incarceration on "easy time" through unity with others in their group, gaining as many amenities as they can without risking a longer stay. To be "in the life" is to be antisocial in prison just as one had been on the outside. Such persons are the habitual offenders who have been involved in prostitution, drugs, numbers, and shoplifting. They have been in prison before and make up about 50 percent of the prison population, interact with others with similar experiences, and find community within the prison. It is important to them to stand firm against authority.[42]

Heffernan's three adaptations to incarceration correspond to criminal identities brought in from the outside. Prisoners who assume these roles group themselves together so that three subsystems, each with its own perspectives, exist within the society. Even divided, the inmates Heffernan studied tried to mitigate the deprivations of imprisonment through the informal social system.

The Importance of Correctional Officers

They may be the most influential persons in institutions simply by virtue of their numbers and their daily intimate contact with offenders. It is a mistake to define them as persons responsible only for control and maintenance. They can, by their attitude and understanding, reinforce or destroy the effectiveness of almost any correctional program. They can act as effective intermediaries or become insurmountable barriers between the inmates' world and the institution's administrative and treatment personnel.

Source: President's Commission on Law Enforcement and Administration of Justice, *Task Force Report: Corrections* (Washington, D.C.: Government Printing Office, 1967), p. 96.

Male versus female subcultures. When one compares the research findings on the subcultures in male and female prisons, one discovers a great deal of correspondence but also a number of major differences. Comparisons are complicated somewhat by the nature of the research, for most studies have been of single-sex institutions. In addition, it seems that theories and concepts have been studied first in male prisons and then replicated in female institutions. Thus the concepts of argot roles, inmate code, indigenous versus imported values, prison economy, and so on are central to this entire body of literature; all have been found to have explanatory value in both types of institution. Heffernan's "square," "cool," and "in the life" are the female counterparts of John Irwin's "square john," "thief," and "convict" in a male prison.[43] In both types of institution, to "make it" is to adapt to prison life in some way that makes the experience as painless as possible. Prisoners who cannot come to terms with incarceration can expect to do "hard time" and suffer from the experience.

A principal difference between these two gender-specific societies lies in interpersonal relations. Male prisoners seem to have a greater sense that they act as individuals and that their behavior is evaluated by the yardstick of the prison culture. As James Fox noted in a comparative study of four male prisons and one women's prison, young men feel compelled to present a macho image, with an emphasis on physical strength and "a conscious avoidance of conduct, speech, or social relationships that may imply a tendency toward homosexuality." The prisoner must gain recognition and status within the convict community by strict adherence to its values. Male prisoners have their gangs or cliques but not the network of "family" relationships that has been found in prisons for women. Men are expected to do their *own* time. The norms stress autonomy, self-sufficiency, and the ability to cope with one's problems. Fox found little sharing.[44]

Surviving in Prison

I was scared when I went to Bedford Hills. But I knew a few things by then. Like if you act quiet and hostile, people will consider you dangerous and won't bother you. So when I got out of isolation and women came up and talked to me, I said, "I left my feelings outside the gate, and I'll pick 'em up on my way out." I meant I wasn't going to take no junk from anyone. I made a promise if anybody hit me, I was gonna send 'em to the hospital.

When you go in, if you have certain characteristics, you're classified in a certain way. First of all, if you are aggressive, if you're not a dependent kind of woman, you're placed in a position where people think you have homosexual tendencies. If you're in that society long, you play the game if it makes it easier to survive. And it makes it easier if people think you're a stud broad. I played the game to make it easier so they would leave me alone. I didn't have money to use makeup and I couldn't see going through any changes. You're in there and the women are looking for new faces. Since I was quiet and not too feminine-looking, I was placed in a certain box in other people's mind. I let them think that's what box I was in—'cause it was a good way to survive. My good friends knew better. But I had three good friends and they were considered "my women"—so they in turn were safe, too. You have to find ways to survive. You cultivate ways to survive. It's an alien world and it has nothing to do with functioning in society better. What I learned there was to survive there.

Source: Kathryn Watterson Burkhart, *Women in Prison* (New York: Doubleday, 1976), pp. 89–90.

Women at the Bedford Hills Correctional Facility in New York were less likely to look toward achievement of status or recognition within the prisoner community or "to impose severe restrictions on the sexual (or emotional) conduct of other members."[45] In prisons for women, close ties seem to exist among small groups of inmates. Within these extended families, some individuals may be involved in a homosexual dyadic relationship while others take the roles of siblings, aunts, or cousins. The family networks provide emotional support and emphasize the sharing of resources.

Some researchers have ascribed the distinctive female prison subculture to the nurturing, maternal qualities of women. Others have criticized this analysis as a stereotype of female behavior, imputing to women sex-specific personality characteristics.

Programs and the female role. A major criticism of women's prisons is that they do not have the variety of vocational and educational programs that is available in male institutions, and that existing programs for women tend to conform to sexual stereotypes of "feminine" occupational roles: cosmetology, food service, housekeeping, sewing. It is suggested that such activities reflect the roles of women before World War II but have little correspondence to the occupations open to women today. Most educational programs for women stop at the secondary level; the larger numbers of male inmates are said to make it more feasible to offer courses at the college level. The importance of vocational and educational opportunities during incarceration is seen by the fact that upon release most women have to support themselves and many are financially responsible for children as well.

Two studies conducted during the 1970s provide most of the information we have about educational and vocational programs in women's prisons. Ruth Glick and Virginia Neto surveyed sixteen prisons, forty-six jails, and thirty-six community-based programs in fourteen states in research funded by LEAA.[46] Editors of the *Yale Law Journal* surveyed forty-seven male and fifteen female institutions that accounted for approximately 30 percent of the male and 50 percent of the female incarcerated populations of the United States. These studies confirm the general understanding about the insufficiencies of programs in women's prisons. The Yale study found that on the average, male institutions had 10.2 vocational programs; female prisons, 2.7. The size of the inmate population is often cited as the reason for the number of programs offered, but it was discovered that although the smallest institution had only 44 inmates and the largest 739, each had at least one program but none had more than three. The following vocational programs were available in at least one of the fifteen institutions for women in the Yale survey: clerical, cosmetology, dental technician, floral design, food service, garment manufacture, housekeeping, IBM keypunch, and nurses' aide.[47]

Critics have pointed out that although the female work force in the broader community has greatly expanded during the past twenty years and women now occupy positions formerly reserved for men, prisoners are not being prepared for such occupations. Not all correctional administrators agree with this assessment. Martha Wheeler of the Ohio Department of Corrections and a past president of the American Correctional Association has contended that some women "are not career-minded and they do not really have it in mind to go out and get a job and be self-supporting."[48] She believes that many inmates want to assume on the outside the traditional role of wife and mother.

The lack of medical, nutritional, and recreational services in women's prisons has also been noted. In particular, the numbers game affects the provision of medical services, with most female institutions sharing physicians and hospital facilities with male prisons. Because the health-delivery system at Bedford Hills Correctional Facility was deficient—no full-time physician or continuous medical care, and inadequate screening for medical problems—a ruling in a lawsuit filed on behalf of the inmates found the institution in violation of the Eighth Amendment's prohibition of cruel and unusual punishments. The court declared that the state had been deliberately indifferent to known medical needs.[49]

Many people believe that the national policies of equal opportunity require that women be given the type and variety of programs and services offered to male inmates. They cite the equal protection clause of the Fourteenth Amendment, the Civil Rights Act of 1964, and the proposed Equal Rights Amendment to buttress their claim.[50] Support for this view can be found in the 1979 case of *Glover* v. *Johnson,* in which the female inmates of the Detroit House of Correction charged that their educational and vocational programs were much inferior to those offered to male prisoners. The court ruled that prison officials had a responsibility to bring the level of services available to women up to that accorded men. The decision was based in part on a New Mexico case, *Barefield* v. *Leach* (1974), in which it was ruled that the equal protection clause "requires parity of treatment, as contrasted with identity of treatment, between male and female inmates with respect to the conditions of their confinement and access to rehabilitation opportunities."[51]

Mothers and their children. Of greatest concern to incarcerated women is the fate of their children. The best available data indicate that about 70 percent of women inmates are mothers, and that on average they have two dependent children. It is thus estimated that on a typical day 21,000 children in the United States—two-thirds of whom are under ten years of age—have mothers who are in jail or prison.[52] As few of the mothers have husbands or male partners who are able or willing to maintain a home for the children, they must be placed with relatives or in state-funded foster care. Because prisoners are predominantly poor and often nonwhite, their anxieties about their children are largely ignored.

Enforced separation of children from their mothers is bad for the children and bad for the mothers. It is one of the great stress-producing experiences that is not fully shared by male prisoners. In most states a baby born in prison must be placed with a family member or social agency within three weeks, to the detriment of the early mother–child bonding thought to be important for the development of a baby. But anxiety about the care of their children is not confined to mothers of infants; it affects all mothers, especially if the children are being cared for by strangers.

Mothers have difficulty maintaining contact with their children because of the distance of prisons from the children's homes, restrictions on visiting hours, only intermittent telephone conversations, and the conditions for interacting with their offspring when they do come to the institution. Some correctional facilities are more advanced than others in devising ways to help mothers retain links to their children and to nurture the relationship; in other institutions, child visitors must abide by the rules governing visits by adults: physical contact is not allowed and visiting time is strictly limited.

Increasingly, programs are being developed to deal with the problems of mothers and their children. In some states, visiting hours and conditions have been changed so that children may meet with their mothers at almost any time, for extended periods, and in playrooms or nurseries where contact is possible. Transportation for visits is arranged in some states, and in some it is even possible for children to stay overnight. In both South Dakota and Nebraska, for example, children may stay with their mothers for up to five days a month. Virginia Neto and LaNelle Marie Bainer found in a study of forty prisons that four had family visiting programs that allow the inmate, her legal husband, and her children to be together, often in a mobile home or apartment, for periods ranging up to seventy-two hours.[53]

Although most states do not allow women to keep their newborns in prison with them for more than a few weeks, some innovative programs make longer periods possible. The emphasis on community corrections as it developed in the 1970s gave rise to programs that permitted mothers and their children to live together in halfway houses. These programs have not expanded as much as it was first thought they might, in part because the presence of children upset the routine of the facility.

Mothers, like other incarcerated women, often have legal problems, and parental rights figure among them. This problem was reviewed in *Los Angeles County Department of Adoptions* v. *Hutchinson* (1977), in which the court upheld an order terminating a mother's parental rights because she was incarcerated—even though she had objected to the order and had tried to make contact with her daughter. During the mother's four and a half years of confinement, the child had lived in six foster homes. The court ruled against the mother because she would not be released immediately, even though the case came to trial only six months before she was to be released.[54]

In view of the gains made by women in the United States during the past decade, one might have expected the differences between men's and women's prisons to diminish. But the proportion of arrested women who are sent to prison is rising, and their offenses are becoming more like those of men. One wonders whether a new generation of researchers will find future female

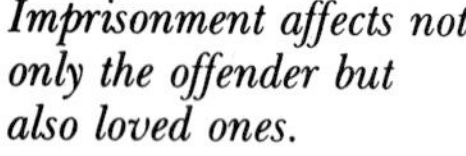
Imprisonment affects not only the offender but also loved ones.

Conditions in some prisons may lead to violence.

inmates engaged in the nurturing enterprise of the pseudofamily and female prisons being run in a different manner.

Prison violence

A recipe for violence: confine in cramped quarters 1,000 men, some of whom have a history of engaging in violent interpersonal acts, restrict their movement and behavior, allow no contact with women, guard them with guns, and keep them in this condition for an indefinite period of time. Although collective violence such as the riots at Attica, Rahway, and Santa Fe, New Mexico, has become well known to the public, little has been said about the interpersonal violence that exists in U.S. prisons. Each year more than 100 inmates die and countless others are assaulted. Still other prisoners live in a state of constant uneasiness, always on the lookout for persons who might subject them to homosexual demands, steal their few possessions, and in general increase the pangs of imprisonment.

It is true that some of the violence is perpetrated by the guards and not always in the performance of their duties. But, most violence in prison occurs among inmates. Although not all institutions have records of violence, and although the correctional systems of some states seem more prone to violence than others, the problem is one that all must face. The presence of assaultive behavior in our correctional institutions raises serious questions for administrators, criminal justice specialists, and the general public. What are the nature and causes of prison violence, and what can be done about it? What is the responsibility of the state to the prisoners whom it holds in these institutions?

Causes of prison violence

Too often explanations of prison violence merely recite the deprivations and injustices of life in penal institutions. Mention is usually made of the rules enforced by brutal guards, the loss of freedom, and the boredom. Although such statements may identify the speaker as humane, they usually do not explain the violence itself. Incarceration is undoubtedly a harsh and painful experience, but it need not be intensified by physical assault or death at the hands of fellow inmates. Data from Western Europe appear to show that incidents of prison violence are relatively few there,[55] a finding that may result from the fact that those countries also have lower rates of violent crime. Hence the relative lack of violence may be explained by the character of the general population and the culture that inmates bring with them to the prison.

Alternatively, the absence of assaultive behavior may stem from a more effective prison management that provides few opportunities for attacks. The open character of European, especially Scandinavian, prisons is given as a reason for the lower incidence of violence; yet many penologists feel that the granting of additional freedoms may in fact raise the probability of violence because contacts with the outside world allow for ease in the smuggling of contraband (drugs, food, weapons) that may spark conflict. In addition, the contrast of freedom with the regimentation of the institution may increase the frustrations of confinement. Obviously, the causes of assaultive behavior in our penal institutions are more complex than simple answers suggest.

Inmate population. The extent to which violent behavior occurs in prisons is partly a function of the types of people who are incarcerated and the characteristics they bring to prison with them. A study of violent and nonviolent prisoners at San Quentin Prison in California revealed that violent prisoners tended to share the following characteristics:

- They were younger than nonviolent prisoners.
- They were predominantly black or Hispanic.
- Their homes had been broken by death or divorce before they reached age 16.
- They had either no father figure in their lives or a succession of father figures; if a father was present, he was alcoholic, abusive, or criminal.
- Their measured grade level was 6.5 or lower.
- They had a history of institutional violence and disciplinary infractions.
- They had been in prison at least once before or had been committed to jail or juvenile detention at least twice.
- They had first been arrested before the age of 12.
- Their first arrest had been for robbery or burglary.[56]

Of the personal characteristics that bear on the problem of violence in prisons, three stand out: age, attitudes, and relationships with the outside world.

Age. Studies have shown that young people, both inside and outside prison, are more prone to violence than their elders. The group most likely to commit violent crimes is made up of males between the ages of fifteen and twenty-four. Not surprisingly, 96 percent of adult prisoners are males with an average age at the time of admission of twenty-seven years.[57] Prisoners committed for crimes of violence are generally a year or two younger than the average. Not only do the young have greater physical strength, they lack those commitments to career and family that are thought to restrict antisocial behavior. In addition, many young men have difficulty defining their position in society; thus many of their interactions with others are interpreted as challenges to their status. "Machismo," the concept of male honor and the sacredness of one's reputation as a man, has a bearing on violence among the young. To be macho is, for one thing, to have a reputation for physically retaliating against those who make slurs on one's honor. The potential for violence among prisoners with these attributes is obvious.

Attitudes. One of the sociological theories advanced to explain crime is that among certain economic, racial, and ethnic groups there is a "subculture of violence."[58] This view argues that persons brought up in such a subculture are accustomed to violent behavior in their families and among their peers. Arguments are settled and decisions made by the fist rather than by verbal persuasion. The environment forms attitudes about the way one should act, and these attitudes are brought into the prison as part of an inmate's heritage.

Relationships with the outside world. In recent years the influence of outside groups on prison violence has been documented. Studies have shown that in some states, many inmates were members of street gangs that engaged in violent rivalry with other gangs. Identification with the gang was maintained in prison because fellow members were often in the same institution. The gang wars of the streets are often continued in prison. In the prison system of California, racial-ethnic gangs have been linked to many acts of violence during the past few years.[59] Although the gangs are small, they are tightly organized and have even been able to kill opposition gang leaders housed in other institutions.

Institutional structure. It is not enough to point to the personal characteristics of inmates as the cause of prison violence. The social and physical environment of the institution also plays a part. Such variables as the physical size and condition of the prison, the pangs of imprisonment, and the relations between inmates and staff all have a bearing on violence.

Physical setting. The gray walls of the fortress prison certainly do not create a likely atmosphere for normal interpersonal relationships. In addition, the prison that houses up to 3,000 inmates presents problems of both crowding and management. The massive scale of some institutions provides opportunities for aggressive inmates to hide weapons, carry out private justice, and engage in other illicit activities free from supervision. As the prison population rises and the personal space of each inmate is decreased, we may expect an increase in antisocial behavior.

Pangs of imprisonment. The many restrictions on freedom make prison a painful experience. The bland diet, absence of the opposite sex, numbing daily routine, physical confinement, and lack of purposive activity are all thought to contribute to aggressive behavior.

Inmate–staff relations. As we have seen, the staff is greatly dependent on the inmate society for the functioning of the prison. The degree to which inmate leaders are allowed to take matters into their own hands may have an impact on the amount of violence among inmates. When prison administrators run a tight ship, security is maintained within the institution so that rapes do not occur in dark corners, "shivs" (knives) are not made in the metal shop, and conflict among inmate groups does not take place. "A prison should be

---

Incident

The guys were fooling around and grabbing me by the ass. He said I was a pussy and he was going to break me. So I picked him up and threw him against the wall. When he came off the wall I just beat the pulp out of him. I kind of just lost my head and I know that if I get in that state I'm really going to break because, you know, after a while it builds up. You can't take it any longer.

Source: Daniel Lockwood, "Maintaining Manhood: Prison Violence Precipitated by Aggressive Sexual Approaches," paper presented at the 1978 annual meeting of the Academy of Criminal Justice Sciences, Dallas, p. 17.

---

the ultimate exemplar of 'defensible space.' It should be an irreducible and primary principle of prison administration that every inmate is entitled to maximum feasible security from physical attack."[60]

In sum, prisons must be made safe places. Because the state puts offenders there, it has a responsibility to prevent violence and maintain order. These purposes may conflict with the goals of correction and restriction of freedom. If violence is to be excluded from prisons, limitations may have to be placed on movement within the institution, contacts with the outside, and the right to choose one's associates. These measures may seem to run counter to the goal of producing men and women who will be accountable when they return to society. Albert Cohen has stated this dilemma well:

> We must acknowledge that prisons contain a lot of people morally prepared and by experience equipped to take advantage of opportunities to dominate, oppress, and exploit others. The problem of the prison—to construct a system of governance that reconciles freedom with order and security—is also the problem of civil society.[61]

Prisoners' rights

The name Martin Sostre can be found in much of the literature of prison reform. A Black Muslim, Sostre has been incarcerated almost continuously in the prisons of the New York State's Department of Correctional Services since 1952. During this period he has been engaged in constant litigation, often while in solitary confinement, to secure religious liberties for Black Muslim prisoners, to limit some of the "more outrageously inhumane" aspects of solitary confinement,[62] and to obtain damages under the Civil Rights Act of 1871[63] for abuses that he has suffered at the hands of prison officials. His persistence is truly amazing because each attempt has brought him into further conflict with the prison administration. As a result, the conditions of his own incarceration have become more restricted. A federal court recognized in

Close-up: . . . *On the Yard*

Just then a line of fish began to enter through the gate at the head of the yard, and they moved closer to search for familiar faces among the new arrivals, as well as to draw some measure of security from the awkward uncertainty of the fish, their skins bleached dead white in the county jail, their hair mutilated from the amateur barbering they practiced on one another. Red saw one man he thought he might know. An old man, wrinkled as a prune, bald except for a few strands still straggling across his white scalp, who moved with the indefinable air of one who had entered many strange jails and prisons, and found them all much the same. His face was oddly familiar to Red, but for a long moment he couldn't summon a name, or place this old con in either space or time, then he suddenly remembered a kid he had always paired off with to chop cane, or pick cotton, his running mate in the Southern prison farm where he'd pulled his first jolt. Anson Meeker. The name came back over the years, and he saw a cocky kid grinning at him from the other side of the row as they worked furiously through the last hours of the afternoon to just make their task, having spent the morning coasting while they planned in excited whispers the big scores they'd take off once they were free.

Source: Malcolm Braly, *On the Yard* (Boston: Little, Brown, 1967). Reprinted by permission of Knox Burger Associates.

1970 that Sostre was sent to solitary confinement and kept there not because of any serious infraction of the rules of prison discipline but rather because of his

> legal and Black Muslim activities during his 1952–1964 incarceration, because of his threat to file a law suit against the Warden to secure his right to unrestricted correspondence with his attorney and to aid his codefendant, and because he is unquestionably a black militant who persists in writing and expressing his militant and radical ideas in prison.[64]

That such prisoners as Sostre, George Jackson, and Eldridge Cleaver were able to obtain judicial notice of the conditions of their incarceration represented a major shift in American law. Until the 1960s, the courts, with few exceptions, took the position that the internal administration of prisons was an executive, not a judicial, function. They maintained a hands-off policy with regard to corrections. Judges accepted the view that they were not penologists and that their intervention would be disruptive of prison discipline. The view was a continuation of a position taken more than a century earlier by a Virginia court that said in *Ruffin* v. *Commonwealth* (1871) that the prisoner "has, as a consequence of his crime, not only forfeited his liberty, but all his personal rights except those which the law in its humanity accords to him. He is for the time being the slave of the state."[65] Even in 1951, in a case involving the "bird man of Alcatraz" (*Stroud* v. *Swope*), a federal circuit judge declared: "We think it well settled that it is not the function of the courts to superintend the treatment and discipline of persons in penitentiaries, but only to deliver from imprisonment those who are illegally confined."[66]

With the civil rights movement of the 1960s and the expansion of due process by the Supreme Court, prisoner groups and their supporters pushed to secure inmate rights. In many ways, some expressed the belief that prisoners were—like blacks, women, and the handicapped—a deprived minority whose rights were not being protected by the government. To achieve such protection, the American Civil Liberties Union and various legal services agencies, including the federally funded Office of Economic Opportunity, began to counsel prisoners. Clinic programs for law students and committees of the American Bar Association soon discovered that their services were needed. Alliances were formed between prisoners and groups outside the institutions that could promote the redress of inmates' grievances in the courts.

The most far-reaching departure from the hands-off policy occurred in 1964 when the Supreme Court ruled in *Cooper* v. *Pate* that prisoners are entitled to the protections of the Civil Rights Act of 1871.[67] Because of this decision, the federal courts now recognize that prisoners are *persons* whose rights are protected by the Constitution, and prisoners in both state and federal institutions may challenge the conditions of their confinement in the federal courts. As James Jacobs has pointed out, "just by opening a forum in which prisoners' grievances could be heard, the federal courts destroyed the custodian's absolute power and the prisoners' isolation from the larger society. And the litigation in itself heightened prisoners' consciousness and politicized them."[68]

As a result of this decision and others, the amount of prisoner-inspired litigation in the courts skyrocketed. In 1969, for example, the Supreme Court ruled (*Johnson* v. *Avery*) that prison officials could not prohibit one inmate from acting as a jailhouse lawyer for another inmate unless the state provided the inmate with free counsel to pursue a claim that rights had been denied.[69] By the mid-1970s inmates and wardens had learned that in the view of the courts "a prisoner is not wholly stripped of constitutional protection when he is imprisoned for crime" and that "there is no iron curtain drawn between the Constitution and the prisoners of this country."[70]

The first successful cases concerning prisoner rights involved the most excessive of prison abuses: brutality and inhuman physical conditions. In 1967, for example, the Supreme Court invalidated the confession of a Florida inmate who had been thrown naked into a "barren cage," filthy with human excrement, and kept there for thirty-five days.[71] Gradually, however, prison litigation has focused more directly on the daily activities of the institution, especially on the administrative rules that regulate inmates' conduct. The result has been a series of court decisions in three general areas of the law. Probably the greatest gains have been made in the upholding of such First Amendment rights as the free exercise of religion. Fourth Amendment protections against unreasonable searches and seizures have been upheld in some circumstances. Courts have found the conditions of confinement in some prisons to be in violation of the Eighth Amendment's protection against cruel and unusual punishments, and have required that some of the elements of due process be included in the disciplinary procedures of institutions. Finally, prisoners have been successful in challenging individual situations in which the conditions of confinement as defined by the Civil Rights Act have been violated.

First Amendment rights

Because the Supreme Court has long maintained that the First Amendment holds a special position with respect to the Constitution, it is not surprising that litigation concerning prisoner rights has been most successful in this area. The First Amendment to the Constitution guarantees freedom of speech, press, assembly, petition, and religion. Many of the restrictions of prison life—access to reading materials, censorship of mail, and some religious practices—have been challenged by prisoners in the courts.

Since 1970 the federal and state courts have extended the rights of free-

---

Freedom of Speech

1. *Mail. Procunier* v. *Martinez* (1974). Censorship of mail is allowed only when there is a substantial governmental interest in maintaining prison security, and when the restrictions are not greater than those necessitated by security.
2. *Media access. Saxbe* v. *Washington* (1974). Rules prohibiting individual interviews with members of the press are justified to prevent the enhancement of the reputations of some inmates.
3. *Association. Jones* v. *North Carolina Prisoners' Labor Union* (1977). Regulations of the department of corrections prohibiting solicitation of membership, group meetings, and bulk mailings to members were upheld as consistent with the legitimate operational considerations of the institution.

---

dom of speech and expression to prisoners and have required correctional administrators to show why restrictions on these rights must be imposed. The result has been that communication between inmates and the outside world has markedly increased. It is only when officials have been able to prove that limitations on speech are necessary and when they have proved that an inmate poses a threat to himself or herself, other inmates, or the staff that courts have supported these institutional rules.

The First Amendment also prevents Congress from making laws respecting the establishment of religion or prohibiting its free exercise. The history of the Supreme Court's interpretation of this clause has been long and complex, and its application to the prison setting is no exception. Freedom of religion is enshrined in the Constitution, and religion itself has been described as an important tool for rehabilitation. Even so, the courts have been cautious. Although freedom of belief has not been challenged, challenges concerning the free exercise of religion have caused the judiciary some problems, especially when the practice may interfere with prison routine.

The arrival of the Black Muslim religion in prisons holding large numbers of urban blacks set the stage for litigation demanding that this group be granted the same privileges as other faiths (special diets, access to clergy and religious publications, opportunities for group worship). Many prison administrators believed that the Muslims were primarily a radical political group posing as a religion, and they did not grant them the benefits accorded to persons who practiced "standard" religions.

In an early case (*Fulwood* v. *Clemmer,* 1962), the U.S. District Court of the District of Columbia ruled that correctional officials must recognize the Muslim faith as a religion and not restrict members from holding services. It did not accept the view of the commissioner of corrections that the Muslims were a "clear and present danger."[72] In the only prisoner-religion case to reach the Supreme Court, *Cruz* v. *Beto* (1972), the justices declared that it was discriminatory and a violation of the Constitution for a Buddhist prisoner to be denied opportunities to practice his faith comparable to those accorded fellow prisoners who belonged to conventional religions.[73]

In many respects, Muslims and other prisoners have succeeded in gaining some of the rights considered necessary for the practice of their religion. There is no accepted judicial doctrine in this area, however, and courts have varied in their willingness to order institutional policies changed to meet Mus-

---

Freedom of Religion

1. *Belief. Theriault* v. *Carlson* (1977). The Church of the New Song, founded by a prisoner, sought to hold services and engage in other practices. The federal court ruled that the First Amendment does not protect so-called religions that tend to mock established institutions and are obvious shams and whose members are devoid of religious sincerity.
2. *Practice. Gittlemacker* v. *Prasse* (1970). The state must give an inmate the opportunity to practice his religion but is not required to provide a clergyman.
3. *Equal protection. Cruz* v. *Beto* (1972). Officials may not discriminate by withholding from prisoners who adhere to other than conventional beliefs the opportunity to practice their religion.

---

lim requests. This one religious minority, however, has managed to break new legal ground in matters dealing with both the First Amendment and other constitutional issues.

Fourth Amendment rights

Upon entering a correctional institution, prisoners surrender most of their rights under the Fourth Amendment. It must be emphasized that the amendment prohibits "unreasonable" searches and seizures; thus regulations reasonable in light of the institutions' needs for security and order may be justified. The courts have not been active in extending Fourth Amendment protections to prisoners. In 1984 the decision in *Hudson* v. *Palmer* upheld the right of officials to search cells and confiscate any materials found.[74]

The Fourth Amendment opinions by the Supreme Court illustrate the difficulty of balancing the right to privacy and institutional needs. Body searches have been harder for administrators to justify than cell searches, for example, but they have been upheld when they are part of a clear policy demonstrably related to an identifiable legitimate institutional need, and when they are not intended to humiliate or degrade. Courts have ruled that staff members may not supervise inmates of the opposite sex during bathing or use of the toilet, or carry out strip searches of the opposite sex. Any inconvenience that administrators may experience in ensuring that the supervisor is of the same sex as the inmate does not justify such intrusion. Yet the right of female guards to "pat down" male prisoners, exclusive of the genital area, has been upheld. These cases illustrate the lack of clear-cut constitutional principles in such matters.

Eighth Amendment rights

The Eighth Amendment's prohibition of cruel and unusual punishments has been tied to prisoners' rights in relation to their need for decent treatment and minimal standards of health. Most claims involving the failure of prison administrators to provide minimal conditions necessary for health, to furnish reasonable levels of medical care, and to protect inmates from assault by other prisoners have taken the form of suits against specific officials. Wardens have been held liable for maintaining an environment that is suitable to prisoners' health and security, but recoveries of damages by inmates have been rare.

Unreasonable Searches and Seizures

1. *Strip searches. Bell* v. *Wolfish* (1979). Strip searches, including body-cavity searches after contact visits, may be carried out when the need for the search outweighs the invasion of personal rights.
2. *Privacy in toilet and shower areas. Lee* v. *Downs* (1981). Staff members may not supervise inmates of the opposite sex in toilets or showers, whether or not this rule is inconvenient to the administration.
3. *Cell searches. United States* v. *Hitchcock* (1972). A warrantless search of a cell is not unreasonable, and documentary evidence found as a result is not subject to suppression. It is not reasonable to accord a prison cell the same level of privacy as a home or automobile.

Three principal tests have been applied by courts to determine whether conditions violate the protection of the Eighth Amendment: whether the punishment shocks the general conscience of a civilized society; whether the punishment is unnecessarily cruel; and whether the punishment goes beyond legitimate penal aims.

There have been several dramatic cases in which prison conditions were shown to be so bad that judges have demanded change. On 13 January 1976 Federal Judge Frank M. Johnson, Jr., issued a precedent-setting order listing a set of minimal standards for the prisons of Alabama and threatened to close all the institutions in that state if the standards were not met. He appointed a special committee empowered to oversee implementation of the standards. Judge Johnson's opinion was that imprisonment in Alabama constituted cruel and unusual punishment because prison conditions were barbaric and inhumane.[75]

In an earlier suit (*Holt* v. *Sarver*, 1970), a federal court cited the notorious Cummins Farm Unit of the Arkansas State Penitentiary as being in violation of the Eighth Amendment. The court cited the use of inmates as prison guards and said that prisoners had a constitutional right of protection by the state while they were incarcerated. As the judges noted, a system that relies on trusties for security and that houses inmates in barracks, leaving them open to "frequent assaults, murder, rape and homosexual conduct," is unconstitutional.[76]

In *Hutto* v. *Finney* (1978), the Supreme Court upheld a lower court decision that confinement in Arkansas's segregation cells for more than thirty days was cruel and unusual. In that decision the Court also summarized three principles with regard to the Eighth Amendment: courts should (1) consider the totality of conditions of confinements, (2) specify in remedial orders each factor that contributed to the violation and for which a change would be necessary to remove the unconstitutionality, and (3) specify, when appropriate, minimum standards that if met would remedy the entire constitutional violation. The Court has also indicated, however, that courts should defer to correctional officials and legislators unless they find that conditions are "deplorable" or "sordid."[77]

Of particular concern to correctional officials have been rulings that overcrowding is in violation of the Eighth Amendment and must be ended. Among the conditions that the courts have found to violate the Constitution is the crowding of inmates into cells that afford each person less than sixty square feet of floor space. These orders have come at a time when the size of prison populations has skyrocketed in most jurisdictions. Many conditions that violate the rights of prisoners may be corrected by administrative action, train-

Cruel and Unusual Punishments

1. *General conditions. Holt* v. *Sarver* (1970). Conditions in the Arkansas State Penitentiary were inherently dangerous and therefore unconstitutional. The state could not protect inmates from injury or abuse.
2. *Medical conditions. Estelle* v. *Gamble* (1976). Deliberate indifference to serious medical needs of prisoners constitutes an unnecessary and wanton inflicting of pain, prohibited by the Eighth Amendment.

ing programs, or a minimal expenditure of funds, but overcrowding requires an expansion of facilities or a dropping of the intake rate. Prison officials have no control over the capacities of their institutions or over the number of offenders that are sent to them by the courts. New facilities are expensive, and they require appropriations by legislatures and, often, approval of bond issues by voters. In some states, reduction of prison overpopulation has only added to jail populations later. In other states, building programs have not been able to keep pace with the number of new prisoners.

Due process in prison discipline

The idea that disciplinary procedures should be carried out according to the dictates of due process of law probably strikes most traditional wardens and guards as absurd. Yet in a series of decisions the Supreme Court began to insist that procedural fairness be included in the most sensitive of institutional decisions: the process by which inmates are sent to solitary confinement and the method by which "good time" credit may be lost because of misconduct.[78]

Administrative discretion in determining disciplinary procedures can usually be exercised within the prison walls without challenge. The prisoner is physically confined, lacks communication with the outside, and is legally in the hands of the state. Further, either formal codes stating the rules of prison conduct do not exist so that all may know them or the rules are written vaguely. Disrespect toward a correctional officer, for example, may be called an infraction of the rules but not be defined. Normally, disciplinary action is taken on the word of the correctional officer, and the inmate has little opportunity to challenge the charges.

In a case concerning welfare recipients (*Goldberg* v. *Kelley,* 1970), the Supreme Court ruled that all citizens have due process rights when there is the possibility that they may suffer loss through arbitrary or erroneous decision making by officials.[79] The Supreme Court has said further that certain procedural rights must be granted to inmates: the rights to receive notice of the complaint, to have a fair hearing, to confront witnesses, to be assisted in preparing for the hearing, to be given a written statement of the decision. The courts have not always been consistent, however, and have emphasized the need to balance the rights of the prisoner against the interest of the state. The Supreme Court has noted the special problems associated with the prison environment, "where tension is unremitting, frustration, resentment, and despair are commonplace." In 1974 (*Wolff* v. *McDonnell*) it issued an opinion guaranteeing prisoners the fundamental rights of due process discussed above.[80]

Due Process in Prison Discipline

1. *Procedures. Wolff* v. *McDonnell* (1974). The basic elements of procedural due process must be present when decisions are made concerning the disciplining of an inmate.
2. *Counsel. Baxter* v. *Palmigiano* (1976). Although due process must be accorded, there is no right to counsel in a disciplinary hearing.
3. *Escape defense. United States* v. *Bailey* (1980). A prisoner who justifies his escape from prison on the grounds of duress or necessity for self-protection must show that he attempted to surrender to an authority.

As a result of the Supreme Court decisions, rules have been established in most prisons to provide some elements of due process in disciplinary proceedings. In many institutions, a disciplinary committee receives the charges, conducts hearings, and decides guilt and punishment. Such committees are usually made up of administrative personnel, but sometimes inmates or citizens from the outside are included. Even with these protections, the fact remains that prisoners are powerless and may fear further punishment if they too strongly challenge the disciplinary decisions of the warden.

Conditions of confinement

One of the major breakthroughs with regard to prisoners' rights was the 1964 decision (*Cooper* v. *Pate*) that inmates have protections under the Civil Rights Act of 1871.[81] This piece of post–Civil War legislation asserts that

> every person who, under color of any statute, ordinance, regulation, custom, or usage, of any State or Territory subjects, or causes to be subjected, any citizen of the United States or other person within the jurisdiction thereof to the deprivation of any rights, privileges, or immunities secured by the Constitution or laws, shall be liable to the party injured in an action at law, suit in equity, or other proper proceedings for redress.

Under this provision prisoners may file suit in a federal district court requesting injunctive and compensatory relief against such abuses as brutality by guards, inadequate nutritional and medical care, theft of personal property, and violence by other inmates. One result of the willingness of the courts to hear these suits has been a startling increase in the number of cases filed in federal courts under this act: from 218 in 1966 to 17,000 in 1983.

Although the number of filings appears extremely high, the number of successful suits is much smaller. One reason is that most cases are *pro se* (without the assistance of counsel) and are often filed in error because of misinterpretations of the law. In some courts, clerks evaluate the complaints and dismiss most without docketing them. In others, all complaints are docketed but most are quickly dismissed following motions by the defense (correctional officials usually) for a summary judgment by the court. As a result of these screening processes, few of the actions filed by prisoners receive significant review. There have nonetheless been many cases in which individual

---

Discipline—Due Process?

Prisoners often have their privileges revoked, are denied right of access to counsel, sit in solitary or maximum security or lose accrued "good time" on the basis of a single, unreviewed report of a guard. When the courts defer to administrative discretion, it is this guard to whom they delegate the final word on reasonable prison practices. This is the central evil in prison. It is not homosexuality, nor inadequate salaries, nor the cruelty and physical brutality of some of the guards. The central evil is the unreviewed administrative discretion granted to the poorly trained personnel who deal directly with prisoners. The existence of this evil necessarily leads to denial of communication, denial of right to counsel and denial of access to the courts. Prison becomes a closed society in which the cruelest inhumanities exist unexposed.

Source: Philip J. Hirschkop and Michael A. Millemann, "The Unconstitutionality of Prison Life," *Virginia Law Review* 55 (1969): 811–12. Reprinted by permission of Fred B. Rothman & Company.

---

inmates have been able to secure redress of their grievances in the courts. Some have received monetary compensation for neglect; others have been given the medical attention they desired; still others have elicited judicial orders that end certain correctional practices.

Courts may respond to prisoners' requests in specific cases, but judges cannot possibly oversee the daily activities within institutional walls. As a result of the increase in conditions-of-confinement cases, correctional authorities have taken steps to ensure that fair procedures are followed and that unconstitutional practices are forgone. Publication of institutional rules, obligations, and procedures is one of the first and most important steps required to meet this goal. In a number of states, correctional ombudsmen—officials who investigate complaints—have been employed. Modeled after an office in Sweden that looks after the interests of individual citizens in their dealings with governmental bureaucracies, the prison ombudsman is usually not a correctional employee but brings the grievances of individual prisoners to the attention of the administrators and often negotiates between competing parties so that a solution may be found. Mediation, arbitration, and other forms of dispute settlement have been used as ways of coming to terms with inmate grievances without resort to formal litigation.

In *Bell* v. *Wolfish* (1979) a majority of the Supreme Court signed an opinion that may signal a return, at least in part, to the hands-off policy.[82] The *Bell* case involved the Metropolitan Correctional Center (MCC) in New York City, a newly constructed federal detention unit designed with the most advanced and innovative features. The inmates, however, complained that soon after it opened it was overcrowded, regulations prevented them from receiving hardcover books from anyone but a publisher, they were not allowed to receive packages containing items available in the jail's commissary, and they were not allowed to be present during shakedown inspections of their quarters. The Supreme Court found no constitutional violations in the conditions at MCC and declared that management of the facility should be left to correctional personnel. It is too early to tell whether the Burger Court intends to sustain the hands-off policy of earlier decades or whether *Bell* v. *Wolfish* was merely a single detour from the trend toward the protection of the constitutional rights of prisoners.

Alternatives to litigation

Although decisions of the U.S. Supreme Court make headlines, they are only the very tip of the iceberg. Almost 17,000 suits are filed annually in the lower federal courts by prisoners contesting aspects of their confinement under the Civil Rights Act of 1871. A very high proportion of these cases are deemed frivolous by the judiciary and are dismissed. Of the remainder, only a few are decided in such a way that their effects extend beyond the individual litigants. It is generally recognized that many prisoners have legitimate claims that must be heard, yet correctional specialists, judges, and even prisoners are raising questions about the suitability of litigation as the means of resolution. Litigation is viewed as a cumbersome, costly, and often ineffective way to handle such claims.

Although most suits filed by prisoners are dismissed before trial, enough remain to give correctional officials pause. They are aware that such suits may require them to expend time and resources in litigation; that they may be sued personally; and that their authority may be eroded. Many nonfrivolous suits concern small monetary sums, and the time devoted to them by administrators and attorneys is disproportionate to the amounts involved. Even if correctional officials are able to "win" the suits against them, leadership may be hurt when wardens, rather than the responsible staff members, are placed on trial. In the adversarial process plaintiff and defendant—prisoner and warden—are legally and symbolically equal, a fact that does not go unnoticed by those whom the warden must supervise.

From the perspective of the prisoner, litigation in the federal courts may be a difficult route to an uncertain outcome. Experience has shown that most prisoners who complain about the unconstitutionality of the conditions of their confinement face three problems: (1) they generally lack representation, (2) constitutional standards are difficult to meet, and (3) implementation of successful suits is formidable.

Given the drawbacks of resolving prisoner grievances in an equitable and effective manner through litigation, it is apparent that there is a need for noncourt mechanisms that can help settle the group of cases that may be called "administrative." These are the nonfrivolous, non-class-action complaints filed by state prisoners under the Civil Rights Act of 1871. They are the cases that may be meritorious yet that under current conditions are being screened out by judicial clerks or that are unable to withstand motions for summary judgment—cases, for example, in which prisoners typically request changes in mail or visiting procedures, compensation for lost personal property, transfer of a guard, a special diet, or any one of the multiple complaints that arise in an institutional environment.

Correctional systems are increasingly instituting alternative means of resolving disputes in the hope of avoiding litigation. With passage in 1980 of the Civil Rights of Institutionalized Persons Act (CRIPA), Congress lent its support to "encouraging the development and implementation of administrative mechanisms for the resolution of prisoner grievances within institutions." The mechanisms include inmate grievance procedures, ombudsmen, mediation, legal assistance, external review bodies, and inmate councils. Experience has shown that such mechanisms are preferable to litigation for several reasons:

- Informal procedures are more appropriate than the complex and often unwieldy judicial process for dealing with the kinds of complaints raised by prisoners.
- Concrete issues underlying abstract complaints may be more thoroughly explored through an informal dispute-resolution mechanism.
- Nonadjudicatory processes are less costly and less time-consuming than litigation.
- The mutual agreement produced by some of the informal mechanisms can have a more meaningful impact than a solution imposed by a court.

Impact of the prisoners' rights movement

Although activists in the prisoners' rights movement have often written despairingly about the possibility of achieving institutional change through litigation, and although individual inmates may feel that after working patiently with a legal services attorney they have been unable to realize an improvement in the conditions of their confinement, there is no question that American corrections has responded to judicial intervention during the past decade. Allen Breed, former director of the National Institute of Corrections, has said, "The role of courts over the past fifteen years in acting as a catalyst for much needed change in our nation's prisons cannot be overemphasized."[83]

It is difficult to measure accurately the impact of the prisoners' rights movement. There are problems in identifying the impact of specific cases and in defining success or failure in many instances. How can one show that correctional bureaucracies have responded to litigation? Individual cases may make only a dent in such organizations, but over time basic shifts may occur.

The prisoners' rights movement can probably be credited with some general changes in American corrections during the past decade. The most obvious are concrete improvements in institutional living conditions and administrative practices. Law libraries and legal assistance are now generally available; communication with the outside is easier; religious practices are protected; inmate complaint procedures have been developed; and due process requirements are emphasized. Prisoners in solitary confinement undoubtedly suffer less neglect, and, although overcrowding in many institutions is still a major problem, one suspects that the conditions described in the film *Brubaker* no longer exist in any U.S. prison. This is not to say that prison life has become a bed of roses, but conditions have been improved and the more brutalizing elements have been diminished.

The prisoners' rights movement has also had an impact on correctional officials. Surely the threat of suit and public exposure has placed many in the correctional bureaucracy on guard. It can be argued that this wariness has merely led to the increased bureaucratization of corrections, with staff now required to "document" their actions as a means of protecting themselves from suits. Jacobs quotes one prison manager as saying that "court-imposed due process requirements have made extensive and time-consuming documentation a necessity."[84] On the other hand, judicial intervention has forced corrections to rethink many of the existing procedures and organizational structures. As part of the wider changes in the "new corrections," new administrators, increased funding, reformulated policies, and improved management procedures were, at least in part, influenced by the prisoners' rights movement.

The extension of constitutional rights to prisoners has by no means been speedy, and the courts have spoken only to limited areas of the law. The impact of these decisions on the actual behavior of correctional officials has not yet been measured, but evidence suggests that court decisions have had a broad effect. Because prisoners and their supporters have asserted their rights, wardens and their subordinates may be holding back from traditional disciplinary actions that might result in judicial intervention.

In sum, after two hundred years of judicial neglect of the conditions under which prisoners are held, courts have begun to look more closely at the situation. Building on some of the decisions of the Warren Court in the civil rights field, the Supreme Court under Chief Justice Burger has taken a particular interest in corrections. Although practices in state prisons have been the object of much litigation in state courts, the judges in the federal courts have been the most active.

The prison law library inspires close attention.

Summary

During the past decade there have been calls for reduced use of imprisonment as a form of the criminal sanction. Some critics have argued that prisons are not humane, that they are schools of crime, that they do not rehabilitate, and that they are used to oppress minorities. Yet the size of the prison population in the United States continues to reach new record levels.

Although the prison facility depicted in old movies remains, many of the characteristics of the convict population, the programs, the guards, and the rules have changed. The social relations of the convict world have therefore changed, too. The most striking feature of many contemporary prisons is the racial composition of the population and the tensions arising from it. In many institutions, convict solidarity against the "screws" has been broken. Instead, observers report, the convict society has divided along racial lines, with resultant societal instability and the potential for intergroup clashes.

Chapter 15 has described life inside adult prisons. A wide variety of correctional institutions exists, and none is exactly the same as another. Each has its own traditions, organization, and environment, though in many respects the characteristics described apply generally to most institutions. Prisons play an important role in the criminal justice system and their operations need to be understood.

That incarceration will continue to be widely used is clear. To reduce the size of the correctional bureaucracy and tear down the physical plants devoted to incarceration would be all but impossible. As the National Advisory Commission has said, "the prison . . . has persisted, partly because a civilized nation could neither turn back to the barbarism of an earlier time nor find a satisfactory alternative."[85]

For discussion

1. You have just accepted a position as a correctional officer. What should be your attitude toward the prisoners?
2. What are some of the problems likely to arise between custodial and treatment staffs?
3. Should prisoners have the right to organize a union? What might the impact of a prisoners' union be on the inmate society?
4. What can be done to reduce prison violence?

5. You have just arrived in a maximum security prison to serve a sentence. What goals and fears are you likely to have? How would you cope with them?

For further reading

Braly, Malcolm. *On the Yard.* Greenwich, Conn.: Fawcett, 1972.
Carroll, Leo. *Hacks, Blacks, and Cons.* Lexington, Mass.: Lexington Books, 1974.
Heffernan, Esther. *Making It in Prison.* New York: Wiley, 1972.
Irwin, John. *The Felon.* Englewood Cliffs, N.J.: Prentice-Hall, 1970.
Jackson, George. *Soledad Brother: The Prison Letters of George Jackson.* New York: Bantam Books, 1971.
Lombardo, Lucien X. *Guards Imprisoned.* New York: Elsevier, 1981.
Sheehan, Susan. *A Prison and a Prisoner.* Boston: Houghton Mifflin, 1978.

Notes

1. John Irwin, *Prisons in Turmoil* (Boston: Little, Brown, 1980), p. 1.
2. Donald Clemmer, *The Prison Community* (New York: Holt, Rinehart & Winston, 1940); Gresham M. Sykes, *The Society of Captives* (Princeton: Princeton University Press, 1958).
3. James Jacobs, *Stateville* (Chicago: University of Chicago Press, 1977).
4. President's Commission on Law Enforcement and Administration of Justice, *Task Force Report: Corrections* (Washington, D.C.: Government Printing Office, 1967), p. 46.
5. Erving Goffman, *Asylums* (Garden City, N.Y.: Anchor Books, 1961).
6. Donald R. Cressey, "Limitations on Organization of Treatment in the Modern Prison," in *Theoretical Studies in Social Organization of the Prison,* ed. Richard A. Cloward, Donald R. Cressey, George H. Grosser, Richard McCleery, Lloyd E. Ohlin, Gresham M. Sykes, and Sheldon L. Messinger (New York: Social Science Research Council, 1960), pp. 78–110.
7. Sykes, *Society of Captives,* p. 49.
8. Ibid., p. 53.
9. Ibid., p. 56; Note, "Bargaining in Correctional Institutions: Restructuring the Relation between the Inmate and the Prison Authority," 81 *Yale Law Journal* 726 (1972).
10. Richard Korn and Lloyd W. McCorkle, "Resocialization within Walls," *Annals* 293 (1954): 191.
11. Edwin H. Sutherland and Donald R. Cressey, *Criminology* (Philadelphia: Lippincott, 1970), p. 536.
12. Sykes, *Society of Captives,* pp. 84–90.
13. Irwin, *Prisons in Turmoil,* p. 32.
14. John Irwin, *The Felon* (Englewood Cliffs, N.J.: Prentice-Hall, 1970), p. 67.
15. Ibid., pp. 67–79.
16. Ibid., p. 78.
17. Ibid., p. 75.
18. Vergil L. Williams and Mary Fish, *Convicts, Codes, and Contraband* (Cambridge, Mass.: Ballinger, 1974), p. 50.
19. Susan Sheehan, *A Prison and a Prisoner* (Boston: Houghton Mifflin, 1978), p. 90.
20. Williams and Fish, *Convicts, Codes, and Contraband,* p. 50.
21. Sheehan, *Prison and a Prisoner,* pp. 92–93.
22. Daniel Glaser, "The Effectiveness of Correctional Education," *American Journal of Correction* 28 (1966): 4–9.
23. Gordon Hawkins, "Prison Labor and Prison Industries," in *Crime and Justice,* ed. Michael Tonry and Norval Morris, vol. 5 (Chicago: University of Chicago Press, 1983), p. 90.
24. National Advisory Commission on Criminal Justice Standards and Goals, *Task Force Report: Corrections* (Washington, D.C.: Government Printing Office, 1973), p. 388.
25. Justice System Improvement Act of 1979, P.L. 96–157, 93 Stat. 1167, 1215.
26. Hawkins, "Prison Labor and Prison Industries," p. 108.
27. Robert Martinson, "What Works? Questions and Answers about Prison Reform," *Public Interest* 35 (Spring 1974): 22; Walter C. Bailey, "Correctional Treatment: An Analysis of One Hundred Correctional Outcome Studies," *Journal of Criminal Law, Criminology and Police Science* 57 (1966): 153–60.
28. Ted Palmer, *Correctional Intervention and Research* (Lexington, Mass.: D. C. Heath, 1978); Francis T. Cullen and Karen E. Gilbert, *Reaffirming Rehabilitation* (Cincinnati: Anderson, 1982).
29. Lucien X. Lombardo, *Guards Imprisoned* (New York: Elsevier, 1981), p. 6.
30. James Jacobs and Norma Crotty, "The Guard's World," in *New Perspectives on Prisons and Imprisonment,* ed. James B. Jacobs (Ithaca, N.Y., Cornell University Press, 1983), p. 135.
31. Cressey, "Treatment in the Modern Prison," p. 103.
32. Jacobs, *Stateville,* pp. 179–80.

33. James B. Jacobs and Harold G. Retsky, "Prison Guard," in *The Sociology of Corrections,* ed. Robert G. Leger and John R. Strattion (New York: Wiley, 1977), p. 54.
34. Leo Carroll, "Race, Ethnicity, and the Social Order of the Prison," in *The Pains of Imprisonment,* ed. Robert Johnson and Hans Toch (Beverly Hills, Calif.: Sage, 1982), p. 185.
35. U.S. Department of Justice, Bureau of Justice Statistics, *Report to the Nation on Crime and Justice* (Washington, D.C.: Government Printing Office, 1983), p. 95.
36. David Duffee, "Careers in Criminal Justice: Corrections," in *Encyclopedia of Crime and Justice,* ed. Sanford H. Kadish (New York: Free Press, 1983), p. 1232.
37. Gordon Hawkins, *The Prison* (Chicago: University of Chicago Press, 1976), p. 106.
38. Josefina Figueira-McDonough, Alfreda Iglehart, Rosemary Sarri, and Terry Williams, *Females in Prison in Michigan, 1968–1978* (Ann Arbor: University of Michigan, Institute for Social Research, 1981), p. 15.
39. U.S. Department of Justice, Bureau of Justice Statistics, *Sourcebook of Criminal Justice Statistics* (Washington, D.C.: Government Printing Office, 1983), p. 145.
40. Esther Heffernan, *Making It in Prison* (New York: Wiley, 1972), p. 88.
41. Rose Giallombardo, *Society of Women: A Study of a Women's Prison* (New York: Wiley, 1966), pp. 102, 103.
42. Heffernan, *Making It in Prison,* pp. 41–42.
43. Irwin, *The Felon,* pp. 67–80.
44. James G. Fox, *Organizational and Racial Conflict in Maximum-Security Prisons* (Lexington, Mass.: Lexington Books, 1982), pp. 100, 102.
45. Ibid., p. 100.
46. Ruth M. Glick and Virginia V. Neto, *National Study of Women's Correctional Programs,* U.S. Department of Justice, National Institute of Law Enforcement and Criminal Justice (Washington, D.C.: Government Printing Office, 1977).
47. Ralph R. Arditi; Frederick Goldberg, Jr.; M. Martha Hartle; John H. Peters; and William R. Phelps, "The Sexual Segregation of American Prisons," *Yale Law Journal* 82 (May 1973):1243n, 1271.
48. Martha Wheeler, "The Current Status of Women in Prisons," in *The Female Offender,* ed. Annette M. Brodsky (Beverly Hills, Calif.: Sage, 1975), p. 87.
49. Judith Resnik, "Should Prisoners Be Classified by Sex?" in *Criminal Corrections: Realities and Ideas,* ed. Jameson W. Doig (Lexington, Mass.: Lexington Books, 1983), p. 111. See Todaro v. Ward, 431 F. Supp. 1129 (S.D.N.Y. 1977).
50. Sharon L. Fabian, "Women Prisoners: Challenge of the Future," in *Legal Rights of Prisoners,* ed. Geoffrey P. Alpert (Beverly Hills, Calif.: Sage, 1980), p. 176; Glover v. Johnson, 478 F. Supp. 1075 (E.D. Mich. 1979).
51. Barefield v. Leach, Civ. No. 10282 (D.C.N.Y. 1974).
52. Brenda G. McGowan and Karen L. Blumenthal, *Why Punish the Children?* (Hackensack, N.J.: National Council on Crime and Delinquency, 1978), p. 3.
53. Virginia V. Neto and LaNelle Marie Bainer, "Mother and Wife Locked Up: A Day with the Family," *Prison Journal* 63 (Autumn–Winter 1983): 124.
54. Fabian, "Women Prisoners," p. 185.
55. John P. Conrad, "Violence in Prison," *Annals* 364 (1966): 113–19.
56. Laurence A. Bennett, "The Study of Violence in California Prisons: A Review with Policy Implications," in *Prison Violence,* ed. Albert K. Cohen, George F. Cole, and Robert G. Bailey (Lexington, Mass.: Lexington Books, 1975), p. 150.
57. Robert M. Carter, Richard A. McGee, and E. Kim Nelson, *Corrections in America* (Philadelphia: Lippincott, 1975), p. 114.
58. Marvin E. Wolfgang and Franco Ferracuti, *The Subculture of Violence: Towards an Integrated Theory in Criminology* (London: Tavistock, 1967).
59. James W. L. Park, "The Organization of Prison Violence," in *Prison Violence,* ed. Cohen et al., p. 89.
60. James B. Jacobs, "Prison Violence and Formal Organization," in *Prison Violence,* ed. Cohen et al., p. 79.
61. Cohen, "Prison Violence," in *Prison Violence,* ed. Cohen et al., p. 19.
62. Sostre v. Rockefeller, 312 F. Supp. 863 (1970).
63. 42 U.S.C., sec. 1983.
64. Hawkins, *The Prison,* p. 139.
65. Ruffin v. Commonwealth, 62 Va. 790 (1871).
66. Stroud v. Swope, 187 F. 2d 850 (9th Circ. 1951).
67. Cooper v. Pate, 378 U.S. 546 (1964).
68. James B. Jacobs, "The Prisoners' Rights Movement and Its Impacts, 1960–1980," in *Crime and Justice,* ed. Norval Morris and Michael Tonry, vol. 2 (Chicago: University of Chicago Press, 1980), p. 433.
69. Johnson v. Avery, 393 U.S. 483 (1969).

70. Pell v. Procunier, 94 S.Ct. 2800 (1974).
71. Brooks v. Florida, 389 U.S. 413 (1967).
72. Fulwood v. Clemmer, 206 F. Supp. 370 (1962).
73. Cruz v. Beto, 92 S.Ct. 1079 (1972).
74. Hudson v. Palmer, 52 L.W. 5052 (1984).
75. Pugh v. Locke, 406 F. Supp. 318 (1976).
76. Holt v. Sarver, 300 F. Supp. 825 (E.D. Ark. 1970).
77. Hutto v. Finney, 98 S.Ct. 1861 (1979).
78. Wolff v. McDonnell, 94 S.Ct. 2963 (1974).
79. Goldberg v. Kelley, 397 U.S. 254 (1970).
80. Wolff v. McDonnell, 94 S.Ct 2963 (1974).
81. Cooper v. Pate, 42 U.S.C. 1983 (1976).
82. Bell v. Wolfish, 99 S.Ct. 1861 (1979).
83. As cited in Jacobs, "Prisoners' Rights Movement," p. 453.
84. Ibid., p. 458.
85. National Advisory Commission on Criminal Justice Standards and Goals, *Task Force Report: Corrections* (Washington, D.C.: Government Printing Office, 1973), p. 343.

Prison and beyond

You can write to your lawyer, your preacher and six other people, the sergeant was saying, only remember—your letters are censored so watch what you say. No. 69656, born Donald Payne, sat half listening in the front row in his gray prison coveralls, his eyes idling over the chapel wall from the flag to the sunny poster—GOOD MORNING WORLD. Nothing controversial about prison in your letters, the sergeant was saying. "Let's keep this personal, fellas, your parents get a lot of this on TV." No sex either—"Let's keep this down to personal matters, fellas, we're not in a Sunday school class but let's keep our hands above the table." No double talk, no jive talk, no hep talk, no profanity. And fellas—don't risk your mail privileges by breaking the rules. "The more mail you get, the easier it will be for you," the sergeant was saying. "It gets depressing in here."

Payne had been marched aboard a black sheriff's bus by early light only a few days before and had been shipped with sixteen other County Jail inmates to Joliet Prison, a 112-year-old yellow-stone fortress on the Des Plaines River forty miles southwest of Chicago. The transfer, typically, was accidental. Payne was to have been held in jail until this month, when he is due in court on charges of having violated his old probation for burglary, but the papers got mixed up and he was bused out early. He didn't really mind, since by then he hated the jail so badly that even the pen seemed preferable. And so, on February 5, he checked into Joliet's diagnostic center, drew his number and his baggy coveralls, was stripped, showered and shorn and began four to six weeks of testing to see which prison he would fit into best and what if anything it could do for him. Coveralls aren't much, but Payne, sharp, flipped the collar rakishly up in back and left the front unbuttoned halfway down his chest. Cool. Good morning, world.

Except in this world, as the sergeant of the guard said, it gets depressing. Illinois's prisons, like most of America's, had fallen over the years into a sorry state of neglect until Richard B. Ogilvie made them a campaign issue at some hazard in his 1968 gubernatorial campaign and got elected. Ogilvie since has trusted the problem to a new director of corrections, Peter Bensinger, the 34-year-old heir to the Brunswick Corp. money and position, and Bensinger—an energetic beginner—has put Joliet and its neighbor, Stateville, under the management of reform-minded pros. The new team has begun upgrading the guard force, putting new emphasis on correction as against punishment and doing away with some of the pettiest dehumanizing practices; now, for example, they no longer shave a man's body hair off when he arrives, and prisoners are called to the visiting room by name, not by number. "We've taken everything else from the man," says Stateville's 33-year-old warden, John Twomey. "If we take his name, too, how can he feel he's a worthwhile human being?"

But money is short and reform painfully slow. "We've moved ahead about fifty years," says Joliet's black warden, Herbert Scott. "We're now up to about 1850." And 1850 dies hard. Donald Payne, a child of the city streets, is rousted from his bunk at 6 A.M., fed breakfast at 7, lunch at 10, dinner at 3 and locked back in his cell before sundown. The language of the place confirms his devalued humanity: men are "tickets," meals are "feeds." The battery of IQ, personality and aptitude tests he is undergoing at Joliet are exhaustive but of uncertain value, since the prisons still lack programs enough to make use of what the tests tell them. So Payne is consigned to his bars and his bitterness. In Joliet at mealtime 900 men sit at long stone tables spooning food out of tin dishes and facing an enormous American flag—"to instill patriotism," a young staff psychologist explained wryly. A visitor asked how the men respond to this lesson. "I imagine," said the psychologist, "that they think, 'F—— the flag.' "

It is here that society has its last chance with the Donald Paynes—and here that the last chance is squandered at least as often as not.

The lesson of People vs. Payne and countless cases like it is that the American "system" of justice is less a system than a patchwork of process and improvisation, of Sisyphean labor and protean inner motives. Payne was arrested on chance and the tenacity of two policemen; was jailed for want of money while better-off men charged with worse crimes went free on bail; was convicted out of court and sentenced in a few minutes' bargaining among overworked men who knew hardly anything about him. It cannot be said that justice miscarried in People vs. Payne, since the evidence powerfully suggests his guilt and the result was a penalty in some relation, however uneven, to the offense. But neither was justice wholly served—not if the end of justice is more than the rough one-to-one balancing of punishments with crimes.

The punishment most commonly available is prison, and prisons in America have done far better at postponing crime than at preventing or deterring it. Joliet is a way station for Payne. He may wind up at Pontiac, where most younger offenders do their time; he would prefer the company of older men at Stateville, a vintage 1925 maximum-security prison with cells ranged in enormous glassed-in circles around a central guard tower. He says that in either event he will stick to his cell and go for early parole. "When I get out," he told his mother once in jail, "I'll be in church every day." Yet the odds do not necessarily favor this outcome: though the Illinois prisons have made progress toward cutting down on recidivism, a fifth to a third of their alumni get in trouble again before they have been out even a year. "Well," said Payne, smiling that half-smile at a visitor during his first days as No. 69656, "I'm startin' my time now and I'm on my way home." But his time will be a long and bleak one, and, unless luck and will and the last-chance processes of justice all work for him, Donald Payne may be home right now.

Source: Peter Goldman and Don Holt, "How Justice Works: The People vs. Donald Payne," *Newsweek,* 8 March 1971, pp. 20–37.

Community Corrections: Probation and Parole

16

It is often said that the way a society deals with its criminals reflects the forces operating in that society. As we have seen, the invention of the penitentiary paralleled and incorporated the values of nineteenth-century religion and culture. Prisons were intended to instill discipline and good work habits and to give inmates an opportunity to reflect on their misdeeds. During the early part of the twentieth century, with the rise of the social and behavioral sciences, correctional institutions became places for treatment of offenders. Reflecting the belief that science could solve the criminal's problems, rehabilitative programs were incorporated into most prison systems. During the social and political turmoil of the late 1960s, a new shift took place in assumptions about how offenders should be handled. The change reflected forces at work both in society and in the criminal justice system—the questioning of the worth of educational, social, and political institutions; the extension of the civil rights movement to prisoners; and the belief that treatment programs have not been successful. This new shift became known as "community corrections"; it emphasized the reintegration of the offender into the community.

The general underlying premise for the new directions in corrections is that crime and delinquency are symptoms of failures and disorganizations of the community as well as of individual offenders.

PRESIDENT'S COMMISSION ON LAW ENFORCEMENT AND ADMINISTRATION OF JUSTICE

American corrections has not underscored incarceration to the exclusion of other forms of the criminal sanction; almost three times as many adult offenders are under supervision in the community as are in prison. Even during the nineteenth-century reform period it was recognized that supervision in the community was a more appropriate means to bring about the desired change in some offenders. The development of probation by John Augustus and the transplantation of parole from England in the 1880s best exemplify this approach. Until the 1950s, however, many states still relied more on incarceration than on probation and parole, and it was not until the 1960s that a variety of community alternatives was developed. Within a decade, the emphasis on community corrections had greatly accelerated.

Often referred to as the "new" corrections, the movement attracted the attention of penological groups and was broadly supported by the President's Commission on Law Enforcement and Administration of Justice. As that body noted, crime results from community disorganization and the inability of some persons to receive and be sustained by the stable influences and resources necessary to live as productive members of society.

> These failures are seen as depriving offenders of contacts with the institutions

that are basically responsible for assuring development of law-abiding conduct: sound family life, good schools, employment, recreational opportunities, and desirable companions. . . . The substitution of deleterious habits, standards, and associates for these strengthening influences contributes to crime and delinquency.[1]

Chapter 16 discusses the assumptions of community corrections and the alternatives to incarceration that have been proposed. Probation and parole, the most widely used means to supervise offenders in the community, will be examined in detail, and the reader should evaluate these approaches in order to decide whether they will succeed where others have failed. Is community corrections the latest penological fad, is it merely something that has developed out of disillusionment with other attempts, or does it appear to have some relevance for the future? With the recent rise in determinate and mandatory sentences, increased prison populations, and less government funding for treatment alternatives, does community corrections have a chance?

Community corrections: assumptions

community corrections Programs designed to rehabilitate offenders through probation, diversion, halfway houses, and parole.

Community corrections aims at building reintegrating ties between the offender and the community: the restoration of family links, help in obtaining employment and education, and development of a sense of place and pride in daily life. The Reintegration Model of corrections assumes that the offender must change, but it also recognizes that factors within the community that might encourage criminal behavior (unemployment, for example) must change too. Where the Rehabilitation Model focuses on social and psychological imperfections in the criminal, the Reintegration Model emphasizes that social conditions in the community have an influence on the criminal as well.

Three factors are usually cited in support of community corrections. First, community supervision is cheaper than incarceration. Varying in cost from state to state, prison is usually estimated to be three to ten times more expensive than community supervision. Second, if rehabilitation is measured by recidivism rates, prison is no more effective than community supervision. In fact, some studies show that just being in prison raises the offender's potential for recidivism. Third, incarceration is more destructive to both the offender and society. In addition to the pangs of imprisonment and the deleteriousness of prison life, there is the suffering of family members, particularly that of the children of women offenders.

Supported by the President's Commission, the National Council on Crime and Delinquency, the Law Enforcement Assistance Administration, and the American Correctional Association, community corrections received a great boost in the late 1960s. Central to this approach is the concept of "least restrictive alternative," the belief that the criminal sanction should be applied only to the minimum extent necessary to meet the community's need for protection, the gravity of the offense, and the rehabilitative needs of the offender. It was argued that personal freedom is so valuable that it is unjust to incarcerate individuals needlessly when community-based alternatives can achieve correctional goals. Supporters of community corrections urged that no new prisons be built, states were given funds to develop halfway houses and work release and furlough programs, and the emphasis of probation and parole shifted from supervision to the provision of services that would help to reintegrate the offender into the community.

Three trends in the new penology reflect the emphasis of community corrections: (1) smaller institutions near urban areas, (2) special programs designed to create links between the offender and the community, and (3) increased use of probation and parole. All of these features of community corrections reflect the belief that actions should be taken to increase offenders' opportunities to succeed in law-abiding activities and to reduce their contact with the criminal world.

Smaller institutions

Massive stone fortress prisons dot the American rural landscape. In some states such institutions hold upwards of 4,000 prisoners. Any institution that large must be run rigidly and impersonally. Critics of the modern prison stress that it is an unnatural environment because social contacts are limited to felons and because the total regulation of life prevents prisoners from making choices and being responsible for their actions. Some argue that treatment programs cannot be effective under these conditions and that offenders cannot acquire the values necessary to remain law-abiding after their release.

As the makeup of the prison population in most states has changed during the past thirty years from white to urban black, the isolated sites of most prisons have created further problems. Guards recruited from the local population have been unable to interact successfully with prisoners whose cultural backgrounds contrast so greatly with their own. In addition, the location of prisons in such places as Attica, New York; Stateville, Illinois; and Soledad, California, makes it almost impossible for inmates to maintain contact with their families, most of whom reside in distant cities.

The new corrections also challenges the accent in American criminal justice on the prolonged incarceration of felons. Reformers argue that only a few convicted felons need to be set apart under maximum security conditions and that most would be candidates for successful rehabilitation if they were placed in smaller institutions in their communities. Toward this end an effort has been made to prevent the construction of new prisons designed in the traditional style.

Services in the community

To ease the transition of released offenders from prison to the community and to assist parolees, the new corrections asserts that a variety of educational, medical, and social services should be available. Provision of these services should involve not only correctional authorities but also public and private agencies. Finally, the services should be made available to those under supervision in the community, such as probationers and parolees, as well as to offenders who are still incarcerated.

Work release, educational release, furloughs, and halfway houses have all been used in community corrections programs to assist both parolees and incarcerated offenders preparing for release. The community correctional center, usually a halfway house in a selected neighborhood, is used in a num-

Halfway house residents meet to discuss a member's problem.

ber of states. Often residents are allowed to work in the community but must return at night. The center is viewed as a place for short-term intensive treatment before release under supervision. In addition, it provides services to parolees who may have employment or other needs.

The provision of services in the community rather than in the prison is believed to be in the interest of both offenders and society. The offender is able to develop community ties at a cost to the taxpayer that is much less than the cost of prison. Further, the presence of offenders in the neighborhood has an important impact on the community because citizens may develop positive attitudes toward inmates, a fact that should assist the reintegration process. Consistent with the belief that corrections should prepare offenders for return to society, the new treatment approach emphasizes services that will help the reintegrative process and provide a gradual adjustment to freedom.

Increased use of probation and parole

Community corrections appeals to people who believe that most prison terms in the United States are too long and that institutionalization has important negative consequences for the offender's reintegration. In this view, incarceration of some types of offenders not only imposes punishment out of proportion to the crime but unnecessarily exposes first-timers to the prison "crime factory," so that the possibility of successful reintegration is reduced. If the objective is to avoid the negative impact of separation from the community, severing of family ties, and the culture of the prison, for many offenders the alternative of probation may be more beneficial. Most probationers do well with minimal supervision. Some penologists therefore suggest that many offenders who are now incarcerated might also succeed under intensive community supervision.

The remainder of this chapter will describe and attempt to evaluate the major alternatives that constitute community corrections: probation, work and educational release, furloughs, residential programs, and parole. Each approach attempts to deal with the problems of a particular type of offender in a somewhat distinctive manner, and each has organizational characteristics of its own. As each mode is discussed, consider its likely contribution to the goals of corrections. Is community corrections effective? What changes might be made?

Probation: correction without incarceration

probation A suspension of the sentence of a convicted offender under conditions that permit the offender to serve the sentence imposed by the court in the community under supervision.

Probation denotes the conditional release of the offender into the community under supervision. The American Bar Association Project on Criminal Justice Standards describes it as "a sentence not involving confinement which imposes conditions and retains authority in the sentencing court to modify the conditions of sentence or to re-sentence the offender if he violates the conditions."[2] Often the sentencing judge imposes a prison term but then suspends execution of it and places the offender instead on probation. Unlike the parolee, the probationer need not enter prison so long as the conditions set by the court are met. Violations of these terms may cause the probation to be revoked and the prison sentence carried out.

One of the most important assumptions of probation is that, given the personal characteristics of the offender and the nature of the crime committed, incarceration would be more damaging to the offender and to the community than permitting the offender to remain in the community under supervision. This belief is supported by studies showing that offenders who have been incarcerated are thereafter labeled "criminals," with the result that recidivism often follows their release. Probation is also supported on the grounds that offenders whose crimes are not serious deserve a second chance—one misstep should not blight their futures. With a probation officer's help, the offender can retain community ties, undergo treatment if there is a medical or psychological basis for the criminality, and continue to be self-supporting and to provide for dependents.

Origins of probation

Although historical antecedents for probation can be found in the procedures of reprieves and pardons of early English courts, John Augustus, a prosperous Bostonian, has become known as the world's first probation officer. By persuading a judge in the Boston Police Court to place a convicted offender in his custody for a brief period, Augustus was able to assist his probationer so that the man appeared to be rehabilitated when he returned for sentencing.

Probation continued to be a voluntary activity in Boston until 1878, when it was formalized; the mayor was given the power to hire officers who would report directly to the criminal courts. Massachusetts developed the first statewide probation system in 1880, and by 1920 twenty-one other states had followed suit. The federal courts were authorized to hire probation officers in 1925, and by the beginning of World War II forty-four states had implemented the concept.

Like the penitentiary, probation is an American contribution to penology. Today over 60 percent of offenders in the United States are placed on probation. At any one time there are an estimated one million probationers. Such groups as the National Council on Crime and Delinquency have urged that probation be the disposition of choice for most first offenders, although several questions have been raised about probation's effectiveness. Some observers say that to place an offender on probation nowadays is to do almost nothing. Given the huge caseloads of probation officers, offenders are given very little guidance, supervision, or assistance. Philadelphia criminal court judge Lois Forer has remarked: "Probation is not a penalty. The offender continues with his life style. . . . If he is a wealthy doctor, he continues with his practice; if he is an unemployed youth, he continues to be unemployed. Probation is a meaningless rite; it is a sop to the conscience of the court."[3]

Organization

Probation may be viewed as a form of corrections, but in many states it is administered by the judiciary, and it is very much a local affair. A study by the National Council on Crime and Delinquency found that although twenty-six states are formally responsible for all probation services (see table 16.1), it is the locally elected county judges who are really in charge. Randy Polisky, first vice-president of the American Probation and Parole Association, asserts, "The state might issue edicts, commands and paychecks but in many places, the judges appoint probation officers, and let's face it, the judges run probation."[4] This controversy persists. Some persons argue that judges know little about corrections and that probation increases the administrative duties of the overworked courts. Others contend that probationers would be unduly stigmatized if they were under the supervision of the corrections department.

Perhaps the strongest argument in favor of judicial control is that probation works best when there is a close relationship between the judge and the supervising officer. Proponents say that judges need to work with probation officers they can trust, whose presentence reports they can accurately evaluate, and whom they can rely on to report on the success or failure of individual

John Augustus

John Augustus (1785–1859) was a Boston bootmaker who became a self-appointed probation officer, thereby developing the concept of probation as an alternative to incarceration. His initial probation effort occurred in the Boston Police Court in 1841 when he posted bail for a man charged with being a common drunkard. Because his philanthropic activities made Augustus a frequent observer in the courts, the judge was willing to defer sentencing for three weeks and the man was released into Augustus' custody. At the end of this brief probationary period, the man convinced the judge of his reform and therefore received a nominal fine. The concept of probation had been born.

Continuing his interest in criminal justice reform, Augustus was frequently present in Boston courts, acting as counsel and furnishing bail. He found homes for juvenile offenders and frequently obtained lodging and employment for adults accused or convicted of violating Boston's vice or temperance laws. Between 1842 and 1858 he bailed out 1,946 people, making himself liable to the extent of $243,235 and preventing these individuals from being held in jail to await trial. He reported great success with his charges and asserted that, with help, most of them eventually led upright lives. Since Augustus belonged to no charitable or philanthropic society, his primary sources of financial support were his own business and voluntary contributions. He never received a salary from any organization. Augustus persisted in his efforts, and as a result, criminal justice gained a practice that has since become commonplace.

TABLE 16.1 Number of state, local, and combined state-local governments responsible for adult probation, by branch of government

	Level of government			
Branch of government	***State***	***Local***	***State and local***	***Total***
Executive	22	0	1	23
Judicial	1	3	3	7
Executive and judicial	3	0	18	21
All branches	26	3	22	51

Source: Belinda Rodgers McCarthy and Bernard J. McCarthy, *Community-Based Corrections* (Monterey, Calif.: Brooks/Cole, 1984), p. 99.

cases. These views have been extensively argued in the literature. At the same time, judges may well be interested also in their ability to appoint probation officers who are responsive to the local political system.

Yet it is in the executive branch of government that corrections and other human service agencies are found. Probation officers have a greater chance of using such services for their clients' benefit if they have direct access to the services. In a number of states this consideration has led to the combining of probation and parole services in the same agency. Proponents of this move argue that it increases effectiveness and efficiency because community supervision is involved with both types of clients. Others point out, however, that probationers are quite different from parolees, for they have not developed criminal lifestyles and do not have the same problems of reintegration with the community.

Probation services

Probation officers are expected to be both police personnel and social workers. In addition to assisting the judiciary with presentence investigations and reports, they are to supervise clients in order to keep them out of trouble and to help them secure treatment and other services. Not surprisingly, individual officers may emphasize one role over the other, and the potential for conflict is great. But studies have shown that most probation officers have backgrounds in social service and are partial to the treatment role.

Probation originated as a humanitarian way of giving first-time and minor offenders a second chance. To this end, probation officers were to use a casework model and intervene in the client's life, guiding him or her toward the "right" path. The offender was not only to refrain from criminal acts but also to behave in a morally acceptable fashion. Early officers were thus actively "involved in all levels of the offender's lifestyle—family, religion, recreation, employment, free time."[5] They were to provide a role model or moral leadership for those who had been in trouble.

With the rise of psychology in the 1920s, the probation officer continued as caseworker, but the emphasis was now on therapeutic counseling in the office rather than on assistance in the field. As Martin Schwartz, Todd Clear, and Lawrence Travis point out, this shift in emphasis brought a number of important changes. First, the officer was no longer primarily a community supervisor charged with enforcing a particular morality. Second, the officer became more of a clinical social worker whose goal was to help the offender

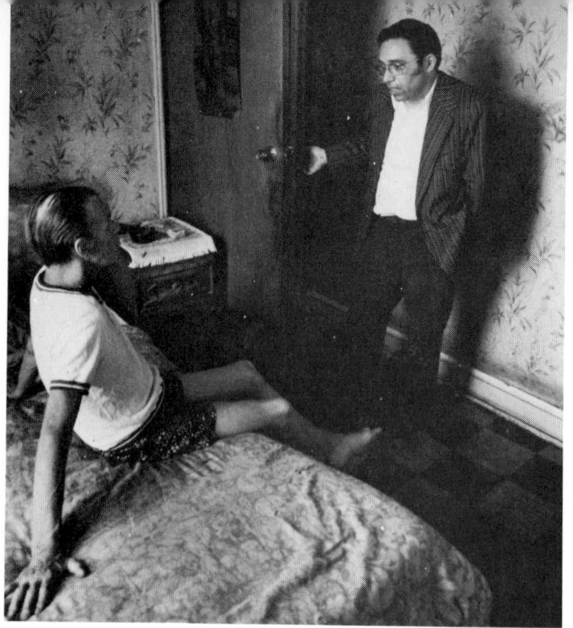

Supervision in the community is a component of parole.

solve psychological and social problems. Third, the offender was expected to become actively involved in the treatment program. As in other aspects of the Rehabilitation Model, the probation officer had to be given extensive discretion to diagnose the problem and treat it.[6]

During the 1960s, perhaps reflecting the emphasis of the "War on Poverty," a third shift occurred in the orientation of probation work. Rather than counseling offenders in their offices, probation officers provided them with concrete social services, such as assistance with employment, housing, finances, and education. Probation officers backed away from direct involvement in the lives of offenders, on the assumption that when offenders exercised more control over their own goals and activities, their chances of adjustment to the community were improved. Finally, instead of being a counselor or therapist, the probation officer was to be an advocate, dealing with private and public institutions on the offender's behalf.

One of the continuing issues related to probation services is the size of the caseload that is both efficient in the use of resources and effective in the guidance of offenders. The oversized caseload is usually identified as one of the major obstacles to successful operation of probation. As the President's Commission pointed out, "differences in individual probationers' needs require different amounts of time and energy from a probation officer."[7] The 50-unit caseload established in the 1930s by the National Probation Association was reduced to 35 by the President's Commission in 1967; yet in some places the average caseload is 150, and in extreme cases it rises to more than 300. Recent evidence seems to indicate, however, that the size of the caseload is less significant than the nature of the supervision experience, the classification of offenders, the professionalism of the officer, and the services available from the agencies of correction.

Because the probation officer is also responsible for filing presentence reports, assistance and supervision have obviously to be on a catch-as-catch-can basis. In some urban areas, probationers are merely required to telephone or mail reports of their current residence and employment. Under such conditions, it must be asked which justification for the criminal sanction—punishment, rehabilitation, deterrence, incapacitation—is being realized. If none is being realized, the offender is getting off free.

Probation is at a crossroads. Some people advocate a continuation of the service-provider orientation; others object that the individual probation officer cannot possibly know all that is required in the specialized fields of human services to be effective. Thus it is urged that the probation unit contract with community agencies for these services and that the probation officer return to supervision. Finally, there is dissatisfaction with probation itself. In many quarters it is argued that, especially in urban areas, it does nothing. Because of huge caseloads and indifferent officers, probation is regarded as a "free ride" by offenders, who can easily avoid supervision and check in only perfunctorily with the officers. Such a situation does little for crime control.

New approaches

The past decade has seen experiments with a number of new approaches to probation. Many of these programs lasted only for the period of their initial funding, while others have been fully incorporated into probation systems. The following examples are given merely to indicate the flavor of the alternatives being tried.

Probation subsidy. Developed originally in California in 1967, probation subsidy has been explored in other jurisdictions as well.[8] Because of the high cost of incarceration, the California correctional authority instituted a financial incentive program to encourage counties to keep offenders on probation and out of institutions. The state gave $4,000 per offender to counties that created "special supervision" caseloads to ensure that the most difficult cases would get more than perfunctory supervision. It has been estimated that during the eleven years of the program, 45,000 individuals were kept out of state institutions and the county probation departments earned more than $200 million, which they were able to use to establish a variety of supervision alternatives.

Special-supervision probation officers were trained in new techniques, given smaller caseloads, and provided with technical resources. Although these measures increased their professional standing and perhaps their effectiveness, other probation officers resented the newly elevated status of their colleagues. In 1978, after prolonged opposition from police chiefs and county sheriffs, the subsidy law was repealed. Evaluators of the project have given it mixed marks, with some questioning the extent to which the subsidy itself reduced the prison population. Research has suggested that the prison population was already starting to drop in 1968 and that incarceration rates in counties that did and did not receive subsidies differed little.

Volunteers in probation. In keeping with one of the original goals of probation outlined by John Augustus, "to befriend," a volunteers-in-probation program was begun in 1959 by Judge Keith Leenhouts in Michigan. Citizens volunteer as sponsors of probationers on a one-to-one basis under the overall supervision of probation officers. This has become one of the most widely copied programs in the nation. Because probation officers with heavy caseloads cannot give individual service, the volunteer assists by serving as a friend to the offender, being an advocate, and seeking out whatever is needed. The program has not escaped controversy; some probation officers see it as an intrusion into their domain. It is also asserted that citizens who want to help are often "taken in" by manipulative offenders.

Pretrial services. As we saw in chapter 10, criminal justice has developed a variety of arrangements for the pretrial release or diversion of individuals arrested but not fully processed through the system. Many cases are diverted through an informal agreement with the prosecutor to withhold the filing of charges, and in some locations formal organizations have been created to assist persons who have been arrested for first or minor criminal offenses. Release on recognizance allows suspects who lack bail money to be free in the community while awaiting trial. Probation officers are assigned in many jurisdictions to do the background investigations, collecting the data the judge needs to make a release decision.

In some localities, probation departments provide counseling and other services to individuals awaiting disposition of their cases so that time will not be lost in efforts to reintegrate them into the community. A person who uses these services and meets individually set goals may have initial arrest charges dropped by the court and the record cleared.

Intensive supervision. In response to research findings indicating that a small core of high-risk offenders commits a disproportionate amount of crime and adds to the overcrowded conditions of prisons, various localities have developed programs for the intensive supervision of certain offenders. It is thought that daily contact between the probationer and officer may cut rearrests and may permit offenders who might otherwise go to prison to be released into the community. Yet programs of intensive supervision have been characterized as "old-style" probation, because one officer has only twenty clients and frequent face-to-face contacts are required. Because the intention is to place in the community high-risk offenders who would normally be incarcerated, it is expected that resources will be saved. But questions have been raised about how much difference constant surveillance can make to probationers who also need help to secure employment and to deal with emotional and family situations as well as their own drug or alcohol problems.

A Georgia program requires probationers to meet with a probation officer or a surveillance officer five times a week and to provide 132 hours of community service work, and except in unusual cases imposes a 10 P.M. curfew. It has been noted that officers engaged in intensive supervision are less likely to take a rehabilitative approach toward their clients and instead look upon their jobs as part of the effort to control crime.

An evaluation of the probation experience of those under intensive supervision by federal officers in the San Francisco area indicated that there was little difference in "success" between offenders who were part of a 20-client caseload and offenders who were assigned to the more "normal" load of 70 to 130 clients. In fact, technical violations of probation were higher among the more closely supervised group, an example of the influence of bureaucratic factors on the program.[9]

Revocation of probation

Probationers who violate the provisions of their sentences may be taken to court for further disposition. Often probation is granted in conjunction with a suspended jail or prison sentence. If the terms of probation are not fulfilled, incarceration may follow. Probation officers and judges have widely varying notions of what constitutes grounds for revoking probation. Certainly arrest and conviction for new offenses are grounds, yet some officers contend that technical violations must be considered in connection with a probationer's general attitude and adjustment to the community. Once the officer has decided to call a violation to the attention of the court, the probationer may be arrested or summoned for a revocation hearing. Although revocation for technical reasons was fairly common in the 1950s and 1960s, the contemporary emphasis is on avoiding incarceration except for flagrant and continual violation of the conditions of probation.

Not until 1967 did the Supreme Court of the United States give an opinion concerning the due process rights of probationers at a revocation hearing. In *Mempa* v. *Rhay* it determined that a state probationer had the right to counsel at a revocation proceeding, but nowhere in the opinion does the Court refer to any requirement for a hearing.[10] This issue was addressed by the Court in *Gagnon* v. *Scarpelli* (1973).[11] Here the justices ruled that revocation demands a preliminary and a final hearing. In the preliminary hearing, such elements of due process as the opportunity to appear and present evidence and to confront witnesses are essential. In the final hearing, the minimum requirements of due process must prevail.

Assessing probation

Although probation is under less attack than parole, its effectiveness is being increasingly questioned. Probation produces less recidivism than incarceration, but researchers now wonder if this effect is a direct result of supervision or an indirect result of the maturation process. Most offenders placed on probation do not become career criminals, their criminal activity is short-lived, and they become stable citizens as they become employed and marry. Even most of those who are arrested a second time do not repeat their mistake again. It is disturbing to some observers that intensive supervision may have little influence on the likelihood of "success." What rallies support for probation is its relatively low cost. Estimates vary, but it takes roughly $700 a year to keep an offender on probation and about $15,000 a year to keep one behind bars. We must remember, however, that the type of person who is granted probation is usually a first-time offender who has committed a misdemeanor or minor felony. Most incarcerations come only after several scrapes with the law and perhaps after several periods of probation. Thus, in the United States today, it is generally the "loser" who finds his or her way to prison. If we are really serious about probation as a form of community corrections, we should return to the original idea of John Augustus—to "advise, assist, and befriend." The real challenge of probation is to find the means to keep this promise within the context of a bureaucratic framework and limited resources.

Community programs following release

Community corrections entails continuous evaluation and testing of the offender to ensure that the least-restrictive-alternative goal is being met and that the individual is steadily moved toward reintegration with the community. In pursuit of the latter goal, programs of partial confinement are used to test the readiness of the offender for full release. Throughout the period of correctional supervision staff members must therefore ask such questions as: "Is it necessary for this offender to be held in a maximum security facility, or is he ready for a less structured environment?" "With only a year remaining before she appears before the parole board, should this offender be moved to a halfway house?" "Is work release an option, given the offender's skills?" Notice that community-based corrections assumes that multiple alternatives to incarceration are available, and that the goal is to choose the least restrictive situation consistent with eventual reintegration.

Among the many programs developed to assist offenders in their return to the community, three are especially important: work and educational release, furloughs, and residential programs. Although they are similar in many ways, each offers a specific approach to helping the formerly incarcerated individual reenter the community. This may be a period of anxiety, for the offender must adjust to changes that have taken place in society while a sentence was served. It is believed to be the period of greatest uncertainty as to whether or not the offender returns to crime; to a great extent this depends upon how well the person adjusts to being free.

Transfer of the offender from prison to the community has taken on a new dimension in the states that have adopted the just deserts model of the criminal sanction, with fixed sentences and the abolition of release on parole. No longer is the decision to release a matter for the parole board to consider; rather, correctional authorities have gained new discretionary powers with regard to the reintegration process. In some states, offenders leave prison upon the expiration of their sentence minus good time, and are then required to live under supervision in the community. In other states, a more gradual process has developed, with release first to a halfway house or community center, and then to supervision status. There are some jurisdictions with "home supervision," under which the former inmate lives with his or her family and has contact with a parole officer on a regular basis. What must be emphasized is that in the jurisdiction with reformed sentencing patterns, community corrections has acquired fresh significance.

Work and educational release

work and educational release
The release of inmates from correctional institutions during the day so that they may work or attend school.

Work and educational release programs were first established in Vermont in 1906, but the Huber Act, passed by the Wisconsin legislature in 1913, is usually cited as the model on which such programs are based. By 1972 most states and the federal government had release programs that allowed inmates to go into the community to work or to attend school during the day and return at night to an institution. Although most of the programs are justifiable in terms of rehabilitation, many correctional administrators and legislators like them because they cost little. In some states, a portion of the inmate's employment earnings may even be deducted for room and board. One of the problems of administering the programs is that the person on release is often viewed by other inmates as being privileged, and such perceptions can lead to social troubles within the prison. Another problem is that in some states organized labor complains that jobs are being taken from "free" citizens. Further, the releasee's contact with the community makes it possible for contraband to be brought into the institution. To deal with such bootlegging and to assist in the reintegration process, some states and counties have built special work and educational release units in urban areas.

Furloughs

Isolation from loved ones is one of the pains of imprisonment. Although conjugal visits have been a part of correctional programs in many countries, they have rarely been used in the United States. Many penologists view the ***furlough*** as a meaningful alternative. Consistent with the focus of community corrections, home furloughs for brief periods of time have come into increasing use in the United States. A 1974 survey conducted by *Corrections Magazine* found that all but eleven states had instituted a furlough program for adult offenders and all but five states had one for juvenile offenders.[12] In some states an effort is made to ensure that all eligible inmates are able to use the furlough privilege on Thanksgiving and Christmas. In other states, however, the program has been much more restrictive, and often only those about to be released are given furloughs.

furlough The temporary release of an inmate from a correctional institution for a brief period, usually one to three days, for a visit home. Such programs are designed to maintain family ties and prepare inmates for release on parole.

Furloughs are thought to offer an excellent means of testing an inmate's ability to cope with the larger society. Through home visits, family ties may be renewed and the tensions of confinement lessened. Most administrators also feel that furloughs are good for morale. To the detriment of the program, the general public is sometimes aroused when an offender on furlough commits another crime or fails to return.

Residential programs

Located in a carefully selected neighborhood, the ***community correctional center*** is an institution designed to reduce the inmate's isolation from community services, resources, and support. It may take a number of forms and serve a variety of offender clients. Throughout the country, halfway houses, prerelease centers, and correctional service centers may be found. Most are residential in that offenders are required to live there, although they may work in the community or visit with their families. Others are designed primarily to provide special services and programs for parolees. Often these facilities are established in former private homes or small hotels, which permit a less institutional atmosphere. Individual rooms, group dining rooms, and other homelike features are maintained whenever possible. Note that we are describing true community correctional centers, not merely former jails that were renamed to give the appearance of progress.

community correctional center A correctional institution, usually located in an urban area, housing inmates soon to be released. Such centers are designed to help inmates maintain community ties and thus to promote their reintegration with society.

Halfway houses. The term *halfway house* has been applied to a variety of community correctional facilities and programs. Halfway houses range from secure institutions in the community with programs designed to assist inmates preparing for release on parole to shelters where parolees, probationers, or persons diverted from the system are able to live with minimal supervision and direction. Some halfway houses are organized to deliver special treatment services, such as programs designed to deal with alcohol, drug, or mental problems. A national survey by Edward Latessa and Harry Allen found that there were about 800 halfway houses in the United States, most operated under contract by private organizations, with an average capacity of twenty-five residents. Eight to sixteen weeks was found to be the average length of stay.[13]

As figure 16.1 indicates, there are three models of release or transfer to halfway houses. The offender may be released on parole either directly to a halfway house (model 1) or into a community where a halfway house is available should the parolee need its services (model 3). In model 2 (an increasingly popular alternative) the halfway house is a way station where the offender stays for a time before being released on parole.

Home detention. As prisoners have become more and more crowded, some states have experimented with sentencing offenders to terms of incarceration *in their own homes.* This variation on community corrections gives supervisors some flexibility in determining the extent to which offenders are allowed to venture beyond their homes for work or recreation. Proponents of home detention argue that ties are maintained with family and friends yet the offender is not a threat to the community. Others, however, believe that home detention lessens the symbolic as well as the actual impact of punishment. It is also said that the terms of the sanction are very difficult to enforce, although electronic surveillance devices have been suggested as a means to alert the police when an offender "escapes." Evaluation of these programs is anticipated in the near future.

Problems of residential programs. Not unexpectedly, few neighborhoods want halfway houses or treatment centers for convicts; community resistance has been an important roadblock and has forced the closing of

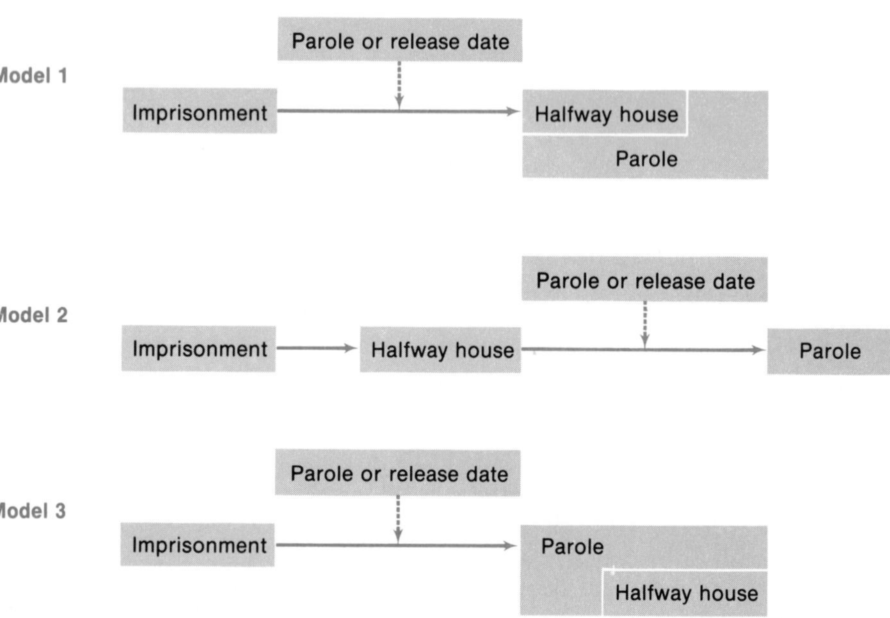

FIGURE 16.1
Three models of release or transfer from prison to halfway house

many facilities. Community corrections, along with programs to deinstitutionalize mental patients and the retarded, has become a major political issue. A 1978 study by the U.S. Bureau of Prisons of approximately 400 private and local-government halfway houses found that 75 percent listed severe to moderate community opposition as the worst problem.[14] One of the results is that the only available facilities are in deteriorating neighborhoods inhabited by the poor, who lack the political power to resist placement of a center in their midst. One wonders whether such locations assist or hinder a former offender.

The future of residential programs is unclear. Originally advocated for both rehabilitative and financial reasons, they do not now seem to be realizing the expected economies. Medical care, education, vocational rehabilitation, and therapy are expensive. Comparisons with incarceration are difficult, but it can probably be said that the costs of quality community programs differ little from those of prisons. The expenditures might be justified if it could be shown that recidivism rates of offenders who have been involved in community treatment were lower, but the available data are not encouraging. One evaluation of a federally administered prerelease guidance center found a recidivism rate of 37 percent among its clients and a 32 percent rate among a control group.[15] The excitement and optimism of the community correctional movement may have been unwarranted. Because of cutbacks in federal funding and resistance by local governments, these programs may be diminished at the very time when they might be helping to relieve the overcrowding in prisons.

Parole: reentry into society

Every year more than 130,000 convicted felons are released from prison and allowed to live, under parole supervision, in the community. Parolees are "the prisoners among us": estimates are that two-thirds of the persons serving criminal sentences are free in the larger society, while only one-third are incarcerated. Seventy-six percent of felons leaving prison are released on ***parole.*** Only felons are released on parole; adult misdemeanors are usually released directly from local institutions on expiration of their sentences. Juvenile offenders are also released under supervision, but the conditions and procedures are markedly different from those for the adult parolee. The importance of parole and its impact on both the criminal justice system and the general public are only now coming to the attention of scholars and planners.

parole
The conditional release of an inmate from incarceration under supervision after a portion of the prison sentence has been served.

Parole is the conditional release of a prisoner from incarceration but not from the legal custody of the state. Offenders who comply with the rules of parole and do not get into further trouble with the law will receive an absolute discharge from supervision at the end of their sentence. If parolees break a rule, parole may be revoked and they will be returned to a correctional facility. Parole rests on three concepts: (1) grace or privilege—the idea that the prisoner could be kept incarcerated but the government extends the privilege of release; (2) contract—the offender promises the government to abide by certain conditions in exchange for being released; and (3) custody—while released from prison the offender is still a responsibility of the government. Parole is thus based on rehabilitative and reintegrative ideals. Most penologists view it as an extension of correctional programs into the community. There is no "right" to parole; it is an earned privilege. Parole authorities are

The parole release decision is made by a "roomful of strangers."

expected to be cautious and return to society only those offenders who are assumed to represent no threat to society.

Parole is often confused with probation. In both, information about offenders is presented to a decision-making authority with power to release them to community supervision under certain specified conditions. If they violate the conditions, they may be placed in or returned to a correctional institution. Parole *differs* from probation in that the parolee has been incarcerated prior to release, while probation is usually granted in place of confinement. The decision to release an offender on parole is usually made by an administrative body; the decision to grant probation is made by the judge who sentences the offender.

Recent changes in parole release

During the past decade a major change has taken place in the manner in which offenders are released from prison into the community. The passage of determinate sentencing laws and the institution of parole guidelines have removed the discretionary aspect of the release decision. In thirty-one jurisdictions—twenty-nine states, the District of Columbia, and the federal system—felons are now released to community supervision as stipulated by law, not at the discretion of the parole board. The new laws are of two types. Eleven states have adopted determinate sentencing, which requires that the felon be released at the conclusion of the period of time stipulated by the judge minus good time and other reductions. Fifteen states and the U.S. Parole Commission require the releasing authority to follow guidelines in regard to the nature of the offense and the characteristics of the inmate in determining the date of release. Three states have both determinate sentencing and guidelines. The guidelines apply equally to all inmates, and thus the parole board has almost no discretion to hold someone beyond the stipulated date.

mandatory release The required release of an inmate from incarceration upon the expiration of a certain time period, as stipulated by a determinate sentencing law or parole guidelines.

discretionary release The release of an inmate from incarceration at the discretion of the parole board within the boundaries set by the sentence and the penal law.

The use of determinate sentences and parole guidelines is referred to as ***mandatory release*** because the paroling authority has little leeway in considering whether the offender is ready for community supervision; release is virtually automatic. Of the 133,000 persons who entered parole supervision in 1981, about 70 percent did so as a result of a parole board decision (***discretionary release***); 26 percent were given mandatory release, as required by determinate sentencing statutes or the use of parole guidelines.[16] As figure 16.2 shows, less than half of the jurisdictions continue to have unlimited discretion in granting release on parole.

Most offenders, whether they are released as a result of a parole board's decision or are given a mandatory release, must spend additional time under supervision. What differentiates mandatory release and release on parole is the action of an official body with discretionary powers in the latter case. For the purpose of this chapter, we will use the familiar term *parole* to describe both procedures.

Although parole may be viewed as a part of corrections, it has an impact on other parts of the criminal justice system. The amount of time to be served has a strong influence on many of the bargaining decisions made throughout the justice system, and in many ways the time to be served is the "currency" of the system. Decisions on guilty pleas are based on a prediction of the length of incarceration, as are decisions on defense and prosecution tactics and regulation of prison populations. New York's Citizens' Inquiry on Parole and Criminal Justice has pointed out:

> Parole is crucial to many parts of the criminal justice system: sentencing schemes are built around it, prosecutors take it into account in charging defendants and participating in plea bargaining, judges' roles in sentencing have been diminished as parole boards' jurisdiction over release has grown. . . . Prison programs may be well or poorly attended depending on whether inmates believe that their participation will improve their chances for parole.[17]

Parole has been justified as a means of providing early release from incarceration consistent with the goal of rehabilitation. It is designed to work in conjunction with the indeterminate sentence so that parole boards may determine the most appropriate time for release on the basis of a diagnosis provided by correctional personnel. Correctional authorities believe that proper timing of the release decision is critical. They argue that premature release of offenders increases the risk of recidivism, while holding them too long only creates bitterness and increases the likelihood of their return to crime. Parole boards are thus faced with a dilemma: they must work to achieve both rehabilitation of the offender and protection of society. Often these two goals are thought to be incompatible.

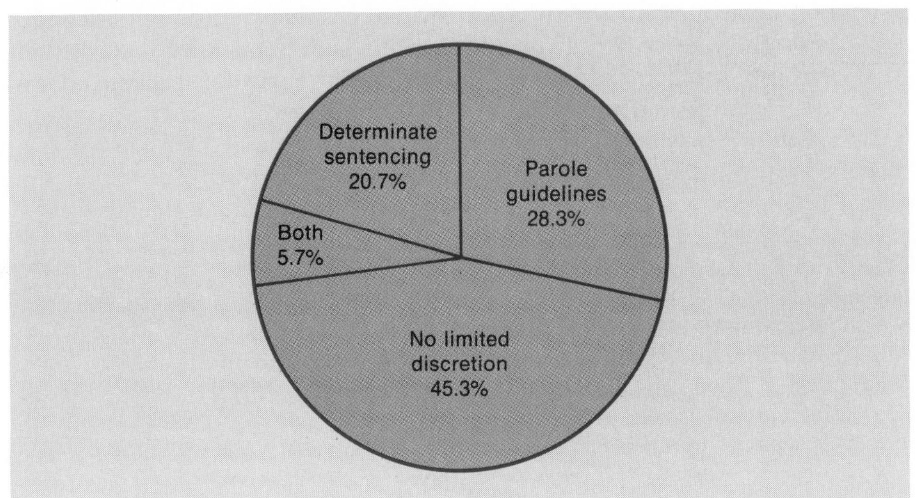

FIGURE 16.2
Proportion of jurisdictions with limited discretion in parole decision making

Parole boards are seen as serving a dual function: acting as a court of leniency that can lessen the harshness of excessive sentences and acting as a panel of persons with clinical expertise who can decide when rehabilitated prisoners can safely be returned to the outside world. The concept of parole involves more than just release; it also assumes that the offender will return to the community only under supervision of a trained agent who will assist in the adjustment and may continue some of the therapeutic endeavors begun in prison. Parole can probably be best summarized as ". . . an extension of a sentence of incarceration served in the community by the grace of God and the parole board under close surveillance, supervision, and guidance."[18]

Origins of parole

Rather than being the product of a single reformer or reform movement, parole in the United States evolved during the nineteenth century as a result of such English, Australian, and Irish practices as conditional pardon, apprenticeship by indenture, transportation of criminals from one country to another, and the issuance of "tickets-of-leave" or license.[19] All these methods have as their common denominator the movement of criminals out of prison, and in most cases such problems as overcrowding, unemployment, and the cost of incarceration appear to have motivated the practice rather than any rationale linked to a goal of the criminal sanction.

As early as 1587 England had passed the Act of Banishment, which provided for the movement of criminals and "rogues" to the colonies as laborers for the king in exchange for a pardon. Although the pardons were initially unconditional, they became conditional on the completion of a period of service after the privilege had been abused. In later periods, especially during the eighteenth century, English convicts were released and indentured to private persons to work in the colonies until the end of a set term, at which time they were freed.

With the independence of the United States, the English were deprived of a major dumping ground for their criminals, and their prisons soon became overcrowded. The opening up of Australia met the need for an outlet when in 1790 the power to pardon felons was granted to the governor there and a system was developed for the transportation of criminals. Although unconditional pardons were at first given to offenders with good work records and good behavior, problems arose—as before—and the pardons became conditional, that is, with the requirement that prisoners support themselves and remain within a specific district. This method of parole became known as a "ticket-of-leave." It was like the modern concept of parole, except that the released prisoner was not under supervision by a government agent.

Reform of Parole Release

Determinate sentencing: Alaska, Arizona, Colorado, Illinois, Indiana, Maine, Missouri, New Jersey, New Mexico, North Carolina, Tennessee.

Parole guidelines: Florida, Georgia, Hawaii, Louisiana, Maryland, Michigan, New York, Ohio, Oregon, Rhode Island, South Carolina, Washington, Virginia, West Virginia, Wisconsin, and U.S. Parole Commission.

Both: California, Minnesota, Pennsylvania.

Source: U.S. Department of Justice, Bureau of Justice Statistics, *Parole Today, 1979* (Washington, D.C.: Government Printing Office, 1980), p. 11.

In the development of parole, two names stand out: Captain Alexander Maconochie and Sir Walter Crofton. In 1840, when Maconochie was in charge of the penal colony on Norfolk Island in the South Pacific, he criticized definite prison terms and devised a system of reward for good conduct, labor, and study. He developed a classification procedure by which prisoners could pass through five stages of increasing responsibility and freedom: (1) strict imprisonment, (2) labor on government chain gangs, (3) freedom within a limited area, (4) a ticket-of-leave or parole resulting in a conditional pardon, and (5) full restoration of liberty. Like modern correctional practices, this procedure assumed that prisoners should be prepared gradually for release.

Although Maconochie's idea of requiring prisoners to earn their early release did not gain immediate acceptance in England, it was used in Ireland, where Sir Walter Crofton had built on Maconochie's idea that an offender's progress in prison and a ticket-of-leave were linked. Prisoners who graduated through Crofton's three successive levels of treatment were released on parole with a series of conditions. Most important, parolees were required to submit monthly reports to the police. In Dublin a special civilian inspector helped releasees find jobs, visited them periodically, and supervised their activities. This concept of assistance and supervision may be viewed as Crofton's contribution to the modern system of parole.

In the United States, parole developed during the prison reform movement of the nineteenth century. Relying on the ideas of Maconochie and Crofton, such American reformers as Zebulon Brockway of Elmira, New York, began to experiment with the concept of parole. Following New York's adoption of indeterminate sentences in 1876, Brockway started to release prisoners on parole. Under the new sentencing law, prisoners could be re-

Alexander Maconochie

A naval officer, geographer, and penal reformer, Alexander Maconochie was born in Edinburgh, Scotland, in 1787. He entered the Royal Navy in 1803 and served in the Napoleonic Wars. A founder of the Royal Geographic Society (1813), Maconochie became private secretary to the lieutenant governor of the colony of Van Diemen's Land (now Tasmania) in 1836. This appointment was to lead to a more important post in the colony's administration, but after completing a report condemning the condition of discipline in the island's penal colony, he was removed from his position.

Maconochie held two views in regard to penology: (1) punishment should be aimed at reform, not at vengeance; and (2) a sentence should be indeterminate, with release depending on the prisoner's industriousness and effort, not on time served. In 1840 he was given an opportunity to apply these principles as superintendent of the Norfolk Island penal settlement in the South Pacific. Under his direction, task accomplishment, not time served, was the criterion for release. Marks of commendation were given to prisoners who performed their tasks well, and they were released from the penal colony as they demonstrated willingness to accept society's rules.

Returning to England in 1844 to campaign for penal reform, Maconochie was appointed governor of the new Birmingham Borough Prison in 1849. But he was unable to institute his reforms there because he was dismissed from his position in 1851 by visiting justices who had power over the prison on the grounds that his methods were too lenient. He died in 1860.

leased when their conduct during incarceration showed that they were ready to return to society. The parole system in New York as originally implemented did not require supervision by the police, as in Ireland; rather, responsibility for assisting the parolees was assumed by private reform groups. With increased use of parole, states replaced the volunteer supervisors with correctional employees who were charged with helping and observing the parolees.

The idea that convicts should be released before they had paid full price for their crimes was opposed by many individuals and groups in the United States. Yet by 1900, twenty states had parole systems; by 1932, forty-four states and the federal government had adopted this method. Today all jurisdictions have some mechanism for the release of offenders into the community under supervision.

Although parole in the United States is now more than one hundred years old, it is still controversial. Once the public opposed the concept because it seemed to allow for lenient treatment of offenders; today it is being attacked for contributing to the unjust exercise of discretion by parole boards and correctional authorities. In contemplating this ongoing debate, remember that parole performs a number of functions unrelated to its rehabilitative effect on the offender. Parole is one means of reducing the actual time served in prison, which has an impact individually and collectively on plea bargaining, sentencing, and the size of prison populations. Questions must be asked about the consequences that changes in parole will have for the various parts of the criminal justice system.

Parole today

Nationally, 76 percent of state and federal adult felons who are released pass into the community through parole. This figure varies among the states, ranging from 95 percent to 12 percent, but the total number of offenders on parole increased by 10 percent in 1979 to more than 221,500. Figure 16.3 presents information concerning the background characteristics of persons who join the parole population. These characteristics correspond very closely to the background data on incarcerated persons, discussed in chapter 14. Of the persons paroled in 1979, 58 percent had had one prior prison commitment, 22 percent had completed two, 11 percent three, and 9 percent four or more commitments.[20]

Impact on sentencing. Although U.S. judges are often said to give the longest prison sentences in the Western world, little attention has been paid to the amount of time that offenders actually serve. One of the important influences of parole is that it allows an administrative body to shorten a judge's sentence. States that have moved to determinate sentencing or to the use of parole guidelines have eliminated the exercise of discretion in release decisions, but various reductions are built into the sentence so that full time is rarely served. To understand the impact of parole on criminal justice, one needs to compare the amount of time actually served in prison with the sentence specified by the judge.

In some jurisdictions up to 80 percent of felons sentenced to the penitentiary are paroled after their first appearance before the board. In most states, eligibility to apply for parole is ordinarily determined by the minimum term of the sentence minus "good time" and "jail time." As we have seen, good time allows the minimum sentence to be reduced for good behavior during incarceration or for exceptional performance of assigned tasks or personal achievement. In some states an inmate is able to earn one day of good time for every four days of good behavior. Jail time—credit given for time spent in jail while the offender awaited trial and sentencing—also shortens the period that must be served before the inmate's first appearance before the parole board.

While there is considerable variation among the states, it is estimated that, on a national basis, felony inmates serve on the average less than two years before their first release. As table 16.2 shows, the amount of time served in prison varies with the nature of the offense. If the data shown in table 16.2 became widely known, most people would probably be shocked to learn that the actual time served is so much less than the sentences announced in court and published in the newspapers.

FIGURE 16.3
Background characteristics of offenders entering parole supervision

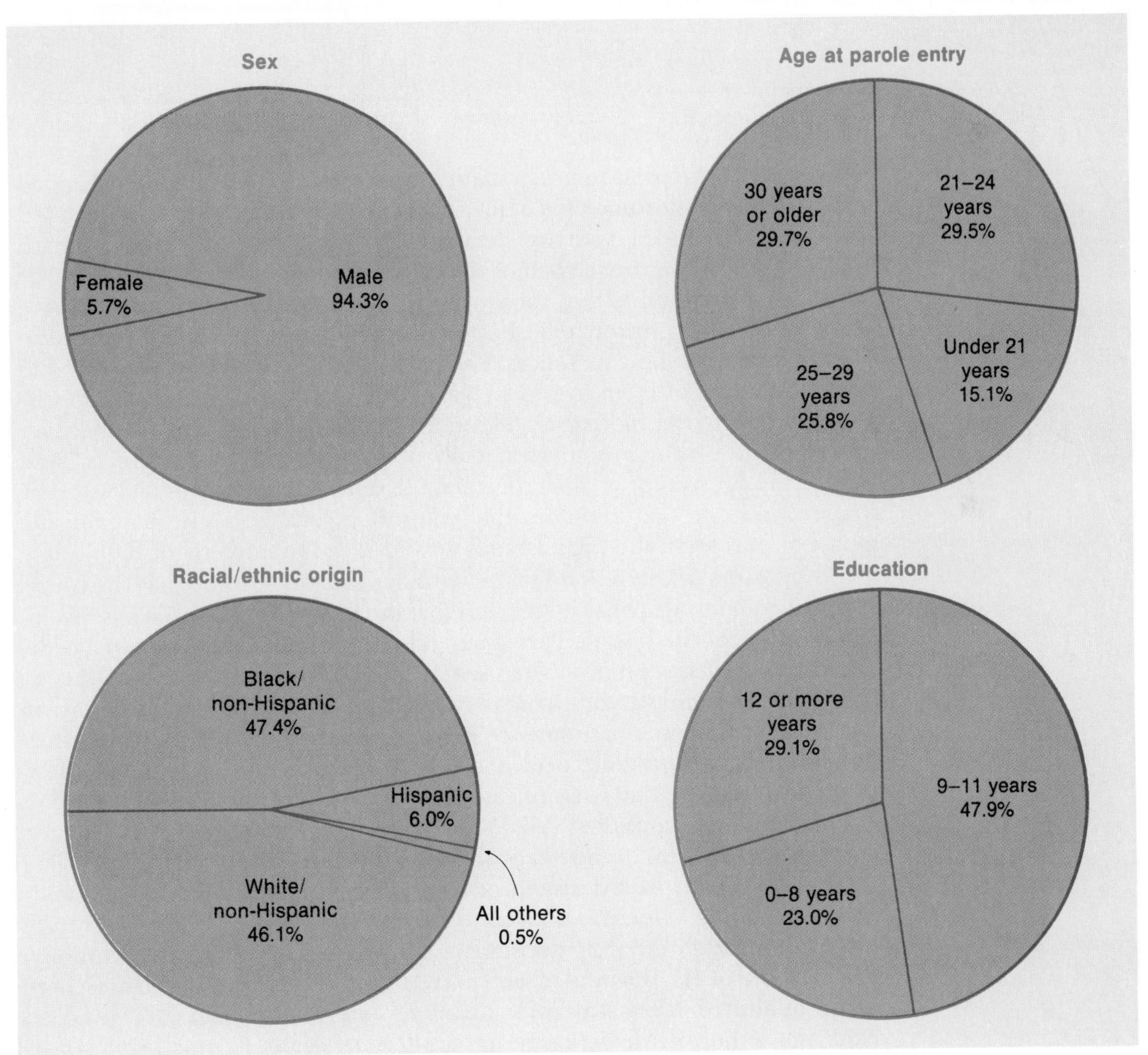

TABLE 16.2 Mean number of months served for nine offenses in twelve states, 1977–1983

State and release period	*Criminal homicide*[a]	*Rape*	*Robbery*	*Aggra-vated assault*	*Burg-lary*	*Larceny*	*Auto theft*	*Arson*	*Drug of-fenses*[b]
Delaware, 1980–82[c]	74.3	25.5	39.3	18.6	15.7	6.5	12.8	9.4	15.0
Illinois, 1978–82	52.1	46.0	29.1	18.7	20.7	14.1	*	*	*
Iowa, 1979–83[c]	72.4	47.1	51.7	33.1	30.5	22.7	15.5	29.9	24.0
Maryland, 1982[c]	63.1	63.7	61.5	30.0	29.2	14.2	20.9	35.6	15.9
North Carolina, 1977–81[c]	51.3	*	40.8	19.7	22.2	*	19.4	*	15.7
Ohio, 1980–81	78.6	50.0	34.9	26.6	27.0	15.4	24.9	22.5	17.3
Oklahoma, 1982	39.3	25.6	29.7	17.4	13.8	11.8	15.1	16.4	11.4
Oregon, 1979–82	41.2	36.0	25.2	23.1	15.3	11.3	11.9	25.5	10.4
Pennsylvania 1981–82[c]	57.4	47.7	33.5	25.4	22.6	16.8	14.8	28.2	18.9
Washington, 7/81–6/82	63.2	36.3	38.8	37.0	*	*	*	*	17.8
Wisconsin, 1/80–5/83	41.8	33.5	42.3	30.7	26.5	22.6	20.6	24.7	22.3
Wyoming, 7/80–6/83[c]	59.5	51.5	29.5	29.4	22.5	15.8	18.2	25.8	15.2

[a] Includes murder and nonnegligent manslaughter.
[b] Includes sale and possession.
[c] Includes credited jail time.
* Data not available.
Source: U.S. Department of Justice, Bureau of Justice Statistics, *Time Served in Prison*, Special Report (Washington, D.C.: Government Printing Office, 1984), p. 3.

Table 16.3 helps us to understand how the indeterminate sentence, good time, and parole shortened the amount of time that inmates were incarcerated in one state, Michigan. Note that the median of the maximum sentence length was 10.6 *years*, while the median of the actual time served was 14.6 *months*. Of further consideration is that those who received longer terms actually were incarcerated a proportionately shorter period of time than were those who received relatively short sentences. For example, 22 percent were sentenced to maximum terms of from five to six years, while only 6 percent were imprisoned for a period of more than 48 months but less than 72 months. Because the defendant is primarily concerned about when he will "hit the streets," and because the prosecutor is concerned about a sentence that the public will view as appropriate to the crime but that will still encourage a plea bargain, the impact of parole on the time actually served is in the interests of both sides.

Supporters of discretion for the paroling authority argue that the courts do not adequately dispense justice and that the possibility of parole has invaluable benefits for the system. Parole mitigates the harshness of the penal code, it equalizes disparities inevitable in sentencing behavior, and it is necessary to assist prison administrators in maintaining order. Supporters also contend that the postponement of sentence determination to the parole stage offers the opportunity for a more detached evaluation than is possible in the atmosphere of a trial and that early release is economically sensible because the cost of incarceration is considerable.

A major criticism of the effect of parole is that it has shifted responsibility for many of the primary decisions of criminal justice from a judge, who holds legal procedures uppermost, to an administrative board, where discretion rules. In most states, parole decisions are made in secret hearings, with only the board members, the inmate, and correctional officers present. Often there are no published criteria to guide decisions, and the prisoners are given no reason for either the denial or granting of their release. Kenneth Culp Davis

TABLE 16.3 Number and percentage of persons incarcerated in Michigan, by maximum length of sentence and actual time served

Maximum sentence length (years)	*Number*	*Percentage*	*Time served (months)*	*Number*	*Percentage*
Total	8,115	100%	Total	8,115	100
Less than 3 years	782	10	Less than 6	1,858	23
3 to less than 4	10	Z	6 to less than 12	1,596	20
4 to less than 5	650	8	12 to less than 18	1,349	17
5 to less than 6	1,783	22	18 to less than 24	811	10
6 to less than 10	35	Z	24 to less than 30	646	8
10 to less than 11	1,402	17	30 to less than 36	385	5
11 to less than 15	153	2	36 to less than 48	527	6
15 to less than 16	1,573	19	48 to less than 72	487	6
16 to less than 20	2	Z	72 to less than 120	276	3
20 to less than 30	635	8	120 or more	174	2
30 to less than 98	499	6	Not reported	6	Z
98 or more, life, or death	591	7	Median		14.6
Median		10.6			

Z = less than 0.5 percent.
Source: Adapted from Law Enforcement Assistance Administration, *Census of Prisoners in State Correctional Facilities, 1973* (Washington, D.C.: Government Printing Office, 1976), p. 106.

asks, "Should any men, even good men, be unnecessarily trusted with such uncontrolled discretionary power?"[21]

Organization of releasing authorities. The authority to release prisoners on parole is granted to the parole board by the legislature. The board tends to be organized either as a part of a department of corrections or as an independent agency of government. It has been argued that the parole board must be autonomous so that members can be insulated from the ongoing activities of the institutional staff. Some people feel that an independent decisional process shields the board members from influence by such staff considerations as reducing the size of the prison population and punishing inmates who do not conform to institutional rules. Recently there has been a movement to locate the parole board within the department of corrections or in a multifunctional human services department. This trend has appeared in response to the criticism that autonomous boards are insensitive to institutional programs and treatment goals. It is believed that when parole decisions are made by persons who are closely connected with corrections, the treatment of a particular offender can be more closely linked with the suitability of release.

Whichever organizational structure is used, the parole board cannot exist in a vacuum, immune to political and organizational influences. The autonomous parole board may develop conflicts with correctional authorities so that the information needed for decision making may be "unavailable" or biased. The board that is closely tied to corrections runs the risk of being viewed by prisoners and the general public as merely the rubber stamp of the department. Both types of boards have to operate under the pressure of public opinion. Members of one parole board said that they had to be very cautious in releasing prisoners because if parolees become involved in further violations of the law, the news media always point to the board as having let them out.

Board members depend on others for the information on which they base decisions. Fragmentation of the decision-making process can mean that the institutional staff and the parole board are working at cross-purposes. Parole boards have often been critical of the information they are given to help them make these crucial decisions. Frequently the data are fitted into a stereotyped format and the individual aspects of a given case are lost, with the result that decisions may be arbitrary and unfair as well as undesirable from a correctional standpoint. Many prisoners say that they would prefer to have the releasing decision made by institutional personnel who know them personally rather than by an outside board.

Membership on the parole board is often based on the assumption that persons with training in the behavioral sciences are able to discern which candidates have been rehabilitated and are ready to return to society; but in many states political considerations dictate that membership include persons with specific racial or geographical qualifications. In the recent past, for example, the Mississippi board consisted of a contractor, a businessman, a farmer, and a clerk; the Florida board included a newspaperman, an attorney, and a man with experience in both business and probation; the state of Washington board had persons with training and experience in sociology, government, law, the ministry, and juvenile rehabilitation.

The decision to release

An inmate's eligibility for parole depends on the requirements set by law and the sentence imposed by the court. In the states with determinate sentences or parole guidelines, release from prison to community supervision is mandatory once the offender has served the required amount of time. In these states, mandatory release becomes a matter of bookkeeping to ensure

Computing Parole Eligibility

Richard Scott was given a sentence of a minimum of five years and a maximum of ten years for the crime of robbery with violence. At the time of sentencing he had been held in jail for six months awaiting trial and disposition of his case. Scott did well in the maximum security prison to which he was sent. He did not get into trouble and was thus able to amass good-time credit at the rate of one day for every four that he spent on good behavior. In addition, he was given thirty days' meritorious credit when he completed his high school equivalency test after attending the prison school for two years. After serving three years and four months of his sentence, he appeared before the Board of Parole and was granted release into the community.

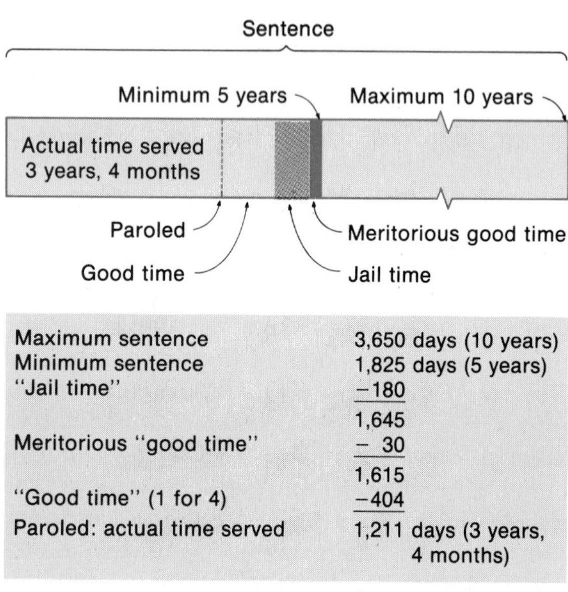

Maximum sentence	3,650 days (10 years)
Minimum sentence	1,825 days (5 years)
"Jail time"	−180
	1,645
Meritorious "good time"	− 30
	1,615
"Good time" (1 for 4)	−404
Paroled: actual time served	1,211 days (3 years, 4 months)

that the correct amount of good time and other credits have been allocated and that the court's sentence has been accurately interpreted so that on expiration of the period, the offender moves automatically into the community. In nearly half of the states, however, the decision to release is discretionary, and the parole board has the authority to establish a date on the basis of the sufficiency of rehabilitation and the individual characteristics of each inmate. Most inmates serving an indeterminate sentence become eligible for parole automatically at the expiration of one-third of the maximum term or three years, whichever comes first.

In 1933 the American Prison Association asserted that the prisoner's fitness for reentry to the community should determine the release time.

> Has the institution accomplished all that it can for him; is the offender's state of mind and attitude toward his own difficulties and problems such that further residence will be harmful or beneficial; does a suitable environment await him on the outside; can the beneficial effect already accomplished be retained if he is held longer to allow a more suitable environment to be developed?[22]

Although parole boards may subscribe to these principles, the nature of the criteria presents difficulties that cannot be resolved by "hard" data. Some boards have used prediction tables specifying the qualities of an inmate that have been shown over time to correlate with parole success. Not only has the reliability of these data been questioned, but civil liberty claims have been raised on the grounds that the described characteristics do not account for individual differences.

What criteria guide board members as they determine whether inmates can be released? Although a formal statement of standards may list such elements as the inmate's attitude toward his family, his insights into the causes of his past conduct, and the adequacy of his parole plan, the decision is a discretionary act that is probably based on a combination of information and moral judgment. It is frequently said that parole boards release only good risks, but as one parole board member has said, "there are no good-risk men in prison. Parole is really a decision of when to release bad-risk persons."[23] Other considerations, such as internal prison control and morale, public sentiment, and the political implications of their decisions, weigh heavily on board members. Former Federal Parole Board chairman Maurice Sigler has observed, "We have this terrible power; we sit up here playing God."[24]

How to win parole. "If you want to get paroled, you've got to be in a program." This statement reflects one of the most controversial aspects of the rehabilitative model: the link between treatment and release. Although penal authorities emphasize the voluntary nature of most treatment services, although clinicians will argue that therapy cannot be successful in a coercive atmosphere, the fact remains that inmates believe they must "play the game" so that they can build a record that will look good before the parole board. Most parole boards stipulate that an inmate's institutional adjustment, including participation and progress in self-improvement programs, is one of the criteria to be considered in a release decision. A Connecticut inmate noted, "The last time I went before the Board they wanted to know why I hadn't taken advantage of the programs. Now I go to A.A. and group therapy. I hope they will be satisfied." Playing the "parole board game" may be the dominant motivation of many inmates. Prisoners believe that if they participate in certain rehabilitative programs their record will look good, the board will be impressed, and they will be released: "When I go to my therapy group I can just play the game as good as the next guy. We sit there and talk about our problems so that the counselor will give us a good report. It's lots better than making hay at the farm out in the hot sun."

Unfortunately, many offenders come up for parole only to find either that they have not done enough to satisfy the board or that they have been in

Close-up: Parole Hearing

Michael Gardner is 22 and looks 16. Frail, narrow-shouldered, quavery-voiced, pale, he seems out of place here. He ought to be at the high school dance, standing uncomfortably against a wall. He grew up in a small textile mill town in the poorest part of the state. Kicked out of school at 16, he retaliated by ransacking the building. At 17 it was larceny, at 18, breaking into a car. A reformatory sentence. An escape. Thirteen more months in the reformatory. Then a string of robberies, finally a sentence of two to eight years. He looks frightened, anxious. He brings out the grandfather in Gates [the parole board chairman].

"This is your first time in prison," Gates begins in a soft voice. "Now you've had some time to think. What's the story? What causes you to do this, do you think?"

Gardner looks at the floor. "I think it was my own stupidity. I didn't stop to think."

"Well, a young fella your age, it's a waste of time if you don't come up with some ideas about where all this is coming from and where you're going. . . ."

Gardner answers slowly, the words measured: "I know where it's coming from and I know where I'm going. I've done something to better myself in here. I've become an apprentice carpenter. And I've taken the time to think. . . ."

Gardner is ringing bells with the board. He's done something to *better himself*. He may be *rehabilitated*. And maybe he is. He wasn't a carpenter when he came in. He was a thief, and not much of one. "If they've got the tiniest bit of smarts they know what this board wants to hear," an ex-inmate has told me. "If you show some inclination to self-help, don't just do your time the old-con way. They want to see you run a little."

Gates seems particularly impressed. He believes in work, and here's a man with a trade. "We live to work, we don't work to live," Gates likes to say. "We've been growing away from that in this country."

Gates is gentle with him, avuncular. "Well, you know you got a long sentence this time, but it's nothing to what you'll get next time."

"Yessir." Gardner almost swallows his reply.

Sacks [a board member] has taken his coat off. He has a sudden thought: "Do you think prison is a good thing for rehabilitation or not? Do you think we ought to close the prisons?" It's time for a commercial.

Gardner sees the opening. "No," he says, "I wouldn't say close the prisons. I may have a different outlook than some of the people in here, but I mean to me it's helped me see myself. I made my apprenticeship."

Rawlins [the third member] is looking thoughtful, puffing on his pipe. Sacks is toying with his glasses. Gates looks like a statue—erect in his chair, not a wrinkle. His eyes have the cool, subdued glow of a distant star. "When was the last time you saw your father?" Sacks asks. They have seen the probation officer's presentence report; Gardner's father has been stepping on him for years.

"About four weeks ago."

"How do you get along with him?"

"I get along with him good now." The answer comes too quickly.

the wrong program. This problem may result from changes in the personnel of the board or the limited number of places in the educational and rehabilitative programs in American prisons. Offenders report that they often must wait long periods before they can gain admission to a program that fits their needs or that will impress the board. Observation of the classification proceedings described in chapter 14 confirms the impression that offenders are assigned to work, education, and rehabilitative programs in keeping with the organizational needs of the institution.

"I mean, we have our arguments like every family does, but . . ."

His last parole officer had reported: "His father and him beat the hell out of each other whenever they saw each other. I couldn't even talk to the old man if I wanted to get anywhere with Mike."

Rawlins senses something: "Did you say you wanted to live with your family?"

"Yes. I figure I owe them something. I mean they done a lot for me."

A week earlier, the father had told me: "The kid's asked me to speak to the parole board for him, but the way I look at it he's on his own now. Why should I lose a day's pay and go down there? He can live here if he wants to, but he's got to behave." The mother was no softer: "The doctor told us when he was 10 that he wasn't getting enough affection at home. He got the same as the rest. He got clothes, food, all a kid could want."

Gardner looks close to tears now. He gets up and leaves the room. The board did not ask his feelings about parole, but the day before Gardner had described it as "a bunch of crap. You got to go out and live like a human being, not with someone watching you all the time. Out there you can't listen to anyone, you gotta look out for yourself."

"I'm going to vote to parole," Gates says. "He's just a youngster, younger than his age. I think this might be the time, prison might have awakened him. This is a kid. He's different from the others with long records and set in their ways."

"I vote for parole," says Sacks. "One thing that impressed me was his answer on what prison does. It made sense."

Rawlins still wonders. "My concern is that he may have problems at home. I see a fragile guy. . . . He may be hurting more deeply than he showed here." ("One of the weaknesses of our operation," Sacks will say later, "is that usually nobody checks out the family, what he's going out to. We should know what it's like.")

All three agreed to parole. Of the seventeen men who come before the board on this day, six will be granted parole, nine denied and the decisions in two cases will be postponed; usually, between 50 and 60 percent win parole.

Gardner is expressionless when he gets the word. "I'll probably still get in trouble if I stay in that little town," he had said. "Everybody knows me there. I gotta get some money and then take off." The old parole officer had said he felt Gardner had a chance "if he can latch onto something for his ego, a good job, a girl, so he can say, 'Look, Dad'. . . ." Now, the board members are saying they want to get Gardner in a work-release program, but they are not sure they can. It means a month's delay in his release. Gardner doesn't understand, and Gates doesn't feel he can explain it. "We think you can stand at least another month because you're learning something." he says instead. "Okay? Now take care of yourself."

Gardner looks uncertain as he walks out.

"Gee," Sacks says quietly, "he looked so downhearted."

"He's a kid," Gates says.

Source: From "Parole Board," by Donald Jackson, *LIFE*. Copyright © 1970 Time, Inc. Reprinted by permission.

Structuring decision making. In response to the criticism that parole boards' release decisions are somewhat arbitrary, the U.S. Board of Parole and similar authorities in at least sixteen states have adopted guidelines to assist their members. As table 16.4 shows, these guidelines include a "severity scale" that ranks crimes according to their seriousness and a "salient factor" score that is based on the offender's characteristics as they are thought to relate to successful completion of parole. By placing the offender's salient factor score next to his or her particular offense on the severity scale, the board, the

TABLE 16.4 U.S. Board of Parole guidelines for adult "normal" time to be served before release: severity of offense and likelihood of recidivism

	Offender characteristics—parole prognosis (salient factor score)			
Offense characteristics—severity of offense behavior (examples)	***Very good (10–8)***	***Good (7–6)***	***Fair (5–4)***	***Poor (3–0)***
Low Alcohol or cigarette law violations, including tax evasion (amount of tax evaded less than $2,000) Property offenses (theft, income tax evasion, or simple possession of stolen property), less than $2,000	6 mo. +	6 to 9 mo. +	9 to 12 mo. +	12 to 16 mo. +
Low moderate Drugs, possession with intent to distribute/sale (very small scale; e.g., less than 200 doses) Property offenses (forgery/fraud/theft from mail/embezzlement/interstate transportation of stolen or forged securities/receiving stolen property with intent to resell), less than $2,000	8 mo. +	8 to 12 mo. +	12 to 16 mo. +	16 to 22 mo. +
Moderate Automobile theft (3 cars or less involved and total value does not exceed $19,999) Drugs, possession with intent to distribute/sale (small scale; e.g., 200–999 doses) Property offenses, $2,000–$19,999	10 to 14 mo. +	14 to 18 mo. +	18 to 24 mo. +	24 to 32 mo. +
High Counterfeit currency or other medium of exchange (passing/possession, $20,000–$100,000) Drugs, possession with intent to distribute/sale (medium scale; e.g., 1,000–19,999 doses) Involuntary manslaughter (e.g., negligent homicide) Mann Act (no force—commercial purposes) Property offenses, $20,000–$100,000	14 to 20 mo. +	20 to 26 mo. +	26 to 34 mo. +	34 to 44 mo. +
Very high Robbery (1 or 2 instances) Breaking and entering/burglary, residence; or breaking and entering of other premises with hostile confrontation with victim Drugs, possession with intent to distribute/sale (large scale) Extortion (threat of physical harm to person or property) Property offenses, more than $100,000 but not exceeding $500,000	24 to 36 mo. +	36 to 48 mo. +	48 to 60 mo. +	60 to 72 mo. +

Note: Specific upper limits are not provided owing to the limited number of cases and the extreme variation possible within each category.
Source: Adapted from 28 *Code of Federal Regulations* 2.20, 1 July 1980, as revised 10 July 1981.

inmate, and correctional officials are able to know the average total time that will be served.

The salient factor score was devised on the basis of research indicating that inmates with certain characteristics—first offenders, for example—have a greater probability of not returning to crime than do those with other characteristics, such as drug addiction. The score is arrived at by adding the points awarded for each item as shown in table 16.5. This aspect of the guidelines may be opposed by civil libertarians and others who feel that to deny freedom

	Offender characteristics—parole prognosis (salient factor score)			
Offense characteristics—severity of offense behavior (examples)	*Very good (10–8)*	*Good (7–6)*	*Fair (5–4)*	*Poor (3–0)*
Greatest I Aggravated felony (e.g., robbery; weapon fired or injury of a type normally requiring medical attention) Drugs, possession with intent to distribute/sale (managerial or proprietary interest and very large scale; e.g., offense involving more than 200,000 doses) Kidnaping (other than listed in Greatest II; limited duration, and no harm to victim; e.g., kidnaping the driver of a truck during a hijacking, driving him to a secluded location, and releasing victim unharmed) Robbery (3 or 4 instances) Sex act—force (e.g., forcible rape or Mann Act [force]) Voluntary manslaughter (unlawful killing of a human being without malice; sudden quarrel or heat of passion)	40 to 52 mo. +	52 to 64 mo. +	64 to 78 mo. +	78 to 100 mo. +
Greatest II Murder Aggravated felony—serious injury (e.g., robbery; injury involving substantial risk of death or protracted disability or disfigurement) or extreme cruelty/brutality toward victim Aircraft hijacking Espionage Kidnaping (for ransom or terrorism, as hostage; or harm to victim) Treason	52 + mo.	64 + mo.	78 + mo.	100 + mo.

TABLE 16.5 Salient factors used in adult parole guidelines

Item A: Prior conviction(s)/adjudications (adult or juvenile)	☐
None	=3
One	=2
Two or three	=1
Four or more	=0
Item B: Prior commitment(s) of more than 30 days (adult or juvenile)	☐
None	=2
One or two	=1
Three or more	=0
Item C: Age at commencement of current offense	☐
26 years or more	=2
20–25 years	=1
19 years or less	=0
Item D: Recent commitment-free period (three years)	☐
No prior commitment of more than 30 days (adult or juvenile) or released to community from last such commitment at least three years prior to commencement of current offense	=1
Otherwise	=0
Item E: Probation/parole/confinement/escape status violator this time	☐
Neither on probation, parole, confinement, nor escape status at time of current offense, nor committed as a probation, parole, confinement, or escape status violator this time	=1
Otherwise	=0
Item F: Heroin/opiate dependence	☐
No history of heroin/opiate dependence	=1
Otherwise	=0
Total score	☐

Source: *Federal Register* 46, no. 132 (10 July 1981): 35639.

on the basis of characteristics over which a person may have no control is at odds with the concepts of equal protection and due process. Others may argue that the guidelines result in fixed and mechanical decisions that do not consider the impact of rehabilitative programs or institutional behavior.

Supervision

Parolees are released from prison on condition that they do not further violate the law and that they live according to rules designed both to help them readjust to society and to control their movements. These rules may require them to abstain from alcoholic beverages, to keep away from bad associates, to maintain good work habits, and not to leave the community without permission. The restrictions are justified on the grounds that people who have been incarcerated must gradually readjust to the community with its many temptations and not easily fall back into their preconviction habits and associations.

A View of the Parole Board

I have not as yet been before the parole board but I am living in constant fear of that day. I do want to better myself but at times I wonder where my motivation lies, like if I'm doing this for myself or for the parole board. I feel that if I know exactly when I could go home then I would give more serious thought as to what I need and to what I would like to do here, but as it stands now, my thoughts seem to be focusing on that day when I'll be walking into that room full of strangers who don't know me, and pray that I have done whatever they expected me to do here.

—Inmate, maximum security prison

Source: George F. Cole and Charles H. Logan, "Parole: The Consumer's Perspective," *Criminal Justice Review* 1 (Fall 1977): 73.

This orientation creates a number of problems not only for the parolee but for the administration of this type of community treatment program. Some people feel that the attempt to impose on parolees standards of conduct that are not imposed on law-abiding persons is absurd.

When they first come out of prison, the parolees' personal and material problems are staggering. In most states they are given only clothes, a token amount of money, the list of rules governing their conditional release, and the name and address of the parole supervisor to whom they must report within twenty-four hours. Although a promised job is often a condition for release, actually becoming employed may be another matter. Most ex-convicts are unskilled or semiskilled, and the conditions of parole may restrict their movement to areas where a job may be available. If the parolee is black and under thirty, he joins the largest group of unemployed in the country, with the added handicap of having ex-convict status. In most states, laws prevent former prisoners from being employed in certain types of establishments—where alcohol is sold, for example—thus placing many jobs automatically off limits. In many trades, union affiliation is a requirement for employment, and there are restrictions on the admission of new members. The situation of the newly released parolee has been described by Mark Dowie, executive director of Transitions to Freedom, a San Francisco convict-help organization:

> He arrives without a job in an urban area, after years in prison, with perhaps $20 or $30 in his pocket. Surviving is a trick, even if he's a frugal person, not inclined to blow his few dollars on drinks and women. The parole agents—with some remarkable exceptions—don't give a damn. He's deposited in the very middle of the city, where all he can find is a fleabag hotel in the Tenderloin. He has an aching determination to make it on the outside, but there are hustlers all over him; gambling con games, dollar poker.[25]

The reentry problems of parolees are seen in the fact that parole violations occur relatively soon after release. Nearly half occur during the first six months and more than 60 percent within the first year.[26] With little preparation, the ex-offender moves from the highly structured, authoritarian life of the institution into a world that is filled with temptations, that presents complicated problems requiring immediate solution, and that expects him to assume responsibilities to which he has long been unaccustomed. The parolee must go through a role change that requires him suddenly to become not only an ex-convict but a workman, father, husband, son. The expectations, norms, and social relations in the free world are quite different from those learned under the threat of institutional sanction. The parolee's adjustment problems are not only material but social and psychological as well.

Parole officer: cop or social worker? After release, a parolee's principal contact with the criminal justice system is through the parole officer. Huge caseloads make effective supervision practically impossible in some states. A national survey has shown that parole caseloads range from 50 to 70—smaller than probation caseloads, but the services required by former inmates are greater. To serve those with the greatest need, most parole officers spend more time with the newly released than with those who have been in the community for some time. As the officer gains greater confidence in the parolee, only periodic check-ins may be required.

Parole officers are asked to play two different roles: cop and social worker. As police officers, they are given the power to restrict many aspects of the parolee's life, to enforce the conditions of release, and to initiate revocation proceedings if violations occur. In many states they have the authority to search the parolee's house without warning, to arrest him or her without the possibility of bail for suspected violations, and to suspend parole pending a

---

Conditions of Parole

This parole is granted to and accepted by you, subject to the following conditions and with the knowledge that the Commissioner of Correction has the authority, at any time, in case of violation of the Conditions of Parole, to cause your detention and return you to his custody pending a review of your case by the Board of Parole, and further, that the Board of Parole has the authority to revoke parole if, in its judgment, you have violated any of the following conditions.

1. Upon release from the institution, you must follow the instructions of the institutional Parole Officer (or other designated authority of the Division of Parole) with regard to reporting to your supervising parole officer, and/or fulfilling any other obligations.
2. You must report to your Parole Officer when instructed to do so and must permit your Parole Officer or any Parole Officer to visit you at your home and place of employment at any time.
3. You must work steadily, and you must secure the permission of your Parole Officer before changing your residence or your employment, and you must report any change of residence or employment to your Parole Officer within twenty-four hours of such change. It is your responsibility to keep your Parole Officer informed at all times concerning your place of residence, your place of employment, and any arrests, convictions, or investigations by law-enforcement officials.
4. You must submit written reports as instructed by your Parole Officer.
5. You must not leave the State of Connecticut without first obtaining permission from your Parole Officer.
6. You must not apply for a Motor Vehicle Operator's License, or own, purchase, or operate any motor vehicle without first obtaining permission from your Parole Officer.
7. You must not marry without first obtaining written permission from your Parole Officer.
8. You must not own, possess, use, sell, or have under your control at any time, any deadly weapons or firearms.
9. You must not possess, use, or traffic in any narcotic, hallucinatory, or other harmful drugs in violation of the law.
10. You must support your dependents, if any, and assume toward them all moral and legal obligations.
11. A. You shall not consume alcoholic beverages to excess.
    B. You shall totally abstain from the use of alcoholic beverages or liquors. (Strike out either A or B, leaving whichever clause is applicable.)
12. You are not to correspond, visit or attempt to contact inmates of correctional institutions or their friends or relatives without the permission of your Parole Officer.
13. You must comply with all laws and conduct yourself as a good citizen. You must show by your attitude, cooperation, choice of associates, and places of amusement and recreation that you are a proper person to remain on parole.

Source: Certificate of Parole, Board of Parole, State of Connecticut.

---

hearing before the board. Like other officials in the criminal justice system, the parole officer has extensive discretion in low-visibility situations. The authoritative component of the parole officer's role relationship with the ex-offender produces a sense of insecurity in the latter that can only hamper the development of mutual trust.

Parole officers are also expected to assist the parolee's readjustment to the community. They must act as social workers by helping the parolee to find a job and restore family ties. Parole officers must be prepared to serve as agent-mediators between parolees and the organizations with which they deal and to channel them to social agencies, such as psychiatric clinics, where they can obtain help. As caseworkers, parole officers must be able to develop a relationship that allows parolees to feel free to confide their frustrations and concerns—something they are not likely to do if they are constantly aware of the parole officer's ability to send them back to prison. It has been suggested that parole officers' conflicting responsibilities of cop and social worker should be separated. Parole officers could maintain the supervisory aspects of the position while other persons performed the casework functions. Alternatively, parole officers could be charged solely with social work duties while local police checked for violations.

Parole is cheaper than confinement, although extensive resources are allocated for case supervision with little evidence that recidivism has been reduced. Parole rules have been increasing in number and complexity, so that it becomes harder for parolees to avoid technical violations. The bureaucratic nature of parole may mean that emphasis is placed on supervision rather than on assistance, with the result that lower caseloads increase the number of parolees returned to prison for rule infractions of a noncriminal nature. The number of parole rules, the amount of time officers have to spend with their clients, and recidivism rates may have important interrelationships.

Revocation of parole

Always hanging over the ex-inmate's head is the potential for revocation of parole because he or she either has committed a crime or has failed to live according to the rules ("technical violations") of the parole contract. Since the paroled person still has the status of inmate, many people believe that parole

---

Criteria for Parole Services

Be known. The parolee must know where to go, or where to find out where to go.

Be open for business. Problems arise at 4:00 A.M., and guidance or temporary remedies must be available around the clock.

Be reachable. Located near clients or with provision for transportation.

Be comprehensive. Whatever the difficulty—money, drugs or alcohol, family problems—a remedial service should exist.

Be trusted. The parolee must feel that he will not be punished or threatened when he reveals a problem.

Be voluntary. The offender has been coerced and told what to do for long enough: forced treatment is unlikely to be effective treatment. In the free community he must make his own choices, and compelling his participation will delay his rehabilitation.

Source: David T. Stanley, *Prisoners among Us* (Washington, D.C.: Brookings Institution, 1976), p. 170. Reprinted by permission.

should be easily revoked without adherence to due process or the rules of evidence. In some states, liberal parole policies have been justified to the public on the grounds that revocation is swift and can be imposed before a crime is committed. The New York statute, for example, provides that if the parole officer has "reasonable cause to believe that [the parolee] has lapsed, or is probably about to lapse, into criminal ways or company, or has violated the conditions of his parole in an important respect," he should report his suspicions to the parole board so that the parolee may be apprehended, or he may retake the parolee himself. The parole officer's power to recommend revocation because the parolee is "slipping" must hang over the parolee like the sword of Damocles, suspended by a thread. The parolee who leaves the state or has been charged with a new offense is usually detained by an arrest warrant until a revocation hearing or a criminal trial is held.

If the parole officer alleges that a technical (noncriminal) violation of the parole contract has occurred, a revocation proceeding will be held. The U.S. Supreme Court, in the case of *Morrissey* v. *Brewer* (1972), distinguished the requirements of such a proceeding from the normal requirements of the criminal trial but held that many of the due process rights must be accorded the parolee.[27] The Court has required a two-step hearing process whereby the parole board determines whether the contract has been violated. The parolee has the right to be notified of the charges against him, to know the evidence against him, to be heard, to present witnesses, and to confront the witnesses against him.

The number of parole revocations is difficult to determine. A combined revocation and recommitment rate of approximately 25 percent has been reported in recent years, but these data do not distinguish between parolees returned to prison for technical violations and those sent back for new criminal offenses. Daniel Glaser believes that most revocations occur only after arrest on a serious charge or when the parolee cannot be located by the parole officer.[28] Given the normal caseload, most parole officers are unable to maintain close scrutiny over parolees and so are not aware of technical violations.

Michael Gardner: Follow-up

Subject was released on parole, July 10, 1970. On October 15, 1970, he was arrested and charged with a number of counts of Breaking and Entering With Criminal Intent and Larceny. He pled guilty and was sentenced December 1, 1970, to serve from three to four years on the first count and four years on the second count making a total effective sentence of three to eight years. Two other counts were nolled. Michael Gardner appeared before the Board on his new sentence on March 22, 1973, and was released on parole July 2, 1973. In August, 1973, he was again arrested and charged with Breaking and Entering, Larceny, and Criminal Trespassing. On December 11, 1973, he pled guilty to one count of Burglary III Degree. The charges of Larceny and Criminal Mischief were nolled. He was sentenced on January 21, 1974, and received a one-year suspended sentence and probation. He was again arrested on December 17, 1974, and charged with Burglary III Degree and Larceny IV Degree. On February 3, 1975, he was sentenced to serve a one-year sentence for the charge of Burglary III, the Larceny IV was nolled. As a result of these new sentences, the Board on April 8, 1975, voted to revoke this subject's parole. . . .

Source: Letter to the author from chairman, Board of Parole, State of Connecticut, 25 April 1975.

Under the new requirements for prompt and fair hearings, parole boards are discouraging the issuance of violation warrants following infractions of parole rules without evidence of serious new crimes.

The effectiveness of corrections is usually measured by rates of recidivism, the percentage of former offenders who return to criminal behavior after release. The rates vary from 5 percent to 70 percent, depending on who does the counting. One of the problems with statistics on recidivism is that the concept means different things to different people. The recidivism rate depends on how one counts three things: the event (arrest, conviction, parole revocation), the duration of the period in which the measurement is made, and the seriousness of the behavior counted. A common analysis of recidivism is based on reimprisonment within one or two years for either another felony conviction or a parole violation.

Although for decades criminology texts repeated the assertion that 50 to 75 percent of former convicts recidivated, recent evidence suggests that this was an exaggeration. Robert Martinson and Judith Wilkes analyzed the histories of about 100,000 criminals and found that the recidivism rate for the 1970s was slightly below 25 percent.[29] Prisoners released under parole supervision had a return rate of 25.3 percent, compared with 31.5 percent for those who were discharged without parole.

A recent study by Howard Sacks and Charles Logan has raised questions about the effectiveness of parole supervision.[30] The court-ordered release of a group of Class D felons from Connecticut prisons permitted a "natural experiment" to be conducted. The researchers compared the recidivism of this group with an identical group under parole supervision. Those discharged by the court without supervision recidivated more quickly, most during the first year of freedom. The group that received parole supervision stayed out of prison for a longer time, but by the third year out 77 percent had recidivated, compared with 85 percent of those discharged directly to the street. The researchers ask if this postponement of a return to prison is worth the effort and cost of parole supervision. Other research, however, has shown that parolees who stay out of trouble for two years after release have a high probability of continuing to live a crime-free life.

The future of parole

At a time of increasing skepticism about rehabilitation as a goal of the criminal sanction, parole has come under attack. Correctional officials, former inmates, and academic penologists have variously argued that rehabilitation as a goal is unrealistic, that parole boards misuse discretion, that parole supervision is oppressive, that the existence of parole has a detrimental effect on sentencing, and that these pressures have culminated in a major shift in parole systems during the past five years. With discretion limited by the shift in some states to determinate sentencing and the use of parole release guidelines, observers believe that prosecutors, judges, and correctional officials will increase their respective parts in the charging process and the allocation of good time.

Although the release decision has become increasingly mechanical, parole officers still have extensive supervisory responsibilities. As the aim of reintegration with the community has gained emphasis, the surveillance activities of parole officers have suffered in proportion to the increase in resources made available to parolees. As prison populations rise, demands that felons be allowed to serve part of their time in the community will undoubtedly mount. Parole provides one of the few mechanisms available to correctional officials to relieve institutional pressures.

Pardon

President Gerald Ford's pardoning of Richard Nixon for crimes that he may have committed in office and President Jimmy Carter's general pardon of Vietnam draft evaders are two recent examples of a very old procedure. References to pardon are found in ancient Hebrew law, and in medieval Europe the

Close-up: On His Own

Lloyd Nieman is white and 36 years of age. He has served two separate terms for forgery, and had been on parole for a short time when interviewed. He is a professional musician and he feels that running with the bar crowd and drinking excessively was in large part responsible for his "overspending."

Lloyd was reared by his mother, who worked in a factory. His friends have usually been cons. He attended school through the 8th grade only, which he has regretted most of his life.

The first few days I was out were about the roughest days of this entire period. I've only been out a short time—five weeks—but the first three days was a hassle . . . no money, no transportation, no job, and no place to live. Now these things have a way of working themselves out in time, but you have to contact the right people, and sometimes it's hard to find the right people. I was lucky enough to make a contact with a fellow at the Service Center and he gave me enough money to tide me over out of a fund that they had. I'd say that I had a pretty rough time. I'd say the first week was rough. A lot of walking, a lot of walking. . . .

I was lucky that I had two friends here, too, that could help me. Nick gave me a place to stay, because I was out of money within four days. They give you $60, and out of that you got to buy your own clothes, and I couldn't just move in without paying something, so I gave him $25, you know, for room and board. He didn't want it, but I think there's a lot of guys getting out that don't particularly want charity. They like to pay their own way. Even a convict's got pride.

I'd met Nick four or five times, and he kind of gave me a little coming home party. There was several people there that we'd call "squares." But he explained the whole thing to them and they just kind of accepted me as a person. They didn't shy away from me because I was an ex-con. Everybody was very nice, very friendly. They didn't go out of their way to please but they were just comfortable, nice. I think that's a big thing, being able to be comfortable.

I put in several job applications when I first got out, and I went through the ex-con bit on the applications. In fact, I thought about going back to music, so I joined a musicians' union. I was hired and fired by a club in 20 minutes because I was an ex-con.

Job training is a farce, as far as the institutions are concerned. I was a musician, but they want you to have a manual trade, so they recommended silk screening, which is fine. I have no objection to silk screening, you know. . . . I might as well learn something while I'm there. So they made a big thing out of this. They programmed me for silk screening. "You got to have this for the [Parole] Board," they say. Well, this is all well and good, but all of a sudden, they have an opening at camp. Now they need me at camp. So they send me to camp and tell me, "This training isn't really necessary. You don't need it to go to the Board." They need bodies up

church and the monarch had the power of clemency. Later, pardon became known as the "royal prerogative of mercy" in England.

Pardons are acts of the executive. In the United States, the president or governors of the states may grant such clemency in individual cases. In each state the executive receives recommendations from the state's board of pardons (often combined with the board of parole) in regard to individuals who are thought to be deserving of the act. In contemporary times, pardons serve three main purposes: (1) to remedy a miscarriage of justice, (2) to remove the stigma of a conviction, and (3) to mitigate a penalty. Although full pardons for miscarriages of justice are rare, newspaper readers are from time to time alerted to the story of some individual who has been released from prison

at camp, so it's not a question of what's good for you, but of what's good for the institution.

Now I'm at State College on the EOP [Equal Opportunities Program]. Whoever thought I'd go to college at 36? My head's kind of all aswivel because I've been away from school for so long. I'm having a hard time studying, a very difficult time because of the problem of getting back with it. I've been away from it for so long a time that nothing seems to sink in. Well, I'm going after my B.A., and we'll work on an M.A. from there. But I want to make it through education. I really do.

Financially, I'm not too bad off. I've got enough money now for about another six weeks, and I hope to get a job to supplement that income. I have a few friends and, right now, things are pretty good.

When I was in the joint, I kind of thought I might have to go back to hanging paper [forgery]. I thought, "I'm not going to get what I want. I'll probably go out and get a job. I don't want to go back to playing in the bars if I can get away from it because I think that's part of my problem." I have always put on a front. I have an 8th grade education and the institution should be proud of the fact that I am in college.

But if this [college] had not come to pass, I probably would have gone back to work in the bars and associate with the middle-class crowd or the high-paid bracket crowd, and invariably, I would go to cashing checks to keep up this front, you know.

I didn't expect it to turn out as well as it has. It's getting better all the time. My major disappointment is trying to do too many things too fast and realizing that I can't. The time that you're locked up is gone, you know, and you want to do all the things you've missed. When you get out, you're three or four years behind, or whatever it happens to be, and you try to make these things up. It's a disappointment when you find out that you can't do it, that it's going to take you a while to catch up. You got to go slow.

I have mixed emotions. I'm happy to be out, but I have a thing about being my own man. I realize it is necessary, but I do resent a parole officer telling me what I can do and what I cannot do. I believe that every man is different, every case is different, and there can be no set policy.

I believe everything should be weighed and judged on the basis of what the man is capable of. I don't think employment's a privilege. I think employment is a right! I believe you have a right to work anywhere you want. You know, you have to put *yourself* to the test. They're keeping you a mental weakling.

Lloyd didn't make it. Shortly after his interview, he jumped parole and left the state. A year later, he still had not been located.

Source: From *Paroled but Not Free*, by R. J. Erickson, W. J. Crow, L. A. Zurcher, and A. V. Connett, pp. 17–20.

after it has been discovered that he or she was incarcerated by mistake. The more typical activity of pardons boards is to expunge the criminal records of first-time offenders—often young people—so that they may enter the professions, obtain certain types of employment, and in general not have to bear the stigma of a single indiscretion. In states that have abolished release on parole and have adopted fixed sentences, the pardons board may become a more important agency for the mitigation of penalties.

Civil disabilities

We may believe that once a person has been released from prison, paid a fine, or been discharged from parole or probation, the punishment has ended; the "debt" to society has been paid. For many offenders, however, a criminal conviction is a lifetime burden. In most states it is not enough to have served time, to have reestablished family ties, to have gotten a job, and otherwise to have become a law-abiding member of the community; certain civil rights are forever forfeited, some fields of employment may never be entered, and some insurance or pension benefits may be foreclosed.

The extent of civil disabilities varies greatly among the states, but generally persons who have been convicted of a felony are treated as a group. In some states, persons who have been convicted of certain crimes are subjected to specific restrictions; forgery, for example, prevents employment in the banking or stock-trading fields. In other states, blanket restrictions are placed on all former felons. The forfeiture of rights can be traced to Greek and Roman times, and American courts have generally upheld the constitutionality of such restrictions.

The right to vote and to hold public office are two civil rights that are limited upon conviction. Thirty-one states have taken away the right to vote from persons convicted of certain offenses. In 1974 the U.S. Supreme Court upheld (*Richardson* v. *Ramirez*) a provision of the California constitution designed to disenfranchise convicted felons.[31] Most states and the federal government also prohibit persons convicted of certain crimes from holding public office.

Ex-offenders: Barriers to Employment

- Discrimination by employers.
- Limited number of job opportunities and poor access to the primary labor market.
- Formal legal or licensing restrictions on employment of ex-offenders.
- Bonding requirements.
- Lack of adequate financial resources for subsistence needs during job search.
- Union membership, civil service tests, and other mechanisms to screen job applicants.
- Correctional policies, procedures, and conditions that inhibit or prohibit access to education, training, or community reintegration programs.
- Blocked or limited access to programs and supportive services necessary to address needs for food, clothing, housing, child care, medical care, education, and employment.

Source: Cicero Wilson, Kenneth J. Lenihan, and Gail Goolkasian, *Employment Services for Ex-Offenders*, U.S. Department of Justice, National Institute of Justice (Washington, D.C.: Government Printing Office, 1981), pp. 23–24.

Although most former felons may not believe that restrictions on their civil rights will make it difficult for them to lead normal lives, limitations on entry into certain fields of employment are a problem. Many observers assert that the restrictions force offenders into menial jobs at low pay that may lead them back to crime. Until the turn of the century, only members of the professions—lawyers, doctors, teachers—were licensed by the state; the withholding of such licenses from felons was quite common. With the rise of the labor movement and the professionalization of many occupations, states began to require licenses to enter hundreds of fields. Originally justified in terms of safety and quality standards, licensing appears now to have been designed primarily to restrict the number of persons in a field so that the fees for services could be kept high.

Occupations that currently restrict the entry of former offenders include nurse, beautician, barber, real estate salesperson, chauffeur, employee of a place where alcoholic beverages are served, cashier, stenographer, insurance agent. Richard Singer has noted: "In all, nearly six thousand occupations are licensed in one or more states; the convicted offender may find the presumption against him either difficult or impossible to overcome."[32] The fact that many prison vocational programs promoted for rehabilitative purposes lead to restricted occupations seems to have been ignored.

Although some states provide no procedures for the restoration of rights, others provide discretionary mechanisms—often through the pardoning process—for the expunging of a criminal conviction after the passage of time. But questions remain as to whether a person may legally deny a conviction on an employment application even after the conviction has been expunged.

Critics of civil disability laws point out that upon fulfilling the penalty imposed for a crime, the former offender should be assisted to full reintegration into society. They argue that it is counterproductive for government to promote rehabilitation with the goal of reintegration while at the same time preventing offenders from fully achieving that goal. Others, however, say that the possibility of recidivism and the community's need for protection justify these restrictions. In the middle ground there is the belief that not all persons convicted of felonies should be treated equally, and that society can be protected adequately by the placement of restrictions on only certain individuals.

Summary

Methods for dealing with criminal offenders have come a long way since the reform activities of Philadelphia's Quakers, but uncertainty remains about the methods that should be used. Although Attica forced Americans to reexamine the correctional system, the violence of that early-morning attack may soon be forgotten. With the rate of recidivism remaining about constant, increased doubts are being expressed about the value of the rehabilitative model. As crime rates continue to rise, questions are raised about the deterrent effect of correctional methods.

Reformers say that rehabilitation has so dominated the thinking of penologists during the past half century that other goals for the criminal sanction have been forgotten. Although some offenders do suffer social and psychological deficits that may be the basis for their criminal behavior, such persons may constitute only a small portion of the offender population. To implement a correctional policy based solely on rehabilitation is to neglect the goals of deterrence, incapacitation, and retributive justice, which are also important elements of the goal of criminal justice—the prevention and control of crime.

The concept of community corrections tied to fixed sentences, good time, and treatment services on a voluntary basis appears to point the way to the future implementation of a policy that seeks to achieve justice for the offender, the victim, and society. Although the thrust of these innovations is found primarily in correctional literature, some states have already begun to implement this approach. Of all the various subsystems of criminal justice, corrections appears to be going through the most sustained soul-searching. Changes made in corrections policy will have an important impact on the way law enforcement and adjudication will pursue their goals in the future.

For discussion

1. You are on the parole board. Before you is a young man with little education and a history of trouble with the law since he was a child. He has been incarcerated for stealing to support a drug habit and is now eligible for parole. What should you consider as you make your decision?
2. What restrictions does your state place on former convicts with regard to occupation?
3. You are a prisoner. You have been sentenced to three to ten years in your prison's maximum security facility. How should you act so that you can win parole at the earliest date? How will you act in relation to your fellow prisoners?
4. What constitutional challenges might be made to the federal parole guidelines?
5. Is community corrections a viable alternative to incarceration? What are its advantages and disadvantages?

For further reading

American Friends Service Committee. *Struggle for Justice.* New York: Hill & Wang, 1971.

Glaser, Daniel. *The Effectiveness of a Prison and Parole System.* Indianapolis: Bobbs-Merrill, 1969.

Stanley, David. *Prisoners among Us.* Washington, D.C.: Brookings Institution, 1976.

von Hirsch, Andrew, and Kathleen J. Hanrahan. *The Question of Parole.* Cambridge, Mass.: Ballinger, 1979.

Notes

1. President's Commission on Law Enforcement and Administration of Justice, *Task Force Report: Corrections* (Washington, D.C.: Government Printing Office, 1967), p. 7.
2. American Bar Association Project on Standards for Criminal Justice, *Standards Relating to Probation* (New York: Institute of Judicial Administration, 1970), p. 9.
3. Quoted in Kevin Krajick, "Probation: The Original Community Program," *Corrections Magazine* 6 (December 1980): 7.
4. Ibid., p. 8.
5. Martin D. Schwartz, Todd R. Clear, and Lawrence F. Travis III, *Corrections: An Issues Approach* (Cincinnati: Anderson, 1980), p. 105.
6. Ibid., pp. 104–8.
7. President's Commission on Law Enforcement and Administration of Justice, *Task Force Report: Corrections,* p. 29.
8. "Probation Subsidy: 'Behavior Modification' for Bureaucracies," *Corrections Magazine* 6 (December 1980): 19.
9. Joseph Banks et al., *Evaluation of Special Probation Projects,* National Evaluation Program, Phase I (Washington, D.C.: Government Printing Office, 1977).
10. Mempa v. Rhay, 389 U.S. 128 (1967).
11. Gagnon v. Scarpelli, 411 U.S. 778 (1973).
12. "A Survey of Furlough Programs," *Corrections Magazine* 1 (July–August 1975): 27.
13. Edward Latessa and Harry Allen, "Halfway Houses and Parole: A National Assessment," *Journal of Criminal Justice* 10 (1982): 156.
14. Kevin Krajick, "Not on My Block," *Corrections* 6 (December 1980): 16.

15. *Treating Youthful Offenders in the Community* (Washington, D.C.: Correctional Research Associates, 1966).
16. U.S. Department of Justice, Bureau of Justice Statistics, *Bulletin,* August 1982, p. 3.
17. Citizens' Inquiry on Parole and Criminal Justice, "Summary Report on New York Parole" (1974), p. 10 (mimeo).
18. Donald J. Newman, "Legal Model for Parole: Future Developments," in *Contemporary Corrections,* ed. Benjamin Frank (Reston, Va.: Reston Publishing Co., 1973), p. 245.
19. Ronald Goldfarb and Linda R. Singer, *After Conviction* (New York: Simon & Schuster, 1973), pp. 257–64.
20. U.S. Department of Justice, Bureau of Justice Statistics, *Parole in the United States, 1979* (Washington, D.C.: Government Printing Office, 1980), p. 10.
21. Kenneth Culp Davis, *Discretionary Justice* (Baton Rouge: Louisiana State University Press, 1969), p. 133.
22. As quoted in Edwin H. Sutherland and Donald R. Cressey, *Criminology* (Philadelphia: Lippincott, 1970), p. 587.
23. As quoted in Newman, "Legal Model for Parole," p. 246.
24. As quoted in Robert Wool, "The New Parole and the Case of Mr. Simms," *New York Times Magazine,* 29 July 1973, p. 21.
25. As quoted in Jessica Mitford, *Kind and Usual Punishment* (New York: Knopf, 1973), p. 217.
26. Goldfarb and Singer, *After Conviction,* p. 292.
27. Morrissey v. Brewer, 408 U.S. 471 (1972).
28. Daniel Glaser, *The Effectiveness of a Prison and Parole System* (Indianapolis: Bobbs-Merrill, 1969).
29. As cited in Selwyn Raab, "U.S. Study Finds Recidivism Rate of Convicts Lower than Expected," *New York Times,* 7 November 1976, p. 61.
30. Howard R. Sacks and Charles H. Logan, "Does Parole Make a (Lasting) Difference?" in *Criminal Justice: Law and Politics,* ed. George F. Cole, 4th ed. (Monterey, Calif.: Brooks/Cole, 1984), p. 362.
31. 418 U.S. 24 (1974).
32. Richard Singer, "Conviction: Civil Disabilities," in *Encyclopedia of Crime and Justice,* ed. Sanford H. Kadish (New York: Free Press, 1983), p. 246.

PART 5

Juvenile Justice System

Crimes committed by juveniles have become a serious national problem. The *Uniform Crime Reports* show that just over a third of the people arrested for an index crime are under eighteen years of age. Children who are charged with crimes, who have been neglected by their parents, or whose behavior is deemed to require official action come in contact with the juvenile justice system, an independent process that is interrelated with the adult system. As chapter 17 will demonstrate, many of the procedures used in the handling of juvenile problems are similar to those used with adults, but the overriding philosophy of juvenile justice is somewhat different and the extent to which the state may intrude into the lives of children is much greater.

Juvenile Justice

There is evidence . . . that there may be grounds for concern that the child receives the worst of both worlds: that he gets neither the protections accorded to adults nor the solicitous care and regenerative treatment postulated for children.

JUSTICE ABE FORTAS

At 10:00 A.M. on Monday, June 8, 1964, fifteen-year-old Gerald Gault and his friend Ronald Lewis were taken into custody by the sheriff of Gila County, Arizona, on the complaint of a neighbor about a telephone call to her in which the caller had made lewd and indecent remarks. On her arrival from work late that afternoon, Gerald's mother became alarmed that her son was not at home. Neighbors told her that the sheriff's car had been at the house earlier in the day. Because Gerald was on probation as a result of an incident in January 1964, when he had been apprehended in the company of another youth who had stolen a woman's purse, Mrs. Gault anxiously called the sheriff's office and learned that her son was being held at the Children's Detention Home for appearance in Juvenile Court the following day.

At hearings conducted before Judge McGhee on 9 and 15 June, Gerald said that he had only dialed the number and that Lewis had done the talking. In attendance at the hearings were only Gerald, his parents, Judge McGhee, and probation officers Flagg and Henderson. The proceedings were informal, no one was sworn, no transcript was made, and no record was prepared. Mrs. Gault asked why the complaining neighbor was not present "so she could see which boy had done the talking." The judge said her presence was not necessary. The only other item that played a role in the hearing was a "referral report" filed with the court by the probation officers; none of the three Gaults was told what it said.

At the end of the hearing, Judge McGhee announced that he was committing Gerald as a juvenile delinquent to the state industrial school "for the period of his majority [that is, until the age of twenty-one], unless sooner discharged by due process of law." Had he been an adult, the maximum punishment for such a telephone call would have been a fine of $5 to $50 or imprisonment for not more than two months. As a minor, Gerald Gault was committed to the state school for six years.

With the aid of Amelia Lewis, an attorney and member of the Arizona Civil Liberties Union, the Gaults appealed the decision on the grounds that the safeguards of due process had not been accorded. They stated that the juvenile court had not given them adequate notice as to the nature of the charges and the hearing; had not advised them of their constitutional rights, including the right to counsel, the right to confront witnesses, and the privilege against self-incrimination; had not made a record of the proceedings; and

had used hearsay testimony from unsworn witnesses.

Appealing to the United States Supreme Court, Mr. and Mrs. Gault argued that their son had not been accorded the procedural guarantees required by the due process clause of the Fourteenth Amendment. Before focusing on these rights, the brief examined the historical background of juvenile court systems. It argued that ***parens patriae***—the legal concept that the state may intervene to protect the welfare of children—had been substituted for procedural due process and had resulted in detrimental effects on many children in juvenile proceedings. Although conceding that the juvenile court movement had led to advances in the treatment accorded juveniles, the brief went on to say that "juvenile court proceedings, which were instituted to protect the young, led in many jurisdictions to findings of delinquency in proceedings that conspicuously failed to protect the child." It further reasoned that neither *parens patriae* nor the theory that a juvenile proceeding was a civil matter dealing with treatment rather than punishment could justify "the refusal to accord Gerald Gault and other juveniles the protection of the Bill of Rights."

parens patriae
The "parent of the country"; the state as guardian and protector of all citizens (such as juveniles) who are unable to protect themselves.

On 15 May 1967, almost three years after Gerald Gault had first been sent to the Children's Detention Home, the Supreme Court reversed the Arizona decision and held that a child in a delinquency hearing must be afforded certain procedural rights, including notice of charges, right to counsel, right to confrontation and cross-examination of witnesses, and protection against self-incrimination. Writing for the majority, Justice Abe Fortas emphasized that due process rights and procedures adhere to juvenile justice. "Under our Constitution the condition of being a boy does not justify a kangaroo court."[1] The opinion went on to specify that juveniles had (1) the right to notice, (2) the right to counsel, (3) the right to confront witnesses, (4) the privilege against self-incrimination, (5) the right to transcripts, and (6) the right to appellate review.

Of the two dissenters, Justice Potter Stewart expressed a more traditional conception of juvenile justice:

> Juvenile proceedings are not criminal trials. They are not civil trials. They are

simply not adversary proceedings. Whether treating with a delinquent child, a neglected child, a defective child, or a dependent child, a juvenile proceeding's whole purpose and mission is the very opposite of the mission and purpose of a prosecution in a criminal court. The object of the one is correction of a condition. The object of the other is conviction and punishment for a criminal act.[2]

The Supreme Court decision points to a constant tension within the juvenile justice system between those who think that children should be given all the due process guarantees accorded adults and those who think that children must be handled in a less adversarial, more treatment-oriented manner so that legal procedures will not interfere with efforts to secure the justice that is in the children's best interest.

The *Uniform Crime Reports (UCR)* indicate that young people make up a substantial and growing portion of the national crime problem. Although the public may believe that juveniles commit only minor violations, the 1983 *UCR* statistics show otherwise. Persons under eighteen years of age, for example, made up about 30 percent of those arrested for all eight index crimes, 17 percent of those arrested for violent crimes, and 34 percent of those arrested for property crimes (see table 17.1).

Some readers may wonder why a chapter on juvenile justice appears in this book, since it is often assumed that the system organized to deal with delinquency and the problems of young people is administrative rather than adversarial, with diagnosis and rehabilitation as its main goals. It is true that the formal processes of juvenile justice differ from those used with adults, but these differences lie primarily in emphasis. The juvenile justice system is a separate but interrelated part of the broader criminal justice system. Whether involved in law enforcement, adjudication, or corrections, one cannot be divorced from the problems of youth. With juveniles composing a significant portion of those who violate the criminal law, serious attention must be paid to this system.

Juveniles and criminal justice

The *Gault* decision was the first major challenge to a system and philosophy of juvenile justice that had its inception in the United States during the period of social reform in the latter part of the nineteenth century. The origin of the idea that children should be treated differently from adults, however, is found in the common law and in the chancery courts of England. The common law had long prescribed that children under seven years of age were incapable of felonious intent and were therefore not criminally responsible. Children aged seven to fourteen could be held accountable only if it could be shown that they understood the consequences of their actions. Under the doctrine of *parens patriae,* which held the king to be the father of the realm, the chancery courts exercised protective jurisdiction over all children, particularly those involved in questions of dependency, neglect, and property. These courts, however, had civil jurisdiction, and juvenile offenders were dealt with by the criminal courts. But the concept of *parens patriae* was important for the development of juvenile justice, for it legitimized the intervention of the state on behalf of the child. The English procedures were maintained in the American colonies. It was not until the early part of the twentieth century that efforts were made to deal with children in special ways and to separate their cases from those of adults. The stages through which the concepts and treatment of delinquent and dependent children have passed from the seventeenth century to the present are outlined in table 17.2.

The child savers

Among the social movements that arose in the United States to cope with the problems associated with rapid industrialization and urbanization in the nineteenth century, reform of the criminal law pertaining to juveniles attracted active supporters. The growing concern about the influence of environmental factors on behavior; the rise of the social sciences, which claimed they could treat the problems underlying deviance; and an awareness of the brutality of the conditions under which children were incarcerated stimulated the reformers.

These middle-class reformers sought to use the power of the state to "save" children from a life of crime. They were concerned primarily with the urban immigrant poor, and sought to have parents declared "unfit" if their children roamed the streets and apparently were "out of control." It was not that the children were engaged in criminal acts (though many were) but—the belief went—that children who were not disciplined and trained by their parents to abide by the rules of society would eventually find themselves in prison. The state's power was to be used to prevent delinquency. The solution was to create institutions for these children where they could learn good work and study habits, live in a disciplined and healthy environment, and develop "character." The first such institution was the House of Refuge of New York, which opened in 1825. It was followed by similar facilities in Boston, Philadelphia, and Baltimore. Children were placed in these homes by court order and often stayed there until they reached the age of majority.

By the middle of the nineteenth century, the more "progressive" states had begun to develop new institutions—reform schools—to provide the discipline needed by wayward youth in a "homelike" atmosphere where education would be emphasized. The first, the Lyman School for Boys, was opened in Westboro, Massachusetts, in 1848. A similar school for girls was opened in Lancaster, Massachusetts, in 1855. Ohio created the State Reform Farm in 1857, and the states of Maine, Rhode Island, New York, and Michigan soon followed suit.

At the same time that some groups were advocating creation of reform schools, other groups, such as the Children's Aid Society of New York, were emphasizing the need to place neglected and delinquent children in private homes. This was a period when the city was viewed as a place of crime and bad influences, in contrast to the clean, healthy, crime-free country. Like the advocates of reform of adult corrections, the children's aid societies of the 1850s emphasized placement in rural areas. The additional hands thus acquired provided an economic incentive for farmers to "take in" these juveniles.

Establishment of the juvenile court

With services to neglected youth widely established in most states by the end of the nineteenth century, the problem of juvenile criminality became the focus of attention during another period of reform. As chapter 14 pointed

TABLE 17.1 Number and percent of arrests of persons under 15, 18, 21, and 25 years of age for index crimes, 1983

	Number of persons arrested					Percent of total, all ages			
Offense charged	*All ages*	*Under 15*	*Under 18*	*Under 21*	*Under 25*	*Under 15*	*Under 18*	*Under 21*	*Under 25*
All offenses	10,287,309	564,983	1,725,746	3,324,558	5,238,328	5.5	16.8	32.3	50.9
Murder and nonnegligent manslaughter	18,064	157	1,345	4,016	7,486	0.9	7.4	22.2	41.4
Forcible rape	30,183	1,332	4,388	8,780	14,985	4.4	14.5	29.1	49.6
Robbery	134,018	9,203	35,219	63,845	91,161	6.9	26.3	47.6	68.0
Aggravated assault	261,421	10,148	33,730	68,482	117,189	3.9	12.9	26.2	44.8
Burglary	415,651	59,400	159,192	246,147	313,236	14.3	38.3	59.2	75.4
Larceny-theft	1,169,066	168,095	377,435	558,779	725,457	14.4	32.3	47.8	62.1
Motor vehicle theft	105,514	8,628	36,497	57,918	75,924	8.2	34.6	54.9	72.0
Arson	17,203	4,113	6,457	8,473	10,661	23.9	37.5	49.3	62.0
Violent crime	443,686	20,840	74,682	145,123	230,821	4.7	16.8	32.7	52.0
Property crime	1,707,434	240,236	579,581	871,317	1,125,278	14.1	33.9	51.0	65.9
Crime Index total	2,151,120	261,076	654,263	1,016,440	1,356,099	12.1	30.4	47.3	63.0

Source: U.S. Department of Justice, *Uniform Crime Reports* (Washington, D.C.: Government Printing Office, 1984), p. 185.

TABLE 17.2 Juvenile justice developments and their impact on conceptions of the relationships of the child, parents, and state

Period	*Major developments*	*Precipitation, influences*	*Child/state*	*Parent/state*	*Parent/child*
Puritan 1646–1824	Massachusetts Stubborn Child Law (1646)	A. Christian view of child as evil B. Economically marginal agrarian society	Law provides: A. Symbolic standard of maturity B. Support for family as economic unit	Parents considered responsible and capable of controlling child	Child considered both property and spiritual responsibility of parents
Refuge 1824–1899	Institutionalization of deviants; New York House of Refuge established (1824) for delinquent and dependent children	A. Enlightenment B. Immigration and industrialization	Child seen as helpless, in need of state intervention	Parents supplanted as state assumes responsibility for correcting deviant socialization	Family considered to be a major cause of juvenile deviancy
Juvenile court 1899–1960	Establishment of separate legal system for juveniles—Illinois Juvenile Court Act (1899)	A. Reformism and rehabilitative ideology B. Increased immigration, urbanization, large-scale industrialization	Juvenile court institutionalizes legal irresponsibility of child	*Parens patriae* doctrine gives legal foundation for state intervention in family	Further abrogation of parents' rights and responsibilities
Juvenile rights 1960–present	Increased "legalization" of juvenile law; *Gault* decision (1966); Juvenile Justice and Delinquency Prevention Act (1974) calls for deinstitutionalization of status offenders	A. Criticism of juvenile justice system on humane grounds B. Civil rights movements by disadvantaged groups	Movement to define and protect rights as well as to provide services to children	Reassertion of responsibility of parents and community for welfare and behavior of children	Attention given to children's claims against parents; earlier emancipation of children

Source: U.S. Department of Justice, *A Preliminary National Assessment of the Status Offender and the Juvenile Justice System,* Reports of the National Juvenile Justice Assessment Centers (Washington, D.C.: Government Printing Office, 1980), p. 29. Copyright held by American Justice Institute, Sacramento, California. Reprinted by permission.

out, the Progressive movement sought to use the power of the state to provide individualized care and treatment of deviants of all kinds—adult criminals, the mentally ill, juvenile delinquents. They pushed for adoption of probation, treatment, indeterminate sentences, and parole for adult offenders, and were successful in establishing similar programs for juveniles. They also campaigned successfully for creation of a juvenile court.

As David Rothman has pointed out, juvenile delinquency created a dilemma for the state. It could either deal with young accused persons under the adult criminal law, calling upon the full powers of the state to prosecute, try, sentence, and imprison them, or it could refrain from such strictness and merely return them to their parents and the community; and both options were viewed as poor policy for juveniles and for society. It was argued that a separate juvenile court system should be created so that the problems of the individual youth could be treated in an atmosphere in which flexible procedures would, as one reformer said, "banish entirely all thought of crime and punishment."[3]

With passage of the Juvenile Court Act by Illinois in 1899 the first comprehensive system of juvenile justice was established. The act brought together under one jurisdiction cases of dependency, neglect, and delinquency ("incorrigibles and children threatened by immoral associations as well as criminal lawbreakers"). Such activists as Jane Addams and Julia Lathrop, of the settlement house movement; Henry Thurston, a social work educator; and the National Congress of Mothers were successful in promoting the juvenile court concept, so that by 1904 ten states had implemented procedures similar to those of Illinois, and by 1920 all but three states provided for a juvenile court.

Undergirding the philosophy of the juvenile court was the idea that the state should deal with a child who broke the law as a wise parent would deal with a wayward child. *Parens patriae* of the English chancery courts helped legitimize the system. Procedures were to be informal and private, records were to be confidential, children were to be detained apart from adults, and a probation and social worker staff were to be appointed. Even the vocabulary and physical surroundings of the juvenile system were changed to emphasize diagnosis and treatment rather than findings of guilt. The term "criminal behavior" was replaced by "delinquent behavior" as it pertained to the illegal acts of children. This shift in terminology serves to underscore the view of these children as wayward; they could be returned to society as law-abiding citizens.

Because procedures were not to be adversarial, lawyers were unnecessary;

Child Saving: An Early View

To save a child from becoming a criminal, or from continuing in a career of crime, to end in maturer years in public punishment and disgrace, the legislatures surely may provide for the salvation of such a child, if its parents or guardians be unable or unwilling to do so, by bringing it into one of the courts of the state without any process at all, for the purpose of subjecting it to the state's guardianship and protection. . . . The act simply provides how children who ought to be saved may reach the court to be saved.

Source: Commonwealth v. Fisher (1905).

psychologists and social workers, who could determine the juvenile's underlying behavior problem, were the main professionals attached to the system. Judge Julian Mack, one of the pioneers of the movement, summarized the questions to be placed before a juvenile court: "The problem for determination by the judge is not, Has this boy or girl committed a specific wrong, but What is he, how has he become what he is, and what had best be done in his interest and in the interest of the State to save him from a downward career."[4]

Juvenile rights

Until the 1960s, the ideology and practices of juvenile justice were dominated by the philosophy expressed by Judge Mack and others, such as Ben B. Lindsey, Denver's juvenile court judge from 1901 to 1929, and Gustav L. Schramm, who served for a long time on the bench of Pittsburgh's juvenile court. During recent years, however, reformers have sought to emphasize a concern for the rights of juveniles and the importance of the family as the means of controlling children's behavior.

The Supreme Court opinion in *Gault* (1967) and the earlier ruling in *Kent* v. *United States* (1966) extended due process rights to children.[5] These cases were followed by *In re Winship* (1970), in which the Court held that proof must be established "beyond a reasonable doubt" before a juvenile may be classified as a delinquent for committing an act that would be a crime if it were committed by an adult.[6] Perhaps signifying the extent to which the Court was willing to extend the concept of due process, the court held in *McKeiver* v. *Pennsylvania* (1971) that "trial by jury in the juvenile court's adjudicative stage is not a constitutional requirement."[7] But, in *Breed* v. *Jones* (1975), the Court extended the protection against double jeopardy to juveniles by requiring that before a

Julian W. Mack

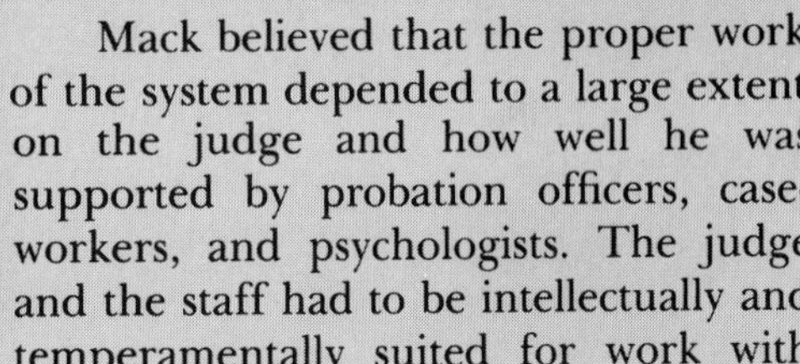

A federal judge for thirty years, Julian Mack (1866–1943) ranks as one of the foremost innovators in juvenile justice. Born in San Francisco, he received his law degree at Harvard and went into practice in Chicago in 1890. He was elected to a judgeship for the Circuit Court of Cook County, Illinois, in 1903, and between 1904 and 1907 he presided over Chicago's juvenile court, the first in the world. This court had been established by the Illinois legislature in 1899. Under Mack, the court dealt with neglected and abused children, runaways, school dropouts, and juveniles who had committed crimes. Juveniles were to be seen as wards of the state, not as criminals, thereby achieving a new legal status. The court was to become a social agency mixing services, discipline, probation, and the use of reformatories.

Mack believed that the proper work of the system depended to a large extent on the judge and how well he was supported by probation officers, caseworkers, and psychologists. The judge and the staff had to be intellectually and temperamentally suited for work with juveniles; they had to be professionals and not political hacks. To this end, Mack supported the founding of the National Probation Officers Association. He sought as much as possible to avoid using reformatories and tried to bring the expertise of social service professionals to work for the courts.

In 1907 Judge Mack was promoted to the Illinois Appeals Court, and in 1911 he was appointed by President William Howard Taft to a seat on the U.S. Court of Appeals for the 7th Circuit, from which he retired in 1941.

case is adjudicated in juvenile court a hearing must be held to determine if it should be transferred to the adult court.[8] However, in 1984 in *Schall* v. *Martin*,[9] the Court significantly departed from the trend toward increased juvenile rights. Noting that any attempt to structure such rights "must be qualified by the recognition that juveniles, unlike adults, are always in some form of custody," the Court confirmed the general notion of *parens patriae* as a primary basis for the juvenile court, equal in importance to the court's desire to protect the community from crime. Thus, juveniles may be detained before trial if they are found to be a "risk" to the community, even though this rationale is not applicable to adult pretrial detention.

The *Schall* decision reflects the ambivalence permeating the juvenile justice system in the 1980s. On one side are the liberal reformers, who call for increased procedural and substantive legal protections for juveniles accused of crime, while on the other side conservatives devoted to crime control policies are alarmed by the rise in juvenile crime. Like the Supreme Court, various state courts have considered issues involving the right to treatment, equal protection, and cruel and unusual punishments, and had to acknowledge the vagueness of certain laws affecting juveniles.

The system has also responded to charges that correctional institutions for children were being operated in ways that reinforced delinquent behavior and that too many children were being incarcerated. During the 1970s there was a movement to attack these problems. In 1972 Massachusetts became the first state to close most of its reformatories and to place the children in group homes and community treatment centers instead. Other states reduced the number of children they held in institutions less dramatically.

Status offenders, as we have seen, are juveniles who have committed acts that are not illegal when they are committed by an adult. Playing truant, running away, or refusing to obey the orders of adults may lead to a correctional term in most states. Efforts have been made to divert such children out of the system, to reduce the possibility of incarceration, and to rewrite the laws with regard to ***status offenses.***

status offense
Any act committed by a juvenile that would not be a crime if it were committed by an adult but that is considered unacceptable for a child, such as truancy or running away from home.

Thus much of the reform effort of the past decade has been directed away from the broad jurisdiction of the juvenile court, with its lack of due process protections and its overarching treatment orientation. At the same time, juvenile crime has become recognized as a serious problem.

Operation of juvenile justice

Juvenile justice operates through a variety of procedures in different states, and even within states, but a national pattern can fairly easily be discerned. In general, the system functions through many of the existing organizations of the adult criminal justice system but often with specialized structures for activities having to do with juveniles. Thus, although some large cities have specialized juvenile sections in their police departments, it is usually the patrol officer who has contact with delinquents when a disturbance or crime has been reported. In many states, special probation officers work with juveniles, but they function as part of the larger probation service. Indeed, there are even some correctional systems that, although they maintain separate facilities for children, are organized under a commissioner who is responsible for both adult and juvenile institutions. The one portion of the system that is distinctive is the jurisdiction and procedures of the juvenile court, where only actions concerning children are heard, where the judge usually has a special concern for such cases, and where many of the processes of the adversarial system are absent. The broad outlines of the juvenile justice system are shown in figure 17.1.

Age normally determines whether a person is processed through the juvenile or adult justice system. The upper age limit for a juvenile varies from sixteen to eighteen: in thirty-eight states and the District of Columbia it is the eighteenth birthday; in eight states, the seventeenth; and in the remainder, the sixteenth. In most states, judges have the discretion to transfer juveniles to adult courts (see table 17.3). Although juveniles may be tried by the adult system when they "are not amenable to treatment in juvenile court" or "not a fit subject" for juvenile court jurisdiction, the severity of the offense and a prior record are the underlying reasons for the transfer. Thus in some states children charged with serious crimes, such as rape, murder, or armed robbery, may be processed in the adult criminal courts; and in a growing number of states, youths charged with a particularly serious offense or who may have a history of repeated offenses may find that charges are filed against them directly in the criminal court, with no process of transfer from the jurisdiction of the juvenile court.

Which cases enter the juvenile justice system? Generally, there are four types: delinquency, status offenses, neglect, and dependency. Delinquent children have committed acts that if committed by an adult would be criminal—for example, auto theft, robbery, and assault. As we have seen, acts that are illegal only if they are committed by juveniles are known as status offenses. Rather than having committed a violation of the penal code, status offenders have behaved in such a way that they conform to descriptions designating them as being ungovernable, incorrigible, runaways, truants, or persons in need of supervision (***PINS***).

Some states do not distinguish between delinquent offenders and status offenders, and label both as juvenile ***delinquents***. Those judged to be ungov-

PINS, CINS, JINS
Acronyms for "person in need of supervision," "child in need of supervision," and "juvenile in need of supervision," terms used to designate juveniles who either are status offenders or are thought to be on the verge of getting into trouble; indicate that the state believes the child is not receiving proper supervision.

delinquent
A child who has committed a criminal or status offense.

TABLE 17.3 Youngest age at which juvenile may be transferred to adult criminal court by waiver of juvenile jurisdiction

No specific age	*10*	*13*	*14*	*15*	*16*
Alaska	South Dakota	Georgia	Alabama	District of Columbia	California
Arizona		Illinois	Colorado	Idaho	Hawaii
Florida		Mississippi	Connecticut	Louisiana	Kansas
Maine			Delaware	Maryland	Kentucky
New Hampshire			Indiana	Michigan	Montana
Oklahoma			Iowa	New Mexico	Nevada
South Carolina			Massachusetts	Ohio	North Dakota
Washington			Minnesota	Tennessee	Oregon
West Virginia			Missouri	Texas	Rhode Island
Wyoming			New Jersey	Virginia	Wisconsin
Federal districts			North Carolina		
			Pennsylvania		
			Utah		

Note: Many judicial waiver statutes also specify offenses that are waivable. This table lists the states by the youngest age for which judicial waiver may be sought without regard to offense.
Source: Hamparian, Donna M., et al. *Youth in Adult Courts: Between Two Worlds* (Columbus, Ohio: The Academy for Contemporary Problems, 1982).

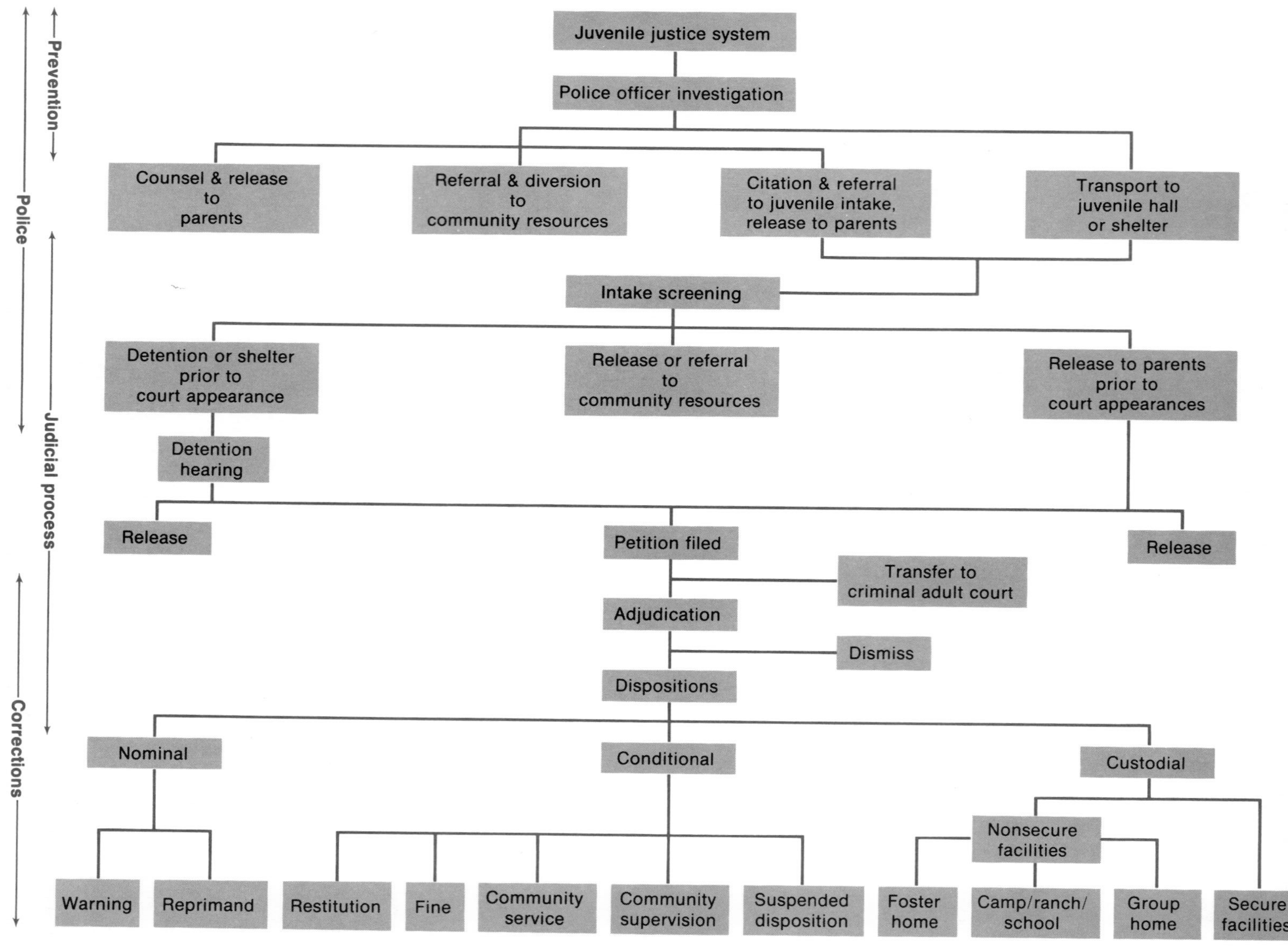

FIGURE 17.1 Juvenile justice system

ernable and those judged to be robbers may find themselves sent to the same correctional institution. Beginning in the early 1960s, many state legislatures attempted to distinguish status offenders and to exempt them from a criminal record. The breadth of the law defining status offenses is a matter of concern because the language is often vague and all-encompassing: "growing up in idleness and crime," "engaging in immoral conduct," "in danger of leading an immoral life," "person in need of supervision." A child may be judged incorrigible and therefore delinquent for "refusing to obey the just and reasonable commands of his parents." The jurisdictional net is so broad in many states that almost any child can be described as requiring the protection of the juvenile justice system.

Juvenile justice also deals with problems of neglect and dependency—situations in which children are viewed as being hurt through no fault of their own, because their parents have failed to provide a proper environment for them. Such situations have been the jurisdictional concern of most juvenile justice systems since the turn of the century, when the idea gained currency that the state should act as a parent to a child whose own parents are unable or unwilling to provide proper care. Illinois, for example, defines a ***neglected child*** as one "who is neglected as to proper or necessary support, education as required by law, or as to medical or other remedial care recognized under State law or other care necessary for his well being, or who is abandoned by his parents, guardians or custodians, or whose environment is injurious to his welfare or whose behavior is injurious to his own welfare or that of others."[10] A ***dependent child*** is either without a parent or guardian or is not receiving proper care because of the physical or mental disability of that person. The jurisdiction here is broad and includes a variety of situations in which the child may be viewed as a victim of adult behavior.

neglected child
A child who is not receiving proper care because of some action or inaction of his or her parent(s).

dependent child
A child whose parent(s) are unable to give proper care.

Nationally about 75 percent of the cases referred to the juvenile courts are delinquency cases, of which a fifth are concerned with status offenses (see table 17.4); about 20 percent are dependency and neglect cases; and about 5 percent involve special proceedings, such as adoption.[11] The system, then, deals with both criminal and noncriminal cases, and a concern has been expressed that juveniles who have done nothing wrong are categorized either officially or in the public mind as delinquents. In some states little effort is made in pre-judicial detention facilities or in social service agencies to keep the classes of juveniles separate.

More discretion is exercised in the juvenile than in the adult justice system. Turn-of-the-century reformers believed that juvenile justice officials should have wide discretion in their efforts to serve the best interests of the

Connecticut: Jurisdiction of the Juvenile Court

Sec. 46b–121. Juvenile matters defined, authority of court. Juvenile matters include all proceedings concerning uncared-for, neglected or dependent children and youth and delinquent children within this state, termination of parental rights of children committed to a state agency, matters concerning families with service needs and contested termination of parental rights transferred from the probate court, but does not include matters of guardianship and adoption or matters affecting property rights of any child or youth over which the probate court has jurisdiction.

Source: Connecticut, *General Statutes,* 1980.

TABLE 17.4 Offenses of juveniles referred to juvenile court (percent)

11% Crimes against persons		***15% Offenses against public order***	
Criminal homicide	1%	Weapons offenses	10%
Forcible rape	2	Sex offenses	6
Robbery	18	Drunkenness	12
Aggravated assault	22	Disturbing the peace	22
Simple assault	52	Escape, contempt, probation, parole	19
Other	5	Other	32
	100%		100%
49% Crimes against property		***20% Status offenses***	
Burglary	26%	Runaway	27%
Larceny	41	Truancy	12
Motor vehicle theft	9	Curfew	7
Arson and vandalism	12	Ungovernable	18
Stolen property offenses	5	Liquor	28
Trespassing	4	Other	8
Other	3		100%
	100%		
6% Drug offenses		***100% Total all offenses***	
Narcotics	9%		
Nonnarcotics	91		
	100%		

Note: Percents may not add to 100 because of rounding.

Source: U.S. Department of Justice, Bureau of Justice Statistics, *Report to the Nation on Crime and Justice* (Washington, D.C.: Government Printing Office, 1983), p. 60.

child. Currently there are pressures to narrow the scope of this discretion, yet to a great extent decision makers may still individualize justice. At the same time, because of the institutional needs of the bureaucracy and the presence of the others with whom they interact, juvenile officials must be attuned to considerations of efficiency, public relations, and the maintenance of harmony and esprit de corps among their underlings.

Juvenile justice is a particular type of bureaucracy that is based on an ideology of social work and is staffed primarily by persons who think of themselves as members of the helping professions. The judge may find that justice must be dispensed in an organizational context in which the public's demand for punishment conflicts with pressures from probation officers and social workers who blame environmental conditions for deviant behavior and urge treatment for the offender. The juvenile court judge does not have the explicit sanctions described in the criminal law to guide decisions and justify actions.

Like the adult criminal justice system, juvenile justice functions within an organizational and political context in which exchange relationships among officials of various agencies influence decisions. The juvenile court must deal not only with children and their parents but also with patrol officers, probation officers, welfare officials, social workers, psychologists, and the heads of treatment institutions. These others all have their own goals, their own perceptions of delinquency, and their own concepts of treatment.

The police interface

Most complaints against juveniles are brought by the police, although they may be initiated by an injured party, school officials, or even the parents. As Ted Rubin notes, the police must make three major decisions with regard to the processing of juveniles: (1) whether to take the child into custody, (2) whether to request that the child be detained following apprehension, and (3) whether to refer the child to court.[12]

As might be expected, the police exercise enormous discretion with regard to these decisions. The police do extensive screening and informal adjustment in the street and the station house. In communities and neighborhoods where law enforcement officials have developed close relationships with the residents or where law enforcement policy dictates, the police may deal with violations by giving warnings to the juveniles and notifying their parents. Figure 17.2 shows that more than half (55.9 percent) of those taken into police custody have their cases handled within the department and are then released; about a third (36.6 percent) are referred to the juvenile court; and 7.5 percent are referred to other agencies or to an adult court.

In a study of four communities in the Pittsburgh metropolitan area, Nathan Goldman found wide variation in the arrest rates and a corresponding variation in the portion of those arrested who were selected for appearance in juvenile court.[13] Only about half of those who come to the attention of the police for law violations are taken to the station house, and only a small proportion of those officially registered on police records (35.4 percent) are referred to the court for action. Thus whether a child is declared a delinquent is to some extent determined by the police officer in selective reporting of juvenile offenders to the court. Such factors as one's attitude toward the juvenile, the juvenile's family, the offense, and the court, the predominant attitude of the community, and one's conception of one's own role as a police officer influence this selection process.

In a study of the police in a metropolitan industrial city of 450,000, Irving Piliavin and Scott Briar found that the choice of disposition of juvenile cases depended very much on the prior record of the child, but second in importance was the offender's demeanor.[14] Juveniles who had committed minor offenses but were respectful and contrite were defined by the officers as worthy candidates for rehabilitation and were given an informal reprimand. Those who were argumentative or surly were defined as "punks" who needed to be taught a lesson through arrest. The researchers found that only 4 percent of the cooperative youths were arrested, in comparison with 67 percent of those who were uncooperative.

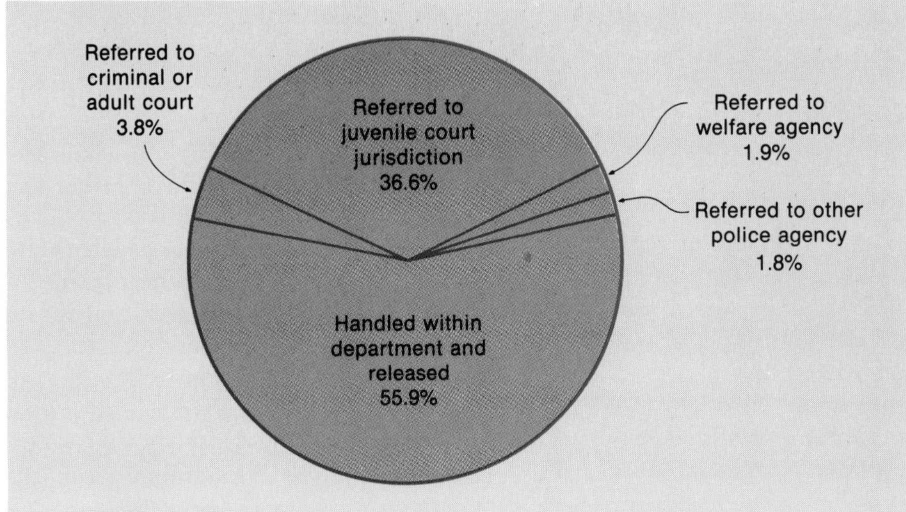

FIGURE 17.2 Percentage distribution of juveniles taken into police custody by method of disposition, 1980

Close-up: Crime at an Early Age: The Violent Streets of Luis Guzman

Luis Guzman is one of tens of thousands of violent youths who prowl the streets of the nation's cities, instilling fear and limiting in countless ways the manner in which urban Americans live.

By this fall, at the age of 16, Luis Guzman had become a familiar figure to the police. He was arrested in September on charges of stealing a teacher's purse at a public school. His history made him a natural suspect for the police in the slaying later that month of a lawyer in a robbery in a riverside park, and he spent two weeks in jail before three other youths were arrested in the crime.

Before the murder charge was dropped, the authorities learned that eight months earlier Luis had violated probation for an armed-robbery conviction by running away from a halfway house for juvenile delinquents in East Harlem. So, for now, he remains in custody at Rikers Island.

Like many other young criminals, Luis has spent much of his life in institutions. Thousands of dollars of public money have been spent on trying to turn him into a responsible member of society. He has had hundreds of hours of group therapy and counseling. He has repeatedly run away from the institutions, most of which had no locked doors or fences.

Luis Guzman is slender and short. He wears his dark hair in a crew cut and looks out at the world through black eyes, his jaw set. His speech is slow and direct.

That afternoon at Rikers Island, Luis described his feelings after a mugging. He would think: " 'Damn, I bet they be telling the cops right now.' I be getting nervous. The cops got my picture, and I be getting nervous that I going to be busted."

What is wrong with robbing, Luis said, is that "you could run into the wrong person. He could turn around and shoot you. That's what I was afraid of. But I still done it anyway. I took big risks for the money. I like to support myself. I do it to support myself, that's why."

About the victims Luis said, "We'd just say, 'We got over. We took the money without getting busted.' I don't be thinking about them. I just think of getting the money and hanging out."

Sometimes Luis mugged with his bare hands, sometimes with an .007 knife with a six-inch blade that he bought for $8.

"Sometimes you run up in the back and yoke 'em," with an arm around the neck, Luis said, "and the other boys take the money out of his pockets."

With a knife, "You just put it in front of them and say, 'Give me your money.' We tell them to walk one way, then we walk the other way. When we get to the corner we run."

Luis's victims were always men. "Women scream. One, I just went up to her, I didn't have my knife out and she started screaming. So I just ran. The men just stop and get scared."

Anyone who tried to rob Luis would have to kill him. If someone resisted him, "I'd probably put them to sleep. My friend would yoke 'em." If he had a knife, he said, "I'll probably stick 'em."

"I don't stick 'em up here," he said, gesturing toward his chest. "I'll probably stick 'em in the leg, down there."

Luis said he had stabbed only one person, his oldest brother, 18-year-old Ramiro, and it was an accident. The day before Luis's latest arrest, he and Ramiro were fighting at their mother's over who got to wear one of Ramiro's shirts. Luis drew a kitchen knife. Ramiro threw a karate kick and hit the tip of the knife with his thigh, just enough to break the skin. Luis ran out the door, and Ramiro hurled a table at him. The next the family heard from Luis, more than 24 hours later, he had been picked up and charged with murder. . . .

Luis's criminal records do not include the jewelry-store robbery he described. Either the information was lost or the case was dropped, or Luis invented it. All are equally plausible in the realm of juvenile delinquency, where prosecution and record-keeping are uneven and where tales of self-aggrandizement are not rare.

Luis passed a few more months in Spofford. Then in late Janury 1980, he went to the Great Valley Youth Camp in the densely wooded foothills of the Allegheny Mountains, near the junction of the New York, Pennsylvania and Canadian borders—about as far from New York City as you can get and still be in New York State. The camp has no locked doors, barred windows or fences.

In the fall of 1980, Luis made a trip to the city on a public bus, and, three days later, returned to Great Valley on schedule. He seemed to be coming along nicely.

While in the city, Luis made an appearance in State Supreme Court in Manhattan before Justice Harold J. Rothwax. There he pleaded guilty to pulling his .007 knife on a man on a subway platform on July 25, 1979, and stealing the man's oversized radio: armed robbery.

Justice Rothwax placed Luis on probation for five years. The judge said in an interview that he had done so in a plea-bargaining arrangement after being assured that Luis would spend the time in a locked facility of the Division for Youth.

Luis did not go to a secure facility. He returned to Great Valley.

Four months later, in February of this year, after he had been at Great Valley for 13 months, Luis was transferred to the state's Judge Harold A. Stevens Youth Development Center No. 2 in East Harlem, an unlocked six-story sandstone-and-brick building at 112th Street and Lexington Avenue. There were 16 boys there. Luis stayed three days before taking flight.

He headed for his father's tenement apartment on the Lower East Side. On March 4, 1981, Felix Guzman returned his son to the center. He still has a tattered receipt for the boy.

"I left the same day," Luis said. This time he went to his mother's apartment on Avenue D.

Law enforcement officials say that a warrant was issued for Luis's arrest, that youth workers searched for him on the Lower East Side, to no avail.

Over the next seven months, Luis made a joke of the attempts to rehabilitate him. He roamed the streets with the "Little Wild Boys" gang, later renamed "The Baddest Boys Around." He snatched gold chains on the Upper East Side, and he went out mugging with "my boys." He drifted in and out of his parents' and friends' apartments.

In April, Luis was arrested and charged with stealing a Father's Day plaque from a card shop on East 14th Street. The charge was conditionally dismissed and Luis went free. No one noticed the outstanding warrant against Luis for running away from the youth center and violating the terms of his probation.

In the summer, a policeman caught Luis trespassing on a construction site, where he had gone to steal sheets of plywood. The policeman took Luis to his mother's apartment and let him go with a warning. That officer was also apparently unaware of the arrest warrant.

Shortly after the start of school in September, the police said, Luis stole a teacher's purse from a classroom at Junior High School 22, where his sister Evelyn is a student. An undercover policeman from the Seventh Precinct saw him sprinting down the street with the purse and took him into custody.

He was taken to Rikers Island for the first time. But in four days he was free again after promising to appear in Criminal Court. Once again, the arrest warrant had been overlooked.

Luis said he had intended to return to court on Oct. 7, but, he added, "then I got busted for this murder, something I didn't do."

"If I did it," he said, "I would admit it. I wouldn't be scared to admit it. Every time I do a robbery I admit it."

At Rikers Island, after talking for more than two hours, sitting still, seldom even moving a hand, Luis began to twist and turn in his straight-backed chair. He was tired of answering questions, he said. He was tired of the way his life had been going, too. He wanted to get out of New York, go to Puerto Rico.

"There's too much trouble around here," he said. "My boys be instigating. If I don't go with them they say, 'You're a sucker.' So I just go with them. But now when I get out of here, if I work this case, I ain't going to hang out with them. My mother's going to try to get me a ticket to Puerto Rico. I ain't never coming back."

Source: Joseph B. Treaster, "Crime at an Early Age: The Violent Streets of Luis Guzman," *New York Times*, 9 November 1981, p. B1.

Because the law specifies that persons classified as juveniles, usually those under eighteen, and adult offenders be treated differently, and because of the belief that prevention should be a dominant goal of efforts to deal with youth crime, most large police departments have specialized juvenile units. The National Advisory Commission has recommended that, depending on the nature and extent of juvenile problems in a given community, a department with more than fifteen employees should have at least one member assigned to deal with youth.[15]

The special juvenile officer is often carefully selected and trained to relate to youths, is knowledgeable about the special laws concerned in these cases, and is sensitive to the special needs of young offenders. Because of the importance accorded the goal of diverting juveniles from the justice system, the juvenile officer is also viewed as an important link between the police and other community institutions, such as the schools, recreational facilities, and organizations serving young people. Because of the emphasis on the prevention of delinquency, many authorities urge that juvenile officers not be involved in the investigation of serious juvenile crimes.[16] Other authorities believe that police resources should not be used to enhance recreational activities as a delinquency-prevention strategy.

Although young people commit many serious crimes, the juvenile function of police work is concerned largely with the maintenance of order. In most incidents of this sort the law is ambiguous and blame cannot easily be assigned. In terms of physical or monetary damage, many offenses committed by juveniles are minor infractions: breaking windows, hanging around the business district, disturbing the peace, adolescent sexual behavior, shoplifting. In such instances the function of the investigating officer is not so much to

---

Factors Influencing Police Selection of Juveniles for Court Appearance

A. The policeman's attitudes toward the juvenile court.
B. The impact of special individual experiences in court, or with different racial groups, or with parents of offenders, or with specific offenses, or an individual policeman.
C. Apprehension about criticism by the court.
D. Publicity given to certain offenses either in the neighborhood or elsewhere may cause the police to feel that these are too "hot" to handle unofficially and must be referred to the court.
E. The necessity for maintaining respect for police authority in the community.
F. Various practical problems of policing.
G. Pressure by political groups or other special interest groups.
H. The policeman's attitude toward specific offenses.
I. The police officer's impression of the family situation, the degree of family interest in and control of the offender, and the reaction of the parents to the problem of the child's offense.
J. The attitude and personality of the boy.
K. The Negro child offender is considered less tractable and needing more authoritarian supervision than a white child.
L. The degree of criminal sophistication shown in the offense.
M. Juvenile offenders apprehended in a group will generally be treated on an all-or-none basis.

Source: Nathan Goldman, "The Differential Selection of Juvenile Offenders for Court Appearance," in *The Ambivalent Force,* ed. Arthur Niederhoffer and Abraham S. Blumberg (Waltham, Mass.: Ginn and Company, 1970), pp. 159–60.

solve crimes as to handle the often legally uncertain complaints involving juveniles. The officer must seek both to satisfy the complainant and to keep the youth from future trouble: "Given this emphasis on settling trouble cases within the community, not on abstract law enforcement, the policeman's power to arrest provides a strategic weapon to be used to cajole and threaten juveniles into better behavior."[17]

It is important not to minimize the amount of serious crime that juveniles perpetrate. At the opening of the chapter it was noted that, according to the *UCR,* 30 percent of those arrested for index crimes were under eighteen. These are the offenses that are of major concern to the public, and in urban areas especially the police must devote more of their resources to these offenses than to the less serious and status offenses of juveniles.

Detention

After the decision is made that some formal action should be taken, should the juvenile be put into ***detention*** until disposition of the case? This decision is usually made by an intake officer of the juvenile court. One of the early reforms of the juvenile justice system was to ensure that children were not held in jails in company with adults who were also awaiting trial or sentencing. To mix juveniles—some of whom are status offenders or under the protection of the court because they are neglected—in the same public facility with adults accused of crimes has long been thought unjust, but in many areas separate detention facilities for juveniles do not exist.

detention
A period of temporary custody of a juvenile before disposition of his or her case.

Children are held in detention for a number of reasons. For some youths, it is the possibility that they will commit other crimes while awaiting trial. For others, it is the possibility of harm from gang members or parents if they are released. For still others, it is the possibility that they may not appear in court as required. Finally, youths are detained when there is no responsible adult who is willing to care for them. These are the formal reasons, but detention may also be used as punishment, to teach a lesson.[18]

Although much attention is focused on the juvenile court and the sanctions imposed by judges as a result of the formal processes of adjudication, many more children are punished through confinement in detention centers and jails before any court action has taken place. An estimated half-million juveniles are detained each year, sometimes for several months; but only about 15 percent are eventually confined to a group home, training school, or halfway house. These figures seem to indicate that detention and intake decisions have a greater impact than the decisions of the court. They may also underscore the belief that a brief period of detention is a good device to "shake up the kid and set him straight." The fact remains: juveniles held in detention have not been convicted.

Intake

In many urban areas the police send formal complaints to a special division of the juvenile probation department for preliminary screening and evaluation. An intake officer looks at the report to determine whether the alleged facts are sufficient to cause the juvenile court to take jurisdiction or if some other action would be in the child's interest. Should it appear that the case warrants formal judicial processing, a formal petition may be filed with the court. If the police referral does not contain sufficient legal evidence or if the juvenile has committed only a minor violation, has no prior record, and is living with a caring parent, the case may be dismissed. Alternatively, a child may be diverted out of the system to an appropriate mental health, educational, or social agency. In some instances, juveniles are put on informal probation by the intake officer so that the department may provide counseling or other services. The intake officer thus has considerable discretion and power. Nationally, between 40 and 50 percent of all referrals from the police are disposed of at this stage, without formal processing by a judge.

The numbers and types of cases sent to the juvenile court are influenced by the decisions of political and enforcement agencies. The size of the court staff and the resources at its disposal depend on the maintenance of cooperative relations with community leaders. The actions of the juvenile court judge must be consistent with local values. Acts of delinquency that outrage the community will inspire pressures on the court to deal severely with transgressors. Politicians feel that they can gain support by advocating a "get tough" policy rather than by pushing for the rehabilitation of offenders. When the sons of influential persons are charged with delinquency, the informality and treatment orientation of the system allow a variety of lenient dispositions, including probation, out-patient care at a psychiatric clinic, and incarceration in a therapeutic community. Not all cases end up in the reform school or industrial school. Robert Emerson observes that

> political efforts to "get a kid off," while they may be compatible with and rationalized in terms of therapeutic goals, grow out of the exigencies of political and personal relations. Hence, such efforts have no necessary or consistent relation to "treatment," although on occasion they may produce lenient dispositions that coincide with the dictates of such policies.[19]

Serious Juvenile Crime: Some Findings

Data from interviews of all residents at least twelve years old in 60,000 U.S. households indicate:

- Rates of personal crimes were higher for juveniles than for adults. Juveniles were also more likely to commit crimes in groups of three or more.
- The seriousness and types of injuries inflicted in crimes committed by juveniles and youthful offenders (18- to 20-year-olds) were similar to those of injuries inflicted by adults.
- No relationship was found between general economic conditions (unemployment rate, consumer price index, and gross national product) and crime. However, juvenile crime rates were higher in urban neighborhoods with high unemployment.
- Use of guns increased with age, but guns were rarely used by juveniles.
- The elderly were more than twice as likely to be victimized by adults as by juveniles. Moreover, offenses committed against the elderly were less serious when juvenile offenders were involved.
- In poor neighborhoods, juveniles and youths, but not adults, were more likely to use weapons than were their counterparts in wealthier neighborhoods.
- Juvenile involvement in robberies of businesses was substantially less than was juvenile participation in robberies of people.
- The highest crime rates were found among offenders between 18 and 20 years old.
- Males committed offenses about 4 to 15 times more frequently than females did, depending on the type of crime.

Source: U.S. Department of Justice, *Justice Assistance News*, September 1981, p. 1.

In most juvenile justice systems the probation officer plays a crucial role during the intake phase. Because intake is essentially a screening process to determine whether a case should be referred to the court or to a social agency, it often takes place without judicial supervision. Informal discussions among the probation officer, the parents, and the child are important means of learning about the child's social situation, of diagnosing behavioral problems, and of recommending treatment possibilities. Table 17.5 shows the findings of a study of intake decisions in seven juvenile courts in four states conducted by the National Assessment of Juvenile Corrections. It has been estimated that nationally about half the delinquency cases each year are settled informally and unofficially during this pre-judicial stage.[20]

With the increased concern about due process and the legal rights of juveniles, prosecuting attorneys are taking a more prominent part in the system.[21] In keeping with the traditional child-saver philosophy, prosecuting attorneys rarely appeared in juvenile court until after the *Gault* decision. Now, with the presence of a defense attorney, it is felt to be important that the state's interest be represented by legal counsel. In many jurisdictions prosecutors are assigned to deal specifically with juvenile cases by advising the intake officer, administering diversion programs, negotiating pleas, and acting as an advocate during judicial proceedings.

Diversion. Although there have always been informal ways of diverting alleged delinquents away from the courts and toward community agencies, the number and types of diversion programs have greatly expanded during the past decade. As Edwin Lemert has written, "if there is a defensible philosophy for the juvenile court it is one of judicious non-intervention."[22] Because of the court's extraordinary powers, many persons believe that it should intervene only as a last resort. When behavioral problems can be identified early, the child should be given access to the necessary remedial resources without being taken before a judge and labeled delinquent. Diversion has also been advocated as one way of reducing the court's workload. Perhaps more important is that children respond more readily to the treatment provided by community-based services than to the correctional services available through the court. Diversion, it is argued, permits the juvenile court to allocate its resources more wisely by concentrating on cases of repeat and serious offenders.

But diversion is not without its critics. Although diversion programs have greatly expanded during the past decade, the number of young people committed to institutions has not decreased appreciably. It appears to many ob-

TABLE 17.5 Intake decisions in seven juvenile courts, by type of offense charged

Offense charged	*Dismissal (percent)*	*Informal handling (percent)*	*Formal handling (percent)*	*Number of cases*
Status	26%	36%	38%	77
Misdemeanor	33	34	33	123
Property	29	34	35	132
Person	16	32	51	37

Source: Mark Creekmore, "Case Processing: Intake, Adjudication, and Disposition," in *Brought to Justice?: Juveniles, the Courts, and the Law,* ed. Rosemary C. Sarri and Yeheskel Hasenfeld (Ann Arbor: University of Michigan, National Assessment of Juvenile Corrections, 1976), p. 127. Reprinted by permission.

servers that the increase in diversion programs has widened the juvenile justice net and that children who in the past would not have been formally handled are so handled now. After evaluating nine diversion programs, Don Gibbons and Gerald Blake noted:

> The police are employing diversion as an alternative action where formerly they would simply counsel and release a youngster. Diversion, growing out of the sociologists' recommendations of "radical nonintervention," "benign neglect," or "judicial nonintervention," has become perverted in practice into a stratagem that swells the population of acted upon offenders.[23]

Adjudication

The questions of attaching the label "delinquent" to a juvenile and determining a sanction are the primary matters before the court. In accordance with the Progressives' belief that adjudication should be informal and noncombative, the normal rules of criminal procedure were modified; the rules of evidence were not strictly followed, hearsay testimony could be admitted, there was no prosecutor (a police or probation officer presented the case), and the sessions were closed to the public. From a formal standpoint, the purpose of the hearing was not to determine a child's guilt or innocence of a specific charge but rather to establish the child's status as either delinquent or not delinquent and to help the child to become law-abiding.

The role of the juvenile court has been described by Ted Rubin, a former judge of the Denver Juvenile Court.

> This court is a far more complex instrument than outsiders imagine. It is law, and it is social work; it is control, and it is help; it is the good parent and, also, the stern parent; it is both formal and informal. It is concerned not only with the delinquent, but also with the battered child, the runaway and many others. . . . The juvenile court has been all things to all people.[24]

The changes in criminal proceedings mandated by the due process decisions of the Supreme Court following *In re Gault* have brought about shifts in the philosophy and actions of the juvenile court. Copies of formal petitions with specific charges must be given to the parents and child, counsel may be present and free counsel appointed if the juvenile is indigent, witnesses may be cross-examined, and a transcript of the proceedings must be kept. In about thirteen states, juveniles have a right to a jury trial.

As with other Supreme Court decisions, the reality of local practice may differ sharply from the stipulations in the opinion. One study of three cities found that juveniles and their parents often waived their rights in response to suggestions made by the judge or probation officer.[25] The lower social status of the offender's parents, the intimidating atmosphere of the court, and judicial hints that the outcome will be more favorable if a lawyer is not present are reasons the procedures outlined in *Gault* are not demanded. The litany of "treatment," "doing what's right for the child," and "working out a just solution" may sound enticing, especially to people who are unfamiliar with the intricacies of formal legal procedures. In practice, then, juveniles still lack many of the protections accorded adult offenders. Some of the differences between the juvenile and adult criminal justice systems are shown in table 17.6.

TABLE 17.6 Adult and juvenile criminal justice compared

	Adult system	*Juvenile system*
Philosophical assumptions	Decisions made as result of adversarial system in context of due process rights	Decisions made as result of inquiry into needs of juvenile within context of some due process elements
Jurisdiction	Violations of criminal law	Violations of criminal law, status offenses, neglect, dependency
Primary sanctioning goals	Punishment, deterrence	Treatment
Official discretion	Widespread	Widespread
Entrance	Official action of arrest, summons, or citation	Official action, plus referral by school, parents, other sources
Role of prosecuting and defense attorneys	Required and formalized	Sometimes required; less structured; poor role definition
Adjudication	Procedural rules of evidence in public jury trial required	Less formal structure to rules of evidence and conduct of trial; no right to public jury trial in most states
Treatment programs	Run primarily by public agencies	Broad use of private as well as public agencies
Application of Bill of Rights amendments		
4th: Unreasonable searches and seizures	Applicable	Applicable
5th: Double jeopardy	Applicable	Applicable (re waiver to adult court)
Self-incrimination	Applicable (*Miranda* warnings)	Applicable
6th: Right to counsel	Applicable	Applicable
Public trial	Applicable	Applicable in half of states
Trial by jury	Applicable	Applicable in half of states
8th: Right to bail	Applicable	Applicable in half of states
14th: Right to treatment	Not applicable	Applicable

Adjudicatory process. In some jurisdictions the adjudication process is more adversarial than it was before the *Gault* and *Winship* decisions. Like adult cases, however, juvenile cases tend to be adjudicated in a style that conforms to the Crime Control (administrative) Model: most are settled in preliminary hearings by a plea agreement, and few go on to formal trial. At the preliminary hearing the youth is notified of the charges and his or her rights, and counsel may be present. Since in most cases the juvenile has already admitted guilt to the arresting or intake officer, the focus of the hearing is on the disposition. In contested cases, a prosecutor presents the state's case and the judge oversees the proceedings, ruling on the admission of evidence and the testimony of witnesses. Because juries are used only sparingly even in states where they are authorized, guilt or innocence is determined by the judge, who then passes sentence.

Disposition. If the court makes a finding of delinquency, a dispositional hearing is required. This hearing may be held immediately following the entry of a plea or at a later date. Typically, the judge receives a social history or predispositional report before passing sentence. Few juveniles are found by the court to be not delinquent at trial since the intake and pretrial processes normally filter out cases in which a law violation cannot be proved. In addition to dismissal of a petition, five other dispositional alternatives are available: (1) suspended judgment, (2) probation, (3) community treatment, (4) institutional care, and (5) waiver to an adult court.

Judges sometimes suspend judgment, or continue cases without a finding, when they wish to put a youth under supervision but are reluctant to apply the label "delinquent." Judgment may be suspended for a definite or indefinite period of time. The court thus holds a definitive judgment in abeyance for possible use should a youth misbehave while under the informal supervision of a probation officer or parents.

Although probation and commitment to an institution are the major dispositional alternatives, judges have wide discretion to warn, to fine, to arrange for restitution, or to refer a juvenile for treatment at either a public or a private community agency. In making this decision the judge relies on the social background report developed by the probation officer. Often it includes reports of other community persons, such as school officials or a psychiatrist. When psychological issues are involved, a disposition may be delayed pending further diagnosis.

Probation may be structured so that the delinquent is under fairly strict supervision, with regular contacts with the probation office, or it can be more open, with only periodic checks required. The choice of probation rather than incarceration depends to a great extent on the availability of resources, the seriousness of the offense, a history of prior offenses, and the attitude of the judge. If community alternatives are few, judges may believe they have no alternative but to send delinquents to an institution. This is particularly true in rural areas, where social agencies and foster homes may be lacking.

Treatment in community-based facilities for youths has greatly expanded during the past decade, just as it has for adults. In particular, the number of private, nonprofit agencies that contract with the states to perform services for troubled youths has grown. Demands for deinstitutionalization emphasized that juveniles could receive better and less costly treatment in the community from private social service agencies.

Incarceration of juveniles has traditionally meant commitment to a state institution often called a training school, reform school, or industrial school. An assumption of the Progressive movement was that juveniles could be helped only if they were removed from "the crowded slum-life of the noisy, disorderly settlement where 70 percent of the population is of foreign parentage." The children were to be "taken away from evil association and temptations, away from the moral and physical filth and contagion, out of the gas light and sewer gas; away out into the woods and fields, free from temptation and contagion; out into the sunlight and the starlight and the pure, sweet air of the meadows."[26] Once in a rural setting, the children were to learn a vocation and be trained to middle-class standards. This usually meant that juveniles were taught outdated farming skills and trades no longer practiced in the urban areas to which they were destined to return. The remoteness of these institutions meant the further loss of meaningful personal and family relationships. Even today, state correctional facilities for children tend to be in rural areas.

Although community and law enforcement leaders may urge punishment for juvenile offenders, the judge must deal with equally compelling pressures by members of the helping professions for treatment dispositions. The number and types of placement alternatives depend on exchange relationships with officials who head community treatment facilities. In most regions there are few state institutions, and they are usually crowded, poorly staffed, and custodial in orientation. The variety of private facilities that will accept dispositions from the court is much wider.

LaMar T. Empey refers to studies that show that "except for juveniles convicted of serious personal crimes, status offenders have been as likely to be sentenced to training schools as criminal property offenders." From 25 to 35 percent of all juveniles in state correctional facilities have been status offenders. Girls who have been adjudged incorrigible or sexually promiscuous tend to be incarcerated longer than boys. At the same time, "only about 11 to 16 percent of the total [juvenile] population in correctional facilities—about 6,000 in all"—are serious criminal offenders.[27] These figures indicate that detention is widely used, that status offenders are disproportionally confined, and that children are incarcerated for acts that would be either legal or lightly sanctioned if they were committed by adults.

Correctional facilities for juveniles

Large custodial training schools located in outlying areas remain the typical institutions to which juveniles are committed, although during the past decade there has been an increase in the number of privately maintained facilities that accept residents sent to them by the courts. The Juvenile Detention and Correctional Facility Census revealed that more than 76,000 individuals were housed in 2,151 public and private centers; 64 percent of the residents were in public facilities.[28]

Figure 17.3 shows that there is a major difference between the public and private facilities, with training schools holding only 13 percent of all juveniles

FIGURE 17.3
Percentage of juvenile residents in long- and short-term facilities in public and private sectors

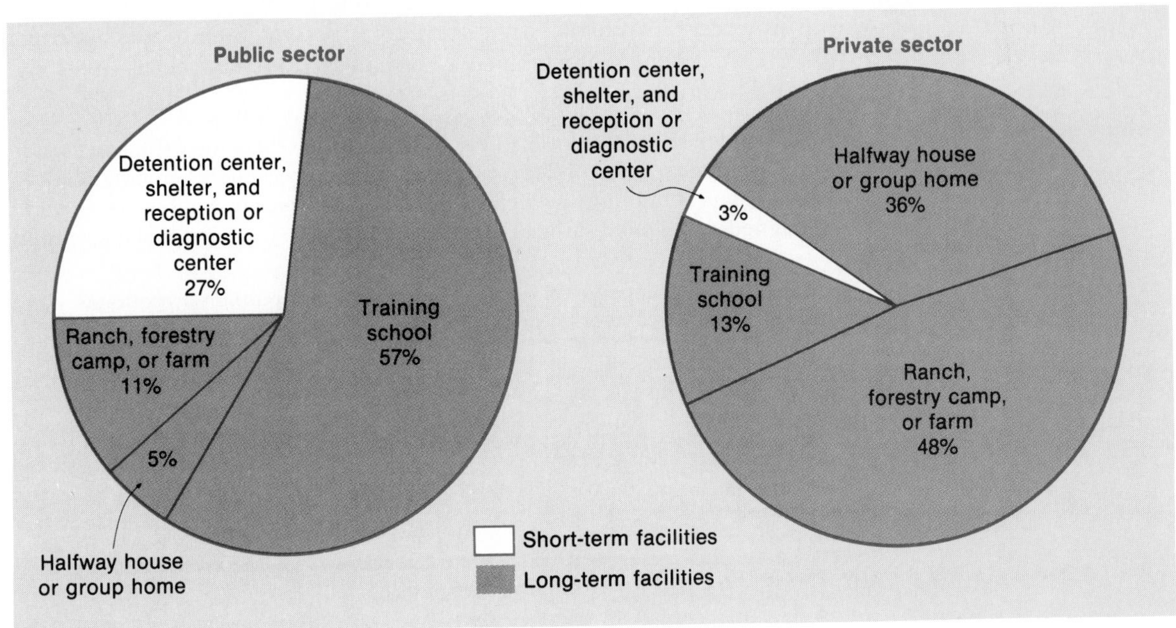

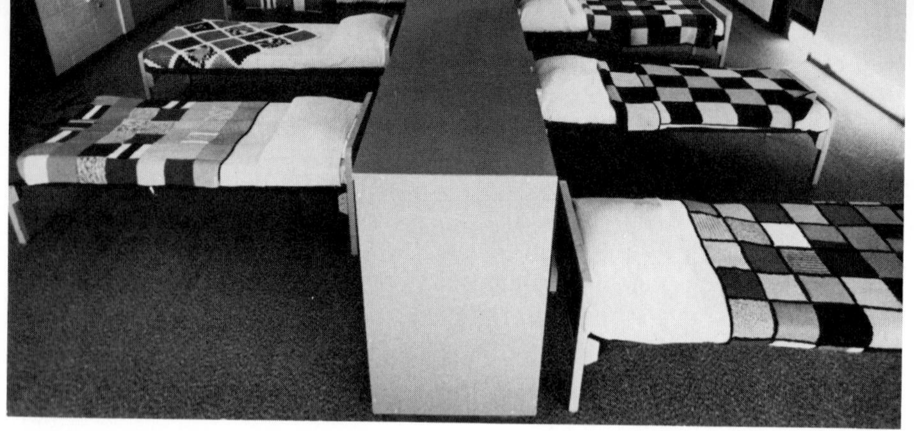

An increasing number of juvenile offenders are detained in private facilities.

in private facilities. The census found that the average age in all facilities was about fifteen years and that boys outnumbered girls three to one. In addition to the juveniles in the institutions named, unknown numbers of children are under the care of the juvenile court but have been placed in noncorrectional private facilities such as schools for the emotionally disturbed, military academies, and even preparatory schools. Although courts usually maintain jurisdiction over delinquents until they attain the age of majority, data from the training schools indicate that nationally the average length of stay is approximately ten months. The percentages of juveniles in the various types of public institutions are shown in table 17.7.

Placement in the more desirable private treatment centers may be sought for preferred juveniles. In the city Emerson studied, the availability of treatment alternatives depended on negotiations between the court and the private agencies. Some private institutions desire referrals as a way of maintaining and expanding their clientele, but they want the "right" type of patients.[29] As Richard Cloward and Irwin Epstein have noted, the private agencies select "motivated" and high-status clients and pass on to public agencies the harder-to-work-with, resistant clients. In return for opening their doors to court referrals, the treatment centers expect to be able to transfer their troublesome cases to state institutions.

> Private residential treatment institutions for juvenile delinquents, having made "errors" in intake, "pass on" their difficult cases to the public training schools; settlement and community agencies arrange to have detached public street workers assigned to the more difficult juvenile gangs. . . . Thus the public programs

TABLE 17.7 Percentage of juveniles committed to public correctional facilities for four categories of offense, by type of facility

Type of facility	*All offenses*	*Felony*	*Status offense*	*Misde-meanor*	*Drug offense*
Detention center	12%	9%	19%	11%	7%
Shelter	Z	Z	Z	Z	0
Reception or diagnostic center	3	3	1	3	3
Training school	63	65	60	67	56
Ranch, forestry camp, or farm	16	18	13	13	28
Halfway house or group home	6	5	7	6	6

Z = less than 0.5 percent.
Source: U.S. Department of Justice, National Criminal Justice Information and Statistics Service, *Children in Custody* (Washington, D.C.: Government Printing Office, 1979), p. 10.

have tended to become the repository for the poor; private agencies have abandoned the neediest segment of society as their chief target.[30]

Because of the emphasis on rehabilitation that has dominated juvenile justice for much of the past fifty years, a wide variety of treatment programs have been used. Counseling, education, vocational training, and an assortment of psychotherapy methods have been incorporated into the juvenile correctional programs of most states. Unfortunately, there is much dissatisfaction with the results. For many offenders, incarceration in a juvenile training institution appears to be mainly preparation for entry into adult corrections. John Irwin's concept of the state-raised youth (chapter 15) is a useful way of looking at children who come in contact with institutional life at an early age, lack family relationships and structure, become used to living in a correctional environment, and are unable to move out of this cycle.

Optimism about treatment and rehabilitation has turned to dismay and soul-searching. During the 1950s and 1960s some experimental programs based on the community-treatment idea were thought to hold much promise. Highfields is a New Jersey program in which a small number of boys live with staff members and in which control is fostered through the development of a group culture. The recidivism rate of Highfields' graduates was lower than that of comparable juveniles who left the Annandale State Reformatory (37 percent versus 53 percent). This rate, the lower cost of Highfields, and the shorter period of confinement seemed to indicate that Highfield's program provided a better form of corrections than total incarceration. Likewise, the Community Treatment Program in California was widely acclaimed in the 1960s. Rather than being sent to an institution, the members of an experimental group were diagnosed, classified, and placed on parole in the community under the close supervision of a parole officer specially trained to meet juveniles' needs. These children were compared with a control group released on regular parole after confinement, and a higher success rate was claimed for the experimental group.[31]

But these and other rehabilitative programs have come under critical examination during the past decade. Reanalysis of the research findings often shows that experimental groups were preselected and would probably have been more successful in leading a crime-free life even without treatment. Some critics argue that the manner in which recidivism has been defined and calculated often leads to a misreading of results. Others concede that experimental therapies do produce positive results but claim that when the particular treatment method is incorporated in the regular correctional program it loses much of its special quality, with the result that resources are diminished,

Youth Custody Costs Compared

A survey by the National Center on Institutions and Alternatives found that the national average cost of keeping a juvenile in an institution was $17,832, while the average cost for a community-based program was $10,928.

Institutions were defined as training schools, youth development centers, residential facilities, reception/diagnostic centers, and detention centers. Community-based programs included shelter care, foster care, group homes, and forestry camps.

Source: U.S. Department of Justice, *Justice Assistance News*, June/July 1981, p. 10.

Close-up: *Scared Straight:* A Second Look

On the night of November 2, 1978, *TV Guide* for the Los Angeles area listed an unusual offering on KTLA, Channel 5: "SCARED STRAIGHT! Special: Inside a maximum security prison. This hour-long program follows 17 juvenile offenders as they learn, at first hand, about the realities of prison life. Using brutally frank and frequently obscene language, 'lifers' at Rahway (N.J.) State Prison tell the young people about the ultimate pay-off for their criminality." It went on to say that about 8,000 juveniles had visited Rahway and that 80% of them had been reformed by the experience—"scared straight." The documentary was narrated by actor Peter Falk, and, to preserve its intensity, was run without commercial interruptions.

Scared Straight! played to a large enthusiastic audience. There had probably never been a television documentary like it: the obscene language, the descriptions of violence and sodomy, the intensity of the prisoners, the resonating sounds of cell doors slamming shut. "Please don't make me hurt you," a lifer spits in the face of a teenage boy, "because if I have to break your face to get my point across, I'll do it, you little dummy. You're here for two hours, you belong to us for two hours." One after another, the prisoners berate, rant, strut, and menace. "I'm bad, you see me, boy, I'm bad," snarls another. "You see them pretty blue eyes of yours? I'll take one out of your face and squish it in front of you." In prison, "the big eat the little."

Later, the 17 boys and girls speak contritely to the camera. They stammer that they are through with crime and violence. Girls and boys alike: a total change of mind. Then Mr. Falk reappears, with the dreary fortress behind him, and tells the audience that six months after the filming all but one of the 17 had gone straight. And, he adds, 80% to 90% of all juveniles in the Rahway program have done the same.

Within 24 hours, *Scared Straight!* had become celebrated. "One of the most riveting hours of television ever produced," said the *Valley News*. "One of the most unusual and powerful television programs ever broadcast," said the *Times*. "The holidays have come early to KTLA Channel 5," the *Times* reported. . . .

In April 1979, *Scared Straight!* received the Academy Award for the year's best documentary. Arnold Shapiro, who wrote, produced, and directed the film, accepted the Oscar.

It wasn't only the drama of *Scared Straight!* that captivated the press and public. There was an almost irresistible allure in the *concept* of the Rahway program. It had the trappings of a morality tale: hardened convicts, realizing the error of their ways, devoting themselves to saving others from the same bitter fate. It wasn't only the youths who were going straight. Mr. Shapiro understood why people like this film: "It has a happy ending. It suggested a path that works—and not only a path that works but one that doesn't cost us any money and can be put into effect immediately. The convicts are there." "*Scared Straight!*" declared a KFWB radio news editorial, "is a story about an idea. The idea is simple. It makes sense. It works." The press and public were excited by the 80% to 90% success rate cited by Mr. Falk in the film, though the *evidence* actually presented was (1) the claim that 16 of the 17 juveniles in the film had gone straight, and (2) that they were a random group of violent or larcenous offenders. The Rahway program was not looked upon as something of a miracle cure for juvenile crime.

In 1977, Dr. James O. Finckenauer, an associate professor in the Rutgers University School of Criminal Justice, submitted a proposal to the State Law Enforcement Planning Agency of New Jersey for a grant to evaluate the Juvenile Awareness Project Help [JAPH] with a team of researchers. The idea was to submit the results of the program to more intense analysis. . . .

The Rutgers researchers' first question was whether exposure to the Juvenile Awareness Project had any effect on the attitude of the juveniles who visited Rahway. Later on would come questions about any effect on behavior.

The research method was to take a random

sample of about 100 juveniles who had been designated for a session with the lifers and randomly divide them into two groups. The "experimental" group would visit Rahway; the "control" group would not. Both groups would be tested twice on their attitudes toward punishing criminals, obeying the law, and concepts such as crime, justice, police, and prison. . . .

The "control" and "experimental" groups were tested to ensure that they were similar. Such factors as age, race, sex and *delinquency probability* were analyzed and the two groups were found to be well matched. The double round of tests began in February, 1978, and ended in November.

Quickly, during the first round, the researchers noticed something odd. There is a "test" for predicting juvenile delinquency called the Glueck Social Prediction Table, developed by Sheldon and Eleanor Glueck in 1950, which classifies subjects into low, medium, and high probability of delinquent behavior. The Rutgers researchers discovered that *over* 70% of the 81 juveniles designated for the Rahway program had a *low probability* of delinquency according to the Glueck Table. About 20% had a medium probability, and *only 8% had a high probability.* "If this is so," they wrote, "it raises several issues: Why do these particular kids need to attend the Project? Why are referring agencies not sending more high probability juveniles who might be more in need of deterrence? If the low probability of delinquency juveniles in fact do not become delinquent, can the JAPH claim credit?"

Training schools are for the worst and most persistent juvenile offenders, but *not one of the 81 had ever been in a training school.*

The researchers tested attitudes toward punishment of criminals with 34 questions. The result: The juveniles in the experimental group who went to Rahway *did not change their attitudes* more than did a comparable control group of juveniles who did not attend the Project.

"Deterrence," the Rutgers researchers began their second report, "has long been one of the fundamental goals of the criminal justice system, and more recently of the juvenile justice system as well. Unfortunately, little is known about the deterrent effects of exposure to these systems." In any case, the researchers went on, studies suggest that the *certainty of punishment* has more impact on crime than the *severity*. The lifers at Rahway can expound on the horrors of the place to their young audiences, but they cannot guarantee them that the kids are going to end up there if they steal a purse or sell some drugs. "Perceived severity," the researchers concluded, "has no particular deterrent effect."

Now, using the same groups of juveniles, 46 who visited Rahway and 35 who had been picked to do so but had not, the researchers went to work studying the juveniles' behavior.

- Nineteen of the 46 who visited Rahway had no prior record. Twenty-one of the second group had none. The behavior of the two groups so far had been about even. But six months after the 46 had gone to Rahway to be scared straight, "a significantly higher proportion of the juveniles who did *not* attend the Project did better in terms of subsequent offenses than did the group which attended." The graduates of JAPH were getting in more trouble than the kids who'd stayed home.
- Among the 27 who had prior records, 14 were successes after their visit to Rahway. That's a recidivism rate of 48.2%, which, as the researchers note, "is not only better than, but in some instances worse than, recidivism rate from other programs designed to prevent or treat juvenile delinquency."
- Six of the 19 who *went* to Rahway *with no prior record* were arrested within the next six months. Only one of the 21 with no prior record who did not go to Rahway was arrested.

"There are no panaceas," Finckenauer's report concludes. "No cure-alls. There are no simplistic solutions. It is not possible to simply scare kids straight."

Source: *Scared Straight: A Second Look* (Washington, D.C.: National Center on Institutions and Alternatives, n.d.).

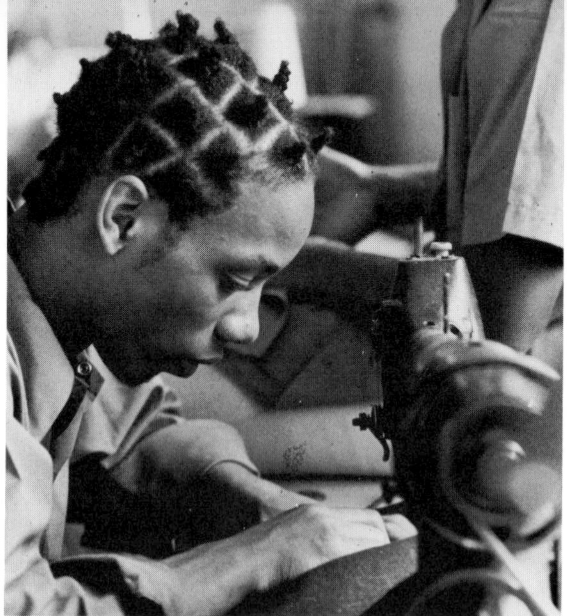

Vocational training must prepare offenders for jobs that will be available to them.

staffs become overburdened, and the bureaucratic milieu deadens the participants' enthusiasm. The warehousing of juveniles until they reach the age of majority may become the underlying goal of many institutions.

Problems and perspectives

Much of the criticism of juvenile justice has emphasized the disparity between the treatment ideal and the institutionalized practices of an ongoing bureaucratic system. Commentators have pointed to the ways in which the language of the social reformers has been used to disguise day-to-day operations in which elements of due process are lacking and custodial incarceration is all too frequent. Other criticisms have stressed the apparent inability of the juvenile justice system to control juvenile crime.

Francis A. Allen reminds us that the juvenile court, in both theory and practice, is a remarkably complex institution called on to perform a wide variety of functions.

> On the one hand, it administers what are essentially welfare functions, such as the exercise of its dependency jurisdiction. On the other hand, it may be required to provide a forum for criminal prosecution, as in cases of adults alleged to have contributed to the delinquency of minors. The juvenile court is a court; but it is also a governmental agency charged with manifold administrative responsibilities, and, in some localities, the performances of clinical services.[32]

Given the range of roles played by the juvenile justice system, it is inevitable that goals and values will collide. In many states the same judges, probation officers, and social workers are asked to deal with neglected children as well as with young criminals. Although departments of social services may deal primarily with neglect cases, the distinction is often not maintained.

In addition to recognizing the organizational problems of the juvenile system, we must acknowledge that our understanding of the causes of delinquency and its prevention or treatment is extremely limited. Over the years, various social and behavioral theories have been advanced to explain delinquency. Where one generation looked to slum conditions as the cause of juvenile crime, another now points to the affluence of the suburbs. Freudians may stress masculine insecurity in a matriarchal family structure, and some sociologists note the peer group pressures of the gang. The array of theories has occasioned an array of proposed—and often contradictory—treatments. With this type of confusion, those interested in the problems of youth may well throw up their hands in despair. What is clear is that additional research is needed to give insights into the causes of delinquency and the treatment of juvenile offenders.

Using a different perspective, other social scientists have deemphasized the importance of juvenile crime. Norval Morris and Gordon Hawkins point out that the majority of juvenile delinquents "both convicted and unconvicted do not subsequently pursue criminal careers; only a minority become recidivists."[33] With this evidence, some authorities maintain that it is inappropriate to say that there are certain "causes" of youth crime. They argue instead that young people go through stages of development and that such earmarks of youth crime as vandalism and auto theft do not necessarily indicate a criminal in the making.[34]

But there remains much concern about the serious offender who recidivates and continues a life of crime as an adult. Barbara Boland argues that the unavailability of juvenile court records to judges in the adult courts means that persons who have already served several periods of time on probation and in juvenile institutions are thought to be first offenders when they reach the age of majority. She believes it is very important that juvenile records be made available and that efforts be made to treat young criminals more severely in order to deter them from future illegal activity.[35]

Five major reforms of the juvenile justice system have been proposed: (1) reduction of the jurisdictional breadth, (2) increase of the due process rights of children, (3) reduced discretion for the juvenile court, (4) greater use of more tangible sanctions, and (5) deinstitutionalization. In many ways these reforms are interrelated because they basically aim at lessening the scope of the system and its impact on individual juveniles. Note also that the changes are quite similar to many of those advanced for the adult system. In 1974 Congress passed the Juvenile Justice and Delinquency Prevention Act, which established a special office within the Law Enforcement Assistance Administration (LEAA) to deal with this problem. For the 1980s the office has listed as its goals: (1) prevention programs for youth, (2) alternatives to incarceration, and (3) deinstitutionalization of status offenders.

Jurisdictional breadth

It has been suggested that juvenile justice concern itself only with law violations rather than with the other, widely divergent problems that are within its legal scope. The court is responsible both for delinquency matters and for cases of child neglect and dependency. The latter are social problems that can probably be more readily treated by other community service agencies. There is no reason why a child in an unstable family environment must have contact with criminal justice actors or agencies, even though they specialize in problems of youth. Too often the nondelinquent child who comes before the court is a victim of the labeling process, viewed by his or her peers and the community as a potential delinquent. A self-fulfilling prophecy is created with discouraging frequency.

It has also been urged that most status offense laws be made more specific and that others be removed from the books. The President's Commission commented: "The provisions on which intervention . . . is based are typically vague and all-encompassing: growing up in idleness and crime, engaging in immoral conduct, in danger of leading an immoral life."[36] The imprecision of these statutes often means that children may be judged delinquent for practically any behavior. From a different perspective, we might ask: Why should children be subject to laws that if contravened by adults would not result in their being labeled criminal? In some states, truancy, curfew violations, and unwed motherhood can lead to a judgment of delinquency. Since the commission spoke, there has been activity with regard to this issue, but in many states the reform effort needs to be continued.

Due process

To repeat, there has been a major change in the extension of due process rights to juveniles since the 1967 *Gault* decision. This has been quite a departure from the earlier belief that the juvenile court should follow informal procedures, that counsel should not be present, and that the judge should have wide discretion to act in the child's best interests. In accord with the opinions of the Supreme Court in the *Gault* and *Winship* cases, it seems only proper that juveniles be given the full protections of the Constitution accorded to adults in a criminal proceeding.

Reduced discretion

Formerly, juvenile court judges had extensive discretion to use the power of the state as a parent in dealing with a problem child, but there are now pressures to reduce this discretion. Much has been accomplished toward this end by the requirement that due process prevail in juvenile court, but legislators are increasingly looking at this portion of the justice system and stipulating the way the process will operate. In some states, limitations have been placed on the length of time that a juvenile may be held in a detention center and on judicial discretion with regard to case disposition, and laws dealing with juvenile delinquency have been revised so that they are less vague.

Use of sanctions

As with adult sentencing, there is increased interest in the use of such tangible sanctions as fines and restitution for juvenile offenders. In addition, perhaps as a reaction to rising crime and the seeming ineffectiveness of rehabilitative methods, legislators in many states have urged that more serious juvenile offenders suffer punishment. Youthful offender acts and mandatory sentencing for those who have committed certain crimes have been incorporated into the laws of some states.

Deinstitutionalization

Reducing the number of juveniles held in state institutions has been the focus of reform for the past decade. Following the pattern advanced by Massachusetts in 1972, there has been a trend in other states toward keeping more delinquents with their families or in group homes or other programs that foster ties with the community. Increased use of probation and diversion to noncorrectional agencies has been advocated. These changes are based on the belief that law violators are not corrected by incarceration. Given all of modern penology's treatment goals, the fact remains that "rehabilitation" has often been carried on in the environment of institutions where confinement, punishment, and submission to authority are omnipresent. A juvenile's self-image can hardly be enhanced or acceptance of society's values encouraged in this atmosphere, nor can the community be better protected when the youth returns home.

Summary

The juvenile justice system has not lived up to its ideals. Its goals have often been subverted by a jurisdictional overreach in an attempt to use the law to solve a host of moral and social problems. Within the bureaucratic context of the system, the needs of the organization have often subverted the needs of the child. After years of neglect, the juvenile justice system is going through a period of rapid change. The case of Gerald Gault and the due process revolution have brought into the open many practices long obscured from public view. Currently the system is under pressure to do something about youth crime. What should be done? Although many reforms have been suggested, it seems that we still know too little about the underlying causes of delinquency to reduce effectively the number of crimes committed by juveniles.

For discussion

1. What are some of the legal and social implications of extending due process rights to minors?
2. Under what circumstances should a juvenile be incarcerated?
3. Should the law consider the acts of young people and those of adults differently? Why?
4. You are the judge. Jane, an eight-year-old, has been placed under the care of the juvenile court because her father has disappeared and her alcoholic mother is unable to care for her. How would you provide for Jane's upbringing?

For further reading

Cicourel, Aaron V. *The Social Organization of Juvenile Justice.* New York: Wiley, 1968.
Emerson, Robert. *Judging Delinquents.* Chicago: Aldine, 1971.
Matza, David. *Delinquency and Drift.* New York: Wiley, 1964.
Murphy, Patrick T. *Our Kindly Parent, the State.* New York: Viking, 1974.
Platt, Anthony. *The Child Savers.* Chicago: University of Chicago Press, 1970.
Rothman, David J. *Conscience and Convenience.* Boston: Little, Brown, 1980.

Notes

1. In re Gault, 387 U.S. 9 (1967).
2. Ibid.
3. David J. Rothman, *Conscience and Convenience* (Boston: Little, Brown, 1980), p. 213.
4. Julian Mack, "The Juvenile Court," 2 *Harvard Law Review* 119 (1909).
5. In re Gault, 387 U.S. 9 (1967); Kent v. United States, 383 U.S. 541 (1966).

6. In re Winship, 397 U.S. 358 (1970).
7. McKeiver v. Pennsylvania, 403 U.S. 528 (1971).
8. Breed v. Jones, 421 U.S. 519 (1975).
9. Schall v. Martin, 82-1248 (1984).
10. H. Ted Rubin, *Juvenile Justice* (Santa Monica: Goodyear, 1979), p. 215.
11. Rosemary C. Sarri and Robert D. Vinter, "Juvenile Justice and Injustice," *Resolution* 1 (Winter 1975): 45.
12. Rubin, *Juvenile Justice,* p. 61.
13. Nathan Goldman, "The Differential Selection of Juvenile Offenders for Court Appearance," in *The Ambivalent Force; Perspectives on the Police,* ed. Arthur Niederhoffer and Abraham S. Blumberg (Waltham, Mass.: Ginn, 1970), p. 156.
14. Irving Piliavin and Scott Briar, "Police Encounters with Juveniles," in *Back on the Street,* ed. Robert M. Carter and Malcolm W. Klein (Englewood Cliffs, N.J.: Prentice-Hall, 1976), pp. 197–206.
15. National Advisory Commission on Criminal Justice Standards and Goals, *Report on Police* (Washington, D.C.: Government Printing Office, 1973), p. 223.
16. George D. Eastman, ed., *Municipal Police Administration* (Washington, D.C.: International City Management Association, 1969), p. 148.
17. Robert M. Emerson, *Judging Delinquents* (Chicago: Aldine, 1971), p. 42.
18. Rubin, *Juvenile Justice,* p. 89.
19. Emerson, *Judging Delinquents,* p. 38.
20. President's Commission on Law Enforcement and Administration of Justice, *Task Force Report: Juvenile Delinquency and Youth Crime* (Washington, D.C.: Government Printing Office, 1967), p. 15.
21. Rubin, *Juvenile Justice,* p. 118.
22. As quoted in President's Commission on Law Enforcement and Administration of Justice, *Juvenile Delinquency and Youth Crime,* p. 96.
23. Don C. Gibbons and Gerald F. Blake, "Evaluating the Impact of Juvenile Diversion Programs," *Crime and Delinquency* 22 (October 1976): 413.
24. H. Ted Rubin, *The Courts: Fulcrum of the Justice System* (Santa Monica: Goodyear, 1976), p. 66.
25. Norman Lefstein, Vaughan Stapleton, and Lee Teitelbaum, "In Search of Juvenile Justice: Gault and Its Implementation," *Law and Society Review* 3 (1969): 491.
26. Ronald Goldfarb and Linda R. Singer, *After Conviction* (New York: Simon & Schuster, 1973), p. 514.
27. LaMar T. Empey, *American Delinquency* (Homewood, Ill.: Dorsey, 1978), p. 460.
28. U.S. Department of Justice, National Criminal Justice Information and Statistics Service, *Children in Custody* (Washington, D.C.: Government Printing Office, 1979), p. 3.
29. Emerson, *Judging Delinquents.*
30. Richard A. Cloward and Irwin Epstein, "Private Social Welfare's Disengagement from the Poor: The Case of the Family Adjustment Agencies," in *Social Welfare Institutions: A Sociological Reader,* ed. Mayer N. Zald (New York: Wiley, 1965), p. 626.
31. Empey, *American Delinquency,* pp. 511–13.
32. Francis A. Allen, *The Borderland of Criminal Justice* (Chicago: University of Chicago Press, 1964), p. 44.
33. Norval Morris and Gordon Hawkins, *The Honest Politician's Guide to Crime Control* (Chicago: University of Chicago Press, 1970), p. 155.
34. Marvin E. Wolfgang, Robert Figlio, and Thorstein Sellin, *Delinquency in a Birth Cohort* (Chicago: University of Chicago Press, 1973).
35. Barbara Boland, "Punishing Habitual Criminals," *Wall Street Journal,* 11 April 1978.
36. President's Commission on Law Enforcement and Administration of Justice, *Juvenile Delinquency and Youth Crime,* p. 4.

Glossary

Accusatory process The series of events that take place from the arrest of a suspect to the filing of a formal charging instrument (indictment or information) with the court.

Actual enforcement Enforcement of the law at a level that reflects such factors as civil liberties, discretion, resources, and community values.

Aggressive patrol A patrol strategy designed to maximize the number of police interventions and observations in the community.

Appeal A request to a higher court that it review actions taken in a completed trial.

Appellate court A court that does not try criminal cases but hears appeals of decisions of lower courts.

Arraignment The act of calling an accused person before the court to hear the charges lodged against him or her and to enter a plea in response to those charges.

Arrest The physical taking of a person into custody on the grounds that there is probable cause to believe that he or she has committed a criminal offense. Police may use only reasonable physical force in making an arrest. The purpose of arrest is to hold the accused for a court proceeding.

Assembly-line justice The operation of any segment of the criminal justice system with such speed and impersonality that defendants are treated as objects to be processed rather than as individuals.

Assigned counsel An attorney in private practice who is assigned by a court to represent an indigent and whose fee is paid by the government that has jurisdiction over the case.

Biopsychological explanations Explanations of crime that emphasize individual biological and psychological conditions as the causes of criminal behavior.

Bureaucracy A form of administrative organization characterized by depersonalized, rule-bound, and hierarchically structured relationships that efficiently produces highly predictable, rationalized results.

Career criminal An individual for whom criminal activity is a way of life; such individuals are thought to be responsible for a large proportion of all crimes.

Challenge for cause To question formally a prospective juror's competency to render a fair verdict by showing bias or some other legal disability. Prospective jurors so challenged are excused. The number of such challenges permitted is unlimited.

Citation A written order issued by a law enforcement officer directing an alleged offender to appear in court at a specified time to answer a criminal charge; referred to as a *summons* in some jurisdictions.

Civilian review board A citizen board independent of the police, established to receive and investigate complaints against law enforcement officers.

Classification The act of assigning a new inmate to a type of custody and treatment appropriate to his or her needs.

Clearance rate The percentage of crimes known to the police that they believe they have solved through an arrest; a statistic used as a measure of a police department's productivity.

Collective bargaining Negotiation between management and a labor union in regard to compensation, working conditions, and other aspects of employment. An agreement is set forth in a contract binding on both parties.

Common law The Anglo-American system of uncodified law, in which judges follow precedents set by earlier decisions when they decide new but similar cases. The substantive and procedural criminal law was originally developed in this manner but was later codified by legislatures.

Community correctional center A correctional institution, usually located in an urban area, housing inmates soon to be released. Such centers are designed to help inmates maintain community ties and thus to promote their reintegration with society.

Community corrections Programs designed to rehabilitate offenders through probation, diversion, halfway houses, and parole.

Conflict Model A legal model that asserts that the political power of interest groups and elites influences the content of the criminal law.

Consensus Model A legal model that asserts that the criminal law, as an expression of the social consciousness of the whole society, reflects values that transcend the immediate interests of particular groups and individuals.

Continuance An adjournment of a scheduled case until a future date.

Copping out Entering a plea of guilty, normally after bargaining (slang). The "copping out ceremony" consists of a series of questions that the judge asks the defendant as to the voluntary nature of the plea.

Count Each separate offense of which a person is accused in an indictment or an information.

Crime A specific act of commission or omission in violation of the law for which a punishment is prescribed.

Crime Control Model A model of the criminal justice system that assumes that freedom is so important that every effort must be made to repress crime; emphasizes efficiency and the capacity to apprehend, try, convict, and dispose of a high proportion of offenders and also stresses speed and finality.

Crime rate The number of reported crimes per 100,000 population as published in the *Uniform Crime Reports.*

Crimes without victims Offenses involving a willing and private exchange of goods or services for which there is a strong demand but which are illegal. Participants do not feel that they are being harmed. Prosecution is justified on the grounds that society as a whole is being injured by the act.

Criminal justice wedding cake A model of the criminal justice process in which criminal cases form a four-tiered hierarchy with a few celebrated cases at the top, each succeeding layer increasing in size as its importance in the eyes of officials and the public diminishes.

Criminogenic factors Factors thought to bring about criminal behavior in an individual.

Critical criminology A school of criminology that holds that criminal law and the criminal justice system have been created to control the poor and have-not members of society.

Custodial Model A model of corrections that emphasizes security, discipline, and order.

Dark figure of crime A metaphor that emphasizes the dangerous dimensions of crime that is never reported to the police.

Defense attorney The lawyer who represents the accused and the convicted offender in their dealings with criminal justice officials.

Delinquent A child who has committed a criminal or status offense.

Dependent child A child whose parent(s) are unable to give proper care.

Detention A period of temporary custody of a juvenile before disposition of his or her case.

Determinate sentence A sentence that fixes the term of imprisonment at a specified period of time.

Deterrence Discouragement of criminal behavior on the part of known offenders (special deterrence) and of the public (general deterrence) by the threat of punishment.

Discovery A prosecutor's pretrial disclosure to the defense of facts and evidence to be introduced at trial.

Discretion The authority to make decisions without reference to specific rules or facts, using instead one's own judgment; allows for individualization and informality in the administration of justice.

Discretionary release The release of an inmate from incarceration at the discretion of the parole board within the boundaries set by the sentence and the penal law.

Diversion An alternative to adjudication by which the defendant agrees to conditions set by the prosecutor (such as to undergo counseling or drug rehabilitation) in exchange for withdrawal of charges.

Double jeopardy The subjecting of a person to prosecution more than once for the same offense, prohibited by the Fifth Amendment.

Dual court system A court system consisting of a separate judicial structure for each state in addition to a national structure. Each case is tried in a court of the same jurisdiction as that of the law or laws broken.

Due process (procedural) The constitutional requirement that all persons be treated fairly and justly by government officials. This means that an accused person can be arrested, prosecuted, tried, and punished only in accordance with procedures prescribed by law.

Due Process Model A model of the criminal justice system that assumes that freedom is so important that every effort must be made to ensure that criminal justice decisions are based on reliable information; emphasizes the adversarial process, the rights of defendants, and formal decision-making procedures.

Durham Rule A test of the defense of insanity which requires it to be shown that the accused is not criminally responsible because the act resulted from mental disease or mental defect.

Exchange A mutual transfer of resources; hence, a balance of benefits and deficits that flow from behavior based on decisions as to the values and costs of alternatives.

Exclusionary rule The principle that illegally obtained evidence must be excluded from a trial.

Felony A serious crime carrying a penalty of death or incarceration for more than one year. Persons convicted of felonies lose the right to vote, to hold public elective office, and to practice certain professions and occupations.

Filtering process A screening operation; hence, a process by which criminal justice officials screen out some cases while advancing others to the next level of decision making.

Fine A sum of money to be paid to the state by a convicted person as punishment for an offense.

Full enforcement A policy whereby the police are given the resources and support to enforce all laws within the limits imposed by the injunction to respect the civil liberties of citizens.

Furlough The temporary release of an inmate from a correctional institution for a brief period, usually one to three days, for a visit home. Such programs are designed to maintain family ties and prepare inmates for release on parole.

General deterrence Punishment of criminals intended to serve as an example to the general public, and thus to discourage the commission of offenses.

Good time A reduction of a convict's prison sentence awarded for good behavior at the discretion of the prison administrator.

Grouping A collectivity of individuals who interact in the workplace but because of shifting membership do not develop into a workgroup.

Habeas corpus A writ or judicial order requesting that a person holding another person produce the prisoner and give reasons to justify continued confinement.

Incapacitation Deprivation of capacity to commit crimes against society by detention in prison.

Incorporation The extension of the due process clause of the Fourteenth Amendment to make binding on state governments the rights guaranteed in the first ten amendments to the U.S. Constitution (the Bill of Rights).

Indeterminate sentence A period set by a judge in which there is a spread between the minimum date for a decision on parole eligibility and a maximum date to completion of the sentence (five to ten years). In holding that the time necessary for treatment cannot be set, the indeterminate sentence is closely associated with the rehabilitative model.

Inmate code The system of values and norms of the prison social system that define for inmates the characteristics associated with the model prisoner.

Interest group A private organization formed to influence government policies so that they will coincide with the desires of its members. Such organized pressure groups operate at all levels of government.

Internal affairs unit A segment of a police department designated to receive and investigate complaints against officers alleging violation of rules and policies.

Irresistible Impulse Test A test of the defense of insanity which requires it to be shown that although the accused knew right from wrong, he or she was unable to control an irresistible impulse to commit the crime.

Jurisdiction The territory or boundaries within which control may be exercised; hence, the legal and geographical range of a court's authority.

Jury A panel consisting of a statutorily defined number of citizens selected according to law and sworn to determine matters of fact in a criminal action and to render a verdict of guilty or not guilty.

Law enforcement The police function of controlling crime by intervening in situations in which it is clear that the law has been violated and only the identity of the guilty needs to be determined.

Legal sufficiency The presence of the minimum legal elements necessary for prosecution of a case. When a prosecutor's decision to prosecute a case is customarily based on legal sufficiency, a great many cases are accepted for prosecution but the majority of them are disposed of by plea bargaining or dismissal.

M'Naghten Rule A test of the defense of insanity which requires it to be shown that at the time of committing the act the accused was unable to distinguish right from wrong because of a disease of the mind.

Mala in se Offenses that are wrong by their very nature, irrespective of statutory prohibition.

Mala prohibita Offenses prohibited by statute but not inherently wrong.

Mandatory release The required release of an inmate from incarceration upon the expiration of a certain time period, as stipulated by a determinate sentencing law or parole guidelines.

Mandatory sentence A type of sentence by which statutes require that a certain penalty shall be imposed and executed upon certain convicted offenders.

Mens rea "Guilty mind" or blameworthy state of mind, necessary for the imputation of responsibility for a criminal offense; criminal as distinguished from innocent intent.

Misdemeanor An offense less serious than a felony and usually punishable by incarceration for no more than a year, a fine, or probation.

Missouri Merit Selection Plan A reform plan in which judges are nominated by a committee and appointed by the governor for a given time period. When the term expires, the voters are asked to signify their approval or disapproval of the judge for a succeeding term. If the judge is disapproved, the committee nominates a successor for the governor's appointment.

Motion An application to a court requesting that an order be issued to bring about a specified action.

National Crime Surveys National surveys of samples of the U.S. population conducted by the Bureau of Justice Statistics to determine the number and types of criminal victimizations and thus the extent of unreported crime.

Necessarily included offense An offense committed for the purpose of committing another offense; for example, trespass committed for the purpose of committing burglary.

Neglected child A child who is not receiving proper care because of some action or inaction of his or her parent(s).

Nolle prosequi An entry made by a prosecutor on the record of a case and announced in court to indicate that the charges specified will not be prosecuted. In effect the charges are thereby dismissed.

Nolo contendere A defendant's formal answer in court in which it is stated that the charges are not contested and which, while not an admission of guilt, subjects the defendant to the same sentencing consequences as a plea of guilty. Often used to preclude civil action against the accused by the victim.

Nonpartisan election An election in which candidates who are not endorsed by political parties are presented to the voters for selection.

Order maintenance The police function of preventing behavior that disturbs or threatens to disturb the public peace or that involves face-to-face conflict between two or more persons. In such situations the police exercise discretion in deciding whether a law has been broken.

Organized crime A social framework for the perpetration of criminal acts, usually in such fields as gambling, narcotics, and prostitution, in which illegal services that are in great demand are provided.

Overcriminalization The use of criminal sanctions to deter behavior that is acceptable to substantial portions of society.

Parens patriae The "parent of the country"; the state as guardian and protector of all citizens (such as juveniles) who are unable to protect themselves.

Parole The conditional release of an inmate from incarceration under supervision after a portion of the prison sentence has been served.

Partisan election An election in which candidates endorsed by political parties are presented to the voters for selection.

Penology A branch of criminology dealing with the management of prisons and treatment of offenders.

Peremptory challenge Removal of a prospective juror without assignment of any cause. The number of such challenges permitted is limited.

PINS, CINS, JINS Acronyms for "person in need of supervision," "child in need of supervision," and "juvenile in need of supervision," terms used to designate juveniles who either are status offenders or are thought to be on the verge of getting in trouble; indicate that the state believes the child is not receiving proper supervision.

Plea bargaining A defendant's pleading of guilty to a criminal charge with the reasonable expectation of receiving some consideration from the state for doing so, usually a reduction of the charge. The defendant's ultimate goal is a penalty lighter than the one formally warranted by the offense originally charged.

Political considerations Matters taken into account in the formulation of public policies and the making of choices among competing values—who gets what portion of the good (justice) produced by the system, when, and how.

Political crimes Acts that constitute threats against the state (as treason, sedition, espionage).

Preplea conference A discussion, in which all parties openly participate, of ways to bring about an agreement on a sentence in return for a plea of guilty.

Presentence investigation An investigation into the background of a convicted offender, which forms the basis of a report prepared to help the judge determine an appropriate sentence.

Preventive patrol The activity of providing regular protection to an area while maintaining a mobile police presence for the purpose of deterring potential criminals from committing crimes.

Proactive Occurring in the absence of a specific external stimulus, as an active search for offenders on the part of police in the absence of reports of violations of the law. Arrests for crimes without victims are usually proactive.

Probation A suspension of the sentence of a convicted offender under conditions that permit the offender to serve the sentence imposed by the court in the community under supervision.

Prosecuting attorney A legal representative of the state with sole responsibility for bringing criminal charges. In some states referred to as *district attorney, state's attorney, county attorney.*

Public defender An attorney employed on a full-time, salaried basis by the government to represent indigents.

Reactive Occurring in response to a stimulus, as police activity in response to notification that a crime has been committed.

Recidivism A return to criminal behavior.

Rehabilitation The process of restoring a convicted offender to a constructive place in society through some form of vocational, educational, or therapeutic treatment.

Rehabilitation Model A model of the criminal sanction based on the view that the offender is suffering from some physical or psychological defect that can be corrected.

Rehabilitation Model (institutions) A model of corrections that emphasizes the provision of treatment programs designed to reform the offender.

Reintegration Model A model of corrections that emphasizes maintenance of the offender's ties to family and the community as a method of reform.

Restitution Compensation for injury one has inflicted, in the form of either a payment of money to the victim or the performance of service to the community.

Retribution (deserved punishment) Punishment inflicted on a person who has infringed the rights of others and so deserves to be penalized. The severity of the sanction should fit the seriousness of the crime.

Self-incrimination The act of exposing oneself to prosecution by being forced to answer questions that may tend to incriminate one, protected against by the Fifth Amendment. In any criminal proceeding the prosecution must prove the charges by means of evidence other than the testimony of the accused.

Sentence disparity Divergence in the lengths and types of sentences imposed for the same crime or for crimes of comparable seriousness when no reasonable justification can be discerned.

Sentencing council A seminar at which judges discuss particular cases before their courts. Recommendations for an appropriate sanction are made to the sentencing judge, who may follow them or not in sentencing the offender.

Sentencing guidelines An instrument developed to indicate to judges the usual sanction given in the past in particular types of cases.

Sentencing institute A seminar designed to acquaint judges with sentencing laws and practices with the objective of reducing disparity in sentences.

Sentencing review A process whereby a board of review may consider the propriety of sentences appealed to it in individual cases. After hearing an appeal, the board may increase or decrease the original sentence.

Service The police function of providing assistance to the public, usually with regard to matters unrelated to crime.

Socialization The process by which the rules, symbols, and values of a group or subculture are learned by its members.

Sociological explanations Explanations of crime that emphasize social conditions that bear on the individual as the causes of criminal behavior.

Special deterrence Punishment inflicted on criminals with the intent to discourage them from repeating their illegal behavior.

Stare decisis The principle that judges should be bound by precedents (decisions made in previous similar cases) when they decide the cases before them.

Status offense Any act committed by a juvenile that would not be a crime if it were committed by an adult but that is considered unacceptable for a child, such as truancy or running away from home.

Statutes Laws passed by legislatures. Statutory definitions of criminal offenses are embodied in penal codes.

Strict liability An obligation or duty whose breach constitutes an offense that requires no showing of *mens rea* to be adjudged criminal; a principle usually applied to regulatory offenses involving health and safety.

Subculture The aggregate of symbols, beliefs, and values shared by members of a subgroup within the larger society.

Substantial Capacity Test A test of the defense of insanity which requires it to be shown that the accused, as a result of mental disease or defect, lacked a substantial capacity to appreciate the wrongfulness of his or her conduct at the time of the act.

System A complex whole consisting of interdependent parts whose operations are directed toward goals and which are influenced by the environment within which they function.

System efficiency Operation of the prosecutor's office in such a way as to effect speedy and early disposition of cases in response to caseload pressures in the system. Weak cases are screened out at intake, and other nontrial alternatives are used as primary means of disposition.

Team policing A police organizational strategy by which teams of generalists and specialists are assigned to defined geographical areas (neighborhoods).

Total enforcement A policy whereby the police are given the resources and support to enforce all laws without regard to the civil liberties of citizens.

Total institution An institution (such as a prison) that completely encapsulates the lives of those who work and live within it. Rules govern behavior, and the group is split into two parts, one of which controls all aspects of the lives of the other.

Trial court of general jurisdiction A criminal court that has jurisdiction over all offenses, including felonies, and that may in some states also hear appeals.

Trial court of limited jurisdiction A criminal court of which the trial jurisdiction either includes no felonies or is limited to some category of felonies. Such courts usually have jurisdiction over misdemeanor cases and probable-cause hearings in felony cases, and sometimes over felony trials that may result in penalties below a specified limit.

Trial sufficiency The presence of sufficient legal elements to ensure successful prosecution of a case. When a prosecutor's decision to prosecute a case is customarily based on trial sufficiency, only cases that seem certain to result in conviction at trial are accepted for prosecution. Use of plea bargaining is minimal; good police work and court capacity are required.

Uniform Crime Reports A statistical summary of crimes reported to the police based on voluntary reports to the FBI by local, state, and federal law enforcement agencies, published annually.

Upperworld crime Conduct in violation of the law engaged in during the course of business activity (as tax evasion, price fixing). Such offenses are often viewed as shrewd business practices that are not really criminal.

Victimization rate The number of victimizations per 1,000 persons or households as reported by the National Crime Surveys.

Victimology A subfield of criminology that examines the role played by the victim in precipitating a criminal incident.

Visible crimes Offenses against persons and property committed primarily by lower-class persons. Often referred to as "street crimes" or "ordinary crimes," these are the offenses most upsetting to the public.

Voir dire An examination of prospective jurors by means of which the prosecution and defense screen out persons who might be biased or incapable of rendering a fair verdict.

Work and educational release The release of inmates from correctional institutions during the day so that they may work or attend school.

Workgroup A collectivity of individuals who interact in the workplace on a continuing basis, share goals, develop norms in regard to the way activities should be carried out, and eventually establish a network of roles that serves to differentiate this group from others.

Working personality The complex of emotional and behavioral characteristics developed by a member of an occupational group in response to the work situation and environmental influences.

Appendix: Constitution of the United States: Criminal Justice Amendments

The first ten amendments to the Constitution, known as the Bill of Rights, became effective on December 15, 1791.

IV. The right of the people to be secure in their persons, houses, papers, and effects, against unreasonable searches and seizures, shall not be violated, and no warrants shall issue but upon probable cause, supported by oath or affirmation, and particularly describing the place to be searched, and the persons or things to be seized.

V. No person shall be held to answer for a capital or otherwise infamous crime, unless on a presentment or indictment of a grand jury, except in cases arising in the land or naval forces or in the militia when in actual service in time of war or public danger; nor shall any person be subject for the same offence to be twice put in jeopardy of life or limb; nor shall be compelled in any criminal case to be a witness against himself, nor be deprived of life, liberty, or property, without due process of law; nor shall private property be taken for public use without just compensation.

VI. In all criminal prosecutions the accused shall enjoy the right to a speedy and public trial, by an impartial jury of the State and district wherein the crime shall have been committed, which district shall have been previously ascertained by law, and to be informed of the nature and cause of the accusation; to be confronted with the witnesses against him; to have compulsory process for obtaining witnesses in his favor, and to have the assistance of counsel for his defense.

VIII. Excessive bail shall not be required, nor excessive fines imposed, nor cruel and unusual punishments inflicted.

The Fourteenth Amendment became effective on July 28, 1868.

XIV. Section 1. All persons born or naturalized in the United States, and subject to the jurisdiction thereof, are citizens of the United States and of the State wherein they reside. No State shall make or enforce any law which shall abridge the privileges or immunities of citizens of the United States; nor shall any State deprive any person of life, liberty, or property, without due process of law; nor deny to any person within its jurisdiction the equal protection of the laws.

Index of Cases

Index

Boldface numbers in this index refer to the page on which the term is defined.

Credits

Photos

CHAPTER 1 **p. 2,** Michael D. Sullivan; **p. 6,** Burt Glinn, Magnum Photos, Inc.; **p. 8,** Magnum Photos, Inc.; **p. 13,** Mimi Forsyth, Monkmeyer Press Photos, Inc.; **p. 18,** Harry Wilks, Stock Boston, Inc.; **p. 23,** Eve Arnold, Magnum Photos, Inc.; **p. 25,** Rhoda Sidney, Monkmeyer Press Photos, Inc.; **p. 29,** University of Connecticut **CHAPTER 2** **p. 36,** Ed Buryn, Jeroboam, Inc.; **p. 38** (both), The Bettmann Archive; **p. 42,** Universita' deglis Studi di Paria; **p. 45,** Indiana University; **p. 50,** Mimi Forsyth, Monkmeyer Press Photos, Inc.; **p. 54,** Barbara Alper, Stock Boston, Inc. **CHAPTER 3** **p. 86,** AP/Wide World; **p. 93,** The Bettmann Archive; **p. 95,** American Bar Association; **p. 98,** Michelle Bogre, Black Star; **p. 101,** John J. Lopinot, Black Star **CHAPTER 4** **p. 109,** Olof Källström, Jeroboam, Inc.; **p. 114,** Alex Webb, Magnum Photos, Inc.; **p. 115,** F.B.I.; **p. 127,** Mary Ellen Mark, Archive Pictures, Inc.; **p. 132,** Michael O'Brien, Archive Pictures, Inc. **CHAPTER 5** **p. 150,** Christopher Morrow, Photo Researchers, Inc.; **p. 157,** The Bettman Archive; **p. 159,** The Bancroft Library, University of California; **p. 167,** Hank Lebo, Jeroboam, Inc.; **p. 184,** Cary Wolinsky, Stock Boston, Inc. **CHAPTER 6** **p. 197,** The Bancroft Library, University of California; **p. 199,** Alex Webb, Magnum Photos, Inc.; **p. 203,** Charles Gatewood, The Image Works, Inc.; **p. 226,** Steven W. Denny; **p. 229,** Ed Cancone, Black Star; **p. 232,** Paul Conklin, Monkmeyer Press Photos, Inc. **CHAPTER 7** **p. 246,** Eve Arnold, Magnum Photos, Inc.; **p. 251,** Charles Gatewood, The Image Works, Inc.; **p. 267,** Sybil Shelton, Monkmeyer Press Photos, Inc.; **p. 271,** Bill Powers, Frost Publishing Group, Inc.; **p. 275,** Owen Franken, Stock Boston, Inc. **CHAPTER 8** **p. 283,** Bettye Lane, Photo Researchers, Inc.; **p. 286,** David R. Frazier; **p. 294,** Tony O'Brien, Frost Publishing Group, Inc.; **p. 302,** Steven W. Denny; **p. 311,** Gilles Peress, Magnum Photos, Inc. **CHAPTER 9** **p. 323,** Sandra Levitz; **p. 331,** Library of Congress; **p. 336,** Michael O'Brien, Archive Pictures, Inc. **CHAPTER 10** **p. 355,** Mimi Forsyth, Monkmeyer Press Photos, Inc.; **p. 361,** James L. Shaffer; **p. 367,** James L. Shaffer **CHAPTER 11** **p. 382** (right), Bill Anderson, Monkmeyer Press Photos, Inc.; **p. 382** (left), William E. Frost, Frost Publishing Group, Inc.; **p. 383,** Harvard College Library; **p. 400,** Michelle Bogre, Black Star **CHAPTER 12** **p. 422,** John J. Lopinot, Black Star; **p. 423,** AP/Wide World Photos; **p. 425,** Michael O'Brien, Archive Pictures, Inc.; **p. 433,** Mimi Forsyth, Monkmeyer Press Photos, Inc.; **p. 450,** Bill Powers, Frost Publishing Group, Inc. **CHAPTER 13** **p. 456,** The Bettmann Archive; **p. 464,** Cornell Capa, Magnum Photos, Inc.; **p. 468** (left), David Powers, Stock Boston, Inc.; **p. 468** (right), Owen Franken, Stock Boston, Inc.; **p. 479,** David R. Frazier **CHAPTER 14** **p. 493,** Library of Congress; **p. 495,** Library of Congress; **p. 496,** Richard Lawson, Illinois State Archives, Southern Illinois University; **p. 498,** American Correctional Association; **p. 509,** Arthur Grace, Stock Boston, Inc.; **p. 519,** Michael O'Brien, Archive Pictures, Inc. **CHAPTER 15** **p. 524,** Bill Powers, Frost Publishing Group, Inc.; **p. 525,** Tony O'Brien, Frost Publishing Group, Inc.; **p. 541** (left), Rose Skytta, Jeroboam, Inc.; **p. 541** (right), Paul S. Conklin, Monkmeyer Press Photos, Inc.; **p. 544,** Earl Dotter, Archive Pictures, Inc.; **p. 546,** Mimi Forsyth, Monkmeyer Press Photos, Inc.; **p. 549,** The Bettmann Archive, Inc.; **p. 554,** Liane Enkelis, Black Star; **p. 555,** Tony O'Brien, Frost Publishing Group, Inc.; **p. 569,** Paul Conklin, Monkmeyer Press Photos, Inc. **CHAPTER 16** **p. 580,** Bruce Kliewe, Jeroboam, Inc.; **p. 582,** From *John Augustus, First Probation Officer;* **p. 584,** Gilles Peress, Magnum Photos, Inc.; **p. 592,** Ethan Hoffman, Archive Pictures, Inc.; **p. 595,** David Redfern Photography **CHAPTER 17** **p. 618,** Charles Harbutt, Archive Pictures, Inc.; **p. 622,** Leonard Freed, Magnum Photos, Inc.; **p. 627,** Painted by Boardman Robinson, Courtesy of Harvard Law Art Collection; **p. 644,** Bill Powers, Frost Publishing Group, Inc.; **p. 648,** Paul S. Conklin, Monkmeyer Press Photos, Inc.

Figures

CHAPTER 1 **p. 17,** Figure 1.1 from U.S., Department of Justice, *Uniform Crime Reports* (Washington, D.C.: Government Printing Office, 1984), p. 179. **p. 19,** Figure 1.2 from *The Gallup Report,* by G. H. Gallup, Report No. 210 (Princeton, N.J.: The Gallup Poll, March 1983), p. 6. Constructed by SOURCEBOOK staff. Reprinted by permission. **p. 22,** Figure 1.3 from U.S., Department of Justice, Bureau of Justice Statistics, *Report to the Nation on Crime and Justice* (Washington, D.C.: Government Printing Office, 1983), p. 21. **CHAPTER 2** **p. 48,** Figure 2.1 from U.S., Department of Justice, Bureau of Justice Statistics, *Report to the Nation on Crime and Justice* (Washington, D.C.: Government Printing Office, 1983), p. 35. **p. 49,** Figure 2.2 from U.S., Department of Justice, Bureau of Justice Statistics, *Report to the Nation on Crime and Justice* (Washington, D.C.: Government Printing Office, 1983), p. 35. **CHAPTER 4** **p. 113,** Figure 4.1 from U.S., Department of Justice, Bureau of Justice Statistics, *Report to the Nation on Crime and Justice* (Washington, D.C.: Government Printing Office, 1983), p. 89. **p. 121,** Figure 4.4 from *Sense and Nonsense about Crime,* by S. Walker (Monterey, CA: Brooks/Cole Publishing Company, 1985), p. 16. **p. 122,** Figure 4.5 adapted from *The Limits of Law Enforcement,* by H. Zeisel (Chicago: University of Chicago Press, 1982), p. 18. **p. 144,** Figure 4.8 adapted from *The Flow of Defendants through the New York City Criminal Courts, 1967,* by J. B. Jennings (New York: New York City Rand Institute, 1970). **CHAPTER 5** **p. 161,** Figure 5.1 adapted from "Police Discretion Not to Invoke the Criminal Process: Low-Visibility Decisions in the Administration of Justice," by J. Goldstein. In G. F. Cole (Ed.), *Criminal Justice: Law and Politics* (Monterey, CA: Brooks/Cole, 1980), pp. 81–100. **p. 173,** Figure 5.2 from *Varieties of Police Behavior,* by J. Q. Wilson (Cambridge, MA: Harvard University Press, 1968), pp. 85–89. **CHAPTER 6** **p. 195,** Figure 6.1 from *Municipal Police Administration,* 7th Ed., by G. and E. Eastman (Eds.) (Washington, D.C.: International City Management, 1971), p. 34. Reprinted by permission. **p. 205,** Figure 6.2 from *Calling the Police: Citizen Reporting of Serious Crime,* by W. Spelman and D. K. Brown (Washington, D.C.: Police Executive Research Forum, 1981), p. 64. Reprinted by permission. **p. 208,** Figure 6.3 from *Calling the Police: Citizen Reporting of Serious Crime,* by W. Spelman and D. K. Brown (Washington, D.C.: Police Executive Research Forum, 1981), p. 29. Reprinted by permission. **p. 215,** Figure 6.4 from President's Commission on Law Enforcement and Administration of Justice, *Task Force Report: Science and Technology* (Washington, D.C.: Government Printing Office, 1967), pp. 8–9. **p. 218,** Figure 6.5 from U.S., Department of Justice, *Uniform Crime Reports* (Washington, D.C.: Government Printing Office, 1985), p. 160. **CHAPTER 7** **p. 248,** Figure 7.1 from *Citizen Attitudes Toward Local Government Services and Taxes,* by F. F. Fowler, Jr. (Cambridge, MA: Ballinger Publishing Co., 1974), p. 168. Reprinted by permission. **p. 268,** Figure 7.2 from U.S., Department of Justice, Bureau of Justice Statistics, *Sourcebook of Criminal Justice Statistics,* 1982 (Washington, D.C.: Government Printing Office, 1983), p. 43. **p. 274,** Figure 7.3 from U.S., Department of Justice, National Institute of Justice, *Research in Brief,* "The Growing Role of Private Security," by W. C. Cunningham and T. H. Taylor (Washington, D.C.: Government Printing Office, 1984), p. 2. **p. 276,** Figure 7.4 from U.S., Department of Justice, National Institute of Justice, *Research in Brief,* "The Growing Role of Private Security," by W. C. Cunningham and T. H. Taylor (Washington, D.C.: Government Printing Office, 1984), p. 3. **CHAPTER 8** **p. 308,** Figure 8.3 from U.S., Department of Justice, Bureau of Justice Statistics, *Report to the Nation on Crime and Justice* (Washington, D.C.: Government Printing Office, 1983), p. 55. **CHAPTER 9** **p. 330,** Figure 9.2 from U.S., Department of Justice, Bureau of Justice Statistics, *Special Report,* August 1984. **CHAPTER 10** **p. 353,** Figure 10.1 from "Bail Revisited," by H. Zeisel, *American Bar Foundation Research Journal,* 1979, p. 774. Reprinted by permission. **CHAPTER 11** **p. 390,** Figure 11.1 from *New York Times,* 13 April 1977, p. 40. © 1977 by The New York Times Company. Reprinted by permission. **CHAPTER 13** **p. 465,** Figure 13.1 from "Setting Prison Terms," (U.S. Bureau of Justice Statistics), *Bulletin,* August 1983. **p. 475,** Figure 13.2 from "Capital Punishment 1983," (U.S. Bureau of Justice Statistics), *Bulletin,* July 1984, p. 4; National Association for the Advancement of Colored People, *Death Row, U.S.A.* (New York: NAACP, December 20, 1984). **p. 481,** Figure 13.3 from *New York Times,* 30 March 1979, p. B3. © by The New York Times Company. Reprinted by permission. **CHAPTER 14** **p. 502,** Figure 14.1 from "Probation and Parole, 1982," (U.S. Bureau of Justice Statistics), *Bulletin,* September 1984, p. 2. **p. 512,** Figure 14.2 adapted from U.S., Department of Justice, Bureau of Justice Statistics, *Pris-*

oners in State and Federal Institutions on June 30, 1981 (Washington, D.C.: Government Printing Office, 1981), p. 2; *Prisoners in 1983*, p. 3. **p. 513,** Figure 14.3 from U.S., Department of Justice, Bureau of Justice Statistics, *Prisoners in 1983* (Washington, D.C.: Government Printing Office, 1984), p. 2. **CHAPTER 16 p. 590,** Figure 16.1 from "Halfway Houses and Parole: A National Assessment," by E. Latessa and H. Allen, *Journal of Criminal Justice* 10 (1982): 156. Copyright © 1982, Pergamon Press, Ltd. Reprinted by permission. **p. 593,** Figure 16.2 from U.S., Department of Justice, Bureau of Justice Statistics, *Parole in the United States, 1979* (Washington, D.C.: Government Printing Office, 1980), p. 10. **p. 597,** Figure 16.3 from U.S., Department of Justice, Bureau of Justice Statistics, *Characteristics of the Parole Population, 1978* (Washington, D.C.: Government Printing Office, 1980), p. 5. **CHAPTER 17 p. 630,** Figure 17.1 from U.S., National Advisory Committee on Criminal Justice Standards and Goals, Task Force on Juvenile Justice and Delinquency Prevention, *Report* (Washington, D.C.: Government Printing Office, 1976), p. 9. **p. 633,** Figure 17.2 from U.S., Department of Justice, *Sourcebook of Criminal Justice Statistics, 1980* (Washington, D.C.: Government Printing Office, 1980), p. 374. **p. 643,** Figure 17.3 from U.S., Department of Justice, National Criminal Justice Information and Statistics Service, *Children in Custody* (Washington, D.C.: Government Printing Office, 1979), p. 6.

TO THE OWNER OF THIS BOOK:

I hope that I've been able to make this book likable. I'd like to learn your reactions to this textbook. Only through your comments and advice and the comments and advice of others can I hope to improve the next edition of *The American System of Criminal Justice.*

School: ______________________________

Your instructor's name: ______________________________

1. What did you like most about *The American System of Criminal Justice?* ______________________________

____

2. What did you like least about the book? ______________________________

____

3. Were all of the chapters of the book assigned for you to read? ______________________________

(If not, which ones weren't?) ______________________________

4. Which special features were most interesting and informative? Why? ______________________________

____

____

____

____

5. If you used the study guide, how helpful was it to understanding concepts and theoretical approaches?

____

____

____

____

6. In the space below or in a separate letter, please let me know what other comments about the book you'd like to make. (For example, were any chapters or concepts particularly difficult?) I'd be delighted to hear from you.

____

____

____

____

____

____

____

____

____

____

Optional:

Your Name: ______________________________ Date: ____________

May Brooks/Cole quote you, either in promotion for *The American System of Criminal Justice* or in future publishing ventures?

Yes _______ No _______

Sincerely,

George F. Cole

CUT PAGE OUT AND FOLD HERE

NO POSTAGE NECESSARY IF MAILED IN THE UNITED STATES

BUSINESS REPLY MAIL

FIRST CLASS PERMIT NO. 84 MONTEREY, CALIF.

POSTAGE WILL BE PAID BY ADDRESSEE

George F. Cole
Brooks/Cole Publishing Company
Monterey CA 93940